CASES AND MATERIALS ON

WATER LAW

Seventh Edition

By

George A. Gould
Professor of Law
University of the Pacific
McGeorge School of Law

Douglas L. Grant
Cord Foundation Professor of Law
University of Nevada, Las Vegas
William S. Boyd School of Law

Gregory S. Weber
Professor of Law
University of the Pacific
McGeorge School of Law

AMERICAN CASEBOOK SERIES®

THOMSON
WEST™

Mat #40259584

610 Opperman Drive
P.O. Box 64526
St. Paul, MN 55164–0526
1–800–328–9352

Printed in the United States of America

ISBN 0–314–15392–6

TEXT IS PRINTED ON 10% POST CONSUMER RECYCLED PAPER

Preface

George A. Gould and Douglas L. Grant welcome Gregory S. Weber as a coauthor of the Seventh Edition of Cases and Materials on Water Law. The first edition, authored by the late Frank J. Trelease, was published in 1965. George Gould joined Frank Trelease as a coauthor of the Fourth Edition, and Douglas Grant joined George Gould for the Fifth and Sixth Editions.

Those who have used prior editions will find the Seventh Edition familiar. Like preceding editions, it is a traditional casebook built around cases and supplemented by notes and statutory materials. It examines water law largely through the perspective of private water rights. Public rights, water quality regulation, and other environmental regulation are covered extensively, but primarily in the context of how they affect long-established systems of private water rights—the appropriation doctrine and the riparian doctrine for streams, and various doctrines for groundwater. This approach illuminates the tension between affording stability and accommodating change that is at the heart of modern water law and policy. Interstate allocation, federal-state relations, and water distribution organizations are also extensively examined.

New principal cases and statutory materials have been added for the Seventh Edition to reflect recent developments in the law. Additionally, new notes have been added and existing notes have been extensively rewritten to incorporate changes in the law.

Cases and statutory citations, as well as footnotes, of courts and commentators have been omitted without so specifying; numbered footnotes are from the original materials and retain the original numbering; lettered footnotes within the cases are those of the authors. Occasionally, paragraph structure has been altered from the original materials and headings and other organizational features have been omitted.

The authors thank Olivia Wright and James Herink, McGeorge students, for their assistance in research, proofreading, cite checking, and similar editorial tasks. Without their skill and diligence, preparation of the book would have been much more difficult.

GEORGE A. GOULD
DOUGLAS L. GRANT
GREGORY S. WEBER

January 2005

Summary of Contents

Table of Contents

Table of Cases

The principal cases are in bold type. References are to pages.

CASES AND MATERIALS ON

WATER LAW

Seventh Edition

*

Chapter 1

INTRODUCTION TO WATER LAW

GEORGE A. GOULD, WATER RIGHTS SYSTEMS

Water Rights of the Eastern United States 8-10 (Kenneth R. Wright ed. 1998).

The function of water law. What is the function of water law? What is society trying to accomplish through water law? Very simply, water law is concerned with resource allocation; water law determines who can use water and for what purposes. Resource allocation is not an end in itself. The end is, or should be, the advancement of social values and needs. Thus, in considering various water law systems from a public policy perspective, one should ask whether a system serves society.

Some persons may object that focusing on resource allocation places too much emphasis on commercial uses of water and minimizes the value of non-commercial uses, such as environmental preservation. This objection is without merit if resource allocation is broadly defined. Focusing on resource allocation does not mean that water cannot or should not be used to provide environmental or other non-commercial values. To be sure, traditional legal rules for allocating water and other resources favored commercial uses, and changes in the law have been required to reflect noncommercial values. Indeed, change in the law to reflect new social values has been the essence of the environmental movement over the last 30 years. Nevertheless, such laws, like traditional legal rules, allocate resources. Whether it involves competition between private parties over water or whether it involves efforts to provide water for public or environmental uses, water law is concerned with difficult choices that must be made about the allocation of a scarce resource.

Water resources. The law must necessarily reflect the nature of the legal problem to be resolved. Usually, the more complex the problem, the more complex must be the legal system. The allocation of water resources—the legal problem of water law—is quite complex. To begin with, rivers and streams are "flow" resources and it is flow, not quantity, that must be allocated. That is, at any point in time, the problem confronting the law is the division of the available flow among the competing demands. Adding to the complexity of the problem, both flow and demands for the flow are variable. By analogy one might envision a water tap discharging a stream of water and a number of persons trying to capture part of the stream with straws. The stream varies as the control valve is turned. Similarly, the number of persons trying to insert straws into the stream varies. The problem is not to allocate glasses or gallons of water; the problem is to determine which persons can have their straws in the stream at any time.

The East and the West have developed very different legal systems to solve this problem. This reflects very different water resources and demands for water. In the East, water resources are relatively abundant. The climate is humid, irrigation is not necessary for successful farming, and demand for water has historically been low. In addition, the flow of eastern streams is much less variable than the flow of western streams.[3] As a consequence, conflict is atypical; it is generally the result of extraordinary uses or exceptional shortages (drought). Applying the analogy to the water tap, the stream from the tap exceeds demand except when attempts are made to place an unusually large straw in the stream or when the valve is turned exceptionally low.

In the West, water resources are scarce and highly variable, both seasonally and from year-to-year. The climate is arid, irrigation is necessary for successful farming, and demand is high, particularly during the irrigation season. Conflict is frequent and predictable; it results from ordinary uses (principally irrigation) and periodic shortage (low, late summer flows). Using the water tap analogy, even in a normal year, the stream from the tap fluctuates widely and is insufficient during part of the year to fill all the straws inserted into the stream.

The role of government. Government plays a variety of roles with regard to water law; it enforces, it creates, and it regulates water rights; it also develops water supplies and uses water. Initially, water rights were created through private acts, and the role of government was simply to enforce such rights. More recently, [state] government has become the creator of water rights through permit systems. * * *

A third role, closely related to government's role as creator, is its role as a regulator of water rights. Government regulation is a widespread feature of modern society and is typically predicated on failure of market forces adequately to address certain problems. Historically, the western system of permits and administrative regulation was directed toward making the operation of the private water rights system more effective and efficient. Recently, however, most western states have become increasingly active in regulating toward other ends. Similarly, [a number of eastern states now regulate water use] motivated by the desire to increase the efficacy of private water rights and the desire to advance other social goals.

---

3. On an eastern stream, flows may vary by a factor of two between the driest and wettest months and a factor of 24 between the driest and wettest years; on western streams these factors may be 40 and 85, respectively. See, New Challenge, New Direction, The Water Policy Report of the Western Governors' Association 7-9 (undated) and National Water Commission, Water Policies for the Future 5 (1973).

Government uses water and develops water supplies for use by its constituents. Municipal governments are particularly active in developing water supplies for their citizens. In the West, the federal government has been a major water developer, primarily in the form of reclamation projects which supply water for irrigation.

The relationship of the federal government and the states also deserves brief mention. Water rights are primarily a subject of state law. Although the federal government has extensive authority to deal with water pursuant to a number of constitutional powers, the federal government has never attempted to create a general system of water rights. Federal law is the source of limited rights held by the federal government and Indian tribes in the western United States. The federal government also regulates some activities related to water use pursuant to its power over interstate commerce and navigable waters. In addition, it has constructed a number of water projects.

Notes

1. **Public policy and water use.** Nat'l Water Comm'n, Water Policies for the Future 2-3 (1973):

"The National Water Commission is convinced that there are few water 'requirements,' except for relatively small amounts for drinking, cleaning, fire fighting in municipalities, and similar other essential social and environmental purposes. But there are 'demands' for water and water-related services that are affected by a whole host of other factors and policy decisions, some in fields far removed from what is generally considered to be water policy. For example, the invention of the kitchen garbage disposal unit greatly increased the load on municipal sewage treatment plants, and the decision to support the price of cotton led to vast increases in irrigated acreage on the High Plains of Texas.

"It is impractical, and in fact undesirable, to attempt to forecast precise levels of future water use on the basis of past water use. How much water will be used, where, and for what purposes will depend on the policies that are adopted. * * *"

Wayne B. Solley et al., U.S. Dep't of the Interior, Circular 1200, Estimated Use of Water in the United States in 1995, at iv (1998):

"As a Nation, we are using less water. Total water withdrawals during 1995 were 10 percent less than during 1980. This is a significant decline considering that population increased 16 percent during the same period. This decline signals that we are managing our water resources more effectively, that water use does respond to economic and regulatory factors, and that the general public has an enhanced awareness about water-resources and conservation issues. * * *"

2. **Changing directions in public policy.** Wayne B. Solley, supra Note 1, at 2:

"Traditionally, water management in the United States has focused on manipulating the country's supplies of freshwater to meet the needs of users. A number of large dams were built during the early 20th century to increase the supply of freshwater for any given time. This era of building large dams to meet water demand in the United States has passed. As we approach the 21st century, the finite water supply and established infrastructure require that demand be managed effectively within the available sustainable supply. * * * [T[he focus on water management is increasingly on the river basin or watershed, often spanning multiple States * * *."

Report of the Western Water Policy Rev. Advisory Comm'n, Water in the West: Challenge for the Next Century 3-51 to -52 (1998):

"The emphasis on the protection of fish and migratory waterfowl is one of the most dramatic changes in federal water policy since 1973 and is leading to a more holistic focus on the restoration and maintenance of healthy aquatic ecosystems. The 1973 [National Water] Commission emphasized the incorporation of fish protection measures and flow release schedules into new projects, rather than the restoration of existing degraded systems. However, the events of the past 20 years have rendered this focus outdated—a key issue today is the potential reoperation of existing projects to help restore aquatic ecosystems * * *.

"The construction of dams and the diversion of water from river systems or basins have contributed to the decline of historic natural fish populations in many river basins throughout the West. Dams and water diversion patterns have also increased predation, reduced wildlife habitat, and increased pollution. * * *

"The immediate dilemmas facing modern water managers concern the preservation of existing native fish species and wildlife habitats, as well as the restoration of degraded habitats to increase their productivity. But there is also a growing recognition that the development of ecological baselines and the maintenance and restoration of health aquatic ecosystems are the best ways to avoid the bitter fish-versus-diversion conflicts that now pervade the West. There are three primary reasons for this. First, the ESA [Endangered Species Act] makes protection of listed fish and wildlife an absolute priority. The ESA directs the Fish and Wildlife Service (Service) or the National Marine Fisheries Service of the Department of Commerce to list species, subspecies, or distinct populations of fish and wildlife as threatened or endangered; the difference reflects the degree of extirpation risk. Once a species is listed federal agencies or permittees may not take any action likely to jeopardize the continued existence of the species, including habitat destruction or modification. Second, the ESA applies to existing activities as well as to future ones. Third, there is increasing recognition that there are few 'natural' aquatic environments to preserve. More and more, the emphasis is on the restoration of degraded systems."

FRANK J. TRELEASE, FEDERAL–STATE RELATIONS IN WATER LAW

National Water Commission, Legal Study No. 5, at 2-8 (1971).

[People use] water in many ways. * * * A boy swims in a neighbor's pond. A trout fisherman casts his fly into the riffles of a mountain stream. A vacationer tows his girl on water skis behind a power boat. The owner of a summer home merely sits and enjoys the view of a lake or brook. The tugs and barges of a navigation company ply a great river. A city discharges the wastes of its people and industries into the river.

* * * A power company's dam builds up the pressure that enables it to turn turbines and generators. A farmer diverts the water from a stream to

irrigate his fields and orchards. A manufacturer withdraws it from an underground source to use as a raw material or to wash and treat other materials. A city pumps large quantities through its mains for use in homes and commercial establishments. Any of these users may store water for future use, or a government agency may build a great multipurpose reservoir project to supply them all.

[T]here is not enough water anywhere on this globe to permit every user to do with it as he pleases. Not even the vast oceans can be mistreated without repercussions. Although the hydrologic cycle endlessly replenishes the fresh water of the earth there is not enough for all to use at will. Water is to this extent a scarce commodity and law is needed to allocate its use * * *. Water law has arisen, as other laws arise, to order * * * activities * * * in relation to water so as to allow and encourage desirable activities and to prevent or restrict undesirable conduct. Like other laws governing scarce things, the institutional framework of American water law is a combination of interacting property rights, economic forces and public regulation.

All of the water uses described in the opening paragraphs are desired by and have utility and value to the users. Not all will be protected by law and given the property status of a "water right." The boy's desire to swim is outweighed by the neighboring landowner's right to full possession of his land. The trout fisherman and motorboater similarly may have no private rights if the stream or lake is on private land but they may have "public rights" and be entitled to protection if the water is open to the public under the governing law. The tugboat also operates under a public right of navigation, but if the captain finds his highway blocked by a dam constructed by the sovereign government he will have no recourse. The owner of the summer home, who receives not only pleasure but also increased land value from the lake or brook, may have a protected interest in the water in some states but not in others. The city which saves money by discharging raw sewage into a stream, spoiling it for others or imposing costs of treatment on them, has no property right to continue its use.

The hydroelectric power company needs legal protection for its substantial investment in dam and power plant. In most jurisdictions it has a perpetual water right, in others a right for a term of years sufficiently long to allow it to amortize its sunk costs. The farmer provides the best illustration of the way in which the law may be varied to reflect the desirability of an activity. In a western state where irrigation reclaimed the desert and is much favored, he has a water right as permanent as the title to his land. In an eastern state where irrigation is still somewhat new and strange, he may have no right at all if his land does not border on the stream, and if it does, his use is theoretically subject to displacement by some other more reasonable use of the water. Under some modern eastern water statutes he has a right that lasts for a term of years, or one that may be cancelled "in the public interest." The manufacturer withdrawing ground water receives different protection in different states, but in one way or another he is assured of a supply. The city supplying the domestic needs of its people has the firmest of water rights, preferred over all others, though it may have to pay damages if it injures other existing rights. Its customers may not have property rights in a strict sense, but they are protected by municipal or public utility law that guarantees them service at reasonable rates. The government has seen to it that its dam has a water right, but the consumers of the water stored behind it may have almost any sort of right ranging from a temporary use until the water is needed for another purpose, through a contract right that may be subject to an infinite number of agreed-upon terms, to a property right in the works.

The allocation of property rights in water resources follows the pattern set for other resources like minerals or like land itself. Since water is a renewable resource producing a flow of benefits, what is allocated is its use, the right to take and use it over a period of time. * * *

Note

Water uses. Nat'l Water Comm'n, Water Policies for the Future 4 (1973):

"Water use consists of (1) intake uses, (2) onsite uses, and (3) instream or flow uses. Intake uses include water for domestic, agricultural, and industrial purposes—uses that actually remove water from its source. Onsite uses consist mainly of water consumed by swamps, wetlands, evaporation from the surface of water bodies, natural vegetation, unirrigated crops, and wildlife. Flow uses include water for estuaries, navigation, waste dilution, hydroelectric power and also some fish and wildlife and recreational uses.

"Water uses are measured in two ways, by amount withdrawn and by amount consumed. Water withdrawn is water diverted from its natural course for use, and may be returned later for further use. Water consumed is water that is incorporated into a product or lost to the atmosphere through evaporation and transpiration, and cannot be reused. Water consumption is the more important indicator, since some part of withdrawn water can usually be reused, although not always near the point where the first withdrawal takes place. Under certain circumstances, therefore, large water withdrawals over a short time period may become critical, adversely affecting onsite and instream uses. * * *"

FRANK J. TRELEASE, NEW WATER LEGISLATION: DRAFTING FOR DEVELOPMENT, EFFICIENT ALLOCATION AND ENVIRONMENTAL PROTECTION

12 Land & Water L. Rev. 385, 408-10 (1977).

[W]hat if there is not enough to satisfy all rights? What physical security does the law provide, what guarantees that the holder of a right will get water? When there is a shortage of water, which water uses get it? These questions go to the heart of the law, indeed, shortages are what the law of water rights is all about. There is little need for water rights if there is plenty of water for all.

The word "shortage" needs to be defined. It is meaningless unless demand is considered as well as supply. On a variable stream there may be an annual shortage if the normal or average low flows cannot support existing uses, although much high water flows to the sea. There may be shortages induced by drought if a usually sufficient supply fails in some years. There may be a shortage although the stream is running full, if the full flow is needed for fisheries, navigation, or environmental concerns. There may be no shortage even though every drop is used if the stream is so controlled that annual and perennial flows are equated by storage and the smoothed-out supply is fully but not over allocated. Such a firm right to a firm supply puts the water user in the best of all worlds.

In all cases, however, the physically available supply limits the water that can be withdrawn and the state, if it is to avoid chaos, must limit the claims to it. * * * When claims equal supply, no more can be granted. New demands for better uses must then be accommodated by some mechanism for flexibility * * *. Such a limit can be easily fixed if the supply is fixed. When the source fluctuates and sometimes can fill all needs but sometimes cannot, some method of allocating or distributing the immediately available water must be devised.

There are at least five ways of doing this. One is to enforce strict temporal priority, as exemplified by American prior appropriation. Another is to apply equal sharing enforced by proportionate reduction, as among some riparian irrigators. A third is to follow a statutory list of preferences, giving priority according to a fixed ranking of the values of different uses. A fourth is to distribute the water as determined by administrative discretion based on various economic and social factors. A fifth is to put up the water for sale or auction, as practiced in some Moslem communities.

Notes

1. **Property right variations.** Many variations can exist in the characteristics of property rights in water. The method of acquisition might be that the right exists as an incident of land ownership, that people are allowed to initiate a right by their own actions in commencing to use water, or that the right is acquired by a grant from the legislature or an administrative agency. The duration of the water right might be perpetual, contingent on continued use, for a term of years, terminable upon a contingency, or terminable at will by a state agency. The right might be personal to the holder, tied inseverably to land, or transferable at will. The water might be free, paid for by an initial lump sum, or paid for by a unit price.

2. **Governmental powers.** Some water uses are made not as an exercise of property rights but as an exercise of governmental powers. The United States, for instance, has no "water rights" for Hoover Dam on the Colorado River, but the Constitution and federal statutes authorize the U.S. Bureau of Reclamation to construct and operate it.

In an exercise of governmental power that crosses straightforwardly into the realm of property rights, many western states have authorized or directed state agencies or officials to acquire water rights to maintain instream flows. The purpose is to protect flow-based environmental values such as scenic beauty, recreational use, and fish and wildlife habitat.

For the most part, however, environmental values in water sources are not protected by assigning property-style water rights. Rather, these values are protected—to the extent they are protected—primarily through the exercise of state and federal regulatory powers. For example, a state permit system might require denial of a permit for any new water right that will have unacceptable environmental consequences. Other measures such as state or federal endangered species legislation might limit not only the acquisition of new private water rights but the future exercise of longstanding private water rights in order to protect fish or wildlife habitat.

3. **Public rights.** Public rights empower members of the public to use certain waters for certain purposes. For example, the public has rights to use navigable waters for navigation, fishing, and recreation. The exercise of these public rights might be protected and enhanced by the minimum streamflow water rights and environmental regulations referenced in Note 2.

4. **Water distribution organizations.** Much water is abstracted or stored by organizations that distribute the water to their ultimate consumers. Institutional law relating to business organizations, cooperatives, public utilities, municipal corporations, and myriad forms of public districts may become "water law," especially insofar as it governs the rights of consumers between themselves, against the distributor, or against the holders of other water rights.

5. **A property-rights viewpoint.** As suggested by Notes 2 through 4 and other preceding materials, water law includes much more than property-style rights to abstract water from its source. Nonetheless, such rights form the basis of most water uses and are central to water allocation issues. For that reason, other water laws and water uses are conveniently studied by examining their impact upon property rights in water. The next three chapters of this book provide detailed exploration of property rights in water. The remaining chapters consider the other elements of water law and their effect upon property rights.

OVERVIEW OF PRIVATE PROPERTY RIGHTS IN WATER

Surface Streams. Rights to abstract and use the water of streams in the United States are based on two quite different doctrines, the law of riparian rights and the law of prior appropriation. Each type of right is a property interest created by or obtained under state law, but they have very different characteristics. Most states recognize only one or the other, though in several states both kinds of rights can exist.

The modern form of the riparian doctrine gives each owner of land bordering on a stream the right to make a reasonable use of the water and imposes liability on an upper riparian owner who unreasonably interferes with that use. The right exists whether or not the water is actually used, and a use may be initiated at any time. The use must usually be made on the riparian land and within the watershed of the stream. A nonriparian who uses water is liable to any riparian injured thereby, and conversely a riparian who initiates a use that interferes with a prior nonriparian use is subject to no liability. Some states do not give effect to attempts of riparian proprietors to grant their water rights to nonriparians.

Under the modern form of the appropriation doctrine, a water right may be described as a state administrative grant that allows the use of a specific quantity of water for a specific beneficial purpose, if water is available in the source free from the claims of others with earlier appropriations. The right is initiated by an application for a permit. The place of use is not restricted to riparian land or even to the watershed. The right may be sold and its use or place of use changed, and it may cease to exist if it is not used.

Riparian law, developed in the green countrysides of England and eastern America, seems to be based on the unspoken premise that if rights to the use of water are restricted to those persons who have access to it through the ownership of the banks and if those persons will restrict their demands on the water to reasonable uses, there will be enough for all. Appropriation law, developed in the arid West, is usually thought of as a system for water-short areas. Where there is not enough for everyone, the rule of priority insures that those who obtain rights will not have their water taken by others who start later. The theory is that as demands arise, water rights to supply them will be given out until the water is exhausted, after which those with new demands must purchase rights. Because western streams fluctuate greatly, appropriation law places much emphasis on distribution of scarce water to the persons entitled to it. This is an ongoing process, while riparian law is more sporadic. While in some western states riparian law has been used to distribute shares of scarce water among riparian irrigators regardless of when they initiated their uses, much of the thrust of riparian law is to adjust uses so that all riparians can be accommodated. The late Professor Jacob Beuscher once said that eastern riparian law is not so much a system of water allocation as a fire fighting device used to settle the few disputes that arise between users of the generally abundant supplies.

In general, then, the appropriation doctrine is western water law, and the riparian doctrine is eastern water law. More specifically, nine western states have pure appropriation law, the "Colorado Doctrine," which has existed from their beginnings. These are Alaska, Arizona, Colorado, Idaho, Montana, Nevada, New Mexico, Utah, and Wyoming. Nine other western states began with the "California Doctrine," which recognizes both riparian rights and appropriations, but all of these are now substantially appropriation states in that that law is the most important today. Only in California, Nebraska, and Oklahoma are there possibilities of initiating new uses by exercising riparian rights; and in each of these states, the new exercise of riparian rights is subject to limitations that did not exist historically. In the other six states—Kansas, North Dakota, Oregon, South Dakota, Texas, and Washington—riparian rights are the historical basis of some uses, but all new uses must be appropriative.

It would be misleading to say that the water law of the other 32 states is common law riparianism. At least 14 of these states control the initiation of substantially all new uses by administrative permits—Connecticut, Delaware, Florida, Georgia, Iowa, Kentucky, Maryland, Massachusetts, Minnesota, Mississippi, New Jersey, North Carolina, Virginia, and Wisconsin. Some permit states allow only riparian uses, but others apparently allow nonriparian uses as well. The remaining mainland states may have the doctrine of riparian rights as their common law, but it has been heavily overlaid with statutes that control dams on navigable streams (hydroelectric dams or all dams), statutes that authorize nonriparian use of water stored in dams, statutes that authorize and control the abstraction of water by cities, districts and state agencies, and more recently, with statutes that control private uses for the protection of minimum flows and environmental values. In most "riparian states," these statutes rather than the common law are the important features of modern water law. Louisiana has riparian rights, though they stem from the Civil Code rather than the common law. Hawaii has a unique blend of ancient customary rights, appurtenant rights, and riparian rights overlaid with a permit system.

Groundwater. The law of underground water forms a somewhat different pattern. Groundwater that can be withdrawn in usable quantities is found in aquifers, which are porous earth formations such as gravel, sandstone, or fractured limestone that hold a substantial amount of water and permit it to move through the formation. Aquifers are usually fed by seepage from the surface, and often discharge water into springs and streams. Some narrowly confined aquifers have been treated as "underground streams," and the law of surface streams is applied to them. Most groundwater in aquifers, however, is so physically different from water in streams that historically it was treated differently. The first common law rule was absolute ownership, under which a landowner is regarded as owner of the water underneath the land and is allowed to take whatever quantity can be captured. The next common law rule to emerge was reasonable use, which requires that the landowner's use of groundwater must be reasonable and connected with use of the overlying land. A third common law rule is a rule of correlative rights similar to riparian doctrines of reasonable sharing. A fourth common law rule is prior appropriation. Many states now have superimposed substantial statutory regulation on the exercise of rights under these various common law doctrines.

Classification of states as to groundwater doctrine is significantly a matter of interpretation that sometimes borders on reading tea leaves, which explains why commentators have disagreed about how particular states should be classified. Classification is especially problematic for a number of eastern states if one seeks to assess whether permit statutes or other regulatory measures have substantially superseded the common law rules. See generally Joseph W. Dellapenna, 3 Waters and Water Rights chs. 20-22 (Robert E. Beck, ed., 2003). Western states are somewhat easier to classify. Arizona applies the reasonable use doctrine but has replaced it in specified management areas with a statutory scheme designed over time to reduce existing pumping to the safe yield of aquifers. California adheres to the correlative rights doctrine. Hawaii used correlative rights for decades, but recent case law and legislation create uncertainty about how much of that doctrine survives. Nebraska uses a combination of the reasonable use and correlative rights doctrines. Oklahoma once applied the reasonable use doctrine but has substantially altered it by statute. Texas follows the absolute ownership doctrine. The remaining western states use the appropriation doctrine. These include Alaska, Colorado, Idaho, Kansas, Montana, Nevada, New Mexico, North Dakota, Oregon, South Dakota, Utah, Washington, and Wyoming. In addition, groundwater districts that exercise many controls on withdrawals exist in California, Colorado, Nebraska, New Mexico, and Texas.

Notes

1. Alternatives to private property rights. Not all economists regard property-style water rights as the ultimate in water law. One sees water as a natural monopoly that requires large public investment in storage and transportation facilities, and he advocates an institutional solution—putting water in the hands of large public utilities that sell the capacity of their facilities at fixed periodic prices. Mason Gaffney, Economic Aspects of Water Resources Policy, 28 Am. J. Econ. & Sociology 131 (1969). Another sees the state as a monopolist, selling water at demand-generated prices determined so that the quantity and quality demanded at that price just equal the available supply. Dudley D. Johnson, An Optimal State Water Law: Fixed Water Rights and Flexible Market Prices, 57 Va. L. Rev. 345 (1971).

2. Water measurement. The unit commonly used to measure the rate of flow of a stream or the rate at which water is diverted from a stream into a ditch is the cubic feet per second, abbreviated to "second foot" or "c.f.s." This unit is the official statutory measure for appropriations in most western states. For example, an appropriation might give its owner a right to divert at the rate of five c.f.s. To determine the flow of a stream or the flow into a diversion ditch in c.f.s., the area of the cross-section of the stream or ditch in square feet is multiplied by the velocity of the water in feet per second. The average velocity of the flow must be computed, since near the sides and bottom and at the surface the water will be slowed by friction and will flow at a lesser rate than at the center of the stream. A wide variety of weirs, flumes, meters and registers is used to measure the flow of water.

The "miner's inch" or "inch of water" is a unit that formerly was widely used to measure small diversions, though it has been to a large extent superseded by the second foot. One miner's inch is the quantity of water that will flow through a one-inch square orifice under a certain pressure. As usually measured, a box or dam containing the orifice is set in the stream or main ditch so that the water stands at a certain height above the orifice, and the water is discharged through it into the ditch, or from the main ditch into a lateral. The vertical dimension of the orifice remains constant at one inch, and as the horizontal dimension is increased the number of miner's inches of water is increased, so that if it measures one inch by ten inches, it will deliver ten miner's inches of water. The head of water above the orifice varied from four to six inches, according to the custom of the locality, and since the greater the head, the higher the pressure and the greater the discharge, the flow described by "one miner's inch" can be translated into cubic feet per second only if the exact conditions of the measurement are known. In an effort to standardize it, many states have adopted legislative definitions. As measured in Colorado, a second foot is equal to 38.4 miner's inches; in Arizona, California, Montana, Nevada, and Oregon, it takes 40 inches to make a cubic foot per second; and in Idaho, Nebraska, New Mexico, North Dakota, South Dakota, and Utah, it takes 50 inches.

When the total volume of water is to be measured, rather than the rate of flow, the common unit is the "acre-foot." This is the amount of water that will cover one acre to a depth of one foot. It is 43,560 cubic feet, or 325,851 gallons.

If gallons were always the measure for stored water, the capacity of large reservoirs would run into astronomical figures. A typical suburban family of five consumes approximately one acre-foot of water per year. The relation of flow to total volume is that one second foot running for 24 hours will deliver 1.98 acre-feet. The flow of streams can be expressed in "acre-feet per year." The right to store water in a reservoir is usually measured in acre-feet, and the total quantity delivered from the reservoir to land is given as "acre-feet per acre."

The usual measure of flow for pumped water, especially from underground sources, is "gallons per minute." It takes 448.8 g.p.m. to equal one cubic foot per second. Municipal uses are often calculated in millions of gallons per day. One million gallons is 3.07 acre-feet, and one m.g.d. is approximately 1.55 cubic feet per second running for 24 hours.

CHARLES J. MEYERS, A HISTORICAL AND FUNCTIONAL ANALYSIS OF THE APPROPRIATION SYSTEM

National Water Commission, Legal Study No. 5, at 3-6 (1971)

Western courts developed a body of law that can be summarized as follows:

> A property right in the use of water is created by diversion of the water from a stream (or lake) and its application to a beneficial use. Water can be used at any location, without regard to the position of place of use in relation to the stream. In the event of a shortage of supply, water will be supplied up to a limit of the right in order of temporal priority: the last man to divert and make use of the stream is the first to have his supply cut off.

The function of this system of law was to ration a scarce resource and to promote economic development. The rationing principle adopted—first come, first served—is a familiar, if unsophisticated, means of allocating the use of a scarce resource. It is often used by parents to settle disputes among children over the use of toys; it is used by sponsors of such public events as football games and operas to allocate tickets; and it is used in some popular restaurants to allocate tables. Queuing, in short, is a familiar response of a simple social organism to the problem of shortage.

The rule of first-come, first-served is also found in the common law. * * * In the case of lost goods, many cases resolved the conflict between two claimants (neither the owner) by awarding the right to the first to take possession. The first possessor of wild animals (e.g., fish and foxes) was similarly protected. And as between trespasser on land owned by another, prior peaceful possession was protected against subsequent intrusion. * * *

This favor bestowed upon the appropriation system in the West cannot be explained solely by the necessity of adopting an elementary rule in a frontier society. The system has endured too long—as society, government and law became increasingly complex—for that explanation to do. It seems, rather, that the reason for the endurance of the appropriation system is found in the economic goals that the system serves. The system promotes investment by giving security of use. Prior appropriation said in effect: Come West, take up land and water, and they shall be yours. Thus the national (as well as regional) goals of settlement and development of the West were served (and continue to be served) by the appropriation system.

Notes

1. **The appropriation doctrine and wise resource allocation.** Frank J. Trelease, Federal-State Relations in Water Law, Nat'l Water Comm'n, Legal Study No. 5, at 5-6 (1971):

"Water uses may add substantially to the value of land, and most require a substantial investment in facilities for withdrawing and using it. The use of water is usually the basis of an enterprise which has a value as a going concern. The purpose behind much of water law is to insure that water users will receive a future water supply that will enable them to continue their uses, plan for the future and realize their expectations. While the law gives absolute and unqualified certainty to few property interests and may ascribe different degrees of security to different interests in or uses of a resource, it generally follows a strong policy of encouraging enterprise and development with a system of property rights that will give some assurance that the activity will not be subjected to premature termination without compensation.

"Another essential of water law is that it should follow and implement a wise policy of resource allocation, one that will insure the use of the resource to produce the maximum benefits for man and for society as a whole. This is generally accomplished by allocating the use of water to individuals who put it to use, so that private initiative is employed to increase the general as well as individual welfare. By giving security to water rights and protection to water uses, investments in water resources development and in enterprises dependent upon water use are encouraged. By permitting the grant and transfer of water rights, the use of water can be changed to higher and more beneficial uses through the economic process of purchase by persons and entities who can pay the price because of the greater value or productivity of the water in the new use. By regulations restricting water uses to those which are reasonable and beneficial, harmful uses and other undesirable effects are minimized. By other regulations restricting water uses that interfere with public uses and are contrary to the public interests, the public good is promoted and protected."

George A. Gould, Conversion of Agricultural Water Rights to Industrial Use, 27B Rocky Mtn. Min. L. Inst. 1791, 1791-92, 1801 (1982):

"There are two general solutions available to an industry needing new water supplies: it can develop new sources of water or it can transfer water from an existing use. While transfers have occurred for years, the more typical response in the past was to develop new sources. * * * The cheaply developed water was taken first. The water which remains consists largely of snowmelt run-off and flood water which require the construction of expensive storage facilities if a dependable supply is to be available. * * * [W]ater reallocation should begin to occur before all water is allocated; reallocation is less costly privately and socially. * * *

"Thus, in developing the appropriation doctrine, western courts viewed a water right as an independent property interest which might be changed or transferred freely, subject only to the limitation that no injury to other appropriators could result from the change. This view undoubtedly resulted from the nature of an appropriation right. Unlike the riparian doctrine which treats water rights as an incident of land ownership—one of the sticks of the bundle, so to speak—the appropriation doctrine treats a water right as an independent property interest which arises as a result of, and only as a result of, the application of water to beneficial use. Since an appropriative right arises independently, it is a separate and independently transferable property interest."

2. **Opposition to treating water as a commodity.** Harrison C. Dunning, Reflections on the Transfer of Water Rights, 4 J. Contemp. L. 109, 109-10 (1977):

"The commodity school of thought regarding water rights transfers has become an increasingly significant one among water resources economists and lawyers in recent years. The commodity school is that which suggests in general that water should be treated as a commodity like any other and points to the advantages of enhanced transferability of the water right.

"In its simplest form, the commodity approach to water resources embraces three principal points: First, the economically most productive uses of water resources are the best uses, provided adequate accounting is made for direct third party impacts. Second, the market, preferably as free a market as possible, will bring about the economically most productive uses, because the price mechanism will direct water resources to those uses most highly valued by various users. Third, certainty in the definition of property rights in water resources and a minimum of legal and institutional barriers to the transferability of those rights are necessary if this market is to be developed. * * *

"The notion that the economically most productive uses of water resources are necessarily the best ones is a difficult one to accept. * * * [T]he heart of the problem is whether economic theory alone should dictate the use of water resources or whether economic theory should be but one factor, among others, which determines how these resources are utilized. It is inadequate to say that a particular resource should be put to a higher valued use rather than to a lower valued use if value means dollar value in the marketplace, and if we know that many benefits from a given pattern of resource utilization are so diffused that they will not be represented in the public bidding. * * *"

Environmentalists opposed to the commodification of water have found an ally in the agricultural community. Pat O'Toole, A Blueprint for Effective Water Policy in the West: An Alternative to the Final Report of the Western Water Policy Review Advisory Commission, in Water in the West: Challenge for the Next Century, supra p. 4, Note 2, at O'Toole-9:

"For decades, agriculture has been the social and economic backbone of many western states. Agriculture utilizes approximately three quarters of the developed water in the western United States, converting that water into an affordable and reliable supply of food and fiber for the nation and the world. * * * Moreover, throughout the West, irrigated agriculture also provides vast quantities of open space, wetlands, and wildlife habitat that will not and cannot be replaced if irrigated agriculture is destroyed. * * * For the farmer or rancher, the current water allocation and reallocation schemes often create economic conditions and a sense disillusionment [sic] and resignation. This sense of uncertainty, combined with rising land values which follow increased population pressure, leads to the sale of agricultural lands and the subdivision of riparian areas. Unquestionably, the benefits of western agriculture accrue to all Americans. A cornerstone of western water policy in the 21st century must be a recognition of the importance of irrigated agriculture and its preservation."

Even if one does not view water as a commodity, water law is about resource allocation, i.e., about how water will be used, using the term "used" broadly.

CHARLES F. WILKINSON, WESTERN WATER LAW IN TRANSITION

56 U. Colo. L. Rev. 317, 321-22, 329, 344 (1985).[a]

[Western water law] has been dominated by themes of appropriation under state law; stable priority for historic uses; concern for private rights over public rights; preference for consumptive, usually commercial, uses; and the provision of subsidized water for irrigators. It goes virtually without saying that this range of nineteenth and early twentieth century priorities is not as broad as the spectrum of considerations that must be accommodated in current water policy.

First, we have become increasingly aware of budgetary restraints on governments. Subsidies of all stripes are increasingly being called into question. Second, the press of the continuing migration to the West has created unprecedented strains on water supplies, thus intensifying the scrutiny of wasteful practices. Third, post-World War II innovations in high-lift pumping equipment have allowed us to begin to tap the potential of the great reservoirs of ground water. But, as shortages have developed, we have learned that many ground water aquifers are not renewable resources in the sense that surface waters are; the annual recharge of some aquifers is so small that they amount to stock resources that can be mined out, much like oil or coal deposits. Further, we have learned that ground water is usually hydrologically related to surface water, so that the traditional system of managing surface water and ground water separately fails to reflect the hydrologic reality; conjunctive management of underground and surface resources is required when the two connect up. Fourth, we have become determined to abate water pollution, an issue given little or no attention in prior appropriation law.

Fifth, we have revolutionized our concept of what western water is. It is no longer simply a commodity to be removed from a watercourse for use on farmland or in a factory. There is life and beauty in water. It is a valid use of water simply to allow it to remain in a stream or lake. In a sense, after first rejecting the riparian rule so resoundingly, we reached a deeply held consensus that there is undeniable merit in some aspects of riparianism: sufficient water absolutely must be available to meet a broad range of public environmental, recreational, ecological, and aesthetic needs.

---

a. Copyright 1985. Reprinted with the permission of the University of Colorado Law Review.

Finally, we have come to recognize that this body of water law and policy bred of the westward expansion must begin to account for the rights of Indians, to whom legally binding promises were made in order to open aboriginal land and resources for those who settled the West. * * *

The primary method for dealing with the critical issue of creating new water supplies will be to conserve water from existing supplies. For generations, water conservation has been defined chiefly as the construction of new water projects. But most of those proposals will have difficulty satisfying the scrutiny of this newly cost-conscious field. In addition, nearly all of the prime dam sites in the West have already been utilized. Even more fundamentally, water storage projects are conservation projects only in the sense that they capture water that would otherwise flow out to sea. True water conservation is a much broader concept requiring users to employ waste-saving practices designed to ensure that all, or a great percentage of, water is actually applied to the intended use and not to leaks, spill, or evaporation. A major source of new water is the conservation of water in existing uses. * * *

The ultimate problem, of course, is that the old doctrine forces us to proceed today according to the values of a century and a quarter ago. The promising young shoots in this time of transition all are nurtured by our determination to decide by contemporary standards, not those of a distant time.

Notes

1. **Last in time, last in right?** David E. Lindgren, The Colorado River: Are New Approaches Possible Now That the Reality of Overallocation Is Here?, 38 Rocky Mtn. Min. L. Inst. 25-1, 25-3 (1992):

"[T]he West has sustained a remarkable transformation. Industry and commerce replaced agriculture as the dominant economic force, and the region's population burgeoned as Americans abandoned the 'rust-belt' of the Northeast and Mid-West, and the environmental movement's growth during the last two decades changed the public's perception of the place environmental protection should occupy in matters of natural resources allocation and development.

"The pressures resulting from these societal changes have placed western water law—largely rooted in the appropriation doctrine of 'first in time, first in right'—in the throes of dynamic, fundamental change. Simply put, the urban and environmental interests who are 'last in time' are not willing to accept the proposition that, as supplies become fully allocated, western water law always places their interests 'last in right.'"

2. **Continuity versus innovation and change.** The ideas and sentiments expressed in the last two principal excerpts (by Meyers and Wilkinson) and the accompanying Notes help to frame much of the current policy debate and ferment affecting water law. Interesting perspective on the debate and ferment comes from famed business management consultant and astute societal observer Peter Drucker. He said he "see[s] as central to society and civilization the tension between the need for continuity and the need for innovation and change." James

W. Michaels, Jane Austen Novels as Management Manuals, Forbes, Mar. 10, 1997, at 14.

3. **Policy options.** Although not an exhaustive list, options for coping with increasing water demands include the following: (1) Increase usable water supplies by conservation in the traditional sense, i.e., constructing more storage and distribution facilities or, perhaps more likely in modern society, by utilizing groundwater storage capacity more effectively. (2) Reduce water demands by reducing subsidies to water users or making water use more costly through pricing, taxation, or regulation. (3) Reduce water demands by conservation in the broader sense, i.e., encouraging existing water users to become more efficient. Greater efficiency might be encouraged by the carrot of facilitating water right transfers and by the stick of legislative, administrative, or common law regulation.

Chapter 2

PRIOR APPROPRIATION

SECTION 1. ORIGIN

IRWIN v. PHILLIPS

Supreme Court of California, 1855.
5 Cal. 140.

HEYDENFELDT, J., delivered the opinion of the Court. MURRAY, C.J., concurred.

The several assignments of error will not be separately considered, because the whole merits of the case depend really on a single question, and upon that question the case must be decided. The proposition to be settled is whether the owner of a canal in the mineral region of this State, constructed for the purpose of supplying water to miners, has the right to divert the water of a stream from its natural channel, as against the claims of those who, subsequent to the diversion, take up lands along the banks of the stream, for the purpose of mining. It must be premised that it is admitted on all sides that the mining claims in controversy, and the lands through which the stream runs and through which the canal passes, are a part of the public domain, to which there is no claim of private proprietorship; and that the miners have the right to dig for gold on the public lands was settled by this Court in the case of Hicks et al. v. Bell et al., 3 Cal. 219.

It is insisted by the appellants that in this case the common law doctrine must be invoked, which prescribes that a water course must be allowed to flow in its natural channel. But upon an examination of the authorities which support that doctrine, it will be found to rest upon the fact of the individual rights of landed proprietors upon the stream, the principle being both at the civil and common law that the owner of lands on the banks of a water course owns to the middle of the stream, and has the right in virtue of his proprietorship to the use of the water in its pure and natural condition. In this case the lands are the property either of the State or of the United States, and it is not necessary to decide to which they belong for the purposes of this case. It is certain that at the common law the diversion of water courses could only be complained of by riparian owners, who were deprived of the use, or those claiming directly under them. Can the appellants assert their present claim as tenants at will? To solve this question it must be kept in mind that their tenancy is of their own creation, their tenements of their own selection, and subsequent, in point of time, to the diversion of the stream. They had the right to mine where they pleased throughout an extensive region, and they selected the bank of a stream from which the water had been already turned, for the purpose of supplying the mines at another point.

Courts are bound to take notice of the political and social condition of the country which they judicially rule. In this State the larger part of the territory consists of mineral lands, nearly the whole of which are the property of the public. No right or intent of disposition of these lands has been shown either by the United States or the State governments, and with the exception of certain State regulations, very limited in their character, a system has been permitted to grow up by the voluntary action and assent of the population, whose free and unrestrained occupation of the mineral region has been tacitly assented to by the one government, and heartily encouraged by the expressed legislative policy of the other. If there are, as must be admitted, many things connected with this system, which are crude and undigested, and subject to fluctuation and dispute, there are still some which a universal sense of necessity and propriety have so firmly fixed as that they have come to be looked upon as having the force and effect of *res judicata.* Among these the most important are the rights of miners to be protected in the possession of their selected localities, and the rights of those who, by prior appropriation, have taken the waters from their natural beds, and by costly artificial works have conducted them for miles over mountains and ravines, to supply the necessities of gold diggers, and without which the most important interests of the mineral region would remain without development. So fully recognized have become these rights, that without any specific legislation conferring or confirming them, they are alluded to and spoken of in various acts of the Legislature in the same manner as if they were rights which had been vested by the most distinct expression of the will of the law makers; as for instance, in the Revenue Act "canals and water races" are declared to be property subject to taxation, and this when there was none other in the State than such as were devoted to the use of mining. Section 2 of Article IX of the same Act, providing for the assessment of the property of companies and associations, among others mentions "dam or dams, canal or canals, or other works for mining purposes." This simply goes to prove what is the purpose of the argument, that however much the policy of the State, as indicated by her legislation, has conferred the privilege to work the mines, it has equally conferred the right to divert the streams from their natural channels, and as these two rights stand upon an equal footing, when they conflict, they must be decided by the fact of priority, upon the maxim of equity, *qui prior est in tempore, potior est in jure.* The miner who selects a piece of ground to work, must take it as he finds it, subject to prior rights, which have an equal equity, on account of an equal recognition from the sovereign power. If it is upon a stream, the waters of which have not been taken from their bed, they cannot be taken to his prejudice; but if they have been already diverted, and for as high and legitimate a purpose as the one he seeks to accomplish, he has no right to complain, no right to interfere with the prior occupation of his neighbor, and must abide the disadvantages of his own selection.

It follows from this opinion that the judgment of the Court below was substantially correct, upon the merits of the case presented by the evidence, and it is therefore affirmed.

Notes

1. **Mining law origin.** "In January of 1848, two Americans, John A. Sutter and James T. Marshall, while building a sawmill on the American River in the mountain regions of California discovered gold in the mill race. * * * Within a period of two or three years the population of California increased from two or three thousand people to two or three hundred thousand people. * * *

"A vast and intricate field of mining law was to develop from these few simple rules as adopted in the early California mining districts. For a quarter of a century and more, mining law was the most significant field of law in the West. But the mining districts are of current significance not only because of the law of mining but also because of the law of water which owes its origin to them. A good many of the mines in California were placer mines. Water is essential to the operation of a placer mine. But a great many of these placer mines were situated a considerable distance from the stream and frequently entirely beyond the drainage of the stream. Just as there were not enough mines for all the people, there was not enough water for all the mines. Now the Anglo-American doctrine of riparian water rights was established on the premise that water belonged to the owner of the land adjacent to the stream and that while each land owner had a right to use the water still he was obligated to return it to the stream undiminished in quality and quantity for his neighboring riparian owner immediately below him on the stream. Such a law was of course worked out to meet the economic needs of a group of eastern factory owners and mill operators. It was a law made in a damp moist country, and simply did not fit the needs of the western miners. Hence, they were again thrown upon their own resources to work out a system wherein the greatest amount of good could be obtained from the limited amount of water.

"The miners met this problem just as they met the problem of adjusting the right to use a limited number of mines among a multitude of people. They applied the doctrine of prior appropriation to the water just as they did to the mining claims, and they limited the amount of water each person could use to the amount that he originally appropriated from the stream to operate his mine. The size of the ditch was used to determine the quantity of water originally taken. They also decreed that a failure to use the water for a given time worked an abandonment of the right to take the water just as a failure to work the mine worked an abandonment of the mine.

"It was soon discovered by those who went to farm that the water law as worked out by the miners was much more appropriate to their needs in such an arid country than the riparian rights which their ancestors had worked out in the humid East. Hence, the law of water, as originally worked out in the mining districts of California, was soon to become the water law of the entire arid west." John D. McGowen, The Development of Political Institutions on the Public Domain, 11 Wyo. L.J. 1, 8-14 (1956).

2. **Mexican origin.** Decisions in Arizona and New Mexico trace statutes adopting the appropriation doctrine in those states to Spanish or Mexican law. See Maricopa County Mun. Water Conservation Dist. No. 1 v. Southwest Cotton Co., 4 P.2d 369 (Ariz. 1931); United States v. Rio Grande Dam & Irrigation Co., 51 P. 674 (N.M. 1898). In contrast, Lux v. Haggin, 10 P. 674 (Cal. 1886), held that the Spanish and Mexican law applicable to territory ceded from Mexico was superseded by statutes adopting the common law. A confusing note was added by Motl v. Boyd, 286 S.W. 458 (Tex. 1926), in which dictum equated the Mexican law with riparian rights. However, some excellent scholarly research led the Texas courts to repudiate this dictum in State v. Valmont Plantations, 346 S.W.2d 853 (Tex. Civ. App. 1961), aff'd, 355 S.W.2d 502 (Tex. 1962). After an exhaustive study of historical and legal materials, it was concluded that a Spanish or Mexican grant of land riparian to the Rio Grande did not carry with it an appurtenant irrigation right, and that the Spanish and Mexican irrigation system was not a system of riparian law, but required a specific grant of the water.

3. **Mormon roots.** Seeds of prior appropriation have also been found in the Mormon settlement of Utah in 1847, six months before the discovery of gold in California. However, initial Mormon practice appears to have reflected a communitarian philosophy:

"During the earliest years, in the absence of political law, the Mormon church approved the custom of diverting water by group effort and applying it to beneficial use, and supervised these operations. Early legislation made grants of water privileges, authorized the making of grants, and vested in the county courts control over appropriations of water. A statute passed in 1880 recognized accrued rights to water acquired by appropriation or adverse use, but did not contain a specific authorization to appropriate water. The principle of priority in time appears to have been recognized by custom before there was any general law on the subject." 1 Wells A. Hutchins, Water Rights Laws in the Nineteen Western States 163 (1971).

4. **Early common law.** Sir William Blackstone, apparently misinterpreting early cases basing the particular litigated water rights on prescription from ancient custom, stated: "If a stream be unoccupied, I may erect a mill thereon, and detain the water; yet not so as to injure my neighbor's prior mill, or his meadow: for he hath by the first occupancy acquired a property in the current." 2 William Blackstone, Commentaries *403. From this, Samuel Wiel, who considered riparian principles more progressive than appropriation principles, argued that prior appropriation was the common law of England before importation from France, via the United States, of "modern" riparian principles in the early nineteenth century. Samuel C. Wiel, Waters: American Law and French Authority, 33 Harv. L. Rev. 133 (1919). Subsequent scholarship exposed the fallacies of Blackstone and Wiel and asserted that early English law was riparian in nature. Arthur Maass & Hiller B. Zobel, Anglo-American Water Law: Who Appropriated the Riparian Doctrine?, 10 Pub. Pol'y 109 (1960). Carol M. Rose has argued that pre-nineteenth century English law was neither riparian nor appropriative but preserved the status quo by protecting "ancient uses." Rose asserts that English law of the early nineteenth century, influenced by Blackstone, vacillated between ancient use principles and prior appropriation before rejecting both in favor of riparian reasonable use principles in mid-century. Carol Rose,

Energy and Efficiency in The Realignment of Common-law Water Rights, 19 J. Legal Stud. 261 (1990).

5. **Colonial law.** The Massachusetts mill acts, dating back to colonial times, gave the riparian owner of a mill dam a superior right over others who might later erect dams that interfered with the first by unreasonably withholding the water above it or backing up water upon it from below. See Smith v. Agawam Canal Co., 84 Mass. (2 Allen) 355 (1861).

6. **Other countries.** Frank J. Trelease, New Water Legislation: Drafting for Development, Efficient Allocation and Environmental Protection, 12 Land & Water L. Rev. 385, 414-16 (1977):

"I think one of those notions is that when a person has taken, used, become accustomed to, and made a livelihood from water, it becomes 'his water,' and that one who takes it from him has 'stolen his water.' I used to think that prior appropriation was an American invention, but now I am convinced it was simply the verbal identification of a very widespread human trait.

"Teclaff, in his survey of 57 countries, tells us that seniority in use is the most common of all bases for distributing water among users.[2] In its most explicit form, prior appropriation exists not only in 19 American states, but also in the four western provinces of Canada, in Taiwan (China), Iran, Rhodesia, Zambia and the Philippines. There are strong elements of it in several South American countries. The 1963 British Water Resources Act creates a 'protected right' indistinguishable from an appropriation, though enforced in an unusual roundabout manner.

"Protection based on temporal priority is to some degree implicit in many other laws. Before state controls came into being, customary water rights, held from time immemorial or for prescriptive periods, were everywhere protected. When state authority to use water was instituted, the notion that a state should not make successive grants of the same water to different people appeared in most such laws. Permits, licenses or concessions, whatever they may be called, are not to be issued to the detriment of existing uses in most of the Spanish American countries, in several of the eastern United States, in Tanzania, and in Italy. Practically every new water code has given some sort of group preference to uses in existence when the code was adopted.

"Some evidence indicates a subliminal recognition of priority even where the law is specifically to the contrary. * * * Even under modern statutes that subject the allocation and distribution of water to administrative discretion, the administrators in Great Britain, Kenya and Mexico have eased their burden by issuing permits that authorize the withdrawal of water only when there is a surplus over the needs of existing users."

7. **Influence of irrigation.** Irrigation, not mining, has been the dominant use of water in the American West. The needs and problems of irrigated agriculture have had a major influence on the development of the appropriation doctrine. To a significant degree, the appropriation doctrine is irrigation law. The influence of irrigation is illustrated by the title *Irrigation Institutions* which

---

2. Abstraction and Use of Water: A Comparison of Legal Regimes—U.N./ST/ECA/154 (1972).

Elwood Mead gave to his 1903 book on western water law. Similarly, V Hutchins, writing in 1942, began his discussion of the appropriation doctri the following sentence: "It is undeniable that in the arid portions of the \ States irrigation is essential to agriculture." Wells A. Hutchins, S Problems in the Law Of Water Rights in the West 64 (1942).

8. **California doctrine.** Despite the application of the appropriation doctrine in Irwin v. Phillips, in a series of subsequent cases, culminating in Lux v. Haggin, 10 P. 674 (Cal. 1886), the California Supreme Court held that a federal patent to riparian land carried with it riparian rights. Thus, California came to recognize both appropriative and riparian rights in a system which came to be known as the "California doctrine." At one time at least nine other states—those on the west coast and the great plains—applied the California doctrine, but all except California, Nebraska, and Oklahoma now apply the appropriation doctrine exclusively.

The California doctrine integrates appropriative and riparian rights essentially as follows. Riparian rights associated with a particular tract of riparian lands are subordinate to all appropriative rights (rights for the use of water on nonriparian lands) which are created before a federal patent for the particular tract is issued and are superior to all appropriative rights created after the riparian lands are patented. Lux v. Haggin and the California doctrine are explored more fully in Chapter 3, Section 5.

9. **Federalism.** Private water rights are almost exclusively a matter of state law. An extensive legal and scholarly debate has raged over the theoretical basis for state jurisdiction over water rights in the West. Central to the debate is the relationship between ownership of western lands by the United States and legal control of water resources associated with those lands. Although frequently conducted with "sound and fury," it is a debate which has "signif[ied] [almost] nothing" where private water rights are concerned.[a] Notwithstanding what it might have done, the federal government left the creation and regulation of private water rights to the states. The debate has only had practical significance when the federal government has asserted rights on its own behalf or in connection with a federal program, project, or activity. Consequently, the debate is left to Chapter 8, Section 2, in which federal powers and federal-state conflicts are developed in depth.

---

a. "[I]t is a tale told by an idiot, full of sound and fury, signifying nothing." William Shakespeare, Macbeth, act 5, sc. 5, line 26 (G. Blakemore Evans ed., Houghton Mifflin Co. 1974)(1623).

SECTION 2. ATTRIBUTES

A. Diversion

IN RE ADJUDICATION OF THE MISSOURI RIVER DRAINAGE AREA

The Supreme Court of Montana, 2002
311 Mont. 327, 55 P.3d 396

JUSTICE W. WILLIAM LEAPHART delivered the Opinion of the Court.

The Montana Department of Fish Wildlife and Parks (DFWP) appeals a ruling by the Chief Water Judge on five pre-1973 water rights claims in the Missouri River basin. The five claims are based on diversions of water for purposes of fish, wildlife or recreation. The Water Court ruling refers to In the Matter of Dearborn Drainage Area (1988), 234 Mont. 331, 766 P.2d 228 *(Bean Lake*) in remarking on the potential invalidity of the claims. * * * To provide guidance to the Water Court, we must resolve the *Bean Lake* confusion and address not only the question of whether fish, wildlife and recreation uses are recognized as beneficial uses for appropriation purposes, but also whether a diversion is required for appropriation purposes. * * *

The common law elements of a valid appropriation are intent, notice, diversion and application to beneficial use. However, in Montana, as in many western states, the flexibility of the prior appropriation doctrine has allowed acquisition of the right to use a specific amount of water through application of the water to a beneficial use. A. Stone, Montana Water Law (1994). Judicial opinions and scholarly commentators have repeatedly stated the rule that application to a beneficial use is the touchstone of the appropriation doctrine. See, e.g., A. Stone, Selected Aspects of Montana Water Law 30 (1978); Thomas v. Guiraud (1883), 6 Colo. 530, 533 ("[t]he true test of appropriation of water is the successful application thereof to the beneficial use designed, and the method of diverting or carrying the same, or making such application, is immaterial").

Bean Lake involved a claim for inlake water rights for fish, wildlife and recreation purposes in a natural pothole lake. * * * To the extent *Bean Lake* suggests that fish, wildlife and recreation are not beneficial uses, it simply misstates Montana precedent and is hereby overruled. We next address whether *Bean Lake* correctly held that non-diversionary water rights for fish, wildlife and recreation purposes were not recognized in Montana under the doctrine of prior appropriation. * * *

After the *Bean Lake* Court concluded that prior to 1973, Montana did not allow appropriation of water for fish, wildlife and recreation purposes, the Court essentially skipped the traditional appropriation analysis. Rather than evaluating whether DFWP had intended to appropriate water and whether DFWP provided notice of its intent, the Court simply stated that because Montana did not recognize water rights for fish, wildlife and recreation purposes, DFWP could not have intended to appropriate water for those purposes, and thus adverse water users could not have had notice of any such intent. It is unclear from the opinion itself, whether the Court denied the appropriation for Bean Lake because there was no diversion or because it found there was no notice of intent to appropriate. To resolve the confusion engendered by *Bean Lake,* we now determine whether a valid appropriation of water may be established without a diversion where no diversion is physically necessary for the intended use.

While most traditional uses necessitated a diversion of water for application to beneficial use, the appropriation doctrine's history of flexibility and practicality support a holding that a diversion is not required where the application to beneficial use does not physically require a diversion. Common sense rebels against a rigid diversion requirement that would refuse to recognize an acknowledged beneficial use simply because application to the use does not require removal from and depletion of the water source. In accordance with the doctrine's flexibility, we find that a diversion is not a requisite element of an appropriation when it is not a physical necessity for application to a beneficial use.

More than one commentator has warned against the strict adherence to traditional elements, such as diversion, when the element no longer serves its original purpose. These scholars also note that beneficial use is the only essential element of a valid appropriation. See, e.g., Tarlock, Appropriation For Instream Flow Maintenance: A Progress Report on "New" Public Western Water Rights, 1978 Utah L. Rev. 211, 221 ("Most western water experts agree that the actual diversion requirement serves no function that cannot be served by other water law doctrines and statutory procedures. Thus the real issue is whether these uses are beneficial"); Christine A. Klein, The Constitutional Mythology of Western Water Law, 14 Va. Envtl. L.J. 343, 351 (1995) ("Rigid adherence to the diversion requirement has increasingly restricted the traditional flexibility of the ideas of beneficial use and waste. Although appropriation to beneficial use is the true measure of a water right, diversion has frequently been substituted as the constitutional requirement").

Under prior appropriation, a diversion traditionally served dual purposes providing notice of a user's intent to appropriate water, and defining the extent of the use. In Wheat v. Cameron (1922), 64 Mont. 494, 210 P. 761, this Court explained that intent to appropriate is to be determined from the specific facts and circumstances pertaining. * * * In accordance with the historical flexibility of the doctrine of prior appropriation, the *Wheat* Court held that although intent could be *presumed* from actual diversion, intent could be proven through other facts and surrounding circumstances. Similarly, in *Bean Lake,* the Court noted that diversion could provide notice or proof of an intent to appropriate. *Bean Lake,* 234 Mont. at 339, 766 P.2d at 233. These decisions do not require a diversion for proof of intent. To the contrary, the opinions suggest that although a diversion may provide proof, intent is the essential element and may be proven through means other than a diversion. In other words, a diversion, although sufficient to prove intent, is not necessary.

Decisions from this Court have not consistently required diversions for water appropriations. Indeed, despite the fact that most traditional beneficial uses of water, such as mining and irrigation, could not occur without a diversion, Montana has specifically recognized appropriations of water without diversions where no diversion was required for the intended beneficial use. See, e.g., Donich v. Johnson (1926), 77 Mont. 229, 250 P. 963 (appropriation recognized for instream reservoir); Axtell v. M.S. Consulting, 1998 MT 64, 288 Mont. 150, 955 P.2d 1362 (domestic use recognized without a diversion). Those cases that do suggest that a diversion is an essential element of an appropriation involve uses that, of practical necessity, require a diversion for the application to beneficial use. See, e.g., Warren v. Senecal (1924), 71 Mont. 210, 220, 228 P. 71, 75 (diversion by ditch for use in mining and irrigation); Sherlock v. Greaves (1938), 106 Mont. 206, 216, 76 P.2d 87, 89 (diversion by pipes and flumes from ditch for irrigation and domestic use). * * *

Ample case law depicting the evolution of the prior appropriation doctrine, and emerging from throughout the west, supports a conclusion that the doctrine should not rigidly demand a diversion where unnecessary to achieve the intended beneficial use. See, e.g., Empire Water & Power Co. v. Cascade Town Co. (8th Cir.1913), 205 F. 123, 129 ("[i]f nature accomplishes a result which is recognized and utilized, a change of process by man would seem unnecessary"); In re Water Rights in Silvies River (1925), 115 Or. 27, 237 P. 322, 336 ("[w]hen no 'ditch, canal, or other structure' is necessary to divert the water from its natural channel, the law does not vainly require such works, prior to an appropriation"); Town of Genoa v. Westfall (1960), 141 Colo. 533, 349 P.2d 370, 378 ("It is not necessary in every case for an appropriator of water to construct ditches or artificial ways through which the water might be taken from the stream in order that a valid appropriation be made. The only indispensable requirements are that the appropriator intends to use the waters for a beneficial purpose and actually applies them to that use"); State, Dept. of Parks v. Idaho Dept. of Water Admin. (1974), 96 Idaho 440, 530 P.2d 924, 933 (Bakes, J., concurring) ("[w]here an appropriative water right does not require a diversion to make it effective and beneficial, in the absence of a statute requiring a diversion there appears to be no practical reason why a diversion should be required"). * * *

Only two short months after our *Bean Lake* decision, the Nevada Supreme Court decided a nearly identical controversy. In State v. Morros, the Nevada Court considered whether "Nevada law absolutely requires a physical diversion of water to obtain a water right" in a controversy involving an inlake appropriation claim for recreation purposes. State v. Morros (1988), 104 Nev. 709, 766 P.2d 263, 265. After noting that the common law had evolved to allow appropriations for stock watering without a diversion when there was no practical need for a physical diversion, the Nevada Court validated an inlake appropriation for recreation purposes. *Morros,* 766 P.2d at 267. In protecting the inlake water right, the court held that just as the common law "conformed to the practical demands of stockwatering," so should it reflect the fact that "[d]iversions are not needed for and are incompatible with many recreational uses." *Morros,* 766 P.2d at 267. We find the Nevada Court's reasoning persuasive.

Any perception that Montana law required a diversion as a *sine qua non* to an appropriation arises from the fact that most traditional uses, such as agriculture and mining, had a practical need for a physical diversion. That necessity combined with the practice of using diversions as evidence of a user's intent to appropriate has undeniably led to confusion in our precedent, which likewise recognizes instream uses of water where no diversion is necessary for the beneficial use. See, e.g., Axtell v. M.S. Consulting, 1998 MT 64, 288 Mont. 150, 955 P.2d 1362; Donich v. Johnson (1926), 77 Mont. 229, 250 P. 963; Montana Coalition, 210 Mont. at 44, 682 P.2d at 166; and *Greely,* 219 Mont. at 91, 712 P.2d at 763. Given Montana's long history of beneficially using water for purposes of agriculture, mining, cattle and sheep ranching, logging, railroading, fishing and recreation, we resolve the confusion in favor of the *Axtell, Donich, Montana Coalition* and *Greely* line of authority and hold that the doctrine of prior appropriation does not require a physical diversion of water where no diversion is necessary to put the water to a beneficial use. Thus, instream/inlake appropriations of water for beneficial uses may be valid when the purpose (e.g., stock-watering, fish, wildlife and recreation) does not require a diversion.

Because beneficial use rather than diversion is the touchstone of the prior appropriation doctrine; because Montana has long recognized as beneficial the use of water for fish, wildlife and recreation; and because Montana has validated non-diversionary appropriations, we now hold that Montana law prior to 1973 did not absolutely require a diversion for a valid appropriation of water. * * *

Notes

1. **Elements of appropriation.** The "common law" elements—intent, notice, diversion, and beneficial use—listed in the principal case are typical of the physical acts used by many pioneer courts to define an appropriation. However, legislation regulating the appropriation process began to be adopted at a fairly early stage in the development of the law of appropriation, and today the appropriation and use of water is subject to extensive statutory regulation. A central feature of such regulation in most states is an administrative permit system. Under this system, a government issued permit is required in order to make an appropriation. The common law elements remain relevant, but the practical importance of some of them has been greatly diminished by the permit system.

The descriptive parameters of an appropriative right, as distinct, from the elements necessary to its creation, typically include the source of supply (e.g., a named stream or river), the point of diversion, the place of use, the purpose of use (e.g., irrigation, domestic use, municipal use), the quantity of water which can be taken, specified by rate of flow (e.g., cubic feet per second) or volume (e.g., acre-feet) or both, and the priority date. Modern appropriative rights are often subjected to additional terms or limitations which are usually imposed to protect the "public interest" or the environment. (See, Chapter 2, Section 3C (Public Interest)). The point of diversion and the place and purpose of use of a right can generally be changed, subject to certain limitations and pursuant to specified procedures. (See Chapter 2, Section 5 (Transfer)).

2. **Defining "diversion."** A dam alone, which caused overflow of a meadow without the aid of ditches, was held sufficient in Thomas v. Guiraud, 6 Colo. 530 (1883). The construction and maintenance of fish ladders, fish passage facilities, a barrier dam, and a fish trap were recognized as a diversion in In re Dearborn Drainage Area, 766 P.2d 228, 232 (Mont. 1988). A so-called "nature dam" designed solely to return a stream to its "historic" channel to preserve the recreational and environmental benefits of flowing water was held to be a diversion in City of Thornton v. City of Fort Collins, 830 P.2d 915 (Colo. 1992). Colorado statutes authorize a "recreational in-channel diversion," defined as "the minimum stream flow as it is diverted, captured, or controlled, and placed to beneficial use between specific points defined by physical control structures * * * for a reasonable recreation experience in and on the water." Colo. Rev. Stat. §§ 37-92-103(7), (10.3).

3. **Early importance of a diversion.** Whether an actual diversion is essential to an appropriation was of some importance in the early days of the West when pioneers took advantage of natural conditions. Nevada, New Mexico, and Utah held that reaping the benefits of natural overflow and percolation irrigation was not an appropriation of the water. Walsh v. Wallace, 67 P. 914 (Nev. 1902); State ex rel. Reynolds v. Miranda, 493 P.2d 409 (N.M. 1972); Hardy v. Beaver County Irrigation Co., 234 P. 524 (Utah 1924). Oregon held that a water right was acquired by natural overflow in In re Silvies River, 237 P. 322 (Or. 1925), although the court suggested that as time passed the necessities of economy might require the appropriator to install a controlled system of diversion. Colorado codified this rule in its "meadow right" statute. See Broad Run Inv. Co. v. Duel & Snyder Improvement Co., 108 P. 755 (Colo. 1910). On the other hand, lack of diversion prevented an appropriation of water seeping from a reservoir, although benefits from subirrigation resulted. Lamont v. Riverside Irrigation Dist., 498 P.2d 1150 (Colo. 1972).

Where horses, cattle and sheep do their own diverting, stockwater appropriations have been upheld in Hunter v. United States, 388 F.2d 148 (9th Cir. 1967); England v. Alley Ong Hing, 459 P.2d 498 (Ariz. 1969); Stevenson v. Steele, 453 P.2d 819 (Idaho 1969); and Steptoe Live Stock Co. v. Gulley, 295 P. 772 (Nev. 1931). In Utah, the animals may drink but the owner obtains no protectable right. Adams v. Portage Irrigation Reservoir & Power Co., 72 P.2d 648 (Utah 1937).

4. **Constitutional claims that a diversion is required.** Several cases raising the diversion issue have involved statutes which expressly provided for "instream" appropriations. Opponents of the appropriations argued that the statutes were unconstitutional because they authorized appropriations having no physical diversions. The opponents cited state constitutional provisions protecting the right to appropriate water, a common feature in western constitutions, and argued that these provisions made a diversion a constitutional requirement of a valid appropriation. The constitutional challenges were rejected and the statutes were all upheld in all cases. See Colo. River Water Conservation Dist.. v. Colo. Water Conservation Bd., 594 P.2d 570 (Colo. 1979); Idaho Dep't of Parks v. Idaho Dep't of Water Admin., 530 P.2d 924 (Idaho 1974); Neb. Game & Parks Comm'n v. The 25 Corp., 463 N.W.2d 591 (Neb. 1990).

5. **Instream appropriation in California.** Two California Courts of Appeal ruled that without a diversion no appropriation of instream flows could be made for fishery purposes. Cal. Trout, Inc. v. State Water Res. Control Bd., 153 Cal. Rptr. 672 (Ct. App. 1979); Fullerton v. State Water Res. Control Bd., 153 Cal. Rptr. 518 (Ct. App. 1979). However, a statute enacted in 1991 allows existing water rights to be changed to environmental uses "whether or not the proposed use involves a diversion of water." Cal. Water Code § 1707.

6. **Intent and notice.** The requirements of intent and notice are seldom an issue today because water rights in most states are initiated by filing an application for a permit accompanied by substantial engineering work. Perhaps clear proof that the application was filed only with intent to establish a paper claim could lead to its rejection. Compare the early case of Power v. Switzer, 55 P. 32 (Mont. 1898), where the turning of Uncle George's Creek out of its banks for no apparent purpose was held not to constitute an appropriation. Intent and notice can also be issues where pre-permit law rights are being adjudicated for the first time, as in the principal case.

In Colorado, which has no permit law, intent and notice are still important. An overt act sufficient to manifest intent and provide notice to interested persons of the proposed demand upon the water supply is sufficient to initiate a water right. This often takes the form of a survey of the land. However, in City of Aspen v. Colorado River Water Conservation District, 696 P.2d 758 (Colo. 1985), the court held that acts "on the land" were not required, reversing its earlier position on this point. In In re the Applications for Water Rights of the Upper Gunnison River Water Conservancy District, 838 P.2d 840 (Colo. 1992), the court held that acts of negotiating and executing a contract relating to reservoir operations were sufficient to manifest intent and provide notice. Some of the uncertainty regarding intent and notice has been removed by present Colorado appropriation procedures, discussed supra p. 124, Note 6, authorizing a prospective appropriator to file an application for a "conditional decree" with a "water court." An application for a conditional decree, accompanied by some other "substantial step" toward appropriation, satisfies the intent and notice requirements. In re Vought, 76 P.3d 906 (Colo. 2003).

B. Beneficial Use

IDAHO DEPARTMENT OF PARKS v. IDAHO DEPARTMENT OF WATER ADMINISTRATION

Supreme Court of Idaho, 1974
96 Idaho 440, 530 P.2d 924

SHEPARD, CHIEF JUSTICE. * * * In 1971 the Idaho Legislature enacted I. C. § 67-4307. In essence the statute directs the Department of Parks of the State of Idaho to appropriate in trust for the people of Idaho certain unappropriated natural waters of the Malad Canyon in Gooding County, Idaho. Additionally, it declares (1) that the preservation of the waters for scenic beauty and recreation uses is a beneficial use of water; (2) that the public use of those waters is of greater priority than any other use save domestic consumption, and (3) that the unappropriated state land located between the highwater marks on either bank of these waters is to be used and preserved in its present condition as a recreational site for the people of Idaho. * * *

Pursuant to the statute the Idaho Department of Parks filed an application for a permit to appropriate the waters specified by the statute. The waters in question arise in part at least from springs in the canyon and are natural waters. There appears no argument but that there is unappropriated water available for appropriation. That application was protested by the Idaho Water Users Association, Twin Falls Canal Company, and North Side Canal Company under the provisions of I.C. § 42-203. Those parties are cross-appellants herein and are hereafter designated "Water Users." * * *

The Water Users * * * assert error in the trial court's determination that the preservation of aesthetic values and recreational opportunities for the citizens of this state is a beneficial use in the sense that they will support an appropriative water right under the Idaho Constitution. The foundation of the Water Users' argument is that the five uses specified in article 15, section 3 of the Constitution, i. e., domestic, agriculture, mining, manufacturing and power are exclusive and thus are the only uses that are cognizable beneficial uses under our Constitution. We reject that argument.

We find no support for the position of the Water Users in the discussions reported in II Idaho Constitutional Convention, Proceedings and Debate 1889 (1912), as pertaining to article 15, section 3. It appears that insofar as particular uses were mentioned in the debates, discussion was confined to the establishment of preferences for certain uses over others under certain circumstances. Such establishment of preferences appears to be a common feature of water law in the west. See 1 Wells A. Hutchins, Water Rights Laws in the Nineteen Western States, supra. While it is well established in western water law that an appropriation of water must be made for a "beneficial use," nevertheless in Idaho at least the generic term "beneficial use" has never been judicially or statutorily defined. Our research does not disclose any case in which any court has attempted to define the term "beneficial use." Comment, Water Appropriation for Recreation, 1 Land and Water Law Review 209, 210 (1966).

Consideration of the statute in question herein indicates clearly that the legislature has declared that "[t]he preservation of water in the area described for its scenic beauty and recreational purposes necessary and desirable for all citizens of the state * * * is hereby declared to be a beneficial use of such water." We note that numerous other western states have recognized through legislation that utilization of water for scenic or recreational purposes is a beneficial use. 1 Wells A. Hutchins, Water Rights Laws in the Nineteen Western States, ch. 8, pp. 542 (1971). Such legislation in other states carries no binding effect on this court but, in the absence of persuasive case law to the contrary, it would appear to indicate that the use of water for providing recreational and aesthetic pleasure represents an emerging recognition in this and other states of social values and benefits from the use of water. See Final Report to the President and to the Congress of the United States by the National Water Commission, Ch. 7, sec. E, p. 271 et seq. (1973). The statute in question herein recognizes aesthetic and recreational values and benefits which will accrue to the people of the state in respect to the waters of Malad Canyon. We find no basis upon which to disturb that declaration of the legislature that in this instance those values and benefits constitute "beneficial uses." The decision of the district court upon this issue is affirmed. * * *

BAKES, JUSTICE (concurring specially). * * * Article 15 of the Idaho Constitution does not concern itself with abstract notions such as the relationship between the citizenry and their government, but instead concerns itself with the very practical question of water rights. I think we should look to very practical considerations in attempting to construe it. Prior to the time that the Constitution was adopted there were a number of common uses of water which were neither domestic, mining, agricultural nor manufacturing. A community would store water in a tank for use in fighting fires. The operator of a livery stable or a stockyard would water the stock kept there. Logging operations used water both to transport logs and for storage in mill ponds. Communities would use water wagons to settle dust on their dirt streets. The railroad used water for its steam engines and other uses related to the operation of the railroad. All of these uses were undoubtedly considered beneficial, but none of them were domestic, mining, agricultural or manufacturing. I do not believe that by adopting Article 15, § 3, of the Idaho Constitution that it was intended that uses such as these could no longer be considered beneficial uses. On the contrary, the universal expectation must have been that such uses could continue and could be the subject of an appropriation. Many of those uses still continue today, and the changing needs of our society are generating new uses for water which are neither domestic, agricultural, mining nor manufacturing. As an example, many privately owned public swimming pools or health facilities have applied for and received licenses to drill their own wells to supply their water needs. Natural hot water springs have been extensively developed into health resorts, e.g., Lava Hot Springs, upon the assumption that they have obtained a valid right to the use of the water in their facilities. Such uses, could not be considered as domestic, mining, agricultural or manufacturing as used in Article 15, § 3, without unduly broadening the definitions of the terms, yet such uses are no doubt beneficial from a societal point of view in that they contribute to the general welfare of the citizenry; and unless a valid water right could be obtained for such a use, not only would society suffer by the loss of such uses, but a great deal of capital which has been invested in reliance upon the validity of a right to such a use for water would be in jeopardy. I therefore conclude that uses other than those enumerated in Article 15, § 3, can be beneficial uses. * * *

With the exception of those uses elevated to beneficial status by Article 15, § 3, of the Constitution, the concept of what is or is not a beneficial use must necessarily change with changing conditions. For example, if we were now presented with a question of whether or not using water to operate a public swimming pool, a fountain, or to flood a tract to provide ice for a skating rink were beneficial uses, a good argument could be presented that such uses, although not domestic, mining, agricultural or manufacturing uses, were nevertheless beneficial. But we cannot say that such uses will always be beneficial because conditions might so change that these uses would be an unjustifiable use of water needed for other purposes. The notion of beneficiality of use must include a requirement of reasonableness. With the exception of the uses implicitly declared to be beneficial by Article 15, § 3, there is always a possibility that other uses beneficial in one era will not be in another and vice versa. * * *

MCFADDEN, JUSTICE (dissenting). * * * It is beyond dispute that scenic beauty and recreation are both of vital importance to modern day life in Idaho. But this does not ipso facto mean the state has the right to promote these beneficial ends by withdrawing waters from appropriation, given the guarantee contained in the Idaho Constitution. I note, however, that the effect of a proposed appropriation upon scenic beauty and recreation can and should be considered in determining whether the use contemplated is "beneficial" within the meaning of the Constitution. Comment, Water Appropriation for Recreation, 1 Land & Water L.Rev. 209, 221 (1966). In other words, where the benefits of a proposed use are outweighed by the attendant detriment to scenic beauty and recreation, the use is not a "beneficial use," and the application for a permit to appropriate public waters for that use should be denied. As always, the question of beneficial use must be determined on a case by case basis, since the benefits of a particular proposed appropriation may outweigh the detriment to recreation and scenic beauty. Whether a use of water is "beneficial" is a question of fact to be resolved upon a consideration of the circumstances present in a particular case. * * *

In conclusion, although I believe that recreation and scenic beauty can and should be taken into consideration on a case by case basis, they cannot be used as an excuse to deny all future appropriation of water for other purposes, at least until the Constitution is amended.

Notes

1. **A core principle.** Beneficial use is a core principle of the appropriation doctrine; many doctrinal rules are refinements or corollaries of the concept. The importance of beneficial use finds expression in judicial opinions and in statutes in many appropriation states. See, e.g., *In re Missouri River*, supra p. 24 referring to beneficial use as the "touchstone" of appropriation and citing with approval a statement by the Colorado Supreme Court that application to beneficial use is the "true test" of appropriation); Ariz. Rev. Stat. § 45-141 (stating that "[b]eneficial use shall be the basis, measure and limit to the use of water"). See also N.M. Const. art. XVI, § 3; Nev. Rev. Stat. 533.035; N.M. Stat. Ann. § 72-1-2; N.D. Cent. Code § 61-04-01.2; S.D. Codified Laws § 46-1-8; Wyo. Stat. Ann. § 41-3-101.

2. **Instream appropriations.** Like Idaho, a number of other states have enacted detailed programs which expressly authorize and regulate instream appropriations. See, e.g., Colo. Rev. Stat. § 37-92-102(3); Neb. Rev. Stat. §§ 46-2,107 et seq.; Or. Rev. Stat. §§ 537.332-.356; Wyo. Stat. Ann. §§ 41-3-1001 to -1014. Instream appropriations have also been recognized in states without express programs. See State v. Morros, 766 P.2d 263 (Nev. 1988); DeKay v. United States Fish & Wildlife Serv., 524 N.W.2d 855 (S.D. 1994). In *Morros*, the court confirmed an instream appropriation for recreation and

fishery purposes by the United States Bureau of Land Management. The court found statutory authorization for an "in situ" appropriation in a 1969 statute recognizing recreation as a beneficial use. In *DeKay,* the court approved an appropriation by the United States Fish and Wildlife Service of the natural flow of six springs to maintain marshes, sloughs, and wet meadows in a wildlife refuge, citing a statute which states that all streams are "assigned beneficial uses of irrigation and wildlife propagation and stock watering."

3. **Private instream appropriations.** Many states restrict instream appropriations to designated public agencies. See, e.g., Colo. Rev. Stat. §37-92-102(3); Neb. Rev. Stat. § 46-2,108; Wyo. Stat. Ann. § 41-3-1002. Should private parties be permitted to make instream appropriations? Consider the following views:

"[I]nstream uses differ from water rights applied to the more traditional beneficial uses in that the public is the real beneficiary of the dedication. * * * Because the benefits of instream uses inevitably redound to the public generally rather than the claimant, only public rather than private bodies should be permitted to claim water for instream uses." A. Dan Tarlock, The Recognition of Instream Flow Rights: "New" Public Western Water Rights, 25 Rocky Mtn. Min. L. Inst. 24-1, 24-3 (1979).

"[T]he benefits [of privately held instream rights] for streamflows could be significant. * * * Parties who have invested significant sums in private rights are likely to be vigilant in seeing that their rights are protected. As these parties pressure watermasters to enforce private instream rights, state instream rights might be better enforced as well. * * * Private parties also can provide an important source of additional funds to supplement state efforts to maintain adequate instream flows for fish. Private parties operating in the free market can use their funds to acquire senior rights on important streams and tributaries, without harming the rights of other users." Jack Sterne, Instream Rights and Invisible Hands: Prospects for Private Instream Rights in the Northwest, 27 Envtl. L. 203, 232-33 (1997).

4. **Transfers to instream use.** In California, instream appropriations are not allowed. See supra p. 29, Note 5. At the same time, Cal. Water Code § 1707(a) states that "[a]ny person entitled to the use of water, whether based upon an appropriative, riparian, or other right, may petition the board pursuant to this chapter * * * for a change for purposes of preserving or enhancing wetlands habitat, fish and wildlife resources, or recreation in, or on, the water." Consider also Or. Rev. Stat. §§ 537.336 and 537.341, limiting new instream appropriations to state agencies, and § 537.348, authorizing private parties to convert existing appropriations to instream rights.

Does it make sense to restrict new instream appropriations but allow transfers of existing rights to instream purposes? The late Frank J. Trelease suggested that one should "think land" when considering policy issues related to water. Frank J. Trelease, The Model Water Code, the Wise Administrator, and the Goddam Bureaucrat, 14 Nat. Resources J. 207 (1974). In the Nineteenth Century and the early part of the Twentieth Century, the United States gave large amounts of public land to private parties—primarily homesteaders, miners, and railroad companies. Much like the appropriation doctrine requirement of beneficial use, private parties were required to invest substantial resources in the development of such land before receiving title. Federal law, however, did not give public land to private parties for public parks, wildlife refuges, and similar reserves, although homesteaders, miners, and railroad companies were not prohibited from dedicating land to such purposes once title had been received from the federal government. Did it make sense to give land to those who would develop it economically but not to those who would preserve it or was this just another example of a bias in favor of consumption over preservation?

5. **Relinquishment of instream rights.** In Aspen Wilderness Workshop v. Colorado Water Conservation Board, 901 P.2d 1251 (Colo. 1995), the court held that the Colorado Water Conservation Board had no authority to unilaterally decrease an instream appropriation. In so holding, the court noted that, unlike other appropriators, the board acts on behalf of the people of the state in making instream appropriations and, thus, has "a unique statutory fiduciary duty to protect the public in the administration of its water rights decreed to preserve the natural environment." Shortly thereafter, the Colorado legislature amended Colorado's instream appropriation statutes to give such authority to the board. Colo. Rev. Stat. § 37-92-102(4)(a). However, a board decision to decrease an instream appropriation must be preceded by public notice and public hearings. The decision is also subject to judicial review to determine that "the decreed appropriation as decreased will preserve the natural environment to a reasonable degree." Id. § 37-92-102(4)(b).

WASHINGTON DEPARTMENT OF ECOLOGY v. GRIMES

Supreme Court of Washington, 1993.
121 Wash.2d 459, 852 P.2d 1044.

SMITH, JUSTICE. This matter is before the court upon direct review after we accepted certification from the Court of Appeals, Division Three, pursuant to RCW 2.06.030(d), raising the question of the legal definition of "reasonable use" of water as an element of "beneficial use" under the Water Code of 1917, RCW 90.03, the Water Resources Act of 1971, RCW 90.54, and other related statutes. Appellants Clarence E. and Peggy V. Grimes (Grimeses) appeal from a decree adjudicating water rights pursuant to RCW 90.03.200 entered by the Pend Oreille County Superior Court. Respondents are Leonard B. and Elsie E. Magart and the State of Washington Department of Ecology (Ecology). We affirm the Superior Court. * * *

The Grimeses submitted five claims for water rights, only the first of which is at issue in this appeal. This claim was for the use of waters for domestic supply, irrigation and recreational purposes. The Grimeses requested an instantaneous flow rate of 3 cubic feet per second (c.f.s.) for irrigation purposes, and a storage right of 1,520 acre feet of water in the Marshall Lake reservoir. The referee recommended that this claim be confirmed, but limited it to an instantaneous flow of 1.5 c.f.s. during irrigation season, and a storage right of 183 acre feet plus 737 acre feet for evaporative loss, for a total storage right of 920 acre feet. * * *

On January 5, 1990, after hearing testimony on the Grimeses' exceptions, the Superior Court entered its "Decree Adjudicating Water Rights Pursuant to RCW 90.03.200." The decree approved the "Report of Referee." * * * The appellants challenge the consideration of evidence by the referee and the trial court, as well as application of the law relating to appropriative water rights. * * *

The Doctrine of Prior Appropriation

The law of prior appropriation was established in this state by the Territorial Legislature in 1873 and recognized by this court in 1897. This court in Neubert v. Yakima-Tieton Irrig. Dist.[32] said * * *:

> The key to determining the extent of plaintiffs' vested water rights is the concept of "beneficial use" * * * An appropriated water right is established and maintained by the purposeful application of a given quantity of water to a beneficial use upon the land. * * *

"Beneficial use" is a term of art in water law, and encompasses two principal elements of a water right. First, it refers to the purposes, or type of activities, for which water may be used. Use of water for the purposes of irrigated agriculture is a beneficial use. The Grimeses' use of water to irrigate alfalfa fields is not at issue in this case.

Second, beneficial use determines the measure of a water right. The owner of a water right is entitled to the amount of water necessary for the purpose to which it has been put, provided that purpose constitutes a beneficial use. To determine the amount of water necessary for a beneficial use, courts have developed the principle of "reasonable use." Reasonable use of water is determined by analysis of the factors of water duty and waste. * * *

We first consider the evidence used by the referee in establishing the factors of water duty and waste. We then consider the test of "reasonable efficiency" employed by the referee, and adopted by the Superior Court, to evaluate these factors.

Water Duty

"[Water duty is] that measure of water, which, by careful management and use, without wastage, is reasonably required to be applied to any given tract of land for such period of time as may be adequate to produce therefrom a maximum amount of such crops as ordinarily are grown thereon. It is not a hard and fast unit of measurement, but is variable according to conditions."[40]

---

32. 117 Wash.2d 232, 237, 814 P.2d 199 (1991).

40. In re Steffens, 756 P.2d 1002, 1005-06 (Colo.1988) (quoting Farmers Highline Canal & Reservoir Co. v. Golden, 129 Colo. 575, 272 P.2d 629 (1954)); see In re Ahtanum Creek, 139 Wash. 84, 96, 245 P. 758 (1926).

The referee based his determination of the volume of water necessary for irrigation in the Marshall Lake basin on a Washington State University Research Bulletin entitled "Irrigation Requirements for Washington—Estimates and Methodology" (Irrigation Report), and on the expert testimony of Jim Lyerla, the District Supervisor for seven Eastern Washington counties, including Pend Oreille County, in the Water Resources Program of the Department of Ecology. Mr. Lyerla testified that as a part of his work in assigning water quantities to new water permittees, he relied on the Irrigation Report to determine the "water duty" for a proposed use of water. The Irrigation Report provides information for water requirements for specific crops, given in inches per acre per irrigation season, in 40 locations around the state, including Newport, Washington, 5 miles south of Marshall Lake.

Based on the testimony of Mr. Lyerla and the Irrigation Report, the referee determined that an irrigated alfalfa crop grown in the Marshall Lake area requires 21 inches or 1.75 acre feet of water per acre during the irrigation season. The referee then applied an efficiency factor and increased this water duty to 2.5 acre feet per acre per year. The referee found this water duty to be "approximately commensurate with the duty utilized by the Department of Ecology in its quantity allocations in this geographic area under the water right permit system."

Because water rights are characterized in both total yearly allowance and instantaneous flow, the referee also established the maximum rate of diversion at 0.0166 c.f.s. per acre under irrigation. The referee first calculated a standard flow of 1 c.f.s. of water per 60 acres as a reasonable instantaneous flow for alfalfa irrigation in the Marshall Lake basin. In considering the Grimeses' claim, he determined that the Grimeses were entitled to sufficient flow to irrigate 73 acres, or a minimum of 1.21 c.f.s. He then calculated in an efficiency factor to increase this flow by 25 percent and awarded the Grimeses an instantaneous flow of 1.5 c.f.s. * * *

Waste

From an early date, courts announced the rule that no appropriation of water was valid where the water simply went to waste. Those courts held that the appropriator who diverted more than was needed for the appropriator's actual requirements and allowed the excess to go to waste acquired no right to the excess. A particular use must not only be of benefit to the appropriator, but it must also be a reasonable and economical use of the water in view of other present and future demands upon the source of supply. The difference between absolute waste and economical use has been said to be one of degree only.

Appellant Clarence E. Grimes acknowledged in his testimony that his existing irrigation system required a water flow of up to 3 cubic feet per second in order to deliver 1 cubic foot per second to the field, and that this system was highly inefficient, causing one-half to two-thirds loss of water. * * * While an appropriator's use of water must be reasonably efficient, absolute efficiency is not required. * * * Relying on a standard efficiency factor for irrigation sprinkler systems found in the irrigation report, [the referee] confirmed in the Grimeses a water right with one-fourth conveyance loss for a total of 1.5 cubic feet per second. * * *

The Reasonable Efficiency Test

In limiting the Grimeses' vested water right, the referee balanced several factors, including the water duty for the geographical area and crop under irrigation, the claimants' actual diversion, and sound irrigation practices. In his report, the referee described his method of calculating the Grimeses' water right as a "reasonable efficiency" test. * * *

Decisions of courts throughout the western states provide a basis for defining "reasonable efficiency" with respect to irrigation practices. While customary irrigation practices common to the locality are a factor for consideration, they do not justify waste of water. As this court stated in a case predating the Water Code of 1917:

> [W]hen rights in such an important element as water is in the arid regions are to be measured by the courts, we cannot lay down a rule that would give to the user an arbitrary right to use water at will. [An irrigator's] rights are to be measured by his necessities * * * and not by any fanciful notion of his own. * * * [C]ustom can fix the manner of use of water for irrigation only when it is founded on necessity * * * [and] an irrigator is entitled to use only so much as he can put to a beneficial use, for the public policy of the people of the United States will not tolerate waste of water in the arid regions.[66]

Local custom and the relative efficiency of irrigation systems in common use are important elements, but must be considered in connection with other statutorily mandated factors, such as the costs and benefits of improvements to irrigation systems, including the use of public and private funds to facilitate improvements. * * * The referee alluded to a test incorporating factors that consider impacts to the water source and its flora and fauna. While consideration of these impacts is consonant with the State's obligations under RCW 90.03.005 and 90.54.010(1)(a) and (2), these factors cannot operate to impair existing water rights.

There is some confusion in the record as to the legal standard used by the referee in determining beneficial use. * * * There is no discussion in the original report of any "reasonable efficiency" test. However, the referee rendered a supplemental report in response to exceptions taken by the Grimeses. * * * [I]n a footnote the referee set forth a detailed "test of reasonable efficiency" which he purportedly used in determining beneficial use. That "test" is stated as follows:

> (1) [C]ustomary delivery and application practices in the area, (2) technology and "practices" improvements feasible and available to reduce water consumptions and financial needs associated with implementation thereof, and (3) impacts of improvements of existing facilities and practices, if

66. Shafford v. White Bluffs Land & Irrig. Co., 63 Wash. 10, 13-16, 114 P. 883 (1911).

initiated, upon (a) the water source from which the diversion takes place, (b) the existing flora and fauna within the area of diversion, conveyance and actual uses, (c) other water rights from said water source, and (d) other water users on other water sources.

There is nothing in the record to support the referee's statement that he employed the reasonable efficiency test. Nowhere in the record does he discuss application of the elements of the so-called "test." If he had in fact applied the "test," it would be necessary for this court to reverse and remand. That test is without statutory authorization in an adjudication proceeding which relates exclusively to confirmation of water rights established or created under "other provisions of state law or under federal laws."

Adjudication proceedings cannot be used "to lessen, enlarge, or modify the existing rights of any riparian owner, or any existing right acquired by appropriation, or otherwise." The suggested test would be contrary to the vested rights of water users. "It has long been settled in this state that property owners have a vested interest in their water rights to the extent that the water is beneficially used on the land." Included in the vested rights is the right to diversion, delivery and application "according to the usual methods of artificial irrigation employed in the vicinity where such land is situated."[75] The Legislature sets a standard clearly contradictory to the suggested test in RCW 90.03.040, which relates to eminent domain over water rights. The test is contrary also to long established principles of Western water law.

While we reject use of the specific test suggested by the referee, we affirm because (1) there is no indication in the record that he in fact applied the factors stated in the "test," and (2) he applied the actual beneficial use made by Grimes, taking into account the actual needs and use and the methods of delivery and application in the vicinity. * * *

The Takings Argument

Appellants Grimes argue that diminishment of their prior appropriation in any way is a "taking" of their property right for which they must be compensated or have the decision of the trial court set aside. A vested water right is a type of private property that is subject to the Fifth Amendment prohibition on takings without just compensation. Nevertheless, the concept of "beneficial use," as developed in the common law and as described earlier in this opinion, operates as a permissible limitation on water rights. * * *

Notes

1. **Duty of water.** Contrary to the suggestion in the principal case, in many states "duty" is a hard and fast measure. See, e.g, Idaho Code § 42-202 (1 c.f.s. for 50 acres); Neb. Rev. Stat. § 46-231; S.D. Codified Laws § 46-5-6 (limiting appropriations for irrigation to 1 c.f.s. for 70 acres and 3 acre-feet per acre per year); Wyo. Stat. Ann. § 41-4-317 (1 c.f.s. for 70 acres); see also Cal. Water Code § 1004 (2 ½ acre-feet per acre per year for the irrigation of uncultivated areas not devoted to cultivated crops). Nevada and New Mexico have repealed their former

---

75. RCW 90.03.040

fixed statutory limitations and have replaced them with flexible standards. Nev. Rev. Stat. 533.070; N.M. Stat. Ann. § 72-5-18. In Kansas, which straddles the boundary between arid and humid zones, the administrative allowance is 2 acre-feet per year in the western section, 1 ½ in the central part, and 1 near the eastern boundary. Robert V. Smrha, Problems of Water Administration in Kansas, 5 Kan. L. Rev. 649, 655 (1957).

2. **Reservoirs.** Reservoirs require special rules. Since the purpose of constructing large reservoirs is to balance out the lean and the fat years, the courts have been liberal in allowing "carryover storage." E. Side Canal & Irrigation Co. v. United States, 76 F. Supp. 836 (Ct. Cl. 1948); Fed. Land Bank v. Morris, 116 P.2d 1007 (Mont. 1941). In Idaho, storage rights for irrigation are limited to 5 acre feet per year. Idaho Code § 42-202. By administrative practice in California, storage in a reservoir in any year is usually limited to the maximum amount stored during the five-year period prior to the issuance of a license.

In most states the quantity which can be stored during a particular water year is governed by the capacity of the reservoir—what it will hold as a result of a single filling, not what it can be made to hold by successive fillings and emptyings. Windsor Reservoir & Canal Co. v. Lake Supply Ditch Co., 98 P. 729 (Colo. 1908). The one-filling rule is usually applied so that if at the beginning of a particular "water year" a reservoir is partly full with carryover storage, only the balance needed to fill it can be taken during that year.

The one-filling rule reflects irrigation practices. Water is usually stored in irrigation reservoirs during the winter or spring, when demand is low and/or flows are high, and is later released to irrigate crops during late summer, when flows are low and demand is high. Thus, the typical irrigation reservoir fills only once each year. If such a reservoir were subsequently allowed to fill and empty several times during the same year under its original priority, the burden on the river would be substantially increased, often to the detriment of parties holding junior rights. The one-filling rule prevents this, and, under such circumstances, the rule works well and fairly. However, the rule can require unnecessary construction of excess storage capacity if the demand for water from the reservoir is constant throughout the year, as for a city or industry, since it prevents the use of a small regulating facility that can be filled, partially drained and refilled to take full advantage of predictable river fluctuations. See Wheatland Irrigation Dist. v. Pioneer Canal Co., 464 P.2d 533 (Wyo. 1970).

In City of Denver v. Northern Colorado Water Conservancy District, 276 P.2d 992 (Colo. 1954), the one-filling rule, added to the pioneer rule that the capacity of the ditch is the top measure of a water right, was used to block an imaginative feat of modern engineering. Denver filed a map and statement showing a diversion from the Blue River of 1600 cubic feet of water per second through a tunnel under the continental divide. This quantity of water was available only during short periods of spring run-off. Later, Denver proposed to save a major portion of construction costs by accumulating water in Dillion Reservoir at the rate of 1600 second feet when that quantity was available and carrying it away through a tunnel with a capacity of 788 second feet; i.e., Denver intended to use Dillion Reservoir for temporary storage until the accumulated water could be drained away by the smaller tunnel. Denver already had a late priority for storage for the full capacity of Dillon Reservoir. "One cannot add water to a full cup, and may not have a second decree for water from the same source to be held at the same time in the same reservoir to which a decree has already been ordered to its full capacity. Further, the rule is elementary that the first essential of an appropriation is the actual diversion of the water with intent to apply to a beneficial use. * * * Water can be actually diverted only by taking it from the stream. The amount so diverted is necessarily limited to the capacity of the ditch or tunnel through which diversion is made. * * * Where water is stored in a channel reservoir, a ditch headed in such reservoir has no right by virtue of direct use decree to deplete such storage. * * * " Id. at 998-99.

Three dissenting judges pointed out that with its junior priority the reservoir, as a practical matter, would never be full when the proposed diversion of 1600 second feet was being made. "Thus the illustration of the 'full cup' fails to hold water. * * * Unquestionably the city of Denver would have the right to appropriate the 1600 cubic feet per second of water by the construction of a tunnel of that capacity. This objective could be obtained with no grounds for opposition by the expenditure of an additional $10,000,000 of the peoples' money. If the same result can be obtained by the substitution of a mechanical operational equivalent to the larger tunnel I am at a loss to understand why the increased burden on the taxpayers should be required. * * * In all normal operations the Dillon Dam would serve two functions: (1) as a headworks for diverting Denver's direct appropriation through the tunnel; and (2) for catching an occasional flood in the late summer. * * * There is no reason why the Dillon Dam cannot fulfill in succession both the diverting and the storage functions." Id. at 1021-22.

The Colorado Supreme Court revisited Dillon Reservoir in 1998 in City of Grand Junction v. City of Denver, 960 P.2d 675 (Colo. 1998). In 1987, Denver sought a refill right for Dillon Reservoir to replace water lost through seepage, evaporation, and releases required by flood control obligations. Grand Junction, which has a junior priority to water from the Blue River, objected, citing a provision of the Blue River Decree which states that "as against junior appropriators * * * only one filling [of Dillon Reservoir] shall be allowed each year." Id. at 680.

Despite this provision, the Colorado Supreme Court affirmed a lower court decree awarding Denver refill rights with a 1987 priority. The court held that the Blue River Decree only prohibited Denver from filling Dillon Reservoir more than once under the priority awarded it in that decree. Thus, the court said, Denver's request for new right with a 1987 priority was entirely consistent with the decree. In a footnote, the court said: "This provision [the one-fill provision in the Blue River Decree] is consistent with other 'one fill' limitations found in our case law. * * * '[T]he statute which provides for these decrees forbids the allowance of more than one filling on one priority in any one year.'" Id. at 683 n.6. The court also noted that the new refill right with a 1987 priority could not be exercised to the detriment of the 1946 priority right awarded Grand Junction in the Blue River Decree.

If a city can later obtain a right to refill a reservoir, why can't it obtain a refill right at the time it makes its original reservoir appropriation in those cases where it is efficient to successively fill, drain, and refill a reservoir several times during the same year? Would other parties who subsequently obtain junior rights be unfairly harmed by such a practice? Did the court overrule its earlier opinion sub silentio?

3. **Vested rights.** In *Grimes* the court stated that an appropriator has "vested rights * * * to diversion, delivery and application 'according to the usual methods of artificial irrigation employed in the vicinity where such land is situated.'" If the "usual methods" become more efficient over time, do an appropriator's rights "vest" in accordance with the "usual methods" on the date the right was initiated? On the date water was applied to beneficial use? On the date of adjudication? The court also noted that beneficial use "operates as a permissible limitation on water rights." As a result of the litigation in the principal case, the Grimeses were adjudicated rights to 1.5 c.f.s. If future improvements reduce the amount of water required for irrigation "according to the usual methods," can this figure be reduced? Justice Bakes, concurring in *Idaho Department of Parks*, supra p. 29, suggests that a use which is beneficial in one era may not be beneficial in another. Can the Grimeses' right be extinguished if their use—irrigation of alfalfa—ceases to be a beneficial use? Consider the following case.

IMPERIAL IRRIGATION DISTRICT v. STATE WATER RESOURCES CONTROL BOARD

California Court of Appeal, 1990.
225 Cal. App. 3d 548, 275 Cal. Rptr. 250.

FROEHLICH, ASSOCIATE JUSTICE. * * * In 1980 a private citizen requested the Department of Water Resources to investigate alleged misuse of water by IID [Imperial Irrigation District] which had resulted in a rise in the level of the Salton Sea, flooding the citizen's farmland. After an investigation, an initial conclusion of water waste, and unproductive communications with IID, the Department of Water Resources referred the matter to the Board for investigation and action. * * * On June 21, 1984, the Board issued its Decision Regarding Misuse of Water by Imperial Irrigation District, designated Decision 1600 (hereafter sometimes referred to as "Board Decision") which consisted of a 71-page review of the history of the proceedings, the evidence taken by the Board, the Board's findings and conclusions, and an order requiring certain action be taken by IID. * * *

[The trial] court undertook to review by writ of mandate the substance of Decision 1600. Using the independent judgment test (as directed by this court, ibid.), the court determined that the Board's findings were supported by the evidence, that its decision was "a reasonable and balanced directive for achieving compliance with Article X, Section 2," and that the writ should be denied. This appeal followed. * * *

As IID concedes in its brief, the essential facts of this case are not in dispute. The experts on any particular issue were never in complete agreement, but their differences were of degree, not kind. For instance, estimates of water lost through "canal spill" ranged from 53,000 to 135,000 acre feet per annum; and water lost through excessive "tailwater" ranged from 312,000 to 559,000 acre feet per annum. There was no dispute, however, that very large quantities of water in each case were being lost. The dispute is whether such loss (and this is but one example of such decisions made by the Board) was or was not reasonable. * * *

[The contentions of IID] are several, and receive different characterization in the briefs of appellant and respondents. Our effort to summarize the contentions results in the following outline of issues: * * * (b) Does the Board have power to interfere with vested water rights? * * *

IID's water rights * * * are the result of federal statute, U.S. Supreme Court decision, and a seven-party agreement allocating water among Southern California users. Water rights within the state of California traditionally were derived from riparian rights or entitlement based upon prior appropriation. (See historical discussion in United States v. State Water Resources Control Bd. (1986) 182 Cal.App.3d 82, 100-102, 227 Cal.Rptr. 161.) It is conceivable that IID's water rights, based as they are upon a unique blend of statutory and contractual origins, could be characterized as somehow more stable or securely vested than water rights from traditional sources. IID does not, however, make this claim. It simply contends that a right to use water, no matter how derived, once vested, becomes a property right which cannot be undermined without due compensation.

Illustrative of IID's broad contention is the following quote from United States v. State Water Resources Control Bd., supra, at page 101, 227 Cal.Rptr. 161: "It is * * * axiomatic that once rights to use water are acquired, they become vested property rights. As such, they cannot be infringed by others or taken by governmental action without due process and just compensation." The essence of IID's contention, therefore, is that the Board was without power to deprive IID of its discretionary power of determination of water use without providing compensation (which the Board admittedly has no power to provide).

As a preliminary matter we should note exactly what the Board did require of IID. * * * IID was required within a period of eight months to submit a plan for reservoir construction and to affirm its intent to construct one reservoir per year. Once a general plan of water conservation was achieved, IID was required to submit progress reports every six months "until the objectives have been achieved." The Board reserved jurisdiction to monitor IID progress and to "take such other action" as might be required to assure compliance with an approved plan. There can be no doubt that the Board's intrusion into IID's previously untrammeled administration of the use of water in its district was substantial. As often stated in water law cases, "what is meant by a water right is the right to use the water. * * *" (Id. at p. 100, 227 Cal.Rptr. 161.) While the Board's decision in no way interfered with IID's contractual and statutory entitlement to Colorado River water, it most certainly presaged an interference with IID's utilization of that water once it traversed the All- American Canal.

Our conclusion that the Board Decision substantially impacted the practical use and administration by IID of its water does not, however, result in our acceptance of IID's contention of unconstitutional interference with "vested" rights. Historic concepts of water "rights" in California were dramatically altered by the adoption in 1928 of the above referenced constitutional amendment. Our Supreme Court, in Gin S. Chow v. City of Santa Barbara (1933) 217 Cal. 673, 22 P.2d 5, acknowledged that the new provision altered previously vested rights. "As already observed the amendment purports only to regulate the use and enjoyment of a property right for the public benefit, for which reason the vested right theory cannot stand in the way of the operation of the amendment as a police measure. A vested right cannot be asserted against it because of conditions once obtaining. It has been long established that all property is held subject to the reasonable exercise of the police power and that constitutional provisions declaring that property shall not be taken without due process of law have no application in such cases."

The concept of the dimension of rights remaining to the water user after the constitutional amendment was fully developed in Joslin v. Marin Mun. Water Dist. (1967) 67 Cal.2d 132, 60 Cal.Rptr. 377, 429 P.2d 889. In that case a lower user attempted to enjoin upstream diversion by a municipal water company upon the contention that the downstream prior use for deposit of sand and gravel was a vested, protectible use. The Supreme Court held that simply because a use is beneficial it does not become "reasonable" under the constitution. Denying the plaintiff's assertion of compensability for its loss of water, the court focused on the nature of water rights after 1928. "While plaintiffs correctly argue that a property right cannot be taken or damaged without just compensation, they ignore the necessity of first establishing the legal existence of a compensable property interest. Such an interest consists in their right to the reasonable use of the flow of water. * * * [While a] vested right as now defined may not be destroyed or infringed upon without due process of law or without just compensation * * * [there is] no provision of law which authorizes an unreasonable use or endows such use with the quality of a legally protectible interest merely because it may be fortuitously beneficial to the lands involved." (Id. at pp. 143-144, 60 Cal.Rptr. 377, 429 P.2d 889; see also * * * National Audubon Society v. Superior Court (1983) 33 Cal.3d 419, 443, fn. 23, 189 Cal.Rptr. 346, 658 P.2d 709 ["After the effective date of the 1928 amendment, no one can acquire a vested right to the unreasonable use of water."])

Put simply, IID does not have the vested rights which it alleges. It has only vested rights to the "reasonable" use of water. It has no right to waste or misuse water. The interference by the Board with IID's misuse (this finding of fact by the Board being accepted for purposes of the present issue) does not constitute a transgression on a vested right. * * *

We note from IID's brief that it has "engaged for three decades in costly and critical litigation about its water rights." It asks that we reverse all the lengthy deliberations that have preceded our hearing and requests even again an "opportunity to more extensively brief the issue."

All things must end, even in the field of water law. It is time to recognize that this law is in flux and that its evolution has passed beyond traditional concepts of vested and immutable rights. In his review of our Supreme Court's recent water rights decision in In re Water of Hallett Creek Stream System (1988) 44 Cal.3d 448, 243 Cal.Rptr. 887, 749 P.2d 324, Professor Freyfogle explains that California is engaged in an evolving process of governmental redefinition of water rights. He concludes that "California has regained for the public much of the power to prescribe water use practices, to limit waste, and to sanction water transfers." He asserts that the concept that "water use entitlements are clearly and permanently defined," and are "neutral [and] rule-driven," is a pretense to be discarded. It is a fundamental truth, he writes, that "everything is in the process of changing or becoming" in water law.[5]

In affirming this specific instance of far-reaching change, imposed upon traditional uses by what some claim to be revolutionary exercise of adjudicatory power, we but recognize this evolutionary process, and urge reception and recognition of same upon those whose work in the practical administration of water distribution makes such change understandably difficult to accept.

Notes

1. **Contrary views?** In Enterprise Irrigation District v. Willis, 284 N.W. 326 (Neb. 1939), the court in dicta suggested that retroactive application of a "duty" statute to reduce the quantity of water that can be diverted would be an unconstitutional interference with vested rights. McDonald v. State of Montana, 722 P.2d 598 (Mont. 1986), involved Mont. Code Ann. § 85-2-234 which required that decrees adjudicating water rights state "the amount of water included in the right." Prior to 1973, water rights in Montana were limited only by rate of flow. The court first held that pre-1973 rights could be limited by volume as well as rate of flow but then seemingly subverted this holding by stating that the amount required for beneficial use, not the volume limit, will control in "rare" cases where the volume specified is insufficient to meet the requirements of beneficial use. Are these cases inconsistent with the principal case? In considering the question, note that the Board did not interfere with IID's contractual or statutory entitlements to water, but rather with the way the water was used.

2. **Relationship to beneficial use.** To what extent is the court's decision dependent on article X, section 2 of the California Constitution which prohibits "waste or unreasonable use or unreasonable method of use of water"? What is the relationship between "reasonable use" and "beneficial use"? In an omitted part of the opinion, IID argued that even the excess water introduced into the district was used for beneficial purposes such as power generation and prevention of excess salinization of the Salton Sea. The court responded:

"IID is also in error in contending that all 'beneficial' uses are 'reasonable.' * * * The fact that a diversion of water may be for a purpose 'beneficial' in some respects (as for desalinization of lakes or generation of electric power) does not make such use 'reasonable' when compared with demands, or even future demands, for more important uses." 275 Cal. Rptr. at 265-66.

Assume that a California farmer is using no more water than is necessary to grow crops. Could the Board, nevertheless, find that the farmer's use was "unreasonable" because there was a more important or more valuable use for the water? See footnote 28, infra p. 540; see also Brian E. Gray, "In Search of

---

5. Freyfogle, Context and Accommodation in Modern Property Law, 41 Stanford Law Review (1989) 1529, 1546-1547.

Bigfoot" The Common Law Origins of Article X, Section 2 of the California Constitution, 17 Hastings Const. L.Q. 225 (1988); Clifford W. Schultz & Gregory S. Weber, Changing Judicial Attitudes Towards Property Rights in California Water Resources: From Vested Rights to Utilitarian Reallocation, 19 Pac. L.J. 1031, 1086-93 (1988).

3. **Defining waste.** Water Policies for the Future, supra p. 3, Note 1, at 304-05: "Substantial savings can be made through improved efficiency in the use of water for irrigation. * * * For example, a statement submitted to the Commission by the Utah-Idaho Sugar Company at its public conference in Spokane indicates that Company achieved substantial reduction in water use when it switched in the early 1960's from gravity-flow irrigation to sprinkler irrigation on its Osgoode Project in Southeastern Idaho. The U-I Osgoode Project consists of approximately 6,000 acres of irrigated land and is not a federal reclamation project. Prior to the change to sprinkler irrigation, the Commission was told, the project had been 'water hungry.' After the change, which included squaring up fields and other modernizations, an additional 1,000 acres of land could be put under irrigation and the usage of water per acre for irrigation crops was cut in half."

A rancher in a high altitude, northern Idaho valley grows one crop of "wild hay" per year to supply winter feed for his cattle, drawing over 2 acre feet per acre in the short irrigating season, using "wild flood" irrigation methods. An equipment salesman tells him that with pumps and sprinklers he could grow the same or a slightly better crop with one-half the water. He does not buy the pumps and sprinklers. Is he wasting water? On the plains downstream from the rancher, the U-I Company could grow sugar beets of higher cash value than the hay grown by the rancher. Because of his early priority, however, the rancher gets the water. Is this waste?

If the irrigator's ditch is long or dug through porous soil, a considerable amount of water—sometimes called "carriage water"—may be lost by evaporation and seepage between the point where it is diverted and the place of use. In *Grimes*, supra p. 34, the referee added twenty-five percent for transportation losses. Is that a waste of water? The duty statutes cited supra p 38, Note 1 appear to make no allowance for carriage water. If a duty statute accurately reflects the minimum quantity of water required for irrigation, an irrigator whose ditch is long and porous will not be able to irrigate all of his land unless he can afford to line his ditch. Is that a waste of land? If he can use carriage water instead of concrete to get the full amount needed on his land, is it a waste of concrete to line the ditch?

4. **Defining waste—third party and environmental benefits.** Water Policies for the Future, supra p. 3, Note 1, at 305: "It must not be assumed, however, that all irrigation water in excess of consumptive use is lost to the system. In many cases, perhaps most cases, the water is returned to the stream as stream flow or serves to recharge ground water. Some excess water is needed in almost all irrigated areas to leach salts from the soil."

As the preceding quote suggests, one person's "waste" is sometimes another's source of supply. In addition, environmental amenities are often produced by inefficient uses of water. For example, a leaky earthen canal may increase stream flows or may create new wetlands; lining the canal may reclaim water previously lost to seepage, but may also damage the environment by decreasing the stream flows or drying up the wetlands. See, e.g., Protect the Historic Amador Waterways v. Amador Water Agency, 11 Cal. Rptr. 3d 104 (Ct.

App. 2004) (holding that an environmental impact report was deficient because it did not adequately assess the affect that replacing an earthen canal with a pipeline would have on late summer stream flows created by canal leakage); Oval Hinojosa-Huerta, et al, Andrade Mesa Wetlands, 42 Nat. Resources J. 899 (2002) (discussing the importance of large wetlands created by leakage from the All-American Canal, which parallels the California/Mexico border, and the damage to the wetlands that will result from lining a 23-mile section of the canal to reclaim approximately 70,000 acre-feet of water); see also J. Roman Calleros, The Impact on Mexico of the Lining of the All-American Canal, 31 Nat. Resources J. 829 (1991); Alfonso Cortez-Lara & Maria Rosa Garcia-Acevedo, The Lining of the All- American Canal: The Forgotten Voices, 40 Nat. Resources J. 261 (2000) (discussing the social and economic injury to Mexican farmers resulting from the elimination of groundwater recharge provided by the canal). Should the benefits of inefficient practices to other water users and the to environment we taken into account in defining waste?

5. **Financial or physical feasibility.** In Colorado v. New Mexico, 459 U.S. 176 (1982), the State of Colorado sought a declaration that some water in the small Vermejo River was available for appropriation in that state, even though essentially all of the water in the stream was diverted and consumed downstream in New Mexico. O'Connor, J., concurring in a judgment sending the case back for further findings, stated:

"In this case, the Special Master has cast an accusatory finger at the Vermejo Conservancy District, concluding that '[t]he system of canals used to transport the water to the fields is inefficient.' Undoubtedly, there is evidence in the record indicating that large losses of water occur through seepage and evaporation in transporting waters of the Vermejo through open ditches for irrigation and stock watering. It is a leap, however, from observing that large losses occur to concluding, as Colorado would have the Court do, that the practices of the Conservancy District are wasteful or unreasonable. As the Court observes, the extent of the duty to conserve that may be placed upon the user is limited to measures that are 'financially and physically feasible,' Wyoming v. Colorado, 259 U.S. 419, 484, 42 S.Ct. 552, 564, 66 L.Ed. 999 (1922), and 'within practicable limits.' Ibid.[1] Nevertheless, in concluding that the Conservancy District's distribution system is 'inefficient,' the Special Master made no factual finding that improved economy in that system is within the practicable means available to the District." Id. at 192.

6. **Eliminating waste through regulation.** Is the elimination of "waste" by government regulation a good policy? Consider the following:

"With careful planning, none of the problems associated with reducing wasteful water rights is insurmountable. Legislatures can formulate measures, if required, to make resource tradeoff decisions and to distribute the cost of modernization through all sectors of the economy. There are indeed prices to be paid, but they must not be allowed to overshadow the need for proper water management. As growth continues in the arid West, the quality of life in the

---

1. It is significant to note that in Wyoming v. Colorado, 259 U.S. 419, 42 S.Ct. 552, 66 L.Ed. 999 (1922), upon which the Court relies for the proposition that an affirmative duty to conserve may be imposed on the States, ante, at 546, the Wyoming appropriators *already* had storage facilities in place for equalizing the river's natural flow.

region will depend on maintaining a reliable water supply and natural streamflows. Without a commitment to efficient water use, not only will segments of the agricultural industry be threatened by increased problems of erosion and salinity, but all sectors of the economy could be undermined by the resulting water constraints. Consequently, the time has come for state governments to implement the move to water conservation." Steven J. Shupe, Waste in Western Water Law: A Blueprint for Change, 61 Or. L. Rev. 483, 521 (1982).

"Many writers seem to view the statutory and judicial prohibition of 'waste' with approval and argue that water should be put to 'beneficial' use. It is somewhat difficult to understand this position. The logic of the situation is the same as in the case of statutory preferences or the loss of water rights through non-use. It is not clear why a person should not be free to use his own property as he sees fit, providing losses are not imposed upon others. If water rights are salable, and if protection is provided to third parties, it is difficult to see how the problem of waste would become important. To deny rationality in the use of one's own water right is to question the basis of private decisions in the use of all resources. The problem here is to define water rights in such a way that they do become real property and susceptible to market allocation by the forces of supply and demand.

"The California case of *Chow v. Santa Barbara*[12] can be used to illustrate judicial judgments on waste of water. Chow, as a riparian water user, had used for many years the flood waters of a stream for leaching purposes on his riparian lands. In 1933 the California Supreme Court declared this use of water to be unreasonable and also wasteful. * * * As a result the city of Santa Barbara was allowed to appropriate the 'waste' waters formerly used by Chow *without* any compensation.

"There is probably little doubt that the economic worth of the water to the city exceeded the value of the water for leaching purposes. What is important here is that (1) the court took the responsibility of saying that the well-established practice of leaching was wasteful and unreasonable, and that (2) Chow was deprived of his use of water without compensation. If Chow's property right had been clearly defined, the city of Santa Barbara could have purchased that right in the ordinary manner of transfer of property. This case invites reflection upon the application of riparian law and upon the efficacy of judicial decision-making." Jerome W. Milliman, Water Law and Private Decisionmaking: A Critique, 2 J.L. & Econ. 41, 50-51 (1959).[b]

7. **Regulation versus the market.** Is there a role for both government regulation and the market in reducing waste of water? Government regulation is usually justified by claims of market failure, and markets in water rights have been a failure. One source of market failure is alluded to in the Milliman article quoted in the preceding note—the lack of clearly defined property rights in water. Indeed, deficiencies in the definition of water rights under existing doctrines is the focus of Milliman's article. This problem and other legal, institutional, and practical

---

12. Chow v. City of Santa Barbara, 217 Cal. 673, 22 P.2d 5 (1933).

b. Copyright 1959 by the University of Chicago.

impediments to the development of water markets are considered elsewhere in the book, particularly in Chapter 2, Section 5 (Transfer).

Although a variety of contemporary efforts are underway to eliminate impediments to transfers and facilitate the development of water markets, progress has been slow and success limited. Until such reforms are in place, government action to eliminate the most egregious instances of waste might be appropriate even in states firmly committed to water markets. In addition, even if most reform efforts are ultimately successful, residual transaction costs may prevent a number of economically positive transactions, particularly where inefficiencies are small individually but large collectively, i.e., where a large number of appropriators engage in inefficient practices. In such cases, government imposition of conservation measures may be appropriate, particularly if care is taken to observe the limitations regarding financial and physical feasibility of such measures suggested by Justice O'Connor in Note 5, supra.

Government regulation can also encourage market solutions. The principal case provides an example. In 1989, IID entered into a contract with the Metropolitan Water District of Southern California (MWD) in which MWD agreed to finance conservation projects in the district in exchange for long-term rights to the water salvaged by the projects. Most observers agree that Decision 1600 of the California Water Resources Control Board—the subject of the principal case—was a significant factor in the consummation of the contract. See Mark Reisner & Sarah Bates, Overtapped Oasis: Reform or Revolution for Western Water 149-66 (1990).

8. **Efforts to eliminate waste.** Only Arizona has made a concerted regulatory effort to eliminate waste. Although Arizona's efforts are aimed at curtailing serious groundwater overdraft problems, the Arizona conservation regulations also affect the use of surface waters. The Arizona conservation regulations are discussed infra p. 368, Note 1. Recent efforts to curtail waste are reviewed and critiqued in Janet C. Neuman, Beneficial Use, Waste and Forfeiture: The Inefficient Search for Efficiency in Western Water Use, 28 Envtl. L. 919 (1998).

CITY OF THORNTON v. BIJOU IRRIGATION CO.

Supreme Court of Colorado, 1996
926 P.2d 1

[The City of Thornton applied for new conditional water rights and for changes in use of existing water rights as part of a long-term project to meet the needs of projected population increases. The trial court awarded Thornton conditional water rights, rejecting objections raised by a several parties. (A "conditional water right" is decreed in Colorado when a party has taken an adequate "first step" toward appropriation but has not "perfected" the appropriation by applying water to beneficial use. A decree of a conditional water right is functionally similar to issuance of a permit to appropriate water in states utilizing a permit system. See infra page 121, Note 6, discussing the Colorado appropriation system.)]

LOHR, JUSTICE. * * * [A]n applicant must establish an intent to appropriate water for application to beneficial use. Pursuant to the anti-speculation doctrine, an applicant's intent to appropriate cannot be based upon the subsequent speculative sale or transfer of the appropriative rights. In the present case, the trial court held that Thornton formed the necessary nonspeculative intent. Objectors NCWCD [Northern Colorado Water Conservancy District] and [City of] Fort Collins appeal this finding and argue that Thornton's plan violates the anti-speculation doctrine. Resolution of the issues raised by NCWCD and Fort Collins requires an examination of the anti-speculation doctrine as it applies to municipalities. Our specific analysis will be informed by a general overview of the anti- speculation doctrine as it has developed in Colorado water law.

Our seminal case in this area is Colorado River Water Conservation District v. Vidler Tunnel Water Co., 197 Colo. 413, 594 P.2d 566 (1979). In that case, Vidler Tunnel Water Company (Vidler), a private corporation, sought a conditional storage decree for a reservoir as part of a planned transmountain diversion project. The corporation planned to sell the water to municipalities on the eastern slope for general municipal use but had not obtained firm contractual commitments binding those municipalities to purchase or receive the water. We held that Vidler's plan, which essentially depended on an unsubstantiated assumption that general population growth would produce a need for more water in the future and that municipalities would seek to satisfy this need from Vidler's supply, did not establish the necessary intent to apply the appropriated water to beneficial use. In the absence of firm contractual commitments for the use of water not intended by Vidler for its own use or of agency relationships between Vidler and the intended users, we held Vidler's application unduly speculative. Because the applicant in Vidler was a private corporation, we did not consider whether these strict requirements applied equally to municipal applicants.

Although *Vidler* has most often been cited as defining the anti-speculation doctrine, we did not articulate a new legal requirement in that case, but rather merely applied longstanding principles of Colorado water law. Thus, we must examine *Vidler's* predecessors to determine the scope of the application of the anti-speculation doctrine to municipal applicants.

The question of a municipality's ability to appropriate water to meet future needs first received significant attention from this court in City & County of Denver v. Sheriff, 105 Colo. 193, 96 P.2d 836 (1939). In Sheriff * * * [w]e emphasized the necessity of preserving the flexibility of municipalities to exercise their managerial judgment in resolving their water supply problems, and made the following statement regarding the unique circumstances of municipal water providers:

> The concern of the city is to assure an adequate supply to the public which it serves. In establishing a beneficial use of water under such circumstances the factors are not as simple and are more numerous than the application of water to 160 acres of land used for agricultural purposes. A specified tract of land does not increase in size, but populations do, and in short periods of time. With that flexibility in mind, it is not speculation but the highest prudence on the part of the city to obtain appropriations of water that will satisfy the needs resulting from a normal increase in population within a reasonable period of time.

The *Sheriff* decision clearly counsels against a strict application of the anti-speculation doctrine to municipalities seeking to provide for the future needs of their constituents.

* * * [I]n City & County of Denver v. Northern Colorado Water Conservancy District, 130 Colo. 375, 276 P.2d 992 (1954) (*Blue River*) * * * [s]everal objectors challenged Denver's application on the ground that the city's water supply was adequate without the claimed Blue River water, and that to base a decree solely on projected future needs would be improperly speculative. We noted the divergent estimates of the future growth and needs of the city but ultimately reached the following conclusion:

> We cannot hold that a city more than others is entitled to decree for water beyond its own needs. However, * * * when appropriations are sought by a growing city, regard should be given to its reasonably anticipated requirements.

Thus, under *Blue River*, a city may appropriate water for its future needs without violating the prohibition on speculation so long as the amount of the appropriation is in line with the city's "reasonably anticipated requirements."

* * * [I]nterpreting *Vidler* in conjunction with *Sheriff* and *Blue River*, we do not read the requirements of firm contractual commitments or agency relationships applied to private parties in *Vidler* to apply with equal force to municipalities. This limited exception to the *Vidler* requirements is supported by actions taken by the General Assembly. In 1979, immediately following the *Vidler* decision, the legislature amended the definition of "appropriation" in the Water Right Determination and Administration Act of 1969 to codify the prohibition on speculation articulated in *Vidler*. Following the amendment, subsection 103(3)(a) now states:

> (3)(a) * * * [N]o appropriation of water, either absolute or conditional, shall be held to occur when the proposed appropriation is based upon the speculative sale or transfer of the appropriative rights to persons not parties to the proposed appropriation, as evidenced by either of the following:
> (I) The purported appropriator of record does not have either a legally vested interest or a reasonable expectation of procuring such interest in the lands or facilities to be served by such appropriation, unless such appropriator is a governmental agency or an agent in fact for the persons proposed to be benefitted by such appropriation.
> (II) The purported appropriator of record does not have a specific plan and intent to divert, store, or otherwise capture, possess, and control a specific quantity of water for specific beneficial uses.

By enacting the above provision, the General Assembly endorsed the *Vidler* holding with respect to private parties but also recognized the need for governmental agencies, which include municipalities and other agencies responsible for supplying water to individual users, to exercise some planning flexibility with respect to future water needs. This exception, however, does not completely immunize municipal applicants from speculation challenges. Rather, as part of the statute codifying *Vidler*, the exception must be read as consistent with the scope of the exception recognized for municipalities in those decisions underlying *Vidler*, such as *Sheriff* and *Blue River*. Thus, under section 37-92-103(3)(a), a municipality may be decreed conditional water rights based solely on its projected future needs, and without firm contractual commitments or agency relationships, but a municipality's entitlement to such a decree is subject to the water court's determination that the amount conditionally appropriated is consistent with the municipality's reasonably anticipated requirements based on substantiated projections of future growth.

* * * We have reviewed numerous challenges to decrees based on the anti-speculation doctrine subsequent to *Vidler* and the enactment of section 37-92-103(3)(a). However, almost all of those cases concerned applications by private parties rather than by municipalities. Our sole post-*Vidler* case addressing speculation in the municipal application context is City & County of Denver v. Colorado River Water Conservation District (CRWCD), 696 P.2d 730 (Colo.1985).

* * * Our holding in Denver v. CRWCD must be viewed as limited to the unique facts of that case. Denver sought the claimed water to sell it for profit to parties outside its own boundaries. The city was acting in the capacity of a water supplier on the open market rather than as a governmental entity seeking to ensure future water supplies for its citizens. Accordingly, the municipal planning exception was simply inapplicable, and Denver was required to comply with the full range of requirements applicable to private parties under *Vidler*. Thus understood, Denver v. CRWCD does not eliminate a municipality's ability to plan for the future, and municipal appropriations for reasonably anticipated future requirements, including requirements for projected growth areas not presently within the municipal boundaries, are valid if the municipality substantiates such need. * * *

In the present case, the trial court evaluated the evidence pursuant to the proper legal standard. Furthermore, the trial court's factual findings that the decreed water is consistent with Thornton's reasonably anticipated water requirements and that the water will eventually be used to satisfy needs within Thornton's boundaries or service areas have an adequate basis in the record. Therefore, we accept these findings and uphold the court's determination that Thornton established a nonspeculative intent to appropriate the claimed water.

Notes

1. **Beneficial use, speculation, and municipal water supply.** A bias against speculation is inherent in the concept of beneficial use, and the views of the principal case on speculation are shared, to a greater or lesser degree, by all appropriation states. Relaxation of anti-speculative policies on behalf of municipalities—sometimes referred to as the "growing communities doctrine"—is also a widely accepted policy. The policy is reflected in judicial decisions, statutory provision, and administrative regulations which give cities special consideration with regard to the completion ("perfection" or "vesting") of new appropriations or which excuse nonuse of water rights by cities. (Completion of new appropriations is examined in Chapter 2, Section 2C (Priority); loss of rights because of non-use—abandonment and forfeiture—is examined in Chapter 2, Section 4. (Loss)). The special treatment which cities receive is examined in Janis

E. Carpenter, Water for Growing Communities: Refining Tradition in the Pacific Northwest, 27 Envtl. L. 127 (1997). See also Frank J. Trelease, Preferences to The Use of Water, 27 Rocky Mtn. L. Rev. 133, 138-40 (1955).

2. **Private suppliers.** A California case, Central Delta Water Agency v. State Water Resources Control Board, 20 Cal. Rptr. 3d 898 (Ct. App. 2004), presented a situation very similar to the *Vidler* case discussed in the principal case, with similar results. A private entity, known as Delta Wetlands Properties, proposed a rather novel project to convert two "islands" in the Sacramento/San Joaquin Delta Estuary into storage reservoirs. Delta Wetlands planned to sell the stored water, but had no specific buyers for the water, relying instead on a general demand for water in California. Despite the lack of specificity regarding where and how the stored water would be used, the California Water Resources Control Board issued appropriation permits which identified potential places of use and purposes of use only generally. However, the permits provided, *inter alia*, that actual buyers had to be identified and that the Chief of the Division of Water Rights had to determine that water would be placed to beneficial use before water could be stored. The Court of Appeal set aside the permits, holding that "a statement of alternative, potential beneficial uses" did not satisfy constitutional and statutory requirements relating to beneficial and reasonable use of water and that the board could not satisfy its obligations by requiring that particular uses be identified and evaluated at a later date. The court also held that the board's obligations regarding beneficial use could not be delegated.

In Department of Ecology v. Theodoratus, 957 P.2d 1241 (Wash. 1998), the Washington Supreme Court refused to extend the growing communities doctrine to a private subdivision developer. The court affirmed a decision by the Department of Ecology (DOE) which held that the quantity of water awarded in a final certificate of appropriation must be based on water actually applied to beneficial use and not on the capacity of the supply system. In rejecting the capacity of the system as the measure of quantification, the court and DOE reversed a long-standing Washington practice. The court noted that DOE could allow additional time to the developer to actually put water to use before seeking a final certificate, but reminded DOE that beneficial use must occur within a "reasonable time." The opinion also suggests that a certificated right previously quantified on the basis of system capacity may be vulnerable to partial forfeiture for nonuse where a number of subdivision lots remain vacant after a long time.

3. **Pueblo rights.** Some municipalities in the Southwest claim "pueblo rights," rights for municipal purpose that are superior to those of agricultural appropriators and that permit a city to expand its uses and take without compensation water put to use long before the city's exercise of the right. Such rights are generally said to be a remnant of the Southwest's Spanish heritage, stemming from Spanish or Mexican grants to agricultural villages which have since grown up into American cities. A document which established the village of Pitic in Sonora, Mexico, is claimed to have granted the inhabitants unrestricted rights to water and provided that pueblos established thereafter were to have like privileges.

Only in California are pueblo rights recognized. Pueblo rights in California are based on a discussion, albeit dicta, of Mexican law in Lux v. Haggin, 10 P. 674 (Cal. 1886). Subsequently, the California Supreme Court held that the cities of San Diego and Los Angeles have paramount rights to the San Diego River and Los Angeles River, respectively, which extend to so much of the waters of the rivers as the expanding needs of the cities require. City of San Diego v. Cuyamaca Water Co., 287 P. 475 (Cal. 1930); Vernon Irrigation Co. v. City of Los Angeles, 39 P. 762 (Cal. 1895). Although modern historical research indicates that the plan of Pitic did not give pueblos the expansive rights claimed in Lux v. Haggin and other decisions, the California Supreme Court reaffirmed the existence of pueblo rights in City of Los Angeles v. City of San Fernando, 537 P.2d 1250 (Cal. 1975), in part because of Los Angeles' long reliance on them. Despite their long recognition in California, only San Diego and Los Angeles have been adjudicated pueblo rights by reported decisions.

In Cartwright v. Public Service Co., 343 P.2d 654 (N.M. 1959), the New Mexico Supreme Court adopted the pueblo rights doctrine in a suit involving the town of Las Vegas. However, in State ex rel Martinez v. City of Las Vegas, 89 P.3d 47 (N.M. 2004), the New Mexico Supreme Court overruled *Cartwright.* While the court concluded that the historical evidence was not sufficiently clear to justify overruling *Cartwright*, the court held that the doctrine was incompatible with the New Mexico system of prior appropriation, particularly the principle of beneficial use. The court also held that protection of the "expanding quality" of pueblo rights was not required by the Treaty of Guadalupe Hidalgo because the treaty does not protect inchoate rights. Although it rejected arguments that *Cartwright* established a "rule of property" which should be adhered to even if wrong or that it should be overruled only prospectively, the court remanded the case to determine an appropriate equitable remedy to balance Las Vegas' reliance on *Cartwright* with the reliance of others on the system of prior appropriation.

Texas, the only other state to consider the doctrine, rejected it, finding no basis for it in the law of New Spain. In re Contests of City of Laredo, 675 S.W.2d 257 (Tex. Ct. App. 1984); see Peter L. Reich, Mission Revival Jurisprudence: State Courts and Hispanic Water Law Since 1850, 69 Wash. L. Rev. 869 (1994) (arguing that the courts deliberately distorted Mexican law in developing the pueblo rights doctrine).

4. **"Can and will doctrine."** Colo. Rev. Stat. § 37-92-305(9)(b), provides that a conditional right cannot be recognized unless it is "established that waters can and will be diverted." This statute—called the "can and will doctrine" in Colorado—focuses on the ability of the applicant to complete the intended appropriation. In FWS Land & Cattle Co. v. Division of Wildlife, 795 P.2d 837 (Colo. 1990), the court held that a conditional decree to enlarge existing reservoirs was properly denied because the applicant lacked the legal ability to acquire lands which enlargement would inundate. Similarly in West Elk Ranch, L.L.C. v. United States, 65 P.3d 479 (Colo. 2002), it held that a conditional right to appropriate water from a spring in a national forest was appropriately denied because the United States Forest Service had refused to grant the applicant the special use permit needed for access. In Gibbs v. Wolf Land Co., 856 P.2d 798 (Colo. 1993), on the other hand, the court held that lack of legal access to a stream does not violate the "can and will" doctrine if the applicant can invoke a statutory right of private condemnation. Accord Lemmon v. Hardy, 519 P.2d 1168 (Idaho 1974). In In re Vought, 76 P.3d 906 (Colo. 2003), the court explained that the applicants in *FWS* and *West Elk* could not invoke the right of condemnation because both involved government lands which could not be condemned.

But in City of Black Hawk v. City of Central, 97 P.3d 951 (Colo. 2004), the court indicated that the can and will doctrine does not always require legal access or the ability to obtain access through condemnation. The court affirmed a lower court decision granting a conditional right to the City of Black Hawk to enlarge a reservoir owned by Central City despite a resolution by the city council of Central City denying Black Hawk access to the reservoir. The court distinguished *FWS* and *West Elk*, observing that, unlike those cases, the resolution did not constitute a final denial of access because it did not bind future Central City city councils. The court found it unnecessary to decide if Black Hawk could condemn access to the reservoir, saying that lack of current access is not typically dispositive of whether the can and will statute is satisfied and that the can and will statute should not be rigidly applied in cases not involving speculation.

The right of non-governmental parties to condemn property to facilitate the appropriation of water is examined in subsection H, infra p. 112.

5. **Economic functions of speculation.** Although "speculation" and "speculator" often carry a pejorative connotation, economists assert that speculation serves important economic functions. See, e.g., Stephen F. Williams, The Requirement of Beneficial Use as a Cause of Waste in Water Resource Development, 23 Nat. Resources J. 7 (1983). Williams argues that the requirement of beneficial use creates economic waste by encouraging uneconomic investments and premature development of resources. He suggests that unappropriated water should be allocated by state auction and that the purchasers should be allowed to hold their rights for speculative profit without beneficial use.

6. **Appropriation for the benefit of others.** Could the Izaak Walton League appropriate water for a reservoir to be stocked with fish and opened for public fishing? See Lake Shore Duck Club v. Lake View Duck Club, 166 P. 309, 310-11 (Utah 1917):

"The vital question, then, to be determined is, can an appropriation of water be made under the laws of this state for the irrigation of unsurveyed, uninclosed, unoccupied public domain of the United States for the sole production of food for wild water fowl, which, when propagated and raised, must, of necessity, be as accessible to capture, destruction, and appropriation to use, by any other person who may see fit to hunt upon the land, as to the person who went through the form of making an appropriation? * * *

"We have searched in vain for any authority in support of appellant's claim of a valid appropriation of the water in controversy. The beneficial use stated in the application is not in question. We are not disposed to hold that any use of water tending to supply man or domestic animals with food is not beneficial. But for the purpose of effecting a valid appropriation of water under the statutes of this state we are decidedly of the opinion that the beneficial use contemplated in making the appropriation must be one that inures to the exclusive benefit of the appropriator and subject to his complete dominion and control."

No other state seems to have placed a similar limitation on appropriations. In Scherck v. Nichols, 95 P.2d 74 (Wyo. 1939), the Wyoming court (in a different context) stated: "[I]t is not contrary to the policy of this state that a man may apply for the diversion of water for the ultimate use of it by another. * * * A man cannot apply for water, or divert it, for idle purposes. He must claim it, if he wants to separate it from the unappropriated body of water. But the claim need not, we think, be personal in the sense that no one else can reap the benefit thereof." Is the Utah rule of exclusive benefit consistent with the instream appropriations confirmed in the cases discussed supra p. 32, Note 2? With the appropriation of water by a district or distributing company for use by its consumers?

Since 1995, the Nevada legislature has attempted to prevent the United States Bureau of Land Management from appropriating water to be used by its grazing lessees to water livestock. These attempts are discussed infra pp. 711-12, Note 5.

C. Priority

CITY OF DENVER v. NORTHERN COLORADO WATER CONSERVANCY DISTRICT

Supreme Court of Colorado, 1954.
130 Colo. 375, 276 P.2d 992.

[Proceedings for the adjudication of water rights to the Blue River. The Blue, Williams Fork and Fraser rivers are tributaries of the Colorado River, having their headwaters on the western slope of the continental divide. Denver is on the eastern slope. As early as 1914, Denver had made a reconnaissance of the western slope as a possible source of future water. In 1921 it employed a consulting engineer, who began surveys for diversions from the Fraser and Williams Fork. In 1922 he made preliminary surveys in the basin of the Blue, and filed with the State Engineer a map and statement for a transmountain diversion of 1200 c.f.s. through a tunnel headed on a tributary of the Blue. In 1926 another survey showed that a lower tunnel from the Blue itself could capture the water of several more tributaries through collection ditches, and in 1927 another filing was made for a 1600 c.f.s. tunnel at the new site. Several years of geological investigations disclosed unfavorable conditions along the line of the second proposed tunnel and plans were drawn for a third tunnel at about the same site but with a different direction. In 1941 further engineering work showed that a dam and reservoir at Dillon on the Blue River would eliminate the need for collection ditches, and a new filing was made showing the reservoir and a new location for the tunnel, 20 feet lower in elevation and 3500 feet farther down stream. Later, the plan of operation was revised to call for storage of water in the reservoir at the rate of 1600 c.f.s., and releases at a slower rate through a smaller tunnel with a capacity of 788 c.f.s. Work was begun on this tunnel in 1946.

In the meantime, Denver had proceeded to construct diversion works and tunnels for the waters of the Fraser and Williams Fork rivers, and reservoirs and works on the eastern slope to hold and distribute the western slope waters. In other proceedings, it was decreed rights to appropriate waters of the Fraser and Williams Fork.

In this proceeding, Denver claimed 1200 c.f.s. with a priority of 1921 and 400 c.f.s. with a priority of 1927. The Conservancy District resisted this claim and filed a claim for its large storage reservoir farther down on the Blue, with a priority of 1937. The district court allowed this claim, and decreed to Denver a right to 788 c.f.s. with a priority of 1946. Denver appeals.]

STONE, CHIEF JUSTICE. * * * [S]erious questions are raised by Denver's challenge to the priority date awarded the Blue River project in the decree. The basic law is not disputed, to wit: (1) that priority of appropriation shall give the better right as between those using the water for the same purpose; (2) that as to the rights here involved a municipal corporation has no different status from that of an individual or any other party to the proceeding; (3) that although an appropriation is not complete until actual diversion and use, still the right may relate back to the time when the first open step was taken giving notice of intent to secure it; * * * (4) that right to relate back is conditional that construction thereafter was prosecuted with reasonable diligence, and conditional further that there was then "a fixed and definite purpose to take it up and carry it through," State of Wyoming v. Colorado, 259 U.S. 419, 42 S.Ct. 552, 567, 66 L.Ed. 999; * * * and (5), that the questions of reasonable diligence and of fixed and definite purpose are questions of fact to be determined by the trial court from the evidence. * * *

There is no evidence that any work even of survey, on the Blue River project was begun on July 4, 1921, or at any time prior to the summer of 1922. The claim for the 1921 date is based solely on the fact that survey was started on that date on Denver's Williams Fork and Fraser River projects and the contention that those two projects and the Blue River project constitute in fact a single irrigation project, and consequently that in the determination of the date when the first step was taken, and also in the determination of reasonable diligence since such date, the three projects should be considered as a single project.

In determining the date "when the first step was taken," a survey made on the Fraser River or on the Williams Fork would of itself be no evidence of intent to appropriate water from the Blue River. Certainly such a survey in a far distant basin supplying water to another stream would constitute no notice to another appropriator of such intent. The filing of a plat of method of diversion from the Fraser or Williams Fork would be no evidence of intent to appropriate water from the Blue or notice of such intent. Therefore, there is nothing to support the contention that the priority should be dated as of July 4, 1921. At most, the priority for the Blue River project could date back only to the time when the first step was taken in construction of a project on the Blue River.

In determining reasonable diligence, also, we find no ground for holding, as urged by Denver, that the Blue River project, the Williams Fork project and Fraser River project are each units of a single project so that the construction work on those projects and the expenses incurred thereon can be considered as part of the construction of the Blue River project. Denver's claim for its Blue River project was made by survey, plat and filing entirely separate from those of its Fraser and Williams Fork projects. It seeks priority to water from an entirely separate stream, not even confluent with the Fraser River or Williams Fork except to the extent that each is ultimately a tributary of the Colorado River. It seeks water to be diverted from an entirely separate drainage basin. It was surveyed and planned after those projects. It directly affects other claimants who are protestants here but not directly affected by those projects. It is to be carried through an entirely separate conduit,—the Fraser River being diverted through the Moffat Tunnel and the Williams Fork through the Jones Pass Tunnel, and the Blue, as now planned, to be carried in the Montezuma Tunnel to be bored through the Continental Divide many miles to the south of the others. Its water rights are here sought to be adjudicated as entirely separate from the rights of those projects. It has even less relation to the Fraser River and Williams Fork projects than to Denver's South Platte water system with which it will share the same river channel and reservoirs. In fact, the only relation between the Blue River project and these other projects is that their several waters may ultimately rest in common filtration and concentration plants, and that by means of exchange they may be used cooperatively for supplying prior rights or filling storage reservoirs such as would be probable in the case of any other independent water right. The priority of appropriation which gives the better right under our Constitution is priority on a stream rather than on a project, and any diligence in construction to permit dating back of priority on the Blue River must be diligence relating to and promoting the Blue River appropriation. No such relation here appears. Therefore, diligence in the prosecution of the Fraser and Williams Fork projects cannot be imputed to the Blue River project. However, the fact that the City of Denver was engaged in the construction of these or other enterprises may properly be considered together with all other evidence as to existing facilities and ability of the city in determination of the issue of reasonable diligence. * * *

During the entire period from 1927 to 1946, substantially all the work done and all the money spent by Denver in connection with its Blue River project was for investigation and exploratory work or work in connection with Eastern Slope reservoirs which were not dependent on any one plan for diversion or even on Blue River water. This and similar evidence before the trial court presented substantial support to the contention of protestants that Denver had no fixed and definite plan and no definite point of diversion prior to * * * 1946, and supported the decree of the trial court consistent therewith.

As to the second question, that of diligence:

In summary, the evidence showed that the * * * plan of 1923 has been abandoned without any construction whatever; that following the filing of the * * * plan in 1927, no evidence of actual excavation work in connection with its proposed tunnel appeared until 1942, some fifteen years later, when a cut was made and a small exploratory tunnel was driven about 400 feet at a place then intended to be the west portal to ascertain the condition of the ground. The proposed location of the portal has since been changed and a part of the excavation has caved in. No other work was performed on the ground until July 1946 when work at the east portal of the tunnel was started. Denver's Chief Engineer testified that "That was the first actual construction work." * * *

It appears that throughout the period from 1936 to 1941 efforts were made by the City to induce the United States Bureau of Reclamation to build the project, but without success. There was no evidence of any effort by Denver to finance the project itself prior to the year 1946, but only of efforts to induce the United States to do so.

To support its contention that this work was sufficient to satisfy the requirements of reasonable diligence, Denver cites Tausig v. Moffat Tunnel Co., 106 Colo. 384, 106 P.2d 363, wherein it was held that surveys, preparation of maps, acquiring of rights of way and options and obtaining a contract for the carriage of water through the Moffat Tunnel, drilling of test holes, clearing of timber along proposed ditch lines and other similar work was sufficient to satisfy the requirement of reasonable diligence in construction of a ditch leading to the Moffat Tunnel. However, there the party seeking diversion of the water was a private company of apparently limited resources. The dating back was apparently for a period of less than five years, and the decision of this court affirmed the finding of the trial court, holding that there was due diligence; while here, we are asked to hold such that expenditures on the part of a great city, without shown limitation upon its financial capacity, spread out over a period of nearly twenty years would require us to reverse the decision of the trial court and say that such expenditures were evidence of reasonable diligence as a matter of law.

Kinney, in his great work on irrigation, says: "Probably the best definition of the word diligence was given by Lewis, C.J., in rendering the opinion in an early Nevada case, Ophir Silver Min. Co. v. Carpenter, 4 Nev. 534. It is there defined as 'the steady application to business of any kind, constant effort to accomplish any undertaking.' 'It is the doing of an act or series of acts with all possible expedition, with no delay except such as may be incident to the work itself.' " Kinney on Irrigation and Water Rights, Vol. 2, § 735. * * *

It is undisputed that during a period of about twenty years, Denver had not even begun the actual construction of its project and had made no effort whatever as appears from the record towards financing it, but only a laudable but fruitless attempt after nine years of inaction to induce the United States Reclamation Service to finance it for the joint use of Denver and the South Platte Water Users Association. Meanwhile others have worked diligently and long to put a part of this water to actual use. The record before us does not show such conclusive evidence of "steady application" to the business of constructing the project or of such "constant effort to accomplish" it as to require us to hold that the trial court erred in refusal to date back Denver's appropriation, to the loss of such prior users. On the contrary, in order to sustain Denver's claim, we should have to establish as a law of Colorado that a great city or a great corporation, by the filing of a plat of a water diversion plan and the fitful continuance of surveys and exploratory operations, could paralyze all development in a river basin for a period of nineteen years without excavating a single shovel full of dirt in actual construction and without taking any step towards bond issue or other financing plan of its own for carrying out its purpose; that for nineteen years no farmer could build a ditch to develop his farm and no other city or industry could construct a project for use of water in that area without facing loss of their water when and if the city or corporation which filed the plat should actually construct its project. This we cannot do. * * *

MOORE, JUSTICE (dissenting). * * * *To what extent can a claimant of water change his plan of development without that change amounting to a relinquishment of his claim?*

As will be seen from the quotation in De Haas v. Benesch, supra, there are some changes which can be made in the plan of a water development which will not constitute a relinquishment of the project. One criterion for determination of this problem was used by the United States Supreme Court in the case of State of Wyoming v. Colorado, 259 U.S. 419, 42 S.Ct. 552, 66 L.Ed. 999, where the changes planned had to do with the determination of "whether" the would-be appropriator would proceed at all with the diversion project. Such changes are to be distinguished from those which go rather to selection of the most economical or effective means to be employed for the accomplishment of a diversion and use of water, concerning which there already is a fixed and definite intention to take. Once the decision has been made to proceed with the project, continuing investigations and changes are simply evidence of diligence and endeavor to accomplish the greatest good at a minimum of cost to the public, not abandonment of the project. * * * Changes undertaken with the apparent intent to improve or make more efficient or less costly the whole work to be undertaken, should be regarded as the natural diligence of a prudent man rather than the want of constancy in the prosecution of the undertaking. * * *

May a claimant of water offer evidence to show that the water claimed is part of an interrelated system involving other water rights, and, if so, is work on various parts of such interrelated system to be considered in determining the diligence with which each of the component water rights in the system is being developed?

This question must be answered in the affirmative. With respect to the development of a water right to irrigate a single piece of land through a single ditch to which water is diverted through one headgate, it would be obvious that diligence could be shown by reference to work on any, or all, of the three component parts: diversion dam, carrying ditch, or distribution laterals.

As the works become more complex, including, several sources of supply, wider spread uses, and a variety of purposes, a project may cross county lines, irrigation district or irrigation division lines, and different jurisdictional lines for adjudicating the water rights involved. It does not appear that there is any point at which a water system becomes so large that its parts no longer relate to each other in such a way that work on one part may not constitute diligence with respect to completion of the whole including its other parts. It may well be that a single entity may have holdings so extensive that many of them are unrelated to others. In such a case, work on one holding would not constitute work on an unrelated holding.

It appears, therefore, that the test of the extent to which work on one part of a water system may properly relate to another for the purpose of determining due diligence, is whether the parts of the work relate to a single integrated purpose intimately enough that progress on one part has a direct bearing upon another part. What we are really considering is whether or not the work done is within the limits of what is reasonably to be considered as customary to an enterprise unified under single management and in which impairment of any part tends to directly impair the remaining parts, or in which construction of one part directly contributes to the whole which is comprised of other parts.

Much of the evidence which was admitted, and that which was erroneously excluded, established the fact that the city of Denver has one interrelated water system which should have been considered as a whole in so far as the question of reasonable diligence of the city in going forward with the Blue River diversion is concerned. Even without the full delineation of fact which might have been presented had the trial court not restricted evidence to the Blue River unit alone, the only evidence in the record concerning Denver's efforts shows a continuing good faith endeavor to accomplish the appropriation for which she now seeks a conditional decree. * * * The majority opinion comments that: "There was no evidence of any effort by Denver to finance the project itself prior to the year 1946, but only of efforts to induce the United States to do so." Unmentioned is the fact, which every citizen then living well knows, that in 1929 the whole nation trembled and lay prostrate in depression; that the public treasuries were empty; that for years thereafter any attempt to finance such a large undertaking upon the local level would have been sheer folly; and that the only hope for resources sufficient to warrant a start at construction was to seek the financial backing of the United States. In those years all business, both public and private, looked only to Washington for rescue from total collapse.

At about the time when another approach to the financial problem might reasonably have been expected to succeed, World War II broke out and thereafter for several years the productive energies of all the people were concentrated on the war effort. Men and materials were not to be had for any development of this kind, which could possibly wait. Just as soon as the conflict ended and war demands relaxed, construction of the tunnel began, and, despite inadequate financing and disappointments, the city has gone forward with the work.

For the foregoing reasons I am of the opinion that the City and County of Denver is entitled to a conditional decree for 1600 cubic feet per second, with a priority date as of October 19, 1927.

Notes

1. **Subsequent developments.** The Colorado legislature defined "reasonable diligence" for the first time in 1990, adopting the views of the dissent in the principal case. Colo. Rev. Stat. § 37-92-301(4)(b):

"The measure of reasonable diligence is the steady application of effort to complete the appropriation in a reasonably expedient and efficient manner under all the facts and circumstances. When a project or integrated system is comprised of several features, work on one feature of the project or system shall be considered in finding that reasonable diligence has been shown in the development of the water rights for all features of the entire project or system." Accord Nev. Rev. Stat. 533.395(5). See also Four Counties Water Users Association v. Colorado River Water Conservation District, 414 P.2d 469 (Colo. 1966), where the court sustained substantial changes in plans and allowed an early priority based on the original plans, quoting the dissenting, not the majority, opinion in the principal case.

2. **Priority date in permit states.** In states where a permit is required for an appropriation (all appropriation states except Colorado), the priority of the appropriation dates from the filing of the application for a permit. See, e.g., Ariz. Rev. Stat. § 45-162B; Utah Code Ann. § 73-3-18; Wash. Rev. Code § 90.03.340; Wyo. Stat. Ann. § 41-4-512. As in the principal case, this priority is retained only if the permittee completes the appropriation by applying water to beneficial use with reasonable diligence. See, e.g., Ariz. Rev. Stat. § 537.160; Utah. Code Ann. § 73-3-12; Wash. Rev. Code § 90.03.320; Wyo. Stat. Ann. § 41-4-506. As discussed supra p. 51, Note 1, diligence requirements are sometimes relaxed for cites or other public entities. See, e.g., Nev. Rev. Stat. 533.395(6) (directing the state engineer to consider reasonably anticipated future needs identified in planning documents when reviewing request for extension of time by political subdivisions and public utilities); Or. Rev. Stat. § 537.410 (exempting permits issued to municipal corporations, irrigation districts, and certain public utilities from cancellation for failure to meet diligence requirements); Wash. Rev. Code § 90.03.320 (directing water officials to undertake special considerations in establishing diligence requirements in permits for municipal water supply purposes).

3. **Policies behind "relation back" and "diligence."** The priority rule of the appropriation doctrine is an application of the principle of "first possession" which finds broad expression in the common law. Like rights to the fox made famous in Pierson v. Post, 3 Cai. R. 175 (N.Y. Sup. Ct. 1805), rights to water are perfected only when water is physically captured (applied to beneficial use). Unlike the fox hunter, an appropriator obtains protected, albeit inchoate, rights to water by taking a "first step" toward appropriation—by beginning the "chase" so to speak—a proposition expressly rejected by the court in Pierson v. Post. This deviation from the rule of Pierson v. Post is explained by the effort necessary to apply water to beneficial use. Application of water to beneficial use, particularly for large projects, requires large investments of capital and labor and may take a substantial time to complete. A party might be reluctant to make such investments if priority to an essential water supply could be lost to a competitor who is able to initiate and complete a project in a shorter time. To assuage such concerns and thereby encourage investments in water development, the appropriation doctrine holds that the priority "relates back" to the "first act" of appropriation. See Dallas Creek Water Co. v. Huey, 933 P.2d 27, 35 (Colo. 1997). At the same time, the principal of "relation back" is tempered by the requirement of "reasonable diligence" to prevent hoarding and speculation. Id.

4. **Codification of "due diligence."** In a number of permit states, the requirement of due diligence has been crystallized by statutes setting forth a specific time within which the work must be commenced, (two years, Ariz. Rev. Stat. § 45-160; six months., Neb. Rev. Stat. § 46-238) the physical works must be

completed, (five years, N.M. Stat. Ann. § 72-5-6, Wyo. Stat. Ann. § 41-4-506) and the water applied to beneficial use (five years, Idaho Code § 42-204). These are often coupled with intermediate standards for testing diligence, such as that one-fifth of the work must be completed within one-half the time allowed. S.D. Codified Laws 46-5-25; see Neb. Rev. Stat. § 46-238 (one-tenth within one year.) In some states, progress reports must be filed with water officials. Nev. Rev. Stat. 533.390. Colorado requires the holder of a conditional decree—the functional equivalent of a permit—to obtain a finding of diligence from the water court every sixth year. Colo. Rev. Stat. §37-92-301(4).

Extensions of these periods may be granted by the state water officials upon a showing of "good cause," which usually amounts to much the same as "due diligence." See Tulkisarmute Native Cmty. Council v. Heinze, 898 P.2d 935 (Alaska 1995); Associated Enters., Inc. v. Toltec Watershed Improvement Dist., 578 P.2d 1359 (Wyo. 1978). In some states, extensions may be granted almost as a matter of course with only minimal showings of good cause. For an extreme case, see Green River Development Co. v. FMC Corp., 660 P.2d 339 (Wyo. 1983), which involved permits that had been extended for more than sixty years without any significant development efforts. See also Carbon Canal Co. v. Sanpete Water Users Ass'n, 353 P.2d 916 (Utah 1960), where the court upheld extensions totaling thirty-six years, and 425 P.2d 405 (Utah 1967), where it finally lost its patience and terminated the permit.

5. **Excusing lack of progress.** In determining reasonable diligence, what is the relevance of financial troubles? See Maricopa County Mun. Water Conservation Dist. No. 1 v. Southwest Cotton Co., 4 P.2d 369 (Ariz. 1931) (pecuniary inability does not dispense with the need to complete an appropriation with diligence). Of economic uncertainty? See Pub. Serv. Co. v. Blue River Irrigation Co., 753 P.2d 737 (Colo. 1988) (economic feasibility of the proposed development is a relevant factor in a diligence proceeding (but see the next paragraph of this Note)). Of pioneer difficulties and slowness of settlement? See In re Hood River, 227 P. 1065 (Or. 1924) (difficulties of clearing land is a relevant factor, and reasonable diligence is exercised if diversions keep pace with area of land brought under cultivation); Campbell v. Wyoming Dev. Co., 100 P.2d 124 (Wyo. 1940) (slow development of state should not count against the appropriator). Of litigation? See Metro. Suburban Water Users Ass'n v. Colo. River Water Conservation Dist., 365 P.2d 273 (Colo. 1961) (applicant satisfies diligence during pendency of adjudication proceedings by seeking to have claim allowed and opposing claims of others); Associated Enters., Inc. v. Toltec Watershed Improvement Dist., 578 P.2d 1359 (Wyo. 1978) (extension of time for completion of appropriation is justified where litigation delayed construction and completion of reservoir). Of efforts to sell water? See Public Serv. Co. v. Blue River Irrigation Co., 829 P.2d 1276 (Colo. 1992) (efforts to sell water are not evidence of reasonable diligence). Of age, psychological stress, and ill health? See In re Application No. 5189-3 to Extend Time, 467 N.W.2d 907 (S.D. 1991) (cumulative impact of such factors might have excused failure to complete construction but did not excuse failure to file for an extension of the permit); *Maricopa County Mun. Water Conservation Dist. No. 1*, supra (ill health does not dispense with the need to complete an appropriation with diligence).

Colo. Rev. Stat. § 37-92-301(4)(c) states: "current economic conditions beyond the control of the applicant which adversely affect the feasibility of perfecting a conditional water right * * * [shall not] be considered sufficient to deny a diligence application, so long as other facts and circumstances which show diligence are present." In Municipal Subdistrict, Northern Colorado Water Conservancy District v. Chevron Shale Oil Co., 986 P.2d 918 (Colo. 1999), the court upheld, pursuant to this section, a 1995 extension of conditional appropriations dating back to the 1950s although no actual construction activities had ever taken place and the applicant's own studies indicated that the appropriations might not be completed until 2085. See also Mun. Subdistrict, N. Colo. Water Conservancy Dist. v. OXY USA, Inc, 990 P.2d 701 (Colo. 1999). In both cases, the rights are to be used in the development of shale oil projects; oil shale is a rock which can be processed to yield petroleum, but production is not currently economically feasible.

Is the statute consistent with Colorado's policy of maximum beneficial use of water? What would cause the Colorado legislature to adopt such a statute? (The legislative history indicates that the statute, enacted in 1990, was adopted at least in part for the benefit of the oil shale industry.) Is it good policy to tie up water for an industry which may not become economically viable for almost 100 years?

6. **Commencement of diligence requirements.** Although the date of permit application fixes the priority, diligence requirements do not commence until the permit is issued. In Wyoming, this led to the practice of "shelf filings" in which the State Engineer held applications for many years without taking action on them, thereby preserving applicants' priority dates without requiring any efforts toward development. Some states remedy this problem by requiring water officials to act on applications within fixed time limits. See, e.g., Mont. Code Ann. § 85-2-310; Nev. Rev. Stat. 533.370. The Wyoming practice is examined and criticized in Jackson B. Battle, Paper Clouds Over the Waters: Shelf Filings and Hyperextended Permits in Wyoming, 22 Land & Water L. Rev. 673 (1987).

7. **Protection of pre-application activities.** Since an application for a permit must be accompanied by detailed maps, plans, and other information, much planning, surveying, and engineering work must be completed before the application can be filed. A small project, inconsistent with a larger and more complex one, could be initiated and the application filed after much preliminary work was done on the larger project but before a filing could be made for it. To protect such pre-application efforts, New Mexico provides that a notice of intention can be filed, which will fix the date of priority if a formal application for a permit is made within a reasonable time. N.M. Stat. Ann. § 72-5-1. In Washington, a preliminary permit can be issued for up to five years (with extensions) to allow an applicant to develop and provide information to remedy deficiencies in the original application. Wash. Rev. Code § 90.03.290.

8. **Notice and Opportunity to be Heard.** If a permittee does not comply with diligence requirements established in a permit and does not apply for an extension, does due process require notice and an opportunity to be heard before the permit is canceled? See In re Application No. 5189-3 to Extend Time, 467 N.W.2d 907 (S.D. 1991) (suggesting that such requirements must be met before cancellation). In Colorado, a person holding a conditional right (one which has not been perfected by application to beneficial use) is required by statute to file an application for a finding of reasonable diligence every six years. Colo. Rev. Stat. § 37-92-301(4)(a)(I). In several cases, the Colorado Supreme Court held that

failure to file before the deadline results in automatic termination of the right. See, e.g., Town of De Beque v. Enewold, 606 P.2d 48 (Colo. 1980). A second statute, Colo. Rev. Stat. §37-92-305(7) directs the water courts to give notice before cancellation or expiration of a conditional right. In In re Double RL Co., 54 P.3d 908 (Colo. 2002), the court held that the second statute prevents automatic termination if notice is not given. However, the court also held that such failure only extends the time for filing a diligence application; it does not relieve the applicant from proving that reasonable diligence occurred during the six-year diligence period.

9. **Priority date in Colorado.** Because of the absence of a permit system, the priority date in Colorado continues to depend, in part, on the "first step" toward appropriation, and disputes regarding the sufficiency of putative "first steps" occur frequently. See In re Vought, 76 P.3d 906 (Colo. 2003); City of Thornton v. Bijou Irrigation Co., 926 P.2d 1 (Colo. 1996); City of Thornton v. City of Fort Collins, 830 P.2d 915 (Colo. 1992). To further complicate the matter, the date of the "first step" does not always determine the priority of an appropriation. Under Colorado's "postponement doctrine," rights filed with the water court in a particular year are junior to all rights filed in previous years, regardless of the dates the "first steps" were taken. See Colo. Rev. Stat. § 37-92-306; Bd. of County Comm'rs v. United States, 891 P.2d 952 (Colo. 1995). See infra p. 124, Note 6, for a discussion of Colorado appropriation procedures.

STATE EX REL. CARY v. COCHRAN

Supreme Court of Nebraska, 1940.
138 Neb. 163, 292 N.W. 239.

CARTER, JUSTICE. This is an action of mandamus brought by a number of irrigators under the Kearney canal, on behalf of themselves and others similarly situated, and by the Central Power Company, which, with the exception of one small user of water, is the owner of the oldest water appropriation on the Platte River and its tributaries. The respondents are the governor, the state engineer, and the chief of the bureau of irrigation and his subordinates. The petition prays for the issuance of a writ of mandamus compelling the proper administration and enforcement of the irrigation laws of the state for the purpose of protecting the irrigation and power rights of the relators from alleged unlawful diversions of water above relators' canal by junior appropriators. The trial court denied the writ and dismissed the petition of the relators. Relators thereupon perfected an appeal to this court.

It is not disputed that the waters of the Platte River and its tributaries are subject to appropriation for irrigation and power purposes upon the principle that priority of time bestows priority of right, and that pursuant to such principle the Central Power Company, through its predecessors in interest, was adjudicated and given a priority upon the Platte River, as of September 10, 1882, of 140 cubic feet per second of flow of water for power purposes, and a further appropriation, as of February 12, 1920, of 485 cubic feet per second for the same purposes. It is also admitted by the pleadings that 22 second-feet of water have been adjudicated to certain lands in Buffalo county for irrigation purposes with a priority dating of September 10, 1882, and which, for the purposes of this suit, will be treated as the property of certain of the relators claiming to be the owners thereof in this litigation. The foregoing appropriations of water, bearing the priority dating of September 10, 1882, are prior in time to all appropriations on the Platte River and its tributaries in Nebraska, except an appropriation to the Nelson Radcliffe canal in Morrill county with a priority dating of June 1, 1882, for 2.77 cubic feet of water per second of time. * * *

The respondents, as officers, agents and employees of the bureau of irrigation, are charged by law with the duty of the administration and enforcement of the irrigation laws of the state and the distribution of the waters of the Platte River and its tributaries within the state in accordance with adjudicated priorities. It is the contention of relators that respondents, in administering and enforcing the irrigation laws of the state and in the distribution of water for irrigation, have continuously permitted and allowed junior appropriators, situated above the headgate of the Central Power Company, to take and use water for irrigation, storage, and other purposes, without regard to priority and to the prejudice and damage of the relators. * * *

Losses from evaporation and transpiration are heavy, due to the wide and shallow character of the river. Changes of temperature and varying types of wind add to the uncertainty of the losses resulting from these changing conditions. Losses from percolation vary along the various sectors of the river. * * * Experts with experience on the river estimate that the loss in delivering water from North Platte to the headgate of the Kearney canal with a wet river bed amounts to three times the amount of delivery, and with a dry river bed that it is almost impossible to get water through without a flood or a large sustained flow. In other words, it requires approximately 700 second-feet of water at North Platte to deliver 162 second-feet at the headgate of the Kearney canal when the river bed is wet. The underlying sand and gravel beds thicken as the river moves east. With the bed of the river on the surface of these sand and gravel deposits, it requires a huge amount of water to recharge the river channel and surrounding water table after the river bed once becomes dry. Until the water table is built up to the surface of the river bed, the river channel will not support a continuous flow. * * *

Appropriations of water are made throughout the length of the river. The priority dates of these appropriations have no relation whatever to their location on the stream. Hence, very early appropriations may be found at the upper and lower ends of the stream, while very late appropriations are likewise found at both ends. In times of water shortage, the later appropriators are the first to be deprived of water. The closing of canals in accordance with the inverse order of their priority dates necessarily requires certain canals to close their headgates all along the stream at the same time. Water moves down the stream at approximately 25 miles per day with the result that it requires approximately ten days to deliver water from the state line to the Kearney headgate under normal conditions. The resulting lag therefore becomes an important factor to be considered. * * *

The real question to be decided, however, is the determination of the duty imposed upon the officers of the state in administering the waters of the stream when the available supply of water at the headgate of the Kearney canal is reduced to an amount less than the 162 second-feet to which the relators are entitled. The rights of relators to the use of this water as against all appropriators subsequent to September 10, 1882, cannot be questioned. It is the duty of the administrative officers of the state to recognize this right and to give force to relators' priority. This requires that junior appropriators be restrained from taking water from the stream so long as such water can be delivered in usable quantities at the headgate of the Kearney canal. If it appear that all the available water in the stream would be lost before its arrival at the headgate of the Kearney canal, it would, of course, be an unjustified waste of water to attempt delivery. Whether a definite quantity of water passing a given point on the stream would, if not diverted or interrupted in its course, reach the headgate of the Kearney canal in a usable quantity creates a very complicated question of fact. It therefore is the duty of the administrative officers of the state to determine from all available means, including the factors hereinbefore discussed, whether or not a usable quantity of water can be delivered at the headgate of the Kearney canal. It necessarily follows that this finding of fact must be determined in the first instance by the officers charged with the administration of the stream. The finding of fact thus made is final unless it appears that it was unreasonable or arbitrarily made. The determination of the facts is an administrative function, and an order or course of conduct based thereon raises only the question whether the administrator was supported in his finding by evidence indicating his action was not unreasonable or arbitrary.

After determination that a given quantity of water passing a certain point on the river would not, even if uninterrupted, reach the headgate of the Kearney canal in usable quantities, the administrative officers of the state may lawfully permit junior appropriators to divert it for irrigation purposes. This results ofttimes in having junior appropriators receiving a head of water at a time when an appropriator farther downstream is getting none, though he is prior in time. Such situations are not therefore conclusive evidence of unlawful diversions.

Amici curiae urges that the doctrine of reasonable use is in force in this state and that it should be applied to the case at bar. We recognize the principle that the public has an interest in the public waters of the state and it is the use thereof only that may be appropriated. Even though an adjudicated appropriation may be vested, it may be subjected to regulation and control by the state by virtue of its police power. It may likewise be circumscribed to the extent that a limited diversion for a specified purpose will not permit of an undue interference with the rights of other appropriators on the stream. But we cannot agree that the doctrine of reasonable use can be applied in a case where delivery of a usable quantity of water can be made, although the losses suffered in so doing are great. To permit the officers of the state the right to say whether prospective losses would or would not justify the delivery of usable quantities of water would clothe such officers with a discretion incompatible with the vested interests of the relators, and destroy the very purpose of the doctrine of appropriation existent in this state. When upstream appropriators applied for and received adjudicated priorities, they did so with the knowledge that there was an earlier appropriator at the lower end of the stream whose rights had to be recognized. When the relators applied for and received their adjudications, they are likewise presumed to have known that other appropriators would obtain inferior rights above them that would have to be recognized. Each is required to respect the vested rights of the others, even though some hardships may be thereby imposed. We therefore hold that the doctrine of reasonable use does not extend so far as to authorize the administrator of the waters of the stream to refrain from delivering a usable quantity of water to a senior appropriator because it might appear to him that excessive losses would result. The duty of the administrator, in administering the waters of the stream by virtue of the police power of the state, is to enforce existing priorities, not to determine, change or amend them. But in regulating the distribution of water it may become incidentally necessary for him to ascertain for that purpose only whether a prior appropriator is injured by a diversion above him. This finding of fact must be made, not to change existing priorities, but in order to determine whether or not a distribution of water may be made to a junior appropriator in accordance with existing priorities. * * *

The administration of the waters of the stream must be in accordance with the law announced in this opinion. The administrator testifies to his willingness to so administer the stream and, in fact, contends that he has so administered it. We doubt not that he will endeavor to so administer it in the future. * * * After a consideration of the pleadings, the evidence, and all the circumstances, surrounding the case, we think the trial court was justified in the exercise of such discretion in denying the writ prayed for. We likewise believe that the action will accomplish the desired end without the issuance of the writ at the time and in the form in which it was asked. We therefore hold that the district court did not err in denying the writ.

Notes

1. **Wisdom of the decision**. The rule of this case has been criticized as an example of waste built into the appropriation doctrine. See Clyde O. Fischer, Jr., Western Experience and Eastern Appropriation Proposals, in The Law of Water Allocation in the Eastern United States 75 (Haber & Bergen eds., 1958); Frank Maloney, Richard Ausness & James Morris, A Model Water Code 77, 158 (1972). But see Frank J. Trelease, The Model Water Code, the Wise Administrator and the Goddam Bureaucrat, 14 Nat. Resources J. 207 (1974):

"The 'waste' caused by the downstream senior on the dwindling stream should concern the easterner not at all. His streams gain water throughout their length, they do not lose it to desert soils. That such waste exists, even in the west, is doubtful. * * * A waste of 538 c.f.s.? The richer lands are at Kearney, and perhaps more can be produced there, at least the North Platte irrigators have never seen fit to buy out the Kearney irrigators. A better explanation is that the 538 c.f.s. feed the alluvial aquifer underlying a vast sea of corn and alfalfa that stretches along the valley, irrigated by thousands of wells. At any rate, the fault is not that of prior appropriation law but of historical accident.[91]"

The rule of the principal case may also provide another benefit not mentioned by Trelease—the preservation of instream flows. Note that the senior right of the Kearney Canal preserves a flow of at least 162 c.f.s. in the Platte River for some 250 miles when such flows are physically available. The existence of downstream senior rights has a similar effect on a number of western streams.

2. **A contrary view?** Would the principal case be followed in California (assuming that the water not reaching the Kearney Canal is wasted)? See *Imperial Irrigation Dist.*, supra p. 41.

3. **Effect of priority.** Frank J. Trelease, Climate Change and Water Law, in Climate, Climatic Change and Water Supply (National Research Council & National Academy of Sciences eds., 1977):

"The rule of priority operates even in a normal year, not only in time of shortage. On an unregulated stream (one without storage dams) from which many irrigators draw water, all may open their ditches in the spring as the mountain snowpacks melt and the stream is high. As the flow decreases during the dry summer, the diversion works are shut off in inverse order of priority. The last ditch is first closed; the first need never be. The entire burden of the lessened flow falls on the junior appropriator. He loses all his water; the senior, none. Some have called this a harsh rule, but it should be remembered that the low flow is insufficient for all, and that equal shares for everybody would be sufficient for none. The rule of priority does guarantee a firm supply to all for whom the source is sufficient, and the senior irrigators can build a stable agriculture unmatched in humid climes. The junior appropriator is not unlike the farmer in a semihumid area who must take his chances on rain. If he can only count on spring flood water, he will grow one crop of wild hay and will not plant a late maturing crop like sugar beets. The senior may grow an orchard or a vineyard, the junior will plant corn, since he may gamble on the loss of an annual crop but not of a permanent investment.

"Since the low flow will accommodate so few users, storage is desirable to detain the spring flood for release in the late summer. The rule of priority also determines who will pay for the dam—it is the junior appropriator who will get the benefit from it. In return for his investment, he will often have a better right than many seniors, since his stored water will carry him late into the year when the base flow becomes insufficient for all but a few. For this reason, seniors will often join in a dam project in order to receive supplemental water to firm up their late season supply. * * *

"Applying the rule of priority to the physical results of drought or climatic change may have some unexpected effects. It is not correct to think that drought will simply fall upon the most junior appropriators and wipe them out. In the long run, of course, the juniors will be those squeezed out, but many holders of senior

---

91. Nebraska was settled from east to west as the homesteaders encroached on Indian territory, so the early priorities are in the downstream east. In Colorado, however, the lands at the foot of the Rockies were settled first so the senior rights are there, and the downstream lands were settled later as the junior appropriators pushed eastward against the Cheyennes of the Smoky Hills.

and intermediate priorities may be affected. It will depend in part on the nature of the change, whether it takes the form of an extraordinarily 'subnormal' water year, an 'unexpectedly long' series of low water years, or a 'permanent' change in climate that reduces the long-term yield to some new norm. In most subnormal years, the high water begins to drop at an earlier date than usual, and as the flow subsides each junior appropriator will 'go out of priority' and must close his intake some indeterminate number of days earlier than he would have if the year had been within the 'normal' range. On an unregulated stream, the odds will be changed on all the bets. The original marginal junior rights become untenable and forfeit, the moderately secure rights are now risky, and the relatively certain are smaller in number. If the subnormality consists of unusually low base flows, the seniors who depend on late summer flows may get hurt the worst. If the drought flattens out the peaks and there is less high water than expected, then junior storage projects bear the brunt. Where large-scale storage has been built to equate the supply, the planners had in mind some combination of bad years to be hurdled. If that 'design drought' were never exceeded, every right would be as good as any other; but if the dams are finally run dry, a substantial block of shares—all of those that depend on the junior project—will fail together.

"Variations in the pattern of multiyear drought will also change the incidence of hardship. The North Platte River, to take an example, is a fully regulated stream on which the annual and perennial fluctuations have been ironed out by two large projects with different priorities. The earliest, Pathfinder Dam, has low storage in proportion to the land it serves, while the more recent project, Seminoe Dam, has large storage but a late priority. A short-term drought with several years of very low flows would dry up Pathfinder but might be well within the carryover capacity of Seminoe, while a long sequence of mediocre years would hardly affect Pathfinder but would ruin the Seminoe project."

4. **Importance of priority.** Priority is the principle most associated with the appropriation doctrine; for example, it is frequently called "the doctrine of *prior* appropriation." But just how important is the principle? Consider:

"The priority of a water right is a * * * the most important stick in the water rights bundle. * * * The security and reliability of water rights turn on the enforceability of priorities when natural supply is not adequate to fill all decreed rights and administration of decreed rights is necessary to ensure the property value of water rights." Empire Lodge Homeowners' Ass'n v. Moyer, 39 P.3d 1139, 1148-49 (Colo. 2001)

"This article addresses the question of whether priority enforcement is in fact the rule of western water law. It argues that priority is an efficient rule of water allocation, but it is often more rhetoric than rule. * * *

"The fact that priority enforcement is more bluff than substance does not undermine the need for consistent and fair allocation rules, but it does call into question the sole reliance on enforcement of priorities to allocate water in temporary and chronic shortages. The principal assumption of this article is that experience will demonstrate that priorities are seldom enforced in practice. In many situations, the strict enforcement of prior appropriation would raise substantial fairness and efficiency concerns. * * * Thus, it is not surprising that states have taken extraordinary steps to ensure that the rule is never applied in practice and that federal, state and local water distribution agencies find alternative ways to ameliorate the rule when droughts occur.

"I do not argue that priority should be abandoned. There are no superior alternatives. Rather, I make a positive and normative argument. The positive one is simply that priority enforcement is generally the exception rather than the norm, and thus there is a need to examine more systematically what happens when scarcity occurs and how large and small systems cope. The normative argument is that the focus of water allocation should be on the actual expectations that lie behind a use, rather than the simple enforcement of the entitlement to understand that alternative ways of satisfying those expectations exist. The core idea of prior appropriation is the protection of investment-backed expectations from the risks of variable water years and perhaps now global climate change, and this idea remains a valid objective. The issue is whether the enforcement of priorities contributes to this objective." A. Dan Tarlock, Prior Appropriation: Rule, Principle, or Rhetoric, 76 N.D. L. Rev. 881, 883-84 (2000)

5. **Ignoring priority—"futile calls."** In Colorado a senior appropriator's complaint to the water commissioner that upstream juniors are taking his water and should be regulated is known as "calling the river." When shutting down the junior does not improve the senior's water supply, a "futile call" has occurred. The Water Right Determination and Administration Act of 1969 deals with the matter both substantively and procedurally: "No reduction of any lawful diversion because of the operation of the priority system shall be permitted unless such reduction would increase the amount of water available to and required by water rights having senior priorities." Colo. Rev. Stat. § 37-92-102(2)(d).

"Each division engineer shall order the total or partial discontinuance of any diversion in his division to the extent the water being diverted is not necessary for application to a beneficial use; and he shall also order the total or partial discontinuance of any diversion in his division to the extent the water being diverted is required by persons entitled to use water under water rights having senior priorities, but no such discontinuance shall be ordered unless the diversion is causing or will cause material injury to such water rights having senior priorities. In making his decision as to the discontinuance of a diversion to satisfy senior priorities the division engineer shall be governed by the following: The materiality of injury depends on all factors which will determine in each case the amount of water such discontinuance will make available to such senior priorities at the time and place of their need. Such factors include the current and prospective volumes of water in and tributary to the stream from which the diversion is being made; distance and type of stream bed between the diversion points; the various velocities of this water, both surface and underground; the probable duration of the available flow; and the predictable return flow to the affected stream. Each diversion shall be evaluated and administered on the basis of the circumstances relating to it and in accordance with provisions of this article and the court decrees adjudicating and confirming water rights. In the event a discontinuance has been ordered pursuant to the foregoing, and nevertheless such does not cause water to become available to such senior priorities at the time and place of their need, then such discontinuance order shall be rescinded." Colo. Rev. Stat. § 37-92-502(2).

6. **Another "futile call."** Seepage and return flows sometimes recharge downstream segments of a stream even though diversions have completely depleted the flow upstream. Baker Ditch Co. v. District Court, Gallatin County, 824 P.2d 260 (Mont. 1992), involved such a situation. In an attempt to protect

instream flows, the water commissioner applied the rule of priority literally and refused to allow a downsteam appropriator to divert water because there was no water available for upstream senior rights. Held, the downstream appropriator could divert water because it would cause no detriment to prior appropriators.

7. **Priority and tributary flows.** Diversions from tributaries may be regulated in favor of senior appropriators from the main stream below the junction, Strickler v. City of Colorado Springs, 26 P. 313 (Colo. 1891), but not infrequently practical considerations lead to separate administration of intermittent tributaries. For example, in Nebraska v. Wyoming, 325 U.S. 589 (1945), the Court entered a decree protecting prior Nebraska appropriators of the North Platte River from violations of priority by Wyoming irrigators from the main stream, but said regarding the tributaries: "Below Pathfinder and above Geurnsey the Special Master dealt only with diversions from the main river. He concluded that the run-off of the tributaries becomes so far exhausted before any shortage of water occurs in the main river that any regulation of the tributary diversions would be of no material benefit. The tributary inflow is greater than the depletion of the river. There is some out-of-priority diversion as we have noted. But * * * practical difficulties of applying restrictions which would reduce the amount of water used by the hundreds of small irrigators would seem to outweigh any slight benefit which senior appropriators might obtain." Id. at 624.

8. **Seasonal priorities.** Seasonal priorities exist in some states. They entitle the appropriator to take water only during certain periods or seasons, so that other persons who initiated their rights at later dates may have a better claim to water during other times of the year. Some courts have rigidly frozen the pioneer pattern of use, restricting the use of the lands to the original crop irrigated, or even incorporating the personal habits of the original appropriator into the water right. Thorne v. McKinley Bros., 56 P.2d 204 (Cal. 1936) (never at night); Santa Paula Waterworks v. Peralta, 45 P. 168 (Cal. 1896) (24 hours per week beginning Saturday noon); Oliver v. Skinner, 226 P.2d 507 (Or. 1951) (an appropriation for irrigating hay lands, never used after July 1st, cannot be used for crops requiring water later in the year).

The more modern rule is that unless the claim, permit or decree upon which the right is founded imposes time limits on its use, the appropriator can take the water at any time he can put it to the beneficial use for which it was appropriated. See Harkey v. Smith, 247 P. 550, 553 (N.M. 1926): "In this connection it is to be observed that the doctrine of seasonal appropriation is not well adapted to general agriculture, such as that in which the parties are here engaged. The right, to be effective, must authorize the rotation of crops and variation of times or methods of the irrigation thereof, from year to year, as experience may dictate, or conditions of the lands, or markets for agricultural products, might seem to render advisable. * * * The farmer must have the water whenever, in pursuance of any reasonable plan, he requires it for his crops, or the preparation of his lands for planting; otherwise his right will be too precarious to be of any practical value."

9. **Reservoir storage.** Usually there is no division of the year into an irrigation season and a storage season, so as to give later direct users a seasonal preference over earlier reservoirs or vice versa. People ex rel. Park Reservoir Co. v. Hinderlider, 57 P.2d 894 (Colo. 1936). But see Neb. Rev. Stat. § 46-241 (forbidding the impounding of water when it is required for direct irrigation).

10. **Priority in a "regulatory drought."** In a physical drought, the rule of priority means that junior appropriators receive nothing while senior appropriators remain untouched. Should the result be the same in a "regulatory drought"—a shortage caused by new laws which reduce the quantity of water available for diversion and consumptive use—or should the shortfall be allocated by different principles? See United States v. State Water Res. Control Bd., infra pp. 580-81, Note 1; Harrison C. Dunning, State Equitable Apportionment of Western Water Resources, 66 Neb. L. Rev. 76 (1987).

PHILLIPS v. GARDNER

Court of Appeals of Oregon, 1970.
2 Or. App. 423, 469 P.2d 42.

SCHWAB, CHIEF JUDGE. The defendant watermaster, who is charged with the duty of distributing water in Yamhill County in accordance with the rights of each user, threatened to cut off plaintiffs' domestic water supply and to empty plaintiffs' impoundment for that purpose to give water to a downstream user who holds the water right for irrigation prior in time to plaintiffs' domestic right. Plaintiffs brought suit to enjoin the defendant watermaster from so doing, claiming a statutory priority for domestic use under ORS 540.140. The trial judge granted the injunction and the defendant watermaster appeals, contending that ORS 540.140 has no application to the facts of this case. The plaintiffs' water certificate has a priority date of June 7, 1947; the downstream property owner's water certificate has a priority date of August 26, 1919.

During the months of August and September 1967, there was not sufficient water to serve both appropriators. The watermaster threatened to cut off plaintiffs' water supply and this gave rise to the suit in question. This controversy relates to surface water only, not to ground water available through wells.

ORS 540.140 was enacted in 1893. It reads:

> "When the waters of any natural stream are not sufficient for the service of all those desiring the use of the same, those using the water for domestic purposes shall, subject to such limitations as may be prescribed by law, have the preference over those claiming such water for any other purpose, and those using the water for agricultural purposes shall have the preference over those using the same for manufacturing purposes."

The statute has never been cited or discussed in any of the numerous opinions of the Oregon Supreme Court dealing with the application of Oregon water laws.

Oregon first adopted a comprehensive water code in 1909. Since then this code has been subject to major amendments. The reasons for the extensive body of statutory law and court rulings relating to the use and conservation of water in Oregon are succinctly set out in the Preface to United States Dep't of Agriculture, Selected Problems in the Law of Water Rights in the West, Misc.Pub. No. 418 (Wells A. Hutchins 1942):

"By and large, water is plentiful east of the tier of States from North Dakota to Texas. Within those six States and their western neighbors, however, water is scarce and provides a limiting factor on the productivity of the soil. It is understandable, therefore, that the water law of these Western States presents a complexity of pattern and a fullness of development not to be found in the law relating to waters in the East * * *."

The 1909 Act established a system for the filing of applications for the appropriation of water with the state engineer in § 47 (ORS 537.130(1)), and provided in § 46 (ORS 537.140), that applications contain, among other information, the nature and amount of proposed use. Section 46 discloses that the legislature had in mind that there were varying uses of water for among the uses to which it there refers are those for agriculture, power, municipal water supply and mining. Section 54 (ORS 537.250(3)) provides "The right acquired by an appropriation shall date from the filing of the application in the office of the State Engineer."

The Act, § 73, provides "All laws and parts of laws so far as in conflict or inconsistent with the provisions of this act are hereby repealed."

The plaintiffs argue that despite the provisions of the 1909 Water Act the holder of a certificate for domestic water use has a preference by virtue of ORS 540.140 over a prior recorded water right for other purposes.

* * * Although the 1909 Act did not directly state that thereafter priorities should be based on priority in time and not on nature of use, the whole thrust of the Act clearly indicates such a purpose. The insufficiency of water in parts of Oregon is what gave rise to Oregon's comprehensive water code commencing with the 1909 Act. Priorities are meaningful only in times of shortage. If we were to apply ORS 540.140 as plaintiffs would have us do, in times of shortage—the only time when there is any reason for priorities—water would be allocated based upon the nature of the various uses involved, not on the basis of the effective date of appropriation. The result would be that the priorities established by the 1909 Act and subsequent additions to it would be effective only as to appropriators within similar categories of use. It is hard for us to conceive that the 1909 and subsequent legislatures could have intended such a result without one word in the statutes to indicate their desire to adopt such a complicated scheme. It may be that ORS 540.140 still has viability as to rights which were perfected prior to 1909 or as to rights bearing the same effective date. Since neither situation is involved in the case at bar, we need not consider those possibilities here.

Appealing as plaintiffs' humanistic arguments may be, if viewed from a single point of view, it is our opinion that the statutory interpretation they seek is in conflict with what we perceive as clear legislative intent—the substitution of priority based on time of appropriation for the pre-1909 statutory preference (ORS 540.140) based on the nature of the use.

Reversed and remanded for the entry of a decree in accordance with this opinion.

Notes

1. **Alternatives for the junior appropriator.** Does this decision mean that Gardner goes thirsty? See Chapter 2, Section 5 (Transfer).

2. **The meanings of "preference."** "Preference" can refer to one of several quite different things: (1) In times of shortage, the water is devoted to the preferred use instead of to a non-preferred purpose although the latter is prior in time—sometimes called a "true preference." (2) Where applicants compete for permits to appropriate a supply of unappropriated water insufficient for all proposed uses, the preferred user gets the water right, regardless of the relative priority of filing the applications. (3) Where a change is needed in the use of appropriated water, the preferred user may condemn and pay for a prior right for a non-preferred use. The principal case involves a putative preference of the first type. Preferences of the second type are discussed infra p. 158, Note 5, of the third at p. 211, Note 3. Other doctrines sometimes result in one or another type of preference existing under certain circumstances. See Frank J. Trelease, Preferences to the Use of Water, 27 Rocky Mtn. L. Rev. 133 (1955).

3. **Subordination of Priority.** Cal. Water Code § 106 provides that "the use of water for domestic purposes is the highest use of water and that the next highest use is for use in irrigation." In implementing this statute, the California authorities not only have chosen applications for preferred uses over presently competing applications, but have subordinated current non-preferred uses to future preferred uses, for example, by inserting into a permit for a hydroelectric power project the condition, "The right to store and use water for power purposes under this permit shall not interfere with future appropriation of said water for agricultural or municipal purposes." This procedure was upheld in East Bay Municipal Utility District v. Department of Public Works, 35 P.2d 1027 (Cal. 1934).

In Benz v. Water Resources Commission, 764 P.2d 594 (Or. Ct. App. 1988), a farmer used groundwater which had a high boron content to irrigate his lands. The accumulation of boron in the soil was detrimental to the farmer's crops, and he sought a permit to appropriate winter stream flows to be used to leach boron from the soil. The Water Resources Commission found that boron leaching was a beneficial use of water. However the commission also found:

"[B]ecause boron leaching will require the application of large quantities of water, boron leaching is of less benefit overall than other potential future uses, junior in priority to the subject application, for which water should be conserved. Accordingly, [the commission] allowed the appropriation for boron leaching on the condition that it be 'subordinate and inferior to both the storage and direct use of water for other consumptive beneficial uses of water.'"

The court affirmed the subordination of the appropriation, citing Oregon statutes requiring the Commission to consider various factors, including "the highest use of the water" and "the maximum economic development of the waters involved," in determining if a proposed use of water will be in the public interest.

A subordination can also be consensual. See, for example, Board of County Commissioners v. Crystal Creek Homeowners' Association, 14 P.3d 325 (Colo. 2000), in which the United States Bureau of Reclamation subordinated certain rights in the Gunnison River to junior rights for in-basin uses, but not to junior rights for out-of-basin uses. Why would an appropriator voluntarily subordinate the priority of a water right?

Is subordination appropriate if the proposed appropriation requires a large capital expenditure? Will an applicant go forward with the project in such a case?

4. **"True preferences"?** S.D. Codified Laws § 46-1-5: "It is the established policy of this state: (1) That the use of water for domestic purposes is the highest use of water and takes precedence over all appropriative rights, if it is exercised in a manner consistent with public interest as provided in § 46-1-2."

Utah Code Ann. § 73-3-21: "Appropriators shall have priority among themselves according to the dates of their respective appropriations, so that each appropriator shall be entitled to receive his whole supply before any subsequent appropriator shall have any right; provided, in times of scarcity, while priority of appropriation shall give the better right as between those using water for the same purpose, the use for domestic purposes, without unnecessary waste, shall have preference over use for all other purposes, and use for agricultural purposes shall have preference over use for any other purpose except domestic use."

Are these "true preferences"? Or are they preferences of the third type, requiring compensation if a senior appropriator is required to relinquish water for a preferred junior use?

CACHE LA POUDRE WATER USERS ASS'N v. GLACIER VIEW MEADOWS

Supreme Court of Colorado, 1976.
191 Colo. 53, 550 P.2d 288.

GROVES, JUSTICE. The applicant Glacier View Meadows, a limited partnership, is a developer of residential lots in the mountains northwest of Fort Collins, Colorado. It filed with the water court two applications for approval of a plan of augmentation. The plans would provide future owners of presently unimproved lots with domestic water from wells to be drilled in the future. * * * The court granted approval of the plan for augmentation in the first two applications. We affirm with some modifications. * * *

The objector, Cache LaPoudre Water Users Association, is a non-profit protective association, whose members own substantial reservoir and direct flow decrees on the Cache LaPoudre River. * * *

The applicant owns 75 "preferred shares" of the Mountain and Plains Irrigation Company, which entitle applicant to both reservoir and direct flow water. Applicant acquired these 75 shares from Ideal Cement Company, Dreher Pickle Company and City of Fort Collins, which historically had made year-around use of their water. Under the plan some of applicant's reservoir rights will be used to replace consumptively used water from proposed wells. The water from the wells will be exclusively devoted to in-house, residential domestic use. Under the two applications which are the subject of the court's decree, there will be a maximum of 1892 single-family residential units. In some cases, one well will furnish water for more than one unit.

The reservoirs containing replacement water and the points of discharge of water therefrom into the stream, as well as all of the residential units and the points of return flow therefrom into the stream, lie above the points of diversion of any water of the objectors.

Of the 1892 units, at ultimate development 105 units are expected to use an evapotranspiration system of sewage disposal. The consumptive use for these 105 units will be 100% of the water diverted from wells. This 100% will be replaced entirely by reservoir water plus enough to account for evaporative losses during transportation in the stream.

The remaining 1787 units, when ultimately developed, will have septic-soil absorption sewage systems. From these latter diversions there will be a consumptive use of not more than 10% and at least 90% will constitute return flow to the stream. Replacement water for the 10%, plus an amount sufficient to embrace transportation losses, will be replenished by the aforementioned releases from the reservoirs.

The rate of flow permitted and claimed for each well will be four gallons per minute for each dwelling unit to be served by any well. The plan is predicated upon the assumption that each dwelling unit will be occupied by 3.5 persons 365 days a year, and that each person will require 80 gallons of well water per day. The entire consumptive use of well water (including those units having 100% consumptive use) will not exceed 89 acre feet per year. 55 of applicant's 75 shares will be devoted to replacement of this consumptively used water. 55 shares represent an amount of 94.71 acre feet per year. After deducting 5% for transportation losses, 89.97 feet remain for replacement. * * *

As mentioned earlier, the applicant acquired the 75 shares from Ideal Cement Company, Dreher Pickle Company and the City of Fort Collins. Historically, only 25% of the water used by these three returned to the stream. The plan allocates the water from 20 of the 75 shares of stock for use in the stream in lieu of the 25% return flow which no longer exists.

It is contemplated by the plan that, so long as its provisions are followed, there will be no injury to the holders of prior rights. However, if there is a call by a right superior to the association's priority rights, that call must be met. The water court concluded that the only thing that will upset the plan will be an extended period of drought. If such a drought causes insufficient water to be available for replacement, the well water users will be obliged to acquire additional water by lease or otherwise, or else to reduce their consumptive use, to the end that water consumptively used under the plan will not exceed that available for replacement. * * *

The principal argument of the objectors is that, except during flood stages, the Cache LaPoudre River is over-appropriated. With this we agree. The argument continues that, unless there is 100% replacement of the water taken from the wells, senior water rights will be injured and there will be a violation of the Water Right Determination and Administration Act of 1969 (section 37-92-101 et seq., C.R.S.1973, hereinafter called the "Act"), and the rules and regulations of the State Engineer's office. * * *

First, we look to the Act, and here quote some of the legislative declaration underlying it and the definition of "plan for augmentation":

"(1) It is hereby declared to be the policy of the state of Colorado that all waters originating in or flowing into this state, whether found on the surface or underground, have always been and are hereby declared to be the property of the public, dedicated to the use of the people of the state, subject to appropriation and use in accordance with law. As incident thereto, it is the policy of this state to integrate the appropriation, use, and administration of underground water tributary to a stream with the use of surface water in such a way as to maximize the beneficial use of all of the waters of this state.

"'Plan for argumentation' means a detailed program to increase the supply of water available for beneficial use in a division or portion thereof by the development of new or alternate means or points of diversion, by a pooling of water resources, by water exchange projects, by providing substitute supplies of water, by the development of new sources of water, or by any other appropriate means." Section 37-92-103(9), C.R.S.1973.

We find that the plan of augmentation has been formulated and approved consonant with, and in furtherance of, the purpose and intent of our recent statutes; and that the plan is valid.

We hold here * * * that under the plans for augmentation involved water is available for appropriation when the diversion thereof does not injure holders of vested rights.

Objectors cite Southeastern Colorado Water Conservancy District v. Shelton Farms, 187 Colo. 181, 529 P.2d 1321 (1974), in which this court ruled that one, who cuts down water-consuming vegetation (phreatophytes) along the Arkansas River, does not have a right to a decree for an equivalent amount of water to that consumed by the vegetation, free of the call of the river. In the opinion it was stated, "Appellees would substitute the priority doctrine with a lack of injury doctrine." The judgment was reversed and the cause remanded to the trial court with directions to vacate the decree. The indication from the foregoing that *Shelton Farms* stands for the proposition that lack of injury does not cause water to be available for appropriation must be analyzed. *Shelton Farms* involved a factual situation which makes it distinguishable from this. * * *

There, the senior rights had adjusted to the loss of the water caused by the growth of phreatophytes; and, once returned to the river, the water would still belong to the senior users in satisfaction of their decrees. In the instant case, the water to be used in replacement never was that of the senior users. Here, there is not displacement "*from the time and place of* their need." Under the findings here, the stream will be the same, irrespective of the well diversions.

Under the circumstances of this case, there is no significant difference between the prior appropriation doctrine, and the lack of injury doctrine. Here, where senior users can show no injury by the diversion of water, they cannot preclude the beneficial use of water by another. Fellhauer v. People, 167 Colo. 320, 447 P.2d 986 (1968), was cited as authority in *Shelton Farms.* It is likewise authority here. As was there said, "As administration of water approaches its second century the curtain is opening upon the new drama of *maximum utilization* and how constitutionally that doctrine can be integrated into the law of *vested rights*."

We rule that, in a matter such as this one, water is available for appropriation if the taking thereof does not cause injury. Therefore, the argument of the objectors, to the effect that water withdrawn from the wells must be replaced 100%, falls.

Notes

1. **Priority and substitution.** "Plan of augmentation" is a Colorado term, but the rule that a senior appropriator can be compelled to accept a substitute source of water or other modifications which allow a junior to use water without harming the senior is widely accepted. See Harrison C. Dunning, The "Physical Solution" in Western Water Law, 57 U. Colo. L. Rev. 445 (1986). More broadly, the rule is a corollary of the principle that the rights of the junior appropriator begin at the limits of the rights of the senior.

2. **Other examples of substitution.** Senior appropriators may claim all the summer flow in the downstream reaches of a stream, while a reservoir site lies above them and undeveloped lands above the site. Junior appropriators may build the reservoir, appropriate the senior's natural flow for the upstream land and substitute the stored water on the downstream land. Reno v. Richards, 178 P. 81 (Idaho 1918). Where senior appropriators claim all the natural flow within a valley, a junior may import water from a different watershed, use the natural flow, and deliver the imported water to the senior. Bd. of Dirs. of Wilder Irrigation Dist. v. Jorgenson, 136 P.2d 461 (Idaho 1943).

3. **Limits of senior rights.** The defining elements of an appropriative right serve not only to "measure" the right but also to limit it, in much the same way that a boundary description both measures and limits the rights of a landowner. Consequently, a senior appropriator has no right, as against a junior appropriator, to waste water, to increase the amount or extend the time of his diversion so as to put it to double use by irrigation of other lands, nor to lend, rent or sell to others the excess water. Enlarged Southside Irrigation Ditch Co. v. John's Flood Ditch Co., 183 P.2d 552 (Colo. 1947). In Colorado, this rule is often phrased in terms of a vested right of the junior appropriator to the continuation of stream conditions as they existed at the time of his appropriation. See Farmers Highline Canal & Reservoir Co. v. City of Golden, infra p. 197.

This rule is an over-simplification that is subject to many exceptions, since the second user of water is not protected against its loss in every case of change in the manner and form of the first use. See Metro. Denver Sewage Disposal Dist. No. 1 v. Farmers Reservoir & Irrigation Co., 499 P.2d 1190 (Colo. 1972). For thirty years Denver had deposited the effluent from its municipal sewage treatment plant into the South Platte River above the headgate of the irrigation company. When the plant became inadequate the sewage was transported to a large new metropolitan plant whose outfall was downstream from the plaintiff's point of diversion. Held, in an action for a declaratory judgment, downstream appropriators have no vested right of control over the works of the upstream appropriator, and a change in the point of return to the stream is not subject to the no-harm rule. See also Chapter 2, Section 6, examining reuse of return flows and rights to imported water.

4. **Senior appropriators not protected from every injury.** A senior appropriator is not protected against every detrimental change caused by junior appropriators. In Colorado's "dirty water case," A-B Cattle Co. v. United States, 589 P.2d 57 (Colo. 1978), complaint was made by irrigators from the Bessemer Ditch that the muddy water of the Arkansas River, which had sealed the ditch with silt, had been replaced by the Bureau of Reclamation with clear, clean reservoir water, which leaked out of the ditch so that less water arrived at the place of use. In a 4-3 decision, the court decided, in effect, that plaintiffs had a water right, not a silt right, and no claim to compensation.

In City of Thornton v. Bijou Irrigation Co., 926 P.2d 1 (Colo. 1996), Thornton proposed to divert water from the Poudre River above a manufacturing plant owned by Eastman Kodak Company and replace it with a substitute supply below Kodak's plant. Although the proposal substantially reduced river flows between the point of diversion and replacement, it left sufficient flows to satisfy Kodak's water rights. Nevertheless, Kodak opposed the proposal because it reduced the quantity of water in the river available to dilute wastewater discharged by Kodak. Kodak asserted that the flow reduction would require it to construct a new treatment facility costing nine to twelve million dollars to meet water quality standards for its discharged wastewater. The court ruled against Kodak, holding that the loss of diluting flows is not an injury against which a senior appropriator is protected. The court said that Kodak was essentially seeking a private instream flow right for the purpose of waste dilution or assimilation, contrary to Colo. Rev. Stat. § 37-92-102(3), which prohibits private parties from holding instream flow rights, and to Colo. Rev. Stat. § 25-8-104(1), which prohibits the use of minimum stream flows to protect water quality. The court also noted that Kodak was not entitled to the diluting flows because it had no appropriation for such a purpose. (The relationship between water rights and water quality regulation is explored further in Chapter 7, Section 2B).

5. **Interconnected surface water and groundwater.** Glacier View Meadows plans to use wells for its water supply. Why then is it concerned with the rights of appropriators from the Cache LaPoudre River? The answer, of course, is that the groundwater and the river are interconnected and are being treated as a single source of supply. In Colorado, such groundwater is labeled "tributary groundwater." The label is an apt one. Like surface tributaries, the groundwater in *Glacier View* feeds the river. Pumping the groundwater will reduce flows in the river *in much the same way* as diversions from surface tributaries would. Because the river is over-appropriated, new diversions from tributary waters, whether surface or underground, are permissible only if the diverted water is replaced, as Glacier View Meadows proposes to do by releasing reservoir water.

As the italicized phrase implies, diversions through wells will usually not have an identical effect to diversions from surface tributaries. Indeed, management of interconnected groundwater and surface water is one of the most complex problems encountered in water law. This problem is explored in detail in Chapter 4, Section 2 C.

6. **"Transfer" v. "Dedication."** The Rio Grande River in New Mexico is fully appropriated. Groundwater in the Rio Grande basin is hydrologically connected to the river. In order to protect senior rights to river flows, the New Mexico State Engineer requires applicants for groundwater permits in the basin

to acquire and "dedicate" (retire) sufficient surface water rights to offset the effects of pumping on the river, a practice which was upheld in City of Albuquerque v. Reynolds, 379 P.2d 73 (N.M. 1963). An alternative for a prospective groundwater user might be to acquire a surface right and transfer its point of diversion to a well. The distinction between "dedication" and "transfer" is explained in Charles T. Dumars, Changing Interpretations of New Mexico's Constitutional Provisions Allocating Water Resources: Integrating Private Property Rights and Public Values, 26 N.M. L. Rev. 367, 375 (1996):

"The distinction * * * is more than academic. The distinction can be summed up in two words—'priority date.' In the transfer of a water right, one seeks to take a water right with a certain priority on the system and move it to a new location—thereby establishing a right to a particular quantity of water, at a particular point of diversion, for a particular use. Theoretically, this transferred right can then be protected by injunction in court. In prior appropriation water law, this priority date is critical because during scarcity that right will continue to be served if it is senior, while junior users go without water.

"The dedication process is quite different. When a person agrees by contract to cease using his water right, he is not moving his priority date to a new location. The groundwater user who is paying him to no longer irrigate is simply committing to the state engineer that a set quantity will remain in the river to offset the impacts of his groundwater diversion. The priority date of the groundwater user is the date of his well. If a call is made on the river in the future because of scarcity, the groundwater user may be shut down. but that was the risk he took when he chose to simply appropriate groundwater."

Why wouldn't a person wishing to drill a well in the Rio Grande basin prefer the early priority obtained through a transfer to the later priority obtained through dedication? Dumars implies that approval of a transfer is more complex and costly than approval of a dedications. ("Requiring all well owners to 'transfer' would * * * add to the external costs associated with groundwater pumping.") Dumars also prefers dedication on policy grounds, arguing that it is more consistent with hydrologic realities and provides better protection to other public and private values associated with a flowing river.

7. **Rotation.** Where there is water enough for each of several small appropriations, each appropriator in turn may take the total share of all for a short interval, in order to give each an "irrigating head" of a manageable quantity of water and to cut down on seepage and evaporation. Such "rotation" does not violate the doctrine of priority, but is a variation in its administration. Most of the western states have statutes permitting and regulating the practice of rotation by agreement. E.g., Wyo. Stat. Ann. § 41-3-612. Sometimes courts have imposed rotation upon appropriators by decree, where more efficient utilization of small flows will result. McCoy v. Huntley, 119 P. 481 (Or. 1911); Big Cottonwood Tanner Ditch Co. v. Shurtliff, 164 P. 856 (Utah 1916); compare Harris v. Harrison, 29 P. 325 (Cal. 1892) (rotation among riparians).

Where water users draw from a community ditch or have shares entitling them to participate in the water right of a mutual ditch company or an irrigation district, so that all rights are of equal dignity, it is usual to rotate the water to them and allow each a specified number of "water days," rather than to distribute the water to all at once and allow small quantities to dribble into many laterals simultaneously.

D. Waters Subject To Appropriation

WATER: THE YEARBOOK OF AGRICULTURE
United States Department of Agriculture, 1955.
pp. 42, 43.

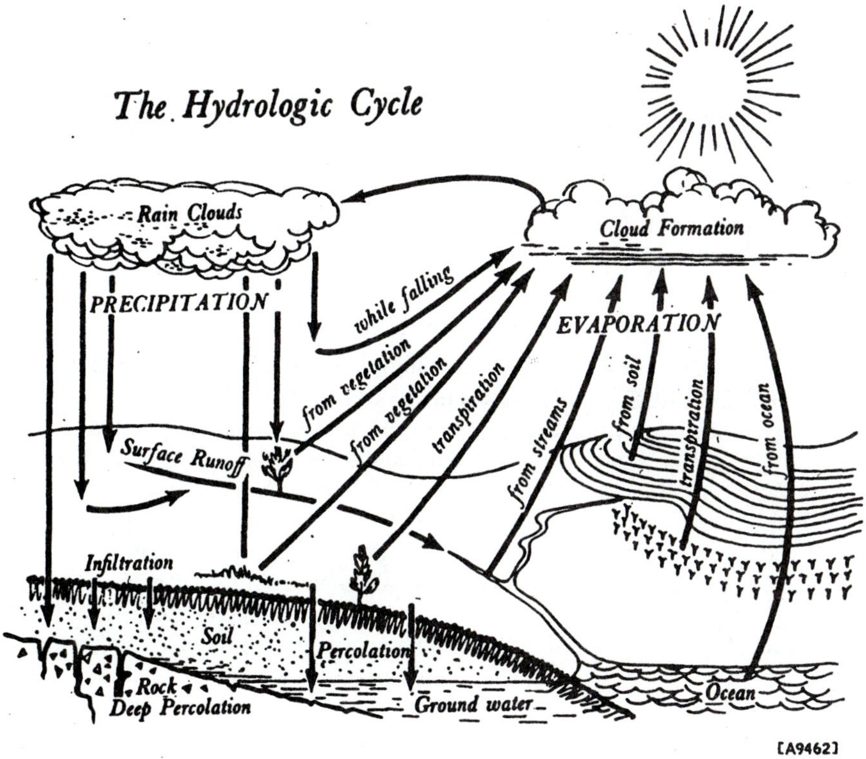

The unending circulation of the earth's moisture and water is called the water cycle. It is a gigantic system operating in and on the land and oceans of the earth and in the atmosphere that surrounds the earth. The cycle has no beginning or ending, but because our discussion must start someplace, we can think of it as beginning with the waters of the oceans, which cover about three-fourths of the earth's surface.

Water from the surface of the oceans is evaporated into the atmosphere. That moisture in turn is lifted and is eventually condensed and falls back to the earth's surface as precipitation. The part of the precipitation that falls as rain, hail, dew, snow, or sleet on the land is of particular concern to man and agriculture. Some of the precipitation, after wetting the foliage and ground, runs off over the surface to the streams. It is the water that sometimes causes erosion and is the main contributor to floods. Of the precipitation that soaks into the ground, some is available for growing plants and for evaporation. Some reaches the deeper zones and slowly percolates through springs and seeps to maintain the streams during dry periods. The streams in turn eventually lead back to the oceans, where the water originated. It is because of this never-ending circulation that the process has become known as the water cycle, or hydrologic cycle.

About 80,000 cubic miles of water are evaporated each year from the oceans. About 15,000 cubic miles are evaporated from the lakes and land surfaces of the continents. Total evaporation is equaled by total precipitation, of which about 24,000 cubic miles fall on the land surfaces. * * *

Rain that reaches the soil surface is wholly or partly absorbed by the soil in the process of infiltration. How much of it enters the soil depends upon the rate of rainfall and the receptiveness or infiltration rate of the soil. When the rainfall rate exceeds the infiltration rate, the excess rain becomes surface flow, which runs off quickly to streams. Surface flow is undesirable because it may erode the soil and also because it often produces damagingly rapid and high flows in streams during storms.

Note

Although scientists regard the hydrologic cycle as a unity, the law has usually applied different rules to different segments of the cycle. Historically, the legal problems of the past arose principally between persons competing for water at the same point in the cycle. Disputes between competitors for ground water or between users or drainers of diffused surface waters were not seen to require rules identical to those developed to settle conflicts over the use of stream flows, and scientific knowledge of the nature of water occurrence and the interrelationship of different classes of water was lacking. Thus each type of case was handled separately, and different bodies of law grew up concerned with different types of water occurrence. It is therefore important to determine the legal classification of an occurrence of water in order to discover the rules which the courts will apply to it.

Disputes between persons using water at different points in the hydrologic cycle have become more frequent, particularly where the use of groundwater has increased significantly. The problems associated with physically connected groundwater and surface water are examined in detail in Chapter 4, Section 2C.

STATE v. HIBER

Supreme Court of Wyoming, 1935.
48 Wyo. 172, 44 P.2d 1005.

[Adamson received a permit from the state to construct a reservoir on a "natural stream" known as Adamson Draw. The draw, described by several witnesses as a "swale," drained about 300 acres, mostly on the lands of Hiber, above Adamson's lands. The dam was partially constructed when Hiber built on his land, without a permit, a dam across the draw 200 feet long and 13 feet high. The state brought this action to abate Hiber's dam as an illegal structure and to enjoin him from interfering with the natural flow of the draw. The lower court found for the defendant. Other facts are stated in the opinion.]

BLUME, JUSTICE. * * * Under section 1, article 8 of the Constitution of the State, "the waters of all natural streams, springs, lakes or other collections of still water, within the boundaries of the state are hereby declared to be the property of the state." * * * The controlling question, accordingly, is as to whether or not the assertion that the draw is a natural stream is correct. Counsel for the state contend that in an arid region the term "natural stream" should be construed liberally. So much we may, for the purposes of this case, concede. But it is further contended that "the proper test of distinction, according to the rule laid down * * * as to what constitutes a natural stream or water course is whether or not the water is in such shape as to make it susceptible to application for beneficial use." The test proposed does not seem to be justified by any authorities, even by Popham v. Holloron, 84 Mont. 442, 275 P. 1099, which was decided under a statute not at all like ours, and which in its facts differs materially from those in the case at bar. * * *

If, then, the water in question here was surface water, or what comes to the same thing, if it was not the water of a natural stream, the court was right in finding for the defendant, as to his right to impound it. As to whether it is the one or the other in a specific case is not always easy to determine, and is generally, or often, a question of fact. * * * "Surface water," it has been said, is that which is diffused over the surface of the ground, derived from falling rains and melting snows, and continues to be such, and may be impounded by the owner of the land, until it reaches some well-defined channel in which it is accustomed to, and does, flow with other waters; or until it reaches some permanent lake or pond, and it then ceases to be surface water and becomes the water of the water course, or a lake or a pond, as the case may be. * * * This, accordingly, brings us directly to the point as to whether or not the waters in controversy reached such definite channel—in other words, whether Adamson Draw was a natural stream or water course. * * *

It is said by Kinney, supra, § 303, that "according to the great weight of authority, the essential characteristics of a water course are: A channel, consisting of a well-defined bed and banks, and a current of water." Some exceptions have been made, the definition has not been applied in all cases, and it may be difficult to give one that is universally applicable. Too much stress ought not, perhaps, be placed upon any one of the elements mentioned, and all should be given due consideration. However, the definition given has been approved in recent cases. * * * In Hutchinson v. Watson Slough Ditch Co., 16 Idaho 484, 101 P. 1059, 1060, 133 Am.St.Rep. 125, which involved appropriation of water, the court held that: "a water course is a stream of water flowing in a definite channel, having a bed and sides or banks, and discharging itself into some other stream or body of water. The flow of water need not be constant, but must be more than mere surface drainage occasioned by extraordinary causes; there must be substantial indications of the existence of a stream, which is ordinarily a moving body of water." In Simmons v. Winters, 21 Or. 35, 27 P. 7, 9, 28 Am.St.Rep. 727, also involving appropriation of water, the Oregon court, after citing and quoting from a number of decisions, finally stated: "The conclusion to be deduced from these decisions is that a water-course is a stream of water usually flowing in a particular direction, with well-defined banks and channels, but that the water need not flow continuously,—the channel may sometimes be dry; that the term 'water-course' does not include water descending from the hills, down the hollows and ravines, without any definite channel, only in times of rain and melting snow; but that where water, owing to the hilly or mountainous configuration of the country, accumulates in large quantities from rain and melting snow, and at regular seasons descends through long deep gullies or ravines upon the lands below, and in its onward flow carves out a distinct and well-defined channel, which even to the casual glance bears the unmistakable impress of the frequent action of running water, and through which it has flowed from time immemorial, such a stream is to be considered a water-course, and to be governed by the same rules."

Courts of other western states have taken the same view; * * * Kinney, supra, § 302, says that: "A water course does not include surface water conveyed from higher to lower levels for limited periods, during the melting of snow, or during or soon after a heavy fall of rain, through hollows or ravines, which at all other portions of the year are entirely dry. These occasional bursts of water, which in times of freshets, or of melting ice or snow, descend from the hills and inundate the country, have none of the characteristics of a water course." The water, as already indicated, need not run through the entire year. On that subject Kinney, supra, says in section 307 that: "Those who are acquainted with the streams and water courses of the arid Rocky Mountain region of this country, draining as they do steep, mountain areas with their swift currents, running over gravelly and rocky bottoms, know that often in a dry summer month many of them are entirely dry, at least upon the surface. All of them, nevertheless, have well defined beds, channels, banks and currents of water, at least the greater portion of the year." Again, it is said that a water course does not include the water flowing in the hollows or ravines in land, which is mere surface water from rain or melting snow (i.e., snow lying and melting on the land) and is discharged through them from a higher to a lower level, but which at other times are destitute of water; that such hollows or ravines are not, in legal contemplation, water courses. * * * Kinney, supra, § 312. And it has been stated that "it is almost the unanimous doctrine that swales are not, in their strict legal sense, water courses." Kinney, supra, § 314. Farnham, supra, § 457, maintains that the source of water which flows in a channel claimed to be a water course is a more satisfactory test than is the presence or absence of a channel. But even he holds that there must be more than surface water, unless it comes from a large area of country, and is so continuous in its flow that it takes upon itself the character of a water course. So it is said in 27 R.C.L. 1064 that a "water course is the condition created by a stream of water having a well defined and substantial existence, and that if this substantial existence is present the fact that the stream is not strong enough to create for itself bed and banks is not sufficient to defeat its character as a water course." Hinkle v. Avery, 88 Iowa 47, 55 N.W. 77, 78, 45 Am.St.Rep. 224, and Miller & Lux v. Madera Canal, etc., Co., 155 Cal. 59, 99 P. 502, 22 L.R.A.,N.S., 391, are cited. In the Iowa case the water in question came from a spring, running continuously, at times in a well-defined channel with banks, at times spreading out several rods, later again coming together again in a narrow, well-defined, and single channel, with the current visible along the entire course. Here the substantial existence of the stream could not be questioned, and the case presents a feature altogether absent in the case at bar. In the California case it was held that where a stream flows in a continuous current, the fact that the water thereof, on account of the level character of the lands, spreads over a large area, without apparent banks, does not affect its character as a water course; the overflow caused by ordinary rainfall is but a part thereof. Other cases, cited in note to 1 L.R.A.,N.S., 757, are of a similar character, and have no application in the case at bar. See in this connection Miller v. Eastern Ry. & Lumber Co., 84 Wash. 31, 146 P. 171. So while too strict adherence to the definition that, to constitute a water course, there must be a stream flowing in a bed with banks, has at times given trouble, that definition is, ordinarily, correct and sufficient. Note 1 L.R.A.,N.S., 757. * * *

Testing the facts in this case by these rules of law, we think we must hold that there was ample testimony to sustain the finding and judgment of the trial court, and that the state has failed, at least by a preponderance of the evidence, to show that Adamson Draw is a natural stream. According to most, if not all, of the evidence, it is dry nearly all the time; the main exception being in the spring. It is covered with grass; it has no banks; it is easily crossed by a vehicle almost everywhere; its main course is confined to the lands of the defendant. Its commencement is but a short distance beyond the north boundary thereof, and it has not been shown that it extends southward to a great length; at least, so far as the evidence shows it has no natural outlet. The run of the water therein is confined to a short period in the spring time when the snows melt; or heavy rains at other times may cause it to run for a short period of time. It is even doubtful, by reason of the porous soil, that any water would in any event reach [Adamson's] reservoir. Judging from the testimony, no one would instantaneously perceive that it is a water course. It is, of course, marked on the ground, as all draws are, but that it has been worn out by the water, in view of its grassy condition and the absence of banks, is not very likely, even though the testimony of the witness Morrow might, in answer to a double and leading question put to him, be understood to the contrary. The watershed is small; at least half of it, if not more, is confined to the lands of the defendant, and it would seem that the case may be said to resolve itself into the question as to whether or not the defendant has the right to impound water coming from melting snows and heavy rains, which fall onto his lands and on a small adjoining area, and which drain into a depression on defendant's lands. We think he has that right under the circumstances disclosed herein, or, at least, the trial court had the right to so find. * * *

The judgment of the trial court should, accordingly, be affirmed, and it is so ordered.

Notes

1. **Approaches to defining a watercourse.** Compare, with the descriptive definition in the principal case, the functional treatment in Hoefs v. Short, 273 S.W. 785 (Tex. 1925). Barilla Creek runs for one or two days after rains fall on its 350 square-mile watershed, from one to twenty-two times a year. The court said: "When it is said that a stream in order to be a natural watercourse to which water rights attach must have bed, banks, a current of water, and a permanent source of water supply, we have only described in detail such physiographic and meteorological characteristics as make the use of the stream for irrigation practicable. When it is once shown that the waters of a stream are so confined and

persistent in their course, and flow with such frequency and volume that it is both practicable and valuable to irrigate therefrom, it is a stream to which such water rights attach. With reference to the phrase 'definite and permanent source of supply of water,' frequently used by the courts as describing a necessary requisite of an irrigable stream, all that is meant is that there must be sufficient water carried by the stream at such intervals as may make it practicable to irrigate from or use the stream."

Did the court in the principal case rely, in part, on a functional test? (See the statement by the court expressing doubt that any of water captured by the defendant would reach the reservoir of the downstream competitor.)

2. **Other exceptional cases.** In addition to the exceptions to the definition of a watercourse discussed in the principal case, consider the Fresno slough, which flows sometimes northward and sometimes southward, held part of a watercourse in Turner v. James Canal Co., 99 P. 520 (Cal. 1909). Consider also Medano Creek, which disappears into sand dunes only to reappear as Big and Little Spring Creeks. See Medano Ditch Co. v. Adams, 68 P. 431 (Colo. 1902).

3. **Extent of "diffused surface waters."** In Oklahoma Water Resources Board v. Central Oklahoma Master Conservancy District, 464 P.2d 748 (Okla. 1968), a city owned the entire watershed of a small creek and, claiming "the right to capture water falling on its property for private use," dammed the stream. Held, an illegal appropriation of the stream: "Diffused surface waters lose their original character when they reach some well-defined channel in which they are accustomed to, and do, flow with other waters, or when they reach some permanent lake or pond. They then become 'a constituent part' of the stream, lake or pond, as the case may be. Diffused surface water may be appropriated by the owner of land over which it flows and become his property *when captured by him before it enters a definite stream.* Thereafter it is no longer subject to appropriation by the landowner." Id. at 754. Accord In re the Adjudication of Water Rights of the Lower Guadalupe River Segment, 730 S.W.2d 64 (Tex. Ct. App. 1987).

4. **Constitutional and statutory provisions.** The constitutions or statutes of several western states define water that is subject to appropriation so as to conform to the watercourse concept. E.g., Colo. Const. art. XVI, § 5 ("natural stream"); N.M. Const. art. XVI, § 2 ("perennial or torrential"). In several statutes waters are defined so as to exclude diffused surface water. See Ariz. Rev. Stat. § 45-141A; N.D. Cent. Code § 61-01-01. On the other hand, the laws of some states refer to "all sources of water supply" or "all waters." Nev. Rev. Stat. 533.025; Or. Rev. Stat. § 537.110; Utah Code Ann. § 73-1-1.

5. **Effect of soil conservation practices.** Harold E. Thomas, Hydrology v. Water Allocation in the Eastern United States, in The Law of Water Allocation in the Eastern United States 165, 173 (Haber & Bergen eds., 1958): "Of all the various 'diffused surface waters,' those that would be most likely to affect streamflow are the waters gathered on or flowing over the surface after precipitation. Such waters contribute materially to storm runoff, and especially to floods. Land owners within any drainage basin, therefore, by holding these 'diffused' waters on their land could reduce the streamflow materially; and if all overland flow could be prevented, the water in watercourses would consist largely of the discharge from ground-water reservoirs. Thus if the landowners have absolute ownership of both the ground water and diffused surface water on their lands, a surface-water appropriator cannot be assured of a secure water right. * * * [I]t

is reported that soil-conservation practices have reduced the flow of many streams in west Texas. At a water conference last September at Texas A & M College it was conceded that, with continuing reduction of base flow and reduction of storm runoff from minor storms, some surface-water appropriators would eventually have rights to nothing but the runoff during major floods."

Cal. Water Code § 1252.1: "An appropriation of water of any stream or other source of water under this part does not confer authority upon the appropriator to prevent or interfere with soil conservation practices above the point of diversion in the watershed in which such stream or other source originates, which practices do not themselves constitute an appropriation for which a permit is required by this part."

6. **Springs and Lakes.** Springs which form a watercourse are usually held to be a part of the watercourse, and their use is governed by the law, riparian or appropriative, applicable to watercourses. In Arizona, "springs on the surface" are appropriable by statute, even though they do not flow beyond the boundary of the land on which they arise. Ariz. Rev. Stat. § 45-141A; Parker v. McIntyre, 56 P.2d 1337 (Ariz. 1936). Although the Oregon statutes appear to require a permit for diversions from all springs, case law holds that a permit is required only when the spring, if undiverted, flows beyond the boundaries on the land on which the spring arises. Or. Rev. Stat. § 537.800; Norden v. State, 973 P.2d 910 (Or. Ct. App. 1999). California follows a similar rule as to springs arising on private lands, but springs which arise on public lands are subject to appropriation even though their waters do not reach living streams. See Wells A. Hutchins, The California Law of Water Rights 407-13 (1956). If a dispute arises long after the diversion and development of spring waters, it may be difficult to determine whether the spring would flow beyond the property boundaries in its natural condition. See *Norden,* supra.

In Melville v. Salt Lake County, 570 P.2d 687 (Utah 1977), the court said, "No one owns or can own water in this state, regardless of whether that water is found in the form of a spring, stream, lake, pond or under the ground. One can only acquire the right to use the water. One's right to use the water is measured by the amount he puts to beneficial use without interfering with another person's right to the use of the water."

Lakes and ponds are mentioned as sources of appropriable water in several state constitutions and statutes, and are generally treated as a part of the watercourse which feeds them or originates from them. A lake may be appropriable though it is not an integral part of a stream, and has neither a visible source of supply nor an outlet. Proctor v. Sim, 236 P. 114 (Wash. 1925).

7. **Glacial ice.** In the 1980s glacial ice became a valuable novelty item for use in drinks because it makes more noise than normal ice. In 1987, the Alaska Attorney General ruled that the Alaska appropriation statutes apply to glacial ice and icebergs. Thomas A. Meacham, 21 Water L. Newsl. No. 3, at 4 (Rocky Mtn. Min. L. Found., Westminster, Colo.) (1988).

R.J.A., INC. v. WATER USERS ASS'N OF DISTRICT NO. 6

Supreme Court of Colorado, 1984.
690 P.2d 823.

LOHR, JUSTICE. R.J.A., Inc. (applicant) appeals from a judgment of the water judge for water division 1 denying its application for a developed water right. The applicant based its claim on a project that will reduce water loss from a marshy mountain meadow by removing the underlying peat moss, thereby eliminating a saturated, seepy condition. This will decrease evaporation from the soil and surface and reduce evapotranspiration from grassy vegetation. We affirm the judgment.

R.J.A., Inc. operates a summer resort business on property located south of Estes Park, Colorado, in a mountain valley approximately 9000 feet above sea level. The property is situated at the headwaters of Tahosa Creek, which flows into St. Vrain Creek, a tributary of the South Platte River. This land originally included a 27-acre peat moss marsh which was approximately 3000 years old and, thus, was in existence long before any water rights were established on the South Platte River system. Historically, water entered this marsh from several surface streams and springs, and the area was much wetter than the surrounding lands. According to the applicant, loss of water to the atmosphere was higher from this peat moss marsh than from a well-drained mountain meadow of equivalent size. This is because the soil was saturated at or near surface level, resulting in relatively high rates of evaporation from the soil and standing water on the surface and evapotranspiration from the grassy vegetation growing throughout the marsh. While substantial amounts of water were lost to the atmosphere in this manner, the remaining water eventually moved through or around the marsh to become the headwaters of Tahosa Creek.

In the early 1970s, the applicant undertook a project to remove the extensive deposits of peat moss underlying the marsh, drain the land, and convert the marsh to a well-drained meadow more suitable for use in the applicant's resort business. At the time of the water court hearing in 1982, R.J.A., Inc. had completed about three quarters of the planned work.

In 1979, R.J.A., Inc. filed an application for a developed water right in the district court for water division 1, seeking a decree for 22.5 acre feet absolute and 20.8 acre feet conditional to be used for augmentation and other specified beneficial uses. See section 37-92-302(1)(a), 15 C.R.S. (1973). The applicant claimed that the drainage of the marsh and elimination of the saturated, seepy condition would reduce the rates of evaporation and evapo-transpiration, and thereby would decrease consumptive use of water by 43.3 acre feet per year. Because this would represent a net gain to the stream, the applicant asserted that its water right should not be subject to administration under the priority system. * * *

The applicant contends that a developed water right for tributary water, free from the priority system, may be recognized where a claimant increases the natural flow of a stream by reducing consumptive uses that existed before the first appropriations were made on the stream. In support of this position, the applicant relies upon a line of cases in which we have recognized rights to developed water based upon addition of water to an existing supply. We hold that reduction of consumptive use of tributary water cannot provide the basis for a water right that is independent of the system of priorities on the stream.

As the trial court found, the water involved in the application before us is tributary to Tahosa Creek. The Water Right Determination and Administration Act of 1969, Article 92 of Chapter 37, 15 C.R.S. (1973) (the 1969 Act), provides a comprehensive scheme for adjudication of rights to tributary water and for administration of the distribution of such water. That act provides for adjudication and administration under a system of priorities, implementing the constitutionally based right of prior appropriation in waters of natural streams. * * * Nowhere in the entire scheme of the 1969 Act is there a suggestion that rights to tributary water independent of the priority system can be obtained.

The applicant urges, however, that we have previously recognized that developed water rights, independent of the priority system, may be established as to tributary water in appropriate circumstances. We have stated on several occasions that one who increases the flow of a natural stream by adding water that otherwise would not reach the stream is entitled to the use of the water to the extent of the increase. * * *

Review of our cases relating to developed water brings us to the same conclusion that we reached in *Shelton Farms* that under prior case law "[no] person has been granted a water right free from the call of the river for water which has always been tributary to a stream." 187 Colo. at 187, 529 P.2d at 1325. Thus, the developed water cases provide no support for the applicant's position.

In *Shelton Farms* we considered an application with many similarities to the one now before us. There, we reversed judgments of the water court awarding water rights free from the call of senior decreed water rights on the Arkansas River. The trial court had decreed these rights based upon the reduction of evaporation and evapotranspiration effected by clearing phreatophytes from the land and filling in a marshy area. We concluded that, since the water in question had always been tributary to the stream and was not water new to the river system, the developed water cases were inapposite. We rejected the argument that demonstration of lack of injury to vested rights could serve as a basis for recognition of a water right outside the priority system and concluded:

> [Present section 37-92-306, 15 C.R.S. (1973) prescribing the ranking of water rights by priorities] cannot be ignored * * *. There is nothing in the plain language of the statute to except appellees' plans [for award of water rights independent of the priority system] from the priority date system. Thus, we hold that all water decrees of any kind are bound to the call of the river, subject to any specific exceptions found within the law. To hold any

other way would be to weaken the priority system, and create a superclass of water rights never before in existence.[7] 187 Colo. at 190, 529 P.2d at 1326.

In *Shelton Farms* we recognized the importance of maximizing beneficial use of Colorado's water. See Fellhauer v. People, 167 Colo. 320, 447 P.2d 986 (1968). We noted, however, that subsequent to *Fellhauer's* strong emphasis on the importance of maximum utilization of this scarce resource, the General Assembly had not authorized the creation of a water right outside the priority system through elimination of a prior consumptive use, as sought by the applicant here.

The applicant argues that *Shelton Farms* is not controlling because the phreatophytes in that case grew after the early water rights had been established on the river. Therefore, the plants were aptly characterized as "water thieves," and we visualized the generation of a new industry of "planting and harvesting trees to create water rights superior to the oldest decrees on the Arkansas * * *." 187 Colo. at 191, 529 P.2d at 1327. In the present case, however, the peat bog existed long before initiation of the earliest water right on the South Platte system. The water lost from the river system by evaporation and evapotranspiration from the seepy bog was never available for utilization by holders of senior rights. While this difference is real, we do not consider it controlling.

A separate strand of analysis supported our decision in *Shelton Farms.* We expressed concern over adoption of a rule of law that would encourage widespread destruction of plant life, with attendant likelihood of irreparable erosion and the creation of a barren wasteland. We said, "the waters of Colorado belong to the people, but so does the land. There must be a balancing effect, and the elements of water and land must be used in harmony to the maximum feasible use of both." 187 Colo. at 191, 529 P.2d at 1327. *Cf. In Re Rules and Regulations,* 674 P.2d 914 (Colo.1984) (environmental concerns are properly to be taken into account in rules and regulations promulgated by the state engineer to govern administration of diversions of tributary water).

The water rights sought here are based upon alterations of long existing physical characteristics of the land. Alteration of natural conditions and vegetation in order to save water carries with it the potential for adverse effects on soil and bank stabilization, soil productivity, wildlife habitat, fisheries production, water quality, watershed protection and the hydrologic

7. We distinguished between "developed" and "salvaged" water. The former is new water not previously part of the river system, i.e., it is imported or nontributary water. The latter is tributary water made available for beneficial use through elimination of waste. Only developed water can be made the basis of a right independent of the priority system. *Shelton Farms,* 187 Colo. at 187, 529 P.2d at 1324-25; see Sweetwater Development Corp. v. Schubert Ranches, Inc., 188 Colo. 379, 383, 535 P.2d 215, 218 (1975). One example of a developed water right described in *Shelton Farms* clearly involves tributary water—the capture, storage and utilization of flood waters. 187 Colo. at 187, 529 P.2d at 1324. There are valid reasons consistent with the priority system for entering a decree in favor of the person capturing such waters. Despite our dicta in *Shelton Farms,* such a decree does not involve a right to developed water independent of the priority system.

cycle. See Harrison and Sandstrom, The Groundwater-Surface Water Conflict and Recent Colorado Water Legislation, 43 U.Colo.L.Rev. 1, 2 (1971); F. Trelease, Water Law: Resource Use and Environmental Protection 59 (2d ed. 1974). Whether to recognize such rights, and thus to encourage innovative ways of reducing historical consumptive uses by modifying conditions found in nature, is a question fraught with important public policy considerations. As such, the question is especially suited for resolution through the legislative process.

In the 1969 Act, the General Assembly has used priority of appropriation as the sole criterion for ranking rights to tributary water. As we recognized in *Shelton Farms,* the general legislative policy of maximizing beneficial and integrated use of surface and subsurface water must be implemented with a sensitivity to the effect on other resources. The General Assembly has addressed the accommodation of the policy of maximum utilization of water and the policy of preservation of natural resources, but only in a limited way. It has expressed its concern that maximum utilization of water be balanced by preservation of the natural environment "to a reasonable degree" by authorizing appropriations on behalf of the people of the state of Colorado for that latter purpose. §§ 37-92-102(3) and 103(4), 15 C.R.S. (1973), the relevant portions of which were adopted in 1973 in Ch. 442, secs. 1 and 2, §§ 37-92-102(3) and 37-92-103(4), 1973 Colo.Sess.Laws 1521, 1521-22.

Then, in 1975, shortly after the *Shelton Farms* case was decided, the General Assembly revised the definition of "plan for augmentation" to affirm that neither the salvage of tributary waters by eradicating phreatophytes nor the increase of runoff by making land surfaces impermeable provides an increased supply of water that may be utilized to support a plan for augmentation. § 37-92-103(9), 15 C.R.S. (1983 Supp.). These partial approaches to the problem reflect a cautious step-by-step legislative approach in addressing the issues. It is noteworthy, however, that in neither of these statutes has the legislature deviated from the basic priority system for tributary water when engrafting refinements upon the system.

The phreatophytes in *Shelton Farms* may have presented a factually more compelling case for rejection of recognition of a developed water right through their eradication than is present here. The larger consideration of achieving maximum feasible use of both land and water, however, is also present here, with the result that we find what we said in *Shelton Farms* equally applicable in this case:

> No one on any river would be adverse to a schematic and integrated system of developing this kind of water supply with control and balancing considerations. But to create such a scheme is the work of the legislature, through creation of appropriate district authorities with right of condemnation on a selective basis, not for the courts. Until such time as the legislature responds, action such as appellees' should not be given court sanction. 187 Colo. at 192, 529 P.2d at 1327.

We affirm the judgment of the water court.

Notes

1. **Phreatophyte eradication.** Phreatophytes (a Greek word meaning "well-plants") literally pump water through their structure and transpire it from their foliage.

"Along many of the river valleys of the West, saltcedars and other generally worthless vegetation (willows, cottonwoods, mesquite, greasewood, and certain reeds and weeds) have crowded onto river bottom land to such an extent that they now cover nearly 16 million acres and discharge into the atmosphere an estimated 20 to 25 million acre-feet of water annually. These plants, having their roots in the ground water, have first call on available water supplies, leaving for man only that which they cannot use. Losses are particularly acute in the water shortage states of Arizona and New Mexico, where the warmer climate leads to greater consumption of water, particularly by the saltcedars. Elimination of the consumptive waste from these plants provides an excellent opportunity for increasing the usefulness of available water supplies." Senate Select Comm. on Nat'l Water Res., Report of the Committee Pursuant to S. Res. 48, S. Rep. No. 29, at 108-09 (1961).

Phreatophyte removal is controversial:

"A case in point is Arizona, where Federal agencies are studying or proposing the removal of phreatophytes—deep rooted vegetation—from the banks of many rivers in the state. The main purpose of the removal is to conserve water in that arid state. * * *

"Bitterly opposing the phreatophyte removal projects, some of which are already under way, are conservationists and wildlife proponents who say that the riverbank vegetation is the only major wildlife habitat in the arid state. Remove it, they say, and the adverse effects on wildlife will be devastating and sometimes irreversible. Some also mention indications, somewhat less supported by scientific evidence, that the effects on fisheries may be equally detrimental. * * *

"The dove, quail, grey hawk and black-bellied tree duck are some of the birds affected, according to Arizona Game and Fish Department. Other types of wildlife are also affected, of course, including deer and javelina. Although waterfowl do not use the plant cover directly, it forms sanctuaries for ducks and geese using the Pacific Flyway. * * * " Richard H. Gilluly, Wildlife Versus Irrigation, 99 Sci. News 184 (1971).

But see People v. Shirokow, 605 P.2d 859 (Cal. 1980), in which the California Water Resources Control Board required the eradication of phreatophytes as a condition for receiving a permit to appropriate water.

2. **Water outside the priority system.** The court's statement in footnote 7 of the principal case that imported water is independent of the priority system should not be misunderstood. The court only means that imported water is outside the priority system in the basin to which it is imported. Such water is subject to the priority system in the basin in which it originates; i.e., water can be diverted from the basin of origin only when the appropriation for such water is in priority. Indeed, as public jurisdiction has been extended to other parts of the hydrologic cycle, it is difficult to find water that is not subject to appropriation or some other form of public administration (other than diffused surface water). For example, in Ripley v. Park Center Land & Water Co., 90 P. 75 (Colo. 1907), water trapped

in abandoned mine shafts was labeled "developed water" and was held to be free of the priority system, but more recently in In re General Determination of the Rights to Use of Surface and Ground Waters of Payette River Drainage Basin, 687 P.2d 1348 (Idaho 1984), it was held that the water emanating from a mine shaft was not "developed water" but was public groundwater subject to appropriation.

3. **Stored water.** In footnote 7 of the principal case the court also notes that it was previously in error in categorizing stored water as developed water—water independent of the priority system. The court's confusion on this point is understandable because stored water has some of the attributes of developed water. An appropriation is required to store water, and, like any appropriation, a storage appropriation is subject to the rule of priority. Thus, water in a stream or river can be captured for storage only when the right to store is in priority—i.e., only when more senior rights do not require the water. However, once lawfully stored, water is no longer subject to the claims of more senior appropriators; it can be held and used by the storing party without regard to "calls" by more senior appropriators. Thus, a right to *store* water is subject to the priority system, but the right to *stored* water is independent of the system.

4. **Augmentation or return flows?** When computing the effect of an appropriation for irrigation or other uses, return flows are generally offset against the amount diverted in Colorado (and elsewhere). See *Glacier View Meadows*, supra p. 75. The return flows are not considered "augmentation," but are simply a factor in determining the net depletion of an appropriation. Quite descriptively, the net depletion of an appropriation is sometimes called the "burden on the river."

Colo. Rev. Stat. § 37-92-103(9), cited in the principal case, provides that increased runoff resulting from making land surfaces impermeable cannot be used to support a plan of augmentation. Land development often replaces the natural terrain with impermeable surfaces, primarily paved roads and building roofs, thereby increasing surface runoff. If a land developer proposes an appropriation for a subdivision water supply, can increased surface runoff resulting from urbanization be used in determining the burden on the river of the proposed appropriation? Or is the use of such water to offset the effects of diversion prohibited under the above statute? I.e., should the increased runoff be classified as "augmentation" or as an incident of use analogous to return flows?

In State Engineer v. Castle Meadows, Inc., 856 P.2d 496 (Colo. 1993), the court found it unnecessary to determine the correct classification. In adopting the prohibition referred to above, the court concluded that the legislature intended to remove the incentive for persons to increase water supplies by replacing natural land conditions with impermeable surfaces. Consequently, the court held that the use of such water to offset the effect of diversions would impermissibly contravene the legislative policy embodied in the statute, whether characterized as augmentation or as an incident of use.

5. **Injury to existing appropriators and water available for appropriation.** Collier v. Arizona Department of Water Resources, 722 P.2d 363 (Ariz. App. 1986), involved a spring which surfaced for the first time in 1979. Prior to surfacing, the water of the spring had been "percolating groundwater" and had contributed to the flow of Kirkland Creek. The Colliers built a dam to intercept the spring flow before it reached Kirkland Creek and applied for an appropriation. The application was protested by appropriators from Kirkland Creek who claimed that their appropriations included the spring water because of its hydrologic

connection to the creek. The Colliers countered that the spring constituted a new source of unappropriated water. They noted that before surfacing it had been percolating groundwater which is not appropriable in Arizona and that after surfacing they had intercepted it before it had ever reached the creek. Thus, they reasoned that the water had never been part of the "appropriated" water of Kirkland Creek. The court agreed with the Colliers' reasoning but rejected the application anyway, basing the result on a statute which prohibits new appropriations which interfere with existing ones.

6. **Artificially induced precipitation.** Although there have been some successes, the ability to significantly increase water supplies through weather modification (cloud seeding) is controversial and largely unproven. See American Meteorological Society, Planned and Inadvertent Weather Modification (A Policy Statement) (1992); Water Policies for the Future, supra p. 3, Note 1, at 348; Neyman, A Statistician's View of Weather Modification Technology (A Review), 74 Proc. Nat'l Acad. of Sci. 4714 (1977).

Most of the litigation has involved unsuccessful attempts to collect damages for the harms allegedly caused by artificial precipitation; most of the legislation is concerned with regulatory and institutional controls of the activity. See Ray Jay Davis, Weather Modification Law Developments, 27 Okla. L. Rev. 409 (1974); Ralph W. Johnson, Federal Organization for the Control of Water Modification, 10 Nat. Resources J. 222 (1970); A. Gregory McKenzie, Weather Modification: A Review of the Science and Law, 6 Envtl. L. 387 (1975). Legal issues associated with inadvertent modification are discussed in Ray J. Davis, Law and Urban-Induced Weather Change, 25 U. Tol. L. Rev. 379 (1994). The last article also reviews legal issues associated with intentional weather modification activities.

From the "water law" standpoint, the best article is John M. Pierce, Legal Aspects of Weather Modification—Snowpack Augmentation in Wyoming, 2 Land & Water L. Rev. 273 (1967), speculating on the rights of the "rain maker" to capture, store, use and sell the water he adds to the natural stream flow. See also Ward H. Fischer, Weather Modification and the Right of Capture, 8 Nat. Resources Law. 639 (1975). Consider Cal. Water Code § 401: "It is hereby declared that atmospheric water within the state which is caused to fall by weather resources management activities shall, for the purpose of water rights determinations, be considered as if it occurred as natural precipitation." Accord N.M. Stat. Ann. §75-3-3; N.D. Cent. Code § 61-04.1-02.

7. **Protection of instream uses.** Instream uses—uses associated with water in a stream, such as recreation, aesthetics, maintenance of fish and wildlife habitat and general environmental preservation—did not fare well historically under the appropriation doctrine because of its emphasis on diversion and consumptive use of water. Although limited acts to protect instream uses can be found in earlier times, the issue did not receive widespread attention until the 1970s. Since then, most western states have adopted legislation which provides for instream uses. In most cases, such legislation effectively withdraws water from appropriation.

The instream appropriation is perhaps the most widely used technique for the protection on instream uses. Essential developments in the utilization of this technique were the elimination of a diversion as a requirement for appropriation and the recognition that the protection of instream values is a beneficial use of water. See In re Adjudication of the Mo. River Drainage Area, supra p. 24; Idaho Dep't of Parks v. Idaho Dep't of Water Admin., supra p.29.

Other techniques include withdrawal of specified streams from appropriation (see Or. Rev. Stat. § 538.200), protection from diversion of minimum flows established by the state (see Wash. Rev. Code §§ 90.22.010-.060, 90.54.005-.920), reservation of water for instream flows by public agencies (see Mont. Code Ann. § 85-2-316), wild and scenic rivers designations to preserve the free-flowing nature of specified rivers (see federal Wild and Scenic Rivers Act, 16 U.S.C. §§ 1271-1287; California Wild and Scenic Rivers Act, Cal. Pub. Res. Code §§ 5093.50-.70), regulation of the appropriation process to deny or condition new appropriations (see Chapter 2, Section 3C), application of the public trust doctrine (see Chapter 7, Section 1B), limitations on diversions pursuant to section 404 of the Clean Water Act (see Chapter 7, Section 2C) and the Endangered Species Act (see Chapter 7, Section 2D), imposition of flow requirements as water quality standards under sections 303 and 401 of the Clean Water Act (see City of Thornton v. Bijou Irrigation Co. and accompanying Notes, infra p, 575; Pub. Utilities Dist. No. 1 v. Wash. Dep't of Ecology and accompanying Notes, infra p. 651), and flow requirements dictated by federal land agencies in use permits issued for water development (see infra p. 594, Note 8).

Various approaches to protecting instream flows are surveyed in Cynthia F. Covell, A Survey of State Instream Flow Programs in the Western United States, 1 U. Denv. Water L. Rev. 177 (1998). See also Ronald A. Kaiser & Shane Binion, Untying the Gordian Knot: Negotiated Strategies for Protecting Instream Flows in Texas, 38 Nat. Resources J. 157 (1998); A. Dan Tarlock, The Recognition of Instream Flow Rights: "New" Public Western Water Rights, 25 Rocky Mtn. Min. L. Inst. 24-1 (1979).

E. Geographic Restrictions On Use

COFFIN v. LEFT HAND DITCH CO.

Supreme Court of Colorado, 1882.
6 Colo. 443.

HELM, J. Appellee, who was plaintiff below, claimed to be the owner of certain water by virtue of an appropriation thereof from the south fork of the St. Vrain creek. It appears that such water, after its diversion, is carried by means of a ditch to the James Creek, and thence along the bed of the same to Left Hand Creek, where it is again diverted by lateral ditches and used to irrigate lands adjacent to the last named stream. Appellants are the owners of lands lying on the margin and in the neighborhood of the St. Vrain below the mouth of said south fork thereof, and naturally irrigated therefrom.

In 1879 there was not a sufficient quantity of water in the St. Vrain to supply the ditch of appellee and also irrigate the said lands of appellant. A portion of appellee's dam was torn out, and its diversion of water thereby seriously interfered with by appellants. The action is brought for damages arising from the trespass, and for injunctive relief to prevent repetitions thereof in the future. The answer of appellants, who were defendants below, is separated into six divisions. * * * But it nowhere appears by sufficient averment that such appropriations of defendants making the same were actually made prior to the diversion of water through appellee's ditch. * * *

It is contended by counsel for appellants that the common law principles of riparian proprietorship prevailed in Colorado until 1876, and that the doctrine of priority of right to water by priority of appropriation thereof was first recognized and adopted in the constitution. But we think the latter doctrine has existed from the date of the earliest appropriations of water within the boundaries of the state. The climate is dry, and the soil, when moistened only by the usual rainfall, is arid and unproductive; except in a few favored sections, artificial irrigation for agriculture is an absolute necessity. Water in the various streams thus acquires a value unknown in moister climates. Instead of being a mere incident to the soil, it rises, when appropriated, to the dignity of a distinct usufructuary estate, or right of property. It has always been the policy of the national, as well as the territorial and state governments, to encourage the diversion and use of water in this country for agriculture; and vast expenditures of time and money have been made in reclaiming and fertilizing by irrigation portions of our unproductive territory. Houses have been built, and permanent improvements made; the soil has been cultivated, and thousands of acres have been rendered immensely valuable, with the understanding that appropriations of water would be protected. Deny the doctrine of priority or superiority of right by priority of appropriation, and a great part of the value of all this property is at once destroyed.

The right to water in this country, by priority of appropriation thereof, we think it is, and has always been, the duty of the national and state governments to protect. The right itself, and the obligation to protect it, existed prior to legislation on the subject of irrigation. It is entitled to protection as well after patent to a third party of the land over which the natural stream flows, as when such land is a part of the public domain; and it is immaterial whether or not it be mentioned in the patent and expressly excluded from the grant.

The act of congress protecting in patents such right in water appropriated, when recognized by local customs and laws, "was rather a voluntary recognition of a pre-existing right of possession, constituting a valid claim to its continued use, than the establishment of a new one." Broder v. Notoma W. & M. Co., 11 Otto, 274.

We conclude, then, that the common law doctrine giving the riparian owner a right to the flow of water in its natural channel upon and over his lands, even though he makes no beneficial use thereof, is inapplicable to Colorado. Imperative necessity, unknown to the countries which gave it birth, compels the recognition of another doctrine in conflict therewith. And we hold that, in the absence of express statutes to the contrary, the first appropriator of water from a natural stream for a beneficial purpose has, with the qualifications contained in the constitution, a prior right thereto, to the extent of such appropriation. * * *

It is urged, however, that even if the doctrine of priority or superiority of right by priority of appropriation be conceded, appellee in this case is not benefitted thereby. Appellants claim that they have a better right to the water because their lands lie along the margin and in the neighborhood of the St. Vrain. They assert that, as against them, appellee's diversion of said water to irrigate lands adjacent to Left Hand Creek, though prior in time, is unlawful.

In the absence of legislation to the contrary, we think that the right to water acquired by priority of appropriation thereof is not in any way dependent upon the *locus* of its application to the beneficial use designed. And the disastrous consequences of our adoption of the rule contended for, forbid our giving such a construction to the statutes as will concede the same, if they will properly bear a more reasonable and equitable one.

The doctrine of priority of right by priority of appropriation for agriculture is evoked, as we have seen, by the imperative necessity for artificial irrigation of the soil. And it would be an ungenerous and inequitable rule that would deprive one of its benefit simply because he has, by large expenditure of time and money, carried the water from one stream over an intervening watershed and cultivated land in the valley of another. It might be utterly impossible, owing to the topography of the country, to get water upon his farm from the adjacent stream; or if possible, it might be impracticable on account of the distance from the point where the diversion must take place and the attendant expense; or the quantity of water in such stream might be entirely insufficient to supply his wants. It sometimes happens that the most fertile soil is found along the margin or in the neighborhood of the small rivulet, and sandy and barren land beside the larger stream. To apply the rule contended for would prevent the useful and profitable cultivation of the productive soil, and sanction the waste of water upon the more sterile lands. It would have enabled a party to locate upon a stream in 1875, and destroy the value of thousands of acres, and the improvements thereon, in adjoining valleys, possessed and cultivated for the preceding decade. Under the principle contended for, a party owning land ten miles from the stream, but in the valley thereof, might deprive a prior appropriator of the water diverted therefrom whose lands are within a thousand yards, but just beyond an intervening divide. * * *

The judgment of the court below will be affirmed.

Notes

1. **Geographic restrictions.** Prior appropriation began with a rejection of the riparian watershed limitation, see Irwin v. Phillips, supra p. 18. Yet, in some states, a strong sectionalism has developed along the lines of basin divides, and local politics have produced inroads on the freedom to transfer water from water-rich areas to water-short areas. Consider the following provisions of the California Water Code, relating to state "appropriations" of water and their assignment or release to actual appropriators and to authorization of the federal Central Valley Project and the California Water Plan:

"Section 10505. No priority under this part shall be released nor assignment made of any application that will, in the judgment of the commission, deprive the county in which the water covered by the application originates of any such water necessary for the development of the county.

"Section 11460. In the construction and operation by the department of any project under the provisions of this part a watershed or area wherein water originates, or an area immediately adjacent thereto which can conveniently be supplied with water therefrom, shall not be deprived by the department directly or indirectly of the prior right to all of the water reasonably required to adequately supply the beneficial needs of the watershed, area, or any of the inhabitants or property owners therein.

"Section 11461. In no other way than by purchase or otherwise as provided in this part shall water rights of a watershed, area, or the inhabitants be impaired or curtailed by the department, but the provisions of this article shall be strictly limited to the acts and proceedings of the department, as such, and shall not apply to any persons or state agencies.

"Section 11462. The provisions of this article shall not be so construed as to create any new property rights other than against the department as provided in this part or to require the department to furnish to any person without adequate compensation therefor any water made available by the construction of any works by the department.

"Section 11463. In the construction and operation by the department of any project under the provisions of this part, no exchange of the water of any watershed or area for the water of any other watershed or area may be made by the department unless the water requirements of the watershed or area in which the exchange is made are first and at all times met and satisfied to the extent that the requirements would have been met were the exchange not made, and no right to the use of water shall be gained or lost by reason of any such exchange."

The preceding statutes apply primarily to water rights held by the federal Central Valley Project and the State Water Project. In 1984, the legislature provided additional "area of origin" protection to designated river systems located in the northern and central part of the state. See Cal. Water Code §§ 1215-1222; see also §§ 12200-12228. In addition, a number of California counties have adopted ordinances restricting or prohibiting the export of groundwater. See discussion infra p. 364, Note 3.

2. **Compensatory storage.** Consider the limitation placed on the powers of Colorado water conservancy districts:

"Any works or facilities planned and designed for the exportation of water from the natural basin of the Colorado river and its tributaries in Colorado, by any district created under this article, * * * shall be designed, constructed and operated in such a manner that the present appropriations of water and in addition thereto prospective uses of water for irrigation and other beneficial consumptive use purposes, including consumptive uses for domestic, mining and industrial purposes, within the natural basin of the Colorado river in the state of Colorado, from which water is exported, will not be impaired nor increased in cost at the expense of the water users within the natural basin. The facilities and other means for the accomplishment of said purpose shall be incorporated in, and made a part of any project plans for the exportation of water from said natural basin in Colorado." Colo. Rev. Stat. § 37-45-118(1)(b)(II).

This statute translates into a requirement for "compensatory storage"; a reservoir which the exporting district must construct on the western slope of the continental divide to replace with stored water the direct flow taken to the eastern slope, even though the water is not needed for present western slope uses. The City of Denver, although a major exporter of Colorado River water, is not bound by this law. Metro. Suburban Water Users Ass'n v. Colo. River Water Conservation Dist., 365 P.2d 273 (Colo. 1961). The Colorado constitutional guarantee that the right to appropriate water "shall never be denied" was held not to proscribe this limitation on the powers of an instrumentality of the state in Central Colorado Water Conservancy District v. Colorado River Water Conservation District, 526 P.2d 302 (Colo. 1974).

3. **Nebraska interbasin diversions.** In Nebraska, an 1895 statute required that unused irrigation water be returned to the river of origin or the Missouri River. Neb. Rev. Stat. § 46-265. In 1936 this was held to prevent interbasin surface water diversions, since it would be impracticable to transport irrigation return flow back across the divide to the river of origin. The decision was perhaps influenced by the drought conditions of the 1930s and a fear that a large irrigation project planned for use of the Platte River in the Blue and Republican river basins might dry up the Platte River valley. Osterman v. Cen. Neb. Pub. Power & Irrigation Dist., 268 N.W. 334 (Neb. 1936). *Osterman* was overruled in Little Blue Natural Resources District v. Lower Platte North Natural Resources District, 294 N.W.2d 598 (Neb. 1980). The Court noted that all of Nebraska is ultimately drained by the Missouri River, and ruled that cross-divide diversions are governed by the general statute permitting appropriations wherever there is unappropriated water and the appropriation would not be otherwise detrimental to the public welfare.

4. **Other restrictions on interbasin diversions.** See Alaska Stat. § 46.15.035 (restricting exports to water which is surplus to the needs of the exporting area); Kan. Stat. Ann. § 82a-1502 (restricting exports to water which is surplus to the needs of the exporting area unless the benefits to the state of exporting water outweigh the benefits of not exporting it); Mont. Code Ann. § 85-2-301 (restricting exports to the Department of Natural Resources and Conservation, thereby forcing users to "lease" the water from the Department); Okla. Stat. tit. 82, § 105.12(4) (requiring the consideration of in-basin needs); Tex. Water Code Ann. § 11.085 (requiring that the benefits to the receiving basin outweigh the detriments to the exporting basin).

5. **Land use restrictions.** In Delta Wetlands Properties v. County of San Joaquin, 16 Cal. Rptr. 3d 672 (Ct. App. 2004), the court rejected a facial challenge to a county land use ordinance requiring a conditional use permit for reservoirs. The plaintiff, Delta Wetlands, held appropriation permits issued by the California Water Resources Control Board for the storage of water in reservoirs to be created by flooding several "islands" in the Sacramento-San Joaquin Delta. The county adopted the ordinance after the board issued the permits because of concerns about various impacts of the project, particularly the loss of farmland resulting from the inundation of the islands.

Citing the expansive regulatory authority given to the water board, Delta Wetlands argued that the state has impliedly preempted local regulation of matters considered by the board in issuing an appropriation permit. The court rejected the argument, holding that the board's exclusive jurisdiction over the appropriation of water and its authority to attach conditions to an appropriation permit in the public interest does not preempt county land use authority over the location of reservoirs. Because Delta Wetlands had not applied for a use permit from the county, the court refused to speculate as to specific county regulations that would be preempted by the appropriation permit. The court also held that the ordinance reflected legitimate land use concerns and was not improperly discriminatory.

In City of Colorado Springs v. Board of County Commissioners, 895 P.2d 1105 (Colo. Ct. App. 1994), a county successfully used its authority to regulate land use to block proposed transbasin diversions by two cities. The court found that the county was justified in denying use permits needed for construction of the projects because the cities failed to satisfy county regulatory criteria regarding wetlands protection and nuisance abatement. The county's regulatory authority was upheld against various statutory and constitutional challenges.

6. **Purpose of geographic restrictions.** What is the purpose of such restrictions? To protect prior appropriators? To protect the future of slower growing regions? Are there any economic justifications for geographic restrictions? See Lawrence J. MacDonnell & Charles W. Howe, Area-of-Origin Protection in Transbasin Water Diversions: An Evaluation of Alternative Approaches, 57 U. Colo. L. Rev. 527 (1986). MacDonnell and Howe suggest that in a market setting like the West such statutes can be a means of assuring "economically efficient transbasin diversions" by making exporters accountable for costs which they impose on an area of origin. They conclude that requiring compensation to an area of origin is the most direct way of assuring economic efficiency. See also Nev. Rev. Stat. 533.438 (authorizing a tax on groundwater that is appropriated for use outside the county of origin and requiring that all money raised by the tax be deposited in a trust fund to be used by the county "for purposes of economic development, health care and education").

7. **Interstate diversions.** In the absence of a statute, an appropriation may be made by diverting water with a ditch that taps the stream in one state and carries the water across a state line to a place of use in another state. The courts of the state where the diversion is made will protect the appropriation. Willey v. Decker, 73 P. 210 (Wyo. 1903). Most of the western states, however, enacted statutes designed to see that the benefits of water use remained within the state of origin. Limitations on exports of water took a number of forms: absolute embargoes, requirements of specific legislative approval, requirements for a discretionary permit, and (alone or in conjunction with permission for export) a requirement that the receiving state grant reciprocal privileges. Some statutes applied to all sources, others only to streams or to groundwater. See Wells A. Hutchins, Water Right Laws in the Nineteen Western States 389-96 (1971); Steven E. Clyde, State Prohibitions on the Interstate Exportation of Scarce Water Resources, 53 U. Colo. L. Rev. 529 (1982). In 1982 this pattern was considerably altered when Sporhase v. Nebraska ex rel Douglas, 458 U.S. 941 (1982), invalidated a Nebraska statute that prevented the owner of a farm lying partly in Nebraska and partly in Colorado from piping water from a well on the Nebraska side across the state line to irrigate the Colorado field. The Court ruled that groundwater is an "article of commerce" subject to the potential, though unexercised, regulatory power of Congress, and held that Nebraska could not build into a water right restrictions that unreasonably burden interstate commerce. The Court discussed a number of factors that might permit some preference for in-state uses. Several states have since amended their laws to give as much protection to local needs as is permissible under the *Sporhase* guidelines. The case and those laws are considered in Chapter 8, Section 1.

F. Appurtenance

SALT RIVER VALLEY WATER USERS' ASS'N v. KOVACOVICH

Arizona Court of Appeals, 1966.
3 Ariz. App. 28, 411 P.2d 201.

EDWIN THURSTON, SUPERIOR COURT JUDGE. These actions, consolidated for purpose of appeal, were brought by appellant in the Yavapai County Superior Court seeking a permanent injunction against appellees to enjoin the use of waters of the Verde River upon certain land situate in Yavapai County, and asking for determination with respect to whether or not valid and existing water rights were legally existing appurtenant to such land. In the basic actions, each of the parties filed motions for summary judgment and each motion submitted to the lower court upon an agreed statement of facts together with supporting memoranda and exhibits. The statement of facts agreed to by the parties is as follows:

1. That the defendants and their predecessors in interest have made valid appropriations of water from the Verde River for irrigation purposes upon a portion of the lands owned by them;

2. That prior to 1933 in the Kovacovich action and prior to 1950 in the Ward action, certain additional lands owned by the respective defendants were not used for farming purposes nor was irrigation water applied thereon;

3. That neither the defendants nor their predecessors in interest ever made application under the Arizona Water Code to appropriate water for these additional lands;

4. That during and after 1933 in the Kovacovich action and during 1950 in the Ward action, the defendants, respectively, undertook in addition the cultivation of approximately thirty-five (35) acres and forty (40) acres of land adjacent to the land upon which the parties already had a valid water appropriation by irrigating said lands with water from the Verde River; and

5. That because of water-saving practices, no more water was thus used by the defendants to irrigate all of their lands here involved than was formerly used upon only their lands with a valid water appropriation.

The lower Court denied injunctive relief in each action and confirmed the right of appellees to beneficially use, as presently used, that quantity of water used by the appellee Kovacovich during or prior to 1933 and by the appellee Ward during or prior to 1950. * * *

In essence this case involves the narrow issue of whether or not an owner of land having a valid appurtenant water right may through water-saving practices apply the water thus saved to immediately adjacent lands owned by that person, without need to apply for the right to use such additional waters under the State Water Code. The further issue is that since the application of such waters would not result in less quantity of water flowing to the use of the appellants herein as owners of lower and subordinate water rights than would have previously occurred, have appellants been damaged whereby they are entitled to injunctive relief?

It was argued that decision of this issue in favor of appellants would result in penalizing persons who, through their industry, effort and expenses, engage in water-saving practices. The water-saving practices here referred to include improvement of ditches and concrete lining of ditches. This Court is of the opinion that the water-saving practices entered into by appellees not only result in conservation of water but also other benefits to appellees such as weed and vegetation growth control along such irrigation ditches and reduction of time and cost of maintenance of such ditches. Certainly any effort by users of water in Arizona tending toward conservation and more economical use of water is to be highly commended. However, commendable practices do not in themself create legal rights.

Historically, the development of water rights in Arizona created confusion by attempts to apply some of the strict concepts of common law riparian rights to the peculiar circumstances of not only the use of water but the need for its economical use prevalent in Arizona. The confusion concomitant with early attempts to apply the law with respect to use of water in Arizona progressed through several stages, including that where the right to use water appeared to be vested in the owner of land whereby same could be traded, leased or sold in much the same manner as other property. In an effort to achieve some degree of order out of the chaos then existing, our Courts through a series of decisions developed and applied what we today refer to as the "Doctrine of Beneficial Use." This doctrine is clearly enunciated in Gillespie Land & Irrigation Co. v. Buckeye Irr. Co. et al., 75 Ariz. 377, 384, 257 P.2d 393, 397, 398 (1953).

> "Slosser v. Salt River Valley Canal Co. [7 Ariz. 376, 65 P. 332], supra; Gould v. Maricopa Canal Co., 8 Ariz. 429, 76 P. 598; Brockman v. Grand Canal Co., 8 Ariz. 451, 76 P. 602; Tattersfield v. Putnam, 45 Ariz. 156, 41 P.2d 228; Olsen v. Union Canal & Irr. Co., 58 Ariz. 306, 119 P.2d 569. The holding in all of these cases is to the effect that a water right is attached to the land on which it is beneficially used and becomes appurtenant thereto, and that the right is not in any individual or owner of the land. It is in no sense a floating right, nor can the right, once having attached to a particular piece of land, be made to do duty to any other land, with certain exceptions, e.g., where the land is washed away."

This doctrine was further implemented by enactment of a series of statutes, today referred to as the State Water Code, wherein matters pertaining to application of waters to new lands or changes in use of waters previously appropriated was placed under the jurisdiction of the Arizona State Land Department. In addition these statutes prescribe certain standards to be followed by the State Land Department with respect to applications for acquisition of change in the use of water. Title 45, Chapter 1, Articles 1-6, Arizona Revised Statutes.

This Court is of the opinion that the Doctrine of Beneficial Use precludes the application of waters gained by water conservation practices to lands other than those to which the water was originally appurtenant. * * * Under the doctrine of beneficial use, the appellees are not entitled under all circumstances to appropriate a given number of acre feet of water per year. Beneficial use is the measure and limit to the use of water. A.R.S. § 45-201, subsec. B. The appellees may only appropriate the amount of water from the Verde River as may be beneficially used in any given year upon the land to which the water is appurtenant even though this amount may be less than the maximum amount of their appropriation. They may not take a quantity of water in excess of their appropriation even though they could beneficially use the same upon water right land. If in a given year, this should constitute an appropriation and use of all the water available at that particular point on the Verde River, subordinate owners of water rights have no cause to complain. However, in those years when water in excess of that which appellees may beneficially use upon the appurtenant land to which their water right attaches, all water which may flow to lower and subordinate owners of water rights is no longer of concern to appellees. Any practice, whether through water-saving procedures or otherwise, whereby appellees may in fact reduce the quantity of water actually taken inures to the benefit of other water users and neither creates a right to use the waters saved as a marketable commodity nor the right to apply same to adjacent property having no appurtenant water rights. It is believed that any other decision would result in commencement of return to the very area of confusion and chaos which gave rise to the development and application of the concept of beneficial use.

The judgment of the lower Court is reversed with instructions to the lower Court to issue an injunction on behalf of appellant as against appellees as prayed for in appellant's complaints.

Notes

1. **Nature of the water right.** What is the nature of the "water right" in *Kovacovich?* A right to divert a quantity of water or a right to irrigate a specific piece of land?

2. **Purpose of appurtenance.** Charles J. Meyers, A Historical and Functional Analysis of the Appropriation System, in Nat'l Water Comm'n, Legal Study No. 1, at 17-18 (1971): "[T]his restriction was an understandable but misguided effort to get at what was regarded as the evil of speculation. Despite adoption of the permit system, it was believed that many pre-permit rights were inflated. In an effort to make more unappropriated water available at zero cost to new settlers—and in this sense, encourage development—statutes were enacted * * * making water rights appurtenant to land and nontransferable (subject to certain exceptions). The theory of these statutes (some since repealed) is that by attaching water rights indissolubly to land, the owner of the inflated right (who is unable to use all the water on his own land) will be unable to sell the excess for use on other land."

3. **Appurtenance and water rights transfers.** The foregoing note suggests that appurtenancy makes water rights nontransferable, "subject to certain exceptions." The exceptions have largely swallowed the rule. In most states today, water rights may by transferred to new places or purposes of use pursuant to statutory procedures, notwithstanding pronouncements of appurtenance. Transfer procedures and substantive limits on transfers to protect other appropria-

tors are examined in Section 5 of this Chapter. Unlike the *Kovacovich* situation, in most transfers the original use is partially or completely discontinued.

4. **Trend away from *Kovacovich*.** Colorado and Utah permit an appropriator to enlarge the lands under irrigation if it can be shown that the expanded use will not result in injury to other appropriators; i.e., if it can be shown that the appropriator's conservation measures have salvaged water that would otherwise be lost to the system and have not merely captured return flows relied on by other appropriators. In both states the statutory transfer procedures are used for this purpose. See Danielson v. Kerbs Ag., Inc., 646 P.2d 363 (Colo. 1982); E. Bench Irrigation Co. v. Deseret Irrigation Co., 271 P.2d 449 (Utah 1954). Several states have codified this approach in an effort to promote conservation. See Cal. Water Code §§ 1010, 1011; Mont. Code Ann. § 85-2-419; Or. Rev. Stat. §§ 537.455-.500; Tex. Water Code Ann. § 11.002 (4), (9). To date, such statutes do not appear to have been widely used, principally, it appears, because of high transaction costs and significant uncertainties associated with demonstrating that others will not be injured. See Mark Honhart, Comment, Carrots for Conservation: Oregon's Water Conservation Statute Offers Incentives to Invest in Efficiency, 66 U. Colo. L. Rev. 827 (1995).

5. **Appurtenance and conveyancing.** In most states, a water right is an "appurtenance" in a conveyancing sense; i.e., water rights pass in a conveyance of land unless expressly reserved. See, e.g., Utah Code Ann. § 73-1-11; Russell, v. Irish, 118 P. 501 (Idaho 1911); Axtell v. M.S. Consulting, 955 P.2d 1362 (Mont. 1998). In Dermody v. City of Reno, 931 P.2d 1354 (Nev. 1997), the court extended the rule to condemnation, holding that Reno acquired appurtenant water rights when it condemned land for airport expansion although the decree made no mention of the rights. In Wayt v. Buerkel, 875 P.2d 499 (Or. Ct. App. 1994), the court applied the rule to contract rights to water, holding that such rights were acquired by a purchaser of land at a foreclosure sale. However, in Colorado the question depends on the intent of the grantor, and in New Mexico the rule applies only to irrigation rights. Bessemer Irrigating Ditch Co. v. Woolley, 76 P. 1053 (Colo. 1904); KRM, Inc. v. Caviness, 925 P.2d 9 (N.M. Ct. App. 1996). In Little v. Greene & Weed Investment, 839 P.2d 791 (Utah 1992), the court ruled that a right does not become appurtenant for conveyancing purposes until the state engineer issues a certificate of appropriation. If the land is divided, the amount appurtenant to each tract is the amount which was beneficially used on the tract prior to division, Stephens v. Burton, 546 P.2d 240 (Utah 1976), or is a proportionate share of the entire right. Crow v. Carlson, 690 P.2d 916 (Idaho 1984); Axtell v. M.S. Consulting, supra; cf. Silverstein v. Carlson, 797 P.2d 856 (Idaho 1990).

In Spears v. Warr, 44 P.3d. 742 (Utah 2002), land developers made oral representations to several buyers that irrigation water rights were included in the purchase price of lots, but deeds conveying the lots made no mention of water rights. Subsequently, the developers refused to convey the promised water rights, and the buyers sued for specific performance. The court ruled for the buyers, holding that proof and enforcement of the oral agreements was not blocked by the merger doctrine, the parol evidence rule, or the statute of frauds. The Utah appurtenance statute noted above was not mentioned, apparently because the rights involved were in the process of being transferred from other lands and were not appurtenant at the time the lots were sold.

G. Protection of Means of Diversion

STATE EX REL. CROWLEY v. DISTRICT COURT

Supreme Court of Montana, 1939.
108 Mont. 89, 88 P.2d 23.

JOHNSON, CHIEF JUSTICE. * * * The suit in question is for damages for alleged interference with plaintiff's use of irrigation water from the Madison River in 1935, 1936 and 1937. There are nine causes of action, which are grouped as to years. The first three relate to 1935, the next three to 1936, and the last three to 1937. Thus there are three causes of action with reference to each of the three years. * * *

The second group, comprising causes 2, 5 and 8, is based upon the allegations that the defendants [Montana Power Company et al] impounded by their dams the entire natural flow of the river so that the water level at plaintiff's point of diversion was so low that he could not divert water into his ditches by his diversion dam, although the latter was suitable and efficient for the purpose and was a reasonably adequate means of diversion, and reasonably constructed and maintained to divert water from the river to plaintiff's land in spite of the fluctuations in flow incidental to the reasonable and lawful use of water by all persons lawfully entitled to use the same. The exact allegations relative to these points will be set forth below. The demurrers to these causes of action numbered 2, 5 and 8 were sustained. * * *

The allegations of the causes are those usual to actions of this kind. Defendants' contentions are that plaintiff has no cause of action merely because their acts so reduced the flow that he could not divert his appropriated water by his reasonably efficient diversion system; that he should have alleged that not enough was left to permit his diversion without leaving any water in the stream. In other words, they contend that plaintiff has no cause of action if there are 200 inches of water at his point of diversion, even though he cannot get the water into his ditches without a pump; that an appropriator's vested interest is only in the use of the quantum of water appropriated by him without reference to his means or manner of diversion, however reasonably efficient; that not reasonable efficiency but absolute efficiency is required. To this theory we cannot assent without doing violence to the entire principle of water rights by appropriation. If it is to be followed, there are few, if any, irrigation water rights in the state of Montana, however long established, which could not in effect be destroyed entirely by subsequent appropriations. One hundred per cent efficiency can be furnished by no system of diversion, and certainly by none financially available to the average water user. The law does not defeat its own end by requiring the impossible. The marginal character of many farming enterprises, and especially of the smaller ones, is well known, and if defendants' argument is followed, vested interests will be seriously affected and rights limited by the necessity of installing diversion systems by which the last drop may be taken from the stream.

There is no question that waste of our water resources must be minimized in the general interest, but it is equally manifest that there is a vanishing point at which the possible waste of water would be more than overcome by the waste incidental to the abandonment of reasonably efficient diversion systems and the establishment of diversion systems whose expense is neither warranted nor permitted by the benefit to be derived from the water.

It is well established that subsequent appropriators take with notice of the conditions existing at the time of their appropriations. In making their appropriation of storage or other water and their expenditures in connection therewith, defendants and their predecessors were chargeable with knowledge of the existing conditions, with reference not only to the amount of prior appropriations, but also to the existing diversion systems of prior appropriators. They cannot now argue that they are limited by the amount but not the means of prior appropriations, however reasonably efficient under the circumstances, or that so long as they leave the exact amount of plaintiff's appropriation in the river at his point of diversion, they have no further duty and that it is his worry and not theirs how or whether he can divert it upon his land. His right is to divert and use the water, not merely to have it left in the streambed; that is the essential difference between riparian and appropriation rights. * * *

Defendants contend that the case of Schodde v. Twin Falls Land & Water Co., 224 U.S. 107, 32 S.Ct. 470, 56 L.Ed. 686, affirming 9 Cir., 161 F. 43, 88 C.C.A. 207, sustains their contention that a prior appropriator has no vested interest in his means of diversion. It cannot be so construed. In that case plaintiff had appropriated 1250 inches of water from Snake River in Idaho, for use on his ranch of 429 acres, and diverted it by means of large waterwheels operated by the stream flow. The defendant thereafter constructed a dam nine miles below to supply water to about 5,000 settlers for the irrigation of approximately 300,000 acres of land. The dam backed the water up beyond plaintiff's waterwheels so that the current was no longer available to operate them. Plaintiff sued for damages in the federal court of Idaho, and defendant's demurrer was sustained. On appeal the Ninth Circuit Court of Appeals affirmed the trial court's action on the ground that there was no attempted appropriation of water to run the wheels, and that there could be none under the laws of Idaho without an actual diversion for the purpose, and upon the further ground that the statute expressly authorizing the use of rams and other machines to lift appropriated water from streams gave a mere license, and not an appurtenance to the water right appropriated. In other words, the right to the flow of the river constituted neither an appropriation of the flow nor an appurtenance to the irrigation water actually appropriated. It also held that where the method of diversion was obviously unreasonable and inefficient it could not be used where it interfered with the reasonable use of water by others. Obviously, of course, under the circumstances of that case, it was unreasonable to prevent the irrigation of 300,000 acres by an unusual and inefficient method of diverting water for 429 acres. The complaint there was not that the defendant had taken water out of the stream so as to interfere with the waterwheels; as a matter of fact, the defendant had confined more water there. What it had deprived plaintiff of was not the water, but the force of the water, which was no part of his appropriation. This can be made clear by an analogy. If, instead of building waterwheels to utilize the force of the stream, he had constructed windmills to employ the force of the wind, it would have been entirely clear that his complaint was not of water right interference, but of something entirely different. If the conditions were such that he could have recovered for an obstruction to the flow of the wind to his windmills, it would still have been something entirely apart from and not appurtenant to his water right. This is clear from the opinion of the Circuit Court of Appeals in 161 F. at page 45, as follows: "It is contended on the part of the plaintiff that the current of the river is necessarily appurtenant to the water location and that the means of utilizing that current is attached as an appurtenance to the appropriation. We have not been referred to any case—and we know of none—where either of these propositions has been upheld. The claim that the right to the current of the river is appurtenant to the water location is contrary to well-established principles of the common law governing such a relation. The water location was an appropriation and diversion of a certain quantity of the flowing water of the stream. The current of the river is part of the stream. There can be no right to the current of a stream as appurtenant to a diversion of the flowing waters of the stream. The two rights in such case would be equal and of the same character and quality, and one such right cannot be appurtenant to the other." The court then went on to show that there had been no diversion or appropriation of water for power purposes, so that plaintiff's asserted right against defendant's interference was not a water right, and concluded by quoting the decision of this court in Fitzpatrick v. Montgomery, 20 Mont. 181, 50 P. 416, 63 Am.St.Rep. 622, to the effect that the tendency and spirit of legislation in the northwest had been to prevent a monopoly of water.

On certiorari the United States Supreme Court, speaking through Mr. Chief Justice White, said: "The trial court recognized fully the right of the plaintiff to the volume of water actually appropriated for a beneficial purpose. It nevertheless dismissed the complaint on the ground that there was no right under the Constitution and laws of the state of Idaho to appropriate the current of the river so as to render it impossible for others to apply the otherwise unappropriated waters of the river to beneficial uses. The court did not find it necessary to deny that power might be one of the beneficial purposes for which appropriations of water might be made, but in substance held that to uphold as an appropriation the use of the current of the river to the extent required to work the defendant's wheels would amount to saying that a limited taking of water from the river by appropriation for a limited beneficial use justified the appropriation of all the water in the river as incident to the limited benefit resulting from the use of the water actually appropriated. The court said: 'It is conceded and is beyond question, that the statute law as well as judicial authority directly protects plaintiff in all water he has actually appropriated, diverted, and used; but there is no statute, nor so far as known, any judicial rulings, protecting him in the establishment and in the use of his water wheels, as he claims to, and must, use them for the diversion of water to his land.' * * * It is unquestioned that what he has actually diverted and used upon his land, he has appropriated; but can it be said that all the water he uses or needs to operate his wheels is an appropriation? As before suggested, there is neither statutory nor judicial authority that such a use is an appropriation. Such use also lacks one of the essential attributes of an appropriation,—it is not reasonable.' " * * *

The rule in this connection is well stated as follows in Long on Irrigation, 2nd ed., 202, 203, sec. 116: "The irrigator may employ any means best suited to the existing physical conditions, and all the circumstances of the case, though undoubtedly he will be required to employ reasonably economical means, so as to prevent unnecessary waste. * * * As already stated, the means of diversion employed must not be unnecessarily wasteful (Doherty v. Pratt, 34 Nev. 343, 124 P. 574), but when ditches and flumes are the usual and ordinary means of diverting water, parties who have made their appropriations by such means cannot be compelled to substitute iron pipes, though they will be required to prevent unnecessary waste by keeping their ditches and flumes in good repair (Barrows v. Fox, 9 Cal. 63, 32 P. 811)." * * *

Plaintiff alleges that he has diverted the water by means of a wing dam of brush, rocks and dirt, and proceeds to allege that the means of diversion was at the time in question "suitable and efficient for the diversion of water," and "a reasonably adequate means of diversion and reasonably constructed and maintained" for the purpose, notwithstanding the fluctuations incidental to the reasonable and lawful use of water by all those entitled, including defendants. These are statements of ultimate facts, and causes numbered 2, 5 and 8 sufficiently state causes of action. It follows that the demurrers should have been overruled. * * *

Notes

1. **Illustration of unreasonable means of diversion.** In *Schodde,* distinguished in the principal case, both the trial court and the Supreme Court used the following illustration: "Suppose from a stream of 1000 inches a party diverts and uses 100, and in some way uses the other 900 to divert his 100, could it be said that he had made such a reasonable use of the 900 as to constitute an appropriation of it? Or, suppose that when the entire 1000 inches are running, they so fill the channel that by a ditch he can draw off to his land his 100 inches, can he then object to those above him appropriating and using the other 900 inches, because it will so lower the stream that his ditch becomes useless? This would be such an unreasonable use of the 900 inches as will not be tolerated under the law of appropriation." 224 U.S. 107, 119 (1912 (quoting the unpublished opinion of the trial court).

2. **Is "reasonableness" static or dynamic?** On remand, what standards will be used to determine if Crowley's means of diversion are "reasonably adequate," the standards at the time Crowley initiated the appropriation or the standards at the time the dispute with the defendant arose?

In Warner Valley Stock Co. v. Lynch, 336 P.2d 884 (Or. 1959), the court refused to protect the use of natural overflow to divert water from a lake for irrigation, although the rights at issue had been previously adjudicated. However, the earlier adjudication had found that the diversions were wasteful and were "privileges," not rights, to be enjoyed only until rendered impractical by fuller use of the stream. In distinguishing cases in which appropriators' means of diversion were protected, including the principal case, the court said simply, "in each of these cases the interest * * * which the court protected was a vested right." If

Crowley has a "vested right" to his means of diversion, as *Warner* suggests, can he be required to adopt more efficient methods if economic changes, advances in irrigation technology, or changes in customary irrigation practices make his "wing dam" obsolete? See *Imperial Irrigation Dist.*, supra p. 41.

3. **Codification.** N.D. Cent. Code § 61-04-06.3: "Priority of appropriation does not include the right to prevent changes in condition of water occurrence, such as the increase or decrease of streamflow, or the lowering of a water table, artesian pressure, or water level, by later appropriators, if the prior appropriator can reasonably acquire his water under the changed conditions."

4. **An economic perspective.** R. H. Coase, The Problem of Social Cost, 3 J.L. & Econ. 1 (1960):

"This paper is concerned with those actions of business firms which have harmful effects on others. The standard example is that of a factory the smoke from which has harmful effects on those occupying neighboring properties. The economic analysis of such a situation has usually proceeded in terms of a divergence between the private and social product of the factory, in which economists have largely followed the treatment of Pigou in *The Economics of Welfare*. The conclusions to which this kind of analysis seems to have led most economists is that it would be desirable to make the owner of the factory liable for the damage caused to those injured by the smoke, or alternatively, to place a tax on the factory owner varying with the amount of smoke produced an equivalent in money terms to the damage it would cause, or finally, to exclude the factory from residential districts (and presumably from other areas in which the emission of smoke would have harmful effects on others). It is my contention that the suggested courses of action are inappropriate, in that they lead to results which are not necessarily, or even usually, desirable.

"The traditional approach has tended to obscure the nature of the choice that has to be made. The question is commonly thought of as one in which A inflicts harm on B and what has to be decided is: how should we restrain A? But this is wrong. We are dealing with a problem of a reciprocal nature. To avoid the harm to B would inflict harm on A. The real question that has to be decided is: should A be allowed to harm B or should B be allowed to harm A? The problem is to avoid the more serious harm. I instanced in my previous article the case of a confectioner the noise and vibrations from whose machinery disturbed a doctor in his work. To avoid harming the doctor would inflict harm on the confectioner. The problem posed by this case was essentially whether it was worth while, as a result of restricting the methods of production which could be used by the confectioner, to secure more doctoring at the cost of a reduced supply of confectionery products. * * *

"The court's decision established that the doctor had the right to prevent the confectioner from using his machinery. But, of course, it would have been possible to modify the arrangements envisaged in the legal ruling by means of a bargain between the parties. The doctor would have been willing to waive his right and allow the machinery to continue in operation if the confectioner would have paid him a sum of money which was greater than the loss of income which he would suffer from having to move to a more costly or less convenient location or from having to curtail his activities at this location or, as was suggested as a possibility, from having to build a separate wall which would deaden the noise and vibration. The confectioner would have been willing to do this if the amount he would have to pay the doctor was less than the fall in income he would suffer if he had to change his mode of operation at this location, abandon his operation or move his confectionery business to some other location. The solution of the problem depends essentially on whether the continued use of the machinery adds more to the confectioner's income than it subtracts from the doctor's. But now consider the situation if the confectioner had won the case. The confectioner would then have had the right to continue operating his noise and vibration-generating machinery without having to pay anything to the doctor. The boot would have been on the other foot: the doctor would have had to pay the confectioner to induce him to stop using the machinery. If the doctor's income would have fallen more through continuance of the use of this machinery than it added to the income of the confectioner, there would clearly be room for a bargain whereby the doctor paid the confectioner to stop using the machinery. That is to say, the circumstances in which it would not pay the confectioner to continue to use the machinery and to compensate the doctor for the losses that this would bring (if the doctor had the right to prevent the confectioner's using his machinery) would be those in which it would be in the interest of the doctor to make a payment to the confectioner which would induce him to discontinue the use of the machinery (if the confectioner had the right to operate the machinery). * * * With costless market transactions, the decision of the courts concerning liability for damage would be without effect on the allocation of resources. * * *

"Judges have to decide on legal liability but this should not confuse economists about the nature of the economic problem involved. * * * The doctor's work would not have been disturbed if the confectioner had not worked his machinery; but the machinery would have disturbed no one if the doctor had not set up his consulting room in that particular place. * * * If we are to discuss the problem in terms of causation, both parties caused the damage. If we are to attain an optimum allocation of resources, it is therefore desirable that both parties should take the harmful effect (the nuisance) into account in deciding on their course of action. It is one of the beauties of a smoothly operating pricing system that, as has already been explained, the fall in the value of production due to the harmful effect would be a cost for both parties. * * *

"Of course, if market transactions were costless, all that matters (questions of equity apart) is that the rights of the various parties should be well-defined and the results of legal actions easy to forecast. But as we have seen, the situation is quite different when market transactions are so costly as to make it difficult to change the arrangement of rights established by the law. In such cases, the courts directly influence economic activity. It would therefore seem desirable that the courts should understand the economic consequences of their decisions and should, insofar as this is possible without creating too much uncertainty about the legal position itself, take these consequences into account when making their decisions. Even when it is possible to change the legal delimitation of rights through market transactions, it is obviously desirable to reduce the need for such transactions and thus reduce the employment of resources in carrying them out. * * *

"The problem which we face in dealing with actions which have harmful effects is not simply one of restraining those responsible for them. What has to be decided is whether the gain from preventing the harm is greater than the loss which would be suffered elsewhere as a result of stopping the action which produces the harm. In a world in which there are costs of rearranging the rights established by the legal system, the courts, in cases relating to nuisance, are, in effect, making a decision on the economic problem and determining how resources are to be employed. It was argued that the courts are conscious of this and that they often make, although not always in a very explicit fashion, a comparison between what would be gained and what lost by preventing actions which have harmful effects. But the delimitation of rights is also the result of statutory enactments. Here we also find evidence of an appreciation of the reciprocal nature of the problem. While statutory enactments add to the list of nuisances, action is also taken to legalize what would otherwise be nuisances under the common law. The kind of situation which economists are prone to consider as requiring corrective Government action is, in fact, often the result of Government action. Such action is not necessarily unwise. But there is a real danger that extensive Government intervention in the economic system may lead to the protection of those responsible for harmful effects being carried too far. * * *

"It would clearly be desirable if the only actions performed were those in which what was gained was worth more than what was lost. But in choosing between social arrangements within the context of which individual decisions are made, we have to bear in mind that a change in the existing system which will lead to an improvement in some decisions may well lead to a worsening of others. Furthermore we have to take into account the costs involved in operating the various social arrangements (whether it be the working of a market or of a Government department), as well as the costs involved in moving to a new system. In devising and choosing between social arrangements we should have regard for the total effect. This, above all, is the change in approach which I am advocating."

5. **Equity.** Note that Professor Coase puts "problems of equity" aside in concluding that it makes no difference in resource allocation whether or not, to translate into our terms, the priority of the first right includes the right to maintain an inefficient means of diversion. If in the *Crowley* situation the loss to Crowley's crops is less than the benefit the power company obtains when the extra water required by the inefficient wing dam is held back, the water will be stored in the company's reservoir, whether the company has to pay Crowley or not. If the benefit to the company is less than the crop loss, the water will be released, either because if the company is liable it will be cheaper to release it than to pay damages, or if not liable the company will make a profit by accepting Crowley's offer to buy the water at a price somewhere between the company's benefit and his loss. Whether an improved dam will be built is similarly independent of the rule of liability. If the water is stored in the reservoir and if the cost of building an improved diversion dam is less than the crop loss, the dam will be built. If Crowley has no claim against the company, he will build it to eliminate his crop loss. If the company is liable, it will build it or pay Crowley to build it rather than continuing to pay the greater damages. If the water is released from the reservoir because it has less value to the company than to Crowley, the new dam will not be built. The "inefficient" wing dam then remains as the most efficient method of utilizing the resource.

What "problems of equity" remain? Assuming maximum efficiency in resource allocation is obtainable under either rule, *ought* the cost of constructing the improved dam be placed on the power company or on the irrigator? Should it make any difference if all the water users are irrigators?

If the prior appropriator's means of diversion is protected, does the relief given by the court make any difference? Crowley asked for damages. If he had sought and obtained an injunction, would the Coasian analysis of the situation change? Suppose there are a number of persons situated similarly to Crowley, all of whose diversion works need to be improved to get the desirable combination of irrigation and power. If each is given the right to an injunction, is the Coasian optimum more or less likely to be reached?

H. Access

HALLAUER v. SPECTRUM PROPERTIES, INC.

Supreme Court of Washington, 2001
143 Wash.2d 126, 18 P.3d 540,

MADSEN, J. Wilbur G. and Josephine Hallauer, who hold a certificated water right to water from a spring on neighboring land, seek to condemn a way across that land for transporting water to their property for domestic use, and to ponds for fish propagation. The Court of Appeals held that because the Hallauers' property is not landlocked and alternative sources of water are available, the Hallauers failed to prove a reasonable necessity for condemnation. We reverse the Court of Appeals and hold that the Hallauers are entitled to proceed with their condemnation action. * * *

Although several other grounds for relief have been argued during litigation between the parties, the only matter before this court is whether the Hallauers are entitled to condemn an easement across the Del Rosarios' property for a pipeline to transport water from the spring to their property for use in the heat pump and cooling system and as a water supply for propagation of fish. The authority to condemn a right of way to transport water has long existed in this state, both by constitutional and statutory provisions. The chief question posed by this case is whether the showing of necessity to condemn a right of way to transport water is identical to the showing required to condemn a private way of necessity. The Court of Appeals held that "necessity" means the same in both contexts, relying on RCW 8.24.010. We disagree because RCW 8.24.010 does not apply in the context here.

As we explain below, RCW 90.03.040 provides the statutory authority for condemnation in this case. Among other things, the statute directs that "property or rights shall be acquired [through condemnation] in the manner provided by law for the taking of private property for public use by private corporations." RCW 90.03.040. Therefore, chapter 8.20 RCW (eminent domain by corporations), rather than chapter 8.24 RCW, provides the procedures for condemnation. * * *

In order to determine whether the Hallauers are entitled to an order of public use and necessity, we examine both public use and necessity * * *. Also, the public interest condition and the necessity condition "are generally subsumed under the definition of 'necessity'." *City of Seattle v. Mall, Inc.*, 104 Wash.2d 621, 623, 707 P.2d 1348 (1985). The interrelatedness of the conditions is particularly apparent where water rights or rights of way to transport water are concerned. This is because of the adoption of the prior appropriation doctrine in this state for acquisition of new water rights; condemnation of rights of way to transport water is an integral component of application of water to beneficial use.

Accordingly, we begin by discussing the public use condition as a predicate to discussion of the necessity condition. Our analysis begins with article I, section 16 of the Washington State Constitution, which provides:

> Private property shall not be taken for private use, except for private ways of necessity, and for drains, flumes, or ditches on or across the lands of others for agricultural, domestic, or sanitary purposes. No private property shall be taken or damaged for public or private use without just compensation having been first made * * *.

As an initial matter, this constitutional provision does not require that condemnation for rights of way to transport water is subject to the same criteria as condemnation for private ways of necessity. The first sentence of article I, section 16 carves out two forms that a condemnation for "private" use may take. The constitution states the exceptions to the rule that private property may not be taken for private uses as: "except *for* private ways of necessity, *and for* drains, flumes, or ditches on or across the lands of others for agricultural, domestic, or sanitary purposes ." Const. art. I, § 16 (emphasis added). * * *

[RCW 90.03.040] was enacted as part of the 1917 water code under which the prior appropriation doctrine became the sole method for acquisition of new water rights. It provides in part that "[t]he beneficial use of water is hereby declared to be a public use, and any person may exercise the right of eminent domain to acquire any property or rights now or hereafter existing when found necessary for the storage of water for, or the application of water to, any beneficial use." RCW 90.03.040.

This statute was needed in order to implement the prior appropriation doctrine. Before adoption of the 1917 water code, two water rights doctrines applied in Washington. Under the doctrine of riparian rights, an owner of land on a stream or other body of water has the right to use the water. Crook v. Hewitt, 4 Wash. 749, 31 P. 28 (1892). The second doctrine, the prior appropriation doctrine, developed in the arid western states, and "provides that a right to water can be established only by putting water to beneficial use and that the first such use in time is the first such use in right." Charles B. Roe & Peter R. Anderson, Water Law, in 1C Kelly Kunsch, Washington Practice: Methods of Practice § 91.4 (4th ed.1997). Both of these types of water rights could be acquired in Washington in its early history.

Where a riparian water right was involved, the water right holder generally had access to sufficient water because water was adjacent to or within the holder's property. However, prior appropriation rights, by definition, do not require that the owner's land abut a stream or other water body. Where appropriative rights are concerned, there "need be no relationship between the source of the water and the locus of use." A. Dan Tarlock, Law of Water Rights and Resources § 5.24, at 5-41 (2000). Accordingly, there must be some means of delivering the appropriated water to the owner's land. The authority to condemn property for rights of way to transport water is thus an essential part of the prior appropriation scheme: "Access to water open to appropriation can generally be acquired by eminent domain. To prevent de facto riparianism, western states passed statutes permitting a water rights claimant to condemn the necessary rights of way to bring the water from the stream to the place of his use." Id. at 5-42.

The constitutionality of these statutes was originally at issue because the power of eminent domain was limited to public uses. *Id.* at 5-43. However, by the time RCW 90.03.040 was enacted the validity of such statutes was settled. In *Clark v. Nash,* 198 U.S. 361, 25 S.Ct. 676, 49 L.Ed. 1085 (1905), the Court upheld a Utah statute granting the right to condemn land for the purpose of conveying water in ditches across that land for irrigation of the condemnor's land alone. The Court observed that

> [w]here the use is asserted to be public, and the right of the individual to condemn land for the purpose of exercising such use is founded upon or is the result of some peculiar condition of the soil or climate, or other peculiarity of the State, where the right of condemnation is asserted under a state statute, we are always, where it can fairly be done, strongly inclined to hold with the state courts, when they uphold a state statute providing for such condemnation. The validity of such statutes may sometimes depend upon many different facts, the existence of which would make a public use, even by an individual, where, in the absence of such facts, the use clearly be private.
>
> * * *
>
> [Water rights] are not the same in the arid and mountainous States of the West that they are in the States of the East. These rights have been altered by many of the Western States, by their constitutions and laws, because of the totally different circumstances in which their inhabitants are placed. * * *.

Clark, 198 U.S. at 367-68, 370, 25 S.Ct. 676. It is now settled that "[e]minent domain may be used to transport water so long as the use is beneficial; beneficial uses are presumed public uses." Tarlock, supra, § 5.24, at 5-42. * * *

In Galbraith v. Superior Court, 59 Wash. 621, 629, 110 P. 429 (1910), the court discussed this principle in the context of beneficial use of water. The court noted that article I, section 16, provides for eminent domain for certain private purposes, including ditches for agricultural purposes. * * * The court explained that the reclamation through irrigation of one small field by an individual promotes the development and adds to the taxable wealth of the state as well as reclamation by irrigation of large areas. *Id.* at 632, 110 P. 429.

> The benefit to the public which supports the exercise of the power of eminent domain for purposes of this character, is not public service, but is the development of the resources of the state, and the increase of its wealth generally, by which its citizens incidentally reap a benefit. Whether such development and increased wealth comes from the effort of a single individual, or the united efforts of many, in our opinion does not change the principal upon which this right of eminent domain rests.

Id. at 631, 110 P. 429; see also, e.g., Prescott Irrig. Co. v. Flathers, 20 Wash. 454, 458-59, 55 P. 635 (1899); White v. Stout, 72 Wash. 62, 66, 129 P. 917 (1913). The same principle was discussed by the United States Supreme Court in *Clark,* quoted above. * * *

The legislative declaration in RCW 90.03.040 that beneficial use of water is a public use must also be viewed in light of other language in article I, section 16, which states that "[w]henever an attempt is made to take private property for a use alleged to be public, the question whether the contemplated use be really public shall be a judicial question, and determined as such, without regard to any legislative assertion that the use is public." This does not mean, however, that the Legislature cannot declare public uses. State ex rel. Andersen, 119 Wash. at 410, 205 P. 1051. "The Legislature can declare in the first instance that the purpose is a public one, and it remains the duty of the court to disregard such assertion if the court finds it to be unfounded." *Id.* A legislative declaration will be accorded great weight. Port of Seattle v. Isernio, 72 Wash.2d 932, 936, 435 P.2d 991 (1967); Miller v. City of Tacoma, 61 Wash.2d 374, 383-84, 378 P.2d 464 (1963). * * *

We conclude that the Legislature's declaration that beneficial uses are public uses, coinciding with its choice of prior appropriation as the sole basis for acquisition of new water rights in this state in 1917, is entitled to deference. Our conclusion accords with the laws of other western states that provide that condemnation of any property or rights necessary to apply water to beneficial use is a condemnation for a public use.

Our discussion of the public use question sets the stage for discussion of the necessity question. RCW 90.03.040 provides that the right of eminent domain may be exercised by any person "to acquire any property ... *when found necessary for* ... the application of water to[ ] any beneficial use." (Emphasis added.) "The word 'necessary,' when used in or in connection with eminent domain statutes, means reasonable necessity, under the circumstances of the particular case." City of Tacoma v. Welcker, 65 Wash.2d 677, 683-84, 399 P.2d 330 (1965) (citing State ex rel. Lange v. Superior Court, 61 Wash.2d 153, 377 P.2d 425 (1963)).

However, rather than determining whether the Hallauers established that a right of way across the Del Rosarios' land was necessary in order to put water from the spring to beneficial use, as RCW 90.03.040 directs, the Court of Appeals applied RCW 8.24.010. That court read RCW 8.24.010 as providing that an easement for transporting water may be condemned only where the land on which the water is to be used is landlocked. * * *

This analysis overlooks the fact that RCW 90.03.040 does more than declare that beneficial use of water is a public use. The statute also provides that any person can condemn a right of way to transport water where necessary to apply the water to beneficial use. * * * Thus, in marked contrast to RCW 8.24.010, RCW 90.03.040 does not require necessity based upon the landlocked nature of the condemnor's property, but expressly states the relevant necessity as "*necessary for* the storage of water for, or *the application of water to, any beneficial use.*" (Emphasis added.) * * * Because RCW 90.03.040 provides for condemnation of rights of way to transport water for application to beneficial use, the Del Rosarios and the Court of Appeals have mistakenly relied on cases involving private ways of necessity where necessity largely turned on the landlocked nature of the land of the party seeking condemnation. * * *

The necessity for the right of way is obvious. The water right that the Hallauers hold allows withdrawal of water from the spring on the Del Rosarios land. The only way in which the water can be conveyed to the Hallauers' property is over or through the Del Rosarios' land. Accordingly, the Court of Appeals' holding that necessity has not been established must be reversed. * * *

Notes

1. **Ditch rights.** A "ditch right" is a separate property interest from a water right. The acquisition of a water right does not automatically result in the acquisition of a right to transport the water across the lands of others. Often the two are linked, and, carrying out the intention of the parties, it has been held that a conveyance of a ditch may carry with it the water right as an appurtenance, Williams v. Harter, 53 P. 405 (Cal. 1898), or that the ditch may be regarded as an appurtenance of the water right and pass with a deed to the latter, Jacob v. Lorenz, 33 P. 119 (Cal. 1893). Often they are sufficiently separate that one can be sold independently of the other, or that abandonment of the water right does not bring the existence of the ditch right-of-way to an end. Ada County Farmers' Irrigation Co. v. Farmers' Canal Co., 51 P. 990 (Idaho 1898). This case also points out that the ditch itself is more than a hole in the ground, that it is a valuable structure, an asset subject to sale.

2. **Acquisition of rights of way.** Rights of way for ditches can be acquired by purchase, or obtained by prescription where their existence and use have been adverse to the servient estate for the period of the statute of limitations. Where oral permission has been given by the owner of the servient estate so that the use is not adverse, the water user may still have a permanent ditch right in the form of an "executed parol license" or a "license by estoppel." See Gustin v. Harting, 121 P. 522 (Wyo. 1912). The owner of an easement for a ditch has a secondary easement to enter and to inspect, repair, maintain or otherwise use the easement. O'Connor v. Brodie, 454 P.2d 920 (Mont. 1969).

3. **Rights of way on federal lands.** Rights of way for canals and ditches over the federal public domain were first authorized in 1866. The first statutes gave the water user general permission to use the land, but later laws required the filing of applications and specific approval, normally in the form of a "use permit." These have been repealed and replaced by section 501 of the Federal Land Policy and Management Act of 1976 (the "BLM Organic Act"): "The Secretary of the Interior, with respect to public lands, and the Secretary of Agriculture with respect to lands within the National Forest system (except wilderness areas) are authorized to grant, issue or renew rights of way under or through such lands for reservoirs, canals, ditches, flumes, laterals, pipes, pipelines, tunnels and other facilities and systems for the impoundment, storage, transportation or distribution of water." 43 U.S.C. § 1761. Rather elaborate procedures are required. Rights of way are limited to a reasonable term and are subject to an annual rental and elaborate conditions and regulations..

4. **Entry on another's land.** In Oregon, a person may enter another's land for the purpose of locating a point of diversion and surveying the line of ditches and sites for reservoirs. Or. Rev. Stat. § 537.320; see also Utah Code Ann. § 73-3-19.

5. **Modification of ditch rights of way.** As western cities expand over former farmlands, irrigation ditches following the contour of the country present problems to subdivision developers. The historic rule is that the location of an easement cannot be changed by either the servient or the dominant owner without the other's consent. This rule was followed in Stamatis v. Johnson, 224 P.2d 201 (Ariz. 1950), but on rehearing the landowner was allowed to install a covered tile pipe on the original right of way of the ditch it replaced. 231 P.2d 956 (Ariz. 1951). In a recent case, Roaring Fork Club, L.P. v. St. Jude's Co., 36 P.3d 1229 (Colo. 2001), the Colorado Supreme Court explicitly rejected the historic rule, adopting instead the rule of the Restatement (Third) of Property (Servitudes) § 4.8, which allows the owner of the servient estate to move an easement provided that the owner of the easement is not damaged. The court held, however, that the burdened owner cannot utilize self-help, but must seek court approval. Idaho Code § 42-1207 provides that the owner of the servient land "shall have the right" to move an irrigation ditch if it can be done without injury to the owner of the ditch, but a later clause requiring the "written permission of the owner" of the ditch seems to deprive the "right"of much utility. In Boz-Lew Builders v. Smith, 571 P.2d 389 (Mont. 1977), a land developer filled in a ditch that had apparently been used since 1866, and built a fourplex apartment over it. The developer was ordered to find a way of getting the water around or through his property, to pay damages, and to pay attorneys' fees.

SECTION 3. REGULATION

A. The Permit System

WYOMING HEREFORD RANCH v. HAMMOND PACKING CO.

Supreme Court of Wyoming, 1925.
33 Wyo. 14, 236 P. 764.

KIMBALL, J. This action involves rights to the use of the waters of Crow creek, a stream rising west of the city of Cheyenne, and flowing in a general easterly direction through that city and through lands owned by the Hammond Packing Company and the Wyoming Hereford Ranch. The plaintiff, the Wyoming Hereford Ranch, and the defendant the Hammond Packing Company are appropriators of the waters of said creek for the purpose of irrigation. * * *

In addition to its rights under the decree of 1888, the plaintiff claimed an appropriation through the Bolln ditch for the irrigation of about 200 acres. The decree of the district court upheld this claim and established the right as prior and superior to the rights of the defendant under its permits of 1909 and 1911, hereinbefore mentioned. It is conceded that whatever right the plaintiff has to divert and use water through the Bolln ditch was acquired since the adoption of the Constitution and the enactment of the state water law of 1890. Article 8 of the Constitution contains the following provisions:

> "Section 1. The waters of all natural streams, springs, lakes or other collections of still water, within the boundaries of the state, are hereby declared to be the property of the state.
>
> "Sec. 2. There shall be constituted a board of control, to be composed of the state engineer and superintendents of the water divisions; which shall, under such regulations as may be prescribed by law, have the supervision of the waters of the state and of their appropriation, distribution and diversion, and of the various officers connected therewith. Its decisions to be subject to review by the courts of the state.
>
> "Sec. 3. Priority of appropriation for beneficial uses shall give the better right. No appropriation shall be denied except when such denial is demanded by the public interest. * * *
>
> "Sec. 5. There shall be a state engineer who shall be appointed by the governor of the state and confirmed by the senate; he shall hold his office for the term of six (6) years, or until his successor shall have been appointed and shall have qualified. He shall be president of the board of control, and shall have general supervision of the waters of the state and of the officers connected with its distribution. No person shall be appointed to this position who has not such theoretical knowledge and such practical experience and skill as shall fit him for the position."

At the first session of the state Legislature, there was enacted a law approved December 22, 1890, "providing for the supervision and use of the waters of the state." Chapter 8, Laws of Wyoming 1890-91. Section 34 of that act provided, among other things, that any one thereafter intending to appropriate any of the public waters of the state should, before commencing construction, enlargement, or extension of any distributing works, or performing any work in connection with said appropriation, make an application to the president of the board of control for a permit to make such appropriation. It requires that the application for a permit shall, among other things, state the source from which the appropriation is to be made, the amount of the appropriation, the location and character of the proposed works, and the time at which the application of water to beneficial purposes shall be made, which time is limited to the time required for the completion of the work when prosecuted with due diligence. If it is intended that the water should be used for irrigation, the application should describe the lands to be irrigated. It is further provided that the application shall state additional facts required by the board of control. On receipt of the application, it is filed and recorded in the office of the state engineer, and if on investigation it is found that there is unappropriated water in the source of supply named in the application, and if the appropriation is not otherwise detrimental to the public welfare, the engineer shall approve the application. The application indorsed with such approval is then returned to the applicant, "who shall, on receipt thereof, be authorized to proceed with such work, and to take such measures as may be necessary to perfect such appropriation." It is further provided that—

> "If there is no unappropriated water in the source of supply, or if, in the judgment of the state engineer, such appropriation is detrimental to public interests, the state engineer shall refuse such appropriation, and the party making such application shall not prosecute such work, so long as such refusal shall continue in force."

There is provision for appeal from the action of the state engineer to the board of control and from the board to the courts. These provisions of section 34 of the Act of 1890 have continued in force to the present day without any amendments material to our present inquiry. Sections 835 to 842, Wyo.C.S.1920.

It is conceded as to the Bolln ditch that the plaintiff has never conformed to the provisions of this law, and we are required to decide whether, under the Constitution and the legislation of 1890, a lawful appropriation of waters can be made without a permit, and without an application therefor. The question is one of considerable importance and of some difficulty. Its solution requires a careful consideration of the foregoing provisions of the Constitution and statutes.

Directing our attention first to statute law of 1890, there would seem to be little need for construction or interpretation. When it is provided that before commencing the construction or enlargement of any distributing works, there must be an application for a permit, and that, if approval of the permit is refused, the party applying therefor shall not prosecute such work, it would seem quite clear, so far as the statute is concerned, that the permit is a condition precedent to the right to divert and appropriate water. If an applicant for a permit has no right to divert waters until the application is approved, it surely was not intended that a person who has never made such application could legally divert and use the waters of the state. Similar statutes seem to have been given their obvious meaning in Nebraska. Castle Rock Irrigation, etc., Co. v. Jurisch, 67 Neb. 377, 93 N.W. 690. It is argued, however, that section 3 of article 8 of the state Constitution, supra, requires a different construction, and that though a permit is necessary in order that the appropriator may have priority as of the date of filing the permit, an "appropriation" can still be made as under previous laws by diversion and use without a permit, with the only difference that such an appropriation will have priority only from the time of the application of the water to the beneficial use. The effect of the contention is that the statutes requiring a permit, if construed as preventing a diversion and use of the waters of the state without a permit, are unconstitutional.

The declaration of section 3, article 8, of the Constitution, that "priority of appropriation for beneficial uses shall give the better right," must be construed in connection with section 1 of the same article, declaring that the waters of all natural streams, etc., are the property of the state; section 2 providing that the board of control shall, under such regulations as may be prescribed by law, have the supervision of such waters and of their appropriation, distribution, and diversion, and the last sentence of section 3, that no appropriation shall be denied except when such denial is demanded by the public interest. In the first place, it is to be noted that the framers of the

Constitution deliberately refrained from including in that instrument any definition of the word "appropriation." Debates of Wyoming Constitutional Convention, pp. 498, 500, 504. This was after the attention of the members of the convention had been called to the fact that some courts had construed an appropriation as being the commencement of work which was diligently pursued until the water was applied to the beneficial use, and other courts had held that it was the actual application of the water to the beneficial use. It is clear, from the reports of the proceedings of the constitutional convention that the precise method and system subsequently embodied in the law of 1890 was within the purpose of the convention. Farm Inv. Co. v. Carpenter, supra, at page 144. A member of the committee of the convention on agriculture, irrigation, and water rights, in reply to an inquiry concerning the meaning of section 3, supra, described in rather forceful language the old and the proposed new system of obtaining water rights, as follows (Debates, pp. 504, 505):

> "Mr. Burritt: I will explain to Mr. Hay. The present system, as the gentleman well knows, is for a man to rush out to the creek, as has been done in the gentleman's own county, and without consulting anybody, finding out anything about whether there is any water there or not, he rushes in and begins a ditch, and rushes into court and begins a lawsuit. Now this system proposes to revise the order of things, and instead of rushing all over the country, and beginning a ditch and taking the chances about getting any water, we propose to have them get permission to construct ditches from the board of control. In other words, all the information necessary to enable a man to do the wise thing in this matter will be with the board of control. This provision is to revise this system from what we have it now, and instead of allowing ditches to be taken out without any system at all, to have a man find out from the board of control just what he can do."

The contemporaneous construction of these provisions of the Constitution by the administrative officers is shown in the report of Mr. Elwood Mead, who was territorial engineer at the time of the adoption of the Constitution, and state engineer upon the admission of the state into the Union. This report, evidently prepared after the adoption of the Constitution, but before the admission of the state, contains the following (2 Ann. Rep. Terr. Eng. Wyo. p. 97):

> "If state ownership is to be anything but a delusion, if it is to be more than nominal, there must be the same authority and control over streams and over diversion of water as is now exercised by the general government over the occupation and settlement of public lands. No diversion or appropriation should be permitted, therefore, until the sanction of the territory, through its constituted authorities, has been obtained, and the beneficial character of the proposed use established. Such oversight and precaution is necessary for the proper protection of public interests (public water supply being of greater agricultural value than public lands) and in order that controversies growing out of extravagant and injurious claims may be avoided.
>
> "Instead of the present absence of supervision over either the nature of the diversion and use or the amount of the claim, I would recommend that each and every intending appropriator be required to make application to the irrigation authorities for a permit to divert and use the public waters and that

approval of such authorities must be had before work is begun. For convenience in recording, and as a matter of economy, I would recommend that all such applications be made to the territorial engineer." * * *

In determining the meaning of a written law, it is proper to consider the evils sought to be remedied. The laws of the territory had permitted the diversion of water without any state supervision of the works and without any adequate notice and record of the amount, purpose, and date of the appropriation. Defective and badly located diversion works often made the use of water wasteful. No right became definite until it was adjudicated in court, and adjudications were often long delayed and then made on inaccurate testimony and without any disinterested measurements of the ditches or of the lands irrigated. Until such an adjudication, no subsequent appropriation could be made with safety, for no one could tell the amount of unappropriated water in the stream. The evils attendant on such a system, and the importance of providing a different system that would give the state the unquestioned right of control, had become well recognized at the time the Constitution was framed. See 2 Annual Rep. Terr. Eng. Wyo. (1889) pp. 3, 12, 16, 37, 41, 58, 69, and 98. To correct these defects in the old system, it was provided by the Constitution not only that the waters of the state are the property of the state but also that those waters, and their appropriation, distribution, and diversion, shall be under the supervision of a state board of control. This supervision, it was hoped, would cure many of the evils of the old system, and we think that hope has been justified by the later events. The constitutional declaration that priority of appropriation for beneficial uses shall give the better right was not intended to prevent the Legislature from prescribing reasonable conditions that must be complied with before a lawful appropriation could be made. Their power in this respect is both recognized and limited by the further provision of the Constitution, carried into the statutes, that "no appropriation shall be denied except when such denial is demanded by the public interests." In interpreting this language, we must give consideration to the contemporaneous recognition not only of the importance of state supervision of the diversion of waters, but also of the fact that such supervision could not be effective, nor intelligently exercised, without accurate and complete information of proposed appropriations. The Legislature has decided that the public interests demand that such information shall be given to the state board by an application for a permit, and that until such an application is approved, no appropriation can be lawfully made. We believe these requirements are reasonable in so far at least as they are questioned in this case. * * *

A different decision would leave prevalent many of the acknowledged evils of the territorial system intended to be superseded by the system of state control contemplated by the Constitution and carried into effect by the law of 1890. The plaintiff is willing in this case to concede that its right under the Bolln ditch would take priority only from the date of the application of the water to the land. Another claimant of a similar right might not be willing to make that concession. If a right may be lawfully acquired by diversion and use since 1890 without compliance with the state laws, it might be impossible to find a sufficient reason for holding that the right would not have priority as of the date of commencement of the work. If that condition should prevail, there would seem to be no advantage to be gained by proceeding under a permit, and we would be thrown back to the confusion incident to the haphazard methods of the old system. * * *

It follows that the part of the decree which gives the plaintiff a priority for use of water through the Bolln ditch cannot be upheld.

Notes

1. **Early procedures.** In the early history of appropriation law, the word "appropriation" was used in its crudest sense—as a taking of possession—and a legal right flowed from the physical acts of constructing a ditch, diverting the water and applying it to use. Nevertheless, a need was felt by the appropriators for improving their legal position, and following the common procedure of staking a mining claim, the custom arose of posting a notice of claim upon the bank of the stream near the point of diversion. The courts recognized such a notice as evidence of the possessory right to the water. Thompson v. Lee, 8 Cal. 275 (1857). Later these procedures were codified in a number of states by statutes which required the posting of a more elaborate notice and its recordation in the county where posted. These systems were optional. A failure to comply did not affect the validity of the rights acquired by diversion and application to beneficial use, though it did affect the date of priority. If an appropriator did not post and file a notice, his priority dated from the time of completion of the appropriation, but if he did, his priority related back to the start of work. Once the application to beneficial use was made, an unfiled appropriation was a complete and vested right, and took precedence over any subsequently initiated appropriations.

The defects in this system are obvious. "Claims are filed in the different counties, and as Montana rivers are long, the water-right records of a single stream are often found in several counties. Musselshell River forms a part of the boundary between Fergus and Meagher, Yellowstone, Dawson, and Custer counties. Ditches on one side of the stream are recorded in one county, and ditches on the other side of the river in another county. It would require a journey of several hundred miles and an examination of five sets of county records to ascertain the extent of the claims to this stream." Elwood Mead, Irrigation Institutions 301 (1903).

2. **Adoption of the permit system.** The permit system of initiating appropriations is now found in all of the states recognizing the appropriation doctrine except Colorado. It is the exclusive method in each state. Although Idaho has long had permits, until 1971 it had a dual system. A "statutory water right" was obtained under permit, but a "constitutional right" could be acquired by diversion and use without any formalities. The principal incentive to go the permit route was that the statutory right had a priority relating back to the date of the application for permit while the constitutional right dated from its completion. The new statute is explicit that the right to use water can be acquired only by permit and not otherwise. Idaho Code §§ 42-103, 42-201; see Phillip M. Barber, Statutory Water Rights and Permits, 9 Idaho L. Rev. 1 (1972).

Until 1973 Montana appropriations on "unadjudicated streams" could be obtained by diversion and use, but their priority would date from completion, not commencement, unless an 1885 statute requiring posting and filing of notice was followed. On "adjudicated streams" a 1921 statute set up what might be called a judicial permit system. An intending appropriator had to file a petition in the court which had entered the decree, all affected appropriators were named as defendants and a final or conditional decree added the new appropriation to the list of water right holders. For some of the difficulties inherent in this procedure, see Albert W. Stone, Are There Any Adjudicated Streams in Montana?, 19 Mont. L. Rev. 19 (1957); Albert W. Stone, The Long Count on Dempsey: No Final Decision in Water Right Adjudication, 31 Mont. L. Rev. 1 (1969).

The 1973 permit procedure (Mont. Code Ann. §§ 85-2-301 to -351) was enacted pursuant to a new state constitution adopted in 1972, which provided, "The legislature shall provide for the administration, control and regulation of water rights * * *." Mont. Const. art. IX, § 3(4).

Not until 1980 did California determine that compliance with the permit system is mandatory. Many early water cases involved claims that persons who took water to irrigate nonriparian land or stored it for future use were violating the riparian rights of downstream landowners (see Chapter 3). The upstream nonriparian uses were validated, however, if they had been exercised for the period of the statute of limitations and the user had obtained prescriptive rights. In these cases the terms "prescriptive rights" and "appropriations" were sometimes used interchangeably and sometimes independently. The 1914 Water Commission Act established a permit system (Cal. Water Code §§ 1201 et seq.), and in 1923 an amendment declared that compliance with this procedure was the exclusive method of acquiring the right to appropriate or use water subject to appropriation (§ 1225). For years lawyers debated whether or not a party who met the requirements for prescription after 1914 must also comply with the statutory permit procedure. People v. Shirokow, 605 P.2d 859 (Cal. 1980), decided that such a party must obtain a permit, concluding that to rule otherwise would substantially impair the water board's ability to comply with the legislative mandate that appropriations be consistent with the public interest and would undermine the effectiveness of the comprehensive regulatory scheme of the Water Commission Act.

3. **Exceptions.** Some statutes contain express exceptions to the requirement of a permit for certain classes of small appropriations or appropriations from some sources. See Cal. Water Code §§ 1228-1229.1; S.D. Codified Laws § 46-5-8; Tex. Water Code Ann. §§ 11.142, 11.143.

4. **Procedures.** The procedures for obtaining a permit and appropriating water are not identical in all states where a permit is required. Although the statutes have a common origin and many basic similarities, they contain many variations, and a person seeking a water right must carefully check and follow the practice of the particular state. The following steps are typical: (1) application to the designated agency or official, accompanied by required supporting documents such as maps and engineering plans, (2) publication of notice of the application and, in some states, notice to designated officials or agencies, such as the Department of Fish and Game, (3) acceptance of protests from interested parties, (4) internal agency processing, including an environmental assessment if required, (5) hearing, if protests have been filed or if the agency has made a preliminary decision to deny or condition the application, (6) issuance or denial of a permit, (7) construction of necessary facilities and application of water to beneficial use, and (8) issuance of a "certificate of appropriation" or other document confirming that the appropriation has been completed.

5. **Stored water.** Several states have a dual permit system for stored irrigation waters. The person intending to impound the waters must make application for a "primary permit" to construct the reservoir; the person intending to use the water on particular land can or must apply for a "secondary permit" to appropriate the stored water to the land. See Ariz. Rev. Stat. § 45-151; Or. Rev. Stat. § 537.400; Wash. Rev. Code § 90.03.370; Wyo. Stat. Ann. § 41-3-301.

6. **Colorado procedures.** Since the Colorado Constitution declares, "[t]he right to divert the unappropriated waters of any natural stream to beneficial uses shall never be denied" (art. XVI, § 6), it has generally been assumed that a permit system is unavailable in that state. Colorado was the first state to create the office of State Engineer, but the engineer's duties are confined to regulating the works of appropriators and distributing water according to decrees entered by courts in proceedings to adjudicate all rights to a stream or segment of a stream. Colorado had an early precursor of a permit system in her "map and statement law," which provided that any person constructing works for an appropriation shall, "within sixty days after the commencement of such construction * * * make a filing in the office of the State Engineer," consisting of an accurate map of the project and detailed information on the works, including the time of commencement of the works or the survey for it. This early attempt to at least record the initiation of rights was emasculated by holdings that the map and statement were evidentiary only and were not required for the validity of an appropriation. An appropriation could be made without compliance with the statute and if a map and statement were filed, the completed appropriation need not conform to them. See De Haas v. Benesch, 181 P.2d 453 (Colo. 1947).

When an adjudication proceeding was initiated all appropriators had to file their claims in court or lose their priority. A person who had commenced an appropriation but had not applied the water to beneficial use received a "conditional right" fixing the priority. If subsequent supplemental adjudications were initiated, the recipient had to establish reasonably diligent efforts to complete the appropriation or prove it had been completed. See Taussig v. Moffat Tunnel Water & Dev. Co., 106 P.2d 363 (Colo. 1940).

The Water Right Determination and Adjudication Act of 1969 introduced a complete new procedure. The Act carves the state into seven water divisions, each covering a major river basin. Colo. Rev. Stat. § 37-92-201. One district judge in the division is designated a "water judge." He is assisted by a "water clerk" who is in charge of all records of water matters and by such "water referees" as may be necessary. §§ 37-92-203, 37-92-204. Since amended in several procedural details, the act in effect makes each water court an administrative agency with complete records of and supervision over newly initiated and incomplete water rights ("conditional rights"). In effect, the act also creates a perpetual suit of adjudication in each water division.

"Any person who desires a determination of a water right or a conditional water right and the amount and priority thereof, including a determination that a conditional water right has become a water right by reason of the completion of the appropriation, * * * [or] finding of reasonable diligence shall file with the water clerk * * * a verified application setting forth facts supporting the ruling sought * * *." § 37-92-302(1)(a). The application must contain a detailed description of the right sought. Elaborate provisions for notice, protests of applications and investigations and rulings by the referee are set out. Twice a year the water judge holds hearings on protests to referees' rulings and orders referred to him by the referee, and enters a judgment and decree embodying his rulings on all cases before him. §§ 37-92-303, 37-92-304. A finding of reasonable diligence is required every sixth year for conditional rights which have not become absolute through the application of water to beneficial use. § 37-92-301(4).

An application for a conditional right is functionally similar to an application for a permit in other appropriation states; likewise the conditional right, if granted, is functionally similar to a permit. The recipient of a conditional right must use reasonable diligence in completing the appropriation in order to retain the priority awarded in the conditional decree, and, as noted above, must obtain periodic finding of diligence until the appropriation is completed. When the necessary work for appropriation is done and water has been put to beneficial use, an absolute right is sought from the water court; if granted, the absolute right is functionally similar to a certificate of appropriation. While theoretically an appropriation can be made without following this process, it can never receive an enforceable priority. Although the relative priorities of all water rights or conditional water rights applied for during a calendar year are determined, all of them must be decreed to be junior to all water rights granted in previous years. § 37-92-306.

B. Availability of Water

LOWER COLORADO RIVER AUTHORITY v. TEXAS DEPARTMENT OF WATER RESOURCES

Supreme Court of Texas, 1984.
689 S.W.2d 873.

KILGARLIN, JUSTICE. We reverse the judgments of the courts below because those courts have misconstrued and misapplied Tex. Water Code Ann. § 11.134. We hold that the term "unappropriated water" means the amount of water remaining after taking into account all existing uncancelled permits and filings valued at their recorded levels.

The Water District applied for a permit to impound over 500,000 acre-feet of water from the Colorado River at the Stacy Dam site southeast of Ballinger, Texas. * * *

The right to impound water had to be obtained by the Water District, through a Department permit. Tex.Water Code Ann. § 11.121. To acquire a permit, the Water District had to satisfy the statutory grounds of Tex. Water Code Ann. § 11.134(b)(2) & (3):

> Action on Application * * *
>
> (b) The commission shall grant the application only if: * * *
>
> (2) unappropriated water is available in the source of supply; and
> (3) the proposed appropriation: * * *
>
> (B) does not impair existing water rights or vested riparian rights; and
>
> (C) is not detrimental to the public welfare.

The Colorado River waters are presently charged with four types of outstanding water rights. There are vested riparian rights, certified filings, permits to appropriate water, and certificates of adjudication. The Colorado is an inconstant stream. There is insufficient water to satisfy the existing rights during drought, but the water supply is capable of supplying additional users during times of abundant rain.

The Department developed a sophisticated computerized model of the seasonally varying inflow to the Colorado at various points along the river. One goal of the computer model was to allow the staff to obtain a reasonably accurate scientific estimate whether there was "unappropriated water" at points along the river, at least during some seasons or months.

The computer model assumed that all existing recorded water rights in the Colorado River basin would be exercised in the maximum amounts authorized, or to the extent of water available from the inflows. The staff study concluded that "very little water would be available for appropriation at the proposed reservoir site. * * * The estimated firm yield of the reservoir for these quantities of appropriable water is 3,120 acre-feet per year * * *." The study also concluded that the proposed reservoir would adversely affect two existing downstream lakes—Lake Travis and Lake Buchanan—by reducing the firm yield of each by approximately fifteen percent.

The Water District rebutted the staff conclusion by expert studies and testimony. The studies used the hydrologic data from the staff report but discounted the recorded filings in a number of ways. As to certified filings, the experts presented historical use data to demonstrate that the maximum amount claimed under the filings had never in fact been used, and that some claims necessarily had not been "perfected." As to riparian rights, many of the riparian claims were invalid because they were based on Spanish and Mexican land grants that did not include riparian rights. Finally, experts testified that demographic projections and historical use data indicated that the full amounts authorized under uncancelled permits would not be used. By subtracting the estimated amounts that would not be used from the recorded filings, the Water District's expert witnesses concluded there was sufficient water available for the proposed Stacy Reservoir. Similarly, they concluded that downstream rights would not be impaired if occasional flow-throughs were allowed.

The Commission made finding 15 that there was "unappropriated water" within the meaning of section 11.134(b)(2).

> After recognizing downstream existing appropriations and claims below Stacy Dam, the Commission finds that there are unappropriated flows in the Colorado River at the dam site sufficient to permit the impoundment of 554,340 acre-feet of water at elevations 1151.5 feet above mean sea level and the diversion and consumptive use of not to exceed 113,000 acre-feet of water per annum without impairing existing water rights, provided releases of water from the reservoir are made from time to time in such quantities as may be necessary to provide water to which all superior and senior water rights are entitled.

The undisputed evidence in this record is that existing uncancelled permits and filings, valued at their recorded levels, leave an insufficient supply of "unappropriated water for Stacy Dam." Sections 11.134(b)(2) & (3) are unambiguous in their statements that the Commission shall grant applications for new water rights only if there is available unappropriated water and the new appropriation does not impair existing water rights or vested riparian rights. Additionally, granting additional permits cannot be detrimental to public welfare. Basically, our decision is that the article prohibits "double permitting" or the stacking of appropriated waters on appropriated waters. * * *

Section 11.134(b)(2) finds its source in section 19 of the 1913 Act and its reenactment in section 24 of the 1917 Act. Representative D.W. Glasscock, a principal author of the 1913 Act, stated that the purpose of the 1913 Act was to prevent overappropriation of rivers and thus to insure the stability necessary to attract development capital. An initial purpose of the permit system has been to insure as much as possible that the water granted in a permit would be available when the project was completed. Section 11.146(e), by providing that water granted under *any* permit is not again subject to a new permit to appropriate until the permit has been canceled in whole or in part, is consistent with the overall legislative purpose.

* * * The court of appeals rationalized that the statement in Motl v. Boyd, 116 Tex. 82, 286 S.W. 458 (1926), that the Board of Water Engineers would merely consult their records to determine the amount of existing appropriations, was not contrary to its holding in this case. "Records," to the court of appeals, included the required annual reports which showed how much water the permittee actually used. The court of appeals reasoned that in consulting its records, to determine whether there existed "unappropriated water," the Board would consider how much of the recorded appropriation was going unused. That rationalization is directly contrary to the legislature's purpose. According to the 1953 Act, even if the records under the existing permit indicated the appropriator had not used any water at all for the last 10 years, it was still necessary to cancel the unused permit before the water covered by it would again be subject to a new appropriation. * * *

The majority of the court of appeals reasoned, through a series of rhetorical questions, that the term, "unappropriated water," included unused waters that were subject to existing permits. The court reasoned that any other construction would mean the Commission and its predecessor agencies had shirked their statutory duty by allowing Texas rivers to become overappropriated. There can be no doubt that the prevention of overappropriation was a principal goal of the legislative scheme. Nineteenth Biennial Report of the Board of Water Engineers 8 (1948-50); Cox, The Texas Board of Water Engineers, 7 Texas L. Rev. 86, 96 (1928). The fact that some rivers are overappropriated does not mean the state's water agencies have failed in their duty. Because of changing circumstances, the vagaries of nature or the possibility of erroneous assumptions about the inflow amounts to the rivers, overappropriation may exist. These circumstances may make any river overappropriated, particularly during a drought period, and thus there can be no substitute for enforcement. The Texas statutes protect senior water rights from actual impairment. No matter how many permits the Commission issues, the action is purely administrative, and it cannot divest or impair prior rights.

Conclusion

Under the law, the Department may not grant permits when its own records show that the supply must come from an existing downstream permittee's water that the Department speculates he will not actually need. Section 11.025 places a limit on the amount of water that can be used beneficially or the amount the senior holders can claim, even though the face amount of their permits may be more. Among other things, that limitation serves to distribute the water appropriately when there is a drought. It does not mean the Department may intentionally overappropriate. A contrary decision would return water rights to the state of chaos that the act is designed to avoid. For example, upstream junior permit holders whose grants depended upon an overappropriation of the stream would suffer the most from deprivation of water in times of drought. The water source they had come to rely upon would be denied them. * * *

We reverse the judgments of the courts below and set aside the permit granted by the Texas Department of Water Resources to the Colorado River Municipal Water District. * * *

RAY, JUSTICE, concurring.

I agree with the court's conclusion that "unappropriated water" must not include water already granted under an existing, uncancelled permit. I do not agree with the court's disposition of setting aside the Commission's order. I would remand the case to the Commission for further proceedings in accordance with the opinion.

* * * The Commission's error was applying the wrong definition of "unappropriated water." This court had not previously expressly addressed the question. Had the water district presented its application under the proper standard, it could have simultaneously sought partial or total cancellations of unused water rights under existing certified filings and permits. Although the district can now file a new application using the proper definition, that action would not be a complete remedy. Both the priority of an appropriation and the claimant's right to use the water date from the filing of the *application* with the Department. Tex.Water Code Ann. § 11.141 (Supp. 1984). Since the misconception of the law caused the Commission to commit error, I believe it is appropriate to preserve the district's priority by remanding to the Commission for proper proceedings under the correct legal standard.

Opinion on Motion for Rehearing

KILGARLIN, JUSTICE.

* * * Because an examination of authorities on the issue demonstrates that a remand is more appropriate than a reversal and rendition, we reverse the judgments of the courts below and remand the cause to the Texas Department of Water Resources pursuant to our power under the Administrative Procedure

and Texas Register Act, Tex.Rev.Civ.Stat.Ann. art. 6252-13a, § 19(e)(4) (Vernon Supp.1984). * * *

Notes

1. **Other states.** Statutes in a number of western states express criteria similar to those in Tex. Water Code Ann. § 11.134(b). See, e.g., Neb. Rev. Stat. § 46-235; Wyo. Stat. Ann. § 41-4-503.

2. **Determining if unappropriated water exists.** In Central Platte Natural Resources District v. Wyoming, 513 N.W.2d 847 (Neb. 1994), the director of the Department of Water Resources used the "historic flows" method to find that there was unappropriated water available for a proposed instream appropriation. The "historic flows" method, which utilized actual flow records from gauging stations along the river, was similar to the method which the Texas Supreme Court rejected in the principal case. An opponent of the proposed appropriations, the State of Wyoming, challenged the finding, arguing that the director should have used a method which assumed that all existing rights would be fully exercised, similar to the method adopted by the court in the principal case. In concluding that the "historic flows" method was permissible the court said:

"The beneficial use requirement limits the amount of water which the holder can actually appropriate. For example, if a landowner had an appropriation right to use 10 cfs for irrigation purposes, and if the landowner needed only 5 cfs in a given month, then the landowner would not be entitled to capture and sell the other 5 cfs. An appropriation right extends only as far as the beneficial use requirement will allow.

"It thus appears that an appropriation right can be measured in two ways. First, the right can be measured with reference to the appropriation limit. This is a fixed and theoretical limit—the most water that a particular holder is authorized to use. Second, the right can be measured with reference to the beneficial use limit. This is a fluctuating and practical limit—the amount of water that a particular holder is entitled to use at any given time.

"We find that the phrase 'subject to an existing appropriation right' refers to the appropriation right measured by the beneficial use limit. That is, when the director considers an instream flow application, the director must find that there is enough water that is not subject to another appropriator's beneficial use. The question then becomes how the director is to measure the water that is not subject to another appropriator's beneficial use.

"We find that the historic flow method is a permissible way of measuring the beneficial use limit. As explained above, the beneficial use limit fluctuates with the appropriators' needs. The appropriators' needs fluctuate with external factors. The most important external factor is the weather; in a dry year, the holders' need to divert water for irrigation increases dramatically. The historic flow method lends perspective to the fluctuations because the data is collected over a span of years. According to Woodward, the historic flow data used in his calculations encompassed almost 30 years and included periods of high precipitation and periods of drought. In short, the amount of water that is actually in the river is a rough approximation of the amount of water not needed for beneficial use elsewhere. Accord Temescal Water Co. v. Dept. of Public Works, 44 Cal.2d 90, 280 P.2d 1 (1955) (stating that the amount of unappropriated water will depend on the stream's flow, the rainfall, and the nonuse of existing rights)." Id. at 855; accord In re Application for Water Rights of the Bd. of County Comm'rs, 891 P.2d 952 (Colo. 1995).

3. **Purpose of the rule.** In unusual situations, a junior appropriation, if allowed, would interfere with senior appropriations. See, for example, Lionelle v. Southeastern Colorado Water Conservancy District, 676 P.2d 1162 (Colo. 1984), in which the court concluded that expansion of a reservoir used to supply water for the generation of hydroelectric power (a nonconsumptive use) would impair the rights of downstream seniors because evaporation would reduce river flows downstream. However, in most cases, a junior appropriation cannot legally harm a senior appropriation; under the rule of priority, the junior appropriator cannot divert water when it is need by the senior. Furthermore, variability in the flow of western streams and in the demand for water makes it likely, if not certain, that there will be times when there are unused flows even on the most heavily appropriated stream. In view of this, is it good public policy to reject an appropriation because there is no unappropriated water? Consider:

"'The Commission is charged with securing the maximum beneficial use and control of the state's water resources. Because streamflows vary greatly from year to year, disallowing further permits once the reliable flow had been appropriated would result in nonuse of the excess water available in years of greater than average water supply. It is the Commission's position that the maximum beneficial use of waters of the state is achieved by issuing a permit to anyone who is willing to attempt appropriation and use of whatever unappropriated water may become available, except where a basin program identifies a need to set aside some amount of unappropriated water for particular future uses.'" Benz v. Water Resources Comm'n, 764 P.2d 594, 599 (Or. 1988) (quoting with approval a decision of the Oregon Water Resources Commission granting an appropriation permit where the evidence was conflicting regarding the availability of unappropriated water).

"While it is true that some unappropriated water is present during times of high flow at the proposed diversion point, to be available in a practical sense the supply of water must be fairly continuous and dependable. The director concluded that based on historical flow records, the appellants would not be able to withdraw any water in a number of years, sometimes consecutive. * * * Although appellants do not quarrel with that factual finding, it is their argument that the director is not entitled, as a matter of law to base his refusal to allow the application on the unlikelihood of success of the irrigation project.

"As early as 1910 in Young & Norton et al. v. Hinderlider, 15 N.M. 666, 110 P. 1045 (1910), the New Mexico court held that it was proper to refuse an appropriation of water for a project which appeared doomed to failure. That court stated:

> If there is available, unappropriated water of the La Plata river for only five or six thousand acres of land, it would be contrary to the public interest that a project for fourteen thousand acres with that water should receive an official approval which would, perhaps enable the promoters of it to market their scheme, to sell stock reasonably sure to become worthless, and land which could not be irrigated, at the price of irrigated land. * * * The failure of any irrigation project carries with it not only disastrous consequences to

it owners and to the farmers who are depending on it, but beside tends to destroy faith in irrigation enterprises generally."

In re Hitchcock & Red Willow Irrigation Dist., 410 N.W.2d 101, 108 (Neb. 1987).

4. **Frequency of unappropriated flows.** The principal case deals with the demand side of the equation. But, of course, the supply side must also be considered, including the fact that the natural flow of western streams fluctuates greatly. On remand, should the Texas Department of Water Resources use flows available in a drought year to calculate whether unappropriated water is available? Flows available in an "average" year? Flows available in a high-flow year? Stated differently, how frequently must be water available for a proposed appropriation in order to find that a requirement of unappropriated water has been met?

"A showing of reasonable availability does not require a demonstration that water will always be available to the full extent applied for in the decree. The applicant need only prove that there is a substantial probability that the appropriation can and will be completed, based upon necessarily imperfect predictions of future conditions. This approach to obtaining a conditional water right decree promotes the development and maximum utilization of Colorado's scarce water resources." Aspen Wilderness Workshop, Inc. v. Hines Highlands L.P., 929 P.2d 718, 724 (Colo. 1996).

In Note 3, supra, the Nebraska Supreme Court stated that the supply must be "fairly continuous and dependable." In Central Platte Natural Resources District v. Wyoming, supra Note 2 at 859, the court elaborated on this standard:

"A determination regarding water availability cannot and should not be divorced from the applicant's purpose. There are two ways in which the applicant's purpose affects the "fairly continuous and dependable" standard.

"First, the nature of a fairly continuous and dependable flow may change depending upon the nature of the application. An application to divert water is not the same as an application for instream flows; an irrigation project is not the same as a habitat project. If an irrigation project fails because insufficient water was available, then there is a loss on the investment and a loss to any junior downstream appropriators who could have used the diverted water. In contrast, if a habitat project fails, then there is minimal, if any, loss of investment, and there is no loss to junior downstream appropriators, because the water was never removed from the stream.

"Second, in the context of instream flow applications, the threshold of a fairly dependable and continuous flow may change depending on the specific goals of the application. A wildlife project is not the same as a recreation project.

"In the context of an instream flow application to maintain existing wildlife habitats, we hold that "fairly continuous and dependable" means the flow regime which the species can bear. Put another way, there is sufficient water available under § 46-2,115(1) when there is enough water to maintain the wildlife habitat sought by an applicant."

5. **Unadjudicated rights.** A number of unadjudicated claims to water exist in many western states. An important example involves Indian and federal reserved rights claims. In several states there are also significant numbers of unadjudicated appropriative claims which pre-date the adoption of mandatory

permit systems. (Adjudication of water rights is discussed in the next section. Indian and federal reserved rights are examined in Chapter 8, Section 3.) The validity and the size (quantity) of unadjudicated claims is often in question. How should such claims be dealt with in deciding whether water is available for new appropriations? In Montana, which had statutory criteria similar to those at issue in the principal case, the Montana Supreme Court held that no permits for new appropriations could be issued until Indian reserved rights claims have been adjudicated. In re Application for Beneficial Water Use Permit No. 66459-76L, 923 P.2d 1073 (Mont. 1995).

The Montana legislature quickly amended the appropriation statute to reverse the decision, which threatened to completely stop the granting of permits for new appropriations in Montana. A showing that "unappropriated waters" are available is no longer required. Instead an applicant is required to show that water for the proposed appropriation is "physically available" and "can reasonably be considered legally available." Mont. Code. Ann. § 85-2-311 (1)(a). To further clarify the matter, the preceding statute states that "[a] permit can be issued * * * prior to the adjudication of existing water rights in a source of supply." A companion statute specifies, however, that all permits issued prior to a final determination of existing water rights are only provisional and are subject to being reduced, modified, or revoked if necessary to protect adjudicated senior rights. § 85-2-313.

Shortly after the legislature adopted the amendment, the Montana Department of Natural Resources and Conservation announced its intent to issue new appropriation permits on the Flathead Reservation although the reserved rights associated with the reservation had not been adjudicated. In Confederated Salish & Kootenai Tribes v. Clinch, 992 P.2d 244 (Mont. 1999), the Montana Supreme Court enjoined the Department from issuing permits on the Flathead Reservation until the tribes' reserved rights are adjudicated, despite the legislative directive that permits can be issued prior to adjudication. The court noted that the term "legally available" in the amended statute is not defined and concluded that it should adopt a construction which would not render the section unconstitutional. The court reasoned that the issuance of permits on the reservation for the use of water which may belong to the tribes would violate Article IX, Section 3(1) of the Montana Constitution, which protects existing water rights whether adjudicated or unadjudicated. Thus, the court concluded that water is "legally available" only if it has not been reserved for the reservation, which, the court held, cannnot be determined until the tribes' reserved rights are adjudicated and quantified.

After adjudication and quantification, the tribes' reserved rights may remain unexercised for years. How should such rights be accounted for in determining if water is "legally available" for appropriation? In adopting the amendments to the appropriation statutes referred to above, the legislature observed: "Because water is a resource that is subject to use and reuse, such as through return flows, and because at most times all water rights on a source will not be exercised to their full extent simultaneously, it is recognized that an adjudication is not a water availability study. Consequently, the legislature has provided an administrative forum for the factual investigation into whether water is available for new uses and changes both before and after the completion of an adjudication in the source of supply." Mont. Code Ann. § 85-2-101 (5). This observation seemingly indicates that the Department of Natural Resources and Conservation should investigate actual uses of water and apply its administrative expertise in determining whether water is available for appropriation. Nevertheless, the opinion in *Confederated Tribes* implies that water required to satisfy Indian reserved rights is not "legally available" even if the Indians are not actually using the water and it appears the Indians may not use it for the forseeable future. In other words, in the court's view, the Department cannot make the factual investigation prescribed by the legislature, but must treat Indian water rights as fully exercised even if that is not actually the case. It is unclear whether this treatment is confined to Indian water rights. See infra p. 690, Note 6, for a discussion of other aspects of *Confederated Tribes*.

6. **Closing streams to further appropriations.** Are there valid administrative reasons for prohibiting additional appropriations when a stream is substantially overappropriated? Is it desirable to expend administrative effort to process applications if there is little likelihood that water will ever be put to use? Should records be cluttered up with appropriations which will seldom, if ever, be exercised? Are enforcement problems exacerbated by creating additional rights to an already inadequate supply? Consider Cal. Water Code §§ 1205-1207. These statutes authorize the Water Resources Control Board to declare streams fully appropriated and close them to further appropriation. The Board has declared some streams fully appropriated year-round and others only during specified months. The effect of closing streams to new appropriations during specified months is to require new appropriators to construct storage reservoirs.

In Postema v. Pollution Control Hearings Board, 11 P.3d 726 (Wash. 2000), the court upheld the authority of the Washington Department of Ecology to close steams to further appropriation, despite the lack of explicit statutory authority. The court cited several provisions giving the Department authority to promulgate rules for the administration of water rights and protection of the environment. The court said: "Stream closures by rule embody Ecology's determination that water is not available for further appropriations." Id. at 742.

C. Public Interest

YOUNG & NORTON v. HINDERLIDER

Supreme Court of the Territory of New Mexico, 1910.
15 N.M. 666, 110 P. 1045.

On the 1st day of October, 1907, M.C. Hinderlider filed with the territorial engineer an application for a permit to appropriate 200 second feet of the flow of the La Plata river in San Juan county, N.M., and for the construction of a storage reservoir with a storage capacity of 12,406 acre feet for the purpose of reclaiming and irrigating about 14,000 acres of land in said county. On December 20, 1907, Messrs. Young & Norton for themselves and others filed with the territorial engineer an application for a permit to appropriate the waters of the same stream in the same county and territory, for the purpose of reclaiming and irrigating about 5,000 acres of land, being a part of the same land covered by the Hinderlider project. This last application included the construction of a storage reservoir with a storage capacity of 10,149 acre feet for the purpose of storing the flood waters of the said river and applying the same to the reclamation of the said 5,000 acres of land. After the publication of the notice required by law and on the 19th day of March, 1908, the said Young, Norton, and others filed with the territorial engineer a protest against the approval of the said Hinderlider application. That after a hearing before the territorial engineer and on July 20, 1908, he rendered an opinion sustaining said protest rejecting the Hinderlider application and approving the application of the protestants. * * *

[The Territorial Engineer found that Hinderlider's filing covered much public land as well as the private land owned by protestants, that his project would cost $40 per acre; that Young and Norton and others they represent are settled on about 5,500 acres of land, their project is for the irrigation of the settled land, and would cost about $20 per acre; that there was water available for about 5,000 to 6,000 acres, that either applicant could and would complete his appropriation, but that Young and Norton's project was more within the water supply. Hinderlider appealed to the Board of Water Commissioners, which ruled that the power of the Engineer to reject an application as contrary to the public interest is limited to cases in which the project would be a menace to the public health and safety, and ordered Hinderlider's application approved. The District Court affirmed, and Young and Norton appealed.]

ABBOTT, J. We think the decision of the district court was justified and probably required by the statement of facts on which it was heard; but we find that statement very incomplete and unsatisfactory as the basis of a decision in such a cause. If it were a matter of private interest alone, a question simply between two rival applicants for the right to use the waters in question, we should content ourselves with affirming the decision of the district court. But the question is much broader than that, and includes the public interest as well, by the terms of the statute under which the territorial engineer, the water commissioners, and the courts have jurisdiction of the subject-matter.

The view apparently adopted by the water commissioners in their decision that the power of the territorial engineer to reject an application, "if in his opinion the approval thereof would be contrary to the public interest" (section 28), is limited to cases in which the project would be a menace to the public health or safety is we think, not broad enough. There is no such limitation expressed in terms of the statute, and we think not by implication. The declaration in the first section of the statute that the waters therein described are "public waters," and the fact that the entire statute is designed to secure the greatest possible benefit from them for the public, should be borne in mind. It is, for instance, obviously for the public interest that investors should be protected against making worthless investments in New Mexico, and especially that they should not be led to make them through official approval of unsound enterprises. If there is available unappropriated water of the La Plata river for only 5,000 or 6,000 acres of land, it would be contrary to the public interest that a project for irrigating 14,000 acres with that water should receive an official approval which would, perhaps, enable the promoters of it to market their scheme, to sell stock reasonably sure to become worthless, and land which could not be irrigated, at the price of irrigated land. Such a proceeding would in the end result only in warning capital away from the territory. The failure of any irrigation project carries with it not only disastrous consequences to its owners and to the farmers who are depending on it, but besides tends to destroy faith in irrigation enterprises generally.

It may be said that the territorial engineer could have approved the Hinderlider project for the number of acres which could be irrigated from it. He makes it clear, however, from his report, that the cost of the works for that project would be much greater than for works fit to irrigate the land which could really be irrigated from the available water there. While that element is not conclusive on the question of public interest, we think it should be taken into account. It may be that, of the 5,000 or 6,000 acres there which it is claimed can be irrigated at an expense of $10 or $12 per acre under the Young-Norton project, a thousand acres could be irrigated at $5 per acre because of its being at a lower level or nearer the water than the other land. But that would not justify refusing the owners of the other 4,000 or 5,000 acres the privilege of irrigating their lands, under a plan which would increase the cost of irrigation to the owners of the thousand acres. And the same may be said of the Hinderlider project as compared with the Young-Norton project. The mere fact that irrigation under the former project would cost more per acre than under the latter is not conclusive that the former project should be rejected. But the attempt to cover too much land may have gone so far that the cost of irrigation under that project would be so excessive that the owners of land under the project could not pay the water rates and farm their lands at a profit. The statute provides that the charges for irrigation shall be "reasonable"; but what is reasonable in any case must depend largely on the cost of constructing and operating the irrigation works.

The agreed statement of facts on which the judgment of the district court is based may be held to include by reference the findings of the territorial engineer and those of the board of water commissioners, although it is not made clear that they are to be a part of the stipulated facts, as it should be if that was the intention of the parties. Even if they are to be considered, we are still without proper material for a conclusion. The territorial engineer finds that the Young-Norton project is "better within the available water supply." But that furnished no reason why he should not have approved the earlier project for the amount of land there is water for. He does not find that the cost of water under the Hinderlider project would be prohibitory or excessive, but only that it would be considerably greater per acre than under the Young-Norton project. The price which the owners of land can afford to pay for irrigation must depend in part on the use to which it can be put.

For ordinary farm crops $40 per acre for water might be prohibitory, while for fruit or garden truck in certain localities it might not be excessive. But neither the territorial engineer nor the water commissioners have touched on that point in their reports. The territorial engineer apparently bases his approval of the latter project as against the former on the fact that Young and Norton and their associates are actual settlers on the land, while Hinderlider is not a resident of the territory. We do not say this circumstance should have no weight in determining the question of the public interest, but we think it should not outweigh the other considerations to which we have referred.

On the other hand, the water commissioners find that there is available unappropriated flood water of the La Plata river, but do not find whether there is enough for 14,000 or any other number of acres, nor whether the cost of the Hinderlider project would be such as necessarily to make the irrigation charges under it prohibitory or excessive. * * *

The cause is therefore remanded to the district court to obtain facts through the water commissioners and territorial engineer, or by agreement of counsel, or otherwise, essential to a satisfactory decision of the cause. It is not meant to limit the district court to the precise points we have named, but to leave the matter open for the introduction of any facts bearing on the question of public interest. And the judgment of the district court is set aside in order that it may on further consideration render such decision as it shall deem proper.

Notes

1. **Extent of public interest review.** Among appropriation states, only Colorado and Oklahoma do not require some form of public interest review of new appropriations. The statute in *Hinderlider* is typical of the older statutes which provide little or no guidance to administrators. At the other extreme is an Alaska statute which lists eight specific criteria to be considered: (1) the benefit to the applicant resulting from the proposed appropriation; (2) the effect of the economic activity resulting from the proposed appropriation; (3) the effect on fish and game resources and on public recreational opportunities; (4) the effect on public health; (5) the effect of loss of alternate uses of water that might be made within a reasonable time if not precluded or hindered by the proposed appropriation; (6) harm to other persons resulting from the proposed appropriation; (7) the intent and ability of the applicant to complete the appropriation; and (8) the effect upon access to navigable or public waters. Alaska Stat. § 46.15.080(b). Between these two extremes are states like California which do not give a comprehensive definition of public interest, but in which substantial guidance is provided. See Cal. Water Code §§ 1243, 1243.5, 1254, 1256-1259. See Douglas L. Grant, infra Note 2, for an extensive discussion of modern public interest statutes.

2. **Purpose of public interest review.** Douglas L. Grant, Public Interest Review of Water Right Allocation and Transfer in the West: Recognition of Public Values, 19 Ariz. St. L.J. 681, 702 (1987):

"In modern society, administrative agencies regulate diverse economic activities. Such regulation typically is predicated on a failure of market forces to deal adequately with particular structural problems. The problems vary with the economic activity regulated. With water resources use, the key problem is externalities. An externality exists when a person's water use affects others, negatively or positively, but the user does not consider those effects in deciding whether to engage in the use. In other words, some of the costs or benefits of the water use activity are external to the user's calculations in deciding whether to make the use. The difficulty with externalities is that they tend to cause resource misallocation. For example, suppose a farmer's diversion of water to irrigate sugar beets reduces opportunities for water-based recreation some distance downstream. The loss of downstream recreation is a cost of the farmer's water use. Suppose further that the law does not require the farmer to take that cost into account in deciding whether to irrigate. From a societal viewpoint, the result may be the use of too much water to produce sugar beets and too little water for downstream recreation use."

3. **Benefit-cost analysis.** In 1973 the State of Washington added an express benefit-cost formula to its statutes: "Allocation of waters among potential uses and users shall be based generally on the securing of the maximum net benefits for the people of the state. Maximum net benefits shall constitute total benefits less costs including opportunities lost." Wash. Rev. Code § 90.54.020(2).

4. **Opportunity costs.** "Opportunity costs" is the economists term for benefits foregone when one alternative development is chosen rather than another. How concrete should the foregone alternative be if the loss of its benefits is to be considered "opportunity costs"? Consider Tanner v. Bacon, 136 P.2d 957, 964-65 (Utah 1943) (Wolfe, Chief Justice, concurring):

"I assume that the State Engineer could not reject an application on the ground that if approved it would 'prove detrimental to the public welfare' because in his mind he conceived some ultimate or remote public project which would need the water. A farsighted person with imagination and bold conceptions may visualize projects which in the future may be most beneficial to the state. Perhaps we should plan a campaign for the most effective use of all unappropriated waters of the state and work to that end, but until such plans are formulated, or at least the water is withdrawn from appropriation for such purposes, I do not conceive that ideal conceptions for future and better public use of water in the State Engineer's head can be the basis for refusing to approve an application. It is not now necessary to draw the line on the degree of concreteness to which plans or projects must have attained to form bases for legal rejections by the Engineer. Suffice it to say in this case that the Deer Creek project reached a point in conception and realization where it could definitely be said to be against public interest to affirm any application which would interfere with its fruition."

5. **Effect of investment in physical works.** Why should a water administrator be concerned with possible future use of water at all? After all, water in a stream or river is a "flow" resource, not a "stock" resource. Current use does not diminish future availability. Because no future benefits are foregone when a present use is made of water, isn't it correct to say that a potential future use cannot be an opportunity cost of a present use? Indeed, shouldn't the law encourage any present use of flowing water so long as present benefits exceed present costs because a present use precludes no future benefits while the benefits lost when a present use is foregone can never be recovered? Except in the case of contemporaneous competing projects or uses, is the concept of opportunity costs even relevant to water in a stream or river? Consider Edgar S. Bagley, Some Economic Considerations in Water Use Policy, 5 Kan. L. Rev. 499, 510 (1957):

"Mention should be made of the fact that water projects often involve large capital investments in permanent or semi-permanent works. Decisions to undertake such works have a certain physical inflexibility and irrevocability which underlines the importance of careful, long-range planning, regardless of the system of water rights in effect and whether water resource development is public or private."

6. **Beneficial use and public interest.** To what extent might the requirement of "beneficial use" substitute for a public interest standard? Is an appropriation which is not in the "public interest" a beneficial use of water? Colorado does not provide for "public interest" review of applications for appropriation of water. In In re Application for Water Rights of the Board of County Commissioners, 891 P.2d 952 (Colo. 1995), the Colorado Supreme Court was asked to hold that a proposed appropriation was not a "beneficial use" of water because of the adverse effects which it would have on the environment, on recreation, and on similar values. The court refused:

"The degree of protection afforded the environment and the mechanism to address state appropriation of water for the good of the public is in the province of the General Assembly and the electorate.

"Conceptually, a public interest theory is in conflict with the doctrine of prior appropriation because a water court cannot, in the absence of statutory authority, deny a legitimate appropriation based on pubic policy. * * * The cross-appellants do not cite any authority that authorizes a water court to deny an application for a conditional decree because of environmental concerns, and we reject the cross-appellants' invitation to create a complex system of common law to balance competing public interests." Id. at 972, 973.

Compare the dissenting opinion of Justice McFadden in *State of Idaho,* supra p. 29.

SHOKAL v. DUNN

Supreme Court of Idaho, 1985
109 Idaho 330, 707 P.2d 441.

[Dunn, the director of the Idaho Department of Water Resources, issued a permit to Trout Co. for an appropriation from Billingsley Creek for fish propagation and hydropower generation. Shokal and others who had protested the issuance of the permit appealed the decision to the district court. Judge Schroeder reversed and remanded Dunn's decision, finding the Department of Water Resources consideration of two issues inadequate: (1) The financial ability of the applicant to complete the project, and (2) the local public interest with respect to the project. On remand, Dunn again approved the permit, after substantial changes were made in the project to comply with water quality standards set by Dunn. An appeal was again taken to the district court, this time before Judge Smith. Judge Smith again reversed and remanded. Judge Smith's decision was appealed to the Idaho Supreme Court.]

BISTLINE, JUSTICE. * * * While we affirm the decision of the district court to remand for a new hearing, we differ on the matters necessary for consideration at the new hearing. We hold that Water Resources used the proper standard for and has adequately dealt with the financing question. In addition, although we in general affirm the district court's order as it related to public interest matters, we modify in part the district court's guidelines. * * *

Since Water Resources's decisions on financing are reinstated, the only matters for the agency to consider on remand are those which relate generally to the local public interest. I.C. § 42-203A(5)(e). We turn first to the interpretation of this provision, a question of first impression before this Court.

Under I.C. § 42-203A(5)(e), if an applicant's appropriation of water "will conflict with the local public interest, where the local public interest is defined as the affairs of the people in the area directly affected by the proposed use," then the Director "may reject such application and refuse issuance of permit therefor, or may partially approve and grant a permit for a smaller quantity of water than applied for, or may grant a permit upon conditions." * * *

The authority and duty of the Director to protect the public interest spring naturally from the statute; the more difficult task for us is to define "the local public interest." Public interest provisions appear frequently in the statutes of the prior appropriation states of the West, but are explicated rarely. I.C. § 42-203A provides little guidance. Fortunately, however, the legislature did provide guidance in a related statute, I.C. § 42-1501. We also derive assistance from our sister states and from the academic community.

In I.C. § 42-1501, the legislature declared it "in the public interest" that:

> the streams of this state and their environments be protected against loss of water supply to preserve the minimum stream flows required for the protection of fish and wildlife habitat, aquatic life, recreation, aesthetic beauty, transportation and navigation values, and water quality.

Not only is the term "public interest" common to both §§ 42-1501 and 42-203A, and the two sections common to the same title 42 (Irrigation and Drainage—Water Rights and Reclamation), but also the legislature approved the term 'public interest' in both sections on the same day, March 29, 1978. Clearly, the legislature in § 42-203A must have intended the public interest on the local scale to include the public interest elements listed in § 42-1501: "fish and wildlife habitat, aquatic life, recreation, aesthetic beauty, transportation and navigation values, and water quality." *Accord*, National Water Commission, *New Directions in U.S. Water Policy* 5 (1973) ("The people of the United States give far greater weight to environmental and aesthetic values than they did when the nation was young and less settled.")

In so intending, the legislature was in good company. Unlike other state public interest statutes, the Alaska statute enumerates the elements of the public interest. The public interest elements of I.C. § 42-1501 are almost precisely duplicated within the Alaska statute. * * *

The Alaska statute contains other elements which common sense argues ought to be considered part of the local public interest. These include the proposed appropriation's benefit to the applicant, its economic effect, its effect "of loss of alternative uses of water that might be made within a reasonable time if not precluded or hindered by the proposed appropriation," its harm to others, its "effect upon access to navigable or public waters," and "the intent and ability of the applicant to complete the appropriation." Alaska Stat. § 46.15.080(b).

Several other public interest elements, though obvious, deserve specific mention. These are: assuring minimum stream flows, as specifically provided in I.C. § 42-1501, discouraging waste, and encouraging conservation. * * *

The above-mentioned elements of the public interest are not intended to be a comprehensive list. As observed long ago by the New Mexico Supreme Court, the 'public interest' should be read broadly in order to 'secure the greatest possible benefit from [the public waters] for the public.' Young & Norton v. Hinderlider, 15 N.M. 666, 110 P. 1045, 1050 (N.M.1910) (Rejects considering only public health and safety; considers relative costs of two projects.). By using the general term 'the local public interest,' the legislature intended to include any locally important factor impacted by proposed appropriations.

Of course, not every appropriation will impact every one of the above elements. Nor will the elements have equal weight in every situation. The relevant elements and their relative weights will vary with local needs, circumstances, and interests. For example, in an area heavily dependent on recreation and tourism or specifically devoted to preservation in its natural state, Water Resources may give great consideration to the aesthetic and environmental ramifications of granting a permit which calls for substantial modification of the landscape or the stream.

Judge Smith provided some specific guidelines, also needful of comment, to which our attention is now drawn.

1. *Finality of Design*

In order to be able to assess a project's impact on the public interest, the project's design must be definite enough to reflect its impacts and implications. Judge Smith held that because the applicant has the burden of proof to show a project is worthy of issuance of a permit, "the design of the proposed facility should be final, detailed and not schematic." He elaborated on the finality issue by stating:

> The department should not have to issue a permit on conditions that the Department review the final plans. The final plans should be presented to the Department with the application for a permit. Thus, all interested parties could review the plans, cross-examine in regard thereto and offer suggestions that might be helpful in reducing any adverse impact. The issuance of the permit, therefore, would also constitute approval of the plan.
>
> Any application for a permit that is not substantially complete in its engineering so that it cannot be properly evaluated for a here-and-now financial commitment or for impact on the public, can be readily denied by the Director. If he cannot grant the permit without establishing substantial conditions, he should deny the permit with leave to amend the application if he so desires affording all interested parties an opportunity to be heard if and when the application is amended. Such process would hopefully preclude some accusations that a Director is acting arbitrarily, capriciously or unreasonably.

In our perception, Judge Smith's language requires an applicant to present "blueprint quality" plans at the outset of seeking a permit, much in the same vein as his "here and now" standard of financing required ready cash. We are not persuaded that blueprint quality plans of a facility are always necessary when applying for a permit to appropriate water. Rather, the design plan for a proposed facility depends on the nature of the facility, the complexity of the proposal, and the extent of the proposed appropriation's impact on the local area. In this particular case, the Department will determine at the hearing on the amended application whether blue print quality plans and drawings are a prerequisite to giving approval. In all cases the plans should be sufficient to generally apprise the public of the efficacy of the proposed use in the planned facility, and of its potential impact.

2. *Dewatering*

The dewatering of Billingsley Creek raises significant public interest and public trust concerns. In his discussion of the issue Judge Smith simply declared that "the rights of an appropriator prevail over riparian rights." Such a statement on its face fails to account for the state's policy of providing for minimum stream flows, and for the public's legitimate interests in the stream environment, wildlife, aesthetics, recreation, and alternative uses. However, after reviewing the record, we agree with Judge Smith that Water Resources has dealt properly with the dewatering issue. Therefore we affirm Judge Smith's holding that there is no "legal basis for reversing the Department decision on the grounds that a portion of Billingsley Creek would be dewatered from 125 CFS to a 25 CFS minimum for an approximate 700 ft. stretch of the creek."

3. *Health Hazard*

Judge Smith opined that the law will not allow Billingsley Creek to become a nuisance or a health hazard, adding also that "a permit cannot issue which would allow construction of a project contrary to the authority of the Board of Health in policing water for pollution." Hence, Judge Smith concluded that the Director had authority to consider whether the design of any particular facility will meet all environmental requirements.

We believe this to be a correct assessment of the law, but add a word of caution regarding the differing functions of Water Resources and the Department of Health and Welfare. Water Resources must oversee the water resources of the state, insuring that those who have permits and licenses to appropriate water use the water in accordance with the conditions of the permits and licenses and the limits of the law. It is not the primary job of Water Resources to protect the health and welfare of Idaho's citizens and visitors—that role is vested in the Department of Health and Welfare, including compliance with the water quality regulations and monitoring effluent discharge in our state's waterways. Nevertheless, although these agencies may have separate functions, Water Resources is precluded from issuing a permit for a water appropriation project which, when completed, would violate the water quality standards of the Department of Health and Welfare. It makes no sense whatsoever for Water Resources to blindly grant permit requests without regard to water quality regulations. Hence, Water Resources should condition the issuance of a permit on a showing by the applicant that a proposed facility will meet the mandatory water quality standards. Under this rule, Water Resources has the authority to withhold a permit application until it receives a proposed design which appears to be in compliance with the water quality standards. Once the conditional permit is granted, Water Resources has continuing jurisdiction over compliance with the conditions of the permit, including suspension or revocation of the permit for proven violations of the permit's conditions regarding water quality.

The Department of Health and Welfare continues to have the primary responsibility for policing water quality control in this state, and can exercise in personam jurisdiction over those who violate the state's water pollution laws. While it often may be both more feasible and more reasonable for Health and Welfare to take remedial steps against one violating the pollution laws, either by forcing compliance or shutting down a facility, than to resist an application for a permit in the first instance, Health and Welfare certainly has the right to be heard in proceedings before Water Resources. And, as appointed guardian of the quality of Idaho water, its views are entitled to consideration.

In sum, we agree with the district court, Judge Smith, that Water Resources cannot issue a permit which would allow construction of a project violative of the laws regulating water quality. However, later compliance with those laws after construction of a facility generally will be a proper concern of the Department of Health and Welfare.

The above elements of the public interest, together with other elements and factors which Water Resources deems relevant, will be considered at the hearing on the amended application. * * *

Notes

1. **Ad hoc approach.** The Nevada appropriation statutes contain a simple directive to the State Engineer to reject any application for appropriation which "threatens to prove detrimental to the public interest." In Pyramid Lake Paiute Tribe of Indians v. Washoe County, 918 P.2d 697 (Nev. 1996), a trial court remanded an approved application to the State Engineer with a directive to provide an administrative definition of the quoted phrase. On remand, the State Engineer did not provide a definition, but instead identified thirteen "guidelines" contained in the Nevada water statutes and, pursuant to the guidelines, again approved the application. The approval was again challenged on the grounds, inter alia, that the guidelines did not adequately define the "public interest." The challengers argued that Nevada should follow the lead of the principal case and define the public interest using criteria from the Alaska statute. They further asserted that the approval of the application was invalid under the Alaska definition because the State Engineer had not considered certain criteria identified in the Alaska statute. The Nevada Supreme Court rejected the argument saying, "we can find no indication that Nevada's legislature intended that the State Engineer determine public policy in Nevada by incorporating another state's statutes * * *." Although the dissent called the guidelines "rambling," "unresponsive," and "a useless summary of readily assessible statutory water law", the court affirmed the State Engineer's decision, finding that the "thirteen guidelines adequately defined the public interest *in this case*." (Emphasis added).

2. **Other approaches.** In addition to the ad hoc approach, Consuelo Bokum, Implementing the Public Welfare Requirement in New Mexico's Water Code, 36 Nat. Resources J. 441 (1996), identifies three approaches that the New Mexico State Engineer might use to define the public welfare: (1) define it sufficiently narrowly that issues regarding its application are essentially avoided, (2) rely solely on definitions that evolve from regional and state water planning processes, and (3) promulgate regulations defining the public welfare broadly and establishing standards for application of the definition. The article concludes that the third alternative would best promote the sound development of public policy.

3. **Statutory directives regarding environmental and recreational considerations.** Cal. Water Code § 1257 directs water officials to consider the "relative benefit to be derived from * * * all beneficial uses of the water concerned including, but not limited to, use for * * * preservation and enhancement of fish and wildlife, [and] recreational * * * uses" in acting on applications to appropriate water. Section 1260(j) requires an application for a permit to appropriate water to set forth all data and information reasonably available to the applicant or that can be obtained from the Department of Fish and Game concerning the extent, if any, to which fish and wildlife would be affected by the appropriation, and a statement of any measures proposed to be taken for the protection of fish and wildlife in connection with the appropriation.

The Alaska Water Use Act requires that in the issuance of a permit one criterion for determining the public interest shall be "the effect on fish and game resources and on public recreational opportunities." Alaska Stat. § 46.15.080.

The Oregon Water Resources Board "shall have due regard for conserving the highest use of the water for all purposes, including * * * public recreation, protection of commercial and game fishing and wildlife, * * * navigation, scenic attraction or any other beneficial use to which the water may be applied for which it may have a special value to the public." Or. Rev. Stat. § 537.170(8)(a).

The Utah State Engineer is directed to reject an application for an appropriation if he has reason to believe that it will "unreasonably affect the public recreation or the natural stream environment." Utah Code Ann. § 73-3-8.

The Washington Water Resources Act of 1971 contains a "general declaration of fundamentals for utilization and management of water of the state," which include the following:

"(3) The quality of the natural environment shall be protected and, where possible, enhanced as follows:

"(a) Perennial rivers and streams of the state shall be retained with base flows necessary to provide for preservation of wildlife, fish, scenic, aesthetic and other environmental values, and navigational values. Lakes and ponds shall be retained substantially in their natural condition. Withdrawals of water which would conflict therewith shall be authorized only in those situations where it is clear that overriding considerations of the public interest will be served." Wash. Rev. Code § 90.54.020.

4. **Environmental policy acts.** In Stempel v. Department of Water Resources, 508 P.2d 166 (Wash. 1973), water officials, relying on previous case law, contended that the term "public welfare" related only to withdrawal of water and not to pollution and health concerns. The court responded:

"These contentions are no longer meritorious in light of the enactment of two significant and far-reaching statutes, the State Environmental Policy Act of 1971 (SEPA) (RCW 43.21C), and the Water Resources Act of 1971 (WRA) (RCW 90.54). These two statutes apply to this case and the department is obligated, under them, to consider the total environmental and ecological factors to the fullest in deciding major matters.

"The mistreatment of the environment has long been a concern in many sectors of our society, but the enactments of SEPA and WRA, as well as their national counterparts, declare a legislative mandate of the ecological ethic. SEPA strongly declares our state environmental policy. RCW 43.21C.010, 43.21C.020. It is a policy recognizing the necessary harmony between humans and the environment in order to prevent and eliminate damage to the environment and biosphere, as well as to promote the welfare of humans and the understanding of our ecological systems. To ensure that these values of ecological health become part of the decision-making process in our rapid, highly commercial and industrial society, SEPA requires various governmental branches and agencies to submit environmental impact statements before pursuing specified actions. RCW 43.21C.030(c)(i). The environmental impact reports require a detailed statement by the responsible official on:

(i) the environmental impact of the proposed action;
(ii) any adverse environmental effects which cannot be avoided should the proposal be implemented;
(iii) alternatives to the proposed action;
(iv) the relationship between local short-term uses of man's environment and the maintenance and enhancement of long-term productivity; and
(v) any irreversible and irretrievable commitments of resources which would be involved in the proposed action should it be implemented.

"Environmental protection has thus become a mandate to every state and local agency and department. Consideration of environmental values is advanced under SEPA. In the preparation of impact statements, SEPA requires consultation with other agencies, the studied development of appropriate alternatives to proposed projects, and recognition of 'the world-wide and long-range character of environmental problems.' See RCW 43.21C.030(d), (e) and (f). All of the foregoing shall '[u]tilize a systematic, interdisciplinary approach * * * in decision making which may have an impact on man's environment.' RCW 43.21C.030(a).

"We recognize SEPA does not demand any particular substantive result in governmental decision making, for it indicates 'other considerations of state policy' (RCW 43.21C.030(2)(a-g)) continue to be the responsibility of the agencies. 'Environmental amenities' will undoubtedly often conflict with 'economic and technical considerations.' In essence, what SEPA requires, is that the 'presently unquantified environmental amenities and values will be given appropriate consideration in decision making along with economic and technical considerations.' RCW 43.21C.030(2)(b). It is an attempt by the people to shape their future environment by deliberation, not default."

Cf. Friends of Mammoth v. Bd. of Supervisors, 502 P.2d 1049 (Cal. 1972). See Chapter 7, Section 2A, for a more detailed examination of federal and state environmental assessment requirements.

5. **Endangered Species Acts.** The Nebraska Nongame and Endangered Species Conservation Act directs all state agencies "to insure that actions authorized * * * by them do not jeopardize the continued existence of * * * endangered species * * *." Neb. Rev. Stat. § 37-435(3) (recodified at § 37-807(3)). In Upper Big Blue Natural Resources District v. City of Fremont, 499 N.W.2d 548 (Neb. 1993), the Nebraska Department of Water Resources rejected several applications for permits to appropriate water because it determined, inter alia, that the proposed projects would jeopardize several endangered species. The applicants challenged the rejection, arguing that the statute deprived them of the right to divert unappropriated waters as guaranteed by Neb. Const. art. XV, §§ 4, 5, and 6. Section 6 states: "The right to divert unappropriated water of every natural stream for beneficial use shall never be denied except when such denial is demanded by the public interest."

The Nebraska Supreme Court rejected the constitutional challenge:

"Whether or not legislation is in the public interest is generally a question for legislative determination; however, under the guise of regulation in the public interest, the Legislature may not impose conditions which are on their face unreasonable, arbitrary, discriminatory, or confiscatory.

"In the legislative declaration to the Nongame and Endangered Species Conservation Act (NESCA), of which § 37-435(3) is a part, the Legislature stated that "nongame, threatened, and endangered species have need of special protection and * * * it is in the public interest to preserve, protect, perpetuate, and enhance such species of this state through preservation of a satisfactory environment and an ecological balance." * * * The stated legislative intent behind NESCA is to conserve wildlife species for human enjoyment, for scientific purposes, and to ensure their perpetuation as viable components of their ecosystems, as well as to assist in the protection of endangered species pursuant to the federal Endangered Species Act.

"In consideration of these legislative declarations and statements of intent, and the unchallenged constitutionality of the federal Endangered Species Act, this court would be hard pressed to hold that there is a clear and palpable absence of a public purpose in state legislation which protects endangered species. Section 37-435(3) provides for the establishment and implementation of conservation programs to effectuate the protection of endangered species as a public interest. The Legislature's determination of a public interest and the corresponding implementing statutes are not unreasonable, arbitrary, discriminatory, or confiscatory. The limitations that § 37-435(3) places on the diversion of unappropriated waters permissibly effectuate the provisions of Neb. Const. art. XV, §§ 4, 5, and 6."

In a subsequent case, Central Platte Natural Resources District v. City of Fremont, 549 N.W.2d 112 (Neb. 1996), also involving permit applications which were denied because of jeopardy to endangered species, the court said:

"[W]e need not at this time formulate a prescriptive definition of the term 'demanded,' for the only way to satisfy the public interest, as declared in § 37-435(3), is by denying permits to appropriate waters when doing so would jeopardize the continued existence of an endangered or threatened species. Consequently, the director's evidentially supported finding that the district's proposed project would jeopardize the continued existence of the endangered whooping crane demanded that the district's applications be denied."

Endangered Species Acts are examined in greater detail in Chapter 7, Section 2D.

6. **Valuation of environmental gains and losses.** Economists would prefer a common denominator for all factors and have long struggled with the problem caused by the lack of a market in which prices are fixed for many experiences and opportunities. In the beginning the emphasis was on "recreation." How can recreational opportunities be fitted into the benefit-cost calculus? Can dollar values be assigned to the intangibles of pleasure? By valuing the facility as an asset, like a painting by an old master? By totaling gross expenditures by sportsmen? By capitalizing "derived values" from admittance fees and user charges for comparable private recreational opportunities? See Frank J. Trelease, Policies for Water Law: Property Rights, Economic Forces and Public Regulation, 5 Nat. Resources J. 1, 18-23 (1965), and materials cited.

A valuable insight, that one measurement of an intangible is its opportunity costs, was offered by Milliman:

"Intangibles are those wants or values which cannot be directly measured by the common denominator of dollars and cents. Major gains and costs to society cannot be ignored just because they are incapable of dollar measurement, because they cannot be bought and sold, or because organized markets for them do not exist. Examples of alleged intangible values in the resources field stem from national defense considerations, the theme of balanced development, the family farm, the saving of human life and the preservation of historical or scenic sites. But market inadequacy for provision of intangibles does not mean that they should be exempt from rational consideration or from at least some economic analysis. No intangible has infinite value. All intangibles have costs. The least that can be done is to specify and to make very clear to all concerned the cost of obtaining the intangible. As a *minimum* the intangible must be worth as much as it costs in terms of alternatives sacrificed if it is to be approved. Second, it is often possible to place a *maximum* value on the intangible if it can be produced by alternative means. For example, the value of a particular facility for preserving human life can be worth no more than the cost of preserving human life in other ways. Such considerations may reduce the common tendency to consider intangibles as exceptions to economic calculus." Jerome W. Milliman, Can People Be Trusted with Natural Resources?, 38 Land Econ. 199, 216 (1962).

7. **Permit conditions.** In addition to the power to deny outright an application for a permit, the agency may grant it subject to public-interest conditions. See Kirk v. State Bd. of Irrigation, 134 N.W. 167 (Neb. 1912):

"We think there is no doubt of the power and duty of the state board of irrigation to determine such questions. 'If there is unappropriated water in the source of supply named in the application, and if such appropriation is not otherwise detrimental to the public welfare, the state board, through its secretary, shall approve the same.' Comp. St. 1911, c. 93a, art. 2, § 28. Thus the state board of irrigation is made the guardian of the public welfare in the appropriation of the public waters of the state, and this necessarily devolves upon that board a large discretion in such matters. If the public welfare demands it, they may grant a qualified and limited right of appropriation and in the beneficial use of the water so appropriated."

Such discretion is not unlimited, however. Bank of America National Trust & Savings Ass'n v. State Water Resources Control Board, 116 Cal. Rptr. 770 (Ct. App. 1974), involved applications for two off-stream reservoirs to be used as water supplies for a large residential development. In approving the applications the Board imposed stream by-pass requirements to protect fish, which had been agreed to by the Bank and the California Department of Fish and Game. In addition, the Board required the applicant to open the reservoirs to public recreational use. The applicant appealed the latter requirement, designated as "condition 11" by the Board. In reversing the Board the court said:

"It becomes clear that the Board's reason for condition 11 was that the approved diversion would reduce the flow of the river which, in turn, would have an uncertain effect on the 'fishery.' Further, the diversion would result in "diminished recreational value" of the Cosumnes because of its lower level downstream. These two factors—the undetermined effect on fish and lessened recreational prospects caused by lower water level—prompted the Board to require as a 'trade-off' public access to the Rancho Murieta recreational reservoirs.

"While Fish & Game's determination that the [by-pass] formula fixed in the agreement is adequate to support fish life is not binding on the Board, Fish & Game's judgment in this matter is entitled to great weight. Charged with a statutory obligation, Fish & Game is the guardian and custodian of the public's deep and continuing interest in the fish and game resources of this state. It has the collective experience and expertise to make the essential determinations in the technical areas of water flows and fish maintenance. The agreed formula was negotiated and approved by Fish & Game and we cannot presume that its conclusions were not carefully reached. Of greater significance is the fact that nowhere in the record does there appear before the Board any evidence that adoption of the formula would adversely affect, diminish, or impair the fishery. We accordingly, conclude that the first basis for imposition of the condition, preservation of the fish life in the Cosumnes downstream from the diversion, has been otherwise adequately assured.

"The remainder of our inquiry relates to whether substantial evidence in the record establishes a 'diminished recreational value' of the Cosumnes warranting a 'trade-off' or exchange for condition 11. Our review of the record discloses no such evidence. There are clear inferences from the record that the water level of the Cosumnes below the diversion during certain times of the year will be lower because of it, but there is no testimony as to its degree or, more importantly, as to its effect in terms of recreational use of the river, present or prospective. No testimony written or oral was presented which in any substantial manner pointed to the specifics of impairment of recreational activities.

"We note that one of the exhibits, a report prepared by the U.S. Department of the Interior, on the Feasibility of Water Supply Development, Cosumnes River Diversion of the Central Valley Project, described general recreational activities around *reservoirs* as 'boating, swimming, waterskiing, and fishing,' and that shoreline activity includes 'camping, picnicking, sightseeing, hiking and related activities.' We envision that the boating and waterskiing activities in a stream like the Cosumnes because of its size and configuration would be very limited with or without the diversion, but the remaining recreational uses will be unimpaired insofar as disclosed by the Board record. No evidence, written or oral, was presented which indicated that the lower water level would change or affect the recreational utilization of the Cosumnes downstream from the diversion.

"We have heretofore underscored the primacy of the 'public interest' in the considerations before the Board and have emphasized the broad discretion vested in it. Nonetheless, we apply a measure of substantiality in reviewing the evidence supporting the Board's action. * * *

"The record, in our view, is barren of evidence which is of 'ponderable legal significance' in support of the conclusion that the diversion would result in a reduction in the recreational value of the Cosumnes. While fully accepting the rule giving primacy to the public interest, we may not leave to speculation the nature of its impairment. Condition 11 constitutes an onerous burden. The Board, in our view, has the jurisdiction and the right to impose a condition requiring public access but only for precise and specific reasons founded on tangible record evidence.

"To summarize, we conclude that the record lacks substantial evidence supporting condition 11 and it must fail."

8. **Permit conditions v. instream appropriations**. "Some states (such as California) authorize retention of water in the source for purposes of fishery protection and recreation on a case-by-case basis when considering new applications to appropriate. This process is less desirable than that of the Model Water Code for two reasons. First, the Code's reservation device provides advance notice of a contemplated appropriation, while the case-by-case procedure does not allow a determination until a project has been fully planned and a specific applicant is before the appropriate administrative agency. Second, the extent of the reservation on a case-by-case basis will necessarily be determined by weighing the utility of the specific project against the value of the instream use instead of basing such reservation on general public policy. It is difficult for noneconomic uses based on such policy to be broadly considered." Ronald B. Robie, Modernizing State Water Rights Laws: Some Suggestions for New Directions, 1974 Utah L. Rev. 760, 770 (1974).

The California Department of Fish and Game has complained that the use of permit conditions provides little permanent protection to instream values. The department has noted that bypass flows required of one appropriator often become a target for subsequent appropriation downstream, forcing it to make its case for instream protection again and again, with the possibility that it may be successful in nine cases only to lose on the tenth. See Anne J. Schneider, Legal Aspects of Instream Water Uses in California, at 44-45 (Governor's Comm'n to Review Cal. Water Rights Law, Staff Paper No. 6, 1978).

Does the following report suggest a means of overcoming the shortcomings described above?

"Nebraska Director of Water Resources John Neuberger has closed two streams in western Nebraska to appropriation. The moratorium was imposed after water right cancellation hearings, field investigations, and Department of Water Resources reports. After reviewing these materials, Director Neuberger determined that issuance of additional stream diversion permits would not be in the public interest, presumably because the water supply is inadequate to support additional uses. In addition, the moratoria will avoid 'additional and unjustifiable administrative costs.' The Department will, however, continue to consider applications to store water and use stored water from Lodgepole and Pumpkinseed Creeks." J. David Aiken, 13 Water L. Newsl., No. 1, at 5 (Rocky Mtn. Min. L. Found., Westminster, Colo.) (1980).

9. **Weighing public interest factors.** Most permit statutes provide little guidance concerning how to weigh various factors in deciding if a proposed appropriation is in the public interest. Is this a deficiency? See Frank J. Trelease, A Water Code for Alaska 17 (1962):

"Making decisions such as these will be very difficult. No law can make them, they must be made by people. No economic formula can solve these problems by push button techniques. Although * * * the proposed Code incorporate[s] the benefit-cost idea, (following the model of some of the Wisconsin Statutes, Sections 31.06(3) and 107.05(3)) the balancing of benefits against cost must be performed by the exercise of judgment. Mathematical equivalents could be used if desired, to insure that some factors are not vastly overweighed. Indeed, the Code could be amended to delete the formula, yet surely the administrators would consider these same factors in determining the public interest. It is believed that the real strength of the Code lies in its procedures, which will enable all viewpoints to be brought together and all factors considered, so that choices will be made, not by action of an appropriator or polluter, and not to further the policy of a single-purpose agency, but on an informed basis by officials responsible to the State for 'maximum use consistent with the public interest', for the 'maximum benefit of (all) its people.'"

10. **Institutional competence and public interest decisions**. Consideration of the public interest in the regulation of water use raises difficult questions regarding the competence of various government institutions to address particular issues. For example, should a particular issue be addressed by an administrative or a legislative body? Should it be addressed at the state level or at a local level? If it is to be addressed by an administrative body, what should be the make up of the body and what should be the scope of its authority? Should its authority be confined to primarily technical issues or should it include broad discretion to choose between conflicting public values? Should it include authority to address matters which are typically addressed by other governmental institutions? Such questions arise in the context of statutory interpretation and in the development of sound public policy; i.e., *does* a water agency have the authority to address particular issues and *should* it have such authority? Obviously, the latter question—should a water agency have such authority—may be relevant in addressing the former question—does it have such authority—particularly when a statute contains a simple, unadorned directive to promote the "public interest."

In re Application of Water Permit No. 4580A-3, South Dakota Water Management Board, discussed in Grant, supra p. 136, Note 2, at 698, illustrates aspects of the problem. In that case, the South Dakota Water Management Board considered the effect on adjacent public recreation areas of odors from a hog farm in determining whether a proposed appropriation for the hog farm was in the public interest. The board concluded that the economic benefits of the facility outweighed the harm to the recreation areas resulting from the occasional presence of unpleasant odors and approved the appropriation.

Did the South Dakota Legislature intend the Water Management Board to consider land-use conflicts in determining the public interest with regard to water matters? Would it have been appropriate for the Board to deny the appropriation if local land use officials had considered the matter and approved the hog farm? Should such a decision be made at the state or local level? See Pyramid Lake Paiute Tribe of Indians v. Washoe County, supra p. 142, Note 1, in which the court concluded that the state engineer appropriately refused to consider alternatives to a proposed county water supply project because the legislature had assigned the responsibility for water supply planning and development to the county, and Serpa v. County of Washoe, 901 P.2d 690 (Nev. 1995), holding that approval of the water supply plans for a proposed subdivision by the state engineer did not preempt the authority of the county to disapprove the subdivision because of its effect on regional water resources. See also City of Colorado Springs v. Board of Commissioners, discussed supra p. 99, Note 5, in which a county blocked a transbasin appropriation through the exercise of its land use authority. Arguments for a stronger local role in water allocation decisions are examined in A. Dan Tarlock & Sarah B. Van de Wetering, Growth Management and Western Water Law: From Urban Oases to Archipelagos, 5 Hastings W.-Nw. J. Envtl. L. & Pol'y 163 (1999). David H. Getches, Changing the River's Course, Western Water Policy Reform, 26 Envtl. L. 157 (1996), argues for the creation of watershed based institutions to determine the public interest in water regulation.

In 2003 the Idaho legislature amended the definition of "local public interest." The relevant section now reads: "'Local public interest' is defined as the interest that the people in the area directly affected by a proposed water use have in the effect of such use on the public water resource," Idaho Code § 42-202B (3). A statement of purpose accompanying the legislation which amended the definition states that the "local public interest" should not be construed to require the consideration of secondary effects of an activity simply because the activity happens to use water. The statement gives an example: "[T]he effect of a new manufacturing plant on water quality, resident fish and wildlife and the availability of water for other beneficial uses is appropriately considered under the local public interest criteria. On the other hand the effect of the manufacturing plant on air quality is not within the local public interest criteria because it is not an effect of the diversion of water but rather a secondary effect of the proposed plant. While the impact of the manufacturing plant is important this effect should be evaluated by [the Department of Environmental Quality under other legislation]." Statement of Purpose/Fiscal Impact of H.O. 284, 57th Leg., 1st Reg. Sess. (Idaho 2003).[c] The statement indicates that the change was prompted by protests based on a broad range of social, economic, and environmental policy issues having nothing to do with impacts on water resources.

In In re Howard Sleeper, discussed infra p. 218, Note 3, a trial judge decided that the protection of cultural values outweighed the economic development which would result from a particular water use. Is a judge "competent" to make such a decision? Is the New Mexico State Engineer, whose decision was being challenged in *Sleeper*, "competent" to make such a decision? If not, what body should address such questions?

11. **Police power regulation of water rights.** Terms and conditions in state-issued permits provide the backbone of modern water rights regulation in

---

c. Available at http://www3.state.id.us/oasis/2003/H0284.html.

most western states. However, a recent California case provides a reminder that administrative permits are not the only basis for the regulation of water rights. In People v. Murrison, 124 Cal. Rptr. 2d 68 (Ct. App. 2002), Murrison claimed a water right based on an appropriation made before the state adopted a permit requirement in 1914. To exercise this right, he constructed a diversion dam in a stream without notifying the California Department of Fish and Game as required by a California statute. When challenged by state authorities, Murrison argued that his water right was not subject to statutory regulation because it was not based on a state permit. The court rejected the argument: "A water right, whether it predates or postdates 1914 is not exempt from reasonable regulation. Just as a real property owner does not have an unfettered right to develop property in any manner he or she sees fit, * * * an owner of a water right may be similarly restricted." Id. at 76.

UNITED PLAINSMEN ASS'N v. NORTH DAKOTA STATE WATER CONSERVATION COMMISSION

Supreme Court of North Dakota, 1976.
247 N.W.2d 457.

PEDERSON, JUSTICE. This is an appeal by the United Plainsmen Association, a North Dakota non-profit corporation, from a decision of the district court of Burleigh County dismissing the complaint for failure to state a claim upon which relief could be granted.

The complaint sought an injunction against the North Dakota State Water Conservation Commission and Vernon Fahy, State Engineer. Should this court find that the trial court erred, then United Plainsmen asks for a temporary restraining order against the Commission and the State Engineer pending trial on the merits. We hold that the district court did err in dismissing the complaint, we deny a temporary restraining order, and remand the case for further proceedings. * * *

The injunction sought by United Plainsmen would have prevented the State Engineer from issuing future water permits for coal-related power and energy production facilities until there is a comprehensive short- and long-term plan for the conservation and development of the State's natural resources, which, United Plainsmen contends, is required by § 61-01-26, NDCC, and the common law Public Trust Doctrine existing in this State. Section 61-01-26 reads as follows:

> "In view of legislative findings and determination of the ever-increasing demand and anticipated future need for water in North Dakota for every beneficial purpose and use, it is hereby declared to be the water resources policy of the state that: * * *
>
> "4. Accruing benefits from these resources can best be achieved for the people of the state through the development, execution and periodic updating of comprehensive, coordinated and well-balanced short- and long-term plans and programs for the conservation and development of such resources by the departments and agencies of the state having responsibilities therefor;
>
> "5. Adequate implementation of such plans and programs shall be provided by the state through cost-sharing and cooperative participation with

the appropriate federal and state departments and agencies and political subdivisions within the limitation of budgetary requirements and administrative capabilities; * * *

"The provisions of this chapter shall not be construed to in any manner limit, impair or abrogate the rights, powers, duties or functions of any department or agency of the state having jurisdiction or responsibilities in the field of water and related land resources conservation, development or utilization."

United Plainsmen argues that the language of subsection 4 of that statute imposes mandatory planning responsibility upon the State Engineer, which constitutes a condition precedent to the issuance of temporary or permanent water permits in this State. We do not agree. In the light of the qualifying proviso at the end of § 61-01-26, we must conclude that subsection 4 thereof is "hortatory and precatory, but not mandatory." See Dathe v. Wildrose School District No. 91, 217 N.W.2d 781, 782 (N.D. 1974).

Although it is not mandatory, § 61-01-26, entitled "Declaration of state water resources policy," is a significant advisory policy statement. The last sentence therein clearly indicates that it is not to be construed to limit, impair or abrogate the rights, powers, duties or functions of any department or agency of the State. This statute provides but little support for United Plainsmen's contention that the State Engineer must complete short- and long-term planning as a condition precedent to the issuance of water permits.

We note, also, that the Legislature has reserved to itself the task of research in the areas of natural resources use and the determination of governmental responsibility for the results or impacts from developments, and to assure that "there shall not be material detrimental deterioration of the environment or quality of life in North Dakota." See Section 4 of Chapter 4, Session Laws of 1975.

The foregoing, however, does not relieve the Commission and State Engineer of mandatory planning responsibilities with respect to the issuance of water permits, and we note that counsel for the Commission emphasized in his argument that the State Engineer and the Commission do have plans and do not reject the concept of prior planning. We agree with United Plainsmen that the discretionary authority of state officials to allocate vital state resources is not without limit but is circumscribed by what has been called the Public Trust Doctrine.

This doctrine was first clearly defined in Illinois Central Railroad v. Illinois, 146 U.S. 387, 13 S.Ct. 110, 36 L.Ed. 1018 (1892), a case in which the United States Supreme Court was called upon to decide the competency of the State of Illinois to convey, by legislative grant, a portion of Chicago's harbor on Lake Michigan to the Illinois Central Railroad.

"That the State holds the title to the lands under the navigable waters of Lake Michigan, within its limits, in the same manner that the State holds title to soils under tide water, by the common law, we have already shown, and that title necessarily carries with it control over the waters above them whenever the lands are subjected to use. * * * It is a title held in trust for the people of the State that they may enjoy the navigation of the waters, carry on commerce over them, and have liberty of fishing therein freed from the obstruction or interference of private parties." 146 U.S. at 452, 13 S.Ct. at 118.

"The State can no more abdicate its trust over property in which the whole people are interested, like navigable waters and soils under them, so as to leave them entirely under the use and control of private parties, except in the instance of parcels mentioned for the improvement of the navigation and use of the waters, or when parcels can be disposed of without impairment of the public interest in what remains, than it can abdicate its police powers in the administration of government and the preservation of the peace." 146 U.S. at 453, 13 S.Ct. at 118. * * *

The Commission, the State Engineer, and the lower court, while acknowledging the existence of this doctrine in North Dakota, interpret it in a narrow sense, limiting its applicability to conveyances of real property. We do not understand the doctrine to be so restricted. The State holds the navigable waters, as well as the lands beneath them, in trust for the public. North Dakota's Constitution, Article XVII, § 210, states:

"All flowing streams and natural water courses shall forever remain the property of the state for mining, irrigating and manufacturing purposes."

Section 61-01-01, NDCC, further defines the public waters of this State:

"All waters within the limits of the state from the following sources of water supply, namely: * * * belong to the public and are subject to appropriation for beneficial use and the right to the use of these waters for such use, shall be acquired pursuant to the provisions of chapter 61-04."

These statutes provide a means by which those who seek use of public waters can petition the State Engineer for water permits. In the performance of this duty of resource allocation consistent with the public interest, the Public Trust Doctrine requires, at a minimum, a determination of the potential effect of the allocation of water on the present water supply and future water needs of this State. This necessarily involves planning responsibility. The development and implementation of some short- and long-term planning capability is essential to effective allocation of resources "without detriment to the public interest in the lands and waters remaining."

We believe that § 61-01-01, NDCC, expresses the Public Trust Doctrine. * * * Confined to traditional concepts, the Doctrine confirms the State's role as trustee of the public waters. It permits alienation and allocation of such precious state resources only after an analysis of present supply and future need.

The Legislature has indicated its desire to see such planning take place, although not in mandatory language. Until the Legislature speaks more forcefully, we think the Public Trust Doctrine requires, as a minimum, evidence of some planning by appropriate state agencies and officers in the allocation of public water resources, and that the Environmental Law Enforcement Act (Chapter 32-40, NDCC) requires more than a plenary dismissal of the action.

United Plainsmen has requested a temporary restraining order, enjoining the further issuance of water permits pending trial on the merits in the lower court. A temporary injunction or restraining order may be granted if it appears by the complaint that the plaintiffs are entitled to the relief requested, and that such relief consists of restraining acts which would, if continued, produce injury to the plaintiffs during the litigation. Section 32-06-02, NDCC. We are not convinced that a temporary restraining order is necessary or advisable in this instance.

During oral argument counsel for appellees stated that, of the total number of water permits considered each year, a very small percentage is in the industrial category relating to energy conversion. Of that small percentage of industrial water-use applications considered, only a few are actually granted and some that are granted will never be used because of other causes which prevent the intended development.

We express no opinion about the ultimate outcome of the trial on the merits, should that point be reached in this case. We acknowledge, however, that there is merit in the argument that the extent of planning is somewhat related to the sums appropriated therefor by the Legislature. It may be that the planning being done by the Commission, according to the oral argument made in this Court, is sufficient.

We hold that the dismissal was premature and improvident under the circumstances. The amended complaint charges a failure to devise any water conservation plan, as well as a failure to consider injury to the public. For the purpose of the motion to dismiss, the trial court and this Court must consider all allegations of the complaint to be true. We hold, accordingly, that the complaint does state a claim upon which relief could be granted, if proved, and, therefore, must be reinstated.

Reversed and remanded for further proceedings.

Notes

1. **Extent of planning.** Most western states have statutes which provide for water planning of some sort. However, a 1988 survey indicated that in about half the states the process was essentially moribund; i.e., plans were never completed or had become outdated and there were no ongoing planning efforts. David H. Getches, Water Planning: Untapped Opportunity for the Western States, 9 J. Energy L. & Pol'y 1, 44-45 (1988). The situation does not appear to have changed appreciably since then.

2. **Modern water planning.** Modern planning statutes establish a dynamic and comprehensive process. E.g., Kan. Stat. Ann:

"§ 82a-901a. Legislative declaration."

"The people of the state can best achieve the proper utilization and control of the water resources of the state through comprehensive planning which coordinates and provides guidance for the management, conservation and development of the state's water resources."

"§ 82a-903. Same; formulation of state water plan; cooperation of state water agencies; advice of general public."

"In accordance with the policies and long-range goals and objectives established by the legislature, the office shall formulate on a continuing basis a comprehensive state water plan for the management, conservation and development of the water resources of the state. Such state water plan shall include sections corresponding with water planning areas as determined by the office. The Kansas water office and the Kansas water authority shall seek advice from the general public and from committees consisting of individuals with knowledge of and interest in water issues in the water planning areas. The plan shall set forth the recommendations of the office for the management, conservation and development of the water resources of the state, including the general location, character, and extent of such existing and proposed projects, programs, and facilities as are necessary or desirable in the judgment of the office to accomplish such policies, goals and objectives. The plan shall specify standards for operation and management of such projects, programs, and facilities as are necessary or desirable. The plan shall be formulated and used for the general purpose of accomplishing the coordinated management, conservation and development of the water resources of the state. The division of water resources of the state board of agriculture, state geological survey, the division of environment of the department of health and environment, department of wildlife and parks, state conservation commission and all other interested state agencies shall cooperate with the office in formulation of such plan."

"§ 82a-907. State water resource planning act; considerations in formulation of state water plan."

"In formulating the state water plan the office shall consider:

(a) The management, conservation and development of the water resources of the state for the benefit of the state as a whole;
(b) the benefits to be derived from development of reservoir sites for the combined purposes of flood control, water supply storage and recreation;
(c) the safeguards to public health, aquatic and animal life established by K.S.A. 65-161 to 65-171t, inclusive, and amendments thereto, and the Kansas water quality management plan approved and adopted as provided by chapter 351 of the 1979 Session Laws;
(d) the water development policies, whenever possible, consistent with the beneficial development of other natural resources;
(e) the public health and general welfare of the people of the state;
(f) all appropriation and other rights to the use of water that exist pursuant to the Kansas water appropriation act and the state water plan storage act;
(g) the interrelationship of groundwater and surface water supplies and the effects of evapotranspiration on water supply;
(h) the alternative plans, programs and projects in the interest of effective water resource management, conservation and development;
(i) the means and methods for the protection of aquatic and other wildlife;
(j) the use of waters to augment the flow of surface streams for the support of aquatic and other wildlife and to improve the water quality of the stream and to protect the public health;

(k) the inclusion of conservation storage in reservoir development and planning for the regulation of streamflow for the purpose of quality control, such inclusion not to serve as a substitute for methods of controlling wastes at their sources;
(l) the maintenance, preservation and protection of the sovereignty of the state over all the waters within the state;
(m) plans, projects and recommendations of public corporations, the federal government and state agencies prepared pursuant to statutory authority;
(n) plans, recommendations and projects of private associations or organizations as they relate to the water resources of the state;
(o) the need of the state to control storage in federal reservoirs by purchase or agreement; and
(p) such other matters as the office deems proper or desirable."

3. **More on modern water planning—California.** The California Water Plan, prepared by the Department of Water Resources in 1957 and approved by the legislature in 1959, was an example of an older, more static, type of plan—a list of 376 dams and related facilities on rivers and streams throughout the state. In effect, the plan was a blueprint for water development projects in the state.

Water planning in California has evolved into a dynamic process. Beginning in 1966, the Department of Water Resources periodically prepared a series of updates to the plan. This process was codified in 1991 with a legislative directive to the Department to update the plan every five years. See Cal. Water Code §§ 10004-10005. Unlike the 1957 plan, the updates do not focus solely or even primarily on water facilities. Instead, the updates collect and analyze extensive regional and statewide data and information on water use, on water management activities and proposals, and on contemporary and future issues and problems confronting water management efforts in California in an effort to assess present and future water supplies and demands and to evaluate progress and options in meeting future water needs. Although the updates make various recommendations, they are not primarily policy documents; they are essentially descriptive and analytic in nature. Indeed, the Water Code specifies that the "Plan" does not itself authorize the construction of any facilities. Cal. Water Code § 10005. It is simply "the master plan" for the state's water resource conservation, management and development.

Although the Plan's updates might not create policy, they, like most else involving water in California, can create a controversy. After the 1998 update was released, it was criticized by many environmentalists and some urban water agencies. Among other matters, the environmentalists disliked the update's continuation of the decades-old "gap analysis." These analyses, employed by many water engineers in many planning processes, displayed an ever-growing "gap" between firm water supplies and increasing demand. "Filling the gap" had been the decades-old justification for new dams and reservoirs. When others tried to replicate the analysis used by the Department of Water Resources, they found it difficult to identify the various assumptions used by the Department. After a series of hearings, the Legislature amended the California Water Plan legislation. Cal. Water Code §§ 10004-10004.6, 10013.

The new legislation makes three principal changes. First, it requires the Department to release, at least a year prior to each update, a "preliminary draft of the assumptions and other estimates upon which the study will be based."

§ 10004.6(c). The legislation details nine major topics that must be included in the report: 1) basin hydrology, 2) groundwater supplies, 3) current and projected land use patterns, 4) environmental water needs, 5) current and projected population, 6) current and projected interior and exterior residential, commercial, industrial and park water use, 7) evapotranspiration rates for major crop types, 8) current and projected adoption of urban and agricultural conservation practices, and 9) current and projected supplies provided by water recycling and reuse. This preliminary report is designed to give interested parties a "heads up" about the key assumptions upon which the Department will be basing its ultimate recommendations. Among other matters, this allows controversy over underlying data to be dealt with in advance of controversy over water conservation, management or development options.

Second, the new legislation mandates that the Department convene an advisory committee. § 10004(b)(2). This codifies a voluntary practice that the Department had begun in 1993. The statute specifies that members must include representatives of "agricultural and urban water suppliers, local government, business, production agriculture, and environmental interests * * *." Advisory committees, an ever increasing fixture of natural resources planning, allow the Department to receive stakeholder input to improve the planning process, as well as to build support for any eventual recommendations.

Finally, the new legislation mandates that the plan contain a region by region analysis of "regional and local water projects * * * to improve water supplies to meet municipal, agricultural and environmental water needs and minimize the need to import water from other hydrologic regions." § 10013. In particular, it mandates that the report study regional efforts to desalinate brackish groundwater and ocean water, reclaim water, improve drinking water treatment, and construct dual water systems and brine lines. The clear import of the section is that water-importing regions, particularly in Southern California, should thoroughly develop their own supplies and reuse capabilities before seeking additional inter-regional water imports.

In January 2000, the Department began its most recent update process. Although the 1999 legislation mandated the production of the "assumptions and estimates" report by the end of 2002 and the release of the new update itself by the end of 2003, neither deadline was met. This was due in part to changes in the plan's content recommended by the duly convened advisory committee; in part to a change in administrations; and in part to controversies over some of the initial draft recommendations. Progress on the current update, and its successor efforts, can be tracked through the Department's web site.[d]

4. **Effect of the water plan.** When one California water district applied for a permit to construct one of the listed dams in the 1957 California Water Plan and another sought approval of an inconsistent project that would displace the listed dam but better use existing facilities, the latter was preferred by the State Water Rights Board and its choice was upheld in Johnson Rancho County Water District v. State Water Rights Board., 45 Cal. Rptr. 589 (Ct. App. 1965). The court noted that the plan itself included a recommendation that more detailed studies of component features were necessary to determine their need, their engineering

---

d. http://www.waterplan.water.ca.gov/b160/indexb160.html.

feasibility and their financial feasibility, and that further investigation might indicate alternative projects. The court also noted that the legislature had not made the plan binding but had merely directed the Board (now the Water Resources Control Board) to "give consideration to any general or coordinated plan * * * including the California Water Plan * * * and any modification thereto * * *."

Should a water plan be binding in water allocation decisions to the extent that it addresses particular issues? Should water officials at least be required to consider a water plan and justify inconsistent allocation decisions? If not, is a plan anything more than an "academic exercise"?

5. **Preference statutes.** Preference statutes are a more static form of planning:

N.D. Cent. Code § 61-04-06.1: "Preference in granting permits. When there are competing applications for water from the same source, and the source is insufficient to supply all applicants, the state engineer shall adhere to the following order of priority: (1) Domestic use. (2) Municipal use. (3) Livestock use. (4) Irrigation use. (5) Industrial use. (6) Fish, wildlife, and other outdoor recreation."

6. **Absolute preferences.** Cal. Fish and Game Code §§ 5937, 5946 create another kind of preference. Section 5937 provides: "The owner of any dam shall allow sufficient water at all times to pass through a fishway, or in the absence of a fishway, allow sufficient water to pass over, around or thorough the dam, to keep in good condition any fish that may be planted or exist below the dam. * * *" Section 5946, states that all permits and licenses issued in a particular region of the state must be conditioned on full compliance with section 5937. Nevertheless, various water rights were issued to Los Angeles without the required conditions. In California Trout, Inc. v. State Water Resources Control Board, 255 Cal. Rptr. 184 (Ct. App. 1989), the court ordered water officials to amend Los Angeles' water rights:

"The legislative mandate of section 5946 was either overlooked or misconstrued in the actions of the Water Board granting the licenses here in issue. We agree with the Water Board that the mandate of section 5946 is a specific legislative rule concerning the public trust. Since the Water Board has no authority to disregard that rule, a judicial remedy exists to require it to carry out its ministerial functions with respect to that rule. The Legislature, not the Water Board, is the superior voice in the articulation of public policy concerning the reasonableness of water allocation. The unfortunate fact that the Water Board did not hear the Legislature's voice in 1974 does not warrant, by the passage of time, its turning a deaf ear now."

Is this absolute preference for fishery protection good public policy? What if the evidence showed only a small number of "trash" fish would be preserved by the flows but that alternate uses of the water were very valuable?

7. **Ecosystem management.** Ecosystem management is a type of planning that is receiving increasing interest. The concept is relatively new and there is not complete agreement about its meaning. Nevertheless, the following description by one of its strongest advocates captures the essence of the ecosystem management:

"The concept of ecosystem management, though still often misunderstood, has now been defined with sufficient precision to constitute a viable natural resource management policy. Drawing heavily upon ecological and biological sciences, particularly the field of conservation biology, ecosystem management views the land and resource base in its entirety, as a holistic or integrated entity. Management focuses on entire ecosystems, not just individual resources such as timber and forage. Recognizing that natural systems often cross jurisdictional boundaries, ecosystem management emphasizes the need for inter-jurisdictional coordination to ensure ecological integrity and sustainable resource systems. The policy is designed to maintain and restore natural processes, including biodiversity levels and natural disturbance regimes. And because ecological systems evolve over time, often unpredictably, ecosystem management is intended to accommodate such instability and change. Human intervention, including commodity production and extraction activities, may be used to accomplish these goals, although this will vary depending upon the managing agency's organic mandate and basic philosophy." Robert B. Keiter, Beyond the Boundary Line: Constructing a Law of Ecosystem Management, 65 U. Colo. L. Rev. 293, 295 (1994).[e]

Ecosystem management is both narrower and broader than traditional water planning. It is narrower because its focus is primarily on environmental protection, particularly the preservation of biological diversity. It is broader because its emphasis is on management of all resources within ecosystems rather than on management of water resources alone. While its proponents can identify a number of efforts at ecosystem management, the concept is not yet widely reflected in the law. If widely adopted, it would have a substantial impact on water management. Water is a major component of most ecosystems; indeed, the watershed is often identified as the logical geographic unit for ecosystem management. Protection of the aquatic ecosystem has already been the central focus of some ecosystem management efforts. See, e.g., Michael C. Blumm, The Amphibious Salmon: The Evolution of Ecosystem Management in the Columbia River Basin, 24 Ecology L.Q. 653 (1997); Henry B. Lacey, Dancing in Place: The Clinton Administration and Aquatic Ecosystem Protection in the Pacific Northwest, 36 Nat. Resources J. 539 (1996).

8. **Public Trust Doctrine.** *Illinois Central Railroad* and other cases dealing with the public trust doctrine are found in Chapter 7, Section 1B.

D. Adjudication and Enforcement

FARM INVESTMENT CO. v. CARPENTER

Supreme Court of Wyoming, 1900.
9 Wyo. 110, 61 P. 258.

POTTER, C.J. This suit was instituted in the district court of Johnson County for the purpose of securing a decree quieting the title of plaintiff to the right to use water from French creek for the irrigation of certain lands, as against each and all of the defendants, who, it is alleged, are asserting prior and superior rights to the plaintiff. An appropriation by plaintiff's grantor in

---

the year 1879, and the continued use and application of the water so appropriated, are set out, and in consequence thereof a right superior to the defendants is alleged to reside in the plaintiff. The answer of but one of the defendants is in the record. Admitting the original appropriation alleged in the petition, and the ownership of plaintiff to the water right acquired thereby, if any, the answer, as a separate defense, after disclosing the claim of the answering defendant to the use of certain of the waters of the stream for irrigation purposes by reason of an appropriation in 1883, sets up an adjudication by the state board of control of the rights of the various claimants to the use of the water of said stream on or about October, 1893, in accordance with the provisions of chapter 8 of the Laws of 1890-91; the same being an act entitled "An act providing for the supervision and use of the waters of the state." It is alleged that all the notices required by said act were duly given and published, and that the plaintiff had actual notice, and that the proceedings were conducted in accordance with the statutory provisions, and that neither the plaintiff nor his grantors appeared or submitted any proof of their alleged rights. It is also alleged that by the order of the said board in that proceeding the defendant was awarded a certain priority for a definite quantity of water, for which a certificate was issued to him, and that "no amount of water whatever was awarded or decreed to the plaintiff or to any other person for use upon the lands described in said plaintiff's petition." Wherefore it is averred that the plaintiff has abandoned its rights, and is now estopped from asserting the same. * * *

[Counsel for plaintiff contended that the statutory provisions for the adjudication were unconstitutional on various grounds. The district court certified the constitutional questions directly to the supreme court for answer.]

The expressions of the constitution relating to irrigation and water rights are as follows: "Water being essential to industrial prosperity, of limited amount, and easy of diversion from its natural channels, its control must be in the state, which, in providing for its use, shall equally guard all the various interests involved." Article 1, § 31. "The waters of all natural streams, springs, lakes, or other collections of still water, within the boundaries of the state, are hereby declared to be the property of the state." Article 8, § 1. "There shall be constituted a board of control to be composed of the state engineer, and superintendents of the water divisions; which shall, under such regulations as may be prescribed by law, have the supervision of the waters of the state and of their appropriation, distribution and diversion, and of the various officers connected therewith. Its decisions to be subject to review by the courts of the state." Id. § 2. * * *

Pursuant to the constitutional requirements, the first state legislature, by an act entitled "An act providing for the supervision and use of the waters of the state," approved December 22, 1890, created the state board of control, divided the state into four water divisions, and provided for the appointment of a superintendent for each division. * * * By the act in question, also, a system of procedure to be inaugurated and conducted by the board is established, wherein and whereby the board is directed and empowered to ascertain, adjudicate, and determine the priorities of rights of the various claimants from the same stream, and the former legislation authorizing such adjudication by a special proceeding in the district court is repealed. * * *

Concerning the proceedings preliminary to an order of determination, it will sufficiently answer our purpose to state that notices are required to be published and sent by registered mail to each person having a recorded claim to waters of the stream or streams embraced in the adjudication proceedings, showing when the engineer will begin a measurement of the stream and the several diverting works, and the time and place when the superintendent will commence the taking of testimony. Accompanying the notice, there is required to be sent to the claimant a blank form, on which the claimant is required to present in writing, under oath, certain specified facts relating to his appropriation. Upon the completion of the testimony the same is to be opened to public inspection at a time and place mentioned in a notice thereof to be previously published and sent by mail to the several claimants. An opportunity is provided for any interested party to contest before the superintendent and the board the claim of any other persons who may have submitted their proof. Upon the completion of the evidence in the original hearing, and in all contests, the same is required to be transmitted to the board of control. In the meantime the engineer or his assistant is required to make an examination and measurement of the stream and the works diverting water therefrom, as well as of the irrigated lands, or lands susceptible of irrigation from the various ditches or canals taking water from the stream then under consideration, and to make a map or plat showing the course of the stream, the location of each ditch, and the lands irrigated or susceptible of irrigation therefrom. Sections 872 and 873 are as follows:

> "Sec. 872. At the first regular meeting of the board of control, after the completion of such measurement by the state engineer, and the return of said evidence by said division superintendent, it shall be the duty of the board of control to make, and cause to be entered of record in its office, an order determining and establishing the several priorities of right to the use of waters of said stream, and the amounts of appropriations of the several persons claiming water from such stream, and the character and kind of use for which said appropriation shall be found to have been made. Each appropriation shall be determined in its priority and amount, by the time by which it shall have been made and the amount of water which shall have been applied for beneficial purposes. * * *
>
> "Sec. 873. As soon as practicable after the determination of the priorities of appropriation of the use of waters of any stream, it shall be the duty of the secretary to issue to each person, association or corporation represented in such determination, a certificate to be signed by the state engineer, as president of the board of control, and attested under seal by the secretary of said board, setting forth the name and post-office address of the appropriator; the priority number of such appropriations; the amount of water appropriated; and if such appropriation be for irrigation a description of the legal subdivisions of land to which said water is to be applied. * * * "

Provision is made for an appeal, by any party feeling himself aggrieved, from the decision of the board to the district court, and from that court to the supreme court.

Counsel for the plaintiff contend that the act of December 22, 1890, is unconstitutional, in so far as it confers upon the board of control authority to determine the priorities of rights to the use of water. * * * The position maintained by counsel is that a determination of the priorities of rights to the use of water involves solely a judicial inquiry into rights to property as between private parties, and that the jurisdiction to undertake such an investigation and adjudicate therein can be constitutionally lodged only in some court which is by article 5 of the constitution vested with judicial power. The statute nowhere attempts to devest the courts of any jurisdiction granted to them by the constitution to redress grievances and afford relief at law or in equity under the ordinary and well-known rules of procedure. A purely statutory proceeding is created, to be set in motion by no act or complaint of any injured party, but which in each instance is to be inaugurated by order of the board,—a proceeding which is to result, not in a judgment for damages to a party for injuries sustained, nor the issuance of any writ or process known to the law for the purpose of preventing the unlawful invasion of a party's rights or privileges; but the finality of the proceeding is a settlement or adjustment of the priorities of appropriation of the public waters of the state, and is followed by the issuance of a certificate to each appropriator, showing his relative standing among other claimants, and the amount of water to which he is found to be entitled. * * *

The other fundamental principles expressed in the constitution are that control of the public waters must be in the state, which, in providing for their use, shall equally guard all the various interests involved. Such control shall consist in a supervision of the waters, their appropriation, distribution, and diversion, by a board of control, to be composed of certain designated officers, with an officer of technical and practical knowledge and experience at its head; and priority of appropriation shall give the better right. Let us inquire into the nature and subject of the supervisory power of the board. * * * It has already been suggested that the supervision of the board affects individual appropriations, and concerns the distribution of water to individual claimants. Any effort to supervise and control the waters of the state, their appropriation and distribution, in the absence of an effective ascertainment of the several priorities of rights, must result in practical failure in times when official intervention is most required. In fact, that had been demonstrated under our former system. In the development of the irrigation problem under the rule of prior appropriation, perplexing questions are continually arising, of a technical and practical character. As between an investigation in the courts and by the board, it would seem that an administrative board, with experience and peculiar knowledge along this particular line, can in the first instance, solve the questions involved, with due regard to private and public interests, conduct the requisite investigation, and make the ascertainment of individual rights, with greater facility, at less expense to interested parties, and with a larger degree of satisfaction to all concerned. In the opinion of an able law writer upon this subject, the powers of the board of control in this respect constitute one of the most praiseworthy features of our legislation. He says: "In the state of Wyoming, at least, there will no longer be the ludicrous spectacle of learned judges solemnly decreeing the right to from two to ten times the amount of water flowing in a stream, or, in fact, amounts so great that the channel of the stream could not possibly carry them; thus practically leaving the questions at stake as unsettled as before." Kin. Irr. § 493. * * *

The determination required to be made by the board is, in our opinion, primarily administrative rather than judicial in character. The proceeding is one in which a claimant does not obtain redress for an injury, but secures evidence of title to a valuable right,—a right to use a peculiar public commodity. That evidence of title comes properly from an administrative board, which, for the state in its sovereign capacity, represents the public, and is charged with the duty of conserving public as well as private interests. The board, it is true, acts judicially; but the power exercised is quasi judicial only, and such as, under proper circumstances, may appropriately be conferred upon executive officers or boards. The jurisdiction bears some resemblance to that of the land department of the government concerning the disposal of the public lands. * * *

We are not persuaded that the act is void, as conferring judicial power upon the board in violation of the constitution. That the board was expected to exercise quasi judicial functions is apparent from that provision of section 2 of article 8 of the constitution requiring its decisions to be subject to review by the courts. * * *

Notes

1. **Limitations of private litigation.** Private litigation has its limitations in adjudicating water rights. In a suit between two appropriators, the trial court decreed that the plaintiff was the owner of the first right to divert the waters of the source and that the defendant was the owner of a large right, subject only to the prior right of the plaintiff. Other appropriators, claiming rights prior to both, sought a writ of prohibition to set aside the decree. Denied. "Although [the decrees are] general in form, and broad enough in language to include the whole world, they can have no such effect. They are binding on the parties to the action and their privies, but upon no one else. As to strangers claiming rights in the waters of the lake the decrees in no manner affect them. The decrees are not even evidence of adverse rights. Strangers may proceed as if the decrees had never been entered." State ex rel. McConihe v. Steiner, 109 P. 57, 60 (Wash. 1910).

The rights of third persons likewise have no effect upon a judgment as to the relative rights of the litigants. "Neither do we think that the trial court was called upon, at the instance of the defendants, entire strangers in every aspect to other appropriators, to inquire into and pass upon the question whether appropriators of water below the mouth of the proposed canal of appellee would be injured by the construction of the canal. The rights of such persons will not, of course, be injuriously affected by the decree in this cause, and *non constat* but that they may yet intervene for their own protection, if they deem that the construction of the canal will be an invasion of their rights, or that they may be willing to forego objection to the construction of the canal." Gutierres v. Albuquerque Land & Irrigation Co., 188 U.S. 545, 556-57 (1903).

Private litigation can even fail to adjudicate the relative rights of all parties to it. In a recent case, predecessors of plaintiff and defendants had been co-defendants in a 1916 adjudication. The trial court enjoined the defendants from diverting more water than was allocated to their predecessors in the 1916 judgment. Reversed. "Although the Poplar case adjudicated the rights of the Poplar Irrigation Company with respect to numerous upstream water users, there are many other users who were not parties to the action. Moreover, the decision does not purport to determine the rights of the various codefendants as among themselves. In short, the Poplar decision suffers from the inherent inability of private lawsuits to provide just the sort of 'comprehensive allocation' of water rights attributed to it by the trial court. As our Supreme Court has noted, 'This method of resolving controversies involving the rights of the users of water on the river is necessarily piecemeal, unduly expensive and obviously unsatisfactory.' It is just these sorts of shortcomings that a statutory streamwide adjudication is designed to overcome." Pleasant Valley Canal Co. v. Borror, 72 Cal. Rptr.2d 1, 17-18 (Ct. App. 1998).

See also State v. Haggerman Water Rights Owners, Inc., 947 P.2d 409 (Idaho 1997), holding that a decree in a private adjudication is not binding in a subsequent comprehensive statutory adjudication.

2. **Development of special procedures.** In 1881, Colorado enacted a special adjudication procedure with a unique round robin feature. All claimants within a water district were joined, any claim could be contested by any party, and the validity, quantity and priority of each water right was settled in relation to all of the others. Since a district covered only a part of a stream system, coordination between districts was accomplished by allowing users in one district to join in the proceedings in another, or to contest within four years the priorities awarded in another. The decrees were brought up to date from time to time and new uses were added to the list in supplemental adjudications, but no priority could be awarded that was earlier than the latest right adjudicated under the prior decree. Rights not brought to completion were awarded a conditional decree which could ripen into an appropriation if the water was later applied to beneficial use in compliance with the requirements for reasonable diligence. The procedures were modified and recodified in 1943. For descriptions of these early procedures, see Moses Lasky, From Prior Appropriation to Economic Distribution of Water by the State—Via Irrigation Administration, 1 Rocky Mtn. L. Rev. 1, 190-98 (1929).

The Colorado procedure served as the inspiration, if not the model, for the administrative and administrative-judicial procedures described in the principal case and in Note 4 below. The Colorado Water Rights Determination and Administration Act of 1969, Colo. Rev. Stat., §§ 37-92-101 to -602, consolidated all decreed water rights into new "tabulations" as described infra p. 168, Note 11.

Montana clung to the classic lawsuit, only slightly modified, until 1973. For the troubles and problems of the embattled and litigious appropriators of Montana, see Albert W. Stone, Are There Any Adjudicated Streams in Montana?, 19 Mont. L. Rev. 19 (1957); Albert W. Stone, Improving Montana Water Law, 20 Mont. L. Rev. 60, 63 (1958); Albert W. Stone, The Long Count on Dempsey; No Final Decision in Water Rights Adjudication, 31 Mont. L. Rev. 1 (1969); Albert W. Stone, Montana Water Rights—A New Opportunity, 34 Mont. L. Rev. 57 (1973). Professor Stone's role changed from that of a voice crying in the wilderness to that of a major prophet with the enactment of the Montana Water Use Act of 1973, Mont. Code Ann. §§ 85-2-101 to -123.

3. **Constitutional barriers to administrative adjudication.** The Wyoming court's views on administrative and constitutional law were quite advanced for the

period. See Lasky, supra Note 2, at 203-16. Texas adopted the Wyoming system in 1917, but it was struck down in Board of Water Engineers v. McKnight, 229 S.W. 301 (Tex. 1921), as unconstitutionally giving an administrative board judicial power over vested property rights. The constitutionality of subsequent legislation, the Texas Water Adjudication Act of 1967, Tex. Water Code Ann. §§ 11.301-11.341, was upheld in In re Adjudication of the Water Rights of the Upper Guadalupe Segment of Guadalupe River, 642 S.W.2d 438 (Tex. 1982). The court noted that prior to the act the water law of Texas had been in a "chaotic state," and ruled:

"A significant difference between the 1917 Irrigation Act and the procedure under the Water Rights Adjudication Act is that the agency does not make the final determination of rights. There is a two-step procedure. The Commission makes its determination which is followed by an automatic and mandatory judicial review. * * *

"By statute, the standard of review under the Adjudication Act is neither a substantial evidence review nor a de novo review. It is a review made independently of the Commission's adjudication, and a review exercised on those parts of the Commission's determination to which exceptions were timely leveled. In passing on the exceptions, the court may, as in the case now before us, hear additional evidence. Tex. Water Code Ann. § 11.321. The exceptions are the pleadings which the court acts upon with or without a jury trial. The burden of proof is upon the one who levels the exceptions. * * * We conclude that the act, unlike the statutes construed in *McKnight,* 111 Tex. 82, 229 S.W. 301, * * * provides a constitutional method for adjudication."

4. **Adjudication systems.** Most states have adopted one of several variations on the Wyoming theme, designed to combine in some degree the efficiency of the administrative action with the sanctity of a court decree. These systems are described and tabulated in Albert W. Stone, Montana Water Rights—A New Opportunity, 34 Mont. L. Rev. 57, 70-71 (1973):

"The Wyoming system authorizes the Board of Control to select streams for adjudication, to publish notice of the investigation and hearing, and (after a hearing by the Division Superintendent) to make the determination of rights which is conclusive and binding upon all. An aggrieved person may appeal to the courts.

"The Oregon system starts out similarly to the Wyoming system, in that the State Engineer publishes and mails notice, conducts an investigation and hearing, and makes a determination of all rights. But then this administrative order of determination is filed in a circuit court, where interested parties may file exceptions, and from which emanates a final court decree of adjudication which is conclusive and binding upon all, subject to appeal to the Supreme Court of Oregon.

"The Bien Code system derives its name from Morris Bien of the U.S. Reclamation Service who drafted this system of stream adjudication in 1903. It provides for an administrator such as the State Engineer to prepare a hydrographic survey and transmit it to the state Attorney General, who then brings an action in court based upon the Engineer's findings and determinations. Some of the states which use the Bien Code provide for publication of notice and a conclusive decree."

The various state adjudication statutes are classified and compared in A. Lynne Krogh, Water Right Adjudications in the Western States: Procedures, Constitutionality, Problems & Solutions, 30 Land & Water L. Rev. 9 (1995).

5. **Problems with comprehensive adjudications.** Modern adjudication statutes have not solved all of the problems:

"Many of the western states have entered into ambitious efforts for the comprehensive adjudication of water rights. Unfortunately, most of these states have encountered serious obstacles in their adjudication efforts. Water right claimants, courts, legislatures, and agencies involved in water right adjudications are deeply frustrated by the complexity and resultant length and cost of these adjudications.

"Montana, Idaho, and Arizona have the largest adjudication efforts currently underway. Montana is currently engaged in a statewide adjudication of water rights that began in 1979. Idaho is currently engaged in an adjudication of the Snake River Basin, including approximately 87% of the state, that began in 1987. Arizona is currently engaged in adjudications of the Little Colorado and Gila Rivers, including approximately 65% of the state, that began in 1978 and 1974 respectively.

"During the pendency of these adjudications, mounting frustration has garnered legislative attention in each of these states. Consideration of statutory revisions of both adjudication procedure and substantive water law is a priority item in the upcoming legislative session in Arizona. Idaho significantly revised its statute in 1994. The Montana adjudication statute has been the subject of revision in every session since the adjudication commenced, and is likely to be the subject of consideration in the next session * * *.

"Given the myriad issues and interests involved in water rights adjudications, it is no surprise that adjudication efforts face some very real problems. There are, however, some real solutions to these problems. The solutions may include enactment of laws to address substantive issues, or adoption of procedures to make adjudications more effective, whether by statute, formal judicial orders or agency rules, or informal judicial or agency practices. But, given the many issues and interests involved in water rights adjudications, complexity is a fact that no amount of substantive or procedural tinkering can make disappear. The real solution thus becomes the collective efforts of all participants to promote an effective adjudication." A. Lynn Krogh, supra Note 4, at 10-11.

6. **Constitutional limits on legislative efforts to streamline adjudications.** In San Carlos Apache Tribe v. Superior Court, 972 P.2d 179 (Ariz. 1999), the Arizona Supreme Court struck down a number of provisions adopted by the legislature in 1995 to expedite the Gila River and Little Colorado River adjudications referred to in the preceding note. The 1995 provisions fell into three general categories: (1) substantive provisions which were intended to clarify ambiguities in the law, (2) evidentiary rules and presumptions which were intended to simplify factual findings and legal determinations, and (3) changes to the adjudication process.

The court invalidated all of the substantive provisions. Although the court noted that the legislature has broad power to define substantive rules prospectively, it found that the provisions in the 1995 legislation were intended to be applied retroactively. The court determined that some of the provisions changed existing law and would, therefore, alter vested rights in violation of the due process clause of the Arizona Constitution. Other substantive provisions which perhaps only resolved ambiguities in the law, as opposed to changing it, were held to be invalid on the grounds that they would deprive the judicial branch of its exclusive power under the Arizona Constitution to define applicable law in a lawsuit. The court held that the substantive provisions were not even entitled to evidentiary consideration in construing ambiguous statutory provisions, noting that the legislature had no special insight into the legislative intent behind statutes that were enacted long ago.

The evidentiary provisions received a more mixed response, but many were stricken on grounds that they impermissibly interfered with the authority of the judicial branch to make factual and legal determinations in litigation. Those provisions that merely created presumptions or specified that certain matters were entitled to evidentiary consideration were generally upheld, but those that dictated factual or legal conclusions, such as a provision defining de minimis uses of water and a provision directing that unchallenged findings of the Arizona water agency must be incorporated into the court's decree, were held unconstitutional. Noting that all the parties agreed that procedural changes may be applied retroactively, the court upheld the changes to the adjudication process.

State ex rel. Higginson v. United States, 912 P.2d 614 (Idaho 1995), involved constitutional challenges to 1994 amendments to the Snake River adjudication statutes. Like the Arizona litigation, the challenges centered on separation of powers issues. Several procedural changes which addressed matters already governed by existing court rules were held to be inconsistent with a provision of the Idaho Constitution which permits the legislature to prescribe procedural rules for the lower courts only "when necessary." The Idaho Supreme Court upheld a provision specifying that the water agency's report constituted prima facie evidence, but like the Arizona Supreme Court, invalidated a provision which stated that unchallenged findings of the agency must be decreed as reported. The court also held that a provision requiring the district court to include provisions in its decree for administration of rights was not an impermissible delegation of executive branch powers to the judiciary.

Fremont-Madison Irrigation District & Mitigation Group v. Idaho Ground Water Appropriators, Inc., 926 P.2d 1301 (Idaho 1996), involved a second challenge to the 1994 amendments. This challenge involved so-called "amnesty statutes" which attempted to protect appropriators who had changed or enlarged their appropriations without complying with mandatory statutory procedures. In effect, the amnesty statutes allowed changes or enlargements which had been made unlawfully to be confirmed in the adjudication process. The amnesty statutes were found to be constitutional, in large part because changes or enlargements could be confirmed only if they did not cause harm to water rights existing at the time of change or enlargement. The court also found no separation of powers violation in a provision which specified the priority given to certain enlargements, stating that the legislature has the power to define the rights of claimants to water and may provide that a court shall decree those rights.

7. **Coordination of rights determined in different adjudications.** As to coordination of the priorities of parties to different adjudications of confluent streams, see Campbell v. Wyoming Development Co., 100 P.2d 124 (Wyo. 1940),

and Alamosa-LaJara Water Users Protection Ass'n v. Gould, 674 P.2d 914 (Colo. 1983).

8. **Adjudications involving federal and Indian water rights..** The United States and Indian tribes have extensive claims to water in the West. Many of these claims are associated with federal land ownership, which averages almost fifty percent in western states. See footnote 3, infra page 704. Adjudications involving water rights of the United States and Indian tribes present unique jurisdictional, procedural, and substantive complications, stemming largely from the sovereign immunity of the United States and Indian tribes and from the basis of rights in federal law, not state law. These complications are examined in Chapter 8, Section 3.

9. **Adjudication of rights in private proceeedings..** In states which provide for administrative adjudication of water rights, administrative agencies are typically not given exclusive jurisdiction, and unadjudicated rights may be litigated in suits between private parties. Territory of Hawaii v. Gay, 32 Hawaii 404 (1932); Crawford Co. v. Hathaway, 93 N.W. 781 (Neb. 1903). In Simmons v. Ramsbottom, 68 P.2d 153 (Wyo. 1937), the Board of Control had given plaintiff's rights a general date of "1884", and defendant's rights a date of "February 1884". Held, the court might determine the relative priorities without first resubmitting the case to the Board of Control. Conceding the power of the legislature to make the administrative proceeding exclusive, the court found no intent to do so in the statute. Similarly, the statutory procedures are not exclusive in states which utilize a judicial process for the general adjudication of water rights, and rights may be adjudicated in private litigation.

Although administrative water agencies do not have exclusive or primary jurisdiction, their decisions are final and binding on collateral attack. "The Board of Control was given complete and exclusive jurisdiction to make general adjudication of the waters of this state as to priority and amount to which the several appropriators are entitled. The jurisdiction of the courts is (aside from appeals) confined to determining the rights of the parties in individual cases to the extent that the Board has not acted." Campbell v. Wyo. Dev. Co., 100 P.2d 124 (Wyo. 1940).

10. **Adjudication of new rights.** After a general adjudication has been held, new rights are typically added to the list of priorities by procedures for separately adjudicating rights acquired by permits. The permit ripens into a license or certificate of appropriation, upon proof of completion of the works and application of the water to beneficial use. See, e.g., Wyo. Stat. Ann. § 41-4-511.

11. **Inaccurate records.** The water records in many states do not accurately reflect actual water use. In some states, many streams have never been adjudicated. In such states, rights which predate the adoption of a mandatory permit requirement are often not reflected in water rights records. Similarly, rights which are not created by appropriation—for example, Indian and federal reserved rights and riparian rights—are usually not reflected in the records of unadjudicated streams. In other cases, the adjudications are old and there is substantial divergence between rights as adjudicated and rights as exercised; e.g., changes in points of diversion or place and purpose of use have been made without following prescribed procedures or rights have been abandoned or forfeited (See Chapter 2, Section 4) but are still carried on the records. In addition, most states do not require that changes in ownership of water rights be recorded with water agencies.

For example, the ownership of a ranch and appurtenant water rights might be transferred from A to B, but there is no requirement to notify water officials that the water rights are now owned by B.

The best procedures for maintaining accurate records are probably found in Colorado. The Colorado Water Right Determination and Adjudication Act of 1969, Colo. Rev. Stat. §§ 37-92-101 to -602, described partially supra p. 124, Note 6, requires a continuous suit of adjudication in each of the state's seven water divisions. This procedure assures that incomplete appropriations (conditional rights) and newly completed appropriations are adjudicated and integrated into the water rights records on an ongoing basis. In addition, each division engineer is required to make periodic tabulations (quadrennially beginning in 1988) in order of seniority of all water rights within his division. These tabulations reflect judgments and decrees entered by the water court since the previous tabulation which determine, change, or otherwise affect water rights. Persons who wish to object to tabulations are permitted to do so, revisions deemed appropriate are made, and the tabulations are filed with the water court. The tabulations form the basis for the administration of water rights by the state engineer and divisions engineers. However, the tabulations are not adjudications and do not themselves alter water rights.

Each division engineer is also required to prepare a periodic abandonment list decennially, listing all rights which appear to have been partially or totally abandoned. After providing for an opportunity for protests and revision, these lists are filed with the water court. Once again, the statutes provide an opportunity for protests and a hearing. Thereafter, the water judge enters a decree which is conclusive as to rights determined to have been abandoned.

Major adjudication efforts underway in several western states will improve water records when completed. See supra p. 166, Note 5. Washington and Idaho established deadlines, under penalty of loss, for registration of claims not represented by permits, certificates, or licenses. See Idaho Code §§ 42-241 to -247; Wash. Rev. Code §§ 90.14.010 to -.121. Registration of a claim does not establish its validity in either state. Utah also provides for registration of pre-permit claims, but registration is not mandatory, and the primary effect of registration appears to be evidentiary. See Utah Code Ann. § 73-5-13. Nevada and Idaho require conveyances of water rights to be recorded with water officials. See Idaho Code § 42-248; Nev. Rev. Stat. 533.382 -.387. Failure to record a conveyance appears not to affect the validity of the water right in either state, but administrative notice of actions affecting water rights need only be given to the record owner. The Nevada statutes also provide that recording imparts notice of a transfer to subsequent purchasers of the water right. Nev. Rev. Stat. 533.383.

RETTKOWSKI v. DEPARTMENT OF ECOLOGY

Supreme Court of Washington, 1993.
122 Wash. 2d 219, 858 P.2d 232.

DURHAM, JUDGE. A group of ranchers who water their cattle at the aptly named Sinking Creek have complained to the Department of Ecology (Ecology) for over two decades about the detrimental effect on the creek's flow of groundwater pumping by irrigation farmers in the surrounding area. After numerous investigations, Ecology determined that there was a connection between the groundwater withdrawals and the diminished flow of the creek. Ecology also decided that the water rights of the various ranchers were superior to those possessed by the irrigation farmers. Accordingly, Ecology issued cease and desist orders which prohibited the irrigation farmers from making any further groundwater withdrawals. Through a complicated procedural history which will be explained below, the dispute was brought to this court to decide if Ecology possesses the authority to issue these orders. We hold that it does not. We also hold that the trial court correctly exercised its jurisdiction in hearing this matter. * * *

The resolution of this case turns on a fundamental rule of administrative law—an agency may only do that which it is authorized to do by the Legislature. The Administrative Procedure Act of 1988 (APA), RCW 34.05, specifically provides that a court "shall grant relief from an agency order * * * if it determines that * * * [t]he order is outside the statutory authority or jurisdiction of the agency conferred by any provision of law". RCW 34.05.570(3)(b).

Under RCW 90.03 (hereinafter the Water Code), a "first in time, first in right" rule is followed for appropriations of both groundwater and surface water. RCW 90.03.010. Ecology claims that it was attempting to follow this rule when it issued the cease and desist orders to the Irrigators. While Ecology cannot point to any statute which specifically authorizes the procedures it followed in issuing these orders, it argues that it derives inherent authority to do so from the penumbra of a number of statutes. Primarily, Ecology rests upon its enabling statute as vesting it with the plenary authority to protect senior water rights from encroachment or diminution by junior appropriators. That statute proclaims that Ecology "shall regulate and control the diversion of water in accordance with the rights thereto". RCW 43.21A.064(3). Ecology additionally points out that it is authorized to issue regulatory orders "whenever it appears to [Ecology] that a person is violating or is about to violate any of the provisions of [the Water Code]." RCW 43.27A.190.

However, these broad enabling statutes are silent as to how Ecology is to determine water rights in a regulatory context. This silence is even more telling when compared to the elaborate general adjudication process for determining water rights entrusted to the superior courts by RCW 90.03. Nowhere in Ecology's enabling statutes was it vested with similar authority to conduct general adjudications or even regulatory adjudications of water rights. An administrative agency cannot modify or amend a statute through its own regulation. The absence of a specific grant to Ecology to determine water rights, coupled with an explicit grant to another branch of government to do exactly that, makes Ecology's determination of such rights seemingly ultra vires.

Since Ecology has no explicit statutory authority to rely upon, it asks instead that we extend a number of previous cases to allow it the authority to make "tentative determinations" of the priorities of existing water rights in order to regulate. Ecology argues that it only "tentatively determined" that the Irrigators' rights were junior to those of the Ranchers, and that a final determination would occur if the PCHB [Pollution Control Hearing Board] hearings were allowed to proceed. [Appeals from Ecology decisions are generally heard by the PCHB]

There are two problems with this argument. First, the concept of "tentative determinations" in the cases cited by Ecology was developed in a different context. Each of those cases dealt with the authority of Ecology (or its predecessor agency) to grant permits to appropriate water. The inquiry in that situation is relatively straightforward: is there water available to apportion, is the proposed use beneficial and not detrimental to the public interest, and is there any conflict with existing water rights. RCW 90.03.290. In the permitting situation, Ecology's determination is limited to tentatively determining whether there are existing water rights with which the proposed use will conflict. Ecology investigates an application for a permit to tentatively determine the existence of water rights and the availability of water. If a conflict exists, it is resolved by denying the permit, not by determining who has the better claim. Ecology does not have to pass upon the validity of such existing or claimed rights in order to determine a potential conflict.

Once the permit has been granted, the situation is significantly different. Permit holders have a vested property interest in their water rights to the extent that the water is beneficially used. Unlike the permitting process, in which Ecology only tentatively determines the existence of claimed water rights, a later decision that an existing permit conflicts with another claimed use and must be regulated necessarily involves a determination of the priorities of the conflicting uses. In order to properly prioritize competing claims, it is necessary to examine when the use was begun, whether the claim had been filed pursuant to the water registration act, RCW 90.14 and whether it had been lost or diminished over time. These determinations necessarily implicate important property rights. It is because of the complicated nature of such inquiries, and their far-reaching effect, that the Legislature has entrusted the superior courts with responsibility therefor. RCW 90.03.110.

The second problem with Ecology's argument that it was only "tentatively determining" water rights is that the PCHB has no jurisdiction to conduct adjudicative hearings regarding such rights. The statute creating the PCHB specifically forbids it to conduct hearings on "[p]roceedings by [Ecology] relating to general adjudications of water rights". RCW 43.21B.110(2)(c). Both Ecology and the PCHB argue that this case did not involve a general adjudication, but rather an appeal of an administrative order issued by Ecology, which would be within the jurisdiction of the PCHB. RCW 43.21B.110(1)(b), (c).

This bootstrap argument is unpersuasive. The administrative orders in question were based upon Ecology's determinations of the existence, quantities, and relative priorities of various legally held water rights. Ecology cannot sustain the argument that it conducted only a little, or a limited, or a tentative, adjudication, so that it is then permitted to have the PCHB conduct a more thorough adjudication. The PCHB cannot adjudicate priorities between water users. Nor can Ecology determine allegedly senior water rights outside of the context of a general adjudication. * * *

Were Ecology allowed to allocate water resources solely on the basis of its own determination of priorities, general adjudications might become unnecessary. Ecology could circumvent the general adjudication process by conducting minor, ad hoc investigations and subsequent piecemeal adjudications throughout the state. This result could prove detrimental to the general adjudication process statewide in light of Ecology's statutory role as the initiator of general adjudications in the superior court. RCW 90.03.110. There would be no reason to grant a petition to initiate a general adjudication if Ecology could conduct its own investigation and solve the conflict as it sees fit. We have previously refused the pleas of potential appropriators to narrow the scope and use of general adjudications, and we can see no reason to treat Ecology differently. * * *

[U]nder the Water Code, a claim which allegedly dates back to the turn of the century may be found, upon closer examination, to be flawed for a variety of reasons. Ecology's orders assumed that the Ranchers' claims were entirely valid without ever undertaking the formal statutory process necessary to make such a determination. * * *

To summarize, we hold that Ecology had no authority to issue these cease and desist orders without first utilizing a general adjudication pursuant to RCW 90.03 in order to determine the existence, amount, and priorities of the water rights claimed in the Sinking Creek basin. The Superior Court properly exercised its authority, and we affirm its order holding the cease and desist orders null and void. Although the conclusion Ecology reached as to the relative priorities of the water rights in the Sinking Creek basin may ultimately prove to be correct, the only method of ascertaining this will be through a general adjudication.

Notes

1. **Effect of *Rettkowski.*** Can the Department of Ecology ever enforce water rights? Even on a fully adjudicated stream, doesn't the enforcement of rights implicitly require an "adjudication" that none of the rights have been abandoned or forfeited? Isn't DOE's enforcement authority even more questionable if there has been an assertion by an appropriator that other rights have been abandoned or forfeited? Wouldn't a determination by DOE that forfeiture has or has not occurred be a forbidden adjudication? Does the case mean that adjudicated rights must be administered as adjudicated?

The court in the principal case stated that DOE can make "tentative determinations" of water rights in connection with the issuance of permits. This concept was extended in Okanogan Wilderness League v. Town of Twisp, 947 P.2d 732 (Wash. 1997), to include determinations regarding beneficial use of water rights made by DOE in ruling on applications for changes in use of water rights. Does the concept of "tentative determinations" as developed by the Washington Supreme Court include the sorts of determinations discussed in the prior paragraph?

2. **Comprehensive administration of rights.** In some western states the actual distribution of water and regulation of headgates and storage works is

performed by a state official, sometimes known as a water commissioner, working under a central state water agency. The Colorado system is typical:

"Here is an entire state * * * divided into districts covering every stream, creek, or runlet from which water is taken. And up and down these streams, creeks and runlets patrol in every irrigating season a small army of commissioners and deputies who have absolutely complete control of all the water. Not a drop may be diverted not only without their consent but without their actually setting the gates and superintending the diversion. All the districts are combined into divisions along drainage lines, and in each division there is an engineer, a captain over the privates; to him come frequent reports, perhaps daily, perhaps telegraphic, of the flow in every creek, of the rainfall in the headwaters and the mountains, from which he calculates the amount of water which will flow into each district on each day, and upon which, knowing from his records who is entitled to water, in what order, and how much, he 'marshals' the water of all the tributaries in the area and orders its distribution, perhaps from day to day, so that those who are entitled to water shall receive it, whether they be ditch or reservoir owners. At the top is the state engineer who commands the whole array. It is a most complete police system, controlling every phase of the distribution; and more." Moses Lasky, From Prior Appropriation to Economic Distribution of Water by the State, 1 Rocky Mtn. L. Rev. 161, 262 (1929).

The water commissioner's acts are ministerial, comparable to those of a sheriff or police officer, so that his regulation of a headgate requires no notice or hearing. Hamp v. State, 118 P. 653 (Wyo. 1911). Disregard of his orders, or opening a headgate closed by him, is in most states a misdemeanor. Persons aggrieved by his acts may appeal to his supervisor and eventually to the central state water agency and to the courts. However, the administrative law doctrine of "exhaustion of administrative remedies" seems to have no application here. The failure to appeal from an adverse decision of the commissioner up through the administrative hierarchy does not make his action binding on the courts in a later proceeding between two appropriators. Ryan v. Tutty, 78 P. 661 (Wyo. 1904). Nor does the doctrine of "prior resort" apply in Wyoming. An appropriator aggrieved by another's unlawful diversion may sue for damages or for an injunction without first calling upon the water commissioner to regulate the ditches. Van Buskirk v. Red Buttes Land & Live Stock Co., 156 P. 1122 (Wyo. 1916). Not so in New Mexico. A downstream senior on a regulated stream "must make his needs known," and cannot sue for damage to crops because upstream juniors took all the water, when he did not serve a demand on either the water master or the State Engineer. Worley v. United States Borax & Chemical Corp., 428 P.2d 651 (N.M. 1967).

3. **Subordination of unadjudicated rights.** For many years Idaho law allowed both "statutory" water rights obtained in compliance with the permit statute and "constitutional" water rights self-initiated by diverting water and putting it to beneficial use. Idaho Code § 42-607 directs watermasters distributing water in time of shortage to treat constitutional rights which have never been adjudicated as "subsequent to any adjudicated, decreed, permit, or licensed right" regardless of alleged priority dates. In Nettleton v. Higginson, 558 P.2d 1048 (Idaho 1977), a plaintiff claiming that his prior unadjudicated right had been subordinated to junior recorded rights challenged the constitutionality of the statute on three grounds: deprivation of property without due process, denial of equal

protection, and taking of property without just compensation. The court found the statute constitutional in all respects.

4. **Procedural problems in suits against water officials.** Suits by an appropriator against water officials raise difficult procedural problems of party joinder and res judicata. In Mitchell Irrigation District v. Whiting, 136 P.2d 502 (Wyo. 1943), a senior appropriator sued for a mandatory injunction requiring the water commissioner to close the headgates of junior ditches above the plaintiff's point of diversion. Held, the junior appropriators were indispensable parties and must be joined in the suit. In Merrill v. Bishop, 237 P.2d 186 (Wyo. 1951), a senior sued for an injunction against the water commissioner closing his headgate for the benefit of downstream juniors. Held, the juniors are not indispensable parties. How can these be distinguished? See also McLean v. Farmers' Highline Canal & Reservoir Co., 98 P. 16 (Colo. 1908). In an action by A against a water commissioner, judgment by default was entered enjoining defendant from closing A's headgate except in favor of prior appropriators named in a particular decree. In a later action by A against B, an appropriator claiming under another decree, it was held that the first suit was not res judicata as to B, even though B had notice of the first action and had been requested to defend it. Lower Latham Ditch Co. v. Louden Irrigating Canal Co., 60 P. 629 (Colo. 1900). On the other hand, where the first action was between appropriators, it was said: "[T]he question cannot be relitigated between the same parties or their privies, and the defendants, water officials, are in privity with the Ft. Lyon Company. They have no interest of their own. They must obey the decree." On application for rehearing this was qualified as follows: "It is urged that the water officials are not privies to the Ft. Lyon Company. Perhaps not technically, but what we mean is that they must turn out the water according to the judgment of the court, and so are bound thereby as if they had been parties thereto." Reorganized Catlin Consol. Canal Co. v. Hinderlider, 253 P. 389 (Colo. 1927).

5. **Reference of matters to water agencies.** In Laramie Rivers Co. v. LeVasseur, 202 P.2d 680 (Wyo. 1949), plaintiff began an action in the district court for a declaratory judgment as to the relative rights of the parties, appropriators from the same stream. Defendant had previously obtained a permit to construct a reservoir, and after the bringing of the action commenced proceedings before the Board of Control for the adjudication of its right. The Board decreed to defendant a right, by relation, prior to plaintiff's right. Plaintiff appealed to the district court, the appeal was consolidated with the action, and the court confirmed the adjudication of the Board and ruled against the plaintiff in the action. On appeal to the supreme court, plaintiff contended that since the district court first acquired jurisdiction of the subject matter, the Board was without jurisdiction.

The court said: "But a not dissimilar point arose in the case of Crawford Co. v. Hathaway, 67 Neb. 325, 93 N.W. 781, 60 L.R.A. 889. There is a board in Nebraska similar to the Board of Control in this state, and in the creation of which the legislature of Nebraska followed the Wyoming laws, as stated in the foregoing case. Wiel on Water Rights, 3rd Ed., at 1106, refers the foregoing case, and states that while it was held that courts have the right to adjudicate water rights, it was also held 'that it is within the discretion of the court to remand the parties to their remedies by application to the board.' See 93 N.W. 793. There is good reason for that. Irrigation matters frequently involve many technicalities in connection with which courts cannot be expected to be experts, while the members of the Board of

Control supposedly are. Now, if the trial court would have had the right to ask the parties to go and have the matters of priorities first determined by the Board of Control, there would be no reason to hold that the parties may not themselves initiate proceedings before it, at least in the absence of the court's objection, if, in the meantime, the action brought in court has not been finally determined, as is true in this case. In other words, we can find no good reason why the court may not avail itself of the aid which may be furnished by having a previous adjudication of the right made by the Board of Control, just as it might refer a case to a referee, and that is in substance the situation in this case." Id. at 694-95.

The California court has repeatedly reminded the trial courts of their power to call upon the state's administrative agencies for expert assistance. In one such case the court said, "The facilities of the commission can, in this manner, be made available to the trial court and that court can thus secure independent and impartial expert advice not colored by personal interest. Incidentally, the procedure outlined in this section will secure representation of the state in such actions, thus insuring the protection of the rights of the public." Tulare Irrigation Dist. v. Lindsay-Strathmore Irrigation Dist., 45 P.2d 972 (Cal. 1935). See also Kans. Stat. Ann. § 82a-725.

What would prompt the reverse practice, of administrative use of the courts to enforce the water laws? See a 1973 Wyoming enactment:

"(a) Upon the request of the state engineer, the attorney general shall bring suit in the name of the state of Wyoming, in the proper district court, to enjoin the unlawful appropriation, diversion or use of the waters of the state, or the waste or loss thereof. A showing of injury in such suits shall not be required as a condition to the issuance of any temporary restraining order, preliminary or permanent injunction. If an appeal is taken from the judgment or decree entered by the district court in such suit, it shall be the duty of the supreme court, at the request of one (1) of the parties, to advance the appeal to the head of its docket and give it precedence over all other civil causes in the hearing and determination thereof." Wyo. Stat. Ann. § 41-2-111.

6. **Jurisictional problems caused by federalism.** The existence of federal and state courts under our federal system sometimes complicates the administration and enforcement of water rights. United States v. Alpine Land & Reservoir Company, 174 F.3d 1007 (9th Cir. 1999), involved an appeal to a state court of a decision of the Nevada State Engineer authorizing the transfer of several water rights which had previously been adjudicated by the United States District Court for Nevada. On a motion by the State Engineer, the United States District Court enjoined the state court proceeding, holding that it had exclusive jurisdiction to hear the appeal. The Ninth Circuit affirmed, relying on the principle that the court which first gains jurisdiction over a "*res,*" exercises exclusive jurisdiction over actions involving that *res.*

State Engineer v. South Fork Band of Te-Moak Tribe of Western Shoshone Indians, 339 F.3d 804 (9th Cir. 2003), involved irrigation water rights adjudicated by the Nevada Sixth Judicial District Court pursuant to the Nevada general adjudication statutes. The irrigated lands and associated rights were later transferred to the United States for use by the Te-Moak Tribe. The Tribe denied Nevada water officials access to its lands to regulate the rights and stopped paying associated regulatory fees, and the water officials initiated contempt proceedings in the Sixth Judicial District Court. The United States, joined as a necessary party, removed the case to federal district court. Eventually, the federal district court abstained in favor of the state court proceedings under Colorado River Water Conservation District v. United States, infra p. 714. On appeal, the Ninth Circuit ruled that the federal district court should have dismissed, rather than abstained, for want of jurisdiction. Applying the principles relied on in *Alpine,* which it labeled the doctrine of "prior exclusive jurisdiction," the Ninth Circuit held that the state court obtained jurisdiction over the water rights when it adjudicated them, thereby precluding the federal court from exercising jurisdiction over the rights.

A critical fact in both of the Ninth Circuit decisions was the explicit or implicit reservation of continuing jurisdiction by the court adjudicating the rights. Consequently, the doctrine of prior exclusive jurisdiction should not be applicable to suits to administer rights which were adjudicated administratively or to suits to administer rights which were adjudicated judicially if the adjudicating court did not explicitly or implicitly reserve continuing jurisdiction. Thus, a federal court would have jurisdiction in a dispute involving administration of water rights adjudicated statutorily in Wyoming, where the process is administrative (assuming other requirements for federal jurisdiction were met), but would not have jurisdiction in an identical situation in Nevada, where a judicial process in which the court retains continuing jurisdiction is used for statutory adjudications. Should the jurisdiction of federal courts depend on the method of statutory adjudication which a state has adopted?

Colorado River Water Conservation District v. United States, infra p. 714, involved concurrent suits in state and federal courts to adjudicate water rights of the federal government. The Supreme Court ruled that both courts had jurisdiction, but held that the federal court should abstain in favor of the state court proceedings even though the federal court proceedings had been commenced first. Is the decision in *Te-Moak*, consistent with *Colorado River?* In reconciling *Colorado River*, the Ninth Circuit said: "[The issue in *Colorado River*] is a question of *adjudication.* In contrast, the question here is one of administration. *Colorado River* stands for the unremarkable proposition that, *before* a res has been seized, both federal and state courts enjoy concurrent jurisdiction and may commence proceedings to decide questions about the allocation of water rights. * * * *Colorado River* is thus entirely consistent with the doctrine of prior exclusive jurisdiction. The doctrine is only triggered after a court has acquired jurisdiction over the res." *Id.* at 813. Is this explanation convincing? Didn't the federal court in *Colorado River* first acquire jurisdiction over the "res"? If not, why not?

7. **Regulation of dam safety.** State regulatory statutes commonly give the state engineer or an equivalent agency control over engineering features affecting the safety of dams, the adequacy of works, etc. It is the responsibility of one who applies for and obtains a water right to provide at his own expense a proper control mechanism and measuring device. Vandehey v. Wheeler, 507 P.2d 831 (Or. Ct. App. 1973).

SECTION 4. LOSS

A. Abandonment

EAST TWIN LAKES DITCHES AND WATER WORKS, INC. v. BOARD OF COUNTY COMMISSIONERS

Supreme Court of Colorado, 2003
76 P.3d 918

RICE, JUSTICE. East Twin Lakes Ditches and Water Works, Inc., ("ETLD") appeals the water court's holding that the water right in the Derry Ditch No. 1, owned by the Lake County Board of County Commissioners ("Lake County"), was not abandoned. ETLD contends that (1) the water right was abandoned due to non-use for approximately thirty years; and (2) the decision by the predecessors of Lake County to not line the ditch was affirmative proof of that abandonment. * * *

The Derry Ditch No. 1 is a senior water right with an appropriation date of 1879 and an adjudication date of 1904 * * * for the irrigation of two hundred acres on what is commonly known as the "Hallenbeck Ranch" in Lake County. * * * In 1972, the Hallenbeck Ranch and all of its water rights were purchased by the Twin Lakes Recreation Land Investment Company ("TLR") * * *. TLR purchased the Hallenbeck Ranch and its water rights with the intent of reselling it for residential development. Despite apparently diligent sales efforts, however, the ranch and its water rights did not sell until 1998 when they were purchased by Lake County.

During the entire twenty-six years that TLR owned the property, the ranch and its water rights were managed by Walter Clotworthy. Throughout this period of time, Clotworthy was unable to get the Derry Ditch No. 1 to carry water more than one-half to one mile down its length. The first section of the ditch was evidently so porous that even the full decree of four cfs would travel only a short distance before it seeped into the bottom of the ditch and disappeared. Clotworthy testified that at various times during his tenure he did grading and shovel work on the ditch in an unsuccessful attempt to improve its carrying capacity. He also made numerous diversions of water into the ditch in a similarly unsuccessful effort to saturate and seal the bottom of the ditch. * * *

[In 1985, Mickelson, one of TLR's general partners,] raised the issue of lining the ditch to the limited partners at a partnership meeting. Because the amount of money that could be assessed the limited partners had already been exhausted, and because it was believed that a sale of the ranch was imminent, Mickelson was unable to secure the partnership funds necessary to line the ditch. As a result, the Derry Ditch No. 1 remained functionally inoperable for approximately another ten years, up until and after the ranch and water rights were sold to Lake County in 1998. * * *

Lake County concedes that the approximately thirty-year period between 1972 and 2002 during which the Derry Ditch No. 1 water right was not applied to beneficial use gave rise to a presumption of abandonment. The county contends, however, that there was no intent to abandon, that the county and TLR engaged in numerous activities that were inconsistent with an intent to abandon, and that the water court correctly concluded that the presumption had been rebutted. We agree. Our examination of the record reveals sufficient evidence to support the trial court's finding of no abandonment

The principles of law governing the issue of abandonment in Colorado are well established. "Abandonment of a water right" is defined as "the termination of a water right in whole or in part as a result of the intent of the owner thereof to discontinue permanently the use of all or part of the water available thereunder." § 37-92-103(2), 10 C.R.S. (2002). This court has consistently held that a finding of abandonment requires the concurrence of two elements: a sustained period of non-use and an intent to abandon. The objector must prove abandonment by a preponderance of the evidence.

Because intent is a subjective element that is difficult for a complainant to prove by direct evidence, Colorado law provides that failure to apply water to a beneficial use for a period of ten years creates a rebuttable presumption of abandonment. § 37-92-402(11), 10 C.R.S. (2002). The presumption of abandonment shifts the burden of going forward to the water rights owner, but is insufficient in and of itself to prove abandonment. Rather, the element of intent remains the touchstone of the abandonment analysis, and the owner of the water right can rebut the presumption of abandonment by introducing evidence sufficient to excuse the non-use or demonstrate an intent not to abandon. Acceptable justifications for an unreasonably long period of non-use are limited, however, and a successful rebuttal requires objective and credible evidence, not merely subjective statements of intent by the water rights owner.

A review of our precedent reveals a number of different factors that Colorado courts have considered as indicative of an intent not to abandon a water right. Significantly, although failure to put the water to beneficial use may give rise to the presumption of abandonment in the first instance, it is not the standard by which the second element, intent to abandon, has been measured. Instead, in determining whether or not an owner intended to abandon his water right, Colorado courts have looked at such factors as: (1) repair and maintenance of diversion structures, (2) attempts to put the water to beneficial use, (3) active diversion records and non-appearance of the water right on the State Engineer's abandonment list, (4) diligent efforts to sell the water right, (5) filing documents to protect, change, or preserve the right, (6) leasing the water right, and (7) economic or legal obstacles to exercising the water right. While none of these factors is necessarily conclusive, their cumulative weight, as assessed by the water court, may be enough to rebut a presumption of abandonment. On the other hand, if these factors are insufficient or nonexistent, only then is the failure to put the water to a beneficial use enough by itself to sustain a finding of abandonment.

Because resolution of an abandonment case is largely based upon the weighing of evidence and assessing the credibility of witnesses, this court has consistently held that the water court's resolution of an abandonment case will not be disturbed on appeal unless the evidence contained in the record is "wholly insufficient to support the decision." *Haystack Ranch,* 997 P.2d at 552; *Danielson,* 775 P.2d at 19. It is therefore incumbent upon this court to search the record for any evidence in support of the decision, and if successful, to uphold the decision even if, had this court been the trier of fact, it might have held differently. With these principles in mind, we now turn to the task of determining whether there was sufficient evidence in the record of this case to support the water court's decision that the Derry Ditch No. 1 was not abandoned in the thirty-year period between 1972 and 2002.

Two of the TLR general partners (Mickelson and Sims), Clotworthy, and a former Lake County Commissioner all testified that despite the problems with the carrying capacity of the Derry Ditch No. 1, it was never the intent of Lake County or TLR to abandon the water right. To the contrary, each asserted that the water rights associated with the Hallenbeck Ranch were exceedingly important assets, and of those rights, the Derry Ditch No. 1 was the most important because it was the most senior. Mickelson and Sims also indicated that all of the Hallenbeck Ranch water rights were critical components of their sales efforts. These statements, although valid evidence to be weighed by the water court, are necessarily subjective and therefore fall well short of the quantum of proof necessary to rebut a presumption of abandonment.

There is, however, an abundance of other objective evidence in the record regarding actions taken by TLR and Lake County that were inconsistent with an intent to abandon the Derry Ditch No. 1. These include attempts to repair the ditch and divert water, the filing of legal documents with regard to the water right, the fact that the water right never appeared on the State Engineer's abandonment list, the lease of the water right, diligent efforts to sell the ranch and water rights, and financial obstacles to exercising the water right. We turn now to an examination of this evidence.

There was a substantial amount of evidence in the record regarding maintenance and repair of the Derry Ditch No. 1. TLR engaged Clotworthy as an on-site ranch manager almost immediately upon TLR's acquisition of the Hallenbeck Ranch in 1972. * * * Clotworthy made a number of attempts during his tenure to maintain the Derry Ditch No. 1 and apply the water to beneficial use. He testified that during the time period from 1985 to 1990, and perhaps earlier, he used a tractor, grader, and shovel in attempts to get the ditch to carry water. * * *

There was also evidence introduced at trial regarding attempts—although unsuccessful—to put the water right to beneficial use in the years between 1972 and 2002. Clotworthy testified that he diverted water into the ditch a number of times over his years at the ranch, either in an attempt to saturate and seal the bottom of the ditch, or to check the success of his grading efforts. * * * The Derry Ditch No. 1 was never listed during this time on the State Engineer's abandonment list.

TLR and Lake County also took legal and investigative actions during their years of ownership that were consistent with the use and protection of their water rights. Sims testified that during his involvement with the partnership, TLR actively investigated several other water rights applications and filed one statement of opposition, to ensure that its water rights were protected. In 1995, TLR filed several applications with the water court to correct invalid points of diversions in its water decrees, including a filing for the Derry Ditch No. 1. In 1998, Lake County filed jointly with the City of Aurora to the water court requesting that the Derry Ditch No. 1 be used as an alternate point of diversion in a change case.

The next evidence presented at trial of an intent not to abandon was the lease of the Derry Ditch No. 1. In 1980, TLR leased the Hallenbeck Ranch and all its water rights to Box Creek Mining Company, a business entity initially owned by Clotworthy. * * * The venture ultimately failed, however, evidently due to partnership squabbles and the failure to obtain financing, and the lease was terminated in 1992. Regardless of the failure of the mining venture, the lease of the Derry Ditch No. 1 by TLR to Box Creek Mining Company, even for an undecreed use, demonstrates an intent to not abandon the water right. * * *

Although not specific to the Derry Ditch No. 1, intent not to abandon was next demonstrated by TLR's consistent efforts to sell the ranch and its water rights throughout the duration of its ownership. * * * TLR introduced a voluminous exhibit at trial detailing the partnership's sales efforts from 1975 through 1998, including documentation of marketing efforts, preliminary letters of interest, sales proposals, two signed option agreements, and two signed sales contracts (which ultimately failed). * * *

The final type of evidence this court has considered in rebutting a presumption of abandonment is the presence of legal or economic obstacles to exercising a water right. * * * Such conditions were arguably present here; testimony indicated that the partnership declined to line the ditch because the amount of money that could be assessed the limited partners had already been exhausted, and because it was believed that a sales contract was imminent.

ETLD argues, however, that the partnership's failure to act, followed by approximately another ten years of non-use is instead affirmative proof of abandonment. The trial court took the opposite view, finding that the request Mickelson made to the limited partners to line the ditch was "indicative of a desire to maintain the ditch and is contrary to an intent to abandon." We find no error in the trial court's conclusion. The task before the court was to determine the intent of the partnership, as an entity, with regard to the use or abandonment of the water right. Such intent would be better evidenced by the general partner's actions than by an investment decision made by limited partners who likely had no familiarity whatsoever with the Derry Ditch No. 1.

In summary, the record indicated that Lake County and TLR took a number of actions inconsistent with an intent to abandon. * * * None of these actions was by itself conclusive nor sufficient to rebut the presumption of abandonment. Indeed, over a period of thirty years, many of these activities were inconsistent, sporadic, and subject to contradictory interpretations. Nevertheless, taken as a whole, we find there was sufficient evidence in the record to support the water court's finding of no abandonment. The water court's findings of fact in an abandonment case are accorded considerable deference and we will not reverse absent a showing of abuse of discretion. There was no such abuse here. * * *

HOBBS, JUSTICE, dissenting: * * * Beneficial use is essential to the establishment of a water right and its perpetuation. Knapp v. Colorado River Water Conservation Dist., 131 Colo. 42, 52, 279 P.2d 420, 425 (1955). "Speculation on the market, or sale expectancy, is wholly foreign to the principle of keeping life in a proprietary right and is no excuse for failure to perform that which the law requires." *Id.* at 56, 279 P.2d at 427; see Southeastern Colo. Water Conservancy Dist. v. Twin Lakes Assocs., 770 P.2d 1231, 1238 (Colo. 1989).

Our cases repeatedly provide that "[c]ontinued and unexplained nonuse of a water right for an unreasonable period of time creates a rebuttable presumption of *intent* to abandon." City & County of Denver v. Snake River Water Dist., 788 P.2d 772, 776 (Colo. 1990)(emphasis added); Here, the nonuse is explained, but this explanation supports abandonment, and not the water court's conclusion that the presumption of abandonment was rebutted. The explanation for nonuse is that the ditch could not deliver the water to its place of use, and the owner did not wish to make the investment an actual water user would be required to make to maintain the priority of the water right. * * *

Affirmatively deciding not to make repairs necessary to utilize a water right is convincing evidence of intent to abandon it. Southeastern Colo. Water Conservancy Dist., 770 P.2d at 1241 (upholding finding of abandonment when ditches deteriorated and were not repaired); Masters Inv. Co. v. Irrigationists Ass'n, 702 P.2d 268, 270 (Colo. 1985) (upholding finding of abandonment where ditch had washed away and was not replaced). Evidence of non-repair is especially persuasive where the owner ignored advice that the repairs were required. *Haystack Ranch,* 997 P.2d at 553. Failure to maintain the entire length of the ditch is also evidence of intent to abandon. Southeastern Colo. Water Conservancy Dist., 770 P.2d at 1236-37.

We have considered economic difficulty a justifiable excuse for nonuse in very limited circumstances. We recognized that the Great Depression, material and labor shortages during World War II, and federal regulatory requirements can provide an excuse for nonuse. Hallenbeck v. Granby Ditch & Reservoir Co., 160 Colo. 555, 568, 420 P.2d 419, 426 (1966). However, run-of-the-mill economic difficulties are not recognized. "Nonuse resulting from present economic difficulties, coupled with an expectation of a more favorable economic climate for future use, will not constitute justifiable excuse." Southeastern Colo. Water Conservancy Dist., 770 P.2d at 1238.

Without doubt, the investment partnership tried repeatedly to sell the ranch and the water rights. However, in *Knapp,* we held that intent to sell a water right, including listing the right with a real estate agent, was not sufficient to overcome the presumption of abandonment raised by a long period of nonuse. 131 Colo. at 55-56, 279 P.2d at 427.

I would distinguish our decision in Danielson v. City of Thornton, 775 P.2d 11 (Colo. 1989), from this case. There, a developer acquired the water rights for use in a central water system for a subdivision it was creating. It sought to obtain a change of point of diversion for the wells to effectuate its use. Upon finding that a centralized water system would be impractical, it diligently and continuously attempted to sell the water rights to a party who would use the water under the water rights. The wells were in good condition and capable of operation throughout the efforts to sell them. Within eight years, the developer sold the water rights. The water court held that, under the circumstances, eight years was a reasonable time period to effectuate sale of the water rights. On appeal, we applied a legal standard that took into account the "totality of the evidence in evaluating whether a water right [had] been abandoned" and concluded that it had not. In contrast, in this case, the investment partnership never had a use for the water, never effectuated a use, and when put on actual notice of the need to maintain the water rights, affirmatively decided not to repair the structure so the right could be utilized under its decree.

As we recognized in *Danielson,* efforts to sell the water right, in light of other evidence in the case, may be sufficient to overcome the presumption of abandonment arising from a prolonged period of nonuse. But, we also said that the presumption of abandonment is a strong one. The *Knapp* anti-speculation basis for the abandonment doctrine continues to be good law, in my view. * * *

I disagree with the Majority conclusion that there is competent evidence in the record to rebut the strong presumption of abandonment arising from the investment partnership's prolonged period of nonuse. The investment partnership's decision not to repair the ditch is factually no different from those cases in which water courts and we have declared abandonment based upon prolonged failure to repair. Here, the evidence of holding the right for speculation is manifest. Like *Knapp,* this case involved twenty-six years of nonuse and "[o]n the whole their conduct is much more indicative of being speculative than operative." 131 Colo. at 51, 279 P.2d at 425. Accordingly, I would reverse the judgment of the water court and, therefore, respectfully dissent.

Notes

1. **Questions on intent.** Can the difference in the positions taken by Justices Rice and Hobbs be explained by concluding that Justice Rice focuses on intent to abandon the water right while Justice Hobbs focuses on intent to abandon the use of water authorized by the right? If so, which approach is most consistent with the principle of beneficial use? If the correct focus is on abandonment of the water right, why would anyone intentionally abandon a valuable right, particularly a "senior water right?" Justice Rice says that "subjective statements of intent" are not sufficient to rebut the presumption of abandonment. Why not, if intent truly is the "touchstone" of abandonment? Certainly, present statements of past intent may be highly suspect from an evidentiary standpoint, but what about past statements? For example, what if an owner has given regular notices to water officials of the intent to retain a right? In terms of evidencing intent, what is the difference between such notices and efforts to sell a water right? Is the difference

between mere statements and the acts relied on by Justice Rice to rebut the presumption of abandonment primarily one of effort rather than intent?

2. **Contrary authority on rebuttal evidence?** In In re Adjudication of the Clark Fork River, the court reaffirmed several recent decisions holding that to rebut the presumption of abandonment a party "must establish 'some fact or condition excusing the long period of nonuse, not mere expression of hope or desire reflecting a 'gleam-in-the eye philosophy' regarding future uses of the water.'" 908 P.2d 1353, 1355 (Mont. 1995), (quoting CF&I Steel Corp. v. Purgatoire River Water Conservancy Dist., 515 P.2d 456 (Colo. 1973)). Can efforts to sell a water right be used to rebut the presumption in Montana? If "must" means must, is intent really an element of abandonment in Montana?

3. **Miscellaneous holdings.** Where an appropriator sold land with a water right, and later repurchased the land and irrigated with water obtained by renting other water rights, he abandoned his prior right. Brockman v. Grand Canal Co., 76 P. 602 (Ariz. 1904). Turning water into another ditch, but not using it, was held a mere pretense not preventing abandonment in Parsons v. Fort Morgan Reservoir & Irrigation Co., 136 P. 1024 (Colo. 1913), but the yearly turning of water into a broken ditch, whence it shortly returned to the stream, was held to negative an intent to abandon in Featherman v. Hennessy, 113 P. 751 (Mont. 1911). In Colorado, "economic, financial or legal difficulties or natural calamities" confronting an appropriator may excuse nonuse, Hallenbeck v. Granby Ditch & Reservoir Co., 420 P.2d 419 (Colo. 1966), but not the present economic infeasibility of a particular use, CF&I Steel Corp. v. Purgatory River Water Conservancy District, supra Note 2. Montana follows Colorado on the latter point, In re Adjudication of the Clark Fork River, supra Note 2, but 79 Ranch, Inc. v. Pitsch, 666 P.2d 215 (Mont. 1983), held that a claim that an appropriator lacks sufficient funds to irrigate is not sufficient to rebut the presumption of abandonment.

In re Adjudication of the Clark Fork River Drainage Area, 833 P.2d 1120 (Mont. 1992), held that the presumption of intent to abandon was not rebutted by carrying unused rights as an asset on the books of a municipal corporation, and Okanogan Wilderness League, Inc. v. Town of Twisp, 947 P.2d 732 (Wash. 1997), held that a municipality's "continuous existence and need for a municipal water supply" was not sufficient to rebut the presumption. United States v. Alpine Land and Reservoir Co., 27 F. Supp. 2d 1230 (D. Nev. 1998), held that the payment of taxes and assessments associated with water rights of an irrigation project can be considered in determining intent to abandon. Including water rights in deeds conveying real property was held not to be sufficient to rebut a presumption of abandonment in Haystack Ranch, LLC v. Fazzio, 997 P.2d 548 (Colo. 2000). The last case also held that removal of water rights from a division engineers abandonment list does not preclude a finding of abandonment, although it may considered along with other evidence in determining abandonment. Nevada, apparently alone among western states, holds that long non-use does not give rise to a rebuttable presumption of abandonment, but is only evidence of intent to abandon. United States v. Orr Water Ditch Co., 256 F.3d 935 (9th Cir. 2001)(applying Nevada law).

4. **Excess water.** Where an appropriator is decreed water far in excess of his needs, the failure to make any attempt to put such excess to use was held to

constitute an abandonment in New Mercer Ditch Co. v. Armstrong, 40 P. 989 (Colo. 1895).

5. **Abandonment as a strategy.** In City of Denver v. Middle Park Water Conservancy District, 925 P.2d 283 (Colo. 1996), Denver found itself in the seemly absurd position of defending its asserted abandonment of certain rights which it had purchased against the claim of Middle Park that Denver had not abandoned the rights. Why would Denver purchase and then attempt to abandon water rights? Denver diverts water for municipal supply upstream from the diversion points for the purchased rights, all of which were senior to Denver's right. By purchasing and abandoning the rights, Denver increased diversions to its project because it no longer had to bypass water to satisfy those rights.

Why would Middle Park object to abandonment of the rights? Middle Park apparently has rights which are junior to Denver's right and which are downstream from the purchased rights. Prior to Denver's purchase, Middle Park received the return flows from the purchased rights. The elimination of the bypass water also eliminated the return flows to Middle Park. Middle Park argued that Denver had not abandoned the purchased rights but was exercising them by diverting them to its municipal supply project. Although it is not discussed by the court, Middle Park's apparent strategy was to force Denver to seek a formal transfer of the purchased rights. Pursuant to principles, discussed in Section 5, infra, Denver might be required in a transfer proceeding to bypass flows equal to the historic return flows of the purchased rights.

The court held that the rights had been abandoned, noting that the evidence showed that Denver intended to abandon the rights and that it had diverted no water under the rights for approximately 40 years. In a footnote, the court said that the proceeding was limited to abandonment and that the effect of abandonment on Denver's other rights was not at issue.

B. Forfeiture

RENCKEN v. YOUNG

Supreme Court of Oregon, 1985.
300 Or. 352, 711 P.2d 954.

CAMPBELL, JUSTICE. This is a review of a decision by the Court of Appeals which affirmed an order of the Director of the Water Resources Department canceling the bulk of a water right owned by Rudolph G. Rencken. The water right had granted Rencken the use of the water from the East Branch of Mud Creek to irrigate 10 acres in Umatilla County. Following an administrative hearing, the Director found that Rencken had not used the water for "five successive years" as required by ORS 540.610(1) and canceled the right for irrigation except for .1 acre. Rencken filed a petition for judicial review with the Court of Appeals which affirmed without opinion. 72 Or. App. 781, 697 P.2d 578 (1985). We remand to the Director with instructions to re-evaluate the evidence in light of this opinion.

Two of the chief issues in this case involve the interpretation of ORS 540.610(1) which provides: "Beneficial use shall be the basis, the measure and the limit of all rights to the use of water in this state. Whenever the owner of a perfected and developed water right ceases or fails to use the water appropriated for a period of five successive years, the right to use shall cease, and the failure to use shall be conclusively presumed to be an abandonment of water right. Thereafter the water which was the subject of use under such water right shall revert to the public and become again the subject of appropriation in the manner provided by law, subject to existing priorities."

* * * In 1979, 1980, 1981 and 1982, [Rencken] did not use the water granted by the right except to irrigate a garden of approximately .1 acre. The factual controversy in this case concerns the year of 1983. * * * During the fall season of 1983, Rencken excavated a small pond or sump near the East Branch of Mud Creek to receive and hold water from the channel of the stream. He then purchased and installed an electric centrifugal pump to pump the water from the sump into the pipeline serving the sprinkler irrigation system. The pump was purchased in September 1983 and a permit which authorized the connection of the electricity to it was obtained from the State of Oregon on October 4, 1983.

Witnesses on Rencken's behalf testified that after the pump was installed, the alfalfa growing on the 10 acres was irrigated in late October or November 1983, with water from the East Branch of Mud Creek. The assistant water master for the area observed the subject land being irrigated with water from the same source on November 21, 1983. Two neighboring orchard owners, who were the proponents of the cancellation and interested witnesses, testified that the irrigation of the subject 10 acres with water from the East Branch of Mud Creek did not commence until after the end of October 1983.

The Water Resources Director found that water from the East Branch of Mud Creek was not used by Rencken in 1983 to irrigate the 10 acres until after the end of the irrigation season on October 31. The Director's ultimate findings of fact in part were: "With the exception of the continued use of water from the East Branch of Mud Creek for irrigation of a garden area of approximately 0.1 acre in area, water from the East Branch of Mud Creek was not diverted and used for irrigation under the provisions of the water right in question during the years of 1979, 1980, 1981, 1982 and 1983, being a period of five successive years of nonuse. The Director then ordered that the right to use the water from the East Branch of Mud Creek for irrigation purposes be canceled as to 9.9 acres.

The principal issues in this case are: (1) Does ORS 540.610(1) provide for the "abandonment" or the "forfeiture" of water rights after a failure to use; (2) Does the term "five successive years" in ORS 540.610(1) mean "five successive calendar years" or "five successive irrigation seasons," and (3) Did the Director properly allocate the burden of proof in evaluating the evidence?

The distinction between "abandonment" and "forfeiture" is important to the correct determination of this case. The Director, relying upon Withers et al. v. Reed, 194 Or. 541, 558, 243 P.2d 283 (1952), held that ORS 540.610(1) is a forfeiture statute. However, if ORS 540.610(1) is an abandonment statute and an intent to abandon the water right is required, the Director might have reached a different result because there is uncontradicted evidence in the record that before the end of the fifth irrigation season, Rencken dug a sump and bought an electrical pump to use the water from the East Branch of Mud Creek.

ORS 540.610(1) was passed by the Oregon Legislature in 1913 as Chapter 279. The language of the statute has remained the same since its enactment except for minor editorial changes. See Or .Laws 1920, ch. 8, § 5776; 3 Oregon Code Annotated (1930) § 47-901; OCLA § 116-437 (Oregon Compiled Laws Annotated). Oregon cases decided after the enactment of this statute have not always drawn a clear distinction between abandonment and forfeiture. * * *

In Withers et al. v. Reed, supra, the sole question was whether OCLA § 116-437, now ORS 540.610(1), applied to the State of Oregon's ownership of lands. * * * During the period of 13 years when the state owned the land, it was not irrigated, although water was available for that purpose. The circuit court affirmed the state engineer's order canceling the water rights. Justice Lusk, writing for this court, held that OCLA § 116-437, now ORS 540.610(1), applied to the state ownership of lands and affirmed the circuit court. The 4-3 opinion of the court said at 194 Or. page 558, 243 P.2d 283:

> Under the statute in question, failure of "the owner of a perfected and developed water right" to use the water appropriated for a period of five successive years works a *forfeiture* of the right, not for the benefit of any individual as in the case of an ordinary statute of limitations—which this is not—but for the benefit of the public, to the end that the "water right shall revert to the public and become again the subject of appropriation in the manner provided by law." Here again, is a statement as clear as words can make it of the public policy behind the statute. (Emphasis added.) * * *

Two law professors and one attorney general agree that ORS 540.610(1) is a forfeiture statute. Professor Chapin D. Clark in Survey of Oregon's Water Laws * * * at page 153 refers to ORS 540.610(1): "This is a statutory declaration that failure to use a water right for five successive years shall cause the right to be forfeited. Intent to abandon, actual or inferred, is not an element of forfeiture." * * *

1942-44 Opinions of Attorney General 48 comments on OCLA § 116-437 (now ORS 540.610(1)): "Although the statute employs the word 'abandonment', it clearly contemplates an involuntary forfeiture through non-user rather than a voluntary abandonment. An intent to relinquish the right is, of course, an essential element of abandonment, but the forfeiture provided by section 116-437 results without regard to the owner's intent."

2 Hutchins, Water Rights Law in the Nineteen Western States (1974), contains the following statement concerning ORS 540.610(1) on page 320: " * * * The controlling sentence in the Oregon statute reads: 'Whenever the owner of a perfected and developed water right ceases or fails to use the water appropriated for a period of five successive years, the right to use shall cease, and the failure to use shall be *conclusively presumed* to be an abandonment of water right.' [Emphasis in original.] This goes beyond the Kansas Legislature's 'shall be deemed abandoned' and makes it clear that if 'conclusively presumed' means anything at all, it completely rules out the element of intent.

Its ingredients are those of forfeiture—nonuse and lapse of time. Although this may purport to be an abandonment statute, it is in effect a forfeiture statute."

Since the 1952 case of Withers et al. v. Reed, supra, this court has consistently indicated that ORS 540.610(1) is a forfeiture statute. The above-cited legal literature agrees with the conclusion. We reaffirm Withers et al. v. Reed, supra.

Next we are requested to determine if the term "five successive years" in ORS 540.610(1) means "five successive calendar years" or "five successive irrigation seasons." * * * Rencken contends that ORS 540.610(1) refers to calendar years. Therefore, even if the Director found that Rencken did not use the water during the fifth irrigation season which ended on October 31, 1983, his undisputed use of the water in November 1983 was within the fifth calendar year and the terms of the statute. Under Rencken's position, this proceeding should be dismissed.

Even if we should decide that ORS 540.610(1) refers to "calendar years" and not "irrigation seasons," it does not help Rencken. His water right from the East Branch of Mud Creek was limited for irrigation to a season from March to October. Rencken's use of the water in November was not "the water appropriated" under the circuit court decree and referred to in ORS 540.610(1). * * * We hold that Rencken's use of the water from the East Branch of Mud Creek during November 1983 was not "appropriated water" within the limits of his adjudicated right. We are dealing with a decree that specifically limits the use of the water for irrigation from March to October of each year * * *.

The Director's findings of fact in part contain the following statement: "The initial burden is on the proponents of cancellation to show that a period of five successive years of nonuse of water under the terms of the water right in question has occurred. With the exception of that portion of the water right in question appurtenant to the 0.1 acre garden area, proponents did meet that burden in regard to the use of water for irrigation. "The burden of proof then shifted to the protestant [Rencken] to refute the showing made by proponents. Protestant did not meet that burden."

The Director is mistaken. The burden of proof does not shift. There is no affirmative defense in this proceeding. "The burden of presenting evidence to support a fact or position in a contested case rests on the proponent of the fact or position." ORS 183.450(2). The proponents of cancellation have the burden to prove by reliable, probative and substantial evidence, ORS 183.450(5), that Rencken had ceased or failed to use the water appropriated for a period of five successive years. * * *

The proceeding is remanded to the Director of Water Resources to re-evaluate the evidence in light of this opinion.

Notes

1. **Legislative clarification?** The critical part of Or. Rev. Stat. § 540.610(1) now reads: "Whenever the owner of a perfected and developed water right ceases or fails to use all or part of the water appropriated for a period of five successive years, the failure to use shall establish a rebuttable presumption of forfeiture of all or part of the water right." Does this change make it clear that forfeiture, not abandonment, is intended? See Hannigan v. Hinton, 97 P.3d 1256 (Or. Ct. App. 2004) (assuming without discussion that the preceding provision is a forfeiture statute).

2. **Unauthorized uses.** United States v. Alpine Land & Reservoir Co., 340 F.3d 903 (9th Cir. 2003) held that the use of rights appurtenant to one part of a farm to irrigate other parts of the farm results in forfeiture. Similarly, Hannigan v. Hinton, supra Note 1, held that the use of water at an unauthorized location does not prevent forfeiture, and Hennings v. Water Resources Department, 622 P.2d 333 (Or. Ct. App. 1981), held that the use of water to wet ground for plowing does not avoid forfeiture when "irrigation" is the authorized use. On the other hand, Russell-Smith v. Water Resources Department, 952 P.2d 104 (Or. Ct. App. 1998) and Salt Lake City v. Silver Fork Pipeline Corp., 5 P.3d 1206 (Utah 2000), held that an unauthorized change in the designated point of diversion does not result in forfeiture.

3. **Forfeiture statutes.** The statutes vary considerably in their language and in the period of nonuse that will result in forfeiture. One common feature is a list of circumstances which excuse nonuse. See, e.g., Or. Rev. Stat. § 540.610(2); Wash. Rev. Code § 90.14.140. As the Oregon experience demonstrates, neither the legislatures nor the courts have been careful to preserve the distinction between abandonment and forfeiture, or to use these words as words of art. See, for example, Scott v. McTiernan, 974 P.2d 966 (Wyo. 1999), in which the court repeatedly and consistently refers to "abandonment" while stating that "intent" to abandon need not be shown under the statute involved. (The statute, Wyo. Stat. Ann. Ann. § 41-3-401, uses both the words "abandoned" and "forfeit.")

4. **Effect of forfeiture statutes on abandonment.** Adoption of a forfeiture statute does not necessarily result in rejection of abandonment. See Crow v. Carlson, 690 P.2d 916 (Idaho 1984); New Mexico ex rel. Martinez v. McDermett, 901 P.2d 745 (N.M. Ct. App. 1995). In Washington, which recognizes both concepts, cities are exempt from forfeiture but not from abandonment. Okanogan Wilderness League, Inc. v. Town of Twisp, 947 P.2d 732 (Wash. 1997).

5. **Involuntary nonuse.** Ramsay v. Gottsche, 69 P.2d 535 (Wyo. 1937), held that a forfeiture must be effected by a "voluntary act," and did not occur when the appropriator was prevented from using water from several years by floods that washed out his diversion dams and ditches. In 1973 the Wyoming legislature amended the forfeiture statute to provide that forfeiture will occur if the appropriator fails "either intentionally or unintentionally" to use water. Wyo. Stat. Ann. § 41-3-401. In Scott v. McTiernan, supra Note 2, the court held that the amendment had not overruled *Ramsay*. The court said that "intent to abandon" need not be shown in order for a right to be extinguished under the statute, but nonuse must still be "voluntary," i.e., not the result of circumstance beyond the owner's control.

6. **Standing.** In Horse Creek Conservation District v. Lincoln Land Co., 92 P.2d 572 (Wyo. 1939), the court required the complaining party to show that he would be appreciably benefitted by a declaration of forfeiture of the earlier rights, and held that a late-priority junior appropriator with a "flood water right," who would receive little water whether the questioned right were used or not, had no standing to initiate the proceedings. A 1985 amendment expressly gives standing to any person having a right which is "equal to or junior in date of priority to the right for which abandonment is sought." Wyo. Stat. Ann. § 41-3-401. Held: A complaining party must still show it will benefit from forfeiture. Joe Johnson Co. v. Wyo. State Bd. of Control, 857 P.2d 312 (Wyo. 1993).

7. **Jurisdiction.** In Louth v. Kaser, 364 P.2d 96 (Wyo. 1961), the court held that the statutory procedure for declaration of forfeiture was not exclusive, and that the question of abandonment and forfeiture could be decided in private litigation. The issue can arise in many types of litigation in which the water right of either plaintiff or defendant is challenged. In Kearney Lake, Land & Reservoir Co. v. Lake De Smet Reservoir Co., 487 P.2d 324 (Wyo. 1971), the Wyoming Supreme Court came to regard this concurrent jurisdiction of administrative agencies and courts as not entirely satisfactory. Held, that primary jurisdiction should rest with the administrative agency, that when an issue of forfeiture or abandonment arises in a civil case the court should ordinarily certify the issue to the State Board of Control, and that the Board should make the initial determination and report its findings and conclusions back to the court. Finally, the Wyoming legislature gave the Board exclusive original jurisdiction over forfeiture proceedings in 1973. Wyo. Stat. Ann. § 41-3-401.

8. **Concentration of water.** Will forfeiture lie if an irrigator concentrates water on only a part of the land included in the appropriation?

N.M. Stat. Ann. § 72-5-28F: "The owner or holder of a valid water right or permit to appropriate waters for agricultural purposes appurtenant to designated or specified lands may apply the full amount of water covered by or included in said water right or permit to any part of the designated or specified tract without penalty or forfeiture."

Wyo. Stat. Ann. § 41-3-401(f): "An appropriation for irrigation use is not subject to partial abandonment for failure of the appropriator to irrigate part of the lands described in his permit or certificate of appropriation during the successive five (5) year period if:

(i) Facilities to divert the water and to apply it to beneficial use upon the lands which were not irrigated existed in usable form during the period of nonuse; and

(ii) There was not a sufficient supply of water available, because of regulation for prior water rights or because shortage of supply resulted in insufficient water to satisfy the appropriation in full, to irrigate the lands for which abandonment is sought provided that a diligent effort was made to use the supply which was available."

In Russell-Smith v. Water Resources Department., 952 P.2d 104 (Or. Ct. App. 1998), the court held that use of water through an unauthorized point of diversion does not result in forfeiture of the right.

9. **Revival by resumption of use.** If the holder of the right does not use the water for the statutory period, but commences to use it again before a declaration of forfeiture, is the right revived? In Town of Eureka v. State Engineer, 826 P.2d 948 (Nev. 1992), the court held that substantial use of water "cures" the forfeiture so long as no forfeiture proceeding has been commenced. In support of its decision, the court cited Carrington v. Crandall, 147 P.2d 1009 (Idaho 1944), and Sturgeon v. Brooks, 281 P.2d 675 (Wyo. 1955), but acknowledged that contrary holdings had been given in Bausch v. Myers, 541 P.2d 817 (Or. 1975), and in In re Cancellation of Stabio Ditch Water Right, 417 N.W.2d 391 (S.D. 1987). See also Affolter v. Rough & Ready Irrigating Ditch Co., 154 P. 738 (Colo. 1916) (suggesting that an abandoned right cannot be revived). The *Eureka* rule is codified in Arizona. See Ariz. Rev. Stat. § 45-188D. Oregon and Utah both provide that forfeiture proceedings must be brought within 15 years after a resumption of use. Or. Rev. Stat. § 540.610(2)(f); Utah Code Ann. § 73-1-4(3)(c). The Idaho Supreme Court reaffirmed the "resumption of use doctrine" in 2003 in Sagewillow, Inc.v. Idaho Department of Water Resources, 70 P.3d 669 (Idaho 2003), but deprived the doctrine of most of its practical significance by holding that a forfeited right may be revived by resuming its use only where there are no junior appropriators who have used water during the forfeiture period.

10. **Due process.** In In re Cancellation of Stabio Ditch Water Right, supra Note 9, the court acknowledged that the forfeiture statute appeared to be self-executing—i.e., nonuse for the statutory period extinguished the right without any judicial or administrative action. Nevertheless, the court concluded that due process requires that there be a hearing before forfeiture and held that a right existed until the hearing on forfeiture was finalized. However, the court seemingly deprived this holding of much of its significance by ruling that a right cannot be revived by resuming use of water after the statutory forfeiture period. Did the court confuse the due process requirements of forfeiture with the requirements of a judicial or administrative determination that forfeiture has occurred? See Texaco, Inc. v. Short, 454 U.S. 516 (1982), in which the Supreme Court held that an Indiana statute which terminates severed mineral rights without notice or a hearing is constitutional. The Court noted, however, that due process notice and hearing requirements are applicable to procedures to determine if termination has occurred.

11. **Conservation and forfeiture.** Prior appropriation law is sometimes criticized as conducive to waste or at least giving no incentive to save water. Cf. *Kovacovich* and notes, supra p. 101. In an effort to promote conservation and efficiency in the use of water, the 1982 California legislature provided that an appropriator may keep for his own benefit water saved by conservation efforts or as a result of using reclaimed or polluted water in lieu of appropriated water. The legislation also provides that cessation or reduction in the use of appropriated water as a result of these activities shall be deemed the equivalent of a reasonable beneficial use of the appropriated water and will not result in forfeiture of the water right. Cal. Water Code §§ 1010, 1011.

12. **Effect on water records.** If vigorously enforced, forfeiture and abandonment procedures can help to reduce the divergence between water records and the actual use of water. In Colorado, each division engineer must prepare a list of unused rights every ten years which serves a basis for abandonment proceedings in the water court. See supra p. 168, Note 11. In Nebraska, the

Department of Water Resources is given the responsibility of making examinations of ditches "as often as necessary" and of initiating cancellation proceedings on its own motion. Neb. Rev. Stat. § 46-229.01; see also Mont. Rev. Code § 85-2-405; Wyo. Stat. Ann. § 41-3-402; Tex. Water Rights Comm'n v. Wright, 464 S.W.2d 642 (Tex. 1971).

13. **Forfeiture and water rights transfers.** Does approval of a change in point of diversion, in place of use, or in purpose of use by a state water rights agency preclude a subsequent claim that the transferred right was forfeited or abandoned prior to its transfer? In Kerivan v. Water Resources Commission, 72 P.3d 659 (Or. Ct. App. 2003), the court answered yes, but in Sagewillow, Inc. v. Idaho Department of Water Resources, 70 P.3d 669 (Idaho 2003), the court held that principles of res judicata and collateral estoppel did not preclude such a challenge unless forfeiture or abandonment was actually raised in the transfer proceeding.

14. **Duration of water rights.** Appropriation statutes are silent on the duration of water rights. The Supreme Court of the United States once said that an appropriation is a "vested right to take and divert from the same source, and to use and consume the same quantity of water annually forever." Arizona v. California, 283 U.S. 423, 459 (1931). Is the tenure of the water right like that of land held in fee simple absolute? Does a forfeiture statute make it more like a fee simple determinable, or a fee simple subject to condition subsequent?

In 1985, Montana enacted leasing legislation which limits the duration of water rights received by private parties. The legislation provides that only the Montana Department of Natural Resources and Conservation may make appropriations if water in excess of 4000 acre-feet a year and 5.5 cubic feet per second is to be consumed or if water is to be transported outside designated river basins. Private parties wishing to use water in these circumstances must lease it from the Department. The term of the leases cannot exceed fifty years. See Mont. Code Ann. §§ 85-2-141, -301.

The Montana legislature apparently believed that the users of large amounts of water should not receive perpetual rights, that such users should pay for the use of water rather than receiving it for free, thereby providing an incentive to conserve, and that leasing would provide greater protection from environmental damage caused by transporting water out of watersheds. In addition, the legislature felt that the state could exercise greater regulatory control over the interstate movement of water by acting as a "proprietor" of water under the leasing statute. See John E. Thorson, Margery H. Brown & Brenda Desmond, Forging Public Rights in Montana's Waters, 6 Pub. Land L. Rev. 1, 43-44 (1985).

C. Prescription

TURNER v. BASSETT

New Mexico Court of Appeal, 2003
134 N.M. 621, 81 P.3d 564

[Turner, as trustee of two trusts, brought suit in 1999 to quiet title to certain water rights which were originally appurtenant to lands purchased by the trusts in 1984. The trial court granted summary judgment against Turner, holding that the water rights had been "severed" from the land prior to its sale to the trusts, and that New Mexico's adverse possession statute precluded the suit if the rights had not been severed. Turner had not exercised the rights since the trusts purchased the lands. It is not clear from the facts whether the defendants had ever exercised the rights to irrigate other lands. The New Mexico Court of Appeal reversed and remanded. It first ruled, as a matter of law, that the defendants had not severed the water rights prior to sale. It then turned to the issue of prescription (adverse possession).]

BESTOWMENT, J. * * * Having determined that the trial court erred in ruling that the water rights were severed, we are now confronted with the question of whether Turner's action to quiet title was time barred by New Mexico's adverse possession statute. See [N.M. Stat. Ann.] § 37-1-22 (providing that adverse possession of any lands, tenements, or hereditaments bars actions by another party seeking to assert title). Unless Section 37-1-22 can be applied to bar the claim, there is no statute of limitations applicable to actions to quiet title. Garcia v. Garcia, 111 N.M. 581, 588, 808 P.2d 31, 38 (1991) (noting that statutes of limitation do not apply to quiet title actions and that such actions can only be barred by our adverse possession statute). * * *

The question of whether or not rights to water may be acquired through adverse possession has never, until now, been answered in New Mexico. See Pioneer Irrigating Ditch Co. v. Blashek, 41 N.M. 99, 102, 64 P.2d 388, 390 (1937) (noting that whether a water right is subject to being acquired by prescription is still an open question); see also State ex rel. Reynolds v. W.S. Ranch Co., 69 N.M. 169, 175, 364 P.2d 1036, 1040 (1961) (passing on question of whether a water right is subject to being acquired by prescription). We now hold that water rights cannot be acquired by adverse possession. We base this holding on established principles of New Mexico law.

All waters within New Mexico belong to the public. N.M. Const. art. XVI, § 2; NMSA 1978, § 72-12-1 (2003). In 1907, the legislature established a comprehensive water code, under which the statutory method of acquiring water rights became the exclusive means for acquiring water rights. NMSA 1978, § 72-1-1 to -10 (1907, as amended through 2003). Water appropriation is, as a result, governed exclusively by the permit system administered by the State Engineer. NMSA 1978, § 72-2-1 (1982); NMSA 1978, § 72-12-3 (2001); see State ex rel. Reynolds v. King, 63 N.M. 425, 428, 321 P.2d 200, 201 (1958).

As the State Engineer observes, our water code contains no provision for the adverse possession of water rights. The omission of such a provision makes particular sense in light of the fact that adverse possession is based partly on the presumption that the owner has abandoned the property. Williams v. Howell, 108 N.M. 225, 227, 770 P.2d 870, 872 (1989). When water rights are abandoned, unlike land, ownership of those rights reverts to the public and is regarded as unappropriated public water. Public water is governed exclusively by the permit system administered by the State Engineer. State ex rel. Reynolds v. S. Springs Co., 80 N.M. 144, 146, 452 P.2d 478, 480 (1969); NMSA 1978, § 72-5-28 (2002); § 72-2-1; § 72-12-3. As there can be no right in an individual to interfere with public rights in water, adverse possession of water rights does not logically follow. See, e.g., Trigg v. Allemand, 95 N.M. 128, 134, 619 P.2d 573, 579 (Ct. App. 1980).

The Bassetts contend that adverse possession of water rights should nonetheless be permitted under the facts of this case, because the adverse possession did not begin with an illegal taking of water. A similar argument was raised in Lewis v. State Board of Control, 699 P.2d 822 (Wyo.1985). The *Lewis* court summarily disposed of the argument, finding such a distinction to be patently inconsistent with the legislature's establishment of a comprehensive water code, under which the statutory method is the exclusive means of acquiring water rights. Wyoming's statutory scheme for water appropriation is similar to our own. As the Wyoming court noted, acceptance of adverse possession, even where the water rights in question were not based on an initial illegal taking of water rights, would effectively cripple the permit procedure and make impossible the efficient administration of water. We find Wyoming's analysis persuasive on this point.

As the State Engineer contends, adverse possession would defeat the requirements established by the legislature to protect water rights from being impaired. See, e.g., NMSA 1978, § 72-5-6 (1985); § 72-5-23; and NMSA 1978, § 72-12-13 (1965) (providing that it is the State Engineer's duty to make findings that a proposed appropriation or change to an existing water right does not impair existing rights, is not contrary to conservation, and will not be detrimental to the public welfare). In enacting the water code, our legislature recognized the importance of state supervision of the appropriation of waters, as well as the fact that such supervision could not be effective, nor intelligently exercised, without accurate and complete information about proposed appropriations. See, e.g., NMSA 1978, § 72-5- 5.1 (1985) (recognizing the importance of public welfare and conservation of water in administering its public waters); § 72-12-3 (requiring application to the State Engineer, in the form prescribed by him, for the appropriation of any underground water, and itemizing information required to be contained in the application).

The notion of adverse possession of water rights is also inconsistent with New Mexico case law. In 1994, this Court held that beneficial use of appurtenant irrigation water rights on other lands for more than twenty years was insufficient to permit the user to retain those rights upon a challenge by the owner of the land to which the water rights were appurtenant. *McCasland,* 119 N.M. at 393-96, 890 P.2d at 1325-28. The Bassetts correctly note that, in

McCasland, this Court was not specifically addressing a claim of adverse possession, but rather an equitable argument that the "long-continued use of such water rights at a different location was sufficient to permit a finding of a de facto transfer of such water rights." *Id.* at 394, 890 P.2d at 1326. However, the issue is sufficiently analogous to an adverse possession claim to be highly informative of this Court's view on the issue. In *McCasland* we stressed the necessity of compliance with the statutory procedures set out in the water code for transfers of water rights to become effective. *Id.* at 394, 890 P.2d at 1326. We now reiterate the necessity of compliance with the statutory procedures set out in the water code for the creation, acquisition, or transfer of water rights. To the extent that the Bassetts contend that public policy alone mandates that we apply a statute of limitations to Turner's quiet title action, this Court's rejection of the equity-based argument in *McCasland* informs this Court otherwise.

In accordance with our established case law, our comprehensive water code, and the public policy concerns noted above, we now determine that water rights cannot be obtained through adverse possession. Accordingly, we reverse the trial court's determination that Section 37-1-22 acts to bar Turner's action.

Notes

1. **Contrary decision overruled by legislature.** In Hammond v. Johnson, 66 P.2d 894 (Utah 1937), the court held that rights could be acquired by prescription. The court concluded that rights to the unappropriated waters of the state could only be acquired by compliance with the statutes regulating appropriations, but that prescription involved the acquisition of rights to appropriated water. In 1939, the Utah legislature overruled the decision. It amended the appropriation statutes by adding the following sentences to the sections relating to permits to appropriate and to abandonment: "No right to the use of water either appropriated or unappropriated can be acquired by adverse use or adverse possession." Utah Code Ann. § 73-3-1. "The provisions of this section are applicable whether such unused or abandoned water is permitted to run to waste or is used by others without right." Utah Code Ann. § 73-4-1(3)(e). An almost exactly parallel development took place in Nevada. Nev. Rev. Stat. 533.060; Application of Filippini, 202 P.2d 535 (Nev. 1949). Alaska and Kansas have similar statutes. Alaska Stat. § 46.15.040(a); Kan. Stat. Ann. § 82a-705.

2. **Problems with prescriptive claims.** In People v. Shirokow, 605 P.2d 859, 866-67 (Cal. 1980), after concluding that the statutory appropriation procedures are mandatory, the court said:

"Even if arguendo we were to hold defendant was not required to comply with the statutory appropriation procedures, his claim of a prescriptive right would fail for two reasons.

"First, public rights cannot be lost by prescription. Defendant alleged and the trial court agreed that as against the state he had perfected a prescriptive right. Both were mistaken. What is being challenged is the state's governmental interest in regulating the use of public waters rather than any proprietary interest in the water claimed by defendant. The stipulated facts do not reveal that the state was using the water; indeed, defendant admits the state, if successful in obtaining the injunction, will not make use of the water. Thus it is undisputed that the state's interest here at stake is nonproprietary.

"More than a century ago, in Hoadley v. San Francisco (1875) 50 Cal. 265, 274-276, we articulated the rule that property held by the state in trust for the people cannot be lost through adverse possession. * * *

"The second reason defendant cannot prevail in his claim of a prescriptive right is that the stipulated facts do not provide the necessary elements. Defendant has not shown his diversion was hostile to the interests of any downstream user; we are told only that there was general community knowledge that the dam and reservoir existed and water was impounded. Since it is axiomatic that common law prescriptive rights are based on adverse use, such rights could not have been obtained by defendant by a taking of excess water which did not invade the interests of another. * * * Not only did defendant fail to identify any downstream users having actual knowledge of his diversion (see Pabst v. Finmand (1922) 190 Cal. 124, 129-130, 211 P. 11), no downstream users were parties to this action. Accordingly, the court lacked jurisdiction to adjudicate their rights vis-a-vis those of defendant."

Compare Mountain Meadow Ditch & Irrigation Co. v. Park Ditch & Reservoir Co., 277 P.2d 527, 528 (Colo. 1954): "[A] water right does not represent actual ownership of any part of the stream, but only the right to claim the amount needed up to the volume of the priority at the headgate of the ditch, and the taking of water from the stream by junior claimants elsewhere or by virtue of other priorities is not hostile to the title of the senior priority but hostile to the stream, that is, to the public. The unappropriated water of every stream is the property of the public against which title by adverse user may not be acquired."

3. **Prescription in California after *Shirokow*.** While *Shirokow*, supra Note 2, seemingly held that a permit is the exclusive method by which a new appropriation may be obtained vis-a-vis the state, prescription may still be viable in disputes between private parties. In Pleasant Valley Canal Co. v. Borror, 72 Cal. Rptr. 2d 1 (Ct. App. 1998), an upstream defendant claimed prescriptive rights against a downstream plaintiff and all other water users on the river, based on excess diversions. The court entertained the claim and discussed the requirements for prescription. The court ruled against the defendant, finding that there was no evidence that defendant's use of water had impaired the plaintiff's rights. The court also rejected the defendant's claim against other users on the river, citing the language of *Shirokow* quoted above.

4. **Right of an adverse possessor.** Suppose a squatter, claiming adversely to the owner of land, obtains title to the land by adverse possession. Does he become the owner of a water right which is appurtenant to the land, and which he used during the period of adverse possession? See Cook v. Hudson, 103 P.2d 137 (Mont. 1940).

5. **Prescriptive rights to diverted water.** Can a right by prescription be obtained by long continued use of water after it has been appropriated, diverted from the stream, and is stored in a reservoir or is running in a ditch? See Grandby Ditch & Reservoir Co. v. Hallenbeck, 255 P.2d 965 (Colo. 1953); Verwolf v. Low Line Irrigation Co., 227 P. 68 (Mont. 1924). Are there policy or doctrinal reasons for treating such situations differently than those involving prescriptive claims to water which has not been diverted?

6. **Out of priority use.** In Lewis v. State Board of Control, 699 P.2d 822 (Wyo. 1985), discussed in the principal case, upstream juniors argued that downstream seniors had abandoned their right by permitting the juniors to divert water out of priority. In rejecting this argument the court said:

"Contestants' original claim before the State Board of Control was for an abandonment or partial abandonment. However, this claim is also premised on an adverse possession theory. * * *

"The evidence is clear that the BQ appropriators utilized all the water that was available to them. In times when less than 16.5 c.f.s. were available, they consistently diverted the full amount that was available, and contacted a water official for administrative regulation. It is the duty of the officers charged with regulating water to make distribution in accordance with established priorities. Quinn v. John Whitaker Ranch Co., 92 P.2d 568 (Wyo. 1939). The BQ appropriators had the right to rely on the water officials to do their jobs. If said officials were not effective in their regulation, that alone will not work to effect a water abandonment, considering the facts herein that (1) the BQ appropriators consistently called for regulation when the flow of water in Twin Creek fell below 16.5 c.f.s.; (2) such regulation was attempted; and (3) such regulation failed primarily due to the refusal of contestants to abide by the lawful orders of the water officials." Accord Coryell v. Robinson, 194 P.2d 342 (Colo. 1948).

On the other hand, in Idaho and Montana such suits were entertained but junior appropriators seldom secured a reversal of priorities. See Note, Prescriptive Rights to the Use of Water in Montana, 3 Mont. L. Rev. 135 (1942). Both states have ended such suits. Mont. Code Ann. § 85-2-301(3): "A right to appropriate water may not be acquired by any other method, including by adverse use, adverse possession, prescription or estoppel. The method prescribed by this chapter is exclusive." Idaho Code § 42-607: "So long as a duly elected watermaster is charged with the administration of the waters within a water district, no water user within such district can adversely possess the right of any other water user."

7. **Legalizing nonconforming uses.** Is there something to be said for confirming and legalizing long-continued uses and practices that do not square with the paper titles to water rights? See Colo. Rev. Stat. § 37-92-401(1)(b)(VI): "If, in the preparation of the tabulations provided for in this section, the application of the preceding principles [for determining priorities] would cause in any particular case a substantial change in the priority of a particular water right to the extent theretofore lawfully enjoyed for a period of not less than eighteen years, then the division engineer shall designate the priority for that water right in accordance with historic practice." For some of the difficulties involved in holding appropriators to their paper titles, see Albert W. Stone, Montana Water Rights—A New Opportunity, 34 Mont. L. Rev. 57, 59-68 (1973). For some of the difficulties involved either in strict enforcement of laws against those who have long ignored them or in "confirming" illegal uses, see Michael V. McIntire, The Disparity Between State Water Rights Records and Actual Water Use Patterns, 5 Land & Water L. Rev. 23, 37-44 (1970).

SECTION 5. TRANSFER

FARMERS HIGH LINE CANAL & RESERVOIR CO. v. CITY OF GOLDEN

Supreme Court of Colorado, 1954.
129 Colo. 575, 272 P.2d 629.

CLARK, JUSTICE. To review a judgment and decree favorable to defendant in error, City of Golden, in an action to change the point of diversion of certain water rights heretofore adjudicated to the Swadley ditch out of Clear Creek upstream a distance of some five miles to the headgate of the Church ditch, plaintiffs in error present the cause in our Court by writ of error. We will herein refer to the parties as they were aligned in the trial court where the City of Golden was petitioner and plaintiffs in error appeared as respondents.

Petitioner claimed ownership of said water rights by recent purchase and conveyance by deed, and sought to have changed, not only the point of diversion, but likewise, the manner of use, said rights having previously been employed under the Swadley ditch in the irrigation of farm lands, and petitioner is now seeking to devote the same to municipal uses by way of increase to the domestic supply of water for the City of Golden as well as for the irrigation of lawns, gardens and similar purposes within the city. The trial court granted the petition, and by its decree authorized the change of 0.844 cubic feet of water per second of time under priority number thirteen, dated May 14, 1861, and 0.92 cubic feet of water per second of time under priority number twenty-one under date June 1, 1862, for a total of 1.764 cubic feet of water per second of time. * * *

With respect to the facts, the parties hereto are in complete disagreement, and the evidence, limited and inadequate, as to us it seems to be, is in serious conflict. With respect to many legal issues, counsel for the respective parties are quite in accord. It is recognized that water is a property right, subject to sale and conveyance, and that under proper conditions not only may the point of diversion be changed, but likewise the manner of use. It further is recognized that such change may be permitted, by proper court decree, only in such instances as it is specifically shown that the rights of other users from the same source are not injuriously affected by such change, and that the burden of proof thereof rests upon petitioner. These principles have been enunciated by our Court time and again in many decisions. Here, there appears no disagreement as to the law but a wide divergence of theory in its applicability.

There is absolutely no question that a decreed water right is valuable property; that it may be used, its use changed, its point of diversion relocated; and that a municipal corporation is not precluded from purchasing water rights previously used for agricultural purposes and thereafter devoting them to municipal uses, provided that no adverse effect be suffered by other users from the same stream, particularly those holding junior priorities.

Equally well established, as we have repeatedly held, is the principle that junior appropriators have vested rights in the continuation of stream conditions as they existed at the time of their respective appropriations, and that subsequent to such appropriations they may successfully resist all proposed changes in points of diversion and use of water from that source which in any way materially injures or adversely affects their rights. * * *

[I]n Enlarged Southside Irrigation Ditch Co. v. John's Flood Ditch Co., 116 Colo. 580, 585, 183 P.2d 552, * * * Mr. Justice Stone declared the principle that the owner of a priority for irrigation has no right, as against a junior appropriator, to waste water, to increase the amount or extend the time of his diversion so as to put it to double use by irrigation of other lands; nor to lend, rent or sell to others the excess water. "The well-recognized right to change either the point of diversion of the water right or its place of use is always subject to the limitation that such change shall not injure the rights of subsequent appropriators." * * *

Under subhead (d) of its findings, the trial court stated that it was convinced that, under no tenable theory of the case would any injury be done if 1.2 cubic feet of water per second of time out of priorities thirteen and twenty-one were allowed to be transferred, as requested by Golden. Then, under subdivision (e), the trial court "determined to authorize the change of point of diversion of Golden's priorities numbered thirteen and twenty-one, but effectuate the relinquishment of its priority number forty-four." True, under subhead (d) of its findings, the trial court further stated that it was not persuaded that water rights of any users appearing as protestants would be injured by granting decree for the full amount of all three priorities, but it specifically found that no injury would result if the diversion point of 1.2 cubic feet of water per second of time were authorized to be changed, and then proceeded to change the whole of the two oldest priorities for 1.764 cubic feet of water per second of time. This inconsistency of itself would be sufficient to justify a remand of the cause to the trial court for correction, but there appears a far more urgent necessity for reversal. As we have hereinbefore stated, the evidence presented before the trial court is conflicting and from our standpoint not altogether satisfactory. The principal witness who testified in behalf of the petitioner was one Wheeler, an engineer; while the principal witness who testified for protestants was one Lowe, likewise an engineer. Their testimony primarily was based upon two conflicting statistical theories, Mr. Wheeler using the Lowry-Johnson method, and Mr. Lowe the Blaney-Criddle method. The testimony of Mr. Wheeler was considerably more favorable to petitioner than was that of respondents' engineer; nevertheless, Mr. Wheeler testified that in his opinion there might be permitted, without injury to the stream, a change of point of diversion for 1.2 cubic feet of water. An effort was made to have him enlarge upon that amount, but he would not so commit himself other than to say that if an amount were transferred in addition to 1.2 cubic feet of water per second of time the effect on the stream would be so infinitesimal that it could not be measured. Mr. Wheeler's testimony was the extreme of all testimony before the court, both as to acreage irrigated under these decrees from the Swadley ditch, and the amount thereof for which point of diversion might properly be changed without injury to junior appropriators.

Regardless of this, the trial court, with no evidence whatever to support him, presumed to enter a finding that no injurious effect would result if the entire amount of the two older priorities, aggregating 1.764 cubic feet of water per second of time, was transferred, and that if any injury did result therefrom, it would be a general injury and could not affect any of the respondents specifically. The fallacy of such presumption is readily apparent. When any injury is permitted under the assumption that it is general to the stream, it immediately becomes clear that such instances multiplied might become very serious. Where general injury would result to the stream by the transfer, the change could not be authorized without injury to junior appropriators because it is their rights, proportionate with senior rights, that consume the whole stream. * * *

Where it appears that the change sought to be made will result in depletion to the source of supply and result in injury to junior appropriators therefrom, the decree should contain such conditions as are proper to counteract the loss, and should be denied only in such instances as where it is impossible to impose reasonable conditions to effectuate this purpose. City of Colorado Springs v. Yust, 126 Colo. 289, 249 P.2d 151. * * * What condition and limitation should be imposed depends upon the facts and surrounding circumstances in each particular instance. In this case it would require a full accounting not only of the amount of water reasonably required for the irrigation of Swadley lands and the proper return flow to the creek therefrom, but also should be taken into account the actual consumptive use of the City of Golden and the probable return flow to Clear Creek from such uses. If the return flow from the City use be shown to be greater than the return flow from the irrigation of farm lands, naturally the period and extent of use might be increased by the petitioner and the conditions imposed would not have to be so severe as where it would appear that the return flow was equal. It is the purpose of the law, both statutory and by decision, to protect all appropriators and holders of water rights; to this end all elements of loss to the stream by virtue of the proposed change should be considered and accounted for; and thereupon such appropriate provisions of limitation inserted in the decree as the facts would seem to warrant. * * *

As it now stands, we regard the judgment unsupported by proper record evidence. In this instance it would be improper to order dismissal of this action; but it should be and is remanded with direction to the trial court to vacate the decree heretofore entered and for further proceedings in conformity with the rules and principles herein set forth.

Notes

1. **Meaning of "transfer."** The term "transfer" as applied to water rights refers primarily to changes in the use of water and not to mere changes in ownership. Transfers of ownership, which typically accompany a transfer of the land on which the right is used, are quite routine and present few legal difficulties. As discussed supra p. 105, Note 5, water rights are usually considered to be

appurtenant to land and are automatically transferred when land is conveyed unless expressly excepted in the deed. It may not even be necessary to notify water officials of a transfer of ownership. Changes in use, on the other hand, present many legal complications, as the principal case illustrates. Such changes include changes in the type of use, changes in the place of use, changes in the point of diversion, and changes from direct diversion and use to storage of water. Most transfers involve irrigation rights, reflecting the fact that 80 to 90 percent of the water in the West is used for irrigation. An essential goal of a water rights transfer is the retention of the priority of the right being transferred.

2. **Importance of transfers.** The transfer of a water right to new uses has been recognized almost from the inception of the appropriation doctrine. See McDonald & Blackburn v. Bear River & Auburn Water & Mining Co., 13 Cal. 220 (1859); Maeris v. Bicknell, 7 Cal. 261 (1857). Until recently, however, transfers have been a relatively rare phenomenon; new users typically developed new supplies to meet their needs. The convergence of a number of factors has led to a marked increase in transfers and an even greater interest in the topic of transfers in recent years. These factors include new demands for water generated by industrialization and urbanization of the West, the declining availability of unappropriated water, and the high cost of developing new supplies, which often require dams for collection and storage or extensive transportation facilities to move water from areas of abundance to areas of shortage. Concern about environmental damage caused by large water projects and parochial opposition to the export of water, manifested in "area of origin" legislation discussed supra p. 97, Note 1, are also factors. Increased interest in transfers is reflected in new labels, such as "water marketing," and "water banking," which refer to efforts to make water transfers more responsive to market forces. Even environmental advocates and others who previously objected to the "commodification" of water implied by water marketing have begun to view water transfers more favorably. Ronald A. Kaiser & Michael McFarland, A Bibliographic Pathfinder on Water Marketing, 37 Nat. Resources J. 881 (1997), provides a useful guide to books, journal articles, technical reports, and conference proceedings on water transfers.

3. **"No-injury rule."** The principal difficulty in attempting to treat a water right as a salable property right is that many water uses are subject to a peculiar interdependency. Since the same water can be used and reused by several persons, all may have water rights that entitle them to receive the same molecules of water. If the sale and transfer of one person's water right will result in making those molecules unavailable to another who also has a right to them, the first user has sold the latter's water as well as his own.

"Return flow is a common phenomenon in Western irrigated regions and many water rights are predicated wholly or partly upon it. For example, on streams such as the Provo in Utah, downstream development occurred first, and return flow from junior upstream diversions not only satisfied the requirements of earlier downstream appropriators but actually benefitted them by prolonging the seasonal supply. On the other hand, on the South Platte in Colorado, upstream development occurred first and the increasing return flow made progressive downstream development possible and eventually added materially to the value of the junior downstream rights." Wells A. Hutchins, Selected Problems in the Law of Water Rights in the West 331 (1942).

A sale that results in the transfer out of the watershed of the total diversion made by a seller whose use produced return flow will reduce the quantity of water available to appropriators below the point of return. If they are senior to the transferred right, the rule of priority protects them; if they are juniors, they are nevertheless protected by the rule against transfers that cause them harm, frequently referred to as the "no-injury rule." This usually results in the rule of thumb that the person making the transfer can take only the amount consumed by the original use. Can a water right for a completely nonconsumptive use such as for power or mining never be sold? Could an irrigator of land on one side of a stream sell his entire diversion to his neighbor who wishes to irrigate the land on the other side? Could an appropriator upstream from both new and old diversion points ever show an injury that would prevent or limit the change? See CF&I Steel Corp. v. Rooks, 495 P.2d 1134 (Colo. 1972).

The principal case, discusses a reduction in the rate of diversion to offset the loss of return flows relied on by junior appropriators. In addition to reducing the diversion rate, recent decisions in Colorado have imposed volumetric limitations (acre-feet) on transferred rights even though the original right contained no such limitation. See Farmers High Line Canal & Reservoir Co. v. City of Golden, 975 P.2d 189 (Colo. 1999). Limitations on diversion dates (e.g. May through October), approximating historic periods of diversion under the original right, are also common. See id.

A decrease in return flows is not the only form of injury which can result from a transfer. Anything which alters quantity, timing, or quality of stream flows at any point on a stream may cause injury unless appropriate conditions are imposed. A change in dates of diversion can cause injury by extending the period of use or shifting diversions from a period of low demand to a period of high demand; moving the point of diversion and place of use downstream of a junior appropriator can deprive the junior of return flows that previously supplied its appropriation; reducing the quantity diverted to compensate for increased consumption, as was done in the principal case, may eliminate late season return flows relied on by downstream appropriators. As the frequency of transfers has increased, junior appropriators and water officials have gotten more sophisticated in identifying potential injuries and in requiring mitigation. When proposed transfers are contested, the dispute frequently centers on the nature and sufficiency of proposed conditions. Problems encountered in transfers and possible solutions are discussed in George A. Gould, infra Note 5.

4. **Historic use.** The Colorado Supreme Court adopted the concept of "historic use" in City of Westminster v. Church, 445 P.2d 52, 56-57 (Colo. 1968):

"It was proper, therefore, for the district court to examine the state engineer's records introduced into evidence to determine the historical use of the Eggleston No. 2 and McKenzie Ditch water rights during the period 1938-59. The purpose and effect of this inquiry was not to readjudicate the issue of Jenkins' abandonment, but simply to ascertain the extent of actual historical usage by Jenkins and the Rodgers.

"Perhaps defendant's allegations of error—because of the trial court's examination into the state engineer's records—stems from the fact that the term 'historical use' is not very prevalent in the prior decisions of this court and the belief that we had not heretofore sanctioned any such yardstick. * * * Precedent for the trial court's limitation of the direct flow rights finds sanction in the apropos language of this court to be found in Enlarged Southside Irrigation Ditch Company v. John's Flood Ditch Company, 116 Colo. 580, 183 P.2d 552, as follows:

'The owner of a priority for irrigation has no right, as against a junior appropriator, to waste it; neither has he the right to increase the amount or extend the time of his diversion to enable him to put it to double use by irrigation of other lands in addition to those for which it was appropriated * * *; nor to lend, rent or sell to others the excess water after irrigation of the land for which it was appropriated, to the detriment of junior appropriators, and such limitation of right of use cannot be circumvented by shifting the use to other lands. The well-recognized right to change either the point of diversion of the water right or its place of use is always subject to the limitation that such change shall not injure the rights of subsequent appropriators.'"

See also Wyo. Stat. Ann. § 41-3-104(a):

"The change in use, or change in place of use, may be allowed, provided that the quantity of water transferred by the granting of the petition shall not exceed the amount of water historically diverted under the existing use, not exceed the historic rate of diversion under the existing use, nor increase the historic amount consumptively used under the existing use, nor decrease the historic amount of return flow, nor in any manner injure other existing lawful appropriators."

The relationship between a decreed right and historic use was explained in Dallas Creek Water Co. v. Huey, 933 P.2d 27, 34 n.3 (Colo. 1997):

"An absolute decree entitles the subsequent operation of the right in the amount of its decreed quantity, so long as the water is applied beneficially. River conditions vary from year to year, as does the need of the appropriator for the water. Over an extended period of time, a pattern of historic diversions and use under the decreed right will mature and become the measure of that right for change purposes."

The New Mexico Supreme Court, on the other hand, insists that the decree, not historic use, fixes the nature and extent of the right to be transferred. W.S. Ranch Co. v. Kaiser Steel Corp., 439 P.2d 714 (N.M. 1968).

In Santa Fe Trail Ranches Property Owners Ass'n v. Simpson, 990 P.2d 46 (Colo. 1999), water rights acquired for manufacturing purpose were leased and used for irrigation for many years, but no judicial approval of the transfers was obtained as required by Colorado law. Subsequently, an attempt was made to transfer the rights to supply an urban subdivision. Held: the rights could not be transferred because no evidence existed regarding the historic use of the rights for manufacturing purposes and the use for irrigation could not be utilized to establish historic use because the transfer to irrigation use had not been judicially approved and, thus, might represent an expansion of the manufacturing use.

City of Westminister v. Church, above, held that a prior unsuccessful abandonment action does not bar an examination of historic use in a transfer proceeding. Conversely, People v. City of Thornton, 775 P.2d (Colo. 1989), held that implied limitations on a water right based on historic use are not relevant in abandonment proceedings.

Transfer proceedings can also raised complex questions regarding claim and issue preclusion. Farmer's High Line Canal & Reservoir Co. v. City of Golden, 975 P.2d 189 (Colo. 1999), involved rights which had been transferred from agricultural use to municipal use in the 1960s. The 1960s transfer decrees contained flow limitations but not volumetric limitations. Junior appropriators later sued, seeking to add volumetric limitations to the original decrees to reflect historic consumptive use. The court concluded that doctrine of claim preclusion barred the addition of volumetric limitations because historic consumptive use had been calculated and relied on in the formation of the earlier transfer decrees, which, as noted, contained no volumetric limitations. However, the court also held that the earlier proceedings did not bar claims that the transferee, the City of Golden, had subsequently enlarged its use of the transferred rights by changing municipal use patterns and increasing lawn irrigation. On appeal after remand, 44 P.3d. 241 (Colo. 2002), the court found that the flow limitations in the 1960s decrees were based on calculations that Golden would not irrigate more than 225 acres of lawn or apply more that 900 acre-feet of transferred water to lawn irrigation and held that these calculations were permissible limits on Golden's use of transferred water.

5. **Factual difficulties associated with no-injury rule.** George A. Gould, Water Rights Transfers and Third-Party Effects, 23 Land & Water L. Rev. 1, 20-21 (1988):

"Determining third-party effect is a complex process, frequently requiring the assistance of various experts and the accumulation of extensive data. For example, the prevention of an increase in consumption is a major concern in most transfer proceedings. * * * Actual data concerning the quantity of water diverted is frequently not available. Return flows may sometimes enter streams as discrete, identifiable, sources, but even so, these flows are seldom measured. More often return flows seep back over a broad stretch of the stream or percolate into groundwater which is tributary to the stream, making direct measurement impossible. Consequently, it is usually necessary to estimate consumption indirectly.

"Techniques such as the Blaney-Criddle method use temperature, sunshine, climatological data, and consumptive coefficients for various crops to estimate consumption. This approach requires the collection of data about the area irrigated and the crops grown. It also requires the assistance of agronomists, agricultural engineers, and other experts. It leads to an inevitable battle of experts concerning factual information and technical issues. Furthermore, this method assumes that only water used in the growing process is "consumed." Because the purpose of the transfer process is to preserve stream flow conditions, however, consumption properly includes all water lost to the stream, not just that used in the growing process. Thus, irrigation water which seeps into deep aquifers not tributary to the stream or which collects on the surface and evaporates is also 'consumed' and should be included in the amount available for transfer. Disputes involving the extent of such losses further complicates the transfer process.

"Although the effect on consumption is typically the central focus of transfer proceedings, other matters must also be evaluated. Like consumption and return flows, information concerning stream conveyance losses, the timing of return flows, the effects of alterations in diversion patterns, water quality changes resulting from a change in use, and other factors which must be evaluated to determine the effects of a proposed transfer, is sketchy or nonexistent and subject to varying interpretations. Gathering this information, evaluating it, and presenting it entail the same delays, expenses, and uncertainties as information concerning consumption."

6. **Burden of proof.** Who has the burden of proof? The Colorado statute requires the applicant for a change to show the "absence of any injurious effect." Colo. Rev. Stat. § 37-92-304(3). While the applicant bears the initial and ultimate burden of showing absence of injury, once the applicant meets the initial burden, objectors have the burden of going forward with evidence of injury. Farmers Reservoir & Irrigation Co. v. Consol. Mut. Water Co., 33 P.3d 799 (Colo. 2001); see also Tanner v. Humphreys, 48 P.2d 484 (Utah 1935) (petitioner is only required to make a general showing of no injury and then rebut specific claims of injury). But see Mont. Code Ann. § 85-2-402(5) (requiring proof of no injury by "clear and convincing evidence" in some cases).

Colorado also allows a trial period: "Any decision of the water judge * * * dealing with a change of water right * * * shall include the condition that the approval of such change * * * shall be subject to reconsideration by the water judge on the question of injury to the vested rights of others for such period * * * as is necessary or desirable to preclude or remedy any such injury." § 37-92-304(6). In Farmers Reservoir & Irrigation Co., above, the court explained that historic consumptive use is to be determined in granting a transfer and that the retained jurisdiction provided by the foregoing statute cannot be used to reopen this determination; rather, the court said, retained jurisdiction provides a period for testing the change plan to determine if it operates as predicted to protect against injury and to make adjustments if it does not.

7. **Economic impact of the no-injury rule.** The transaction costs and the uncertainty generated by the no-injury rule substantially impede the transfer of water rights and the development of water markets. Some economists suggest that the no-injury rule would be unnecessary if water rights were redefined in terms of consumptive use of water. See Timothy D. Tregarthen, Water in Colorado, Fear and Loathing of the Marketplace, in Water Rights, Scare Resource Allocation, Bureaucracy and the Environment 125-30 (Terry Anderson ed., 1983); Ronald N. Johnson, Micha Gisser & Michael Werner, The Definition of a Surface Water Right and Transferability, 24 J.L. & Econ. 273 (1981); Jerome W. Milliman, Water Law and Private Decisionmaking: A Critique, 2 J.L. & Econ. 41, 46, 58 (1959). For an argument that redefinition is impractical and would only provide a marginal solution, see George A. Gould, supra Note 5.

8. **Transfers involving water companies and irrigation districts.** A great deal of western water is supplied by mutual water companies and public irrigation districts which have constructed large dams and canals or have contracted for delivery of large quantities of water from U.S. Bureau of Reclamation projects. The ability of a water user to sell the user's share of the district supply may depend upon conceptual notions of who owns the water right or whether the water is appurtenant to land, rather than on questions of the desirability of the change and whether injury would befall anyone. In some states the district may have a veto over the change; it must give its approval to such a transfer. The power of the district to sell its water outside its service area may depend upon the same considerations, as well as on the terms of the statute under which it was formed or the documents of incorporation, and on whether the water is "surplus" or in use.

A recent article concludes that the reallocation of water among users within the service areas of mutual water companies and irrigation districts occurs with much greater ease and frequency than formal transfers of water rights and plays a much more important role in local water transfers than is typically recognized. The article attributes this to the standardized, interchangeable nature of water entitlements created by such institutions, the availability of the institutions as clearinghouses to match potential buyers and sellers, the existence of distribution systems to redirect water within the service areas, and the fact that intra-institution transfers typically do not require the approval of state water officials. See, e.g., Dep't of Ecology v. Acquavella, 935 P.2d 595 (Wash. 1997) (holding that the trial court had correctly specified that water rights held by an irrigation district were appurtenant to all irrigable lands within the district rather than the lands actually irrigated because an irrigation district water right can be transferred and applied to any land within the district without administrative approval).

The same article concludes that transfers outside service areas by members of mutual water companies occur with some frequency, that transfers by irrigation districts outside their service areas occur, but less frequently than might be expected, and that transfers by members of irrigation district outside service areas are virtually nonexistent. Barton H. Thompson, Jr., Institutional Perspectives on Water Policy and Markets, 81 Cal. L. Rev. 673 (1993). The transfer of water by members of mutual water companies and irrigation districts is discussed in greater detail in Chapter 5.

The transferability of Bureau of Reclamation water varies from project to project and may depend on the legislation authorizing it, whether the project is paid out, and upon the residency of the parties. A 1971 study described the matter as "extraordinarily murky." Charles J. Meyers & Richard A. Posner, Toward an Improved Market in Water Resources, in Nat'l Water Comm'n, Legal Study No. 4, 1971); see also Bruce C. Driver, The Effect of Reclamation Law on Voluntary Water Transfers, 33 Rocky Mtn. Min. L. Inst. 26-1 (1987). More recently, administrative and legislative steps have been taken to clarify and simplify the transfer of Reclamation water. These developments are discussed infra p. 679, Note 4.

9. **Transfer of permits and applications.** In Green River Development Co. v. FMC Corp., 660 P.2d 339 (Wyo. 1983), the court held that an inchoate permit cannot be transferred, reasoning that only water which has been beneficially used is subject to transfer. Accord Hansen v. Turney, 94 P.3d 1 (N.M. Ct. App. 2004) (citing *Green River*). In United States v. Alpine Land & Reservoir Co., 965 F.2d 731 (9th Cir. 1992), a federal court held that the reference to "water already appropriated" in the Nevada statutes precludes transfers if water has not been put to beneficial use. This holding was contrary to a long-standing practice of the Nevada state engineer and cast into doubt many such transfers previously approved. In response the Nevada Legislature enacted Nev. Rev. Stat. 533.324, which states that "'water already appropriated' includes water for whose appropriation the state engineer has issued a permit but which has not been applied to the intended use." The act adopting the statute states that the section is to clarify rather than change existing law and that the legislature ratifies the transfers previously approved by the state engineer. In Catherland Reclamation District v. Lower Platte North Natural Resources District, 433 N.W.2d 161 (Neb. 1988), the court held that an application for a permit cannot be transferred, reasoning that until a permit is issued an applicant has no transferable property interest. See also City of West Richland v. Dep't of Ecology, 103 P.3d 818 (Wash. Ct. App. 2004)

(holding that the Wash. Rev. Code § 90.44.100 prohibits transfers of inchoate groundwater rights to new purposes of use).

10. **Transfer procedures.** In most states, the administrative agencies that regulate the appropriation and distribution of water have the power to approve or disapprove transfers after proceedings at which all interested parties are represented. Ariz. Rev. Stat. § 45-172; Cal. Water Code §§ 1700-1707; Idaho Code § 42-222; Kan. Stat. Ann. § 82a-708b; Mont. Code Ann. §§ 85-2-402, -403; N.M. Stat. Ann. § 72-5-24; N.D. Cent. Code § 61-04-15; Or. Rev. Stat. § 540.510; Utah Code Ann. § 73-3-3; Wash. Rev. Code § 90.03.380; Wyo. Stat. Ann. § 41-3-104. In Texas the same result was reached by a decision which required an amended permit when such a change was made, and gave the water officials power to approve the amended permit just as the original permit is approved. Clark v. Briscoe Irrigation Co., 200 S.W.2d 674 (Tex. Civ. App. 1947).

In Colorado, the former "change in point of diversion" procedure illustrated in the principal case has been abolished and an application for a change is handled by the Water Judge under the Water Right Determination and Adjudication Act of 1969. Colo. Rev. Stat. §§ 37-92-101 to -602. A contrast between judicial and administrative regulations is found in Don Seastone & L.M. Hartman, Alternative Institutions for Water Transfers: The Experience in Colorado and New Mexico, 39 Land Econ. 31 (1963).

11. **Miscellaneous.** The lack of facilities to transport water is often a barrier to water transfers. In 1986, California enacted legislation to alleviate this problem. Cal. Water Code §§ 1810-1814. This legislation attempts to make available to transferees the unused capacity of water transportation facilities owned or operated by public agencies. This legislation and some of the difficulties encountered in applying it are discussed in Brian E. Gray, The Shape of Transfers to Come: A Model Water Transfer Act for California, 4 Hastings W.-Nw. J. Envtl. L. & Pol'y 23 (1996).

In Desert Irrigation, Ltd. v. State, 944 P.2d 835 (Nev. 1997), the Nevada State Engineer canceled permits to transfer irrigation water rights to residential land development after numerous extensions. The land developer argued that the water represented by the canceled transfer permits should revert to the original rights. The court ruled otherwise, holding that canceled rights revert to the public and are available for further appropriation.

Paloma Investment L.P. v. Jenkins, 978 P.2d 110 (Ariz. Ct. App. 1998), is certain to revive unpleasant memories of the first year of law school for many law students and lawyers. Jenkins acquired a contract right to purchase a ranch and appurtenant water rights. Jenkins later assigned the contract, and, at the same time, entered into an agreement with the assignee giving Jenkins twenty per cent of all proceeds from the sale or lease of the appurtenant water rights. A subsequent purchaser of the ranch sued to quiet title, alleging that he was not bound by the agreement. The court ruled that the agreement did not create a equitable mortgage or lien, nor did it constitute a covenant running with the land. Instead, the court held Jenkins had retained a "royalty interest" which was binding on the subsequent purchaser.

BONHAM v. MORGAN

Supreme Court of Utah, 1989.
788 P.2d 497.

PER CURIAM: Plaintiffs appeal from a summary judgment which denied them standing to pursue count one of their complaint against the state engineer. * * * Plaintiff Stanley B. Bonham, who is not a water user, protested against a permanent change application filed under Utah Code Ann. § 73-3-3 (1980) in the office of the defendant state engineer (state engineer) in June of 1984 by defendants Salt Lake County Water Conservancy District and Draper Irrigation Company (applicants). Applicants sought to change the point of diversion, place, and nature of use of certain water rights in Bell Canyon, Dry Creek, Rocky Mouth Creek, and Big Willow Creek. At a subsequent hearing, Bonham produced evidence of substantial flooding and damage to plaintiffs' properties and adjacent public lands during 1983 and 1984. Bonham informed the state engineer that the flooding was the result of applicants' construction of a screw gate, pipeline, and diversion works after they obtained preliminary approval of their change application. According to Bonham, the flooding had occurred and would recur on a yearly basis whenever the applicants closed their screw gate, allowing the waters to be diverted down the hillside onto plaintiffs' properties and nearby property contemplated for use as a public park. Bonham objected that the proposed structures and improvements contemplated after final approval would detrimentally impact the public welfare.

The state engineer conducted on-site inspections but eventually issued his memorandum decision in which he concluded that he was without authority to address Bonham's claims in ruling on the permanent change application, as Bonham was not a water user, that the state engineer's authority was limited to investigating impairments of vested water rights, and that there was no evidence before him to indicate that the implementation of the change application would impair those rights. The state engineer then granted the permanent change application.

Plaintiffs sued in the district court in compliance with Utah Code Ann. § 73-3-14 (1980), which provides in pertinent part:

> In any case where a decision of the state engineer is involved any person aggrieved by such decision may within sixty days after notice thereof bring a civil action in the district court for a plenary review thereof * * *

Plaintiffs alleged that the state engineer's disclaimer of any authority to consider, in connection with a permanent change application, any damages caused to plaintiffs as a result of his approval of the application, was contrary to the clear mandate of section 73-3-8, which requires an evaluation of the factors there set out, including any and all damage to public and private property and the impact the application will have on the public welfare. * * *

Before any discovery was conducted, the district court granted the state engineer's motion for summary judgment after concluding that the change application process under section 73-3-3 did not contemplate a consideration of all the factors listed in section 73-3-8; that the issues raised by plaintiffs were outside the limited criteria governing approval and rejection of change applications contained in section 73-3-3; and that plaintiffs were, therefore, not "aggrieved persons" within the meaning of section 73-3-14 and could not bring an action to review the decision of the state engineer under section 73-3-3. * * *

Plaintiffs appealed. This Court granted the request of the National Parks and Conservation Association (NPCA) to intervene as amicus curiae and granted a like request by Weber Basin Water Conservancy District, Weber River Water Users Association, Davis and Weber Counties Canal Company, Draper Irrigation Company, Sandy City, Central Utah Water Conservancy District, Salt Lake County Water Conservancy District, and Provo River Water Users Association (the water users).

* * * At oral argument, the parties conceded that the question of whether plaintiffs are aggrieved persons within the meaning of section 73-3-14 turns on whether the scope of the considerations appropriate for the state engineer under a section 73-3-3 proceeding for a permanent change application is the same as that listed in section 73-3-8. If it is, the state engineer concedes that plaintiffs are aggrieved persons; if it is not, plaintiffs concede that they are not aggrieved persons and that summary judgment was proper. The issues before us may therefore be reduced to the question of whether in permanent change applications (section 73-3-3) the state engineer has the same duties with respect to approval or rejection of applications as he has when considering appropriation applications (section 73-3-8). We hold that the state engineer's duties under the two statutes are the same and that plaintiffs therefore are aggrieved persons entitled to a trial on the merits of count one of their complaint. * * *

Utah Code Ann. § 73-3-3 (1980), at the time the state engineer rendered his decision, read in pertinent part:

> Any person entitled to the use of water may change the place of diversion or use and may use the water for other purposes than those for which it was originally appropriated, but no such change shall be made if it impairs any vested right without just compensation. Such changes may be permanent or temporary. Changes for an indefinite length of time with an intention to relinquish the original point of diversion, place or purpose of use are defined as *permanent changes*. *Temporary changes* include and are limited to all changes for definitely fixed periods of not exceeding one year. Both permanent and temporary changes of point of diversion, place or purpose of use of water including water involved in general adjudication or other suits, shall be made in the manner provided herein and not otherwise. No permanent change shall be made except on the approval of an application therefor by the state engineer. * * * *The procedure in the state engineer's office and rights and duties of the applicants with respect to applications for permanent changes of point of diversion, place or purpose of use shall be the same as provided in this title for applications to appropriate water*; * * * No temporary change shall be made except upon an application filed in duplicate with the state engineer. * * * The state engineer shall make an investigation and *if such temporary change does not impair any vested rights of others he shall make an order authorizing the change*. (Emphasis added.)

Section 73-3-8 (1985), at the time the state engineer rendered his decision, read in pertinent part:

> (1) It shall be the duty of the state engineer to approve an application if: (a) there is unappropriated water in the proposed source; (b) the proposed use will not impair existing rights or interfere with the more beneficial use of the water; (c) the proposed plan is physically and economically feasible, unless the application is filed by the United States Bureau of Reclamation, and would not prove detrimental to the public welfare; (d) the applicant has the financial ability to complete the proposed works; and (e) the application was filed in good faith and not for purposes of speculation or monopoly. *If the state engineer, because of information in his possession obtained either by his own investigation or otherwise, has reason to believe that an application to appropriate water will interfere with its more beneficial use for irrigation, domestic or culinary, stock watering, power or mining development or manufacturing, or will unreasonably affect public recreation or the natural stream environment, or will prove detrimental to the public welfare, it is his duty to withhold his approval or rejection of the application until he has investigated the matter. If an application does not meet the requirements of this section, it shall be rejected.* (Emphasis added.)

Although the two statutes before us have remained virtually unchanged in their substantive provisions for over fifty years, the issue whether the state engineer must consider all the factors listed in section 73-3-8 when passing on a permanent change application under section 73-3-3 is one of first impression in this Court. * * * The language critical to our determination was added to section 100-3-3 in 1937. The amendment removed provisions addressing notice requirements and added for the first time language defining permanent and temporary changes. After setting out procedures relating to applications for permanent changes, the 1937 amendment continued:

> The procedure in the state engineer's office *and the rights and duties of the applicant with respect to application for permanent changes* of point of diversion, place, or purpose of use *shall be the same as provided in this title for applications to appropriate water*. (Emphasis added.)

The appropriations statute, section 100-3-8, to which the amendment made cross-reference, contained then, as section 73-3-8 does now, a specification on the duties of the state engineer when acting on appropriation applications. These were to be granted if, and only if, they did not interfere with more beneficial use, public recreation, the natural stream environment, or the public welfare, as more specifically set out in the statute. In contrast to the cross-reference between *permanent change* applications and appropriations, the 1937 amendments prescribed different and very summary procedures for *temporary changes*, under which the state engineer "shall make an investigation and *if such temporary change does not impair any vested rights of others, he shall make an order authorizing the change.*" See also § 73-3-3 (1980). From these contrasting references and procedures, we draw the rational inference that in temporary change applications the review criteria (now contained in section 73-3-8) did not apply, but in considerations of permanent change applications they did. * * *

Plaintiffs and the NPCA * * * rely on those general provisions to underscore their position that neither the right to appropriate water nor the right to permanently change its use or place of use is absolute. The conditioning of that right, they say, was acknowledged by our Supreme Court in United States v. Caldwell, 64 Utah 490, 502-03, 231 P. 434, 439 (1924), when it stated:

> [A]ppellants' right to change the place of diversion is not an absolute or vested right, but is only a conditional or qualified one. No such change can be made if thereby the public, or any other appropriator, prior or subsequent, is adversely affected. * * *

Even were we convinced, which we are not, by the state engineer's argument that the "procedure in the state engineer's office" in section 73-3-3 refers only to his ministerial duties, the lack of precision in the cross-reference is of little avail to the state engineer. The further mention in that section of the "rights and duties" of the applicants and the reference to section 73-3-8 are sufficient by themselves to show that the legislature meant to require more than similar procedures alone. The only reasonable meaning to read into section 73-3-3 is that the state engineer must investigate and reject the application for either appropriation or permanent change of use or place of use if approval would interfere with more beneficial use, public recreation, the natural stream environment, or the public welfare. It is unreasonable to assume that the legislature would require the state engineer to investigate matters of public concern in water appropriations and yet restrict him from undertaking those duties in permanent change applications. Carried to its logical conclusion, such an interpretation would eviscerate the duties of the state engineer under section 73-3-8 and allow an applicant to accomplish in a two-step process what the statute proscribes in a one-step process. For all that an applicant would need to do to achieve a disapproved purpose under section 73-3-8 would be to appropriate for an approved purpose and then to file a change application under section 73-3-3. * * *

We hold that the state engineer is required to undertake the same investigation in permanent change applications that the statute mandates in applications for water appropriations and that plaintiffs are aggrieved persons who have standing to sue him pursuant to Utah Code Ann. § 73-3-14 (1980) for a review of his decision approving the subject change application. The summary judgment in favor of the state engineer is vacated, and plaintiffs' complaint against him reinstated for trial on the merits.

Notes

1. **Other decisions.** Accord Clark v. Briscoe Irrigation Co., 200 S.W. 2d 674 (Tex. Civ. App. 1947). Contra In re Application of Sleeper, 760 P.2d 787 (N.M. Ct. App. 1988); but see N.M.Stat. Ann. §§ 72-5-23, 5-24, -12-7, -12B-1).

2. **Expansion of public interest review.** Douglas L. Grant, Public Interest Review of Water Right Allocation and Transfer in the West: Recognition of Public Values, 19 Ariz. St. L.J. 681, 684-85 (1987):

"Public interest review of water right transfers * * * has grown rapidly in recent years. In 1971, Nevada was the only state with a permit statute requiring denial of proposed transfers that would be detrimental to the public interest. Now, eight states have such statutes.[21] Two more states have statutes that require consideration of certain public effects of proposed transfers."[22]

In Colorado there is no public interest review of appropriations or transfers. Nevertheless, in City of Thornton v. Bijou Irrigation Co., 926 P.2d 1 (Colo. 1996), the water court conditioned a proposed transfer on "revegetation" of lands which would be removed from irrigation pursuant to a transfer of water from agricultural to urban use. The revegetation requirements reflected statutory requirements found in legislation adopted in 1992. Colo. Rev. Stat. § 37-92-305(4.5). However, by its own terms, the 1992 legislation was not applicable to the Thornton applications because they had been filed before its adoption. Thornton asserted that the revegetation requirements were invalid, arguing that prior to the enactment of the statute the water court only had authority to impose conditions to prevent injury to other appropriators. The Colorado Supreme Court disagreed. It held that the legislation merely codified existing powers of the water courts. Reviewing past decisions, the court found that, in addition to promoting maximum beneficial use and protecting water rights, water judges must give consideration to the potential impact of the utilization of water on other resources.

3. **Transfer restrictions.** Wyoming's "no change" statute, enacted in 1909, laid down the rule that water rights could not be detached from the land, place or purpose for which they were acquired. The provision, codified at Wyo. Stat. Ann. § 41-3-101, is so riddled with exceptions as to be almost meaningless. See Frank J. Trelease & Dellas W. Lee, Priority and Progress—Case Studies of the Transfer of Water Rights, 1 Land & Water L.Rev. 1 (1966) and Frank J. Trelease, Transfer of Water Rights—Errata and Addenda—Sales for Recreational Purposes and to Districts, 2 Land & Water L. Rev. 321 (1967).

In three states, restrictions on transfers of water rights have been adopted by substantially identical statutes providing that a water right shall remain appurtenant to the land on which it is used, but if for any reason it should at any time become impracticable to beneficially or economically use the water on the land to which it is appurtenant, the right may be severed from the land and transferred to other land without loss of priority, if such change has the approval of the state water authorities and can be made without detriment to existing rights. Nev. Rev. Stat. 533.040, .325; Okla. Stat. tit. 82, § 105.22; S.D. Codified Laws §§ 46-5-34 to -36. In Nevada the statute applies to all water rights, in the other states, only to rights for irrigation, leaving other rights freely transferable upon compliance with procedures for obtaining approval. The South Dakota statute does not affect water rights vested prior to its enactment in 1907. Jewett v. Redwater Irrigating Ass'n, 220 N.W.2d 834 (S.D. 1974).

---

21. See Idaho Code § 42-222(1)(Supp. 1986); Kan. Stat. Ann. § 82a-708b (Supp. 1986); Mont. Code Ann. § 85-2-402(3)(1985) * * * Neb. Rev. Stat. § 46-290, -294 (1984); Nev. Rev. Stat. § 533.370(3) (1985); N.M. Stat. Ann. § 72-5-23, 5-24, -12-7, -12B-1 (1985 & Supp. 1986); N.D. Cent. Code § 61-04-15.1 (1985); S.D. Codified Laws Ann. § 46-2A-12 (1983). * * *

22. Cal. Water Code §§ 1725 (temporary change), 1735 (trial transfer), 1738 (long-term transfer) (Deering Supp. 1987) (all requiring consideration of the impact on instream uses); Wyo. Stat. § 41-3-104 (1977) (requiring consideration of the economic effect on the community).

In North Dakota a transfer may be made only to a "superior" use, as defined in the preference statute, N.D. Cent. Code § 61-04-15.1. The Washington Family Farm Water Act, Wash. Rev. Code §§ 90.66.010-.910, adopted by initiative in 1977, substantially restricts the transfer of agricultural water rights. See Wash. Rev. Code § 90.66.065. The transfer restrictions were applied in City of West Richland v. Department of Ecology, 103 P.3d 818 (Wash. Ct. App. 2004). Arizona and Kansas at one time had statutes prohibiting or severely restricting transfers and changes of water rights. 1919 Ariz. Sess. Laws, c. 64, § 48; 1891 Kan. Sess. Laws, c. 133, art. 2, § 5.

4. **Temporary Transfers.** A number of states have statutes which authorize temporary transfers. See N.M. Stat. Ann. §§ 72-6-1 to -7; Wash. Rev. Code § 90.03.390; Wyo. Stat. Ann. § 41-3-110. California has a particularly impressive array of such statutes. See Cal Water Code §§ 1725-1732 (temporary changes); §§ 1735-1737 (long-term transfers); §§ 1435-1442 (temporary urgency changes); §§ 1020-1031 (water leases). Colorado recently adopted legislation authorizing expedited approval of "interruptible water supply agreements," Colo. Rev. Stat. § 37-93-309, and both Colorado and Oregon authorize loans or leases of water for instream uses, Colo. Rev. Stat. § 37-83-105; Or. Rev. Stat. § 537.348. Like the Utah statute in the principal case, these statutes attempt to create greater flexibility in water use by facilitating short-term changes in use to meet temporary or one-time needs. In general, these statutes provide for simplified or expedited transfer processes and for automatic reversion to the right to its prior use at the end of the transfer period.

5. **Criticism of prior appropriation.** M. Mason Gaffney, Economic Aspects of Water Resource Policy, 28 Am. J. Econ. & Soc. 131, 140 (1969) (a very critical review of all water law, treating prior appropriation only slightly less roughly than riparian rights):

"Rationing under scarcity. Under the 'first in time, first in right' doctrine, appropriators are senior and junior to one another along a scale from the first to the last. When water falls low, the juniors drop out first and lose everything before the next senior appropriator loses anything. In result, there is no pooling of risk whatever. The top senior has a 100 per cent firm supply; the last junior has a supply so uncertain it is unusable. Two basic economizing principles are denied. One is marginal productivity. The junior appropriator who loses all his water obviously loses marginal units of high productivity, while the senior retains marginal units of low productivity. The other is pooling of risk. The doctrine is conceived in terms of an assumed necessity for vertical integration: that is, there is no market for the raw material, water, but every user rather owns his own supply. His supply is a piece of the larger common supply, but his piece is defined in such a way as greatly to increase the aggregate variability of supply above that which nature imposes; to increase the uncertainty as well; and, finally, to distribute these risks unequally."

To what extent can water rights transfers alleviate Gaffney's criticisms?

6. **Water Banking.** The State of California turned to "water banking" to deal with drought conditions in 1991. In February 1991, precipitation for the water year, which began on October 1, 1990, was only 25 per cent of normal statewide. In addition, four prior years of drought had substantially depleted reservoir storage. In response, the governor directed the Department of Water Resources, which operates the massive State Water Project, to establish a water bank to purchase

water from willing sellers for reallocation to urban areas, critical agricultural uses such as orchards and vineyards, environmental protection, and carryover storage.

Through the bank, more than 800,000 acre-feet of water were transferred to buyers from farmers, who either fallowed land or pumped groundwater to replace surface water sold to the bank. The bank was operated on a greatly reduced scale in 1992, and the Department of Water Resources subsequently developed a permanent water drought water bank program.

Although there have been some critics, the California drought water bank is generally considered a success. However, a number of factors may make it difficult to duplicate elsewhere. First, the extreme severity of the drought in California in 1991 created a climate of cooperation in which legal and political barriers which might otherwise have impeded the bank were suppressed. Second, the Department of Water Resources, which operates the State Water Project, provided funds to capitalize the bank and took the financial risks inherent in the bank. Third, because of idiosyncracies in California law, most of the transfers did not have to be approved by the Water Resources Control Board. Finally, California has unparalleled facilities to move large quantities of water around the state.

Colorado, Kansas, Idaho, and Texas have adopted water banking legislation, Colo. Rev. Stat. §§ 37-80.5-102 to -107 (expires in 2007), Kan. Stat. Ann. §§ 82a-762 to -769, Idaho Code §§ 42-1761 to -1765A; Tex. Water Code Ann. §§ 15.701 to .708, but water banking is not yet greatly utilized in these states. Arizona has also created a state operated water bank. Ariz. Rev. Stat. §§ 45-2401 to -2472. A primary purpose of this legislation is to allow Arizona to use its entire allocation of Colorado River Water by storing ("banking") water in depleted groundwater basins. However, the legislation does provide a mechanism for the transfer of some water to users in California and Nevada. The interstate functions of the bank must operate under federal regulations adopted by the Secretary of Interior. See 43 C.F.R. pt. 414. Colorado River issues are examined more fully in Chapter 6, Section 3.

CITY OF THORNTON v. FARMERS RESERVOIR & IRRIGATION CO.

Supreme Court of Colorado, 1978.
194 Colo. 526, 575 P.2d 382.

GROVES, JUSTICE. The City of Thornton ("Thornton"), a home rule municipality, on November 14, 1973 brought a proceeding in eminent domain against The Farmers Reservoir and Irrigation Company ("Farmers"). The property sought to be condemned may be described generally as the water and water rights, ditches and ditch rights of the Standley Lake Division of Farmers. * * *

Farmers is a mutual ditch company, organized and acting under sections 7-42-101 et seq., C.R.S.1973. The Standley Lake Division is one of four divisions of Farmers' extensive water distribution system. The legal title of the property sought to be condemned is in Farmers. At the time the action was brought Farmers had 1105 shareholders, 271 of whom held shares allocated to the Standley Lake Division. * * *

On June 29, 1975 the Water Rights Condemnation Act was adopted, to become effective on July 1, 1975. Sections 38-6-201 through 216, C.R.S.1973 (1976 Supp.). This legislation is here referred to as the 1975 Act. With notable exceptions, the 1975 Act contains the same provisions as sections 38-6-101 through 118, C.R.S.1973 (Eminent Domain Proceedings by Cities and Towns).

We now consider some of these exceptions. The 1975 Act provides that, in its petition for condemnation filed in the district court, the municipality shall pray for the appointment of three commissioners "to determine the issue of the necessity of exercising eminent domain as proposed in the petition." The 1975 Act further states that no municipality shall be allowed to condemn water rights for any anticipated or future needs in excess of 15 years. The 1975 Act further specifies that the municipality shall prepare a "community growth development plan" and a detailed statement concerning the proposed condemnation of water rights and the effect of the taking of the same. The plan and statement are to be presented to the commissioners. * * *

The 1975 Act contains the following provisions relating to the commission:

> The municipality's petition for condemnation of a water right "shall pray for the appointment of three disinterested commissioners appointed by the court * * * to determine the issue of the necessity of exercising eminent domain as proposed in the petition and, if the condemnation is to be allowed, to appraise the award of damages." Section 38-6-202(1), C.R.S.1973 (1976 Supp.).
>
> Prior to any hearing of condemnation the municipality shall prepare and update a community growth development plan and a detailed statement describing: (1) the water rights to be required and their present uses; (2) the effects from the change of the use of the water to the proposed use, including economic and environmental effects; (3) unavoidable adverse and irreversible effects from the taking; and (4) alternative sources of water supply that might be acquired. These statements shall be presented to the commission. Section 203.
>
> It is the duty of the commissioners to "[e]xamine and assess the growth development plan and statement provided by the municipality * * * obtain necessary information pursuant to powers granted * * * and make a determination as to the necessity of exercising the power of eminent domain for the proposed purposes." The commissioner shall provide "one of the following recommendations to the court, based upon their findings: (I) There exists no need and necessity for condemnation as proposed." Section 207(1).
>
> The commissioners shall, after hearing, certify the proper compensation to be made to the owners of property to be taken but, if "the commissioners find there exists no need and necessity for the condemnation proposed, they shall make no finding as to the value of the condemned property." Section 207(3) and (4).
>
> After filing of the report of the commissioners, written objections may be made thereto. "Any party interested in said proceeding may introduce such evidence as may tend to establish the right of the matter. The burden of

proof to change any finding, award, or assessment of said commissioners shall be upon the person objecting thereto. * * * The court, for good cause shown, may modify, alter, change, annul, or confirm the report of the commissioners, or any part thereof, or may order a new appraisement and assessment as to any of the property affected in the proceeding by the same commissioners or by other commissioners appointed by the court." Section 210.

The provisions of the 1975 Act relating to the appointment, action and effect of a commission to determine the issue of necessity of exercising eminent domain are unconstitutional as applied to Thornton as a home rule municipality. These provisions are in conflict with the express grant of eminent domain powers to home rule cities by Colo. Const. Art. XX, Sec. 1.

The 1975 Act does not state specifically the effect of a finding by the commission that there exists no need or necessity for condemnation as proposed. It is to be implied from the Act, however, that such a finding of the commission prevents the proposed condemnation; or, with the burden of proof upon a person objecting thereto, such finding is subject to judicial review. * * *

We quote with approval this statement from the brief of the amicus curiae, Colorado Municipal League:

> "The power of eminent domain is an inherent attribute of sovereignty limited only by applicable portions of the state and federal constitutions, and the exercise of the right of eminent domain is the exercise of the sovereign power. People of Colorado v. District Court, 207 F.2d 50 (10th Cir.1953). A portion of that sovereign power is granted directly by the people of the state of Colorado to the citizens of home rule municipalities through the adoption of Sections 1 and 6 of Article XX of the Colorado Constitution."

Colo. Const. Art. XX, Sec. 1 provides in part that a home rule municipality:

> "*shall have the power, within or without its territorial limits, to* construct, *condemn and purchase,* purchase, acquire, lease, add to, maintain, conduct and operate, *water works,* light plants, power plants, transportation systems, heating plants, and any other public utilities or works or ways local in use and extent, in whole or in part, *and everything required therefore* * * * and * * * the same or any part thereof may be purchased by said city and county which may enforce such purchase by proceedings at law as in taking land for public use by right of eminent domain." (emphasis added.)

By the adoption of Article XX, and particularly the above quoted provisions thereof, the people of Colorado intended to, and in effect did, delegate to home rule municipalities full power to exercise the right of eminent domain in the effectuation of any lawful, public and municipal purpose, including particularly the acquisition of water rights. Toll v. Denver, 139 Colo. 462, 340 P.2d 862 (1959); and Fishel v. Denver, 106 Colo. 576, 108 P.2d 236 (1940).

The determination of necessity is an essential part of the power of eminent domain and, once necessity is determined by legislative act, no further finding or adjudication is required. Londoner v. Denver, 52 Colo. 15, 119 P. 156 (1911). The determination of necessity by Thornton was not reviewable by the judiciary absent a showing of fraud or bad faith. Colorado State Board of Land Commissioners v. District Court, 163 Colo. 338, 430 P.2d 617 (1967); Dallasta v. Department of Highways, 153 Colo. 519, 387 P.2d 25 (1963); Mack v. Highway Commission, 152 Colo. 300, 381 P.2d 987 (1963); Denver v. Board of Commissioners, 113 Colo. 150, 156 P.2d 101 (1945); and Lavelle v. Town of Julesburg, 49 Colo. 290, 112 P. 774 (1911).

Relying on cases such as Denver v. Sweet, 138 Colo. 41, 329 P.2d 441 (1958), the respondents argue that the determination of necessity is a matter of statewide concern and, as a result, a home rule municipality is subject to statutory limitations in this area. We fully recognize that, generally, the legislative powers of a home rule municipality are superior with respect to local and municipal matters; and that, in cases of conflict between a statute and the ordinance of a home rule city relating to a matter of statewide concern, the statute must govern. Here, however, there is involved a specific constitutional power granted to home rule municipalities and, even though the matter may be of statewide concern, the General Assembly has no power to enact any law that denies a right specifically granted by the Colorado Constitution. * * *

The judgment of the district court is reversed and the cause remanded with directions to vacate the order of dismissal and to proceed not inconsonant with the views herein expressed.

ERICKSON, JUSTICE, dissenting. The majority opinion concludes that the City of Thornton is not subject to the provisions of the Water Rights Condemnation Act of 1975, section 38-6-201 through 216, C.R.S.1973 (1976 Supp.), because Thornton is a home rule city with the power of eminent domain, as provided in Article XX, Section 1 of the Colorado Constitution. The Colorado Constitution, however, grants a home rule municipality exclusive control only over matters of local and municipal concern. Matters of statewide concern remain subject to statewide regulation. Spears Free Clinic and Hospital For Poor Children v. State Board of Health, 122 Colo. 147, 220 P.2d 872 (1950); People v. McNichols, 91 Colo. 141, 13 P.2d 266 (1932).

A municipality's election to exercise eminent domain powers to condemn water rights is a matter of statewide concern, subject to statutory regulation by the General Assembly. Expanding water requirements of growing municipal populations are causing much of Colorado's scarce water, previously devoted to agricultural use, to be acquired for municipal use. Municipal condemnation of water rights necessarily has a tremendous impact upon the economies of agricultural areas and disrupts farm operations which are far distant from the condemning city. Therefore, I cannot accept the majority's conclusion that this area of statewide concern cannot be regulated on a statewide basis by the Water Rights Condemnation Act of 1975. * * *

I would, therefore, affirm the district court's dismissal.

Notes

1. **Economic and social effects of water rights transfers.** Gray & Nobe, Water Resource Economics, Externalities and Institutions in the United States, 1975 Proc., Int'l Conf. on Global Water Systems, Valencia, Spain.

"[A] brief historical perspective is in order. Thornton had developed rapidly during the 1950s as a suburb of Denver, the major metropolitan center of the intermountain region of the nation. Since its incorporation in 1956, the City of Thornton has grown so that it now encompasses 17 square miles and has a population of 27,000 people. During its period of rapid growth, the City of Denver provided adequately for its municipal water requirements so no serious thought was given to whether or not it would continue to do so indefinitely. In recent years, however, proposed additional trans-mountain diversions for augmenting Denver's water supply have been opposed because of adverse environmental impacts. Faced with a potential future limit to its growth due to an upper limit on its source of Denver water, the City of Thornton set out to satisfy its needs from alternative sources. This decision led in turn to the condemnation proceedings filed against the irrigation water users in the vicinity.

"The fact that the City of Thornton has resorted to condemnation proceedings is a clear indication of the great difficulty and high cost of obtaining alternative, new water supplies in its region. Thus, it can be inferred that such an option also does not exist for the irrigators if they lose their existing water rights. What are the adverse implications of this situation? First of all, it must be recognized that farmers in the area would not necessarily be forced out of agriculture. They could revert to dryland farming and continue to grow most of the crops now being produced. But yields will decline drastically and so will net incomes per acre (in the order of magnitude of dropping from a long term average of $200/acre under irrigation to $40/acre under dryland farming). In the short run, yields will drop even lower because, under irrigation, plant nutrients are applied in excess of the levels plants can utilize under dryland conditions, and it will take several years to leach out the excess.

"In addition, indirect—but nonetheless significant—adverse effects of the transfer of water rights in these cases would result. These are as follows:

1. Since real estate taxes are unlikely to decline in response to lower income yields under dryland farming, there would be abandonment of some farm land (presumably to other uses).

2. There will certainly be a displacement or loss of sunk capital invested by farmers in their irrigation systems, land leveling, and in equipment utilized in irrigated farming in excess of that required in dryland farming.

3. There will be a broadbased reduction in secondary benefits that have been accruing from irrigated agriculture to others in the vicinity, including farm labor jobs, farm machinery and fertilizer sales, plus lower sales volume in the food processing sector.

4. The farms affected are primary grain producers; the Front Range area of Colorado is already grain deficient and subsequent reduction in production will particularly affect a large number of grain dependent industries, including breweries, beef cattle feedlots, feed mills, and elevators.

5. Finally, there will be loss of open space as some of the agricultural area is built up in residential and industrial uses which will adversely affect the quality of life of the area via increased pollution and congestion (and will trigger another round of increasing water demand)."

The social and economic effects of fallowing land was of some concern in the operation of the California Water Bank, discussed supra p. 212, Note 6. One county filed an unsuccessful claim with the Department of Water Resources for increased welfare costs allegedly resulting from sales of water to the bank.

2. **Policy concerns.** Should the law require consideration of the negative social and economic effects associated with water rights transfers? Resource shifts are common in our economy and are the source of much economic growth. One economist has argued that there is little the government can or should do about the indirect economic and social dislocations which result from water transfers beyond existing wealth redistribution programs such as unemployment compensation and welfare. B. Delworth Gardner, The Untried Market Approach to Water Allocation, in New Courses for the Colorado River 166-67 (Gary Weatherford & F. Lee Brown eds., 1986). Another writer has objected that the consideration of such factors dulls market incentives because it increases the risk that a transfer will not be approved and makes the expectation of revenues from a transfer less certain. Stephen F. Williams, A Market-Based Approach to Water Rights: Evaluating Colorado's Water System, in Tradition, Innovation and Conflict: Perspectives on Colorado Water Law 113 (Lawrence J. MacDonnell ed., 1986).

Other writers have argued that water is a social good in which the interest of the public is paramount; to treat it as a commodity and allocate it on the basis of economic efficiency alone is a mistake. See Helen M. Ingram, Lawrence A. Scaff & Leslie Silko, Replacing Confusion with Equity: Alternatives for Water Policy in the Colorado River Basin, in New Courses for the Colorado River 177, 195, (Gary Weatherford & F. Lee Brown eds., 1986); Santos Gomez & Penn Loh, Communities and Water Markets: A Review of the Model Water Transfer Act, 4 Hastings W.-Nw. J. Envtl. L. & Pol'y 63 (1996); see also Joseph L. Sax, Understanding Transfers: The California Water Torture, in California Water Transfers: Gainers and Losers in Two Northern Counties (Raymond H. Coppock & Marcia Krieth, eds. 1992) (arguing that those who suffer economic loss as the result of water transfers should be compensated and that a transfer tax is the most expedient means to accomplish this); A. Dan Tarlock, Can Cowboys Become Indians? Protecting Western Communities as Endangered Cultural Remnants, 31 Ariz. St. L.J. 539 (1999) (examining community cultural claims and arguing that they should be considered in dealing with the effects of water reallocating).

In 1991, Arizona enacted legislation to mitigate the loss of tax base caused by the transfer of groundwater from rural areas. The legislation requires cities to pay a "transportation fee," ranging from $3 to $30 per acre-foot, to counties in which groundwater originates. Ariz. Rev. Stat. § 45-556.

3. **A celebrated case.** In re Application of Sleeper, Rio Arriba County, Cause No. RA 84-53 (C) (N.M. 1st Jud. Dist. April 16, 1985), involved a proposal to transfer water from irrigation to a recreational lake associated with a ski area. On appeal from a decision of the state engineer, the district court denied the transfer application, holding that it was not in the public interest. The court, noting that the development would produce mostly menial jobs for local residents, said:

"[I]t is simply assumed by the Applicants that greater economic benefits are more desirable than the preservation of a cultural identity. This is clearly not so. Northern New Mexicans possess a fierce pride over their history, traditions and culture. This region of northern New Mexico and its living culture are recognized at the state and federal levels as possessing significant cultural value, not measurable in dollars and cents. The deep-felt and tradition bound ties of northern New Mexico families to the land and water are central to maintenance of that culture. * * *

"I am persuaded that to transfer water rights, devoted for more than a century to agricultural purposes, in order to construct a playground for those who can pay is a poor trade, indeed."

Did the court strike the appropriate balance between economic benefits and social costs? Should judges be deciding such issues? Should water officials, selected primarily for technical expertise, be deciding such issues? Which official, agency, or institution is most competent to undertake this balancing process?

The New Mexico Court of Appeals reversed the district court on the grounds that transfer statutes in effect at that time precluded the state engineer from considering the public interest. In re Application of Sleeper, 760 P.2d 787 (N.M. 1988). The statutes, later amended, now require the state engineer to deny transfers which are not in the public interest. See footnote 21, supra p. 211.

4. **Condemnation powers.** In each western state, cities and towns are given the power to condemn water rights for the purpose of obtaining a municipal supply, and hence have a preferred right in this sense, although most of the statutes conferring the power are found in the laws relating to municipal governments and not in the water codes. Statutes granting a preference for domestic use are also construed as conferring the power of eminent domain. See Town of Sterling v. Pawnee Ditch Extension Co., 94 P. 339 (Colo. 1908).

In Nebraska and Idaho the constitutions give an order of precedence between various uses when the waters of a stream are not sufficient for all, and each expressly provides for condemnation and compensation as the means of acquiring the water of the non-preferred user. Neb. Const. art. XV, § 6; Idaho Const. art. XV, § 3. Wyoming's statutory list of preferences is carried into execution by a combination of eminent domain and an administrative procedure authorizing the change of use. Wyo. Stat. Ann. §§ 41-3-102, -103.

SECTION 6. REUSE

DEPARTMENT OF ECOLOGY v. UNITED STATES BUREAU OF RECLAMATION

Supreme Court of Washington, 1992.
118 Wash.2d 761, 827 P.2d 275.

EN BANC. The Washington State Department of Ecology (Department) granted to J.M. Hanson a permit to appropriate water from a stream running across his property. Hanson's property is located within the boundaries of a federal irrigation project and the stream carries, at least in part, water that the project diverted from the Columbia River pursuant to the federal government's own rights of appropriation. * * *

The Columbia River Basin Irrigation Project is a massive federal project providing irrigation water for lands along the Columbia River. * * * The federal government, through the United States Bureau of Reclamation, contracted with local irrigation districts to operate and maintain the facilities and to deliver the water to the basin's farmlands. * * * Certain farmlands (known as "farm units") receive a direct water supply from the irrigation districts. In return, the farm units pay a proportionate share of the cost of the facilities.

After these farm units use the water for irrigation, significant amounts of the water seep through the land and accumulate, either above or below ground, within the project's borders. The parties refer to this water as "waste, seepage or return flow water", abbreviated as "WSRF water". * * *

Although some of the WSRF water returns to the Columbia River without being used for further irrigation, the project does recapture and reuse a portion of the used water. The irrigation districts enter into "water service contracts" with area landowners granting the landowners the right to divert the previously used water for purposes of further irrigation. These landowners pay a portion of the project's construction and maintenance costs, but a smaller portion than that charged to the landowners who used the water initially. The landowners entering into water service contracts pay for their own costs of capturing and diverting the runoff water.

J.M. Hanson owns farmland within the boundaries of the federal project and he receives water from the project to irrigate portions of his land. In the early 1980's, Hanson became interested in obtaining more water to irrigate an additional 30 acres of his land. Particularly, he wanted to divert water from an unnamed stream flowing across his property.

A significant portion of the water in Hanson's stream is WSRF water from other project lands. * * * The stream carries the water across Hanson's land and then, within a mile of his proposed point of diversion, empties into the Columbia River. The land downstream from Hanson's is undeveloped and currently has no use for project waters. The project currently has no facilities in place along this stream with which it could recapture this WSRF water, and it currently has no intention of building such facilities in the future. * * *

Hanson * * * applied to the Department of Ecology in order to obtain his own independent rights of appropriation in the stream. The United States Bureau of Reclamation opposed Hanson's application. The Bureau argued that the WSRF water in Hanson's stream had already been appropriated to the federal government, thereby precluding any further reappropriation.

The Department investigated Hanson's application and the Bureau's objection. It determined that the statutory requirements for granting the permit were met * * *. Accordingly, the Department granted Hanson's permit application.

* * * At particular issue is whether the water in Hanson's stream is still subject to the federal government's prior right of appropriation. If the federal right still applies to this water, then the Department may not grant any conflicting appropriation rights in the water.

The holder of a water right owns no title to any molecules of water until that water is diverted. Once an appropriator diverts water and brings it under his control and possession, the appropriator owns it as personal property. This principle is generally held throughout the Western States. See 1 S. Wiel, Water Rights in the Western States § 35 (3d ed. 1911); 2 C. Kinney, Irrigation and Water Rights and the Arid Region Doctrine of Appropriation of Waters §§ 773, 774 (2d ed. 1912); 1 W. Hutchins, Water Rights Laws in the Nineteen Western States 144 (1971).

The appropriator's rights in the particular molecules of diverted water do not necessarily end when the water has been used once for irrigation. See Ide v. United States, 263 U.S. 497, 506, 44 S.Ct. 182, 185, 68 L.Ed. 407 (1924). An appropriator has a right to recapture and reuse this WSRF water, even under certain circumstances, when the water has left the appropriator's land and entered a natural watercourse.

This much the parties agree on. Where the parties differ is with regard to when the appropriator's rights in particular molecules of water end.[6]

The irrigation districts cite to a line of cases holding that an appropriator's rights in particular water molecules extend at least as long as the water remains within the boundaries of the appropriator's property. We refer to this theory as the "geographical" test. In Miller v. Wheeler, 54 Wash. 429, 434-35, 103 P. 641 (1909), the court stated that landowners who irrigate using appropriated water retain the right to WSRF water while it remains on their land. This rule is also the law in other jurisdictions. One of the clearest statements of this rule is from Nevada:

> *So long as [waste] water exists upon [the plaintiffs'] lands, it is their property*, and they may consent to others acquiring rights therein upon their property and in ditches thereupon for the purpose of conveying such waters to the lands of such other parties. These waters, while upon the lands of the plaintiffs Bidleman, were certainly not subject to appropriation by the defendants. * * *

(Citation omitted. Italics ours.) Bidleman v. Short, 38 Nev. 467, 471, 150 P. 834 (1915). Similar pronouncements are found in cases from other Western States. See Barker v. Sonner, 135 Or. 75, 79, 294 P. 1053 (1931) (water is not even considered waste water until it has left the land of the original appropriator); Smithfield West Bench Irr. Co. v. Union Cent. Life Ins. Co., 105 Utah 468, 472-73, 142 P.2d 866 (1943); Jones v. Warmsprings Irr. Dist., 162 Or. 186, 198-99, 91 P.2d 542 (1939) (an irrigation district's water becomes free, unappropriated water when it leaves lands within an irrigation district and returns to the stream from which its was diverted, absent any attempt by landowners in the district to control it).

---

6. As the Department of Ecology stresses in its brief, we are not being asked to determine whether the federal government has abandoned its water rights. Abandonment of water rights has broader consequences than abandonment of water molecules. Abandoning water molecules, as opposed to abandoning water rights, does not affect the party's right to change its practices so as to recapture future supplies of diverted water. See Stevens v. Oakdale Irr. Dist., 13 Cal.2d 343, 350, 90 P.2d 58 (1939).

Here, the water in Hanson's stream is still within the boundaries of the irrigation project. Therefore, under the irrigation districts' theory, the water would still be appropriated to the project.

The Department counters that an appropriator's rights do not depend on the water's geographical location. It instead cites a number of authorities for the proposition that the duration of an appropriator's rights in particular molecules of water depends on continued control and possession of the water. One of the cases cited by the Department describes the test as follows:

> When possession of the actual water, or corpus, has been relinquished, or lost by discharge without intent to recapture, property in it ceases. This is not the abandonment of a water right, but merely an abandonment of specific portions of water, i.e., the very particles which are discharged or have escaped from control.

(Italics omitted.) Stevens v. Oakdale Irr. Dist., 13 Cal.2d 343, 350, 90 P.2d 58 (1939). General statements of this standard seem to be fairly well accepted in the Western States. See 1 S. Wiel, Water Rights in the Western States § 37 (3d ed. 1911).

The Department of Ecology argues that under its theory the water molecules in Hanson's stream are no longer appropriated to the federal government. According to the Department, once the water reaches Hanson's proposed point of diversion, the irrigation project has discharged the water without intent to recapture, as the water is headed toward the project's outer boundary and the project has no current plans to recapture this water.

It appears that both the Department's "control and possession" test and the irrigation districts' geographical test are wellfounded in the water law of the Western States. We therefore strive to construe these lines of authority so as to give greatest possible effect to each. We conclude that an appropriator's rights in particular molecules of water do not end while the water remains within the boundaries of the appropriator's property, and that after water has left those boundaries, the termination of the appropriator's rights depends on the "control and possession" test. Accordingly, once an appropriator has discharged water from his or her own property, then the issue becomes whether the appropriator nevertheless retains an intent to recapture that water, whether downstream on another piece of property or otherwise. * * * Thus, the theories may be fully reconciled by applying the geographical test until the water has left the appropriator's lands and the "control and possession" test after that point.

[W]e conclude the Department abused its discretion in granting Hanson's permit application. We cannot uphold the Department's interpretation of the law when doing so would run counter to the most directly applicable principle of western water law. * * *

Notes

1. **Policy behind the decision.** What policy does the decision serve? Isn't the court simply allowing the Bureau to play the role of "dog in the

manger"—denying the water to others although the Bureau has no use for it? In an omitted part of the opinion the court said:

"Additional support for our decision flows from the fact that the original appropriator here is a federal irrigation project that was formed for the very purpose of supplying farmers like Hanson with irrigation water. Supplying this water is an expensive undertaking, and each farmer using the water—even those using WSRF water—is required to pay a share of the costs of building and maintaining the project's facilities. Under the Department's theory, Hanson would be able to obtain the water without having to pay his fair share of the system's costs.

"Moreover, if Hanson is allowed to obtain water rights without paying his portion of the system's costs, others similarly situated would have to be similarly treated. Even those landowners who currently obtain WSRF water through water service contracts—and who therefore currently contribute toward the payment of the system's costs—could potentially do so as well, for the water service contracts are terminable by landowners at the end of each year. The irrigation districts fear these landowners too would seek to avoid the system's true costs. The Bureau of Reclamation has gone so far as to maintain that the potential loss of repayment from these sources 'seriously jeopardizes the successful completion of the project.' While we cannot independently determine if this last assertion overstates the impact on the project, the potential for disruption to the system certainly is present." 827 P.2d at 281.

Is this case an example of a "hard case" making "bad law"? Is there some narrower legal basis on which Hanson might be forced to pay for project water like other irrigators? Does the answer lie in some other method of charging for project benefits? For example, instead of entering into "water service contracts," could the irrigation district assess the lands of those who use or could use WSRF water, including Hanson, for the benefits which the availability of WSRF water provides? See infra p. 419, Note 4. Would the court have the authority to impose such a charge if the enabling legislation in Washington does not provide for it?

If the court had held that Hanson could appropriate the WSRF water, would that have prevented the Bureau from recapturing and reusing the water at a future time? See the next case.

2. **More on the right to recapture.** In Binning v. Miller, 102 P.2d 54 (Wyo. 1940), the right to recapture waste water still on the original land and to reuse it on that land was apparently regarded as existing indefinitely, without time limit. Jones v. Warmsprings Irrigation District, 91 P.2d 542 (Or. 1939), held that the intent to recapture must exist at the time the water is appropriated, and that the water is abandoned to downstream users if that intent is not exercised within a reasonable time. In United States v. Haga, 276 F. 41 (D. Idaho 1921), the principal requisite was that the first appropriator be able to identify the recaptured water as that added by his operations.

3. **"In lieu diversion."** Nebraska v. Wyoming, 325 U.S. 589 (1945), involved the Bureau of Reclamation's Kendrick Project, under construction on the North Platte River in Wyoming. The project would be supplied almost entirely by water stored in Seminoe Dam and diverted at Alcova Dam to the project lands in Wyoming. Return flows from the project were estimated to be 96,000 acre feet, 46,000 during the irrigation season. The Bureau did not wish to use the water

below the point where it returned to the river, but could use it to enlarge the project. It therefore proposed to divert an amount equivalent to this return flow through the canal at Alcova "in lieu of" recapturing the actual return flow.

The Court refused to permit the diversion. "But we think the proposal is basically not in accord with the principle underlying [Ide v. United States, 263 U.S. 497 (1924)]. That principle is that although the water rights belong to the landowners, the owner of the irrigation project has an interest in the appropriative rights to the extent of obtaining the fullest use of the water for the project. It may therefore, retain control over the water until abandonment. We think it goes too far to say that when the return flows are abandoned, they may nevertheless be exchanged for upstream diversions by the same amount. When the return flows are abandoned, they become subject to appropriation downstream. See 2 Kinney, Irrigation and Water Rights (2d Ed. 1912) § 1114. They no longer remain subject to control for further use in the project. Any claim to them or their equivalent under the form of an 'in lieu of' diversion is lost." 325 U.S. at 636-37.

FUSS v. FRANKS

Supreme Court of Wyoming, 1980.
610 P.2d 17.

[Waste-water from the plaintiffs' lands collected in a drainage ditch built by the Goshen County Irrigation District (G.I.D.) in the borrow pit of a "ditch-rider" road, which ran along the lower end of the plaintiffs' lands. The water was carried by the drainage ditch to the borrow pit of a state highway where it flowed for some distance, eventually crossing the highway in an underground pipe constructed by G.I.D. After the water crossed the highway, one of the plaintiffs, Fuss, had for many years used it to irrigate a piece of land. Fuss held no appropriation to use the water on this piece of land. The defendant, Franks, received an appropriation permit to construct a dam in the highway borrow pit to intercept the water and use it as a supplemental supply for his lands.]

ROSE, JUSTICE. * * * We will address these following issues, which we find to be dispositive of all material questions raised by the appellants:
* * *

Point 1: Was the water from the highway borrow pit lawfully appropriated by Franks?

Whether or not Franks' appropriation was lawful is resolved by answering whether or not the State Engineer had authority to approve the Franks permit in July of 1979. In this case, there was testimony that the seepage water in contest here would, if uninterrupted, flow into a natural stream. This is a qualifying requirement for appropriation. Binning v. Miller, 55 Wyo. 451, 102 P.2d 54 (1940).

In *Binning* we said:

> " * * * And so it is held in a number of cases that seepage water which, if not intercepted, would naturally reach the stream, is just as much a part of the stream as the waters of any tributaries and must be permitted to return thereto, if the owner cannot make beneficial use thereof. Rock Creek Ditch Co. v. Miller, 93 Mont. 248, 17 P.2d 1074, and note thereto in 89 A.L.R.

218-227; 67 C.J. 1006, 1015. That would seem to be the more reasonable rule in irrigating states * * *."

This concept was reaffirmed in Bower v. Big Horn Canal Association, 77 Wyo. 80, 307 P.2d 593 (1957).

The permit having been issued to Franks, this constituted prima facie evidence of his right to take the water. Hunziker v. Knowlton, 78 Wyo. 241, 322 P.2d 141 (1958). This being so, it fell to appellants to allege facts sufficient to show that they had a right to the water superior to that of Franks, the permittee.

Appellants say in their brief:

> "* * * The appropriator who captures upon his land waters not fully used for irrigation, sometimes referred to as waste water, may recapture the water for beneficial *use upon his premises for which the water had been appropriated.* * * *" (Emphasis supplied.)

That is a correct statement of law. It cannot, however, inure to the favor of appellants under the facts of this case.

We commented upon *Binning,* supra, where the facts were uniquely similar to those to be found here, when, in *Bower,* supra, we said:

> "* * * The real question in the case [*Binning*] was whether the prior appropriation of what was termed in the original application as 'waste and seepage water' was good as against the owner of the land *from which said water came.* The court held that the seepage water which formed a natural stream might be appropriated, subject to the right of the land owner to use the water for beneficial purposes *upon the land for which the water forming the seepage was originally appropriated.*" (Emphasis and bracketed matter supplied.)

This language means that the owner of land upon which seepage or waste water rises has the right to use and reuse—capture and recapture—such waste waters for use only "upon the land for which the water forming the seepage was originally appropriated." When the water leaves the land for which it was appropriated and would, if left to flow uninterrupted, reach a natural stream, it becomes eligible to other and separate appropriation for other and different uses. It leaves the landowner upon which the seepage rose, and from which it has escaped, without any superior right to such water by reason of its having been utilized upon the land to which it was first appropriated.

We recognized this concept in *Bower,* supra, when we said:

> "* * * Additionally, it is equitable, in accordance with the constitutional provisions of this State, and in line with our previous holdings, that we here decree seepage water arising on Bower's land to be subject *to appropriation* by him (subject to prescribed procedures) for lands *other than those upon which the seepage arises.* * * *" (Emphasis supplied.)

The "prescribed procedures" referred to are the application requirements for a water permit under the statutes. The rationale for this rule finds its genesis in the doctrine long since established in this state to the effect that waters become appurtenant to the lands for which they are acquired and, unless the statutes are followed with respect to change of use, the waters cannot be detached and assigned to other land without the loss of priority.

The water which accumulates in the collection ditch separating the Franks land from Bremers, Fusses and Baumgartner in Section 5, and which thereafter runs into the highway right-of-way originates on the land of the last three mentioned owners and is adjudicated in the name of the individual landowners for use upon their particular land tracts. This fact statement is undisputed. Therefore, once the water escapes the aforementioned Bremers, Fusses and Baumgartner lands in Section 5 and finds its way to the collection ditch and thence to the highway right-of-way, it must be regarded as having escaped the land to which it is appropriated and, since it would, if undisturbed, have flowed to a natural stream, it, therefore, becomes eligible for other appropriation.

Franks' permit was valid because the Fusses, Bremers and Baumgartner had no superior right to the water after it left their properties to accumulate in the collection ditch and from there flow to the highway right-of-way borrow pit. * * *

Notes

1. **Rights of junior appropriators.** Comstock v. Ramsey, 133 P. 1107 (Colo. 1913), is the leading case holding that return flow seeping from the lands of a senior appropriator cannot be intercepted and reused *on different lands* when the water is tributary to the stream and junior appropriators have relied on it to serve their ditches downstream from the point of reentry. The same rule relied on in Farmers High Line Canal & Irrigation Co. v. City of Golden, supra p. 197—that junior appropriators are entitled to have conditions on the stream maintained as they were when the junior appropriations were made—was relied on in *Comstock*.

Why are junior appropriators entitled to have stream conditions maintained when a senior appropriator transfers water (*High Line Canal*) or tries to recapture water for use on different lands (*Comstock*) but not when the senior recaptures it for use on the same land? I.e., can the rule of *Comstock* and *High Line Canal* be reconciled with the rule permitting a senior appropriator to recapture return flows for reuse on the land for which it was initially appropriated to the detriment of junior appropriators who have come to rely on them?

2. **Appropriating return flows at the inception of a water right.** In Water Supply & Storage Co. v. Curtis, 733 P.2d 680 (Colo. 1987), an applicant for a water right requested a ruling that "the water may be used and reused and put to a succession of uses until totally consumed." In effect, the applicant attempted to appropriate its own return flows for future unspecified uses at the same time that it made the initial appropriation, thereby avoiding the problems encountered by Fuss in the principal case. The court indicated that such a ruling might be proper in a suitable case but denied the request because the applicant had no concrete plans for reuse of return flows and, thus, lacked the requisite "intent to appropriate."

3. **Protecting seepage with the law of servitudes.** A Californian court found a method of compelling the continuance of the source of the water. What kind of a right did the servient owner have in Krieger v. Pacific Gas & Electric

Co., 173 Cal. Rptr. 751 (Ct. App. 1981)? The Utica Ditch originally crossed public land that was later patented to Krieger's predecessor. By federal statute the patented land was subject to a right of way for the ditch. When PG&E acquired the water right it began to line the ditch with liquid concrete ("gunite"). Krieger sought an injunction. PG&E cross-complained against Krieger for siphoning water from the ditch with a hose. The court held that the original earthen ditch "fixed the extent of the servitude," and enjoined further guniting as an enlargement of the easement, not within the "secondary easement" to make repairs. The "riparian vegetation" subsisting on the leakage was a benefit enjoyed by the landowner, said the court, and its loss would be an increase in the burden of the easement. No waste was involved, in the court's mind, the seepage was said to be beneficial to the riparian vegetation. Although the injunction against the siphon was held appropriate, the final declaration of the rights of the parties was, "The water flowing in the ditch is the property of PG&E, and [Krieger] has no right to that water; however, water which percolates, leaks or seeps through the ditch to [Krieger's] property thereby becomes his property."

4. **Tort liability for drainage.** "Waste water" or "tail water," surface return flow from irrigation, is a common phenomenon in irrigated country. Common law or civil law rules of drainage of natural surface waters do not apply to waters artificially brought upon the land. The owner of the upper irrigated land must acquire from the owner of the lower land permission or an easement to drain the waste water across the land. Loosli v. Heseman, 162 P.2d 393 (Idaho 1945). The upper owner may, however, discharge into a watercourse on the lower land such reasonable quantities of excess waters as can be carried away without injury to the lower lands. Provident Irrigation Dist. v. Cecil, 271 P.2d 157 (Cal. Ct. App. 1954). It has been said that every irrigation project eventually becomes a drainage project. Ditches for the collection of waste water and its redistribution to other users, and for the drainage of what would otherwise become seeped and boggy lands, are commonly constructed as part of modern projects, or as additions to older projects, by drainage districts or by the irrigation district that distributes the water.

THAYER v. CITY OF RAWLINS

Supreme Court of Wyoming, 1979.
594 P.2d 951.

ROSE, JUSTICE. This appeal concerns the rights of the defendant water users to effluent water discharged by the City of Rawlins. By virtue of water rights dating from 1900, the City of Rawlins has imported all of its municipal water supplies from the North Platte River and from Sage Creek, a tributary of the North Platte River. After using the water for municipal purposes, the City has historically discharged the resulting effluent into a channel, known as Sugar Creek, which connects with the North Platte River. In the past, the point of this discharge was above the points at which the defendants diverted the effluent for irrigation, stock water and other purposes. Defendants diverted the effluent pursuant to certificates of appropriations giving them priorities to the Sugar Creek effluent dating from 1914. To be in compliance with state and federal water-quality laws, the City must now meet certain minimum-quality standards before discharging water into Sugar Creek. To meet these standards, the City of Rawlins proposes to establish an aerated lagoon system at a location which will cause the purified water to reach Sugar Creek at a point below the defendants' point of diversion. In an effort to determine the legal effect of this proposal, the City sought and was granted a judgment declaring that the defendants were not entitled to compensation for the loss of this water. We will affirm the district court's judgment. * * *

Defendants premise their claim to compensation on the belief that Sugar Creek below the City of Rawlins has, due to the passage of a long period of time, become a natural stream subject to appropriation, thus entitling the defendants to protections afforded to other holders of water rights in the state. * * *

More than fifty years ago, this court stated, in Wyoming Hereford Ranch v. Hammond Packing Co., 33 Wyo. 14, 236 P. 764, 772 (1925):

> " * * * Even in this state, where the conservation of water for irrigation is so important, we would not care to hold that in disposing of sewage the city could not adopt some means that would completely consume it. It might, we think, be diverted to waste places, or to any chosen place where it would not become a nuisance, without any consideration of the demands of water users who might be benefitted by its disposition in some other manner. * * * "

While we may not rely on the Wyoming Hereford Ranch decision for a disposition of the present case—due to significant factual distinctions—it is somewhat prophetic with respect to the clash, between concepts of western water law and the directives of environmental-protection statutes, now before us. We will not, however, attempt to decide all of the potential questions that are bound to arise as the demands for cleaner environment begin to impinge on the availability of sufficient supplies of water. For example, we are not asked in this case to theorize with respect to the rights of water users on the North Platte River in the event that the City had gone ahead with its original plan to entirely consume, through treatment, the waters it imports from the North Platte and its tributaries. These questions and others related thereto are bound to arise, but it is important to understand that they are not now before the court. See, gen., Comment, "Water Law—Cessation of Return Flow as a Means of Complying With Pollution Control Laws," 12 Land & Water L.Rev. 431 (1977); and Muys, "Quality v. Quantity: The Federal Water Pollution Control Act's Quiet Revolution in Western Water Rights Administration," 23 Rocky Mtn. Min. L. Inst. 1013 (1977). As a result, our discussion and disposition of this case will be narrowly drawn.

The fundamental question becomes: Do the defendants have a right to compensation for a loss occasioned by the City's change in the point of discharge of imported waters? It has been stated that generally junior appropriators have vested rights in a continuation of stream conditions existing at the time of their appropriations, thus entitling them to resist changes in points of diversion or use which materially affect their rights. However, an importer of water—at least insofar as these defendants are concerned—has the right to reuse, successively use and make disposition of imported waters. See, City and County of Denver Bd. of Water Commissioners v. Fulton Irrigating Ditch Co., Colo., 179 Colo. 47, 506 P.2d 144 (1972). Even though, at the time of the Fulton Irrigation Ditch decision, there was a statute authorizing the conclusion reached, the Colorado Supreme Court opined that the rule would be the same without the statute, subject to contrary contractual obligations.

The right of the City to use such imported waters finds its roots in the common law of property and the Puritan ethic: One who by his own effort adds to the supply of a stream, is entitled to the water even though a senior priority might be without water. A person should reap the benefit of his own efforts, and a priority relates only to the *natural* supply of the stream at the time of appropriation.

These concepts are not new to Wyoming water law, since they have been applied to protect the right of a senior appropriator to recapture waste and seepage water. See, Binning v. Miller, 55 Wyo. 451, 102 P.2d 54 (1940). The lower landowner using such water merely takes his chances as to future supplies, no matter how long he uses such water.

Defendants seem to want this court to declare that the City has abandoned its right to make a change in the point of discharge of these imported waters. We indicated in Binning v. Miller, supra, that if the senior appropriator had allowed the lower landowner to use waste water for 35 years, but then legitimately began to use it himself, the lower landowner would have no right to complain—"The water is always different from year to year." This question, in its broad sense, was raised but not answered in the Fulton Irrigation Ditch case, supra. See, gen., Stephen F. Williams, "Optimizing Water Uses: The Return Flow Issue," 44 U. Colo. L. Rev. 301, 318-321 (1973). We hold that in the imported-water context—which gives the importer the unrestricted right to reuse, successively use and make disposition—the importer's right to do these things is not subject to abandonment insofar as these defendants are concerned. It must be remembered that any other holding would be inconsistent with the fact that the defendants depend entirely on the City's sufferance—it is always free to terminate the importation. Under such circumstances, we are reluctant to declare an abandonment. * * *

We turn, then, to the statutory provisions which purportedly vest the State Engineer or Board of Control with primary jurisdiction over the City's proposed actions. Defendants claim that the City's water-treatment proposal constitutes either a change or expansion in use—because the water will be used as a purifying agent, instead of only as a flushing agent—or a change in the place of use, because the sewage will be transported for treatment to a place outside the city limits. The City, on the other hand, contends that there will be no change in use since the use will still be for municipal purposes, and that the place of use will remain with the City of Rawlins. The only change, according to the City, is a change in the place of discharge.

The difficulty in attempting to classify the changes required by water-pollution-control laws has been noted. Comment, supra, 12 Land & Water L.Rev. 431, 448. The Colorado Supreme Court has indicated that changes in points of discharge of sewage are not governed by the same rules as changes in points of diversion. Metropolitan Denver Sewage Disposal Dist. No. 1 v. Farmers Reservoir and Irrigation Co., 179 Colo. 36, 38, 499 P.2d 1190, 1193 (1972). This conclusion has, in turn, been severely criticized. Williams, supra, at 304-311. We find no need, however, to put a label on what the City of Rawlins proposes to do, in order to determine whether the City must file a petition under § 41-3-104.

The purpose of § 41-3-104 is to provide a procedure for those wishing to change a water right *and* to place limitations on the quantity of water that can be transferred. We must ask why the City's proposal should be subjected to these procedures. The manifest result of a § 41-3-104 proceeding is the entry of a Board of Control order limiting the amount of water transferred by a change in use or a change in the place of use. Insofar as these defendants are concerned, we have already held that the City has the *unrestricted* right to reuse, successively use and make disposition of these imported waters. If these rights are not subject to restriction, it would be anomalous to require the City to submit to a procedure that assumes that restrictions are permissible and, indeed, required. As a result, we hold that the State Engineer and Board of Control have no jurisdiction, by virtue of § 41-3-104 over the controversy between these parties. * * *

ROONEY, JUSTICE, dissenting, with whom RAPER, CHIEF JUSTICE joins.

I dissent. I agree with the contention of the defendants that this matter is prematurely in the courts, and that the board of control should first apply its expertise in passing on the issues. * * *

The necessary expertise and experience in water matters are with the board of control and the office of the state engineer. They are conversant with the new problems occasioned by increased industrial and municipal needs for water; additional use of water for recreational purposes; transbasin diversions; interstate aspects of water availability and control; intrusion into underground aquifers; diversions of underground streams; development of chemical and physical methods for control of initial flow, for control of return flow and for control of storage of water; pollution; and waste. And they are conversant with the interplay of these new problems on customary and historical use of water. * * *

Portions of § 2 of Art. 8, Wyoming Constitution, are emphasized as follows:

> "There shall be constituted a board of control, to be composed of the state engineer and superintendents of the water divisions; which shall, under such regulations as may be prescribed by law, have the supervision of the waters of the state and of their *appropriation, distribution and diversion,* and of the various officers connected therewith. Its decisions to be *subject to review by the courts* of the state." (Emphasis supplied.)

Supervision of "distribution and diversion" includes supervision of water which is not appropriated, and it includes supervision of appropriated water at times and places other than those involved at the initial distribution or diversion. It includes supervision of individual appropriations, of trans-basin appropriations, of trans-state deliveries, of underground water—in short, of all water. * * *

The majority opinion overlooks this primary jurisdiction and the extensive control of quantity and quality of water in the board of control for the purpose of securing beneficial use of it. The majority opinion lays its cornerstone on the proposition that an importer of water has the unobstructed right to reuse, successively use and make disposition of imported waters. The importer, then, would have supervision over the appropriation, distribution and diversion of such water. Imported water is no less precious than any other kind of water. The mere fact that it is transported from one basin to another does not make it more subject to waste, more subject to the whims of any private citizen, less subject to the requirement of beneficial use, or less subject to the constitutional supervision of the board of control. If there is case law to the contrary, I would reverse it. If there is statutory law to the contrary, I would hold such to be unconstitutional. * * *

This case had its origin in a very worthy direction to the City of Rawlins to clean up its discarded water. To do so will cost money. It would be incongruous, in view of the value of water in Wyoming, to not also direct the city to preserve the water as it cleans it—preserve it for additional beneficial use. This may cost more money. Cleaning water is no more worthy than preserving it. The board of control should determine the relation of beneficial use to other aspects of the project. The board may authorize the project as now planned. It may direct pumping to the original place of discharge. It may direct a different method of cleaning. It may require payment of just compensation to the damaged appropriators. It may require change in reservoir construction to provide for a deeper but less extensive body of water so as to reduce evaporation. It may reach the same conclusion as did the district court. * * *

I would reverse and remand with directions that the plaintiff be ordered to submit the plans for the project to the state engineer for review and approval.

Notes

1. **Abandonment and intent to reuse.** In City of Thornton v. Bijou Irrigation Co., 926 P.2d 1 (Colo. 1996), the Colorado Supreme Court answered the question which the principal case notes it had previously raised but not answered regarding the abandonment of imported water. The court joined Wyoming in holding that the rights to reuse, to successively use, and to dispose of imported water are not subject to abandonment. *Bijou* also held that "intent" to reuse at the time of initial appropriation and importation is not a precondition to the these special rights in imported water.

2. **Use of natural facilities to transport and store imported water.** The City of Los Angeles brings water from the Owens River Valley to the San Fernando Valley where it spreads part of it in gravel pits and spreading grounds with the object of having it sink beneath the surface to join other water in the gravels of the valley floor. It sells other parts of it to farmers of the San Fernando Valley, 27 1/2% of which also sinks beneath the surface. Both the induced recharge and the return flows join waters normally present in the valley and eventually become part of the surface flow of the Los Angeles River, from which the city takes its water. The cities of Glendale and Burbank pump water from

wells in the valley. Held, Los Angeles has a prior right to both the recharge and the return flow. City of Los Angeles v. City of Glendale, 142 P.2d 289 (Cal. 1943). The court, per Traynor, J., stated:

"Plaintiff had a prior right to the use of the water brought to the San Fernando Valley. It did not abandon that right when it spread the water for the purpose of economical transportation and storage. It used a similar storage system at the source of this supply in the Owens River Valley. By availing itself of these natural reservoirs, it spared its citizens the cost of financing the construction of additional dams, if, indeed, appropriate sites were available at the lower end of the aqueduct. Early in the history of the state, this court recognized the advantage of permitting the use of natural surface facilities, stream beds, dry canyons and the like, for the transportation of water (Hoffman v. Stone, 7 Cal. 46; Butte Canal & Ditch Co. v. Vaughn, 11 Cal. 143, 70 Am.Dec. 769) for 'It would be a harsh rule * * * to require those engaged in these enterprises to construct an actual ditch along the whole route through which the waters were carried, and to refuse them the economy that nature occasionally afforded in the shape of a dry ravine, gulch, or cañon.' Hoffman v. Stone, 7 Cal. at page 49. The rule of these cases was incorporated into section 1413 of the Civil Code. In codifying this rule, designed to encourage the use of natural facilities, the Legislature could hardly have intended to abrogate the right to use other natural facilities for similar purposes. Under these circumstances, the maxim expressio unius alterius exclusio est is inapplicable. * * * It would be as harsh to compel plaintiff to build reservoirs when natural ones were available as to compel the construction of an artificial ditch beside a stream bed. In making water available for irrigation, plaintiff sought not only to increase cultivation of the land, but to convey some of the water into the underground reservoir of the valley. Thus, in selling water to the farmers, as in spreading water, plaintiff was interested in its economical transportation and storage.

"The use by others of this water as it flowed to the subterranean basin does not cut off plaintiff's rights. * * *

"It is immaterial whether the farmers who use the imported water acquire their rights through a transfer of land that includes a water right (United States v. Ide, supra) or by some other means. See Stevens v. Oakdale Irr. Dist., supra. In any event the importer brings the water to the land of the farmer, and the farmer uses it. Nothing would be gained by requiring plaintiff to change the form of its contracts from a 'sale' of the water to a transfer of the right to its use. In making water available, plaintiff selected an area where it could recover as much water as possible from seepage, and it should not be deprived of the benefit of its foresight."

3. **When is water "imported?"** City of Thornton v. Bijou Irrigation Co., supra Note 1, at 81:

"Through its use of the Larimer County Canal, Thornton transports water from the Poudre River to an area that the river otherwise would not have reached. However, the area to which the water is carried is not within an entirely different watershed or drainage area. The water was initially diverted from the Poudre River, a tributary of the South Platte River, and the aquifer fed by the return flows from irrigation with this water remains a part of the tributary system of these rivers. Thus, unlike water imported from across the Continental Divide, Thornton's irrigation water is not new to the system; Thornton essentially changed only the place of use of that water. This type of diversion is common in Colorado and users downstream from these diversions have every reason to believe that they are among those protected against injury. Therefore, we decline to extend the special treatment afforded imported and developed water to the 'transbasin' diversion within the same general water system at issue here."

Would the Colorado Supreme Court treat the water in the principal case as imported water? Note that Sugar Creek is a tributary of the North Platte River, the source of the water "imported" by Rawlins.

4. **Artificially stored groundwater.** In Jensen v. Department of Ecology, 685 P.2d 1068 (Wash. 1984), the court held that imported irrigation water which percolates into an aquifer is "artificially stored groundwater." As such, the court held the water is not subject to appropriation by another as public groundwater. The court rejected the argument that the importer, the Bureau of Reclamation, had abandoned or forfeited the water, finding that the Bureau intended to recapture it from the inception of the irrigation project and had, in fact, utilized natural and artificial systems to control and channel it. The court also rejected the argument that the water had lost its identity as artificially stored groundwater by being commingled with natural groundwater. Neb. Rev. Stat. § 46-226.01 essentially codifies the approach of the *Jensen* case by authorizing a permit to recapture groundwater which is "incidentally" stored as a result of an appropriative use. The statute was construed and upheld in Central Nebraska Public Power & Irrigation District v. Abrahamson, 413 N.W.2d 290 (Neb. 1987).

5. **Appropriation of unrecaptured return flows from imported water.** May others appropriate return flows from foreign water which are not recaptured by the importer? In Dodge v. Ellensburg Water Co., 729 P.2d 631 (Wash. Ct. App. 1986), the court held that foreign water abandoned by the developer does not become public water and is not subject to appropriation. Rather, the water may be used without appropriation by the "first taker," that is, by the first person to get physical control of the water at any point in time. The court also held that prescriptive rights could not be acquired in foreign water. But as to the first point above see Arizona Public Service Co. v. Long, 773 P.2d 988 (Ariz. 1989).

6. **Sale of return flows from transferred rights.** Employment of the right to sell newly-produced return flows is urged as a partial solution to the problem faced by a purchaser who must buy all of a former user's diversion yet will acquire only his consumptive use when transferring the right to a new use. The discrepancy between what the former user sells and what the new user gets may be 50%. If the purchaser can in turn sell return flows from the new use, part of this loss can be recouped. See L. M. Hartman & Don Seastone, Efficiency Criteria for Market Transfers of Water, 1 Water Resources Res. 165 (1965). The National Water Commission has joined in the suggestion, Water Policies for the Future, supra p. 3, Note 1, at 269.

7. **Right in sewage effluent.** Compare Pulaski Irrigating Ditch Co. v. City of Trinidad, 203 P. 681 (Colo. 1922), with the principal case. The municipal supply for the City of Trinidad was taken from the Las Animas River. After use, the water was deposited as raw sewage into settling pits, from which it seeped back into the river. When the city built a treatment plant, it proposed to sell the purified water to the owners of the Model Ditch. Senior appropriators downstream protested.

"It is elementary that the waters of the public streams of this state belong to the people, and that appropriators acquire only a right of use. It is also settled law that an appropriator is limited in his use of water to his actual needs. He must not waste it, and if there is a surplus remaining after use it must be returned to the stream whence it came. * * *

"The use of water in cities by which it is contaminated is principally as a vehicle for carrying away noxious matter; and when that duty has been discharged and the city, under its obligations to prevent the sewage becoming obnoxious, has withdrawn the solid matter from the water, the water should be returned to the stream. It has performed the service required of it as truly as has water which has passed over a millwheel. * * *

"It is said, however, that the city might have disposed of the sewage by evaporating the water from it, from which it is argued that it had a right to destroy the water; hence it could not belong to the public.

"It would seem that, according to the established public policy of this state, this right to destroy the water by evaporation can exist only when there is no other practicable method of disposing of the sewage; that is to say, if all other methods were very expensive as compared with the cost of evaporation, public policy might, in the interest of the community producing sewage, permit its disposal by the evaporation of the water. That case, however, is not before us. We are dealing with water which the city is voluntarily purifying.

"To turn this water back into the river will not increase the river's flow above what it would have been had the water not been diverted, and it is not therefore developed water. Applying the principle heretofore laid down, it seems clear that the water here in question does not belong to the city, and that it has no right to sell it." Id. at 682-83.

Cal. Water Code § 1211: "Prior to making any change in the point of discharge, place of use, or purpose of use of treated wastewater, the owner of any wastewater treatment plant shall obtain the approval of board for that change. The board shall review the changes pursuant to the provisions [relating to changes in use]." If the source of treated waste water was imported water could the board refuse to permit a change in use because it would deprive downstream junior appropriators of water they have come to rely on? See Stuart L. Somach, Who Owns Reclaimed Wastewater?, 25 Pac. L.J. 1087 (1994).

In Arizona Public Service Co. v. Long, 773 P.2d 988 (Ariz. 1989), the Arizona Public Service Company entered into contracts to purchase sewage effluent from several Arizona cities. The effluent, which had previously been discharged into the Gila River after treatment, was transported by pipeline some fifty miles for use in cooling a nuclear power plant. Downstream irrigators who relied on the sewage effluent sued, alleging that the cities must continue discharging the effluent into the river. Although the court rejected the cities' argument that they owned the effluent, the court, nevertheless, concluded that effluent is neither surface water nor groundwater under Arizona statutes and is not subject to statutory regulation. Consequently, the court held, cities are free to sell the effluent. The court refused to create a regulatory system for sewage effluent by judicial decision but invited the legislature to do so. See also Arizona Water Co. v. City of Bisbee, 836 P.2d 389 (Ariz. Ct. App. 1991), holding that the city was not illegally competing in a water utility's service area by selling sewage effluent.

In City of San Marcos v. Texas Commission on Environmental Quality, 128 S.W.3d 264 (Tex. Ct. App. 2004), the court held that the City of San Marcos did not retain ownership of sewage effluent after discharging it into the San Marcos River and, thus, could not divert the water for reuse at a downstream location without obtaining an appropriation permit. The court reached this holding despite the fact that the source of the effluent was groundwater, which under the Texas rule of capture is privately owned (see infra p. 332, Note 1), and despite prior Texas case law recognizing the right to use a natural watercourse to transport captured groundwater. The court said that the right to transport is based on retaining physical control of the transported water. Where the transported water is "fungible" with the receiving water, physical control is maintained if the amount of discharged water is tracked while it is transported. In language reminiscent of Arizona Public Service Co. v. Long, supra, the court said that although the effluent was "groundwater-derived," it was no longer groundwater and, thus, was not fungible with the receiving waters of the San Marcos River. Because it was not fungible, the court reasoned, the City did not maintain control by tracking the amount of discharged water. Rather, the court held, when the City discharged its effluent into the river where it commingled with the state's water, the City abandoned control over the identifying characteristics of its property, resulting in abandonment of the effluent as a matter of law.

Was the City of San Marcos simply being stubborn when it refused to apply for an appropriation permit? Who do you suppose objected to the City's plans to recapture the discharged effluent without a permit? The victory of the objectors appears to have been short-lived. Legislation passed while the case was pending authorizes reuse projects similar to the San Marcos project. Tex. Water Code Ann. §11. 042(b).

8. **Rights to reservoir water.** Should an appropriator who stores water in a reservoir have the right to reuse, successively use, and dispose of the water without regard to the injury caused other appropriators? Don't the reasons which the court gives in *Thayer* for allowing unrestricted uses of imported water apply equally to stored water? In City of Westminster v. Church, 445 P.2d 52 (Colo. 1968), the Colorado Supreme Court seemed to so hold, but in Southeastern Colorado Water Conservancy District v. Fort Lyon Canal Co., 720 P.2d 133 (Colo. 1986), the court clarified its earlier decision and held that changes in the use of stored water are limited by historical use to prevent injury to other appropriators.

Chapter 3

RIPARIAN RIGHTS

SECTION 1. BASIS OF RIGHT

ANAHEIM UNION WATER CO. v. FULLER

Supreme Court of California, 1907.
150 Cal. 327, 88 P. 978.

SHAW, J. This is an action to enjoin the defendants from diverting water from the Santa Ana river. Judgment in favor of the plaintiffs as prayed for was given in the court below. The defendants appeal from the judgment, and from an order denying their motion for a new trial.

The plaintiffs own lands through which the Santa Ana river flows. They have been accustomed for many years to irrigate this land with waters from the river, and for that purpose there is required, during the irrigating season, a continuous flow of 400 miners' inches of water. The defendants, or some of them, own land on the river, situated above the land of the plaintiffs, and upon it they had built a dam in the river and were thereby diverting water from the stream, which, by means of a ditch, they were conducting to other lands owned by them and were there using it for irrigation. The plaintiffs claim, and the court found, that the land which the defendants were thus irrigating with water from the river was not riparian thereto. * * *

Some distance below the land of the plaintiffs a tributary, known as "Chino creek," enters the Santa Ana river. Chino creek also has a tributary, known as "Mill creek," which enters Chino creek 1 1/2 miles above the confluence of the latter with the Santa Ana river. The defendants take the water from the river, above the land of the plaintiffs, in a ditch which extends across the low bottom to the high land or bluff, and then extends along the bluff, at a grade less than that of the river, gradually getting further above and away from the river until it reaches and crosses the divide, or summit of the elevated land, between the watershed of the river and that of Mill creek. The court found that the land irrigated with water from this ditch lies beyond this divide, and is wholly within the watershed of Mill creek, and that it does not abut upon the stream of the Santa Ana, and is not riparian thereto. Land which is not within the watershed of the river is not riparian thereto, and is not entitled as riparian land, to the use or benefit of the water from the river, although it may be part of an entire tract which does extend to the river. * * *

shed of the river is not riparian thereto, and is not entitled as riparian land, to the use or benefit of the water from the river, although it may be part of an entire tract which does extend to the river. * * *

The defendants claim that these findings are contrary to the evidence, and that this rule does not apply to the land they seek to irrigate, because, while it is wholly within the Mill creek watershed, it is also within the general watershed of the Santa Ana river, considered as an entirety including the valley from its sources to its mouth. This fact does not affect the case, at least so far as the land of the plaintiffs is concerned. The principal reasons for the rule confining riparian rights to that part of lands bordering on the stream which are within the watershed are that, where the water is used on such land, it will, after such use, return to the stream, so far as it is not consumed, and that, as the rainfall on such land feeds the stream, the land is in consequence entitled, so to speak, to the use of its waters. Where two streams unite, we think the correct rule to be applied, in regard to the riparian rights therein, is that each is to be considered as a separate stream, with regard to lands abutting thereon above the junction, and that land lying within the watershed of one stream above that point is not to be considered as riparian to the other stream. The fact that the streams are of different size, or that both lie in one general watershed, or drainage basin, should not affect the rule, nor should it be changed by the additional fact that the two watersheds are separated merely by the summit or crown of a comparatively low table land, or "mesa," as it is called in the evidence, and not by a sharp or well-defined ridge, range of hills, or mountains. The reasons for the rule are the same in either case. In some cases it may be difficult to distinguish the line of separation. This seems to have been a case of that sort. Nevertheless, we think there is evidence sufficient to support the finding of the court that there is a dividing line between the two watersheds, and that the land irrigated by defendants lies upon the slope which descends into Mill creek. It is not necessary to discuss this evidence in detail.

The evidence also supports the finding that the land irrigated by the defendants does not abut upon, or extend to, the river. If the owner of a tract abutting on a stream conveys to another a part of the land not contiguous to the stream, he thereby cuts off the part so conveyed from all participation in the use of the stream and from riparian rights therein, unless the conveyance declares the contrary. Land thus conveyed and severed from the stream can never regain the riparian right, although it may thereafter be reconveyed to the person who owns the part abutting on the stream, so that the two tracts are again held in one ownership. * * * All the land belonging to the defendants, including the Smith tract, which was in part irrigated, was originally a part of the Jurupa rancho, which abutted upon the river. The original owner of that rancho subdivided it by arbitrary lines, corresponding to the government surveys, and sold and conveyed it in parcels according to that survey. Under the rule above stated the conveyance by him of a tract not contiguous to the stream would sever such tract from the riparian interest and deprive it of subsequent participation in the use of the water of the river, the right to which previously attached to the entire rancho. The tract which includes the irrigated land of the defendants is not at any point contiguous to the river. At the time the action was begun it was owned by the defendant Smith. He was not the owner of any adjoining land which lay contiguous to the river. After the action was begun he conveyed this land, to certain of the other defendants, some of whom owned adjoining lands extending from the Smith land to the river. This subsequent conveyance gave those defendants a continuous ownership of land extending from the river to and including the Smith land. This contiguous ownership, however, did not confer upon the Smith land the riparian rights of which it was deprived, when Smith, or his predecessors, obtained it by a conveyance which severed it from the portion of the Jurupa rancho abutting upon the river. * * *

It is further contended that the plaintiffs' land is in no wise damaged by the diversion complained of, and hence that the diversion cannot be enjoined. * * *

On this point the defendants cite several cases in which it is held that a lower riparian owner cannot enjoin a diversion by another riparian proprietor above, unless he can show that such diversion works damage to him, and that it is more than a just proportion of the water to which the upper owner is entitled. Such decisions are not applicable to this case. Riparian owners have correlative rights in the stream, and neither is a trespasser against the other until he diverts more than his share and injures and damages the other thereby. Here the defendants were not, with respect to the land irrigated, riparian owners, but were trespassers on plaintiffs' property rights from the beginning, and the continuance of the trespass for a sufficient time would divest the right of the plaintiffs with respect to the water diverted. * * *

The defendants urge that inasmuch as the plaintiffs need but 400 inches of water for their land, and there remained in the stream, after defendants' diversion, more than 2000 inches, which flows down to and beyond the plaintiffs' land, and which is more than they can possibly use thereon, that it therefore follows that no damage can ever ensue, even if the diversion is unlawful and should ripen into a prescriptive right by continuance; and hence that their diversion should not be enjoined. The theory of the law of riparian rights in this state is that the water of a stream belongs by a sort of common right to the several riparian owners along the stream; each being entitled to sever his share for use on his riparian land. The fact that a large quantity of water flows down the stream by and beyond the plaintiffs' land does not prove that it goes to waste, nor that the plaintiffs are entitled to take a part of it, as against other riparian owners or users below. Nor can it be said that plaintiffs, on account of the present abundance, could safely permit defendants to acquire, as against them, a right to a part of the water. The riparian right is not lost by disuse, and other riparian owners above may take or others below may be entitled to take, and may insist upon being allowed to take, all of the stream, excepting only sufficient for the plaintiffs' land. In either alternative, the taking of a part of the water by the defendants would not leave enough for the plaintiffs' use. There is nothing in this case to show how much water is required above and below by those having rights in the stream. In view of the well-known aridity of the climate, and the high state of cultivation in the vicinity, the court could almost take judicial notice that in years of ordinary rainfall there is no surplus of water in the stream over that used by the various owners under claim of right. But, however this may be, it is settled by the decisions above cited that a party, situated as the plaintiffs are, can enjoin an unlawful diversion, in order to protect and preserve his riparian right.

The findings support the judgment, and we are unable to perceive any substantial or material conflict in them. We find no error in the record.

The judgment and order are affirmed.

Notes

1. **Source of title test.** The "source of title" test of the extent of riparian lands was summarized in Boehmer v. Big Rock Creek Irrigation District, 48 P. 908 (Cal. 1897), by saying that the riparian right extends only to the smallest tract held under one title in the chain of title leading to the present owner. Accord Yearsley v. Cater, 270 P. 804 (Wash. 1928) and Watkins Land Co. v. Clements, 86 S.W. 733 (Tex. 1905). Under this rule, the amount of riparian land can only diminish. Express or implied preservation of riparian rights when a riparian tract is subdivided is discussed in Thompson v. Enz, infra p. 242 and accompanying Note 1.

2. **Unity of title test.** A contrasting theory is that of "unity of title." In Jones v. Conn, 64 P. 855, 858 (Or. 1901), the court said, "It would seem, therefore, that any person owning land which abuts upon or through which a natural stream of water flows is a riparian proprietor, entitled to the rights of such, without regard to the extent of his land, or from whom or when he acquired his title. The fact that he may have procured the particular tract washed by the stream at one time, and subsequently purchased land adjoining it, will not make him any the less a riparian proprietor, nor should it alone be a valid objection to his using the water on the land last acquired. The only thing necessary to entitle him to the right of a riparian proprietor is to show that the body of land owned by him borders upon a stream." This rule was approved in Clark v. Allaman, 80 P. 571 (Kan. 1905), and is adopted by the American Law Institute in Restatement (Second) of Torts, § 843, cmt. c (1979).

3. **Government subdivision test.** In Crawford Co. v. Hathaway, 93 N.W. 781 (Neb. 1903), the court suggested that since the government disposed of the public domain in 40 acre tracts, riparian rights should be limited to such subdivisions, but in computing damages for loss of riparian rights by condemnation, the court later decided that damage to entire sections (640 acres) should be considered. McGinley v. Platte Valley Pub. Power & Irrigation Dist., 271 N.W. 864 (Neb. 1937).

4. **Extent of riparian lands in eastern states.** Questions of the extent of riparian lands have not often been litigated in the eastern states. The watershed limitation clearly finds acceptance, see William H. Farnham, The Permissible Extent of Riparian Land, 7 Land & Water L. Rev. 31 (1972). Farnham argues for the adoption of a "reasonable limit" rule that can be supported by an analysis of some cases. Neither the "smallest tract" rule of *Boehmer*, supra Note 1, nor the "government subdivision" rule of *Crawford*, supra Note 3, seem to have been adopted by eastern courts. A Wisconsin administrative agency which issues permits to riparian irrigators construed the term riparian land to mean that land

bordering on a lake or stream which has been in the same ownership in an uninterrupted chain of title from the original government patent. Harold H. Ellis, et al., Water-Use Law and Administration in Wisconsin 17 (1970).

5. **Necessity of bed ownership.** It was once thought that land to be riparian had to include a part of the bed of the watercourse or border on public watercourse whose bed is in private ownership. Restatement of Torts, § 843 (1939). The Restatement (Second) of Torts § 843 (1979), now takes the position that ownership of the bed is immaterial.

Some powers and privileges relating to the stream and commonly denominated as riparian rights may require either ownership of the bed or public access to the water. These include the building of dams and probably the commercial cutting of ice. But cases prohibiting an adjacent land owner from performing these acts deal with trespasses on another's land and not directly with the rights of the contiguous owner to use the water if he can do so without trespass. The possibilities of such uses are many. A number of early California and Washington cases have held that there is a riparian right to the natural overflow of a stream which annually goes out of its banks. Lux v. Haggin, 10 P. 674 (Cal. 1886); Still v. Palouse Irrigation & Power Co., 117 P. 466 (Wash. 1911). There are many cases which hold that a riparian owner may go upstream on the land of another and with permission divert water to the riparian land. Rose v. Mesmer, 75 P. 905 (Cal. 1904); Redwater Land & Canal Co. v. Jones, 130 N.W. 85 (S.D. 1911). Where the bank is vertical it is possible for a contiguous owner who does not own the stream bed to cut a ditch in the bank and divert water without committing any trespass on the bed itself. A case expressly holding that ownership of the bed is not a requisite is Bouris v. Largent, 236 N.E.2d 15 (Ill. App. 1968).

The rule requiring ownership of or public access to the bed was thought to be justified by several cases. One clearly supported the rule: Rockwell v. Baldwin, 53 Ill. 19 (1869). Several involved a trespass to the bed: Jewett v. Gardner, 12 Mass. 309 (1815); Whittier v. Montpelier Ice Co., 96 A. 378 (Vt. 1916); Adams v. Barney, 25 Vt. 225 (1853). Another involved the commercial cutting of ice: Allen v. Weber, 50 N.W. 514 (Wis. 1891). One was based on the old rule that boating over another's land is a trespass: Kilgo v. Cook, 295 S.W. 355 (Ark. 1927).

As to the status of the bed itself as riparian land, see the omitted portions of the opinion in *Anaheim* (bottom lands, apparently sometimes overflowed). A statute granting riparian owners bordering on tidal waters the sole right of planting and gathering oysters in front of their lands for 500 yards to seaward gives rights which are protected from private infringement, though subject to superior rights of the public and the state. Crary v. State Highway Comm'n, 68 So.2d 468 (Miss. 1953). There are no cases dealing directly with the status as riparian proprietors of persons who have rights to tidelands affected by river water, but who own no uplands. However, such a status may be inferred from Grant v. United States, 192 F.2d 482 (4th Cir. 1951), which held that a person holding a lease from the state for cultivation of oysters on lands beneath tidal waters may complain of stream pollution which destroys the beds.

6. **Nonriparian use.** The principal case holds that a nonriparian use, even one that causes no harm, may be enjoined by a downstream riparian. The more typical holding is that a nonriparian use may be enjoined if it causes "actual

perceptible damage to the present or potential enjoyment" of a downstream riparian. Stratton v. Mt. Hermon Boys' School, 103 N.E. 87 (Mass. 1913). See also Elliot v. Fitchburg Ry. Co., 64 Mass. (10 Cush.) 191 (1852); Garwood v. N.Y. Cent. & H. R. R.R., 83 N.Y. 400 (1881). In the context of the doctrine of reasonable use, discussed in the next section, this translates to a rule that a non-riparian use which causes injury is "per se" unreasonable. A related corollary holds that a downstream nonriparian use is per se unreasonable and not entitled to protection against the acts of an upstream riparian. See Kennebunk, Kennebunkport & Wells Water Dist. v. Maine Turnpike Auth., 71 A.2d 520 (Me. 1950).

Perhaps no feature of riparian law has received more adverse and critical comment than the concept that the waters are reserved for the benefit of the lands along the stream, and that rights to the use of water are special privileges of the owners of such lands. See William L. Zeigler, Water Use under Common Law Doctrines, in Water Resources and the Law 49, 70–72 (1958):

"With the growth of population numbers and the ever-expanding industrial and irrigative developments, the demand for water has increased continually. These demands come from the nonriparian as well as the dweller along the stream; from the city dweller as well as the riparian farmer. * * *

"Apart from the problem of uncertainty and instability of a riparian's right to use water, there is the problem of supplying water to non-riparian land. It is impossible for all people to be riparians. The increasing population and industrial expansion require the utilization of lands which are not adjacent to surface water supplies. In most [riparian] states, use of stream or lake water on non-riparian land is prohibited. This is considered as unreasonable or as unlawful per se. The water of a stream or lake is for the riparians only. * * * The prohibition on non-riparian uses precludes the distribution of water from areas of plenty to areas of drought or great demand, and the water, where available, may be wasted. * * *

"The social and economic disadvantages presented by the riparian doctrine as applied to present day living conditions appear substantial and worthy of legislative attention."

Compare John E. Cribbet, Illinois Water Rights Law 28 (1958): "This does not appear to be a major problem. Practically, water can be most efficiently used close to its source and land with riparian rights can always be purchased just as one purchases oil land, gravel pits, etc. This is largely a matter of economics rather than a serious legal problem."

Which would be the preferable rule for determining the extent of riparian land, source of title or unity of title? Would it make a difference whether the land were located in California, where appropriators may make non-riparian uses, but new riparian uses are superior to them, or in a midwestern state where riparian rights are the only source of water titles?

7. Nonriparian use by a riparian proprietor. The Restatement (Second) of Torts § 855 (1979), takes the position that a nonriparian use *by a riparian proprietor* is not per se unreasonable, although the comments to the section state that the fact that the use is on a nonriparian parcel is an additional factor to be considered in determining reasonableness. The comments state that this rule follows the policy that riparian law should be utilitarian and should place no artificial or absolute restrictions on the use of water. In contrast, the Restatement (Second) takes the position that the use of water by a nonriparian which causes harm to a riparian is per se unreasonable unless (1) the nonriparian's use is pursuant to a grant from another riparian, (2) the nonriparian is exercising a right created by governmental authority, or (3) the nonriparian is exercising a public right. See Restatement (Second) of Torts §§ 856, 857. See also Pyle v. Gilbert, 265 S.E.2d 584 (Ga. 1980), citing the Restatement (Second) in holding that a nonriparian use is not per se unreasonable.

Is the distinction which the Restatement (Second) makes between a nonriparian use by a riparian proprietor and a nonriparian use by a nonriparian proprietor a valid one? How can there ever be a nonriparian use by a nonriparian proprietor? In order to get access to a stream wouldn't a nonriparian proprietor need a grant from a riparian and would not the grant either convey riparian lands, making the nonriparian a riparian, or convey riparian rights to the nonriparian?

8. **Extent of the watershed limit.** Where plaintiff's land is situated below the junction of two branches of a stream, he cannot complain of the transportation, by a defendant who has riparian lands above the forks, of water out of one branch for irrigation use in the watershed of the other branch. Rancho Santa Margarita v. Vail, 81 P.2d 533 (Cal. 1938).

9. **Characterization of riparian rights.** Riparian rights have been described as part and parcel of the land itself, corporeal hereditaments, incorporeal hereditaments, easements, appurtenances and as tenancies in common in the stream. What are the characteristics of these species of property? What is the value of approaching a problem concerning riparian rights in this manner? See John K. Bennett, Some Uncertainties in the Law of Water Rights, 21 S. Cal. L. Rev. 344 (1948); John K. Bennett, Some Fundamentals of Legal Interests in Water Supplies, 22 S. Cal. L. Rev. 1 (1948).

In Stewart v. Bridges, 292 S.E.2d 702 (1982), one lakeshore proprietor sued another to enjoin use of the water for irrigation. It was held error for the trial court to instruct the jury (1) that the parties had a tenancy in common in the water of the lake and the defendant irrigator therefore had no superior right to use the water to the exclusion of the plaintiff, and (2) that the plaintiff, as the owner of the part of the lake bed, was entitled to possession and control of the water vertically above his land, and hence to "lateral support" for that water.

THOMPSON v. ENZ

Supreme Court of Michigan, 1967.
379 Mich. 667, 154 N.W.2d 473.

KAVANAGH, JUSTICE. Plaintiffs filed a complaint in the Barry county circuit court against defendants claiming violation of their rights as riparian owners on Gun Lake and seeking a declaratory judgment to that effect. Both parties moved for summary judgment. Plaintiffs were granted the relief requested. * * *

This case concerns certain property rights in and around Gun Lake, which is situated partly in Barry county and partly in Allegan county. The parties agree that this lake has approximately 2,680 acres of surface area and approximately 30 miles of shore line. The defendant corporation is a contract purchaser of a riparian parcel of land having approximately 1,415 feet of frontage on said lake, and the individual defendants are the sole stockholders of the corporation. Plaintiffs are riparian owners of other property abutting Gun Lake. * * *

Defendants are in the process of developing and subdividing their parcel of land into from 144 to 153 lots. Of these lots, approximately 16 will abut on the natural shore line of the lake. The remainder of the lots will front on canals. To give the back lot purchasers access to the lake the defendants' plan calls for excavating across riparian lots Nos 13 and 76. The defendants purport to grant to the purchasers of those lots fronting on the canals riparian rights to the lake and rights of access through the excavation to the lake. The back lots would have frontage on the canals of approximately 11,000 feet.

The following questions are raised on appeal:

1. May a right of access to Gun Lake be created by dredging an artificial canal from the lake through lots having frontage on Gun Lake to back lots having no frontage thereon, and may ownership of such lots carry with it riparian rights? * * *

"Riparian land" is defined as a parcel of land which includes therein a part of or is bounded by a natural watercourse. 4 Restatement, Torts, § 843, p. 326. * * * Artificial watercourses are waterways that owe their origin to acts of man, such as canals, drainage and irrigation ditches, aqueducts, flumes, and the like. 4 Restatement, Torts, § 841, subd. h., p. 321.

Land abutting on an artificial watercourse has no riparian rights. * * * We, therefore, conclude that parcels of land to be subdivided from the main tract of land bordering on Gun Lake have no riparian rights as: (1) they neither include therein a part of nor are they bounded by Gun Lake, and (2) the canal itself would be an artificial watercourse giving rise to no riparian rights.

The remaining question for decision is whether or not riparian rights may be conveyed to a grantee or reserved by the grantor in a conveyance which divides a tract of land with riparian rights into more than one parcel, of which parcels only one would remain bounded by the watercourse.

In the case of Harvey Realty Co. v. Borough of Wallingford, supra, Justice Hinman, writing for the Court, stated (150 A. p. 63):

> "It is clear that the grantees or contractees, from the plaintiff, of lots separated from and not bordering on Pine Lake can have, of their own right, no riparian privileges in its waters. *And any attempted transfer of the right made by a riparian to a nonriparian proprietor is invalid.*" (Citing cases.) (Emphasis supplied.) * * *

We hold that riparian rights are not alienable, severable, divisible or assignable apart from the land which includes therein or is bounded by a natural watercourse.

Judgment of the Court of Appeals reversed.

BRENNAN, JUSTICE. * * * Here, the developer wishes to subdivide his property and convey back lots by deeds which will expressly grant easements for rights of way, permitting access to the lake through the canal. There is no doubt that a riparian owner can grant an easement over his land to permit a nonriparian owner to have access to the water.

A great many inland lakes in Michigan have been developed in this fashion, where cottages or homes do not have actual lake frontage, but do enjoy, in common with other property owners, the use of a granted or reserved easement providing for access to the water for recreational purposes. If the easement proposed in this case were a road, rather than a canal, no serious issue would be raised concerning the defendants' right to convey back lots with such an easement included in the grant. * * *

Notes

1. **Preservation of riparian status when land is subdivided.** Where a portion of riparian lands, not contiguous to the stream, was conveyed with "the same rights to the use of water that appurtained to said land in the hands of the party of the first part", it was held that the non-riparian land retained the riparian rights. Strong v. Baldwin, 97 P. 178 (Cal. 1908). Where a land company which owned a large tract of riparian land organized another corporation to which it transferred the water right, and then sold the land in small parcels, giving with each parcel a certificate of stock in the water corporation which declared that the holder was entitled to a certain part of the water, the purchaser of each parcel became vested with a proportionate part of the riparian right originally held by the land company. Copeland v. Fairview Land & Water Co., 131 P. 119 (Cal. 1913). The partition of a riparian tract among tenants in common does not destroy the riparian character of the plots lying away from the stream. Rancho Santa Margarita v. Vail, 81 P.2d 533 (Cal. 1938). Where a right-of-way for a road was granted across a riparian tract it was held that the part of the tract which was separated from the stream by the right-of-way retained its riparian status. Pleasant Valley Canal Co. v. Borror, 72 Cal. Rptr. 2d 1 (Cal. Ct. App. 1998). A conveyance of an upland portion of a riparian tract was held not to carry with it a portion of the riparian right in Harvey Realty Co. v. Borough of Wallingford, 150 A. 60 (Conn. 1930).

As for the status and rights of landowners on man-made bodies of water, see Alvin E. Evans, Riparian Rights in Artificial Lakes and Streams, 16 Mo. L. Rev. 93 (1951).

2. **Riparian rights to continued access to watercourse**. The riparian right includes reasonable access to the watercourse even though the bed may belong to the state under the equal footing or public trust doctrines. E.g., Romeo v. Sherry, 308 F. Supp. 2d 128 (E.D.N.Y. 2004) (New York law). This can include the right to build a wharf out to the navigable portion of the water. See infra p. 522, Note 2. The principal case held that riparian rights could not be extended to nonriparian parcels by dredging an access channel. Where, however, siltation or other natural changes in a watercourse affect a riparian's continued access to the watercourse, courts have concluded that riparian rights may be *preserved* by dredging. Town of Oyster Bay v. Commander Oil Corp., 759 N.E. 2d 1233 (N.Y. 2001).

3. **Conveyance of Easement.** As the dissenting opinion in the principal case noted, many courts will allow a riparian owner to grant an easement to nonriparians to allow access to the watercourse. Little v. Kin, 644 N.W.2d 375 (Mich. App. 2002).

4. **Riparian rights of cities.** Under the majority rule, a city lying on a river bank or fronting a lake is not regarded as a riparian proprietor with a riparian right to take water for public water supply, City of Emporia v. Soden, 25 Kan. 588 (1881), Town of Purcellville v. Potts, 19 S.E.2d 700 (Va. 1942); but see City of Canton v. Shock, 63 N.E. 600 (Ohio 1902).

The water rights of cities, public utilities, and public agencies furnishing domestic and municipal water supply in "riparian rights states" that follow the majority rule are examined Chapter 3, Section 3C. In several cases cities have been treated, without discussion and perhaps inadvertently, as if they were riparian proprietors. See, e.g., Sayles v. Mitchell, 245 N.W. 390 (S.D. 1932).

5. **Riparian rights to diffused surface water.** Riparian rights relate to watercourses, including springs and lakes, but not to every source in other phases of the hydrologic cycle. See State v. Hiber, supra p. 82 and accompanying Notes, for other materials on what constitutes a watercourse. Diffused surface water resulting from precipitation may be captured and used, or dammed and redirected, by the owner of the land on which the waters are found, even though the water would otherwise reach a stream and these activities diminish the flow of the stream with adverse effects on riparian proprietors below. Broadbent v. Ramsbotham, 156 Eng.Rep. 971 (Exch. 1856). See also Joseph A. Dellapenna, The Legal Regulation of Diffused Surface Water, 2 Vill. Envtl. L.J. 285 (1991).

6. **Drainage of diffused surface water.** Many controversies over surface water arise because the landowners are trying to get rid of it, rather than to capture and use it. In the law of drainage two rules have competed for acceptance by the courts, and a third has developed. Some courts follow the "common enemy" rule, under which the possessor of land may protect himself against surface water as best he can, building dikes to keep the water off his land or drains to cast it down onto lower lands. Argyelan v. Haviland, 435 N.E.2d 973 (Ind. 1982); Johnson v. Whitten, 384 A.2d 698 (Me. 1978); Grundy v. Brack Family Trust, 67 P.3d 500 (Wash. App. 2003) (review granted) (seawater). Others apply the "civil law" rule, borrowed from European countries, which subjects each piece of land to a servitude for the natural flow of water across it, so that a landowner cannot prevent water from coming to his land, nor may he collect it so it flows from his land in unusual quantities, or change the direction of the natural drainage. Dekle v. Vann, 182 So.2d 885 (Ala. 1966); Robinson v. Belanger, 52 N.W.2d 538 (Mich. 1952).

Each of these rules has obvious disadvantages and both have been modified in some states by statute or decision. Thus some courts applying the civil law rule have held that the natural flow may be changed if damage is slight, or if the landowner is protecting himself from extraordinary flood water. McManus v. Otis, 143 P.2d 380 (Cal. Ct. App. 1943); Bolinger v. Murray, 137 So. 761 (La. Ct. App. 1931). Some courts have imposed liability despite the common enemy rule where the upper owner has discharged unusually large flows on the lower. Clark v. City of Springfield, 241 S.W.2d 100 (Mo. Ct. App. 1951). Others restrict the upper owner from collecting the diffuse waters and discharging them "as a body." Bulldog Battery Corp. v. Pica Investments, Inc., 736 N.E.2d 333 (Ind. App.

2000). These modifications have been merged into a rule of "reasonable use," which is gaining increasing acceptance. This rule allows a landowner to modify natural drainage patterns provided the alteration does not unreasonably injure adjacent landowners. Page Motor Co. v. Baker, 438 A.2d 739 (Conn. 1980); Von Henneberg v. Generazio, 531 N.E.2d 563 (Mass. 1988); Whorton v. Malone, 549 S.E.2d 57 (W.Va. 2001). The distinction between surface water and water in watercourses is equally important here, for these rules do not permit an obstruction of a watercourse or its diversion into a new channel.

Most drainage is performed today by drainage districts, which are public bodies established to build common works to drain a large area of land. They are formed with the approval of a court or county board when the majority of the landowners in the area desire the improvement. They are financed by assessments on all improved lands, and these assessments can be levied and enforced regardless of whether a minority landowner desires to participate. The actions of such public districts are not limited by the laws of private drainage, and if damage is done to others the district may nevertheless proceed, making compensation payments where necessary and adding them to the costs of the project.

See Joseph A. Dellapenna, supra p. 245, Note 5, and Wendy B. Davis, Reasonable Use has Become the Common Enemy: An Overview of the Standards Applied to Diffused Surface Water and the Resulting Depletion of Aquifers, 9 Alb. L.J. Envir. Outlook 9 (2004), for recent examinations of the subject.

7. **Drainage of wetlands.** Drainage and filling of swamps and marshes to produce farmland and residential sites was once "reclamation," encouraged and subsidized by the United States Department of Agriculture's Soil Conservation Service and Agricultural Conservation Program. Now it is "destruction of wetlands" and of the wilderness and wildlife habitat that wetlands provide. Protection of the environmental and ecological features of wetlands is now a function of water quality control, and is regulated by discharge permits and "dredge and fill" permits under sections 402 and 404 of the Federal Clean Water Act. See Chapter 7, Section 2.

SECTION 2. REASONABLE USE

HARRIS v. BROOKS

Supreme Court of Arkansas, 1955.
225 Ark. 436, 283 S.W.2d 129.

WARD, JUSTICE. The issues presented by this appeal relate to the relative rights of riparian landowners to the use of a privately owned nonnavigable lake and the water therein.

Appellant, Theo Mashburn, lessee of riparian landowners conducts a commercial boating and fishing enterprise. In this business he rents cabins, sells fishing bait and equipment, and rents boats to members of the general public who desire to use the lake for fishing and other recreational purposes. He and his lessors filed a complaint in chancery court on July 10, 1954 to enjoin appellees from pumping water from the lake to irrigate a rice crop, alleging that, as of that date, appellees had reduced the water level of the lake to such an extent as to make the lake unsuitable "for fishing, recreation, or other lawful purposes." After a lengthy hearing, the chancellor denied injunctive relief, and this appeal is prosecuted to reverse the chancellor's decision.

Factual Background. Horseshoe Lake, located about 3 miles south of Augusta, is approximately 3 miles long and 300 feet wide, and, as the name implies, resembles a horseshoe in shape. Appellees, John Brooks and John Brooks, Jr., are lessees of Ector Johnson who owns a large tract of land adjacent to the lake, including three-fourths of the lake bed. For a number of years appellees have intermittently raised rice on Johnson's land and have each year, including 1954, irrigated the rice with water pumped from the lake. They pumped no more water in 1954 than they did in 1951 and 1952, no rice being raised in 1953. Approximately 190 acres were cultivated in rice in 1954.

* * * In March 1954 Mashburn leased * * * a relatively small camp site on the bank of the lake and installed the business above mentioned at a cost of approximately $8,000, including boats, cabins, and fishing equipment. Mashburn began operating his business about the first of April, 1954, and fishing and boat rentals were satisfactory from that time until about July 1st or 4th when, he says, the fish quit biting and his income from that source and boat rentals was reduced to practically nothing.

Appellees began pumping water with an 8 inch intake on May 25, 1954 and continued pumping until this suit was filed on July 10, and then until about August 20th. They quit pumping at this time because it was discovered fish life was being endangered. The trial was had September 28, 1954, and the decree was rendered December 29, 1954.

The Testimony. * * * The years 1952, 1953 and 1954 were unusually dry and the water levels in similar lakes in the same general area were unusually low in August and September of 1954. During August 1954 Horseshoe Lake was below "normal", but it is not entirely clear from the testimony that this was true on July 10 when the suit was filed. It also appears that during the stated period the water had receded from the bank where Mashburn's boats were usually docked, making it impossible for him to rent them to the public. There is strong testimony, disputed by appellees, that the *normal* level of the lake is 189.67 feet above sea level and that the water was below this level on July 10. Unquestionably the water was below normal when this suit was tried the latter part of September, 1954.

On the part of appellees it was attempted to show that; they had used the water for irrigation several years dating back to 1931 and Mashburn knew this when he rented the camp site; although they had been pumping regularly since May 25, 1954 the water did not begin to fall in the lake until July 1st or 4th; an agent of the Arkansas Game and Fish Commission examined the lake and the water about July 2nd and found no condition endangering fish life, and similar examinations after suit was filed showed the same condition and; they stopped pumping about August 20th when they first learned that fish life was being endangered.

Issues Clarified. In refusing to issue the injunction the chancellor made no finding of facts, and did not state the ground upon which his decision rested. * * * If it be conceded that the testimony does show and the chancellor should have found that the water in Horseshoe Lake was at or below the normal level when this suit was filed on July 10th, then appellants would have been entitled to an injunction provided this case was decided strictly under the uniform flow theory mentioned hereafter. However as explained later we are not bound by this theory in this state. It appears to us there might have been some confusion as to the ground upon which appellants based their contention for relief. Under the pleadings it appears that they may be asking for relief on two separate grounds: (a) The right to fish and (b) The right to conduct a commercial boating enterprise. It was incumbent upon appellants to show that one or both rights were unreasonably interfered with when the water level sank below "normal". It is difficult to tell whether the testimony establishes this fact in either instance. (a) The only testimony in the first instance is that fish quit biting somewhere about the 4th of July but there was no conclusive evidence that this was caused by the lake being below "normal" level. It is common knowledge that fish quit biting some time for no apparent good reason. There was no testimony that fish life was endangered before July 10th but on the other hand there was positive testimony to the contrary. (b) Likewise there was no conclusive testimony showing that it was impractical to dock or run boats on the lake prior to July 10th. Moreover it would be pure conjecture to say that the same water level, whether normal or otherwise, controlled both fishing and boating. Certainly appellants made no attempt to make any distinction either in the pleadings or by the testimony between the two causes of action.

In view of the above situation it is urged by appellees that the case should therefore be affirmed, but we have concluded that the best interest of the parties hereto and the public in general will be served by concluding this case in the light of the announcements hereafter made and the conclusions hereafter reached. Before attempting such conclusion it appears proper to make some general observations relative to the law regulating the use of water in lakes and streams. * * *

Riparian Doctrine. This doctrine, long in force in this and many other states, is based on the old common law which gave to the owners of land bordering on streams the right to use the water therefrom for certain purposes, and this right was considered an incident to the ownership of land. Originally it apparently accorded the landowner the right to have the water maintained at its normal level, subject to use for strictly domestic purposes. Later it became evident that this strict limitation placed on the use of water was unreasonable and unutilitarian. Consequently it was not long before the demand for a greater use of water caused a relaxation of the strict limitations placed on its use and this doctrine came to be divided into (a) the natural flow theory and (b) the reasonable use theory.

(a) *Natural Flow Theory.* Generally speaking again, under the natural flow theory, a riparian owner can take water for domestic purposes only, such as water for the family, live stock, and gardening, and he is entitled to have the water in the stream or lake upon which he borders kept at the normal level. There are some expressions in the opinions of this court indicating that we have recognized this theory, at least to a certain extent.

Reasonable Use Theory. This theory appears to be based on the necessity and desirability of deriving greater benefits from the use of our abundant supply of water. It recognizes that there is no sound reason for maintaining our lakes and streams at a normal level when the water can be beneficially used without causing unreasonable damage to other riparian owners. The progress of civilization, particularly in regard to manufacturing, irrigation, and recreation, has forced the realization that a strict adherence to the uninterrupted flow doctrine placed an unwarranted limitation on the use of water, and consequently the court developed what we now call the reasonable use theory. This theory is of course subject to different interpretations and limitations. In 56 Am.Jur., page 728, it is stated that "The rights of riparian proprietors on both navigable and unnavigable streams are to a great extent mutual, common, or correlative. The use of the stream or water by each proprietor is therefore limited to what is reasonable, having due regard for the rights of others above, below, or on the opposite shore. In general, the special rights of a riparian owner are such as are necessary for the use and enjoyment of his abutting property and the business lawfully conducted thereon, qualified only by the correlative rights of other riparian owners, and by certain rights of the public, and they are to be so exercised as not to injure others in the enjoyment of their rights." It has been stated that each riparian owner has an equal right to make a reasonable use of waters subject to the equal rights of other owners to make the reasonable use, United States v. Willow River Power Co., 324 U.S. 499, 65 S.Ct. 761, 89 L.Ed. 1101. The purpose of the law is to secure to each riparian owner equality in the use of water as near as may be by requiring each to exercise his right reasonably and with due regard to the rights of others similarly situated. Meng v. Coffey, 67 Neb. 500, 93 N.W. 713, 60 L.R.A. 910.

This court has to some extent recognized the reasonable use theory. Thomas v. La Cotts, 222 Ark. 171, 257 S.W.2d 936; Harrell v. City of Conway, 224 Ark. 100, 271 S.W.2d 924, but we have also said in the City of Conway case that the uniform flow theory and the reasonable use theory are inconsistent and, further that we had not yet made a choice between them. It is not clear that we made a choice in that case. The nucleus of this opinion is, therefore, a definite acceptance of the reasonable use theory. We do not understand that the two theories will necessarily clash in every case, but where there is an inconsistency, and where vested rights may not prevent, it is our conclusion that the reasonable use theory should control.

In embracing the reasonable use theory we caution, however, that we are not necessarily adopting all the interpretations given it by the decisions of other states, and that our own interpretation will be developed in the future as occasions arise. Nor is it intended hereby that we will not in the future, under certain circumstances, possibly adhere to some phases of the uniform flow system. It is recognized that in some instances vested rights may have accrued to riparian landowners and we could not of course constitutionally negate those rights. * * *

The result of our examination of the decisions of this court and other authorities relative to the use by riparian proprietors of water in non-navigable lakes and streams justifies the enunciation of the following general rules and principles:

(a) The right to use water for strictly domestic purposes—such as for household use—is superior to many other uses of water—such as for fishing, recreation and irrigation.

(b) Other than the use mentioned above, all other lawful uses of water are equal. Some of the lawful uses of water recognized by this state are: fishing, swimming, recreation, and irrigation.

(c) When one lawful use of water is destroyed by another lawful use the latter must yield, or it may be enjoined.

(d) When one lawful use of water interferes with or detracts from another lawful use, then a question arises as to whether, under all the facts and circumstances of that particular case, the interfering use shall be declared unreasonable and as such enjoined, or whether a reasonable and equitable adjustment should be made, having due regard to the reasonable rights of each.

Application to This Case. Some of the questions, therefore, which must be considered are these:

(a) Had appellees on July 10, 1954, by the continued use of water from Horseshoe Lake, destroyed appellants' right to fish and conduct the boating enterprise? If so, the injunction should be granted.

(b) If it is found however that appellants' rights had only been impaired at the stated time, then it must be judged, under all the facts and circumstances as before mentioned, whether such impairment is unreasonable. If it is so found then the injunction should issue. If it is found that appellants' rights have not been unreasonably impaired, having due regard to all the facts and circumstances and the injury which may be caused appellees as weighed against the benefits accruing to appellants, then the injunction should be denied.

We do not minimize the difficulties attendant upon an application of the reasonable use rule to any given set of facts and circumstances and particularly those present in this instance. It is obvious that there are no definite guide posts provided and that necessarily much must be left to judgment and discretion. The breadth and boundaries of this area of discretion are well stated in Restatement of the Law, Torts, § 852c in these words: "The determination in a particular case of the unreasonableness of a particular use is not and should not be an unreasoned, intuitive conclusion on the part of the court or jury. It is rather an evaluating of the conflicting interests of each of the contestants before the court in accordance with the standards of society, and a weighing of those, one against the other. The law accords equal protection to the interests of all the riparian proprietors in the use of water, and seeks to promote the greatest beneficial use of the water, and seeks to promote the greatest beneficial use by each with a minimum of harm to others. But when one riparian proprietor's use of the water harmfully invades another's interest in its use, there is an incompatibility of interest between the two parties to a greater or lesser extent depending on the extent of the invasion, and there is immediately a question whether such a use is legally permissible. It is axiomatic in the law that individuals in society must put up with a reasonable amount of annoyance and inconvenience resulting from the otherwise lawful activities of their neighbors in the use of their land. Hence it is only when one riparian proprietor's use of the water is unreasonable that another who is harmed by it can complain, even though the harm is intentional. Substantial intentional harm to another cannot be justified as reasonable unless the legal merit or utility of the activity which produces it outweighs the legal seriousness or gravity of the harm."

In all our consideration of the reasonable use theory as we have attempted to explain it we have accepted the view that the benefits accruing to society in general from a maximum utilization of our water resources should not be denied merely because of the difficulties that may arise in its application. In the absence of legislative directives, it appears that this rule or theory is the best that the courts can devise.

Our Conclusion. After careful consideration, an application of the rules above announced to the complicated fact situation set forth in this record leads us to conclude that the Chancellor should have issued an order enjoining appellees from pumping water out of Horseshoe Lake when the water level reaches 189.67 feet above sea level for as long as the material facts and circumstances are substantially the same as they appear in this record. We make it clear that this conclusion is not based on the fact that 189.67 is the normal level and that appellees would have no right to reduce such level. Our conclusion is based on the fact that we think the evidence shows this level happens to be the level below which appellants would be unreasonably interfered with. * * *

We think the conclusion we have reached is not only logical but practical. Although appellees had quit using water from the lake when this case was tried yet they testified that they intended to use water therefrom in 1955. We might assume that they would want to also use water in subsequent years, so it would seem to be to the best interest of all parties concerned to have a definite level fixed at which pumping for irrigation must cease in order to avoid useless litigation.

Appellees make the point that the Chancellor should be sustained because they have acquired a prescriptive right to the unlimited use of the water in Horseshoe Lake, and, to the same effect, that appellants are estopped from asserting any rights to the contrary. We cannot sustain this contention. Although appellees, according to the record, have used this water for irrigation purposes on several occasions in previous years, dating back for more than seven years, yet it appears that appellants had not been disturbed in the exercise of their riparian rights previous to 1954. Prior to that year appellees had merely been exercising their lawful rights as riparian owners and their exercise of those rights was in no way adverse to the rights of any one. (56 Am.Jur. p. 730, § 343) In the City of Conway case, supra, where the same contention was made that appellees here make the contention was denied, the court saying [271 S.W.2d 927]: "We are unable to find any act or acts on the part of Conway of an adverse claim or nature, or such as would put appellants on notice of any adverse claim." The court then followed with citations which are applicable here.

Reversed with direction to the trial court to enter a decree in conformity with this opinion.

Notes

1. **Historical development.** Restatement (Second) of Torts, Chapter 41, Interference with the Use of Water ("Riparian Rights"), Introductory Note on the Nature of Riparian Rights and Legal Theories for Determination of the Rights:[a]

"*Riparian rights—history.* In the early English common law there was little litigation over the private use of water. * * * With the advent of the Industrial Revolution there came a marked increase in the use of water for powering machinery, and industrial wastes added a new dimension to pollution problems. In the resulting increase of litigation over water use the underlying principle was brought forth and clearly stated: each riparian proprietor has a right to use the stream as it passes his property, but no riparian proprietor has a right to use water to the injury of another. This developed into what has been called the natural flow theory, which required the stream to be left substantially unchanged except for minor effects of reasonable means of harnessing and using it as it passed.

"As American industry grew it became obvious that many economically and socially desirable uses of water could not fit this pattern of leaving the streams substantially unchanged. A large mill required not merely a small dam to create a head of water but a reservoir for storage of water. The consumption of water increased as steam power freed the mills from the river banks, irrigation expanded and railroads and other industries multiplied. The idea of preserving the natural stream gave way to the need to alter it materially in order to enable the water to be put to these beneficial uses. The use, not the stream, came to be the thing protected by law, and injury to a reasonable use became the tort. * * * Under the reasonable use theory the primary or fundamental right of each riparian proprietor on a watercourse or lake is to be free from unreasonable uses that cause harm to his own reasonable use of the water. Emphasis is placed on a full and beneficial use of the advantages of the stream or lake, and each riparian proprietor has a privilege to make a reasonable use of water for any purpose, provided that his use does not cause harm to the reasonable uses of others. Each riparian must make his use in a manner that will accommodate as many other uses as possible. * * * The major advantage of this theory is that it tends to promote the beneficial use of water resources.

"The reasonable use theory has won an almost complete victory in the American courts, although a considerable amount of natural flow language can still be found. Some cases do not require a clear distinction, since the natural flow

---

theory allows many reasonable accommodations between users and the reasonable use theory sometimes results in holdings that the maintenance of a stream or lake in its natural condition is reasonable under particular circumstances. Even when the reasonable use rule is applied in its strictest form, the natural flow preference for 'natural wants' is preserved in the form of a preference for domestic uses. Some courts have applied the reasonable use theory in cases between riparians and the natural flow theory in cases between a riparian and a nonriparian. In some western states the streams were regarded merely as sources for irrigating the arid land and the courts applied the reasonable use theory to its ultimate extreme and permitted the streams to be dried up completely. In eastern states, however, where a stream is regarded as an amenity that may add value to land though it remains unused, courts that usually apply the reasonable use rule will sometimes use natural flow language to preserve a living stream, although what is preserved is the minimum flow required to protect its values, not the full natural flow."

2. **Civil law origins?** Samuel C. Wiel, Waters, American Law and French Authority, 33 Harv. L. Rev. 133 (1919), argued that the riparian doctrine stems from the civil law, was imported into the United States in the early nineteenth century, and then found its way to England. More recent research has pretty well exploded it. See supra p. 21, Note 4.

3. **Determination of reasonableness.** Restatement (Second) of Torts § 850A. Reasonableness of the Use of Water:[a]

"The determination of the reasonableness of a use of water depends upon a consideration of the interests of the riparian proprietor making the use, of any riparian proprietor harmed by it and of society as a whole. Factors that affect the determination include the following: (a) The purpose of the use, (b) the suitability of the use to the watercourse or lake, (c) the economic value of the use, (d) the social value of the use, (e) the extent and amount of the harm it causes, (f) the practicality of avoiding the harm by adjusting the use or method of use of one proprietor or the other, (g) the practicality of adjusting the quantity of water used by each proprietor, (h) the protection of existing values of water uses, land, investments and enterprises, and (i) the justice of requiring the user causing harm to bear the loss.

"Comment: *a. Determination of reasonable or unreasonable use.* The reasonableness or unreasonableness of a use of water by a riparian proprietor must be determined by a court or jury from a number of points of view and upon the consideration of a number of factors. A conflict arising out of a claim of harm to one riparian proprietor caused by the water use of another proprietor involves an examination of the use or interest alleged to be harmed, the use causing the harm, the effect that the latter has upon the former and the effects upon society, the economy and the environment of making the uses and of resolving the conflict.

"In a suit between two riparian users of water the reasonableness of both uses is in issue. The plaintiff, in order to show he has a right that has been violated, must establish that his use of the water is reasonable. * * * "

4. **Application of reasonableness principles in Harris v. Brooks.** The court in *Harris*, quoting the Restatement of Torts, states that a determination of

---

a. Copyright 1979. Reprinted with the permission of the American Law Institute.

unreasonableness should not be an "unreasoned, intuitive conclusion" but should involve "an evaluating of the conflicting interests of each of the contestants and a "weighing of those, one against the other." Did the court engage in such a process in *Harris*? The quoted language also provides that substantial harm to another riparian may not be unreasonable if the utility of the activity outweighs the gravity of the harm. Did the court follow this directive?

5. **Domestic use preference.** The preference for domestic use, referred to in *Harris*, permits an upper riparian to take the full flow of the stream even though such use would deprive a lower riparian of any use of the water whatever. This preference for "natural uses," had its origin in a dictum from Evans v. Merriweather, infra p. 263:

"Now the question fairly arises, is that a reasonable use of running water by the upper proprietor, by which the fluid itself is entirely consumed? To answer this question satisfactorily, it is proper to consider the wants of man in regard to the element of water. These wants are either natural or artificial. Natural are such as are absolutely necessary to be supplied, in order to his existence. Artificial, such only, as by supplying them, his comfort and prosperity are increased. To quench thirst, and for household purposes, water is absolutely indispensable. In civilized life, water for cattle is also necessary. These wants must be supplied, or both man and beast will perish. The supply of man's artificial wants is not essential to his existence; it is not indispensable; he could live if water was not employed in irrigating lands, or in propelling his machinery. In countries differently situated from ours, with a hot and arid climate, water doubtless is absolutely indispensable to the cultivation of the soil, and in them, water for irrigation would be a natural want. Here it might increase the products of the soil, but it is by no means essential, and cannot therefore be considered a natural want of man. So of manufacturers, they promote the prosperity and comfort of mankind, but cannot be considered absolutely necessary to his existence; nor need the machinery which he employs be set in motion by steam."

The suggestion of a natural use preference for irrigation in areas where that practice is necessary for the successful cultivation of crops was rejected in Watkins Land Co. v. Clements, 86 S.W. 733 (Tex. 1905) and Meng v. Coffey, 93 N.W. 713 (Neb. 1903). In City of Canton v. Shock, 63 N.E. 600 (Ohio 1902), expressing the minority view that a city may be a riparian proprietor, it was held that the city's domestic use would be entitled to a preference over manufacturing uses. In Prather v. Hoberg, 150 P.2d 405 (Cal. 1944), the court held that the preference for domestic uses might extend to a hotel or resort, although it indicated that the preference might be lost if the use was too extensive. In United States v. Fallbrook Public Utility District, 108 F.Supp. 72 (S.D. Cal. 1952), the use of water for domestic purposes by 50,000 soldiers in a military camp was held a proper and reasonable riparian use, on the authority of the *Prather* case. However, the court did not accord it a preferred status, and in a later phase of the case, 109 F.Supp. 28 (S.D. Cal. 1952), the court limited the use of water for the military purposes of the camp to the maximum amount allowable for agricultural use on the ranch which had been purchased for the camp.

6. **Adjustment of conflicting uses.** *Harris* also suggests that an equitable adjustment of uses may resolve the conflict between two riparians in some cases. See also Restatement (Second) of Torts § 850A(f) above. Did the court utilize this principle in resolving the case?

Hazard Powder Co. v. Somersville Mfg. Co., 61 A. 519 (Conn. 1905), involved a conflict between the operators of two mill dams. The upstream defendant stored the entire flow of the stream during the night and used the water during the day. The downstream plaintiff, who operated day and night, objected to this practice because it was deprived of water for night operations. The court held for the defendant, finding that the conflict was caused by the inadequacy of storage capacity in the plaintiff's mill pond and that it would be feasible for the plaintiff to increase the capacity of its pond. Rancho Santa Margarita v. Vail, 81 P.2d 533 (Cal. 1938), involved a stream which was inadequate to meet the needs of two riparian ranchers during the summer months. The court said it was the duty of a trial court to work out a "physical solution" to accommodate the needs of both riparians if possible and suggested the construction of storage reservoirs as a possible solution.

Where a physical solution is possible, who should bear the costs? See Chapter 2, Section 2G. See also Restatement (Second) of Torts § 850A, cmt. h.

7. ***De minimus* harm.** Many cases which purport to balance the relative reasonableness of plaintiff's existing use and of defendant's new use and which are resolved in favor of the defendant seem in fact to be holding that the harm to the plaintiff is not substantial in economic terms or is the type of inconvenience that is the inevitable result of progress and development. For example, in Gehlen v. Knorr, 70 N.W. 757 (Iowa 1897), the plaintiff complained of defendant's new dam for an ice pond, yet it was filled in two days and neither removal of ice nor seepage and evaporation from the dam materially affected plaintiff's mill. *De minimus non curat lex* and *damnum absque injuria* are important principles in riparian law, although the courts have not always identified them as such or distinguished the two. See also Heise v. Schulz, 204 P.2d 706 (Kan. 1949); City of Louisville v. Tway, 180 S.W.2d 278 (Ky. 1944); Elliot v. Fitchburg Ry. Co., 64 Mass. (10 Cush.) 191 (1852); Meyers v. Lafayette Club, 266 N.W. 861 (Minn. 1936); Montelious v. Elsea, 161 N.E.2d 675 (Ohio Ct. C.P. 1959).

BOTTON v. STATE

Supreme Court of Washington, 1966.
69 Wash.2d 751, 420 P.2d 352.

HILL, JUDGE. The State of Washington, through its Department of Game, acquired by purchase a waterfront lot on Phantom Lake (nonnavigable) which it has developed to be used as a public fishing access area. Its use or abuse, for that purpose, has resulted in the present action by other owners of waterfront property on the lake, asking that the state be enjoined from maintaining its public access area.

The trial court made very comprehensive findings of fact:

> Since the defendant, through its Game Department, put in the public access area, the plaintiffs have suffered the following as a result of it:
>
> 1. The fair market value of plaintiffs' property has been decreased.
>
> 2. Thievery on the lake has greatly increased, particularly the stealing of boats, oars, outdoor furniture, tools and miscellaneous items of personal property of all kinds. In many of the cases it was definitely ascertained that the thieves gained access to the lake from the public access area.

> 3. Persons relieving themselves in the lake as well as on the property and front yards of various of the plaintiffs, to the considerable embarrassment and annoyance of the plaintiffs, their families and guests.
>
> 4. Beer cans, worm cans, sandwich bags, pop bottles, rafts, and other assorted trash has been deposited in the lake and on the plaintiffs' beaches in considerable quantity.
>
> 5. Repeated and frequent trespasses on the plaintiffs' front yards, docks, beaches and property. In addition to the trespasses by persons coming in by the access area, numerous other trespassers have crossed the plaintiffs' yards, docks, beaches and property from other adjoining residential areas, and which trespassers, when confronted by the plaintiffs, have justified their actions by saying to the effect that, "Well, now, it's a public lake, isn't it."
>
> 6. Numerous of the plaintiffs, their children and grandchildren, have severely and frequently been cut by broken beer bottles left on the beaches.
>
> 7. Fishermen using plaintiffs' docks, and fishing immediately adjacent to their beaches and front yards, would refuse to leave when requested and would stare and make remarks when plaintiffs, their wives and daughters would try to use their beaches for sun bathing, swimming or the entertainment of guests. The plaintiffs, as a result of this, cut down very considerably in their use of their front yards and beaches.
>
> 8. Although hunting and shooting on the lake are illegal, hunters come in and hunt and shoot on the lake. Persons also come in and shoot at ducks with air rifles.
>
> 9. Speed boating on the lake has greatly increased. In some cases it has increased to the extent that it has become a danger to the plaintiffs' children.
>
> 10. The public use of the lake has interfered with the plaintiffs' use of the lake for boating, swimming, fishing and recreational purposes.
>
> 11. The noise on the lake has substantially increased.

From these findings, the trial court drew the legal conclusions that the state's opening up of the lake to public use through its access area, without resorting to eminent domain, constituted a taking and damaging of private property without compensation to the owners thereof; and that the state's opening up of the lake to public use constituted an unreasonable interference with the rights of the plaintiffs.

Based on these conclusions, the trial court entered an injunction enjoining the state

> from maintaining its public access area on Phantom Lake as a public access area and from admitting the public to Phantom Lake and across the access area until such time as it condemns the plaintiffs' property and property rights in the manner provided by law.

The state appeals, urging that as a riparian owner on a nonnavigable lake it can permit the public to enjoy the right to fish from boats over every portion of the lake so long as this does not constitute an unreasonable interference with the rights of the other riparian owners. This implies an obligation to police and control the use of the nonnavigable lake by the public to prevent such use becoming an unreasonable interference with the rights of the other riparian owners thereon.

The lake is small and shallow, covering 63.2 acres, and with depths running from extremely shallow to a maximum of 47 feet near the middle. The shore of the lake is partly surrounded with nice homes (most of the homeowners reside on the lake the year-round) and partly by as yet undeveloped properties. It lies between Lake Washington and Lake Sammamish (within only a few hundred feet of the latter), both of which are large, navigable lakes with many public access areas, parks, and beaches. There are no commercial establishments, resorts or public beaches on Phantom Lake. Nor were there any public streets, roads, or street ends which would give the public an access to the lake, until the state, acting through its Department of Game, acquired approximately a hundred feet of lake frontage, extending back some 800 feet to a public thoroughfare, and developed it to provide an access for fishermen and their boats.

There has been no serious attempt by the state to limit access to the lake to fishermen; and the trial court found that this access area had been open to any member of the public. We do not question the right of the state, as a riparian owner, to ignore the county's zoning regulations and to permit the public, as its licensees, access to the lake over its property. There is, however, a limitation, and that is that it cannot permit such use of its property as constitutes an unreasonable interference with the rights of the other riparian owners.

We have stated the law applicable in the present case quite succinctly in Snively v. Jaber, 48 Wash.2d 815, 821, 296 P.2d 1015, 1019, 57 A.L.R.2d 560 (1956):

> We hold that with respect to the boating, swimming, fishing, and other similar rights of riparian proprietors upon a nonnavigable lake, these rights or privileges are owned in common, and that any proprietor or his licensee may use the entire surface of a lake so long as he does not unreasonably interfere with the exercise of similar rights by the other owners. This rule does not have the effect of making the nonnavigable lake public, since a stranger has no right to enter upon the lake without the permission of an abutting owner. The rule we have announced affords equal protection to the interest of all riparian owners in the use of the water and seeks to promote the greatest beneficial use by each with a minimum of harm to other owners.

In that case, the defendant Jaber had a dance hall, picnic grounds, and a swimming area on Angle Lake (nonnavigable) and rented some 30 rowboats to the public. The conduct of the licensees in rented rowboats was such that the trial court found it necessary to enjoin that operation for a 2-year period, and this we affirmed.

The depredations and conduct of Jaber's licensees, which warranted an injunction in that case, could be characterized as a Sunday-school picnic as compared with the indecencies and obscenities to which the other riparian owners on Phantom Lake have been subjected. Added to this is the physical danger to other riparian owners, their children and grandchildren from broken beer bottles left on the beaches and from the operation of speed boats dangerously close to bathers and swimmers near the shore. While the trial court's injunction was justified at the time of trial, it was too extensive in time and was not properly conditioned as to termination.

The dedicated people who make up the great fishing fraternity in this state should not be deprived of the opportunity and pleasure of fishing for perch, crappie, and the like (the water is too warm for trout) because of the conduct of a relatively few hooligans.

The state, as a riparian owner, does not have to acquire by condemnation the rights of the other riparian owners before it permits fishermen in reasonable numbers access to the waters of Phantom Lake; but it does have the obligation, and counsel for the state so concede, to so regulate the number and conduct of its licensees as to prevent any undue interference with the rights of other riparian owners.

The injunction should be continued only until the state, through its Department of Game, presents a plan for the controlled operation of its property that satisfies the trial court that the rights of other riparian owners will be adequately safeguarded. The state is entitled to all the rights of a riparian owner, but it should also accept the responsibility of a riparian owner for the conduct of its licensees.

We are in accord with the trial court's conclusion, from the facts in this case, that there has been an unreasonable interference by the state's licensees with the rights of other riparian owners and that an injunction was properly granted, but it should be modified and limited as indicated herein; and the cause is remanded for that purpose. * * *

FINLEY, JUDGE (concurring specially in the majority opinion). We are confronted in this appeal with a complex natural resources problem certain to become more and more acute in this age of a geometrically increasing demand by more and more people for outdoor recreational and leisure time activities. The problem is one of insuring that the greatest possible number of Washingtonians, and others, are able to utilize reasonably the natural resources of our state for recreational activity. * * *

If the problem is approached strictly in the sense of the legal concept of "riparian rights," its solution will be a restricted and limited one, and probably inadequate, in terms of its recognition of either the rights of the public or the rights of the individual lakefront owners. The same kind of danger or limitation is apparent in approaching the problem solely in terms of the legal concept of state ownership of the waters of nonnavigable lakes. Again, in the best tradition of the common law, some gloss upon the legal concept of "riparian rights" and upon the legal concept of state ownership of the waters of the lake seems indicated and necessary for a juristic accommodation of the conflicting interests and rights of members of the public and the private owners of water front on Phantom Lake. Without employing or adverting to the foregoing nomenclature, or characterization, it seems to me the reasoning of the majority opinion by Judge Hill resolves the problem in a common-sense, practicable way—again, in the best tradition of the common law—and that the results reached constitute an adequate and highly desirable solution of the problem involved. * * *

OTT, JUDGE (concurring in part and dissenting in part). Phantom Lake has been open for public fishing continuously since 1926. It is not a popular fishermen's lake because it is stocked only with spiny ray fish. On opening day in 1963, only 50 fishermen appeared, who caught a total of 9 fish. The evidence was undisputed that seldom were more than 6 boats on the lake at any one time. It is this limited use by the public that the riparian owners wish to exclude entirely.

The majority sustain the injunction until such time as the Department of Game "presents a plan for the controlled operation of its property that satisfies the trial court that the rights of other riparian owners will be adequately safeguarded." With this holding, I do not agree for the following reasons:

(1) One who builds his home on the shore of public waters of this state is aware that the public will use those waters for recreational purposes, and that such use may be abused by relatively few members of the public and by other riparian owners. The debits of such living must be measured against the credits of the scenic beauty and the many recreational pleasures enjoyed by those who are the owners of waterfront property.

(2) The majority do not suggest what type of "plan" will be acceptable to this court. Are 50 boats on opening day and less than 6 boats a day thereafter too many on this 63-acre lake? I do not believe that this use is excessive or that regulations limiting the number of boats on Phantom Lake have been shown to be necessary.

Should the "plan" of the game department require that the Sheriff of King County station a deputy on Phantom Lake from daylight until dark to keep under surveillance the operators of the 6 boats in order to arrest the offenders if the general misdemeanors complained of are committed? I doubt whether the sheriff could find, much less afford, sufficient officers to police so intensively the myriad lakes in King County.

Should the "plan" require that the game department be authorized to police all of the lakes of this state, including Phantom Lake, to prevent violation of the general misdemeanor laws? Such a plan must be submitted to the legislature, not to the courts. The legislature has vested in the game protectors of this state limited authority to enforce only the game laws. RCW 77.12.070. A game protector has no more authority to arrest a person for general misdemeanors than has a riparian owner.

The legislature, in the exercise of its discretion, has vested solely in the local authorities power to enforce the general misdemeanor laws. The record before us establishes that the riparian owners on Phantom Lake never sought the aid of such officers when they observed these laws being violated. Any "plan" which the game department might suggest would be advisory only to those authorities whose duty it is to enforce the general misdemeanor laws of this state.

Notes

1. **Use of the surface above beds owned by another.** A number of cases have held that swimming or boating on the surface of the water above that portion of the bed owned by another are trespasses. Sanders v. De Rose, 191 N.E. 331 (Ind. 1934); Berger Farms, Inc. v. Estes, 662 N.E.2d 654 (Ind. Ct. App. 1996); Shandalee Camp v. Rosenthal, 233 N.Y.S. 11 (1929); Lembeck v. Nye, 24 N.E. 686 (Ohio 1890); Decker v. Baylor, 19 A. 351 (Pa. 1890). Some of these courts, however, will not presume that the non-riparian use is adverse to the riparians' interests. Rather, they will require clear and convincing evidence of an adverse use. Carnahan v. Moriah Prop. Owners Ass'n, 716 N.E.2d 437 (Ind. 1999). Beginning with Beach v. Hayner, 173 N.W. 487 (Mich. 1919), the common use rule adopted in *Botton* has taken hold in a number of states where water recreation is of special importance. Duval v. Thomas, 114 So.2d 791 (Fla. 1959); West Michigan Dock & Market Corp. v. Lakeland Investments, 534 N.W.2d 212 (Mich. Ct. App. 1995); Johnson v. Seifert, 100 N.W.2d 689 (Minn. 1960); Improved Realty Corp. v. Sowers, 78 S.E.2d 588 (Va. 1953).

2. **Limits on filling privately owned beds.** In Bach v. Sarich, 445 P.2d 648 (Wash. 1968), the parties were riparians surrounding Bitter Lake, a small 19-acre non-navigable lake in Seattle. The bed was privately owned, and a zoning ordinance designated the defendant's portion of the bed as open for apartment use. Defendant started construction on an apartment building that would extend 180 feet into the lake, built partly on lake fill and partly on piers. Plaintiffs, claiming a common right to use the surface, obtained an objection. The court said that the building could not be considered a reasonable use of the lake surface by the defendant since it was not a riparian use at all, it was not "intimately associated with the water." See Ralph W. Johnson & G. Richard Morry, Filling and Building on Small Lakes—Time for Judicial and Legislative Controls, 45 Wash. L. Rev. 27 (1970).

3. **Protection of aesthetic values.** A "right to view" was recognized in City of Los Angeles v. Aitken, 52 P.2d 585 (Cal. 1935). The city, condemning littoral rights to lands surrounding a lake to be drained for municipal supply, objected to substantial damages being awarded persons who withdrew no water from the lake.

"The lake has no outlet. It is situated in a volcanic mountainous region east of the Yosemite Valley. It has an elevation of 6,426 feet above the level of the sea. This elevation has remained substantially the same during all of the time of which we have knowledge. The lake is unique in its character, occupying a depression in the midst of lofty mountains and extinct volcanic cones. It is ten miles in width and fifteen miles in length with a maximum depth of 150 feet. In the middle of the lake are two small islands. The water of the lake is permeated with mineral salt and alkali to such an extent that it is unfit for domestic use or for irrigation.

"Mono Lake is situated on the now famous Tioga Highway connecting Los Angeles with Lake Tahoe. From Mono a frequently traveled thoroughfare extends through a timbered country to the Yosemite Valley. The picturesque beauty, the highly colored rocks and precipitous walls and the rare surroundings of Mono Lake attract an increasing number of tourists to its popular resorts. John Muir, the late famous exploring scientist, half a century ago said of this locality: 'This beauty * * * is of a still higher order, enticing us lovingly on through gentian meadows and groves of rustling aspen to Lake Mono, where, spirit-like, our happy stream vanishes. * * * Mountains, red, gray, and black, rise close at hand on the right, whitened around their bases with banks of enduring snow; on the left swells the huge red mass of Mount Gibbs, while in front the eye wanders down the shadowy canon, and out on the warm plain of Mono, where the lake is seen gleaming like a burnished metallic disk, with clusters of lofty volcanic cones to the south of it.'

"But this limitation of riparian rights of owners of land to a necessary use for beneficial purposes does not mean that the water must be actually used in irrigating the land or consumed for domestic purposes. It does not authorize the appropriation of littoral rights to land bordering on the margin of a lake without the payment of just compensation therefor, when the very value of the land depends on the maintenance of the lake in its natural condition. Irrigation and household uses of water are not the only reasonable or beneficial purposes for which it may be employed, even though the presence of mineral salts or alkali in the water renders it unfit for human consumption or domestic use.

"For the reason that the existence of Mono Lake in its natural condition, with all of its attractive surroundings, is the vital thing that furnishes to the respondents' marginal land almost its entire value, and that the draining of the lake will nearly destroy the value of their properties and the incident littoral rights thereto, it seems clear that the lake is not being used by the respondents for an unreasonable or nonbeneficial purpose, but, upon the contrary, that their use of the lake in its natural condition is reasonably beneficial to their land, and the littoral rights thereof may therefore not be appropriated, even for a higher or more beneficial use for public welfare, without just compensation therefor."

Other cases protecting riparians from the loss of land values resulting from drying up a stream or lowering lake levels include Collens v. New Canaan Water Co., 234 A.2d 825 (Conn. 1967) and Taylor v. Tampa Coal Co., 46 So.2d 392 (Fla. 1950).

4. **Protection of public values.** As is true of prior appropriation law, riparian law, although concerned with private rights, can serve to some degree the objectives of enhancing and producing recreational opportunities available to the public. In Snively v. Jaber, cited in the principal case, and in *Botton* itself, the Washington court permits riparian proprietors operating a commercial resort and a public park to invite the public to share in their riparian rights to recreational uses of water. In a famous eastern case, McCord v. Big Brothers Movement, 185 A. 480 (N.J. Ch. 1936), the use of water for a swimming pool used by a large number of boys at a summer camp was enjoined. "Riparian rights can be claimed only by the owner thereof, and they include the use of the waters of a stream for ordinary and reasonable bathing privileges, which extend only to the owner, his family, and inmates and guests of his household. The transfer to a large number of invitees of the bathing use of transported waters exceeds the reasonable use to which the riparian owner is entitled."

The rules of riparian law that preserve living streams, restrict the extent of riparian land and restrict non-riparian uses offer a form of blunt-instrument protection of some environmental values. For a more finely tuned provision, see Cal. Water Code § 1707. That provision allows both riparian and appropriative rights holders to dedicate their water rights to preserve or enhance "wetlands habitat, fish and wildlife resources, or recreation in, or on, the water." The transfers require approval of the State Water Resources Control Board. The Board may approve the petition if it neither will "increase the amount of water the petitioner is entitle to use" nor will "unreasonably affect any legal user of water." Cal. Water Code § 1707(b)(1) & (2). Petitioners may also indicate the extent to which such dedications are meant "to satisfy any applicable federal, state, or local regulatory requirements governing water quantity, water quality, instream flows, fish and wildlife, wetlands, recreation, and other instream beneficial uses." Through this latter provision, the Board serves as a clearinghouse, recording credits towards petitioners' externally imposed legal obligations.

5. **Regulation of water levels in lakes.** The water level in natural lakes, and often as well in man-made reservoirs, has important implications for residential, recreational and environmental values. Several states have imposed extensive controls on fluctuations and minimum levels. Reservoir levels may be fixed in Minnesota, Minn. Stat. § 103G.401, and Michigan (by county boards of commissioners), Mich. Comp. Laws §§ 324.30701 et seq. Natural lake levels are the subject of regulation in Vermont, Indiana, and Michigan. Vt. Stat. Ann. tit. 10 §§ 905, 1421-1426; Ind. Code § 14–26–2–6; Mich. Comp. Laws, §§ 324.30701 et. seq. The Michigan statutes were construed in Wortelboer v. Benzie County, 537 N.W.2d 603 (Mich. Ct. App. 1995). See Richard W. Bartke, Navigability in Michigan in Retrospect and Prospect, 16 Wayne L. Rev. 409, 440 (1970).

6. **Reasonableness and equality.** Upon retrial and second appeal of Thompson v. Enz, supra p. 242, the Michigan supreme court ruled that the developer's canals that would give boat access to the lake from 128 back lots created by subdivision of the defendant's riparian tract would be unreasonable and a violation of the riparian rights of other lakefront property owners. The evidence showed, however, that several other large tracts had been similarly subdivided and canalized. The trial court had said, "Defendants contend that plaintiffs and others are contributing their share to the congestion. * * * The answer to this is that the others were there before the breaking point was reached." The supreme court approved the trial judge's finding but held that the injunction could not issue, the plaintiffs being estopped because, with notice of the dredging, they had stood by while nearly all the defendants' canals had been excavated before seeking preventive relief. The dissenting judge stated, "These defendants do not propose to exercise any rights or inaugurate any uses which are in the slightest fashion more detrimental to the lake than the existing uses of other lake owners. * * * The trial court would brand these defendants' use as the 'straw that broke the camel's back,' and in the name of preserving to these plaintiffs a quasi-monopoly to use a lake which belongs to the people of Michigan, our Court would approve the arbitrary, unlawful and unconstitutional confiscation of the defendants' property without payment of compensation therefor." Thompson v. Enz, 188 N.W.2d 579 (Mich. 1971).

It is often said that all riparian proprietors have "equal rights." How equal are the rights of Botton and the state to use Phantom Lake? But for estoppel, how equal would be the rights of plaintiff and defendants in Thompson v. Enz?

7. **Character and capacity of the watercourse.** Mason v. Hoyle, 14 A. 786 (Conn. 1888): "In the next place, a reasonable use is one adapted to the character and capacity of the stream, * * * The other fact found, that five days' detention of the water has enabled the defendant to run [his mill] only five hours

shows still more forcibly the enormous disproportion of his machinery to the capacity of the stream during the dry season." The court also emphasized that prior to the time the defendant enlarged his mill the custom had been to use run-of-the-river power, using the dams only to provide a head of water. This long established mode of running the mills was considered as an element in determining that the intermittent use by the enlarged dam was unreasonable.

8. **Use of a stream to transport artificial flows.** Does an upstream riparian have a right to use a stream as an artificial conduit to transport water? No, said the Pennsylvania Supreme Court in Alburger v. Philadelphia Elec. Co., 535 A.2d 729 (Pa. 1988). The court enjoined the electric company from using a small stream having a median flow of 1.4 cfs to transport 71 cfs of water from the Delaware River to a nuclear generating plant. The court noted that Pennsylvania is a reasonable use jurisdiction but held that the flowage easement which an upstream riparian enjoys over a downstream riparian extends only to waters naturally originating on the upstream lands.

9. **Disruption of natural flows.** In theory, in a pure natural flow jurisdiction, any retention of water infringes on the rights of downstream riparians. Thus, in City of Waterbury v. Town of Washington, 800 A.2d 1102 (Conn. 2002), the court stated that the existence of an upstream dam put downstream riparians on notice that a prescriptive right was accruing in favor of the dam owner.

Given the harsh and inefficient consequences of the pure natural flow doctrine, many courts modified it to permit substantial interference with such flows. J. H. Beuscher, Appropriation Water Law Elements in Riparian Doctrine States, 10 Buff. L. Rev. 448, 453 (1961):

"Dams often disrupt the natural flow of the stream, especially in dry periods when water flowing down the stream is held behind the dam to maintain the head or power potential. Cases from mill dam and logging dam days willingly (and understandably) sustained as reasonable the complete retention of the full flow of the river for days at a time. Economic needs dictated these blows at "natural flow" ideals. Far from protecting a bare technical right to the natural flow of the watercourse,[25] courts permitted complete disruption of the flow for sustained periods of time. Nor have the legislatures failed to react to similar pressures. A Wisconsin statute, for example, requires the hydro-dam proprietor to let by, not the entire natural flow, but as little as 25% of it."

EVANS v. MERRIWEATHER

Supreme Court of Illinois, 1842.
3 Scam. (4 Ill.) 492.

LOCKWOOD, JUSTICE, delivered the opinion of the court: This was an action on the case, brought in the Greene Circuit Court, by Merriweather against Evans, for obstructing and diverting a water course. The plaintiff obtained a verdict, and judgment was rendered thereon. On the trial the defendant excepted to the instructions asked for and given, at the instance of

---

25. In United States v. Gerlach Live Stock Co., 339 U.S. 725 (1950), Mr. Justice Jackson said that such riparianism pressed to the limits of its logic enables one to play dog-in-the-manger.

the plaintiff. The defendant also excepted, because instructions that were asked by him, were refused. After the cause was brought into this court, the parties agreed upon the following statement of facts, as having been proved on the trial, to wit: "It is agreed between the parties to this suit, that the following is the statement of facts proved at the trial in this case, and that the same shall be considered as part of the record by the court, in the adjudication of this cause. Smith and Baker, in 1834, bought of T. Carlin six acres of land, through which a branch ran, and erected a steam mill thereon. They depended upon a well and the branch for water in running their engine. About one or two years afterwards, John Evans bought of T. Carlin six acres of land, on the same branch, above and immediately adjoining the lot owned by Smith & Baker, and erected thereon a steam mill, depending upon a well and the branch for water in running his engine.

> "Smith & Baker, after the erection of Evans' mill, in 1836 or 1837, sold the mill and appurtenances to Merriweather, for about $8,000. Evans' mill was supposed to be worth $12,000. Ordinarily there was an abundance of water for both mills; but in the fall of 1837, there being a drought, the branch failed, so far that it did not afford water sufficient to run the upper mill continually. Evans directed his hands not to stop, or divert the water, in the branch; but one of them employed about the mill did make a dam across the branch, just below Evans' mill, and thereby diverted all the water in the branch into Evans' well. Evans was at home, half a mile from the mill, and was frequently about his mill, and evidence was introduced conducing to prove that he might have known that the water of the branch was diverted into his well. After the diversion of the water into Evans' well, as aforesaid, the branch went dry below, and Merriweather's mill could not and did not run, in consequence of it, more than one day in a week, and was then supplied with water from his well. Merriweather then brought this suit, in three or four weeks after the putting of the dam across the branch for the diversion of the water, and obtained a verdict for $150. This suit, it is admitted, is the first between the parties litigating the right as to the use of the water. It is further agreed, that the branch afforded usually sufficient water for the supply of both mills, without materially affecting the size of the current, though the branch was not depended upon exclusively for that purpose. Furthermore, that at the time of the grievances complained of by the plaintiff below, the defendant had water hauled in part for the supply of his boilers. That the dam was made below the defendant's well, across the branch, which diverted as well the water hauled and poured out into the branch above the well, as the water of the branch, into the defendant's well."

Upon this state of facts, the question is presented, as to what extent riparian proprietors, upon a stream not navigable, can use the water of such stream? The branch mentioned in the agreed statement of facts, is a small natural stream of water, not furnishing, at all seasons of the year, a supply of water sufficient for both mills. There are no facts in the case showing that the water is wanted for any other than milling purposes, and for those purposes to be converted into steam, and thus entirely consumed. * * *

Each riparian proprietor is bound to make such a use of running water as to do as little injury to those below him as is consistent with a valuable benefit to himself. The use must be a reasonable one. Now the question fairly arises, is that a reasonable use of running water by the upper proprietor, by which the fluid itself is entirely consumed? * * * But where the water * * * is not sufficient for each proprietor living on the stream, to carry on his manufacturing purposes, how shall the water be divided? We have seen that, without a contract or grant, neither has a right to use all the water; all have a right to participate in its benefits. Where all have a right to participate in a common benefit, and none can have an exclusive enjoyment, no rule, from the very nature of the case, can be laid down, as to how much each may use without infringing upon the rights of others. In such cases, the question must be left to the judgment of the jury, whether the party complained of has used, under all the circumstances, more than his just proportion.

It appears, from the facts agreed on, that Evans obstructed the water by a dam, and diverted the whole into his well. This diversion, according to all the cases, both English and American, was clearly illegal. For this diversion, an action will lie. * * *

For these reasons I am of opinion that the judgment ought to be affirmed, with costs.

Notes

1. **Difficulties of sharing.** Sharing of shortages has an egalitarian appeal but entails a number of difficulties. If competing uses are incompatible in the sense that they cannot both exist in a reduced amount, an equal sharing of the supply might effectively destroy one or both uses. An irrigator of annual crops might reduce the acreage he waters so long as he will have water enough to mature the remainder of his crop, but if reducing his share means that he would be cut off completely in mid season, he may lose the entire crop. Cutting the supply of a fruit grower could result in loss of part of the orchard. The reduction of water power below a certain point may stop a mill completely. A reduced water supply may allow one enterprise to continue operation at reduced levels of production and profit, while it may put another out of business if profitability depends upon maintenance of a high level of production because of fixed costs. The irrigator who takes his share by lowering a lake level may spoil for a summer some recreational features on which a resort depends and may induce ecological changes which have an even more lasting effect on fishing.

2. **Sharing v. over-development.** When do the virtues of sharing become the evils of "common pool exploitation?" What is a shortage? Suppose a drought of the same severity in 1830 had reduced the branch to the 1837 flow. Was there then a shortage? Suppose another drought in 1835, after the Smith & Baker mill was erected but before Evans' was in operation? How many more mills will (or should) riparian law allow to be built on the branch?

3. **Unreasonable sharing.** What happens if a shortage becomes so acute or demand so large that the shares are sufficient for no one? The riparian vineyardists of the Napa Valley ward off frost damage by pumping water from the Napa River and spraying their vines with a fine mist. In a cold snap all spray together, which threatens to dry up the river and create a water shortage for all the wine growers. The State Water Resources Control Board sought to force construction of a storage reservoir on the river by obtaining a declaratory judgment

that the simultaneous diversion of unstored water in this manner was an unreasonable use and method of use proscribed by the California Constitution. (See *Joslin,* infra p. 270, Note 5). Held, the Board's complaint states a cause of action and the case should proceed to a determination of whether, under the facts and circumstances of the case, these simultaneous uses of unstored water were unreasonable. People ex rel. State Water Resources Control Bd. v. Forni, 126 Cal. Rptr. 851 (Cal. Ct. App. 1976).

4. **Allocation among riparian irrigators.** In the West, where shortage is common even in the absence of drought, the courts have sometimes allocated fixed proportions of water among riparian irrigators. For example, Hunter Land Co. v. Laugenour, 250 P. 41 (Wash. 1926), involved three riparians who owned 133, 70 and 2 acres respectively, in a basin containing 1040 irrigable riparian acres. They were decreed rights to 133/1040, 70/1040 and 2/1040 of the water of the stream. This method of allocation was approved in Wiggins v. Muscupiabe Land & Water Co., 45 P. 160, 163-64 (Cal. 1896): "The right of a riparian owner to the use of the water is not, however, measured by the amount which he actually uses, and it is not to be assumed that the same amount of land will be cultivated in every succeeding year. The amount of irrigable land belonging to each party, rather than the amount of land already under cultivation, would be properly made a controlling element in adjusting their respective rights to the flow of the stream; otherwise a readjustment would be necessary whenever either party should cultivate a greater or less area." See also Harris v. Harrison, 29 P. 325 (Cal. 1892), in which the court approved an order which allowed to riparian irrigators to each use the full flow of the small stream for 3 1/2 days per week, and Southern California Inv. Co. v. Wilshire, 77 P. 767 (Cal. 1904), in which it was held error to divide the water solely on the basis of the proportion of the frontage of the owners' lands upon the stream. However, a decree apportioning proportionate shares among riparians is binding only so long as the conditions on which it is based remain unchanged. See City of Los Angeles v. Baldwin, 53 Cal. 469 (1879) (Rhodes J., concurring specially).

Compare Lone Tree Ditch Co. v. Cyclone Ditch Co., 128 N.W. 596, 598 (S.D. 1910): "It will also be seen from the foregoing that the amount of water, in inches, to which a riparian owner may be entitled for irrigation as against other riparian owners, is absolutely impossible of estimation, as it must continually vary, not only from the varying volume of water flowing down the stream at different times of the year or during different years, but also from the amount of land that may have been settled upon; and the extent of the use of water for the so-called ordinary or natural purposes which in itself varies with the population of the riparian district and the number of domestic animals kept thereon." See also Seneca Consol. Gold Mines Co. v. Great Western Power Co., 287 P. 93, 98 (Cal. 1930), holding that a riparian right does not entitle one to "any specific concrete amount of water" and stating that "[t]he moment a right * * * is defined in a concrete inflexible amount, at that moment the right becomes one of priority and not riparian." The rule of *Seneca Consolidated Gold Mines* was recently applied in Pleasant Valley Canal Co. v. Borror, supra p. 244, Note 1, to hold that a prior suit had adjudicated only appropriative rights, not riparian rights, because the decree awarded specific quantities of water.

5. **Sharing of water power.** Warren v. Westbrook Manufacturing Co., 33 A. 665 (Me. 1895): "To make water power of economic value, the rights to its use

and the division of its use, according to those rights, should be determined in advance. This prior determination is evidently essential to the peaceful and profitable use by the different parties having rights in a common power. To leave them in their uncertainty, to leave one to encroach upon the other, is to leave the whole subject matter to possible waste and destruction."

6. **Sharing in appropriation states.** Sharing of shortages by persons similarly situated is widely practiced in western irrigation districts, which take water wholesale and retail it to consumers. When stream flow or storage is insufficient to supply in full the district's appropriation, the shortage is shared *pro rata* by the irrigators. See infra p. 438, Note 6.

FARRELL v. RICHARDS

New Jersey Court of Chancery, 1879.
30 N.J.Eq. 511.

THE CHANCELLOR. The bill is filed by the owners and lessee of the property in Atlantic county long known as the Pleasant Mills, but now, also, as the Nescochague Mills, against Augustus H. Richards, to restrain him from diverting, to the damage of the complainants, as owners and lessee of the mill property, a stream known as the Forge stream, by which one of the two ponds of the complainants, known as the Forge pond, is supplied with water. From that pond the other, called the Pleasant Mills pond, and on which their mills are, draws part of its supply; and the mills, which are driven by water-power, depend wholly on the ponds for their power. The two ponds are connected by a ditch or canal. This connection between the ponds, and the use of the water in both of them to drive the machinery of the mills, have existed for over fifty years, though there was an interval of about ten years from the time when the mills were burned to the time when they were rebuilt (which was in or about 1860) when the mill site was not used.

The defendant, by various conveyances to him from the year 1858, has become the owner of a large tract of land, of about two thousand five hundred acres, extending from the head of the Forge stream up and along that stream for about three miles and a half. This property, or a considerable part of it, is used by him for the production of cranberries. In 1876 (according to the evidence it was probably in the summer and fall), he dug a large ditch, extending from the upper part of that tract to the Forge pond. His object in digging the ditch was, to irrigate his land. He also, at the same time, for the purpose of diverting the water of the stream into the ditch, constructed, with stones, brickbats and pieces of fence-rails driven into the bottom of the stream by way of piling, a dam in the stream. He and his witnesses say that it extended only partially across the stream; but some of the complainants' witnesses testify that it is entirely across the main body of the stream.

In the summer of 1877, the complainants, William E. Farrell (he is the owner of two undivided thirds of the Pleasant Mills property) and Lucius H. Warren (lessee of the other third), were operating the mills as partners. They then, in the month of August, perceived a sudden and very considerable diminution of their water-power, which was found to be due to the decrease of the water in the Forge pond. The season being an unusually wet one, and they being unable to account for the diminution of the water, set on foot investigations which resulted in the discovery of the existence of the dam and ditch. The ditch was then found to be draining the water from the Forge stream in large quantities. In January, 1878, they filed their bill in this cause for relief, praying that the defendant may be restrained from interfering in any way with the natural and ancient flow of the water down the Forge stream, and from storing or retaining the water of the stream, and that the dam built by him, or so much of it as may be found to interfere with the natural, ancient flow of the water in the stream, may be decreed to be a nuisance. They show, by the bill, a case of irreparable injury. On the filing of the bill, an order to show cause why an injunction should not be issued was made, and under it numerous affidavits were taken on both sides, which have been read without objection.

* * * The proof is that, as soon as the ditch began to withdraw the water from the stream the effect was perceived at the mills, and in August, 1877, the effect was so great that the operations of the mills were seriously affected. These facts are conclusive as to the amount withdrawn, and the consequent injury to the complainants. The defendant has no right to so use the water as to diminish its quantity to the prejudice of the complainants. While every riparian owner has a right to use the water flowing through his land for the proper irrigation of his land, his use for that purpose must be such as not essentially to interfere with the natural flow of the stream, or essentially and to the material injury of the proprietors below to diminish the quantity of water that goes to them. * * *

I do not deem it necessary to discuss the evidence. A careful consideration of it leads me to the conclusion that the defendant, by means of the dam and ditch, has withdrawn from the stream so much water as seriously to affect the complainants' water-power, and to do them irreparable injury. He still claims the right to divert the water, but insists that, in so doing, he does the complainants no injury, and causes no diminution whatever of the water in the pond. The evidence satisfies me that, by the withdrawal of the water, he not only causes diminution of the water in the pond, but diminishes it to such an extent as to cause very serious injury to the complainants. The complainants, when he began to divert the water, had enjoyed the unquestioned right of the water for over half a century. They are entitled to the protection of this court. * * *

The defendant should be restrained from diverting the water and maintaining the dam. There will be an injunction accordingly.

Notes

1. **Priority in the riparian doctrine.** Is *Farrell* merely a "natural flow" decision since overruled by "reasonable use" cases? Or does it bear out Professor Beuscher's dictum, supra p. 263, Note 9, "There is actually much more protection given to the prior user of water as against a subsequent water claimant than one would have any reason to expect from a mere recitation of black-letter riparianisms?" Recall also the answer given by the Michigan Supreme Court in Thompson v. Enz, supra p. 262, Note 6, when the defendants pointed out that their

proposed development, which the court had decided was "unreasonable," created no more congestion that several existing developments: "The answer to this is that the others were there before the breaking point was reached."

The typical expression of the reasonable use rule omits any reference to temporal priority and there are some cases that expressly say it is immaterial, e.g., Tyler v. Wilkinson, 24 Fed.Cas. 472 (C.C.R.I. 1827); McCarter v. Hudson County Water Co., 65 A. 489 (N.J. Ch. 1906). Nevertheless, it is occasionally stated as a factor to be considered: "It is also material, sometimes, to ascertain which party first erected his works and began to appropriate the water." Strobel v. Kerr Salt Co., 58 N.E. 142, 147 (N.Y. 1900).

2. **Mill dams and priority.** "Mill dam acts gave a private eminent domain power to entrepreneurs who chose to construct dams on streams flowing through riparian lands, a power to build the dam, flow the lands of an upstream riparian and be free of any obligation except to pay the value of the flowage right if the damaged landowner sued in time. More striking, for our purposes, however, is the express guarantee of appropriative status given to the riparian who first constructed a dam. No subsequent dam could be erected to the injury of any mill lawfully existing. As a matter of fact, independent of legislation or prescriptive rights, American courts have protected the earlier dam against upstream or downstream structures which threatened to impair the power potential. Similar protections are accorded hydroelectric dams erected in accordance with state-granted permits or franchises." J.H. Beuscher, supra p. 263, Note 9.

3. **Priority v. sharing.** Priority (in time) and sharing are not necessarily incompatible concepts. Priority might be used to limit the demand to the dependable supply; i.e., new uses might be prohibited once the limits of the dependable supply are reached. But, sharing, not priority, might be used to allocate water among permitted uses when an atypical shortage makes the supply inadequate.

The leading cases requiring riparian irrigators to restrict withdrawals were all triggered by drought or unusually low flows. Half Moon Bay Land Co. v. Cowell, 160 P. 675 (Cal. 1916); Frizell v. Bindley, 58 P.2d 95 (Kan. 1936); Clark v. Allaman, 80 P. 571 (Kan. 1905); Meng v. Coffey, 93 N.W. 713 (Neb. 1903); Nesalhous v. Walker, 88 P. 1032 (Wash. 1907). When flows are above the normal level each riparian may take as much as he wants as long as he causes no harm. Half Moon Bay Land Co. v. Cowell, supra.

The concept of dependable flow as the basis for making an equitable apportionment between states was developed in Wyoming v. Colorado, 259 U.S. 419 (1922). Some indication that the courts will stop further development when the capacity of the stream has been reached is found in the following excerpts from Mason v. Hoyle, 14 A. 786 (Conn. 1888): "Every owner improving a mill privilege has a right to consider the law as protecting him against any unfair use by any other owner who may establish a mill above him. * * * It is for the public interest that all our streams be improved as far as they can be. * * * These men of moderate capital, investing their means in mills upon our lesser streams should be protected against such a use of the streams by mills disproportioned to their capacities as would practically deprive them of water and ruin their privileges. * * * Now, may we not advance a step, and adopt the principle that if seasons of great scarcity occur so regularly, and continue so long, as to fix the character of the stream in that regard, the upper proprietor must adapt the running of his machinery to that condition?"

4. **Contrasting views of the first and second Restatements on priority.** The first Restatement says that a riparian whose use of water causes substantial harm to another riparian's use is liable for the harm caused "unless the utility of use outweighs the gravity of the harm." Restatement of Torts §§ 851, 852 (1939). Under this rule a new, more valuable use can apparently displace an otherwise reasonable established use. Indeed, the flexibility to replace old uses with new ones is sometimes considered to be one of the virtues of the riparian doctrine. See Frank J. Trelease, A Model State Water Code for River Basin Development, 22 Law and Contemp. Probs. 302, 314 (1957).

The Restatement (Second) states that one of the factors to be considered in determining if a riparian use is reasonable is the protection of "existing values" in water uses, land, investments and enterprises. Restatement (Second) of Torts § 850A. This translates to a rule of priority, although the comments to the section indicate that the rule is not as absolute as that found in the doctrine of prior appropriation: "The effect given to priority by the law of riparian rights is very different from its effect under the western law of appropriation. That law not only protects uses of the normal flow from harm caused by new withdrawals, but also protects the elder uses in times of temporary shortage. The senior appropriator may withdraw the total quantity allowed by his appropriation even thought this might leave the junior appropriator none at all. In contrast, similarly situated riparians would normally be required to share the reduced supply without regard to priority of use." Restatement (Second) of Torts § 850A, cmt. k (1979)[c]. See also the Restatement (Second) of Torts § 850A, associate reporter's notes to comment k (1982), indicating that the priority factor may be "of little moment" if the other factors of § 850A (see supra p. 253, Note 3) are present.

The Restatement (Second) acknowledges that only a few cases have expressly mentioned priority, but states that it can be deduced from the results of cases which favor the prior user in almost every case in which a new use threatens a substantial investment of a the prior user. See supra comment k and associate reporter's notes. But see Joseph W. Dellapenna, Introduction to Riparian Rights, 1 Water and Water Rights § 703(d) (Robert E. Beck ed., 1991), asserting that outside dual-system states virtually all authority rejects priority as relevant except perhaps in otherwise evenly balanced cases.

5. **An uncompensated reallocation of water.** Joslin v. Marin Municipal Water District, 429 P.2d 889 (Cal. 1967), is a rare case in which an established riparian use was extinguished without compensation in favor of a new, more valuable use, albeit an appropriative (nonriparian) use. The water district constructed a municipal water supply reservoir upstream from Joslin's gravel operation. The reservoir obstructed flows which had replenished Joslin's supply of sand and gravel prior to its construction. Despite Joslin's allegations of substantial damages, the court sustained the trial court's grant of summary judgment in favor of the district. The court held that Joslin had no property interest in continued replenishment of sand and gravel by the stream. Relying on a 1928 amendment to the California constitution (Art. X, § 2), which prohibits all

---

c. Copyright 1979. Reprinted with the permission of the American Law Institute.

unreasonable uses of water, the court said: "Is it 'reasonable' then, that the riches of our streams, which we are charged with conserving in the great public interest, are to be dissipated in the amassing of mere sand and gravel which for aught that appears subserves *no* public policy? * * * We are satisfied that in the instant case the use of such water as an agent to expose or to carry and deposit sand, gravel and rock, is as a matter of law unreasonable within the meaning of the constitutional amendment."

Is "reasonableness" under the California constitution the same as "reasonableness" under the common law doctrine of riparian rights? The court said that the purpose of the constitutional amendment was to extend to disputes between an appropriator and a riparian "the rule of reasonableness of use as a measure of water rights which had theretofore been applied between [riparian] claimants."

6. **The remedy when a prior use is displaced.** The Handy Horsecollar Company manufactures harnesses, using the waters of the small stream on its property to tan leather. Horse harnesses are of very little utility today, demand is low, and the company is barely getting along. General Motors acquires the land upstream and builds a $40,000,000 plant to manufacture emission control devices for its new compact cars. It takes all the water for drinking, sanitary and processing purposes in its plant, and pipes all its waste water to a metropolitan sewage treatment plant so that none of it returns to the stream. The Handy Company sues General Motors for damages. What result? The Handy Company sues for an injunction. What result?

7. **The compensation principle.** "The Pareto criterion says that a change that makes at least one individual better off and leaves no individual worse off represents an increase in welfare. This criterion is usually interpreted to mean that welfare is increased by a change rendering it 'possible' to make at least one individual better off and leave no individual worse off by compensating the losers. Most of the discussion in the new welfare economics deals with this compensation principle." S. V. Ciriacy-Wantrup, Concepts Used as Economic Criteria for a System of Water Rights, in The Law of Water Allocation in the Eastern United States 531, 546 (Haber and Bergen eds., 1958).

The compensation principle has respectable support in the law. The leading riparian rights case is Strobel v. Kerr Salt Co., 58 N.E. 142, 145-47 (N.Y. 1900): "[The defendant's acts] would amount to a virtual confiscation of the property of small owners in the interest of a strong combination of capital. * * * We have never adopted that rule [of destroying one water use by another which would produce greater wealth] in this state and no public necessity exists therefor, even if it would ever warrant the courts in relaxing rules for the protection of property of small value in the interests of some business required to develop the resources of the state and in which much capital had embarked, giving employment to a great number of people." A leading case protecting a riparian right against public impairment without compensation is United States v. Gerlach Live Stock Co., 339 U.S. 725 (1950). A California riparian's use of water was destroyed by the Friant Dam built by the United States Bureau of Reclamation as part of the great Central Valley Project. The United States Supreme Court held, "But the public welfare, which requires claimants to sacrifice their benefits to broader ones from a higher utilization, does not necessarily require that their loss be uncompensated any more than in other takings where private rights are surrendered in the public interest. * * * No reason appears why those who get the waters should be spared from making whole those from whom they are taken. Public interest requires appropriation: it does not require expropriation." The Court also emphasized the loss distribution factor and pointed out that the project beneficiaries could well afford to reimburse the riparian for his loss of irrigation.

A classic statement is that of Baron Bramwell in Bamford v. Turnley, 122 Eng.Rep. 25, 33 (Ex.Ch. 1862): "The public consists of all the individuals of it, and a thing is only for the public benefit when it is productive of good to those individuals on the balance of loss and gain to all. So that if all the loss and all the gain were borne and received by one individual, he on the whole would be a gainer. But whenever this is the case—whenever a thing is for the public benefit, properly understood—the loss to the individuals of the public who lose will bear compensation out of the gains of those who gain. It is for the public benefit there should be railways, but it would not be unless the gain of having the railway was sufficient to compensate the loss by the use of the land required for its site; and accordingly, no one thinks it would be right to take an individual's land without compensation to make a railway. It is for the public benefit that trains should run but not unless they pay their expenses."

8. **Water rights and water pollution.** The various forms of the reasonable use rule (and the original 1939 Restatement rule) were applied both to water supply cases and to pollution cases. The utility-harm formula of § 852 of the original Restatement is exactly the same as the formula applied to determine a nuisance under § 826. The Restatement (Second) of Torts (1979) includes water pollution in the chapter on nuisances and restricts the operation of its chapter on riparian rights to acts affecting the physical volume of the water, such as a diversion, withdrawal, obstruction, storage, or consumption that interferes with a beneficial use of water. Chapter 41, Scope Note.

SECTION 3. NONRIPARIAN USES: PRESCRIPTION, GRANT, AND MUNICIPAL SUPPLY

A. Prescription

PABST v. FINMAND

Supreme Court of California, 1922.
190 Cal. 124, 211 P. 11.

LENNON, J. This action was instituted by the plaintiffs, Charlie Lee Pabst and the Priors, against H.H. Finmand and N.H. Finmand and the Cambrons, to quiet title to the waters of Eagle creek, in the county of Modoc, state of California. Eagle creek, rising in the Warner Mountains, west of the lands of both plaintiffs and defendants, flows in a single channel until just before it reaches the land of the plaintiffs, Priors, and the defendant, N.H. Finmand. There it forks and the north branch flows across the northwest corner of N.H. Finmand's lands and across the Prior lands. The south branch flows across the south portion of N.H. Finmand's lands and thence onto and across the lands of plaintiff Pabst.

The lands of the other defendant, H.H. Finmand, are not riparian to the creek. They lie to the west of the lands of the plaintiffs Priors and to the northwest of the lands of the plaintiff Pabst and the defendant N.H. Finmand, and are irrigated by means of two ditches, the "Gee" and the "Grider" ditches, which run from the main channel of Eagle creek before it forks, northerly to the lands of H.H. Finmand.

The trial court found that the lands of the defendant N.H. Finmand were riparian to Eagle creek, and that the defendant N.H. Finmand was entitled, as an appropriator, to a first right to 300 inches of the water of Eagle creek, measured under a 4-inch pressure, and that said defendant also had a prescriptive right to said quantity of water. The court found that the defendant H.H. Finmand was entitled to a first right of 200 inches of water from Eagle creek through what is known as the "Gee" ditch, and a first right to 200 inches of water through what is known as the "Grider" ditch, both under a right by prior appropriation and by prescription. Judgment was accordingly rendered and entered in favor of the defendant N.H. Finmand for 300 miner's inches of water under a 4-inch pressure, and in favor of H.H. Finmand for 400 miner's inches of water under a 4-inch pressure, for the irrigation of his lands through the Gee and Grider ditches. It is from this judgment that plaintiffs appeal.

The N.H. Finmand lands being riparian, whereas the H.H. Finmand lands are nonriparian, the rights arising from the use of water on these different tracts are necessarily based upon different principles, and for this reason these different tracts of lands will be considered separately.

As to the rights of the N.H. Finmand lands, it is conceded by counsel for defendants that the right to the amount of water awarded to the defendants by the judgment of the trial court must rest upon a prescriptive right alone. This is so for the reason that, as admitted by defendants, the right by appropriation is not supported by the evidence, and, while the trial court found that N.H. Finmand was a riparian owner, no judgment was given such defendant based upon his right as a riparian owner, and no attempt was made to apportion the waters among the plaintiffs and defendants as riparian owners.

The judgment for a prescriptive right was given in favor of the N.H. Finmand lands against both the Prior lands and the Pabst lands. The N.H. Finmand lands claimed this right, and it was adjudged to those lands upon the theory that said lands had gained it by adverse use of the water which was taken from the south fork of the creek. As to the Prior lands no right could be gained by prescription. This is so because the water used on the N.H. Finmand lands was taken from the south fork of the stream, which runs below and does not border the Prior lands, whereas the water diverted for use on the Prior lands is taken from the north fork of the creek, which runs by a small portion of the northwest corner of the N.H. Finmand lands and on to the Prior lands. The Prior lands, therefore, are riparian only to the north fork of the stream. A right can be gained by prescription only by acts which operate as an invasion of the rights of the person against whom the right is sought and which afford a ground of action by such party against such claimant, and it is a rule of law so well settled by decisions in this and other states as to scarcely need any citation to support it that a lower use, since it interferes in no way with the flow above, constitutes no invasion of the upper riparian owner's right, and cannot, therefore, afford any basis for a prescriptive right. * * *

As to the Pabst lands, the N.H. Finmand lands are the upper riparian lands, and the Pabst lands are lower riparian lands. It is the contention of defendants that the continuous use of a certain amount of water each year for the statutory period of time gave to them a prescriptive right to that certain quantity of water so used by them, and this in spite of the fact that the use of the water by the lower riparian owner was never in any manner interrupted or interfered with by such use, and in the absence of any indication or bringing of knowledge home to the lower riparian owner that the upper riparian owner was claiming such right, not as a riparian owner, but adversely to him. This contention cannot be maintained. In the absence of a showing that the upper owner is using the water under a claim of prescriptive right, the lower owner has the right to presume that such owner is only taking that to which he is entitled as a riparian owner by virtue of his riparian right. * * * Such use was not hostile unless there was an actual clash between the rights of the respective owners. While there was sufficient water flowing down the stream to supply the wants of all parties, its use by one was not an invasion of the rights of the other. * * *

A riparian owner is entitled to a reasonable amount of water for use on his riparian lands. What is a reasonable amount varies with the circumstances of each particular case and also varies from year to year, for the amount which might be reasonable in a season of plenty might be manifestly unreasonable in a season of drought. Nor is the question of reasonableness to be tested solely by the needs of the upper riparian proprietor. The rights of riparian proprietors are correlative, and the "reasonable" amount to which any one riparian owner is entitled is to be measured by comparison with the needs of the other riparian proprietors. The fact that there was always sufficient water coming down the creek for the Pabst lands with the exception of the two years prior to the trial is undisputed by any evidence offered by the defendants. And, so long as defendants left sufficient water in the stream for the use of the lower riparian proprietors, it cannot be said that they were using an unreasonable amount, and, so long as they were not using an "unreasonable" amount, the plaintiffs had no cause to complain, nor was any right of theirs invaded. * * *

The adverse use must be such as to raise a presumption of a grant of an easement as the only hypothesis on which to account for the other party's failure to complain thereof. * * * In the absence of any facts showing an actual knowledge by plaintiffs of the adverse nature of defendants' claim or of any facts sufficient to create a presumption of a knowledge of that claim, it cannot be said that a failure of plaintiffs to assert their rights by bringing an action against the defendants was such a submission as could be accounted for only on the hypothesis of a grant. Indeed, defendants have not shown such an unreasonable use of the water on their lands as to put plaintiffs on notice of their claim. We do not mean to hold that a right may not be gained by an upper riparian proprietor by prescription, but to do so it must be clearly shown either that actual notice of the adverse claim of such owner has been brought home to the other party, or that the circumstances are such, as, for instance, the use of all of the water of the creek, that such party must be presumed to have known of the adverse claim. In the instant case there was nothing to indicate to the lower riparian owners that the owners of the N.H. Finmand lands were exercising, or attempting to exercise, any more than their riparian rights, and, in the absence of such indication to plaintiffs that the owners of the N.H. Finmand lands were asserting a right hostile to the rights of the plaintiffs, no prescriptive title was acquired. Even if the upper riparian owner is using all the water of the stream, still, if the lower riparian owner is not then using any and has no desire to do so, such use by the upper riparian owner would not be adverse, and, and if continued five years, would not gain him a prescriptive right. * * *

It is the contention of plaintiffs that there was no invasion of plaintiffs' riparian rights by the nonriparian owners of the H.H. Finmand lands by the diversion by such nonriparian owners of water which the riparian owners did not need, and therefore no prescriptive right to the use of the water could be acquired in the absence of a showing of actual damage to the lands of the riparian owners caused by a deprivation of the water. As to a nonriparian owner the riparian owner is under no duty to share the waters of the creek, and the slightest use by such nonriparian owner diminishes to some extent the flow of the stream. Obviously, there is no question of reasonable use in the sense in which that term is applied to the rights of respective riparian owners, since a riparian owner, as against a nonriparian owner, is entitled to the full flow of the stream without the slightest diminution. The initial step in the diversion of the water by the nonriparian owner is therefore an invasion of the right of the lower riparian owner, and every subsequent diversion is a further invasion of that right. Against a person who seeks to divert water to nonriparian lands, the riparian owner is entitled to restrain any diversion, and he is not required to show any damage to his use. Although no damage to the present use of the riparian owner results from the diversion, yet damage to the future use may result, and an injunction will be granted to prevent the diversion from growing into a right by the lapse of the statutory period. * * * In the instant case the adverse use of the water on nonriparian lands was continued "openly and notoriously" for a period longer than five years, and, the slightest use by the owners of these lands being notice to all the lower riparian owners that a hostile right was being asserted, a prescriptive right was acquired by such adverse use on those lands. * * *

Judgment reversed.

Notes

1. **Noninjury, injunctive relief, and prescription**. A 1928 amendment to the California constitution, now found at Article X, Section 2, limits riparian rights to reasonable beneficial use and removes the right of a riparian owner to enjoin a nonriparian use which is not causing present injury. Logically, the amendment should have eliminated the acquisition of prescriptive rights through a nonriparian use which causes no present injury. However, the California courts exhibited confusion on the point before arriving at this conclusion. While acknowledging

that a riparian owner could no longer enjoin a nonriparian use that was causing no present injury, some cases held that to protect future uses a riparian owner was entitled to declaratory relief to prevent the nonriparian use from ripening into a prescriptive right. See Peabody v. City of Vallejo, 40 P.2d 486 (Cal. 1935) and Tulare Irrigation Dist. v. Lindsay-Strathmore Irrigation Dist., 45 P.2d 972 (Cal. 1935). Other cases continued to hold that a nonriparian use is adverse to a lower riparian owner whether or not the lower riparian is damaged. See Moore v. California Oregon Power Co., 140 P.2d 798 (1943). Finally, in 1949 the court held "[p]rescriptive rights are not acquired by the taking of surplus or excess water, since no injunction may issue against a taking and the appropriator may take the surplus without giving compensation." City of Pasadena v. City of Alhambra, 207 P.2d 17, 29 (Cal. 1949).

2. **Harmless use rule.** If a nonriparian use causes no present harm but is enjoined to prevent the acquisition of a prescriptive right, a "dog in the manger" situation results in which desirable uses of water resources are inhibited. New York solved this problem by the enactment of the "harmless use law," N.Y. Envtl. Conserv. Law § 15–0701:

"An alteration (whether or not it causes water to cover or permeate land previously dry) in the natural flow, quantity, quality or condition of a natural watercourse or lake situated in this state and either on or below the surface of the earth, effected by the use either on or off riparian land, withdrawal, impoundment, or obstruction of the water in such watercourse or lake, or by the addition of water thereto, or by changes in the banks, bed, course or other physical characteristics of such watercourse or lake, is reasonable and lawful as against any person, as defined in subdivision two of section 15–0107, having an interest in such watercourse or lake, unless such alteration is causing harm to him or it, or would cause him or it immediate harm if and when begun. No action for nominal damages or for an injunction shall be maintainable because of such an alteration against any person or corporation, whether a riparian owner or not, on the ground that such alteration is an infringement of the plaintiff's private rights and privileges in the waters of, or with respect to, such watercourse or lake unless such alteration is causing plaintiff harm, or would cause him or it immediate harm if and when begun. This subdivision shall apply to such an action regardless of whether the alteration sought to be made the basis of it was caused before or after the effective date of this section. * * *

"The cause of action essential to the initiation and creation of a prescriptive right or privilege against a private riparian owner to continue an alteration in the natural condition of such a watercourse or lake shall not be supplied by such an alteration until it shall have caused such riparian owner harm and then only if it is unreasonable."

The necessity for and constitutionality of this law is discussed in William H. Farnham, The Improvement and Modernization of New York Water Law Within the Framework of the Riparian System, 3 Land & Water L. Rev. 377, 382-388 (1968).

If the rule allowing a riparian landowner to enjoin a harmless nonriparian use is so obviously bad policy, why did the California courts cling to it until forced to abandon it by the 1928 constitutional amendment? Was the rule merely a archaic vestige of the natural flow theory which the California courts felt compelled to follow out of misguided loyalty to stare decisis? Was the rule completely one-sided, favoring only riparian landowners? Or did it sometimes favor nonriparian appropriators? Who benefitted from the rule in *Pabst*, the riparian landowner or the nonriparian appropriator? See infra p. 320, Note 2.

3. **Prescription against upstream riparians.** Since in most cases a downstream use causes no harm to an upstream riparian, a long-continued downstream nonriparian use does not create a prescriptive right that can receive protection against a new upstream use that causes harm to it. Kennebunk, Kennebunkport & Wells Water Dist. v. Maine Turnpike Auth., 84 A.2d 433 (Me. 1951). In the West this rule has become epitomized as "prescription does not run upstream." But see Dontanello v. Gust, 150 P. 420 (Wash. 1915).

4. **Extent of prescriptive rights.** "[W]hen a party has, for the prescriptive period, diverted all the water from a watercourse, it has established a prescriptive easement to divert all the water, regardless of whether the diversion was later reduced, or the scope of the diversion fluctuated. Second, if a party has, for that period, not diverted all, but only a portion, of the water from a watercourse, however, then it will have established an easement only for an amount that has become customary between the parties. Finally, if there is subsequently a significantly increased change in usage, that new use may be considered unreasonable, and a new prescriptive period would start to run as to that increased usage." City of Waterbury v. Town of Washington, 800 A.2d 1102, 1154 (Conn. 2002).

Should the extent of a prescriptive right be fixed in terms of a specific quantity of water, or should it be measured by the proportion of the total flow of the stream that was diverted? In Mally v. Weidensteiner, 153 P. 342 (Wash. 1915), the court put both limitations on an adverse claimant who had diverted and used 1 1/2 c.f.s., but never more than one-third of the stream. However, in Akin v. Spencer, 69 P.2d 430 (Cal. Ct. App. 1937), an adverse user of six inches of water was held to be absolutely entitled to this quantity as against downstream riparians, and could not be compelled to prorate very low flows with the riparians.

5. **Right to compel continuation of use by another party.** Can principles of prescription or estoppel create a right to the continuation of a long-existing use by another? In Kray v. Muggli, 86 N.W. 882 (Minn. 1901), the court enjoined the removal of 40-year old mill dam:

"The dam in question, having been erected for the purpose of developing power to operate mill machinery, must be taken to be a permanent obstruction; and, it having existed and been maintained as such for so great a length of time, the artificial conditions created thereby must be deemed to have become the natural conditions. * * * The authorities all hold, as far as our examination has extended, that in such cases the conditions arising from the permanent obstruction, though artificial to begin with, become by long lapse of time the natural conditions, and interested parties are bound by the rules of law applicable to such conditions. In the case at bar even nature herself became adapted to the new surroundings. A native growth of hard-wood timber sprang up along the shore of the lakes formed by the raise of the river, thus giving a natural effect and appearance to the conditions created by the dam. The government, in the survey of the lands in that vicinity, recognized the artificial as the natural state, and surveyed the public lands with reference to the lakes, meandering them precisely as other natural bodies of water are surveyed and meandered."

But see Kiwanis Club Foundation Inc. of Lincoln v. Yost, 139 N.W.2d 359 (Neb. 1966).

Some states may require the owners of dams to maintain them against their will. See Minn. Stat. § 103G.401; Wis. Stat. § 31.185. How can these be enforced perpetually? In New Jersey, a dam 20 years old or older, upon which other landowners have made permanent improvements, may be ordered maintained, but if the expense would be an undue burden on the owner the landowners around the reservoir may be ordered to pay part or all of it. N.J. Stat. Ann. § 58:4–10.

B. Grant

DUCKWORTH v. WATSONVILLE WATER & LIGHT CO.

Supreme Court of California, 1910.
158 Cal. 206, 110 P. 927.

[Plaintiff Duckworth is the owner of lands riparian to Pinto Lake, formerly owned by McKinley, who deeded to defendant company all the water rights pertaining to the land. Defendant is diverting water and selling it to persons who use it on nonriparian lands. Plaintiff is now irrigating his lands from the lake, and brings this action to quiet his title to the water. Held, defendant has a right superior to the plaintiff's, to take water from the lake in any quantity, for any purpose.]

SHAW, J. I concur. * * * Perhaps something more should be said regarding the effect of a conveyance, by the owner of riparian land, of his riparian right therein, to another for nonriparian use. The court below seems to have been of the opinion that the riparian right consisted of the ownership of a definite quantity of the water of the lake, a quantity equal only to the amount which could be beneficially used on the riparian land concerned, and that the conveyance merely transferred to the grantees that quantity from the lake, leaving the riparian grantor free to take thereafter an equal or greater quantity therefrom and use it on the identical land, provided only that he must leave enough to furnish to the grantees the definite quantity which, by this theory, was conveyed, or if the grantees were using less, then enough to provide for their actual use from time to time. This was not the legal effect of the conveyance. The riparian right exists solely because the land abuts upon the water. It is parcel of the land. It extends to all the water which may be reached from the land, and not to any specific particles or definite quantity or area of it. It is the right to make reasonable use and consumption of the water on the adjoining land and to a reasonable use of the water, in place, in connection with and for the benefit of the land. The water cannot be severed from the land and transferred to a third person so as to give him the title and right to remove it, as against other riparian owners. The grantor alone will be estopped by such a conveyance. The estoppel against him, with respect to the use and consumption of the water, or diversion from its natural position, must be as complete and extensive as was the right he conveyed. The McKinley deeds conveyed the entire right to use this water for irrigation on these lands to the defendant's predecessors, and it now belongs to the defendant, and not to Duckworth. A man may not eat his cake and have it. A man who sells a right to do a thing cannot thereafter exercise the right himself, except by permission of the buyer, and it is immaterial that the buyer may not be using or exercising it. If the water company had obtained similar deeds from the owners of all the lands abutting upon the lake and its tributaries, it would have obtained a complete estoppel against such landowners which would have prevented them from interfering with any use it saw fit to make of the water, and such estoppel would undoubtedly extend to all the water of the lake. If, having this right of estoppel, it chose to use only a part of the water, or none of it, this neglect to use it would not give any of the owners the right to take that which the company suffered to remain unused. A judgment which purported to give such owners the unqualified right to use the water on their respective tracts, as against the company, would operate to deprive the company of the property which it had bought and paid for and to return that property to the person who sold it and received payment of the price. The same principle must apply when the estoppel has been obtained as to one, only, of the riparian owners. He is absolutely estopped to use any part of the water on the land, except as specified in the deed by which he is bound. These propositions are fully established by the * * * authorities. * * *

Notes

1. **Other Cases.** Other cases giving no effect, as against other riparians, to a grant from a riparian to a non-riparian are Williams v. Wadsworth, 51 Conn. 277 (1884); Hendrix v. Roberts Marble Co., 165 S.E. 223 (Ga. 1932); Kennebunk, Kennebunkport & Wells Water Dist. v. Maine Turnpike Auth., 71 A.2d 520 (Me. 1950); Roberts v. Martin, 77 S.E. 535 (W. Va. 1913);.

2. **Statutory Proscription of Transfers.** In Stoesser v. Shore Drive P'ship, 494 N.W.2d 204, 208 (Wisc. 1993), the Wisconsin Supreme Court concluded that "riparian rights can be conveyed to non-riparian owners by easement." In response, the Wisconsin Legislature adopted Wisconsin Statutes § 30.133. That section bars transfers of riparian rights "by easement or by a similar conveyance . . . except for the right to cross the land in order to have access to the navigable water." The statute does not bar a transfer of the rights if they are accompanied by a transfer of the real property interests to which they are appurtenant. ABKA, L.P. v. Wisconsin Dept. of Natural Resources, 648 N.W.2d 854 (Wis. 2002).

PYLE v. GILBERT

Supreme Court of Georgia, 1980.
245 Ga. 403, 265 S.E.2d 584.

HILL, JUSTICE. This is a water rights case involving a non-navigable watercourse. It presents a confrontation between the past and the present. Plaintiffs are the owners of a 140-year-old water-powered gristmill. They emphasize the natural flow theory. Defendants are upper riparians using water to irrigate their farms. They emphasize the reasonable use theory of water rights.

The plaintiffs, Willie and Arlene Gilbert, own property commonly known as Howard's Mill located on Kirkland's Creek, a non-navigable stream in Early County which goes into the Chattahoochee River. They acquired a partial interest in the property in 1974. The other interest was acquired at the same time by their daughter and son-in-law. In 1977, they purchased the other interest and now own the fee. Until August 31, 1978, the Gilberts owned and operated a water-powered gristmill on their property. They also rented boats for profit and permitted fishing and swimming in the 40-acre pond. * * *

On July 7, 1978, the Gilberts filed a complaint against Sanford Hill, who is an owner of property that is upper riparian in relation to the Gilbert's property, alleging that since 1975 he has been diverting and using water from Kirkland's Creek for irrigation, * * *

The testimony at a hearing on July 18, 1978, revealed to plaintiffs that other upper riparian owners also had irrigated with water from the creek. The plaintiffs subsequently added four defendants: George Edgar Pyle, Jimmy Doster, Philip Buckhalter and Vinson Evans.[2] Following discovery, the trial court made an extensive examination of our water law and granted the plaintiffs' motions for summary judgment as to liability against all defendants, holding that the defendants' use of the water for irrigation constituted a diversion, a trespass, a nuisance and an unreasonable use as a matter of law, and enjoining any future use. The issue of damages was reserved for trial. The defendants appeal. * * *

We do not find that the record supports the conclusion that the uses complained of were unreasonable as a matter of law. Whether the use of water for irrigation is reasonable or unreasonable presents a triable question. White v. East Lake Land Co., supra, 96 Ga. at 417, 23 S.E. 393; Price v. High Shoals Mfg. Co., supra, 132 Ga. at 249, 64 S.E. 87. It was error to grant summary judgment to the plaintiffs.

In its detailed analysis of Georgia water law, the trial court had to apply Hendrix v. Roberts Marble Co., 175 Ga. 389, 394, 165 S.E. 223, 226 (1932), to the effect that "* * * riparian rights are appurtenant only to lands which actually touch on the watercourse, or through which it flows, and that a riparian owner or proprietor can not himself lawfully use or convey to another the right to use water flowing along or through his property * * *." Thus *Hendrix* held water could only be used on riparian lands. Yet four years later, in reversing the denial of an injunction against the use of water on non-riparian land, the court did not rely heavily on *Hendrix,* supra. Instead the court (Russell, C.J., writing the opinion in both cases) based its decision more on general riparian water law principles than on the non-riparian use. Robertson v. Arnold, 182 Ga. 664, 671, 186 S.E. 806 (1936). To the extent that Robertson v. Arnold might reflect ambivalence as to the rule announced in *Hendrix,* that concern is well-founded.

---

2. Vinson Evans owns non-riparian property which he admits having irrigated with the alleged permission of a riparian owner. The evidence does not show that he owns any riparian property. The second and fourth findings of fact by the trial court must be reversed to the extent that they imply he is an upper riparian landowner to the plaintiffs.

A major study of Georgia water law concluded that "Another disadvantage of this doctrine is that it permits the use of stream water only in connection with riparian land." Institute of Law and Government, University of Georgia Law School, A Study of the Riparian and Prior Appropriation Doctrines of Water Law (1955), p. 104. Likewise, the American Law Institute now recommends allowing use of water by riparian owners on non-riparian land, Rest. Torts 2d § 855, as well as allowing non-riparian owners to acquire a right to use water from riparian owners. Id., § 856(2), (see also 7 Clark, Waters and Water Rights 71–72, § 614.1 (1976)). The Restatement relies on two principles: that riparian rights are property rights and as such could normally be transferred, and that water law should be utilitarian and allow the best use of the water. Id., Comment b. Also, the Institute considers the acquisition of water rights by condemnation a "grant of riparian right." Id., Comment c.

Georgia recognizes the power to condemn riparian rights; in fact, this court relied on that principle in affirming an injunction in City of Elberton v. Hobbs, 121 Ga. 749(2), 49 S.E. 779 (1905) (see also the second City of Elberton v. Hobbs, 121 Ga. 750, 49 S.E. 780 (1905)). City of Elberton, in turn, was relied on by the court in *Hendrix* for the proposition that water could not be used on non-riparian lands. In our view, City of Elberton is not good authority for that rule; rather, it established that the right to use water on non-riparian lands can be acquired by condemnation. We agree with the American Law Institute that the right to use water on non-riparian land should be permitted and if that right can be acquired by condemnation, it can also be acquired by grant. Thus we find that the right to the reasonable use of water in a non-navigable watercourse on non-riparian land can be acquired by grant from a riparian owner. The contrary conclusion in Hendrix v. Roberts Marble Co., supra, will not be followed.

In summary, the grant of summary judgment, and the permanent injunction based thereon, against each of the defendants must be reversed. On remand, the issues must be tried in accordance with the foregoing decision, looking always to see if, insofar as injunctive relief is concerned, all the uses of the creek and pond can be accommodated.

Judgment reversed.

Notes

1. **Accord.** Elliot v. Fitchburg Ry. Co., 64 Mass. (10 Cush.) 191 (1852); St. Anthony Falls Water-Power Co. v. City of Minneapolis, 43 N.W. 56 (Minn. 1889); Gillis v. Chase, 31 A. 18 (N. H. 1892); Concord Mfg. Co. v. Robertson, 25 A. 718 (N.H. 1890); Doremus v. City of Paterson, 52 A. 1107 (N.J. Ch. 1902); Lawrie v. Silsby, 56 A. 1106 (Vt. 1904); Thurston v. City of Portsmouth, 140 S.E.2d 678 (Va. 1965).

2. **Lease of water.** In Smith v. Stanolind Oil & Gas Co., 172 P.2d 1002 (Okla. 1946), the riparian owner leased water to the company for use in drilling operations on nonriparian lands. A lower riparian sought an injunction. Held, the company's right to use water was a derivative right to be measured by the extent of the rights of the riparian owner who granted it. Since the use by a riparian

owner on non-riparian lands would not be unreasonable per se, the nonriparian grantee could similarly use the water so long as the plaintiff's present uses for domestic and stock water were not substantially impaired.

STATE v. APFELBACHER

Supreme Court of Wisconsin, 1918.
167 Wis. 233, 167 N.W. 244.

Action by George Apfelbacher against the State of Wisconsin and others. Judgment for plaintiff, and defendants bring error. Affirmed.

The appeal in this case (no bill of exceptions being before us in the record), presents only the pleadings, findings, and judgment for review. From these findings it appears:

That the defendant Humphrey and his predecessors have for many years operated a gristmill at the outlet of Lake Nagawicka in Waukesha county. Lake Nagawicka has an area of 1.41 square miles, and its waters are held and maintained, to a certain extent, by a dam owned and controlled by defendant Humphrey at this outlet. The stream forming the inlet and outlet to this lake is Bark river. One mile below Lake Nagawicka and on Bark river plaintiff and his predecessors had for many years also maintained a dam and operated a similar mill. The millpond at this point was about 25 acres in extent and held only sufficient water supply to run plaintiff's mill for a few hours. The mill and water power of defendant Humphrey was the elder of the two.

In 1906 the State of Wisconsin established a fish hatchery just below Nagawicka Lake with ponds numbered 1, 2, and 3 just below the lake and on the north side of the Bark river, and ponds numbered 4, 5, and 6 south thereof. Ponds 1, 2, and 3 were supplied with water from a spillway on Lake Nagawicka; ponds 4, 5, and 6 by a 12-inch pipe running from the waters of Lake Nagawicka through or under ponds 1, 2, and 3 and the Bark river. The waters from these six ponds, save such as is lost by seepage or evaporation, ultimately find their way into Bark river above the plaintiff's dam. The total fall between the two dams is 10 1/2 feet.

That for upwards of 20 years prior to 1906, as the two water powers were being operated by their respective owners, and with the natural flow of the Bark river between them, the upper mill had been operated practically every day continuously, and the plaintiff was thereby enabled to also operate his mill continuously.

By a written contract made in 1906 between the defendant Humphrey and the State of Wisconsin it was agreed that the state might place and maintain in Lake Nagawicka, for the purpose of drawing water for use in the fish hatchery, the 12-inch pipe connected with the ponds numbered 4, 5, and 6, and might use for the hatchery so much of the waters of Lake Nagawicka as could be drawn through such pipe, and that, if at any time such use by the state and by defendant Humphrey in connection with his mill should lower the waters in the lake to a point 12 inches below a certain high-water mark, then the said Humphrey, his heirs and assigns, would absolutely desist and refrain from using any water from said lake for the running of the mill property, or for any other purpose, until the waters of said lake should again reach a point within 12 inches below such high-water mark.

That the defendant state by reason of such agreement claimed to have the right to, and did, exercise practical control over the waters at said dam, and did at several times subsequent to 1906 shut off the outflow of the waters in Lake Nagawicka so that for periods of one or two weeks each the plaintiff was practically deprived of the use of the waters of Bark river and forced thereby to shut down his mill. That the natural flow of water from Lake Nagawicka into Bark river and from thence on into Upper Nemahbin Lake is sufficient to operate the two mills in question, and that each of such mills is reasonably adapted to such water course and the ordinary operation of the fish hatchery maintained by the state of Wisconsin is also a reasonable use of the natural flow of Bark river. That it is not necessary for the maintenance of the fish hatchery and its efficient operation that the defendant state of Wisconsin should avail itself of the attempted grant of power under the agreement between itself and the defendant Humphrey, and that the exercise of such attempted grant of power on its part is to impair the power and destroy the use of the mill of plaintiff in dry or low water seasons. The operation of plaintiff's mill prior to the agreement between defendants in 1906 was of substantial value to him, but by the exercise by the state of such claim of right under the agreement there has been a substantial interference with, if not destruction of, the plaintiff's business. * * *

That the mill of the defendant Humphrey may be efficiently operated, although not to its full capacity, when the waters of Lake Nagawicka are down as low as a point 15 inches below such high-water mark. By lowering the water in Lake Nagawicka proportionally more and more water is needed to generate the same amount of power in Humphrey's mill, and that, therefore, as riparian owner, defendant Humphrey has the optional right, when the water in the millpond is as low as 12 inches below high-water mark, to either close his mill so that more water and power may be accumulated or to run his mill under low-water pressure.

As conclusions of law the court found that the defendant state of Wisconsin has made an unreasonable use of the waters of Lake Nagawicka and Bark river, and that both defendant state and the defendant Humphrey should be restrained from exercising or attempting to exercise, the power attempted to be given under the agreement between them so far as it affected the detaining of the water from Bark river in such manner as theretofore done under such claim of right and except only when such detention is a reasonable one having relation to the correlative rights and duties existing between the plaintiff and the defendant Humphrey as riparian owners. From such judgment the defendants appeal.

ESCHWEILER, J. (after stating the facts as above). * * * In this state the owner of an upper dam has the right to withhold the waters of the stream at certain periods in order that there may be thereby created a sufficient storage of water to more properly and efficiently carry out the purpose to which he, as riparian owner, may put the waters of the stream. Mabie v. Matteson, 17 Wis. 1; Timm v. Bear, 29 Wis. 254; Coldwell v. Sanderson, 69 Wis. 52, 28

N.W. 232, 33 N.W. 591; Lawrence v. Am. W.P. Co., 144 Wis. 556, 563, 128 N.W. 440.

But the right to detain for a time, as well as every other right which a riparian owner acquires as such, to the waters of the stream flowing through or by his land is restricted always to that which is a reasonable detention or a reasonable use, and these terms are to be measured and determined by the extent and capacity of the stream, the uses to which it is and has been put, and the rights that other riparian owners on the same stream also have. There can be no absolute or fixed standard for the measure of such relative rights. The essential question to be determined by the court or jury trying the issues between the parties in each particular case is what is reasonable under the circumstances there presented. This was the view adopted by the trial court, and his finding, therefore, that the state's withholding at times the flow of water from Lake Nagawicka was not a reasonable or necessary use of the waters of Lake Nagawicka and the Bark river for the proper carrying on of the fish hatchery, is the controlling fact in this case. * * *

The right that defendant Humphrey has to hold back the waters of Lake Nagawicka for a time when below the high-water mark so that the supply of water may thereby be increased is one that is necessarily also within the limitation prescribed for all riparian rights of being kept within the boundaries of what is reasonable, and it cannot be severed from his entire rights as riparian owner so that this particular element of those rights that is, to withhold the natural flow of the Bark river, can be, in a measure, carved out therefrom and transferred to some one else, and by that person used in a manner that would be unreasonable if the use were by Humphrey himself. The conveyance by Humphrey to the state confers no greater right with reference to these flowing waters than Humphrey himself had. The condition of reasonable use attached to it before he conveyed it, and remained with it after such conveyance. The state stands in no better position with reference to its exercise than did or would the defendant Humphrey.

Note

Compare Farmers Highline Canal & Reservoir Co. v. Golden, supra p. 197.

C. Municipal Supply

ADAMS v. GREENWICH WATER CO.

Supreme Court of Errors of Connecticut, 1951.
138 Conn. 205, 83 A.2d 177.

INGLIS, JUDGE. The plaintiffs, who are riparian owners along the Mianus River in Greenwich, instituted this action to enjoin the defendant from diverting, and from attempting to take by condemnation, any of the waters of that stream. The defendant filed a cross complaint claiming a declaratory judgment determining whether it has the right to condemn the water rights although part of the benefits may accrue to inhabitants of Port Chester, New York. * * *

The defendant is a corporation specially chartered by the Connecticut General Assembly in 1880. 8 Spec.Laws 406. By virtue of its charter and amendments thereof, it has the franchise to furnish water for public and domestic use in the town of Greenwich, in a small portion of the town of Stamford adjacent to the Mianus River, in the town of Rye, New York, including Port Chester, and in Westchester County, New York, whenever that use in Westchester County will not curtail the supply adequate for the inhabitants of Connecticut. * * *

A period of extreme drought occurred in the summer of 1949. The defendant's water supply diminished rapidly. By August 1 its reservoirs were only about 60 per cent full. Notice was received that the Stamford Water Company would have to reduce the amount of water to be furnished by it below the four million gallons daily called for by the contract. Thereupon, on August 9, 1949, the defendant began pumping water, at the rate of about a million gallons daily, from the Mianus River at Farms Road into a pipe line which led into one of its reservoirs. When this came to the attention of the plaintiff Altschul, inquiries were made of the defendant on her behalf and a series of conferences and letters between the parties ensued. The defendant acknowledged that it had no legal right to divert the water as it was doing without purchasing or condemning the water rights but took the position that conditions required it to do so. * * * On January 1, 1950, the defendant had less than forty days' supply of water on hand, and on February 4 the Stamford Water Company cut off its supply completely. This necessitated the installation of an additional pump and the pumping of a greater quantity of water from the Mianus. Between August 9, 1949, and June 1, 1950, the approximate date of the trial of this case, the defendant diverted from the river an average of 1.56 million gallons daily. During that same period the average flow of the river was 16.2 million gallons daily. At no time did the defendant cut off the flow in the river completely, although during the driest period of the diversion the defendant was taking more than half of the flow. During most of the period the flow of the river was in such quantity that the diversion resulted in no inconvenience or detriment to the plaintiffs. Even during the driest periods the plaintiffs suffered no actual or substantial damage.

The original charter of the defendant granted it the right to take by eminent domain any land or water in the town of Greenwich for its corporate purpose. 8 Spec.Laws 406. In 1927, after its franchise had been extended in 1925 to include the furnishing of water to Rye, 19 Spec.Laws 848, the General Assembly granted it authority, for the purpose of supplying water for public or private use, to take by eminent domain, purchase or otherwise all or any part of the waters of the Mianus River, to construct such reservoirs as it might deem necessary to impound such water, and to take by eminent domain, purchase or otherwise such property as it might deem necessary for the construction of reservoirs, the protection of its watershed or any other corporate purpose. * * *

A water company in the situation of the defendant should plan for a supply of water to meet conditions as they will be at least ten and preferably fifteen or twenty years in the future. The safe yield of the defendant's present water supply system, not including the water it receives under its contract with the Stamford Water Company, based on experience during the dry year June 1, 1949—June 1, 1950, is only about four million gallons daily. In 1949 Greenwich consumed about five million gallons daily and Port Chester and Rye about four million. It is estimated that in 1960 there will be required for Greenwich 6.8 million gallons a day and for Port Chester and Rye 4.3 million, while in 1970 Greenwich will take 8.75 million gallons daily and Port Chester and Rye 4.65 million. Thus it appears that the safe yield of the defendant's own system without aid from the Stamford company was not adequate in 1948-49 to take care of the needs of the defendant's Connecticut customers alone, and as time goes on this yield will become less able to do so. To meet this condition, the defendant plans to construct a reservoir by damming the Mianus River above Farms Road. This will give the defendant additional storage capacity of approximately 2,200 million gallons. From this reservoir certain quantities of water will be conducted through the present pipe line into Rockwood Lake. The defendant will be bound to allow enough water to flow down the river to meet the needs of the New York, New Haven and Hartford Railroad Company, and its plan is to release sufficient water down the stream to equalize the flow over the entire year. A portion of the proposed reservoir and a major portion of its watershed will be in New York state, and the land for that portion will be acquired by the Port Chester Water Works, Inc. The defendant has no permanent source of water storage available to it other than the Mianus River.

On the foregoing facts the trial court concluded that, because the damage suffered by the plaintiffs from the diversion of the water of the river was far outweighed by the utility of the defendant's conduct and the interests of the public therein, no injunction should issue against future diversion. It also decided, with reference to the prayer for a declaratory judgment, that the defendant may exercise its right of eminent domain in respect to lands and water rights on the Mianus River, "including those of the plaintiffs," in order to increase its water supply storage, although a portion of such additional supply may be delivered to and used by those inhabitants of the state of New York to whom the defendant may supply water under existing legislative grants. It followed from this that the prayer for an injunction against such condemnation was denied.

We will first consider the question whether the defendant has the power to condemn the water rights of the plaintiffs for the purpose of constructing its proposed reservoir. Clearly, the General Assembly, by the amendment of the defendant's charter in 1927, purported to grant it that right. The taking of water by a water company chartered to supply water to the public is a taking for a public use. * * * When the legislature endows a public utility company with the power to take by eminent domain such property as is necessary to fulfill its corporate purposes without restriction, the determination of what is necessary to be taken lies in the discretion of the company. The courts will interfere with the exercise of that discretion only in cases of bad faith or unreasonable conduct. * * * On the question of the necessity of a taking, needs which will arise in the reasonably foreseeable future must be taken into consideration. * * * Upon the subordinate facts found, there can be no question that it is reasonably necessary for the defendant to acquire water rights for the construction of a reservoir in the Mianus River in order to continue to furnish an adequate supply of water to its customers in Connecticut, to say nothing of the users of its water in New York state. The court would not be warranted in concluding the contrary. * * *

We turn now to a consideration of the plaintiffs' prayer for an injunction restraining the defendant from further diverting the water of the Mianus by pumping. It is well established that a riparian owner is entitled to have the water of the stream upon which he borders continue to flow in its wonted manner. * * * Any infringement of that right entitles him to relief, at least by way of damages, even though the actual, provable damage is small. * * * It does not necessarily follow, however, that he is entitled to relief by way of injunction, for the granting of such relief lies in the sound discretion of the court. * * *

The trial court denied the injunction in this case because it concluded that to grant it would result in damage to the defendant disproportionate in amount to the damage refusal of the injunction would cause the plaintiffs and would be detrimental to the public interest. * * *

The limitations on the propriety of the denial of an injunction on the theory of comparative damage between the parties do not apply to the refusal of an injunction which, if issued, would seriously affect public interest. It is well within a court's discretion to deny an injunction against the infringement of riparian rights if to grant it would adversely affect the interest of the public. * * * The subordinate facts found amply supported the court's conclusion in the instant case that the issuance of the injunction prayed for would seriously and adversely affect the public interest at the time the case was tried. Except for one consideration, therefore, the denial of the plaintiffs' prayer for that injunction was correct.

That consideration is this: The plaintiffs do have property rights to the accustomed flow of the Mianus River. In the emergency of a drought the public interest may require the court to refuse to protect those rights by way of injunction. However, the riparian owners ought not to be deprived permanently of those rights without compensation. If the judgment of the trial court stands in its present form, there is nothing to prevent the defendant from continuing indefinitely to pump water from the river as the most economical way of getting its required supply. By doing this it might well be able to avoid the building of its proposed reservoir. The result would be that the plaintiffs would for many years continue to be deprived of their rights without any compensation except that which they might recover by a multiplicity of actions. It is obviously not doing equity to leave them in such a position. Under the circumstances of this case, equity demanded that the defendant be allowed a reasonable time within which to make adequate compensation to the plaintiffs for the permanent taking of their water rights if it intends to acquire them, and, if that compensation is not made within such reasonable time, the defendant should be enjoined from further diversion of the waters of the stream. * * * Although the granting or withholding of an injunction lies in the discretion of a trial court, when the only reasonable conclusion is that a plaintiff is, in equity, entitled to an injunction in a given form, it is competent for us to order such an injunction even though the trial court has refused it. * * * The trial court was in error in unconditionally denying the injunction against the diversion of the waters of the stream.

There is error in part, the judgment is set aside and the case is remanded with direction to hear the parties and determine what will be a reasonable time to be allowed to the defendant to acquire the water rights of the plaintiffs by condemnation or otherwise—that to be the sole issue of fact to be tried—and then to enter a judgment which shall (1) direct that unless compensation is made within that reasonable time the defendant shall be enjoined from further diversion of the waters of the stream as prayed, (2) deny the prayer for an injunction against condemning such water rights of the plaintiffs as will be taken for the construction of the proposed reservoir, and (3) deny the prayer of the cross complaint for a declaratory judgment.

Notes

1. **Aftermath.** What will the city acquire by condemning such water rights of the plaintiffs as will be taken for the construction of the proposed reservoir? We are told that in subsequent eminent domain proceedings no claims for compensation were pressed because the riparian owners felt they would collect only nominal damages. Robert L. Leonard, An Economic Evaluation of Connecticut Water Law: Water Rights, Public Water Supply and Pollution Control, Report No. 11, Institute of Water Resources, University of Connecticut 11 (1970).

2. **Inverse condemnation.** In most states the procedure of "inverse condemnation" is available. Ferguson v. Village of Hamburg, 5 N.E.2d 801 (N.Y. 1936), was a suit for injunction brought by downstream riparians claiming injury from a diminution caused by a reservoir built and operated by defendant village. The lower court granted alternative relief in the form of an injunction which would go into effect unless the village commenced an action to acquire the rights. The Court of Appeals reversed, with orders to the lower court to ascertain the damages and issue an injunction unless within a reasonable time the defendant paid or tendered to the plaintiff the damages so fixed. A simpler form of inverse condemnation is the ordinary damage action brought against the city for injury to the plaintiff's riparian rights. See Pernell v. City of Henderson, 16 S.E.2d 449 (N.C. 1941).

3. **Application of riparian principles.** Cases involving cities and water companies in New Jersey are handled simply on a riparian basis. City of Paterson v. East Jersey Water Co., 70 A. 472 (N.J. Ch. 1908), aff'd 78 A. 1134 (N.J. 1910).

4. **Basis of municipal authority.** Cities and public water supply companies were originally given powers to procure their supplies by special acts or by the charters incorporating them. See, e.g., statutes recited in principal case. More commonly today, the power is given in general statutes applicable to all municipalities or water companies.

5. **Special municipal rights in public waters.** On some public waters (see Chapter 7) cities have been held to partake of the superior rights of the public and to have power to take water without compensating injured riparians. Watuppa

Reservoir Co. v. City of Fall River, 18 N.E. 465 (Mass. 1888) (great ponds); Minneapolis Mill Co. v. Board of Water Comm'rs of St. Paul, 58 N.W. 33 (Minn. 1894) (navigable waters).

HUDSON RIVER FISHERMAN'S ASS'N v. WILLIAMS

New York Supreme Court, Appellate Division, 1988.
139 A.D.2d 234, 531 N.Y.S.2d 379.

YESAWICH, J. Respondent Spring Valley Water Company, Inc. (hereinafter Spring Valley) provides water for approximately 88% of the residents of petitioner Rockland County and various industrial users from four major sources: (1) 57 wells, (2) the Lake De Forest Reservoir and Filter Plant, (3) the Ramapo Valley Well Field, and (4) the Stony Point Reservoir and Filter Plant. In 1979, Spring Valley submitted a water supply application to respondent Department of Environmental Conservation (hereinafter DEC) for permission to construct an additional water source named the Ambrey Pond project on a 364-acre site near the Town of Stony Point, Rockland County, including a reservoir with a nearly two-billion-gallon capacity, a filtration plant, and a diversion pipeline to bring water to the reservoir from a nearby brook; acquisition of land to construct the reservoir and filtration plant is contemplated by the first stage of this multistage undertaking. The project, capable of adding a dependable yield of approximately 7.5 million gallons per day (mgd) to the utility's water distribution capacity, was sought to meet three perceived needs: (1) a present water supply deficit in the Haverstraw-Stony Point area of the Spring Valley system that is currently being met with releases of water from Lake Tiorati, pursuant to an agreement with the Palisades Interstate Park Commission, a circumstance which is not expected to continue, and by pumping water from lower elevations in the system at a substantial cost; (2) an anticipated inability to meet peak demand throughout the system in the short-term future; and (3) a projected system-wide inability to meet average demand further into the future. A primary factor requiring a new supply is the growth of Rockland County's population, though other factors include the contamination of six wells, the antiquation of the Stony Point treatment facility, the unavailability of water from the Ramapo Valley Well Field during periods of drought, and the aforementioned loss of water supply from Lake Tiorati.

During the course of extensive hearings, the inevitability of the need for an additional water supply became obvious; there was, however, a great deal of disagreement as to when this need would become manifest. The inherent uncertainty in determining precisely when the project would be necessary prompted Spring Valley and the Department of Public Service, which had expressed interest in increasing the peaking capacity of Spring Valley's system, to suggest that a "trigger mechanism" tying the date of the project's implementation to the demand for water be utilized. So that preliminary steps could be taken without authorizing premature construction and yet avoid a redundant new hearing which might perilously delay development of the proposed water supply, respondent Commissioner of Environmental

Conservation (hereinafter the Commissioner) approved the project but "triggered" issuance of construction permits upon Spring Valley's experiencing an average demand of 27.9 mgd for two consecutive years. * * * Although Spring Valley expects to reach its maximum peak demand capacity well before it approaches the limit of its average demand capacity, the "trigger mechanism" was linked to the average demand because it more accurately reflects the relatively smooth trend of increased demand than the erratic peak demand which is heavily influenced by such vagaries as the weather. The point at which Spring Valley's current peak demand capacity would be exhausted was approximated by divining an appropriate ratio between average and peak demands to determine at which average demand level the peak demand capacity would be exhausted; that average demand figure was then adjusted downwards to allow for the three to four years' construction time required for the project. A regrettable and apparently inescapable consequence of the Ambrey Pond project is the likely destruction of a major naturally reproducing trout population due to the diversion of most of the flow from Rockland County's best trout stream into the Ambrey Pond Reservoir. * * *

Petitioners argue initially that Spring Valley failed to demonstrate the "public necessity" which ECL 15-1503 (2) requires as a precondition to construction of a water supply project. Citing Matter of Country Knolls Water Works v. Reid, 52 A.D.2d 284, 383 N.Y.S.2d 661, they assert that because Spring Valley concedes that it does not have a present need for which the proposed source will be developed in the "immediate future", the application should have been denied (see, id., at 288, 383 N.Y.S.2d 661). This argument is flawed in several respects. First, ECL 15-1503 (2) authorizes the granting of permits based on a number of factors including "future needs for sources of water supply". It is also important to note the posture of the Country Knolls case. There we held that the DEC could deny a permit because a present need was not sufficiently shown; we did not concomitantly hold that the DEC must wait for the need to become dire and then only issue permits belatedly. Second, aside from the present water supply deficit in the Haverstraw-Stony Point area, there is substantial evidence of an unavoidable, if not imminent, necessity for greater peak demand capacity. Third, the trigger mechanism itself insures that the construction permits will not be issued until the need for an expanded water supply is close at hand, at least to the extent that such a demand can be foretold. The time required to construct dams, a filtration plant and a diversion pipeline necessitates that some sort of predictive mechanism be used. Given the many variables affecting the demand for water, it is hardly surprising that there was great divergence in the trigger proposals advanced by the various parties or that the figures relied upon have changed over the course of the long application process. Nevertheless, this does not equate to a showing of irrationality for the Commissioner's decision to conditionally authorize the project

Petitioners maintain further that the Commissioner's choice of the crucial 27.9 mgd trigger which actuates the process for issuing the construction permits was irrational; specifically that there is no historical foundation for relying on average demand to forecast peak demand. Reliance on average demand is undeniably a logical indicator here because of its stability and, though not faultlessly predictive of peak demand, the ratio between the two has remained between 1.4 and 1.9, thus providing the Commissioner with a rational and not unreasonable means of judging when to authorize additional water supply construction.

* * * Viewed in the context of the problems facing Spring Valley and considering that the basic dispute is one of timing, the trigger mechanism was a particularly apt resolution, for it postpones costly construction if the water demand does not grow as expected while allowing Spring Valley to acquire property in the inevitable reservoir basin, and yet allows it adequate time to construct the project when the demand for water begins pressing the limits of the existing system. * * *

The last of petitioners' arguments, which though lacking in merit calls for comment, is their contention that compliance was not had with SEQRA. The fact that Spring Valley's offer to mitigate the damage to the trout stream by increasing the flow past its diversion structure from 0.3 mgd to 0.8 mgd was not given consideration in the final environmental impact statement is understandable inasmuch as there was expert testimony that a stream flow of 7.3 mgd was essential to sustain the trout. A flow of that level would effectively subvert the project. In light of the high priority of domestic and municipal water uses (see, ECL 15-0105[5]; see also, ECL 8-0103[7]), the trout stream must unfortunately give way to the predictable and unrelenting growth in human water demands.

Notes

1. **Regulation of public water supply projects.** R.I. Gen. Laws § 46–15–2: "No municipal water department or agency, public water system, including special water districts or private water company, or the water resources board, engaged in the distribution of water for potable purposes shall have any power: (1) To acquire or take a water supply or an additional water supply from an existing approved source * * * until the municipal water department or agency, special water district, or private water company has first submitted the maps and plans therefor to the director of the department of health, the commissioner of environmental protection for the department of the environment, the state planning council and the board, as hereinafter provided, and until the director of the department of the environment, after receiving the recommendations of the director of the department of health and the commissioner for environmental protection and the division of statewide planning, shall have approved the recommendations or approved the recommendation with modifications as he or she may determine to be necessary; provided, however, this subsection shall not apply to any area presently served by any municipal water department or agency, or special water district."

2. **Priority applied to competing public water supply projects.** In 1939 Pennsylvania created a priority system among public water supply agencies, 32 Pa. Cons. Stat. §§ 631–641. Unused water rights of any such agency were declared null and void, § 632, and all other water rights had to be registered with and their validity determined by the Water and Power Review Board, §§ 633 and 634. Compliance with the Act was made the exclusive method of acquiring water

rights, § 635. A permit to acquire (by purchase, eminent domain, payment of damages, etc.) designated water rights (of riparians) must be applied for, § 636. "However, if the board finds that the proposed new source or additional supply will not conflict with the rights to such water or to water rights held by any other public water supply agency which are reasonably necessary for its present purposes or future needs, and that the water or the water rights proposed to be acquired are reasonably necessary for the present purposes and future needs of the public water supply agency making application, that the taking of said water or the exercise of said water rights will not interfere with navigation, jeopardize public safety, or cause substantial injury to the Commonwealth, then, and in that case, the board shall approve the application and shall issue a permit therefor." § 637. If the rights are not acquired within one year or the water is not actually taken within four years, the permit may be revoked, but, "if the project required for the taking of water has been commenced in good faith or if the commencement thereof has been prevented by events beyond the control of the permittee, the board shall have the power, upon application of the permittee, to grant such extensions of said period as the board deems to be necessary to enable the permittee to complete the project required for the taking of water." § 638.

3. **Other rules governing competition between water supply agencies.** There has been little litigation on the question of the relative rights of eastern cities that are competing for the same water, but in it the courts have given a rule for every taste. In Massachusetts priority was the basis of the decision. The legislature in 1926 authorized the town of Somerset "to take by eminent domain * * * or acquire by purchase or otherwise * * * the waters of the Segreganset River." Prior to 1961 the only use of the river was to recharge the town's well field by flooding it in dry years. In that year a survey was undertaken for a diversion of water from the stream to an off-stream reservoir, money was appropriated to purchase land for the project, and bonds for construction funds were authorized. Meanwhile, the Dighton Water District had been established by legislative act in 1950 and authorized to acquire water from any stream within its service area "not already appropriated and used for the purpose of public water supply." Learning of Somerset's plans in 1962, the District hastily recorded an "order of taking" which purported to appropriate all the water of the Segreganset not already appropriated and used for public water supply. Held, the District's authority should be construed to mean that it could not take water "appropriated *or* used" for public supply, and that "appropriated" meant "permitted by legislative authority to be taken." Town of Somerset v. Dighton Water Dist., 200 N.E.2d 237 (Mass. 1964).

In New York, an "administrative allocation" was made. The City of Syracuse long ago was given legislative authority to take from Skaneateles Lake, through a 30 inch pipe, water not needed for the Erie Canal. In the twentieth century it almost doubled its withdrawals under authority of an order of the Water Power and Control Commission that contained the following clause, "The Commission reserves the right from time to time to authorize the amount of water found reasonably necessary for the supply of other parts of the state and the inhabitants thereof to be taken from Skaneateles Lake and applicant shall have no claim for compensation to the water so diverted unless it shall render a service in connection therewith * * *." In 1935 the Commission ordered the city to share its supply with the village of Jordan, which had no water works of its own. On appeal, affirmed. "The city accepted the determination and acted upon it, necessarily assumed and agreed to any burdens it imposed and is not now in any position to question the propriety of the limitations, conditions, or restrictions fixed or the power of the Commission to impose them." The order was held reasonable and fully sustained by the evidence. City of Syracuse v. Gibbs, 28 N.E.2d 835 (N.Y. 1940).

An interstate case was decided on riparian sharing. The Hackensack River flows from New York into New Jersey. In New York it is used by defendant Village of Nyack and several neighboring villages. Once used, the water is not returned to the Hackensack but is released into the Hudson. In New Jersey the plaintiff Hackensack Water Company diverts most of the water to serve 800,000 people in several cities. The plaintiff has several dams, some built in New York under authority of the New York Water Resources Commission, some in New Jersey, approved by that state's Department of Commerce and Development, Division of Water Policy and Supply. When Nyack took steps to increase its supply, claiming the right to do so under the terms of the New York Commission's orders allowing the dams, the plaintiff claimed that as builder of the dams it was entitled to the undiminished flow of the regulated river, and brought this action to determine its right to compensation for the proposed "withdrawal without return." The case came up on a motion for a summary judgment. In the stated facts it appeared that the plaintiff company owned 90% of the riparian land in New Jersey, but the defendant Village's holdings, if any, were not mentioned, and the reason for treating both parties as riparian proprietors was not discussed. Nevertheless the court set out at some length the "respective rights of upstream and downstream riparian owners," and discussed riparian principles applicable to diversions without return to the stream, domestic consumption and reasonable use. "From the foregoing it is apparent that the right of the plaintiff to the undiminished flow of the Hackensack River cannot be established as a matter of law. On the other hand, it is by no means clear that as a matter of fact the defendant's use of water of the Hackensack River is reasonable." The court overruled the motion and set these issues of fact for trial. Hackensack Water Co. v. Village of Nyack, 289 F.Supp. 671 (S.D.N.Y. 1968).

4. **Federal regulation of public water supply projects.** The Ambrey Pond project in the principal case probably required a permit from the Army Corp of Engineers under section 404 of the Clean Water Act, regulating the discharge of "dredge and fill materials" in most waters. (See Chapter 7, Section 2C). Could the Corp refuse to issue the permit because of the effect which the project will have on the trout fishery even though New York authorities have apparently concluded that the need for public water supplies outweighs the damage to the fishery? See infra p. 591, Note 3. Could the Administrator of the U.S. Environmental Protection Agency veto a permit for the project because of its effects on the fishery without considering local water supply needs? See James City County v. Environmental Protection Agency, infra p. 593, Note 4. How would the authority and responsibilities of the Corp and EPA be affected if the trout were a listed species under the federal Endangered Species Act. See Riverside Irrigation Dist. v. Andrews, infra p. 583, and Chapter 7, Section 2D.

SECTION 4. STATE REGULATION

MUENCH v. PUBLIC SERVICE COMMISSION

Supreme Court of Wisconsin, 1952.
261 Wis. 492, 53 N.W.2d 514.

On March 8, 1950, the Namekagon Hydro Company (hereinafter referred to as the "Company") filed an application with the Public Service Commission to construct, operate, and maintain a hydro-electric dam on the Namekagon River in Washburn county. The Conservation Commission entered its appearance and objected to construction of the dam on the ground that it was violative of public rights and in particular the right declared by sec. 31.06(3), Stats., to *"the enjoyment of natural scenic beauty"*. The Conservation Commission was represented at the hearing by the attorney general acting on the express direction of the governor of the state. * * *

Under date of September 29, 1950, the commission issued its findings, conclusions, and certificate of permit to the Company. The effect of the Public Service Commission's findings was to determine that the statutory requirements entitling the Company to a permit to construct the dam existed, and that there were no public rights which required denial of the application.

After the permit was issued both the Conservation Commission and the petitioner Muench filed motions for rehearing before the Public Service Commission, which motions were denied by an order entered December 6, 1950. Muench, a private citizen who is also president of the state division of the Izaak Walton League, had appeared as a party at the original hearing before the Public Service Commission. * * *

CURRIE, JUSTICE. We are concerned in this case with the problem of the nature of public rights in the navigable streams of the state and the beds underlying the same, and the protection of such rights. A review of the historical background and a sketching of the development of the recognition of these public rights in the court decisions and statutes of this state should prove to be helpful in passing upon the specific issues presented by the appeals therein.

After the Revolutionary War, the original thirteen states were impoverished and were confronted with the problem of paying the debts created by the war. States without western lands demanded that Virginia and other states claiming such lands to the west should cede the same to the Confederation to be sold to pay such debts. In 1783 the Virginia legislature authorized the ceding of the Northwest Territory to the Confederation, and the actual deed of conveyance was executed March 1, 1784. This cession was made upon two conditions: (1) The new states to be admitted as members of the Federal Union were to have the same rights to sovereignty as the original states; and (2) The navigable waters flowing into the Mississippi and the St. Lawrence rivers, and the carrying places between them were to be forever free public highways. These conditions were incorporated into the Northwest Ordinance of 1787, which set up the machinery for the government of the Northwest Territory.

Art. IX, sec. 1, of the Wisconsin Constitution, adopted by the Territorial Convention on February 17, 1848, and approved by the act of Congress admitting Wisconsin into the Union, incorporated verbatim the wording of the Northwest Ordinance with respect to navigable waters, such section reading as follows:

> "The state shall have concurrent jurisdiction on all rivers and lakes bordering on this state so far as such rivers or lakes shall form a common boundary to the state and any other state or territory now or hereafter to be formed, and bounded by the same; and the river Mississippi and the navigable waters leading into the Mississippi and St. Lawrence, and the carrying places between the same, shall be common highways and forever free, as well to the inhabitants of the state as to the citizens of the United States, without any tax, impost or duty therefor." * * *

One of the early cases which established the "saw-log" test of navigability in the state is that of Olson v. Merrill, 1877, 42 Wis. 203, 212. * * *

It will thus be seen that Wisconsin, in adopting the saw-log test of navigability, based the same on commercial considerations. * * * In Diana Shooting Club v. Husting, 1914, 156 Wis. 261, 271, 145 N.W. 816, 820, * * * the defendant Paul O. Husting (later United States Senator from Wisconsin) entered his hunting boat floating upon the waters of Rock river, and with the aid of a pole and paddle propelled it down the river to the place of the alleged trespass for the purpose of shooting wild ducks * * *. This case is significant in that the navigability was established not through any commercial use, such as floating of logs, but through the use of shallow draft boats for purposes of recreation. * * *

In 1911 Wisconsin enacted the first Water Power Act, ch. 652, Laws of 1911, which contained a new definition of navigable streams and rivers which was very similar in wording to our present sec. 30.01(2), Stats., which reads:

> "All rivers and streams which have been meandered and returned as navigable by the surveyors employed by the government of the United States, and all rivers, streams, sloughs, bayous and marsh outlets, whether meandered or nonmeandered *which are navigable in fact for any purpose whatsoever* are hereby declared navigable to the extent that no dam, bridge, or other obstruction shall be made in or over the same without the permission of the legislature."

Therefore, since 1911 it is no longer necessary in determining navigability of streams to establish a past history of floating of logs, or other uses of commercial transportation, because any stream is *"navigable in fact"* which is capable of floating any boat, skiff or canoe, of the shallowest draft used for recreational purposes. * * *

Our present Water Power Law dates from 1915, ch. 380, Laws of 1915, and such act contained a provision, sec. 1596–7, Stats.1915, which required the Railroad Commission (predecessor to the Public Service Commission), in granting a permit to construct a dam upon a navigable stream, to find that "the proposed dam will not materially obstruct existing navigation *or violate other public rights*." This same provision is now contained in sec. 31.06(3), Stats.

The nature of these *"other public rights"* referred to in sec. 31.06(3) Stats., is elucidated in the opinion of this court in Nekoosa-Edwards Paper Co. v. Railroad Comm., 1930, 201 Wis. 40, 46-47, 228 N.W. 144, 147, 229 N.W. 631. * * *

> "Many of the meandered lakes and streams of this state, navigable in law, have ceased to be navigable for pecuniary gain. They are still navigable in law; that is, subject to the use of the public for all the incidents of navigable waters. As population increases, these waters are used by the people for *sailing, rowing, canoeing, bathing, fishing, hunting, skating and other public purposes.* While the public right may have originated in the older use or capacity of the waters for navigation, such public right having once accrued, it is not lost by the failure of pecuniary profitable navigation, but resort may be had thereto for any other public purpose. Our state has for many years been extensively engaged in the propagation of fish and the stocking of the waters of the state with fish fry in order that the public may more fully enjoy the sport and recreation of fishing. By reason of the state's enterprise in behalf of the public, the small streams of the state are fishing streams to which the public have a right to resort so long as they do not trespass on the private property along the banks." * * *

The 1929 legislature enacted ch. 523, Laws of 1929, which amended sec. 31.06, Stats., so as to provide that *the enjoyment of scenic beauty is a public right* to be considered by the Public Service Commission in making findings as to whether a permit for a proposed dam shall be issued. Thus we have a further public right in navigable streams recognized by legislative enactment which is highly illustrative of the trend to extend and protect the rights of the public to the recreational enjoyment of the navigable waters of the state. * * *

The second question to be passed upon is whether the petitioner Muench is a person *"aggrieved"* and *"directly affected"*, under the provisions of sec. 227.16(1), Stats., by the decision of the Commission in this instance which is reviewable under sec. 227.15, Stats. The Company contends that Muench is not directly affected by the Commission's decision because he has no direct pecuniary interest which would be jeopardized by the issuance of a permit to erect the dam. The right of the citizens of the state to enjoy our navigable streams for recreational purposes, including the enjoyment of scenic beauty, is a legal right that is entitled to all the protection which is given financial rights. * * *

Such rights would be severely limited, curtailed, or endangered if we did not hold that any citizen who has appeared at a hearing of the Public Service Commission, held under sec. 31.06 with respect to an application to erect a dam in a navigable stream is *"aggrieved"* and *"directly affected"* by a decision of the Commission finding that public rights will not be violated by erection of a proposed dam so as to entitle him to petition for review under sec. 227.15, Stats. We conclude that petitioner Muench was therefore entitled to petition the circuit court for review.

Our holding in this respect is in keeping with the trend manifested in the development of the law of navigable waters in this state to extend the rights of the general public to the recreational use of the waters of this state, and to protect the public in the enjoyment of such rights. * * *

The state contends that the Namekagon river, on which the proposed dam is to be erected, is famous throughout the eastern half of the United States because of its scenic beauty, desirability for float trips and canoeing, and for a type of fishing water which the Federal Fishing and Wildlife Service has described as rapidly disappearing from the state of Wisconsin. The Public Service Commission will be required to make findings as to whether public rights for the recreational enjoyment of this stream in its present natural condition outweigh the benefits to the public which would result in the construction of the dam.

Judgment reversed with directions to remand the cause to the Public Service Commission for further proceedings in accordance with this opinion.

Notes

1. **Origins of state regulation.** Much of the movement for statutory regulation of water uses in the eastern states is directed at environmental protection. The State of Wisconsin was a leader in this regard as its legislature and courts built on the "public rights" concept, and *Muench* (case and man) should not be forgotten.

2 **Basis of state regulation.** Many early water regulation statutes and special acts authorized the construction of dams, operation of log booms and diversions to canals. For the most part these were limited, as is the statute in the principal case, to navigable waters over which the state as the embodiment of the public has clear powers. This was not a particularly limiting factor in Wisconsin, which has so broad a definition of navigability that it applied to quite small streams such as Buena Vista Creek, involved in the next case. As one official of the Wisconsin Conservation Commission said, "If a perch can swim in it—even on his side like a flounder—it's navigable, and we'll take charge."

Some of the earliest statutes, however, were directed at the use of private water. The mill dam statutes of New England gave the privilege of erecting dams across streams which were not navigable and gave the power to lawfully flood the lands of upper riparians. "From these provisions it is an inevitable implication, that, although the right is given indiscriminately to all riparian proprietors, he who first erects and establishes his mill does, by his priority of occupation, acquire to that extent a title to the use of the water in the stream prior and superior to that of any other person, and a right to maintain his dam against all proprietors of lands both above and below his own." Smith v. Agawam Canal Co., 84 Mass. (2 Allen) 355, 357 (1861).

Today it is generally recognized that state powers over public waters are not the only source of water legislation and that the general police power is the basis for statutes affecting all types of waters.

3. **Regulation of particular uses**. Many eastern states have long had limited permit systems for certain uses, like Wisconsin's Water Power Law. Another Wisconsin statute requires a permit for the diversion of surplus water (not

beneficially used by riparians) to maintain the normal level or natural flow of a lake or stream in a watershed. Non-surplus water may be diverted for irrigation use only with the consent of injured riparians. In essence, this means the irrigator must buy water from power companies with run-of-the-river low head hydroelectric power plants. See Nekoosa-Edwards Paper Co. v. Pub. Service Comm'n, 99 N.W.2d 821 (Wis. 1959), and Harold H. Ellis, et al., Water Use Law and Administration in Wisconsin 223–316 (1970). The Indiana Flood Control and Water Resources Commission may grant any person, including a non-riparian owner, the right to divert flood waters from a watercourse for any useful purpose, provided such diversion does not cause injury to landowners in the watershed in which the watercourse is located and the diversion does not limit any existing right. Ind. Code § 14–25–1–7.

Many other eastern states have statutes regulating the construction of dams, e.g., Conn. Gen. Stat. §§ 22a–401 to 22a–410; W. Va. Code. §§ 22–14–1 to 22–14–18. Some are applicable only to navigable rivers, many deal only with safety licensing and inspection. For many years Wisconsin has not only licensed the initial construction of dams but engaged in extensive regulation of the relations between power companies, between power companies and riparians, and between power companies and the public. Wis. Stat. §§ 31.01-31.39, 196.91-196.93. The Arkansas Soil and Water Conservation Commission not only controls and regulates the building of dams, but also some relations between water users. A permit is required, but only surplus water may be impounded by virtue of it. "Surplus" is whatever remains in excess of a continuous discharge, fixed by the Commission in amount to protect lower riparian rights and fish and wildlife. The person constructing the dam under a permit has an exclusive right to the use of the water impounded. Ark. Code Ann. § 15–22–210.

VILLAGE OF TEQUESTA v. JUPITER INLET CORP.

Supreme Court of Florida, 1979.
371 So.2d 663.

[The Jupiter Inlet Corporation owned property on which it planned to build a 120 unit condominium project, supplied with water from an underlying shallow aquifer. The property was less than a quarter of a mile from the well field that supplied the Village of Tequesta with water from seven wells which pumped more than one million gallons per day from a depth of 75 to 90 feet. This is the entire "safe yield" of the shallow aquifer, since greater withdrawals would induce the intrusion into the aquifer of salt water from the nearby Intercoastal Waterway, a canal connected to the Atlantic Ocean. The only other nearby source of fresh water is a deep artesian aquifer which can be tapped only by 1200 foot wells, at greatly increased drilling and pumping costs.

Florida's common law applicable to ground water gave the overlying landowner a right to reasonable use of the water, modified by the correlative rights of adjacent landowners to use the same water, if it could move freely through the land of one owner to the land of the other. Reasonableness of a landowner's particular use was determined in much the same way as the reasonableness of a riparian use of water in a water course. As explained in the opinion, the Florida Water Resources Act of 1972 applies to both stream water and ground water, requires a permit for all substantial new withdrawals and provides for regularizing existing common law withdrawals by issuing permits for them. Tequesta applied for and received permits for its wells. When Jupiter applied for a permit to take water from the shallow aquifer, its application was denied. Jupiter now sues Tequesta in inverse condemnation, claiming that Tequesta had deprived Jupiter of the beneficial use of its property rights and thereby effected a taking of the property. The legal problem is essentially identical to that which would exist if Jupiter's property were riparian to a small stream, upstream from a point where Tequesta took the entire flow for municipal supply.]

ADKINS, JUSTICE. * * * The State of Florida operates under an administrative system of water management pursuant to the terms of the Florida Water Resources Act. Ch. 373, Fla.Stat. (1972). The law prior to the Florida Water Resources Act did not allow ownership in the corpus of the water, but only in the use of it. Even then, the use was bounded by the perimeters of reasonable and beneficial use. Legislation limiting the right to the use of the water is in itself no more objectionable than legislation forbidding the use of property for certain purposes by zoning regulations. Village of Euclid v. Ambler Realty Co., 272 U.S. 365, 47 S.Ct. 114, 71 L.Ed. 303 (1926); 54 A.L.R. 1016 (1928).

The Florida Water Resources Act, in recognizing the need for conservation and control of the waters in the state (Section 373.016, Fla.Stat. (1973)) makes all waters in the state subject to regulation, unless otherwise specifically exempt. § 373.023(1) Fla.Stat. (1973). The Department of Environmental Regulation and the various water management districts are given the responsibility to accomplish the conservation, protection, management, and control of the waters of the state. § 373.016(3) Fla.Stat. (1973). In order to exercise such controls a permitting system is established which requires permits for consumptive use of water, exempting only "domestic consumption of water by individual users" from the requirements of a permit. § 373.219(1) Fla.Stat. (1973). Jupiter, in serving a 120-unit condominium, does not qualify as an individual user and thus must secure a permit in order to draw water from beneath its property. Without a permit Jupiter has no such property right to the use of water beneath its land for which, upon deprivation, it must be compensated through inverse condemnation.

The Water Resources Act of 1972 recognizes a right to use water under the common law as separate from the right to use water under a permit granted pursuant to the act. This is done by a provision concerning the termination of the common-law right and a transitional procedure. The holder of such a common-law water-use right was given two years to convert the common-law water right into a permit water right. § 373.226(3) Fla.Stat. (1973). In order to qualify for the initial permit under section 373.226(2) Florida Statutes (1973), the right must have been exercised prior to the implementation of the Florida Water Resources Act by a water management district with geographical jurisdiction in that area. Otherwise the right is abandoned and extinguished requiring a new application for a permit. Tequesta had acquired the permit and Jupiter was merely a proposed user. The Florida Water Resources Act makes no provision for the continuation of an *unexercised* common-law right to use water. Jupiter had perfected no legal interest to the use of the water beneath its land which would support an action in inverse condemnation.

Section 373.1961 Florida Statutes (1975) provides additional powers and duties for the governing boards of the water management district. Subsection (7) provides that the governing board:

> May acquire title to such interest as is necessary in real property, by purchase, gift, devise, lease, eminent domain, or otherwise, *for water production and transmission* consistent with this section. However, the district shall not use any of the eminent domain powers herein granted to acquire water and water rights already devoted to reasonable and beneficial use or any water production or transmission facilities owned by any county, municipality, or regional water supply authority. [Emphasis supplied].

Condemnation of "water rights" is not granted in the first sentence of this subsection. The authority granted is specifically limited to the acquisition of land for the purpose of constructing and operating well fields and other withdrawal facilities and for the right-of-way necessary for the transmission of water to consumers. The second sentence prohibits the use of eminent domain to acquire such "water rights" which were *already* being put to a reasonable and beneficial use. The statutory prohibition of the use of eminent domain in one situation cannot be used as authority for its use by implication in another, as the statute must be strictly construed. Canal Authority v. Miller, 243 So.2d 193 (Fla.1970). All that Section 373.1961(7) Florida Statutes (1975) accomplishes is to further protect presently existing legal uses of water. No implication can be drawn that this section intends to include any "water right" other than the permit that may be granted by a water management district. After all, if a use of water is both preexisting and also reasonable and beneficial, after two years, it must be either under permit or it is conclusively presumed to be abandoned. There was no necessity for the Water Resources Act to provide for the condemnation of an unexercised right to use water, as the owner became subject to the permit provisions of the law. There was no "taking" of this right.

Jupiter's remedy is only through proper application for a permit under the Florida Water Resources Act.

Notes

1. **Comprehensive permit systems ("regulated riparianism").** At least seventeen eastern states have adopted more or less comprehensive permit systems. See Ala. Code §§ 9–10B–1 to –30; Ark. Code Ann. §§ 15–22–201 to –622; Conn. Gen. Stat. §§ 22a–365 to –380; Del. Code Ann. tit. 7, §§ 6001-6031; Fla. Stat. §§ 373.013 to -.71; Ga. Code Ann. §§ 12–5–20 to –31, 12–5–43 to –53; Iowa Code §§ 455B .261 to -.281; Ky. Rev. Stat. Ann. §§ 151.010 to -.600; Md. Nat. Res. Code Ann. §§ 8–101 to –204, 5–501 to –514; Mass. Gen. Laws ch. 21G, §§1 -19; Minn. Stat. §§ 103G.255 to -.315; Miss. Code Ann. §§ 51–1–5 to –3–55; N.J. Stat. Ann. §§ 58:1A–1 to –17; N.Y. Envtl. Conserv. Law §§ 15–1501 to –1529;

N.C. Gen. Stat. §§ 143–215.11 to –215.22; Va. Code Ann. §§ 62.1–242 to –253; Wis. Stat. §§ 30.18, 30.28, 30.292, 30.294, 30.298. See also Haw. Rev. Stat. §§ 174C–1 to –101, and, infra p. 323, Note 6. Professor Joseph W. Dellapenna used the term "regulated riparianism" to describe such systems and the use of that term seems to be receiving increasing acceptance. See Joseph W. Dellapenna, Owning Surface Water In the Eastern United States, 6 Proc. E. Min. L. Found. 1–1, 1–33 to 1–34 (1985); American Society of Civil Engineers, The Regulated Riparian Model Water Code (Joseph W. Dellapenna, ed. 1997).

Although they vary greatly in detail, the common theme of these statutes is government regulation of water use through an administrative permit system. While this theme is shared by western permit systems under the appropriation doctrine, the eastern permit systems differ substantially from those in the West. Notably, the role of priority in time is greatly reduced (typically, it receives no explicit mention), permits expire after a specified period or may be canceled administratively, and administrative officials are given greater discretion to allocate water in time of shortage and to reallocate water to new (presumably better) use as needs and values change. Descriptions and analyses of eastern permit systems are found in Joseph W. Dellapenna, Introduction to Riparian Rights, 1 Waters and Water Rights, ch. 9 (Robert E. Beck ed., 1991); Richard Ausness, Water Rights Legislation in the East: A Program for Reform, 24 Wm. & Mary L. Rev. 547 (1983); Peter N. Davis, Eastern Water Diversion Permit Statutes: Precedents for Missouri, 47 Mo. L. Rev. 429 (1982); George W. Sherk, Eastern Water Law: Trends in State Legislation, 9 Va. Envtl. L.J. 287 (1990).

2. **Reasons for eastern permit systems.** The rise of eastern permit systems is due to perceived inadequacies in common law riparian rights. Critics charge that riparian rights are vague, inherently unstable, and do not provide a sound basis for investment in water development, that, because the system is "litigation driven," determination and enforcement of rights are slow, expensive, and the outcomes are unpredictable, that the riparian doctrine does a poor job of protecting environmental and public values associated with water, that the doctrine does a poor job of allocating water in times of drought, and that limiting the use of water to riparian lands is unsound economic policy. See M. Mason Gaffney, Economic Aspects of Water Resource Policy, 28 Am. J. Econ. & Soc. 131; Richard Ausness, supra Note 1, at 552-553.

3. **Aspects of the Florida permit system.** The Florida permit system has been a substantial success in two respects, in the registration and quantification of preexisting uses and in the control of the initiation of new withdrawals. The applicant for a permit must demonstrate that the proposed use will be "reasonable-beneficial," that it will not interfere with any presently existing legal water use, and that it will be consistent with the public interest. Fla. Stat. § 373.223(1). The reasonable-beneficial standard limits water use to the quantity needed for economic and the efficient utilization for a purpose and in a manner which is both reasonable and in the public interest. § 373.019(13). The new use must comport with the state's water plan which may not only provide for development, protection and management of water resources but may also prohibit or restrict uses on designated streams that might impair public recreation or harm fish and wildlife. § 373.036(3). Further environmental protection is given by minimum flow requirements setting the limit at which further withdrawals would be significantly harmful to the water resources or ecology of the area. § 373.042.

Priority. In practice, the success of the permit granting process seems largely attributable to putting as much priority into the system as possible. The requirement of non-interference with existing uses is heavily stressed. Some permits have been conditioned to coordinate withdrawals, rotating the pumping of different users, scheduling withdrawals to avoid depletion of minimum flows or fluctuation of lake levels, and when visual effects are offensive by allowing pumping only at night. Some actual priority is practiced—some permits forbid withdrawals when they would interfere with the supply of an existing permit holder, and some permittees have been required to build retaining ponds to store water for use during times of peak demand. See Harloff v. City of Sarasota, 575 So.2d 1324 (Fl. Dist. Ct. App. 1991) (priority to existing user). Cf. § 373.223(1)(b) (protection of existing uses).

The permit statutes of other states prohibit the water agency from issuing new permits that impair the rights of existing water users or indicate that the effect on existing uses is a factor in issuing new permits. See Conn. Gen. Stat. § 22A–373(b)(2); Ga. Code Ann. § 12–5–31(g); Ky. Rev. Stat. Ann. § 151.170(2); Mass. Gen. Laws ch. 21G, § 7(4). Nearly all of the eastern statutes provide for registration and quantification of pre-existing uses.

Nonriparian uses. The Florida statutes apparently authorize permits for nonriparian uses: "The governing board or department may authorize the holder of a use permit to transport and use ground or surface water beyond overlying land, across county boundaries, or outside the watershed from which it is taken * * *." Fla. Stat. § 373.223(2). Transfer of water between water management districts, although not expressly permitted, was approved in Osceola County v. St. Johns River Water Management District, 504 So.2d 385 (Fla. 1987). See also Ark. Code. Ann. § 15–22–304(b), specifically authorizing the transfer of "excess surface water" to nonriparians, and Wis. Stat. § 30.18(6)(b), permitting the irrigation of contiguous nonriparian lands. Although most states do not specifically authorize nonriparian uses, none of them expressly limit permits to riparian proprietors. A few early statutes were administered as if the permits were merely regulatory measures affecting the exercise of riparian rights. See Nekoosa-Edwards Paper Co. v. Pub. Serv. Comm'n, 99 N.W.2d 821 (Wis. 1959).

For a recent summary of the Florida law, in the context of the law of its neighboring states, see Joseph W. Dellapenna, The Law of Water Allocation in the Southeastern States at the Opening of the Twenty-First Century, 25 U. Ark. Little Rock L. Rev. 9 (2002)

4. **Administrative discretion.** The Florida statute is taken almost verbatim from Frank Maloney, Richard Ausness & James Morris, A Model Water Code (1972). A severely critical review of the book raised strong objections to administrative distribution of water among users in times of shortage. Frank J. Trelease, The Model Water Code, The Wise Administrator and the Goddam Bureaucrat, 14 Nat. Resources J. 207 (1974):

"Reduction, restriction, changes in permits, suspension of permits, apportionment, rotation, limitation, prohibition—these are what the water user may expect. The Code's solution to the legal uncertainties of riparian rights is the substitution of these administrative uncertainties.

"To what end? Protection of the public, the environment? No—that is all taken care of. To understand the choice between property rights and administrative distribution, it must be very clearly kept in mind that all we are talking about is water already allocated to private use, that the state and its administrators have issued permits for its use, that every use is reasonable-beneficial, that all the uses can be made in times of water plenty. It must be remembered that all minimum flow requirements are met, that all other environmental factors are protected, and that the state water plan is observed and even furthered. The 'public interest' stands neutral, and the only question is, which people get to use the water. The choice is between giving people, industries and cities water rights that entitle them to water under stated conditions, rights that they may use as they see fit and adjust among themselves as they may agree, or giving the regulatory official the power to determine in his discretion which water users get water in times of shortage, and to shift water between uses and users as time progresses."

Since that article was written the shortage plans of the decentralized water management districts have been revised and adopted and many of these terrible things have not occurred. Each district is required by Fla. Stat. § 373.246(1) to prepare a shortage plan. These extensive documents are essentially plans for droughts, for periods of subnormal precipitation that require temporary cutbacks when the supply drops below the level usually sufficient for all. The shortage plans all follow a pattern, although all are not identical. The Water Shortage Plan of the St. Johns River Water Management District is typical (Fl. Admin. Code Ch. 40C–21). Uses are classified by source of water, type of use, and method of abstraction or diversion. Shortages are classified as moderate, severe, extreme and critical, or as emergencies. Target cutbacks are set at 15% through 30%, 45% and 60%. Voluntary reductions in use are primarily relied on in the early stages. As the shortage deepens strict provisions against waste and careless or profligate use are instituted, fountains are shut off, and irrigation of lawns, trees and golf courses is limited by day of the week, hour of use, and time of day. Car washing and street and sidewalk flushing are restricted. Overhead spray irrigation of agricultural crops is restricted by day, hour and length, flood irrigation to a few days a month, and frost protection to forecasts of severe freeze.

Essentially, these shortage plans set up mechanisms for sharing a temporary drought in a usually abundant supply. Sharing, of course, occurs among householders during droughts in cities of other states, and among irrigators in western irrigation districts when project supplies are below normal. Sharing among persons similarly situated is functional as long as the shares do not become too small for everyone. When not all uses are the same, however, less than a full supply may stop some processes. Perhaps for this reason the Florida shortage plans typically contain very specific rules for mines and processing plants.

Areas of bureaucratic rule over the fortunes of water users may remain. The system of classification allows uses and users to be ranked according to official notions of which are least essential and can be cut off first. Farmers, however, are the most vulnerable. Irrigated agriculture is the largest water user and receives the brunt of the cutbacks. In an extreme shortage or emergency, an overall allocation is made to each class of water. The total agricultural irrigation allocation is set, but it is not necessarily shared equally. "The share available to each user will be based on any prioritization among crops the District establishes based on economic loss and equity considerations and the acreage and quantity of withdrawals for which the user has been permitted." Fla. Admin. Code §§ 40C–21.641(2)(a)(6); 40C–21.651(2)(a)(6).

In other states administrators are given wide discretionary powers in times of shortage to determine who gets water and who does not, guided only by vague and general criteria such as "the best interests of the public" (Ky. Rev. Stat. Ann. § 151.200(1); giving priority to "(1) sustaining life; (2) maintaining health; and (3) increasing wealth" (Ark. Code Ann. § 15–22–217(c)); "to protect adequately such citizens or water resources" (Ga. Code Ann. § 12–5–31(l)); or allocating to each user "an equitable portion of available water" (Ark. Code Ann. § 15–22–217(a)).

5. **Inadequate control of over-development.** In the eastern states, a "shortage" seems to be conceived of as a one-sided phenomenon, a temporary subnormal supply of natural origin. There appears to be little recognition that demands upon normal supplies can exceed the available quantity and thus create a shortage. Although in the *Tequesta* case a new permit was refused because increased drafts on the supply would ruin the entire source for everyone, there are no statutes or cases which recognize that too many permits can produce a permanent shortage or that on a fluctuating source each new permit will cause the next "shortage" to cut deeper, and will bring the one after that sooner. There is no apparent recognition that as the permit-granting process continues the existing uses will be impaired by having their shares reduced during the next below-normal year. There are no statutory requirements that call for halting the issuance of permits when some limit of safe yield or dependable supply is reached. The Florida shortage plans mention no reduction in future use or restrictions on new permits, but seem to assume the resumption of business as usual with the return of the rains.

6. **Flexibility and reallocation.** Some method must be devised to accommodate new demands and uses and to reallocate water in use to different and more productive purposes if the limits of supply are reached. See Frank J. Trelease, The Model Water Code, the Wise Administrator and the Goddam Bureaucrat, 14 Nat. Resources J. 207 (1974):

"Under the Model Code [and most eastern codes], the mechanism to accomplish these shifts is the issuance of new permits to newly-favored users upon the expiration of old and now-to-be-discarded uses. I see several difficulties with this process. First, to the extent that the 'normal' permit lasts twenty years, flexibility is surrendered during its life. If the application for the new use does not coincide with permit expirations, the new user may have to wait a fairly long time before water becomes available. Second, the investment may have been only partly amortized during the 20-year (or shorter) period. Third, the holder will in most cases lose an asset more valuable than his investment, that is, the going concern value of his enterprise, the continuing opportunity to make a profit, which is presumably a contribution to the economy. Fourth, if it were my enterprise, I would suspect that some Bureaucrat might solve the first problem and aggravate the second and third by simply granting the permit and squeezing the water out of me and other less favored users under the shortage plans and emergency measures."

How transferable is a 20-year water right in its 17th year? Suppose an irrigation system of pumps and sprinklers, which initially cost $40,000, hopelessly breaks down in the 15th year. Will it be replaced?

A mid-western farmer with sandy soils can, under normal rainfall, grow small grain that brings him $50 per acre. With irrigation, he can grow vegetable crops that bring in $200 per acre. He obtains an irrigation permit, borrows $40,000 from the bank, and buys pumps, pipes and sprinklers. After ten years the mortgage is paid off. His permit is then canceled, or expires and is not renewed. Has he suffered a loss? Suppose a western appropriator whose permit runs "in perpetuity" sells his land with appurtenant water right at $500 per acre when dry land in the neighborhood is selling at $100 per acre. Has he made a "windfall profit?" Suppose he sells an acre's worth of water right at $400?

Suppose an Iowa farmer has a permit to irrigate 160 acres, and that withdrawals under it often reduce the stream to its minimum flow. A downstream cannery needs a water supply, and could pay the farmer more than he realizes through irrigation. Iowa Code § 455B.273 provides, "A permittee may sell, transfer, or assign a permit by conveying, leasing, or otherwise transferring the ownership of the land described in the permit * * *." Will the water move to its "highest and most productive use?"

7. **Other criticisms of eastern permit systems.** Others besides Frank Trelease (supra Notes 3 and 5) have criticized eastern permit systems. Professor Richard Ausness, one of the draftsmen of the Model Water Code, has criticized such statutes (1) because there is no coordination between water resource planning and administration of the permit system, (2) because permits are of short duration, have no certainty of renewal, and leave the allocation of water during shortages uncertain, thereby undermining the confidence of permit holds and discouraging capital investments, and (3) because there is no explicit mechanism for reallocation of water. Richard Ausness, supra Note 1. Professor Robert Abrams identifies three evident drawbacks of a standard permit system: its rigidity, its tendency to overregulate, and its lack of articulated policy objectives. Robert H. Abrams, Replacing Riparianism in the Twenty-First Century, 36 Wayne L. Rev. 93 (1989). See also Joseph W. Dellapenna, Adapting Riparian Rights to the Twenty-First Century, 106 W. Va. L. Rev. 539 (2004).

8. **Constitutional objections.** Constitutional objections to eastern permit systems are discussed infra p. 322, Note 3.

SECTION 5. ABOLITION AND COMBINATION (INCLUDING THE "CALIFORNIA DOCTRINE")

COFFIN v. LEFT HAND DITCH CO.

Supreme Court of Colorado, 1882.
6 Colo. 443.

[See opinion, supra p. 95.]

Notes

1. **Cases rejecting the doctrine in other jurisdictions.** The leading cases in other states that have extinguished riparian rights to the use of water and adopted the "Colorado doctrine" are Van Dyke v. Midnight Sun Mining & Ditch Co. (Alaska) 177 F. 85 (9th Cir. 1910); Clough v. Wing, 17 P. 453 (Ariz. 1888); Drake v. Earhart, 23 P. 541 (Idaho 1890). See also Hutchinson v. Watson Slough Ditch Co., 101 P. 1059 (Idaho 1909); Mettler v. Ames Realty Co., 201 P. 702

(Mont. 1921); Jones v. Adams, 6 P. 442 (Nev. 1885); Albuquerque Land & Irrigation Co. v. Gutierrez, 61 P. 357 (N.M. 1900), aff'd 188 U.S. 545 (1903); Stowell v. Johnson, 26 P. 290 (Utah 1891); Moyer v. Preston, 44 P. 845 (Wyo. 1896).

2. **Meaning of statutes adopting the common law.** In Boquillas Land & Cattle Co. v. Curtis, 213 U.S. 339 (1909), a riparian, seeking to protect his unused right against an upstream appropriation, argued that the Arizona statute adopting the common law of England conferred upon him property rights not subject to legislative change. Mr. Justice Holmes disposed of this contention with one of his famous aphorisms, that this statute " * * * is far from meaning that patentees of a ranch on the San Pedro are to have the same rights as owners of an estate on the Thames."

3. **Riparian rights in appropriation jurisdictions.** The phrase "riparian rights" frequently describes rights to ownership of land, such as the bed of a stream or fast land created by accretion, rights to protect the bank from stream erosion, rights to fish in waters, and rights to access to waters. For the status of these rights in Colorado doctrine states, see Note, Riparian Rights in Appropriation States, 9 Wyo. L.J. 130 (1955).

LUX v. HAGGIN

Supreme Court of California, 1886.
69 Cal. 255, 10 P. 674.

[Henry Miller, the "Cattle King," head of the firm of Miller & Lux, owned land for 120 miles on both sides of the San Joaquin River and other streams of California's Central Valley. In the southern end of his domain vast areas of "grass lands" were naturally irrigated by annual spring floods of the Kern River, which split into numerous channels and sloughs. When the floods subsided, the water was spread over the land by dams thrown across the sloughs. Huge quantities of native hay were produced in this fashion. The lands had been purchased in 1872 from the State of California, which had acquired them from the federal government in 1850 under the terms of the Federal Swamp Land Act, granting overflowed lands to the states.

Haggin was the promoter of the Kern River Land & Canal Company, a large irrigation project. In 1875 he and the company acquired an appropriation of 74,000 inches of the Kern. His point of diversion was on federal public lands upstream from the land of Miller & Lux. Some of these facts, and more interesting background on the case, are found in Samuel Wiel, Fifty Years of Water Law, 50 Harv. L. Rev. 252, 256 (1937).

Miller & Lux brought suit against Haggin and the company to enjoin the proposed diversion on the ground that it would interfere with their riparian rights to the overflow. The trial court denied relief. The Supreme Court of California reversed by a four to three decision. The majority opinion on rehearing, by McKinstry, J., from which the following excerpts are taken, dealt very extensively with the development of water law in the West, and covered 200 pages in the California reports and 110 in the Pacific Reporter.]

A grant of public land of the United States carries with it the common-law rights to an innavigable stream thereon, unless the waters are expressly or impliedly reserved by the terms of the patent, or of the statute granting the land, or unless they are reserved by the congressional legislation authorizing the patent or other muniment of title. * * *

It has often been held by this court and its predecessors that a grant of a tract of land bounded by a river or creek not navigable, conveys the land to the thread of the stream; and from a very early day the courts of this state have considered the United States government as the owner of such running waters on the public lands of the United States, and of their beds. Recognizing the United States as the owner of the lands and waters, and as therefore authorized to permit the occupation or diversion of the waters as distinct from the lands, the state courts have treated the prior appropriator of water on the public lands of the United States as having a better right than a subsequent appropriator, on the theory that the appropriation was allowed or licensed by the United States. It has never been held that the right to appropriate waters on the public lands of the United States was derived directly from the state of California as the owner of innavigable streams and their beds; and, since the act of congress granting or recognizing a property in the waters actually diverted and usefully applied on the public lands of the United States, such rights have always been claimed to be deraigned by private persons under the act of congress, from the recognition accorded by the act, or from the acquiescence of the general government in previous appropriations made with its presumed sanction and approval. * * *

It has never been held by the supreme court of the United States, or by the supreme court of this state, that an appropriation of water on the public lands of the United States (made after the act of congress of July 26, 1866, or the amendatory act of 1870) gave to the appropriator the right to the water appropriated as against a grantee of riparian lands, under a grant made or issued prior to the act of 1866, except in a case where the water so subsequently appropriated was reserved by the terms of such grant.

Since, as before, September 28, 1850, the United States has been the owner of lands in California, with power to dispose of the same in such manner, and on such terms and conditions, (not interfering with vested rights derived from the United States,) as it deemed proper. But neither the legislation of congress with respect to the disposition of the public lands, nor its apparent acquiescence in the appropriation by individuals of waters thereon, *subsequent* to the act of September, 1850, granting the swamp lands to the state, can affect the title of the state to lands and waters granted by that act. Neither the supreme court of the United States, nor the supreme court of California, has ever held in opposition to this view. * * *

In Broder v. Water Co., 101 U.S. 274, it appeared: In the year 1853 the defendant completed a canal, through which it had continuously conducted waters and distributed them for mining, agricultural, and other uses; that a portion of the land through which the canal ran was included in the land granted to the Pacific Railroad (under whom plaintiff claimed) by the act of July 2, 1864; that the plaintiff also claimed as a pre-emptor, the inception of his claim as such being a declaratory statement filed August 6, 1866. The court held that the plaintiff was not entitled to have the canal running through his land abated as a nuisance by reason of his pre-emption right, because previous to the initiation of proceedings to secure pre-emption, on the twenty-sixth of July, 1866, (14 St. at Large, 251,) congress had enacted a statute, the ninth section of which contained the declaration "that wherever, by priority of possession, rights to the use of water for mining, agricultural, manufacturing, or other purposes have vested and accrued, and the same are recognized and acknowledged by the local customs, laws, and the decisions of courts, the possessors and owners of such vested rights shall be maintained and protected in the same; and the right of way for the construction of ditches and canals, for the purposes aforesaid, is hereby acknowledged and confirmed." The court also held that the plaintiff was not entitled to relief under his deraignment of title from the railroad company, because the grant to the company of July 2, 1864, contained the following reservation:

> "Any lands granted by this act, or the act to which this is an amendment, shall not defeat or impair any pre-emption, homestead, swamp-land, or other *lawful claim,* nor include any government reservation or mineral lands, or the improvements of any *bona fide* settler on any lands returned or denominated as mineral lands, and the timber necessary to support his said improvements as a miner or agriculturist."

In the opinion of the court the section of the act of 1866 above quoted "was rather a voluntary recognition of a pre-existing right of possession, constituting a valid claim to its continued use, than the establishment of a new one," and that the claim of the defendant to the right of way was such a "lawful claim" as was unaffected by the grant to the railroad company made before the act of 1866 was passed. * * *

In Broder v. Water Co. the claim of the appropriator was recognized in the grant to the railroad company, and prior to the initiation by the plaintiff of proceedings to secure a pre-emption. In the case at bar the grant of the lands to the state (containing no reservation of the waters of flowing streams, express or to be implied from its terms) was made nearly 30 years before the first appropriation of water by the defendant, which was *after* the act of congress of July, 1866, and the amendatory act of 1870. Copp, Min.Dec. 1873–74, 296.

In Osgood v. Water Co., 56 Cal. 571, it was held that where a person acquired a right, by appropriation, to water upon the public lands of the United States, *before* the issuance of a patent to another for lands through which the stream ran, the patentee's rights were, "by express statutory enactment, subject to the rights of the appropriator." The court cited the amendatory act of congress above referred to, the seventeenth section of which reads:

> "That all patents granted, or pre-emptions or homesteads allowed, shall be subject to any vested and accrued water-rights, or rights to ditches and reservoirs used in connection with such water-rights, as may have been acquired under or recognized by the ninth section of the act of which this is amendatory." * * *

Both Broder v. Water Co. and Osgood v. Water Co. are (by strongest implication) authority for the statement that one who acquired a title to riparian lands from the United States prior to the act of July 26, 1866, could not (in the absence of reservation in his grant) be deprived of his common-law rights to the flow of the stream by one who appropriated its waters after the passage of that act.

Much stress is laid by counsel on the language used in Broder v. Water Co., supra, with reference to the clause in the act of 1866, that water-rights recognized or acknowledged by the local customs, etc., "shall be maintained and protected," "was rather a recognition of a pre-existing right of possession, constituting a valid claim to its continued use, than the establishment of a new one." But this language is to be interpreted in view of the context. The language cannot be construed as a recognition by the court of vested rights in appropriators of water, created by mere appropriation and independent of statute. The case proceeds on the assumption that neither the plaintiff nor the defendant had any rights except such as were granted or recognized by acts of congress. It holds that appropriators of water from streams on (or flowing to) the lands granted by the act of 1864 were "recognized" or admitted to have rights which were protected by that act, because the act by its terms reserved from the grant to the railroad company every "lawful claim;" that one who had been permitted to divert water from those lands had a claim which was not in itself unlawful; and that the reservation included *"every honest claim* evidenced by acts of possession." There is no statement in the opinion in Broder v. Water Co., that except for the reservation found in the act of 1864, and the provision in the act of 1866, the defendant would have any right to the water as against the grantees named in the act first named, or their successors in interest. The court holds that Broder acquired no right by virtue of his preemption, because his proceedings to secure it were begun after the act of 1866, which recognized the prior appropriation of the water as being a right in the appropriator, and that Broder acquired no right under the railroad grant, because the water previously appropriated was reserved in that grant. * * *

It may be suggested, however, that the rulings of the courts of California with reference to possessory rights on the public mineral lands enter into, and in some manner limit, the effect of grants of land by the government of the United States, made, as is assumed, under statutes enacted in view of the local law, and of the varying rules and regulations of mining districts. The statutes passed long afterwards cannot affect rights acquired by the state by virtue of a grant made in 1850, nor can the subsequent *policy* of the United States (which is supposed to be indicated by a failure, by express laws, to prohibit the occupation of portions of its lands for mining, etc., and by the omission of the executive officers to attempt to remove miners and other occupants by force) be held to affect the rights acquired by the state through the grant of 1850. * * *

[Reversed.]

Notes

1. **California Doctrine.** This is the "California Doctrine" in its purest form, though the term is often applied to any system recognizing both riparian and appropriative rights. Since the early appropriations had been from streams "on the public domain," the California courts later seized upon this phrase and gave it new significance, requiring that the actual diversion of the water must take place on public land. Thus, the California rule came to be that where an appropriator diverted the water from the stream at a point where it touched private land, no rights were acquired that were superior to the later uses of upstream riparians who subsequently acquired their lands. San Joaquin & Kings River Canal & Irrigation Co. v. Worswick, 203 P. 999 (Cal. 1922). See Thorne v. McKinley Bros., 56 P.2d 204 (Cal. 1936); compare Brown v. Baker, 65 P. 799 (Or. 1901) and Offield v. Ish, 57 P. 809 (Wash. 1899).

2. **Relationship between federal land patents and local law.** Is an analysis of the federal land statutes necessary to a determination of whether a patentee of a parcel of land from the public domain acquires riparian rights? Or whether a state may authorize an appropriation of water? Or whether, as between holders of private rights, one type of right is superior to the other? See Connecticut v. Massachusetts, 282 U.S. 660 (1931). Compare Sturr v. Beck, 133 U.S. 541 (1890) with Boquillas Land & Cattle Co. v. Curtis, 213 U.S. 339 (1909), as to the effect of local law on the incidents of ownership of land acquired by patent. In neither case does the Court make a direct connection, but is it merely coincidence that in Dakota, where the Territory had codified riparian law, the patentee had riparian rights, while in Arizona, where neither the Territory nor the preceding Mexican State of Sonora recognized such rights, the patentee acquired none?

In California Oregon Power Co. v. Beaver Portland Cement Co., 295 U.S. 142 (1935), the Supreme Court gave some credence to the notion that the federal land laws control the question of whether a parcel of riparian land patented by the government had an appurtenant federally created riparian right, but concluded that those laws left to the states the "power * * * to legislate in respect of waters and water rights as they deemed wise in the public interest * * * with the right in each to determine for itself to what extent the rule of appropriation or the common law rule in respect to riparian rights should obtain. For since 'Congress cannot enforce either rule upon any state,' State of Kansas v. Colorado, 206 U.S. 46, 94, the full power of choice must remain with the state." Compare also Borax, Consol. v.City of Los Angeles, 296 U.S. 10 (1935) and Oregon ex rel. State Land Bd. v. Corvallis Sand and Gravel Co., 429 U.S. 363 (1977).

As to the extent to which the federal laws reserve to the national government a residuum of "title to unappropriated water" and of power to dispose of the water as a part of the public domain, see Chapter 8, Section 2B.

3. **Riparian rights in Texas.** Texas, by statute, established a cut-off date after which a person acquiring public land would not receive riparian rights. Tex. Water Code Ann. § 11.001. Another important limitation in Texas is that Spanish and Mexican grants of land along the lower Rio Grande have no appurtenant riparian rights. State v. Valmont Plantations, 346 S.W.2d 853 (Tex. Civ. App. 1961), aff'd 355 S.W.2d 502 (Tex. 1962). This ruling was modified to some extent in State v. Hidalgo County Water Control & Improvement District No. 18, 443 S.W.2d 728 (Tex. Civ. App. 1969), the case from which *Valmont Plantations*

was spun off. The court recognized "equitable" water rights of several types, including some held by owners of riparian tracts in Spanish land grants whose land had been irrigated under the claim to riparian rights rejected in *Valmont.* The decision was motivated by the "unprecedented situation" resulting from the fact that two large reservoirs (Falcon and Amistad) had been constructed on the Rio Grande by the federal government pursuant to a treaty with Mexico, which had made large quantities of water available for use in Texas at no expense to irrigators. On "water-short Cibolo Creek," however, an attempt by the owner of a riparian Spanish land grant tract to claim an "equitable right" was not successful. In re Water Rights of Cibolo Creek Watershed, 568 S.W.2d 155 (Tex. Civ. App. 1978).

In 1895 Nebraska passed a comprehensive water code, which the court held prevented by implication the acquisition of any riparian rights in lands thereafter acquired. Crawford Co. v. Hathaway, 93 N.W. 781 (Neb. 1903). Nevertheless, in Brummund v. Vogel, 168 N.W.2d 24 (Neb. 1969), the owner of farm property which abutted on a creek claimed the right to use water from this stream for domestic purposes superior to an appropriator's right to build a dam upstream. The landowner was held to have this riparian right despite the fact that he neither pleaded nor proved that he or his predecessors had owned the land before the cutoff date of April 4, 1895.

4. **Additional limitations on riparian rights.** Although riparians are generally regarded as having rights in navigable waters, the Supreme Court of Washington held that since that state's constitution declares that the state owns the bed and shores of all navigable waters up to the line of ordinary high water, an owner of the shore of a navigable lake cannot make a riparian claim to the waters of the lake for irrigation that is good against the state, or against one who appropriates water in pursuance of the laws of the State. State ex rel. Ham v. Superior Court, 126 P. 945 (Wash. 1912).

A similar approach in Texas confined riparian rights to low-water flows, with the result that large quantities of the annual flow of variable streams were reserved for use by appropriators. In Motl v. Boyd, 286 S.W. 458 (Tex. 1926), the court said that riparian rights could attach only to waters below the line of highest ordinary flow, which it defined as the highest line of flow which the stream reaches and maintains for a sufficient length of time to become characteristic when its waters are in their ordinary normal and usual condition, uninfluenced by recent rainfall or surface runoff. The Texas water officials, in an attempt to introduce a measure of certainty into the rule as a guide to determining the availability of water for appropriation, translated the court's definition of "highest ordinary flow" into "modal flow," that level of water most frequently occurring in daily measurements of the actual flow of the stream. Carter, Proceedings, Water Law Conferences, University of Texas School of Law, 194 (1954).

5. **Economic efficiency in the California Doctrine.** Until the 1928 constitutional amendment on reasonable use, discussed supra p. 275, Note 1, the California Supreme Court generally held that a riparian landowner could enjoin an upstream appropriation even though it caused no present injury. See Anaheim Union Water Company v. Fuller, supra p. 236 and Pabst v. Finmand, supra p. 272. Nevertheless, there were cases prior to the amendment in which the California Supreme Court refused to enjoin an upstream appropriation. E.g., Gin S. Chow v. City of Santa Barbara, 22 P.2d 5 (Cal. 1933); E. Clemens Horst Co. v. New

Blue Point Mining Co., 171 P. 417 (Cal. 1918). In Chowchilla Farms v. Martin, 25 P.2d 435, 450 (Cal. 1933), the court reconciled these two lines of cases by distinguishing ordinary and extraordinary floodwaters: "A consideration of the authorities upon this subject leads to the conclusion that flood waters in a stream which can be put to a reasonably beneficial use by riparian owners on the stream are not subject to appropriation by an upstream claimant. On the other hand, *if the flood waters are not being used by riparians and cannot be put to any beneficial use by them,* then, under the doctrine of Gallatin and Gin Chow cases, they are, to the extent that the riparian owners cannot put them to any beneficial use, subject to appropriation." (emphasis added)

Mark T. Kanazawa, Efficiency in Western Water Law: The Development of the California Doctrine, 27 J. Legal Stud. 159 (1998), suggests a different reconciliation of these cases. The author tentatively concludes that the court selectively applied these two lines to promote economic efficiency. He hypothesizes that injunctions without regard to injury make economic sense when the number of competing riparians is small because they pave the way for voluntary transfers from riparians to appropriators by giving well-defined property right to the riparians; i.e., the appropriator can pay the riparians to have the injunction lifted if the appropriator's use is sufficiently valuable. This is exactly what happened after the decision in Lux v. Haggin according to the author; the parties in that case negotiated an exchange in which Miller/Lux gave Haggin water and Haggin paid part of the costs of a dam to augment the supply. However, when the number of competing riparians is large, Kanazawa hypothesizes, voluntary transfers are much less likely because of the greater transaction costs associated with negotiating with more parties. In such cases, a court concerned with economic efficiency would not automatically enjoin diversions by appropriators but would enjoin them selectively depending on the damage caused to downstream riparians. Reviewing the California Supreme Court cases involving conflicts between appropriators and riparian landowners and the settings in which the cases occurred, the author concludes that they support the forgoing hypothesis; i.e., when there were only a few riparian landowners downstream from an appropriator, the author says that the court usually enjoined diversions by the appropriator, but was less likely to do so when there were a large number of riparian landowners downstream.

6. **Reassessment of Lux v. Haggin.** Lux v. Haggin is reassessed in Eric T. Freyfogle, Lux v. Haggin, The Common Law Burden of Modern Water Law, 57 U. Colo. L. Rev. 485 (1986). Professor Freyfogle suggests that the case was burdened by 19th century views of property rights and the common law which continue to dominate modern water law.

FRANCO-AMERICAN CHAROLAISE, LTD. v. OKLAHOMA WATER RESOURCES BOARD

Supreme Court of Oklahoma, 1990.

855 P.2d 568.

OPALA, JUSTICE. This appeal challenges the constitutionality of the 1963 amendments to Oklahoma's water law insofar as the amendments regulate riparian rights. * * * We hold that the Oklahoma riparian owner enjoys a vested common-law right to the reasonable use of the stream. This right is a valuable part of the property owner's "bundle of sticks" and may not be taken for public use without compensation. We further hold that, inasmuch as 60 O.S.1981 § 60, as amended in 1963, limits the riparian owner to domestic use and declares that all other water in the stream becomes public water subject to appropriation without any provision for compensating the riparian owner, the statute violates Art. 2 § 24, Okl. Const. * * *

Since 1897, both the common law and the statutes have operated in Oklahoma to confer riparian and appropriative rights. Though these rights have coexisted in the State for almost 100 years, they are theoretically irreconcilable.[15] The common-law riparian right extends to the reasonable use of the stream or to its natural flow, depending on the jurisdiction; the appropriative right attaches to a fixed amount. The last riparian use asserted has as much priority as the first; the appropriator who takes first has the senior right. In 1963 the legislature attempted to reconcile the two doctrines. * * *

[T]he 1963 amendments provided a validation mechanism as a method for protecting pre-existing beneficial uses, including those of the riparian owner and pre-existing appropriators. All subsequent rights to the use of stream water, except for riparian domestic uses, are to be acquired by appropriation. The stream's natural flow is considered public water and subject to appropriation. The riparian owner may not assert his (or her) common-law right to the use of stream water other than for the domestic uses. * * *

The issue here is whether the legislature can validly abrogate the riparian owner's right to initiate non-domestic reasonable uses in stream water without affording compensation. Art. 2, § 24, Okl. Const. provides in part: "Private property shall not be taken or damaged for public use without just compensation. * * *" Private property protected by Art. 2, § 24 includes "easements, personal property, and *every valuable interest which can be enjoyed and recognized as property*."[42] Further, In Oklahoma Water Resources Board v. Central Oklahoma Master Conservancy District[43] we held: "A 'vested right' is the power to *do certain actions* or possess certain things lawfully, and is substantially a property right. It may be created by common law, by statute or by contract. Once created, it becomes absolute, and is protected from legislative invasion * * * " Therefore, the common-law riparian right to use stream water, as long as that use is reasonable, has been long recognized in Oklahoma law as a private property right.

The general rule is that the legislature may restrict the use of private property by exercise of its police power for the preservation of the public, health, morals, safety and general welfare without compensating the property

---

15. This dual system of water rights is known nationally as the "California Doctrine" and at one time was the rule in all West Coast states and the tier of the Great Plains from North Dakota to Texas. Only California and Nebraska retain it. Most dual-system states have since adopted the appropriation doctrine as controlling all rights to stream water. * * *

42. Graham v. City of Duncan, Okla., 354 P.2d 458, 461 (1960).

43. Okla., 464 P.2d 748, 755 (1969) (Emphasis added).

owner. In Phillips Petroleum Co. v. Corporation Comm'n[46] this court defined the permissible exercise of police power: "[T]he police power is usually exerted merely to regulate the use and enjoyment of property by the owner, or, if he is deprived of his property outright, it is not taken for public use, but rather destroyed in order to promote the general welfare. * * * " Therefore, in C. C. Julian Oil & Royalties Co. v. Capshaw [145 Okl. 237, 292 P. 841 (1930)] we declared that the legislature could regulate a landowner's use and enjoyment of natural resources to prevent waste and infringement on the rights of others. Thus, a statutory regulation of the methods to be used in extracting hydrocarbons was a constitutional exercise of police power where none of the hydrocarbons was taken for public use. Then, in Frost v. Ponca City[48] we held that in the interest of health and safety, the city could exercise its police power to restrict the plaintiff's right to capture hydrocarbons underlying his property, but the city could not remove the hydrocarbons and sell them without compensating the plaintiff.

We, therefore, hold that the 1963 water law amendments are fraught with a constitutional infirmity in that they abolish the right of the riparian owner to assert his (or her) vested interest in the prospective reasonable use of the stream. The riparian owner stands on equal footing with the appropriator. His ownership of riparian land affords him *no right* to the stream water except for limited domestic use. * * *

The OWRB argues the 1963 amendments are a permissible exercise of the police power just as a zoning ordinance would be. That contention is inapposite when, as here, the use of stream water is *not just restricted but is taken for public use*.

Although the 1963 water law amendments provided a mechanism for a riparian owner to "perfect" all beneficial uses initiated prior to the legislation, that mechanism falls short of protecting the riparian owner's common-law appurtenant right. The mechanism is constitutionally inadequate first of all because the full sweep of the riparian right is much broader than the validation mechanism could ever shield. The heart of the riparian right is the right to assert a use at *any time* as long as it does not harm another riparian who has a corresponding right. Further, yesterday's reasonable use by one riparian owner may become unreasonable tomorrow when a fellow riparian owner asserts a new or expanded use. After the 1963 amendments, the riparian owner who wants to expand a use or assert a new use may do so *only as an appropriator*. His use is not judged by its reasonableness but only by its priority in time.

Furthermore, the validation mechanism attempted to forever set in stone the maximum amount of stream water the landowner, *as a riparian owner*, can use. Any use asserted by the landowner, *as an appropriator*, is either denied because no water is available or is given a lower priority than all other uses,

---

46. Okla., 312 P.2d 916 (1956) (quoting 29 C.J.S. §6); * * *.

48. Okla., 541 P.2d 1312, 1324 (1975).

including those of appropriators who are non-riparian to the stream. It matters not that the riparian owner's use is reasonable when compared with prior uses. This result is antithetical to the very nature of the common-law riparian right, which places no stock in the fact of past use, present use, or even non-use. * * *

To assure that the state's resources are put to the most reasonable and beneficial use, we adopt the approach of the Supreme Court of Nebraska in Wasserburger v. Coffee.[54] *Wasserburger* holds that the rights of the riparian owner and the appropriator are to be determined by relative reasonableness. On remand, the trial court shall balance the riparian owners' uses against those of the City, with due consideration to be given to the factors listed earlier in this opinion. * * *

LAVENDER, VICE CHIEF JUSTICE, concurring in part; dissenting in part:

I must respectfully dissent from that part of the majority opinion holding the 1963 legislative amendments to our State's stream water law unconstitutional under the guise the amendments effected a taking of property without just compensation in violation of Okla. Const. art. 2, § 24. In reaching this result the majority makes several errors.

Initially, it misperceives that future, unquantified use of stream water by a riparian is a vested property right that can only be limited or modified pursuant to judicially mandated common law factors that were generally used to decide piecemeal litigation between competing riparians in water use disputes. Secondly, it misinterprets the plain and unambiguous legislation at issue and it fails to recognize that even assuming a vested property right is at issue, such rights in natural resources like water, may be subject to reasonable limitations or even forfeiture for failure to put the resource to beneficial use. Thirdly, its analysis of the law as to what constitutes a taking of private property requiring just compensation is flawed. In my view the majority errs in such regard by failing to view the legislation as akin to zoning regulation, which although may limit a riparian's open-ended common law right to make use of the water to benefit his land and thereby effect the value of his land, does not deprive him of all economic use of his land or absolutely deprive him of water. The lack of water to a riparian, if it occurs, is caused by his own neglect or inaction by years of failure either to put the water to beneficial use or failure to gain an appropriation permit from the Oklahoma Water Resources Board (OWRB) for uses being made prior to passage of the 1963 amendments or uses made or sought to be made between passage of the amendments and the City of Ada's appropriation at issue here. This mistake of the majority is particularly egregious because it wholly ignores the virtually admitted fact that neither riparians or appropriators own the water they are being allowed to use. All of the people in this State own the water and that ownership interest by the legislation before us is merely being channeled by the Legislature, for the benefit of those owners (i.e. the people), to those uses deemed wise.

---

54. 180 Neb. 149, 141 N.W.2d 738, 743 (1966).

The majority has failed to consider persuasive case law from the highest courts of other jurisdictions upholding analogous legislation over similar attacks and pronouncements of the United States Supreme Court which lead me to conclude the legislation *on its face* is constitutional. * * * In place of the statutory scheme drafted by the Legislature after years of study and debate the majority acts as a super-legislature by rewriting the water law of this State in accord with its views of prudent public policy, something neither this Court or any court has the power to do. The foundation of this judicial "legislation", relying as it does on the so-called California Doctrine, is illusory at best because the majority ignores pronouncements from the California Supreme Court which has itself recognized the common law doctrine of unquantified future riparian use of stream water is not a vested right, even in the face of a California constitutional provision specifically interpreted to protect it, *when it may impair the promotion of reasonable and beneficial uses of state waters and, in effect, constitute waste of the resource.*[2] * * *

In order to understand the erroneous nature of the majority opinion it is first necessary to understand the "property" right of riparians it purportedly protects and the central rationale given for holding the 1963 water law amendments unconstitutional. The "property" interest is supposedly the prospective or future reasonable use of stream water. The opinion posits that this unquantified *prospective* or *future use* is a vested right.

* * * In my view only preexisting uses (i.e. uses initiated prior to passage of the amendments and subject to validation thereunder) can be said to be property in any real or actual sense. *Such uses the majority admits were subject to validation under the 1963 amendments.* As to any common law claim to use an unquantified amount of water in the future such open-ended claim was lost or forfeited because it was determined to be wasteful by the Legislature and was properly limited to domestic use. Furthermore, riparians, just as other potential future water users, may obtain their future needs of water in addition to domestic use by applying for an appropriation under our water laws. If the water is not then available it is their own inaction or neglect which deprives them of water and not action of the State under the involved legislation. In effect, all the legislation at issue did was to put water users in this State on an equal footing (except for a statutory preference in favor of riparian domestic use) and provide a statewide *unitary* system for the acquisition of water rights.

* * * In essence, the majority indicates it relies on the so-called California Doctrine for its position. It, however, nowhere discusses recent

---

2. In re Waters of Long Valley Creek Stream System, 25 Cal. 3d 339, 158 Cal. Rptr. 350, 355, fn. 3, 599 P.2d 656, 661, f.n. 3 (1979). In said case the California Supreme Court said: [A]ppellant also asserts that these common law cases disclose his future right to an unquantified amount of water has become "vested." The assertion is without merit. As discussed post, riparian rights are limited by the concept of reasonable and beneficial use, and they may not be exercised in a manner that is inconsistent with the policy declaration of article X, section 2 of the [California] Constitution. Thus, to the extent that a future riparian right may impair the promotion of reasonable and beneficial uses of state waters, it is inapt to view it as vested. (emphasis added)

authority from California that sheds serious doubt on its analysis. In the case of In Re Waters of Long Valley Creek Stream System[40] the California Supreme Court was not so generous. There it held that the state, through its water board, *may subordinate any future unexercised riparian right below any appropriation awarded prior to user by the riparian when conducting stream wide adjudications because doing so will promote the state's interest in fostering the most reasonable and beneficial uses of scarce water resources.* This view was recently reaffirmed in a unanimous decision by the California Supreme Court.[42] In my view our Legislature has accomplished nothing more than that approved by the California Supreme Court via the legislation at issue here and its limitations and modifications in regard to the common law reasonable use doctrine.

[E]ven if it be assumed the majority is correct that the riparian had a protectible property interest to some unquantified right to make use of the water at some unspecified time in the future, this common law right could be lost or forfeited by nonuse or, at least, limited to domestic use and appropriative uses granted by the OWRB as sought to be accomplished by the legislation under review. To rule otherwise simply places a common law doctrine as an impenetrable barrier to efficient management of a natural resource never deemed to be owned by private landowners.

The majority further fails in its analysis in the area of just compensation law. It relies on the case of Frost v. Ponca City[57] which ruled although a city may exercise its police power to restrict a landowner's right to capture hydrocarbons underlying his property in the interest of health and safety, if a city (or a public entity) itself removes the hydrocarbons and sells them the private landowner must be compensated. The majority fails to see at least two significant distinguishing factors between the situation involved in Frost and that facing us today. One, Frost relied on the fact hydrocarbons, such as oil and gas underlying a landowner's property, were subject to the law of capture, i.e. the landowner had the exclusive right to drill for, produce, or otherwise gain possession of such substances and when reduced to actual possession, the landowner obtained an absolute ownership interest in the substance. After the ownership interest was established the landowner could sell the hydrocarbons. *Riparians were never deemed to have such exclusive rights in regard to stream water as shown above and the majority admits this.*

Secondly, in *Frost* the landowners were *totally restricted from removing the hydrocarbons themselves or reducing them to actual possession under the law of capture. Here Appellee riparians are not totally restricted from gaining the use of stream water in the future.* The only requirement is that they apply for an appropriation permit. Of course they also may use the water

---

40. 25 Cal. 3d 339, 158 Cal. Rptr. 350, 599 P.2d 656 (1979), * * *.

42. In Re Water of Hallet Creek Stream System, 44 Cal. 3d 448, 243 Cal. Rptr. 887, 899-901, 749 P.2d 324, 336-338 (1988), cert. denied, 488 U.S. 824, 109 S.Ct. 71, 102 L.Ed.2d 48 (1988).

57. 541 P.2d 1321 (Okla. 1975).

for domestic purposes without a permit and the legislation provided an opportunity to protect preexisting uses. No State or public law prohibits their use of stream water, but only inaction on their part. In view of these differences it is inapposite for the majority to rely on *Frost*.

Instead of placing unwarranted reliance on *Frost* to strike down the legislation under review I would uphold it by ruling it is akin to zoning regulations which have long been upheld by the courts. When one properly determines riparians have no property right to insist that the law remain as it was under the common law the attack on the amendments is nothing more then a facial assault that the amendments have an adverse impact on riparian land values and detrimentally effect the ability of riparians to use stream water in connection with their land. I believe such attack is without merit, although it does point out it is *use of the water upon the land or, at least, in relation to the land that is the property interest potentially affected.* In my view, when the constitutional attack is analyzed in proper perspective the just compensation challenge must fail in regard to any facial attack on the legislation.

The United States Supreme Court has long recognized that land use regulations normally do not effect a taking of property as long as the regulations at issue substantially advance legitimate state interests and do not deny a landowner economically viable use of his land. No one argues here, including the majority, that the statutory scheme under review does not substantially advance legitimate state interests. The State interests advanced are numerous. Among them are direct promotion of the efficient management of our State's water resources by preventing waste. It provides a semblance of certainty in the area of water rights and distributes this valuable resource *which is owned by all the public* in response to demonstrated need. Therefore, the only real question in the taking context is whether the legislation has deprived riparians of the economically viable use of their land. I do not think it has nor from my review of the record herein do I read Appellees submissions to assert otherwise.

Nowhere is there evidence in this record that the legislation itself has rendered the use of riparian land economically unviable. Riparians are not estopped from using their land for any purpose or gaining water rights in connection therewith as specified above. * * * In sum, I would hold the legislation on its face did not constitute a taking of private property for which compensation is required just as land use regulation does not constitute a taking of private property when the owner is not denied economically viable use of his land. * * *

Notes

1. **Abolition of riparian rights in other states.** Oregon was the first "California Doctrine" state to attempt to incorporate riparian rights into its appropriation system. The Water Code of 1909 made all waters within the state appropriable for beneficial use, provided no "vested rights" were taken away or impaired. The vested rights of riparian proprietors were defined to include only the actual application of water to a beneficial use prior to the passage of the Act. Or. Laws 1909, ch. 216, p. 319. The "Oregon plan" has been upheld as

constitutional. California-Oregon Power Co. v. Beaver Portland Cement Co., 73 F.2d 555 (9th Cir. 1934), aff'd on other grounds 295 U.S. 142 (1935); In re Hood River, 227 P. 1065 (Or. 1924). The statute made no provision for compensating the riparian owner for the loss of his unused rights. A similar Kansas statute was upheld in State ex rel. Emery v. Knapp, 207 P.2d 440 (Kan. 1949). It was also upheld by a three-judge federal court, in a decision affirmed without opinion by the United States Supreme Court. Baumann v. Smrha, 145 F.Supp. 617 (D. Kan. 1956), aff'd 352 U.S. 863 (1956).

In re Adjudication of Water Rights in the Upper Guadalupe River, 642 S.W.2d 438 (Tex. 1982), upheld that part of the Texas Water Adjudication Act that limited riparian claimants to the quantity of water actually beneficially used during one of the five years between 1963 and 1967. The court held that after notice and upon reasonable terms, the statute's termination of the riparians' continuous nonuse of water is not a taking of their property. The court cited the Oregon and Kansas cases, and drew additional support from Texaco, Inc. v. Short, 454 U.S. 516, 530 (1982), in which the Supreme Court said:

"We have concluded that the State may treat a mineral interest that has not been used for 20 years and for which no statement of claim has been filed as abandoned; it follows that, after abandonment, the former owner retains no interest for which he may claim compensation. *It is the owner's failure to make any use of the property*—and not the action of the State—that causes the lapse of the property right; there is no 'taking' that requires compensation. The requirement that an owner of a property interest that has not been used for 20 years must come forward and file a current statement of claim is not itself a 'taking.'"

Although Washington adopted a water code in 1917 which provided for appropriation through a permit system and stated that "any right [to water] * * * shall be hereafter acquired * * * in the manner provided and not otherwise," it was not until 1985 that it was clearly decided that the code terminated riparian rights which had not been exercised within a reasonable time after the adoption of the code. In re Deadman Creek Drainage Basin, 694 P.2d 1071 (Wash. 1985). The court determined that 15 years was a reasonable time and held that all riparian rights not exercised by 1932 were relinquished.

Unused riparian rights have been effectively abolished and the post-statute water user must go the appropriation route in all of the other "California Doctrine" states, except California, Oklahoma, and Nebraska. See text accompanying footnote 54 of the principal case. The Oregon system was expressly adopted in South Dakota (except for domestic uses), S.D. Codified Laws § 46–1–9. The same result was reached by N.D. Cent. Code § 61–01–01.1 (since repealed), after a rather garbled legislative process described in 1 Wells A. Hutchins, Water Rights Laws in the Nineteen Western States 198, 213-215 (1971).

Under the South Dakota statutes, S.D. Codified Laws §§ 46–1–9(2), 46–1–5(1), 46–1–6(7), a riparian owner has vested rights to use stream water for irrigation purposes only to the extent of previous beneficial use, but he has the further right to take and use water for domestic use (irrigation of gardens, trees, shrubbery or orchards and stock watering), and such use takes precedence over all appropriative rights. Belle Fourche Irrigation Dist. v. Smiley, 204 N.W.2d 105 (S.D. 1973).

In Alaska, usually classified as a Colorado doctrine state, some quasi-riparian rights attached to mining claims existing under a territorial statute. All of these rights in use were simply converted into appropriations when the state enacted a comprehensive water code. Alaska Stat. § 46.15.060; Frank J. Trelease, Alaska's New Water Use Act, 2 Land & Water L. Rev. 1 (1967).

2. **Diminished importance of riparian rights in California.** California, which gave the doctrine its name, remains the quintessential "California Doctrine" or "dual-system" state. Nevertheless, a variety of factors has diminished the practical importance of riparian rights and have reduced the theoretical primacy which riparian rights enjoy over appropriative rights. Such factors include use of the "source of title" test for riparian lands, discussed in supra p. 239, Note 1, which produces a continuing contraction in riparian lands. Similarly, the rule that storage of water in one season for use in another season is not a riparian use in California and can only be accomplished by appropriation is a significant limitation on riparian rights because seasonal storage is often necessary where dependability is important. See Colorado Power Co. v. Pacific Gas & Elec. Co., 24 P.2d 495 (Cal. 1933).

Ironically, however, it has been a rule that seemingly gave riparian rights the greatest primacy which has in fact most undermined that primacy. This is the rule which held that a riparian proprietor could enjoin an appropriative use even though the appropriative use caused no injury. See Anaheim Union Water Co. v. Fuller, supra p. 236. This rule made it easier for appropriators to acquire prescriptive rights against riparians because any appropriative use started the statute running against downstream riparian proprietors. See Pabst v. Finmand, supra p. 272. More significantly, reaction to a particularly egregious application of the rule in Herminghaus v. Southern California Edison Co., 252 P. 607 (Cal. 1926), produced an amendment to the California constitution which has significantly altered the relationship between riparian and appropriative rights. The amendment, referred to in footnote 2 of Justice Lavender's dissenting opinion in the principal case, requires all uses to be "reasonable." Thus, in a conflict between a riparian use and an appropriative use, the riparian use will prevail only if it is "reasonable."

Initially, it appeared that the amendment, now found at Article X, Section 2, was purely remedial in nature; that is, it appeared that a riparian proprietor could not enjoin an upstream appropriation which interfered with the riparian's "unreasonable" use of water but could obtain damages. See Peabody v. City of Vallejo, 40 P.2d 486 (Cal. 1935); United States v. Gerlach Live Stock Co., 339 U.S. 725 (1950). However, in Joslin v. Marin Municipal Water District, 429 P.2d 889 (Cal. 1967), the court held that the amendment was a substantive modification of riparian rights which precludes an award of damages to a riparian proprietor whose use is unreasonable. In addition, although early cases interpreting the amendment, such as *Peabody*, supra, equated "unreasonable" uses with "waste," *Joslin* seems to hold that a riparian use may become "unreasonable" simply because socially or economically more valuable uses develop. The case involved a sand and gravel operator who sued for damages caused by an upstream reservoir which prevented the stream from replenishing the supply of rocks and gravel. The court contrasted "unanimous" policy pronouncements regarding the conservation of water with the lack of such pronouncements regarding sand and gravel and said:

"Is it 'reasonable.' then, that the riches of our streams, which we are charged with conserving in the great public interest, are to be dissipated in the amassing of mere sand and gravel which for aught that appears subserves *no* public policy? We cannot deem such a use to be in accord with the constitutional mandate that our limited water resources be put only to those beneficial uses 'to the fullest extent of which they are capable,' that 'waste or unreasonable use' be prevented, and that conservation be exercised 'in the interest of the people and for the public welfare.' (Cal. Const., [Art. X, § 2] XIV, § 3.) We are satisfied that in the instant case the use of such waters as an agent to expose or to carry and deposit sand, gravel and rock, is as a matter of law unreasonable within the meaning of the constitutional amendment."

See Clifford W. Schulz & Gregory S. Weber, Changing Judicial Attitudes Towards Property Rights in California Water Resources: From Vested Rights to Utilitarian Reallocations, 19 Pac. L.J. 1031 (1988); Eric T. Freyfogle, Context and Accommodation in Modern Property Law, 41 Stan. L. Rev. 1529 (1989).

The amendment has had a significant impact on unexercised riparian rights. In Tulare Irrigation District v. Lindsay-Strathmore Irrigation District, 45 P.2d 972 (Cal. 1935), the court found that the amendment protects the "prospective reasonable beneficial use" of riparians and held unconstitutional a statutory provision which terminated riparian rights after ten years of nonuse. Nevertheless, in the *Long Valley* case, decided in 1979, the California Supreme Court held that unexercised riparian rights can be "subordinated" to appropriations in a statutory streamwide adjudication of water rights conducted by the state water board. See the text accompanying footnote 40 of the dissenting opinion. "Subordination" can include a loss of priority to appropriations existing at the time of adjudication and to any future appropriations which are authorized before riparian rights are exercised. For all practical purposes, "subordination" is equivalent to extinguishment of unexercised riparian rights, albeit subordination can result only from a statutory adjudication by the state water board, not from private litigation. See Pleasant Valley Canal Co. v. Borror, 72 Cal. Rptr. 2d 1 (Cal. Ct. App. 1998); Wright v. Goleta Water Dist., 219 Cal. Rptr. 740 (Cal. Ct. App. 1985). In reaching its conclusion, the court in *Long Valley* relied heavily on the amendment's directive to foster reasonable uses of water, finding that unexercised riparian rights unreasonably deter water development, foster costly piecemeal litigation, and impair state administration of water rights.

3. **Alteration of riparian rights by eastern permit systems.** In the eastern states which adopted permit systems, most exercises of riparian rights initiated in the future (in the areas where the statutes apply) must be made by virtue of a permit, the issuance of which is to some degree discretionary. Permits are not specifically limited to riparians in most states. See Del. Code Ann. tit. 7, §§ 6003, 6004; Fla. Stat. § 373.219; Iowa Code § 455B.264; Ky. Rev. Stat. Ann. § 151.140; Md. Code Ann., Nat. Res. § 5–502; N.J. Stat. Ann. § 58:1A–5; N.C. Gen. Stat. § 143–215.15.

It is not clear in all of these states just what effect the statutes have on existing uses under riparian law. In some states it is specifically stated that the uses must be confirmed by a permit. Fla. Stat. § 373.226; N.J. Stat. Ann. § 58:1A–6. All of the other statutes are subject to the interpretation that a permit is required for continuation of an existing use, and all permits are subject to denial on various grounds of administrative discretion. All are issued for short terms and many are subject to discretionary cancellation. In many cases the quantity of water a riparian may withdraw and the arrangement for distribution of water among permit holders in times of shortage may be changed from what would have been allowable under common law.

These fairly extensive changes in the nature and attributes of riparian rights may be thought to raise constitutional questions. A great deal of discussion of constitutional issues has occurred, but no courts have decided the questions. Few commentators seem to have many qualms as to the validity of these acts. Fisher, Due Process and the Effect of Eastern Appropriation Proposals on Existing Rights, in The Law of Water Allocation in the Eastern United States 441 (Haber & Bergen eds., 1958); William N. Hines, A Decade of Experience Under the Iowa Water Permit System—Part II, 8 Nat. Resources J. 21 (1968); Dominic B. King, Regulation of Water Rights Under the Police Power, Water Resources and the Law 269 (1958); Theodore E. Lauer, The Riparian Right as Property, Water Resources and the Law 131 (1958); Jeffrey O'Connell, Iowa's New Water Statute—The Constitutionality of Regulating Existing Uses of Water, 47 Iowa L. Rev. 549 (1962); National Water Commission, Water Policies for the Future, supra p. 1, at 282–283.

4. **Purchase of unused riparian rights.** One way to get rid of unused riparian rights is for the appropriators to buy them. In *Tulare,* supra p. 321, Note 2, the court said, speaking of the powers of condemnation enjoyed by public districts, "as to prospective uses, however, it is obvious that when, as here, the appropriator takes the water and devotes the same to a public use, prior to the time such prospective needs arise, a public use has intervened as to the quantity required for such future uses. The appropriator may not desire to appropriate the water and to construct large and expensive works with the possibility constantly in the offing that the riparians, who have been protected by a declaration of their rights in the water for future purposes will increase their reasonable and beneficial use of the water, so that ultimately, perhaps, none is left for appropriation. The appropriator may and probably would desire to condemn the riparians' right to use of the water in the stream for these prospective purposes. No good reason suggests itself why the appropriator should not be permitted to do this in the injunction suit by means of an inverse condemnation. The same compelling reasons that exist for permitting such a procedure when the entire riparian right is sought to be condemned likewise exists where the appropriator simply desires to condemn the right of the riparian to whatever additional water he may later need for prospective reasonable beneficial purposes. In both cases, the all important fact must exist that a public use has attached, but once that is present, this procedure seems to us sensible and well calculated to prevent multiplicity of suits and interminable delays." 45 P.2d at 990-91.

5. **Resolving riparian/appropriation conflicts by augmenting supply.** Some of California's riparian-appropriation controversies have been given the "California solution" under which water problems are solved by pouring water on them, i.e., by augmenting supply rather than regulating demand. The United States Bureau of Reclamation's Central Valley Project and the State Department of Water Resource's State Water Project annually release water from Shasta Dam and Oroville Dam to supply 370,300 acre feet to Sacramento River riparians and 295,000 acre feet for use on land riparian to the Feather, Yuba and Bear Rivers, in addition to releases of appropriated water for delivery pursuant to contracts with districts serving non-riparian irrigated land. David B. Anderson, Riparian Water

Rights in California 6-8 (Staff Paper No. 4, Governor's Comm'n to Review California Water Rights Law (1977).

6. **A reversal of the historic trend.** In somewhat of a reversal of the usual historic pattern, the Hawaii Supreme Court in 1973 sua sponte overruled territorial case law establishing a system of water rights based on ancient Hawaiian customs and adopted common law riparian rights. McBryde Sugar Co. v. Robinson, 504 P.2d 1330 (Haw. 1973). Subsequently, several large irrigators sued, alleging that enforcement of the *McBryde* decision would terminate their existing transbasin diversions of water and would result in a taking of property contrary to the federal constitution. In Robinson v. Ariyoshi, 753 F.2d 1468 (9th Cir. 1985), the Ninth Circuit agreed. The Ninth Circuit assumed that the Hawaii Supreme Court was free to overrule the territorial cases and adopt a new water law. However, the court ruled that the new law could only be applied prospectively and could not "divest" rights that were "vested" before the *McBryde* decision. Finding that the plaintiffs' transbasin diversions were vested rights, the court held that these rights could not be divested except through the state's exercise of its powers of eminent domain. Subsequently, the United States Supreme Court vacated the judgment and remanded the case to the Ninth Circuit for reconsideration on ripeness grounds. 477 U.S. 902 (1986). Ultimately, the Ninth Circuit dismissed the case. Finding that the state, to that date, had not interfered with the plaintiffs' diversions, the court held that the "inchoate and speculative cloud" created by the *McBryde* decision was insufficient to make the controversy ripe. 887 F.2d 215 (9th Cir. 1989).

In 1987 Hawaii adopted a water code, Haw. Rev. Stat. 174C. The code requires all existing users to file a declaration of use, § 174C–27; except for personal domestic use, permits are required of all users in water management areas (designated water short regions), § 174C–48. Water use is not regulated outside water management areas, but riparian principles, including restrictions on transbasin diversions, apparently apply. Within water management areas, the code allows permits to be issued for transportation and use of water outside the watershed of origin "the common law of the State to the contrary notwithstanding." § 174C–49(c). The law of water rights in Hawaii and the affect of the water code are examined in Douglas W. MacDougal, Testing the Current: The Water Code and the Regulation of Hawaii's Water Resources, 10 U. Haw. L. Rev. 205 (1988).

7. **Water rights and constitutional "takings."** For a recent case exploring the application of takings principles to water rights, see Tulare Lake Basin Water Storage Dist. v. United States, 49 Fed. Cl. 313 (2001), discussed at the end of Ch. 7 (contractual entitlements). For a general discussion of constitutional "takings" and water rights see Joseph L. Sax, The Constitution, Property Rights and the Future of Water Law, 61 U. Colo. L. Rev. 257 (1990); see also Jan G. Laitos, Regulation of Natural Resource Use and Development in Light of the "New" Takings Clause, 34 Rocky Mtn. Min. L. Inst. 1 (1988). On the question of whether courts "take" property in overruling earlier decisions and altering property rights see Williamson Chang, Unraveling Robinson v. Aroyoshi: Can Courts "Take" Property, 2 U. Haw. L. Rev. 57 (1979); Bradford H. Lamb, Robinson v. Ariyoshi: A Federal Intrusion Upon State Water Law, 17 Envtl. L. 325 (1987); Barton H. Thompson, Jr., Judicial Takings, 76 Va. L. Rev. 1449 (1990).

8. **Critique of *Franco-American Charolaise.*** The principal case is reviewed and critiqued in Frano-American Charolaise: The Never Ending Story, 30 Tulsa L.J. 1 (1994).

Chapter 4

GROUNDWATER

SECTION 1. DOCTRINES

JAMES W. CROSBY, III, A LAYMAN'S GUIDE TO GROUNDWATER HYDROLOGY

Charles E. Corker, Groundwater Law, Management and Administration, National Water Commission, Legal Study No. 6, Chapter II, 38-45, 65, 68-70 (1971).

A. What is Groundwater

[W]e adopt the definition of groundwater employed by Professor William C. Walton (1970, p. 29) in Groundwater Resource Evaluation:

> "Water that exists in the interstices of rocks is called *subsurface water* * * *; that part of subsurface water in interstices completely saturated with water is called groundwater." [Emphasis in original.]

This definition is useful both for its simplicity and because it accurately identifies the bulk of the subsurface water about which managerial and legal decisions are made—most typically the decision either to withdraw or to permit withdrawal of water from the ground or to leave it in the ground available for later withdrawal or discharge. The subsurface water which Walton excludes from his definition of groundwater is * * * water above the zone of saturation, not generally capable of withdrawal through wells but available, in part, to plant life. * * *

To understand the groundwater environment, one needs only to consider the void spaces, or *porosity*, of an accumulation of sand or gravel; or to view the fractures and crevices in the granites or limestones that form the walls of a road cut; or to note the open spaces that occur between the successive lava flows exposed in the walls of a valley. Picture then, the environment that would exist if these unconsolidated or consolidated rock masses were partially submerged beneath water, perhaps by rising waters of a lake or reservoir. The air occupying the different types of openings would be displaced by water which, in the natural setting, would be called groundwater. The upper surface of the water-saturated zone, or the air-water interface, would be called the water table. Should impermeable materials be present at the normal position of the upper surface of the zone of saturation, no water table exists. Groundwater sometimes is confined under pressure between or under impermeable or semi-permeable rocks in much the same manner that water is pressurized in a pipeline network. Water in wells penetrating through impermeable material into the underlying permeable materials may rise above the top of the aquifer or water-bearing formation. Such groundwater is said to be under artesian pressure. The pressure is from gravity, just as is the water the water pressure on a dam impounding water in a surface reservoir.

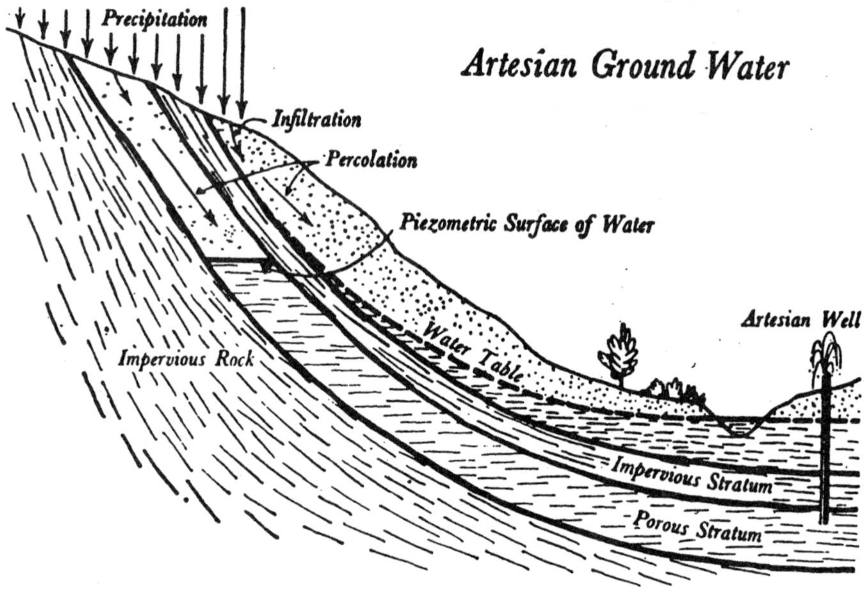

Depending upon the type of rock material saturated, the voids or empty spaces can be expected to range from about one percent to more than 30 percent. At saturation, in other words, such rocks can contain between one and 30 or more percent of their total volume as water. Much of this water might be contained in voids so small that, even given the opportunity, it could never drain out; it would be retained as though the rock were a blotter. Such water would not flow into wells, and hence it could not be extracted from the ground by any normal means.

The capacity of a rock to transmit water through its interconnected pore spaces is called its *permeability*. The capacity of a porous material to store water need have no bearing on its capacity to transmit water. Thus, a clay usually has high porosity but low permeability. On the other hand, an unconsolidated gravel may have both high porosity and high permeability.
* * *

The relatively small size of rock openings and the tortuous nature of the tunnel-like interconnected pore spaces present tremendous frictional resistance to the movement of groundwater. This factor is dominant in establishing the permeability of a porous material. Frictional limitations to flow, coupled with the typically low gradients (or slopes), contribute to the very low flow velocities prevalent in the groundwater environment. Normal flow velocities range from five feet per day to five feet per year. However, velocities as high as 100 feet per day have been reported.

The saturated, permeable earth materials from which significant quantities of water can be produced are called *aquifers*. This term, like permeability, is purely relative and must be considered within the framework of the local hydrogeology. Thus, a farmer drilling a domestic well in the basalts of eastern Washington might consider a well producing a gallon or two per minute a totally successful well. To his neighbor, who needs 500 gallons per minute for irrigation, any lesser quantity is for practical purposes a dry hole. * * *

[W]e must distinguish still further between unconfined (water table) aquifers and confined (artesian) aquifers. The water level in wells penetrating water table aquifers will stand at the level of the water table where the pressure is that of the atmosphere. On the contrary, the water level in an artesian well will stand at the elevation of an imaginary pressure surface, some distance above the aquifer.

When water table wells are pumped, stored waters are removed by physically dewatering the pore spaces, first those in the immediate cone of depression. This is not true for confined conditions. When an artesian well flows or is pumped, a cone of depression is created in the pressure surface but no physical dewatering of aquifer pore volume occurs. The pores remain at full saturation as long as confinement exits, and throughout the confined portion of the aquifer. Waters released from storage are derived entirely from elastic rebound of the aquifer, from expansion of the aquifer skeleton and from expansion of the water. Each of these, in turn, is attributable to the relief of pressure. Because neither rock material nor water is notably compressible it is obvious that the quantities of stored waters made available by their expansion will be small. The amount of water released from storage for each foot of water level decline in the artesian case is much less than for the comparable water table case.

The astute layman will immediately wonder about the circumstance in which the pressure surface of an artesian aquifer drops below the bottom of the confining stratum. Will not physical dewatering of the aquifer then occur? Obviously, yes. When the confining pressure is dissipated, the system reverts to the water table condition and removal of waters from the interstices follows. Associated with this change, the quantity of water available from storage per foot of water level decline increases greatly. However, the pumping lifts also increase to the extent that the pressure head or water level has been reduced.

[A] special class of hydrogeologic conditions are known as perched water bodies and have perched water tables. Perched waters form whenever the conditions of geologic structure and permeability restrict the free gravitational seepage of * * * waters, causing their build-up in local accumulations at elevations above the regional water table. An analogous condition would be presented by a porcelain saucer buried in a tank of sand through which waters are allowed to seep. Some of the downward moving water would be captured by the saucer and would form a suspended zone of saturation.

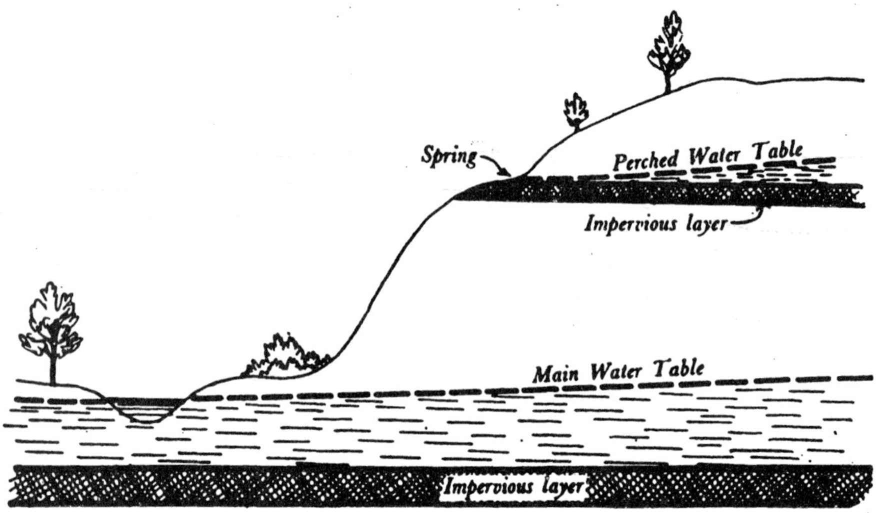

Underground rivers flowing through caverns are rare * * *. However, moving water which is groundwater in one location, surface water in another location, and again groundwater is a very common phenomenon which complicates water "ownership." Nearly all groundwater originates from surface sources and is subject to just such a succession of metamorphoses. Depending upon the fluid circulation pattern, the time sequence can be measured in minutes, days, years, or geologic periods.

Note

Importance of groundwater. Devin L. Galloway et al., U.S. Geological Survey Circular No. 1247, Evolving Issues and Practices in Managing Ground-Water Resources: Case Studies on the Role of Science 1 (2003):

"Ground water is among the Nation's most important natural resources. It is the source of drinking water to more than 140 million residents, or about half of the Nation's population. It is the primary source of drinking water for nearly all of the rural population, as well as for some of our largest metropolitan areas. Nearly 50 billion gallons of ground water are used each day in support of the Nation's agricultural economy. In several midwestern states, ground water provides more than ninety percent of the water used for irrigation. Ground water also plays a crucial role in sustaining streamflow, particularly during droughts and other low-flow periods. Moreover, in recent years, increased attention has been given to the integral role of ground water in maintaining the health of riparian, aquatic, and wetland ecosystems."

STATE v. MICHELS PIPELINE CONSTRUCTION, INC.

Supreme Court of Wisconsin, 1974.
63 Wis. 2d 278, 217 N.W.2d 339.

WILKIE, JUSTICE. This case involves the unrestrained use of percolating ground water to the alleged detriment of owners of neighboring land. In 1972 Michels Pipeline Construction, Inc., contracted with the Metropolitan Sewerage Commission of Milwaukee county to install a 60-inch-diameter sewer in the Root River Parkway, Greenfield, Wisconsin. * * * The complaint alleged that in September of 1972 the defendants began pumping water from wells in the city of Greenfield at a rate of 5,500 gallons per minute in order to dewater the soil to a depth sufficient to permit tunneling for the sewer, approximately 40 feet beneath the ground surface. The complaint alleged that numerous citizens were caused great hardship by the drying up of wells, decreasing capacity and water quality in others, and by the cracking of foundations, basement walls and driveways, due to subsidence of the soil. The State asked that the defendants be ordered to conduct construction of the sewer so as not to create a nuisance and to take action to eliminate or ameliorate the hardship and adverse effect imposed upon state citizens.

The defendants demurred to the complaint on the ground that it did not state facts sufficient to constitute a cause of action. * * *

The trial court granted the demurrer of the defendants-respondents on the basis that the case of Huber v. Merkel[14] established that there is no cause of action for interference with ground water. This is a correct statement of the holding of that case. In Huber v. Merkel an owner of real estate attempted to have another landowner in his vicinity enjoined from wasting and unreasonably using water from artesian wells on the person's property. The defendant allowed his wells to flow continuously, the excess simply spilling on the ground and this adversely affected the artesian pressure of all the wells which tapped the same aquifer. This court held that it was the almost universal consensus of judicial opinion that:

> "* * * If the waters simply percolate through the ground, without definite channel, they belong to the realty in which they are found, and the owner of the soil may divert, consume, or cut them off with impunity. If, on the other hand, the subterranean waters flow in a defined channel, the rules which govern the use of surface streams apply; but the presumption is that the waters are percolating waters until it is shown that they are supplied by a definite, flowing stream."

* * * The basis for this rule of absolute ownership of percolating ground water was a feeling that the ways of underground water were too mysterious and unpredictable to allow the establishment of adequate and fair rules for regulation of competing rights to such water. So the English courts adopted the position that everyone was permitted to take and use all of which they could get possession.

---

14. (1903), 117 Wis. 355, 94 N.W. 354.

In Acton v. Blundell[22] the English courts held the law of surface waters did not apply to percolating ground water because:

> "* * * no man can tell what changes these underground sources have undergone in the progress of time * * * therefore, * * * there can be no ground for implying any mutual consent or agreement, for ages past * * * which is one of the foundations on which the law as to running streams is supposed to be built * * *."

[T]oday scientific knowledge in the field of hydrology has certainly advanced to the point where a cause and effect relationship can be established between a tapping of underground water and the level of the water table in the area so that liability can be fairly adjudicated consonant with due process. Our scientific knowledge also establishes the interdependence of all water systems.

> "* * * The hydrologic cycle traces all existing water from the oceans to the atmosphere, to the land and ultimately back to the oceans. In nature, there is an inseparable relationship between all water, whether in the atmosphere, on the earth's surface, or under the earth's surface."

* * * The Huber v. Merkel case certainly gives no explanation of why a property right in ground water should be an exception to the general maxim—*sic utere tuo ut alienum non laedas*.

Also, although at the time of the decision of Huber v. Merkel the English rule did probably prevail, it was not a common-law rule of venerable, entrenched and ancient origin. The first decisions which enunciated the doctrine were decided in the early 1840's only a short time before Wisconsin achieved statehood. * * *

For the reasons discussed above, we overrule our decision in Huber v. Merkel and for that reason we find it necessary to adopt a rule of law more in harmony with present scientific and legal principles.

What rule should this court now adopt as to the use of percolating ground water? There are three distinct doctrines applied in various American jurisdictions regarding rights in percolating water:

(a) The English or common-law rule:

> "* * * the person who owns the surface may dig therein, and apply all that is there found to his own purposes at his free will and pleasure; and if, in the exercise of such right, he intercepts or drains off the water collected from underground springs in his neighbor's well, this inconvenience to his neighbor falls within the description of damnum absque injuria, which cannot become the ground of an action. * * *"

There is one limitation that the actions may not be motivated by malice and waste of water can be actionable. Although framed in property language this doctrine is really a rule of capture. The landowner may sell and grant his right to withdraw the water to others.

22. (Ex. 1843), 12 Mees. & W. 324, 350, 351, 152 Reprint 1223.

(b) Reasonable Use:

As stated in Corpus Juris Secundum:

"In some states, the rule of the common law followed in early decisions has given way to the doctrine of reasonable use limiting the right of a landowner to percolating water in his land to such an amount of water as may be necessary for some useful or beneficial purpose in connection with the land from which it is taken, not restricting his right to use the water for any useful purpose on his own land, and not restricting his right to use it elsewhere in the absence of proof of injury to adjoining landowners. * * *"

(c) Correlative rights:

Again Corpus Juris Secundum defines this doctrine as:

"Under the rule of correlative rights, the rights of all landowners over a common basin, saturated strata, or underground reservoir are coequal or correlative, and one cannot extract more than his share of the water, even for use on his own land, where others' rights are injured thereby."

In many early cases the two doctrines of reasonable use and correlative rights seem to have been mixed together as the "American rule." However, as Corpus Juris Secundum makes clear, they are two distinct doctrines. According to the appellant's brief only three states adhere to the correlative rights doctrine. This doctrine applies the basic rules of the reasonable use doctrine, but calls for apportionment of underground water where there is not a sufficient supply for all reasonable uses. We are not shown here that water conditions in Wisconsin are so critical as to necessitate the adoption of this doctrine. Also the administrative difficulties of a court trying to make such an apportionment would militate against its adoption.

The "reasonable use" doctrine has been widely adopted in the United States. However, a close reading of the language of the doctrine shows that it is not a very radical departure from the common-law rule. It still contains quite a broad privilege to use ground water. * * * This is because the term "reasonable" has a very special restricted meaning. * * * [A] use of water that causes harm is nevertheless reasonable if it is made in connection with the overlying land. The withdrawal of water for use elsewhere for beneficial purposes such as municipal supply or domestic supply is not "reasonable" in this special sense, but such removal may be made without liability if no harm results.

* * * One may sink a well for domestic use or other use on his land without liability to his neighbors for effects on their wells as long as he acts without malice and is not wasting water to their detriment.

The "reasonable use" rule basically only affords protection from cities withdrawing large quantities of water for municipal utilities. The rule forces cities to pay those affected by such excessive use damages or the cost of new wells and pumping equipment and is very much in accord with policies of loss distribution and requiring the beneficiaries of harmful activities to pay the costs thereof. However, under the rule there is no apportionment of water as between adjoining landowners. If water is withdrawn for a beneficial use on the land from which it is taken there is no liability for any harm to adjoining property owners. In effect, the rule gives partial protection to small wells against cities or water companies, but not protection from a large factory or apartment building on the neighboring land.

We choose not to adopt any of the three rules here discussed, but rather to adopt the rule set forth in Tentative Draft No. 17 of the Restatement of the Law Second, Torts, as proposed on April 26, 1971, for adoption by the American Law Institute. * * *

The proposed section of the Restatement Second reads as follows:

> "Sec. 858A. NON-LIABILITY FOR USE OF GROUND WATER—EXCEPTIONS.
>
> "A possessor of land or his grantee who withdraws ground water from the land and uses it for a beneficial purpose is not subject to liability for interference with the use of water by another, unless
>
> "(a) The withdrawal of water causes unreasonable harm through lowering the water table or reducing artesian pressure, * * *"

Thus the rule preserves the basic expression of a rule of nonliability—a privilege if you will—to use ground water beneath the land. The formulation of the exception to this basic rule recognizes that there is usually enough water for all users so that apportionment is not necessary but that the problem is who shall bear the costs of deepening prior wells, installing pumps, paying increased pumping costs, etc., necessitated by a lowering of the water table by a large user. The common law placed the burden of making improvements on each user. The "reasonable use" rule gives protection to existing wells if the water withdrawal is taken off the land for use elsewhere but not if the water is used for beneficial purposes on the overlying land. The proposed rule of the Restatement Second would place the matter of cost on the same rational basis as the rule applicable to surface streams, the reasonableness of placing the burden upon one party or the other.

The comment on the meaning of "unreasonable harm" as used in the Restatement rule explains that as in other situations, reasonableness will vary with the circumstances. Later users with superior economic resources should not be allowed to impose costs upon smaller water users that are beyond their economic capacity. The comment also address itself to the fear of the respondents that a change in the rule concerning use of percolating water will allow the first user to dictate the depth of wells and the water table to all later users. The comment explains that it is usually reasonable to give equal treatment to persons similarly situated and to place similar burdens on each.

In adopting the rule proposed in the Restatement of Torts, we necessarily overrule the order of the trial court sustaining the demurrer here, and we remand for further proceedings in the trial court.

Notes

1. **Absolute ownership doctrine.** The English doctrine of absolute ownership survives in some eastern states and Texas. The Maine Supreme Court

refused to depart from the doctrine in Maddocks v. Giles, 728 A.2d 150 (Me. 1999). The court gave several reasons: the Maddockses had not shown that the absolute ownership doctrine interfered with water use in the state or resulted in unwise water policy; they had not persuaded the court that it, rather than the state legislature, "should be weighing the heavy policy considerations involved in this issue, not the least of which is the reliance of land owners on the present property laws"; and the legislature recently had chosen not to act on the recommendation of a study it commissioned that urged it to adopt reasonable use principles.

Texas has long supplemented the absolute ownership doctrine with legislation, repeatedly modified, providing for local groundwater conservation districts. For decades, few districts were created, and those that did exist had limited powers and engaged in little groundwater management. In 1997, the Texas Legislature enacted Senate Bill 1 to facilitate creating local districts in areas anticipated to experience groundwater problems, to require permits from districts for large wells, and to give districts authority to regulate water transfers outside their boundaries.

In Sipriano v. Great Spring Waters of America, Inc., 1 S.W.3d 75, 78-80 (Tex. 1999), the Texas Supreme Court rejected an argument that it should replace the absolute ownership doctrine with the reasonable use doctrine:

"[I]t is important that this case comes to us on the heels of Senate Bill 1 * * *. [There] the Legislature expressly stated that '[g]roundwater conservation districts * * * are the state's preferred method of groundwater management.' * * * [B]y Senate Bill 1 the Legislature has chosen a process that permits the people most affected by groundwater regulation in particular areas to participate in democratic solutions to their groundwater issues. It would be improper for courts to intercede at this time by changing the common-law framework within which the Legislature has attempted to craft regulations to meet this state's groundwater-conservation needs. Given the Legislature's recent actions to improve Texas's groundwater management, we are reluctant to make so drastic a change as abandoning our rule of capture and moving into the arena of water-use regulation by judicial fiat. It is more prudent to wait and see if Senate Bill 1 will have its desired effect, and to save for another day the determination of whether further revising the common law is an appropriate prerequisite to preserve Texas's natural resources and protect property owners' interests."

In 2001, the Legislature enacted Senate Bill 2 to strengthen the regulatory powers of local groundwater conservation districts. For example, districts may regulate the spacing of wells and limit groundwater production based on tract size to minimize well interference, prevent land subsidence, protect water quality, and minimize as far as practicable the drawdown of a water table or reduction of artesian pressure. Tex. Water Code Ann. § 36.116. Senate Bill 2 addresses conflict between rights under the absolute ownership doctrine and conservation district regulation by stating that landowners' rights in groundwater "are hereby recognized * * * except as those rights may be limited or altered by rules promulgated by a district." § 36.002.

2. **Reasonable use doctrine.** *Michels Pipeline* reported that the reasonable use doctrine has been widely adopted in the United States. This statement is more of eastern states than western states.

In Arizona, the state supreme court reaffirmed its longstanding adherence to the reasonable use doctrine in In re General Adjudication of All Rights to Use

Water in Gila River System, 857 P.2d 1236 (Ariz. 1993), but a 1980 groundwater management act supplanted the doctrine in large parts of the state designated as groundwater management areas. See infra p. 368, Note 1. Even in the parts of Arizona where the doctrine still applies, there have been significant statutory modifications, e.g., to allow freer transportation of water and generally prohibit irrigation of new overlying acreage in Irrigation Non-Expansion Areas. Ariz. Rev. Stat. §§ 45-437, -453, -544.

Many cases adopting the reasonable use doctrine are titled "_____ v. City of ______." Why?

3. **Correlative rights doctrine.** The leading correlative rights state is California, where the doctrine traces back to Katz v. Walkinshaw, 74 P. 766, 772 (Cal. 1903):

"The controversies arising will naturally divide into classes. There will be disputes between persons or corporations claiming rights to take such waters from the same strata or source for use on distant lands. There is no statute on this subject, as there now is concerning appropriations of surface streams; but the case is not without precedent. * * * The principles which, before the adoption of the Civil Code, were applied to protect appropriations and possessory rights in visible streams, will, in general, be found applicable to such appropriations of percolating waters, either for public or private use, and will suffice for their protection as against other appropriators. Such rights are usufructuary only, and the first taker who with diligence puts the water in use will have the better right. * * * In controversies between an appropriator for use on distant land and those who own land overlying the water-bearing strata, there may be two classes of such landowners—those who have used the water on their land before the attempt to appropriate, and those who have not previously used it, but who claim the right afterwards to do so. Under the decision in this case the rights of the first class of landowners are paramount to that of one who takes the water to distant land, but the landowner's right extends only to the quantity of water that is necessary for use on his land, and the appropriator may take the surplus. As to those landowners who begin the use after the appropriation, and who, in order to obtain the water, must restrict or restrain the diversion to distant lands or places, it is perhaps best not to state a positive rule. Such rights are limited at most to the quantity necessary for use, and the disputes will not be so serious as those between rival appropriators. Disputes between overlying landowners, concerning water for use on the land, to which they have an equal right, in cases where the supply is insufficient for all, are to be settled by giving to each a fair and just proportion. And here again we leave for future settlement the question as to the priority of rights between such owners who begin the use of the waters at different times. The parties interested in the question are not before us."

The California Supreme Court soon supplied the two rankings missing from *Katz*. In Burr v. Maclay Rancho Water Co., 98 P. 260 (Cal. 1908), it held that an overlying landowner who has not yet used groundwater on the land can obtain a declaratory judgment to protect the paramount right to do so as against an appropriator who has previously put the water to use. In Hudson v. Dailey, 105 P. 748 (Cal. 1909), it said without mentioning priority of use that the rights of overlying landowners are equal and correlative. Among overlying owners, however, uncertainty remains about the specifics of what *Katz* called a "fair and just proportion" for each.

An overlying city's withdrawal for municipal supply is not a correlative right but an appropriation; the city does not become substituted as administrator of the rights of its inhabitants owning overlying land. City of San Bernadino v. City of Riverside, 198 P. 784 (Cal. 1921).

4. **Judicial mixing of the reasonable use and correlative rights doctrines and legislative modification.** *Michels Pipeline* noted that many early cases seemed to mix together the reasonable use and correlative rights doctrines. It is a matter of interpretation whether the courts in some states adhere more to the one doctrine or the other.

Courts sometimes have interjected notions that shortages should be shared under a rule of correlative rights into cases that did not require an apportionment. See Jones v. Oz-Ark-Val Poultry Co., 306 S.W.2d 111 (Ark. 1957); Erickson v. Crookston Waterworks Power & Light Co., 117 N.W. 435 (Minn. 1908); Higday v. Nickolaus, 469 S.W.2d 859 (Mo. Ct. App. 1971); Meeker v. City of East Orange, 74 A. 379 (N.J. 1909); Eva H. Hanks & John L. Hanks, The Law of Water in New Jersey: Groundwater, 24 Rutgers L. Rev. 621, 639 (1970).

In MacArtor v. Graylyn Crest III Swim Club, Inc., 187 A.2d 417 (Del. Ch. 1963), a large well that supplied the club's swimming pool lowered the water table below a neighboring householder's shallow well. Apparently both parties were overlying users. Applying what it called the "doctrine of reasonable use," the court said the club's abnormally large withdrawal compared to the householder's domestic use "was not unqualifiedly reasonable," and it required the club to share equally in the cost of deepening the householder's well.

According to dicta in Olson v. City of Wahoo, 248 N.W. 304 (Neb. 1933), the Nebraska rule combines the doctrine of reasonable use on overlying land and the correlative rights principle that "if the natural underground supply is insufficient for all owners, each is entitled to a reasonable proportion of the whole." This rule is modified by legislation creating a preference for domestic use over all other uses and for agricultural use over manufacturing and industrial uses. Neb. Rev. Stat. § 46-613; Prather v. Eisenmann, 261 N.W.2d 766 (Neb. 1978). It is further modified by legislation that authorizes groundwater use on nonoverlying in certain circumstances for agricultural or environmental remediation purposes, Neb. Rev. Stat. § 46-691, authorizes public water suppliers to transport water for use on nonoverlying land, § 46-638(1), and provides for natural resources districts with broad water and related land management powers over entire basins, §§ 2-3203, -3229. Each district must prepare a groundwater management plan, "including a proposed ground water reservoir life goal for the district." § 46-656.12. Districts can limit withdrawals, adopt well spacing requirements, and impose rotation of use. See Bamford v. Upper Republican Natural Res. Dist., 512 N.W.2d 642 (Neb. 1994) (upholding district regulations limiting the amount of groundwater that can be used per acre for irrigation).

5. **Restatement.** Proposed Restatement (Second) of Torts § 858A set forth in part in *Michels Pipeline* was revised by the American Law Institute and became Official Draft § 858.[a]

"§ 858. Liability for Use of Ground Water

"(1) A proprietor of land or his grantee who withdraws ground water from the land and uses it for a beneficial purpose is not subject to liability for interference with the use of water by another, unless

---

a. Copyright 1979. Reprinted with the permission of the American Law Institute.

"(a) the withdrawal of ground water unreasonably causes harm to a proprietor of neighboring land through lowering the water table or reducing artesian pressure,

"(b) the withdrawal of ground water exceeds the proprietor's reasonable share of the annual supply or total store of ground water, or

"(c) the withdrawal of the ground water has a direct and substantial effect upon a watercourse or lake and unreasonably causes harm to a person entitled to the use of its water.

"(2) The determination of liability under clauses (a), (b) and (c) of Subsection (1) is governed by the principles stated in §§ 850 to 857."

The official comment to section 858 elaborates as follows: A "grantee" is one to whom a proprietor has assigned the right to extract groundwater; the grantee need not acquire the overlying land. Clause (1)(a) protects owners of small wells using water on overlying land against harm from large municipal or industrial wells supplying water to nonoverlying lands (making it, in this respect, like the common law reasonable use doctrine). Clause (1)(a) also extends protection to owners of small wells against harm from unreasonably large wells supplying water for use on overlying lands (making it, in this respect, unlike the common law reasonable use doctrine). Subsection 2, by referencing §§ 850-857, incorporates the reasonableness concept of riparian law for surface waters. Subsection 2 thus rejects what *Michels Pipeline* called the "very special restricted meaning" of reasonableness under the common law reasonable use doctrine for groundwater.

Section 858 was followed in Maerz v. United States Steel Corp., 323 N.W.2d 524 (Mich. Ct. App. 1982), and Cline v. American Aggregates Corp., 474 N.E.2d 324 (Ohio 1984). It was rejected in favor of continued adherence to the absolute ownership doctrine in Maddocks v. Giles, supra Note 1, and Wiggins v. Braz. Coal & Clay Corp., 452 N.E.2d 958 (Ind. 1983).

6. **Underground streams.** The *Michels Pipeline* opinion begins by noting that the case involved percolating groundwater. That statement relates to a distinction in the common law between percolating groundwater and underground streams. The common law doctrines discussed in *Michels Pipeline*—absolute ownership, reasonable use, and correlative rights—apply only to percolating groundwater. In contrast, underground streams are governed by the common law doctrine that a state applies to surface streams, whether that be the riparian doctrine or the appropriation doctrine. Pima Farms Co. v. Proctor, 245 P. 369 (Ariz. 1926); Verdugo Canon Water Co. v. Verdugo, 93 P. 1021 (Cal. 1908).

Like a surface stream, an underground stream must have a bed and banks and a current of water. This usually means only that the groundwater must be in a narrow confined aquifer, not that it must flow freely in a cavernous opening. At the same time, however, most states rebuttably presume underground waters are percolating. Woodsum v. Township of Pemberton, 412 A.2d 1064 (N.J. Super. Ct. Law Div. 1980). One form of an underground stream is the subflow of a surface stream, which is water beneath the stream that supports it or feeds it and moves generally in a direction corresponding with the surface flow. Montecito Valley Water Co. v. City of Santa Barbara, 77 P. 1113 (Cal. 1904); City of Los Angeles v. Pomeroy, 57 P. 585 (1899).

The division of groundwater into underground streams and percolating waters ignores physical reality and has been criticized on the ground that although hydrogeological fictions may have some utility, they do more harm than good because the law cannot develop rationally when so divorced from actuality. Charles E. Corker, Groundwater Law, Management and Administration, Nat'l Water Comm'n, Legal Study No. 6, at 147 (1971).

STATE ex rel. BLISS v. DORITY

Supreme Court of New Mexico, 1950.

55 N.M. 12, 225 P.2d 1007.

BRICE, CHIEF JUSTICE. The State of New Mexico, upon relation of its State Engineer John H. Bliss, brought separate suits against Bert Troy Dority, Loman Wiley and S. A. Lanning, Jr., the purpose of which was to enjoin the respective defendants from unlawfully using for irrigating lands, waters drawn from what is known as the Roswell Artesian Basin, and the valley fill above it, which plaintiff asserts under Ch. 131, N.M.L. 1931, 1941 Comp. § 77-1101 et seq., are subject to appropriation as provided therein. * * *

Defendants' lands are situated in Chaves County, New Mexico, and are located within the external boundaries of two underground water sources, one of which is an artesian basin lying between confining strata, the waters of which are commonly referred to as artesian water; and the other, plaintiff asserts, is an underground reservoir or lake in the valley fill overlying such artesian basin, the waters of which are commonly referred to as shallow ground water. About 45,000 acres are irrigated from shallow ground water and 55,000 acres from artesian water.

[T]he plaintiff asserts that the defendant Dority is irrigating 96.7 acres of land illegally, in that he has not been granted the right to so use the water; that the defendant Wiley was in like manner illegally using water to irrigate 48.7 acres of land; and the defendant Lanning was illegally using water to irrigate 120 acres. The defendants admit that they have been using, and will continue to use, the water without a permit unless enjoined from so doing. They deny that their use of it is in violation of law. The principal contention is that the New Mexico statutes providing for the appropriation of sub-surface water is unconstitutional upon several grounds stated.

The statutes of New Mexico declaring that the artesian and shallow ground water from which defendants obtained the water to irrigate their land belongs to the public and providing for their appropriation for beneficial use, are as follows:

> "The waters of underground streams, channels, artesian basins, reservoirs, or lakes, having reasonably ascertainable boundaries, are hereby declared to be public waters and to belong to the public and to be subject to appropriation for beneficial use."
>
> * * *
>
> "Any person, firm or corporation desiring to appropriate for irrigation or industrial uses any of the waters described in this act shall make application to the state engineer * * *."
>
> "Existing water rights based upon application to beneficial use are hereby recognized. Nothing herein contained is intended to impair the same or to disturb the priorities thereof."
>
> "Any person using or appropriating water without a permit, contrary to the provisions of * * * section 77-1103 of the New Mexico Statutes

* * * shall be guilty of a misdemeanor and, on conviction thereof in any court of competent jurisdiction, shall be punished * * *."

The state engineer has the jurisdiction and authority to determine the boundaries of any of the underground waters declared to be public waters, and no judicial determination is necessary to the jurisdiction given him by the laws in question.

No right to the use of water from such sources was obtained by its use by defendants in violation of law, nor can it be. The statutory manner of securing such rights is exclusive. * * *

The principal question raised is whether the Act of 1931, which we have quoted, that declared the ownership of the waters in question to be in the public, violates the 14th Amendment to the Constitution of the United States and Sec. 18 of Art. 2 of the Constitution of New Mexico, in that it authorizes the state to deprive its citizens and others of their property without due process of law, and denies them the equal protection of the laws; and violates Sec. 20 of Art. 2 of the Constitution of New Mexico in that it authorizes the taking of private property for public use without just compensation.

The whole argument is based on the assumption that the water described in Sec. 1 of the Act of 1931 belongs to the owners of the overlying land. Each of the defendants claims that the underground water under his land is his property acquired through mesne conveyances from the United States, beginning with the patent from the Government and that such patent and mesne conveyances transferred to him the water underlying the land conveyed. In other words, that the common law, or at least the law of correlative rights in such waters, is the law of this state. * * * The substance of the contention of each of the appellants is that he has a vested interest in the title to the water under his lands, to the center of the earth, of which he cannot be deprived by any legislative act.

This question was settled by this court in Yeo v. Tweedy, [286 P. 970 (N.M. 1929)]. It was held in that case that the title to the water described in Sec. 1 of the 1931 Act belonged to the public and was subject to appropriation for beneficial uses. * * * It was stated in Yeo v. Tweedy that Sec. 1 of Ch. 182, N.M.L. 1927, almost identical with the 1931 Act, had always been the law in this jurisdiction. [Yeo v. Tweedy invalidated the nearly identical 1927 groundwater act because of a technical defect in the legislative process by which it was passed.]

There is another consideration which requires the affirmance of the trial court's decree. The decision of Yeo v. Tweedy, supra, has become a rule of property. In the nineteen years since that decision it may be assumed that many thousands of acres of the one hundred thousand irrigated with water from the Roswell Artesian basin and the valley fill have been sold to purchasers who relied on that decision as determining title to the right to use the water here involved, and the water rights to which would be injured or destroyed if Yeo v. Tweedy is overruled. Whether it stated the correct rule of law (and we are of the opinion that it did), it is now a rule of property that we will not disturb. * * *

The patents to defendants' lands carried no right to the use of water, except as to that actually applied to the reclaiming of land * * * and not thereafter abandoned. All other water belonged to the State as trustee for the public. * * *

The decree of the district court is affirmed, and it is so ordered.

Notes

1. **Legislative adoption of the appropriation doctrine.** Twelve western states now have appropriation doctrine legislation for groundwater. Generally these states apply that doctrine to all groundwater, thus avoiding the false dichotomy in the common law between underground streams and percolating groundwater. Some of them have a separate code for groundwater. Idaho Code §§ 42-226 to -239; Nev. Rev. Stat. 534.010-.350; N.M. Stat. Ann. §§ 72-12-1 to -28; Or. Rev. Stat. §§ 537.505-.796; S.D. Codified Laws Ann. §§ 46-6-1 to -31; Wash. Rev. Code §§ 90.44.020-.450; Wyo. Stat. Ann. §§ 41-3-901 to -938. The others have a single code for surface water and groundwater. Alaska Stat. §§ 46.15.010-.270; Kan. Stat. Ann. §§ 82a-701 to -734; Mont. Code Ann. §§ 85-2-101 to -520; N.D. Cent. Code §§ 61-01-01, 61-04-01 to -04-32; Utah Code Ann. §§ 73-3-1 to -29.

The state codes typically require a permit to appropriate groundwater. New Mexico still does not require a permit, however, for wells in basins not declared by the state engineer to have reasonably ascertainable boundaries. N.M. Stat. Ann. § 72-12-20. A common permit exemption, found in practically every water code, exists for small domestic wells. This exemption apparently derives from the premise that it is not worth the time and trouble to require a permit for uses that appear to be de minimis. That premise is challenged in Robert Jerome Glennon & Thomas Maddock, III, The Concept of Capture: The Hydrology and Law of Stream/Aquifer Interactions, 43 Rocky Mtn. Min. L. Inst. 22-1 (1997), where the authors report the existence of almost two and one-half million domestic wells in western states many of which probably are in close proximity to rivers. They argue: "It is not sound policy to address the problem of large capacity groundwater wells interfering with surface flow and at the same time exempt small capacity wells which, cumulatively, may have an equally dramatic effect. The exemption of small domestic wells is a loophole of significant proportion that the states need to eliminate."

2. **Constitutionality of appropriation doctrine legislation.** Knight v. Grimes, 127 N.W.2d 708 (S.D. 1964), took a more direct approach than *Dority* to the constitutionality of superimposing a groundwater appropriation statute upon the rule of absolute ownership of percolating waters. South Dakota had recognized the absolute ownership doctrine by statute since territorial days, and the court acknowledged that the new appropriation statute invaded a pre-existing right or interest. Nonetheless, the court ruled that the legislature was fully justified in finding that the public welfare requires maximum protection and utilization of the water supply, and that the police power permitted adoption of a statute imposing regulations that are not unreasonable or arbitrary. The new statute validated existing groundwater uses and abolished only unexercised absolute ownership rights.

See also Baumann v. Smrha, 145 F. Supp. 617, 624-25 (D. Kan.), aff'd mem., 352 U.S. 863 (1956), upholding a Kansas statute adopting the appropriation doctrine for groundwater that validated existing groundwater uses and adversely affected only unexercised rights: "[W]e do not regard a landowner as having a vested right in underground waters underlying his land which he has not appropriated and applied to beneficial use." Compare statutory abolition of unexercised riparian rights in streams, *Franco-American*, supra p. 313 and accompanying Notes.

3. **Colorado groundwater law.** Colorado avoids the common law false dichotomy between underground streams and percolating groundwater but instead uses a unique scheme that recognizes four categories: tributary groundwater, designated groundwater, nontributary groundwater outside of a designated basin, and Denver Basin groundwater. Colorado Groundwater Comm'n v. N. Kiowa-Bijou Groundwater Mgmt. Dist., 77 P.3d 62 (Colo. 2003).

a. Tributary groundwater. This is groundwater that is tributary to a surface stream. It is administered as part of the stream under the appropriation doctrine. Water Right Determination and Administration Act, Colo. Rev. Stat. §§ 37-92-101 to -602. Tributary groundwater was involved in Cache La Poudre Water Users Ass'n v. Glacier View Meadows, supra p. 75, where new wells were approved for operation under augmentation plans designed to avoid injury to senior surface appropriations. Tributary groundwater also was involved in Alamosa-La Jara Water Users Protection Ass'n v. Gould, infra p. 396.

b. Designated groundwater. This is groundwater located within the boundaries of a basin that has been designated by the Colorado Groundwater Commission. Generally designated basins are in the eastern plains of the state. In addition to being in such basin, the groundwater (i) must not be available to and required to fill surface rights or (ii) must be in areas not adjacent to a natural stream wherein groundwater withdrawals have constituted the principal water usage for fifteen years prior to the first hearing on proposed designation of the basin. Colo. Rev. Stat. § 37-90-103(6)(a). Designated groundwater is administered under appropriation principles "modified to permit the full economic development of designated ground water resources." § 37-90-102(1). Designated groundwater was involved in Fundingsland v. Colorado Ground Water Commission, infra p. 347.

c. Nontributary groundwater outside of a designated basin. This is groundwater "located outside the boundaries of any designated basins * * *, the withdrawal of which will not, within one hundred years, deplete the flow of a natural stream * * * at an annual rate greater than one-tenth of one percent of the annual rate of withdrawal." Colo. Rev. Stat. § 37-90-103(10.5). It is administered under a version of the reasonable use doctrine that allows withdrawals by overlying owners based on an aquifer life of 100 years. § 137-90-137(4).

d. Denver Basin groundwater. The Denver Basin underlies the most populous area of the state, extending from the foothills west of Denver eastward for fifty miles or more to Limon, and from near Greeley on the north to Colorado Springs on the south. The basin contains four deep, mostly confined, aquifers that lie one under another. Some of the groundwater in the Denver Basin aquifers is within a designated groundwater basin; some is not. Either way, unless the groundwater is tributary to a surface stream, it is allocated based on overlying land ownership and an aquifer life of 100 years. §§ 37-90-137(4)(b)(I), (II), 37-90-111(5). To determine whether Denver Basin groundwater is tributary or nontributary, the one-hundred-year/one-tenth-of-one-percent depletion standard noted above is used, but the standard is applied in a relaxed way that fictionally expands the waters regarded as nontributary. Colo. Ground Water Comm'n v. N. Kiowa-Bijou Ground Water Mgmt. Dist., 77 P.3d 62, 73 (2003). Furthermore, even if the relaxed depletion standard is exceeded, the groundwater is not treated as tributary and administered under the appropriation doctrine if it is located outside of a designated basin. Rather, it is classified as "not nontributary" and administered on the basis of land ownership as if it were nontributary provided an augmentation plan is devised to avoid injury to surface water rights. Colo. Rev.

Stat. § 37-90-103(10.7); N. Kiowa-Bijou Groundwater Mgmt.Dist., 77 P.3d at 73-74.

4. **Permits in nonappropriation states.** Appropriation doctrine states are not the only ones that require permits. A number of other states now have legislation requiring permits. As in appropriation doctrine states, some of these codes apply only to groundwater while others apply to both surface water and groundwater. See A. Dan Tarlock, Law of Water Rights and Resources §§ 4:30 to -:31 (2003).

5. **Regulation of wells.** Most states have statutes that require the capping, casing, and controlling of artesian wells and that control well specifications and license well drillers.

6. **Geothermal energy.** Geothermal energy is heat that occurs in the earth's interior. Most geothermal resources in the United States are located in western states. One method of utilizing geothermal energy is to extract naturally occurring geothermal fluids (steam or heated water) through a well. Some states treat geothermal resources as groundwater, some treat them as minerals, and some treat them as sui generis. Laura MacGregor Bettis, Comment, In Hot Water: Can Idaho's Ground Water Laws Adequately Govern Low Temperature Geothermal Resources?, 39 Idaho L. Rev. 113 (2002).

SECTION 2. PROBLEMS

PHYSICAL DIFFERENCES BETWEEN GROUNDWATER AND SURFACE WATER

Groundwater and surface water differ markedly in physical occurrence. Four differences particularly affect groundwater law and should be borne in mind as the materials in this section are studied.

First, groundwater is hidden from sight. The physical characteristics of an aquifer are not visible, and the effects of pumping cannot easily be observed. The science of hydrology has made great progress in understanding the principles that determine groundwater behavior. Typically, however, it is necessary to monitor existing wells and to drill and monitor additional wells over a broad geographical area for an extended period before these principles can be applied to a particular aquifer. Because this process is expensive and time consuming, adequate data are often unavailable. This is reflected in the lawyer's adage that in groundwater litigation, the person with the burden of proof loses. The advent of computers has enabled the construction of models in which the physical characteristics of a groundwater system are translated into mathematical language and the effects of groundwater withdrawals can be simulated. Groundwater modeling is discussed in Robert E. Schween & Steven P. Larson, Groundwater Modeling: Capabilities and Limitations, Use and Abuse, 32 Rocky Mtn. Min. L. Inst. 22-1 (1986). As one court observed, however, these models are "vulnerable to 'garbage in, garbage out,' that is, computer computations [are] only as good as the validity of the data supplied." Sorensen v. Lower Niobrara Natural Res. Dist., 376 N.W.2d 539, 543 (Neb. 1985). Consequently, the uncertainties in a particular situation can remain substantial due to inadequate data about the physical system.

Second, surface streams are primarily a flow resource. Annual water use is limited by the streamflow in a given year, except for possible carryover storage in reservoirs that is often modest relative to total streamflow. In contrast, the water available in most aquifers consists of both annual recharge and water accumulated in significant quantity over many years. Annual groundwater use is not physically limited to annual recharge when significant accumulated storage is available. The ratio of average annual recharge to accumulated storage varies from one aquifer to another, but overall for the forty-eight contiguous states, average annual recharge totals perhaps one billion acre-feet while the groundwater supply that can be withdrawn with modern technology totals about forty-six billion acre-feet. Nat'l Water Comm'n, Water Policies for the Future 230 (1973). The presence in aquifers of large quantities of accumulated storage available for withdrawal presents opportunities, creates problems, and raises policy issues not arising with surface streams.

Third, because groundwater is below the surface, wells must be drilled and often pumps must be installed if the water is to be used. The expense associated with groundwater use varies directly with the depth at which it is available. Although the legal issue of protecting a water user's means of diversion can arise with surface streams, see Chapter 2, Section G, this issue tends to be more prominent with groundwater.

Fourth, groundwater flows much more slowly than surface water. As noted in the excerpt from Crosby, supra p. 325, normal flow velocities for groundwater range from five feet per day to five feet per year. In contrast, the North Platte River was reported in State ex rel. Cary v. Cochran, 292 N.W. 239 (Neb. 1940), to be flowing at the rate of twenty-five miles per day. The physical effects of pumping groundwater may spread outward from a well more rapidly that the groundwater flow velocity itself. See, e.g., Dist. 10 Water Users Ass'n v. Barnett, 599 P.2d 894 (Colo. 1979) (recounting expert testimony that pumping groundwater tributary to a stream from a particular well would affect the streamflow in 40 years, while the groundwater if left undisturbed would take about 171 years to proceed from the location of the well to the stream). Nonetheless, it typically takes much longer for groundwater pumping to adversely affect other users from the supply than for a surface stream diversion to affect downstream users. Similarly, when an adverse impact is occurring, closure of the interfering well typically takes much longer to restore the supply to the other users than is true of closure of a surface stream diversion. Time lag complicates groundwater management.

A. Managing Storage: Mining, Safe Yield, and Related Concepts

JAMES W. CROSBY, III, A LAYMAN'S GUIDE TO GROUNDWATER HYDROLOGY

Charles E. Corker, Groundwater Law, Management and Administration, National Water Commission, Legal Study No. 6, Chapter II, 56-67, 68, 72-74 (1971).

C. Where Does Groundwater Come From?

For all practical purposes, the origin of groundwater can be regarded as meteoric, meaning that it comes from the atmosphere. There is also water derived from sources within the earth which is not associated with the hydrologic cycle but which may accrue from geologic processes. While the subject has not been without controversy, the consensus of professional opinion is that such water is not added in useful quantify and quality. The important sources of groundwater are:

1. Precipitation

This is indirectly the source of all fresh groundwater, except for the water just mentioned, and directly the source of much groundwater. Much of the precipitation falling on the earth's surface infiltrates the soil zone where it is utilized by plants and satisfies the capillary requirements (soil moisture deficiency) of the soil. Infiltrating precipitation in excess of these requirements tends to move downward through the zone of aeration under the influence of gravity until it reaches the water table. Some of the excess precipitation moves directly or indirectly by flow over the land surface to streams, from which it may, in part, move into a groundwater body.

2. Stream Flow

Surface streams are sometimes classified as gaining streams or losing streams (or, in the language of the technologist, effluent streams or influent streams, respectively). That is, they acquire water from or lose water to the groundwater body, depending on whether the stream is incised below or elevated above the water table. * * *

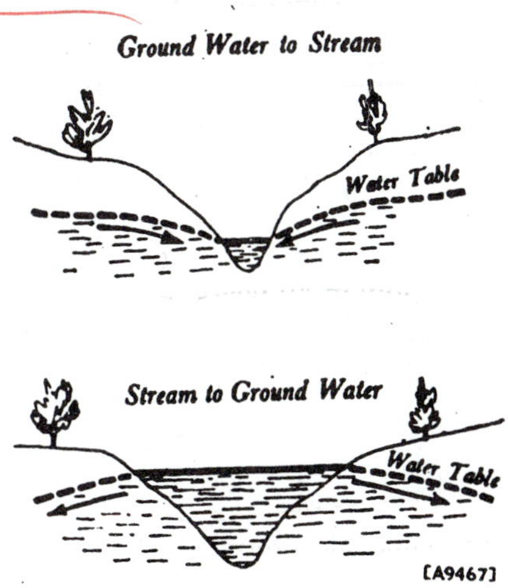

3. Return Flow to Groundwater

Most diversions of groundwater for use are not totally consumed and may return, in part, to some groundwater aquifer. Because irrigation is the major consumptive use of groundwater, it warrants special attention. Depending upon the physical setting and the quantity of groundwater pumped for irrigation, as much as half the diversion, including that of local surface waters, may also contribute return flow to the groundwater resource. Surface waters often are imported in tremendous quantities for irrigation and substantial percentages ultimately accrue to groundwater. The large available quantities of return flow of sewage in urban areas have prompted their ever increasing use, after treatment, in artificial groundwater recharge. In these operations soil mechanisms are called upon to further upgrade partially treated sewage. Any, or all, of these return flows can be important sources of recharge to a given groundwater basin. * * *

4. Artificial Recharge

Water may be imported to a drainage basin or existing basin waters may be allocated for the express purpose of storage underground. Or this storage may be an incidental and, ordinarily, welcomed circumstance, even when not undertaken for the specific purpose. Groundwater recharge may be induced or facilitated by spreading over areas of high infiltration capacity or by injection into deep wells under pressure. * * *

D. How is Groundwater Discharged?

Groundwater does not cease its movement after reaching an underground reservoir or aquifer. However, in rare instances groundwater may reach a closed basin from which no outflow other than evapotranspiration is possible. Such basins must be lower than all possible avenues of outflow or isolated by impermeable geologic barriers. Otherwise, groundwater is eventually discharged to the surface. The rate of movement varies widely, depending on the permeability of the underground material and the slope of the water table or hydraulic gradient. Discharge can occur by natural or artificial means or a combination of both.

1. Natural Discharge

Outflow of groundwater by seepage to lakes, streams, and oceans has already been described. Outflow visibly concentrated in a single location is a spring. Groundwater near enough to the surface to be penetrated by roots of plants is consumed by natural processes of evaporation and transpiration and loss to the atmosphere. * * *

Springs, like surface streams, flow under the influence of gravity. A spring is formed at a point of natural groundwater discharge from an aquifer. Such discharges occur where the land surface intersects a perched or general water table, usually in a valley wall or a hillside slope. More rarely springs are formed where fractures or similar openings in the earth intersect and release confined, or artesian, waters. Hydraulic head, or potential, induced by gravity produces the outflow in all but a few rare spring types characterized by thermal driving mechanisms.

2. Artificial Discharge

Water is produced from underground aquifers by wells which are dug, drilled, or bored. * * *

3. Interconnecting Aquifers

Within any groundwater basin some natural communication between the individual aquifers can be expected under undisturbed conditions. Transfer of water between aquifers can be increased when wells are drilled which penetrate two or more water-bearing zones. Such transfers can be controlled by casing requirements for each well. Failure to provide such controls usually results in dewatering of the upper aquifers and the "drying up" of shallow water supplies. * * *

F. What is the Nature of Groundwater Storage

An unconfined aquifer may be viewed as an underground reservoir. As with a surface reservoir, one important characteristic of an aquifer is the quantity of withdrawable water which it contains. Still more pertinent is the amount of water that can be withdrawn from storage for each foot of water-level decline. Another characteristic is the capacity of the reservoir to contain water, regardless of whether at a given time it is full, partly full, or empty. In an unconfined groundwater reservoir capacity to store water is a function of the volume of the water-bearing materials, and the percentage of those materials which consist of voids or spaces capable of receiving water. * * *

The water remaining in storage at a given time is a resultant of the extent to which portions of the water-bearing material have been dewatered. It can be estimated from driller's and geophysical well logs, from depths to groundwater in various portions of the aquifer, and from comparative quantities of inflow and outflow. Available storage capacity of an aquifer can change with time and further complicate storage calculations. As water-bearing sediments are dewatered, they tend to undergo compaction, which reduces pore volume. Recharge may or may not restore some or all of the lost storage capacity lost by compaction.

Notes

1. **Aquifer equilibrium, capture, and storage reduction.** Under natural conditions, water in an aquifer moves slowly from areas of recharge to areas or points of discharge. Over millennia, the aquifer achieves a state of equilibrium in which the average natural recharge over a climatic cycle approximately equals the natural discharge. The introduction of wells disrupts the natural equilibrium in one or more of three ways, as explained by the following definition of the hydrologic term "capture" in S.W. Lohman et al., U.S. Geological Survey, Water-Supply Paper No. 1988, Definitions of Selected Groundwater Terms—Revisions and Conceptual Refinements 3 (1972) (citations omitted): "Water withdrawn artificially from an aquifer is derived from a decrease in storage in the aquifer, a reduction in the previous discharge from the aquifer, an increase in the recharge, or a combination of these changes. The decrease in discharge plus the increase in recharge is termed *capture*. Capture may occur in the form of decreases in the ground-water discharge into streams, lakes, and the ocean, or from decreases in that component of evapotranspiration derived from the saturated zone." Capture is a key concept in the management of groundwater storage because withdrawals by wells in excess of capture will reduce storage.

An analogy is used to clarify how pumping disrupts aquifer equilibrium in Robert Jerome Glennon & Thomas Maddock, III, The Concept of Capture: The Hydrology and Law of Stream/Aquifer Interactions, 43 Rocky Mtn. Min. L. Inst. 22-1, 22-11 to -12 (1997): Suppose you are a consumer whose income and expenditures are equal (groundwater recharge and discharge are in equilibrium). You decide to purchase a new Porsche (extract water by wells). You have three options to cover the payments: increase your income by moonlighting (increase recharge), decrease your expenditures by foregoing fancy restaurants (decrease discharge), or withdraw money from your savings (reduce storage).

The effects over time of continued groundwater pumping are explained in U.S. Geological Survey, Water-Supply Paper 2250, National Water Summary 1983—Hydrologic Events and Issues 36 (1984):

"As water is withdrawn from storage, ground-water levels decline; this in turn causes a reduction in the natural discharge to streams, to the sea, or to evapotranspiration, and may sometimes also bring about increases in recharge. As natural discharge diminishes and as recharge increases, the amount of water that must be withdrawn from storage to supply the pumpage decreases. In effect, water that was formerly directed toward natural avenues of discharge is now diverted to the pumping centers, and increases in recharge may provide an additional source to sustain the pumpage. Ultimately, withdrawal from storage may cease, and a new equilibrium may be established in which the new rate of recharge balances the pumpage and the remaining natural discharge. On the other hand, if the pumping rate exceeds the reductions in natural discharge and the increases in recharge that can be effected in the system, withdrawal from storage will continue until falling water levels force a reduction in pumping rates. An equilibrium is then established in which the remaining natural discharge and this reduced pumping rate are balanced by the recharge. In many applications, of course, a part of the pumpage is returned to the aquifer or to streams after a cycle of use. To the extent that this occurs, the impact of the pumpage on water supply is reduced; however, it frequently is replaced by an impact on water quality."

The Porsche analogy can be extended to parallel the effects over time of pumping groundwater. Suppose initially you cover the payments on your new Porsche by dipping into savings (decreasing storage). Later you forego fancy restaurants or take a second job, or both,(decrease discharge, increase recharge, or both) in order to bring your income and expenditures into balance (recharge/discharge equilibrium). You thereby cease depleting your savings account. On the other hand, if you do not sufficiently increase your income or decrease your expenditures (increase recharge or decrease discharge), your savings account will continue to shrink (water levels will continue to decline), and at some point economics may force you to get rid of the Porsche (quit pumping).

2. **Adverse consequences of groundwater mining.** The sustained withdrawal of groundwater that depletes storage is called mining. A physical consequence of groundwater mining is water level decline, which in turn has the economic consequence of increasing the cost of withdrawing water as wells need to be deepened. Water level decline may have additional physical consequences depending on the circumstances. These include land surface subsidence; aquifer compaction that results in loss of transmissivity and storage capacity; intrusion into the aquifer of oceanic saltwater or poor quality water from a neighboring aquifer; and depletion of surface lakes, streams, and wetlands.

After noting some of these potential consequences, the National Water Commission concluded: "Mining ground water is not inherently wrong. It is wrong, however, when the water is mined out without taking account of the future value of the water and the storage capacity of the reservoir." Nat'l Water Comm'n, Water Policies for the Future 239 (1973).

3. **Controlling groundwater mining.** Absent controls, overdepletion or overrapid withdrawal of storage is likely because of the typical "common pool" nature of groundwater. If a groundwater pool is shared by users, as it usually is, there is little incentive for individual users to conserve the water in storage for future use because water not pumped now will be taken by someone else. This results in the parties undervaluing and overusing water presently.

As one means of controlling withdrawals, the National Water Commission suggested that pump taxes should be imposed at a rate equal to the predicted future value of the water discounted to present value. Id. at 240-41. But pump taxes are a far less common means of controlling withdrawals than regulation. The principal cases and notes that follow illustrate various regulatory approaches taken by courts, legislatures, and administrative agencies. These materials reveal both different substantive policies on managing storage and different approaches to calculating whether withdrawals exceed the substantive policy.

FUNDINGSLAND v. COLORADO GROUND WATER COMMISSION

Supreme Court of Colorado, 1970.
171 Colo. 487, 468 P.2d 835.

PRINGLE, JUSTICE. On September 2, 1966, Mr. Fundingsland (hereinafter referred to as the plaintiff) filed an application with the Colorado Ground Water Commission (hereinafter referred to as the commission) for a permit to drill a well on certain property located in the Northern High Plains Designated Ground Water Basin in Kit Carson County. No objections to the application were filed. On February 27, 1967, the plaintiff's application was denied by the commission on the basis that there was over appropriation in the area where the well was to be drilled. The plaintiff objected to the ruling of the commission, and a hearing was held before the commission * * *. [O]n May 15, 1968 the commission published an order denying the plaintiff's application

The plaintiff appealed the decision of the commission to the district court, and a trial de novo was held * * *. The trial judge entered a judgment denying the plaintiff's application, and the plaintiff brings writ of error to this Court from that judgment. [Plaintiff] alleges as grounds for reversal (1) that the denial of his application was not supported by the evidence and was arbitrary and capricious * * *. This Court finds no error, and we affirm the judgment of the district court.

The court and the commission derive their authority to pass on the plaintiff's application from 1965 Perm. Supp., C.R.S. 1963, 148-18-1 et seq. * * * Under 148-18-6 the commission is empowered to deny an application if it finds that the proposed appropriation will unreasonably impair existing water rights from the same source, or will create unreasonable waste. The act further provides in 148-18-6(5):

> "In ascertaining whether a proposed use will create unreasonable waste or unreasonably affect the rights of other appropriators, the commission shall take into consideration the area, and geologic conditions, the average annual yield and recharge rate of the appropriate water supply, the priority and quantity of existing claims of all persons to use the water, the proposed method of use, and all other matters appropriate to such questions. With regard to whether a proposed use will impair uses under existing water rights, impairment shall include the unreasonable lowering of the water level, or the unreasonable deterioration of water quality, beyond reasonable economic limits of withdrawal or use."

[T]he trial court made detailed findings of fact concerning the proper tests to be used in determining whether the proposed use of water by the plaintiff would unreasonably impair existing water rights from the same source or create unreasonable waste. And after making those findings, the court determined that they supported a denial of the plaintiff's application.

Among these findings, the trial court determined that a so-called three mile test provided a reasonable basis for assessing the effect of a proposed use on other users in the district. The three mile test was developed for use in the

Northern High Plains. It is partly based on policy and partly based on fact and theory. Using that test, a circle with a three mile radius is drawn around the proposed well site. A rate of pumping is determined which would result in a 40% depletion of the available ground water in that area over a period of 25 years. If that rate of pumping is being exceeded by the existing wells within the circle, then the application for a permit to drill a new well may be denied.

The three mile test takes into account all of the considerations specified in the statute. The factors involved in the three mile test were explained to the court by Mr. Erker, senior engineer in the ground water section of the State Engineer's office. He testified that the three mile circle represents the area over which a well, located at the center, would have an effect if permitted to pump intermittently for 25 years. Intermittent pumping, he explained, meant approximately 100 days per year. Other factors which are considered are the saturated thickness of the aquifer within the three mile circle, the number of wells located within the circle, and the yield of those wells. Multiplying the number of wells within the circle times the yield of those wells gives the total, present appropriation within the three mile circle.

Mr. Romero, an assistant water resource engineer for the State of Colorado Division of Water Resources, testified that the modified Theiss equation was used in determining what the draw down effect on the water in the aquifer would be within the three mile circle. He further testified that in determining the balance of water in the aquifer, he considered the fact that there was only intermittent pumping, the amount of recharge to the aquifer due to precipitation and ground water inflow from outlying areas, recharge due to excess irrigation, and possibly recharge from some other source such as leakage from ditches or rivers.

There does not seem to be any contention that the 40% depletion figure is unreasonable or irrational. The assumption in the three mile test is that a 40% depletion of the aquifer within that area would constitute lowering of the water balance beyond reasonable economic limits of withdrawal or use for irrigation.

Likewise, the selection of 25 years as the period during which the 40% depletion is to be allowed is not contested. Mr. Leslie, a farm and ranch loan representative for Northwestern Mutual Life Insurance Company, testified that 25 years was a reasonable, average period in which a loan for the construction of well facilities would have to be repaid.

The testimony and other evidence in the record before the district court support the reasonableness of the three mile test and establish that the three mile test takes into account the factors specified by the statute. If the three mile test was a proper method for the court to use in determining the effect of plaintiff's proposed use on the ground water supply in the district, then the decision of the district court must be upheld.

[I]t was admitted on both sides that the commission is dealing in a complex area about which little is known. Experts testifying for the commission stated that the three mile test is the best tool they presently have to work with, and that it will be refined as they continue to learn more about the area.

The plaintiff's application did not present the court with a close question of whether the granting of a new permit would work unreasonable injury to existing wells. According to the three mile test, seventeen wells in the three mile circle pumping intermittently with a 1,000 gallon capacity per minute would deplete the water resource 40% in 25 years. There were 28 registered wells within the three mile circle encompassing the plaintiff's proposed well site. These 28 wells had a registered yield of 29,700 gallons per minute while the maximum yield allowable under the three mile test would be 17,000 gallons per minute. * * *

Ground water existing in designated underground water basins is made subject to the doctrine of prior appropriation by 1965 Perm. Supp., C.R.S. 1963, 148-18-1. The statute further provides:

> "* * * While the doctrine of prior appropriation is recognized, such doctrine should be modified to permit the full economic development of designated ground water resources. Prior appropriations of ground water should be protected and reasonable ground water pumping levels maintained, but not to include the maintenance of historical water levels. * * *"

Underground water basins require management that is different from the management of surface streams and underground waters tributary to such streams. In the case of the latter waters, seasonal regulation of diversion by junior appropriators can effectively protect the interests of more senior appropriators and no long range harm can come of over appropriations since the streams are subject to seasonal recharge. The underground water dealt with by 148-18-1 is not subject to the same ready replenishment enjoyed by surface streams and tributary ground water. It is possible for water to be withdrawn from the aquifer in a rate in excess of the annual recharge creating what is called a mining condition. Unless the rate of pumping is regulated, mining must ultimately result in lowering the water balance below a level from which water may be economically withdrawn. Due to the slow rate at which underground waters flow through and into the aquifer, it may be many years before a reasonable water level may be restored to a mined aquifer.

It is clear that the policies of protecting senior appropriators and maintaining reasonable ground water pumping levels set forth by the underground water act require management which takes into account the long range effects of intermittent pumping in the aquifer. In this case all of the experts testifying before the commission and the district court were in agreement that a mining condition exists in the Northern High Plains Designated Ground Water Basin. The commission has determined that proper use of the ground water resource requires that the mining be allowed to continue. However, the maximum allowable rate of depletion, at least when considering applications for permits to drill new wells, has been set at 40% depletion in 25 years. We have pointed out that the depletion rate in the area which would be affected by the plaintiff's proposed well is in excess of the rate allowed by the commission and approved by the district court.

If the plaintiff were permitted to proceed on his theory of "unappropriated water" and pump water from his proposed well until such time as it was no longer economically feasible to withdraw water from the aquifer, then no subsequent regulation of his pumping could protect senior appropriators, and all pumping from the basin within the area of influence of the plaintiff's well would have to cease until a reasonable pumping level was restored through the slow process of recharge. This is not the concept of appropriation contained in the statute, and not the one this Court will follow.

When, as in this case, water is being mined from the ground water basin, and a proposed appropriation would result in unreasonable harm to senior appropriators, then a determination that there is no water available for appropriation is justified. * * *

The judgment is affirmed.

Notes

1. **Controlled mining of storage.** *Fundingsland* illustrates controlled mining of stored groundwater. The policy allowed 40% of the available groundwater within a three-mile circle to be depleted over twenty-five years. The Groundwater Commission later increased the period for 40% depletion to 100 years. Rules and Regulations for the Management and Control of Designated Ground Water, 2 Colo. Code Regs. § 5.2.2.

In Kansas, Southwest Kansas Groundwater Management District No. 3 closes townships to new appropriations in certain circumstances, one of which is that existing wells will cause depletion of 40% or more over twenty-five years. Kan. Admin. Regs. § 5-23-4a. Generally townships are squares six miles on each side.

The first case on controlled mining was Mathers v. Texaco, Inc., 421 P.2d 771 (N.M. 1966). Texaco was given a permit to appropriate 350 acre-feet per year from the Lea County underground water basin to use for water flooding an oil field. The fresh water in the basin is found in the Ogallala formation, which varies in thickness from a thin edge to over 200 feet. The water in the formation is replenished only by a very limited surface precipitation that is just about equaled by natural discharge from the basin. The state engineer calculated the amount of water that could be withdrawn from a township of overlying land and still leave one-third of the water in storage at the end of forty years, at which point it would no longer be economically feasible to withdraw water for agricultural and most other purposes. Existing appropriators using water for agricultural purposes protested the issuance of the permit. In upholding the permit in the face of a statute protecting existing water rights against impairment from new wells, the court said:

"The administration of a non-rechargeable basin, if the waters therein are to be applied to a beneficial use, requires giving to the stock or supply of water a time dimension, or, to state it otherwise, requires the fixing of a rate of withdrawal which will result in a determination of the economic life of the basin at a selected time.

"The very nature of the finite stock of water in a non-rechargeable basin compels a modification of the traditional concept of appropriable supply under the appropriation doctrine. * * *

"The rights of the protestants to appropriate water from this basin are subject to this time limitation, just as are the rights of all other appropriators. A lowering of the water level in the wells of protestants, together with the resulting increase in pumping costs and the lowering of pumping yields, does not constitute an impairment of the rights of protestants as a matter of law. These are inevitable results of the beneficial use by the public of these waters." Id. at 243-44, 246.

An interesting sidelight to the *Mathers* case is supplied by Charles E. Corker, Groundwater Law, Management and Administration, Nat'l Water Comm'n, Legal Study No. 6, at 176 (1971): "According to S.E. Reynolds, State Engineer, forty years was selected because it is two generations, and forty years corresponds to provisions in federal reclamation law for repayment by irrigator beneficiaries."

2. **Refinement of the *Fundingsland* test.** Thompson v. Colorado Ground Water Commission, 575 P.2d 372 (Colo. 1978), modified the *Fundingsland* three-mile circle when it would have extended across the Nebraska state line. The Commission looked only at the portion of the circle located in Colorado and water development in Colorado, and determined that the area around plaintiff's proposed well was overappropriated. If the Groundwater Commission had considered the entire circle and Nebraska development within it, the area would not have been overappropriated. The court upheld the Commission's state-line policy, saying, "Expert testimony supported the Commission's position that over-appropriation of the aquifer at the state line, with the intent to stabilize or reverse the aquifer flow to the benefit of Colorado, would seriously injure vested Colorado rights far west of the state line and could ignite a destructive aquifer depletion race with Nebraska, an adjoining state. Evidence that a portion of Colorado's groundwater naturally flows into adjoining states, when considered in the context of the Commission's overall groundwater policy, does not establish a breach of statutory duty by the Commission in its determination."

Further refinement of *Fundingsland* was reported in Berens v. Colorado Ground Water Commission, 614 P.2d 352, 354-55 (Colo. 1980):

"According to testimony by the Commission's expert witness, Leonard Mercer, the standard three-mile formula did not, in practice, result in a 40% depletion rate in 25 years. Mercer stated that, because a small shift in a proposed well site could eliminate from consideration those senior wells lying on the perimeter of a fully-appropriated circle, and cause the acceptance of the proposed well, the circle could, as a result, be overappropriated. In support of his position, Mercer cited Commission studies suggesting that a number of fully-appropriated townships were actually overappropriated by about 40%. * * * As a result, the Commission has recently modified its standard three-mile formula to take into account the percentage of overappropriation thought to be inherent in that formula. Based on the Commission studies suggesting that a 40% over-appropriation resulted from the use of the Commission's standard formula, the Commission modified the formula to achieve a 40% reduction in its estimate of the amount of available ground water for each three-mile circle."

3. **When available groundwater is depleted.** What happens to existing groundwater users when uneconomic pumping depths are reached? One possibility is that irrigators will simply quit pumping and return to dry land farming or allow the land to revert to prairie. Another solution is to supplement supplies by importing water. For example, much of the early growth of Los Angeles was based on groundwater drawn from overdrafted aquifers. This provided Los Angles with cheap water on which to develop the economic strength to begin importing water in 1913 from the Owens Valley 300 miles away.

Critics of groundwater mining argue that frequently it creates a crisis situation, leading to demands for a "rescue project" to supply supplemental water at subsidized prices. An example is the Central Arizona Project, which transports Colorado River water to Central Arizona. Although not originally conceived as a rescue project, when finally approved by Congress in 1968, its purpose was exactly that. As the project neared completion a quarter century later, it had to be restructured to accommodate the inability of various irrigation districts to pay for water at the originally scheduled, subsidized rates. Even lower rates were provided for agricultural users, though eventually this water will be shifted to municipal and industrial users at higher rates.

4. **Depletion deduction.** Internal Revenue Code § 611(a) allows a cost depletion deduction for mines, oil and gas wells, "and other natural deposits." United States v. Shurbet, 347 F.2d 103 (5th Cir. 1965), ruled that an irrigator obtaining water from the Ogallala formation under the Southern High Plains of Texas was entitled to the depletion deduction. The court noted that under Texas law, an irrigator "owns the soil and the percolating water which is part of the soil." Shortly after that decision, the Internal Revenue Service announced it would allow the depletion deduction also for irrigators using water from the Ogallala formation in the Southern High Plains of New Mexico (where the appropriation doctrine, rather than the absolute ownership doctrine, applies). Rev. Rul. 65-296, 1965-2 C.B. 181. Later, the Internal Revenue Service announced its willingness to allow the depletion deduction for persons taking water from the Ogallala formation outside the Southern High Plains where it can be shown that the groundwater is being depleted and recharge is so low that, once extracted, the groundwater will be lost to the taxpayer and immediately succeeding generations. Rev. Rul. 82-214, 1982-2 C.B. 115; see also Priv. Ltr. Rul. 82-26-022 (Mar. 10, 1982).

DOHERTY v. OREGON WATER RESOURCES DIRECTOR

Supreme Court of Oregon, 1989.
308 Or. 543, 783 P.2d 519.

FADELEY, JUSTICE. This is a judicial review of the state Water Resources Director's amended order, entered in 1986, declaring 274 square miles in Umatilla and Morrow counties a critical ground water area. Several agricultural irrigators challenge the order which can lead to controls on volume of water pumped from area wells. The Court of Appeals upheld the declaration of the Butter Creek Critical Ground Water Area with subareas, as well as the order that no new applications be accepted to appropriate ground water or to expand or change existing uses. * * *

Petitioners contend that one statutory policy standard—providing that "depletion of ground water supplies below economic levels * * * be prevented or controlled within practicable limits"—should be interpreted to permit, not restrict, use of water whenever that use results in profitable agriculture. In short, they assert that holders of water right certificates or registrations have the right to pump a reservoir dry so long as the holders may profitably irrigate crops.

* * * ORS 537.730 and ORS 537.735 authorized the director to establish a critical ground water area if the available supply is "being or about to be overdrawn," water levels "are declining or have declined excessively," or if wells "interfere substantially with one another." * * * The statute provides that, after hearing, the director "shall" by order declare an area to be a critical ground water area if "any" of the statutory factors exist and he further finds that public welfare, health, and safety require that corrective controls be adopted. * * *

The director entered * * * "findings of fact" * * * as follows:

> "The record indicates that approximately 500 wells serve as the source of water needed for domestic and stock water use by residents within the subject area. Although the volume of water withdrawn * * * for domestic and stock water needs is not large in comparison to the amount withdrawn for irrigation and other permitted uses, maintaining adequate and safe supplies of ground water in the subject reservoir for continuing these necessary uses is of considerable significance to the health, safety and welfare of the residents of the area. * * *
>
> "The sustained yield of a ground water basin is the amount of water that can be withdrawn from it annually without exceeding the long-term mean annual water supply to the reservoir. Withdrawals exceeding this supply must come from storage within the reservoir which results in long-term water level declines.
>
> "Any draft in excess of the sustained yield of the basalt ground water reservoir in the proposed Butter Creek Critical Ground Water Area is overdraft."

The director found that testimony and evidence in the hearing record established both overdraft and excessive decline in water levels during the period for which records of well levels have been kept in the Butter Creek area. The director found that "existing developments have reached or exceeded the sustained yield capacity of the reservoir" in each subarea.

The "opinion" portion of the director's order related the facts found to the statutory policy stated in the Ground Water Act of 1955 as follows:

> "ORS 537.525(1)[,(3),] and (9) provide the declared policy of the Oregon Legislature to be that the beneficial use of the available ground water resource be limited to the 'capacity of the available sources' and that 'whenever * * * overdrawing of the ground water supplies * * * exists or impends, controlled use of the ground water concerned be authorized or imposed * * *.' This declared policy requires that the ground water be managed to provide for development and use of the resource within the sustained yield capacity of the ground water reservoir. The sustained yield concept of ground water

management is further supported by ORS 537.525(7) which provides, 'Reasonably stable ground water levels be determined and maintained.'"

* * *

Petitioners argue that public welfare is best served if they are permitted to pump as much as they can use on crops which may be sold at a profit after pumping and other costs are paid. * * *

Petitioners further argue that the statutes permit any amount of drawdown or any level of depletion of the underground water resource, if a current farmer can clear a profit on an irrigated crop. * * * Petitioners contend that the portion of ORS 537.525(8) which states "Depletion of ground water supplies below economic levels * * * be prevented or controlled within practicable limits" supports their claim that economic feasibility must be read into all other policy subsections of the ground water act as a limiting factor. The water should be looked at as a resource similar to gold in a mine and withdrawn totally so long as it is economically feasible to do so, they urge. Writers, whom they cite in support of this concept, advocate that the government establish a time period, such as 25 years, for using up all of the water.

This argument would say that the statutory words of "overdraft" and "excessive decline" in water levels cannot be interpreted to apply to the practice of progressively lowering water levels or permanent depletion of the resource in annual steps if the practice nonetheless provides profitable agriculture today. That is, if the farmer can afford the electricity to pump the water from greater depth and still raise a profitable crop, it cannot be overdraft or excessive decline. In that circumstance, they contend, there is no interference with public health, safety, and welfare, even though no irrigating agriculturalist has suggested that a profit can only be made by pumping the reservoir dry within the next 25 years or any other short-term period. A logical corollary of this mining-analogy argument is that the public health, welfare, and safety are simply not involved where the current generation profitably extracts all of the resource and leaves agricultural ghost towns.

The statutory scheme in the Ground Water Act of 1955 does not support this argument. Instead, the act is designed to prevent that result. The act established the critical area mechanism to assure a reasonably stable, adequate water supply which may be beneficially used only within the capacity of the available resource and is protected against overdrawing, declining water levels, and interference among wells.

We agree with the director and the Court of Appeals that ORS 537.525(8) does not mandate depletion to the lowest water level from which irrigation water may be profitably pumped today. A fair reading of subsection (8) casts it as a restriction on, rather than a justification for, depletion of ground water. The water-mining theory fails because it is inconsistent with the legislative act.

Petitioners assert that the director used an annual reservoir recharge rate as the guideline by which he interpreted the statutory term "overdrawn." They invite our inquiry on review to whether an annual overdraft standard is too stringent. The petitioners are equally dissatisfied with the 15-year study and, were the director to select a 50-year period, apparently would still assert error.

They contend that the proper period for determining whether an overdraft in excess of reservoir recharge is occurring would be in the thousands of years. They assert that present day recharge comes from the Blue Mountains only intermittently, sometimes arriving at the reservoir thousands of years after the precipitation supplying the recharge fell there.

The argument is not supported by the record. Absent evidence needed to support the assertion that a cycle of millennial recharge exists, neither we nor the director should speculate upon that theory. In any event, the director determined overdraft by relying on cumulative overdraft over a 15-year period, not by an annual recharge standard. Moreover, the legislative direction under which he acted gives no hint that it is designed to accommodate pumping the reservoir dry on an expectation of refilling sometime within the next few thousand years. We need not reach any issue about whether "overdrawn" may be interpreted to mean overdraft for only one year. The opinion portion of the director's order does define overdrawing in terms of annual recharge to the reservoir. However, the director did not rely upon annual overdraft but rather the "sustained yield * * * concept" in interpreting and applying ORS 537.525(7), which provides that "reasonably stable ground water levels be determined and maintained."

The director found that precipitation in the area in recent years was higher than long-term averages, but that cumulative decline in water levels continued. He also found that the sustained yield of the ground water basin should be defined in terms of "the long-term mean annual water supply to the reservoir." We agree with the director that a sustained yield concept is consistent with the words of ORS 537.525(7) and the policy of ORS 537.525. The claim of error fails because the director's approach is consistent with the statute.

Petitioners point out that the Butter Creek area is only a part of the Umatilla structural basin [consisting of more than 2,200 square miles] and that others, outside the Butter Creek area, are using up the same general underground reservoir but are not being subjected to the usage controls which the critical area designation threatens to visit upon them. They contend that no critical area may be formed unless all irrigators using the interconnected underground water source are similarly regulated. They argue that partial regulation would be ineffective and ineffective regulation does not promote public welfare. The Ground Water Act of 1955 appears to contemplate an area-by-area enforcement, especially because interference among wells is one ground for creating a critical area. Simultaneous enforcement throughout a basin is not required by statute. The record does not show that partial regulation would be ineffective and thereby does not show that partial regulation fails to promote public welfare, health, or safety. [The record indicated that there were "a number of separate, interconnected subpools within the aquifer."]

* * * The decision of the Court of Appeals is affirmed.

Notes

1. **Phased implementation of the sustained yield policy.** The Oregon Water Resources Commission issued administrative rules for the Butter Creek Critical Ground Water Area designed to reduce pumping to the "sustainable annual yield,"

which was defined as "the volume of water that can be pumped on an annual basis while maintaining reasonably stable water levels." Instead of immediately implementing the policy, however, the rules provided for reduction of the existing overdraft to be phased in over five years. In Waterwatch of Oregon v. Oregon Water Resources Department, 852 P.2d 902 (Or. Ct. App. 1993), the petitioner argued that phased rather than immediate reduction of overdraft violated the statutory requirement that "[r]easonably stable ground water levels be determined and maintained." The court disagreed. After noting that another statutory provision states that the depletion of groundwater supplies below economic levels should be "prevented or controlled within practicable limits," the court concluded: "The problem with petitioner's argument is that it focuses on only one objective of the statute and disregards other statutory objectives. The challenged rules strike a balance between stabilization of water supplies and providing an interim during which agricultural practices can be accommodated to the regulatory stabilization mechanism."

2. **Safe yield.** Some states limit groundwater withdrawals to safe yield. E.g., Kan. Admin. Regs. § 5-22-7 (Equus Beds Groundwater Management Dist. No. 2); Nev. Rev. Stat. 533.371; N.J. Stat. Ann. § 58:1A-15. That standard is neither unambiguous nor physically simple to implement.

Crosby, supra p. 325, at 75-77:

"Safe yield has been variously defined. Todd (1959) states, 'The safe yield of a groundwater basin is the amount of water which can be withdrawn from it annually without producing an undesired result.' * * * Meinzer (1923b, p. 55) had earlier defined safe yield as, 'the rate at which water can be withdrawn from an aquifer without depleting the supply to such an extent that withdrawal at this rate is harmful to the aquifer itself, or to the quality of the water, or is no longer economically feasible.'

"[The term] is inherently ambiguous because it may or may not invite subjective and/or economic judgments above the gravity of the risk from a water shortage. It has the additional disadvantage that decisions made in good faith may prove to be, in time, poorly considered. A regimen of totally 'safe' operation which avoided all risks would utilize much less than the optimum usable storage capacity."

Charles L. McGuinness, U.S. Geological Survey, Circular No. 117, Water Law, with Special Reference to Ground Water 11 (1951):

"Regulation of water use to prevent over-development of an aquifer, or a part of it, involves the determination of a safe or optimum rate of withdrawal and the holding of withdrawals to it. This is true whether the doctrine of prior appropriation or that of correlative rights is applied. Such a determination generally is much more difficult for a ground-water reservoir than for a surface stream or reservoir, for it inevitably involves the economic feasibility of a given means of withdrawal or a given pumping lift, not only in an aquifer as a whole but in different parts of it. * * * [I]n most aquifers the distribution of wells affects the perennial yield significantly. With a given distribution of wells, an enforced reduction in pumping by cutting off the later appropriators (or, under correlative rights, by reducing the pumpage of all in proportion to the estimated perennial yield of the aquifer and to the amount of land owned by each user) may not prevent local overdevelopment. Reducing the pumpage in one part of an aquifer may not result in an equivalent addition to the supply for other wells, either for a long time or, if the reduction simply results in an increase in the natural discharge from the aquifer, possibly not at all."

U.S. Geological Survey, Water Supply Paper No. 2250, National Water Summary 1983—Hydrologic Events and Issues 36 (1983):

"As it is often used, 'safe yield' seems to refer to the pumpage that can be sustained at equilibrium, without continued withdrawal from storage. However, sustained withdrawal from storage, or as it is often termed 'ground-water mining,' is no more 'unsafe' than the mining of any other mineral resource, provided it is recognized and planned. Neither should pumpage at equilibrium necessarily be considered 'safe,' unless the attendant impacts, such as reduced streamflow or degradation of water quality, are deemed acceptable. The expression 'safe yield' can, in fact only be defined in terms of specific impacts of pumpage. The consequences of pumpage must be assessed for each level of development, and 'safe yield' must be taken as the maximum pumpage for which the consequences are considered acceptable. The term 'overdevelopment' then implies pumpage beyond that maximum."

3. **Average annual recharge.** A variation of the safe-yield standard limits groundwater withdrawals to the average annual recharge to a groundwater source. Idaho Code § 42-237a(g) ("the reasonably anticipated average rate of future natural recharge"); S.D. Codified Laws § 46-6-3.1 ("the average estimated annual recharge").

Baker v. Ore-Ida Foods, Inc., 513 P.2d 627 (Idaho 1973), involved twenty irrigation wells pumping from an aquifer and causing the water level to drop by 20 feet per year. The average annual recharge was 5500 acre-feet. The court ruled that Idaho's statute limiting annual withdrawals to average natural recharge prohibits mining, which the court defined as "perennially withdrawing ground water at rates beyond the recharge rate." The court affirmed a decree that enjoined pumping by all but the four most senior wells, which together consumed the entire average annual recharge. (If the four senior wells continued to withdraw 5500 acre-feet, would not storage be mined to whatever extent natural discharge still occurred?)

The *Baker* court assigned further administration of water rights in the aquifer to the Idaho Department of Water Resources. The department then recalculated the parties' rights under the principle that appropriations should be quantified by actual historical use instead of the maximum amount that could have been pumped. Rather than assume that well owners had pumped at their full licensed rates for 24 hours a day 180 days per year, as the court apparently had done, the department examined power company records for each pump to determine the hours and days each year that the pump was operated. It found that the actual length of the pumping season was from 150-160 days per year, and it fixed the annual water right of each well at the highest five-year average withdrawal, expressed in acre-feet per year. This reduced the water rights by 28% to 38% and allowed more appropriators to pump. Then, based on the premise that in a dry year good farming practice might require the use of more than the annual water right, while in a wet year an irrigator might not need the total water right, the department allowed each water user to pump any amount of water necessary in a given year so long as the water user did not pump over five times the annual water right in any consecutive five-year period. The case was again appealed on a narrow point, Briggs v. Golden Valley Land & Cattle Co., 546 P.2d 382 (Idaho 1976), where the above findings are recited but not reviewed.

The Idaho Legislature later amended the statute limiting groundwater withdrawals to average natural recharge to relax the no-mining interpretation of *Baker.* The Legislature retained the average-natural-recharge provision as a basic limit on groundwater withdrawals but added language allowing withdrawals in excess of average natural recharge if (1) the director finds such withdrawals will be in the public interest, (2) a program exists or will exist to increase recharge or decrease withdrawals within a time period acceptable to the director to bring withdrawals into balance with recharge, and (3) senior groundwater appropriators will not be required to pump from below reasonable pumping levels.

The concept of average annual recharge is a less definitive management tool than may first appear: "[A]verage recharge does not imply any particular average water level. When natural discharge is reduced as much as pumpage the level will stabilize. This may occur at many levels and the maximum may be near the original level or it may not be reached until the stored water is largely depleted. Moreover, lowering the level may bring increased recharge." Edgar S. Bagley, Water Rights Law and Public Policies Relating to Ground Water "Mining" in the Southwestern States, 4 J. Law & Econ. 144, 166 n.78 (1961).

As indicated by Note 1, supra p. 345, withdrawals by wells must come either from aquifer storage or from capture, i.e., induced greater recharge or induced lesser natural discharge. Given the physical unity of the hydrologic cycle, induced greater recharge might come from (that is, deplete) surface water supplies to the detriment of senior stream appropriators or environmental interests. Similarly, induced lesser natural discharge from an aquifer might well translate into less flow in a surface stream, which might be fully appropriated, or a loss of wetlands. The average-natural-recharge limit on withdrawals, standing alone, fails to address the policy question of the desirability of aquifer drawdown and surface water depletion.

A further complication is the reality that the physical consequences of pumping, in terms of aquifer drawdown and stream depletion, will vary with local conditions: "There is no valid generic rule, such as pumping the natural recharge, that will lead to a desirable economic or stable (non-depleting) level of groundwater development. Subject to local permeability and storage conditions, such a rule can cause either greatly excessive and increasing drawdown or costly constraints on resource use regardless of the rate of natural recharge. * * * The effects of concern to water policy are primarily aquifer diffusivity, location [of wells in relation to each other and to any surface stream], and time of pumpage. The natural recharge rate is unrelated to any parameters controlling the primary water policy concerns." W.P. Balleau, Water Appropriation and Transfer in a General Hydrogeologic System, 28 Nat. Resources J. 269, 280 & n.26 (1988); see also Gregory S. Weber, Twenty Years of Local Groundwater Export Legislation in California: Lessons from a Patchwork Quilt, 34 Nat. Resources J. 657, 672-77 (1994) (discussing hydrologists' criticisms of the groundwater management concepts of mining, overdraft, safe yield, and average recharge).

4. **Implementing a reduction in groundwater withdrawals.** If withdrawals by wells need to be reduced to comply with governing policy on managing storage, how should the reduction be accomplished? In an appropriation doctrine state, must priorities be strictly enforced as in *Baker*? Compare Wyo. Stat. Ann. § 41-3-915:

"(a) * * * If the state engineer finds after the hearing, and after receiving the advice of the control area advisory board, that the underground water in the control area is insufficient for all of the appropriators, he may by order adopt one or more of the following corrective controls:

> (i) * * *
>
> (ii) He may determine the permissible total withdrawal of underground water in the control area for each day, month or year, and, insofar as may be reasonably done, he shall apportion such permissible total withdrawal among the appropriators holding valid rights to the underground water in the control area in accordance with the relative dates of priority of such rights.
>
> (iii) If he finds that withdrawals by junior appropriators have a material and adverse effect upon the supply available for and needed by senior appropriators, he may order such junior appropriators to cease or reduce withdrawals forthwith.
>
> (iv) If he finds that cessation or reduction of withdrawals by junior appropriators will not result in proportionate benefits to senior appropriators, he may require and specify a system of rotation of use of underground water in the control area.

"(b) * * *

"(c) Appropriators of underground water from a control area may agree to any method or scheme of control of withdrawals, apportionment, rotation or proration of the common supply of underground water. The state engineer shall encourage and promote such agreements and supply the parties with information and advice. When the state engineer, with the advice of the control area advisory board, shall find that any such agreement, executed in writing and filed in his office, is consistent with the intent, purposes and requirements of this act, and would not be detrimental to the public interest or to the rights of other persons not parties to the agreement, he shall approve the agreement, and thereafter such agreement shall control, until terminated as hereinafter provided, in lieu of any order issued pursuant to subsection (a) of this section."

In Kansas, another appropriation doctrine state for groundwater, pumping had to be reduced in the Walnut Creek Intensive Groundwater Use Control Area because it was about twice the safe yield. The chief engineer of the state water agency did not accomplish this by strictly enforcing priorities. Instead, he divided appropriators into two groups, those with priorities of October 1, 1965 or earlier and those with later priorities. He ordered irrigators in the senior group to cut back by 22 or 33 percent, depending on their location, on the rationale that they needed to be more reasonable and efficient. He ordered irrigators in the junior group to cut back by 64 or 71 percent, depending on their location. Dissatisfied irrigators appealed the administrative action asserting inverse condemnation, but the matter was settled before judicial resolution of the takings issue. John C. Peck, Property Rights in Groundwater—Some Lessons from the Kansas Experience, 12 Kan. J.L. & Pub. Pol'y 493, 499-500, 503, 504-05 (2003) (reporting these facts and arguing that "if one accepts the proposition that the chief engineer has the power to control and reduce waste, the [administrative order] might stand.".

Under the correlative rights doctrine, a court may not impose pumping reductions in an overdrafted basin using equitable principles that ignore the superiority the doctrine gives to water rights for overlying land compared to those for nonoverlying land. City of Barstow v. Mojave Water Agency, 5 P.3d 853 (Cal. 2000).

CITY OF PASADENA v. CITY OF ALHAMBRA

Supreme Court of California, 1949.

33 Cal. 2d 908, 207 P.2d 17.

[Numerous persons, municipalities, and water companies had pumped water for many years from a forty square mile aquifer known as the Raymond Basin. The City of Pasadena brought this action to determine the rights to groundwater in the basin and to enjoin an alleged overdraft. The trial court found that the safe annual yield of the Western Unit of the basin was 18,000 acre-feet per year, and that annual withdrawals totaled 24,000 acre-feet. This condition had existed since about 1913, and the water table had been steadily lowered toward the point of unreasonable depletion and possible destruction of the source. Most of the parties entered into a stipulation restricting total withdrawals to the annual yield, and the trial court entered a judgment substantially enforcing the stipulation against all parties, allocating to each about two-thirds of the amount previously pumped, and enjoining all pumping in excess of the rights decreed to each party. The California-Michigan Land and Water Company, not having joined in the stipulation, appealed.]

GIBSON, CHIEF JUSTICE. * * * The question of who shall bear the burden of curtailing the overdraft, and in what proportion, depends upon the legal nature and status of the particular water right held by each party. Rights in water in an underground basin, so far as pertinent here, are classified as overlying, appropriative, and prescriptive. Generally speaking, an overlying right, analogous to that of a riparian owner in a surface stream, is the right of the owner of the land to take water from the ground underneath for use on his land within the basin or watershed; the right is based on ownership of the land and is appurtenant thereto. The right of an appropriator depends upon an actual taking of water. Where a taking is wrongful, it may ripen into a prescriptive right. * * *

In the present case some of the parties, including owners of ranches, golf clubs, and cemeteries, have pumped water solely for use on their own land, and their rights at the outset were overlying. The principal takers of water, however, are public utility corporations and municipalities which have either exported water or have used it within the Western Unit for municipal purposes or for sale to the public, and their taking, when commenced, was entirely appropriative. * * *

It follows from the foregoing that, if no prescriptive rights had been acquired, the rights of the overlying owners would be paramount, and the rights of the appropriators would depend on priority of acquisition under the rule that the first appropriator in time is the first in right. The latest in time of the appropriations would then be the first to be curtailed in limiting total production of the area to the safe yield. If such were the case, the overdraft could be eliminated simply by enjoining a part of the latest appropriations, since the record shows that there is ample water to satisfy the needs of all the overlying users and most of the appropriators * * *.

The principal dispute between appellant and respondents, however, concerns whether any water rights in the Western Unit have become prescriptive and, if so, to what extent. Respondents assert that the rights of all the parties, including both overlying users and appropriators, have become mutually prescriptive against all the other parties and, accordingly, that all rights are of equal standing, with none prior or paramount. * * *

The record shows that there has been an actual adverse user of water in the Western Unit. There was an invasion, to some extent at least, of the rights of both overlying owners and appropriators commencing in the year 1913-1914, when the overdraft first occurred. Each taking of water in excess of the safe yield, whether by subsequent appropriators or by increased use by prior appropriators, was wrongful and was in injury to the then existing owners of water rights, because the overdraft, from its very beginning, operated progressively to reduce the total available supply. Although no owner was immediately prevented from taking the water he needed, the report demonstrates that a continuation of the overdraft would eventually result in such a depletion of the supply stored in the underground basin that it would become inadequate. The injury thus did not involve an immediate disability to obtain water, but, rather, it consisted of the continual lowering of the level and gradual reducing of the total amount of stored water, the accumulated effect of which, after a period of years, would be to render the supply insufficient to meet the needs of the rightful owners. * * *

The lowering of the water table resulting from the overdraft was plainly observable in the wells of the parties * * *. This evidence is clearly sufficient to justify charging appellant with notice that there was a deficiency rather than a surplus and that the appropriations causing the overdraft were invasions of the rights of overlying owners and prior appropriators. The elements of prescription being present in the record, the statute of limitations ran against the original lawful holders of water rights to whatever extent their rights were invaded. * * *

[A]t first glance it would seem to follow that the parties who wrongfully appropriated water for a period of five years would acquire prior prescriptive rights to the full amount so taken. The running of the statute, however, can effectively be interrupted by self help on the part of the lawful owner of the property right involved. * * * [A]lthough the pumping of each party to this action continued without interruption, it necessarily interfered with the future possibility of pumping by each of the other parties by lowering the water level. The original owners by their own acts, although not by judicial assistance, thus retained or acquired a right to continue to take some water in the future. The wrongdoers also acquired prescriptive rights to continue to take water, but their rights were limited to the extent that the original owners retained or acquired rights by their pumping.

Adoption of appellant's position that the water must be allocated, at least as between the municipalities and public utility companies, strictly on the basis of priority in time of appropriation * * * would result in an unequal sharing of the burden of curtailing the overdraft in that all pumping conducted under authority of certain of the later appropriations would be completely eliminated, whereas no restriction in amount would be imposed upon pumping based on earlier appropriations. Such a result does not appear to be justified where all of the parties have been producing water from the underground basin for many years, and none of them have acted to protect the supply or prevent invasion of their rights until this proceeding was instituted. Moreover, it seems probable that the solution adopted by the trial court will promote the best interests of the public, because a pro tanto reduction of the amount of water devoted to each present use would normally be less disruptive than total elimination of some of the uses.

We hold, therefore, that prescriptive rights were established by appropriations made in the Western Unit subsequent to the commencement of the overdraft, that such rights were acquired against both overlying owners and prior appropriators, that the overlying owners and prior appropriators also obtained or preserved, rights by reason of the water which they pumped, and that the trial court properly concluded that the production of water in the unit should be limited by a proportionate reduction in the amount which each party had taken throughout the statutory period. * * * [Affirmed.]

Notes

1. **Limitations on the mutual prescription doctrine.** The California Supreme Court later recognized a difficulty with the doctrine of mutual prescription: "A possible undesirable side effect of the so-called mutual prescription doctrine is that it may encourage a 'race to the pumphouse' after overdraft commences, each party endeavoring to increase the volume of continuous use on which his prescriptive right will be based." City of Los Angeles v. City of San Fernando, 537 P.2d 1250 (Cal. 1975).

Perhaps this difficulty accounts for the court's adoption in *San Fernando* of several limitations on the mutual prescription doctrine. First, the court interpreted a state statute, as amended in 1935, to exempt cities from loss of their water rights by prescription. Cities can still acquire prescriptive rights against other pumpers but cannot have their own rights cut down by prescription. (A 1968 amendment to the statute extends the exemption to public utilities.) Second, the court ruled that times of groundwater surplus break the running of the five-year prescriptive period. The prescriptive period must consist of five consecutive years of overdraft. Third, the court made it clear that the commencement of overdraft is only one prerequisite for the prescriptive period to commence running. Another prerequisite is that the persons against whom prescription is asserted must have notice of the overdraft. Mere notice that others are pumping is not sufficient because their pumping might be drawing from surplus. Fourth, the court suggested that unexercised overlying rights would not necessarily be subject to loss by prescription. 537 P.2d at 1318 n.100.

Further limitation came in Tehachapi-Cummings County Water District v. Armstrong, 122 Cal. Rptr. 918 (Cal. Ct. App. 1975), which held that if all the parties in a groundwater basin adjudication are overlying owners using the water for overlying uses, the mutual prescription doctrine does not apply. The rights of each overlying user must be calculated under the correlative rights doctrine, and if the water quantity is insufficient, each user is limited to a proportionate share of the total amount available based upon his reasonable need. The share "is predicated not on his past use over a specified period of time, nor on the time he commenced pumping, but solely on his current reasonable and beneficial need for water."

2. **Overdraft, surplus, and safe yield.** *Pasadena* predicated running of the prescriptive period on the occurrence of basin overdraft. *San Fernando* elaborated on overdraft and the connected concepts of surplus and safe yield.:

"A ground basin is in a state of surplus when the amount of water being extracted from it is less than the maximum that could be withdrawn without adverse effects on the basin's long term supply. * * * Overdraft commences whenever extractions increase, or the withdrawable maximum decreases, or both, to the point where the surplus ends. * * *

"The trial court defined 'surplus' and overdraft' in terms of 'safe yield.' The findings state that '[s]urplus is that condition which exists when the draft on the ground water supply is less than the safe yield,' and that overdraft exists when such draft 'exceeds the safe yield.' 'Safe yield' is defined as 'the maximum quantity of water which can be withdrawn annually from a ground water supply under a given set of conditions without causing an undesirable result.' The phrase 'undesirable result' is understood to refer to a gradual lowering of the ground water levels resulting eventually in depletion of the supply.

"Although the parties differ sharply over the correct meanings of 'surplus' and 'overdraft' under the present facts, they are in accord over the concept of 'safe yield' and the essential correctness of the method by which the referee and the expert witnesses computed the safe yield of the ULARA [Upper Los Angeles River Area] and its component basins for particular years. Basically, safe yield was deemed equivalent to an adjusted figure for net ground water recharge, consisting of (A) recharge from (1) native precipitation and associated runoff, (2) return flow from delivered imported water, and (3) return flow from delivered ground water less (B) losses incurred through natural ground water depletions consisting of (1) subsurface outflow, (2) excessive evaporative losses in high ground water areas and through vegetation along streams, (3) ground water infiltration into sewers, and (4) rising water outflow, or water emerging from the ground and flowing past Gauging Station No. F57 down the river channel to the sea. The component figures for the particular safe yield year being determined were adjusted to eliminate the effect of fluctuations extraneous to the long range calculation. The adjustment of chief importance here was the use of a 29-year base period, consisting of the water years 1928-1929 through 1956-1957, for the computation of all items dependent upon precipitation. This 29-year period was selected as one for which (1) adequate hydrological data was available and (2) precipitation figures were representative, in both average level and fluctuations, of the 85 years for which weather records were relatively complete.

"Plaintiff contends that the trial court's definition of overdraft as a condition in which draft exceeds safe yield, although consistent with the *Pasadena* decision, is insufficient for the facts of the present case. According to plaintiff, overdraft commenced in the ULARA only when (1) total extractions exceeded safe yield and (2) the available water storage capacity of the basin was sufficient to permit cycling of the safe yield throughout the 29-year base period of wet and dry years without causing a waste of water in the wet years. The referee's report as well as other evidence showed that when ground basin levels were relatively high, and storage space correspondingly diminished, waste occurred. Ground basin levels tended to vary in accordance with wide fluctuations in precipitation. Thus if a rising level of extractions were halted at the point of the safe yield based on the 29-year average, ensuing heightening of ground water levels during years of higher-than-average precipitation would cause waste. Since this waste would constitute a loss of basin water in addition to the safe yield extractions, it would eventually create enough additional storage space to stop further similar waste, but the wasted water itself would be lost to any beneficial use. On the other hand, a withdrawal of water from the basin over and above its safe yield in the amount necessary to create the storage space sufficient to prevent the waste would result in a net addition to the beneficially used supply.

"We agree with plaintiff that if a ground basin's lack of storage space will cause a limitation of extractions to safe yield to result in a probable waste of water, the amount of water which if withdrawn would create the storage space necessary to avoid the waste and not adversely affect the basin's safe yield is a temporary surplus available for appropriation to beneficial use. Accordingly, overdraft occurs only if extractions from the basin exceed its safe yield plus any such temporary surplus."

3. **Departures from safe-yield management in California.** Hi-Desert County Water District v. Blue Skies Country Club, Inc., 28 Cal. Rptr. 2d 909 (Ct. App. 1994), reported a stipulated judgment in a judicial adjudication whereby the parties contracted out of the safe-yield limit on groundwater withdrawals implicit in *Pasadena* and *San Fernando*. The judgment adjudicated overlying and appropriative rights totaling 2,303 acre-feet per year in a high desert basin with an estimated safe yield of only 200 acre-feet per year (later revised to 900 acre-feet per year). Reciting a need to allow "controlled mining" to enable development of the resource, the stipulated judgment allows the parties to pump their full adjudicated rights but calls for an appointed watermaster to devise a "physical solution" to the overdraft, under which water would be imported into the basin and the money to pay for it would be raised by assessing the parties.

The lack of state administrative regulation of groundwater extraction has resulted in serious overdraft of a number of groundwater basins in California despite the safe-yield limit that is implicit in *Pasadena* and *San Fernando*. In the absence of enforcement of the safe-yield limit by the state or by private litigation, some local governments decided to regulate groundwater withdrawals. A common feature of these regulatory schemes has been the prohibition of groundwater withdrawals for export and use elsewhere. Ellen Hanak & Caitlin Dyckman, Counties Wresting Control: Local Responses to California's Statewide Water Market, 6 U. Den. Water L. Rev. 490 (2003); Gregory S. Weber, Twenty Years of Local Groundwater Export Legislation in California: Lessons from a Patchwork Quilt, 34 Nat. Resources J. 657 (1994). Baldwin v. County of Tehama, 36 Cal. Rptr. 2d 886 (Cal. Ct. App. 1994), held that a county ordinance regulating the extraction of groundwater for use on land other than where the extraction occurs was not preempted by state law.

4. **Unexercised overlying rights.** In re Waters of Long Valley Creek Stream System, supra p. 316, footnote 2, held that in administrative adjudication of a stream system, unexercised riparian rights could be subordinated to existing riparian and appropriative water uses. In private groundwater litigation, could a court subordinate unexercised overlying rights to existing overlying and appropriative water uses? No, according to Wright v. Goleta Water District, 219 Cal. Rptr. 740 (Ct. App. 1985). The court viewed *Long Valley* as limited to statutory adjudications of streams by the State Water Resources Control Board. It ruled that *Long Valley* could not be extended to groundwater because no similar statutory scheme exists for the comprehensive determination of all groundwater rights in a basin.

TOWN OF CHINO VALLEY v. CITY OF PRESCOTT

Supreme Court of Arizona, 1981.
131 Ariz. 78, 638 P.2d 1324.

STRUNKMEYER, CHIEF JUSTICE. This appeal is from an order of the Superior Court of Yavapai County dismissing the Town of Chino Valley's complaint to enjoin the City of Prescott from withdrawing groundwater from the Granite Creek Critical Groundwater Area. Order of the Superior Court affirmed.

The Town of Chino Valley lies approximately fifteen miles north of the City of Prescott in Yavapai County, Arizona. Prescott owns 164 acres of land in the Chino Valley. In 1948, it drilled wells on some of its Chino Valley property and began transporting groundwater through a seventeen-mile pipeline to its municipal customers. In 1962, * * * the State Land Department established the Granite Creek Critical Groundwater Area. On September 20, 1970, the Town was incorporated. It was within the Granite Creek Critical Groundwater Area and it owned lands and was withdrawing groundwater from the same underground basin as Prescott. Prescott, itself, was not within the Granite Creek Critical Groundwater Area.

This action was filed on August 21, 1972, seeking to enjoin the pumping of groundwater by Prescott. It did not seek damages for the unlawful pumping or transportation of groundwaters. The lawsuit proceeded at a desultory pace until the order of dismissal on November 3, 1980. * * *

[I]n June of 1980, the Legislature enacted the Groundwater Management Act, herein called the Act or the 1980 Act.* It * * * abolished critical

* The 1980 Act provided for the establishment of Active Management Areas which are geographical areas where groundwater supplies are imperiled. Active Management Areas encompass a whole groundwater basin or basins. Groundwater basins are areas designated as enclosing a relatively hydrologically distinct body or related bodies of groundwater. Groundwater sub-basins are areas designated so to enclose a smaller hydrologically distinct body of groundwater found within a groundwater basin. The 1980 Act provides limitations on use of groundwater in Active Management Areas. In general the Act restricts new uses of water drawn from Active Management Areas. The Act sets up a system of determining grandfathered rights to use groundwater in Active Management Areas, defining certain usages of groundwater previously being made and allowing these usages to continue. The Act also establishes the rights of cities, towns, private water companies and irrigation districts in Active Management Areas to withdraw as much groundwater as is needed from within their service areas to serve their customers although restrictions are provided on extensions of service areas and the types of service that may be provided by these entities. The Act also specifies a few other new uses of groundwater that may be made in Active Management Areas. It allows limited new withdrawals for domestic purposes. It also sets up a system for obtaining permits to withdraw new amounts of water for certain specific purposes.

Provided withdrawal is permitted under any of the provisions of the Act, transportation of groundwater within the same sub-basin may be made without payment of damages. Transportation of groundwater between sub-basins or away from Active Management Areas is also authorized if the groundwater is allowed to be withdrawn under the Act's provisions, but damages must be paid for any injury caused. Rules for determining damage are set out. The transportation rules apply whether in or outside of Active Management Areas, although the restrictions on new uses of groundwater do not apply outside of Active Management Areas.

The Act provides for conservation for all uses of groundwater in Active Management Areas. The Act ends with provisions governing the drilling and registering of wells for with-

groundwater areas, substituting geographic units of groundwater management called Active Management Areas and Irrigation Non-Expansion Areas. Certain areas which had been declared critical groundwater areas under former laws were included in the Active Management Areas. By A.R.S. § 45-411(A)(3), the Prescott Active Management Area was established. It includes the Little Chino and Upper Agua Fria Sub-basins. Both the Town of Chino Valley and Prescott are within the Little Chino Sub-basin of the Prescott Active Management Area.

By A.R.S. § 45-541(A) of the 1980 Act, transportation of groundwater is allowed within a sub-basin of an Active Management Area. Prescott, being within the Little Chino Sub-basin from which it was drawing water, moved for dismissal of the Town's complaint for injunctive relief. The Superior Court granted Prescott's motion, but ordered that the Town have twenty days in which to file an amended complaint specifying any damages. The Town's appeal from that portion of the trial court's order dismissing appellants' claim for injunctive relief is based upon the asserted unconstitutionality of the Act of 1980 since the Act, by permitting the transportation of groundwater, legitimatizes the prospective withdrawal of groundwater from the Little Chino Sub-basin by Prescott. Appellants' principal attack is that the Act takes property without due process of law and without just compensation. * * *

[I]n 1919, the Arizona Legislature provided that the water of all sources falling in streams, canyons, ravines, natural channels or definite underground channels belonged to the public and were subject to appropriation for beneficial use. Waters percolating beneath the soil were not included among those subject to appropriation. Appellants rely on the cases of Howard v. Perrin, 8 Ariz. 347, 76 P. 460 (1904), and Maricopa County Water Conservation District No. 1 v. Southwest Cotton Co., 39 Ariz. 65, 4 P.2d 369 (1931), for their basic proposition that they own the water percolating beneath their lands under the doctrine of reasonable use. * * *

Appellants urge that the 1980 Act denies them due process of law and just compensation. The question therefore is, what are a landowner's rights in the water percolating under his lands?

In our recent case of Town of Chino Valley v. State Land Dept., 119 Ariz. 243, 580 P.2d 704 (1978), we said: "Under the doctrine of reasonable use property owners have the right to capture and use the underground water beneath their land for a beneficial purpose on that land * * *." This statement we think is supported by the better reasoned decisions in this country. In the absolute sense, there can be no ownership in seeping and percolating waters until they are reduced to actual possession and control by the person claiming them because of their migratory character. Like wild animals free to roam as they please, they are the property of no one. * * *

We therefore hold that there is no right of ownership of groundwater in Arizona prior to its capture and withdrawal from the common supply and that the right of the owner of the overlying land is simply to the usufruct of the water.

---

drawing groundwater, and financial and enforcement provisions to carry out the legislation.

This brings us to conclude that appellants' position that the 1980 Act violates the Fifth and Fourteenth Amendments to the Constitution of the United States and art. 2, § 17 of the Constitution of the State of Arizona as a taking of private property without due process of law and just compensation cannot be sustained.

The Legislature, in Ch. 2 of the 1980 Act, A.R.S. § 45-401, declared:

> "A. The legislature finds that the people of Arizona are dependent in whole or in part upon groundwater basins for their water supply and that in many basins and sub-basins withdrawal of groundwater is greatly in excess of the safe annual yield and that this is threatening to destroy the economy of certain areas of this state and is threatening to do substantial injury to the general economy and welfare of this state and its citizens. The legislature further finds that it is in the best interest of the general economy and welfare of this state and its citizens that the legislature evoke its police power to prescribe which uses of groundwater are most beneficial and economically effective.
>
> "B. It is therefore declared to be the public policy of this state that in the interest of protecting and stabilizing the general economy and welfare of this state and its citizens it is necessary to conserve, protect and allocate the use of groundwater resources of the state and to provide a framework for the comprehensive management and regulation of the withdrawal, transportation, use, conservation and conveyance of rights to use the groundwater in this state."

We do not doubt but that the overdraft of groundwater in this state is a serious problem which has no chance of correcting itself, and that it is necessary for comprehensive legislation to both limit groundwater use and allocate its use among competing interests.

More than twenty-five years ago, this Court decided that the Legislature might choose between competing interests where the supply of groundwater was limited. In Southwest Engineering Co. v. Ernst, 79 Ariz. 403, 291 P.2d 764 (1955), we said in holding constitutional the groundwater act of 1948:

> "The legislative finding that the exhaustion of ground water by excessive withdrawals threatens to destroy one of the principal economic resources of the state to the consequential serious injury of all is not disputed. Such a conclusion is obviously justified because unrestrained use must inevitably result either in complete exhaustion of the state's ground water so that in the end the lands dependent thereon will revert to their desert state or in the lowering of water tables so that the increased cost of pumping will reduce these lands to a marginal or submarginal condition." Id. at 408-09, 291 P.2d at 768 (footnote omitted).

We held that there was a preponderant public interest in the preservation of lands then in cultivation as against lands potentially reclaimable "and that where as here the choice is unavoidable because a supply of water is not available for both, we cannot say that the exercise of such choice, controlled by considerations of social policy which are not unreasonable, involves a denial of due process." Id. at 410, 291 P.2d at 769. The Legislature in the Act of 1980 again recognized that the supply of groundwater is limited and again exercised a choice for the preservation and use of groundwater.

Legislation which denies or restricts rights to use property necessarily results in a diminution of that property's value. Yet the United States Supreme Court has on numerous occasions upheld under the state's police power regulations of land use which have virtually destroyed private interests. * * * In the present case, appellants may make such use of their property as they choose, except that their lands may not be irrigated if they were not legally irrigated in the last five years. The 1980 Act furthers legitimate state interests.

Legislatures of various states have from time to time abolished the prevailing uses of groundwater and substituted other plans for its use. State courts have uniformly rejected the idea that groundwater percolating through the soil may not be limited and regulated and must be acquired by eminent domain. * * *

The order of the court below is affirmed.

Notes

1. **The Arizona Groundwater Management Act.** The Arizona Legislature passed the enormous and enormously complicated groundwater act in a single-day special session, and the governor signed it into law the next day. The truly amazing story of the Groundwater Study Commission that prepared the first draft, the federal pressure on the state to enact a code, and the negotiations, concessions, and compromises of the cities, mining companies, and farmers whose "hired guns" hammered out the final bill in a lengthy "rump session" preceding the legislative session is told in Desmond D. Connall, Jr., A History of the Arizona Groundwater Management Act, 1982 Ariz. St. L.J. 313. The next two excerpts provide further details on the genesis and key substantive provisions of the act.

Frank J. Trelease, Conjunctive Use of Groundwater and Surface Water, 27B Rocky Mtn. Min. L. Inst. 1853, 1877-78 (1982):

"The 1980 Arizona Groundwater Management Act is the culmination of a long struggle to bring some order out of the chaos resulting from the disastrous judicial adherence to the so-called 'reasonable use rule' that allowed every landowner unrestricted pumping for use on his land, but severely limited the transportation of water to places where it was needed for municipal and industrial use. The rate of overdraft was checked by the [earlier] legislative restriction of new wells in critical areas, but cities, mining companies, and farmers hacked away at Arizona's very slowly recharging aquifers until overdraft of groundwater reached 2.2 million acre-feet per year. The Act is an enormously complex piece of regulation, carefully designed to impose strict controls on previously unregulated groundwater withdrawals with the least possible disruption. All existing uses of groundwater are converted into 'grandfathered rights' and adjusted in quantity to meet new standards of conservation. The law's main design is to reduce overdraft, so it requires maximum use of surface water before groundwater is used. 'Surface water' will include a very large block of Colorado River water imported under the Central Arizona Project (CAP) * * *."

U.S. Advisory Comm'n on Intergovernmental Relations, Coordinating Water Resources in the Federal System: The Groundwater-Surface Water Connection 33-35 (1991):

"The importation and use of water, when CAP is operating at its full capacity of 1.2 million acre-feet per year, is expected to reduce reliance on groundwater supplies in central and southern Arizona enough to cut the overdraft by as much as two-thirds. * * * [N]o new agricultural lands may be brought into production using CAP water (except on Indian lands), and existing agricultural users of groundwater who receive water from the CAP must reduce pumping by equivalent amounts. In times of shortages, municipal and industrial uses of CAP water have an absolute priority over agricultural uses. * * *

"The remaining one-third or more of the statewide overdraft is to be solved by management and conservation methods. The Groundwater Management Act * * * designates four active management areas (AMAs) and two irrigation non-expansion areas (INAs) with boundaries approximately coterminous with those of major groundwater areas * * *. Eighty percent of Arizona's population and 70 percent of its water consumption are located within the four AMAs. [Later, the Act was amended to create a fifth AMA out of part of one of the original four, and a third INA was designated by administrative action.] The goal of the legislation is to establish a balance between water supply and demand within the AMAs by 2025 (except in the predominantly agricultural Pinal AMA, where a controlled mining operation will be pursued). Within each AMA, a director is responsible for the implementation of the act, with the recommendations of a five-member AMA advisory council. * * *

"The act established a formal decisionmaking structure that centralizes authority in the governor and the Department of Water Resources (DWR) and its director, and creates weaker authority in the local agencies. * * * The governor appoints the DWR director as well as the local AMA advisory council members. The DWR director appoints the AMA directors and is responsible for making a series of 10-year management plans for each AMA (with tighter water use restrictions during each period). The director is authorized to determine maximum water duties for irrigation and water conservation requirements for municipalities and industries within the AMAs, review the plans of local authorities for reducing groundwater withdrawals in critically overdrafted areas, file for civil and criminal penalties for violators of regulations promulgated under the act, set water withdrawal fees, and, ultimately, take land out of agricultural production if necessary.

"The 45-year period from 1980 to 2025 has been divided into five management periods to establish step-by-step control and eventual elimination of groundwater overdrafting. In the first period, from 1980 to 1990, the Department of Water Resources registered wells and defined groundwater rights through an application-and-permit program, with different classes of withdrawal rights but without many requirements or restrictions. The intention was to bring the implementation of the Code along relatively slowly at first, to try to heighten compliance with the first stages before the more restrictive provisions are applied. * * *

"[Apart from some de minimis uses that are not heavily regulated, the act recognizes and regulates three types of rights to withdraw groundwater within AMAs: grandfathered rights, service area rights, and withdrawal permit rights. Although nonirrigation grandfathered rights are recognized, the major grandfathered rights are for irrigation.] Lands that were not irrigated at some time between January

1, 1975, and January 1, 1980, do not qualify for a grandfathered irrigation right and may not be brought into irrigated agricultural production. The clear intention is to freeze the level of irrigated agricultural production that existed in 1980. Reductions in irrigated agricultural acreage and water consumption are reserved for later management periods.

"Grandfathered irrigation rights remain with the land and can be used by a new owner. The groundwater may be used only on the overlying land, however, and the rights remain with the land. If lands with grandfathered irrigation rights are sold for uses other than irrigated agriculture, the rights transfer at a predetermined rate of 3 acre-feet per year. * * *

"Municipalities, water companies, and irrigation districts apply for permits for service area rights to withdraw, transport, and distribute groundwater, provided they remain within per capita water conservation requirements set by the DWR director. Persons not eligible for grandfathered * * * rights or service area rights may apply for groundwater withdrawal permits for [certain] nonirrigation purposes.

"Within the irrigation non-expansion areas, no new land may be brought into irrigated agricultural production. * * * Water withdrawal and consumption for other types of uses [that are reasonable and beneficial, Ariz. Rev. Stat. Ann. § 45-453] may develop [largely] without restriction. * * *

"Groundwater management activities are financed on a 50-50 basis with appropriations from the state General Fund and funds raised from water withdrawal fees assessed against groundwater pumping. Groundwater users who are required to meter their wells and annually report their pumpage are also required to pay the 'pump tax.' The withdrawal fee is set by the DWR director within the guidelines of the law, with a cap of $5.00 per acre-foot. Up to $1.00 of the withdrawal fee may be used to meet operating costs of DWR. Up to another $2.00 may be used for water supply augmentation after the director has established an augmentation plan for the AMA * * *. The remaining $2.00 of the fee is for the purchase and retirement of agricultural land, and cannot be levied until after 2006.

"The 1990-to-2000 management period calls for the implementation of a plan to augment water supplies. The director may propose any means of augmentation from artificial recharge to weather modification. The 2000-to-2010 management period includes the possibility, after 2006, of purchasing and retiring agricultural land to meet water conservation goals and ensure a balance between demand and supply."

The Arizona Legislature has supplemented the 1980 Act years with measures designed to promote water conservation and water supply augmentation. A study done near the end of the second ten-year management period finds, however, that the Act will not likely achieve the goal of safe yield by 2025 that it sets for the Prescott, Phoenix, and Tucson AMAs. This is because of numerous grandfathered rights that cannot be reduced significantly and because of restrictions on DWR's regulatory authority, e.g., DWR must issue groundwater permits for industrial and mineral extraction uses if the applicants meet certain criteria. Auditor General, Report No. 99-8, Performance Audit of the Arizona Department of Water Resources (1999). See also Robert J. Glennon, "Because That's Where the Water Is": Retiring Current Water Uses to Achieve the Safe-Yield Objective of the Arizona Groundwater Management Act, 33 Ariz. L. Rev. 89 (1991) (arguing that water conservation programs and water supply augmentation from CAP and other sources will be insufficient to achieve the safe-yield goal, and proposing a program for retiring current agricultural water rights to meet the goal).

2. **Condemnation.** Sorensen v. Lower Niobrara Natural Resources District, 376 N.W.2d 539 (Neb. 1985), concerned condemnation of the exercised and *unexercised* groundwater rights of an overlying owner under Nebraska's doctrine of "reasonable use and correlative rights," as the court called it. The court said that "the right to use ground water does not float in a vacuum of abstraction but exists only in reference to and results from ownership of the overlying land." It reasoned that the because the right is "a proprietary appurtenance inseparable from the land benefited," the right constitutes property protected by the takings clause of the Nebraska constitution. The court indicated that just compensation could be measured by the difference in land value to a well-informed buyer immediately before and after the taking.

In an appropriation doctrine state, suppose unappropriated water in quantities usable by City *Y* underlies *X*'s irrigable land, and the city desires to drill a well on the land and build a pipeline across it. What would the city buy or condemn from *X*, and how would just compensation be measured? Suppose alternatively (a) that the city's withdrawals will not prevent *X* from obtaining a permit for a groundwater appropriation to irrigate the land, or (b) that because of well-spacing requirements or safe-yield restrictions, the city's well will prevent *X* from obtaining an appropriation to irrigate the land.

On measuring just compensation, see John C. Peck & Kent Weatherby, Condemnation of Water and Water Rights in Kansas, 42 Kan. L. Rev. 827, 854-66 (1994).

3. **Another approach to managing storage.** Oklahoma changed in 1949 from reasonable use to a statutory form of prior appropriation and in 1973 changed again to a unique groundwater act, Okla. Stat. tit. 82, §§ 1020.1-.22. The 1973 act, as amended, distinguishes between major and minor groundwater basins, differentiated by the basinwide average yield of wells. The act directs the state water resources board to determine the maximum annual yield of each basin or subbasin based on hydrologic surveys. The maximum annual yield in a major basin or subbasin must be based on a minimum life of twenty years; in a minor basin or subbasin, it must be based on the present and reasonably foreseeable use of water, the recharge and total discharge, and other relevant factors. Permits from the board are required to use groundwater for all but domestic purposes. The board can issue a permit only to the owner or lessee of the land on which the well is to be located (or under Ricks Exploration Co. v. Oklahoma Water Resources Board., 695 P.2d 498 (Okla. 1984), to the owner of a mineral estate who needs water for mining). In a basin or subbasin where the board has determined the maximum annual yield, a permittee is allocated a proportionate share of the yield. The share equals the percentage of the total land overlying the basin or subbasin that the permittee owns or leases. In a basin or subbasin where the board has not yet determined maximum annual yield, it issues only temporary permits, which must be revalidated annually, and limited quantity permits. The act prohibits waste but allows groundwater to be taken off the land from which it is produced. Okla. Water Resources Bd. v. Texas County Irrigation & Water Resources Ass'n, 711 P.2d 38 (Okla. 1984).

DEVIN GALLOWAY ET AL., LAND SUBSIDENCE IN THE UNITED STATES

4 (U.S. Geological Survey Circular No. 1182, 1999).

We begin with five case histories in which overdraft of susceptible aquifer systems has resulted in regional, permanent subsidence and related ground failures. In alluvial aquifer systems, especially those that include semi-consolidated silt and clay layers (aquitards) of sufficient thickness, long-term ground-water-level declines can result in a vast one-time release of "water of compaction" from compacting aquitards, which manifests itself as land subsidence. Accompanying this release of water is a largely nonrecoverable reduction in the pore volume of the compacted aquitards, and thus an overall reduction in the total storage capacity of the aquifer system. This "water of compaction" cannot be reinstated by allowing water levels to recover to their predevelopment status. * * *

The five case studies demonstrate how agricultural and municipal-industrial ground-water use have combined to deplete critical ground-water resources and create costly regional-scale subsidence. We begin in the "Silicon Valley" in northern California, where early agricultural ground-water use contributed to subsidence that has increased flood risks in the greater San Jose area. Silicon Valley (properly the Santa Clara Valley) was the first place in the United States where subsidence due to ground-water pumpage was recognized; since the late 1960s, the ground-water resource there has been successfully managed to halt subsidence. In nearby San Joaquin Valley, the single largest human alteration of the Earth's surface topography resulted from excessive ground-water pumpage to sustain an exceptionally productive agriculture. In the Houston-Galveston area in Texas, early production of oil and gas, and a long history of ground-water pumpage, have created severe and costly coastal-flooding hazards and affected a critical environmental resource—the Galveston Bay estuary. In Las Vegas Valley ground-water depletion and subsidence have accompanied the conversion of a desert oasis into a thirsty and fast-growing metropolis. Finally, in south-central Arizona, importation of Colorado River water and conversion of water-intensive agriculture to lower-water-demand urban land uses has [sic] helped to partly arrest subsidence and forestall further fissuring of the Earth's surface.

Notes

1. **Liability for subsidence damage.** Friendswood Development Co. v. Smith-Southwest Industries, Inc., 576 S.W.2d 21 (Tex. 1978):

"[I]n 1975 the Legislature undertook to retard further subsidence in Harris and Galveston Counties by creating a subsidence district with power to prevent future [location of wells too close together] and excessive pumping of the nature alleged to have occurred in this case. Previously, in 1949 the Legislature provided for the creation of districts for the purpose of 'conservation, preservation, protection, recharging, and prevention of waste of underground water * * *.'" In 1973, the Legislature added to such purposes the authority "to control subsidence caused by withdrawal of water * * *."

"It is of some importance to note that in the laws authorizing these regulatory Underground Water Districts and the Harris-Galveston Coastal Subsidence District, the Legislature specifically confirmed private ownership of underground water. It provided: "The ownership and rights of the owner of land and his lessees and assigns in underground water are hereby recognized, and nothing in this Act shall be construed as depriving or divesting the owner or his lessees and assigns of the ownership or rights * * *," subject only to the regulatory rules to be promulgated by the districts. See Vernon's Tex. Water Code Ann. § 52.002 and Sec. 29, Ch. 284, Acts 64 Leg.1975.

"[No] Texas case has dealt specifically with land subsidence resulting from * * * pumping of underground waters. In other jurisdictions adhering to the English ground water rule, liability for neighboring land subsidence has been denied. * * *

"We agree that some aspects of the English or common law rule as to underground waters are harsh and outmoded, and the rule has been severely criticized since its reaffirmation by this Court in 1955. Most of the critics, however, recognize that it has become an established rule of property law in this State, under which many citizens own land and water rights. The rule has been relied upon by thousands of farmers, industries, and municipalities in purchasing and developing vast tracts of land overlying aquifers of underground water. Approximately 50,000 wells are used to irrigate 2,800,000 acres in the thirteen county High Plains area of West Texas. As shown in the official reports cited earlier in this opinion, over 2,600 water wells have been drilled in Harris County alone while this rule of immunity from liability was in effect. The very wells which brought about this action were drilled after the English rule had been reaffirmed by this Court in 1955. * * *

"As heretofore mentioned, the Legislature has entered the field of regulation of ground water withdrawals and subsidence. This occurred after geologists, hydrologists, and engineers had developed more accurate knowledge concerning the location, source, and measurement of percolating underground waters, and after legislators became aware of the potential conflicts inherent in the unregulated use of ground water under the English rule of ownership. With a rule that recognizes ownership of underground water by each individual under his own land, but with no limitation on the manner and amount which another individual landowner might produce (absent willful waste and malicious malice), legislative action was essential in order to provide for conservation and protection of public interests.

"The legislative policy * * * of the Texas Water Code is designed to limit the exercise of that portion of the English rule which has been interpreted as giving each landowner the right to take all the water he pleases without regard to the effect on other lands in the same area. * * * Providing policy and regulatory procedures in this field is a legislative function. It is well that the Legislature has assumed its proper role, because our courts are not equipped to regulate ground water uses and subsidence on a suit-by-suit basis.

"This case, however, gives the Court its first opportunity to recognize, and to encourage compliance with, the policy set forth by the Legislature and its regulatory agencies in an effort to curb excessive underground water withdrawals and resulting land subsidence. It also affords us the opportunity to discard an objectionable aspect of the court-made English rule as it relates to subsidence by stating a rule for the future which is more in harmony with expressed legislative policy. We refer to the past immunity from negligence which heretofore has been afforded ground water producers solely because of their "absolute" ownership of the water.

"As far as we can determine, there is no other use of private real property which enjoys such an immunity from liability under the law of negligence. This ownership of underground water comes with ownership of the surface; it is part of the soil. Yet, the use of one's ground-level surface and other elements of the soil is without such insulation from tort liability. Our consideration of this case convinces us that there is no valid reason to continue this special immunity insofar as it relates to future subsidence proximately caused by negligence in the manner which wells are drilled or produced in the future. It appears that the ownership and rights of all landowners will be better protected against subsidence if each has the duty to produce water from his land in a manner that will not negligently damage or destroy the lands of others.

"Therefore, if the landowner's manner of withdrawing ground water from his land is negligent, willfully wasteful, or for the purpose of malicious injury, and such conduct is a proximate cause of the subsidence of the land of others, he will be liable for the consequences of his conduct. The addition of negligence as a ground of recovery shall apply only to future subsidence proximately caused by future withdrawals of ground water from wells which are either produced or drilled in a negligent manner after the date this opinion becomes final."

What does the negligence standard of *Friendswood* mean for pumpers who cause subsidence? Compare Olin L. Browder et al., Basic Property Law 187-88 (5th ed. 1989) (might approach strict liability), with David Todd, Common Resources, Private Rights and Liabilities: A Case Study on Texas Groundwater Law, 32 Nat. Resources J. 232, 253 (1992) (might require high levels of negligence or foreseeability).

2. **Interference with water use versus land subsidence.** The absolute ownership and reasonable use doctrines originated in cases where the defendant's groundwater pumping interfered with the plaintiff's water uses. In the foundational absolute ownership cases in both England and the United States, the defendants pumped water from mines to enable mining, and that interfered with the plaintiffs' springs or wells. Acton v. Blundell, 152 Eng. Rep. 1223 (Ex. Ch. 1843); Wheatley v. Baugh, 25 Pa. 528 (1855). In the leading case establishing the reasonable use doctrine, the parties were competing water users. Forbell v. City of New York, 58 N.E. 644 (N.Y. 1900). Thus, despite variation as to whether the defendant was a land user who extracted groundwater only to facilitate the land use or was a competing water user, the plaintiffs in these cases were water users complaining of impaired supply.

The more recent cases adopting the Restatement approach were factually similar to the foundational absolute ownership cases. In *Michels Pipeline*, supra p. 392, the defendants pumped groundwater to enable tunneling for a sewer line, causing the plaintiffs wells to go dry (though also causing land subsidence). The two Restatement cases in Note 5, supra pp. 335-36, involved the dewatering of quarries that interfered with the wells of neighboring landowners.

In contrast to all these cases, *Friendswood* was purely a land subsidence case. The plaintiffs were not asserting impairment of their water rights. And the governing legal doctrine changed. Rather than apply the absolute ownership doctrine, the Texas court decided that negligence law should govern prospectively. Similarly, although Alabama uses the reasonable use doctrine to govern disputes between competing water users, Martin v. City of Linden, 667 So. 2d 732 (Ala. 1995), nuisance law governs when the dewatering of a quarry causes subsidence damage to a neighboring house. Henderson v. Wade Sand & Gravel Co., 388 So. 2d 900 (Ala. 1980). In both states, tort law—negligence or nuisance—rather than a groundwater property right doctrine governs when the only injury from pumping is land subsidence.

Indiana, which has the absolute ownership doctrine for groundwater rights, adds yet another legal theory to make a groundwater pumper liable for subsidence damage. In City of Valparaiso v. Defler, 694 N.E.2d 1177 (Ind. Ct. App. 1998), the court analogized to Indiana cases holding miners liable for subsidence caused by their removal of subjacent support from overlying land. The court expressly left open, however, whether to borrow the rule of strict liability from mineral cases or to use another standard of liability (presumably negligence) when subsidence is caused by the removal of groundwater rather than the removal of minerals.

California uses the correlative rights doctrine for water use disputes, but a city whose groundwater pumping caused subsidence damage to neighboring buildings was held liable under the theory of inverse condemnation. Los Osos Valley Assocs. v. City of San Luis Obispo, 36 Cal. Rptr. 2d 758 (Ct. App. 1994). The court relied on Restatement (Second) of Torts § 818: "One who is privileged to withdraw subterranean water, oil, minerals or other substances from under the land of another is not for that reason privileged to cause a subsidence of the other's land by the withdrawal."

3. **Regulation of mine dewatering.** Natural Resources Commission v. AMAX Coal Co., 638 N.E.2d 418 (Ind. 1994), held that the absolute ownership doctrine does not preclude a state agency from conditioning issuance of a permit to strip mine upon proof that the permit applicant's dewatering plans will not harm neighboring landowners. A few western states have legislation that regulates mine dewatering. For example, New Mexico requires a dewatering permit, and the miner must provide replacement water to groundwater users whose rights are impaired by dewatering. N.M. Stat. Ann. §§ 72-12A-1 to -13. The laws of selected western states are discussed in Michael F. Browning, Mine Dewatering: Water Right and Water Quality Issues, 38 Rocky Mtn. Min. L. Inst. 24-1 (1992).

B. Protection of Means of Diversion

JAMES W. CROSBY, III, A LAYMAN'S GUIDE TO GROUNDWATER HYDROLOGY

Charles E. Corker, Groundwater Law, Management and Administration, National Water Commission, Legal Study No. 6, Chapter II, 45-47, 95 (1971).

[1]. Wells and Well Hydraulics

Wells are the instruments through which groundwater is generally produced. Wells may be dug, bored, or drilled, and they may be virtually any depth or diameter that proves to be economical. In hard rocks, wells are frequently open holes, whereas in unconsolidated materials support in the form of lengths of pipe or casing may be required. So that groundwater can enter the casing, a screen or section of perforated casing is generally emplaced opposite the productive aquifer.

Water in a properly-constructed well will rise to the level of the water table. If artesian, or pressure conditions exist, the water will rise to the level of the *pressure surface*. If the pressure surface is above ground surface, the well will flow freely unless capped. * * *

As pumping is commenced in a well, a quantity of water is discharged by the pump, lowering the water level in the well and nearby formation below the initial water surface in the formation. A gradient, therefore, is created between the nearby water table and the more distant water table. This gradient causes additional water to flow toward the well under the influence of gravity. The water table near the well takes the form of a hole or depression formed in the groundwater surface. Because it appears as an inverted cone around the pumping well, it is appropriately called the *cone of depression*. When the cones of depression of two or more wells overlap, interference results and decline of the water table is accelerated.

If the water-bearing formation has a high permeability, only a small gradient is required to produce a relatively large quantity of water. However, if the permeability is low, it may be found that the gradient required to produce a desired quantity of water exceeds the limit established by the depth at which the pump intake is set. The capacity of the well is exceeded and the pump soon starts sucking air. It is well to note that although the well is sucked dry in this situation, the pump can be turned off and after a period of recovery, the water in the well will return to nearly its original level. The groundwater has in no way been exhausted by the pumping. Rather, the well went dry temporarily and only because the formation was expected to release its stored water at a rate in excess of its physical capabilities.

[2]. Well Interference

* * * A groundwater reservoir requires serious consideration of well spacings to accommodate well interference effects. These phenomena become problems when the cones of depression (cones of pressure relief) of two or more nearby producing wells overlap. Where such overlaps occur the rate of water level decline is substantially increased. The total quantity of water in storage may be quite adequate, but its availability to pumps at particular locations may be inadequate without incurring excessive pumping lifts. These effects can vary greatly and depend in large part on the transmissivity of the aquifer.

[3]. What is a "Reasonable" Pump Lift?

The groundwater statutes of certain states prescribe protection of a prior appropriator to a "reasonable pump lift" or terms of similar import. Herein lies one of the single greatest obstacles to groundwater management in states recognizing appropriative doctrines.

What is a reasonable pump lift? Is it based upon economic or social criteria? What may be reasonable to an irrigator may be totally unacceptable to a farmer dependent upon groundwater for his domestic supply and yet these people must share the fruits of the same resource. All too frequently the development of deep, highly productive irrigation wells has had a detrimental effect upon shallower domestic wells, occasionally causing them to go completely dry. Proper management, however, might provide adequate protection for the shallow production or replacement by supplemental sources.

Notes

1. **Causes of interference with means of diversion: mining and overlapping cones.** The term "mining" is occasionally used to refer to any removal of water from storage, including that associated with a cone of depression around a well even though, as Crosby notes, the water table may recover around the well nearly to its original level during nonpumping periods. More commonly, however, "mining" refers only to sustained overdraft that permanently depletes storage. See, e.g., U.S. Geological Survey, Water-Supply Paper No. 2250, supra pp. 345-46, Note 2; Baker v. Ore-Idaho Foods, Inc., supra p. 357, Note 3.

Obviously, mining in the sense of sustained overdraft of a basin or subbasin can render the means of diversion of existing wells inadequate. A state's decision to allow mining in that sense, even on a controlled basis, implies that existing diversion methods will not be protected against water level decline in a well due to mining. When the New Mexico court in Mathers v. Texaco, Inc., supra pp. 350-51, Note 1, allowed two-thirds of the water in a basin receiving very limited recharge to be mined over forty years, it stated: "A lowering of the water level in the wells of protestants, together with the resulting increase in pumping costs and the lowering of pumping yields, does not constitute an impairment of the rights of protestants as a matter of law. These are inevitable results of the beneficial use by the public of these waters."

Mining in the sense of sustained overdraft is not the only possible cause of interference with the means of diversion of existing wells. As the Crosby excerpt points out, a new well's cone of depression (or pressure relief in a confined aquifer) might interfere with existing wells if the new well is too large and too close to the existing ones given the transmissivity of the aquifer. This happens even though, as Crosby puts it, "[t]he groundwater has in no way been exhausted by the pumping." Such interference with existing wells can often be avoided or at least minimized by well spacing requirements.

2. **Legal theories to protect a means of diversion.** If a well goes dry because of sustained overdraft in violation of state policy on mining, the well owner can seek enforcement of that policy. But if an overlap of cones of depression is the cause, the well owner would need a different legal theory. The next principal case and some of the Notes following it explore possibilities.

CURRENT CREEK IRRIGATION CO. v. ANDREWS

Supreme Court of Utah, 1959.
9 Utah 2d 324, 344 P.2d 528.

WADE, JUSTICE. * * * The central problem is whether prior appropriators of water from an underground basin, who receive it by means of flowing wells and springs, have a vested right to continue receiving water by artesian pressure; and whether subsequent appropriators, whose withdrawals of water lower the water table and reduce the flow of prior wells, must restore the pressure or bear the expense of replacing the water of prior appropriators.

All of the wells and springs belonging to the parties are in a single broad alluvial fan, which slopes westward from the Wasatch Mountains, in north Juab Valley. * * *

Fowkes are owners of 11 artesian wells and one spring which are located well up eastward on the alluvial fan and toward its northern part: the use is for domestic purposes and for irrigation of approximately 115 acres of land. * * *

Andrews are the owners of a spring and five flowing wells located roughly one-half mile southeast of the Fowkes wells and therefore higher on the fan, which are used to irrigate about 150 acres of land. They date to 1915 or before but are later in priority than the Fowkes wells. Andrews also own the right to use water from a number of seeps and springs which irrigate meadow land and which also have been so used since before 1903. They have further initiated a claim as of March 14, 1950, for a pump well which produces six second feet of water. This was by application to the State Engineer and use is permitted only during the irrigation season.

Current Creek Company's main water source is known as Mona Reservoir, which lies at the center of the valley near its north end. The water is transported about 12 miles to the south for irrigation. The company has also initiated a claim to appropriate 18 second feet of underground water to be pumped from three wells near the reservoir to augment its supply. However, when these wells were drilled they did not produce the anticipated flow, and Current Creek applied for and received approval from the State Engineer to change the location of these wells eastward and higher up on the fan, and to add two additional wells. Thereafter Current Creek contracted with Andrews to permit the drilling of two wells on the latter's property. The new wells produced a better flow of water. The priority date of application for these wells is 1951, although they were not drilled until 1954. They flow by natural pressure about 2.74 second feet of water and are allowed to flow during the entire year for storage in the Mona Reservoir.

This basin upon which all of the wells are situated is classified as a sensitive "cone of influence," because the wells readily affect each other. That is, when the Andrews' pump well is started, the water level drops and the pressure ceases in Andrews' other wells, and in the wells owned by Fowkes; when the pump well is turned off the level pressure rises in the others. Opening and closing the Current Creek Company's wells has the same, although somewhat less, effect. The evidence indicates that the hydrostatic pressure in the Fowkes' and Andrews' flowing wells decreased from about 11 feet above ground in the beginning of 1953 to about 8.5 feet below ground in October, 1956. During the summer of 1956, studies by the State Engineer and the U. S. Geological Survey showed that operation of the Current Creek Company's wells diminished the flow of other wells in the area.

When the operation of the Current Creek wells resulted in stopping the flow in the Fowkes' and Andrews' flowing wells, which had never occurred before, Andrews closed the Current Creek wells on their land and insisted that they be kept closed or damages paid. This is in accordance with Andrews contention as to the terms of their contract. Current Creek's rejoinder is that it was not their wells, but Andrews' own pump well that depleted the Andrews' and Fowkes' flowing wells, and they also assert that Andrews and Fowkes have no absolute rights to artesian pressure, but must use reasonable means and pumping equipment to get their water.

The trial court found that the relative time priorities of the parties to the water in the basin were: (1) springs owned by Andrews and Fowkes, (2) the flowing wells of Andrews and Fowkes, (3) the Andrews' pump well, and (4) the Current Creek Company wells. * * * The court found that there is unappropriated water within the basin. * * *

The court further found that the pump wells of both Andrews and Current Creek interfered with the flow of the flowing wells of Andrews and Fowkes. As to Andrews, it refused to find that the interference in their flow well was caused by the Current Creek wells, as distinguished from the effect caused by their own pump well, and therefore refused to allow them any redress. The decree required Andrews and Current Creek Company to replace for Fowkes 1.775 second feet of water during the irrigation season and 27.11 gallons of water per minute during the nonirrigation season to be supplied by furnishing and installing pumps and sources of power, the cost to be shared equally between them. It further prohibited Andrews and Current Creek from using their pump wells and required them to desist from pumping water until and unless they replaced the water to Fowkes as just stated. * * *

Prior appropriators of this underground water who have beneficially used it through the natural flow of springs or artesian wells are entitled to have the subsequent appropriators restrained from drawing the water out of and lowering the static head pressure of this underground basin unless they replace the quantity and quality of the water by pumping or other means to the prior appropriators at the sole cost of the subsequent appropriators. The same rule should apply to all junior appropriators present and future. They can appropriate water to a beneficial use from the underground basin if it is available but they must replace the flow of the wells and springs at the prior appropriator's place of diversion solely at their own cost. * * *

There can be no doubt that the above is a correct statement of the rules governing this situation. Section 73-3-23, U.C.A. 1953, expressly grants the right of replacement to any junior appropriator whose appropriation diminishes the quantity or quality of previously appropriated underground water at the sole cost or expense of the junior appropriator. The wording of this statute is clear, unambiguous and positive. This court has the highest duty to enforce it and not repeal it by judicial legislation. This section was added by the 1935 Legislature with other sections in order to adapt the law to the new concepts that underground waters are subject to appropriation in accordance with the then very recent decisions of Wrathall v. Johnson and Justesen v. Olsen. * * *

Prior to 1935 we held that percolating waters are a part of the soil and not subject to appropriation, and that underground artesian basins are percolating waters. Still all of our decisions have protected the rights to have the static head pressure maintained. We have consistently enjoined the lowering of the static head pressure which had the effect of preventing a prior user from continuing a beneficial use of underground waters. * * *

The facts of our present case do not indicate that less water will be beneficially used if we continue to follow the right to static head pressure theory. Before the static head pressure was lowered Fowkes received their water without pumping. Now Current Creek gets more water than Fowkes claims from a lower elevation without pumping. There is no reason to believe that the cost of replacement to Current Creek will be prohibitive but that the cost of pumping to Fowkes will be otherwise. So far as this case is concerned, we have the choice between protecting a junior or senior appropriator with nothing whatever to indicate that more water will be beneficially used one way or the other. It would be a mistake to change an age-old system merely in the hope that in some future case more water may be used beneficially under a different system. This court should not completely change the law and ignore an express statute without a showing that such change would cause more water to be beneficially used.

Judgment affirmed. Costs to respondents.

CROCKETT, CHIEF JUSTICE (dissenting). * * * I doubt the wisdom of seeking solutions to problems such as the instant ones in such a generality as a rule that a prior user has the absolute right not only to the water, but to have preserved to him the pressure and the means of diversion under all circumstances. Such a rule may seem easy for the court to apply to rid itself of immediate problems, but it is far from easy in practical operation. More important, it does not serve the fundamental purpose of our water law of providing for the fullest conservation and the highest development of water by making it available to all users in the most convenient and economical way. * * *

The difficulty with preserving to the prior user the absolute right to water and also to the pressure and means of diversion is that projecting its application to basins where there are a great number of users reveals that it does not work to serve the necessary purpose of maximum development and use of water. The evidence indicates and it is a well-known and observable fact, that when the water table of an underground basin is maintained at a high enough level to sustain pressure in flowing wells in the higher areas, there will be water above and near the surface in the lower areas forming ponds, marshes and swamps. This results in wasteful losses from surface evaporation and from consumption by water-loving plants, tules, reeds and rushes, indigenous to such areas, which are of little or no value. There is often further wastage from drainage of the basin by streams or by leakage and seepage out of it.

Under a rule of absolute right to water and pressure, there are other difficulties to be encountered in allocating all the usable water to users. * * * The administrative problems relating to the determination of costs of maintaining pressure for prior users, and allocation against later users, would be insuperable. In addition thereto the cost imposed upon the initiator of a new well might be prohibitive, so that even where there was unused water in the basin it would not be put to use. The various difficulties just discussed make it apparent that it is quite impractical to insure to prior appropriators not only the amount of water they claim, but also the right to have the same pressure maintained as when they made the original appropriation. * * *

In fairness I must concede that the language of Sec. 73-3-23, U.C.A. 1953: "* * * In all cases replacement shall be at the sole cost and expense of the applicant" may reasonably be given the meaning espoused by the majority opinion. * * * However, the preceding language, which provides the foundation for "replacement," states that "the right of replacement is hereby *granted* to any junior appropriator whose appropriation may diminish the quantity or injuriously affect the quality of [prior] appropriated underground water. * * * " (Emphasis added.) Thus *granting* the junior appropriator the *right* of replacement does not necessarily make it mandatory that he maintain pressure and means of diversion under all circumstances. * * * My interpretation of [Utah precedents] is that the prior appropriator gets the right to use the water and to such means of diversion as is reasonably efficient and does not cause undue waste of water.

Notes

1. **A different policy—protection of a reasonable means of diversion.** In City of Colorado Springs v. Bender, 366 P.2d 552 (Colo. 1961), owners of a well used to irrigate approximately fifty acres sued to enjoin interference by the larger, junior wells of a municipality, a hotel, and a water company—all of whom transported the water for use at places remote from the aquifer. The court said:

"At his own point of diversion on a natural water course, each diverter must establish some reasonable means of effectuating his diversion. He is not entitled to command the whole or a substantial flow of the stream merely to facilitate his taking the fraction of the whole flow to which he is entitled. This principle applied to diversion of underflow or underground water means that priority of appropriation does not give a right to an inefficient means of diversion, such as a well which reaches to such a shallow depth into the available water supply that a shortage would occur to such senior even though diversion by others did not deplete the stream below where there would be an adequate supply for the senior's lawful demand. * * *

"In determining [the water level in the aquifer at which a junior appropriator must cease diverting water in order to meet the demands of a senior appropriator,] the conditions surrounding the diversion by the senior appropriator must be examined as to whether he has created a means of diversion from the aquifer which is reasonably adequate for the use to which he has historically put the water of his appropriation. * * *

"A determination of these questions is necessary. The court must determine what, if anything, the plaintiffs should be required to do to make more efficient the facilities at their point of diversion, due regard being given to the purposes for which the appropriation had been made, and the 'economic reach' of plaintiffs. The plaintiffs cannot reasonably 'command the whole' source of supply merely to facilitate the taking by them of the fraction of the entire flow to which their senior appropriation entitles them. On the other hand, plaintiffs cannot be required to improve their extraction facilities beyond their economic reach, upon a consideration of all the factors involved." Id. at 555-56.

2. **Retreat from *Current Creek*?** In Wayman v. Murray City Corp., 458 P.2d 861 (Utah 1969), five householders within the city had small artesian wells that diminished in flow when the city changed its diversion from seven old wells with rights aggregating 750 g.p.m. to a new large well from which it drew the 750 g.p.m. The artesian basin had a natural outflow of 34,000 acre feet per year, so it appeared that there was enough water for all users. A statute provided that no change in point of diversion could be made that would impair any vested right of another without just compensation. The district court directed the state engineer to include in his order approving the change in point of diversion a requirement that the city must at its sole cost replace the plaintiffs' water in an amount and quality equal to their former use. The Utah Supreme Court reversed. It distinguished *Current Creek* because there junior wells interfered with senior wells, while in *Murray City* some of the city's old wells had priorities senior to the householders' wells and those senior priorities transferred to the new city well. The court remanded the case and directed the district court to apply a 'rule of reasonableness," requiring it to analyze the total situation and balance individual rights in relationship to each other in a reasonable way that would best serve the overall objective of seeing all available water put to beneficial use. The court said that, to some degree, the rights of each individual should be subordinate to and correlated with reasonable conditions and limitations established by law for the general good. It thus concluded that all users must, where necessary, employ reasonable and efficient means in taking their own waters in relation to the others.

3. **Domestic wells.** The owners of domestic wells have gotten mixed results in seeking protection of their means of diversion against the owners of newer, higher-capacity wells providing water for nondomestic purposes:

> Erickson v. Crookston Waterworks Power & Light Co., 117 N.W. 435 (Minn. 1908) (correlative rights doctrine): the domestic well owner was obligated "to suffer a reasonable inconvenience for the common good of others equally dependent upon the same gift of nature" and thus had to bear the full cost of deepening his well if the water company could not feasibly get the water it needed for nondomestic use from another source.
>
> MacArtor v. Graylyn Crest III Swim Club, Inc., supra p. 335, Note 4 (reasonable use doctrine): the domestic well owner and the swim club, which apparently also was an overlying user, were required to share equally in the cost of deepening the domestic well or providing replacement water from the swim club's well.
>
> Prather v. Eisenmann, supra p. 335, Note 4 (reasonable use/correlative rights doctrine supplemented by a statute giving preference to domestic wells over all other wells): the owners of artesian domestic wells were entitled to impose on the owners of an interfering irrigation well the full cost of restoring their water supply.
>
> Bishop v. City of Casper, 420 P.2d 446 (Wyo. 1966) (appropriation doctrine supplemented by a statute protecting "adequate" domestic wells against unreasonable interference): the owner of a domestic well twenty-four feet deep was not protected against interference by the city's junior deep wells because the domestic well was not adequate.
>
> Fraser v. Water Rights Commission, 294 N.W.2d 784 (S.D. 1980) (appropriation doctrine as supplemented by a statute declaring a purpose of "protecting

water for reasonable domestic use, without the necessity of requiring maintenance of artesian head pressure"): although the statute precludes absolute protection of artesian pressure for domestic wells, it does not to give the state water agency unbridled power to approve irrigation wells without considering the maintenance of artesian head pressure for domestic wells; a balancing of interests is required.

Parker v. Wallentine, 650 P.2d 648 (Idaho 1982) (appropriation doctrine): the owner of a domestic well with a 1964 priority was absolutely protected in his historic means of diversion, but the owner of an interfering deep junior irrigation well had a right of replacement, as in *Current Creek*, though no statute specifically authorized that; a longstanding statute protecting appropriators only in the maintenance of reasonable pumping levels was held not to apply to domestic wells, and a 1978 amendment thereto clearly subjecting domestic wells to the reasonable pumping level rule was held not to apply to domestic wells predating its enactment.

Restatement (Second) of Torts § 858(1)(a), supra pp. 335-36, Note 5, imposes liability if a well "unreasonably" harms another well by lowering the water table or artesian pressure. According to comment f, interference by a large well with the diversion method of a domestic well making small withdrawals "usually" will be unreasonable when the large well produces water "for more lucrative purposes."

Nev. Rev. Stat. 534.110(5) states that when a permit is sought to pump one-half cubic foot per second or more for municipal, quasi-municipal, or industrial use, "the state engineer shall include as a condition of the permit that pumping water pursuant to the permit may be limited or prohibited to prevent any unreasonable adverse effects on an existing domestic well located within 2,500 feet of the well, unless the holder of the permit and the owner of the domestic well have agreed to alternative measures that mitigate those adverse effects."

4. **Who should pay?** Suppose A, B, C, and D sequentially drill wells in an aquifer, each one month after the last. B imposes added pumping costs on A, C on A and B, and D on A, B, and C. In time, as a result of capture, a new condition of equilibrium is reached in which pumping and natural discharge are in balance with recharge. All of them can continue thereafter to pump from the new, lower level. Did B "cause harm" to A, C to B and A, etc.? Review Ronald H. Coase, The Problem of Social Cost, supra pp. 109-11, Note 4. In a Coasian costless market, which rule, "junior pays senior's added costs" or "each pays his own costs," will optimize social welfare, the amount and value of product from the water that just equals the costs of producing the water? Is there any other criterion which tells which rule is "best"?

Edgar S. Bagley, Water Rights Law and Public Policies Relating to Ground Water "Mining" in the Southwestern States, 4 J.L. & Econ. 144, 161 (1961):

"In some cases the value of the water to a junior appropriator would be great enough to warrant his compensating or supplying the senior appropriator. This might be true if there are not many senior appropriators and if the supply available to the junior appropriator is large. But if there are many hundreds or thousands of prior appropriators who must be compensated for falling water levels additional appropriations may be effectively blocked. Under these conditions unappropriated parts of the perennial yield might go to waste. Considerations of economic effects as well as equity dictate, however, recognition of the fact that falling water levels create burdens on water users. The mere fact that water may be wasted unless junior appropriators are allowed to take supplies without compensating senior appropriators as long as perennial yield is not exceeded or economic pumping limits not yet reached does not imply that allowing such appropriations will enlarge net economic benefits. The higher pumping costs to prior appropriators is a real cost—and there is a question whether cheap methods of obtaining the water with some waste are more economical than more expensive methods which utilize supplies more completely. On the other hand, there may also be a difficult, if not impossible, administrative task which entails expensive costs in measuring the amount of damage additional withdrawals will inflict on prior appropriators. The best policy from an economic standpoint will depend on the facts of the case and would not necessarily always be one way or the other."

5. **What is a "reasonable" means of diversion?** Statutes in most appropriation doctrine states reject the idea that senior groundwater appropriators are absolutely protected in their historical diversion methods. Although the statutes vary, they typically provide that priority in time either does not protect an appropriator against reasonable lowering of static water level or protects an appropriator only in the maintenance of a reasonable pumping lift. In general, these statutes give little specific guidance on what is a "reasonable" water level or pumping lift. But an important theme—explicit in some statutes and likely implicit in the others—is tension between two economic considerations. One is concern about protecting senior appropriators against water level decline that drops below what the *Bender* court, supra Note 1, called their "economic reach." The other is Bagley's concern, supra note 4, that full economic development should not be blocked by burdening new appropriators with liability for the increased withdrawal costs of existing appropriators. Douglas L. Grant, Reasonable Groundwater Pumping Levels Under the Appropriation Doctrine: The Law and Underlying Economic Goals, 21 Nat. Resources J. 1 (1981). A companion article, Douglas L. Grant, Reasonable Groundwater Pumping Levels Under the Appropriation Doctrine: Underlying Social Goals, 23 Nat. Resources J. 53 (1983), discusses policy considerations other than economics and concludes as follows:

"The earlier article opened by quoting the following statement about the reasonable pumping level concept from a National Water Commission study: 'No definitive guidelines exist as to what the measure of reasonableness is or how it will be applied.' Although the reasonable pumping level statutes incompletely enumerate factors that should bear on the measure of reasonableness, the root cause of the uncertainty lies deeper. Additional factors can be ascertained from study of appropriation doctrine laws and traditions, albeit with varying degrees of clarity. Definitive guidelines in the sense of rules that will yield mechanical answers, however, are impossible or at least unwise. Unless one is willing to accept a simplistic, tunnel vision approach, the need is inevitable to weigh potentially competing concerns about economic efficiency, wealth and merit good distribution, and (perhaps) other social goals.

"The task then is to develop procedures to achieve knowledgeable and responsible weighing of such concerns. The essence of the problem is captured by the following commentary upon water management under the Alaska water code. That code allows new appropriations only for uses that will be in the public interest, and it enumerates a number of factors bearing on the public interest. Despite the enumeration Frank Trelease, the code's principal draftsman, has commented:

> Making decisions such as these will be very difficult. No law can make them. They must be made by people. No economic formula can solve these problems by push button techniques. * * * It is believed that the real strength of the Code lies in its procedures, which will enable all viewpoints to be brought together and all factors considered, so that choices will be made, not by action of an appropriator or polluter, and not to further the policy of a single purpose agency, but on an informed basis by officials responsible to the State for 'maximum use consistent with the public interest' for the 'maximum benefit of (all) its people.'

"Similarly, the strongest approach to the pumping level problem seems to be to use procedures which will enable all viewpoints to be brought together and all factors considered, so that choices will be made on an informed basis by officials responsible to the state for the maximum benefit of all its people. The reasonable pumping level statutes are readily adaptable to that approach." Id. at 74-75.

6. **The full statutory mosaic.** Whatever a statute protecting reasonable static water level or reasonable pumping lift might mean in isolation, it will not necessarily operate independently of other elements of the state's water or groundwater code. In *Fundingsland*, supra p. 347, the Colorado court construed a statute calling for "full economic development" of groundwater and protecting existing appropriators in the maintenance of "reasonable groundwater pumping levels," rather than historical water levels, to allow depletion of 40% of the available groundwater supply over twenty-five years. But in *Baker*, supra p. 357, Note 3, the Idaho court read a similar statute calling for "full economic development" of groundwater and protecting existing appropriators in "the maintenance of reasonable groundwater pumping levels" to prohibit mining. The court decided that this statute did not supersede or modify another statute limiting withdrawals to average natural recharge. Similarly, in *Doherty*, supra p. 352, the Oregon court held that a statute calling for "[d]epletion of ground water supplies below economic levels [to] be prevented or controlled within practicable limits" did not implicitly authorize mining down to the economic reach of irrigators because it had to be read in the context of other statutes requiring sustained-yield management and reasonably stable groundwater levels.

C. Physically Connected Groundwater and Surface Water

NATIONAL WATER COMMISSION, WATER POLICIES FOR THE FUTURE

233 (1973).

Ground water is often naturally interrelated with surface water: ground water feeds springs and surface streams, and surface water charges ground water reservoirs. Nevertheless, there persists in the laws of many States myths (long ago abandoned by hydrologists) that ground water is separate from and unrelated to surface water. * * *

As a consequence of the faulty perception of hydrology that ground water is separate from and unrelated to surface water, different legal regimes were applied to surface water and ground water, and only recently and in only a few water-short Western States has an effort been made to coordinate the administration of the integrated surface water-ground water supply. As Colorado and New Mexico have discovered, when the coordination effort comes late—after an economy has been developed in reliance on two different legal systems for one interrelated supply—achieving coordinated administration is very difficult. The problem in those two States is that surface water users generally came first, followed by ground water users pumping from aquifers interdependent with the surface stream. Over time, depletion of the underground aquifer reduced surface flow so that senior surface users were deprived of water by junior pumpers. Untangling this confusion has been a persistent problem in parts of the West.

Notes

1. **The Texas struggle with the myth of separateness.** The separate legal treatment of groundwater and surface water is epitomized by Pecos County Water Control & Improvement District No. 1 v. Williams, 271 S.W.2d 503, 504-06 (Tex. App. 1954):

"The controversy arose by virtue of the fact that plaintiff claims and alleges that the properties serviced by it have used and enjoyed the waters of Comanche Springs for some ninety years, and that prior to the institution of this lawsuit about 1951 the defendants, owners of land south and west of said springs, drilled various water wells and began pumping them with mechanical pumps, and that as a result Comanche Springs ceased flowing and plaintiffs were unable to use the waters therefrom for irrigation, as they had done for many years. * * *

"We deal first with the laws of Texas insofar as they relate to percolating waters. It seems clear to us that percolating or diffused and percolating waters belong to the landowner, and may be used by him at his will. There has been no allegation in this case that the defendants have been wasting any of the water. * * *

"With reference to plaintiffs' claim of appropriation it is clear on the authority of the Texas cases cited above that its appropriation, if any, could extend only to the waters of Comanche Springs at and after their emergence from the ground, and the same is true of riparian rights."

The hydrologically unrealistic *Pecos County* approach led to serious problems regarding the Edwards Aquifer in south central Texas. The Edwards Aquifer is a confined aquifer underlying 3600 square miles. It discharges primarily through large springs at its eastern end, which in turn feed surface streams. The aquifer is the sole or primary source of water for many pumpers, including the City of San Antonio, and the spring-fed surface streams also supply many water users. Around 1989, environmental interests began to complain that unregulated pumping decreased water flow in the springs and threatened several endangered species.

In 1991, the Sierra Club sued the Secretary of the Interior and the U.S. Fish and Wildlife Service in federal district court under the Endangered Species Act (ESA) to require them to take measures to maintain the water level in the aquifer high enough to provide sufficient spring flows for critical species habitat. The court ordered the U.S. Fish and Wildlife Service to determine the minimum spring flows needed to protect the listed species and then advise other federal agencies of its findings so they could perform their duties under the ESA should Texas fail to regulate aquifer withdrawals as needed to protect listed species. Sierra Club v.

Lujan, 36 Env't Rep. Cas. (BNA) 1533 (W.D. Tex. 1993), appeal dismissed, Sierra Club v. Babbitt, 995 F.2d 571 (5th Cir.).

Responding to this federal pressure, the Texas Legislature passed the Edwards Aquifer Act. The act created the Edwards Aquifer Authority (EAA) and charged it with developing and implementing a mandatory permit system for groundwater withdrawals and a plan for comprehensive management to ensure minimum spring flows needed to protect threatened and endangered species. Activity by the EAA was stalled first by a U.S. Justice Department ruling that the method of selecting EAA board members violated the federal Voting Rights Act and then by state trial court rulings against the constitutionality of the Edwards Aquifer Act that eventually were overturned on appeal.

In 1994, with a drought occurring and no functioning EAA board, the *Sierra Club* federal district court appointed a monitor to develop an emergency plan for staged reductions of pumping. Fall rains eliminated the need to implement the plan. In 1996, the Sierra Club brought another lawsuit, and the federal district court again appointed a monitor to develop an emergency plan to reduce pumping. The court later entered a preliminary injunction activating the plan, but the Fifth Circuit vacated the injunction under the Burford abstention doctrine, which calls for federal court abstention to allow a state's comprehensive regulatory scheme to operate without the risk of competing attempts by the federal courts to exercise control over the same entity. Sierra Club v. City of San Antonio, 112 F.3d 789 (5th Cir. 1997).

The Edwards Aquifer Act caps withdrawals by nonexempt wells at 450,000 acre-feet through 2007 and 400,000 acre-feet thereafter. Schizophrenically, the Act also entitles pumpers to obtain permits for withdrawals based on their maximum historical use, which has led to permits being issued that in total exceed the caps. Resolution of this difficulty remains for the future. However, the EAA can assess water users fees to raise funds to retire permitted rights. Further details of the Edwards Aquifer story are reported in Todd H. Votteler, The Little Fish that Roared: The Endangered Species Act, State Groundwater Law, and Private Property Rights Collide Over the Texas Edwards Aquifer, 28 Envtl. L. 845 (1998), and Todd H. Votteler, Raiders of the Lost Aquifer? Or, the Beginning of the End to Fifty Years of Conflict Over the Texas Edwards Aquifer, 15 Tul. Envtl. L.J. 257 (2002).

Apart from the Edwards Aquifer Act, 1997 Senate Bill 1 acknowledges the reality of frequent hydrologic connection between groundwater and surface water. It requires the Texas Commission on Environmental Quality when processing permits to appropriate surface waters to consider the effects, if any, or groundwater or groundwater recharge. Tex. Water Code Ann. §§ 11.134, .151. It also requires groundwater conservation districts, in coordination with surface water management entities on a regional basis, to develop comprehensive management plans that address, inter alia, conjunctive surface water management issues. Id. § 36.1071.

2. **The Arizona struggle with the myth.** Arizona applies the reasonable use doctrine to percolating groundwater (except in Active Management Areas, supra pp. 368-70, Note 1) but applies the appropriation doctrine to streams and their subflow. The Arizona Supreme Court long ago defined subflow as "waters which slowly find their way through the sand and gravel constituting the bed of the stream, or the lands under or immediately adjacent to the stream," and which cannot be extracted without tending "to diminish appreciably and directly the flow of the surface stream." Maricopa County Mun. Water Conservation Dist. No. 1 v. Southwest Cotton Co., 4 P.2d 369, 380 (Ariz. 1931). More recently, in an adjudication of the Gila River

system, the trial court adopted a 50%/90-day test for determining whether wells in the younger alluvium of the valley should be treated as pumping subflow. The test stated that a well should be presumed to take subflow (and thus be governed by the appropriation doctrine) if 90 days of continuous pumping would deplete the stream by 50% or more. The Arizona Supreme Court rejected this test as an impermissible broadening of its longstanding definition of subflow, a definition that it said had served as the backdrop for vast investments in the state and thus should not be altered. In re General Adjudication of All Rights to Use Water in Gila River System & Source, 857 P.2d 1236 (Ariz. 1993). The court stated further:

"Whether a well is pumping subflow does not turn on whether it depletes a stream by some particular amount in a given period of time. * * * [I]t turns on whether the well is pumping water that is more closely associated with the stream than with the surrounding alluvium. For example, comparison of such characteristics as elevation, gradient, and perhaps chemical makeup can be made. Flow direction can be an indicator. If the water flows in the same general direction as the stream, it is more likely related to the stream. On the other hand, if it flows toward or away from the stream it likely is related to the surrounding alluvium." Id. at 1246.

On remand, the trial court applied the "more closely associated with the stream" standard, guided by the Arizona Supreme Court's examples of relevant characteristics, and ruled that the subflow consisted of the saturated younger alluvium located in the floodplain. The trial court also ruled that wells outside this area should be treated as taking appropriable water if their cones of depression reach the subflow and their drawdown appreciably affects the volume of subflow and surface stream flow. The Arizona Supreme Court affirmed both rulings. It observed that subflow "is a purely legal, not scientific, term" and said that the descriptions of subflow in its earlier decisions "should not serve as a straitjacket that restricts us from reaching in the direction of the facts and, so far as possible under those decisions, conforming to hydrological reality." In re General Adjudication of All Rights to Use Water in Gila River System & Source, 9 P.3d 1069, 1076, 1079 (Ariz. 2000).

3. **Coordinated administration when the appropriation doctrine governs groundwater and surface water.** Most western states that apply the appropriation doctrine to both groundwater and surface water now have statutes or case law adopting, at least to some degree, the principle of coordinated administration. The next three principal cases illustrate issues that arise under that approach.

POSTEMA v. POLLUTION CONTROL HEARINGS BOARD

Supreme Court of Washington, 2000

142 Wash.2d 68, 11 P.3d 726.

MADSEN, J. These two consolidated cases, one of which involves four consolidated cases, present numerous issues arising from the Department of Ecology's denial of applications for groundwater appropriation permits on the basis that the groundwater sources are in hydraulic continuity with surface water sources and further appropriations are foreclosed under the criteria of RCW 90.03.290 [one of which prohibits issuance of a permit for an appropriation that will "impair existing rights"]. In the five individual cases before this court, the Pollution Control Hearings Board [PCHB] upheld Ecology's denial of the groundwater applications. * * *

No attempt is made here to fully explain hydrogeological cycles and the science relating to impact of groundwater withdrawals. In general, water can move from groundwater to surface water, as well as from surface water to groundwater. How groundwater moves and where it moves to depend on several factors, including gravity, saturation of the ground materials, the hydraulic gradient, the level of the groundwater, and the type of material through which it moves. * * * The interrelationship can be quite complex and effects are sometimes difficult or impossible to measure in the field. Also, pumping groundwater may not have a discernable effect on surface water until considerable time has passed, depending upon the conditions.

Ecology's understanding of hydraulic continuity has altered over time, as has its use of methods to determine hydraulic continuity and the effect of groundwater withdrawals on surface waters. In 1996, the United States Geologic Services published a report by Morgan and Jones regarding three-dimensional computer modeling for the complex geologic and hydrogeologic basins of Puget Sound. The report concluded that the effects of pumping always reaches some of the surface water boundaries, and can do so over many square miles. Prior to issuance of this report, there was no such model. Ecology maintains that in a complex hydrologic system, use of a three-dimensional computer model is the best method for determining the effects groundwater withdrawals will have on surface water flow and senior surface water right holders. Ecology concluded that the Morgan and Jones model could be used in decisions on the Jorgensen appellants' applications because the climate, topography, and geology in the Green-Duwamish, Snohomish, and Cedar-Sammamish watersheds were similar.

The primary issues common to these appeals concern the impact of groundwater withdrawals on surface waters having minimum flow requirements set by rule which are unmet a substantial part of the year, and on surface waters closed to further appropriation. * * * Appellant Postema contends that there must be a significant measurable effect on surface waters before a groundwater application may be denied even though hydraulic continuity between the ground and surface waters is established. In general, the appellants in the Jorgensen cases argue that minimum flows are limited rights, and that Ecology's regulations require a direct and measurable effect of groundwater withdrawal on surface waters using standard stream measuring equipment, which has effective limits of about five percent of stream flow, before hydraulic continuity has any legal significance vis-a-vis minimum flow rights. If, using these methods, no effect is measurable, these appellants reason, Ecology has no authority to deny a groundwater application because of any affect on or relationship to surface waters. * * *

Once established, a minimum flow constitutes an appropriation with a priority date as of the effective date of the rule establishing the minimum flow. RCW 90.03.345. Thus, a minimum flow set by rule is an existing right which may not be impaired by subsequent groundwater withdrawals. * * *

The appellants' arguments that there must be measurable effects on stream flows raise the question of how impairment must be determined. There seems to be no dispute that Ecology has revised its view of the interconnection of groundwater and surface water in hydraulic continuity as new information has become available. There is also no dispute that Ecology has altered the methods by which it determines the impact of groundwater withdrawal on surface waters. Ecology points to PCHB decisions upholding use of qualitative analysis, such a hydrological studies and conceptual modeling, and quantitative modeling, such as analytical equations or numeric models.

Ecology may use new methods to determine impairment as they are developed. Also, as the King County Superior Court reasoned [when reviewing the Jorgensen cases], logically one cannot actually measure the impact of a well which does not yet exist. That court said that the statutes and regulations do not prohibit use of modeling, and modeling may be the only means of quantifying effect, impact or conflict. * * *

We reject the Jorgensen appellants' claim that a direct and measurable impact on surface water must be shown using standard stream measuring devices before an application for a groundwater permit may be denied. We also reject Postema's argument that a significant measurable effect on stream flows is required. * * * The statutes do not authorize a de minimis impairment of an existing right. RCW 90.03.290 plainly permits no impairment of an existing right. This does not mean, however, that there is no need to show any impact on the surface water resource, nor does it mean that measurement is irrelevant to the inquiry. As explained, though, Ecology is entitled to use more advanced techniques as they become available and scientifically acceptable. Applicants should then be provided the opportunity to challenge Ecology's factual determinations.

We also reject the Board's holding that hydraulic continuity, where minimum flows are unmet a substantial part of the year, equates to impairment of existing rights as a matter of law. As the King County Superior Court noted, existing rights may or may not be impaired where there is hydraulic continuity depending upon the nature of the appropriation, the source aquifer, and whether it is upstream or downstream from or higher or lower than the surface water flow or level, and all other pertinent facts.

Additionally, we reject the premise that the fact that a stream has unmet flows necessarily establishes impairment if there is an effect on the stream from groundwater withdrawals. The Board held that the number of days the minimum flow levels are not met may be considered in determining water availability, but declined to rule on whether it can be the sole consideration. * * * The conclusion is correct. While the number of days minimum flows are unmet is a relevant consideration, it may be, for example, that due to seasonal fluctuations and time of withdrawal, groundwater withdrawal affecting the stream level will not impair the minimum flow rights. However, where minimum flows would be impaired, then an application must be denied.

We hold that hydraulic continuity of an aquifer with a stream having unmet minimum flows is not, in and of itself, a basis for denial of a groundwater application * * *. However, where there is hydraulic continuity and withdrawal of groundwater would impair existing surface water rights, including minimum flow rights, then denial is required. Ecology may use new information and scientific methodology as it becomes available and scientifically acceptable for determining hydraulic continuity and effect of groundwater withdrawals on surface waters.

In each of the rulings in the cases consolidated in Jorgensen, the Board ruled that as a matter of law Ecology could not grant a groundwater application for consumptive use where the groundwater is in hydraulic continuity with surface water which has been closed by rule. The King County Superior Court disagreed, holding that as in the case of streams with minimum flow rights, hydraulic continuity is a factual question which does not satisfy any of the criteria in RCW 90.03.290 for denying a water application. The Jorgensen appellants argue, as they do with respect to minimum flow rights, that hydraulic continuity alone is an insufficient ground for denial. Insofar as they contend that standard stream measuring devices, with five percent limits, must establish a direct and measurable impact on the surface water flow or levels, we disagree for the reasons discussed above. * * *

Notes

1. **Other tests for coordinated administration under the appropriation doctrine.** Colorado applies the appropriation doctrine to surface streams and tributary groundwater, and it integrates the priorities. Colo. Rev. Stat. § 37-92-102(1)(a). Although Colorado does not require a permit to appropriate surface water or tributary groundwater, it requires a permit from the state engineer to construct a well. § 37-90-137(1) (wells outside designated groundwater basins). The state engineer cannot issue a permit if operation of the well "will materially injure the vested water rights of others." § 37-90-137(2)(b). Similarly, the state engineer cannot shut down an existing well under the priority principle unless it "is causing or will cause material injury" to a senior water right. § 37-92-502(2).

Utah has the appropriation doctrine for surface water and groundwater. In Salt Lake City v. Silver Fork Pipeline Corp., 5 P.3d 1206 (Utah 2000), SFPC claimed the right to approximately .5 c.f.s. of groundwater that it intercepted in a mine and transported for residential use. Previously Salt Lake City had appropriated nearly the entire flow of a creek to which the groundwater was tributary, and it responded to SFPC's claim by suing to quiet title to the .5 c.f.s.. The court said "[q]uieting title to source waters requires not only a finding that these waters are naturally tributary to an appropriated creek, but also that interception of these waters substantially interferes with the quantity or quality of water that would otherwise reach the appropriator of the creek." Id. at 1214.

Then the court turned to the adequacy of Salt Lake City's proof of substantial interference:

"SFPC argues that the district court erred in finding substantial interference without requiring Salt Lake to proffer actual measurements of water flowing in the creek at the mouth of the canyon, illustrating that diversion of water at the mine significantly diminished the flow in the creek. We disagree that a court must premise its finding of substantial interference on actual measurements reporting flow before and after interception of the water at its source. Measurements of water flow are often not available to prove interference, and when they are, their value is limited to the extent that other environmental factors dictate flow, such as season and amount of precipitation. It is especially difficult to demonstrate by empirical evidence the extent to which interception of percolating water interferes with a surface body of water to which it is tributary. Hydrogeological characteristics in a particular area may extend to decades the time it takes for underground water to percolate through the soil before reaching the surface, only then making the effect of interception evident based on diminished water levels.

"Given the difficulty in obtaining reliable measurements of water flow that accurately reflect the effects of interception of underground source waters, we cannot agree that a finding of interference must be premised on this type of evidence. If nearly .5 c.f.s. of water intercepted in the mine would naturally flow into the creek but for the existence of the mine, it is reasonable to infer that Salt Lake has suffered, or will eventually suffer, a diminution in its water right of approximately 362 acre-feet of water each year. This evidence is sufficient to support the trial court's finding of substantial interference." Id. at 1215.

2. **The Restatement.** The Restatement of Torts imposes liability on a well owner whose "withdrawal of groundwater has a direct and substantial effect upon a watercourse or lake and unreasonably causes harm to a person entitled to the use of its water." See supra pp. 335-36, Note 5.

TEMPLETON v. PECOS VALLEY ARTESIAN CONSERVANCY DISTRICT

Supreme Court of New Mexico, 1958
65 N.M. 59, 332 P.2d 465.

H. VEARLE PAYNE, DISTRICT JUDGE. This is an appeal from a judgment of the District Court of Chaves County. The appellees filed with the State Engineer their applications to drill wells in the Roswell Shallow Water Basin. Although these were on the usual forms for applications to appropriate underground waters, it was agreed by all of the parties that in effect these applications constituted applications for the changing of the point of diversion of waters from points in the Rio Felix to points in the Valley Fill of the Roswell Shallow Water Basin. The applications were denied by the State Engineer, and an appeal was perfected to the District Court of Chaves County. Upon hearing before the District Court, judgment was entered in favor of the applicants from which the Pecos Valley Artesian Conservancy District and S.E. Reynolds, State Engineer of the State of New Mexico, have appealed. * * *

* * * The water rights of the appellees were to irrigate certain land out of the Rio Felix. The amount of water in the Rio Felix has decreased in recent years for the reasons hereinafter mentioned, so that the water in the river is insufficient to irrigate the land of the appellees and they have applied for permits to drill wells to supplement this water to the extent necessary to produce the amount of water originally appropriated. * * *

The Rio Felix is a small water course which crosses Chaves County from the west toward the east, and empties into the Pecos River. There are two underground bodies of water in this area. The deepest one is known as the Roswell Artesian Basin, and the upper body of water is known as the Roswell Shallow Water Basin. These two bodies of water are separated by impervious red shale and gypsum, known as the Pecos Red Beds. Below the Pecos Red

Beds is the body of artesian water and above the Pecos Red Beds is the Roswell Shallow Water Basin. Above the Pecos Red Beds and spreading over the basin is what is known as the Valley Fill which consists of topsoil, sand, gravel, shale, clay, and boulders which have been washed in and deposited through the centuries. The Shallow Water Basin is held in this Valley Fill and varies in thickness from nothing on the west to two hundred and fifteen feet or more on the east.

The Rio Felix channel passes across this Valley Fill and at places is as deep as twenty-five feet or more into the Valley Fill. The water flow of this river, except for flood waters, rises into the channel from the Valley Fill wherever the waters of the Shallow Basin are higher than the bed of the river.

The Rio Felix is a stream that heads in the foothills of the Sacramento Mountains and runs down to the Pecos River. It is not a continuous stream except in flood times. The waters that fall on the headwaters of the stream run for a distance and then they lose themselves in the ground. In other words, the headwaters of the Rio Felix sink and become a part of the Valley Fill except for the times when the stream is in flood stage. * * *

Until the year 1952, the flow of the Rio Felix supplied enough water for the irrigation of the lands involved, but about that time the water table began to lower materially, and thus decreased the amount of water which, except for floods, flowed into the Rio Felix, so that the appellees have been unable to secure sufficient waters from the river to properly irrigate their lands. This decrease in the water table was due to the pumping of water from irrigation wells which have been drilled into the Shallow Water Basin in later years, aggravated by several years of drouth. * * *

Witness Brown is an Engineer with many years of experience. He testified as follows:

> "Q. Is there any difference in the water that is produced by the shallow wells, or wells in the shallow basin, from the Felix water? A. No, and I would like to explain that this way. In a natural state, the shallow ground water is discharged into the Felix, as described by prior witnesses, because the Felix is cut down below the ground water table. When the first shallow wells were drilled and pumped, the effect of withdrawal of water from the shallow wells was to intercept the ground water that was migrating toward the Felix, so that it reduced the discharge into the Felix, but as the wells were pumped, and the levels of the ground water was lowered, the water level in the wells got down to where they were below the bed of the Felix, and when water is withdrawn under that condition, instead of intercepting water which is going to the Felix, it actually diverts water from the Felix, just as certainly as if it was pumped out of the river, or as if a person had built a dam and taken it off through a canal. Likewise, these appellants, when their wells are put down and water is pumped from them, they will be withdrawing water from the Felix to some extent, the same as these shallow waters in the surrounding area are now doing."
>
> * * *

The Court concluded that the water of appellees appropriated from the natural flow of the Rio Felix included the waters in the Valley Fill that would have naturally reached the river, except for the acts of subsequent appropriators. The Court further concluded that the restoration to the appellees of the quantity of water originally appropriated by means of wells sunk into the Valley Fill at the locations designated by the appellees, cannot and does not impair any other water right. * * *

[T]he appellants [contend] that the proposed change of point of diversion amounts to a new appropriation in an underground basin that is fully appropriated. This proposition is based on the assumption that there is no connection between the surface flow of the Rio Felix and the underground water basin. The findings of the lower court do not support this assumption. The lower court found that the headwaters of the Rio Felix sank into the ground and became a part of the Valley Fill and then rose again into the river and that the appropriations made by the appellees amounted to appropriations out of the Valley Fill.

In 93 C.J.S. Waters § 170, p. 909, is found the following: "An appropriation when made follows the water to its original source, whether through surface or subterranean streams or through percolations."

In the case of Richlands Irrigation Company v. Westview Irrigation Company, 96 Utah 403, 80 P.2d 458, 465, the Supreme Court of Utah had the following to say:

> "The entire watershed to its uttermost confines, covering thousands of square miles, out to the crest of the divides which separate it from the adjacent watersheds, is the generating source from which the water of a river comes or accumulates in its channel. Rains and snows falling on this entire vast area sink into the soil and find their way by surface or underground flow or percolation through the sloping strata down to the central channel. This entire sheet of water, or water table, constitutes the river and it never ceases to be such in its centripetal motion towards the channel. Any appropriator of water from the central channel is entitled to rely and depend upon all the sources which feed the main stream above his own diversion point, clear back to the farthest limits of the watershed."

In the later case of Little Cottonwood Water Company v. Sandy City, 123 Utah 242, 258 P.2d 440, 443, the Supreme Court of Utah stated:

> "Also, no one can interfere with the source of supply of this stream, regardless of how far it may be from the place of use, and whether it flows on the surface or underground, in such a manner as will diminish the quantity or injuriously affect the quality of the water of these established rights."
>
> * * *

Applying the foregoing principles to this case would lead to the conclusion that the appellees were entitled to the waters of the Valley Fill that flowed into the Rio Felix at the time of their appropriation. It seems that there is nothing in the law that would prevent them from following this water through an application for a change of point of diversion, provided that it does not impair any other existing rights. In other words, their applications do not amount to a request for a new appropriation in the underground water basin, but merely a request to follow the source of their original appropriation. * * *

The appellants argue that this amounts to a change from a river or surface water right to an underground water right. If the river and the underground waters had two separate sources of supply and if there were no connection between them, this argument might be sound, but under the facts set forth above, the Valley Fill was the source of the flow of the river.

The next contention of the appellants, was that the change of point of diversion would impair existing rights. This was a question of fact which was determined by the lower court against the appellants * * *. The appellants objected that [this] finding of fact * * * is contrary to [another finding by the lower court that] "the shallow waters of the Roswell Basin were closed to further appropriation on August 1, 1937, by Order of the State Engineer, which recited that all of said waters were fully appropriated."

Apparently this [objection] is based on the assumption that the appellees are seeking a new appropriation. As pointed out above, they are not seeking a new appropriation but merely seeking a change in the point of diversion. Previously the water flowed from the Valley Fill into the Rio Felix and was then lifted on to the land by means of dams or pumping plants. The appellees now intend to lift the water directly out of the Valley Fill, due to the fact that the water table has been lowered. This does not mean that it is a new appropriation at all, but merely a change in the method of extracting the water from the Valley Fill. * * *

[Affirmed.]

Notes

1. **Extension and limitation of *Templeton*.** In Langenegger v. Carlsbad Irrigation District, 483 P.2d 297 (N.M. 1971), the court extended *Templeton* one step further back in the hydrologic cycle. The Pecos River was supplied partly by base flows that passed through the Valley Fill shallow aquifer and partly by flood flows from precipitation within the river drainage. The Red Beds that supported the Valley Fill and confined the underlying artesian Roswell Underground Basin in this area leaked water upwards from the artesian basin into the overlying shallow aquifer. Thus, the base flows supplying the river included some water from the artesian basin. The court held that a senior appropriator from the Pecos River could drill a supplemental well through the Valley Fill and the Red Beds and tap the artesian water under his original priority. Moreover, the court allowed him to take water from the new artesian wells as needed to satisfy his full right, rather than take only that percentage of historically available streamflow coming from the artesian basin or even from base flows.

In State ex rel. Martinez v. City of Roswell, 844 P.2d 831 (N.M. Ct. App. 1992), the court held that a surface water appropriator from an arroyo supplied solely by flood flow could not switch to a well and keep the surface priority under *Templeton*. After reviewing a series of cases interpreting *Templeton*, the court said a surface appropriator cannot switch to a well that captures water anywhere in the watershed. It formulated the *Templeton* doctrine as follows: "A supplemental well priority date may properly 'relate back' to the priority date of the antecedent surface right to which it is supplemental only upon a showing of the *Templeton* factual predicates. The factual showing must demonstrate that the water sought or captured by the supplemental well is water that would otherwise reach the main channel of the surface source and that such water is a source of flow at the point of surface diversion." Id. at 838-39.

The latter requirement also prevents a stream appropriator from changing to a well located below the point of diversion on the stream. "A downstream ground water well necessarily draws on seepage and percolation that occurs after, i.e., downstream from, the surface water diversion. That seepage and percolation could not have been a source of the surface water to which the applicant has a right * * *." Herrington v. State ex rel. Office of the State Engineer, 92 P.3d 31, 35 (N.M. Ct. App. 2004).

2. **Voluntary versus mandated switching from a surface water to a groundwater diversion.** The question in *Templeton* was whether a surface water appropriator could switch voluntarily to a groundwater diversion. A key issue in the next principal case is whether a surface water appropriator could ever be *required* to switch to a groundwater diversion rather than insist that junior wells be shut down to restore stream flow.

ALAMOSA-LA JARA WATER USERS PROTECTION ASS'N v. GOULD

Supreme Court of Colorado, 1983.
674 P.2d 914.

DUBOFSKY, J. This is an appeal from a judgment of the district court for Water Division 3 regarding rules promulgated by the Colorado State Engineer limiting the use of surface and underground water in the San Luis Valley. Curtailment of water use in the valley is required by the terms of an interstate stipulation under which Colorado must meet its Rio Grande Compact obligation to deliver scheduled amounts of Rio Grande water at the Colorado-New Mexico border on an annual basis. The dispute over the proposed rules concerns the distribution of that curtailment * * * between well owners and surface diverters. The water court * * * disapproved rules which phased out all wells in the San Luis Valley unless each well owner could demonstrate a lack of material injury to senior surface water users or provide a plan of augmentation to replace the water taken by a well. * * *

The upper 6000 feet of fill below the valley surface consists of unconsolidated clay, silt, sand, and gravel, and interbedded lava flows, containing an estimated two billion acre-feet of underground water. Some of the underground water is in an unconfined aquifer system at shallow depths. Beneath the unconfined aquifer are relatively impermeable beds of clay and basalt and beneath these confining layers are substantial quantities of water which comprise the confined aquifer. The confining clay layer generally does not exist around the valley's perimeter, and the confined aquifer system is recharged from surface flow to the underground water system at the edges of the valley. Because the recharge areas are higher in elevation than the floor of the valley, the confined aquifer is under artesian pressure, resulting in the free flow of water from some artesian wells and springs at natural breaks in the confining layer. In some places, where the confining layer is less thick and more transmissive, water from the confined aquifer will leak upward through the confining clay layers into the unconfined aquifer. The unconfined aquifer is directly connected with the surface streams in some places. To varying degrees, the surface streams, the unconfined aquifer, and the confined aquifer are hydraulically connected.

The first appropriations from streams in the valley began in the 1850s on the Conejos River. The first appropriation on the Rio Grande mainstem was in 1866, and the most extensive development for irrigation purposes on both rivers was between 1880 and 1890. By 1900, the natural flow of all surface streams in the valley was over-appropriated. High spring runoff and low summer flows in valley streams, coupled with years of severe drought, resulted in undependable water supplies for irrigation; thus, farmers turned to wells and reservoirs to supplement and regulate their water supply.

Well construction in the valley began as early as 1850. Between 1880 and 1891, about 2,000 artesian wells were drilled. Withdrawals from the confined aquifer by wells remained relatively constant until the early 1950s when a number of large capacity wells were constructed. In 1972, the state engineer ceased issuing permits for wells to be drilled into the confined aquifer after determining that both aquifers were tributary to the surface streams in the valley. * * *

Governed by the [interstate] stipulation, the state engineer is required to administer the Conejos River and Rio Grande mainstem on the basis of projected annual runoff. Since 1968, when the state engineer began enforcing the stipulation, water users on both the Conejos and Rio Grande have experienced substantial curtailments of their diversions. Between 1969 and 1975, the state engineer developed annual operating criteria to deliver water to the state line.

In 1975, the state engineer promulgated the proposed rules * * *. [T]he underground water rules provide for phasing out of underground water diversions unless the underground water user submits proof to the division engineer that the user's well is operating under a decreed plan of augmentation or has a decree as an alternate point of diversion, or that the underground water appropriation can occur without impairing the right of a senior appropriator. Numerous protests to the proposed rules were filed, requiring a hearing before a water judge. * * *

At trial, * * * all parties agreed that historical hydrologic patterns in the valley have changed dramatically, particularly since 1950, because of a combination of natural and man-made causes, resulting in an overall reduction in surface water supplies. The state and the Conejos District asserted that the primary cause of the reduction is increased well pumping, but there was also evidence that decreased snowpack runoff and more efficient irrigation are responsible causes. The theories were supported by studies, which contrasted stream system inflow and outflow, and computer modelling, which estimated overall stream depletions from well withdrawals. Farmers testified to the effect of loss of surface water on their ability to grow crops and the need for supplemental well water when surface supplies are undependable. Finally, evidence was presented that the natural consumptive use of water by evapotranspiration from native grasses and phreatophytes, such as cottonwood, greasewood and rabbitwood, accounts for a large portion of the annual loss of water in the valley. Expert testimony indicated, and the water court found, that when wells are pumped, lowering the water table below phreatophyte root zones, the result is a substantial salvage of water, perhaps as much as one million acre-feet a year, that would otherwise be lost through evapotranspiration. * * *

The water court disapproved the underground water rules, suggesting that section 37-92-502, C.R.S. requires that the state engineer must determine that each well causes material injury to a senior appropriator before that well may be curtailed and holding the rules to be inconsistent with the statutory and judicial policy of maximum utilization of water. The court held * * * that in some instances senior appropriators may be required to drill new wells to augment or replace their surface water diversions before curtailment of junior rights can be required. * * * The state and the Conejos District appeal the water court's disapproval of the underground water rules. * * *

The proposed underground water rules tie tributary underground water administration in the valley to regulation for compact requirements by integrating tributary underground water diversions into the priority system for surface streams. The rules are intended over a five-year period to curtail well diversions unless individual well owners prove that their wells do not cause injury to senior water rights or remedy such injury through plans for augmentation.

In support of the underground water rules, the state engineer introduced voluminous exhibits which showed that well pumping decreases artesian pressure, resulting in increased recharge to the confined aquifer from the streams in the recharge areas and decreased flow into surface streams from springs fed from the confined aquifer, and ultimately, in streamflow depletion. The state engineer estimated that well diversions from both aquifers annually deplete the Rio Grande mainstem by 17,700 acre-feet and the Conejos River by 16,400 acre-feet. He concluded that junior well diversions were causing material injury to senior water rights throughout the valley.

The water court found that the underground water was tributary to the surface streams; that surface decrees were experiencing increasing curtailment; and that underground water withdrawals had accelerated in recent years, affecting surface flows. The court also found that the effect of underground water withdrawals had not been specifically quantified and had not been attributed to individual wells. None of the parties take issue with the water court's general factual findings. Instead the rules' proponents challenge the legal bases of the water court's disapproval of the underground water rules. * * *

In disapproving the underground water rules, the water court looked to language in section 37-92-502(2), C.R.S. which prohibits the curtailment of a diversion unless the diversion is causing material injury to senior water rights. The water court stressed the statutory reference to "each case" and "each diversion" and concluded that the materiality of injury must be determined individually for each well * * *. To the extent that the water court ruling disapproves the rules because they presume material injury to senior rights from all junior groundwater diversions in the valley, and to the extent that the ruling requires the division engineer to reprove in each individual well determination the existence of material injury which has already been proven on a valley-wide basis, the ruling is in error. * * * The purpose of the materiality of injury requirement is to prevent the futile curtailment of underground water diversions, not to erect a procedural roadblock to effective regulation of wells. * * *

[W]here, as here, streams are over-appropriated and underground water diversions from an aquifer have been found to significantly affect stream flow, it may be presumed that each underground water diversion materially injures senior appropriators. The state engineer, therefore, will not be required to repeat for every well curtailed the painstaking analysis which led to the aquifer-wide determination of material injury. * * *

The water court disapproved the well regulations because they did not contain a requirement that stream appropriators tap the enormous supply of water underlying the surface of the valley. Relying upon the reasonable-means-of-diversion requirement adopted in Colorado Springs v. Bender, 148 Colo. 458, 366 P.2d 552 (1961) and codified in section 37-92-102(2)(b), C.R.S.; the policy of "maximum utilization" of the State's water as recognized in Fellhauer v. People, 167 Colo. 320, 447 P.2d 986 (1968); and the requirement under section 37-92-102(1), C.R.S., of integration of administration of underground water tributary to a stream with the use of surface water, the water court held that, under certain circumstances, surface stream appropriators have a duty to withdraw underground water tributary to the stream in order to satisfy their surface appropriations. The court observed that this may take the form of requiring senior appropriators to drill new wells to augment or replace their surface water diversions before they can require curtailment of junior rights, and that *Bender* provides that the sole limitation on seniors' duty to effectuate reasonable means of diversion is that senior appropriators cannot be required to improve their extraction facilities beyond their economic reach.

The state engineer asserts that the proposed rules properly place the burden of remedying the injury caused to senior appropriators on junior water users and that the water court's ruling is a misapplication of law. The state engineer relies upon the principle, codified in section 37-92-102, C.R.S., that the priority system governs water allocation and that junior water rights from whatever source are not entitled to divert water that otherwise would be available for use by senior water rights. Under the prior appropriation doctrine, it is argued, the burden of integrating surface and groundwater rights falls upon junior water users, primarily through plans for augmentation under section 37-92-103(9), C.R.S. The state engineer also relies upon Kuiper v. Well Owners Conservation Association, 176 Colo. 119, 490 P.2d 268 (1971), in which this court held: "[I]t is not the present state of the law that the State Engineer is required to compel a person with a senior surface priority to use his ground water to apply on that priority before he makes a call." Id. at 283. * * *

Here, several witnesses testified that the water in storage in the valley's aquifers provides the support for the water above it to move to the streams. The well owners and the communities argue that it is not unreasonable to require surface diverters to deepen their headgates if the water from the stream is beneath their feet. The argument continues that the surface owners have lost nothing except a gravity flow source of supply which is cheaper and easier to divert, and that the loss only occurs at times when the surface stream is inadequate to fill the surface diverters' priorities. A reasonable means of diversion in this case, it is argued, is one that eliminates the need for supporting the surface stream, thereby freeing the underground water for maximum beneficial use.

The Conejos District * * * argues that augmentation is one of the means provided to achieve maximum utilization under the 1969 [Water Right Determination and Administration] Act, and that because the proposed rules require junior wells to augment, the rules are consistent with the policy of maximum utilization. Evaluation of different means of achieving maximum utilization, however, is a matter of policy, and therefore a task to be performed by the state engineer after full consideration of the available alternatives. In proposing the instant rules, the state engineer, relying upon the narrow construction of the 1969 Act in *Well Owners,* excluded consideration of the reasonableness of surface diversions, concluding that the prior appropriation doctrine prevented any means of maximizing utilization of the waters of the San Luis Valley other than what could be accomplished by augmentation plans developed by junior well owners.

We believe that *Well Owners* construed the 1969 Act too narrowly. The prior appropriation doctrine is not a legal barrier to the concurrent consideration by the state engineer of the various methods of implementing the state policy of maximum utilization set out in the 1969 Act. See Trelease, Conjunctive Use of Ground Water and Surface Water, 27 Rocky Mtn. Min. L. Inst. 1853 (1982); Harrison & Sandstrom, The Ground Water Surface Water Conflict and Recent Colorado Water Legislation, 43 U. Colo. L. Rev. 1 (1971). Therefore, to the degree *Well Owners* precludes consideration of a reasonable-means-of-diversion requirement as a method of maximizing utilization of integrated underground and surface waters, we overrule *Well Owners.*

The water court held that, under certain circumstances, surface stream appropriators may be required to withdraw underground water tributary to the stream in order to satisfy their surface appropriations. We affirm this legal conclusion and return the proposed well rules to the state engineer for consideration of whether the reasonable-means-of-diversion doctrine provides, in this case, a method of achieving maximum utilization of water—a consideration which the state engineer erroneously believed was foreclosed. We note that the policy of maximum utilization does not require a single-minded endeavor to squeeze every drop of water from the valley's aquifers. Section 37-92-501(e) makes clear that the objective of "maximum use" administration is "optimum use." Optimum use can only be achieved with proper regard for all significant factors, including environmental and economic concerns. See section 37-92-102(3), C.R.S. (recognizing the need to correlate the activities of mankind with reasonable preservation of the natural environment); Harrison & Sandstrom, supra, at 14-15 (An increase of well diversions at the expense of maintenance of a surface flow would increase the efficiency of irrigation at the expense of other environmental and economic values.). See also Trelease, supra, at 1866-1872 (Determination of what constitutes a reasonable means of diversion may be more a question of the proper allocation of the costs of more efficient diversion than of the quantity of water ultimately diverted.). The water court observed that the state engineer's reconsideration might take the form of requiring senior appropriators to drill new wells before requiring curtailment of junior rights and listed a number of suggestions for increasing utilization. Similarly, the state engineer's reconsideration might result in assessment to junior appropriators of the cost of making those improvements to seniors' diversions which are necessitated by junior withdrawals. Selection among these and other possibilities, including retention of the scheme of the proposed rules, is a policy decision to be made by the state engineer, after consideration of all relevant factors.

* * * For the reasons set forth * * * we affirm the water court's disapproval of the underground water rules. Although we approve the water court's findings of fact on this issue, * * * we remand the rules for the state engineer's consideration of the policy of maximum utilization and the reasonable-means-of-diversion doctrine. * * *

Notes

1. **Complexities of integrating priorities under the appropriation doctrine.** Integrated administration of groundwater and surface water rights under the appropriation doctrine can be complicated. One complication is described in David L. Harrison & Gustave Sandstrom, Jr., The Groundwater-Surface Water Conflict and Recent Colorado Water Legislation, 43 U. Colo. L. Rev. 1, 18 (1971):

"It is worthwhile to emphasize the time dimension of this problem. * * * When a user or water official discovers that a senior right is being damaged by a well far away in terms of [the time lag between pumping and impact on streamflow], it may be too late to cure the situation. The well pumping can be shut down immediately but it may be days before the effect of the shutdown is felt. For the irrigator the water must be delivered at a crucial time; a delay may mean crop destruction."

Another complication is noted in In re Arkansas River, 581 P.2d 293, 295-96 (Colo. 1978):

"When water in the aquifer is brought to the surface by a well and there is a consumptive use of that water * * *, generally the surface supply is depleted by the amount of such consumptive use. The evidence and findings in this case demonstrate, however, that the restriction of wells does not necessarily result in a comparable increase in the supply of surface water. There are countereffects which offset or modify the depletive use of well water. Some of these are: variations in the amount of river flow; more winter irrigation; reduction in evaporation and phreatophyte losses as a result of lowering of water tables; changes in ground water storage; extent of alluvium recharge occurring during wet cycles or as a result of widespread winter irrigation practices; and increased irrigation efficiencies. Other factors which may also be involved are increased ground water storage, stock ponds, municipal sewage lagoons, potholes, changes in side channel inflows, and cyclical fluctuations through wet and dry periods."

See also Douglas L. Grant, The Complexities of Managing Hydrologically Connected Surface and Groundwater Under the Appropriation Doctrine, 22 Land & Water L. Rev. 63, 64-65 (1987).

2. **Coordinated administration when different legal doctrines govern groundwater and surface water.** In City of Lodi v. East Bay Municipal Utilities District, 60 P.2d 439 (Cal. 1936), the city had a right under the correlative rights doctrine to pump from an aquifer recharged by percolation from the Mokelumne River. The city was a nonoverlying user. Under the correlative rights doctrine, a nonoverlying user's water right is inferior to all overlying uses but is governed by the "first in time, first in right" principle with respect to other nonoverlying uses. See supra p. 334, Note 3. The utility district had a water right under the appropriation doctrine to take water from the river. Its surface water right was junior in time to the city's groundwater water right. The city obtained an injunction prohibiting the utility district from making stream diversions that would lower the water table around its wells.

On appeal, the California Supreme Court observed that the injunction required the utility district to release tremendous amounts of water from its storage reservoir on the river, and the releases, after "forcing a relatively small quantity of water into the surrounding underground water table, for the most part waste into the sea." The court found this to be contrary to a 1928 California constitutional amendment that prohibits the waste or unreasonable use or unreasonable method of use of water. It therefore remanded the case with the following instructions:

"The [plaintiff] city's method of diversion appears to be reasonable, and the use to which the water is put is a reasonable beneficial one. * * * One of the expert witness called by the plaintiff conceded that its wells could go down at least 25 feet below their present levels without danger or substantial injury to the plaintiff. Assuming a lowering of one foot a year by the District's operations, as found by the trial court, it is apparent that the plaintiff's water supply is in no immediate danger. What, then, should the trial court have done or now do in such circumstances? * * * In our opinion the cause should be sent back to the trial court to permit it to take evidence as to the levels to which plaintiff's wells may be lowered without substantial danger to the city's water supply. In fixing this danger level an adequate safety factor in favor of the city should be allowed. * * * The decree should then be reframed to provide that the duty rests upon the District to maintain the levels of the plaintiff's wells above the danger level so fixed by the trial court; that in the event the levels of the wells reach the danger points, the duty be cast upon the District to supply water to the city, or to raise the levels of the wells above the danger mark; and if the District does not comply with this order within a reasonable time, then the injunction decree already framed, or upon a proper showing as modified by the court under its continuing jurisdiction, shall go into effect. * * * Such a decree would adequately meet the requirements of the Constitution by preventing an unreasonable waste of the waters of the stream and at the same time would adequately protect the priority rights of the city of Lodi." Id. at 451-52.

Suppose the plaintiff had not been the city but an overlying rather than nonoverlying user of groundwater. Should it have fared any worse for lack of an appropriative right that could be compared in priority with the district's appropriation?

Nebraska is another state with different legal doctrines for groundwater and surface water. It allocates groundwater under a reasonable use/correlative rights doctrine with a statutory preference for domestic use (see supra p. 335, Note 4), and it allocates surface water primarily under the appropriation doctrine. Many municipalities in the Platte Valley have wells located near the Platte River that capture water from the river. When the cities of Lincoln and Omaha began wellfield expansions costing over $250 million, they sought security for their investments. In the 1960s, they tried unsuccessfully to change state law to allow cities to acquire wellfield appropriations. Decades later, in 1993, a compromise between agricultural and municipal interests resulted in legislation allowing public water suppliers (PWSs) to appropriate stream waters that supply their wells through induced groundwater recharge. However, PWS priorities were backdated so that PWS wells, some of which had been operating since the 1930s, generally were junior to Platte Valley irrigation projects in existence when the legislation was enacted. Neb. Rev. Stat. §§ 46-233, -235 to -235.004. Specifics of the legislation and background facts are explained in J. David Aiken, Nebraska, 26 Water Law Newsl. No. 2 (Rocky Mtn. Min. L. Found., Westrminster, Colo.) (1993).

The 1993 legislation largely ignored the hydrologic reality of significant physical connection between some groundwater and surface water sources in the state. In 1996, the Nebraska Legislature laid a foundation for dealing with that reality. It gave local natural resources districts the authority and primary responsibility to regulate *groundwater activities* that contribute to conflicts between groundwater and surface water users, and it gave the Department of Water Resources (DWR) the authority and responsibility to regulate *surface water activities* that contribute to such conflicts. It also gave DWR the power to approve or disapprove local district management plans and in certain circumstances the power, alone or jointly with districts, to prepare plans for integrated management. It charged local districts and DWR with working out the specifics of integration within a framework of broad legislatively declared policies. The legislation specified cumbersome and time-consuming procedures for accomplishing this, which led a commentator to conclude that "any integrated management will be in the distant future." Stephen D. Mossman, "Whiskey Is for Drinkin' But Water Is for Fightin' About": A First-Hand Account of Nebraska's Integrated Management of Ground and Surface Water Debate and the Passage of L.B. 108, 30 Creighton L. Rev. 67 (1996). An overhaul of the legislation in 2004 sets out further directives on the preparation and modification of integrated management plans and, in a measure that could prove highly important, provides for an Interrelated Water Review Board to resolve conflicts that arise between DWR and local districts over the content, implementation, and enforcement of the plans. Nebraska Ground Water Management and Protection Act §§ 46-701 to -753.

3. **Hydrologic and policy considerations in coordinated management.** W.P. Balleau, Water Appropriation and Transfer in a General Hydrogeologic System, 28 Nat. Resources J. 269, 271-74, 278-80 (1988):

[In the West, generally] the reliable baseflow of streams was diverted early for irrigation. * * * Reclamation projects later stored the winter and peak flows and claimed much of the remaining yield from the river systems. Groundwater development followed in the 20th century and has reduced the baseflow of many streams. * * *

"The degree of effect on a stream due to groundwater development varies in each case. The effects on some streams are insignificant, while other stream reaches have changed from perennial to intermittent flow because the regional water table has declined below the stream bed. * * * With wells nearby the surface streams, the total system yield may be expanded in the short term. The system then rapidly adjusts to a new equilibrium with little net gain in the system yield. At greater distances from the surface water bodies, the spacing of the wells and the groundwater hydraulics may allow major expansion of the total supply for centuries. In all cases, the eventual reduction in surface water supply as a result of groundwater development creates an issue in water rights administration.

"The administration of groundwater in the priority system is not straightforward because the source of groundwater has two components: groundwater storage and induced recharge of surface water. Development of aquifer storage interjects an additional source of water into the otherwise well-ordered surface water scheme. Groundwater storage is relatively large. Variation in supply is not a consideration until the decline in water level becomes an economic problem. Diversions from wells, however, are physically linked to surface depletions in the form of induced recharge from the surface streams. * * *

"The timing of effects on adjacent streams caused by groundwater withdrawal depends upon the aquifer diffusivity and the distance from the wells to the surface water body. The major factor in determining the rate of effects on surface supplies is the distance of withdrawals from the surface sources. For radial flow of groundwater, a 10-fold increase in distance from the surface water body causes a 100-fold delay in the response time, whereas a change in diffusivity is linearly proportional to the response time.

"Every groundwater development * * * begins with 100 percent of withdrawals being derived from storage. The timing of the change from storage depletion (mining) to induced recharge from surface water bodies is key to the water policy question. * * * The management category of mineable, nontributary or unrechargeable water is a reasonable one to apply to wellfield areas that would not progress beyond the earliest stages of [transition from storage depletion to induced recharge from surface supplies] within a reasonable planning horizon. * * *

"The rate at which dependence on groundwater storage converts to dependence on surface water depletion is highly variable and is peculiar to each case. * * * The distinct category of groundwater mining depends entirely upon the time frame. All groundwater developments initially mine water, and finally do not."

Balleau makes the important point that groundwater pumping may expand the total system yield significantly during the period that storage is being consumed, but over the long term a new equilibrium will be reached with little net gain in the system yield. His focus is on the induced recharge element of capture. (To review the concept of capture, see supra p. 345, Note 1.) Another possible element of capture is reduced natural discharge. In *Gould,* for example, the district court found that lowering the water table below phreatophyte root zones through pumping would capture perhaps one million acre-feet per year by reducing natural discharge in the form of evapotranspiration from the saturated zone. Would Balleau's point—that groundwater pumping will produce little net gain in system yield over the long term—be valid for an area like the San Luis Valley, where pumping would reduce natural discharge substantially?

The answer is yes, if the "total system yield" before the water table was lowered is understood to encompass not only artificial discharge through wells but all natural discharge, including the one million acre-feet of natural discharge annually to phreatophytes in the San Luis Valley. If the junior wells in *Gould* were allowed to continue to operate, the annual system yield would increase during the period that storage is depleted. But once storage depletion ceases because of capture (whether in the form of greater induced recharge or decreased natural discharge) and a new equilibrium is reached, the total annual system yield will return more or less to what it was. But part of the total system yield will have been reallocated: The one million acre-feet annually that phreatophytes used to consume will go instead to junior wells. Moreover, senior stream appropriators will have to take their shares of the system yield from underground through wells rather than from surface sources that have dried up.

Balleau says the timing of the transition from storage depletion to capture is key to the water policy question. Suppose the transition will occur within the planning horizon. Then a key to deciding upon policy would be comparing (a) the benefits of permanently depleting some storage and (b) the costs of such depletion in the form of increased pumping expenses, phreatophyte and streamflow losses, and other possible adverse consequences such as land subsidence and loss of wetlands—all calculated over the planning horizon and discounted to present value. How long should a planning horizon be? What should the discount rate be? How should the policy maker deal with the need to compare costs and benefits in the absence of perfect economic and hydrologic data?

D. Conjunctive Management of Groundwater and Surface Water

INTRODUCTION

Conjunctive management, though universally praised, has no exact meaning. Different people use the phrase to mean different things, depending on the water supply problem being addressed. Frank J. Trelease, Conjunctive Use of Groundwater and Surface Water, 27B Rocky Mtn. Min. L. Inst. 1853, 1853-54 (1982). In perhaps its narrowest usage, the phrase refers to administering rights in physically connected groundwater and surface water under the same legal doctrine and on an integrated basis. E.g., Musser v. Higginson, 871 P.2d 809 (Idaho 1994). In broader usage, the phrase encompasses a wide variety of measures to coordinate the use of available water supply sources and storage capacity, including underground storage capacity, in an effort to maximize the net benefits from them over time. This might include coordinated management of surface and underground water sources that are not even physically connected. And whether or not the sources are connected, it might involve the use of some creative management ideas and tools. The notes that follow illustrate different techniques of coordinating the use of available water supplies to maximize the benefits from them.

Notes

1. **Purchase and retirement of surface rights.** In City of Albuquerque v. Reynolds, 379 P.2d 73 (N.M. 1962), the city applied for permits to appropriate 6000 acre-feet per year from a groundwater basin physically connected with the fully

appropriated Rio Grande River. Over a seventy-five year period, about half the water the city proposed to pump would come from basin storage and about half from depletion of surface flows. The state engineer found that the proposed wells would impair existing surface rights in violation of state statute. He ruled that the permits could issue, however, upon the condition that the city would have to purchase and retire enough surface water rights to offset the effects of its groundwater pumping on the river. The court upheld the state engineer's power to impose the condition:

"Having found legislative authority in the state engineer to deny the city's applications on the ground that their granting would result in impairment of the rights of Rio Grande River appropriators, we next consider the argument that the state engineer exceeded his power and jurisdiction by establishing and promulgating rules and regulations requiring the retirement of surface water rights as a condition to new appropriations of underground water from the Rio Grande Underground Water Basin. [If] the underground waters in question cannot be taken without impairment to the rights of the river appropriators, even though there are unappropriated underground waters in the basin, then it would seem to follow that some method should be devised, if possible, whereby the available unappropriated water can be put to beneficial use. * * *

"We feel constrained to hold that the state engineer adopted the only known plan to avoid impairment to existing rights and that his requirement, that surface rights be retired to the extent necessary to protect prior stream appropriators as a condition of the granting of an application to appropriate from the basin, is within the lawful power and authority of the state engineer." Id. at 80-81.

In the years after *City of Albuquerque*, the state engineer issued various other groundwater permits conditioned upon the permittee's future purchase and retirement of existing surface rights to offset the effects of pumping. In issuing these permits, the state engineer developed the practice of not identifying or quantifying the surface rights to be retired in the future. Instead, a permit would only specify a date by which surface rights must be retired. Later, as the specified date approached, the permittee would file a proposed dedication with the state engineer identifying and quantifying the specific surface rights it wished to purchase and retire to comply with the permit condition. In N.M. Op. Att'y Gen. No. 94-07 (Dec. 23, 1994), the state attorney general ruled that this practice of deferred identification and quantification of the surface rights to be retired was illegal. There was no specific statutory authority for it, and the attorney general concluded that it violated various statutory rules for new appropriations and water right transfers, e.g., it did not comply with a statute requiring scrutiny of whether a proposed appropriation would impair existing rights, would be contrary to the conservation of water within the state, or would be detrimental to the public welfare. The attorney general also concluded that the failure to provide notice of what surface rights would be retired and an opportunity to protest during the initial permit proceeding violated the procedural due process rights of people whose water rights might be impaired.

2. **Exchanges, by-pass pumping, and artificial recharge.** A discussion of conjunctive management tools thought to be available under Colorado law is found in David L. Harrison & Gustave Sandstrom, Jr., The Groundwater-Surface Water Conflict and Recent Colorado Water Legislation, 43 U. Colo. L. Rev. 1, 37-48 (1971). Although this article is now somewhat dated, it still provides a useful explanation of different physical tools. These include water exchanges, in which water stored in a surface reservoir is released to replace stream flow that is

diminished by groundwater by pumping (as in *Glacier View Meadows*, supra p. 75); "by-pass pumping," in which a fraction of the groundwater pumped is passed on to the stream to replace natural flow; and artificial recharge of groundwater, including storage of stream water during periods of high flows in aquifer-reservoirs for later withdrawal by wells during low flow seasons or drought years. For three case studies of conjunctive management in Colorado, see Lawrence J. MacDonnell, Colorado's Law of "Underground Water": A Look at the South Platte Basin and Beyond, 59 U. Colo. L. Rev. 579 (1988).

3. **Economic tools.** Nat'l Water Comm'n, Water Policies for the Future 234-36 (1973):

"Different management tools can be used in different circumstances. Where a basin has already undergone adjudication and many private rights have been decreed, management may amount to little more than administration of the decreed rights and regulation of new withdrawals. On the other hand, the management agency might use economic tools in lieu of, or in addition to, regulatory ones. A water management agency having the power to impose pump charges would be able to introduce incentives to affect decisions of water users in the interest of the best use and conservation of the resource. Through taxing or pricing mechanisms a management agency may, in effect, efficiently ration ground and surface water.

"An illustration is provided by the management scheme employed by the Orange County Water District in Southern California. The District can buy imported water from the Metropolitan Water District of Southern California. Ground water is also available, but sole reliance on it would cause an overdraft, as it has in the past. Each year the Orange County Water District determines how much of the water demand shall be supplied from ground water and how much from imported water. The determination of the amount of ground water withdrawal is based in part on the quantity in storage in the aquifer and the anticipated recharge, including artificial recharge.

"Suppose in a given year that the District decides to meet demand with 60 percent ground water and 40 percent surface water; these percentages establish each user's 'fair share' of basin supply. Then the District establishes the cost differential between pumped water and imported water. Suppose imported water costs $14 per acre-foot more than pumped water. If a water user takes a total of 100 acre-feet of water during the year, pumping 60 percent and taking imported water for the other 40 percent, he pays no special charge, although he has, of course, paid a premium of $14 per acre-foot for the imported water. If the user takes the full 100 acre-feet in ground water, he must pay a Basin Equity Assessment of $14 per acre-foot on 40 of the 100 acre-feet that he pumped. If another user takes his 100 acre-feet all in imported water (paying the $14 per acre-foot premium on the total imported), the District will credit him with $14 per acre-foot for the 60 acre-feet he could have pumped from the aquifer. As a consequence, all water users in the District pay approximately the same price per acre-foot for water no matter what the source, and all water users pay part of the costs for importing water even though some may use no part of it. Even in the absence of a supply of imported water, a similar pricing system can be used to apportion withdrawals between indigenous surface supply and ground water supply."

4. **California's mix of tools.** U.S. Advisory Comm'n on Intergovernmental Relations, Coordinating Water Resources in the Federal System: The Groundwater-Surface Water Connection 36-37 (1991):

"California has not adopted a comprehensive statewide groundwater management law, but has pursued a policy of encouraging local water users to develop governance structures for water management (usually through the combined efforts of special water districts and water users' associations) with the support of state agencies such as the Department of Water Resources. * * *

"Artificial recharge projects in southern California, using groundwater basins to store surface waters for later use, date back at least to the 1920s. Flood waters were moved out of stream channels, diked and ponded in permeable areas, and allowed to sink into the underground strata. Temporary dams were constructed in more permeable stream channels to obstruct surface flows and increase recharge to groundwater basins, which could then serve both storage and transmission purposes. In the 1980s, over 2 million acre-feet of water per year were placed in underground storage by local water agencies.

"In some locations, extensive spreading grounds were constructed, some of which were designed to recharge the groundwater supply while providing surface recreational opportunities for local residents. The Orange County Water District was a leader in this multipurpose facility development. Groundwater pumping was taxed by local special water districts to provide the funds for artificial replenishment programs that primarily benefited pumpers and consumers. Later innovations included 'in-lieu replenishment' (whereby water users in basins with access to both surface and groundwater supplies are encouraged to take surface water in lieu of pumping groundwater when surface supplies are plentiful) and the use of reclaimed water for basin recharge and sea water barrier projects. * * *

"Through the 1980s, in the aftermath of the severe drought of the late 1970s, as population growth continued apace and as the allotment of Colorado River Water for California declined with the beginning of operations of the Central Arizona Project, still more emphasis has been placed on wiser water management, conservation, and reuse of wastewaters. Environmental concerns and budgetary constraints have largely eliminated the prospect of future water development projects. Local water agencies have focused increasingly on the use of pricing to regulate the demand side of the water supply equation, on reaping new supply availability from conservation, and on interlocal agreements and water rights transfer to move water from wasteful and lower valued uses to higher valued uses."

BOARD OF COUNTY COMMISSIONERS v. PARK COUNTY SPORTSMEN'S RANCH, L.L.P.

Supreme Court of Colorado, 2002.

45 P.3d 693.

[Park Country Sportsmen's Ranch (PCSR) owned 2,037 acres in a high mountain valley. It sought a conditional permit for a groundwater recharge and extraction project that would store water in the saturated and unsaturated space of aquifers underlying approximately 115 square miles of the mountain valley. PCSR planned to construct six surface reservoirs to artificially recharge the aquifers and twenty-six wells to extract water from them for transport to a distant municipality. The Park County Board of Commissioners and two persons owning land in the valley (Landowners) sued for a declaration that PCSR's use of aquifer storage space under their lands would constitute trespass and could not be done without their consent or condemnation of an easement.

None of PCSR's surface reservoirs or wells would be located on the Landowners' land, and the Landowners did not allege the use and enjoyment of their property would be compromised in any way. Instead, the Landowners claimed trespass based on the common law doctrine "cujus est solum ejus est usque ad coelum et ad inferos," which translates "to whomsoever the soil belongs, he owns also to the sky and to the depths." The water court ruled the movement of recharge water through aquifers underlying Landowners' lands would not constitute a trespass. The Colorado Supreme Court affirmed.]

JUSTICE HOBBS delivered the opinion of the Court. * * * To support their theory, the Landowners invoke our decisions in Walpole v. State Board of Land Commissioners, 62 Colo. 554, 163 P. 848 (1917) and Wolfley v. Lebanon Mining Co., 4 Colo. 112 (1878). [*Walpole* and *Wolfley* invoked the common law cujus doctrine in holding that a landowner owns minerals under the surface of the land.] The Landowners invoke *Walpole* and *Wolfley* for the assertion that their "fee ownership includes the space underneath the land" and therefore they have a right to withhold consent and require compensation for PCSR's project.

* * * The Ohio Supreme Court has rejected a very similar contention in Chance v. BP Chemicals, Inc., 77 Ohio St.3d 17, 670 N.E.2d 985 (1996). In that case, a property owner claimed that the migration of injected liquid into portions of a very deep aquifer underlying its property constituted a trespass. Determining that the injectate mixed with "waters of the state" in the aquifer, the Ohio Supreme Court rejected the property owner's claim of ownership and trespass based on the cujus doctrine. It stated:

> Our analysis above concerning the native brine illustrates that appellants do not enjoy absolute ownership of waters of the state below their properties, and therefore underscores that their subsurface ownership rights are limited. As the discussion in *Willoughby Hills* [Willoughby Hills v. Corrigan, 278 N.E.2d 658, 664 (Ohio 1972)], makes evident, ownership rights in today's world are not so clear-cut as they were before the advent of airplanes and injection wells.
>
> Consequently, we do not accept appellants' assertion of absolute ownership of everything below the surface of their properties. Just as a property owner must accept some limitations on the ownership rights extending above the surface of the property, we find that there are also limitations on property owners' subsurface rights. We therefore extend the reasoning of *Willoughby Hills*, that absolute ownership of air rights is a doctrine which "has no place in the modern world," to apply as well to ownership of subsurface rights.

We find the Ohio Supreme Court's discussion of state waters and limitations upon absolute subsurface ownership rights to be of particular significance to the case before us, in light of Colorado's strong constitutional, statutory, and case law holding all water in Colorado to be a public resource and allowing holders of water rights decrees the right of passage for their appropriated water through and within the natural surface and subsurface water-bearing formations. * * *

Under the Landowners' property ownership theory, each landowner would have a cause of action against PCSR or any other person attempting to pursue a conditional water rights application for storage of water in the aquifer. However, we determine that the General Assembly, in authorizing the use of aquifers for storage of artificially recharged waters pursuant to decreed conjunctive use projects, has further supplanted the Landowners' common-law property ownership theory. * * *

When parties have use rights to water they have captured, possessed, and controlled, they may place that water into an aquifer by artificial recharge and enjoy the benefit of that water as part of their decreed water use rights, if the aquifer can accommodate the recharged water without injury to decreed senior water rights. This authority resides in a number of statutory sections that implement the "Colorado Doctrine," which is that all water in the state is a public resource dedicated to the beneficial use of public and private agencies, as prescribed by law. Sections 37-92-305(9)(b) and (c) provide that the Water Court may issue a conditional decree for storage of water in underground aquifers if the applicant can and will lawfully capture, possess, and control water for beneficial use which it then artificially recharges into the aquifer. Section 37-87-101(1) provides that the right to store water of a natural stream is a right of appropriation in order of priority, and section 37-87-101(2) provides that underground aquifers can be used for storage of water that the applicant artificially recharges into the aquifer pursuant to a decreed right. * * *

We now turn to water use rights and property ownership rights under Colorado law. Colorado law differs fundamentally from the English common law [of riparian rights for streams and absolute ownership for groundwater that] it replaced. * * * Advancing the national agenda of settling the public domain required abandonment of the pre-existing common-law rules of property ownership in regard to water and water use rights. Reducing the public land and water to possession and ownership was a preoccupation of territorial and state law from the outset. A new law of custom and usage in regard to water use rights and land ownership rights, the "Colorado Doctrine," arose from "imperative necessity" in the western region. * * * When first announcing the Colorado Doctrine, we said that "rules respecting the tenure of private property must yield to the physical laws of nature, whenever such laws exert a controlling influence." Yunker v. Nichols, 1 Colo. 551, 553 (1872) (Hallett, C.J.). * * *

Accordingly, by reason of Colorado's constitution, statutes, and case precedent, neither surface water, nor ground water, nor the use rights thereto, nor the water-bearing capacity of natural formations belong to a landowner as a stick in the property rights bundle. Section 37-87-103, 10 C.R.S. (2001), for example, codifies this longstanding aspect of the Colorado Doctrine. It provides that water appropriated by means of a reservoir impoundment and then released for travel to its place of beneficial use shall enjoy the right of passage through the natural formation in the administration of water use rights. * * *

[T]he the Landowners claim a common-law property right to require consent or just compensation for an easement to use the subsurface estate for artificial recharge and storage of water in aquifers extending through their properties, asserting that "fee ownership includes the space underneath the land" which the water occupies. The Landowners rely on *Walpole* and *Wolfley* for this proposition, but these are mineral cases which are clearly distinguishable from water cases * * *.

Allowing property owners to control who may store water in natural formations, or charging water right use holders for easements to occupy the natural water bearing surface or underground formations with their appropriated water, would revert to common-law ownership principles that are antithetical to Colorado water law and the public's interest in a secure, reliable, and flexible water supply made available through the exercise of decreed water use rights. It would disharmonize Colorado's historical balance between water use rights and land ownership rights. It would inflate and protract litigation by adding condemnation actions to procedures for obtaining water use decrees. It would counter the state's goals of optimum use, efficient water management, and priority administration. * * * [36]

Notes

1. **Other theories why artificial recharge does not constitute trespass or a taking.** In Niles Sand & Gravel Co. v. Alameda County Water District, 112 Cal. Rptr. 846 (Ct. App. 1974), the county water district artificially recharged the Niles Groundwater Basin with water it diverted from Alameda Creek. The recharge raised the water table enough to flood the gravel company's deep pits even though the water table was still below its natural level prior to any pumping in the basin. To enable quarrying, the gravel company pumped the water out of its pits and dumped it back into Alameda Creek. The court enjoined the gravel company from continuing to do that because it was a waste of water in violation of the correlative rights doctrine and the company's land use permits. The court rejected the company's claim of inverse condemnation because the correlative rights doctrine made the company's overlying land subject to a "public servitude" that prevented it from discharging more than its reasonable share of groundwater.

Central Nebraska Public Power & Irrigation District v. Abrahamson, 413 N.W.2d 290 (Neb. 1987), involved "incidental recharge" due to seepage from the district's 600-mile system of irrigation canals that entered an aquifer. The district filed an application under a Nebraska statute allowing an appropriator to obtain "recognition of incidental underground water storage associated with [its] appropriation." Some landowners overlying the storage area challenged the constitutionality of the statute, arguing that it took their exclusive right to the empty storage space under their lands without just compensation. They offered no evidence, however, of harm to their lands. The court rejected their challenge, reasoning that a statute cannot deprive a person of property unless it prevents the person from making a desired use of the property or diminishes profit the person would otherwise derive from the property.

---

36. We are not presented here with a cause of action in tort for interference with surface uses due to recharge that raises the groundwater table or with any claim to interference with the use and enjoyment of the Landowners' surface or subsurface estates. Our opinion should not be read as altering the otherwise applicable law regarding injury caused by alteration of natural surface drainage patterns.

West Maricopa Combine, Inc. v. Arizona Department of Water Resources, 26 P.3d 1171 (Ariz. Ct. App. 2001), concerned the process by which recharge water is introduced into the ground. At issue was a 1986 Arizona statute allowing a recharger to turn imported water into the channel of a natural stream where gravity will cause it to infiltrate into an aquifer. A riparian landowner who owned the stream bed objected that such use of the channel would interfere with its property rights, particularly its right to exclude others. The court held that there would be neither a trespass nor a taking because the landowner never had the "right" at issue. It said Arizona policy since before statehood encouraged full use of scarce water resources, and the statute merely codified a longstanding background principle of Arizona law regarding the rights water users have in the natural channel that delivers their appropriation.

2. **Recharge statutes.** Most western states have legislation authorizing recharge projects. For example, Nebraska legislation addresses not only incidental recharge, as noted above, but the appropriation of water for intentional recharge and recovery, and it allows a recharger to levy a reasonable fee for withdrawals by others. Neb. Rev. Stat. §§ 46-233, -240 to -242, -295, -296, -299 to -2,106. The California Water Code declares that the storage of water underground is a beneficial use for which stream water can be appropriated if the stored water will thereafter be applied to some beneficial use. § 1242. The Water Code also authorizes various public entities, including water replenishment districts covering more than one county, to store water for future use. §§ 60000-60622. If the storage operation is performed by a water replenishment district, no person can acquire any property or right in the waters, § 60351; and the district may charge water rates to cover operating expenses, § 60245, may tax real property to the extent water rates fail to cover expenses, §§ 60250, 60252, and may levy replenishment assessments on pumpers, § 60325.

Arizona has extensive recharge legislation. One chapter of the state code creates an elaborate system of permits for activities involving underground water storage, savings, and replenishment. Ariz. Rev. Stat. §§ 45-801.01 to -.898.01. Other chapters authorize—or in some cases, obligate—various districts to engage in and finance groundwater recharge activities, e.g., §§ 48-3771 to -3783 (multi-county water conservation districts), §§ 48-4401 to -4575 (groundwater replenishment districts). In addition, the Arizona Legislature established a water banking authority empowered to recharge depleted aquifers with Colorado River water transported through the Central Arizona Project. §§ 45-2401 to -2472. An important motivation for creating the authority was Arizona's expected inability to use its full Colorado River apportionment of 2.8 million acre-feet annually until 2035. Groundwater recharge by the water banking authority enables Arizona to store unused water from its annual apportionment, rather than having to stand by and let California take the unused part. The water banking authority is also authorized to enter into interstate banking agreements, under which water can be stored in Arizona aquifers on behalf of California and Nevada. Such storage would enable those two states thereafter to divert water from the Colorado River in excess of their annual apportionments and in exchange water previously stored in Arizona aquifers on their behalf would go to replace water that Arizonans otherwise would be entitled to take from the Colorado River. Margaret Bushman La Bianca, Note, The Arizona Water Bank and the Law of the River, 40 Ariz. L. Rev. 659 (1998). Bureau of Reclamation rules establish a framework for the Secretary of the Interior to consider, participate in, and administer interstate storage and release agreements among the

Lower Basin states. 43 C.F.R. pt. 414. In 2002, Arizona, Nevada, and the United States signed an agreement providing for the storage in Arizona of up to 200,000 acre-feet per year on behalf of Nevada, to a cumulative total of 1.2 million acre-feet. Storage and Interstate Release Agreement, http://www.awba.state.az.us/annc/2003/sira_agreement_12-18-02.pdf; see also Agreement for the Development of Intentionally Created Unused Apportionment, http://www. awba.state.az.us/annc/2003/icua_agreement_12-18-02.pdf.

3. **Allocation of aquifer storage space.** In Central & West Basin Water Replenishment District v. Southern California Water Co., 109 Cal. App. 4th 891, 135 Cal. Rptr. 2d 486 (Cal. Ct. App. 2003), the 148 entities who collectively held all the rights to pump water from a groundwater basin extending over 277 square miles wanted to use subsurface space to store imported water. About 645,000 acre-feet of storage space was available. The pumpers sought a decree allocating the unused storage space to them on a pro rata basis, e.g., a pumper holding 5% of the rights to extract water would also have 5% of the available storage space. Their efforts were opposed by a water replenishment district created and operating under California legislation referenced in Note 2. The court ruled that extraction and storage rights are not linked, that the storage space is a public resource not owned by the pumpers, and that the legislature authorized the water replenishment district, not the pumpers, to store waters in the space for conjunctive use.

The Nevada recharge legislation creates a three-tiered permit system—a permit to operate a recharge and recovery project, a permit to appropriate the water that will be used for recharge, and a permit for the recovery wells. Nev. Rev. Stat. 534.0145, -.250 to -.340. A permit to operate a recharge and recovery project requires (1) the technical and financial capability to construct and operate the project and (2) an approved appropriation of water for recharge.

Chapter 5

WATER DISTRIBUTION ORGANIZATIONS

SECTION 1. PRIVATE CORPORATIONS

JACOBUCCI v. DISTRICT COURT

Supreme Court of Colorado, 1975.
189 Colo. 380, 541 P.2d 667.

ERICKSON, JUSTICE. On November 14, 1973, the City of Thornton instituted an action in eminent domain in the Jefferson County District Court against Farmers Reservoir and Irrigation Company, the City of Westminster, a shareholder in Farmers, the Treasurer of Jefferson County, the Treasurer of Boulder County, and other unknown persons claiming any interest in the proceeding. Farmers Reservoir and Irrigation Company (Farmers) is a mutual ditch company, organized pursuant to section 7–42–102 et seq., C.R.S. 1973, as a Colorado corporation.

The petitioners here are Victor L. Jacobucci, Dorothy Jacobucci, Paul Jacobucci, Mary J. Jacobucci, Jean J. Jacobucci, Albert Sack, Anne Sack, Casper Sack, Katherine Sack, and Yoxall Farms, Inc. The petitioners, all shareholders in Farmers, filed a cross-petition * * * in order to intervene as defendants in the condemnation proceedings. This motion was denied by the District Court on February 11, 1975, after the court concluded that the shareholders of Farmers were not indispensable parties to the proceeding. Thereafter, this court was petitioned, pursuant to its original jurisdiction under C.A.R. 21, to grant the petitioners relief. The petition requested an order permitting the shareholders to intervene and compelling their joinder as parties in the condemnation proceeding. We issued a rule to show cause why the relief requested should not be granted.

The issue we address in this original proceeding, which renders the other issues moot, is whether the individual shareholders of a mutual ditch company are indispensable parties in an action to condemn the shareholders' decreed water priorities. We hold that they are.

Farmers, a mutual ditch company, administers an extensive water distribution system divided into four divisions. The Standley Lake Division includes a storage reservoir known as Standley Lake located in Jefferson County. The decreed water rights of this reservoir are used to irrigate approximately 15,000 acres of land situated in Jefferson, Adams, and Weld Counties. Property rights administered by the Standley Lake Division are the subject of the condemnation action which created the issues in this proceeding.

At the time of the institution of the condemnation proceeding, Farmers represented a total of 1,105 shareholders, 271 of whom owned shares allocated to the Standley Lake Division of Farmers. * * * The record title to the physical properties of the ditches, reservoir, lands, and rights-of-way stands in the name of Farmers.

In order to determine whether the shareholders of Farmers are indispensable parties to the condemnation proceedings, we must define the nature of their relationship to the mutual ditch company and to the rights and properties administered by the corporation. The history behind the growth and purposes of mutual ditch companies is necessary to an analysis of the issue which is before us.

The rapid development and expansion of agriculture in the arid regions of the west led to the increased importance of irrigation. Irrigation itself, however, proved to be a great obstacle to farmers in need of irrigation water. The construction and maintenance of canals and ditches required the outlay of large sums of money. The average farmer did not have sufficient means to construct, own, or operate an irrigation ditch to convey water to his land. The most economical solution was to convey the water over a great distance through a single large main and laterals and then distribute it to consumers by means of smaller laterals.

In response to the enormous task of supplying water to the parched farmlands, farmers banded together and formed mutual ditch companies for the express purpose of storing and conducting water for irrigation purposes. Farmers who may have previously owned ditches as tenants-in-common would transfer their ownership rights to mutual ditch companies and in return receive stock representing their water rights. This made possible the distribution of water over large areas of land, often remote from the source of supply, and increased the availability of irrigated farmland at reasonable costs. Not only was the management of the ditches and reservoirs made more efficient, but capital was made more available through the operation of these companies.

Mutual ditch companies in Colorado have been recognized as quasi-public carriers. Farmers is not organized for profit or hire and exists primarily for the benefit of its shareholders. Farmers is engaged in the business of storing and transporting water to shareholders who own the right to use the water.

Mutual ditch companies like Farmers were formed expressly for the purpose of furnishing water to shareholders, not for profit or hire. Delivery of water to the consumers is conditioned upon the payment of an annual assessment levied by the company to meet operating expenses and, if they exist, debt installments. These companies are not organized under the general Colorado corporation statutes, but under special legislation for ditch and reservoir companies. * * *

The relationship between the mutual ditch corporation and its shareholders arises out of contract, implied in a subscription for stock and construed by the provisions of a charter or articles of incorporation.

* * * The corporation is not only obligated to furnish a proper proportion of water to each of its shareholders, but it is liable in damages for the failure to do so. The corporation must protect and preserve the interests of the shareholders by keeping the ditches, canals, reservoir, and other works in good repair, the expense of which is paid from the special assessment. Sections 7–42–104, 7–42–107, 7–42–108, C.R.S. 1973.

The shares of stock in a mutual ditch corporation represent the "'consumer's interest in the reservoir, canal and water rights.'" Beaty v. Board of County Comm'rs. of Otero County, 101 Colo. 346, 73 P.2d 982 (1937). The benefit derived from the ownership of such stock is the right to the exclusive use of the water it represents, the water being divided pro-rata according to the number of shares of stock held by each shareholder. Billings Ditch Co. v. Industrial Comm'n., 127 Colo. 69, 253 P.2d 1058 (1953). The shareholders have the right to change the place of the use of the water if other users are not injured thereby.

As a mutual ditch company, Farmers is "merely the vehicle by which its owners operate and manage its affairs." Billings Ditch Co. v. Industrial Comm'n., supra. The corporation, like other mutual ditch companies, was organized solely for the convenience of its members in the management of the irrigation and reservoir systems. The ownership of the shares of stock is merely incidental to the ownership of the water rights by the shareholders. We wish to emphasize that the shares of stock owned by Farmers' shareholders represent a definite and specific water right, as well as a corresponding interest in the ditch, canal, reservoir, and other works by which the water right is utilized.

The City of Thornton seeks to analogize the position of the shareholders in Farmers to that of the shareholders in any other corporation. On this basis, they argue that the shareholders in Farmers are not necessary parties to this litigation, because the corporation, under principles of corporation law, is bound to protect their interests. We have held that a mutual ditch corporation is responsible for maintaining actions in the corporate name to secure or protect the consumers' water rights or other property and to represent the shareholders in civil actions. Inasmuch as Farmers holds legal title to the physical properties sought to be condemned, Thornton argues that Farmers is the real party in interest, not the shareholders.

In the first place, as petitioners rightly point out, a mutual ditch corporation is not organized under the general corporation laws, but under a separate and independent statutory provision. We find that the unique character of these corporations mandates different treatment which is not fully in accord with the principles applicable to corporations in general. As noted above, the shares of stock held by the consumers in a mutual ditch corporation represent a specific property interest in a water right. The interest of these shareholders cannot be "defeated or altered by any action of the ditch company or its other shareholders." United States v. 508.88 Acres of Land, U.S. District Ct. (D. Colo. May 8, 1973, Unpublished); Bent v. Second Extension Water Co., 51 Cal. App. 648, 197 P. 657 (1921). While the "naked title" may stand in the name of Farmers, the ditch, reservoir and water rights are actually owned by the farmers who are served thereby. The shareholders are the real parties in interest in the condemnation action, not the corporation.

In our view, shareholders are indispensable parties. C.R.C.P. 19. * * * The shareholders of Farmers are so situated that their ability to protect their interest in the beneficial application of the water to their land is, as a practical matter, impaired. * * * The condemnation action here in issue has the potential of seriously disrupting the shareholders' property interests. That the water rights owned by Farmers' shareholders are property rights is well established by Colorado law. Billings Ditch Co. v. Industrial Comm'n., supra.

At least 271 shareholders, as of the date of the petition in condemnation, are faced with the prospect of having their farmlands denied a substantial source of water. The productivity and value of their lands, as well as the assurance of their livelihoods, is in many cases entirely dependent upon the continuing flow of water from Standley Reservoir. No court can ignore the magnitude of disruption which would result in a successful condemnation action by the City of Thornton. Moreover, each shareholder stands in a different position from the others and is likely to be affected differently by the condemnation action. Their ability to protect those individualized interests would surely be impaired if this action were allowed to proceed in their absence.

The evidence in the present case does not suggest that joinder would be infeasible. All shareholders of Farmers similarly situated to the petitioners herein are subject to service of process. * * * Therefore, * * * the District Court should join as parties to the condemnation action those shareholders in the Standley Lake Division of Farmers whose water rights would be affected by the condemnation action of Thornton as of the date of the initiation of the condemnation action and all parties in interest.

Accordingly, the rule to show cause is made absolute, and we remand to the District Court for further proceedings consonant with the views expressed in this opinion.

Notes

1. **Just compensation and the indispensable parties.** In the third-to-last paragraph of *Jacobucci*, the court said that each shareholder was likely to be affected differently by the condemnation action and that the ability of shareholders to protect their individualized interests would be impaired if the condemnation action were to proceed without them. In pondering what the court meant, consider how just compensation for the condemnation would be measured and to whom it would be payable. In City of Boulder v. Snyder, 396 F.2d 853 (10th Cir.

1968), a municipal paving project destroyed a small mutual company ditch that carried water to a shareholder-landowner. She sued the municipality for taking her water supply. The court treated the loss of water as a partial taking of her property, for which the measure of just compensation was the difference in the value of her property before the taking (land with appurtenant water) and its value after the taking (land without water). Before-and-after valuation is a standard measure of just compensation for partial takings. 4A Julius L. Sackman, Nichols' the Law of Eminent Domain § 14.02[1].

2. **Mutual companies.** Private associations of irrigators that provide water at cost to their members are called variously mutual water companies, mutual ditch companies, or mutual irrigation companies. Like the Farmers Reservoir and Irrigation Company in *Jacobucci*, most of them are organized as nonprofit corporations. *Jacobucci* reports that in Colorado such companies are incorporated under special legislation rather than under the state's general corporation laws. In some states, they are organized under the general corporation laws, though where that is so typically there are supplemental special provisions limiting formation of the companies and regulating shareholder relations.

The specific characteristics of mutual water companies vary widely, depending on the physical nature of the project, the purpose of the incorporators, the powers granted to the corporation by statute and charter, and the arrangement between the corporation and its stockholders. Sometimes much of the land irrigable by the corporation's works was already irrigated under existing individual water rights, and the mutual company was formed to construct a new, more efficient ditch as a substitute method of carrying water to the farmers. In this situation, the farmers might either have retained their old water rights or have conveyed them to the company and obtained rights as stockholders to a share of the company's water rights.

Other mutual water companies were organized prior to settlement by the farmers. In fact, many mutual companies were created as subsidiaries of land promotion companies. A "land company" or "land and water company," financed as a commercial venture with private capital (often from eastern states, England, and Europe) purchased or obtained control of a large area of land and constructed irrigation works, subdivided the land, and sold to settlers farms and shares in a subsidiary "water company" or "ditch company."

Still other mutual water corporations were formed to replace commercial enterprises originally organized to profit from the sale of water. The failure of such ventures, and their abandonment by their managers, forced the consumers to take over the system on a cooperative basis, either by purchase in bankruptcy or by more informal methods.

A few "Carey Act corporations" still exist. To encourage the reclamation of arid western lands, Congress enacted the Carey Act, 28 Stat. 372 (1894), as amended, 43 U.S.C. § 641. The Act provided that 1,000,000 acres of arid lands of the public domain would be donated to each of the western "public land states," if those states would see to its reclamation and settlement. Most of these states undertook to carry out the obligation of the Act by contracting with private companies to build and operate the reclamation works necessary to bring the water to the lands. The state sold the lands to settlers who bought their water rights from the construction company in the form of stock in a mutual water corporation formed to operate the works. The water corporation stock was usually bought under contract secured by a mortgage on the land in favor of the construction company. Many of the projects were not carefully planned and were economically infeasible so that the settlers were in trouble from the start, and many Carey Act corporations have been reorganized into irrigation districts.

Another form of mutual water company is the "water users' association," a corporation formed to contract with the Secretary of the Interior for the repayment to the government of the reimbursable costs of a federal reclamation project. Formed under the corporation law of the state in which it was located, the association issued stock in proportion to the irrigable acreage of the settlers. It levied assessments against the landowners, secured by liens on both stock and land, thus collecting on behalf of the United States the costs of construction, operation, and maintenance of the project. Today the Bureau of Reclamation prefers to deal with irrigation districts, and many of these associations have changed their form, though they are still used to a considerable extent in Arizona and Utah.

Mutual water companies are discussed and contrasted with other forms of organization in U.S. Dep't of Agric., Circular No. 934, Irrigation-Enterprise Organizations (1953); Theodore W. Russell, Mutual Water Companies in California, 12 S. Cal. L. Rev. 155 (1939); Raphael J. Moses, Irrigation Corporations, 32 Rocky Mtn. L. Rev. 527 (1960).

3. **Mutual company stock.** Usually mutual water companies issue shares based on the number of acres a stockholder irrigates, e.g., one share of stock for each acre of land, and each irrigator is entitled to a pro rata share of the water available to the company based on the amount of his land (or stock) relative to the total held by all stockholders. Shares in some companies, however, entitle the holder to a specific quantity of water or to a specific fraction of the water available to the company regardless of the acreage irrigated. For example, if existing water users formed the company to construct a ditch to replace their individual works, shares might well have been issued according to the quantities of the individual water uses and with no provision for pro rata sharing during shortage.

A mutual water company might hold more than one appropriation due to enlargements of its facilities from time to time. In that situation, the company might have issued a different class of stock for each appropriation. Idaho Code § 42–904 states that the rights of shareholders in the same class shall be equal. The statutory equality within a class applies only until stockholders can get their individual priorities adjudicated. Brose v. Nampa & Meridian Irrigation Dist., 118 P. 504 (Idaho 1911), 132 P. 799 (Idaho 1913). Usually, however, the company's articles of incorporation or bylaws will mandate pro rata sharing of water within a class during times of shortage. Then there can be no individual priorities among shareholders in the same class. Sanderson v. Salmon River Canal Co., 200 P. 341 (Idaho 1921).

4. **Assessments.** Mutual water companies generally have statutory authority to levy assessments against their stockholders to raise funds for operation and maintenance, and for other proper charges such as for making improvements or for paying off bonds or other indebtedness. By statute or by the corporate articles or bylaws, stockholder assessments might have to be levied on a pro rata basis. This requirement is met if the assessment on each share in a given class is the same and if the company's costs are equitably apportioned among the classes of

stock, taking into account that the classes represent different water rights and one class might have a less dependable water supply and thus might use the ditch less than another class. Robinson v. Booth-Orchard Grove Ditch Co., 31 P.2d 487 (Colo. 1934) (upholding a higher assessment on class A and class B shares than on class C shares).

Payment of an assessment is enforced in the first instance by the simple process of denying water to the nonpaying stockholder. The stockholder has no right to damages or affirmative relief if he has not fulfilled his part of the bargain. Henderson v. Kirby Ditch Co., 373 P.2d 591 (Wyo. 1962). In addition, the company articles, bylaws, or stock certificates typically provide that an unpaid assessment shall be a lien upon the stock, which may be forfeited to the company for nonpayment or sold to other water users. By agreement between the company and its stock subscribers, assessments may be made a lien upon the water user's land or a personal obligation as well. However, if state statutes provide for stock liens as the exclusive method of enforcing the payment of assessments, the imposition of a land lien or personal liability is beyond the corporate powers and ultra vires. Thirty Mile Canal Co. v. Carskadon, 70 N.W.2d 432 (Neb. 1955).

In Aberdeen-Springfield Canal Co. v. Peiper, 982 P.2d. 917 (Idaho 1999), two canal company stockholders, the Peipers, sought to defend against foreclosure of an assessment lien on their land by arguing they owed no assessment because they had forfeited their right to water due to nonuse for more than thirty years. The court held the state's five-year forfeiture statute did not apply. It reasoned that the company was the appropriator and to find forfeiture "where the appropriator did nothing to cause the nonuse of the water would have troubling consequences for all Carey Act operating companies. * * * If the Peipers' argument were valid, the [canal company] could only watch helplessly while its water right was lost." Id. at 922.

5. **Other private organizations.** Although the incorporated mutual company is the major form of private water distribution organization, other forms exist. Ditches shared by several people under more informal arrangements are called variously joint, common, and partnership ditches. The relationships between these persons, their interests in the water, and their responsibilities for maintenance costs generally are governed by the law of property, contract, or partnership. E.g., Moss v. Rose, 41 P. 666 (Or. 1895). In some states, however, these matters are elaborately regulated by statute. E.g., Wyo. Stat. §§ 41–3–604, 41–5–102, 41–5–103, 41–6–301 to –308.

Another private organization is the commercial, or for-profit, company that contracts to distribute water to users for a fee. The company might sell water it owns to customers, Willis v. Neches Canal Co., 16 S.W.2d 266 (Tex. Comm'n App. 1929). Alternatively, it might be regarded as providing the service of carrying water to persons who own the water right, Denver v. Brown, 138 P. 44 (Colo. 1914). The carrier-ditch concept reached its high point in Slosser v. Salt River Valley Canal Co., 65 P. 332 (Ariz. 1901). The Arizona court analogized the delivery ditch to a public road. The facts of the case bring out the validity of this comparison: Slosser first drew his water from the Chivari Ditch; when that ditch was washed out by a flood, he switched to the Farmers' Ditch; and when the great Salt River Valley Canal was built above the small ditches, encircling and capable of serving all the land, he drew his water from it, paying an annual charge to the company that built it. Clearly, he was the owner of his own water right, and the canals carried his water, much as a railroad might carry his goods.

Private commercial companies are rare today. Many of the early ones made contracts for permanent service at fixed rates, and rising costs forced most of them into bankruptcy and reorganization as mutual corporations or irrigation districts. A number still exist, however, in Colorado and Texas. For some of the Texas problems, see R. Richard Roberts, Problems Connected with the Distribution of Irrigation Water in Texas, Proceedings, Water Law Conferences 79 (Univ. of Tex. 1952, 1954).

6. **Acequias.** Acequias, or community ditches, are a unique feature of New Mexico and Colorado law. Acequias derived from a mixture of Indian customs and Moorish-Spanish institutions brought by the first colonists, though early Mormon settlers added some features of the mutual ditch company. Acequias are found in the Upper Rio Grande watershed. Typically, land ownership in acequia communities is organized around gravity fed earthen irrigation ditches that give each landowner arable, irrigated land. The ditches and the water flowing through them are supervised by elected mayordomos (ditch bosses) and comisionados (commissioners.) See, e.g., Wilson v. Denver, 961 P.2d 153 (N.M. 1998) (describing election principles under New Mexico law.) Water users contribute labor. In times of shortage, water will be shared under a variety of arrangements.

A tension exists between the preservation of traditional practices and their viability under contemporary water law. These tensions are explored in Gregory A. Hicks & Devon G. Peña, Community Acequias in Colorado's Rio Culebra Watershed: A Customary Commons in the Domain of Prior Appropriation, 74 U. Colo. L. Rev. 387 (2003). As described by Professors Hicks and Peña, contemporary acequia members are "acutely aware" of their relative priorities to water under Colorado water law. Indeed, they insist on recognition of these priorities. At the same time, they are also aware of the tradition and necessity of sharing if their communities are to survive in a land where short-term scarcity often occurs.

Accommodation of these principles—priority and necessity—can lead to creative arrangements. For example, Hicks and Peña describe one instance where during a period of scarcity, a junior rights holder, with an inadequate priority for an insufficient water supply, agreed to pay to farm a portion of a senior rights holder's land. The arrangement recognized the senior's priority but also allowed the junior to plant a crop. The senior received less money from the junior than the senior would have earned from planting his land himself, but both farmers made something.

For recent discussions of New Mexican acequia organization, see Christopher J. DeLara, Note, Who Controls New Mexico's Acequias? Acequia Government and Wilson v. Denver, 40 Nat. Resources J. 727 (2000); Jose A. Rivera, Irrigation Communities of the Upper Rio Grande Bioregion: Sustainable Resource Use in the Global Context, 36 Nat. Resources J. 731, 736 (1996). Cf. Robert E. Clark, New Mexico Water Resources Law 47-52 (1964).

BADGER v. BROOKLYN CANAL CO.

Supreme Court of Utah, 1996.
922 P.2d 745.

STEWART, ASSOCIATE CHIEF JUSTICE. * * * The dispute at issue arises out of a decision by the Brooklyn Canal Company to change its method of agricultural irrigation from a "flood" method to a high-pressure sprinkler method. Brooklyn is a nonprofit mutual water corporation formed for the purpose of distributing water to its shareholders in Sevier County. Brooklyn has traditionally distributed its water by means of the Brooklyn Canal to individual shareholders who have employed ditches and furrows to water their crops. The canal draws most of Brooklyn's water right directly from the Sevier River, but a small portion has also been drawn from several artesian wells. In early 1992, it was proposed that the irrigation method be changed.[2] At a shareholders' meeting held on February 18, 1992, the plan to switch to a pressurized sprinkler method was approved, with 72% of the shareholders present voting in favor of it.

Switching to a pressurized sprinkler system apparently necessitated transferring water to an underground pipe linked to a diversion point several miles upstream from the diversion point that supplies the Brooklyn Canal. The State Engineer must approve any adjustment in a point of diversion of a water right. Consequently, Brooklyn filed a change application for approval of the proposed upstream diversion point. In that change application, Brooklyn proposed to divert its entire water right of 31.27 cubic feet per second from the Sevier River at the new upstream diversion point. Brooklyn has conceded that this change would require abandonment of the artesian wells.

[Dissident Brooklyn shareholders filed protests with the State Engineer asserting impairment of their vested rights.] After receiving evidence submitted by Brooklyn and the various protestants, the State Engineer issued a memorandum decision approving the change in Brooklyn's diversion point. In that decision, the State Engineer referred to two concerns expressed by some of the protestants. First, they were concerned about the cost of constructing the new distribution system and purchasing the high pressure sprinkler equipment required under the new method, and second, they were concerned that they would be deprived of artesian sources of warm water for stock watering during the winter months. The State Engineer considered these arguments and ruled that "[Brooklyn] has a valid right with which to make this change and that if the change is approved with conditions, downstream rights will not be impaired." The State Engineer did not directly address the protestants' concerns with respect to winter stock watering except to opine "that the applicant has the responsibility to deliver water to its stockholders."

---

2. Brooklyn claims that a central reason for switching to a sprinkler irrigation system is that it is more efficient than traditional flood irrigation. * * *

A number of the protestants then filed for de novo review before the district court * * *. Relying solely on the pleadings, Brooklyn moved for summary judgment, asserting that plaintiffs had no standing as shareholders to contest Brooklyn's corporate decisions.[5] [After a hearing, the trial court] granted Brooklyn's summary judgment motion, subsequently issuing a written order * * * stating * * * the shareholder plaintiffs did not have "standing" to protest Brooklyn's change application * * *. Plaintiffs now appeal the grant of summary judgment * * *.

With respect to their claims of vested rights, the shareholder plaintiffs assert that they possess "vested real property rights which are represented by their individual shares of water stock." They thus claim to hold an independent water right apart from their status as mere shareholders in a mutual water corporation. * * *

Our holding in East Jordan Irrigation Co. v. Morgan, 860 P.2d 310, 316 (Utah 1993), * * * directly addressed the issue of a shareholder's rights to act in derogation of a water corporation's policy. *East Jordan* held that a shareholder did not have the right to file a change application without corporate consent. We quoted with approval a California case which summarized the difficulties inherent in treating shareholder rights as independent water rights:

> "[I]t would seem to be too clear for argument that neither one nor any number of such stockholders would or could possess the legal right to take or receive the amount of water to which [they] may be entitled by another manner or means than those supplied by the corporation itself." To recognize such a right "would necessarily be to admit the possession of similar rights in each and every stockholder in each of said corporations to go and do likewise, and it is too plain for argument that such an admission would result in a state of inextricable discord and confusion among the owners of water rights of various sorts. . . . The creation or threatened danger of such a consequence would of itself supply a sufficient reason for the use of the injunctive processes of the court in the way of its prevention."

Id. at 315 (citations omitted) (quoting Consolidated Peoples Ditch Co. v. Foothill Ditch Co., 205 Cal. 54, 269 P. 915, 920-21 (1928)).

Given these prudential concerns, there is no reason for drawing a distinction, as the shareholder plaintiffs request us to do, between the right to file a change application and the right to contest one. Permitting either would lead to the same "state of inextricable discord and confusion" and would nullify the ability of mutual water or irrigation corporations to act as a cohesive unit for the benefit of their shareholders.

* * * [T]he legal relationship of a water company and its shareholders necessarily implicates both benefits and burdens. Where individual holders

---

5. The parties to this litigation have generally characterized this issue as a question of whether plaintiffs have "standing" before the State engineer or the district court. More accurately, however, the question addresses the authority or jurisdiction of the office of the State Engineer to consider and resolve the claims presented to it.

of water rights might meet insuperable obstacles in attempting to maintain their own diversion points and canal or pipe systems for distribution, the pooling of resources under a contractual corporate system permits many individuals to benefit from the resources available through unified action.

Unified action also necessarily entails a certain sacrifice of the autonomy an individual shareholder could retain by refusing to take on the burdens and obligations accompanying the benefits of participating in a corporate body. Where, for instance, the governance of a mutual water corporation dictates that a majority vote of the shareholders will control the obligations of all, individuals who do not agree with the majority will always suffer a certain detriment simply by virtue of their position in the minority. That is the nature of the legal relationship undertaken. Were we to adopt the reasoning proposed by plaintiffs, shareholders could evade their obligations, which would result in an unacceptable interference with the constitution and maintenance of mutual water corporations.

Perhaps even more critical, adoption of the shareholder plaintiffs' argument would impermissibly expand the authority of the State Engineer. Assuming Brooklyn has violated any enforceable obligations it owes to its shareholders with respect to manner, mode, or quantity of delivery, then those shareholders possess a cause of action in a court of competent jurisdiction. Apparently, the plaintiffs in this case have already filed such an action. See Badger v. Madsen, 896 P.2d 20, 21-22 (Utah Ct. App. 1995). Although the State Engineer would not necessarily be required to adjudicate the specific obligations of the corporation vis-à-vis its shareholders, the Engineer's treatment of the shareholders' rights in any context would necessarily interfere with the authority of the court that was required to adjudicate those obligations. For example, assume hypothetical plaintiffs take their case before a district court and that court determines that the corporation has not violated its obligations. If the State Engineer simultaneously or subsequently determines that plaintiffs have suffered an impairment of their rights, then the effect of the district court's ruling could be called into question. We cannot require the State Engineer's office to assume a role which thus undermines the jurisdiction of the courts.

These prudential policy concerns also accord with the intent and the language of the statute at issue. The context of the entire statute makes it clear that the State Engineer does not have the authority to adjudicate all the issues that may arise in the context of a change application. A change application is required for a change in place of diversion, place of use, or purpose of use, but no such change may be made "if it impairs any vested right without just compensation." Utah Code Ann. § 73-3-3(2). The Code further provides, "The state engineer shall follow the same procedures, and the rights and duties of the applicants with respect to applications for permanent changes of point of diversion, place, or purpose of use shall be the same, as provided in this title for applications to appropriate water." Id. § 73–3-3(5)(a). With respect to change applications, the jurisdiction of the State Engineer's office is thus circumscribed by the criteria upon which the statute permits it to base its decisions. Those criteria are largely set forth in § 73-3-8(1), which states in relevant part: "It shall be the duty of the state engineer to approve an application if: * * * (b) the proposed use will not impair existing rights or interfere with the more beneficial use of the water * * *." In this respect, the shareholder plaintiffs essentially argue that they possess individual rights which are protected as "existing rights" by § 73-3-8(1).

Clearly, the shareholder plaintiffs' rights are necessarily intertwined with the rights of the corporation of which they are shareholders and to which they have contractually delegated the authority to act on their behalf. The right and ability of the majority of shareholders to manage their own rights in a collective manner is dependent upon the ability of the corporation to function as a unified organization. If we were to accept the interpretation proposed by the shareholder plaintiffs, minority shareholder "existing rights" would be elevated above the "existing rights" of majority shareholders. We do not believe that the legislature intended such an anomalous result. We therefore hold that in the context of mutual water or irrigation corporations, "existing rights," as that term is employed by § 73–3–8, refers to the right held by the corporation representing its shareholders as a body. Therefore, the statutory authority of the State Engineer does not extend to the resolution of disputes between shareholders and their corporations regarding the distribution of their shares. It follows that because the statutory authority of the State Engineer does not include jurisdiction over cases more properly presented in other forums, the district court correctly refused to address plaintiffs' shareholder rights on de novo review. * * *

Notes

1. **Ownership.** Whether the water distribution organization or the consumer "owns" the water right often presents perplexing problems of semantics. Doctrines of ownership in the consumer seem to have arisen from the necessity of protecting the water user by giving the user a permanent right to the water, instead of leaving the user to the mercy of the distributor.

Whether the private water distribution entity is organized as a mutual company, a commercial company, or a community ditch, three types of cases can be identified: (1) the water users might squabble among themselves, (2) a water user might be at odds with the distribution organization, and (3) the organization might dispute with other appropriators outside the organization over priorities and shares of the stream. In results, a surprisingly uniform pattern has arisen.

Between water users, one user is protected against any attempt by another to increase the latter's share at the expense of the former. Between a water user and the distributor, the most frequent problem arises when the company tries to stop delivering water to the user. Courts throughout the West have been quick to find some sort of enforceable right in the user to have the service continued, since the user's livelihood is at stake. In disputes involving the outside world in the shape of other appropriators from the stream, the usual solution is to leave the defense of the water right to the diverter-distributor as the representative of all its consumers.

As noted earlier, irrigators supplied by a mutual company might have had individual pre-existing rights that they retained when the company was organized, which of course protects them from other users seeking to take more than their share from the ditch. When there were no individual pre-existing rights or they did not survive formation of the mutual company, the company usually distributes water in proportion to shareholdings; and shareholder rights under corporation laws or corporate bylaws prevent one consumer from encroaching on the other. When the interests of consumers of water carried by one mutual company conflict with the interests of consumers under another ditch, the company is regarded as the representative of its consumers; and a decree defining the company's appropriation is binding not only on it but on the consumers of water under its ditch. Combs v. Farmers Highline Canal & Reservoir Co., 88 P. 396 (Colo. 1907). For external purposes, then, the distributing company is the "owner."

Commercial water companies, which seek to make a profit, might naturally be expected to come in conflict with their customers. Denver v. Brown, 138 P. 44 (Colo. 1914), held that farmers supplied with water by a commercial company were appropriators permanently entitled to water supply, but since that seemed to run counter to *Combs*, the court later described *Brown* as establishing that the company was "*in effect* * * * the proprietor of the appropriation" (emphasis added). People ex rel. City & County of Denver v. District Court, 168 P. 260 (1917). Here, too, between the company and its consumers, the consumers have property rights that the court will protect against arbitrary action by the company; but in external relations between the project and outside interests, the distributing entity is the "owner."

In carrier-ditch and community-acequia cases, the rule that the consumer owns the water right applies. Slosser v. Salt River Valley Canal Co., 65 P. 332 (Ariz. 1901); Snow v. Abalos, 140 P. 1044 (N.M. 1914). In *Slosser*, the rule protected a consumer against the distributor. In *Snow*, it protected a consumer against outside appropriators.

Other solutions to the problem of protecting the irrigator have been found without declaring the irrigator to be the owner of the appropriation. In some states, constitutional and statutory rights perform this function instead of property rights. Idaho avoided the "ownership" bog in Hard v. Boise City Irrigation & Land Co., 76 P. 331 (Idaho 1904), by citing Idaho Constitution Art. 15, § 4, which makes a sale, rental, or distribution of water for agricultural purposes an exclusive dedication to such use and gives the irrigator protection against being deprived of the annual use of water as long as the irrigator pays for it and complies with terms prescribed by law. A Texas court held that the distributor, rather than its customers, owns the appropriation, Willis v. Neches Canal Co., 16 S.W.2d 266, 269 (Tex. Comm'n App. 1929); but a Texas statute recognizes the concept of a permanent customer right that can be exercised according to the terms of the delivery contract or, if there is no contract, at a reasonable and nondiscriminatory price. Tex. Water Code Ann. § 11.040.

In several states, ownership of the right to water stored in a reservoir is vested in the landowner by a device known as a "secondary permit." The organization receives a "primary permit" to construct the dam and store the water. The consumer applies for a "secondary permit" to apply the stored water to beneficial use upon the land, and the water right is eventually adjudicated to the consumer. Ariz. Rev. Stat. Ann. § 45–161; Nev. Rev. Stat. § 533.440; Or. Rev. Stat. § 537.400; Wash. Rev. Code Ann. § 90.03.370; Wyo. Stat. §§ 41–3–301, –302.

The role of ownership in the context of water distribution organizations is discussed in Barton H. Thompson, Jr., The Relevance of "Ownership" to Water Markets and Other Issues, in WATER ORGANIZATIONS IN A CHANGING WEST (Nat. Resources L. Center, U. Colo. School of Law, 14th Annual Summer Program, June 14-16, 1993).

2. **Relation of stock and land.** When stock is issued based on the number of acres a stockholder irrigates, it usually is made appurtenant to the land. The stock certificate for appurtenant stock will specifically describe the land. Appurtenant stock may be made inseverably appurtenant by a provision in the corporate articles or bylaws. Riverside Land Co. v. Jarvis, 163 P. 54 (Cal. 1917) (reasonable restrictions on stock transfer are valid, and a provision for inseverable appurtenance is reasonable). Alternatively, stock may be made severable from the land despite its appurtenancy, so that while it would pass with a conveyance of the land if not mentioned, it can be retained upon a sale of the land.

3. **Stock transfers.** Mutual company stock that is not appurtenant or is appurtenant but severable can be sold separately from land. Such sales can be a means of transferring water from land to land. Mutual company stockholders have a common law right, absent any governing statute, to inspect the company's books and records in an effort to locate parties possibly interested in buying or renting their shares. Left Hand Ditch Co. v. Hill, 933 P.2d 1 (Colo. 1997) (en banc).

The corporate articles or bylaws of some mutual companies restrict stock transfers. That was the case in In re Water Rights of Fort Lyon Canal Co., 762 P.2d 1375 (Colo. 1988) (en banc). A bylaw stated that the place where water is delivered to a stockholder could be changed only if, *in the opinion of the company's board of directors*, the change would not injure the company, its canal, or its other stockholders. The court held this restriction was valid, though it imposed a requirement beyond those found in state statutes governing transfer, but limited the board's discretion to find injury. The court said that a finding of injury by the board would be subject to judicial review of whether the board acted arbitrarily or capriciously or abused its discretion.

Uniform Commercial Code (U.C.C.) § 8–204 provides that a corporate restriction on the transfer of a certificated security is ineffective against a purchaser of the security without knowledge of the restriction unless it is noted on the security certificate. The term "certificated security" includes instruments, whether in bearer or registered form, that are "commonly recognized * * * as a medium for investment." U.C.C. § 8–102(1)(a). In Salt Lake City v. Cahoon & Maxfield Irrigation Co., 879 P.2d 248 (Utah 1994), two cities bought outstanding shares of a mutual company whose articles of incorporation stated that "[n]o transfer of stock shall be permitted without the approval, in advance, by the vote of a majority of the members of the Board of Directors." This restriction was not noted on the stock certificates, and the cities were not otherwise aware of it. Not surprisingly, the cities did not seek advance approval from the board. The irrigation company refused for that reason to register the stock transfer and issue new shares to the cities. The court denied the cities the protection of U.C.C. § 8–204. It held that mutual water company stock is not a certificated security because the stock is not a medium for investment, but rather represents an interest in real property. The Utah Legislature responded to this decision by providing that U.C.C. article 8, including of course § 8–204, shall apply to mutual water company stock. Utah Code Ann. §§ 70A–8–409, 73–1–10.

4. **Statutes regulating water transfers.** Mutual company stock transfers that involve the transfer of water from land to land might be limited not only by the corporate articles and bylaws but by state statutes on water right transfers. In *East Jordan*, discussed in the principal case, a city purchased mutual company shares that were not restricted as to transfer by the company's articles or bylaws. The city then applied to the state engineer for permission to change the point of diversion to a city-owned well, from which it wanted to take water for year-round municipal use. Utah Code Ann. § 73–3–3(2) allows a "person entitled to the use of water" to change the point of diversion, place of use, or purpose of use if the vested rights of others will not be impaired. The court ruled that the city was not a person entitled to the use of water within the meaning of the statute. Only the mutual company was eligible to file the transfer application, though the court did indicate that judicial relief would be available to the city should the mutual company unreasonably refuse to apply for a transfer.

5. **Other limits on transfer.** Are there any limits on transfer apart from those found in a corporation's articles and bylaws and in state water transfer statutes? In *Consolidated People's Ditch Co.*, the California decision quoted in the principal case, a purchaser of outstanding mutual company shares was enjoined from changing the point of diversion upstream from the company's ditch. The shares were nonappurtenant, and the court did not mention any statute or any corporate article or bylaw preventing the change. But to avoid what it called inextricable discord and confusion, the court ruled that a stockholder has a right to a proportionate share of the available water supplied *through company facilities*, not a right to receive that amount of water through some other means. In contrast, the Colorado court allowed a mutual company stockholder to transfer water to lands beyond the service area of the company's ditch and transport it through another ditch, so long as he continued to bear his proportionate share of the cost of maintaining the company's ditch. Wadsworth Ditch Co. v. Brown, 88 P. 1060 (Colo. 1907).

YUCAIPA WATER CO. NO. 1 v. PUBLIC UTILITIES COMMISSION

Supreme Court of California, 1960.
54 Cal.2d 823, 357 P.2d 295.

TRAYNOR, JUSTICE. In this proceeding Yucaipa Water Company No. 1 attacks an order of the Public Utilities Commission determining that it is a public utility water corporation subject to the jurisdiction of the commission and directing it to file a financial report and cease and desist from increasing its rates to the Yucaipa Domestic Water Company pending further commission action.

No. 1 is organized as a nonpublic utility mutual water company and has not heretofore been regulated by the commission. Domestic is a regulated public utility water corporation. It secures all of its water from No. 1 and owns approximately 5 percent of No. 1's stock. In 1959 a dispute arose between the two companies over a substantial increase in the rate No. 1 proposed to charge Domestic and extensions of service by Domestic into areas served by No. 1. * * * The parties stipulated that the commission should first determine whether or not No. 1 is a public utility subject to its jurisdiction, and its determination of that issue is the only question before us for review. The commission found that No. 1 is a public utility that has dedicated its property to public use and that it is not exempt from regulation under section 2705 of the Public Utilities Code. No. 1 attacks both of these findings.

No. 1 operates in an area of about 3,500 acres including Yucaipa township. It was organized in 1910 and initially supplied water primarily for irrigation purposes. At the present time, however, about 74 percent of its sales are to domestic users. It also provides service to the Yucaipa Domestic Water Company, poultry farms, trailer parks, scheduled water users, and special users at specified rates. Special users include hospitals, schools, churches, parks, and other large users. With the exception of one domestic user, it supplies water only to its shareholders and lessees of shares from its shareholders. Its shares are freely transferable and are not appurtenant to the land, and users may obtain water in addition to the per-share entitlement by paying special rates. In 1959 No. 1 had about 2,000 domestic users and supplied water to over 100 lessees of shares. It maintained a list of shareholders who were willing to lease shares and referred nonshareholder applicants for service to them. It billed lessees of shares directly, but held the shareholder liable for any unpaid bill. In each of the years 1956, 1957, and 1958 it added 80 to 100 new domestic users to its system, and to increase the number of permissible service connections, it split its stock to permit a connection for each half share instead of each share.

No. 1 contends that since it is organized as a nonpublic utility mutual water corporation that supplies water only to its shareholders, lessees of shares from its shareholders, and one other person, it has not held itself out as willing to supply water to the public or any portion thereof and that it has not therefore dedicated its property to public use. No. 1's organization as a mutual and its formal limitations on its services do not preclude a finding of dedication, however, if it has held itself out as willing to supply water to the public or any portion thereof. * * *

The evidence supports the commission's finding of dedication in this case. It is true that No. 1 did not expressly offer service to everyone in its service area on condition that prospective consumers purchase shares of stock from it. Had it done so, its holding itself out to serve the public would be patent, and the attaching of a condition that any member of the public could meet would not affect its offer. Dedication may also be shown by implication, however, and in the present case, it may clearly be inferred. Thus, No. 1 steadily increased the number of its service connections; it split its shares to double the permissible number of such connections; it supplied water to a substantial number of lessees of shares; and it expedited the leasing of shares to those who wished water service. There is no evidence that anyone in its service area who wished water service could not obtain it by purchasing or leasing half a share or more. Under these circumstances, the commission could reasonably infer that No. 1 supplied its shareholders and lessees of its shares not merely for the reason "peculiar and particular to them" that they were such, but primarily for the reason that they were members of the public in No. 1's service area who accepted its offer of service by becoming shareholders or lessees of shares.

No. 1 contends that even if it has dedicated its property to public use, it is exempted from public utility regulation by section 2705 of the Public Utilities Code. That section provides:

> "Any corporation or association which is organized for the purpose solely of delivering water to its stockholders or members at cost, and which delivers water to no one except its stockholders or members, or to the State or any agency or department thereof, or to any school district, or to any other mutual water company, at cost, is not a public utility, and is not subject to the jurisdiction, control or regulation of the commission."
> * * *

The exemption created by section 2705 indicates a legislative determination that when a mutual water corporation is substantially customer-controlled and delivers water at cost, the usual judicial contract remedies available to those who deal with it are an adequate substitute for public utility regulation. That determination applies when the customers include a public utility as much as when they do not. * * *

The commission contends, however, that a utility is at the mercy of a mutual when, as in this case, the mutual is the utility's sole source of supply and that commission regulation of the mutual is therefore essential. The utility is no more at the mercy of the mutual than any individual customer who has no other source of water, and as to individual customers, the Legislature has clearly determined that public utility regulation is not essential. Moreover, neither an individual shareholder nor a utility shareholder is at the mercy of a mutual because the mutual is the only source of water. They not only have a voice in the management of the mutual, but they may invoke the jurisdiction of the commission if the mutual has stepped outside of the exemption provided by section 2705, and they may enforce their water rights in court if it has not. * * *

In the present case, however, the evidence supports the commission's finding that No. 1 delivered water to others than stockholders; it delivered water to over 100 lessees of shares of stock and one other person. Even if it is assumed that the latter delivery was *de minimis,* the deliveries to lessees were not. Lessees of shares are not stockholders, and to interpret the word "stockholders" in section 2705 to mean "stockholders or lessees of stock" would not only require reading into the statute words that are not there but violate the basic principle of customer control on which the exemption is based. * * * No. 1 was not obligated to deliver water to lessees of shares, for it could have insisted, in accord with its declared corporate purpose, on delivering water only to shareholders. Instead, however, it actively expedited the leasing of shares to those who wished water service, and such activity coupled with its other activities set forth above clearly supported the commission's finding that it had dedicated its property to public use. * * *

The order is affirmed.

Notes

1. **Public utility status.** A companion case, Corona City Water Co. v. Public Utilities Commission, 357 P.2d 301 (Cal. 1960), dealt with whether the Temescal Water Company was subject to regulation as a public utility. Temescal was organized as a nonpublic mutual water company. Nineteen percent of its shares were owned by Corona, a public utility that received its entire water supply from Temescal as a shareholder of Temescal. Temescal completely dominated Corona through majority ownership of Corona's stock and interlocking boards of directors and officers. The water delivery operations of the two companies were closely integrated, with each company sometimes using the other's facilities. Held: Temescal dedicated its property to public use by virtue of its close collaboration with an admitted public utility. Moreover, the exemption of section 2705 did not apply because Corona was a "captive" stockholder with no voice in the management of the mutual company and in no position to enforce its rights as a stockholder: "[T]he intercorporate relationship is fraught with hazards to Corona and its customers. Thus, the largely agricultural independent stockholders of Temescal are in a position to subsidize their water service at the expense of Corona and to prevent Corona's objecting by their control of it." Id. at 304.

In the following session of the legislature, section 2705 was amended to permit a mutual company to keep its nonpublic status though it delivers water at cost to a lessee of its stock, or to land leased by a stockholder to another, or in an emergency to nonstockholders within or adjacent to its service area, or pursuant to a pre-existing contract in settlement of litigation involving disputed water rights or in consideration of the conveyance of a well or water right.

2. **Regulation of public utilities.** Public utility status subjects many of a company's financial and operational matters to public regulation. In many states, a water utility must procure a certificate of convenience and necessity, i.e. a license, to enter the business. E.g., Cal. Pub. Util. Code § 1001. It can be compelled to render service to consumers within its service area, Olsen v. Union Canal & Irrigation Co., 119 P.2d 569 (Ariz. 1941), within the limits of its water supply, Butte County Water Users' Ass'n v. Railroad Commission, 196 P. 265 (Cal. 1921). It cannot discriminate between its customers by giving preferred services or rates to some. Id; Live Oak Water Users' Ass'n v. Railroad Commission, 219 P. 65 (Cal. 1923). Its transactions with other companies and its acquisitions or dispositions of property are subject to scrutiny by the regulatory commission for conformity with the public interest. Corona City Water Co. v. P.U.C., supra Note 1. It cannot discontinue its services, even by going out of business, without the permission of the commission. Van Hoosear v. Railroad Comm'n, 194 P. 1003 (Cal. 1920).

Most important, the rates a utility charges for services are regulated. Rates are fixed to cover operating expenses, including depreciation on company properties, and a fair return on the value of the properties devoted to public use. Where the company merely is a carrier of water belonging to the consumers, it cannot include a value for the water rights in its rate base; but in figuring a fair return on the base, the priority of the water rights may be considered since this affects the value of the securities of the utility as investments. Board of Comm'rs v. Rocky Mountain Water Co., 79 P.2d 373 (Colo. 1938); 103 P.2d 686 (Colo.

1940). In California, no holder of a permit or license to appropriate may assign or claim any value in excess of the actual amount paid to the state for the water right in proceedings for the regulation of the price of the services. Cal. Water Code §§ 1392, 1629.

In most states, rates are fixed by a state public utility commission. In Colorado, though, county commissioners can establish reasonable maximum rates to be charged for the use of water, whether furnished by individuals or corporations. See Farmers Water Dev. Co. v. Barrett, 376 P.2d 693 (Colo. 1962). In Texas, rate-setting power is given to the Texas Natural Resource Conservation Commission. Tex. Water Code Ann. §§ 11.002(1), 12.013(a).

3. **Municipal water supply.** A water company supplying a municipality is not necessarily a public utility, unless declared so by statute. Junction Water Co. v. Riddle, 155 A. 887 (N.J. Ch. 1931). Most such companies are declared so in the statutes establishing public service commissions.

A water company's contract with a city may give the city power to require service and to this extent supersede the powers of the state public utility commission. Portsmouth, Berkley & Suffolk Water Co. v. Portsmouth, 70 S.E. 529 (Va. 1911). A city's charter may empower it to impose regulations in lieu of the public service commission. New York v. New York Water Serv. Corp., 8 N.E.2d 294 (N.Y. 1937).

Residents of a city who consume water that is diverted, stored, and distributed by a public utility company do not own appropriations of water or water rights of any kind. Instead they have rights to service arising under public utility law.

SECTION 2. PUBLIC AGENCIES

SULLIVAN v. BLAKESLEY

Supreme Court of Wyoming, 1926.
35 Wyo. 73, 246 P. 918.

Plaintiff, E.J. Sullivan, brings this action, on behalf of himself and others similarly situated, against Lou Blakesley, county treasurer of Big Horn county, and the commissioners of the Greybull Valley irrigation district. The petition alleges the due organization of said irrigation district under the laws of this state; that an assessment against the lands in said district was made in 1925 to meet the expenses of the district for the current year; that plaintiff is the owner of lands affected by such assessment, and that the county treasurer of said county threatens to sell such land for the nonpayment of such assessment; that the commissioners of said irrigation district threaten to issue and sell the bonds of said district, said bonds to be paid by assessments levied against the property of plaintiff and others similarly situated; that the irrigation district law of this state is unconstitutional for various specified reasons, and plaintiff accordingly seeks an injunction against the collection of said tax and the issuance of the bonds aforesaid. The case comes to this court upon reserved constitutional questions, and we are asked to answer whether or not the irrigation district law of this state is in conflict with * * * the Constitution of this state. * * *

The irrigation district law [was] passed by the Legislature of this state in 1920. * * * For the purposes of this case, it will be sufficient to state the following provisions of the law: A certain number of owners or holders of land in the district may sign and present to the district court a petition, stating therein the name of the proposed district, the necessity of the proposed work, the object and purpose thereof, a general description of the lands proposed to be included in the district, the names of the freeholders owning lands therein, and a prayer for the organization of the district. A preliminary engineering report of the feasibility of the project must accompany the petition. The court or the judge thereof must cause notice to be given of the presentation of the petition, fixing the date for the hearing thereon. Upon the hearing, the district court may approve and confirm the petition, define the boundaries of the district, and establish it as a corporation by the name proposed with powers to sue and be sued, adopt a corporate seal, have perpetual succession, exercise the power of the eminent domain and generally carry out the purposes of the organization. Commissioners are appointed by the court, who are required to organize, who constitute the corporate authority of the district, who are declared to be public officers, and for whom successors are provided by election. Other lands may subsequently be included in the district, and lands originally embraced therein may be excluded therefrom. Immediately after the organization of the district, the commissioners thereof are required to cause surveys, a map, plans, and specifications to be made of the proposed work, and determine, as near as may be, the cost of said work. They must assess against the lands embraced within the district the total amounts of benefits, such benefits to constitute the basis of all assessments; apportion and assess the cost of construction with certain exceptions which need not be noted here, against the several benefited tracts in the irrigation district, in proportion to the benefits which have been assessed against the same, and apportion the water right, expected to be acquired by the proposed work, to each tract of land assessed. A report of such action must be made to the court. Notice of the hearing thereon must be given to all parties interested. Upon such hearing, the court may confirm the report of the commissioners and the assessments made as aforesaid, which assessments may be made payable in installments, as fixed by the court. Additional assessments may be made subsequently, to be confirmed by the court upon due notice given to the interested parties. The assessments become a lien upon the various tracts assessed, and may be enforced in the same manner as a judgment, or may be assessed and collected as taxes. The commissioners may borrow money and issue the bonds of the district therefor and such bonds are declared to be a lien upon the assessments for the repayment of the principal and interest thereof. More specific provisions as to some of these matters will be set forth in the opinion.

BLUME, J. (after stating the facts as above). 1. An irrigation district, reclaiming as it does, desert lands in the state, and accordingly, conferring a benefit, not alone upon the private individuals within the district, but also upon the people of the state as a whole, is a public rather than a private, corporation. * * * Such districts have at times been designated as municipal corporations, and they might be such within the meaning of laws or constitutional provisions not now under consideration, but it is clear that they are not municipal corporations as generally understood. They are merely special state organizations for state purposes with limited powers, created to perform certain work which the policy of the state requires or permits to be done, and to which the state has given a certain degree of discretion in reclaiming desert lands. * * *

There is no special constitutional limitation that we know of limiting the mode or method of the establishment of such districts provided that it is done under a general law. It may be left to a board or commission, or the court. The Legislature has seen fit to cause such districts to be created upon petition of a certain number of people owning or holding lands therein, and upon a hearing, after due notice, upon such petition by the district court. The method of thus establishing the districts is, we think, constitutional.

* * * The exactions authorized to be made by such districts may, in a broad sense, be termed taxes, but they are distinguishable therefrom, for they are levied for local benefits to be spread on the property in the districts in proportion to the peculiar advantages accruing to each parcel therein from the improvement made. Whether in the form of special assessments or in the form of taxes, they are essentially assessments for local benefits, and not levied for general governmental purposes. * * *

2. We come, then, to the consideration as to whether or not the legislation in question is in violation of section 13, art. 15, of the Constitution, which provides that no tax shall be levied except in pursuance of law, and that each law imposing a tax shall state distinctly the object of the same, to which only it shall be applied. * * * The argument is far afield. * * * We might accordingly very well pass this subject without anything further; but inasmuch as we are also asked whether the irrigation district law is in violation of section 33, article 1, that "private property shall not be taken or damaged for public or private use without just compensation," and inasmuch as a complete answer perhaps involves the subject-matter referred to by counsel, we shall discuss it somewhat at length. * * * It has been held [by several courts] that bonds issued by an irrigation district constitute a general lien obligation of the district. The contrary has been held in the case of Interstate Trust Co. v. Montezuma, 66 Colo. 219, 181 P. 123, and Nelson v. Board, 62 Utah 218, 218 P. 952. And the Supreme Court of Colorado in the case just cited holds that to consider such bonds as general lien obligations of the district would be violative of both state and federal Constitutions, presumably because of taking property without due process of law or taking property without just compensation. * * * The difference in opinion as to the character of such bonds may, to some extent at least, be accounted for by the difference in the laws of the several states, and, in order to arrive at the proper conclusion herein, it will be necessary to consider the laws of this state that bear upon the point in question. * * *

We do not think, as contended by counsel, that these provisions leave in doubt the character or extent of the lien of the various assessments. * * *

The Legislature evidently intended to make the assessments a general lien against all of the assessed property in the district, within the limitation * * * hereafter mentioned, since it has provided for the levy in each year of an amount sufficient to meet the principal and interest that may fall due during that year, to be apportioned to all the lands to which benefits are assessed, just as payments of principal and interest are met on general municipal bonds. But there is a limitation. The assessments cannot be in excess of the benefits assessed against the several parcels of land in the district. The objection accordingly urged by the Colorado Supreme Court in the case of Interstate Trust Company v. Montezuma Valley Irrigation District, supra, does not, we think, hold good under the laws of this state even if it were true that the principle there stated would apply in the absence of such limiting provisions of the statute. Made as the assessments are, because and on the theory that they equal the amount of the benefits, they do not constitute a taking of property without due process of law or without just compensation, in the case of irrigation districts any more than under a like situation in the case of municipal improvements generally, and it is well settled that in the latter case there is no violation of constitutional provisions in that regard. It was held in Re Drainage District, 24 Wyo. 143, 161, 156 P. 610, that assessments made for the purpose of constructing drains are not in violation of section 33, article 1, of our Constitution. Assessments made in drainage districts are similar in kind to assessments in irrigation districts. They are all based upon the same underlying principle. It may, possibly, happen, as suggested that the benefits assessed to all or part of the lands within the irrigation district by reason of the construction of improvements, may become exhausted before the full amount of the cost of such improvement is paid. But it is not shown that such contingency will arise, and we are not called upon to anticipate it any more than we are called upon to anticipate that the total cost of making the improvements might happen to be greater than the total amount of the benefits. We answer, accordingly, that the irrigation district law of this state is not in conflict with either of the two constitutional provisions last herein discussed. * * *

Notes

1. **Formation of a district.** All seventeen contiguous western states have laws authorizing the formation of irrigation districts, though some are called water conservation, water improvement, or reclamation districts. Historically, they all stem from California's Wright Act, Cal. Stat. 1887, ch. 34. In most states, the petition for formation of a district is presented to the board of county commissioners, rather than to a court as in the principal case, and a citizen vote on formation is held. There are variations from state to state in eligibility to vote (electors, landowners, owners of agricultural lands) and in the majorities required. In some states, approval of the state irrigation officials is required for the project or the engineering aspects of it.

2. **Bonds and liens.** An irrigation district that wants to construct facilities such as a dam and a canal system usually will need to issue bonds to fund the construction. As indicated in the principal case, the commissioners of a Wyoming irrigation district may proceed to issue bonds after formation of the district has been approved. More commonly, statutes require the submission of proposed

bond issues to the electors at a special election. Also common are statutory proceedings initiated by the governing officers of the district, in which all questions relating to the organization of the district and the proceedings of the board with respect to the issue and sale of the bonds may be judicially approved and confirmed. These proceedings are in rem and are conclusive as to the validity of the bonds but not, of course, as to subsequent negotiation or transfer of the bonds.

The principal case discusses the concept of a general lien against land in the district to provide security for the bondholders. A true general lien has been described as follows: "The district thus may impose assessments on all assessable lands in the district until a bond * * * is retired. By this means, cumulative assessments may be made against district lands to meet deficiencies arising from nonpayment of assessments by some landowners." 3 Report of the President's Water Resources Policy Comm'n, Water Resources Law 173 (1950). In contrast, a specific lien makes each parcel of land subject only to its proportionate share of the debt; recurring assessments on a parcel to make up for delinquencies by other landowners are not allowed.

3. **Assessments and water charges.** The principal case also gives the rule that assessments levied by the district against land must be apportioned among the landowners in accordance with the actual benefits received by the property. Under this rule, it is illegal to treat all land as equal and levy an equal assessment against each acre. Wheatland Irrigation Dist. v. Short, 339 P.2d 403 (Wyo. 1959). It is permissible, however, to divide land into classes according to size, topography, soil classification, etc., fix a value for each class, and apply the formula to all acres in the district. Kansas-Bostwick Irrigation Dist. No. 2 v. Mizer, 270 P.2d 261 (Kan. 1954).

Not all states require assessments to be apportioned according to benefits received. Some allow assessment to be levied on an ad valorem basis, at a standard rate against property valued at market or cash value. See Reed v. Oroville-Wyandotte Irrigation Dist., 304 P.2d 731 (Cal. Dist. Ct. App. 1956). Others allow assessment according to area, whereby an equal charge is levied against each irrigable acre.

Another source of revenue for districts is a direct charge for water delivered: "The statutes of various States authorize the obtaining of revenue through tolls or charges for use of water. These tolls or charges are fixed by the board of directors, either in addition to the levying of assessments or in lieu thereof. * * * Tolls are used by many California districts, usually in addition to assessments. They are used to a lesser extent in some of the other Western States. * * * One irrigation district in California relied entirely upon toll charges for the use of water to cover expenses for operation and maintenance and for bond service as well. As rice was the only major crop grown in the district, this method was preferred because of the large area of rice land idle each year. But the power to assess the land is available in case the toll system proves inadequate to meet the district's financial requirements." U.S. Dep't of Agric., Circular No. 934, Irrigation-Enterprise Organizations 39 (1953).

4. **Federal reclamation projects.** Many irrigation districts were organized primarily as fiscal agents for the United States Bureau of Reclamation. Reclamation projects are built with federal financing, obviating an irrigation district's issue of bonds for construction funds. Certain construction costs of

reclamation projects are "reimbursable," however, and must be repaid to the United States. The irrigation district will enter into a repayment contract with the Secretary of the Interior in which it agrees to collect assessments from water users supplied by the project to cover operation and maintenance costs and construction charges.

5. **Ownership.** Usually there is no controversy over whether an irrigation district or other public agency that distributes water "owns" the water rights as against the consumer. The relations and duties of districts to their consumers are fixed by the statutes under which they are created, and those statutes without exception clearly empower the districts to appropriate or purchase water rights. California has invented a special property right to protect the consumer, but it is not a water right. A California irrigation district or other public agency that distributes water "owns" the water rights as against the consumer, but this ownership is construed to be a trusteeship for the beneficial owners, the water users. Lindsay-Strathmore Irrigation Dist. v. Wutchumna Water Co., 296 P. 933 (Cal. Dist. Ct. App. 1931).

Recently, this ownership interest has been the subject of litigation. In California's Imperial Valley, some farmers who purchase their water from the Imperial Irrigation District have sought to block a large transfer of irrigation to San Diego under a 2002 agreement reached by the District. Under that agreement, large areas of land would be taken out of agricultural production. In 2003, 94 plaintiffs filed a "reverse validation" suit against the District to challenge the agreement. In particular, they sought a determination that the farmers have rights: 1) to transfer water within the District without the District's approval; 2) to receive a proportionate share of the District's water; and 3) to receive a proportionate share of the money received from San Diego. Morgan v. Imperial Irrig. Dist., Nos. L–01510 (Imperial County Super. Ct. filed July 18, 2003) & ECU 01646 (Imperial County Super. Ct. filed Nov. 3, 2003) (transferred to Sacramento County Coordinated Case No. JC 4353). The original complaint was dismissed in November 2003 for plaintiffs' failure to publish timely notice of the pendency of the suit. The second complaint, a class action, has continued without resolution through 2005.

The Washington statutes on water adjudications require personal service of process or publication of notice to all persons claiming the right to divert the water involved, who must then appear in the proceeding or be subject to loss of their rights. Wash. Rev. Code Ann. § 90.03.120 provides, however, that persons claiming the right to use water by virtue of a contract with a claimant of the right to divert the water shall not be necessary parties. The Yakima River adjudication covered 6062 square miles, 475,000 irrigated acres, and over 40,000 people. Most water users were served by irrigation districts, canal companies, ditch companies, and municipalities. In State, Department of Ecology v. Acquavella, 674 P.2d 160 (Wash. 1983), the court acknowledged that individual landowners receiving water from a distribution entity have a vested interest in the water right to the extent that the water is beneficially used on their lands. Nonetheless, the court held that due process did not require service on such individual water users because of the extremely large scale of the proceeding and an identity of interest between the distributor and its water users. The court suggested that its holding might not apply to a smaller adjudication and that even in the Yakima River adjudication, due process might at some point require "service of process, or some other remedy, to protect the interests of water users not adequately represented by their distributing entities."

Landowners served by an irrigation district do not have water rights appurtenant to their land independent from the district. Where individual landowners opt out of a district and vote to form their own district, they do not take with them a share of the original district's water right. Madera Irrigation Dist. v. All Persons, 306 P.2d 886 (Cal. 1957), rev'd on other grounds, Ivanhoe Irrigation Dist. v. McCracken, 357 U.S. 275 (1958).

6. **Allocation among users.** What powers do districts have to allocate their water among the water users within their service areas? The statutes of many states are silent about allocation, in which case it seems to be generally assumed that all landowners are to be treated equally. Some statutes do address allocation. Mont. Code Ann. § 85–7–1911(2) requires proportionate reduction in times of shortage. Or. Rev. Stat. § 545.221 may give districts some degree of discretion by granting them equitable powers to establish rules and regulations for the distribution and use of water. Utah Code Ann. § 17A–2–728 provides that in case of shortage, district officials should distribute the water "upon certain or alternate days to different localities as they may in their judgment think best for the interest of all parties concerned." Ariz. Rev. Stat. Ann. § 48–2991 has this same language but adds, "so that the available water is distributed in as nearly equal proportions as possible to all lands of the district subject to the laws of priorities."

California has an elaborate statutory structure on allocation. The main distributors of irrigation water there are "irrigation districts" and "California water districts." In many of these districts, annual arrangements need to be made to meet variable water requirements of irrigators. The basic statute for each of these two kinds of districts provides that the water they distribute "for irrigation purposes shall except when otherwise provided in this article be apportioned ratably to each landowner upon the basis of the ratio which the last assessment against his land for district purposes bears to the whole sum assessed to the district for district purposes." Cal. Water Code §§ 22250, 35420. Other statutes, however, authorize a district's board of directors to require irrigators to file applications, by a date the board sets, to receive water during the ensuing irrigation season (either for all crops or only for annual crops and new plantings). The board can require a cash deposit that is subject to forfeiture for water not used by the applicant if the district has water available. In case of shortage, the board may "give preference to or serve only the land for which application was filed prior to the date set and the land for which no application was required." Id. §§ 22252.1, 35450-35453.

In 1977, during an extreme drought, the California Legislature added the following provisions:

"In districts where meters or other volumetric measuring instruments or facilities are not available or are inadequate to measure substantially all agricultural water deliveries, the district may establish annual water requirements in the district for growing each type of crop grown in the district, accept such applications for water based on proposed crops to be grown and acreage of each proposed crop, and determine the quantity of water apportioned under [the above statutes] expressed in terms of acreage of each type of proposed crop to be served. In such a district, the district may refuse to deliver water to, or assess penalties on, the landowner who uses such water on a greater acreage of such crops than such landowner's share of the estimated available water will bring to maturity based on the requirements established for growing such crops in the district.

"In establishing annual water requirements for growing particular types of crops, as authorized in this section, the district, with respect to those crops which ordinarily require periodic irrigation, may designate the number of irrigation runs and the amount of water to be allocated to each run with respect to each crop, and may give the water user water credits measured by the designated irrigation runs with respect to each such crop as to which the water user has notified the district he intends to underirrigate.

"This section provides a means of measuring the allocation of water to land based on the type of crop grown and does not authorize a district to designate, the crops to be grown on such land." Id. §§ 22252.3, 35454.5.

Although sponsors of this legislation insisted that it is "a measurement statute," not an "allocation statute," it seems inescapable that the effect of the law is to establish a comprehensive allocation scheme for providing water according to crop and acreage. The practice seems to have been to give preference to needs of perennial plants (orchards, vineyards) over annual crops. Apparently if a district has accurate metering devices, this newer legislation does not apply.

Another kind of public water distribution agency in California, namely, county water districts, may have even broader powers. These districts are authorized "to restrict the use of district water during any emergency caused by drought, or other threatened or existing water shortage, and to prohibit the wastage of district water during such periods, for any purpose other than household uses or such other restricted uses as may be determined to be necessary by the district and may prohibit the use of such water during such periods for specific uses which the district may from time to time find to be nonessential." Cal. Water Code § 31026.

7. **Transfers—by districts and by district members.** Many states have statutes authorizing water districts to sell or lease surplus water for use outside the district. E.g., Colo. Rev. Stat. Ann. § 37–42–135 (can lease for up to twenty years); Mont. Code Ann. § 85–7–1911(3) (can sell or dispose of); Utah Code Ann. §§ 17A–2–711 (can lease for up to five years). California has one of the more detailed statutory schemes. Local and regional public water agencies can sell, lease, exchange or otherwise transfer for use outside the agency water that is surplus to the needs of its water users and water that its users voluntarily forego the use of during the transfer period. Cal. Water Code § 382. They are forbidden, however, to transfer water for use within the boundaries of another agency that furnishes the same water service without the consent of the latter agency. Id. § 385. And they are forbidden to make any transfer that will unreasonably affect instream beneficial uses or the overall economy of the area from which the water is transferred. Id. § 386.

A number of states also allow district members to transfer their rights to receive water if the district consents. E.g., Ariz. Rev. Stat. Ann. § 45–172A(4); Idaho Code § 42–108; Utah Code Ann. § 17A–2–711 (limited to one year at a time; new place of use must be in the district). A district's water right typically is appurtenant to all the irrigable lands within its borders, in which case a transfer by one irrigator to another within the district does not constitute a change in place of use that triggers usual statutory limits on transfer such as the no-injury rule.

E.g., Nev. Rev. Stat. Ann. § 539.230(3); State, Dep't of Ecology v. Acquavella, 935 P.2d 595 (Wash. 1997).

For further discussion of transfers by districts and by district members, see Barton H. Thompson, Jr., Institutional Perspectives on Water Policy and Markets, 81 Cal. L. Rev. 671 (1993). The article also proposes reforms to facilitate transfers for use beyond district boundaries.

IN RE RENO PRESS BRICK CO.

Supreme Court of Nevada, 1937.
58 Nev. 164, 73 P.2d 503.

TABER, JUSTICE.

Respondent corporation is the owner of 33 acres of land included within the boundaries of appellant irrigation district. Acting under the provisions of section 44 of the Irrigation District Act, as amended, respondent, on April 30, 1936, applied in writing to appellant's board of directors for the exclusion from the district of said piece of land. After considering the application, the board of directors of the irrigation district, on July 9, 1936, rejected respondent's application in whole. Thereafter, respondent petitioned the district court to set aside said order of appellant's board of directors, and to direct that said land be excluded from the district. The matter was later tried, and, in December, 1936, the district court granted respondent's application, and adjudged that said land be excluded from the irrigation district. This appeal is taken from said judgment, and from an order of said district court denying a motion for a new trial.

The portion of said section 44 of the Irrigation District Act with which we are primarily concerned, reads as follows: "The board of directors of any district now or hereafter formed under the provisions of this act, either upon its own initiative or upon the application in writing of any holder of title or of evidence of title to land in the district, may, by a majority vote, exclude from the district any land or lands theretofore included in the district, and change the boundary lines of the district so as to exclude or leave out certain tracts or portions of tracts when the proposed system or systems of irrigation cannot practically include land or lands, or when such land or lands would not be benefited by the district or by any improvement it might make." Respondent's application for exclusion of its land was and is based upon the contention that said land would not be benefited by certain improvements contemplated by the district.

The tract of land sought to be excluded from the irrigation district adjoins the city of Reno on the north. No part of it is within the city limits, but its southern boundary line is identical along its whole length with a portion of the northern boundary line of the city of Reno. The land has been irrigated for the past twenty or twenty-one years. For the first five or six years, two crops of alfalfa were grown upon it annually. After that, it was allowed to go to pasture. With an ample supply of water, it will produce good pasturage crops. * * *

During the three or four years that Parker Brick Company owned this property, it was used for the manufacture of brick, and to that extent the statement heretofore made, that this land has been irrigated for some twenty or twenty-one years, must be qualified. The buildings and machinery which had been used by Parker Brick Company in the manufacture of brick on said premises were of small value at the time the property was purchased by respondent. The premises have not been used for brick making at any time since respondent has owned them. * * *

Without water the land in controversy would be valueless for agricultural purposes. With an adequate water right it would be worth from $125 to $150 per acre for agricultural purposes. With the exception of about three and one-half acres, the land is susceptible of irrigation by gravity. * * * It is estimated that this property would be worth about $400 an acre if subdivided for residential purposes. * * *

There is no substantial conflict in the testimony in this case. The question we have to determine is the interpretation to be put on the word "benefited" as applied to the undisputed facts disclosed by the testimony. Upon respondent rests the burden of proving by a fair preponderance of evidence that the Truckee river upstream storage project will not benefit its 33-acre tract of land.

Appellant contends that this court should follow the decisions of courts of other states in holding that the benefit to the land, as contemplated by said amended section 44 of the Irrigation District Act, may be indirect as well as direct. * * * Respondent takes the position that, in Nevada, land within an irrigation district should be excluded therefrom on application of the owner when such land will not be directly benefited by the district or by any improvement it might make. * * *

We find it unnecessary to decide whether, in Nevada, an indirect benefit to land, within the meaning of amended section 44 of the Irrigation District Act, may be sufficient to justify a refusal to exclude such land from an irrigation district, because the uncontradicted evidence satisfies us that respondent has not met the burden imposed upon it by the statute to show that its said land will not be directly benefited by the Truckee river upstream storage project. We shall proceed to set forth some of the reasons which have influenced us in reaching this conclusion.

The land is not now being used for the manufacture of clay products, and will probably not be so used for at least ten or twelve years, because the supply of superior clay where respondent company is now manufacturing its products will, it is estimated, last that long, and respondent has other clay deposits superior in quality to that in its said 33-acre tract. * * *

It will not be necessary for respondent to go to any considerable expense in irrigating this land, because a neighboring farmer has offered to allow respondent to carry water through his ditch for a very small consideration. * * *

If the land were not susceptible of any use for agriculture * * *; if irrigation would constitute a detriment to the clay content of the land; or if the land were now being used for the manufacture of clay products, or definite plans were now being made to use it for that purpose within a reasonably short time, we might well have decided to affirm the judgment of the district court.

It does not result from the refusal to allow respondent's 33-acre tract to be excluded from the district that respondent must irrigate the land. It need not exercise that right unless it so chooses, and, so far as the court can see, respondent may rent or otherwise dispose of it. * * *

The court is not to be understood as holding that respondent may not at some future time be entitled to have this land excluded from the district; but viewing the situation, as we must, as it existed at the time of the filing of respondent's application and at the time of the trial in the district court, it is the court's opinion that, under the law, respondent is not entitled at this time to have said tract excluded from appellant conservation district. We find nothing in the law which would prevent respondent's filing another application for exclusion of this land from the district at a time when conditions may be different from those shown by the evidence to exist in this case.

The judgment and order appealed from are reversed.

Notes

1. **Grounds for exclusion of land.** The fact that land is irrigated from another water source is a common statutory ground for exclusion of the land from the district, unless district facilities are used to transport the water to the land or the district furnishes supplemental water to the land. However, if a district is formed to protect future as well as present underground water resources, or if one of its purposes is to replenish ground waters, any overlying land may be considered benefited by the district. Atchison, Topeka & Santa Fe Ry. v. Kings County Water Dist., 302 P.2d 1 (Cal. 1956); Hobe v. Madera Irrigation Dist., 274 P.2d 874 (Cal. Dist. Ct. App. 1954).

Can land be excluded if it is physically irrigable but cannot legally be irrigated by the landowner? Under the federal Reclamation Act, no water right from a federal project can accrue to more than 960 acres of land held by an individual or small corporation, or to 640 acres owned by a larger corporation. See infra p. 670, Note 6. What if an individual or corporation owns more land within the district?

2. **Contractual assessment obligations.** In Foster v. Sunnyside Irrigation District, 687 P.2d 841 (Wash. 1984), a farmer owning land in an irrigation district contracted with the district's predecessor in interest, the U.S. Bureau of Reclamation, to pay an annual assessment for all irrigable acres, whether irrigated or not. Later, the farmland was subdivided into residential lots, and no provision was made for rights of way or pipelines to bring water to the lots. The Fosters purchased one of the lots. The district continued to levy an assessment on it. A state statute required assessments to be levied in proportion to benefits accruing to the lands assessed, but also stated that this requirement should not be construed to impair the obligation of any existing water supply contract. The Fosters petitioned to be excluded from the district. The court upheld the district's denial of the petition because the contract obligation to pay an annual assessment ran

with the land, and that obligation was not excused by the land's present unirrigable condition since Foster's predecessor in interest caused the condition. The court said that a change of conditions can excuse a contract obligation under the doctrine of frustration of purpose, but only when the change is not the fault of the promisor.

3. **Third-Party Beneficiaries.** In several cases, farmers have wished to sue the Bureau of Reclamation for alleged violations of the Bureau's contracts to deliver water to districts from which the farmers purchased irrigation water. In H.F. Allen Orchards v. United States, 749 F.2d 1571 (Fed. Cir. 1984), farmers belonging to an irrigation district in Washington alleged that the Bureau had breached its contractual duty to accurately estimate the amount of water it expected to supply. The court concluded that the farmers were intended third party beneficiaries of the contract at issue, and permitted the suit to proceed. In contrast, in two Ninth Circuit opinions, that court has rejected third-party beneficiary status under the language of the contracts in issue. Orff v. United States, 358 F.3d 1137 (9th Cir. 2004); Klamath Water Users Protective Ass'n v. Patterson, 204 F.3d 1206 (9th Cir. 1999).

PEOPLE EX REL. ROGERS v. LETFORD

Supreme Court of Colorado, 1938.
102 Colo. 284, 79 P.2d 274.

KNOUS, JUSTICE. This is an original proceeding in quo warranto upon information of the Attorney General to try the right of respondents to occupy the office and exercise the duties of directors of Northern Colorado Water Conservancy District, organized under the provisions of the Water Conservancy Act of Colorado, by the findings and decree of the district court of the Eighth judicial district sitting in and for Weld county. * * *

The Colorado act was passed by the Thirty-First General Assembly and became effective on May 13, 1937. It was intended to make possible the organization of what is designated as "Water Conservancy Districts." Section 1 of the act states the purpose of the Legislature in passing the law in the following words:

> "It is hereby declared that to provide for the conservation of the water resources of the State of Colorado and for the greatest beneficial use of water within this state, the organization of water conservancy districts and the construction of works as herein defined by such districts are a public use and will:
>
> "a. Be essentially for the public benefit and advantage of the people of the state of Colorado.
>
> "b. Indirectly benefit all industries of the state.
>
> "c. Indirectly benefit the State of Colorado in the increase of its taxable property valuation.
>
> "d. Directly benefit municipalities by providing adequate supplies of water for domestic use.
>
> "e. Directly benefit lands to be irrigated from works to be constructed.
>
> "f. Directly benefit lands now under irrigation by stabilizing the flow of water in streams and by increasing flow and return flow of water to such streams.

"g. Promote the comfort, safety and welfare of the people of the State of Colorado, and it is therefore declared to be the policy of the State of Colorado: * * * 3. To cooperate with the United States under the Federal Reclamation laws now or hereinafter enacted and other agencies of the United States Government for the construction and financing of works in the State of Colorado as herein defined and for the operation and maintenance thereof."

The act is general in its nature, and upon compliance with its terms a water conservancy district can be formed at any place within the State of Colorado. * * *

Pursuant to this act * * *, the district court of Weld county, on September 20, 1937, entered its findings and decree organizing the Northern Colorado Water Conservancy District, which includes generally the lands in the agricultural areas in the vicinity of the St. Vrain, Big Thompson, Cache la Poudre rivers, and of the Platte river from Platteville to the eastern line of Colorado. The approximate present total valuation of these farm lands and improvements thereon within the district is alleged to be $40,000,000, in addition to which it is said there has been an economic development within the district of approximately $100,000,000, making a total assessed valuation of all property within the district, both real and personal, of approximately $140,000,000. This economic development has resulted from the building of the cities of Greeley, Eaton, Boulder, Fort Collins, Longmont, Loveland, Fort Morgan, Brush, Sterling and Julesburg, and numerous other towns and hamlets of various size. In this economic development is also embraced a number of sugar factories, extensive public carrier and utility developments, and other large and prosperous businesses, all of which is due principally to the agricultural development which has been made in the district by application of water for the irrigation of the lands therein. The projected further development of this section by the construction of what is commonly known as the "Colorado-Big Thompson Project" allegedly is the motivating cause for the formation of the Northern Colorado Water Conservancy District. The Colorado-Big Thompson Project contemplates the construction of a number of large reservoirs on the western slope of the Continental Divide on the Colorado river and its tributaries, and the diversion of the waters of that river through the Continental Divide by means of canals and tunnels to the Big Thompson river on the eastern slope of the Continental Divide, from whence, through a series of reservoirs, canals, and other facilities, the water ultimately is destined for delivery to the municipalities and lands in the district. As an integral part of the project, the construction of a reservoir on the Blue river on the western slope for the purpose of replacement of water diverted to the eastern slope and to compensate and stabilize the flow of the Colorado river is included. After a detailed survey made under its auspices, with funds provided by the United States, the Bureau of Reclamation has approved the feasibility of the project. * * *

Preliminary to the consideration of the various constitutional questions involved and as decisive of many of these points, it is necessary to determine the legal nature and character of the corporation intended to be created under the Water Conservancy Act. The act itself, in section 7, declares that: "The district shall be a political subdivision of the State of Colorado and a body corporate with all the powers of a public or municipal corporation." While a legislative declaration of this nature is not conclusive upon a court, it must be seriously regarded in the construction of an act. In this connection also must be considered the purpose of the law, not only as disclosed by its words, but also in the light of the physical conditions of the state, its needs, and the character and extent of the projected benefits. * * *

These circumstances demonstrate, and we conclude, as the language of the act states, that its objects are of sufficient public benefit and advantage to the people of Colorado as a whole to constitute a public purpose and that the water conservancy districts authorized thereby are state agencies and public corporations. * * *

Our Legislature did not confer the ordinary functions of local governments enjoyed by towns and cities on the Water Conservancy Districts contemplated, but did vest in them powers which have come to be associated with true municipal corporations, including the power of taxation to further its purpose. * * *

Section 15 of our Conservancy Act is as follows:

> "Section 15. *Classification of Taxes and Assessments—Powers.*
>
> "In addition to the other means of providing revenue for such districts as herein provided, the Board shall have power and authority to levy and collect taxes and special assessments for maintaining and operating such works and paying the obligations and indebtedness of the district by any one or more of the methods or combinations thereof, classified as follows:
>
> "Class A. To levy and collect taxes upon all property within the district as hereinafter provided.
>
> "Class B. To levy and collect assessments for special benefits accruing to property within municipalities for which use of water is allotted as hereinafter provided.
>
> "Class C. To levy and collect assessments for special benefits accruing to lands within irrigation districts for which use of water is allotted as hereinafter provided.
>
> "Class D. To levy and collect assessments for special benefits accruing to lands for which use of water is allotted as hereinafter provided."

Under class A the Legislature has authorized districts to levy and collect general taxes on all property, real and personal, within the district, and in classes B, C, and D to levy and collect assessments for special benefits.

The express authorization for power to levy taxes conferred by the Legislature upon the district here involved is found in article 10, § 7, of the Colorado Constitution, which reads as follows: "*Municipal taxation.*—The general assembly shall not impose taxes for the purposes of any county, city, town or other municipal corporation, but may by law, vest in the corporate authorities thereof respectively, the power to assess and collect taxes for all purposes of such corporation."

In this grant of power lies the distinction between a water conservancy district under this act and the irrigation districts authorized by the Colorado

Irrigation District Act of 1905, as amended. The public character of the water conservancy district is the occasion for this difference. * * *

The relator contends that the due process clauses of the Federal Constitution, the Fourteenth Amendment, and the Colorado Constitution, art. 2, § 25, are contravened by numerous provisions of the Water Conservancy Act.

Under this head it is said the act is fatally defective because no appraisal of benefits or hearing thereon is provided either as to the general mill levy or special assessments.

Our determination that the general tax authorized is for a public purpose and is not a special assessment in effect disposes of the specially urged contention, based generally upon the objection last discussed as to lack of benefits, that the order of court creating the district and the act itself violate the due process clauses as to the owners of: (1) Real property within the limits of incorporated cities and towns lying within the district; (2) lands not susceptible of irrigation; (3) lands already having an adequate water supply; and (4) personal property. All of these owners are subject to the general ad valorem tax by reason of the situs of their property in the same manner as property owners in ordinary political subdivisions are liable for taxation to support the diversified activities of such subdivisions, which liability is not contingent upon direct benefits, and, as to such tax, as we have indicated, the due process clauses have no application. Under the terms of the act, personal property under no circumstances can be directly liable for the special assessments therein contemplated. The liability of landowners under classes 2 and 3 for special assessments can arise only by a contractual relation initiated by them, and those in class 1 can be affected solely when the town or city in which they reside assumes the special assessments by agreement, in which event the urban landowner, in common with his fellow residents, is subject only to a corporate tax imposed by the authorities of said city or town to pay the special assessment for the domestic water supply contracted for, and for which a general liability would exist if domestic water was secured. To this situation, * * * the due process clauses have no application.

We now refer to the power conferred by the Water Conservancy Act to levy special assessments. As a general proposition, special assessments are permitted by authorized governmental agencies upon the theory that the property against which they are levied derives some peculiar benefit by reason of the projected improvement different from that enjoyed by other property in the community in which the improvement is to be made. The so-called assessments for special benefits provided for in classes B, C, and D of section 15 of the act are unique in character and are not directly analogous to special assessments as they generally are known in ordinary local improvement districts. This difference lies in the fact that under the act the liability for these assessments can arise only by the voluntary act of the individuals and corporations affected, whereas in ordinary cases the special assessments are imposed upon the property owners involuntarily on the basis of the benefit fixed by some public board or authority. In effect, the individuals, cities, towns, irrigation districts, and mutual ditch companies who become liable for such special assessments through agreement with the water conservancy district themselves ascertain the amount of the benefit and the extent of their liability in applying for the water which they deem necessary for their purposes. These contracts are the basis for the lien created by the act against the property of the applicant for water. The terms of an act authorizing such assessments cannot be held violative of due process of law, as each individual landowner and designated corporation agrees to process before he or it becomes subject to any special assessment. * * *

The demurrer of relator is overruled and the writ discharged.

Notes

1. **Ad valorem taxation.** Other cases have sustained districts with ad valorem taxing powers against attacks on state constitutional grounds. Santa Barbara County Water Agency v. All Persons, 306 P.2d 875 (Cal. 1975), rev'd on other grounds, Ivanhoe Irrigation Dist. v. McCracken, 357 U.S. 275 (1958); Nebraska Mid-State Reclamation Dist. v. Hall County, 41 N.W.2d 397 (Neb. 1950); In re Arch Hurley Conservancy Dist., 191 P.2d 338 (N.M. 1948); Patterick v. Carbon Water Conservancy Dist., 145 P.2d 503 (Utah 1944), overruled on another point by Timpanogos Planning & Water Management Agency v. Central Utah Water Conservancy Dist., 690 P.2d 562 (Utah 1984).

The Colorado River Storage Project legislation, which deals with comprehensive development of the water resources of the Upper Colorado River Basin, requires that "prior to construction of irrigation distribution facilities, repayment contracts shall be made with an 'organization' * * * which has the capacity to levy assessments upon all taxable real property located within its boundaries to assist in making repayments." 43 U.S.C. § 620c.

2. **Varieties of water districts.** Many states have statutes authorizing multipurpose districts that control water not only for irrigation but also for purposes such as drainage, flood control, municipal water supply, production of hydroelectric power, control of ground water withdrawals, and ground water replenishment. When the production of hydroelectric power is a feature, a common financial device is the issuance of revenue bonds secured by a pledge of income from the sale of electric energy.

In a number of states, general statutes provide for many types of single purpose and multipurpose districts having water as their central object. These give the careful legal shopper a choice of organizations, powers, and financial arrangements. In some states, most notably Texas and California, the legislatures have created many districts by special acts tailored to meet particular situations. According to one study, "California has * * * 38 general acts establishing water districts of different kinds with different powers, and 100 special acts, each of which creates a single district for a specified area. California contains approximately 1,000 of all types of local water districts engaged in all types of functions." U.S. Advisory Comm'n on Intergovernmental Relations, Coordinating Water Resources in the Federal System: The Groundwater-Surface Water Connection 59 (1991).

3. **State projects.** States have extensive taxing and other financing powers, but states themselves—as distinguished from districts created under state law—have not been particularly active in building or operating water storage and

delivery projects. See Western States Water Council, State/Federal Financing and Western Water Resource Development 16-86 (1984). California is the most notable exception, with its large State Water Project (SWP) that impounds surplus northern California water and distributes it to the San Francisco Bay area, the San Joaquin Valley, and Southern California. A key feature of the SWP, which is operated by the Department of Water Resources, is the impoundment of water in the Feather River watershed behind Oroville Dam in Butte County. From there it flows through natural channels to the Sacramento-San Joaquin Delta. The North Bay Aqueduct and South Bay Aqueduct divert water to the San Francisco Bay area for agricultural, municipal, and industrial use. Water is pumped from the Delta into the California Aqueduct, which runs south into the San Joaquin Valley and supplies agriculture and cities there. The remaining water in the California Aqueduct is pumped over the Tehachapi Mountains to flow into Southern California, with a west branch serving Los Angeles and other coastal cities and an east branch serving the Antelope Valley and San Bernardino, Riverside, Orange, and San Diego Counties.

As once conceived, the SWP was expected to deliver 4.2 million acre-feet annually to 31 contracting agencies through nearly 700 miles of canals, pipelines, and tunnels. As presently constructed, its delivery capacity is about 2.4 million acre-feet annually. Future deliveries are likely to be constrained by the need to leave more water in the Delta to solve water quality and endangered species problems. See infra p. 581, Note 1.

Various types of financing have been used for the SWP. Funds derived from the sale of California Water Resources Development Bonds and a portion of the state's tideland oil and gas revenues are deposited in the California Water Fund as authorized by the Burns-Porter Act, Cal. Water Code §§ 12930-12944. Revenue bond financing was authorized by the Central Valley Project Act, id. §§ 11100-11925. Authority to issue revenue bonds was confirmed in Warne v. Harkness, 387 P.2d 377 (Cal. 1963). The fund also receives miscellaneous receipts derived from payments and appropriations authorized by a variety of legislative actions and special contracts and cost-sharing agreements.

The history of the SWP is told in Norris Hundley, Jr., The Great Thirst: Californians and Water, 1970s-1990s, at 272-98, 309-30, 369-73 (1992).

MILLIS v. BOARD OF COUNTY COMMISSIONERS

Supreme Court of Colorado, 1981.
626 P.2d 652.

LOHR, JUSTICE. The appellants are nonresidents of Colorado who own vacation property in the High Drive Water District (District) near Estes Park. On August 13, 1975, the Larimer County Board of County Commissioners (Board) adopted a formal resolution approving the modified service plan submitted by the District to provide domestic water for district residents. The appellants filed suit against the Board and the District, seeking relief * * * on the basis that the Board's approval exceeded its jurisdiction and was an abuse of discretion. The appellants suffered an adverse judgment in the trial court and brought this appeal. We affirm that judgment.

* * * The District consists of approximately 120 to 130 residences or parcels eligible for service, only 9 of which are owned by persons who utilize

their property year-around. The majority of the parcels are owned by persons who, like the appellants, live out of state. * * * [T]he District was organized in 1974. The petition for organization carried by a vote of 27 to 21. * * *

The District's board of directors proposed to issue general obligation bonds in the amount of $350,000 to finance the construction and installation of a water system. Pursuant to section 32–4–124, C.R.S. 1973, the question of issuing the bonds was submitted to the qualified voters of the District, and the measure passed.

As part of the procedure for formation of the District, a service plan projecting the sale of bonds totaling $350,000 and bearing interest at 7% per annum had been submitted to and approved by the Board. Subsequent to the organization of the District, bond market rates rose. It appeared that the bonds could not be sold at a 7% interest rate and, upon recommendation of the underwriter of the proposed bond issue, the District's board of directors proposed a modified service plan raising the authorized interest on the bonds to 9%. Pursuant to section 32–1–209(3), C.R.S. 1973, the District submitted the modified service plan to the Board for approval. A public hearing was held on that plan, after which the Board approved it.

The appellants then filed a complaint in the Larimer County district court, claiming principally that the modified service plan was economically unfeasible. * * * The appellants also challenged the Board's approval of the modified service plan as a taking of property without due process of law. They apparently claim that the ad valorem tax burden necessary to finance the proposed water system is confiscatory and will not benefit the appellants, for they use their property only in the summer months. We do not agree with this analysis.

A water district is organized not for the improvement of land or to benefit only landowners. Such a district is created to "promote the health, safety, prosperity, security and general welfare" of its inhabitants. Section 32–4–101, C.R.S. 1973. The statute with respect to creation and operation of water districts is to be liberally construed to effect its purposes. Section 32–4–130, C.R.S. 1973. The District's board of directors therefore has the power to levy general ad valorem taxes upon property within the District without according a benefit in proportion to the tax burden imposed. Section 32–4–114, C.R.S. 1973. The fact that the appellants' property may be taxed according to its value regardless of whether the appellants choose to participate in the proposed water system, therefore, does not have any constitutional significance. The United States Supreme Court has held that the Fourteenth Amendment does not "prohibit unwise taxes, merely because they are unwise, or unfair or burdensome taxes, merely because they are unfair or burdensome." International Harvester Co. v. Wisconsin Department of Taxation, 322 U.S. 435, 444, 64 S. Ct. 1060, 1065, 88 L. Ed. 1373, 1381 (1944). * * *

Although the due process guarantee may not impose a significant limitation on the District's power to levy ad valorem taxes in order to finance the proposed water system, section 32–1–205, C.R.S. 1973, does require that the service plan for the District reflect an ability to provide economical and sufficient service to the area and that the area included within the District have sufficient financial ability to discharge any proposed indebtedness on a reasonable basis. The Board was charged with assessing these criteria when it approved the modified service plan. It is to the validity of that approval which we now turn.

A water district may not provide domestic water to its inhabitants except pursuant to a service plan which has been approved by the Board and, with respect to an original service plan, by the district court. Sections 32–1–202 to 209, C.R.S. 1973. * * *

Section 32–1–205, C.R.S. 1973, sets forth the reasons for which a service plan or modification thereof may be disapproved. For purposes of this challenge subsections (d) and (e) are relevant. Respectively, these allow disapproval of the modified plan if:

> "(d) The proposed special district is incapable of providing economical and sufficient service to the area within its proposed boundaries; or
> (e) The area to be included in the proposed district does not have, or will not have, the financial ability to discharge the proposed indebtedness on a reasonable basis."

The primary dispute over the modified plan concerned projections as to how many persons would "tap in" to the proposed water system. It was conceded that a decrease in the income from tap fees and water charges caused by a smaller number of persons utilizing the system would have to be made up by increases in the ad valorem tax burden on all District property, increases in tap fees and water charges to those who were on the system, or a combination of such increases. Witnesses for the District, nevertheless, testified that such a decrease would not render the plan economically unfeasible. Although there was testimony at the hearing that some District landowners would not tap in, there was no proof that a substantial number would not do so.

The district court may not substitute its judgment for that of the Board, nor may we. * * * Upon review of the record, we conclude that the district court's finding that competent evidence exists to support the Board's decision is correct. The judgment of the district court is affirmed.

Notes

1. **Domestic water districts.** Practically all states authorize the creation of various districts for the purpose of supplying water for domestic and household purposes outside of incorporated areas. For the most part, these districts depend on fees and charges for water delivered to obtain revenue for operation and maintenance and for bond retirement, though some have general taxing powers.

The Colorado Legislature repealed the statutes discussed in *Millis*, along with separate statutes governing various other quasi-municipal corporations serving purposes unrelated to water, and it replaced them all with a single Special District Act. The new act governs entities ranging alphabetically from ambulance districts to water districts. Colo. Rev. Stat. §§ 32–1–101 to –1605. The *Millis* statutes all have counterparts in the new act, including a provision allowing the county commissioners to approve a service plan only if the district can provide "economical and sufficient service" and the area included in the district will have "the financial ability to discharge the proposed indebtedness on a reasonable basis." Id. § 32–1–203(2).

2. **Moratorium on hookups.** In Lockary v. Kayfetz, 917 F.2d 1150 (9th Cir. 1990), a public utility district's moratorium on water hookups was challenged by the owners of undeveloped lands zoned for residential use. The court ruled that a landowner's interest in receiving water for real estate development is not a fundamental right, and thus to be constitutionally valid a moratorium on hookups need only bear a rational relation to some legitimate state interest, such as coping with a water shortage. It noted that the moratorium might be a regulatory taking of the plaintiffs' property if the district had water available and the lack of hookups prevented all economically viable use of their lands. But it said that the denial of hookups due to a water shortage would not be arbitrary and would not constitute a regulatory taking, a denial of equal protection, or a denial of substantive due process.

3. **Farmers Home Administration financing.** Districts that supply domestic water in rural areas may be eligible for grants and low interest loans from the Farmers Home Administration (FmHA). See 7 U.S.C. § 1926(a). If a district serving an unincorporated area has a FmHA loan and then some of the land it serves is annexed by a city, the district's right to provide water service to the land is protected against encroachment by the city during the term of the loan. Id. § 1926(b).

BALL v. JAMES

Supreme Court of the United States, 1981.
451 U.S. 355, 101 S. Ct. 1811, 68 L. Ed. 2d 150.

JUSTICE STEWART delivered the opinion of the Court.

This appeal concerns the constitutionality of the system for electing the directors of a large water reclamation district in Arizona, a system which, in essence, limits voting eligibility to landowners and apportions voting power according to the amount of land a voter owns. The case requires us to consider whether the peculiarly narrow function of this local governmental body and the special relationship of one class of citizens to that body releases it from the strict demands of the one-person, one-vote principle of the Equal Protection Clause of the Fourteenth Amendment.

The public entity at issue here is the Salt River Project Agricultural Improvement and Power District, which stores and delivers untreated water to the owners of land comprising 236,000 acres in central Arizona. The District, formed as a governmental entity in 1937, subsidizes its water operations by selling electricity, and has become the supplier of electric power for hundreds of thousands of people in an area including a large part of metropolitan Phoenix. Nevertheless, the history of the District began in the efforts of Arizona farmers in the 19th century to irrigate the arid lands of the Salt River Valley, and, as the parties have stipulated, the primary purposes of the District have always been the storage, delivery, and conservation of water. * * *

This lawsuit was brought by a class of registered voters who live within the geographic boundaries of the District, and who own either no land or less than an acre of land within the District. The complaint alleged that the District enjoys such governmental powers as the power to condemn land, to sell tax-exempt bonds, and to levy taxes on real property. It also alleged that because the District sells electricity to virtually half the population of Arizona, and because, through its water operations, it can exercise significant influence on flood control and environmental management within its boundaries, the District's policies and actions have a substantial effect on all people who live within the District, regardless of property ownership. * * *

Reynolds v. Sims, [377 U.S. 533, 84 S. Ct. 1362, 12 L. Ed. 2d 506 (1964)], held that the Equal Protection Clause requires adherence to the principle of one-person, one-vote in elections of state legislators. * * * In Hadley v. Junior College District, 397 U.S. 50, 90 S. Ct. 791, 25 L. Ed. 2d 45, the Court extended *Reynolds* to the election of trustees of a community college district because those trustees "exercised general governmental powers" and "perform[ed] important governmental functions" that had significant effect on all citizens residing within the district. But in that case the Court stated: "It is of course possible that there might be some case in which a State elects certain functionaries whose duties are so far removed from normal governmental activities and so disproportionately affect different groups that a popular election in compliance with *Reynolds* * * * might not be required * * *."

The Court found such a case in [Salyer Land Co. v. Tulare Lake Basin Water Storage Dist., 410 U.S. 719, 93 S. Ct. 1224, 35 L. Ed. 2d 659 (1973).] The Tulare Lake Basin Water Storage District involved there encompassed 193,000 acres, 85% of which were farmed by one or another of four corporations. Under California law, public water districts could acquire, store, conserve, and distribute water, and though the Tulare Lake Basin Water Storage District had never chosen to do so, could generate and sell any form of power it saw fit to support its water operations. The costs of the project were assessed against each landowner according to the water benefits the landowner received. At issue in the case was the constitutionality of the scheme for electing the directors of the district, under which only landowners could vote, and voting power was apportioned according to the assessed valuation of the voting landowner's property. The Court recognized that the Tulare Lake Basin Water Storage District did exercise "some typical governmental powers," including the power to hire and fire workers, contract for construction of projects, condemn private property, and issue general obligation bonds. Nevertheless, the Court concluded that the district had "relatively limited authority," because "its primary purpose, indeed the reason for its existence, is to provide for the acquisition, storage, and distribution of water for farming in the Tulare Lake Basin." The Court also noted that the financial burdens of the district could not but fall on the landowners, in proportion to the benefits they received from the district, and that the district's actions therefore disproportionately affected the voting landowners. The *Salyer* Court thus held that the strictures of *Reynolds* did not apply to the Tulare District * * *.

* * * [T]he services currently provided by the Salt River District are more diverse and affect far more people than those of the Tulare Lake Basin Water Storage District. Whereas the Tulare District included an area entirely devoted to agriculture and populated by only 77 persons, the Salt River District includes almost half the population of the State, including large parts of Phoenix and other cities. Moreover, the Salt River District, unlike the Tulare District, has exercised its statutory power to generate and sell electric power, and has become one of the largest suppliers of such power in the State. Further, whereas all the water delivered by the Tulare District went for agriculture, roughly 40% of the water delivered by the Salt River District goes to urban areas or is used for
nonagricultural purposes in farming areas. Finally whereas all operating costs of the Tulare District were born by the voting landowners through assessments apportioned according to land value, most of the capital and operating costs of the Salt River District have been met through the revenues generated by the selling of electric power. Nevertheless, a careful examination of the Salt River District reveals that * * * these distinctions do not amount to a constitutional difference.

First, the District simply does not exercise the sort of governmental powers that invoke the strict demands of *Reynolds*. The District cannot impose ad valorem property taxes or sales taxes. It cannot enact any laws governing the conduct of citizens, nor does it administer such normal functions of government as the maintenance of streets, the operation of schools, or sanitation, health, or welfare services.

Second, * * * even the District's water functions, which constitute the primary and originating purpose of the District, are relatively narrow. The District [does] not own, sell, or buy water, nor [does it] control the use of any water [it has] delivered. The District simply stores water behind its dams, conserves it from loss, and delivers it through project canals. It is true * * * that as much as 40% of the water delivered by the District goes for nonagricultural purposes. But the distinction between agricultural and urban land is of no special constitutional significance in this context. The constitutionally relevant fact is that all water delivered by the Salt River District, like the water delivered by the Tulare Lake Basin Water Storage District, is distributed according to land ownership, and the District does not and cannot control the use to which the landowners who are entitled to the water choose to put it. As repeatedly recognized by the Arizona courts, though the state legislature has allowed water districts to become nominal public entities in order to obtain inexpensive bond financing, the districts remain essentially business enterprises, created by and chiefly benefiting a specific group of landowners. As in *Salyer*, the nominal public character of such an entity cannot transform it into the type of governmental body for which the Fourteenth Amendment demands a one-person, one-vote system of election.

Finally, neither the existence nor size of the District's power business affects the legality of its property-based voting scheme. As this Court has noted in a different context, the provision of electricity is not a traditional element of governmental sovereignty, and so is not in itself the sort of general or important governmental function that would make the government provider subject to the doctrine of the *Reynolds* case. In any event, since the electric power functions were stipulated to be incidental to the water functions which are the District's primary purpose, they cannot change the character of that enterprise. * * *

The appellees claim * * * that the sheer size of the power operations and the great number of people they affect serve to transform the District into an entity of general governmental power. But no matter how great the number of nonvoting residents buying electricity from the District, the relationship between them and the District's power operations is essentially that between consumers and a business enterprise from which they buy. * * *

The functions of the Salt River District are therefore of the narrow, special sort which justifies a departure from the popular-election requirement of the *Reynolds* case. And as in *Salyer*, an aspect of that limited purpose is the disproportionate relationship the District's functions bear to the specific class of people whom the system makes eligible to vote. The voting landowners are the only residents of the District whose lands are subject to liens to secure District bonds. Only these landowners are subject to the acreage-based taxing power of the District * * *.

As in the *Salyer* case, we conclude that the voting scheme for the District is constitutional because it bears a reasonable relationship to its statutory objectives. Here, according to the stipulation of the parties, the subscriptions of land which made * * * the District possible might well have never occurred had not the subscribing landowners been assured a special voice in the conduct of the District's business. Therefore, as in *Salyer*, the State could rationally limit the vote to landowners. Moreover, Arizona could rationally make the weight of their vote dependent upon the number of acres they own, since that number reasonably reflects the relative risks they incurred as landowners and the distribution of the benefits and the burdens of the District's water operations. * * *

JUSTICE WHITE, with whom JUSTICE BRENNAN, JUSTICE MARSHALL, and JUSTICE BLACKMUN join, dissenting. * * *

The District involved here clearly exercises substantial governmental powers. The District is a municipal corporation organized under the laws of Arizona and is not, in any sense of the word, a private corporation. * * * The District's bonds are tax exempt, and its property is not subject to state or local property taxation. This attribute clearly indicates the governmental nature of the District's function. The District also has the power of eminent domain, a matter of some import. * * *

The District here also has authority to allocate water within its service area. It has veto power over all transfers of surface water from one place or type of use to another, and this power extends to any "watershed or drainage area which supplies or contributes water for the irrigation of lands within [the] district. * * * " Ariz. Rev. Stat. Ann. § 45-172.5 (Supp. 1980-1981).

* * * [P]rivate utilities in Arizona are subject to regulation by public authority. The Arizona Corporation Commission is empowered to prescribe

"just and reasonable rates" as well as to regulate other aspects of the business operations of private utilities. See Ariz. Rev. Stat. Ann. § 40-321 (1974). The rate structure of the District now before us, however, is not subject to control by another state agency because the District is a municipal corporation and itself purports to perform the public function of protecting the public interest that the Corporation Commission would otherwise perform. Its power to set its own rates and other conditions of service constitutes important attributes of sovereignty. When combined with a consideration of the District's wide-ranging operations which encompass water for agricultural and personal uses, and electrical generation for the needs of hundreds of thousands of customers, it is clear that the District exercises broad governmental power. With respect to energy management and the provision of water and electricity, the District's power is immense and its authority complete. * * *

With these facts in mind, it is indeed curious that the Court would attempt to characterize the District's electrical operations as "incidental" to its water operations, or would consider the power operations to be irrelevant to the legality of the voting scheme. The facts are that in *Salyer* the burdens of the Water District fell entirely on the landowners who were served by the District. Here the landowners could not themselves afford to finance their own project and turned to a public agency to help them. That agency now subsidizes the storage and delivery of irrigation water for agricultural purposes by selling electricity to the public at prices that neither the voters nor any representative public agency has any right to control. Unlike the situation in *Salyer*, the financial burden of supplying irrigation water has been shifted from the landowners to the consumers of electricity. * * *

It is apparent in this case that landowning irrigators are getting a free ride at the expense of the users of electricity. It would also seem apparent that except for the subsidy, utility rates would be lower. Of course, subsidizing agricultural operations may well be in the public interest in Arizona, but it does not follow that the amount of the subsidy and the manner in which it is provided should be totally in the hands of a select few.

Notes

1. ***Ball* and *Salyer* in the lower courts.** Two California water district cases on permissible voting schemes illustrate the confusion created by *Ball* and *Salyer*. In Moores v. Edelbrock, 272 Cal. Rptr. 919 (Cal. Ct. App. 1990), the First District Court of Appeal upheld a statute allowing only landowners to vote to elect directors and apportioning votes according to the assessed valuation of the land. In Bjornestad v. Hulse, 272 Cal. Rptr. 864 (Cal. Ct. App. 1990), the Third District Court of Appeal struck down a law allowing only one designated landowner per parcel to vote to elect directors because it violated the equal protection guarantees of the state and federal constitutions. The cases are not necessarily inconsistent because they involved water districts organized under different statutes, possessing different powers, and having different voting schemes. Nevertheless, the two courts clearly took different views of the scope of the exception to the "one person, one vote" principle delineated in *Ball* and *Salyer*.

While *Bjornestad* was pending on appeal to the California Supreme Court, the state legislature narrowed the water district's governmental powers, stripping it of all powers relating to sanitation services, recreational facilities, and fire protection facilities. The supreme court remanded the case to the district court of appeal for reconsideration in light of this change. The latter court found that the primary purpose of the restructured district was to provide domestic water and sewer services to residents. Nonetheless, it ruled that voting could not be limited to landowners because the district served nonlandowning as well as landowning residents, and thus still did not meet the *Ball* and *Salyer* requirement of being "a special limited-purpose district that disproportionately affects landowners as a group." 281 Cal. Rptr. 548 (Cal. Ct. App. 1991).

2. **Voting by nonresident landowners.** The *Bjornestad* remand involved another legislative change, one allowing both residents and nonresident landowners to vote in future district elections. The question presented was whether enfranchising nonresident landowners unconstitutionally diluted the votes of residents. Although the district was not a special land-serving district of limited purpose and powers, the court concluded that the district lacked general purposes and powers. The court therefore decided it was appropriate to test the constitutionality of the voting scheme by applying the "rational basis" test rather than the more demanding "compelling interest" test. The court concluded that the legislature had a rational basis to allow nonresident landowners to vote along with residents, given that the district was not a governmental entity of general purpose and powers, that the area served was primarily a second-home, vacation community in a mountain area with a relatively low number of permanent residents, and that the district's financial burdens were borne largely by landowners.

The High Drive Water District in *Millis*, supra p. 448, also served mountain vacation property—though in Colorado rather than California. The district financed its facilities by general obligation bonds payable out of ad valorem taxes levied on property within its boundaries. The Colorado statute on voting in elections for formation of the district and for approval of its plans enfranchised only "taxpaying electors," which term was defined to exclude nonresidents of the state. Consequently, landowners in the district who did not reside there could vote if they resided elsewhere in Colorado but not if they resided in another state. In a federal case concerning this differential voting scheme for nonresident landowners, the United States Supreme Court affirmed without opinion a federal district court decision finding no violation of the Equal Protection Clause of the Fourteenth Amendment. Millis v. High Drive Water Dist., 439 U.S. 802 (1978).

3. **State constitutional provisions.** Apart from Fourteenth Amendment equal protection, state constitutional provisions may need to be considered in assessing the validity of water district voting rules. After the United States Supreme Court upheld the High Drive Water District's voting scheme under the Fourteenth Amendment though it disenfranchised nonresident landowners, the Colorado Supreme Court (in a portion of its *Millis* opinion omitted earlier) ruled that the scheme did not violate the equal protection guarantee of the Colorado Constitution either:

"Having determined that the special district voting scheme involves no suspect classification and infringes no fundamental right, the appropriate test of its validity is whether it is rationally related to a legitimate state interest. * * *

The appellants contend that there is no rational reason for granting district voting rights to Colorado residents who own land but do not reside within the district, while denying electoral participation to district landowners who live out of state. The federal district court found that Colorado residents are more likely to share a common concern regarding urban development, and its effect on this state's natural environment, than are residents of other states. Because the formation and operation of a water district affects this concern the federal court concluded that a rational basis exists for excluding nonresidents from direct political participation in water district matters. * * * Similarly, the creation of adequate water supply and distribution systems and the provision of adequate sewage collection and disposal facilities implicate important public health considerations. These too are concerns which the legislature rationally might have considered to affect Colorado residents more directly than nonresidents. We can also conceive that the legislature wishes to decrease the chance that nonresidents would control the formation and operation of water districts to the detriment of those who are full-time district residents."

After *Salyer* but before *Ball*, the California Supreme Court struck down a statute making landownership a qualification to be elected to the board of directors of the Imperial Irrigation District—an entity serving 500,000 acres and 100,000 residents with irrigation and domestic water, electric power, drainage, flood control, sewage disposal, and recreational facilities. Choudhry v. Free, 552 P.2d 438 (Cal. 1976). The court distinguished *Salyer* by pointing out differences between the powers and the revenue sources of the districts in the two cases. Some of the differences that the court noted may be of questionable Fourteenth Amendment significance after *Ball*. But as in *Bjornestad*, supra p. 455, Note 1, the court's ruling was based not only on equal protection under the Fourteenth Amendment but on the equal protection clause of the California Constitution.

In Foster v. Sunnyside Irrigation District, 687 P.2d 841 (Wash. 1984), the court held that a statute enfranchising the owners of agricultural or horticultural lands but not other landowners in an irrigation district violated the state constitutional guarantee of "free and equal" elections. The court said that the irrigation district lacked general governmental powers that would trigger the "one person, one vote" rule of *Reynolds v. Sims,* but it ruled that the state constitution goes further to safeguard the right to vote than does the Equal Protection Clause of the Fourteenth Amendment.

4. **Voting Rights Act.** The federal Voting Rights Act prohibits states and their political subdivisions from imposing any voting qualification that denies the right to vote on account of race or color. 42 U.S.C. § 1973. The effect of this act upon the Arizona district involved in *Ball* was addressed in Smith v. Salt River Project Agricultural Improvement & Power District, 109 F.3d 586 (9th Cir. 1997). The court ruled that the district, though a limited-purpose entity, is a political subdivision of the state for purposes of the Voting Rights Act. The court concluded, however, that the district's land ownership requirement for voting did not violate the act despite the fact that only 40% of African-American heads-of-households within the district own homes while 60% of white heads-of-households do. There was no violation because the district had no history of racial politics and the land ownership qualification for voting had been established and continued in force for reasons unrelated to race.

5. **Symposia.** A symposium on the changing form and evolving functions of western water districts appears in Special Project: Irrigation Districts, 1982 Ariz. St. L.J. 345-527. Another symposium, focusing primarily on the social and political aspects, is found in Special Water Districts: Challenge for the Future (James N. Corbridge, Jr., ed., 1983).

FULGHUM v. SELMA

Supreme Court of North Carolina, 1953.
238 N.C. 100, 76 S.E.2d 368.

[Selma Mill Village is a small unincorporated community just outside the town of Selma, North Carolina. In 1946 the town contracted to sell water to plaintiff Fulghum for distribution to the inhabitants of the village through Fulghum's pipes. The water was delivered at a meter just inside the town limits, at the same rate charged to residents of the town. Fulghum charged somewhat higher rates to the inhabitants of the village.

The contract had no fixed duration. In 1952 the town passed an ordinance amending its water rates, charging $.20 per 1,000 gallons for water consumed within the town but $1 per 1,000 gallons for water supplied for consumption outside the town limits. Fulghum brought suit to have the ordinance declared void and to enjoin the city from shutting off his water supply. The trial court dismissed the action.]

ERVIN, JUSTICE. There may be more than a modicum of truth in the assertion of the plaintiffs that the defendant enacted the ordinance and its amendment for the coercive purpose of inducing Fulghum to abandon his water service to the inhabitants of Selma Mill Village and transfer his pipe lines to the defendant at less than their value. Be this as it may, we must remember that hard cases are the quicksands of the law and confine ourselves to our appointed task of declaring the legal rights of the parties.

The crucial question raised by the appeal is this: Does the evidence of the plaintiffs suffice to show that Fulghum has the legal right to compel the Town of Selma to supply water to him at the rates charged consumers within its corporate limits for resale beyond its boundaries?

The plaintiffs insist initially that this question must be answered in the affirmative on the ground that the contract made by Fulghum with the Town of Selma in 1946 gives Fulghum this legal right. * * * Where the parties to a contract calling for a continuing performance fix no time for its duration and none can be implied from the nature of the contract or from the surrounding circumstances, the contract is terminable at will by either party on reasonable notice to the other. * * *

The plaintiffs maintain secondarily that their evidence is sufficient to establish a legal right in Fulghum to the relief sought irrespective of the matter of contract right. They argue in this connection that when the Town of Selma established its waterworks and undertook to distribute water for compensation, it became the legal duty of the Town of Selma to supply Fulghum water for any purpose at the same rates as those charged consumers residing within its corporate limits. * * *

A municipality which operates its own waterworks is under no duty in the first instance to furnish water to persons outside its limits. It has the discretionary power, however, to engage in this undertaking. G.S. § 160–255. When a municipality exercises this discretionary power, it does not assume the obligations of a public service corporation toward nonresident consumers. G.S. § 62–30(3). It retains the authority to specify the terms upon which nonresidents may obtain its water. In exerting this authority, it "may fix a different rate from that charged within the corporate limits". G.S. § 160–256.

The rates fixed by the ordinance and the amendment for water supplied by the Town of Selma for consumption outside its corporate limits are not discriminatory in a legal sense. They apply alike to all nonresidents who purchase town water. The Town of Selma was empowered by law to make these rates different from those charged within its corporate limits. Since a nonresident must pay the uniform rates fixed by the Town of Selma for other nonresidents in order to obtain town water, it is immaterial that he deems such rates to be exorbitant or unreasonable. * * *

When a municipality engages in supplying water to its inhabitants, it owes the duty of equal service in furnishing water only to consumers within its corporate limits. It is under no legal obligation to supply water to a resident for resale to others either within or without its municipal limits.

Fulghum does not seek to have the water in controversy furnished to him as a consumer residing within the boundaries of the Town of Selma. His sole purpose is to resell the water to persons living outside its corporate limits. This being true, he cannot complain of the refusal of the Town of Selma to furnish him the water in controversy at the same rate charged resident consumers of the same quantity of water. * * * [Affirmed.]

Notes

1. **Municipal supply to nonresidents.** Municipal corporations generally have express or implied authority to supply water to consumers outside the corporate limits. See Richards v. City of Portland, 255 P. 326 (Or. 1927); Corporation of Mt. Jackson v. Nelson, 145 S.E. 355 (Va. 1928). Even an express grant of authority to supply water extraterritorially, however, might be construed narrowly as applying only to surplus water not needed by municipal residents. Crandall v. Safford, 56 P.2d 660 (Ariz. 1936).

Whether a municipality (or a municipally owned public service company) with legal authority to supply nonresidents can be compelled to do so is a different question. *Fulghum* illustrates the usual view that nonresidents have no enforceable right to service from the city. Accord, Fairway Manor Inc., v. Board of Comm'rs, 521 N.E.2d 818 (Ohio 1988); Five Mile Prairie v. City of Spokane, 755 P.2d 836 (Wash. Ct. App. 1988). Indeed, a city may be under no obligation even to provide service to all *residents*. Sunset Cay, LLC v. City of Folly Beach, 593 S.E.2d 462 (S.C. 2004) (city not obliged to give sewer service to all residents just because it gives it to some).

In some states, a city that undertakes to serve nonresidents in a given area becomes subject to public utility commission regulation and must serve other nonresidents in the same area. Milwaukee v. Public Serv. Comm'n, 66 N.W.2d

716 (Wis. 1954); Recent Cases, 101 U. Pa. L. Rev. 160 (1952). But see Dateline Builders v. City of Santa Rosa, 194 Cal. Rptr. 258 (Cal. Ct. App. 1983) (in contrast to privately owned utilities, no legislative authority exists for public utility commission jurisdiction over municipal utilities); County Water Sys. v. Salt Lake City, 278 P.2d 285 (Utah 1954) (municipalities are exempt from commission jurisdiction not only in supplying water to their residents but in supplying surplus water to nonresidents). Even in states where extraterritorial service can subject a municipality to public utility commission regulation, incidental service to a small number of nonresidents does not give rise to an obligation to render additional nonresident service that would jeopardize service within the municipality. Mongiello v. Hightstown, 112 A.2d 241 (N.J. 1955).

2. **Terms of nonresident service.** *Fulghum* illustrates the traditional rule that since a municipality is under no duty to supply nonresidents, it is free to set its own rates and other terms in contracting for extraterritorial service. Accord, Hobby v. Sonora, 298 P.2d 578 (Cal. Ct. App. 1956); Childs v. Columbia, 70 S.E. 296 (S.C. 1910). This rule does not apply in states where extraterritorial service triggers public utility commission jurisdiction to regulate rates. Elsewhere, courts increasingly are departing from the traditional rule by requiring that nonresident rates be reasonable and nondiscriminatory, though this does not necessarily mean that nonresident rates must be the same as for residents. Barr v. First Taxing Dist. of Norwalk, 192 A.2d 872 (Conn. 1963); Texarkana v. Wiggins, 246 S.W.2d 622 (Tex. 1952); Platt v. Town of Torrey, 949 P.2d 325 (Utah 1997) (suggesting that higher nonresident rates could be justified by increased costs to serve nonresidents, by greater resident contributions to water system costs through general fund tax payments, or by greater potential resident responsibility for tort liability or replacement of the system). In Bennett Bear Creek Farm & Water Sanitation District v. City & County of Denver, 928 P.2d 1254 (Colo. 1996), the court treated rate classifications as legislative in nature and thus judicially reviewable under the rational basis test. More specifically, it said rates must be rationally related to legitimate governmental utilities purposes such as making additional development pay its way and providing a reasonable rate of return on investment based on plant value. Where the service provider makes the appropriate showing, courts have upheld nonresident surcharges of 100%. Usher v. City of Pittsburg, 410 P.2d 419 (Kan. 1966).

Joseph L. Sax, Municipal Water Supply for Non-residents: Recent Developments and a Suggestion for the Future, 5 Nat. Resources J. 54 (1965), found that the modern trend toward requiring reasonable rates for nonresidents helps them very little in practice and suggested imposing disclosure duties on municipalities designed to help nonresidents prove unreasonableness.

High rates are not the only potential problem for nonresidents. Cities sometimes use a monopoly position to exact terms not germane to water supply or distribution, such as requirements that the nonresidents desiring water accept other city services or agree to annexation. See Wayne v. Village of Sebring, 36 F.3d 517 (6th Cir. 1994); Five Mile Prairie v. City of Spokane, supra p. 459, Note 1; Carvalho v. Levesque, 191 A.2d 165 (R.I. 1963).

Chapter 6

INTERSTATE ALLOCATION

SECTION 1. EQUITABLE APPORTIONMENT

KANSAS v. COLORADO

Supreme Court of the United States, 1907.
206 U.S. 46, 27 S. Ct. 655, 51 L. Ed. 956.

On May 20, 1901, * * * upon leave obtained, the State of Kansas filed its bill in equity in this court against the State of Colorado. To this bill the defendant demurred. * * * In delivering the opinion of the court [185 U.S. 125, 22 S.Ct. 552, 46 L.Ed. 838 (1902)] the Chief Justice disclosed in the following words the general character of the controversy, and the conclusions arrived at (p. 145, S.Ct. p. 559, L.Ed. p. 846):

> "The gravamen of the bill is that the State of Colorado, acting directly herself as well as through private persons thereto licensed, is depriving and threatening to deprive the State of Kansas and its inhabitants of all the water heretofore accustomed to flow in the Arkansas River through its channel on the surface, and through a subterranean course across the State of Kansas; that this is threatened not only by the impounding and the use of the water at the river's source, but as it flows after reaching the river. Injury, it is averred, is being, and would be, thereby inflicted on the State of Kansas as an individual owner, and on all the inhabitants of the State, and especially on the inhabitants of that part of the State lying in the Arkansas Valley. The injury is asserted to be threatened, and as being wrought, in respect of lands located on the banks of the river; lands lying on the line of a subterranean flow; and lands lying some distance from the river, either above or below ground, but dependent on the river for a supply of water. And it is insisted that Colorado, in doing this, is violating the fundamental principle that one must use his own so as not to destroy the legal rights of another.
>
> "The State of Kansas appeals to the rule of the common law that owners of lands on the banks of a river are entitled to the continual flow of the stream; and while she concedes that this rule has been modified in the Western states so that flowing water may be appropriated to mining purposes and for the reclamation of arid lands, and the doctrine of prior appropriation obtains, yet she says that that modification has not gone so far as to justify the destruction of the rights of other states and their inhabitants

altogether; and that the acts of Congress of 1866 and subsequently, while recognizing the prior appropriation of water as in contravention of the common-law rule as to a continuous flow, have not attempted to recognize it as rightful to that extent. In other words, Kansas contends that Colorado cannot absolutely destroy her rights, and seeks some mode of accommodation as between them, while she further insists that she occupies, for reasons given, the position of a prior appropriator herself, if put to that contention as between her and Colorado. * * *"

* * * The issue between these several parties having been perfected by replications, a commissioner was appointed to take evidence, and after that had been taken and abstracts prepared, counsel for the respective parties were heard in argument, and upon the pleadings and testimony the case was submitted. * * *

MR. JUSTICE BREWER delivered the opinion of the court: * * *

[T]he Supreme Court is granted jurisdiction of all controversies between the States which are justiciable in their nature. * * *

One cardinal rule, underlying all the relations of the states to each other, is that of equality of right. Each state stands on the same level with all the rest. It can impose its own legislation on no one of the others, and is bound to yield its own views to none. Yet, whenever * * * the action of one state reaches through the agency of natural laws, into the territory of another state, the question of the extent and the limitations of the rights of the two states becomes a matter of justiciable dispute between them, and this court is called upon to settle that dispute in such a way as will recognize the equal rights of both and at the same time establish justice between them. In other words, through these successive disputes and decisions this court is practically building up what may not improperly be called interstate common law. This very case presents a significant illustration. Before either Kansas or Colorado was settled the Arkansas River was a stream running through the territory which now composes these two States. Arid lands abound in Colorado. Reclamation is possible only by the application of water, and the extreme contention of Colorado is that it has a right to appropriate all the waters of this stream for the purposes of irrigating its soil and making more valuable its own territory. But the appropriation of the entire flow of the river would naturally tend to make the lands along the stream in Kansas less arable. It would be taking from the adjacent territory that which had been the customary natural means of preserving its arable character. On the other hand, the possible contention of Kansas, that the flowing water in the Arkansas must, in accordance with the extreme doctrine of the common law of England, be left to flow as it was wont to flow, no portion of it being appropriated in Colorado for the purposes of irrigation, would have the effect to perpetuate a desert condition in portions of Colorado beyond the power of reclamation. Surely here is a dispute of a justiciable nature which might and ought to be tried and determined. If the two States were absolutely independent nations it would be settled by treaty or by force. Neither of these ways being practicable, it must be settled by decision of this court. * * *

In deciding this case on demurrer we said:

> "As will be perceived * * * the mere fact that a state had no pecuniary interest in the controversy would not defeat the original jurisdiction of this court, which might be invoked by the state as *parens patriae,* trustee, guardian, or representative of all or a considerable portion of its citizens; * * *.
>
> "In the case before us, the State of Kansas files her bill as representing and on behalf of her citizens, as well as in vindication of her alleged rights as an individual owner, and seeks relief in respect of being deprived of the waters of the river accustomed to flow through and across the State, and the consequent destruction of the property of herself and of her citizens and injury to their health and comfort. The action complained of is state action, and not the action of state officers in abuse or excess of their powers."

It is the State of Kansas which invokes the action of this court, charging that, through the action of Colorado, a large portion of its territory is threatened with disaster. In this respect it is in no manner evading the provisions of the 11th Amendment to the Federal Constitution.[a] It is not acting directly and solely for the benefit of any individual citizen to protect his riparian rights. Beyond its property rights it has an interest as a state in this large tract of land bordering on the Arkansas River. Its prosperity affects the general welfare of the State. The controversy rises, therefore, above a mere question of local private right and involves a matter of state interest, and must be considered from that standpoint. * * *

It cannot be denied, in view of all the testimony * * * that the diminution of the flow of water in the river by the irrigation of Colorado has worked some detriment to the southwestern part of Kansas, and yet, when we compare the amount of this detriment with the great benefit which has obviously resulted to the counties in Colorado, it would seem that equality of right and equity between the two States forbids any interference with the present withdrawal of water in Colorado for purposes of irrigation.

Summing up our conclusions, we are of that opinion that * * * the appropriation of the waters of the Arkansas by Colorado, for purposes of irrigation, has diminished the flow of water into the State of Kansas; that the result of that appropriation has been the reclamation of large areas in Colorado, transforming thousands of acres into fertile fields, and rendering possible their occupation and cultivation when otherwise they would have continued barren and unoccupied; that while the influence of such diminution has been of perceptible injury to portions of the Arkansas Valley in Kansas, particularly those portions closest to the Colorado line, yet, to the great body of the valley it has worked little, if any, detriment, and regarding the interests of both States, and the right of each to receive benefit through irrigation and in any other manner from the waters of this stream, we are not satisfied that Kansas has made out a case entitling it to a decree. At the same time it is

a. The Eleventh Amendment provides: "The judicial power of the United States shall not be construed to extend to any suit in law or equity, commenced or prosecuted against one of the United States by Citizens of another State * * *."

obvious that if the depletion of the waters of the river by Colorado continues to increase there will come a time when Kansas may justly say that there is no longer an equitable division of benefits, and may rightfully call for relief against the action of Colorado, its corporations and citizens, in appropriating the waters of the Arkansas for irrigation purposes.

The decree which, therefore, will be entered, * * * will also dismiss the bill of the State of Kansas as against all the defendants, without prejudice to the right of the plaintiff to institute new proceedings whenever it shall appear that, through a material increase in the depletion of the waters of the Arkansas by Colorado, its corporations or citizens, the substantial interests of Kansas are being injured to the extent of destroying the equitable apportionment of benefits between the two States resulting from the flow of the river. * * *

Notes

1. **Supreme Court jurisdiction.** The Supreme Court's jurisdiction of controversies between states is original and exclusive. U.S. Const. art. III, § 2, cl. 2; 28 U.S.C. § 1251(a). In Kansas v. Colorado, the Court appointed a commissioner to take testimony and prepare abstracts of it. Later, the Court settled on the practice of appointing a special master to take evidence and submit a report that typically contains findings of fact, conclusions of law, and a recommended disposition of the case.

2. **Private interstate water suits.** Litigation concerning the allocation of interstate waters has not been confined to suits between states in the Supreme Court. Individual water users from different states have tried allocation disputes in lower courts.

Private interstate allocation suits raise issues of judicial jurisdiction. A court lacks power to issue an in rem decree affecting a water right situated outside its territorial jurisdiction. But the court may obtain personal jurisdiction over the holder of the right if that person either appears voluntarily, is served while present in the forum state, or is served elsewhere under a long-arm statute. Then the court can issue an in personam decree that regulates the person's water use. Vineyard Land & Stock Co. v. Twin Falls Salmon River Land & Water Co., 245 F. 9 (9th Cir. 1917). The decree can be enforced by contempt proceedings. Brooks v. United States, 119 F.2d 636 (9th Cir. 1941).

Private interstate allocation suits also raise issues of choice of law. The doctrine of equitable apportionment plays no role in allocating water between individual litigants in different states if the Supreme Court has not yet decreed an apportionment between the states. *Vineyard Land & Stock Co.*, supra. Instead, if the private litigants are from states that both follow the appropriation doctrine, courts have determined and enforced priorities across the state boundary. E.g., Bean v. Morris, 221 U.S. 485 (1911); Albion-Idaho Land Co. v. Naf Irrigation Co., 97 F.2d 439 (10th Cir. 1938); U.S. v. Walker River Irrigation Dist., 11 F. Supp. 158 (D. Nev. 1935); Willey v. Decker, 73 P. 210 (Wyo. 1903). If the litigants are from states with different water law doctrines, neither existing water cases nor general choice-of-law principles provide much guidance on what law should govern. See Douglas L. Grant, Private Interstate Suits, in 4 Waters and

Water Rights §§ 44.05(b)-.05(b)(2) (Robert E. Beck ed., repl. vol. 2004) (suggesting approaches to the choice-of-law issue).

3. **Further Arkansas River apportionment litigation.** When Kansas commenced the principal case in 1901, the land irrigated from the Arkansas River system totaled approximately 300,000 acres in Colorado and approximately 22,000 acres in Kansas. M.C. Hinderlider & R.I. Meeker, Interstate Water Problems and Their Solutions, 90 Transactions Am. Soc'y Civ. Eng'rs 1035, 1041-42 (1927). Although that pattern of use did not result in an inequitable division of benefits, the Court indicated that additional Colorado diversions could do so at some point.

The dispute returned to the Court in Colorado v. Kansas, 320 U.S. 383 (1943). Colorado asked the Court to enjoin private suits brought by Kansas citizens in lower courts asserting claims that Colorado alleged were inconsistent with the principal case. Kansas responded by arguing Colorado users continued to increase their diversions to the detriment of Kansas, and it again asked the Court to apportion the Arkansas River. The Court enjoined the lower court suits and again denied Kansas an equitable apportionment decree. The Court noted that although Colorado diversions had exceeded the dependable flow of the river ever since 1901, the usable flow passing the state line increased in following years due to return flows from Colorado irrigation. Also, while the acreage in Colorado irrigated from the river had increased since the Court first denied relief, the acreage in Kansas irrigated from the river had increased in greater proportion (albeit in smaller amount). The Court refused to speculate about how much more land might have been irrigated in Kansas under more favorable river flow conditions. Important equities it found in Colorado's favor were that (1) Colorado had built extensive storage for flood and winter flows but Kansas had not, and (2) Kansas could develop additional irrigation from available groundwater, while cutting back the Colorado appropriations probably would cause the abandonment of improvements and migration from farms.

The Court also stated: "The reason for judicial caution in adjudicating the relative rights of states in such cases is that, while we have jurisdiction of such disputes, they involve the interests of quasi-sovereigns, present complicated and delicate questions, and, due to the possibility of future change of conditions, necessitate expert administration rather than judicial imposition of a hard and fast rule. Such controversies may appropriately be composed by negotiation and agreement, pursuant to the compact clause of the Federal constitution. We say of this case, as the court has said of interstate differences of like nature, that such mutual accommodation and agreement should, if possible, be the medium of settlement, instead of invocation of our adjudicatory power." Id. at 392. Taking a cue from this statement, Kansas and Colorado negotiated an apportionment in the Arkansas River Compact. 63 Stat. 145 (1949).

4. **The Laramie River decree.** The Court's first apportionment of an interstate river came in Wyoming v. Colorado, 259 U.S. 419 (1922). The Laramie River begins in northern Colorado and flows north into Wyoming, where it turns northeast and eventually empties into the North Platte River. Wyoming sued to prevent a large new diversion from the Laramie River in Colorado. Both states applied the appropriation doctrine internally, and a key issue was whether the Court should base the equitable apportionment on priority of appropriation, which

would give Colorado less water than it desired for the new project. The Court said:

"We conclude that Colorado's objections to the doctrine of appropriation as a basis of decision are not well taken, and that it furnishes the only basis which is consonant with the principles of right and equity applicable to such a controversy as this is. The cardinal rule of the doctrine is that priority of appropriation gives superiority of right. Each of these States applies and enforces this rule in her own territory, and it is the one to which intending appropriators naturally would turn for guidance. The principle on which it proceeds is not less applicable to interstate streams and controversies than to others. Both States pronounce the rule just and reasonable as applied to the natural conditions in that region, and to prevent any departure from it the people of both incorporated it into their Constitutions. It originated in the customs and usages of the people before either State came into existence, and the courts of both hold that their constitutional provisions are to be taken as recognizing the prior usage rather than as creating a new rule. These considerations persuade us that its application to such a controversy as is here presented cannot be other than eminently just and equitable to all concerned."

The Court did not directly enforce priorities, however. It found that the Laramie River had an average dependable flow of 312,250 acre-feet per year and that the existing water right priorities were as follows: first, 20,000 acre-feet for Colorado diversions out of the basin, second, 4,250 acre-feet for use in Colorado on meadow lands in the basin adjacent to the river, third, 272,500 acre-feet for Wyoming rights. This left only 15,500 acre-feet of the average dependable flow for the new Colorado diversion, and the Court's decree was in form an injunction against diversion of more than this amount. 259 U.S. 496 (1922). In practical operation, the decree guaranteed Colorado 39,750 acre-feet (20,000 + 4,250 + 15,500 = 39,750) and awarded Wyoming the remaining actual flow each year, so Wyoming's share would vary depending on how much the flow in any given year exceeded or fell below the average dependable flow. The Court later described the fixed award to Colorado as a "mass allocation." Nebraska v. Wyoming, 325 U.S. 589 (1945). By consent of the parties, the Court later increased Colorado's mass allocation to 49,375 acre-feet annually. 353 U.S. 953 (1957).

During the irrigation season immediately following entry of the original decree in 1922, the flow of the Laramie River was far below average . Wyoming appropriators with priorities as early as 1883 had to go without water while the new Colorado project got its 15,500 acre-feet though the Court had recognized only a 1909 priority for it. Wyoming's top water official remarked: "Why this situation? Simply because the Court of last resort in its wisdom granted to Colorado rights [to] a certain volume of water for use each year, regardless of the seasonal flow of the river. * * * What was heralded as a victory for Wyoming was indeed an empty one." Frank C. Emerson, Discussion, 90 Transactions Am. Soc'y Civ. Eng'rs 1052, 1052-53 (1927).

5. **Effect of an apportionment decree on individual rights.** During a year of very low flow in the Laramie River, could a Wyoming appropriator with an 1883 priority circumvent the Court's decree by bringing a private suit to enjoin diversion upstream by a 1909 priority Colorado appropriator? The Court addressed this in later litigation between the two states. 286 U.S. 494 (1932). It said that although individual water users were not parties to the action that

resulted in the apportionment decree, they were represented by their respective states and were bound by the decree.

NEW JERSEY v. NEW YORK

Supreme Court of the United States, 1931.
283 U.S. 336, 51 S. Ct. 478, 75 L. Ed. 1104.

MR. JUSTICE HOLMES delivered the opinion of the Court.

This is a bill in equity by which the State of New Jersey seeks to enjoin the State of New York and the City of New York from diverting any waters from the Delaware River or its tributaries, and particularly from the Neversink River, Willowemoc River, Beaver Kill, East Branch of the Delaware River and Little Delaware River, or from any part of any one of them. The other rivers named are among the headwaters of the Delaware and flow into it where it forms a boundary between New York and Pennsylvania. The Delaware continues its course as such boundary to Tristate Rock, near Port Jervis in New York, at which point Pennsylvania and New York are met by New Jersey. From there the river marks the boundary between Pennsylvania and New Jersey until Pennsylvania stops at the Delaware state line, and from then on the river divides Delaware from New Jersey until it reaches the Atlantic between Cape Henlopen and Cape May.

New York proposes to divert a large amount of water from the above-named tributaries of the Delaware and from the watershed of that river to the watershed of the Hudson River in order to increase the water supply of the City of New York. New Jersey insists on a strict application of the rules of the common law governing private riparian proprietors subject to the same sovereign power. Pennsylvania intervenes to protect its interests as against anything that might be done to prejudice its future needs.

We are met at the outset by the question what rule is to be applied. [A] more liberal answer may be given than in a controversy between neighbors members of a single State. Different considerations come in when we are dealing with independent sovereigns having to regard the welfare of the whole population and when the alternative to settlement is war. In a less degree, perhaps, the same is true of the quasi-sovereignties bound together in the Union. A river is more than an amenity, it is a treasure. It offers a necessity of life that must be rationed among those who have power over it. New York has the physical power to cut off all the water within its jurisdiction. But clearly the exercise of such a power to the destruction of the interest of lower States could not be tolerated. And on the other hand equally little could New Jersey be permitted to require New York to give up its power altogether in order that the River might come down to it undiminished. Both States have real and substantial interests in the River that must be reconciled as best they may. The different traditions and practices in different parts of the country may lead to varying results but the effort always is to secure an equitable apportionment without quibbling over formulas.

* * * The removal of water to a different watershed obviously must be allowed at times unless States are to be deprived of the most beneficial use on

formal grounds. In fact it has been allowed repeatedly and has been practiced by the States concerned.

New Jersey alleges that the proposed diversion will transgress its rights in many respects. That it will interfere with the navigability of the Delaware without the authority of Congress or the Secretary of War. That it will deprive the State and its citizens who are riparian owners of the undiminished flow of the stream to which they are entitled by the common law as adopted by both States. That it will injuriously affect water power and the ability to develop it. That it will injuriously affect the sanitary conditions of the River. That it will do the same to the industrial use of it. That it will increase the salinity of the lower part of the River and of Delaware Bay to the injury of the oyster industry there. That it will injure the shad fisheries. That it will do the same to the municipal water supply of the New Jersey towns and cities on the River. That by lowering the level of the water it will injure the cultivation of adjoining lands; and finally, that it will injuriously affect the River for recreational purposes. The bill also complains of the change of watershed, already disposed of; denies the necessity of the diversion; charges extravagant use of present supplies, and alleges that the plan will violate the Federal Water Power Act, 16 U.S.C.A. §§ 791–823, interfere with interstate commerce, prefer the ports of New York to those of New Jersey and will take the property of New Jersey and its citizens without due process of law. * * *

With regard to water power the Master concludes that any future plan of New Jersey for constructing dams would need the consent of Congress and of the States of New York and Pennsylvania and though possible as a matter of engineering probably would not pay. He adds that there is no such showing of a present interest as to entitle New Jersey to relief. We have spoken at the outset of the more general qualifications of New Jersey's rights as against another State. The Master finds that the taking of 600 millions of gallons daily from the tributaries will not materially affect the River or its sanitary condition, or as a source of municipal water supply, or for industrial uses, or for agriculture, or for the fisheries for shad. The effect upon the use for recreation and upon its reputation in that regard will be somewhat more serious, as will be the effect of increased salinity of the River upon the oyster fisheries. The total is found to be greater than New Jersey ought to bear, but the damage can be removed by reducing the draft of New York to 440 million gallons daily; constructing an efficient plant for the treatment of sewage entering the Delaware or Neversink (the main source of present pollution) thereby reducing the organic impurities 85%, and treating the effluent with a germicide so as to reduce the Bacillus Coli originally present in the sewage by 90%; and finally, subject to the qualifications in the decree, when the stage of the Delaware falls below .50 c.s.m. [cubic feet per second per square mile of drainage] at Port Jervis, New York, or Trenton, New Jersey, by releasing water from the impounding reservoirs of New York, sufficient to restore the flow at those points to .50 c.s.m. We are of opinion that the Master's report should be confirmed and that a decree should be entered to the following effect, subject to such modifications as may be ordered by the Court hereafter.

1. The injunction prayed for by New Jersey so far as it would restrain the State of New York or City of New York from diverting from the Delaware River or its tributaries to the New York City water supply the equivalent of 440 million gallons of water daily is denied, but is granted to restrain the said State and City from diverting water in excess of that amount. The denial of the injunction as above is subject to the following conditions.

(a) Before any diversion shall be made an efficient plant for the treatment of sewage at Port Jervis, New York, shall be constructed and the sewage of Port Jervis entering the Delaware or Neversink Rivers shall be treated to such an extent as to effect a reduction of 85% in the organic impurities. And the effluent from such plant shall be treated with a chemical germicide, or otherwise, so that the B. coli originally present in the sewage shall be reduced by 90%.

Untreated industrial waste from plants in said town of Port Jervis shall not be allowed to enter the Delaware or Neversink Rivers, and the treatment of such industrial wastes shall be such as to render the effluent practically free from suspended matter and non-putrescent; and said treatment of sewage and industrial waste shall be maintained so long as any diversion is made from the Delaware River or its tributaries.

(b) At any time the stage of the Delaware River falls below .50 c.s.m. at Port Jervis, New York, or Trenton, New Jersey, or both (.50 c.s.m. being equivalent to a flow of 1535 c.f.s. at Port Jervis and 3400 c.f.s. at Trenton), water shall be released from one or more of the impounding reservoirs of New York City in sufficient volume to restore the flow at Port Jervis and Trenton to .50 c.s.m., provided, however, that there is not required to be released at any time water in excess of 30% of the diversion area yield, and the diversion area yield having been ascertained to be 2.2 c.s.m., the maximum release required shall be 30% of that amount, or .66 cubic feet per second per square mile of the areas from which water is diverted. * * *

2. The diversion herein allowed shall not constitute a prior appropriation and shall not give the State of New York and City of New York any superiority of right over the State of New Jersey and Commonwealth of Pennsylvania in the enjoyment and use of the Delaware River and its tributaries. * * *

Note

1. **Modification of the Delaware River decree.** Later, the Court modified the apportionment to allow New York to construct a new reservoir and divert a total of 800 million gallons per day, subject to a duty to deliver a minimum flow to New Jersey of 1,750 c.f.s. at Montague. 347 U.S. 995 (1954).

NEBRASKA v. WYOMING

Supreme Court of the United States, 1945.
325 U.S. 589, 65 S.Ct. 1332, 89 L.Ed. 1815.

MR. JUSTICE DOUGLAS delivered the opinion of the Court.

Nebraska brought this suit in 1934 against Wyoming, invoking our original jurisdiction * * *. Colorado was impleaded as a defendant. The United States was granted leave to intervene. * * *

The controversy pertains to the use for irrigation purposes of the water of the North Platte River, a non-navigable stream. * * * The North Platte River rises in Northern Colorado in the mountainous region known as North Park. It proceeds in a northerly direction on the east side of the Continental Divide, enters Wyoming west of Cheyenne, and continues in a northerly direction to the vicinity of Casper. There it turns east across the Great Plains and proceeds easterly and southerly into and across Nebraska. About 40 miles west of the Nebraska line it is joined by the Laramie River. At North Platte, Nebraska, it is joined by the South Platte, forming the Platte River. It empties into the Missouri River at Plattsmouth, near the western border of Iowa. * * *

[The earliest water development from the river occurred in the vicinity of the Nebraska-Wyoming line. Some of the early canals were diverting water in Wyoming and serving Wyoming land. Several others, known as the State Line canals, were diverting water in Nebraska at the Tri-State Dam, located about a mile east of the state line, and serving Nebraska land. The French Canal was diverting in Wyoming but supplying land in both states.

In 1904 the United States Bureau of Reclamation started the North Platte Project with construction of Pathfinder Reservoir, located just above Casper, Wyoming. Later it built Guernsey, a small auxiliary reservoir below Casper. Water from these reservoirs was being released into the river and diverted in eastern Wyoming at Whalen Dam into the Interstate Canal and the Fort Laramie Canal. These canals extend far into Nebraska. They were irrigating some land in Wyoming and a very large acreage in Nebraska. Below Whalen Dam, the principal crops were alfalfa, sugar beets, potatoes and grain.

Above Pathfinder, Wyoming ranchers were irrigating about 168,000 acres of hay lands, mostly from tributaries, and Colorado ranchers were irrigating about 131,000 acres of hay lands. Most of these water rights were junior to the State Line Canals, and about half of them were junior to Pathfinder.

In 1931 the Bureau of Reclamation started the Kendrick Project, consisting of Seminoe Reservoir above Pathfinder and Casper Canal to take water to 35,000 acres of Wyoming land. A few years later, it added Alcova Reservoir, just below Pathfinder.]

Prior to the time when the North Platte project went into operation there was a serious shortage of water for irrigation in western Nebraska and to some extent in eastern Wyoming. Many irrigation enterprises were closed. After the North Platte Project had been in operation for a while most of the projects which had been abandoned were reopened. From then until 1931 the supply was reasonably adequate for most of the canals. But the year 1931 started the driest cycle or swing in the North Platte and Platte River valleys of which there is any record. * * * The flow for each of the years between

1931 and 1940 as compared with the mean of the flow for the 37 year period ending in 1940 was as follows:

1931 ----- 55 per cent	1936 ----- 81 per cent
1932 ----- 116 per cent	1937 ----- 87 per cent
1933 ----- 89 per cent	1938 ----- 103 per cent
1934 ----- 30 per cent	1939 ----- 54 per cent
1935 ----- 54 per cent	1940 ----- 44 per cent

Since 1930 only one year equalled the mean of the 1904 to 1930 period. Previous droughts had not exceeded two or three years. The present cycle has persisted for 13 years.

The commencement of this dry cycle plus the initiation of the Kendrick project precipitated the present controversy. Nebraska rests her case essentially on evidence of shortage and of misappropriation of water by the upper States since 1930 and of threats of more serious shortage and diversions in the future. * * *

* * * Colorado moves to dismiss the proceeding. She asserts that the pleadings and evidence both indicate that she has not injured nor presently threatens to injure any downstream water user. * * * And she emphasizes that during the drought there was a divertible flow passing Tri-State Dam during the irrigation season. The argument is that the case is not of such serious magnitude and the damage is not so fully and clearly proved as to warrant the intervention of this Court under our established practice. * * *

We fully recognize those principles. But they do not stand in the way of an entry of a decree in this case.

The evidence supports the finding of the Special Master that the dependable natural flow of the river during the irrigation season has long been overappropriated. A genuine controversy exists. The States have not been able to settle their differences by compact. * * *

What we have then is a situation where three States assert against a river, whose dependable natural flow during the irrigation season has long been over appropriated, claims based not only on present uses but on projected additional uses as well. * * *

Colorado's motion to dismiss is accordingly denied. * * *

The equitable apportionment which Nebraska seeks is based on the principle of priority of appropriation applied interstate. Colorado and Wyoming have the rule of priority of appropriation as distinguished from the rule of riparian rights. * * * The rights asserted by Nebraska in this suit are based wholly on appropriations which have been obtained and recognized under Nebraska law. The appropriation system is dominant in the regions of Nebraska which are involved in the present litigation. Hence we, like the Special Master, treat the case as one involving appropriation rights not only in Colorado and Wyoming but in Nebraska as well. * * *

* * * The Special Master recommended a decree based on that principle. That was indeed the principle adopted by the Court in State of

Wyoming v. Colorado, where an apportionment of the waters of an interstate stream was made between two States, each of which had the rule of appropriation. * * * Since Colorado, Wyoming, and Nebraska are appropriation States, that principle would seem to be equally applicable here.

That does not mean that there must be a literal application of the priority rule. We stated in State of Colorado v. Kansas, supra, that in determining whether one State is "using, or threatening to use, more than its equitable share of the benefits of a stream, all of the factors which create equities in favor of one state or the other must be weighed as of the date when the controversy is mooted." 320 U.S. page 394, 64 S.Ct. 181, 88 L.Ed. 116. That case did not involve a controversy between two appropriation States. But if an allocation between appropriation States is to be just and equitable, strict adherence to the priority rule may not be possible. For example, the economy of a region may have been established on the basis of junior appropriations. So far as possible those established uses should be protected though strict application of the priority rule might jeopardize them. Apportionment calls for the exercise of an informed judgment on a consideration of many factors. Priority of appropriation is the guiding principle. But physical and climatic conditions, the consumptive use of water in the several sections of the river, the character and rate of return flows, the extent of established uses, the availability of storage water, the practical effect of wasteful uses on downstream areas, the damage to upstream areas as compared to the benefits to downstream areas if a limitation is imposed on the former—these are all relevant factors. They are merely an illustrative not an exhaustive catalogue. They indicate the nature of the problem of apportionment and the delicate adjustment of interests which must be made.

Colorado. Practical considerations of this order underlie Nebraska's concession that the priority rule should not be strictly applied to appropriations in Colorado, though some are junior to the priorities of appropriators in Wyoming and Nebraska. As the Special Master points out the flowage time of water from North Park to Bridgeport, Nebraska is between two and three weeks. If a canal in North Park were closed to relieve the shortage of a senior appropriator in Nebraska, it would be highly speculative whether the water would reach the Nebraska appropriator in time or whether the closing of the Colorado canal would work more hardship there than it would bestow benefits in Nebraska. Moreover, there is loss of water in transit from the upper to the downstream sections, increasing with the distance. The lower appropriator thus receives less than the upper appropriator loses. And there is evidence that a river-wide priority system would disturb and disrupt long established uses. * * *

We are satisfied that a reduction in present Colorado uses is not warranted. The fact that the same amount of water might produce more in lower sections of the river is immaterial. State of Wyoming v. Colorado, supra, page 468, 42 S.Ct. page 558, 66 L.Ed. 999. The established economy in Colorado's section of the river basin based on existing use of the water should be protected. Cf. State of Colorado v. Kansas, supra, 320 U.S. page 394, 64 S.Ct. page 181, 88 L.Ed. page 116. Appropriators in Colorado junior to Pathfinder have made out-of-priority diversions of substantial amounts. Strict application of the priority rule might well result in placing a limitation on Colorado's present use for the benefit of Pathfinder. But as we have said, priority of appropriation, while the guiding principle for an apportionment, is not a hard and fast rule. Colorado's countervailing equities indicate it should not be strictly adhered to in this situation. * * *

Colorado State Line to Pathfinder and Guernsey. The Special Master recommends that Wyoming be enjoined from diverting water from the main river above Guernsey and from its tributaries above Pathfinder for the irrigation of more than 168,000 acres. * * * [M]ost of the land under irrigation in the section above Pathfinder is irrigated from tributaries. The rights are small but very numerous. The total acreage under irrigation is 153,000 acres, allowing for a margin of error. Below Pathfinder and above Guernsey the Special Master dealt only with diversions from the main river. He concluded that the run-off of the tributaries becomes so far exhausted before any shortage of water occurs in the main river that any regulation of the tributary diversions would be of no material benefit. The tributary inflow is greater than the depletion of the river. There is some out-of-priority diversion as we have noted. But possibilities for future developments are largely nonexistent. The Special Master concluded that if Wyoming were limited to the irrigation of 15,000 acres (which is the extent of present irrigation with a margin of error) natural conditions would militate against this section getting more than its equitable share of the water.

We think that is a practical and fair adjustment. So far as the tributaries above Pathfinder are concerned, practical difficulties of applying restrictions which would reduce the amount of water used by the hundreds of small irrigators would seem to outweigh any slight benefit which senior appropriators might obtain. This does not seem to be denied. * * *

Pathfinder, Guernsey, Seminoe and Alcova Reservoirs and the Casper Canal. The priority of Pathfinder is December 6, 1904 and of Guernsey April 20, 1923. Between Pathfinder and the Nebraska state line there are 32 canals on the main river which have priorities senior to Pathfinder. The State Line Canals in Nebraska also are senior to Pathfinder. And Guernsey is junior to all canals below it down to the Nebraska line. * * * Under Wyoming law reservoirs in storing water must observe the priority of all senior, Wyoming canals below them on the main river. * * * Seminoe Reservoir has a priority of December 1, 1931; Casper Canal, July 27, 1934 (natural flow); Alcova Reservoir, April 25, 1936. Apart from minor exceptions Seminoe is junior to every appropriator from Alcova to the Tri-State Dam. The project is expected to operate chiefly on storage water. * * * The Special Master found * * * that without violating the Pathfinder priority, the Kendrick Project [the Seminoe and Alcova Reservoirs and the Casper Canal] could have stored no water since 1930 and can store none in the future if present conditions continue. He also found that under the average conditions which prevailed from 1895 to 1939 water could be conserved by Seminoe and Alcova without violation of the priorities between Pathfinder and Tri-State Dam and in sufficient quantities to supply Kendrick and to leave considerable return flow to the river in the irrigation season. * * * The Special Master recommends that Wyoming be enjoined from the storage of water in these four reservoirs and from the diversion of natural flow water through the Casper Canal for the Kendrick Project, between and including May 1 and September 30 of each year, otherwise than in accordance with the rule of priority in relation to the appropriations of the Nebraska lands supplied by the French Canal and by the State Line Canals; that all those Nebraska appropriations for that purpose be adjudged senior to those four reservoirs and to Casper Canal. * * *

We have noted the priorities of Pathfinder and Guernsey, as well as those of the Kendrick Project. We have noted that their priorities make them junior to many downstream appropriators including the State Line Canals. While the four reservoirs in question are Wyoming appropriators, Pathfinder and Guernsey were designed more for the benefit of Nebraska than of Wyoming lands. Recognition of the priorities interstate makes obvious the propriety of an interstate apportionment. * * *

The Special Master recommends that Wyoming be enjoined to respect the rule of priority of these reservoirs in respect to each other and that the order of seniority as between them be defined as follows: (1) Pathfinder, (2) Guernsey, (3) Seminoe, and (4) Alcova. * * * [The Court accepted these recommendations.]

Whalen to Tri-State Dam. This is the pivotal section of the river around which the central problems of this case turn. Apart from the Kendrick project, the demand for water is as great in this short section of the river as in the entire preceding 415 miles from North Park to Whalen. The lands irrigated from the river in this section total 326,000 acres as compared with 339,200 acres in the upper valley—main river and tributaries. The consumptive use on this 326,000 acres far exceeds that of the upper sections combined. * * *

As respects priority, the canals * * * fall into thirteen groups, seven in Wyoming and six in Nebraska. The earliest in priority are some canals in Wyoming, then some in Nebraska, then others in Wyoming and so on. * * *

[The Special Master] proposes that the natural flow water in this section between May 1 and September 30 each year be apportioned [daily] on the basis of 25 per cent to Wyoming and 75 per cent to Nebraska. He recommends that Nebraska be given the right to designate from time to time the portion of its share which shall be delivered to the Interstate, Ft. Laramie, French and Mitchell Canals for use on Nebraska lands served by them and that Wyoming be enjoined from diversions contrary to this apportionment.

None of the parties agrees to this apportionment. * * *

Wyoming argues for a mass allocation, e.g. 705,000 acre feet to be allocated to Nebraska for diversion in this section during the irrigation season for Nebraska lands. The Special Master rejected that method. He concluded that it was based on an assumption of dependability of flow which would be bound to result in injustice to one or other of the States * * *. We [conclude] that the inadequacy of the supply is too clear to permit adoption of Wyoming's formula. * * *

The United States and Nebraska advance as their preferred alternative a strict priority apportionment in which the rights of each appropriator would be fixed. Wyoming says that may not be done since the appropriators are not parties to this proceeding. The Special Master had serious doubts on that score. He also felt that an interstate priority schedule for this section, while not open to all the objections which would be present if it were applied to the whole river, would have other objections. Those were (1) that it would deprive each State of full freedom of intrastate administration of her share of the water and (2) that it would burden the decree with administrative detail beyond what is necessary to an equitable apportionment. Our judgment is that these latter considerations without more are sufficient justification for rejection of the strict priority allocation advanced by the United States and Nebraska. An equitable apportionment may be had without fashioning a decree of that detail. And greater administrative flexibility may be achieved within the respective States by choice of another alternative.

* * * Our problem is not to determine what allocation would be equitable among the canals in Nebraska or among those in Wyoming. That is a problem of internal administration for each of the States. Our problem involves only an appraisal of the equities between the claimants whom Wyoming represents on the one hand and those represented by Nebraska on the other. We conclude that the early Wyoming uses, the return flows, and the greater storage water rights which Nebraska appropriators have in this section as compared with those of Wyoming appropriators tip the scales in favor of the flat percentage system recommended by the Special Master. It should be noted, moreover, that that method of apportionment, though not strictly adhering to the principle of priority, gives it great weight and does not cause as great a distortion as might appear to be the case. * * *

Accordingly, we conclude that the flat percentage method recommended by the Special Master is the most equitable method of apportionment. * * *

[The dissenting opinion of JUSTICE ROBERTS, joined by JUSTICES FRANKFURTER and RUTLEDGE is omitted.]

Notes

1. **Modification and interpretation of the North Platte River decree.** In 1953, the Court modified the apportionment based on the parties' stipulation to account for construction of a dam in Wyoming serving land both there and in Nebraska. 345 U.S. 981 (1953). In 1993, it awarded a 1904 priority to several off-channel reservoirs the Bureau of Reclamation operated as part of the North Platte Project and ruled that the original decree did not cap diversions by individual Nebraska canals in the pivotal river section between Whalen and the Tri-State Dam because the decree expressly gave Nebraska freedom to allocate its seventy-five percent share of the flow among its canals as it might see fit. 507 U.S. 584 (1993).

2. **Modification versus enforcement of a decree.** In the 1993 North Platte River litigation, Nebraska sought modification of the original decree to prevent proposed Wyoming storage projects on North Platte tributaries that it claimed

would adversely affect downstream wildlife habitat within its borders. The Court distinguished between modification and enforcement of a decree:

"In an enforcement action, the plaintiff need not show injury. When the alleged conduct is admitted, the only question is whether that conduct violates a right established by the decree. To be sure, the right need not be stated explicitly in the decree. * * * [W]hen the decree is silent or unclear, it is appropriate to consider the underlying opinion, the Master's Report, and the record in the prior proceedings to determine whether the Court previously resolved the issue. The parties' course of conduct under the decree also may be relevant. But the underlying issue primarily remains one of interpretation. In a modification proceeding, by contrast, there is by definition no pre-existing right to interpret or enforce. At least where the case concerns the impact of new development, the inquiry may well entail the same sort of balancing of equities that occurs in an initial proceeding to establish an equitable apportionment. See Nebraska v. Wyoming, 325 U.S., at 618, 65 S.Ct., at 1350 (listing equitable considerations). * * * [W]hen the plaintiff essentially seeks a reweighing of equities and an injunction declaring new rights and responsibilities, we think the plaintiff still must make a showing of substantial injury to be entitled to relief. That is so not only because a new injunction would work a new infringement on sovereign prerogatives, but also because the interests of certainty and stability counsel strongly against reopening an apportionment of interstate water rights absent considerable justification." 507 U.S. at 592-93.

In a follow-up opinion, the Court said adverse wildlife or wildlife habitat effects in Nebraska, if proved, would be a relevant factor in balancing the equities. 515 U.S. 1 (1995).

3. **Barriers to Supreme Court apportionment.** The Court has issued apportionment decrees for only the Laramie, Delaware, and North Platte Rivers. It has declined to apportion several other rivers under a principle stated as follows in New York v. New Jersey, 256 U.S. 296 (1921): "Before this court can be moved to exercise its extraordinary power under the Constitution to control the conduct of one state at the suit of another, the threatened invasion of rights must be of serious magnitude and it must be established by clear and convincing evidence." See Colorado v. Kansas, supra p. 465, Note 3; Washington v. Oregon, 297 U.S. 517 (1936); Connecticut v. Massachusetts, 282 U.S. 660 (1931).

Another potential barrier to Supreme Court apportionment is that the United States might have sufficient interest in a river to require its presence in an equitable apportionment suit, but its sovereign immunity prevents it from being sued without its consent. In Arizona v. California, 298 U.S. 558 (1936), Arizona petitioned for leave to sue the other states in the Colorado River basin for apportionment of the unappropriated water in the river. The Court dismissed the petition on the ground that the United States was an indispensable party because of its paramount power over the unappropriated waters for the purpose of controlling navigation. Similarly, the Court dismissed Texas v. New Mexico, 352 U.S. 991 (1957) (a suit for breach of an interstate water compact), after six years of litigation, including two references to a special master, because of the absence of the United States as an indispensable party. There, the interest of the United States arose from its role as trustee for Indian tribes.

Although the United States cannot be compelled to appear in a water apportionment suit between states, it may appear voluntarily. For example, the United States intervened in Arizona v. California, 344 U.S. 919 (1953).

Federal interests in a river do not always raise a sovereign immunity bar to equitable apportionment. The principal case, Nebraska v. Wyoming, involved the nonnavigable North Platte River. Wyoming moved to dismiss on the ground that the Secretary of the Interior was an indispensable but absent party. The Court responded: "The bill alleges, and we know as [a] matter of law, that the Secretary and his agents, acting by authority of the Reclamation Act and supplementary legislation, must obtain permits and priorities for the use of water from the State of Wyoming in the same manner as a private appropriator or an irrigation district formed under the state law. His rights can rise no higher than those of Wyoming, and an adjudication of the defendant's rights will necessarily bind him. Wyoming will stand in judgment for him as for any other appropriator in that state. He is not a necessary party." Nebraska v. Wyoming, 295 U.S. 40 (1935).

Congress has consented to the joinder of the United States, as a defendant or otherwise, in a suit by any state of the Colorado River Basin to enforce compliance by the Secretary of the Interior with water compacts and federal laws in storing and releasing water from reservoirs in the basin. Colorado River Storage Project Act § 14, 43 U.S.C. § 620m.

COLORADO v. NEW MEXICO

Supreme Court of the United States, 1982.
459 U.S. 176, 103 S. Ct. 539, 74 L. Ed.2d 348.

JUSTICE MARSHALL delivered the opinion of the Court. * * *

The Vermejo River is a small, nonnavigable river that originates in the snow-belt of the Rocky Mountains in southern Colorado and flows southeasterly into New Mexico for a distance of roughly 55 miles before it joins the Canadian River. The major portion of the river is located in New Mexico. The Colorado portion consists of three main tributaries that combine to form the Vermejo River proper approximately one mile below the Colorado-New Mexico border. At present there are no uses of the water of the Vermejo River in Colorado, and no use or diversion has ever been made in Colorado. In New Mexico, by contrast, farmers and industrial users have diverted water from the Vermejo for many years. In 1941 a New Mexico state court issued a decree apportioning the water of the Vermejo River among the various New Mexico users.

In 1975, a Colorado corporation, Colorado Fuel and Iron Steel Corporation ("C.F. & I."), obtained in Colorado state court a conditional right to divert 75 cubic feet per second from the headwaters of the Vermejo River. C.F. & I. proposed a transmountain diversion of the water to a tributary of the Purgatoire River in Colorado to be used for industrial development and other purposes. * * *

The Special Master found that most of the water of the Vermejo River is consumed by the New Mexico users and that very little, if any, reaches the confluence with the Canadian River. He thus recognized that strict application of the rule of priority would not permit Colorado any diversion since the entire available supply is needed to satisfy the demands of appropriators in New Mexico with senior rights. Nevertheless, applying the principle of equitable apportionment established in our prior cases, he recommended permitting Colorado a transmountain diversion of 4,000 acre-feet of water per year from the headwaters of the Vermejo River. * * *

Explaining his conclusion, the Special Master noted that any injury to New Mexico would be restricted to the [Vermejo] Conservancy District, the user in New Mexico furthest downstream, since there was sufficient water in the Vermejo River for the three other principal New Mexico water users, Vermejo Park, Kaiser Steel, and Phelps Dodge. He further found that the "Vermejo Conservancy District has never been an economically feasible operation." * * *

Equitable apportionment is the doctrine of federal common law that governs disputes between states concerning their rights to use the water of an interstate stream. It is a flexible doctrine which calls for "the exercise of an informed judgment on a consideration of many factors" to secure a "just and equitable" allocation. Nebraska v. Wyoming, 325 U.S. 589, 618, 65 S.Ct. 1332, 1350–1351, 89 L.Ed. 1815 (1945). * * *

In reaching his recommendation the Special Master did not focus exclusively on the rule of priority, but considered other factors such as the efficiency of current uses in New Mexico and the balance of benefits to Colorado and harm to New Mexico. New Mexico contends that it is improper to consider these other factors. It maintains that this Court has strictly applied the rule of priority when apportioning water between states adhering to the prior appropriation doctrine, and has departed from that rule only to protect an existing economy built upon junior appropriations. Since there is no existing economy in Colorado dependent upon the use of water from the Vermejo River, New Mexico contends that the rule of priority is controlling. We disagree with this inflexible interpretation of the doctrine of equitable apportionment.

Our prior cases clearly establish that equitable apportionment will protect only those rights to water that are "reasonably acquired and applied." Wyoming v. Colorado, 259 U.S. 419, 484, 42 S.Ct. 552, 564, 66 L.Ed. 999 (1922). Especially in those Western states where water is scarce, "[t]here must be no waste * * * of the 'treasure' of a river * * *. Only diligence and good faith will keep the privilege alive." Washington v. Oregon, 297 U.S. 517, 527, 56 S.Ct. 540, 544–545, 80 L.Ed. 837 (1936). Thus, wasteful or inefficient uses will not be protected. Similarly, concededly senior water rights will be deemed forfeited or substantially diminished where the rights have not been exercised or asserted with reasonable diligence. Washington v. Oregon, 297 U.S., at 527-528, 56 S.Ct., at 544-545 (1936); Colorado v. Kansas, 320 U.S. 383, 394, 64 S.Ct. 176, 181, 88 L.Ed. 116 (1943).

We have invoked equitable apportionment not only to require the reasonably efficient use of water, but also to impose on states an affirmative duty to take reasonable steps to conserve and augment the water supply of an interstate stream. In Wyoming v. Colorado, Wyoming brought suit to prevent a *proposed* diversion by Colorado from the Laramie River. This Court calculated the dependable supply available to both states, subtracted the senior Wyoming uses, and permitted Colorado to divert an amount not exceeding the balance. In calculating the dependable supply we placed on each state the duty to employ "financially and physically feasible" measures "adapted to *conserving and equalizing* the natural flow." 259 U.S., at 484, 42 S.Ct., at 564 (emphasis added). * * *

We conclude that it is entirely appropriate to consider the extent to which reasonable conservation measures by New Mexico might offset the proposed Colorado diversion and thereby minimize any injury to New Mexico users. Similarly, it is appropriate to consider whether Colorado has undertaken reasonable steps to minimize the amount of diversion that will be required.

In addition, we have held that in an equitable apportionment of interstate waters it is proper to weigh the harms and benefits to competing states. In Kansas v. Colorado, supra, where we first announced the doctrine of equitable apportionment, we found that users in Kansas were injured by Colorado's upstream diversions from the Arkansas River. 206 U.S., at 113-114, 117, 27 S.Ct., at 674, 675-676. Yet we declined to grant any relief to Kansas on the ground that the great benefit to Colorado outweighed the detriment to Kansas. Similarly, in Nebraska v. Wyoming, we held that water rights in Wyoming and Nebraska, which under state law were senior, had to yield to the "countervailing equities" of an established economy in Colorado even though it was based on junior appropriations. 325 U.S., at 622, 65 S.Ct., at 1352. We noted that the rule of priority should not be strictly applied where it "would work more hardship" on the junior user "than it would bestow benefits" on the senior user. Id., at 619, 65 S.Ct., at 1351. The same principle is applicable in balancing the benefits of a diversion for *proposed* uses against the possible harms to existing ones.

We recognize that the equities supporting the protection of existing economies will usually be compelling. The harm that may result from disrupting established uses is typically certain and immediate, whereas the potential benefits from a proposed diversion may be speculative and remote. Under some circumstances, however, the countervailing equities supporting a diversion for future use in one state may justify the detriment to existing users in another state. This may be the case, for example, where the state seeking a diversion demonstrates by clear and convincing evidence that the benefits of the diversion substantially outweigh the harm that might result.[13]

---

13. Our cases establish that a state seeking to prevent or enjoin a diversion by another state bears the burden of proving that the diversion will cause it "real or substantial injury or damage." Connecticut v. Massachusetts, supra, 282 U.S., at 672, 51 S.Ct., at 290. See also Colorado v. Kansas, 320 U.S., at 393-394, 64 S.Ct., at 180-181. This rule applies even if the state seeking to prevent or enjoin a diversion is the nominal defendant in a lawsuit. * * *

New Mexico must therefore bear the initial burden of showing that a diversion by Colorado will cause substantial injury to the interests of New Mcxico. In this case New Mexico

In the determination of whether the state proposing the diversion has carried this burden, an important consideration is whether the existing users could offset the diversion by reasonable conservation measures to prevent waste. This approach comports with our emphasis on flexibility in equitable apportionment and also accords sufficient protection to existing uses. * * *

We conclude, therefore, that in the determination of an equitable apportionment of the water of the Vermejo River the rule of priority is not the sole criterion. While the equities supporting the protection of established, senior uses are substantial, it is also appropriate to consider additional factors relevant to a just apportionment, such as the conservation measures available to both states and the balance of harm and benefit that might result from the diversion sought by Colorado.

Applying the doctrine of equitable apportionment, the Special Master recommended that Colorado be permitted to divert 4,000 acre-feet of water per year from the headwaters of the Vermejo River. Because all of the water of the Vermejo River is currently consumed by New Mexico appropriators, the recommended diversion would necessarily reduce the amount of water available to New Mexico.

In explaining the basis for his recommendation, the Special Master stated that the diversion would not "materially affect" existing New Mexico appropriations. This conclusion appears to reflect certain assumptions about the ability of New Mexico users to implement water conservation measures. The Special Master also concluded that any injury to New Mexico would be "more than offset" by the benefits to Colorado. Both the availability of conservation measures and a weighing of the harm and benefits that would result from the diversion are factors relevant to the determination of a just and equitable apportionment. However, the Special Master did not clearly state the factual findings supporting his reliance on these factors. * * * We remand for specific factual findings relevant to determining a just and equitable apportionment of the water of the Vermejo River between Colorado and New Mexico.

It is so ordered.

[The concurring opinion of CHIEF JUSTICE BURGER, joined by JUSTICE STEVENS, is omitted.]

---

has met its burden since *any* diversion by Colorado, unless offset by New Mexico at its own expense, will necessarily reduce the amount of water available to New Mexico users.

The burden has therefore shifted to Colorado to establish that a diversion should nevertheless be permitted under the principle of equitable apportionment. Thus, with respect to whether reasonable conservation measures by New Mexico will offset the loss of water due to Colorado's diversion, or whether the benefit to Colorado from the diversion will substantially outweigh the possible harm to New Mexico, Colorado will bear the burden of proof. It must show, in effect, that without such a diversion New Mexico would be using "more than its equitable share of the benefits of a stream." Id., at 394, 64 S.Ct., at 181. Moreover, Colorado must establish not only that its claim is of a "serious magnitude," but also that its position is supported by "clear and convincing evidence." Connecticut v. Massachusetts, 282 U.S., at 669, 51 S.Ct., at 289.

JUSTICE O'CONNOR, with whom JUSTICE POWELL, joins, concurring in the judgment.

The doctrine of prior appropriation includes the requirement that the appropriator's use of water be beneficial and reasonable. What is reasonable, of course, does not admit of ready definition, being dependent upon the particular facts and circumstances of each case. In this case, the Special Master has cast an accusatory finger at the Vermejo Conservancy District, concluding that "[t]he system of canals used to transport the water to the fields is inefficient."

Undoubtedly, there is evidence in the record indicating that large losses of water occur through seepage and evaporation in transporting waters of the Vermejo through open ditches for irrigation and stock watering. It is a leap, however, from observing that large losses occur to concluding, as Colorado would have the Court do, that the practices of the Conservancy District are wasteful or unreasonable. As the Court observes, the extent of the duty to conserve that may be placed upon the user is limited to measures that are "financially and physically feasible," Wyoming v. Colorado, 259 U.S. 419, 484, 42 S.Ct. 552, 564, 66 L.Ed. 999 (1922), and "within practicable limits." Ibid.[1] Nevertheless, in concluding that the Conservancy District's distribution system is "inefficient," the Special Master made no factual finding that improved economy in that system is within the practicable means available to the District.

Colorado would have the Court assess the Conservancy District's "waste" and "inefficiency" by a new yardstick—i.e., not by comparing the economic gains to the District with the costs of achieving greater efficiency, but by comparing the "inefficiency" of New Mexico's uses with the relative benefits to Colorado of a new use. The Special Master has succumbed to this suggestion. His recommendation that Colorado be permitted a diversion embodies the judgment that, because Colorado can, in some *unidentified* sense, make "better" use of the waters of the Vermejo, New Mexico may be forced to change her present uses.

Today the Court has also gone dangerously far toward accepting that suggestion. The Court holds that it is appropriate in equitable apportionment litigation to weigh the harms and benefits to the competing States. It does so notwithstanding its recognition that the potential benefits from a *proposed* diversion are likely to be speculative and remote, and therefore difficult to balance against any threatened harms, and its concession that the equities supporting protection of an existing economy will usually be compelling.

This case therefore highlights the restraint with which the Court should proceed in apportioning interstate waters between a State seeking a *future* use

---

1. It is significant to note that in Wyoming v. Colorado, 259 U.S. 419, 42 S.Ct. 552, 66 L.Ed. 999 (1922), upon which the Court relies for the proposition that an affirmative duty to conserve may be imposed on the States, the Wyoming appropriators already had storage facilities in place for equalizing the river's natural flow. * * *

and a State with an existing economy dependent upon the waters to be apportioned. * * *

COLORADO v. NEW MEXICO

Supreme Court of the United States, 1984.
467 U.S. 310, 104 S. Ct. 2433, 81 L. Ed.2d 247.

JUSTICE O'CONNOR delivered the opinion of the Court.

* * * Last Term, because our initial inquiry turned on the factors relevant to determining a just apportionment, the Court explained in detail the law of equitable apportionment. This Term, because our inquiry turns on the evidentiary material Colorado has offered in support of its complaint, we find it necessary to explain the standard by which we judge proof in actions for equitable apportionment. * * *

Last Term, the Court made clear that Colorado's proof would be judged by a clear-and-convincing-evidence standard. * * * Requiring Colorado to present clear and convincing evidence in support of its proposed diversion is necessary to appropriately balance the unique interests involved in water rights disputes between sovereigns. The standard reflects this Court's long-held view that a proposed diverter should bear most, though not all, of the risks of erroneous decision: "The harm that may result from disrupting established uses is typically certain and immediate, whereas the potential benefits from a proposed diversion may be speculative and remote." Colorado v. New Mexico, 459 U.S., at 187, 103 S.Ct., at 547. In addition, the clear-and-convincing-evidence standard accommodates society's competing interests in increasing the stability of property rights and in putting resources to their most efficient uses: "[T]he rule of priority [will] not be strictly applied where it 'would work more hardship' on the junior user 'than it would bestow benefits' on the senior user * * * [, though] the equities supporting the protection of existing economies will usually be compelling." Id., at 186, 103 S.Ct., at 547. In short, Colorado's diversion should and will be allowed only if actual inefficiencies in present uses or future benefits from other uses are highly probable. * * * Upon our independent review of the record, we find that Colorado has failed to meet its burden.

To establish whether Colorado's proposed diversion could be offset by eliminating New Mexico's nonuse or inefficiency, we asked the Master to make specific findings concerning existing uses, supplies of water, and reasonable conservation measures available to the two States. After assessing the evidence both States offered about existing uses and available supplies, the Master concluded that "current levels of use primarily reflect failure on the part of existing users to fully develop and put to work available water." Moreover, with respect to reasonable conservation measures available, the Master indicated his belief that more careful water administration in New Mexico would alleviate shortages from unregulated stockponds, fishponds, and water detention structures, prevent waste from blockage and clogging in canals, and ensure that users fully devote themselves to development of available resources. He further concluded that "the heart of New Mexico's water problem is the Vermejo Conservancy District," which he considered a failed "reclamation project [that had] never lived up to its expectations or even proved to be a successful project, * * * and [that] quite possibly should never have been built." Though the District was quite arguably in the "middle range in reclamation project efficiencies," the Master was of the opinion "that [the District's] inefficient water use should not be charged to Colorado." Furthermore, though Colorado had not submitted evidence or testimony of any conservation measures that C.F. & I. would take, the Master concluded that "it is not for the Master or for New Mexico to say that reasonable attempts to conserve water will not be implemented by Colorado."

We share the Master's concern that New Mexico may be overstating the amount of harm its users would suffer from a diversion. Water use by appropriators along the Vermejo River has remained relatively stable for the past 30 years, and this historic use falls substantially below the decreed rights of those users. Unreliable supplies satisfactorily explain some of this difference, but New Mexico's attempt to excuse three decades of nonuse in this way is, at the very least, suspect. Nevertheless, whatever the merit of New Mexico's explanation, we cannot agree that Colorado has met its burden of identifying, by clear and convincing evidence, conservation efforts that would preserve any of the Vermejo River water supply.

For example, though Colorado alleged that New Mexico could improve its administration of stockponds, fishponds, and water detention structures, it did not actually point to specific measures New Mexico could take to conserve water. * * *

Colorado's attack on current water use in the Vermejo Conservancy District is inadequate for much the same reason. Our cases require only conservation measures that are "financially and physically feasible" and "within practicable limits." See, e.g., Colorado v. New Mexico, supra, 459 U.S., at 192, 103 S.Ct., at 550; Wyoming v. Colorado, 259 U.S. 419, 484, 42 S.Ct. 552, 564, 66 L.Ed. 999 (1922). New Mexico submitted substantial evidence that the District is in the middle of reclamation project efficiencies and that the District has taken considerable independent steps—including, the construction, at its own expense and on its own initiative, of a closed stockwater delivery system—to improve the efficiency of its future water use. * * * Colorado has not identified any "financially and physically feasible" means by which the District can further eliminate or reduce inefficiency and, contrary to the Master's suggestion, we believe that the burden is on Colorado to do so. A State can carry its burden of proof in an equitable apportionment action only with specific evidence about how existing uses might be improved, or with clear evidence that a project is far less efficient than most other projects. Mere assertions about the relative efficiencies of competing projects will not do.

Finally, there is no evidence in the record that "Colorado has undertaken reasonable steps to minimize the amount of the diversion that will be required." Colorado v. New Mexico, supra, 459 U.S., at 186, 103 S.Ct., at 547. Nine years have passed since C.F. & I. first proposed diverting water from the Vermejo River. Yet Colorado has presented no evidence concerning C.F. & I.'s inability to relieve its needs through substitute sources. Furthermore, there is no evidence that C.F. & I. has settled on a definite or even tentative construction design or plan, or that it has prepared an economic analysis of its proposed diversion. * * *

Society's interest in minimizing erroneous decisions in equitable apportionment cases requires that hard facts, not suppositions or opinions, be the basis for interstate diversions. In contrast to Justice Stevens, we do not believe Colorado has produced sufficient facts to show, by clear and convincing evidence, that reasonable conservation efforts will mitigate sufficiently the injury that New Mexico successfully established last Term that it would suffer were a diversion allowed. No State can use its lax administration to establish its claim to water. But once a State successfully proves that a diversion will cause it injury, the burden shifts to the diverter to show reasonable conservation measures exist. Colorado has not carried this burden.

We also asked the Master to help us balance the benefits and harms that might result from the proposed diversion. The Master found that Colorado's proposed interim use is agricultural in nature and that more permanent applications might include use in coal mines, timbering, power generation, domestic needs, and other industrial operations. The Master admitted that "[t]his area of fact finding [was] one of the most difficult [both] because of the necessarily speculative nature of [the] benefits * * *" and because of Colorado's "natural reluctance to spend large amounts of time and money developing plans, operations, and cost schemes * * *." Nevertheless, because the diverted water would, at a minimum, alleviate existing water shortages in Colorado, the Master concluded that the evidence showed considerable benefits would accrue from the diversion. * * *

Again, we find ourselves without adequate evidence to approve Colorado's proposed diversion. Colorado has not committed itself to any long-term use for which future benefits can be studied and predicted. Nor has Colorado specified how long the interim agricultural use might or might not last. All Colorado has established is that a steel corporation wants to take water for some unidentified use in the future.

By contrast, New Mexico has attempted to identify the harms that would result from the proposed diversion. New Mexico commissioned some independent economists to study the economic effects, direct and indirect, that the diversion would have on persons in New Mexico. * * * No doubt, this economic analysis involved prediction and forecast. But the analysis is surely no more speculative than the generalizations Colorado has offered as "evidence." New Mexico, at the very least, has taken concrete steps toward addressing the query this Court posed last Term. Colorado has made no similar effort.

Colorado objects that speculation about the benefits of future uses is inevitable and that water will not be put to its best use if the expenditures necessary to development and operation must be made without assurance of future supplies. We agree, of course, that asking for absolute precision in forecasts about the benefits and harms of a diversion would be unrealistic.

But we have not asked for such precision. We have only required that a State proposing a diversion conceive and implement some type of long-range planning and analysis of the diversion it proposes. Long-range planning and analysis will, we believe, reduce the uncertainties with which equitable apportionment judgments are made. If New Mexico can develop evidence to prove that its existing economy is efficiently using water, we see no reason why Colorado cannot take similar steps to prove that its future economy could do better. * * *

As a final consideration, the Master pointed out that approximately three-fourths of the water in the Vermejo River system is produced in Colorado. He concluded, therefore, that "the equities are with Colorado, which requests only a portion of the water which it produces." Last Term, the Court rejected the notion that the mere fact that the Vermejo River originates in Colorado automatically entitles Colorado to a share of the river's waters. Both Colorado and New Mexico recognize the doctrine of prior appropriation, and appropriative, as opposed to riparian, rights depend on actual use, not land ownership. It follows, therefore, that the equitable apportionment of appropriated rights should turn on the benefits, harms, and efficiencies of competing uses, and that the source of the Vermejo River's waters should be essentially irrelevant to the adjudication of these sovereigns' competing claims. To the extent the Master continued to think the contrary, he was in error. * * *

Accordingly, we sustain the State of New Mexico's exceptions to the Special Master's Report and Additional Factual Findings, and dismiss the case. * * *

Note

Foundation of the doctrine of equitable apportionment. In Idaho ex rel. Evans v. Oregon, 462 U.S. 1017 (1983), Idaho sought an equitable apportionment of anadromous fish (chinook salmon and steelhead trout) that migrate from the Pacific Ocean up the Columbia River and then the Snake River to spawning grounds in Idaho. The Court held that the doctrine of equitable apportionment governs disputes between states over the allocation of fish as well as water. In justifying extension of the doctrine to fish, the Court added a new thought about the foundation of equitable apportionment:

"The doctrine of equitable apportionment is neither dependent on nor bound by existing legal rights to the resource being apportioned. The fact that no State has a pre-existing legal right of ownership in the fish does not prevent an equitable apportionment. Conversely, although existing legal entitlements are important factors in formulating an equitable decree, such legal rights must give way in some circumstances to broader equitable considerations. * * *

"At the root of the doctrine is the same principle that animates many of the Court's Commerce Clause cases: a State may not preserve solely for its own inhabitants natural resources located within its borders. Consistent with this principle, States have an affirmative duty under the doctrine of equitable apportionment to take reasonable steps to conserve and even to augment the natural resources within their borders for the benefit of other States. Even though

Idaho has no legal right to the anadromous fish hatched in its waters, it has an equitable right to a fair distribution of this important resource." Id. at 1025.

While the Court found that Washington and Oregon had allowed some overfishing of the Columbia River, it agreed with the Special Master that Idaho failed to carry its burden of proving a substantial likelihood of future injury. The Court dismissed the action without prejudice to new proceedings should it later appear that Idaho is being deprived of its equitable share of the fish.

SECTION 2. INTERSTATE COMPACTS

HINDERLIDER v. LA PLATA RIVER & CHERRY CREEK DITCH CO.

Supreme Court of the United States, 1938.
304 U.S. 92, 58 S. Ct. 803, 82 L. Ed. 1202.

MR. JUSTICE BRANDEIS delivered the opinion of the Court.

The La Plata River & Cherry Creek Ditch Company, a Colorado corporation, owns a ditch by which it diverts from that river in Colorado water for irrigation. On July 5, 1928, it brought in the district court for La Plata county a suit which charged that since June 24, 1928, the defendants, Hinderlider, State Engineer of Colorado, and his subordinates, have so administered the water of the river as to deprive the plaintiff of water which it claims the right to divert. A mandatory injunction was sought.

The defendants admit that in administering the water of the stream during the period named they shut the headgate of the Ditch Company so as to deprive it of water for purposes of irrigation; but assert that they did so pursuant to the requirements of the La Plata River Compact entered into by the States of Colorado and New Mexico with the consent of the Congress of the United States [in 1925].

The Compact provides that each State shall receive a definite share of water under the varying conditions which obtain during the year, and, among other things: * * *

> "3. Whenever the flow of the river is so low that in the judgment of the State engineers of the States the greatest beneficial use of its waters may be secured by distributing all of its water successively to the lands in each State in alternating periods, in lieu of delivery of water as provided in the second paragraph of this article, the use of the waters may be so rotated between the two States in such manner, for such periods, and to continue for such time as the State Engineers may jointly determine."

* * * During the ten days commencing June 24, 1928, all the water of the river (except small amounts diverted in Colorado for domestic and stock requirements was thus allowed to pass to New Mexico; and during the succeeding ten-day period all the water in the stream was similarly allowed to be diverted in Colorado. The defendant water officials contend that in so rotating the water of the stream they administered it as required by the Compact and wisely. * * *

The relative rights of all claimants to divert in Colorado water from the La Plata River were adjudicated in a proceeding under the Colorado statutes. By decree therein of January 12, 1898 (and later amended), the Ditch Company was declared entitled to divert 393 cubic feet of water per second, subject to five senior priorities aggregating 19 second feet. On June 24, 1928, there was in the stream, at the recognized Colorado gauging station, 57 second feet of water. The Ditch Company claimed that by reason of the 1898 decree it was entitled to all the water in the stream except that required to satisfy the Colorado priorities. If it had been permitted to draw all that water, none would have been available to the New Mexico water claimants, who, under similar laws, had made appropriations. Some of them were earlier in date than the Ditch Company's.

[Colorado courts rejected the compact defense and ordered the defendants to permit the plaintiff to divert water whenever there was water in the stream not subject to prior Colorado appropriations. The United States Supreme Court reversed on the following rationale:]

First. As the La Plata River flows from Colorado into New Mexico and in each State the water is used beneficially, it must be equitably apportioned between the two. The decision below in effect ignores that rule. It holds immaterial the fact that the acts complained of were being done in compliance with the Compact, and does so on the ground that the Compact authorizing diversion and rotation violated rights awarded by the January 12, 1898 decree in the Colorado water proceeding * * *.

It may be assumed that the right adjudicated by the decree of January 12, 1898 to the Ditch Company is a property right, indefeasible so far as concerns the State of Colorado, its citizens, and any other person claiming water rights there. But the Colorado decree could not confer upon the Ditch Company rights in excess of Colorado's share of the water of the stream; and its share was only an equitable portion thereof. * * *

Second. The declared purpose of the Compact was, as the preamble recites, equitable apportionment. * * * The extent of the existing equitable right of Colorado and of New Mexico in the La Plata River could obviously have been determined by a suit in this Court, as was done in Kansas v. Colorado, in respect to rights in the Arkansas River and in Wyoming v. Colorado, in respect to the Laramie. But resort to the judicial remedy is never essential to the adjustment of interstate controversies, unless the States are unable to agree upon the terms of a compact, or Congress refuses its consent. The difficulties incident to litigation have led States to resort, with frequency, to adjustment of their controversies by compact, even where the matter in dispute was the relatively simple one of a boundary. * * *

Third. Whether the apportionment of the water of an interstate stream be made by compact between the upper and lower States with the consent of Congress or by a decree of this Court, the apportionment is binding upon the citizens of each State and all water claimants, even where the State had granted the water rights before it entered into the compact. That the private rights of grantees of a State are determined by the adjustment by compact of a disputed boundary was settled a century ago in Poole v. Fleeger, 11 Pet. 185, 209, 9 L.Ed. 680. * * *

Fourth. As the States had power to bind by compact their respective appropriators by division of the flow of the stream, they had power to reach that end either by providing for a continuous equal division of the water from time to time in the stream, or by providing for alternate periods of flow to the one State and to the other of all the water in the stream. To secure "the greatest beneficial use of" the water in the stream, the Compact provided that the water may be "rotated between the two States, in such manner for such periods, and to continue for such time as the State Engineers may jointly determine." That such alternate rotating flow was then a more efficient use of the stream than if the flow had been steadily divided equally between the Colorado and the New Mexico appropriators was conclusively established by the evidence. That is, the rotating supply which the Compact authorized, and the two State Engineers agreed upon, was clearly more beneficial to the Ditch Company than to have given to it and other Colorado appropriators steadily one-half of the water in the river. The delegation to the State Engineers of the authority to determine when the waters should be so rotated was a matter of detail clearly within the constitutional power. There is no claim that the authority conferred was abused.

Fifth. As Colorado possessed the right only to an equitable share of the water in the stream, the decree of January 12, 1898, in the Colorado water proceeding did not award to the Ditch Company any right greater than the equitable share. Hence the apportionment made by the Compact can not have taken from the Ditch Company any vested right, unless there was in the proceedings leading up to the Compact or in its application, some vitiating infirmity. No such infirmity or illegality has been shown. * * *

Notes

1. **Formation and significance of water apportionment compacts.** Article I, Section 10, Clause 3 of the United States Constitution provides: "No State shall, without the Consent of Congress, * * * enter into any Agreement or Compact with another State * * *." The interstate compact has become far more popular among states than equitable apportionment litigation for allocating interstate waters. See Douglas L. Grant, Water Apportionment Compacts Between States § 46.01, in 4 Waters and Water Rights (Robert E. Beck ed., repl. vol. 2004) (table listing each water allocation compact, the signatory states, and the Statutes at Large citation to it).

The most detailed study of interstate water compacts is Jerome C. Muys, Interstate Water Compacts: The Interstate Compact and Federal-Interstate Compact (National Water Comm'n, Legal Study No. 14, 1971). All the water allocation compacts, as well as various other compacts pertaining to water resources, are reprinted in George William Sherk, Dividing the Waters: The Resolution of Interstate Water Conflicts in the United States (2000).

2. **The Supreme Court's role in compact disputes.** In Oklahoma v. New Mexico, 501 U.S. 221 (1991), which concerned the Canadian River Compact, the Special Master recommended to the Court that states should not be allowed to

invoke its original jurisdiction in compact disputes without certifying they had negotiated in good faith to try to resolve their differences. The Court declined, however, to set forth any jurisdictional prerequisites beyond those already in existence.

Texas v. New Mexico, 462 U.S. 554 (1983), was as suit to enforce the Pecos River Compact. The compact states that New Mexico "shall not deplete by man's activities the flow * * * at the New Mexico-Texas state line below an amount which will give to Texas a quantity of water equivalent to that available to Texas under the 1947 condition." To implement this apportionment, the compact included a detailed inflow-outflow formula for quantifying New Mexico's delivery obligation under varying levels of annual precipitation and inflow to the river. The compact created a commission and empowered it to adopt any other "more feasible method" for quantifying New Mexico's obligation and to determine the occurrence of any shortfall in the flow promised to Texas. The commission consisted of one voting representative from each state and a nonvoting federal member. Soon after the compact became operative, the detailed inflow-outflow formula proved to be based on badly flawed data and assumptions. The two state commissioners were unable to agree on the cumulative shortfalls under the flawed inflow-outflow formula or on an improved method of calculating them.

The Special Master recommended to the Supreme Court that it break the deadlock between the states by rewriting the compact to include a tie-breaking mechanism, such as allowing the federal commissioner to vote. The Court rejected the recommendation on the ground that since "congressional consent transforms an interstate compact * * * into a law of the United States, * * * no court may order relief inconsistent with its expressed terms." Id. at 564.

The Court then had to decide its proper role in resolving the deadlock. New Mexico argued that the compact commission was the exclusive forum for resolving disputes between the states, and that the Court's only role was to review actions by the commission under the deferential model of judicial review of administrative action. This meant the Court would have to dismiss the case because with the commissioners deadlocked, there was no commission action to review. The Court responded: "[T]he mere existence of a compact does not foreclose the possibility that we will be required to resolve a dispute between the compacting States. * * * It is difficult to conceive that Texas would trade away its right to seek an equitable apportionment of the river in return for a promise that New Mexico could, for all practical purposes, avoid at will. In the absence of an explicit provision or other clear indication that a bargain to that effect was made, we shall not construe a compact to preclude a state from seeking judicial relief when the compact does not provide an equivalent method of vindicating the state's rights." The Court concluded that "[u]nder the Compact as it now stands the solution for impasse is judicial resolution of such disputes as are amenable to judicial resolution, and further negotiation for those disputes that are not." Id. at 565.

The Court returned the case to the Special Master to determine how the flawed inflow-outflow formula should be modified and to calculate whether New Mexico had fulfilled its water delivery obligation. The Special Master recommended a modified inflow-outflow methodology, and the Court approved it. 467 U.S. 1238 (1984).

3. **Breach of compact: defenses and burden of proof.** Under the modified inflow-outflow methodology for the Pecos River Compact, New Mexico's shortfall in delivering water to Texas from 1950 through 1983 totaled 340,100 acre-feet. New Mexico sought to avoid liability for breach by arguing the shortfall resulted from good-faith misunderstanding of its compact obligation. The Court rejected that defense because "[a] Compact is, after all, a contract," and under contract law, good-faith differences about the scope of contractual undertakings do not relieve either party from performance.

In Kansas v. Colorado, 514 U.S. 673 (1995), Colorado sought to defend a suit for breach of the Arkansas River Compact by arguing that Kansas was barred by laches. The Court responded:

"The defense of laches requires proof of (1) lack of diligence by the party against whom the defense is asserted, and (2) prejudice to the party asserting the defense. This Court has yet to decide whether the doctrine of laches applies in a case involving the enforcement of an interstate compact. Cf. *Illinois v. Kentucky*, 500 U.S. 380, 388 (1991) (in the context of an interstate boundary dispute, 'the laches defense is generally inapplicable against a State'); *Block v. North Dakota*, 461 U.S. 273, 294 (1983) (O'Connor, J., dissenting) ('The common law has long accepted the principle "*nullum tempus occurrit regi*"—neither laches nor statutes of limitations will bar the sovereign'); *Colorado v. Kansas*, 320 U.S., at 394 (in the context of a suit seeking an equitable apportionment of river flows, facts demonstrating a delay in filing a complaint 'might well preclude the award of the relief requested. But in any event, they gravely add to the burden the plaintiff would otherwise bear'). We need not, however, foreclose the applicability of laches in such cases, because we conclude that Colorado has failed to prove an element necessary to the recognition of that defense [namely, lack of diligence by Kansas in asserting its claim]." Id. at 687-88.

Colorado also argued Kansas should have to prove breach by clear and convincing evidence. The Court responded:

"The Special Master, relying upon *Nebraska v. Wyoming*, 507 U.S. 584, 113 S.CT. 1689, 123 L.Ed.2d 317 (1993),[b] concluded that the proper burden of proof for enforcing an interstate compact is the preponderance of the evidence standard. The Special Master noted that the *Nebraska* Court had distinguished between actions seeking to 'modify' a judicial apportionment decree and actions seeking to 'enforce' such a judicial decree. See *Nebraska*, supra, at 592, 113 S.Ct. at 1695. ('[W]e find merit in [the] contention that, to the extent that Nebraska seeks modification of the decree rather than enforcement, a higher standard of proof applies'). The Special Master concluded that an action seeking to enforce an interstate compact stood on the same footing as an action enforcing a judicial decree, and therefore was subject to the 'preponderance of the evidence' standard.

"We need not, however, resolve this issue. The Special Master concluded that 'regardless of which burden of proof applies' he had 'no difficulty in concluding that [post-Compact] pumping in Colorado has caused material depletions of the usable Stateline flows of the Arkansas River, in violation of the

b. Supra pp. 475-76, Note 2.

Arkansas River Compact.' We agree with this determination, and thus overrule Colorado's exception." Id. at 693-94.

4. **Breach of compact: remedies.** In Texas v. New Mexico, where New Mexico shorted Texas on water compact deliveries by 340,100 acre-feet between 1950 and 1983, the Special Master recommended that New Mexico be ordered to make up the deficit by delivering an additional 34,010 acre-feet annually for ten years. Although he thought money damages might be better for the parties, the compact called for the delivery of water, and he concluded relief inconsistent with the compact could not be ordered. The Court disagreed, ruling that the lack of a specific compact provision for money damages did not preclude that remedy. The Court returned the case to the Master to determine if New Mexico should be allowed to pay money damages and, if so, the amount. 482 U.S. 124 (1987).

The Special Master also recommended that the Court appoint a river master to calculate New Mexico's future annual water delivery obligations under the compact. Although the Court noted that it generally is reluctant to appoint continuing agents to administer its decrees, it agreed that such an agent was needed. This was because the compact apportionment formula was not mechanical but would require the exercise of judgment, and the Court wished to forestall repeated litigation arising from "the natural propensity of the two states to disagree if an allocation formula leaves room to do so." Id. at 134. The Court added, however, that its decree did not displace the authority of the compact commission to agree upon what it had been unable to agree upon before, namely, a more feasible method for quantifying New Mexico's water delivery obligation.

The two states settled the liability issue for $14 million. Texas v. New Mexico, 494 U.S. 111 (1990). To enable future compliance with its compact water delivery obligation, New Mexico undertook a $70 million program to purchase irrigated land in the state and retire the water rights. In view of *Hinderlider*, supra p. 486, was it legally necessary for the state to spend public funds on a purchase program? The reasons the program was adopted, and the ensuing difficulties with it, are described in G. Emlen Hall, High and Dry: The Texas-New Mexico Struggle for the Pecos River ch. 7 (2002) (other chapters relate the fascinating story of the compact litigation and its key players).

In Kansas v. Colorado, 533 U.S. 1 (2001), the Court continued to develop the law on damages for breach of compact. After Kansas twice failed to get an equitable apportionment of the Arkansas River from the Supreme Court, see supra p. 461 and p. 465, Note 3, the two states formed the Arkansas River Compact in 1949. The compact provides that "the Arkansas River * * * shall not be materially depleted in usable quantity or availability for use to the water users in Colorado and Kansas [by] future development." Colorado breached the compact by allowing new wells that pumped groundwater tributary to the Arkansas River and materially depleted the stream flow available for use in Kansas.

The Court approved the Special Master's recommendation of money damages for Kansas running from 1950 when the stream depletion began. The damages were based on Kansas's losses, not Colorado's profits. The damage award included compensation for reduced crop yields suffered by Kansas farmers though the money was payable to the state to use as it wished and thus would not necessarily end up in the farmers' pockets.

The damage award also included prejudgment interest though Colorado's liability was unliquidated prior to judgment. Three Justices opposed any prejudgment interest because they thought that when the states formed the compact, federal common law had not yet abandoned the rule barring prejudgment interest on unliquidated claims, and therefore Colorado had no reason to anticipate such liability. Four Justices thought federal common law had evolved by compact formation to allow prejudgment interest on unliquidated claims if fairness demanded it. They thought fairness justified awarding prejudgment interest from 1969 when Colorado knew or should have known postcompact wells were depleting the stream flow. The remaining two Justices, who did not explain their rationale but perhaps applied the fairness standard differently, thought prejudgment interest should run only from the time Kansas filed suit in 1985. To enable entry of a judgment, the four Justices who favored 1969 joined the two who favored 1985 to produce a majority for the latter date. See also Kansas v. Colorado, 125 S. Ct. 526 (2004) (clarifying that prejudgment interest accrued only on damages that arose after suit was filed in 1985, and did not start accruing in 1985 on damages from earlier years).

5. **Federal-interstate compacts.** A variation of the interstate compact is the federal-interstate compact, in which the United States joins as a party along with the states. Two federal-interstate water compacts have long been operative. The first is the Delaware River Basin Compact—among Delaware, New Jersey, New York, Pennsylvania, and the United States. The second, which is closely patterned after the first, is the Susquehanna River Basin compact—among Maryland, New York, Pennsylvania, and the United States. Jerome C. Muys, supra Note 1, gives a full history of the negotiations for both compacts.

The Delaware River Basin Compact established the Delaware River Basin Commission comprised of the governor of each state (or a delegate) and a federal member. The commission's main charge was to produce a comprehensive plan for development and use of the basin's waters and then to adopt annually a six-year water resources program based on the plan. The commission licenses each project to be undertaken and can itself construct and operate projects. It has "power from time to time as need appears, in accordance with the doctrine of equitable apportionment, to allocate the waters of the basin to and among the states signatory to this compact and to and among their respective political subdivisions, and to impose conditions, obligations and release requirements related thereto." § 3.3. The commission can also regulate withdrawals of surface and ground waters in areas of shortage and cases of emergency. §§ 10.4, 10.5. It exercised these powers during an extended drought that reached the emergency stage in 1965, curtailing New York City's withdrawals and Philadelphia's water intakes.

Few legal problems are created by adding the United States as a party to a compact. The power of the United States to enter into permanent agreements with states, ceding to them federal works and powers, was first recognized in Searight v. Stokes, 44 U.S. (3 How.) 151 (1845). The major legal concern with the Delaware compact was the relationship of the Commission's comprehensive plan to federal programs. Conflicts with the federal power over navigation were seen as difficult, and were avoided by leaving that subject outside the scope of the Commission's activities. The compact provides that for all projects, including federal projects, no expenditures or construction shall occur if the project is not included in the comprehensive plan. The federal government has only one vote on the five-member Commission, so that as the compact is written, state members on the Commission could veto a federal project. This was unacceptable to the federal government, so in the congressional consent legislation a reservation recites that while nothing in the compact shall impair the constitutional authority of the United States or any of its rights or authority under existing or future legislation, the exercise of those federal powers shall not substantially conflict with a Commission plan concurred in by the federal member. Also, the President may suspend any provision of the plan in the national interest. See Jerome C. Muys, supra Note 1, at 206a-225.

In addition to the Delaware and Susquehanna compacts, the United States became a signatory party more recently to two abortive water compacts—the Apalachicola-Chattahoochee-Flint River Basin Compact, Pub. L. No. 105-104 111 Stat. 2219 (among Alabama, Florida, and Georgia) and the Alabama-Coosa-Tallapoosa River Basin Compact, Pub. L. No. 105-105, 111 Stat. 2233 (1997) (between Alabama and Georgia). These similarly structured compacts did not themselves allocate water between states but created a commission charged with developing an allocation formula for equitably apportioning basin waters while protecting water quality, ecology and biodiversity. Each state had one vote on the compact commission, and unanimity of the states was required for all decisions. A federal commissioner had no vote but could veto an allocation formula the states developed upon giving reasons based on federal law. The compacts provided for their automatic termination should the states fail to develop an allocation formula by December 31, 1998, unless the states agreed to extend the deadline. After numerous extensions, both compacts terminated for lack of agreement on either an allocation formula or any further deadline extension.

6. **River basin federalization.** A very different approach from the interstate compact or the federal-interstate compact is the complete federalization of a river basin program and unification of all functions in an agency such as the Tennessee Valley Authority (TVA). The TVA is a federal corporation enjoying substantial independence from other federal agencies and reporting directly to the President and the Congress. See Roscoe C. Martin, The Tennessee Valley Authority: A Study of Federal Control, 22 Law & Contemp. Probs. 351 (1957); Joseph C. Swidler & Robert H. Marquis, TVA in Court: A Study of TVA's Constitutional Litigation, 32 Iowa L. Rev. 296 (1947). The TVA has been much copied in foreign countries as the most suitable institutional form for river basin development, but it seems unlikely to be used again in the United States.

7. **Northwest Power Planning Council.** Several unsuccessful proposals were made during the 1940s and 1950s to extend the TVA model to the Columbia River basin. But the regional entity that was ultimately created, the Northwest Power Planning Council, is not a federal entity. The Council was established under an interstate compact that Congress authorized in the Pacific Northwest Electric Power Planning and Conservation Act, 16 U.S.C. §§ 839-839h. The Council is headed by two gubernatorial appointees from each of the four basin states—Idaho, Montana, Oregon, and Washington. Unlike the TVA, the Council lacks direct operating or regulatory powers. Its focus is limited to the electrical energy needs of the region and the well-being of fish and wildlife on the Columbia River and its tributaries. A major issue for the Council is the effect of hydroelectric dams on anadromous fish. The Council is charged with developing

a regional conservation and electric power plan and a regional program to protect and enhance fish and wildlife, including related spawning grounds and habitat. The Act states that the Council's fish and wildlife program shall not "alter, modify, or affect in any way the laws applicable to rivers or river systems * * * or affect the rights and obligations of any agency, entity, or person under such laws." § 839b(h)(1)(B). However, federal agencies operating in the region—such as the Bonneville Power Administration, the Army Corps of Engineers, and the Bureau of Reclamation—must take the Council's fish and wildlife program "into account at each relevant stage of decisionmaking processes to the fullest extent practicable." Id. § 839b(h)(11)(A)(ii). See Northwest Envtl. Def. Center v. Bonneville Power Admin., 117 F.3d 1520 (9th Cir. 1997); John M. Volkman, Testing New Forms of River Basin Governance: Implication of the *Seattle Master Builders Case*, 17 Envtl. L. 835 (1987).

SECTION 3. CONGRESSIONAL APPORTIONMENT

ARIZONA v. CALIFORNIA

Supreme Court of the United States, 1963.
373 U.S. 546, 83 S. Ct. 1468, 10 L. Ed.2d 572.

MR. JUSTICE BLACK delivered the opinion of the Court.

In 1952 the State of Arizona invoked the original jurisdiction of this Court by filing a complaint against the State of California and seven of its public agencies. Later, Nevada, New Mexico, Utah, and the United States were added as parties either voluntarily or on motion. The basic controversy in the case is over how much water each State has a legal right to use out of the waters of the Colorado River and its tributaries. After preliminary pleadings, we referred the case to George I. Haight, Esquire, and upon his death in 1955 to Simon H. Rifkind, Esquire, as Special Master to take evidence, find facts, state conclusions of law, and recommend a decree, all "subject to consideration, revision, or approval by the Court." * * * Following many motions, arguments, and briefs, the Master in a 433-page volume reported his findings, conclusions, and recommended decree, received by the Court in January 16, 1961. The case has been extensively briefed here and orally argued twice, the first time about 16 hours, the second, over six. As we see this case, the question of each State's share of the waters of the Colorado and its tributaries turns on the meaning and the scope of the Boulder Canyon Project Act passed by Congress in 1928. That meaning and scope can be better understood when the Act is set against its background—the gravity of the Southwest's water problems; the inability of local groups or individual States to deal with these enormous problems; the continued failure of the States to agree on how to conserve and divide the waters; and the ultimate action by Congress at the request of the States creating a great system of dams and public works nationally built, controlled, and operated for the purpose of conserving and distributing the water.

The Colorado River itself rises in the mountains of Colorado and flows generally in a southwesterly direction for about 1,300 miles through Colorado, Utah, and Arizona and along the Arizona-Nevada and Arizona-

California boundaries, after which it passes into Mexico and empties into the Mexican waters of the Gulf of California. On its way to the sea it receives tributary waters from Wyoming, Colorado, Utah, Nevada, New Mexico, and Arizona. The river and its tributaries flow in a natural basin almost surrounded by large mountain ranges and drain 242,000 square miles, an area about 900 miles long from north to south and 300 to 500 miles wide from east to west—practically one-twelfth the area of the continental United States excluding Alaska. Much of this large basin is so arid that it is, as it always has been, largely dependent upon managed use of the waters of the Colorado River System to make it productive and inhabitable. The Master refers to archaeological evidence that as long as 2,000 years ago the ancient Hohokam tribe built and maintained irrigation canals near what is now Phoenix, Arizona, and that American Indians were practicing irrigation in that region at the time white men first explored it. In the second half of the nineteenth century a group of people interested in California's Imperial Valley conceived plans to divert water from the mainstream of the Colorado to give life and growth to the parched and barren soil of that valley. As the most feasible route was through Mexico, a Mexican corporation was formed and a canal dug partly in Mexico and partly in the United States. Difficulties which arose because the canal was subject to the sovereignty of both countries generated hopes in this country that some day there would be a canal wholly within the United States, an all-American canal.

During the latter part of the nineteenth and the first part of the twentieth centuries, people in the Southwest continued to seek new ways to satisfy their water needs, which by that time were increasing rapidly as new settlers moved into this fast-developing region. But none of the more or less primitive diversions made from the mainstream of the Colorado conserved enough water to meet the growing needs of the basin. The natural flow of the Colorado was too erratic, the river at many places in canyons too deep, and the engineering and economic hurdles too great for small farmers, larger groups, or even States to build storage dams, construct canals, and install the expensive works necessary for a dependable year-round water supply. Nor were droughts the basin's only problem; spring floods due to melting snows and seasonal storms were a recurring menace, especially disastrous in California's Imperial Valley where, even after the Mexican canal provided a more dependable water supply, the threat of flood remained at least as serious as before. Another troublesome problem was the erosion of land and the deposit of silt which fouled waters, choked irrigation works, and damaged good farmland and crops.

It is not surprising that the pressing necessity to transform the erratic and often destructive flow of the Colorado River into a controlled and dependable water supply desperately needed in so many States began to be talked about and recognized as far more than a purely local problem which could be solved on a farmer-by-farmer, group-by-group, or even state-by-state basis, desirable as this kind of solution might have been. * * *

The prospect that the United States would undertake to build as a national project the necessary works to control floods and store river waters for irrigation was apparently a welcome one for the basin States. But it brought to life strong fears in the northern basin States that additional waters made available by the storage and canal projects might be gobbled up in perpetuity by faster growing lower basin areas, particularly California, before the upper States could appropriate what they believed to be their fair share. These fears were not without foundation, since the law of prior appropriation prevailed in most of the Western States. Under that law the one who first appropriates water and puts it to beneficial use thereby acquires a vested right to continue to divert and use that quantity of water against all claimants junior to him in point of time. "First in time, first in right" is the short hand expression of this legal principle. * * * In view of California's phenomenal growth, the Upper Basin had particular reason to fear that California, by appropriating and using Colorado River water before the upper States, would, under the interstate application of the prior appropriation doctrine, be "first in time" and therefore "first in right." Nor were such fears limited to the northernmost States. Nevada, Utah, and especially Arizona were all apprehensive that California's rapid declaration of appropriative claims would deprive them of their just share of basin water available after construction of the proposed United States project. It seemed for a time that these fears would keep the States from agreeing on any kind of division of the river waters. Hoping to prevent "conflicts" and "expensive litigation" which would hold up or prevent the tremendous benefits expected from extensive federal development of the river, the basin States requested and Congress passed an Act on August 19, 1921, giving the States consent to negotiate and enter into a compact for the "equitable division and apportionment * * * of the water supply of the Colorado River."

Pursuant to this congressional authority, the seven States appointed Commissioners who, after negotiating for the better part of a year, reached an agreement at Santa Fe, New Mexico, on November 24, 1922. The agreement, known as the Colorado River Compact, failed to fulfill the hope of Congress that the States would themselves agree on each State's share of the water. The most the Commissioners were able to accomplish in the Compact was to adopt a compromise suggestion of Secretary of Commerce Herbert Hoover, specially designated as United States representative. This compromise divides the entire basin into two parts, the Upper Basin and the Lower Basin, separated at a point on the river in northern Arizona known as Lee Ferry. Article III(a) of the Compact apportions to each basin in perpetuity 7,500,000 acre-feet of water a year from the Colorado River System, defined in Article II(a) as "the Colorado River and its tributaries within the United States of America." In addition, Article III(b) gives the Lower Basin "the right to increase its beneficial consumptive use of such waters by one million acre-feet per annum." Article III(c) provides that future Mexican water rights recognized by the United States shall be supplied first out of surplus over and above the aggregate of the quantities specified in (a) and (b), and if this surplus is not enough the deficiency shall be borne equally by the two basins. Article III(d) requires the Upper Basin not to deplete the Lee Ferry flow below an aggregate of 75,000,000 acre-feet for any 10 consecutive years. Article III(f) and (g) provide a way for further apportionment by a compact of "Colorado River System" waters at any time after October 1, 1963. While these allocations quieted rivalries between the Upper and Lower Basins, major differences between the States in the Lower Basin continued. Failure of the Compact to determine each State's share of the water left Nevada and Arizona with their fears that the law of prior appropriation would be not a protection but a menace because California could use that law to get for herself the lion's share of the waters allotted to the Lower Basin. Moreover, Arizona, because of her particularly strong interest in the Gila, intensely resented the Compact's inclusion of the Colorado River tributaries in its allocation scheme and was bitterly hostile to having Arizona tributaries, again particularly the Gila, forced to contribute to the Mexican burden. Largely for these reasons, Arizona alone, of all the States in both basins, refused to ratify the Compact.

Seeking means which would permit ratification by all seven basin States, the Governors of those States met at Denver in 1925 and again in 1927. As a result of these meetings the Governors of the upper States suggested, as a fair apportionment of water among the Lower Basin States, that out of the average annual delivery of water at Lee Ferry required by the Compact—7,500,000 acre-feet—Nevada be given 300,000 acre-feet, Arizona 3,000,000, and California 4,200,000, and that unapportioned waters, subject to reapportionment after 1963, be shared equally by Arizona and California. * * * This proposal foundered because California held out for 4,600,000 acre-feet instead of 4,200,000 and because Arizona held out for complete exemption of its tributaries from any part of the Mexican burden.

Between 1922 and 1927 Congressman Philip Swing and Senator Hiram Johnson, both of California, made three attempts to have Swing-Johnson bills enacted, authorizing construction of a dam in the canyon section of the Colorado River and an all-American canal. * * *

Finally, the fourth Swing-Johnson bill passed both Houses and became the Boulder Canyon Project Act of December 21, 1928, 45 Stat. 1057. The Act authorized the Secretary of the Interior to construct, operate and maintain a dam and other works in order to control floods, improve navigation, regulate the river's flow, store and distribute waters for reclamation and other beneficial uses, and generate electrical power. The projects authorized by the Act were the same as those provided for in the prior defeated measures, but in other significant respects the Act was strikingly different. The earlier bills had offered no method whatever of apportioning the waters among the States of the Lower Basin. The Act as finally passed did provide such a method, and, as we view it, the method chosen was a complete statutory apportionment intended to put an end to the long-standing dispute over Colorado River waters. To protect the Upper Basin against California should Arizona still refuse to ratify the Compact, § 4(a) of the Act as finally passed provided that, if fewer than seven States ratified within six months, the Act should not take effect unless six States including California ratified and unless California, by its legislature, agreed "irrevocably and unconditionally * * * as an express covenant" to a limit on its annual consumption of Colorado River water of "four million four hundred thousand acre-feet of the waters apportioned to the lower basin States by paragraph (a) of Article III of the Colorado River compact, plus not more than one-half of any excess or surplus waters unapportioned by said compact." Congress in the same section showed its continuing desire to have California, Arizona, and Nevada settle their own differences by authorizing them to make an agreement apportioning to Nevada 300,000 acre-feet, and to Arizona 2,800,000 acre-feet plus half of any surplus waters unapportioned by the Compact. The permitted agreement also was to allow Arizona exclusive use of the Gila River, wholly free from any Mexican obligation, a position Arizona had taken from the beginning. Sections 5 and 8(b) of the Project Act made provisions for the sale of the stored waters. The Secretary of the Interior was authorized by § 5 "under such general regulations as he may prescribe, to contract for the storage of water in said reservoir and for the delivery thereof at such points on the river and on said canal as may be agreed upon, for irrigation and domestic uses * * *." Section 5 required these contracts to be "for permanent service" and further provided, "No person shall have or be entitled to have the use for any purpose of the water stored as aforesaid except by contract made as herein stated." Section 8(b) provided that the Secretary's contracts would be subject to any compact dividing the benefits of the water between Arizona, California, and Nevada, or any two of them, approved by Congress on or before January 1, 1929, but that any such compact approved after that date should be "subject to all contracts, if any, made by the Secretary of the Interior under section 5 hereof prior to the date of such approval and consent by Congress."

The Project Act became effective on June 25, 1929, by Presidential Proclamation, after six States, including California, had ratified the Colorado River Compact and the California legislature had accepted the limitation of 4,400,000 acre-feet as required by the Act. Neither the three States nor any two of them ever entered into any apportionment compact as authorized by §§ 4(a) and 8(b). After the construction of Boulder Dam the Secretary of the Interior, purporting to act under the authority of the Project Act, made contracts with various water users in California for 5,362,000 acre-feet, with Nevada for 300,000 acre-feet, and with Arizona for 2,800,000 acre-feet of water from that stored at Lake Mead.

The Special Master appointed by this Court found that the Colorado River Compact, the law of prior appropriation, and the doctrine of equitable apportionment—by which doctrine this Court in the absence of statute resolves interstate claims according to the equities—do not control the issues in this case. The Master concluded that, since the Lower Basin States had failed to make a compact to allocate the waters among themselves as authorized by §§ 4(a) and 8(b), the Secretary's contracts with the States had within the statutory scheme of §§ 4(a), 5, and 8(b) effected an apportionment of the waters of the mainstream which, according to the Master, were the only waters to be apportioned under the Act. The Master further held that, in the event of a shortage of water making it impossible for the Secretary to supply all the water due California, Arizona, and Nevada under their contracts, the burden of the shortage must be borne by each State in proportion to her share of the first 7,500,000 acre-feet allocated to the Lower Basin, that is, $^{4.4}/_{7.5}$ by

California, $^{2.8}/_{7.5}$ by Arizona, and $^{.3}/_{7.5}$ by Nevada, without regard to the law of prior appropriation.

Arizona, Nevada, and the United States support with few exceptions the analysis, conclusions, and recommendations of the Special Master's report. * * * California is in basic disagreement with almost all of the Master's Report. * * *

ALLOCATION OF WATER AMONG THE STATES AND DISTRIBUTION TO USERS

We have concluded, for reasons to be stated, that Congress in passing the Project Act intended to and did create its own comprehensive scheme for the apportionment among California, Arizona, and Nevada of the Lower Basin's share of the mainstream waters of the Colorado River, leaving each State its tributaries. Congress decided that a fair division of the first 7,500,000 acre-feet of such mainstream waters would give 4,400,000 acre-feet to California, 2,800,000 to Arizona, and 300,000 to Nevada; Arizona and California would each get one-half of any surplus. Prior approval was therefore given in the Act for a tri-state compact to incorporate these terms. The States, subject to subsequent congressional approval, were also permitted to agree on a compact with different terms. Division of the water did not, however, depend on the States' agreeing to a compact, for Congress gave the Secretary of the Interior adequate authority to accomplish the division. Congress did this by giving the Secretary power to make contracts for the delivery of water and by providing that no person could have water without a contract.

A. *Relevancy of Judicial Apportionment and Colorado River Compact.*—We agree with the Master that apportionment of the Lower Basin waters of the Colorado River is not controlled by the doctrine of equitable apportionment or by the Colorado River Compact. It is true that the Court has used the doctrine of equitable apportionment to decide river controversies between States. But in those cases Congress had not made any statutory apportionment. In this case, we have decided that Congress has provided its own method for allocating among the Lower Basin States the mainstream water to which they are entitled under the Compact. Where Congress has so exercised its constitutional power over waters courts have no power to substitute their own notions of an "equitable apportionment" for the apportionment chosen by Congress. Nor does the Colorado River Compact control this case. Nothing in that Compact purports to divide water among the Lower Basin States nor in any way to affect or control any future apportionment among those States or any distribution of water within a State. * * *

B. *Mainstream Apportionment.*—The congressional scheme of apportionment cannot be understood without knowing what water Congress wanted apportioned. Under California's view, which we reject, the first 7,500,000 acre-feet of Lower Basin water, of which California has agreed to use only 4,400,000, is made up of both mainstream and tributary water, not just mainstream water. Under the view of Arizona, Nevada, and the United States, with which we agree, the tributaries are not included in the waters to be divided but remain for the exclusive use of each State. Assuming 7,500,000 acre-feet or more in the mainstream and 2,000,000 in the tributaries, California would get 1,000,000 acre-feet more if the tributaries are included and Arizona 1,000,000 less. * * *

C. *The Project Act's Apportionment and Distribution Scheme.*—The legislative history, the language of the Act, and the scheme established by the Act, for the storage and delivery of water convince us also that Congress intended to provide its own method for a complete apportionment of the mainstream water among Arizona, California, and Nevada. * * *

In the first section of the Act, the Secretary was authorized to "construct, operate, and maintain a dam and incidental works * * * adequate to create a storage reservoir of a capacity of not less than twenty million acre-feet of water" for the stated purpose of "controlling the floods, improving navigation and regulating the flow of the Colorado River, providing for storage and for the delivery of the stored waters thereof for reclamation of public lands and other beneficial uses * * *," and generating electrical power. The whole point of the Act was to replace the erratic, undependable, often destructive natural flow of the Colorado with the regular, dependable release of waters conserved and stored by the project. Having undertaken this beneficial project, Congress, in several provisions of the Act, made it clear that no one should use mainstream waters save in strict compliance with the scheme set up by the Act. Section 5 authorized the Secretary "under such general regulations as he may prescribe, to contract for the storage of water in said reservoir and for the delivery thereof at such points on the river * * * as may be agreed upon, for irrigation and domestic uses * * *." To emphasize that water could be obtained from the Secretary alone, § 5 further declared, "No person shall have or be entitled to have the use for any purpose of the water stored as aforesaid except by contract made as herein stated." The supremacy given the Secretary's contracts was made clear in § 8(b) of the Act, which provided that, while the Lower Basin States were free to negotiate a compact dividing the waters, such a compact if made and approved after January 1, 1929, was to be "subject to all contracts, if any, made by the Secretary of the Interior under section 5" before Congress approved the compact.

These several provisions, even without legislative history, are persuasive that Congress intended the Secretary of the Interior, through his § 5 contracts, both to carry out the allocation of the waters of the main Colorado River among the Lower Basin States and to decide which users within each State would get water. The general authority to make contracts normally includes the power to choose with whom and upon what terms the contracts will be made. When Congress in an Act grants authority to contract, that authority is no less than the general authority, unless Congress has placed some limit on it. * * *

APPORTIONMENT AND CONTRACTS IN TIME OF SHORTAGE

We have agreed with the Master that the Secretary's contracts with Arizona for 2,800,000 acre-feet of water and with Nevada for 300,000, together with the limitation of California to 4,400,000 acre-feet, effect a valid apportionment of the first 7,500,000 acre-feet of mainstream water in the Lower Basin. There remains the question of what shall be done in time of shortage. The Master, while declining to make any findings as to what future supply might be expected, nevertheless decided that the Project Act and the Secretary's contracts require the Secretary in case of shortage to divide the burden among the three States in this proportion: California ${}^{4.4}/_{7.5}$; Arizona ${}^{2.8}/_{7.5}$; Nevada ${}^{.3}/_{7.5}$. While pro rata sharing of water shortages seems equitable on its face, more considered judgment may demonstrate quite the contrary. Certainly we should not bind the Secretary to this formula. We have held that the Secretary is vested with considerable control over the apportionment of Colorado River waters. And neither the Project Act nor the water contracts require the use of any particular formula for apportioning shortages. While the Secretary must follow the standards set out in the Act, he nevertheless is free to choose among the recognized methods of apportionment or to devise reasonable methods of his own. This choice, as we see it, is primarily his, not the Master's or even ours. And the Secretary may or may not conclude that a pro rata division is the best solution.

It must be remembered that the Secretary's decision may have an effect not only on irrigation uses but also on other important functions for which Congress brought this great project into being—flood control, improvement of navigation, regulation of flow, and generation and distribution of electric power. Requiring the Secretary to prorate shortages would strip him of the very power of choice which we think Congress, for reasons satisfactory to it, vested in him and which we should not impair or take away from him. For the same reasons we cannot accept California's contention that in case of shortage each State's share of water should be determined by the judicial doctrine of equitable apportionment or by the law of prior appropriation. These principles, while they may provide some guidance, are not binding upon the Secretary where, as here, Congress, with full power to do so, has provided that the waters of a navigable stream shall be harnessed, conserved, stored, and distributed through a government agency under a statutory scheme.

None of this is to say that in case of shortage, the Secretary cannot adopt a method of proration or that he may not lay stress upon priority for use, local laws and customs, or any other factors that might be helpful in reaching an informed judgment in harmony with the Act, the best interests of the Basin States, and the welfare of the Nation. It will be time enough for the courts to intervene when and if the Secretary, in making apportionments or contracts, deviates from the standards Congress has set for him to follow, including his obligation to respect "present perfected rights" as of the date the Act was passed. At this time the Secretary has made no decision at all based on an actual or anticipated shortage of water, and so there is no action of his in this respect for us to review. Finally, as the Master pointed out, Congress still has broad powers over this navigable international stream. Congress can undoubtedly reduce or enlarge the Secretary's power if it wishes. Unless and until it does, we leave in the hands of the Secretary, where Congress placed it, full power to control, manage, and operate the Government's Colorado

River works and to make contracts for the sale and delivery of water on such terms as are not prohibited by the Project Act. * * *

MR. JUSTICE HARLAN, whom MR. JUSTICE DOUGLAS and MR. JUSTICE STEWART join, dissenting in part.

I dissent from so much of the Court's opinion as holds that the Secretary of the Interior has been given authority by Congress to apportion, among and within the States of California, Arizona, and Nevada, the waters of the mainstream of the Colorado River below Lee Ferry. * * * (In all other respects MR. JUSTICE STEWART and I—but not MR. JUSTICE DOUGLAS—agree with and join in the Court's opinion * * *.)

* * *

The Court professes to find this extraordinary delegation of power principally in § 5 of the Project Act, the provision authorizing the Secretary to enter into contracts for the storage and delivery of water. But § 5 * * * had no design resembling that which the Court now extracts from it. Rather it was intended principally as a revenue measure, and the clause *requiring* a contract as a condition of delivery was inserted at the insistence not of the Lower but of the Upper Basin States in an effort to insure that nothing would disturb that basin's rights under the Colorado River Compact. There was no thought that § 5 would give authority to apportion water among the Lower Basin States. * * *

It is manifest that § 4(a), on which the Court so heavily relies, neither apportions the waters of the river nor vests power in any official to make such an apportionment. The first paragraph does not *grant* any water to anyone; it merely conditions the Act's effectiveness on seven-state ratification of the Compact or on six-state ratification, plus California's agreement to a limitation, *i.e.*, a *ceiling,* on her appropriations. The source of authority to make such appropriations must be found elsewhere. And the second paragraph of § 4(a), suggesting a particular interstate agreement, similarly makes no apportionment of water among the States and delegates no power to any official to make such an apportionment. * * *

MR. JUSTICE DOUGLAS, dissenting. * * * [The Court uses the present litigation] as a vehicle for making a wholly new apportionment of the waters in the Lower Basin and turning over all unresolved problems to the Secretary of the Interior. The Court accomplishes this by distorting both the history and language of the Project Act.

The Court relies heavily on the terms and history of a proposed tri-state compact, authorized by § 4(a) *but never adopted by the States concerned, viz., Arizona, California and Nevada.* The proposed tri-state compact provided for a division of tributary waters identical to that made by the Court, insofar as the Gila is awarded to Arizona. The Court in reality enforces its interpretation of the proposed tri-state compact and imposes its terms upon California. * * *

Notes

1. **Commentary.** The principal case is discussed thoroughly in Frank J. Trelease, Arizona v. California: Allocation of Water Resources to People, States and Nation, 1963 Sup. Ct. Rev. 158, 166–83. Congressional apportionment is praised as superior to Supreme Court apportionment in Charles J. Meyers, The Colorado River, 19 Stan. L. Rev. 1 (1966). Dean Meyers argued apportionment by Congress is likely to be more expeditious and better coordinated with federal plans for river basin development. He also thought Congress is institutionally better suited to deal with the mass of technical data and the unavoidable political dimensions of interstate water allocation. Finally, he preferred congressional apportionment over apportionment by interstate compact in view of the failure of states to reach agreement by compact "in a significant number of cases."

2. **Congressional revision of the Lower Basin apportionment.** The Court's decision in the principal case left California vulnerable to reduction of its annual supply below 4.4 m.a.f. in a year of shortage. California was protected against the risk of receiving less than 4.4 m.a.f., however, so long as Arizona was using much less than its full 2.8 m.a.f. annually. Moreover, Arizona was incapable of greatly increasing its use of Colorado River water unless Congress funded construction of the Central Arizona Project to bring the water to the Phoenix and Tucson areas. Not surprisingly, California opposed federal funding for that project. Arizona had little chance of obtaining such funding over opposition by California's congressional delegation. To gain California's support for the project, Arizona had to agree to congressional revision of the Court's decision regarding allocation among the Lower Basin states in times of shortage. The Colorado River Basin Project Act of 1968, § 301, 43 U.S.C. § 1521, authorized construction of the Central Arizona Project but also included a provision guaranteeing California 4.4 m.a.f. annually in times of shortage.

3. **Continuing Colorado River controversy.** Competition for the waters of the Colorado River has resulted in a complex body of state, federal, and international law known as the "law of the river" that governs their use. One report lists no less than forty-six "major components" of the law of the river. Dale Pontius, Colorado River Basin Study: Final Report, Report to Western Water Policy Review Advisory Comm'n, app. B (1997). Of course, the list includes the Colorado River Compact, 70 Cong. Rec. 324 (1928), the Boulder Canyon Project Act, 43 U.S.C. §§ 617-617t, and the Arizona v. California decree. Some other items on the list are the Treaty with Mexico Respecting Waters of the Colorado and Tijuana River, Feb. 3, 1944, 59 Stat. 1219, T.S. No. 994, the Upper Colorado River Basin Compact, 63 Stat. 31 (1949), the Colorado River Storage Project Act, 43 U.S.C. §§ 620-620o, the Colorado River Basin Project Act, 43 U.S.C. §§ 1501-1556 (referred to in Note 2); and the Colorado River Basin Salinity Control Act, 43 U.S.C.A. §§ 1571-1599.

Despite this extensive body of law, controversy over the river persists. In part, this is because of ambiguities and inconsistencies in the documents making up the law of the river. In addition, fundamental errors in the assumptions on which the law of the river is based have produced unanticipated problems and have caused some writers and officials to question the fairness and validity of various aspects of the law. Most notable is an error in the assumption about the flow of the Colorado River on which the Colorado River Compact was based. The compact negotiators assumed an average annual virgin flow at Lee Ferry,

Arizona, of at least 16.4 m.a.f. More recent studies suggest that the quarter century immediately preceding negotiation of the compact was unusually wet and that the long-term average annual flow is only about 13.5 m.a.f.. Tree ring studies that reveal climate and precipitation on an annual basis spanning centuries indicate there have been cycles when the annual flow was much less than that.

For years after the compact became operative, the errors, ambiguities, and inconsistences surrounding the law of the river produced much speculation but few actual disputes because water supply generally exceeded water demand. Recently, however, dissatisfaction with the law of the river has intensified due to various factors. First, the compact allocates 7.5 m.a.f. per year for consumptive use in each basin and allows the Lower Basin to consume an additional 1 m.a.f. in years of surplus flow. But great disparity has developed between Upper and Lower Basin water demands. In recent years, Upper Basin consumptive use has been about 4 m.a.f. while Lower Basin consumptive use has surpassed its basic 7.5 m.a.f. allotment.

Second, although California is allocated only 4.4 m.a.f. of the first 7.5 m.a.f. available in the Lower Basin, its consumptive use has long exceeded that. In 2002, California's consumption reached a high point of about 5.3 m.a.f. Oversupply to California was possible because for decades the other two Lower Basin states underused their shares of the first 7.5 m.a.f. In fact, it was once thought Arizona and Nevada would never use all their allocations of 2.8 m.a.f. and 300,000 acre-feet respectively. However, completion of the Central Arizona Project and reliance on the Colorado River to supply an exploding population in the metropolitan Las Vegas area have all but eliminated the underuse. For example, Nevada's consumptive use was 294,000 acre-feet in 2001, 325,000 acre-feet in 2002, and 270,000 acre-feet in 2003, with the decrease in 2003 being due to new conservation measures that soon will be overtaken by continuing population growth in the Las Vegas area.

Third, Colorado River Indian tribes hold unexercised rights to large quantities of river water, and they are interested in realizing an economic return from this water through leasing or sale. Finally, environmental forces are calling for steps to remedy environmental problems on the Colorado River, including instream flows to protect a number of endangered species under federal law.

California, Nevada, the Indian tribes, environmental forces, and congressional critics of the Bureau of Reclamation have been among the principal parties calling for changes in the law of the river. In general, they have advocated more flexibility in the operation of the river. The various proposals, some of which have been implemented in recent years, include loans of system water in drought years to be repaid from future allocations, banking (storage) for use in future years of unused annual allocations made available through fallowing land and conservation measures, interstate banking mechanisms which allow users not needing water in a particular year to transfer that water to other users elsewhere in the Colorado River basin, and perhaps ultimately leasing or other transfer arrangements through which Upper Basin states and Indian tribes could make unused water available to Lower Basin states on a long-term basis. See David E. Lindgren, The Colorado River: Are New Approaches Possible Now That the Reality of Overallocation Is Here?, 38 Rocky Mtn. Min. L. Inst. 25-1 (1992).

An ambitious cooperative endeavor in the Lower Basin is development of the Lower Colorado River Multi-Species Conservation Plan, which has the goals of (1) conserving habitat and working towards recovery of endangered and sensitive species dependent on the river and (2) accommodating current water diversions and power production and optimizing opportunities for future water and power development consistent with the law. The participants working on the plan are the affected states, regional entities, federal agencies, and private groups including conservation groups.

4. **The Secretary of Interior as Lower Basin watermaster.** The Secretary of Interior continues to be is a key player in allocating Lower Basin waters. Dale Pontius, supra Note 3: "The Boulder Canyon Project Act of 1928, as interpreted by the Supreme Court in Arizona v. California, vested extraordinary authority with the Secretary to serve as 'water master' for the Lower Basin. * * * The Secretary has the authority to define what is 'reasonable beneficial use,' to contract for the disposition of hydropower, to develop an annual operating plan for the reservoirs, and to establish surplus and shortage criteria, among other things."

Recently, the Secretary used the authority to establish surplus criteria to pressure California into developing a plan to reduce its use of Colorado River water from 5.3 m.a.f. to its basic allotment of 4.4 m.a.f. When Arizona and Nevada uses reach 2.8 m.a.f. and 300,000 acre-feet respectively, California can consume more than 4.4 m.a.f. only in years when there is a surplus above 7.5 m.a.f. for Lower Basin. In 2001, the Secretary issued Interim Surplus Guidelines that set out liberal criteria for finding the existence of a surplus, but conditioned operation of the Guidelines upon California's commitment to cut its consumptive use gradually to 4.4 m.a.f. by 2016. California initially resisted meeting the condition, so the Secretary suspended the Guidelines and declared there was no surplus. Faced with the prospect of having to cut its use of Colorado River water to 4.4 m.a.f. immediately, California developed the necessary plan to reduce its overuse of Colorado River water gradually.

5. **The Truckee-Carson-Pyramid Lake congressional apportionment.** Whether Congress apportioned Lower Basin waters in the Boulder Canyon Project Act was a hotly contested issue in Arizona v. California. The only indubitable exercise by Congress of its power to apportion interstate waters came in the 1990 Truckee-Carson-Pyramid Lake Water Rights Settlement Act, which is Title II of the Fallon Paiute Shoshone Indian Tribes Water Rights Settlement Act, Pub. L. No. 101-618, 104 Stat. 3289.

The Settlement Act provides for apportionment between California and Nevada of the waters of the Truckee River, the Carson River, and Lake Tahoe. More broadly, it seeks to resolve more than a century of complex interstate and intrastate controversies and litigation about these waters. The various conflicts involve claims and needs of Indian tribes, a federal wildlife refuge, a large federal reclamation project, and municipalities in the Reno-Sparks area. Further complicating the picture is the presence in Pyramid Lake of two species of fish listed under the Endangered Species Act, the cui-ui and Lahontan cutthroat trout.

Between 1969 and 1971, California and Nevada ratified a compact apportioning the Truckee and Carson Rivers and Lake Tahoe. The states immediately began to abide by its provisions. However, Congress refused several times to consent to the compact because of opposition from the United States Departments of Justice and Interior. Those agencies objected primarily because they thought the compact did not adequately protect Indian and federal claims.

Although the two states eventually gave up on obtaining congressional consent, they continued voluntarily to abide by the compact water allocation.

The Settlement Act incorporates parts of the failed compact, including its allocation of the waters of the Tahoe basin. The act allocates the Truckee and Carson Rivers based largely on earlier water right decrees. It attempts to address objections federal officials had to the failed compact and to resolve the longstanding disputes and problems that plagued the area. It provides for payments to the Pyramid Lake Paiute Tribe that will create a fisheries fund and an economic development fund. It also requires measures to protect wetlands, wildlife, and the endangered fish species. Because solutions to many of the problems necessarily involve the operation of reservoirs and other facilities, the Settlement Act contemplates adoption by the two states and the United States of an operating agreement for such facilities. The operating agreement must resolve a number of complex issues, and its adoption was not assured. Therefore, the Settlement Act states that its interstate water apportionment is not effective until the operating agreement has been adopted and until several other conditions precedent are met.

In the spirit of the Arizona v. California majority opinion, which recounted the enormous and intractable Colorado River problems in order to explain why Congress decided to apportion the river, the U.S. Senate committee report on the Settlement Act traced the long history of conflict and unsuccessful efforts at resolving problems in the Truckee-Carson-Pyramid Lake area. The report characterized the problems as involving "special and unique circumstances" warranting the exercise by Congress of its apportionment power. S. Rep. No. 101-555 (1990). This characterization perhaps was designed to pacify those members of Congress who generally oppose interstate water apportionment by that body. To further justify the exercise of congressional power, the report described the Act as making a "voluntary" apportionment—indicating that Congress would not be forcing anything upon either state against its will.

5. **Congressional apportionment of the Missouri River?** The Missouri River straddles the 98th meridian—the line between East and West, between humid and arid zones. In the upstream western part of the basin, the primary water uses have been diversions from the river for farms, municipalities, and energy development. In the downstream eastern part of the basin, the primary water use is instream flow to transport freight by barge and tugboat. In the Flood Control Act of 1944, 33 U.S.C. §§ 701-709b, Congress authorized the Pick-Sloan Plan, which actually is an amalgam of competing plans—the Pick Plan for U.S. Army Corps of Engineers dams to provide flood control, hydroelectric power, and navigation to downstream cities and states, and the Sloan Plan for Bureau of Reclamation dams upstream to supply water for irrigation, municipal and other uses. The Pick Plan is practically complete. Significant parts of the Sloan Plan remain unbuilt, and some parts of it may never be built. The Flood Control Act and its history are analyzed in John P. Guhin, The Law of the Missouri, 30 S.D. L. Rev. 346 (1985).

The O'Mahoney-Milliken Amendment to the Flood Control Act, 33 U.S.C. § 701-1(b), provides that "use for navigation * * * of waters arising in States lying wholly or partly west of the ninety-eighth meridian shall be only such use as does not conflict with any beneficial consumptive use, present or future, in [those] States * * * of such waters for domestic, municipal, stock water, irrigation, mining, or industrial purposes." South Dakota contended that this provision apportions water for upstream consumptive uses over navigation uses in downstream states, and that the apportionment includes water for irrigation projects still to be built. During the 1980s, the Supreme Court twice denied South Dakota leave to file a complaint asserting this theory against downstream states. South Dakota v. Nebraska, 485 U.S. 902 (1988); 475 U.S. 1093 (1986). The Court did not explain its denials, but a commentator suggested the probable reason was that the Court viewed the basic controversy as being not between South Dakota and the other states but between South Dakota and the United States over the operation of federal dams on the Missouri River. Vincent L. McKusick, Discretionary Gatekeeping: The Supreme Court's Management of its Original Jurisdiction Docket Since 1961, 45 Me. L. Rev. 185, 199, 207 (1993).

Later, South Dakota sued the Corps of Engineers to enjoin it from releasing water stored in a reservoir in that state to maintain downstream navigation. Shifting its strategy, South Dakota asserted the release would interfere with fish spawning , and it argued the Flood Control Act obligates the Corps to maximize all river interests, including recreation in the form of fishing. The Eighth Circuit denied a preliminary injunction, saying the Flood Control Act "provides little guidance about what priority the Corps can or must give to different interests" but the available evidence "indicates the Corps's primary concerns should be flood control and navigation." South Dakota v. Ubbelohde, 330 F.3d 1014 (8th Cir. 2003).

In a further round of litigation, various parties filed suits in different federal district courts regarding the Corps's management of dams on the Missouri River. These suits were consolidated in a single federal district court, and that court ruled neither the Pick Plan nor the Sloan Plan ranks any river interest above another; rather, Congress intended the Corps should strike a balance among the different interests to secure maximum benefits. Interestingly, however, the court also ruled the O'Mahoney-Milliken Amendment "requires that when a conflict between upstream consumptive uses and downstream navigation exists, upstream consumptive uses receive deference." In re Operation of the Missouri River System Litigation, No. 03-MD-1555, 2004 WL 1402563 (D. Minn. June 21, 2004), appeal docketed, No. 04-2878 (8th Cir. July 8, 2004).

6. **Implicit apportionment by federal water project legislation?** The Colorado River Compact allocated 7.5 million acre feet per year to the Upper Basin states but did not make any allocation among those states. At the close of World War II, the Bureau of Reclamation announced a plan to develop the Upper Basin that listed a number of possible projects in each state. However, the Secretary of the Interior announced he would not push for congressional authorization of the projects until the Upper Basin states reached agreement on their respective shares of the water allocated to that basin. H.R. Doc. No. 80-419, The Bureau had no wish to construct a project within a state and later find that the state did not have a legal claim to sufficient water for it. Since the 1963 opinion in Arizona v. California, however, it has been clear that Congress has power to apportion water between states and that such an apportionment places the water beyond the power of the Court to reassign. Could it now be inferred that Congress intends an implicit allocation of water among states whenever it provides for construction of federal projects on interstate rivers? In other words, could it be said that Congress surely would not want to waste money constructing a project that lacks an adequate water supply, and therefore Congress must have

intended an apportionment by the legislation authorizing the project (or if that alone is not enough, by the authorizing legislation plus the appropriation of construction funds)?

7. **Federal regulatory legislation affecting water use between states.** The Water Resources Development Act of 1986 does not directly apportion water between states, but it contains provisions bearing on water use as between states. It prohibits all federal agencies from studying any river basin plan or future federal project involving the transfer of water from the Columbia River basin to another region, unless the study is approved by the governors of all affected states. 33 U.S.C. § 2265. It also bars anyone from exporting water from any portion of the Great Lakes within the United States for use outside the Great Lakes basin, unless the study is approved by all the governors of the Great Lakes states; and it bars federal agencies from studying the feasibility of such export, unless all the Great Lakes governors approve. 42 U.S.C. § 1962d-20(d), (e).

Modern federal environmental statutes, while not aimed at apportioning interstate streams between states, may give a downstream state new procedural and substantive tools to block or modify proposed water development upstream in another state that would reduce flows in the downstream state. This potential is illustrated by Roanoke River Basin Association v. Hudson, 940 F.2d 58, (4th Cir. 1991). The Roanoke River flows southeasterly from Virginia into North Carolina. A Virginia city planned to divert up to 60 million gallons of water daily from the river system for municipal use. To implement the plan, the city needed a permit from the Army Corps of Engineers under Rivers and Harbors Act § 10, 33 U.S.C. § 403, and Clean Water Act § 404, 33 U.S.C. § 1344. When the Corps issued a permit, North Carolina sued and argued that the permit was issued in violation of the two sections cited above and the National Environmental Policy Act. North Carolina expressed concern that the city's water diversion would damage downstream water quality and striped bass. Although the Fourth Circuit upheld issuance of the permit, North Carolina's efforts did result in the addition to the permit of a mitigation requirement designed to maintain adequate downstream flow during bass spawning season.

See also Riverside Irrigation District v. Andrews, infra p. 583, where the federal environmental statutes involved were the Endangered Species Act and Clean Water Act § 404, and the habitat needs of an endangered species along an interstate river in Nebraska prevented an upstream Colorado appropriator from qualifying for a nationwide dredge and fill permit under § 404.

Chapter 7

PUBLIC RIGHTS AND ENVIRONMENTAL PROTECTION

SECTION 1. PUBLIC RIGHTS

A. Navigation

KANSAS v. MEEK

Supreme Court of Kansas, 1990.
246 Kan. 99, 785 P.2d 1356.

LOCKETT, JUSTICE. Jasper R. Hays constructed a fence across Shoal Creek, in part to prevent canoeists and others from using that portion of the stream which flows through his land located in southeast Cherokee County. Christopher Y. Meek, the Cherokee County Attorney, filed a petition for declaratory judgment seeking to confirm the public's right to use Shoal Creek for recreational purposes. On June 11, 1988, the district court ordered Hays to remove the fence pending a hearing on the State's petition. On September 22, the district court denied the State's petition and dissolved its temporary restraining order. * * *

The State appeals, claiming that (1) Shoal Creek is a navigable stream; (2) the public has acquired the right to use Shoal Creek by prescriptive easement; and (3) the public has the right to use Shoal Creek under the public trust doctrine. * * *

Navigability. If Shoal Creek is a navigable stream, the Hays' ownership extends only to the banks. If the stream is nonnavigable, the Hays own the bed of the stream by the same title that they own the adjoining land. If the stream is nonnavigable, the Hays, who own the land adjoining both sides of the stream, may put a fence across the stream to prevent trespassers upon their property.

In England, streams were considered navigable only in so far as they partook of the sea, and to the extent that their waters were affected by the ebb and flow of the tide, and only so far was the title of the riparian owner limited to the bank; above such point, even though the stream was large enough to be used, and in fact was used, for purposes of navigation, the riparian owner owned the soil ad medium filum aquae—to the middle thread of the stream. * * * [T]he better and more generally accepted rule in this country is to apply the term "navigable" to all the streams which are in fact navigable; and in such case to limit the title of the riparian owner to the bank of the stream. This is true in Kansas and most states where the lands have been surveyed and patented under the federal law.

To determine navigability, the first question is whether title to the riverbed passed to the State upon admittance into the Union. The critical case on this point is United States v. Holt Bank, 270 U.S. 49 (1926), which established that ownership of the beds of navigable streams and lakes is a federal question to be resolved according to principles of federal law and under federal definitions. *Holt Bank* also established the specific criteria to be used in determining whether particular bodies of water are deemed navigable for purposes of vesting the state with title to the beds. Under this test, bodies of water are navigable and title to the beds under the water are vested in the state if: (1) the bodies of water were used, or were susceptible of being used, as a matter of fact, as highways for commerce; (2) such use for commerce was possible under the natural conditions of the body of water; (3) commerce was or could have been conducted in the customary modes of trade or travel on water; and (4) all of these conditions were satisfied at the time of statehood. 270 U.S. at 55-56, 46 S.Ct. at 199.

The last navigability case to come before this court was Webb v. Neosho County Comm'rs, 124 Kan. 38, 257 P. 966 (1927). * * * The *Webb* court found the Neosho River was not navigable. * * * As Professor Wadley notes, [the definition applied in *Webb*] "appears to track the [Holt Bank] federal title test in all relevant areas except for the requirement that the criteria be satisfied as of the time of statehood." Wadley, Recreational Use of Nonnavigable Waterways, 56 J.K.B.A. 27, 31 (Nov./ Dec. 1987).

In its analysis, the *Webb* court first stated that navigability "is a question of fact to be determined from the evidence." * * * Did title to the Shoal Creek stream bed pass to the State upon entry into the Union or is there sufficient evidence to declare Shoal Creek navigable? The trial court made these findings of fact: "(10) Shoal Creek cannot be floated without getting out of the canoe or boat at various locations. (11) John Link, Jr., owner of Ozark Quality Products, Inc., travels Shoal Creek several times a year collecting plants used in his business. * * * (12) There is no evidence that Shoal Creek has ever been used for valuable floatage in transportation to market of the products of the country through which it runs. (13) During times of drouth, portions of Shoal Creek are impassable by even a canoe or small boat. * * * (14) Shoal Creek has been used for recreational purposes for more than fifteen years. (15) A canoe rental business exists, known as Holly Haven, which rents canoes to be used on Shoal Creek. The point of entry is near Joplin, Missouri, with the point of exit at Schermerhorn Park, Galena, Kansas, where the business picks up the canoes and their occupants for the return trip to Holly Haven." Based on these findings, the district court held that Shoal Creek did not meet the *Webb* standard for navigability.

The State does not challenge the trial court's findings; rather, it argues that findings (11) and (15) indicate that the stream is susceptible of being used for commerce, thus meeting the *Webb* standard for navigability. The Kansas Wildlife Federation adds: "Because Shoal Creek is in the same natural condition as it was at the time of statehood, any commercial use of the river today conclusively demonstrates that the river was 'susceptible of use' at the time Kansas was admitted to the Union."

Based on the trial court's finding of facts, Shoal Creek is less "navigable" than the Neosho River. Under both the federal (*Holt Bank*) and current state (*Webb*) tests for navigability, title to the Shoal Creek stream bed did not pass to the State upon entry into the Union.

Though federal and state laws set the criteria to determine the issue of navigability for purposes of determining state title, individual states are relatively free to regulate the consumptive and nonconsumptive use of water within their borders. State regulatory concerns may depart from state ownership of the beds of navigable bodies of water as the primary criterion by which public need or access to water is secured.

Based on the public's increasing desire to use water for nonconsumptive recreational purposes, the State urges us to adopt a "modern" view of navigability which would not affect landowners' title to the riverbeds. Other states have taken such action.

In Day v. Armstrong, 362 P.2d 137, 145-46 (Wyo.1961), the court determined that, under the Wyoming Constitution, title to the water is in the State. Neither the Wyoming Constitution nor the act of Congress admitting the state into the Union limited the kind or type of use the State may make of its waters. Therefore, the legislature had the power to allow persons to float on the streams. In addition, the court determined that the public, while floating on the state's waters, may hunt, fish, or do anything which is not otherwise made unlawful.

In People v. Mack, 19 Cal.App.3d 1040, 1045-46, 97 Cal.Rptr. 448 (1971), the California court recognized that under the prior California law, a stream is navigable if it is susceptible to the useful commercial purpose of carrying the products of the country (citing Wright v. Seymour, 69 Cal. 122, 10 Pac. 323 (1886)) or when declared navigable by the legislature. A navigable stream may be used by the public for boating, swimming, fishing, hunting, and all recreational purposes. The court then discussed the modern tendency of several other states to allow the public to use any stream capable of being used for recreational purposes. It then determined that a stream that can be boated or sailed for pleasure is also navigable.

In Southern Idaho F. & G. Ass'n v. Picabo Livestock, Inc., 96 Idaho 360, 362-63, 528 P.2d 1295 (1974), the Idaho court found that, while the federal test of navigability determines the title to stream beds, as the present action did not involve title to the bed of a navigable stream, the federal test of navigability does not preclude a less restrictive state test of navigability. It upheld the legislature's enactment that any stream which, in its natural state, will float logs or any other commercial or floatable commodity, or is capable of being navigated by oar or motor propelled small craft, for pleasure or commercial purposes, is navigable. The Idaho court concluded that, where a stream is navigable, the public's right to use the stream for fishing extended to boating, swimming, hunting, and all recreational purposes.

In State v. McIlroy, 595 S.W.2d 659, cert. denied 449 U.S. 843 (1980), landowners along the Mulberry River brought suit because their privacy was being interrupted by people trespassing on their property, littering the stream, and generally destroying their property. The Arkansas Supreme Court, after recognizing that the criterion for determining the navigability of a stream depended upon the usefulness of the stream for carrying out farm and forest products and bringing in merchandise during some seasons of the year, expanded navigability to include the use of streams for recreational purposes, such as fishing in flatbottomed boats, canoeing, or floating.

The Arkansas court recognized that the landowners have a right to prohibit the public from crossing their property to reach the stream. In addition, the state government has a duty to protect the landowners' rights and the responsibility to keep navigable waters in their natural and unblemished state.

The Hays claim the adoption of a "modern" test for navigability by this court would be a radical change in current state law, citing People v. Emmert, 597 P.2d 1025 (1979), where the Colorado Supreme Court held that the defendants did not have any right under the state constitution to float on nonnavigable streams within boundaries of privately owned property without the consent of the property owner. In that case, Emmert and two others were convicted of criminal trespass after they rafted down a nonnavigable stream without first obtaining the riparian landowner's permission. They challenged the convictions, claiming a right to use the stream under the following state constitutional provision:

> "The water of every natural stream, not heretofore appropriated, within the state of Colorado, is hereby declared to be the property of the public, and the same is dedicated to the use of the people of the state, subject to appropriation as hereinafter provided." Colo. Const. art. XVI, § 5.

In affirming the convictions, the Colorado Supreme Court held that this provision, which appeared under a section entitled "Irrigation," did not open state waters for public recreational use. The court found support for this interpretation in state statutes which: (1) codified the common—law rule of cujus est solum, ejus est usque ad coelum—he who owns the surface of the ground has the exclusive right to everything which is above it; (2) authorized the State Wildlife Commission to contract for public hunting and fishing on private land; and (3) made unauthorized entry upon private land a crime.

The Colorado court in *Emmert* concisely summarized the Hays' position: "'If a change in long established judicial precedent is desirable, it is a legislative and not a judicial function to make any needed change.'" 198 Colo. at 141, 597 P.2d 1025. Our legislature's current view on the recreational use of water is discussed with the last issue.

Prescriptive Easement. The State also claims that the public has acquired the right to use Shoal Creek by prescriptive easement. Though we have never determined whether an individual can acquire a prescriptive easement to use the nonnavigable waterways of this state, in State, ex rel., Akers, 92 Kan. 169, Syl. P 4, 140 P. 637, we found that title to the waters or bed of a navigable stream cannot be acquired through private use or occupancy, whether adverse or by permission, however long continued, or by prescription. * * *

We agree that the doctrine of prescriptive easement for public highways extends to streams and rivers of this state. * * * For the public to obtain a prescriptive easement for recreational travel, both the *Shanks* test [adverse use for the prescriptive period] and *Kratina* requirement for official public action are required. Neither occasional use of the creek by a large number of canoeists nor frequent use by a small number of canoeists gives rise to a prescriptive right in the public to use nonnavigable streams. A public prescriptive right arises during the prescribed period when public use becomes so burdensome that government must regulate traffic, keep the peace, invoke sanitary measures, and insure that the natural condition of the stream is maintained. Because public officials have taken no such action, there is no public prescriptive easement on Shoal Creek.

The Public Trust Doctrine. The State finally contends that the public is entitled to use Shoal Creek under the public trust doctrine. The essence of the public trust doctrine was articulated by Professor Sax: "When a state holds a resource which is available for the free use of the general public, a court will look with considerable skepticism on any government conduct which is calculated either to reallocate that resource to more restricted uses or to subject public uses to the self-interest of private parties." Sax, The Public Trust Doctrine in Natural Resource Law: Effective Judicial Intervention, 68 Mich.L.Rev. 473, 490 (1970). See Illinois Central Railroad v. Illinois, 146 U.S. 387 (1892). * * *

At least one state, Montana, has applied the public trust doctrine under facts similar to those presented by this case. The Montana Supreme Court determined that, under the public trust doctrine and the 1972 Montana Constitution, "any surface waters that are capable of recreational use may be so used by the public without regard to streambed ownership or navigability." Montana Coalition for Stream Access v. Curran, 210 Mont. 38, 53, 682 P.2d 163 (1984). The constitutional provision to which the Montana court referred, Mont. Const. art. IX, § 3, provides: "All surface, underground, flood and atmospheric waters within the boundaries of the state are the property of the state for the use of its people and subject to appropriation for beneficial uses as provided by law."

The State analogizes the Montana constitutional provision with K.S.A. 82a-702, which provides:

> "Dedication of use of water. All water within the state of Kansas is hereby dedicated to the use of the people of the state, subject to the control and regulation of the state in the manner herein prescribed."

While the broad language in 82a-702 is similar to that which appears in the Montana Constitution and others, it is clear that our legislature did not intend to incorporate the State's position when it passed that statute. A thorough discussion of the history behind 82a-702 and related statutes appears in Williams v. City of Wichita, 190 Kan. 317, 331-36, 374 P.2d 578 (1962). Here, it is sufficient to note that these statutes were intended to address problems related to the consumptive use of water, and not nonconsumptive, recreational use. Statutory provisions concerned with consumptive appropriation cannot be applied to subvert a riparian landowner's right to exclusive surface use of waters bounded by his land.

Further evidence of our legislature's disinclination toward the State's position can be seen in the treatment of three bills introduced during the 1986 and 1987 legislative sessions. House Bill 2835, which was introduced in 1986, sought to amend K.S.A. 82a-702 by adding the following language:

> "All water of the state which can serve a beneficial purpose is hereby declared to be public waters, and the public shall have a right to make a nonconsumptive use of such water without obtaining an appropriation. The public character of the water shall not be determined exclusively by the proprietorship of the underlying, overlying or surrounding land or on whether it is a body or stream of water which was navigable in fact or susceptible of being used as a highway for commerce at the time this state was admitted to the Union."

This bill was killed in the House Energy and Natural Resources Committee on February 27, 1986.

House Bill 3038 was also introduced during the 1986 session. Known as the Kansas Recreational River Act, this bill would have allowed the legislature to designate "selected rivers within this state [which possess] outstanding fish and wildlife, recreational, geologic or scenic values" as recreational rivers. This designation would have allowed the public "to enjoy and use such rivers through noncontact river recreation." Noncontact river recreation was defined as "the public use of a recreational river by means of a vessel." This bill died in the House Energy and Natural Resources Committee without action.

House Bill 3038 was resurrected in 1987 as Senate Bill 94 and was killed by the Senate Energy and Natural Resources Committee on February 6, 1987.

Owners of the bed of a nonnavigable stream have the exclusive right of control of everything above the stream bed, subject only to constitutional and statutory limitations, restrictions, and regulations. Where the legislature refuses to create a public trust for recreational purposes in nonnavigable streams, courts should not alter the legislature's statement of public policy by judicial legislation. If the nonnavigable waters of this state are to be appropriated for recreational use, the legislative process is the proper method to achieve this goal.

The public has no right to the use of nonnavigable water overlying private lands for recreational purposes without the consent of the landowner.

Notes

1. **Decoupling public use and navigability.** The principal case discusses the Colorado Supreme Court's decision in People v. Emmert. That court upheld a trespass conviction where public users of a nonnavigable waterway leave their boats and step ashore. The rights of public users in Colorado to simply float over nonnavigable waterways remains an open question. See Lori Potter, Steve Marlin & Kathy Kanda, Legal Underpinnings of the Right to Float Through Private Property in Colorado: A Reply to John Hill, 5 U. Denv. L. Rev. 457 (2002).

A Wyoming case, Day v. Armstrong, also discussed in the principal case, decouples the issue of public use from the question of navigability and adopts the reasoning rejected by the Colorado Supreme Court in Emmert. After holding that the waters involved are nonnavigable and after noting that the Wyoming Constitution declares that the state is the owner of all streams, rivers and lakes, the court said:

"The title to waters within this State being in the State, in concomitance, it follows that there must be an easement in behalf of the State for a right of way through their natural channels for such waters upon and over lands submerged by them or across the bed and channels of streams or other collections of waters. * * * The waters not being in trespass upon or over the lands where they naturally appear, they are available for such uses by the public of which they are capable. When waters are able to float craft, they may be so used."

In Parks v. Cooper, 676 N.W.2d 823 (S.D. 2004), the South Dakota Supreme Court concluded that, under the South Dakota public trust doctrine, the public had rights to use nonnavigable surface waters overlying private lands, but only the state legislature could determine the scope of those uses.

In several other cases in which courts have found that the public has a right to use any stream which is capable of being used for recreational purposes, it is debatable whether the court is decoupling the issue of public use from navigability or whether the court is merely adopting a new test of navigability. See Montana Coalition for Stream Access v. Curran, 682 P.2d 163 (1984); Montana Coalition for Stream Access v. Hildreth, 684 P.2d 1088 (Mont. 1984); Elder v. Delcour, 269 S.W.2d 17 (Mo. 1954). Cf. Madison v. Graham, 126 F. Supp. 2d 1320 (D. Mont. 2001).

2. **Massachussets Bay Colony Ordinance.** Another form of nonnavigable public water goes back to the very origins of American history. The Massachusetts Bay Colony Ordinance of 1641–1647 provides, "And for great ponds lying in common, though within the bounds of some town, it shall be free for any men to fish or foul there, and may pass and repass on foot through any man's property for that end, so they trespass not upon any man's corn or meadow." Today this concept is broadened to include most fields of water recreation, and is still applicable to most fresh water lakes in Maine, Massachusetts and New Hampshire. See Leighton L. Leighty, Public Rights in Navigable State Waters—Some Statutory Approaches, 6 Land & Water L. Rev. 459, 471–472 (1971).

3. **Legislative declarations.** Some states have made certain waters public by the ipse dixit of the legislature. Minnesota has declared eleven categories of water to be "public waters." Minn. Stat. Ann. § 103G.005(15)(a). It has also declared that the determination of the public or private status of a watercourse should not depend exclusively on bed ownership or watercourse navigability.

Minn. Stat. Ann. § 103G.005(15)(b). Indiana has claimed control of all lakes "used by the public with the acquiescence of a riparian owner" for use by all its citizens for fishing, boating, swimming and the storage of water to maintain water levels. Ind. Code Ann. §§ 14–26–2–3, 14–26–2–5. Iowa Code Ann. § 456A.24 provides for the condemnation of access to all water suitable for hunting, fishing and trapping, without distinguishing between navigable and non-navigable waters. The Iowa Supreme Court has indicated that the state may use this authority to condemn access ways to any waters overlying private beds entirely surrounded by private property. See Peck v. Olsen Constr. Co., 245 N.W. 131 (Iowa 1932). "Takings" arguments which might be raised by legislative expansion of public rights in waters are assessed in Chris A. Shafer, Public Rights in Michigan's Streams: Toward A Modern Definition of Navigability, 45 Wayne L. Rev. 9 (1999).

California adds to public waters in two ways. Article I, § 25 of the California Constitution provides: "The people shall have the right to fish upon and from the public lands of the State and in the waters thereof, excepting upon lands set aside for fish hatcheries, and no land owned by the State shall ever be sold or transferred without reserving in the people the absolute right to fish thereupon; * * *." Cal. Fish & Game Code § 5943(a) provides: "The owner of a dam shall accord to the public for the purpose of fishing, the right of access to the waters impounded by the dam during the open season for the taking of fish in the stream or river, subject to the regulations of the commission." Both provisions were involved in State v. San Luis Obispo Sportman's Ass'n., 584 P.2d 1088 (Cal. 1978).

4. **Use of privately owned beds of public waterways.** Where the bed is privately owned but the public has a right to use a waterway, what right does the public have to use the bed? Compare Day v. Armstrong with Montana Coalition for Stream Access v. Curran, both cited in the principal case. In *Day* the court held that the public can float the stream, can touch or scrape the bed when incidental to floating, and can even disembark and walk on the bed when necessary to get watercraft around shoals, rapids, and obstacles, but that the public has no right to wade or walk the stream except as is incident to floating. In *Curran* the court held that the public could use the bed and banks up to the ordinary high water mark and could even go above the high water mark if necessary to get around obstacles. But see Galt v. State Department of Fish, Wildlife, and Parks, 731 P.2d 912 (Mont. 1987), in which the court stated that use of beds and banks must be related to use of the water itself and held that statutes giving the public the right to build duck blinds and boat moorages, to camp, and to engage in big game hunting on private lands below the ordinary high water mark were an unconstitutional confiscation of property. The court also held unconstitutional a statute requiring landowners to bear the cost of constructing portage routes around artificial barriers. *Curran* expressly held that the public has no right to cross privately owned lands to gain access to streams and a similar holding is implicit in *Day*.

5. **Wild rivers.** The federal government and several states have adopted "wild rivers" legislation. See, e.g., federal, California, and Oklahoma acts, supra p. 94, Note 7, and Wis. Stat. Ann. § 30.26. In many cases, the waters affected would be considered public waters before such designation and the methods of preservation consist largely of land use planning and zoning of the banks.

Nevertheless, the expressed purpose of these statutes is to preserve the designated rivers in their free-flowing condition and to protect them from development, and the implementation of this policy restricts riparian uses to the end of greater public use.

6. **State ownership of beds of navigable waters.** State ownership of the beds of navigable waters is rooted in constitutional theory. Upon achieving independence, the original colonies, as successors to the rights of the English Crown, became the owners of the beds of navigable bodies of water. The Constitution requires that new states be admitted to the Union on an "equal footing." See Coyle v. Smith, 221 U.S. 559 (1911). Under the "equal footing doctrine," the United States held the title to territorial lands under navigable waters in trust for future states and such lands passed automatically to new states upon admission to the Union (Pollard's Lessee v. Haggin, 44 U.S. (3 How.) 212 (1845); Utah v. United States, 403 U.S. 9 (1971)), except in very rare cases where title to such lands was conveyed to someone prior to the state's admission or where there was a clear congressional intent to withhold title from the state at admission. See United States v. Cherokee Nation, 480 U.S. 700 (1987); Montana v. United States, 450 U.S. 544 (1981). The equal footing doctrine passes title to navigable intrastate water courses, as well as water courses which are part of a navigable interstate or international highway. United States v. Utah, 283 U.S. 64 (1931). But see James R. Rasband, The Disregarded Common Parentage of the Equal Footing and Public Trust Doctrines, 32 Land & Water L. Rev. 1 (1997). Professor Rasband argues that state ownership of submerged lands is not constitutionally required and is better explained as a principle of federal common law. He notes that the principle was essentially codified by the Submerged Lands Act of 1953, which confirms state ownership of all land under navigable waters not expressly reserved or granted by the United States prior to statehood. See 43 U.S.C. §§ 1301(a), 1311(b)(1), 1313(a).

7. **Title and state tests of navigability.** Some states developed their own tests of navigability for title before the Supreme Court made it clear that the test is a federal one. For example, the Wisconsin Supreme Court held that the beds of lakes navigable under the state but not the federal test are owned by the state but the beds of streams navigable only by state law are held by the riparian owner subject to public rights. Illinois Steel Co. v. Bilot, 84 N.W. 855 (Wis. 1901); Ne-pee-nauk Club v. Wilson, 71 N.W. 661 (Wis. 1897); Baker v. Voss, 259 N.W. 412 (Wis. 1935). The Iowa Supreme Court once held that the state owned the beds of all nonnavigable waters, but later concluded that the state owned only the beds of "meandered" non-navigable waters (marked and identified by the public land survey). Shortell v. Des Moines Elec. Co., 172 N.W. 649 (Iowa 1919).

Now that it is clear that navigability for title is a federal test, what is the effect in title disputes of more liberal state tests of navigability for title? What if the lands involved were previously the subject of litigation in which the state test was applied? What if the lands have not been the subject of such litigation? Does it matter if the rival claimant to the submerged lands is the federal government or is a private party whose title originated in a federal patent? Would the same problems exist if the state has adopted a more stringent test of navigability for title? See Borax, Consol., Ltd. v. Los Angeles, 296 U.S. 10 (1935); Oregon ex rel. State Land Bd. v. Corvallis Sand & Gravel Co., 429 U.S. 363 (1977).

For an analysis of the cases on navigability for title and their effect on public use see Ralph W. Johnson & Russell A. Austin Jr., Recreational Rights and Titles to Beds on Western Lakes and Streams, 7 Nat. Resources J. 1 (1967). A shorter and more general treatment is Leighton L. Leighty, The Source and Scope of Public and Private Rights in Navigable Waters, 5 Land & Water L. Rev. 391 (1970). More recent cases are reviewed in Chris A. Shafer, supra p.516, Note 3, and Richard M. Frank, Forever Free: Navigability, Inland Waterways, and the Expanding Public Interest, 16 U.C. Davis L. Rev. 579 (1983).

8. **Float planes.** In Alaska v. United States, 754 F.2d 851 (9th Cir. 1985), Alaska claimed title to the bed of Slopbucket Lake, based on its use as a landing and take off site for floatplanes. Alaska argued that floatplane use was a customary mode of trade and travel on water at the time of statehood in 1959. Noting that the central theme of navigability is the movement of people or goods from point to point on the water, the court rejected the claim: "The floatplanes go to and from the lake; they do not travel on the water." Id. at 854.

9. **Title to nonnavigable tidal waters.** As noted in the principal case, navigability under the federal title test is not restricted to waters which are subject to the ebb and flow of the tide, but extends to all waters which are "navigable in fact." But what of the title to lands under waters which are subject to the ebb and flow of the tide but which are not navigable in fact? In Phillips Petroleum Co. v. Mississippi, 484 U.S. 469 (1988), the Supreme Court affirmed "long-standing precedents" which hold that upon admission to the Union a state received ownership of all lands under waters which are subject to the ebb and flow of the tide whether navigable in fact or not.

10. **Northwest Ordinance.** As for the Northwest Ordinance as a source of public rights, see G. Graham Waite, Public Rights to Use and Have Access to Navigable Waters, 1958 Wis. L. Rev. 335; G. Graham Waite, The Dilemma of Water Recreation and a Suggested Solution, 1958 Wis. L. Rev. 542.

11. **Bed ownership and private rights.** Bed ownership can be important for reasons other than as a source of public rights. If the bed is exposed by natural or man-made causes, it may have value for surface uses. More commonly, bed ownership is important for purposes of determining title to minerals lying under the bed. See, e.g., United States v. Louisiana, 470 U.S. 93 (1985), which concerned a dispute between the United States on the one hand and the states of Mississippi and Alabama on the other hand over the ownership of the seabed, minerals, and other natural resources underlying Mississippi Sound. An extensive discussion of these problems in inland bodies of water is found in Kemp Wilson, Ownership of Mineral Interests Underlying Inland Bodies of Water and the Effects of Accretion and Erosion, 30 Rocky Mtn. Min. L. Inst. 14–1 (1984).

Somewhat similar questions arise when waterways form the boundaries between parcels of land. The common law rule for nonnavigable bodies puts the boundary at the thread of the stream. If the location of a body shifts or recedes slowly ("accretion," "reliction," or "erosion") there is general agreement that the boundary shifts with it. Similarly, it is generally agreed that the boundary does not shift if the body of water shifts location rapidly ("avulsion"). However, there is no uniform treatment of what qualifies as a rapid or slow shift. These matters and related complications are discussed in Kemp Wilson, supra.

12. **Title problems.** In most states, there has been no systematic effort to determine the ownership of submerged lands. Consequently, title to submerged lands is often unresolved unless a particular watercourse has been the subject of litigation regarding its navigability. The potential "equal footing" claim of the state to the bed tends to cloud the title of upland riparian owners, even where the watercourse is almost certainly nonnavigable. In 1987, Arizona adopted legislation to reduce such clouds in response to aggressive assertion of equal footing claims by state officials. The legislation relinquished outright the state's equal footing claims to waters where navigability was doubtful—all waters except the Colorado River and three other rivers. Where navigability was somewhat more viable—the named rivers other than the Colorado—the legislation provided that the state's claims would be relinquished to the upland owners upon receipt of a nominal fee. In Arizona Center for Law in the Public Interest v. Hassell, 837 P.2d 158 (Ariz. Ct. App. 1992), the court struck down these and related provisions of the legislation, holding that they violated the public trust doctrine and a constitutional prohibition against gifts of state property.

The *Hassell* court indicated that litigation to resolve the state's claims was not constitutionally required and suggested that an administrative process which provided for a systematic investigation and evaluation of each of the state's claims would be acceptable. In response, the legislature in 1992 created the Arizona Navigable Stream Adjudication Commission to collect evidence, make an initial determination of navigability, and make recommendations to the legislature. The legislature disclaims title to the beds if it concurs with the commission's recommendation that a particular watercourse is nonnavigable. Conversely, it directs the State Land Department to claim title and bring a quiet title action if it concurs with a recommendation of navigability. See Ariz. Rev. Stat. Ann. §§ 37–1101 to –1131. Pursuant to this process, the legislature disclaimed title to the beds of a number of rivers in 1998 and 1999. See Ariz Rev. Stat. Ann. §§ 37–1129 to –1129.09.

In Defenders of Wildlife v. Hull, 18 P.3d 722 (Ariz. Ct. App. 2001), the Arizona Court of Appeal found that these disclaimers also violated both the public trust doctrine and the Arizona Constitution's gift clause. In addition, the court found that the statutes' requirements of "clear and convincing" evidence of navigability was preempted under the federal law. In Arizona Laws 2001, Ch. 166, the Arizona legislature enacted new disclaimer provisions to address the court's concerns.

13. **Application of "navigability" in other contexts.** Navigability can be legally significant in a number of other contexts besides public rights and title to beds. Navigability has historically provided a basis for state and federal regulatory activities involving water. See Muench v. Pub. Service Corp. and accompanying Notes, supra p. 294 and Kaiser Aetna v. United States and accompanying Notes, infra p. 632. A related context is the "navigation servitude" under which the federal and state governments can sometimes "take" private property without paying compensation. See United States v. Rands and Kaiser Aetna v. United States, and accompanying Notes, infra pp. 626-36. The public trust doctrine, discussed briefly in the principal case and explored more fully in the next subsection, had its origins in navigable bodies of water and is still tied to navigable waters in many jurisdictions. Admiralty jurisdiction involves yet another application of navigability. See Propeller Genesee Chief v. Fitzhugh, 53

U.S. (12 How.) 443 (1851). The test of navigability can vary depending on the context even within a single jurisdiction; thus, a body may be navigable in one context but not in another.

STATE v. BLECK

Supreme Court of Wisconsin, 1983.
114 Wis.2d 454, 338 N.W.2d 492.

WILLIAM A. BABLITCH, JUSTICE. This is a review of an unpublished decision of the court of appeals, 109 Wis.2d 694, 326 N.W.2d 783 (1983), affirming judgments of the circuit court for Dane county, Honorable Moria Krueger, Judge. Martin Bleck, Bryan Keleny and William Prince (petitioners) were convicted of violating sec. 30.15(1)(d), Stats., which provides that anyone who constructs or places any structure or deposits any material in navigable waters in violation of secs. 30.12 or 30.13, is subject to a forfeiture not to exceed $50. * * *

In the spring of 1980, the petitioners placed a water ski jump on Bass Lake, which is located in Dane county. The ski jump measured twenty-two feet by fourteen feet by six feet, and either rested on the lake bed or was secured to the lake bottom by ropes connected to four sixteen-gallon drums filled with concrete.

In May, 1980, the petitioners, who are not riparian owners, applied to the department of natural resources (DNR) for a permit to place the ski jump on Bass Lake, pursuant to sec. 30.12, Stats. * * *

DNR rejected the application because it was not made by a riparian owner, as required by sec. 30.12, Stats. The petitioners left the ski jump on Bass Lake during the summer of 1980, even though DNR had not issued a permit. On September 17, 1980, a warden from DNR observed the ski jump still on the lake. He issued citations to the petitioners pursuant to sec. 30.15(1)(d) for violation of sec. 30.12.

After a trial to the circuit court, the court found the petitioners guilty of violating sec. 30.15(1)(d), Stats., and imposed a forfeiture of $50 on each. The court found that Bass Lake is a navigable lake within the meaning of sec. 30.10(1). The court also determined that sec. 30.12 is applicable to the petitioner's ski jump, and it concluded that sec. 30.12 did not violate the public trust doctrine or the equal protection guarantees of the Wisconsin and United States Constitutions.

The petitioners contend that the application of sec. 30.12, Stats., to their placement of the ski jump is contrary to the public trust doctrine because the result is that only riparian owners may seasonally moor recreational water facilities on the beds of navigable waters. The petitioners base this conclusion on the fact that only riparians may obtain permits under sec. 30.12. The petitioners argue that this result contravenes the public trust doctrine, which they contend is designed to protect the recreational use of navigable waters by all citizens.

Although the public trust doctrine safeguards interests of all members of the public in navigable waters, Wisconsin has also recognized the existence of certain common law rights that are incidents of riparian ownership of property adjacent to a body of water. See, e.g., Mayer, 29 Wis.2d at 174, 138 N.W.2d at 22; Note, Riparian Water Law—Lakeshore Developments, 1966 Wis.L.Rev. 172, 173. Such riparian rights include the use of the shoreline of the riparian owner's property, the reasonable use of the water, and the privilege to use a lake for bathing, swimming and boating. A riparian who owns property abutting navigable lakes has been held to have a right of access to and from the lake upon his land, a right to build wharves and piers in aid of navigation, and a right to have water flow to his land without artificial obstruction. The traditional distinction between riparian owners and nonriparians was noted in The Attorney General ex rel. Askew v. Smith, 109 Wis. 532, 85 N.W. 512 (1901), in which this court indicated that a riparian owner could construct a pier in a lake in aid of navigation if not prohibited by state law. The construction of a pier by a nonriparian, however, was considered to be an unauthorized invasion of the public's rights because the right to place a pier is merely an incident of riparian ownership.

The common law distinction between riparians and nonriparians is also reflected throughout ch. 30, Stats., which governs navigable waters, harbors, and navigation, and of which sec. 30.12 is a part. Section 30.11(4), provides that riparian proprietors may place solid structures or fill up to a bulkhead line established under sec. 30.11(1). Section 30.13(1), permits riparian proprietors to construct a wharf or pier in a navigable water without a sec. 30.12 permit if certain conditions are satisfied. Neither provision grants the same right to nonriparians.

We conclude that the application of sec. 30.12, Stats., to the petitioners' placement of a ski jump does not violate the public trust doctrine. The fact that sec. 30.12 allows only riparians to apply for permits is simply an acknowledgment by the legislature of certain common law riparian rights that are incidents of their ownership of property abutting the water. Such rights, however, are still subject to the public's paramount right and interest in navigable waters. Under sec. 30.12(2), DNR may grant a permit to a riparian to place a structure only if that structure does not materially obstruct navigation, or reduce the effective flood flow capacity of a stream, or if it is not detrimental to the public interest. There is, therefore, no guarantee that a riparian owner who applies for a permit would obtain a permit under sec. 30.12 to place the type of ski jump the petitioners installed. * * *

Notes

1. **Public access to navigable waters.** A recurring problem where riparians own the shores of navigable waters is the question of how the public can get access to them. A Wisconsin statute provides that the county board may condemn a right of way for any public highway to any navigable stream or lake. In Branch v. Oconto County, 109 N.W.2d 105 (Wis. 1961), Branch had purchased a 100-foot strip completely around a 390-acre lake which was two to four feet deep and while not suitable for fishing or swimming was excellent for duck hunting. The county condemned a road to the lake. Held, Branch was not entitled to the diminution of the value of his property due to loss of exclusive use.

In State v. Bollenbach, 63 N.W.2d 278 (Minn. 1954), the court held that a similar statute, permitting condemnation of access to "public waters * * * upon which the public has a right to hunt and fish" had no application to private non-navigable waters. The lake involved was considerably bigger than the lake in *Oconto County,* but the Minnesota court limited public waters to those navigable by the federal test.

In Iowa, the public trust doctrine, discussed in the next subsection, has been expanded to include the public's right of access to public waters. However, access is protected only to the extent that the land providing access is owned by the state; i.e., the state must protect the public's right of access when disposing of such lands. See Larman v. Iowa, 552 N.W.2d 158 (Iowa 1996). See also Cal. Const. art. I, § 25, supra p. 516, Note 3, protecting the right of the public to fish on state owned lands.

2. **Right to wharf out.** For the right of the riparian to "wharf out" into navigable waters, see Sheldon J. Plager, Interference with the Public Right of Navigation and the Riparian Owners' Claim of Privilege, 33 Mo. L. Rev. 608 (1968). For other access issues, see supra p. 244, Note 2.

3. **Public rights in artificial extensions of navigable waters.** Wilbour v. Gallagher, 462 P.2d 232 (Wash. 1969), dealt with Lake Chelan, a long scenic navigable lake that had been converted into a hydroelectric power reservoir by a dam at its mouth. Gallagher's land, "Blocks Two and Three, Plat of Lake Park," abutted the original shoreline and a part of it was annually submerged as 21 feet of water was stored behind the dam in the spring and released during the fall and winter. Gallagher filled the land to 5 feet above the artificial highwater mark so that he might use it. Wilbour, whose land adjoined Gallagher's on the upland side, brought suit, complaining of loss of ability to use the water. Held, the fill must be removed as an obstruction to navigation. While the defendant can prevent trespass on his land between high and low water marks when it is not submerged, when it is covered by the navigable water the public has rights of fishing, boating, swimming, water skiing and other recreational activities in that water. Compare California v. Superior Court, 625 P.2d 256 (Cal. 1981).

Wilbour was received with mixed reactions. In Charles E. Corker, Thou Shalt Not Fill Public Waters without Public Permission—Washington's Lake Chelan Decision, 45 Wash. L. Rev. 65 (1970), it was hailed as a significant victory for the public, applicable to all waters of the state, with broad implications for all privately owned shore lands and tide lands. On the other hand, in Edward A. Rauscher, The Lake Chelan Case—Another View, 45 Wash. L. Rev. 523 (1970), it was urged that *Wilbour* is narrowly restricted to its facts as an unusual case in which the customary fee title to intermittently flooded land was not acquired by the person flooding it. Hence, Rauscher argued, the case is not applicable to property flooded by naturally fluctuating water and does not affect the property rights of the owners of such lands or their rights to fill.

B. Public Trust Doctrine

ILLINOIS CENTRAL RAILROAD v. ILLINOIS

Supreme Court of the United States, 1892.
146 U.S. 387, 13 S.Ct. 110, 36 L.Ed. 1018.

MR. JUSTICE FIELD delivered the opinion of the court.

This suit was commenced on the 1st of March, 1883, in a circuit court of Illinois, by an information or bill in equity filed by the attorney general of the state, in the name of its people, against the Illinois Central Railroad Company, a corporation created under its laws, and against the city of Chicago. * * *

The object of the suit is to obtain a judicial determination of the title of certain lands on the east or lake front of the city of Chicago, situated between the Chicago river and Sixteenth street, which have been reclaimed from the waters of the lake, and are occupied by the tracks, depots, warehouses, piers, and other structures used by the railroad company in its business, and also of the title claimed by the company to the submerged lands, constituting the bed of the lake, lying east of its tracks, within the corporate limits of the city, for the distance of a mile, and between the south line of the south pier near Chicago river, extended eastwardly, and a line extended in the same direction from the south line of lot 21 near the company's roundhouse and machine shops. The determination of the title of the company will involve a consideration of its right to construct, for its own business, as well as for public convenience, wharves, piers, and docks in the harbor. * * *

We proceed to consider the claim of the railroad company to the ownership of submerged lands in the harbor, and the right to construct such wharves, piers, docks, and other works therein as it may deem proper for its interest and business. The claim is founded upon the third section of the act of the legislature of the state passed on the 16th of April, 1869, the material part of which is as follows:

> "Sec. 3. The right of the Illinois Central Railroad Company under the grant from the state in its charter, which said grant constitutes a part of the consideration for which the said company pays to the state at least seven per cent of its gross earnings, and under and by virtue of its appropriation, occupancy, use, and control, and the riparian ownership incident to such grant, appropriation, occupancy, use, and control, in and to the lands submerged or otherwise lying east of the said line running parallel with and 400 feet east of the west line of Michigan Avenue, in fractional sections ten and fifteen, township and range as aforesaid, is hereby confirmed; and all the right and title of the state of Illinois in and to the submerged lands constituting the bed of Lake Michigan, and lying east of the tracks and breakwater of the Illinois Central Railroad Company, for a distance of one mile, and between the south line of the south pier extended eastwardly and a line extended eastward from the south line of lot twenty-one, south of and near to the roundhouse and machine shops of said company, in the south division of the said city of Chicago, are hereby granted in fee to the said Illinois Central Railroad Company, its successors and assigns: provided,

> however, that the fee to said lands shall be held by said company in perpetuity, and that the aid company shall not have power to grant, sell, or convey the fee to the same, * * *."

The act of which this section is a part was accepted by a resolution of the board of directors of the company at its office in the city of New York, July 6, 1870, but the acceptance was not communicated to the state until the 18th of November, 1870. A copy of the resolution was on that day forwarded to the secretary of state, and filed and recorded by him in the records of his office. On the 15th of April, 1873, the legislature of Illinois repealed the act. The questions presented relate to the validity of the section cited, of the act, and the effect of the repeal upon its operation. * * *

The act, if valid and operative to the extent claimed, placed under the control of the railroad company nearly the whole of the submerged lands of the harbor, subject only to the limitations that it should not authorize obstructions to the harbor, or impair the public right of navigation, or exclude the legislature from regulating the rates of wharfage or dockage to be charged. With these limitations, the act put it in the power of the company to delay indefinitely the improvement of the harbor, or to construct as many docks, piers, and wharves and other works as it might choose, and at such positions in the harbor as might suit its purposes, and permit any kind of business to be conducted thereon, and to lease them out on its own terms for indefinite periods. The inhibition against the technical transfer of the fee of any portion of the submerged lands was of little consequence when it could make a lease for any period, and renew it at its pleasure; and the inhibitions against authorizing obstructions to the harbor and impairing the public right of navigation placed no impediments upon the action of the railroad company which did not previously exist. A corporation created for one purpose, the construction and operation of a railroad between designated points, is by the act converted into a corporation to manage and practically control the harbor of Chicago, not simply for its own purpose as a railroad corporation, but for its own profit generally. * * *

The question, therefore, to be considered, is whether the legislature was competent to thus deprive the state of its ownership of the submerged lands in the harbor of Chicago, and of the consequent control of its waters; or, in other words, whether the railroad corporation can hold the lands and control the waters by the grant, against any future exercise of power over them by the state.

That the state holds the title to the lands under the navigable waters of Lake Michigan, within its limits, in the same manner that the state holds title to soils under tide water, by the common law, we have already shown; and that title necessarily carries with it control over the waters above them, whenever the lands are subjected to use. But it is a title different in character from that which the state holds in lands intended for sale. It is different from the title which the United States hold in the public lands which are open to pre-emption and sale. It is a title held in trust for the people of the state, that they may enjoy the navigation of the waters, carry on commerce over them, and have liberty of fishing therein, freed from the obstruction or interference of private parties. The interest of the people in the navigation of the waters and in commerce over them may be improved in many instances by the erection of wharves, docks, and piers therein, for which purpose the state may grant parcels of the submerged lands; and, so long as their disposition is made for such purpose, no valid objections can be made to the grants. It is grants of parcels of lands under navigable waters that may afford foundation for wharves, piers, docks, and other structures in aid of commerce, and grants of parcels which, being occupied, do not substantially impair the public interest in the lands and waters remaining, that are chiefly considered and sustained in the adjudged cases as a valid exercise of legislative power consistently with the trust to the public upon which such lands are held by the state. But that is a very different doctrine from the one which would sanction the abdication of the general control of the state over lands under the navigable waters of an entire harbor or bay, or of a sea or lake. Such abdication is not consistent with the exercise of that trust which requires the government of the state to preserve such waters for the use of the public. The trust devolving upon the state for the public, and which can only be discharged by the management and control of property in which the public has an interest, cannot be relinquished by a transfer of the property. The control of the state for the purposes of the trust can never be lost, except as to such parcels as are used in promoting the interests of the public therein, or can be disposed of without any substantial impairment of the public interest in the lands and waters remaining. It is only by observing the distinction between a grant of such parcels for the improvement of the public interest, or which when occupied do not substantially impair the public interest in the lands and waters remaining, and a grant of the whole property in which the public is interested, that the language of the adjudged cases can be reconciled. General language sometimes found in opinions of the courts, expressive of absolute ownership and control by the state of lands under navigable waters, irrespective of any trust as to their use and disposition, must be read and construed with reference to the special facts of the particular cases. A grant of all the lands under the navigable waters of a state has never been adjudged to be within the legislative power; and any attempted grant of the kind would be held, if not absolutely void on its face, as subject to revocation. The state can no more abdicate its trust over property in which the whole people are interested, like navigable waters and soils under them, so as to leave them entirely under the use and control of private parties, except in the instance of parcels mentioned for the improvement of the navigation and use of the waters, or when parcels can be disposed of without impairment of the public interest in what remains, than it can abdicate its police powers in the administration of government and the preservation of the peace. In the administration of government the use of such powers may for a limited period be delegated to a municipality or other body, but there always remains with the state the right to revoke those powers and exercise them in a more direct manner, and one more conformable to its wishes. So with trusts connected with public property, or property of a special character, like lands under navigable waters; they cannot be placed entirely beyond the direction and control of the state.

The harbor of Chicago is of immense value to the people of the state of Illinois, in the facilities it affords to its vast and constantly increasing commerce; and the idea that its legislature can deprive the state of control over its bed and waters, and place the same in the hands of a private corporation, created for a different purpose,—one limited to transportation of passengers and freight between distant points and the city,—is a proposition that cannot be defended.

The area of the submerged lands proposed to be ceded by the act in question to the railroad company embraces something more than 1,000 acres, being, as stated by counsel, more than three times the area of the outer harbor, and not only including all of that harbor, but embracing adjoining submerged lands, which will, in all probability, be hereafter included in the harbor. It is as large as that embraced by all the merchandise docks along the Thames at London; is much larger than that included in the famous docks and basins at Liverpool; is twice that of the port of Marseilles, and nearly, if not quite, equal to the pier area along the water front of the city of New York. And the arrivals and clearings of vessels at the port exceed in number those of New York, and are equal to those of New York and Boston combined. Chicago has nearly 25 per cent. of the lake carrying trade, as compared with the arrivals and clearings of all the leading ports of our great inland seas. In the year ending June 30, 1886, the joint arrivals and clearances of vessels at that port amounted to 22,096, with a tonnage of over 7,000,000; and in 1890 the tonnage of the vessels reached nearly 9,000,000. As stated by counsel, since the passage of the lake front act, in 1869, the population of the city has increased nearly 1,000,000 souls, and the increase of commerce has kept pace with it. It is hardly conceivable that the legislature can divest the state of the control and management of this harbor, and vest it absolutely in a private corporation. Surely an act of the legislature transferring the title to its submerged lands and the power claimed by the railroad company to a foreign state or nation would be repudiated, without hesitation, as a gross perversion of the trust over the property under which it is held. So would a similar transfer to a corporation of another state. It would not be listened to that the control and management of the harbor of that great city—a subject of concern to the whole people of the state—should thus be placed elsewhere than in the state itself. All the objections which can be urged to such attempted transfer may be urged to a transfer to a private corporation like the railroad company in this case.

Any grant of the kind is necessarily revocable, and the exercise of the trust by which the property was held by the state can be resumed at any time. Undoubtedly there may be expenses incurred in improvements made under such a grant, which the state ought to pay; but, be that as it may, the power to resume the trust whenever the state judges best is, we think, incontrovertible. The position advanced by the railroad company in support of its claim to the ownership of the submerged lands, and the right to the erection of wharves, piers, and docks at its pleasure, or for its business in the harbor of Chicago, would place every harbor in the country at the mercy of a majority of the legislature of the state in which the harbor is situated.

We cannot, it is true, cite any authority where a grant of this kind has been held invalid, for we believe that no instance exists where the harbor of a great city and its commerce have been allowed to pass into the control of any private corporation. But the decisions are numerous which declare that such property is held by the state, by virtue of its sovereignty, in trust for the public. The ownership of the navigable waters of the harbor, and of the lands under them, is a subject of public concern to the whole people of the state. The trust with which they are held, therefore, is governmental, and cannot be alienated, except in those instances mentioned, of parcels used in the improvement of the interest thus held, or when parcels can be disposed of without detriment to the public interest in the lands and waters remaining.

This follows necessarily from the public character of the property, being held by the whole people for purposes in which the whole people are interested. * * *

The soil under navigable waters being held by the people of the state in trust for the common use and as a portion of their inherent sovereignty, any act of legislation concerning their use affects the public welfare. It is therefore appropriately within the exercise of the police power of the state.

In Newton v. Commissioners, 100 U. S. 548, it appeared that by an act passed by the legislature of Ohio in 1846 it was provided that upon the fulfillment of certain conditions by the proprietors or citizens of the town of Canfield the county seat should be permanently established in that town. Those conditions having been complied with, the county seat was established therein accordingly. In 1874 the legislature passed an act for the removal of the county seat to another town. Certain citizens of Canfield thereupon filed their bill setting forth the act of 1846, and claiming that the proceedings constituted an executed contract, and prayed for an injunction against the contemplated removal. But the court refused the injunction, holding that there could be no contract and no irrepealable law upon governmental subjects, observing that legislative acts concerning public interests are necessarily public laws; that every succeeding legislature possesses the same jurisdiction and power as its predecessor; that the latter have the same power of repeal and modification which the former had of enactment,—neither more nor less; that all occupy in this respect a footing of perfect equality; that this is necessarily so, in the nature of things; that it is vital to the public welfare that each one should be able at all times to do whatever the varying circumstances and present exigencies attending the subject may require; and that a different result would be fraught with evil.

As counsel observe, if this is true doctrine as to the location of a county seat, it is apparent that it must apply with greater force to the control of the soils and beds of navigable waters in the great public harbors held by the people in trust for their common use and of common right, as an incident to their sovereignty. The legislature could not give away nor sell the discretion of its successors in respect to matters, the government of which, from the very nature of things, must vary with varying circumstances. The legislation which may be needed one day for the harbor may be different from the legislation that may be required at another day. Every legislature must, at the time of its existence, exercise the power of the state in the execution of the trust devolved upon it. We hold, therefore, that any attempted cession of the ownership and control of the state in and over the submerged lands in Lake Michigan, by the act of April 16, 1869, was inoperative to affect, modify, or in any respect to control the sovereignty and dominion of the state over the lands, or its ownership thereof, and that any such attempted operation of the act was annulled by the repealing act of April 15, 1873, which to that extent was valid and effective. There can be no irrepealable contract in a conveyance of property by a grantor in disregard of a public trust, under which he was bound to hold and manage it.

Notes

1. **Federal law or state law.** Did the Supreme Court apply state law or federal law in *Illinois Central*? The opinion has the tone of a constitutional decision. Yet in Appleby v. City of New York, 271 U.S. 364, 395 (1926), the Court stated that the "conclusion reached [in *Illinois Central*] was necessarily a statement of Illinois law." In 1988, in Phillips Petroleum Co. v. Mississippi, 484 U.S. 469 (1988), the Court seemingly reaffirmed this conclusion, saying that the states have the authority "to recognize private rights in [public trust] lands as they see fit." See also Weber v. Board of Harbor Comm'rs, 85 U.S. (18 Wall) 57, 65-66 (1873); Shively v. Bowlby, 152 U.S. 1, 58 (1894).

Why was the grant of trust lands by the Illinois legislature to the railroad invalid? Was not the Illinois legislature competent to "recognize private rights in [trust] lands" by its grant to the railroad? What principles of Illinois law did the legislative grant contravene? A principle found in the Illinois Constitution? In the common law? Could the common law invalidate an act of the Illinois Legislature?

2. **More on the jurisprudential basis of the doctrine.** The jurisprudential basis of the public trust doctrine remains elusive. Its historical origins are clearly in English law and courts and commentators usually assume that it is a common law doctrine, often without much examination. This assumption is problematic, particularly when the doctrine is construed as a constraint on the power of state legislatures to dispose of trust resources. One writer has argued that the public trust doctrine is rooted in the commerce clause of the federal constitution and that the states are prohibited from entirely abrogating the doctrine. See Charles F. Wilkinson, The Headwaters of the Public Trust: Some Thoughts on the Source and Scope of the Traditional Doctrine, 19 Envtl. L. 425 (1989). However, Professor Wilkinson states that he does not wish to make "too much" of this point because he concludes that the states have such broad discretion in determining the content of the trust that the constitutional limitation will seldom be called into play.

Another writer has found support for the doctrine in the due process and equal protection clauses of the Constitution. Richard A. Epstein, The Public Trust Doctrine, 7 Cato J. 411 (1987). Emphasizing "property" principles, Professor Epstein draws parallels to the "takings" doctrine which protect private property from legislative actions. He argues that both doctrines provide protection against those who seek to manipulate political process to redistribute property to themselves.

Others have suggested that the doctrine is rooted in sovereignty. According to this view, state ownership of submerged lands is a fundamental attribute of "sovereignty" which cannot be abrogated except pursuant to trust purposes. See Coxe v. State, 39 N.E. 400, 402 (N.Y. 1895) and Michael C. Blumm, Harrison C. Dunning, & Scott W. Reed, Renouncing the Public Trust Doctrine: An Assessment of the Validity of Idaho House Bill 794, 24 Ecology L.Q. 461 (1997).

The authors of the last cited article also argue that the public trust doctrine is a federal requirement, based on principles of the equal footing doctrine. Like Professor Wilkinson, they acknowledge that the states have great discretion in the management of trust resources but are not free to entirely abrogate the doctrine. James R. Rasband, supra p. 517, Note 6, stresses the common parentage of the public trust and the equal footing doctrines but draws very different conclusions. Professor Rasband notes that conveyances of the beds of navigable waters receive disparate treatment under the two doctrines. The equal footing cases treat pre-statehood conveyances by Congress of such beds as a question of congressional intent, not congressional power, while the public trust cases treat post-statehood conveyance by state legislatures of the same lands as a question of power, not intent. He argues that consistency requires that both types of cases be treated similarly; that is, that both be treated as questions of intent or as questions of power. He concludes that it would be preferable to treat both as questions of intent because that permits judges to do that which they do best—determine legislative intent—and preserves for the legislative branch the "quintessential legislative task" of determining how public resources should be used.

More recently, Professor Douglas Grant has argued that the reserved powers doctrine best explains the decision. In Underpinnings of the Public Trust Doctrine: Lessons from Illinois Central Railroad, 33 Ariz. St. L.J. 849 (2001), Professor Grant develops his thesis that "*Illinois Central*, at its core, concerned the Contract Clause of the Federal Constitution and the reserved powers doctrine that the Court used to reduce the ambit of that clause. When *Illinois Central* is read in light of this widely neglected point, the public trust doctrine applied by the Court is seen to fit within the broader reserved powers doctrine. A search for the underpinnings of the public trust doctrine thus becomes a search for the underpinnings of the reserved powers doctrine." Id. at 852. Rejecting the federal law basis advanced by others, he argues that "the reserved powers doctrine is grounded in widely found state constitutional provisions on 'legislative power.'" Id.

According to Professor Grant, a critical passage to understanding *Illinois Central* comes in the last three paragraphs set out above in the case excerpt:

> By establishing the public character of state-owned navigable waters and their beds, he implicitly distinguished the submerged land in the Chicago harbor from state-owned nonpublic land, such as a farm acquired by escheat from an intestate decedent. The legislature could freely convey state-owned nonpublic land to a private grantee, but that was not true of state-owned navigable waters and their beds. The public character of navigable waters and their beds enabled Field to invoke the well-established reserved powers doctrine of the Contract Clause cases. In full context, the reference at the end of the above quotation to a public trust does not rely on the concept of trust ownership alone to explain why the legislature was incompetent to grant the submerged land to the railroad company. Rather, that reference is

> a link in the chain of reasoning that brings the case within the broader reserved powers doctrine. Id. at 868-69.

He continues:

> *Illinois Central* has been unjustly criticized for relying on cases that were inapposite and for not making its reasoning explicit. Although Justice Field rightly acknowledged a lack of direct authority, the case represents a reasoned extension of the reserved powers doctrine applied in *Newton.* Field's discussion of cases concerning state ownership of navigable waters and their beds in trust was not intended by itself to justify the conclusion that the legislature was incompetent to grant the submerged land to the railroad company. Rather, that discussion was intended to lay the foundation for extending the established reserved powers doctrine from the public welfare concern involved in *Newton* (public access to the seat of government) to the public welfare concern involved in *Illinois Central* (public access to navigable waters). Id. at 872.

He concludes that the reserved powers' "theoretical bases indicate that the * * * doctrine is not confined to Contract Clause cases and has continuing vitality to support the public trust doctrine notwithstanding the modern decline in importance of the Contract Clause." Id. at 852.

3. **Illinois Central re-examined:** In The Origins of the American Public Trust Doctrine: What Really Happened in Illinois Central, 71 U. Chi. L. Rev. 799 (2004), Professors Joseph S. Kearney and Thomas W. Merrill exhaustively reexamined the Chicago waterfront land grants, development proposals, title issues, and lobbying campaigns that were the context for the Illinois Legislature's 1869 and 1873 enactments. Professors Kearney and Merrill rejected what they describe as "the standard *Illinois Central* narrative"—"monopoly privilege subverting the public interest." Id. at 806. They concluded that, at least up to 1869, the railroad acted legitimately and purely defensively to protect the substantial investments it had made in the face of efforts by rival Chicago interests to obtain their own title to the waterfront in question.

Along the way, they sought to debunk what they concluded are two myths: 1) the 1869 legislation gave the railroad monopoly control over the entire waterfront, and 2) the waterfront grants promoted no public interest. As to the monopoly charge, the 1869 legislation, they countered, gave the railroad no control over either the entrance to the Chicago River or the extensive harbor facilities located on that River. The authors believe that, instead of considering the legislation as an exclusive license to an entire harbor, it is better analogized to a license to build a private road that would parallel an existing public right of way. The second "myth"—that there was no public interest in the legislative license—the authors ascribed to Professor Sax's comments in his seminal article, The Public Trust Doctrine in Natural Resource Law: Effective Judicial Intervention, 68 Mich. L. Rev. 471 (1970). See infra p. 541, Note 1. Contrary to Sax's assertions, they found no suggestion in any of the legislative debates or newspaper accounts they exhaustively examined that either public funding or public willingness existed to build the needed new, outer harbor on the areas encompassed by the legislative grant.

The authors did find some evidence of improper efforts to influence some legislators. These efforts notwithstanding, the authors concluded that the state legislators who overwhelmingly voted in favor of the grant to the railroad could do so with a clean conscience, reasonably believing that they were voting in the public's true interest. As Professors Kearney and Merrill see it, the legislative battle was between the City of Chicago and the State of Illinois over who would benefit financially from the power to grant private development rights to the waterfront. The City of Chicago opposed the legislation because it would have precluded city leaders' desires to award lucrative development contracts to their cronies in a deal that would have provided no tax revenues to anyone other than Chicagoans. In contrast, the Illinois Central proposal included a 7% tax upon the railroad's gross receipts, payable into the state's coffers. For a legislator from outside of Chicago, the railroad's proposal easily beat the City's.

4. **Loss of government control.** In *Illinois Central*, the Court is primarily concerned with the loss of government control over the harbor and not with the loss by the state of legal title to the submerged beds. Was it necessary to invalidate the grant to preserve the state's regulatory power over the harbor? See Harrison C. Dunning, The Public Trust Doctrine and Western Water Law: Discord or Harmony? 30 Rocky Mtn. Min. L. Inst. 17–1 (1984) and Richard J. Lazarus, Changing Conceptions of Property and Sovereignty in Natural Resources: Questioning the Public Trust Doctrine, 71 Iowa L. Rev. 631 (1986), suggesting that *Illinois Central* can be explained by the limited view which courts took of the police power at the time the case was decided. But see Eric Pearson, Illinois Central and the Public Trust Doctrine in State Law, 15 Va. Envtl. L.J. 713 (1996), arguing that at the time *Illinois Central* was decided it was well established under Illinois law that a grantee of state property is not immunized from police power regulation.

5. **Standards for valid grants of submerged lands.** The Court indicates in the principal opinion that grants of submerged lands which promote or which do not substantially impair trust values are valid. Subsequent cases have dealt with these exceptions in various ways. According to one scholar, who made an extensive study of trust cases, the decisions gravitate around three types of standards: (1) a requirement that the grant satisfy trust purposes, which in some cases may mean little more than that it satisfy some public purpose; (2) a requirement that the grant occur only after consideration of its impact on trust resources and then only if the impact is minimal or necessary; and (3) a requirement that there be specific legislative authorization for the grant. Richard J. Lazarus, supra Note 4.

A North Dakota statute provides that the owners of lands bordering navigable waters take title to the low watermark. N.D. Cent. Code § 47–1–15. In State ex rel. Sprynczynatyk v. Mills, 523 N.W.2d 537 (N.D. 1994), North Dakota asserted that it owned title to lands between the low and highwater marks of navigable water under the equal footing and public trust doctrines, notwithstanding the statute. Conversely, the landowner asserted absolute ownership of such lands under the statute. Held: neither party has absolute title; they have coexistent, overlapping interests in the area. Accord California v. Superior Court, 625 P.2d 239 (Cal. 1981).

6. **Are trust grants void or voidable?** Did the Court hold the grant was "void" or "voidable?" Does it make a difference? The state could have used its power of eminent domain to recover the lands from the railroad. How would its use of eminent domain have been different from its use of the public trust

doctrine? Cf. National Ass'n of Home Builders v. New Jersey Dep't of Envtl. Prot., 64 F. Supp. 2d 354 (D.N.J. 1999) (distinguishing police power and public trust exactions from regulatory takings).

7. **Compensation for improvements.** The implications of Justice Field's statement that when taking back trust lands a state "ought to pay" for improvements made by the grantee are explored in James R. Rasband, Equitable Compensation for Public Trust Takings, 69 U. Colo. L. Rev. 331 (1998). Professor Rasband concludes that both the supporters and the detractors of the public trust doctrine should be able to concur on the principle of equitable compensation for the grantee when grants of trust resources are revoked.

8. **Application to federal property.** To what extent is the federal government subject to state public trust limitations? In some states, such as California, a grant of trust lands is not invalid but the property is impressed with a "public trust easement" which restricts the uses which the grantee may make of the property. See People v. California Fish Co., 138 P. 79 (Cal. 1913). In United States v. 11.037 Acres of Land, 685 F. Supp. 214 (N.D. Cal. 1988), the United States filed an action to condemn trust lands conveyed by the state to the City of Oakland. The California Lands Commission asserted that condemnation by the United States would not, and could not, extinguish the public trust easement, arguing that the public trust is an attribute of state sovereignty. Citing the Supremacy Clause of the U.S. Constitution, the court said that the state was powerless to frustrate or limit the federal power of eminent domain and held that the public trust easement was extinguished by the condemnation action. But see United States v. 1.58 Acres of Land, 523 F. Supp. 120 (D. Mass. 1981).

NATIONAL AUDUBON SOCIETY v. SUPERIOR COURT

Supreme Court of California, 1983.
33 Cal. 3d 419, 189 Cal. Rptr. 346, 658 P.2d 709.

BROUSSARD, JUSTICE. Mono Lake, the second largest lake in California, sits at the base of the Sierra Nevada escarpment near the eastern entrance to Yosemite National Park. The lake is saline; it contains no fish but supports a large population of brine shrimp which feed vast numbers of nesting and migratory birds. Islands in the lake protect a large breeding colony of California gulls, and the lake itself serves as a haven on the migration route for thousands of Northern Phalarope, Wilson's Phalarope, and Eared Grebe. Towers and spires of tufa on the north and south shores are matters of geological interest and a tourist attraction.

Although Mono Lake receives some water from rain and snow on the lake surface, historically most of its supply came from snowmelt in the Sierra Nevada. Five freshwater streams—Mill, Lee Vining, Walker, Parker and Rush Creeks—arise near the crest of the range and carry the annual runoff to the west shore of the lake. In 1940, however, the Division of Water Resources, the predecessor to the present California Water Resources Board, granted the Department of Water and Power of the City of Los Angeles (hereafter DWP) a permit to appropriate virtually the entire flow of four of the five streams flowing into the lake. DWP promptly constructed facilities to divert about half the flow of these streams into DWP's Owens Valley aqueduct. In 1970 DWP completed a second diversion tunnel, and since that time has taken virtually the entire flow of these streams.

As a result of these diversions, the level of the lake has dropped; the surface area has diminished by one-third; one of the two principal islands in the lake has become a peninsula, exposing the gull rookery there to coyotes and other predators and causing the gulls to abandon the former island. The ultimate effect of continued diversions is a matter of intense dispute, but there seems little doubt that both the scenic beauty and the ecological values of Mono Lake are imperiled.

Plaintiffs filed suit in superior court to enjoin the DWP diversions on the theory that the shores, bed and waters of Mono Lake are protected by a public trust. Plaintiffs' suit was transferred to the federal district court, which requested that the state courts determine the relationship between the public trust doctrine and the water rights system, and decide whether plaintiffs must exhaust administrative remedies before the Water Board prior to filing suit. The superior court then entered summary judgments against plaintiffs on both matters, ruling that the public trust doctrine offered no independent basis for challenging the DWP diversions, and that plaintiffs had failed to exhaust administrative remedies. Plaintiffs petitioned us directly for writ of mandate to review that decision; in view of the importance of the issues presented, we issued an alternative writ.

This case brings together for the first time two systems of legal thought: the appropriative water rights system which since the days of the gold rush has dominated California water law, and the public trust doctrine which, after evolving as a shield for the protection of tidelands, now extends its protective scope to navigable lakes. Ever since we first recognized that the public trust protects environmental and recreational values (Marks v. Whitney (1971) 6 Cal. 3d 251, 98 Cal. Rptr. 790, 491 P.2d 374), the two systems of legal thought have been on a collision course. They meet in a unique and dramatic setting which highlights the clash of values. Mono Lake is a scenic and ecological treasure of national significance, imperiled by continued diversions of water; yet, the need of Los Angeles for water is apparent, its reliance on rights granted by the board evident, the cost of curtailing diversions substantial. * * *

1. Background and history of the Mono Lake litigation. DWP supplies water to the City of Los Angeles. * * * After purchasing the riparian rights incident to Lee Vining, Walker, Parker and Rush Creeks, as well as the riparian rights pertaining to Mono Lake,[4] the city applied to the Water Board in 1940 for permits to appropriate the waters of the four tributaries. At hearings before the board, various interested individuals protested that the city's proposed appropriations would lower the surface level of Mono Lake

---

4. Between 1920 and 1934, the city purchased lands riparian to creeks feeding Mono Lake and riparian rights incident to such lands. In 1934, the city brought an eminent domain proceeding for condemnation of the rights of Mono Lake landowners. (City of Los Angeles v. Aitken (1935) 10 Cal. App .2d 460, 52 P.2d 585.)

and thereby impair its commercial, recreational and scenic uses.

The board's primary authority to reject that application lay in a 1921 amendment to the Water Commission Act of 1913, which authorized the board to reject an application "when in its judgment the proposed appropriation would not best conserve the public interest." (Stats.1921, ch. 329, § 1, p. 443, now codified as Wat. Code, § 1255.) The 1921 enactment, however, also "declared to be the established policy of this state that the use of water for domestic purposes is the highest use of water" (id., now codified as Wat. Code, § 1254), and directed the Water Board to be guided by this declaration of policy. Since DWP sought water for domestic use, the board concluded that it had to grant the application notwithstanding the harm to public trust uses of Mono Lake.[6]

The board's decision states that "[i]t is indeed unfortunate that the City's proposed development will result in decreasing the aesthetic advantages of Mono Basin but *there is apparently nothing that this office can do to prevent it.* The use to which the City proposes to put the water under its Applications * * * is defined by the Water Commission Act as the highest to which water may be applied and to make available unappropriated water for this use the City has, by the condemnation proceedings described above, acquired the littoral and riparian rights on Mono Lake and its tributaries south of Mill Creek. This office therefore has *no alternative but to dismiss all protests based upon the possible lowering of the water level in Mono Lake and the effect that the diversion of water from these streams may have upon the aesthetic and recreational value of the Basin.*" * * *

2. The Public Trust Doctrine in California. * * *

(a) The purpose of the public trust. The objective of the public trust has evolved in tandem with the changing public perception of the values and uses of waterways. As we observed in Marks v. Whitney, supra, 6 Cal. 3d 251, 98 Cal. Rptr. 790, 491 P.2d 374, "[p]ublic trust easements [were] traditionally defined in terms of navigation, commerce and fisheries. They have been held to include the right to fish, hunt, bathe, swim, to use for boating and general recreation purposes the navigable waters of the state, and to use the bottom of the navigable waters for anchoring, standing, or other purposes." We went on, however, to hold that the traditional triad of uses—navigation, commerce

---

6. DWP calls our attention to a 1940 decision of the Water Board involving Rock Creek, a tributary of the Owens River, in which the board stated that "the Water Commission Act requires it to protect streams in recreational areas by guarding against depletion below some minimum amount consonant with the general recreational conditions and the character of the stream." (Div.Wat.Resources Dec. 3850 (Apr. 11, 1940), at p. 24.) The decision concluded that the board had insufficient information to decide what conditions, if any, to place upon DWP's application to divert water from Rock Creek for hydroelectric generation.

We do not know why the board was seemingly more willing to limit diversions to protect recreational values for Rock Creek than for the creeks flowing into Mono Lake. (Neither do we know the eventual outcome of the Rock Creek application.) The language of the board's opinions suggests that the crucial distinction was that the application for the Mono Lake streams was for domestic use, the highest use under the Water Code, while the Rock Creek application was for power generation.

and fishing—did not limit the public interest in the trust res. In language of special importance to the present setting, we stated that "[t]he public uses to which tidelands are subject are sufficiently flexible to encompass changing public needs. In administering the trust the state is not burdened with an outmoded classification favoring one mode of utilization over another. There is a growing public recognition that one of the most important public uses of the tidelands—a use encompassed within the tidelands trust—is the preservation of those lands in their natural state, so that they may serve as ecological units for scientific study, as open space, and as environments which provide food and habitat for birds and marine life, and which favorably affect the scenery and climate of the area."

Mono Lake is a navigable waterway. It supports a small local industry which harvests brine shrimp for sale as fish food, which endeavor probably qualifies the lake as a "fishery" under the traditional public trust cases. The principal values plaintiffs seek to protect, however, are recreational and ecological—the scenic views of the lake and its shore, the purity of the air, and the use of the lake for nesting and feeding by birds. Under Marks v. Whitney, supra, 6 Cal. 3d 251, 98 Cal. Rptr. 790, 491 P.2d 374, it is clear that protection of these values is among the purposes of the public trust.

(b) The scope of the public trust. Early English decisions generally assumed the public trust was limited to tidal waters and the lands exposed and covered by the daily tides; many American decisions, including the leading California cases, also concern tidelands. (See, e.g., City of Berkeley v. Superior Court (1980) 26 Cal.3d 515, 162 Cal. Rptr. 327, 606 P.2d 362; Marks v. Whitney, supra, 6 Cal. 3d 251, 98 Cal. Rptr. 790, 491 P.2d 374; People v. California Fish Co. (1913) 166 Cal. 576, 138 P. 79.) It is, however, well settled in the United States generally and in California that the public trust is not limited by the reach of the tides, but encompasses all navigable lakes and streams. * * *

Mono Lake is, as we have said, a navigable waterway. The beds, shores and waters of the lake are without question protected by the public trust. The streams diverted by DWP, however, are not themselves navigable. Accordingly, we must address in this case a question not discussed in any recent public trust case—whether the public trust limits conduct affecting nonnavigable tributaries to navigable waterways. * * *

We conclude that the public trust doctrine, as recognized and developed in California decisions, protects navigable waters from harm caused by diversion of nonnavigable tributaries.[19]

(c) Duties and powers of the state as trustee. In the following review of the authority and obligations of the state as administrator of the public trust,

---

19. In view of the conclusion stated in the text, we need not consider the question whether the public trust extends for some purposes—such as protection of fishing, environmental values, and recreation interests—to nonnavigable streams. For discussion of this subject, see Walston, The Public Trust Doctrine in the Water Rights Context: The Wrong Environmental Remedy (1982) 22 Santa Clara L.Rev. 63, 85.

the dominant theme is the state's sovereign power and duty to exercise continued supervision over the trust. One consequence, of importance to this and many other cases, is that parties acquiring rights in trust property generally hold those rights subject to the trust, and can assert no vested right to use those rights in a manner harmful to the trust.

In summary, the foregoing cases amply demonstrate the continuing power of the state as administrator of the public trust, a power which extends to the revocation of previously granted rights or to the enforcement of the trust against lands long thought free of the trust (see City of Berkeley v. Superior Court, supra, 26 Cal. 3d 515, 162 Cal. Rptr. 327, 606 P.2d 362). Except for those rare instances in which a grantee may acquire a right to use former trust property free of trust restrictions, the grantee holds subject to the trust, and while he may assert a vested right to the servient estate (the right of use subject to the trust) and to any improvements he erects, he can claim no vested right to bar recognition of the trust or state action to carry out its purposes.

Since the public trust doctrine does not prevent the state from choosing between trust uses (Colberg, Inc. v. State of California, supra, 67 Cal. 2d 408, 419, 62 Cal. Rptr. 401, 432 P.2d 3; County of Orange v. Heim (1973) 30 Cal. App. 3d 694, 707, 106 Cal. Rptr. 825), the Attorney General of California, seeking to maximize state power under the trust, argues for a broad concept of trust uses. In his view, "trust uses" encompass all public uses, so that in practical effect the doctrine would impose no restrictions on the state's ability to allocate trust property. We know of no authority which supports this view of the public trust, except perhaps the dissenting opinion in Illinois Central R. Co. v. Illinois, supra, 146 U.S. 387, 13 S.Ct. 110, 36 L.Ed. 1018. Most decisions and commentators assume that "trust uses" relate to uses and activities in the vicinity of the lake, stream, or tidal reach at issue. The tideland cases make this point clear; after City of Berkeley v. Superior Court, supra, 26 Cal. 3d 515, 162 Cal. Rptr. 327, 606 P.2d 362, no one could contend that the state could grant tidelands free of the trust merely because the grant served some public purpose, such as increasing tax revenues, or because the grantee might put the property to a commercial use.

Thus, the public trust is more than an affirmation of state power to use public property for public purposes. It is an affirmation of the duty of the state to protect the people's common heritage of streams, lakes, marshlands and tidelands, surrendering that right of protection only in rare cases when the abandonment of that right is consistent with the purposes of the trust.

3. The California Water Rights System. "It is laid down by our law writers, that the right of property in water is usufructuary, and consists not so much of the fluid itself as the advantage of its use." (Eddy v. Simpson (1853) 3 Cal. 249, 252.) Hence, the cases do not speak of the ownership of water, but only of the right to its use. (Rancho Santa Margarita v. Vail (1938) 11 Cal. 2d 501, 554–555, 81 P.2d 533; see generally Hutchins, The Cal. Law of Water Rights (1956) pp. 36–38; 1 Rogers & Nichols, Water for Cal. (1967) p. 191.) Accordingly, Water Code section 102 provides that "[a]ll water within the State is the property of the people of the State, but the right to the use of water may be acquired by appropriation in the manner provided by law." * * *

"[In 1913 the state enacted] the Water Commission Act, which created a Water Commission and provided a procedure for the appropriation of water for useful and beneficial purposes. The main purpose of the act was 'to provide an orderly method for the appropriation of [unappropriated] waters.' (Temescal Water Co. v. Department Public Works (1955) 44 Cal. 2d 90, 95 [280 P.2d 1]; Bloss v. Rahilly (1940) 16 Cal. 2d 70, 75 [104 P.2d 1049].) By amendment in 1923, the statutory procedure became the exclusive means of acquiring appropriative rights. (§ 1225, Stats.1923, ch. 87.) The provisions of the Water Commission Act, as amended from time to time, have been codified in Water Code, divisions 1 and 2. (Stats.1943, ch. 368.)"

According to the courts, the function of the Water Board was restricted to determining if unappropriated water was available; if it was, and no competing appropriator submitted a claim, the grant of an appropriation was a ministerial act. (Tulare Water Co. v. State Water Com. (1921) 187 Cal. 533, 202 P. 874.)

In 1926, however, a decision of this court led to a constitutional amendment which radically altered water law in California and led to an expansion of the powers of the board. In Herminghaus v. South California Edison Co. (1926) 200 Cal. 81, 252 P. 607, we held not only that riparian rights took priority over appropriations authorized by the Water Board, a point which had always been clear, but that as between the riparian and the appropriator, the former's use of water was not limited by the doctrine of reasonable use. That decision led to a constitutional amendment which abolished the right of a riparian to devote water to unreasonable uses, and established the doctrine of reasonable use as an overriding feature of California water law. * * *

Article X, section 2 (enacted in 1928 as art. XIV, § 3) reads in pertinent part as follows: "It is hereby declared that because of the conditions prevailing in this State the general welfare requires that the water resources of the State be put to beneficial use to the fullest extent of which they are capable, and that the waste or unreasonable use or unreasonable method of use of water be prevented, and that the conservation of such waters is to be exercised with a view to the reasonable and beneficial use thereof in the interest of the people and for the public welfare. The right to water or to the use or flow of water in or from any natural stream or water course in this State is and shall be limited to such water as shall be reasonably required for the beneficial use to be served, and such right does not and shall not extend to the waste or unreasonable use or unreasonable method of use or unreasonable method of diversion of water * * *. This section shall be self-executing, and the Legislature may also enact laws in the furtherance of the policy in this section contained."

This amendment does more than merely overturn *Herminghaus*—it establishes state water policy. All uses of water, including public trust uses, must now conform to the standard of reasonable use. * * *

The 1928 amendment itself did not expand the authority of the Water Board. The board remained, under controlling judicial decisions, a ministerial body with the limited task of determining priorities between claimants seeking to appropriate unclaimed water. More recent statutory and judicial developments, however, have greatly enhanced the power of the Water Board to oversee the reasonable use of water and, in the process, made clear its authority to weigh and protect public trust values. * * *

[T]he function of the Water Board has steadily evolved from the narrow role of deciding priorities between competing appropriators to the charge of comprehensive planning and allocation of waters. This change necessarily affects the board's responsibility with respect to the public trust. The board of limited powers of 1913 had neither the power nor duty to consider interests protected by the public trust; the present board, in undertaking planning and allocation of water resources, is required by statute to take those interests into account.

4. The relationship between the Public Trust Doctrine and the California Water Rights System. As we have seen, the public trust doctrine and the appropriative water rights system administered by the Water Board developed independently of each other. Each developed comprehensive rules and principles which, if applied to the full extent of their scope, would occupy the field of allocation of stream waters to the exclusion of any competing system of legal thought. Plaintiffs, for example, argue that the public trust is antecedent to and thus limits all appropriative water rights, an argument which implies that most appropriative water rights in California were acquired and are presently being used unlawfully. Defendant DWP, on the other hand, argues that the public trust doctrine as to stream waters has been "subsumed" into the appropriative water rights system and, absorbed by that body of law, quietly disappeared; according to DWP, the recipient of a board license enjoys a vested right in perpetuity to take water without concern for the consequences to the trust.

We are unable to accept either position. In our opinion, both the public trust doctrine and the water rights system embody important precepts which make the law more responsive to the diverse needs and interests involved in the planning and allocation of water resources. To embrace one system of thought and reject the other would lead to an unbalanced structure, one which would either decry as a breach of trust appropriations essential to the economic development of this state, or deny any duty to protect or even consider the values promoted by the public trust. Therefore, seeking an accommodation which will make use of the pertinent principles of both the public trust doctrine and the appropriative water rights system, and drawing upon the history of the public trust and the water rights system, the body of judicial precedent, and the views of expert commentators, we reach the following conclusions:

a. The state as sovereign retains continuing supervisory control over its navigable waters and the lands beneath those waters. This principle, fundamental to the concept of the public trust, applies to rights in flowing waters as well as to rights in tidelands and lakeshores; it prevents any party from acquiring a vested right to appropriate water in a manner harmful to the interests protected by the public trust.

b. As a matter of current and historical necessity, the Legislature, acting directly or through an authorized agency such as the Water Board, has the power to grant usufructuary licenses that will permit an appropriator to take water from flowing streams and use that water in a distant part of the state, even though this taking does not promote, and may unavoidably harm, the trust uses at the source stream. The population and economy of this state depend upon the appropriation of vast quantities of water for uses unrelated to in-stream trust values. California's Constitution (see art. X, § 2), its statutes (see Wat. Code, §§ 100, 104), decisions (see, e.g., Waterford I. Dist. v. Turlock I. Dist. (1920) 50 Cal. App. 213, 220, 194 P. 757), and commentators (e.g., Hutchins, the Cal. Law of Water Rights, op, cit. supra, p. 11) all emphasize the need to make efficient use of California's limited water resources: all recognize, at least implicitly, that efficient use requires diverting water from in-stream uses. Now that the economy and population centers of this state have developed in reliance upon appropriated water, it would be disingenuous to hold that such appropriations are and have always been improper to the extent that they harm public trust uses, and can be justified only upon theories of reliance or estoppel.

c. The state has an affirmative duty to take the public trust into account in the planning and allocation of water resources, and to protect public trust uses whenever feasible.[27] Just as the history of this state shows that appropriation may be necessary for efficient use of water despite unavoidable harm to public trust values, it demonstrates that an appropriative water rights system administered without consideration of the public trust may cause unnecessary and unjustified harm to trust interests. As a matter of practical necessity the state may have to approve appropriations despite foreseeable harm to public trust uses. In so doing, however, the state must bear in mind its duty as trustee to consider the effect of the taking on the public trust (see United Plainsmen v. N.D. State Water Con. Commission (N.D.1976) 247 N.W.2d 457, 462–463), and to preserve, so far as consistent with the public interest, the uses protected by the trust.

Once the state has approved an appropriation, the public trust imposes a duty of continuing supervision over the taking and use of the appropriated water. In exercising its sovereign power to allocate water resources in the public interest, the state is not confined by past allocation decisions which

---

27. Amendments to the Water Code enacted in 1955 and subsequent years codify in part the duty of the Water Board to consider public trust uses of stream water. (See, ante, p. 363 of 189 Cal. Rptr., p. 726 of 658 P.2d). The requirements of the California Environmental Quality Act (Pub. ResourcesRes. Code, § 21000 et seq.) impose a similar obligation. (See Robie, op. cit. supra, 2 Ecology L.Q. 695.)

These enactments do not render the judicially fashioned public trust doctrine superfluous. Aside from the possibility that statutory protections can be repealed, the noncodified public trust doctrine remains important both to confirm the state's sovereign supervision and to require consideration of public trust uses in cases filed directly in the courts without prior proceedings before the board.

may be incorrect in light of current knowledge or inconsistent with current needs.

The state accordingly has the power to reconsider allocation decisions even though those decisions were made after due consideration of their effect on the public trust.[28] The case for reconsidering a particular decision, however, is even stronger when that decision failed to weigh and consider public trust uses. In the case before us, the salient fact is that no responsible body has ever determined the impact of diverting the entire flow of the Mono Lake tributaries into the Los Angeles Aqueduct. This is not a case in which the Legislature, the Water Board, or any judicial body has determined that the needs of Los Angeles outweigh the needs of the Mono Basin, that the benefit gained is worth the price. Neither has any responsible body determined whether some lesser taking would better balance the diverse interests. Instead, DWP acquired rights to the entire flow in 1940 from a water board which believed it lacked both the power and the duty to protect the Mono Lake environment, and continues to exercise those rights in apparent disregard for the resulting damage to the scenery, ecology, and human uses of Mono Lake.

It is clear that some responsible body ought to reconsider the allocation of the waters of the Mono Basin. No vested rights bar such reconsideration. We recognize the substantial concerns voiced by Los Angeles—the city's need for water, its reliance upon the 1940 board decision, the cost both in terms of money and environmental impact of obtaining water elsewhere. Such concerns must enter into any allocation decision. We hold only that they do not preclude a reconsideration and reallocation which also takes into account the impact of water diversion on the Mono Lake environment. * * *

This opinion is but one step in the eventual resolution of the Mono Lake controversy. We do not dictate any particular allocation of water. Our objective is to resolve a legal conundrum in which two competing systems of thought—the public trust doctrine and the appropriative water rights system—existed independently of each other, espousing principles which seemingly suggested opposite results. We hope by integrating these two doctrines to clear away the legal barriers which have so far prevented either the Water Board or the courts from taking a new and objective look at the water resources of the Mono Basin. The human and environmental uses of Mono Lake—uses protected by the public trust doctrine—deserve to be taken into account. Such uses should not be destroyed because the state mistakenly thought itself powerless to protect them.

---

28. The state Attorney General asserts that the Water Board could also reconsider the DWP water rights under the doctrine of unreasonable use under article X, section 2. DWP maintains, however, that its use of the water for domestic consumption is prima facie reasonable. The dispute centers on the test of unreasonable use—does it refer only to inordinate and wasteful use of water, as in Peabody v. City of Vallejo, supra, 2 Cal.2d 351, 40 P.2d 486, or to any use less than the optimum allocation of water? (On this question, see generally Joslin v. Marin Mun. Water Dist., supra, 67 Cal. 2d 132, 138–141, 60 Cal. Rptr. 377, 429 P.2d 889.) In view of our reliance on the public trust doctrine as a basis for reconsideration of DWP's usufructuary rights, we need not resolve that controversy.

Let a peremptory writ of mandate issue commanding the Superior Court of Alpine County to vacate its judgment in this action and to enter a new judgment consistent with the views stated in this opinion.

Notes

1. **Development of the modern public trust doctrine.** Until 1970, the public trust doctrine was an arcane principle confined mostly to issues involving ownership of submerged lands. In that year, an article by Professor Joseph Sax infused the doctrine with new vigor. Joseph L. Sax, The Public Trust Doctrine in Natural Resource Law: Effective Judicial Intervention, 68 Mich. L. Rev. 471 (1970). Professor Sax urged wider application of the doctrine by courts reviewing legislative and administrative action alleged to be detrimental to the environment. Sax saw the public trust doctrine largely as a procedural device used by the courts to "mend perceived imperfections in the legislative and administrative process." Sax argued that sometimes legislatures and agencies ignore broad based public interests because a well-organized minority is able to gain political advantage over a diffuse, disorganized majority. Thus, Sax asserted, the courts use the public trust doctrine as an instrument for democratizing decision-making in these situations. Frequently, he said, courts accomplish this by moving a decision from one constituency to another. For example, a court may find that an agency cannot divert trust property to a use which lessens public use without specific legislative authority, thereby moving the decision from the agency, with its narrow constituency, to the legislature, with its broad constituency. Despite the procedural emphasis of this article, later Sax gave the doctrine greater substantive content, stating that its function is to protect public expectations against destabilizing changes. Joseph L. Sax, Liberating the Public Trust Doctrine, 14 U.C. Davis L. Rev. 185, 188 (1980).

Sax's views were enthusiastically received by writers and courts. The period since the publication of the first article has seen a remarkable expansion in the doctrine, both as to the scope of resources subjected to it and the interests protected by it. Although many states still require some connection to navigable waters, the doctrine is no longer confined to waters which are navigable for title purposes. It has been extended to bodies navigable only under more liberal state tests, to nonnavigable waters, and to resources which have no direct connection to water. See Wade v. Kramer, 459 N.E.2d 1025 (Ill. 1984) (wildlife); Save Ourselves, Inc. v. Louisiana Envtl. Control Comm'n, 452 So.2d 1152 (La. 1984) (noting state constitution's extension of doctrine to all natural resources); Gould v. Greylock Reservation Comm'n, 215 N.E.2d 114 (Mass. 1966) (state parks); Montana Coalition for Stream Access, Inc. v. Curran, 682 P.2d 163 (Mont. 1984) (all waters which are capable of recreational use); Matthews v. Bay Head Improvement Ass'n, 471 A.2d 355 (N.J. 1984) (dry sand area of beaches). As *National Audubon* illustrates, the interests protected have been extended from the public's historic rights of navigation, commerce, and fishing to include recreation, esthetics, and environmental preservation.

2. **Scholarly support for the modern public trust doctrine.** The weight of scholarly comment favors the expansion of the public trust doctrine as a means of furthering environmental protection. Articles focusing on the public trust doctrine and water rights include Michael C. Blumm & Thea Schwartz, Mono Lake and the Evolving Public Trust in Western Water, 37 Ariz. L. Rev. 701

(1995); Michael L. Blumm, Public Property and the Democratization of Western Water Law: A Modern View of the Public Trust Doctrine, 19 Envtl. L. 573 (1989); Harrison C. Dunning, The Public Trust Doctrine and Western Water Law: Discord or Harmony, 30 Rocky Mtn. Min. L. Inst. 17–1 (1985); Harrison C. Dunning, The Significance of California's Public Trust Easement for California Water Rights Law, 14 U.C. Davis L. Rev. 357 (1980); Helen Ingram & Cy R. Oggins, The Public Trust Doctrine and Community Values in Water, 32 Nat. Resources J. 515 (1992); Ralph W. Johnson, Public Trust Protection For Stream Flows and Lake Levels, 14 U.C. Davis L. Rev. 233 (1980); Jan S. Stevens, The Public Trust and Instream Uses, 19 Envtl. L. 605 (1989). See also other articles included in Symposium: The Public Trust Doctrine in Natural Resources Law and Management, 14 U.C. Davis L. Rev. 181 (1980); Symposium: The Public Trust and The Waters of the American West: Yesterday, Today and Tomorrow, 19 Envt. L. 425 (1989).

3. **Criticisms of the public trust doctrine.** Not everyone views the public trust doctrine positively:

"Most simply put, the historic function of the public trust doctrine has been to provide a public property basis for resisting the exercise of private property rights in natural resources deemed contrary to the public interest. In recent decades, however especially during the last ten years, modern trends in natural resources law have increasingly eroded traditional concepts of private property rights in natural resources and substituted new notions of sovereign power over those resources. These trends, reflected in a wide variety of legal contexts, ranging from federal environmental protection statutes, new state resource allocation laws, to evolving common law principles of tort law, are currently weaving a new fabric for natural resources law that is more responsive to current social values and the physical characteristics of the resources. By continuing to resist a legal system that is otherwise being abandoned, the public trust doctrine obscures analysis and renders more difficult the important process of reworking natural resources law. Of even broader concern, the doctrine threatens to fuel a developing clash in liberal ideology between furthering individual rights of security and dignity, bound up in notions of private property protection, and supporting environmental protection and resource preservation goals, inevitably dependent on intrusive governmental programs designed to achieve longer-term collectivist goals. * * *

"Assessment of the public trust doctrine on this basis [on the basis that the doctrine is a legal fiction] leads to the conclusion that the day of "final reckoning" for the doctrine is here, or soon will be, and reliance upon it is no longer in order. As shown in the following sections, the law of standing, tort law, property law, administrative law, and the police power have all evolved in response to increased societal concern and awareness of environmental and natural resources problems and are weaving a new and unified fabric for natural resources problems. Whether these developments are viewed as totally independent of the doctrine or, alternatively as somehow having subsumed the doctrine's principles is no matter. The conclusion is the same viewed from either perspective: Much of what the public trust doctrine offered in the past is now, at best, superfluous and, at worst, distracting and theoretically inconsistent with new notions of property and sovereignty developing in the current reworking of natural resources law. * * *

"In sum, the apparent litigation achievements of the public trust doctrine dim considerably, if not diminish altogether, when studied in light of independent developments in more generally applicable areas of the law, such as standing, nuisance, the police power, and administrative law. The doctrine's successes in various cases amount to little more than isolated reflections of these more fundamental trends, but with a public trust label prominently attached. In addition, the basic force of the public trust doctrine rests on legal theories fundamentally inconsistent with current notions of property and sovereignty in natural resources. The doctrine's only independent role remains much where it began in this country, with the narrow concern of access to beaches and beds of navigable waters."

Lazarus, supra p. 531, Note 4. See also Richard Delgado, Our Better Natures: A Revisionist View of Joseph Sax's Public Trust Theory of Environmental Protection, and Some Dark Thoughts on the Possibility of Law Reform, 44 Vand. L. Rev. 1209 (1991); George A. Gould, The Public Trust Doctrine and Water Rights, 34 Rocky Mtn. Min. L. Inst. 25–1 (1988); James L. Huffman, A Fish out of Water: The Public Trust Doctrine in a Constitutional Democracy, 19 Envtl. L. 527 (1989); James L. Huffman, Trusting the Public Interest to Judges: A Comment on the Public Trust Writing of Professors Sax, Wilkinson, Dunning and Johnson, 63 Denv. U. L. Rev. 565 (1986).

4. **Outcome of the principal case.** In 1994, after a number of procedural twists, turns, and delays, the California Water Resources Control Board modified Los Angeles's licenses in the Mono Basin to protect public trust resources and to establish fishery protection flows in tributaries feeding Mono Lake. California Water Resources Control Bd., Water Rights Decision 1631 (1994). The order is the culmination of extensive proceeding by the Water Board to implement the decisions of *National Audubon* and California Trout, Inc. v. State Water Resources Control Board, discussed supra p. 158, Note 6.

The order limits diversions from the Mono Basin to restore Mono Lake to an average elevation of 6392 feet in approximately 20 years. The elevation of Mono Lake was approximately 6417 feet in 1941 when Los Angeles commenced its diversions. The historic low was 6372 feet, and the elevation was 6375 feet in 1994. During the 20-year transition period, diversions by Los Angeles are expected to average 12,300 acre-feet per year. After the transition period, diversions are expected to average 30,900 acre-feet per year. By comparison, Los Angeles's diversions averaged 83,000 acre-feet per year from 1974 to 1989.

The impact of the order is dramatic; it reduces diversions during the transition period to about 15% of the pre-1989 average; after the transition period it reduces diversions to about 37% of the pre-1989 average. The Water Board estimated that it will cost about $27.8 million annually to replace lost water during the transition period and $17.9 million annually thereafter. However, the order is not based solely on the public trust doctrine, and the significance of the doctrine in the outcome is unclear. The 6392-foot restoration elevation was selected as much to meet ambient air quality standards under the Clean Air Act as to protect public trust resources. In addition, mandatory fishery protection flows required in the tributaries by provisions of the Fish and Game Code and the decision in *California Trout* will reduce diversion by an average of 35,200 acre-feet per year. These flows would have restored the lake to an elevation of 6388 to 6390 feet, although the restoration period would have been considerably longer had additional public trust requirements not been imposed. During the transition period, public trust requirements reduce Los Angeles's diversions by an additional 32,300 acre-feet per year. However, after the transition period, public trust requirements only reduce Los Angeles's diversions by an additional 8,500 acre-feet per year.

5. **Development of the public trust doctrine in California.** Gregory S. Weber, Articulating the Public Trust: Text, Near-Text, and Context, 27 Ariz. St. L.J. 1155 (1995), is an in-depth study of the application of the public trust doctrine to water rights in California in the first dozen years after *National Audubon.* Professor Weber observes that the handful of California appellate decisions which have considered the doctrine have added almost nothing of substance to *National Audubon* and have not produced a single reallocation of water to trust uses. In contrast, he notes that the California Water Resources Control Board has developed a sizeable body of pronouncements regarding the trust's meaning and its relationship to the system of water rights and has ordered several reallocations of water to trust uses. He concludes that the Water Board has articulated a vision of accommodation which gives it the fullest possible power to allocate surface water, places practical limits on the ability of other parties to invoke these powers, and acknowledges the necessity of permitting continued diversions of water.

6. **Legislative renunciation of the public trust doctrine.** The Idaho Supreme Court has expressed an expansive view of the public trust doctrine in relation to the law of water rights on several occasions, albeit always in dicta. See, e.g., Idaho Conservation League, Inc. v. State, 911 P.2d 748 (Idaho 1995); Shokal v. Dunn, 707 P.2d 441 (Idaho 1985). In reaction, the Idaho legislature adopted H.B. 794, codified as Idaho Code § 58–1203, in 1996. H.B. 794 states that the public trust doctrine is "solely a limitation on the power of the state to alienate or encumber the title to the beds of navigable waters." More pointedly, the legislation states that the public trust doctrine shall not apply to "[t]he appropriation or use of water, or the granting, transfer, administration, or adjudication of water or water rights * * * or any other procedure or law applicable to water rights in the state of Idaho." See Michael C. Blumm, et al, supra p. 528, Note 2, questioning the authority of the Idaho legislature to abrogate the public trust doctrine. Compare supra p.519, Note 12, addressing the Arizona legislature's repeated efforts to disclaim title to ownership of trust-bound submerged lands.

7. **Impact of the public trust doctrine on water rights in other western states.** Although a number of western courts have recognized the public trust doctrine in disputes involving rights to submerged lands and public use of waters, the doctrine has very limited application to water rights outside California. Only the North Dakota, Idaho and Hawaii supreme courts have explicitly declared that the doctrine applies to water rights. The North Dakota Supreme Court actually preceded the California Supreme Court in applying the doctrine to water rights, United Plainsmen Ass'n v. North Dakota State Water Conservation Commission, supra p. 151. However, that case involved new appropriations, not reallocations of water already appropriated, the doctrine was only used to impose water planning, and the result could have been reached on other grounds. The Idaho Supreme Court's expansive embrace of the doctrine and the subsequent legislative renunciation are discussed in the preceding note.

The Hawaii Supreme Court has also given a broad reading to the trust's application. In In re Water Use Permit Application, 9 P.3d 409 (Haw. 2000), commonly cited as the "*Waiahole Ditch*" case, the court concluded that the trust's application in Hawaii was even broader than its application in California under *National Audubon Society*. For example, the court applied the doctrine to both surface and subsurface water. In reaching its decision, the court was aided by both aboriginal Hawaiian law as well as a state constitutional provision.

A 1993 Washington decision, Rettkowski v. Department of Ecology, 858 P.2d 232 (Wash. 1993), held that the doctrine does not support nonstatutory regulation of water rights by the Department of Ecology.

The North Dakota, Idaho and Washington decisions are reviewed in Michael C. Blumm and Thea Schwartz, supra p. 541, Note 2. The Hawaii decision is reviewed in Denise E. Antolini, Water Rights and Responsibilities in the Twenty-First Century: A Foreward to the Proceedings of the 2001 Symposium on Managing Hawaii's Public Trust Doctrine, 24 U. Haw. L. Rev. 1 (2001).

8. **Assertion of public trust issues in general adjudications.** Statutes in Idaho and Arizona precluding the adjudication of public trust issues in general stream adjudications met very different fates. In Idaho Conservation League, Inc. v. State, 911 P.2d 748 (Idaho 1995), the Idaho Supreme Court denied the petition of environmental groups to intervene in the Snake River Basin Adjudication to assert public trust issues. The Supreme Court held that the SRBA court is a separate division of the district courts which exercises unique jurisdiction given it by the legislature to adjudicate "proprietary" water rights. Noting that all water rights are impressed with the public trust doctrine, the court found that the doctrine is not an element of a water right for purposes of determining competing proprietary claims. Conversely, legislation in Arizona which expressly precludes the consideration of public trust issues in stream-wide adjudications was struck down by the Arizona Supreme Court. While the court noted that the applicability of the public trust doctrine to the claims before the trial court has not been decided, it held that the doctrine is a constitutional limitation on the legislature and, thus, the legislature lacks the power to make the doctrine inapplicable in judicial proceedings.

9. **Applicability to water rights of the United States.** The United States holds a number of water rights in California which were acquired pursuant to state law, most notably those held by the Bureau of Reclamation in connection with the massive Central Valley Project. Are these rights subject to reconsideration and readjustment to protect public trust values under the principles set out in *National Audubon*? See supra p. 532, Note 8, and California v. United States, infra p. 659. Are federal water rights which were not created by state law, such as federal reserved water rights (see Chapter 8, Section 3) subject to state public trust restrictions?

SECTION 2. ENVIRONMENTAL PROTECTION

INTRODUCTORY NOTE

Environmental law covers many facets of the relation of man to nature—land, air, water, plants and creatures. Environmental law is a much broader subject than water law, but the two touch at many points. Earlier materials in the book examine laws that enhance or preserve recreation, scenic enjoyment, fish and wildlife habitat, and other environmental values. However, the environmental provisions examined earlier are part of the *water law* of particular jurisdictions; that is, they are a component of the law regulating the allocation of water and the acquisition of water rights. This section examines the impact of general environmental statutes on the law of water allocation. The statutes presented here are not water laws per se, but are laws which can have a significant effect on water allocation and water rights. Most of the laws considered in this section are federal statutes, but many states have adopted comparable state statutes. Furthermore, the federal environmental statutes often rely heavily on state administration and enforcement.

A. Environmental Assessment

NATIONAL ENVIRONMENTAL POLICY ACT OF 1969

Public Law 91–190, 42 U.S.C. §§ 4331–4335.

PURPOSE

Sec. 2. [42 U.S.C. § 4321] The purposes of this Act are: To declare a national policy which will encourage productive and enjoyable harmony between man and his environment; to promote efforts which will prevent or eliminate damage to the environment and biosphere and stimulate the health and welfare of man; to enrich the understanding of the ecological systems and natural resources important to the Nation; and to establish a Council on Environmental Quality.

Title I

Declaration of National Environmental Policy

Sec. 101. [42 U.S.C. § 4331] (a) The Congress, recognizing the profound impact of man's activity on the interrelations of all components of the natural environment, particularly the profound influences of population growth, high-density urbanization, industrial expansion, resource exploitation, and new and expanding technological advances and recognizing further the critical importance of restoring and maintaining environmental quality to the overall welfare and development of man, declares that it is the continuing policy of the Federal Government, in cooperation with State and local governments, and other concerned public and private organizations, to use all practicable means and measures, including financial and technical assistance, in a manner calculated to foster and promote the general welfare, to create and maintain conditions under which man and nature can exist in productive harmony, and fulfill the social, economic, and other requirements of present and future generations of Americans.

(b) In order to carry out the policy set forth in this Act, it is the continuing responsibility of the Federal Government to use all practicable means, consistent with other essential considerations of national policy, to improve and coordinate Federal plans, functions, programs, and resources to the end that the Nation may—

(1) fulfill the responsibilities of each generation as trustee of the environment for succeeding generations;

(2) assure for all Americans safe, healthful, productive, and aesthetically and culturally pleasing surroundings;

(3) attain the widest range of beneficial uses of the environment without degradation, risk to health or safety, or other undesirable and unintended consequences;

(4) preserve important historic, cultural, and natural aspects of our national heritage, and maintain, wherever possible, an environment which supports diversity and variety of individual choice;

(5) achieve a balance between population and resource use which will permit high standards of living and a wide sharing of life's amenities; and

(6) enhance the quality of renewable resources and approach the maximum attainable recycling of depletable resources.

(c) The Congress recognizes that each person should enjoy a healthful environment and that each person has a responsibility to contribute to the preservation and enhancement of the environment.

Sec. 102. [42 U.S.C. § 4332] The Congress authorizes and directs that, to the fullest extent possible: (1) the policies, regulations, and public laws of the United States shall be interpreted and administered in accordance with the policies set forth in this Act, and (2) all agencies of the Federal Government shall—

(A) utilize a systematic, interdisciplinary approach which will insure the integrated use of the natural and social sciences and the environmental design arts in planning and in decisionmaking which may have an impact on man's environment;

(B) identify and develop methods and procedures, in consultation with the Council on Environmental Quality established by title II of this Act, which will insure that presently unquantified environmental amenities and values may be given appropriate consideration in decisionmaking along with economic and technical considerations;

(C) include in every recommendation or report on proposals for legislation and other major Federal actions significantly affecting the quality of the human environment, a detailed statement by the responsible official on—

(i) the environmental impact of the proposed action,

(ii) any adverse environmental effects which cannot be avoided should the proposal be implemented,

(iii) alternatives to the proposed action,

(iv) the relationship between local short-term uses of man's environment and the maintenance and enhancement of long-term productivity, and

(v) any irreversible and irretrievable commitments of resources which would be involved in the proposed action should it be implemented.

Prior to making any detailed statement, the responsible Federal official shall consult with and obtain the comments of any Federal agency which has jurisdiction by law or special expertise with respect to any environmental impact involved. Copies of such statement and the comments and views of the appropriate Federal, State, and local agencies, which are authorized to develop and enforce environmental standards, shall be made available to the President, the Council on Environmental Quality and to the public as provided by section 552 of title 5, United States Code, and shall accompany the proposal through the existing agency review processes;

(D) study, develop, and describe appropriate alternatives to recommended courses of action in any proposal which involves unresolved conflicts concerning alternative uses of available resources;

(E) recognize the worldwide and long-range character of environmental problems and, where consistent with the foreign policy of the United States, lend appropriate support to initiatives, resolutions, and programs designed to maximize international cooperation in anticipating and preventing a decline in the quality of mankind's world environment;

(F) make available to States, counties, municipalities, institutions, and individuals, advice and information useful in restoring, maintaining, and enhancing the quality of the environment;

(G) initiate and utilize ecological information in the planning and development of resource-oriented projects; and

(H) assist the Council on Environmental Quality established by title II of this Act. * * *

Sec. 104. [42 U.S.C. § 4334] Nothing in Section 102 or 103 shall in any way affect the specific statutory obligations of any Federal agency (1) to comply with criteria or standards of environmental quality, (2) to coordinate or consult with any other Federal or State agency, or (3) to act, or refrain from acting contingent upon the recommendations or certification of any other Federal or State agency.

Sec. 105. [42 U.S.C. § 4335] The policies and goals set forth in this Act are supplementary to those set forth in existing authorizations of Federal agencies.

CALVERT CLIFFS' COORDINATING COMMITTEES, INC., v. UNITED STATES ATOMIC ENERGY COMMISSION

United States Court of Appeals, District of Columbia Circuit, 1971.
449 F.2d 1109.

[The AEC adopted rules for incorporating NEPA requirements into its procedures for licensing atomic power plants that limited the scope and time of considering environmental impacts, relied on the parties and intervenors to raise environmental issues and supply information, and relied on determinations and standards supplied by other agencies. In disapproving these, Circuit Judge J. Skelly Wright issued a directive to all federal agencies:]

In these cases, we must for the first time interpret the broadest and perhaps most important of the recent statutes: the National Environmental Policy Act of 1969 (NEPA). We must assess claims that one of the agencies charged with its administration has failed to live up to the congressional mandate. Our duty, in short, is to see that important legislative purposes, heralded in the halls of Congress, are not lost or misdirected in the vast hallways of the federal bureaucracy.

NEPA, like so much other reform legislation of the last 40 years, is cast in terms of a general mandate and broad delegation of authority to new and old administrative agencies. It takes the major step of requiring all federal agencies to consider values of environmental preservation in their spheres of activity, and it prescribes certain procedural measures to ensure that those values are in fact fully respected. * * * Section 101 sets forth the Act's basic substantive policy: that the federal government 'use all practicable means and measures' to protect environmental values. Congress did not establish environmental protection as an exclusive goal; rather, it desired a reordering of priorities, so that environmental costs and benefits will assume their proper place along with other considerations. In Section 101(b), imposing an explicit duty on federal officials, the Act provides that "it is the continuing responsibility of the Federal Government to use all practicable means, consistent with other essential considerations of national policy," to avoid environmental degradation, preserve "historic, cultural, and natural" resources, and promote "the widest range of beneficial uses of the environment without * * * undesirable and unintended consequences."

Thus the general substantive policy of the Act is a flexible one. It leaves room for a responsible exercise of discretion and may not require particular substantive results in particular problematic instances. However, the Act also contains very important "procedural" provisions—provisions which are designed to see that all federal agencies do in fact exercise the substantive discretion given them. These provisions are not highly flexible. Indeed, they establish a strict standard of compliance.

NEPA, first of all, makes environmental protection a part of the mandate of every federal agency and department. * * * Perhaps the greatest importance of NEPA is to require the Atomic Energy Commission and other agencies to *consider* environmental issues just as they consider other matters within their mandates. * * *

The sort of consideration of environmental values which NEPA compels is clarified in Section 102(2)(A) and (B). In general, all agencies must use a "systematic, interdisciplinary approach" to environmental planning and evaluation "in decisionmaking which may have an impact on man's environment." In order to include all possible environmental factors in the decisional equation, agencies must "identify and develop methods and procedures * * * which will insure that presently unquantified environmental amenities and values may be given appropriate consideration in decisionmaking along with economic and technical considerations." "Environmental amenities" will often be in conflict with "economic and technical considerations." To "consider" the former "along with" the latter must involve a balancing process. In some instances environmental costs may outweigh economic and technical benefits and in other instances they may not. But NEPA mandates a rather finely tuned and "systematic" balancing analysis in each instance.

To ensure that the balancing analysis is carried out and given full effect, Section 102(2)(C) requires that responsible officials of all agencies prepare a "detailed statement" covering the impact of particular actions on the environment, the environmental costs which might be avoided, and alternative measures which might alter the cost-benefit equation. The apparent purpose of the "detailed statement" is to aid in the agencies' own decision making process and to advise other interested agencies and the public of the environmental consequences of planned federal action. Beyond the "detailed statement," Section 102(2)(D) requires all agencies specifically to "study, develop, and describe appropriate alternatives to recommended courses of action in any proposal which involves unresolved conflicts concerning alternative uses of available resources." This requirement, like the "detailed statement" requirement, seeks to ensure that each agency decision maker has before him and takes into proper account all possible approaches to a particular project (including total abandonment of the project) which would alter the environmental impact and the cost-benefit balance. Only in that fashion is it likely that the most intelligent, optimally beneficial decision will ultimately be made. Moreover, by compelling a formal "detailed statement" and a description of alternatives, NEPA provides evidence that the mandated decision making process has in fact taken place and, most importantly, allows those removed from the initial process to evaluate and balance the factors on their own. * * *

Unlike the substantive duties of Section 101(b), which requires agencies to "use all practicable means consistent with other essential considerations," the procedural duties of Section 102 must be fulfilled to the "fullest extent possible." * * * Thus the Section 102 duties are not inherently flexible. They must be complied with to the fullest extent, unless there is a clear conflict of *statutory* authority. Considerations of administrative difficulty, delay or economic cost will not suffice to strip the section of its fundamental importance.

We conclude, then, that Section 102 of NEPA mandates a particular sort of careful and informed decisionmaking process and creates judicially enforceable duties. The reviewing courts probably cannot reverse a substantive decision on its merits, under Section 101, unless it be shown that the actual balance of costs and benefits that was struck was arbitrary or clearly gave insufficient weight to environmental values. But if the decision was reached procedurally without individualized consideration and balancing of environmental factors—conducted fully and in good faith—it is the responsibility of the courts to reverse. * * * Compliance to the "*fullest*" possible extent would seem to demand that environmental issues be considered at every important stage in the decision making process concerning a particular action—at every stage where an overall balancing of environmental and nonenvironmental factors is appropriate and where alterations might be made in the proposed action to minimize environmental costs. * * *

NEPA establishes environmental protection as an integral part of the Atomic Energy Commission's basic mandate. The primary responsibility for fulfilling that mandate lies with the Commission. Its responsibility is not simply to sit back, like an umpire, and resolve adversary contentions at the hearing stage. Rather, it must itself take the initiative of considering environmental values at every distinctive and comprehensive stage of the process beyond the staff's evaluation and recommendation. * * *

NEPA mandates a case-by-case balancing judgment on the part of federal agencies. In each individual case, the particular economic and technical benefits of planned action must be assessed and then weighed against the environmental costs; alternatives must be considered which would affect the balance of values. The magnitude of possible benefits and possible costs may lie anywhere on a broad spectrum. Much will depend on the particular magnitudes involved in particular cases. In some cases, the benefits will be great enough to justify a certain quantum of environmental costs; in other cases, they will not be so great and the proposed action may have to be abandoned or significantly altered so as to bring the benefits and costs into a proper balance. The point of the individualized balancing analysis is to ensure that, with possible alterations, the optimally beneficial action is finally taken.

Certification by another agency that its own environmental standards are satisfied involves an entirely different kind of judgment. Such agencies, without overall responsibility for the particular federal action in question, attend only to one aspect of the problem: the magnitude of certain environmental costs. They simply determine whether those costs exceed an allowable amount. Certifying agencies do not attempt to weigh that damage against the opposing benefits. Thus the balancing analysis remains to be done. It may be that the environmental costs, though passing prescribed standards, are nonetheless great enough to outweigh the particular economic and technical benefits involved in the planned action. The only agency in a position to make such a judgment is the agency with overall responsibility for the proposed federal action—the agency to which NEPA is specifically directed.

Notes

1. **Applicability of NEPA.** NEPA is a statement of federal policy and its directives only apply to federal agencies. Compliance with the environmental assessment requirements of NEPA can be triggered by a federal project, but it will more often be triggered by a private project or activity for which a federal permit or license is required, as in the principal case. Because water rights are primarily a subject of state law, acquisition of a water right alone will not usually activate NEPA, although utilization of the water right may trigger the act. For example, construction of a diversion structure by the owner of a water right may require a section 404 dredge and fill permit from the Army Corps of Engineers (See subsection C), thereby triggering NEPA. Similarly, water development in western states often occurs on federal lands. Diversion works and transportation facilities on federal lands require rights-of-way or special use permits from federal agencies, compelling the issuing agency to observe the environmental assessment provisions of NEPA.

2. **State environmental policy acts.** A number of states have adopted environmental policy acts, patterned generally after NEPA, which express a similar policy and which contain directives to state agencies similar to the directives to federal agencies found in NEPA. See, e.g., The California Environmental Policy Act, Cal. Pub. Res. Code §§ 21000-21177; Washington Environmental Policy Act, Wash. Rev. Code, ch. 43.21C. In states which require a permit or license to create water rights, the issuance of the permit or license can activate the state environmental assessment process. See Stempel v. Dept. of Water Res., supra p. 143, Note 4; Friends of Mammoth v. Mono County, 502 P.2d 1049 (Cal. 1972).

DINAH BEAR, NEPA AT 19: A PRIMER ON AN "OLD" LAW WITH SOLUTIONS TO NEW PROBLEMS

19 Envtl. L. Rep. 10060, 10061-10065 (1989).

The Environmental Impact Assessment Process Under NEPA

Background. As one means of implementing the goals of the Act's national environmental policy, Congress included the well-known §102(2)(C), directing all federal agencies to include, in proposals for legislation and other major federal actions significantly affecting the quality of the human environment, a "detailed statement" by the responsible official. * * *

Title II of NEPA created the Council on Environmental Quality (CEQ) in the Executive Office of the President, composed of three Members appointed by the President with the advice and consent of the Senate. CEQ has a number of responsibilities, including preparation of an annual report on environmental quality, developing and recommending to the President national environmental policies, and documenting and defining environmental trends.

CEQ Guidance and Regulations. * * * [T]he environmental impact assessment process, or "NEPA process," as it frequently is referred to in the federal establishment, acquired some unfortunate "barnacles" during the mid-1970s. The most frequent complaints were the length of EISs and the delays that the NEPA process was perceived to cause in the decisionmaking process. Observers believed that the lack of uniformity throughout the government and uncertainty about what was required accounted to a large degree for these problems. Consequently, in 1977 President Carter issued Executive Order 11991, directing CEQ to issue binding regulations to federal agencies in an effort to make the process more uniform and efficient. The regulations were to cover all procedural provisions of NEPA, and to include procedures for referral to CEQ of conflicts between agencies concerning the environmental impacts of proposed major federal actions. * * *

Regulatory Structure. The CEQ regulations implementing the procedural provisions of NEPA apply to all federal agencies of the government, excluding Congress and any of its institutions, the judiciary, and the President, including the performance of staff functions for the President. The CEQ regulations are generic in nature, and do not address the applicability of the various procedural requirements to specific agency actions. Instead, each federal department and agency is required to prepare its own NEPA procedures that address that agency's compliance in relation to its particular mission. CEQ reviews and approves all agency procedures and amendments to those procedures.

The agency procedures are required to establish specific criteria for and identification of three classes of actions: those that require preparation of an environmental impact statement; those that require preparation of an environmental assessment; and those that are categorically excluded from further NEPA review. Additionally, agencies are required to address NEPA compliance for actions initiated outside of the federal government that require federal approval, the introduction of supplemental EISs into the administrative record, the integration of NEPA analysis into the agency decisionmaking process, and to name a contact office for further information or documents prepared under NEPA.

Categorical Exclusions. "Categorical exclusions" refer to acts falling within a pre-designated category of actions that do not individually or cumulatively have a significant effect on the human environment. Thus, no documentation of environmental analysis is required. Agencies may list either very specific actions, or a broader class of actions with criteria and examples for guidance. However, federal officials must be alert to extraordinary circumstances in which a normally excluded action may have a significant environmental effect. A categorical exclusion is not an exemption from compliance with NEPA, but merely an administrative tool to avoid paperwork for those actions without significant environmental effects.

Environmental Assessments. An environmental assessment (EA) is supposed to be a concise public document that may be prepared to achieve any of the following purposes: to provide sufficient evidence and analysis for determining whether to prepare an EIS; to aid an agency's compliance with NEPA when no EIS is necessary; and to facilitate preparation of an EIS if one is necessary. An EA should include a brief discussion of the need for the proposal, of alternatives as required by NEPA § 102(2)(E), and of the environmental impacts of the proposed action and alternatives. It should list agencies and persons consulted. An EA is followed by one of two conclusions: either a Finding of No Significant Impact (FONSI) or a decision to prepare an EIS. A FONSI briefly presents the reasons why an action, not otherwise categorically excluded, will not have a significant effect on the human environment. It may include a summary of the EA, or simply be attached to the EA. Neither EAs nor FONSIs are filed in a central location (unlike EISs, which are filed with the Office of Federal Activities in the Environmental Protection Agency). However, they are public documents, and the agency responsible for their preparation must involve the public in an appropriate manner. * * *

Environmental Impact Statements. The primary purpose of an EIS is to serve as an action-forcing device to ensure that the policies and goals defined in NEPA are infused into the ongoing programs and actions of the federal government. It must provide full and fair discussion of significant environmental impacts and shall inform decisionmakers and the public of the reasonable alternatives that would avoid or minimize adverse impacts or enhance the quality of the human environment. In preparing EISs, agencies should focus on significant environmental issues and alternatives and reduce paperwork and the accumulation of extraneous background data. Texts should be concise, clear, and to the point, and should be supported by evidence that the agency has made the necessary environmental analyses. An EIS is more than a disclosure document; it should be used by federal officials to plan actions and make decisions.

The threshold requirement for preparation of an EIS is, of course, the statutory threshold of a "major federal action significantly affecting the quality of the human environment." As interpreted by the CEQ regulations and case law, "major federal actions" include a wide range of actions, certainly much more than the construction projects most commonly associated with NEPA compliance. For example, "actions" include adoption of rules, regulations, and interpretations of policy under the Administrative Procedure Act (APA), legislative proposals, treaties and international conventions or agreements, and adoption of programs. Actions include circumstances where the responsible official fails to act and that failure to act is reviewable by courts or administrative tribunals under the APA or other applicable law as agency action. The only items specifically excluded as "actions" under NEPA are judicial or administrative enforcement actions (both civil and criminal) and funding assistance solely in the form of general revenue sharing funds distributed under the State and Local Financial Assistance Act of 1971, with no federal agency control over the subsequent use of such funds.

The question of what is "significant," thus making EIS preparation necessary, has often been a difficult one. In fact, disagreement about whether a proposed action has "significant effects" has been the most frequent reason for NEPA litigation over the past 19 years. CEQ's regulations do not define which particular federal actions are "significant" for purposes of NEPA; rather, they provide a discussion of the factors that should be considered by each agency when drafting their own NEPA procedures and when considering proposed actions. The regulations emphasize the need to consider "significantly" in terms of both context and intensity. "Context" means that the significance of the proposed action must be analyzed in relation to the societal and environmental framework in which the action would occur. Factors to be considered in evaluating "intensity" include the degree to which the proposed action affects public health and safety, unique characteristics of the geographic area involved, the degree of controversy about the environmental impacts, the degree to which the possible effects on the human environment are highly uncertain or involve unique or unknown risks, the precedential value of the action, the presence of cumulative effects, the possible effects on historic, scientific, or cultural resources, the degree to which the action may adversely affect an endangered or threatened species or its habitat, and whether the proposed action would be a violation of a federal, state, or local law. One frequently overlooked point is that the NEPA standard of significance applies to both beneficial and adverse impacts.

Few federal courts have attempted to formulate a definition of the phrase "significantly affecting" that goes beyond the factual circumstances of a particular case. Instead, a review of the cases shows that almost all have been decided by the court determining whether the evidence in a given case pointed to the presence of potentially significant environmental effects and then deciding whether the agency's decision not to prepare an EIS was reasonable under the circumstances. Generally, however, the courts have rejected specific size or monetary factors as a guide to determining the significance of an action. Courts are also increasingly concerned with adequate consideration of cumulative and indirect effects. Although social and economic impacts alone do not trigger the requirement to prepare an EIS under NEPA, the courts have required the inclusion of such impacts once the threshold requirement for preparation of an EIS has been reached.

Two types of EISs that have received less attention than the typical project-specific EIS are the programmatic EIS and the legislative EIS. Programmatic EISs must be prepared prior to an agency's decision regarding a major program, plan, or policy with significant environmental impacts. It may be broad in scope, followed by site-specific EISs or EAs prepared at subsequent stages. The process of preparing a broad statement and subsequent, more narrowly focused NEPA documents is referred to as tiering. Legislative EISs meet the statutory requirement for a "detailed statement on proposals for legislation which would significantly affect the quality of the human environment." Although there are some modifications, the procedures for preparation of legislative EISs are similar to EISs prepared for proposals for executive branch action.

Once the decision is made to prepare an EIS of any type, the proponent federal agency publishes a Notice of Intent (NOI) in the Federal Register. The NOI should describe the proposed action and possible alternatives, the agency's intent to prepare an EIS, the agency's proposed scoping process, and any planned scoping meetings and the name and address of a contact person in the agency.

The agency must then engage in the "scoping process," a process to determine the scope of issues to be addressed in the EIS and for identifying the significant issues related to a proposed action. Scoping may or may not include meetings, but the process should involve interested parties at all levels of government, and all interested private citizens and organizations. Scoping is also the appropriate point to allocate responsibilities among lead and cooperating agencies,[49] identify other environmental requirements that are applicable to the proposal, set any time and page limits, and, in general, structure the process in such a way that all identifiable participants are informed and involved at appropriate points. A well designed scoping process can have an extremely positive ripple effect throughout the rest of the NEPA process.

The next step is preparation of a draft EIS. The EIS may be prepared either by the lead agency, with assistance from any cooperating agencies, or by a contractor. However, if a contractor prepares the EIS, the contractor should be chosen by the agency and must execute a disclosure statement prepared by the lead agency, specifying that the contractor has no financial or other interest in the outcome of the project. The agency may accept information from any party, including the applicant, but it always has the duty to independently evaluate such information.

The content requirements of an EIS, from cover sheet to appendices, are set out in the CEQ regulations. The "heart" of the EIS is the alternatives analysis, which inevitably leads to the question of which alternatives must be analyzed. The answer to that, like the answer to the question of what is "significant," is addressed on a case-by-case basis, with the key judicial standard being that of reasonableness.

If the proposed action is the subject of a request for a federal permit or regulatory approval for a proposed action, the federal agency must consider both public and private purpose and need. Courts have stressed the need to consider the objectives of the permit applicant, but they have also emphasized the requirement for the agency to exercise independent judgment as to the appropriate articulation of objective purpose and need. Thus, NEPA requires the agency to consider both public and private purpose and need in formulating the alternatives to be examined in an EIS.

Once the draft EIS is prepared, it must be circulated for at least 45 days for public comment and review. Federal agencies with jurisdiction by law or special expertise with respect to any of the relevant environmental impacts are expected to comment, although this may take the form of a "no comment" letter. At the conclusion of the comment period, the agency must evaluate the comment letters and respond to the substantive comments in the final EIS. The final EIS is sent to all parties who commented on the draft EIS. No decision may be made concerning the proposed action until at least 30 days

---

49. "Lead agency" and "cooperating agency" designations are used when there is more than one federal agency either proposing an action or involved in the same action or group of actions. Federal, state, or local agencies, including at least one federal agency, may act as joint lead agencies. For criteria and responsibilities of lead and cooperating agencies, see 40 C.F.R. §§ 1501.5 and 1501.6. For resolution of disputes over which agency should be lead agency, see 40 C.F.R. § 1501.5(c).

after the Notice of Availability of the final EIS or 90 days after the publication of the Notice of Availability of the draft EIS, whichever is later.

At the time of decision, the decisionmaker must sign a Record of Decision (ROD). The ROD states what the decision is, identifies which alternatives were considered by the agency in making the decision, specifies which alternatives were considered to be environmentally preferable, and discusses factors that were balanced by the decisionmaker. Further, the ROD states whether all practical methods to avoid or minimize environmental harm are being adopted, and if not, why not. The ROD also includes a description of any applicable enforcement and monitoring programs.

Notes

1. **CEQ guidelines.** The CEQ guidelines referred to in the principal article are found at 40 C.F.R. §§ 1500.1–1508.28. The regulations have remained largely unchanged since their adoption in 1978.

2. **Responsibilities of the Environmental Protection Agency.** The EPA also has some responsibilities for the implementation of NEPA. Section 309 of the Clean Air Act, 42 U.S.C. § 7609, directs the Administrator of EPA to review and comment in writing on the environmental impact of various activities taken by federal agencies including Environmental Impact Statements. The Administrator is further directed to publish his determination and refer to CEQ any activity which he determines is "unsatisfactory from the standpoint of public health or welfare or environmental quality." EPA is also the repository for all EISs. Pursuant to this authority, EPA has developed a system for reviewing and rating actions and underlying EISs. See William H. Rodgers, Jr., Environmental Law, Second Edition § 9.2B (1994).

STRYCKER'S BAY NEIGHBORHOOD COUNCIL v. KARLEN

Supreme Court of the United States, 1980.
444 U.S. 223, 100 S.Ct. 497, 62 L.Ed.2d 433.

[In 1962 the New York City Planning Commission and the United States Department of Housing and Urban Development began formulating a plan for the West Side Urban Renewal Area. Originally the plan called for a mix of 70% middle-income and 30% low-income housing. In 1969, when plans were substantially complete, local agencies urged the need for more low-income units and in 1972 HUD approved an amendment that would add a 160 unit highrise apartment building. Neighborhood groups attacked this decision in the United States District Court, which in 1974 found compliance with NEPA. In 1975 the Second Circuit reversed on the ground that consideration by HUD of alternatives to placing low income housing on the site was either highly limited or nonexistent. A lengthy report was prepared in 1977, which evaluated nine alternatives and rejected all of them on the ground that any relocation of the units would entail an unacceptable delay of two years or more. The district court again upheld the agency.]

PER CURIAM: * * * On appeal, the Second Circuit vacated and remanded again. Karlen v. Harris, 590 F.2d 39 (1978). The appellate court focused upon that part of HUD's report where the agency considered and rejected alternative sites, and in particular upon HUD's reliance on the delay such a relocation would entail. The Court of Appeals purported to recognize that its role in reviewing HUD's decision was defined by the Administrative Procedure Act (APA), 5 U.S.C. § 706(2)(A), which provides that agency actions should be set aside if found to be "arbitrary, capricious, an abuse of discretion, or otherwise not in accordance with law * * *." Additionally, however, the Court of Appeals looked to "[t]he provisions of NEPA" for "the substantive standards necessary to review the merits of agency decisions * * *." 590 F.2d, at 43. The Court of Appeals conceded that HUD had "given 'consideration' to alternatives" to redesignating the site. Id., at 44. Nevertheless, the court believed that "'consideration' is not an end in itself." Ibid. Concentrating on HUD's finding that development of an alternative location would entail an unacceptable delay, the appellate court held that such delay could not be "an overriding factor" in HUD's decision to proceed with the development. Ibid. According to the court, when HUD considers such projects, "environmental factors, such as crowding low-income housing into a concentrated area, should be given determinative weight." Ibid. The Court of Appeals therefore remanded the case to the District Court, instructing HUD to attack the shortage of low-income housing in a manner that would avoid the "concentration" of such housing on Site 30. Id., at 45.

In Vermont Yankee Nuclear Power Corp. v. NRDC, 435 U.S. 519, 558, 98 S.Ct. 1197, 1219, 55 L.Ed.2d 460 (1978), we stated that NEPA, while establishing "significant substantive goals for the Nation," imposes upon agencies duties that are "essentially procedural." As we stressed in that case, NEPA was designed "to insure a fully informed and well-considered decision," but not necessarily "a decision the judges of the Court of Appeals or of this Court would have reached had they been members of the decisionmaking unit of the agency." Ibid. *Vermont Yankee* cuts sharply against the Court of Appeals' conclusion that an agency, in selecting a course of action, must elevate environmental concerns over other appropriate considerations. On the contrary, once an agency has made a decision subject to NEPA's procedural requirements, the only role for a court is to insure that the agency has considered the environmental consequences; it cannot "interject itself within the area of discretion of the executive as to the choice of the action to be taken." Kleppe v. Sierra Club, 427 U.S. 390, 410, n. 21, 96 S.Ct. 2718, 2730, n. 21, 49 L.Ed.2d 576 (1976). See also FPC v. Transcontinental Gas Pipe Line Corp., 423 U.S. 326, 96 S.Ct. 579, 46 L.Ed.2d 533 (1976).[2]

---

2. If we could agree with the dissent that the Court of Appeals held that HUD had acted "arbitrarily" in redesignating the site for low-income housing, we might also agree that plenary review is warranted. But the District Court expressly concluded that HUD had not acted arbitrarily or capriciously and our reading of the opinion of the Court of Appeals satisfies us that it did not overturn that finding. Instead, the appellate court required HUD to elevate environmental concerns over other, admittedly legitimate, considerations. Neither NEPA nor the APA provides any support for such a reordering of priorities by a reviewing court.

In the present litigation there is no doubt that HUD considered the environmental consequences of its decision to redesignate the proposed site for low-income housing. NEPA requires no more. The petitions for certiorari are granted, and the judgment of the Court of Appeals is therefore reversed.

MR. JUSTICE MARSHALL, dissenting. * * *

The issue before the Court of Appeals, therefore, was whether HUD was free under NEPA to reject an alternative acknowledged to be environmentally preferable solely on the ground that any change in sites would cause delay. This was hardly a "peripheral issue" in the case. Whether NEPA, which sets forth "significant substantive goals," Vermont Yankee Nuclear Power Corp. v. NRDC, supra, 435 U.S., at 558, 98 S.Ct., at 1219, permits a projected two-year time difference to be controlling over environmental superiority is by no means clear. Resolution of the issue, however, is certainly within the normal scope of review of agency action to determine if it is arbitrary, capricious, or an abuse of discretion. The question whether HUD can make delay the paramount concern over environmental superiority is essentially a restatement of the question whether HUD in considering the environmental consequences of its proposed action gave those consequences a "hard look," which is exactly the proper question for the reviewing court to ask. Kleppe v. Sierra Club, supra, 427 U.S., at 410, n. 21, 96 S.Ct., at 2730, n. 21. * * *

Notes

1. **Reiteration of NEPA's procedural emphasis.** In 1989, the Supreme Court again held that the judicially enforceable commands of NEPA are primarily procedural, not substantive. Robertson v. Methow Valley Citizens Council, 490 U.S. 332 (1989). The case originated in a U.S. Forest Service decision to issue a special use permit for a ski area in central Washington. Adverse effects identified in the Forest Service EIS included the impact of the ski area and associated development on a 30,000 animal deer herd and on air quality. The EIS contained vague discussions of mitigation measures to reduce these effects, but adopted no mitigation plans, in part because many of the adverse effects would result from activities on private lands over which the Forest Service had no control. The Supreme Court held that NEPA requires a discussion of mitigation measures in the EIS, but reversed a Ninth Circuit decision holding that the Forest Service had a duty under NEPA to develop mitigation plans before issuing the permit. The Court said:

"The sweeping policy goals announced in § 101 of NEPA are thus realized through a set of 'action forcing' procedures that require that agencies take a 'hard look' at environmental consequences, and that provide for broad dissemination of relevant environmental information. Although these procedures are almost certain to affect the agency's substantive decision, it is now well settled that NEPA itself does not mandate particular results, but simply prescribes the necessary process. If the adverse environmental effects of the proposed action are adequately identified and evaluated, the agency is not constrained by NEPA from deciding that other values outweigh the environmental costs. In this case, for example, it would not have violated NEPA if the Forest Service, after complying with the Act's procedural prerequisites, had decided that the benefits to be derived from skiing at Sandy Butte justified the issuance of a special use permit, notwithstanding the loss of 15 percent, 50 percent, or even 100 percent of the mule deer herd. Other statutes may impose substantive environmental obligations on federal agencies, but NEPA merely prohibits uninformed—rather than unwise-agency action." (internal quotation marks omitted).

2. **Mandate to consider the environment.** Although NEPA may not require federal agencies to provide any level of substantive protection to the environment, NEPA is substantive in at least one regard; it authorizes, indeed requires, agencies to consider environmental consequences in their decisionmaking. In the words of Judge Skelly Wright in *Calvert Cliffs,* supra p. 549, NEPA "makes environmental protection a part of the mandate of every federal agency." See also Zabel v. Tabb, 430 F.2d 199 (5th Cir. 1970). State environmental policy acts have a similar effect. See, e.g., Stempel v. Dept. of Water Res., supra p. 143, Note 4, holding that the Washington Department of Water Resources was required by the state environmental policy act to consider environmental effects in issuing a water right permit, although prior to the adoption of the act the Department had no such authority under a water law statute directing it to consider the "public welfare."

However, NEPA does not expand a federal agency's regulatory powers. Thus, in Natural Resources Defense Council, Inc. v. Environmental Protection Agency, 859 F.2d 156 (D.C. Cir. 1988), the court held that while the EPA's authority to regulate the discharge of pollutants under the Clean Water Act allows it to impose "NEPA-inspired" conditions on discharges, NEPA does not expand EPA's authority to regulate discharges into a mandate to regulate plants and facilities producing the discharges.

3. **Utility of nonsubstantive environmental policy acts.** If an environmental policy act does not provide substantive protection to the environment, what is the utility in requiring the identification and exposition of environmental effects? As the Court suggests supra p. 559, Note 1, identification of environmental effects may cause the agency to change a project or decision, to pursue alternatives, or to abandon it altogether. Pressure from other governmental agencies who review the EIS or public reaction to the disclosures of the EIS may result in modification or abandonment of the proposed action. The environmental consequences revealed in the EIS may also trigger the application of substantive environmental statutes, such as the Endangered Species Act, discussed in subsection D. Finally, the NEPA process itself is fertile ground for administrative and judicial challenges (e.g., is preparation of an EIS required? Is the timing of the EIS appropriate? Does the EIS adequately discuss the environmental effects? Should the EIS discuss cumulative effects? Does it adequately discuss alternatives or mitigation measures? Is a supplemental EIS or a programmatic EIS required?) which can be used to delay agency decisions or force their reconsideration.

4. **Effectiveness of NEPA.** Kathleen A. McGinty, *transmittal letter* to Council on Environmental Quality, The National Environmenatl Policy Act, A Study of Its Effectiveness After Twenty-five Years, at iii (1997):

"Overall, what we found is that NEPA is a success—it has made agencies take a hard look at the potential environmental consequences of their actions, and it has brought the public into the agency decision-making process like no other statute. * * * Despite these successes, however, NEPA's implementation at times has fallen short of its goals. For example, this NEPA Effectiveness Study finds that agencies may sometime confuse the purpose of NEPA. Some act as if the detailed statement called for in the statute is an end it itself, rather than a tool to enhance and improve decision-making. * * * The Study finds that agencies sometimes engage in consultation only after a decision has—for all practical purposes—been made. * * * Other matters of concern to participants in the Study were the length of NEPA processes, the extensive detail of NEPA analyses, and the sometime confusing overlay of other laws and regulations."

5. **Substantive state environmental policy acts.** Many of the state environmental policy acts are more substantive than NEPA. Where feasible, several state acts require that an agency minimize or mitigate environmental effects or that it adopt less destructive alternatives. See Cal. Pub. Res. Code § 21081; N.Y. Envtl. Conserv. Law § 8–0109; Minn. Stat. § 116D.04, subd. 6. The Minnesota statute states that "economic considerations alone" shall not justify agency action where a less destructive alternative exists. Although the Washington Supreme Court said that the state's environmental policy act (SEPA) did not mandate any particular substantive result in Stempel v. Department of Water Resources, supra p. 560, Note 2, a later decision by the Washington Court of Appeals said that if there are no important benefits to offset severe environmental consequences the courts would be warranted in holding that government action violates the substantive policies of SEPA. Ullock v. City of Bremerton, 565 P.2d 1179 (Wash. Ct. App. 1977); see also Polygon Corp. v. City of Seattle, 578 P.2d 1309 (Wash. 1978). See Jeffrey T. Renz, The Coming of Age of State Environmental Policy Acts, 5 Pub. Land L. Rev. 31 (1984), for a discussion of the substantive force of state environmental policy acts.

6. **Wild and Scenic Rivers Act.** Balancing costs and benefits project by project, even with careful consideration of environmental factors, may keep a river in constant jeopardy and subject to small incursions that may add up to ruin. Congress opted for absolutes in the Wild and Scenic Rivers Act of 1968, 16 U.S.C. § 1271, which declared a policy that certain selected rivers, and their immediate environments, which possess outstandingly remarkable scenic, recreational, geologic, fish and wildlife, historic, cultural or similar values, should be preserved in free-flowing condition and their environment protected for the benefit and enjoyment of present and future generations. Congress declared that the established national policy of dam and other construction on rivers needed to be complemented by a policy that will preserve other selected rivers or sections thereof. Section 3 of the Act identified three types of eligible streams: (1) wild rivers, free of impoundments and generally inaccessible except by trail, "vestiges of primitive America," (2) scenic rivers, free of impoundments with shoreline or watersheds largely primitive and undeveloped, but accessible in places by roads, and (3) recreational rivers, already accessible by road or railroad, that have some developments and impoundments upon them. 16 U.S.C. § 1273. The Act designated eight rivers as the National Wild and Scenic River System, and named more for further study. Others may be studied by the Secretary of the Interior (or the Secretary of Agriculture if they flow through national forest) and, if the Secretaries so recommend, may be included in the system by Congress. States may nominate still others, which will be recommended to the Congress if approved by the Secretary of the Interior. By 1995 over 150 rivers were included and many more were under study.

The principal effect of designation as a component of the National Wild and Scenic River System is the institution of a land use planning and management system for the banks and environs of the river. In addition, the Act prohibits the Federal Energy Regulatory Commission from licensing the construction of any dam, powerhouse, or transmission line on or directly affecting the rivers in the system or designated for study, and no other federal department may assist by loan, grant, license or otherwise in the construction of any water resources project that would have a direct and adverse effect on the values for which the river was established, except with the express permission of the Secretary of the Interior or Secretary of Agriculture, whichever is in charge of administering the particular river. The Act provides interim protection for rivers under study by the Secretaries. As to whether temporary protection is extended to rivers recommended by the states, see North Carolina v. Federal Power Commission, 533 F.2d 702 (D.C. Cir. 1976), cert. granted, vacated and remanded 429 U.S. 891 (1976). For a case involving both the Wild and Scenic Rivers Act and NEPA, see Oregon Natural Res. Council v. Harrell, 52 F.3d 1499 (9th Cir. 1995).

B. Water Quality Regulation

INTRODUCTORY NOTE

Relation to Water Law. Water quality control is an important part of environmental law, but presents only a peripheral aspect of water law. As traditionally defined, water law is concerned primarily with the allocation of water, i.e., with quantity, not quality. A person who gets rid of a noxious or offensive substance by discharging it into water receives a benefit of a sort, and the discharge may make the water as unavailable to another as if it had been consumed. Conversely, a person who reduces the flow of a stream that dilutes a downstream influx of foreign matter may increase the concentration of the substance to intolerable limits. (See, e.g, Colorado Wild, Inc. v. United States Forest Service, 122 F. Supp. 2d 1190 (D. Colo. 2000) (ski resort's diversions for artificial snowmaking would increase concentration of toxic metals).) Nevertheless, there has been little interplay between water law and pollution control law, historically. The discharger was seldom treated as a water user, and while the diverter might be restrained, it would be by water law, not pollution law.

Sometimes a riparian proprietor was said to have the right to freedom from harmful water pollution, Sandusky Portland Cement Co. v. Dixon Pure Ice Co., 221 F. 200 (7th Cir. 1915); sometimes an upper riparian's use of a stream for waste disposal was said to be an unreasonable exercise of his riparian rights; and sometimes a polluter has defended his fouling the stream as a privileged exercise of his riparian rights, Hazeltine v. Case, 1 N.W. 66 (Wis. 1879). In many cases, however, these property theories had no application. In some the polluter was not a riparian, in some the plaintiff had no status as a riparian although he suffered serious harm. See Kennebunk, Kennebunkport & Wells Water Dist. v. Maine Turnpike Auth., 71 A.2d 520 (1950); Thomas v. Clear Lake, 72 N.W.2d 541 (Wis. 1955).

In the western states similar problems are raised by attempts to apply appropriation law to pollution problems. An appropriator may complain of pollution of his water supply, Game & Fish Comm'n v. Farmer's Irrigation

Co., 426 P.2d 562 (Colo. 1967), but can a riparian who is not an appropriator complain of water pollution in an appropriation state? See Conley v. Amalgamated Sugar Co., 263 P.2d 705 (Idaho 1953). Does an appropriator obtain a prior right to water quality that cannot be impaired by later upstream users of the stream? See Dripps v. Allison's Mines Co., 187 P. 448 (Cal. 1919). Does an appropriator whose use deteriorates the quality of water returned to the stream obtain a prior right to continue this "use" although it prevents beneficial use by subsequent downstream appropriators? Compare State v. California Packing Corp., 141 P.2d 386 (Utah 1943), with Suffolk Gold Mining & Milling Co. v. San Miguel Consol. Mining & Milling Co., 48 P. 828 (Colo. 1897).

Riparian and appropriation law did not produce very satisfactory or predictable results in pollution cases. The emphasis on property doctrines tended to obscure the real factors of decision. Better results were obtained when the courts applied nuisance theories, as in Middlestadt v. Waupaca Starch and Potato Co., 66 N.W. 713 (Wis. 1896); American Cyanamid Co. v. Sparto, 267 F.2d 425 (5th Cir. 1959). In western states which gave no recognition to riparian rights, the concept of nuisance was often used to determine cases of water pollution. See North Point Consol. Irrigation Co. v. Utah & Salt Lake Canal Co., 52 P. 168 (Utah 1898); Wilmore v. Chain O'Mines, Inc., 44 P.2d 1024 (Colo. 1934). The American Law Institute has taken the firm position that "[t]he pollution of water by a riparian proprietor that creates a nuisance by causing harm to another proprietor's interest in land or water is not the exercise of a riparian right." Restatement (Second) of Torts, § 849(2) (1979).

Pollution of surface and groundwaters was a fertile field for litigation, and there were many suits for redress of wrongs and injunctions against permanent damage. These cases built up a substantial body of doctrine. Nuisance law has its intricacies—balancing utility against harm, public nuisance, and coming to the nuisance. There are questions of standing, of proper parties, of joinder of parties, of class actions, problems of irreparable harm, balancing the equities, discretionary jurisdiction and conditional injunctions. None of this litigation had much effect upon the overall quality of water, and all these questions of torts, remedies and procedure lie outside the field of water law as such.

THE CLEAN WATER ACT

Prior to 1948 pollution control was almost entirely a state effort. The first Water Pollution Control Act, 62 Stat. 1155 (1948), offered the state agencies a comprehensive program of investigations, research and funds for operations and treatment works. It set up a complex enforcement system of notices, conferences, hearings and legal proceedings to abate pollution of interstate waters, but this was so chary of state responsibilities and sensibilities as to be completely ineffective. As amended in 1961, the Act was extended to all navigable waters, and in 1965 more amendments required the states to establish water quality standards for interstate streams. To simplify enforcement, federal abatement proceedings could be brought against persons who violated the standards even though no harm or threat to health was shown. Where numbers of polluters were involved, however, problems of proof were difficult, and practical and economic difficulties were excuses for non-compliance and variances.

The sleeping beauty of federal water pollution control turned out to be section 13 of the Rivers and Harbors Act of 1899, 33 U.S.C. § 407, which made it unlawful to throw, discharge or deposit any refuse of any kind or description, other than that flowing from streets and sewers in a liquid state, into navigable waters without a permit from the Secretary of the Army. For years this provision was applied only to discharges that threatened to impede navigation. Dusted off in 1970, rechristened the "Refuse Act," applied to all industrial discharges, administered by the Corps of Engineers under guidelines and standards issued by the Environmental Protection Agency, the Act became the basis of the first effective federal regulation of water pollution. The model of efficient, enforceable permits specifically regulating each discharger, coupled with a rising tide of pollution that in some places reached almost crisis proportions, led to the comprehensive Federal Water Pollution Control Act Amendments of 1972. The "amendments" rewrote the old Act completely and replaced the Refuse Act, and have since been renamed the Clean Water Act. The Clean Water Act is codified at 33 U.S.C. §§ 1251 et seq.

The 1972 amendments were a sharp departure from prior federal efforts in policy and approach. First, Congress made a philosophical shift regarding pollution. Prior to 1972, pollution was unacceptable only if it threatened the health or welfare of people or violated water quality standards, based on federally required, state-promulgated "receiving water standards." In contrast, the 1972 amendments indicate that it is no longer acceptable to use waterways to dispose of waste. This policy is embodied in section 101(a)(1), 33 U.S.C. § 1251(a)(1), which states that "it is the national goal that the discharge of pollutants be eliminated." The amendments recognized that some pollution would continue, at least for the short term, not because it was acceptable but because it was technologically impossible to eliminate all pollution. Second, the 1972 amendments "federalize" water pollution control efforts; federal law and federal agencies have the dominant role, although the states remain important participants. Third, the principal focus of the amendments is on the pollutants, not on the harm done or the water itself. "Effluent limitations," based on technologically achievable treatment, are imposed on all "point source" discharges into surface waters. A system of permits transforms the general effluent limitations into specific treatment and clean-up requirements for each discharger.

Point Source Pollution. The Clean Water Act makes its most vigorous and successful attack on "point source pollution." The act defines a "point source" as "any discernible, confined, and discrete conveyance, including but not limited to any pipe, ditch, channel, tunnel, conduit, well, discrete fissure, container, rolling stock, concentrated animal feeding operation, or vessel or other floating craft from which pollutants are or may be discharged." 33 U.S.C. § 1362(14). With limited exceptions, it is illegal to discharge pollutants from a point source unless a permit issued pursuant to the National Pollution Elimination Discharge System (NPDES) has been obtained. See 33 U.S.C. §§ 1311 and 1342. The NPDES permit sets maximum discharge levels for various pollutants based on uniform national effluent limitations that reflect various levels of technological capabilities. Id. The permit also establishes monitoring and reporting requirements and delineates the permittee's obligations. 33 U.S.C. § 1342(a)(2).

While the act provides for the consideration of economic factors in some situations, technology provides the basic determinant in setting the limitations. The act sets various general standards (e.g., "best available technology economically achievable," "best conventional pollutant control technology," called "BAT" and "BCT" respectively) for existing sources of various types of pollutants (e.g., "toxic pollutants," "conventional pollutants,") and establishes deadlines for achieving the standards. See 33 U.S.C. § 1311. The standards and deadlines have been modified several times since adoption of the 1972 amendments. Toxic pollutants and new sources of pollution are required to meet separate standards. 33 U.S.C §§ 1316, 1317. The general standards have limited intrinsic meaning and must be translated into specific limitations which are established for various industries or for classes or categories within a particular industry. Effluent limitations may be expressed in various ways, including maximum allowable concentrations (e.g., pounds per day), maximum rates of discharge (e.g., parts per million), or maximum discharges per unit of production (e.g., pounds per ton of steel produced).

Nonpoint Source Pollution. Much water pollution originates from nonpoint sources, such as farm lands, city streets, construction sites, road building, logging operations, cleared lands, junkyards, and dumps. In general, nonpoint source pollution is generated by land use activities, is discharged into waters by natural processes, such as runoff and precipitation, rather than being deliberately discharged, and is not susceptible to "end-of-pipe" treatment. Congress recognized that the number and variety of nonpoint sources of pollution, the site-specific nature of such pollution, the lack of known control technologies, and the perception that many of the problems could only be addressed through land use control, a traditional state function, made nonpoint source pollution unsuited to the NPDES.

In the 1972 amendments, Congress chose to address nonpoint source pollution through the section 208 planning process. 33 U.S.C. § 1288. Section 208 requires the governor of each state to designate a local planning agency to develop a "continuing areawide waste treatment management process" for areas that have substantial water quality control problems. Id. § 1288(a)-(b). As one of its components, a section 208 plan is to identify nonpoint source pollution. Id. § 1288(b)(2)(F). The plan is also required to identify procedures and methods to control nonpoint source pollution, primarily through "best management practices" or other land use controls. Id. Section 319, 33 U.S.C. § 1329, added in 1987, directed states to submit to EPA an assessment report describing nonpoint source problems and to develop and submit a management plan for controlling nonpoint source pollution.

Water Quality Standards. Although effluent limitations are the primary control device, the Clean Water Act retains water quality standards in a secondary role. The act requires states to establish and periodically review water quality standards, pursuant to regulations developed by EPA. 33 U.S.C. § 1313. Water quality standards consist of "designated uses" for each body of water and "water quality criteria" sufficient to protect such uses. 33 U.S.C. §§ 1313(c)(2)(A), 40 C.F.R. § 130.2(d). Waste transport and waste assimilation are not permissible designated uses, 40 C.F.R. § 131.10; an antidegradation policy is required, 40 C.F.R. § 131.12(a); where actual quality exceeds the fishable/swimmable goal, that quality must be maintained "except to accommodate economic or social development in the locality," Id. § 131.12(a)(2); water quality of "outstanding natural resources" must be maintained and protected. Id § 131.12(a)(3).

States are required to identify and prioritize waters for which the uniform effluent limitations are not stringent enough to implement applicable water quality standards, known as "water quality limited segments." 33 U.S.C. § 1313(d)(1)(A), 40 C.F.R. §§ 130.2 (j), 131.3(h). States are required to establish the "total maximum daily load" (TMDL) for various pollutants in each water quality limited segment. 33 U.S.C. § 1313(d)(1)(C), 40 C.F.R. § 130.7(c)(1). A TMDL is the maximum amount of a pollutant that a water can receive without violating water quality standards. 33 U.S.C. § 1313(d)(1)(C), 40 C.F.R. § 130.2(e)-(i). TMDLs are allocated to contributing point and nonpoint sources of pollution, 40 C.F.R. § 130.2(g)-(h), and can result in the application of more stringent effluent limitations through the NPDES process. See 33 U.S.C. § 1313(e)(3)(A), 40 C.F.R. §130.7. Unlike the NPDES process, which focuses on individual discharges, the TMDL process focuses on the cumulative effect on a water body of all sources of pollution. More stringent effluent limitations can also be imposed to meet the CWA's fishable/swimmable goal under section 302, 33 U.S.C. § 1312.

Federal and State Roles. The Environmental Protection Agency has initial responsibility for administering the NPDES program. 33 U.S.C. § 1342(a). A state may assume administration if it has an approved program meeting specified criteria, and most have done so. Id. § (b). EPA retains the authority to review each permit and veto those it determines are not incompliance with the act. Id. § (d). EPA may withdraw approval of a state program if it determines the program is not being administered in accordance with the act. Id. § (c)(3). EPA also establishes NPDES effluent limitations. 33 U.S.C. § 1314(b). The states initially set water quality standards, but EPA must review and approve the standards and can itself set them if a state fails to do so or if it sets unsatisfactory standards. 33 U.S.C. §1313(a)-(c). EPA identifies pollutants that are suitable for the TMDL approach, 33 U.S.C. § 1314(a)(2), and must review and approve state identified water quality limited segments and established TMDLs. 33 U.S.C. § 1313(d)(2). Although the states have primary responsibility for nonpoint source pollution, EPA must approve section 208 plans and section 319 assessment reports and management plans. 33 U.S.C. §§ 1288(b)(3), 1329(d); see also section 303(e), 33 U.S.C. § 1313(e). Cf. American Wildlands v. Browner, 260 F.3d 1192 (10th Cir. 2001) (reviewing EPA role under TMDL program.)

SOUTH FLORIDA WATER MANAGEMENT DISTRICT v. MICCOSUKEE TRIBE

Supreme Court of the United States, 2004
541 U.S. 95, 124 S.Ct. 1537, 158 L.Ed.2d 264.

JUSTICE O'CONNOR delivered the opinion of the Court.

Petitioner South Florida Water Management District operates a pumping facility that transfers water from a canal into a reservoir a short distance away. Respondents Miccosukee Tribe of Indians and the Friends of the Everglades brought a citizen suit under the Clean Water Act contending that the pumping facility is required to obtain a discharge permit under the National Pollutant Discharge Elimination System. The District Court agreed and granted summary judgment to respondents. A panel of the United States Court of Appeals for the Eleventh Circuit affirmed. Both the District Court and the Eleventh Circuit rested their holdings on the predicate determination that the canal and reservoir are two distinct water bodies. For the reasons explained below, we vacate and remand for further development of the factual record as to the accuracy of that determination.

The Central and South Florida Flood Control Project (Project) consists of a vast array of levees, canals, pumps, and water impoundment areas in the land between south Florida's coastal hills and the Everglades. Historically, that land was itself part of the Everglades, and its surface and groundwater flowed south in a uniform and unchanneled sheet. Starting in the early 1900's, however, the State began to build canals to drain the wetlands and make them suitable for cultivation. These canals proved to be a source of trouble; they lowered the water table, allowing salt water to intrude upon coastal wells, and they proved incapable of controlling flooding. Congress established the Project in 1948 to address these problems. It gave the United States Army Corps of Engineers the task of constructing a comprehensive network of levees, water storage areas, pumps, and canal improvements that would serve several simultaneous purposes, including flood protection, water conservation, and drainage. These improvements fundamentally altered the hydrology of the Everglades, changing the natural sheet flow of ground and surface water. The local sponsor and day-to-day operator of the Project is the South Florida Water Management District (District).

Five discrete elements of the Project are at issue in this case. One is a canal called "C-11." C-11 collects groundwater and rainwater from a 104 square-mile area in south central Broward County. * * * The area drained by C-11 includes urban, agricultural, and residential development, and is home to 136,000 people. At the western terminus of C-11 is the second Project element at issue here: a large pump station known as "S-9." When the water level in C-11 rises above a set level, S-9 begins operating and pumps water out of the canal. The water does not travel far. Sixty feet away, the pump station empties the water into a large undeveloped wetland area called "WCA-3," the third element of the Project we consider here. WCA-3 is the largest of several "water conservation areas" that are remnants of the original South Florida Everglades. The District impounds water in these areas to conserve fresh water that might otherwise flow directly to the ocean, and to preserve wetlands habitat. * * *

Using pump stations like S-9, the District maintains the water table in WCA-3 at a level significantly higher than that in the developed lands drained by the C-11 canal to the east. Absent human intervention, that water would simply flow back east, where it would rejoin the waters of the canal and flood the populated areas of the C-11 basin. That return flow is prevented, or, more accurately, slowed, by levees that hold back the surface waters of WCA-3. Two of those levees, L-33 and L-37, are the final two elements of the Project at issue here. The combined effect of L-33 and L-37, C-11, and S-9 is artificially to separate the C-11 basin from WCA-3; left to nature, the two areas would be a single wetland covered in an undifferentiated body of surface and ground water flowing slowly southward. * * *

Rain on the western side of the L-33 and L-37 levees falls into the wetland ecosystem of WCA-3. Rain on the eastern side of the levees, on the other hand, falls on agricultural, urban, and residential land. Before it enters the C-11 canal, whether directly as surface runoff or indirectly as groundwater, that rainwater absorbs contaminants produced by human activities. The water in C-11 therefore differs chemically from that in WCA-3. Of particular interest here, C-11 water contains elevated levels of phosphorous, which is found in fertilizers used by farmers in the C-11 basin. When water from C-11 is pumped across the levees, the phosphorous it contains alters the balance of WCA-3's ecosystem (which is naturally low in phosphorous) and stimulates the growth of algae and plants foreign to the Everglades ecosystem.

The phosphorous-related impacts of the Project are well known and have received a great deal of attention from state and federal authorities for more than 20 years. A number of initiatives are currently under way to reduce these impacts and thereby restore the ecological integrity of the Everglades. Respondents Miccosukee Tribe of Indians and the Friends of the Everglades (hereinafter simply Tribe), impatient with the pace of this progress, brought this Clean Water Act suit in the United States District Court for the Southern District of Florida. They sought, among other things, to enjoin the operation of S-9 and, in turn, the conveyance of water from C-11 into WCA-3.

Congress enacted the Clean Water Act (Act) in 1972. Its stated objective was "to restore and maintain the chemical, physical, and biological integrity of the Nation's waters." 86 Stat. 816, 33 U.S.C. § 1251. To serve those ends, the Act prohibits "the discharge of any pollutant by any person" unless done in compliance with some provision of the Act. § 1311(a). The provision relevant to this case, § 1342, establishes the National Pollutant Discharge Elimination System, or "NPDES." Generally speaking, the NPDES requires dischargers to obtain permits that place limits on the type and quantity of pollutants that can be released into the Nation's waters. The Act defines the phrase "'discharge of a pollutant'" to mean "any addition of any pollutant to navigable waters from any point source." § 1362(12). A "'point source,'" in turn, is defined as "any discernible, confined and discrete conveyance," such as a pipe, ditch, channel, or tunnel, "from which pollutants are or may be discharged." § 1362(14).

According to the Tribe, the District cannot operate S-9 without an NPDES permit because the pump station moves phosphorous-laden water from C-11 into WCA-3. The District does not dispute that phosphorous is a pollutant, or that C-11 and WCA-3 are "navigable waters" within the meaning of the Act. The question, it contends, is whether the operation of the S-9 pump constitutes the "discharge of [a] pollutant" within the meaning of the Act. * * *

In its opening brief on the merits, the District argued that the NPDES program applies to a point source "only when a pollutant originates from the point source," and not when pollutants originating elsewhere merely pass through the point source. * * *

This initial argument is untenable, and even the District appears to have abandoned it in its reply brief. A point source is, by definition, a "discernible, confined, and discrete conveyance." § 1362(14) (emphasis added). That definition makes plain that a point source need not be the original source of the pollutant; it need only convey the pollutant to "navigable waters," which are, in turn, defined as "the waters of the United States." § 1362(7). Tellingly, the examples of "point sources" listed by the Act include pipes, ditches, tunnels, and conduits, objects that do not themselves generate pollutants but merely transport them. § 1362(14). In addition, one of the Act's primary goals was to impose NPDES permitting requirements on municipal wastewater treatment plants. See, e.g., § 1311(b)(1)(B) (establishing a compliance schedule for publicly owned treatment works). But under the District's interpretation of the Act, the NPDES program would not cover such plants, because they treat and discharge pollutants added to water by others. We therefore reject the District's proposed reading of the definition of "'discharge of a pollutant'" contained in § 1362(12). That definition includes within its reach point sources that do not themselves generate pollutants.

Having answered the precise question on which we granted certiorari, we turn to a second argument, advanced primarily by the Government as amicus curiae in merits briefing and at oral argument. For purposes of determining whether there has been "any addition of any pollutant to navigable waters from any point source," ibid., the Government contends that all the water bodies that fall within the Act's definition of "'navigable waters'" (that is, all "the waters of the United States, including the territorial seas," § 1362(7)) should be viewed unitarily for purposes of NPDES permitting requirements. Because the Act requires NPDES permits only when there is an addition of a pollutant "to navigable waters," the Government's approach would lead to the conclusion that such permits are not required when water from one navigable water body is discharged, unaltered, into another navigable water body. That would be true even if one water body were polluted and the other pristine, and the two would not otherwise mix. See Catskill Mountains Chapter of Trout Unlimited, Inc. v. New York, 273 F.3d 481, 492 (C.A.2 2001); Dubois v. United States Dept. of Agriculture, 102 F.3d 1273 (C.A.1 1996). Under this "unitary waters" approach, the S-9 pump station would not need an NPDES permit.

The "unitary waters" argument focuses on the Act's definition of a pollutant discharge as "any addition of any pollutant to navigable waters from any point source." § 1362(12). The Government contends that the absence of the word "any" prior to the phrase "navigable waters" in § 1362(12) signals Congress' understanding that NPDES permits would not be required for pollution caused by the engineered transfer of one "navigable water" into another. It argues that Congress intended that such pollution instead would be addressed through local nonpoint source pollution programs. Section 1314(f)(2)(F), which concerns nonpoint sources, directs the Environmental Protection Agency (EPA) to give States information on the evaluation and control of "pollution resulting from . . . changes in the movement, flow, or circulation of any navigable waters or ground waters, including changes caused by the construction of dams, levees, channels, causeways, or flow diversion facilities."

We note, however, that § 1314(f)(2)(F) does not explicitly exempt nonpoint pollution sources from the NPDES program if they also fall within the "point source" definition. And several NPDES provisions might be read to suggest a view contrary to the unitary waters approach. For example, under the Act, a State may set individualized ambient water quality standards by taking into consideration "the designated uses of the navigable waters involved." 33 U.S.C. § 1313(c)(2)(A). Those water quality standards, in turn, directly affect local NPDES permits; if standard permit conditions fail to achieve the water quality goals for a given water body, the State must determine the total pollutant load that the water body can sustain and then allocate that load among the permit-holders who discharge to the water body. § 1313(d). This approach suggests that the Act protects individual water bodies as well as the "waters of the United States" as a whole. * * *

Finally, the Government and numerous amici warn that affirming the Court of Appeals in this case would have significant practical consequences. If we read the Clean Water Act to require an NPDES permit for every engineered diversion of one navigable water into another, thousands of new permits might have to be issued, particularly by western States, whose water supply networks often rely on engineered transfers among various natural water bodies. * * * Many of those diversions might also require expensive treatment to meet water quality criteria. It may be that construing the NPDES program to cover such transfers would therefore raise the costs of water distribution prohibitively, and violate Congress' specific instruction that "the authority of each State to allocate quantities of water within its jurisdiction shall not be superseded, abrogated or otherwise impaired" by the Act. § 1251(g). On the other hand, it may be that such permitting authority is necessary to protect water quality, and that the States or EPA could control regulatory costs by issuing general permits to point sources associated with water distribution programs. See 40 CFR § § 122.28, 123.25 (2003). Indeed, that is the position of the one State that has interpreted the Act to cover interbasin water transfers. * * *

Because WCA-3 and C-11 are both "navigable waters," adopting the "unitary waters" approach would lead to the conclusion that the District may operate S-9 without an NPDES permit. But despite its relevance here, neither the District nor the Government raised the unitary waters approach before the Court of Appeals or in their briefs respecting the petition for certiorari. As a result, we decline to resolve it here. Because we find it necessary to vacate the judgment of the Court of Appeals with respect to a third argument presented by the District, the unitary waters argument will be open to the parties on remand. * * *

Accordingly, the judgment of the United States Court of Appeals for the Eleventh Circuit is vacated, and the case is remanded for further proceedings consistent with this opinion.

Notes

1. **Jurisdictional scope of the Clean Water Act.** As the principal case indicates, the key sections of the Clean Water Act make it unlawful to discharge "any pollutant" into "navigable waters" without a permit. The principal case addresses both components.

As for "any pollutant," the Court concludes that the conveyance of contaminated water, even without further adulteration by the conveyer, from one watercourse for discharge into another, involves the discharge of a "pollutant." As the Court notes, the implications of this holding for water conveyers in general, and voluntary water transfers in particular, are potentially sweeping. See, e.g., Peter D. Nichols, Miccosukee: The Potential for Clean Water Act Discharge Permits for Water Transfers, 33 Colo. Lawyer 119 (2004).

As for "navigable waters," the Act variously refers to the waters protected as "the Nation's water," "the navigable waters" and "the waters of the United States." These are essentially all water courses in the United States, not merely the classically "navigable waters of the United States" discussed infra pp. 621-624, Notes 1-3. In the principal case, because of the parties' failure to raise the issue below, the Court declined to rule on the United States' novel "unitary" theory of "waters of the United States." As indicated in the principal case, this more nuanced reading of the statute would have allowed the Court to conclude that the "discharge" in question was not a "point source," governed by the NPDES permit system, but rather a "nonpoint source," governed by the TMDL process. As the Court noted, however, the issue remains alive for future cases, including the principal case on remand. See also Catskill Mountains Chapter of Trout Unlimited v. City of New York, 244 F. Supp. 2d 41 (N.D.N.Y. 2003) (raising similar issues).

2. **Failure of nonpoint source controls.** The NPDES program has made significant progress in reducing point source pollution. In contrast, little progress has been made in controlling nonpoint source pollution. George A. Gould, Agriculture, Nonpoint Source Pollution and Federal Law, 23 U.C. Davis L. Rev. 461, 463-64 (1990):

"Nonpoint sources cause the predominant amount of pollution in sixty-five percent of streams and rivers in the United States not meeting water quality standards. In all but seventeen states, nonpoint sources exceed any other category of pollution in water quality impaired rivers and streams and account for more than ninety percent of the problem in five states. Nonpoint sources cause the predominant pollution in seventy-six percent of lake acres not meeting water quality standards. In all but eight states, nonpoint sources exceed any other category of pollution in water quality impaired lakes and cause one hundred percent of the problem in six states. Nonpoint sources account for forty-five percent of impaired estuarine waters and cause the predominant effects in nine of sixteen states reporting impaired estuarine waters."

In part, the lack of success in controlling nonpoint source pollution stems from the complexity of the problem. Nonpoint source pollution cannot be controlled simply by attaching end-of-pipe treatment devices to production facilities, as can be done with point source pollution. Control of nonpoint source pollution requires fundamental changes in the activities and practices that generate the pollution. Such changes are not easy to induce. However, the failure to control nonpoint source pollution also stems from the lack of effective regulation. The act does not directly regulate nonpoint source pollution. Rather, it leaves it to the states to develop controls. See, e.g., American Wildlands v. Browner, 260 F.3d 1192 (10th Cir. 2001) (EPA has no direct authority over nonpoint sources). The states have relied primarily on voluntary strategies, and neither sections 208 nor 319 provide effective provisions to induce or require the states to implement mandatory controls.

3. **Implementation of the TMDL process.** The TMDL process, ignored until recently, has become the centerpiece of efforts to resolve the remaining water pollution problems. Initially, EPA made only limited efforts to discharge its responsibilities regarding the TMDL provisions, in large part because implementation of the point source provisions of the 1972 amendments consumed most of its energy. In addition, postponing vigorous implementation of the TMDL provisions was not wholly inconsistent with the CWA. The act requires that TMDLs be developed only for those waters for which application of uniform effluent limitations will not achieve water quality standards. Thus, it made some sense to delay implementation of the TMDL provisions until effluent limitations had been developed and the effect of their application on water quality through the NPDES process was clearer.

Completed implementation of the NPDES program freed EPA to focus on the TMDL provisions in the early 1990s, and the persistence of serious water pollution problems, particularly those resulting from nonpoint sources, indicated that additional pollution control efforts were needed. However, EPA did not fully embrace the TMDL process until several lawsuits successfully challenged its failure to require the states to designate water quality limited segments and develop TMDLs and to assume responsibility for such activities when state efforts were inadequate. See Idaho Sportsmen's Coalition v. Browner, 951 F. Supp. 962 (W.D. Wash. 1996); Sierra Club v. Hankinson, 939 F. Supp. 865 (N.D. Ga. 1996); 939 F. Supp. 872 (N.D. Ga. 1996). Between 1996 and 2000, EPA provided new policy guidance to the states and EPA regions, took steps to force state compliance with TMDL provisions, appointed a federal advisory committee to develop consensus among the states, environmental groups and affected dischargers about the future form of the TMDL process, and developed new regulations to clarify and strengthen TMDL regulatory requirements. See 64 Fed. Reg. 46,012 (1999). Additional regulations proposed by the Clinton administration in 2000, however, were withdrawn by the Bush administration. See 68 Fed. Reg. 13,608 (2003). Not surprisingly, the pace of TMDL implementation has been the subject of continued legal challenges by environmentalists. See, e.g.,

Pronsolino v. Nastri, 291 F.3d 1123 (9th Cir. 2002); American Littoral Soc'y v. United States Envtl. Prot. Agency, 199 F. Supp. 2d 217 (D.N.J. 2002); San Francisco Baykeeper, Inc. v. Browner, 147 F. Supp. 2d 991 (N.D. Cal. 2001).

EPA's recent focus on the TMDL process is supported, indeed demanded, by many environmental advocates. Because of its emphasis on the effects of all sources of pollution on receiving waters, they argue that the TMDL process is more "holistic" than the effluent limitation approach of the NPDES program. They, like EPA, are hopeful that the TMDL process will provide a successful attack on nonpoint source pollution. Although EPA has consistently taken the position that the TMDL provisions apply to nonpoint sources, agricultural groups and others whose activities are major sources of point source pollution, and some federal agencies with close ties to such groups, argue that the TMDL provisions do not apply to nonpoint source pollution. On the other hand, many state officials and industry representatives favor the TMDL approach because of its emphasis on local control.

The history of the TMDL provisions and the difficulties confronting their successful application are discussed in a series of articles by Oliver A. Houck, TMDL: The Resurrection of Water Quality Standards-Based Regulation Under the Clean Water Act, 27 Envtl. L. Rep. 10329 (1997); TMDLs, Are We There Yet?: The Long Road Toward Water Quality-Based Regulation under the Clean Water Act, 27 Envtl. L. Rep. 10391 (1997); TMDLs III: A New Framework for the Clean Water Act's Ambient Standards Program, 28 Envtl. L. Rep. 10415 (1998); TMDLs IV: The Final Frontier, 29 Envtl. L. Rep. 10469 (1999). Professor Houck observes that the emphasis on state-dominated, water quality-based regulation, represented by the TMDL process, is a throwback to the pre-1972 approach to water pollution control. He notes that the TMDL process is beguilingly simple to describe and frustratingly difficult to implement. It is, he says, expensive, site-specific, and heavily reliant on science, monitoring, and the will and ability of states and local governments. While he notes many significant problems which make the success of the TMDL approach far from certain, he concludes that TMDLs hold the best prospect for coming to grips with the last major sources of water pollution.

4. **Agricultural drains and dam-induced water quality changes.** Natural Resources Defense Council, Inc. v. Train, 396 F. Supp. 1393 (D.D.C. 1975), held that EPA had exceeded its authority in exempting agricultural return flows from the NPDES program. Congress responded by amending the definition of point source to exclude "return flows from irrigated agriculture." 33 U.S.C. § 1362(14). Congress also prohibited EPA from requiring a permit for discharges "composed entirely of return flows from irrigated agriculture." 33 U.S.C. § 1342(l)(1).

National Wildlife Federation v. Gorsuch, 693 F.2d 156 (D.C. Cir. 1982), held that dam-induced water quality changes, such as changes in dissolved oxygen, temperature, or sediment loads do not involve the discharge of a pollutant, defined in the act as the "*addition* of any pollutant to navigable water from any point source." See 33 U.S.C. § 1362(12) (emphasis added).

5. **Criteria for delegation of NPDES program to states.** In American Forest & Paper Association v. Environmental Protection Agency, 137 F.3d 291 (5th Cir. 1998), the court struck down conditions imposed by EPA in delegating NPDES permitting responsibility to the state of Louisiana. As a condition of

delegation, EPA required the Louisiana Department of Environmental Quality (LDEQ) to submit proposed permits to the U.S. Fish and Wildlife Service and the National Marine Fisheries Services for review. If the federal agencies agreed that the proposed permit would not threaten endangered species, LDEQ could issue the permit. However, if either service determined that a proposed permit would threaten an endangered species and LDEQ refused to modify the permit to the service's satisfaction, EPA declared it would veto the permit.

The court held that EPA is required to approve a delegation of the NPDES process to a state if its program meets nine requirements enumerated in section 402(b) of the CWA, 33 U.S.C. § 1342(b), and has no discretion to add additional requirements. The court rejected EPA's arguments that its added conditions were required by the Endangered Species Act or that EPA could impose the conditions under its authority to promulgate "guidelines establishing the minimum procedural and other elements" of a state program under section 304(i), 33 U.S.C. § 1314(i). Compare American Forest and Paper Ass'n v. Envtl. Prot. Agency, 154 F.3d 1155 (10th Cir. 1998) (holding that the Association lacked standing to challenge similar conditions imposed in the Oklahoma delegation).

6. **Control of injection wells.** The Safe Drinking Water Act of 1974, 42 U.S.C. §§ 300h to 300h–7, includes requirements for state programs to control underground injections in order to protect public water systems from contamination, pursuant to regulations issued by EPA. Id. at § 300h. See Frank B. Friedman, Environmental Problems Relating to Uranium Mining and Milling, 9 Nat. Resources Law. 277 (1978). The act places emphasis on protection of recharge zones of aquifers and on permits to control waste injection wells that might damage drinking water supplies. See David H. Getches, Controlling Groundwater Use and Quality: A Fragmented System, 17 Nat. Resources Law. 623, 631 (1985).

7. **Other approaches.** Section 304(e) of the CWA, 33 U.S.C. § 1314(e), gives EPA authority to require best management practices for toxic and hazardous pollutants. These include methods for control of plant site runoff, spillage or leaks, sludge or waste disposal, and drainage from raw material storage when these might contribute significant amounts of pollutants to waters.

In the struggle to protect the people against harm from toxic substances, the emphasis has shifted away from protection of waters to management and control of the substances themselves. The Toxic Substances Control Act, 15 U.S.C. §§ 2601 et seq., regulates the testing, manufacture and distribution of chemicals that present a risk of injury to health and the environment. The Resources Conservation and Recovery Act, 42 U.S.C. §§ 6921 et seq., regulates the current and future handling, storage, treatment, transportation and disposal of hazardous wastes. The Comprehensive Environmental Response, Compensation, and Liability Act, 42 U.S.C. §§ 9601 et seq., establishes four measures directed toward cleanup of existing uncontrolled dump sites. It requires owners of hazardous sites to notify EPA of their existence and nature; it gives EPA authority to clean up the dump if the owner cannot be found or does not act; it establishes the "superfund" for cleanup, replenished by a tax on petrochemical plants and crude oil importers; and it creates liability for cleanup and restitution costs.

The Safe Drinking Water Act, 42 U.S.C. § 300f–j, attacks in still another direction, by preventing the use of contaminated supplies. Most water destined for domestic use is treated to some degree before being delivered to consumers.

The act empowers EPA to set maximum levels for contaminants in delivered water and to establish standards for monitoring, delegating enforcement to states with approved programs. All water delivered from public water suppliers (serving more than 25 persons or having 15 service connections) must meet the national standards. If standard treatment techniques cannot produce the required level, a variance or exception may be granted unless it will result in an unreasonable risk to health. In case of emergency, in which a contaminant present in or likely to enter a public water system may present an imminent and substantial endangerment to the health of persons, the appropriate state or federal authorities may take steps necessary to protect health, which may include requiring the provision of alternative supplies. The act was substantially amended in 1996. The amendments preserve the basic structure of the act, but they introduce cost/benefit considerations into the process of setting standards and give the states greater flexibility in adopting protection strategies. See David W. Schnare, Environmental Rationality and Judicial Review: When Benefits Justify Costs Under the Safe Drinking Water Act Amendments of 1996, 5 Hastings W.-N.W. J. Envtl. L. & Pol'y 65 (1998); A. Dan Tarlock, Safe Drinking Water: A Federalism Perspective, 21 Wm. & Mary Envtl. L. & Pol'y Rev. 233 (1997).

CITY OF THORNTON v. BIJOU IRRIGATION CO.

Supreme Court of Colorado, 1996
926 P.2d 1

[The City of Thornton applied for a water exchange as part of a large water development project. See page 48 for other aspects of this case]

LOHR, JUSTICE. * * * We turn now to issues relating to the potential water quality impacts of the Northern Project. The first of these issues on appeal concerns the water court's resolution of certain water quality issues raised by objector Eastman Kodak Company, Colorado Division (Kodak). Kodak operates a manufacturing plant on the Poudre River near Windsor, Colorado. As part of its industrial processes, Kodak uses between 1.1 and 1.3 million gallons of water per day. Kodak receives this water pursuant to an allotment contract with [the Northern Colorado Water Conservancy District], and the water is delivered after treatment by the City of Greeley. Following the use of this water at the plant, it is collected and treated at Kodak's on-site industrial wastewater treatment plant. After treatment, Kodak discharges the water into the Poudre River.

Kodak's discharge of treated wastewater is conducted under a wastewater discharge permit issued by the Colorado Department of Health Water Quality Control Division (Water Quality Division or Division). Pursuant to this permit, Kodak's discharge must meet or remain below certain effluent limits for various chemicals, including ammonia. These effluent limits are based in part on an average low-flow value in the river in the vicinity of Kodak's discharge point,[80] and Kodak has consistently met these current limitations through operation of its existing treatment facility.

Thornton's proposed Poudre River exchange will have a negative, if indirect, impact on Kodak's waste treatment operations. The exchange proposed by Thornton contemplates the diversion of water from the Poudre River above the location of Kodak's plant and return of the substitute supply into the Poudre below the plant. The water being exchanged upon is not water necessary to satisfy Kodak's appropriative rights—i.e., the amount of water remaining in the river after the exchange diversion will be sufficient to allow Kodak to divert the full amount of its appropriative right. Furthermore, as a consequence of the location of the point chosen for return of the substitute supply, none of the substituted water even passes by the Kodak facility. The effect of the exchange about which Kodak complains, however, is the substantial depletion of Poudre River flows at Kodak's plant. Kodak presented evidence that this depletion in flow will affect the average low-flow rates on which Kodak's effluent limits are based and result in stricter unionized ammonia limits on Kodak's discharged water. Kodak alleges that such more stringent standards would require the construction of an entirely new treatment facility at a cost of between nine and twelve million dollars. Kodak objected to Thornton's exchange, seeking imposition by the water court of unspecified terms and conditions to protect the company against these negative impacts on its treatment operations.

In its Memorandum of Decision, the trial court interpreted Kodak's request for protective terms and conditions as a request for a minimum instream flow right for waste dilution purposes, and held that it was forbidden to decree such a right except as specifically authorized by statute. The court noted that "issues relating to water quality are primarily the concern of the appropriate federal and state administrative agencies." The court ultimately approved the exchange subject to various conditions designed to provide protection of water quality. However, these conditions assure that the substitute supply to be introduced into the river below Kodak's plant will meet statutory standards, and do not provide any relief to Kodak. Accordingly, Kodak appeals the trial court's decision to approve the Poudre River exchange without specifically addressing the impact of the exchange on Kodak's water treatment operations.

1. Relation Between Appropriation Doctrine and Quality Issues

From the earliest cases, Colorado courts have given at least some recognition to water quality concerns, holding, for example, that a water right

---

80. * * * The effluent limits are calculated to ensure that water quality standards developed by the Water Quality Commission will be met in each relevant area of the stream. One controlling variable in calculating effluent limits is the volume of water in the stream just upstream of the discharge point. The volume of water is measured as a statistically determined, biologically based average low flow, termed the 30 E 3 flow. Should a detrimental change in stream flow occur, the Division is authorized to impose stricter effluent limits to maintain the water quality standards. Thus, a reduction in average low-flow conditions in a stream may result in stricter effluent limits in a discharge permit.

does not include the right to discharge pollutants that detrimentally affect downstream users. However, beyond recognition of this general prohibition on unreasonable discharges, the system of water quality regulation in Colorado reflects a continued conflict with and subordination to the prior appropriation system. Rather than consolidating the power to regulate water quantity and water quality in the same body, Colorado divides responsibilities for these matters between two very distinct entities. The prior appropriation system, embodied in the adjudication of appropriative rights to water, is presided over by the judiciary in general and the water court in particular. See Water Right Determination and Administration Act of 1969, §§ 37–92–101 to –602, 15 C.R.S. (1990 & 1995 Supp.). Operating under the constitutional and statutory policy of maximum beneficial use, the water court reviews applications for adjudication of appropriative rights and evaluates compliance with the statutorily mandated components of diversion and beneficial use. Although the water court must consider the effects on other water users when a water right owner seeks a change of water right, water court protection of such other users has traditionally been limited to ensuring that they do not suffer a decrease in the quantity of water available through exercise of their rights. The court is explicitly required to consider water quality issues only in the case of an exchange whereby water is being actively substituted into the stream for the use of other appropriators. The water court's primary concern is thus limited to aspects of appropriations unrelated to water quality.

In the Colorado Water Quality Control Act, §§ 25-8-101 to -703, 11A C.R.S. (1989 & 1995 Supp.), the legislature delegated authority over water quality regulation to the Water Quality Control Commission and the Water Quality Division. These agencies were created to develop and enforce water quality standards across the state. Although these agencies exercise considerable authority over water users, the legislature made clear its intention that this authority cannot be exercised in a manner that significantly compromises the appropriative rights of present or future water users. The Water Quality Control Act states in pertinent part:

> No provision of this article shall be interpreted so as to supersede, abrogate, or impair rights to divert water and apply water to beneficial uses in accordance with the provisions of sections 5 and 6 of article XVI of the constitution of the state of Colorado, compacts entered into by the state of Colorado, or the provisions of articles 80 to 93 of title 37, C.R.S., or Colorado court determinations with respect to the determination and administration of water rights. Nothing in this article shall be construed, enforced, or applied so as to cause or result in material injury to water rights.

§ 25-8-104(1), 11A C.R.S. (1989). Water quality regulation that affects water rights without causing material injury or impairment is not necessarily prohibited. However, section 25-8-104(1) serves notice that despite the importance of water quality regulation, the legislature's primary emphasis in enacting this scheme is to maximize beneficial use and to minimize barriers to further beneficial appropriation. The result of this policy decision is essentially to focus water quality regulation on uses culminating in unreasonable discharges, as such discharges are not part of any appropriative right under common law.

For better or worse, this dual system limits the ability of both the water court and the water quality control agencies to address certain water quality issues. The plight of appropriators in Kodak's situation, who allege quality impacts as a result of appropriative depletion rather than substandard discharge or supply water, is a prime example of the limitations of the present system to provide remedies for all types of injuries. The statutory scheme governing water exchange proposals places a clear limitation on the "discharge" aspect of all exchanges—i.e., the provision of the substituted supply of water. See § 37-80-120(3) ("Any substituted water shall be of a quality and continuity to meet the requirements of use to which the senior appropriation has normally been put."); § 37-92-305(5) ("Any substituted water [in the case of plans for augmentation including exchange] shall be of a quality and quantity so as to meet the requirements for which the water of the senior appropriator has normally been used * * *."). These statutory provisions are intended to protect the quality of the substitute supply for those senior appropriators who receive this water. To ensure compliance with this requirement in the present case, the trial court included these conditions in the decree to be administered by the state engineer. Neither the statute nor the decree, however, provides relief to an appropriator in Kodak's situation. Under the decreed operation of the Poudre River exchange, Thornton will return the substitute supply water to the river below the location of Kodak's plant. Kodak is physically unable to receive any of this substitute supply. Thus, the discharge-oriented water quality provisions relating to exchanges fail to protect appropriators in Kodak's position.

2. Relation Between Quality and Cognizable Injury

Kodak argues, however, that under the "no-injury" statute, § 37–92–305(3), 15 C.R.S. (1990), the trial court can and must take into account quality impacts not related to substitute supply and impose any terms and conditions necessary to ensure that operation of the exchange will not "injuriously affect" Kodak's water rights. Accordingly, Kodak takes issue with the trial court's decision not to include any conditions in the decree to protect Kodak against increases in its wastewater treatment costs. Whether section 37-92-305(3) applies to all water exchange projects is not clear from the statutory language. However, we need not decide that issue in the present case. Even assuming that "no-injury" review of Thornton's exchange was required, we agree with the trial court that the legislative water quality scheme is not designed to protect against quality impacts unrelated to discharges or substitute water and specifically prohibits the water court from imposing the protective measures necessary to remedy depletive impacts of upstream appropriations on an appropriator in Kodak's situation.

Kodak does not allege that operation of the Poudre River exchange will reduce the quantity of water available in the river to a volume less than the amount of its appropriative right. Kodak also cannot contend that the substitute supply provided by Thornton in the Poudre River exchange will affect the quality of the water diverted to its plant. The sole negative impact of the Poudre River exchange on Kodak's treatment operations results from a diminution in the flow of excess river water—i.e., water that would otherwise flow by Kodak's plant but that is in excess of the amount that can be diverted under Kodak's water right. Because the volume of water in a stream just upstream of the discharge point is a controlling variable in the formula to set effluent limits, Kodak contends that diminution in flow caused by operation of the exchange will necessarily result in more stringent effluent limits for Kodak. However, to avoid this impact on Kodak's treatment operations, the trial court would have had to impose conditions that required maintenance of sufficient volume in the stream to preserve the average low-flow values that determine Kodak's effluent limits. Despite Kodak's arguments to the contrary, such protection would necessarily require the imposition of conditions creating a private instream flow right for Kodak for the purpose of waste dilution or assimilation.

3. Relation Between Quality and Minimum Stream Flow

The legislature expressed a clear intent to prohibit private parties from adjudicating instream flow rights. Pursuant to section 37-92-102(3), 15 C.R.S. (1990), the General Assembly vested exclusive authority in a state entity, the Colorado Water Conservation Board (CWCB), to appropriate minimum stream flows and limited the purpose for these appropriations to "preserv[ation of] the environment to a reasonable degree." The same provision reinforces this exclusivity with the following prohibition:

> In the adjudication of water rights pursuant to this article and other applicable law, no other person or entity shall be granted a decree adjudicating a right to water or interests in water for instream flows in a stream channel between specific points * * * for any purpose whatsoever.

§ 37-92-102(3), 15 C.R.S. (1990). The meaning of this exclusive delegation of authority is clear—the judiciary is without authority to decree an instream flow right to any private entity.

The legislature similarly prohibited the Colorado Water Quality Commission and the Water Quality Division from imposing minimum instream flows in the course of their water quality protection activities. These agencies must perform their duties subject to the following restriction: "Nothing in this article shall be construed to allow the commission or the division to require minimum stream flows * * * ." § 25-8-104(1), 11A C.R.S. (1989). This language reinforces the legislative intent expressed in the water right adjudication provisions that minimum stream flows are not a valid tool for protecting water quality.

Even in the absence of a specific legislative prohibition, the type of right sought by Kodak is inconsistent with Colorado law and policy concerning appropriations. Kodak currently diverts the full amount of its appropriative right, which it exercises pursuant to its water allotment contract with NCWCD, and the company does not argue that Thornton's exchange will affect its future ability to divert its maximum appropriated amount. Instead, Kodak claims an additional amount of water, above that amount which it can lawfully divert, to ensure the less expensive exercise of its right. Because this additional water exceeds the amount to which Kodak is entitled under its water right, Kodak cannot claim such water as part of its original appropriation. See Rominiecki v. McIntyre Livestock Corp., 633 P.2d 1064, 1067 (Colo.1981) (appropriative right is limited to amount of water actually diverted and put to beneficial use). Without an appropriative right or otherwise established beneficial use, Kodak is not entitled to protection of its incidental use of this water against lawful appropriations by other users. See Colo. Const. art XVI, § 6 ("The right to divert the unappropriated water of any natural stream to beneficial uses shall never be denied."); see also Bender, 148 Colo. at 462, 366 P.2d at 555 ("[An appropriator] is not entitled to command the whole or a substantial flow of the stream merely to facilitate his taking the fraction of the whole flow to which he is entitled.") (citing Schodde v. Twin Falls Water Co., 224 U.S. 107, 119, 32 S.Ct. 470, 472, 56 L.Ed. 686 (1912)). Absent a new appropriation, Kodak cannot establish a protected right to waters in excess of its current appropriation. We decline Kodak's invitation to avoid the effect of the specific prohibition on private instream flow rights by creating such a right in the guise of a condition imposed on the lawful appropriations of others. Under the current system, with its emphasis on maximum beneficial use, Kodak's reliance on unappropriated water in excess of its appropriative right is subject to the risk that a lawful appropriator will appropriate that excess water.

4. Conclusion

We are not unaware of the interrelationship between water quantity and water quality concerns or the specific impact that Thornton's exchange will have on Kodak's operations. However, exchanges in the nature of Thornton's proposal are innovative methods of increasing the beneficial use of the state's waters. Under the current legislative scheme, the impact of which Kodak complains is tolerated as a consequence of the policy of maximum beneficial use. The decision whether further to integrate the consideration and administration of water quality concerns into the prior appropriation system is the province of the General Assembly or the electorate. Thus, we affirm the trial court's decision not to include conditions in the final decree designed to protect Kodak's waste treatment operations.

Notes

1. **Different views.** The Sacramento-San Joaquin Delta in California is the setting for one of the most complex and long-running conflicts between water quality and water rights laws. The Delta is an important environmental resource, it is a source of water supply for several adjacent communities, and it serves as a transit facility for two large water projects, the federal Central Valley Project (CVP) administered by the Bureau of Reclamation and the California Water Project. Both projects store water in reservoirs in northern California. When needed, the water is released into rivers which flow into the Delta and is pumped from the Delta for transportation to central and southern California via large canals. The Delta has serious water quality problems, primarily consisting of salt water intrusion from San Francisco Bay. The intrusion of salt water can be controlled only by regulating water flows into and pumping from the Delta.

In 1978, the California Water Resources Control Board, which administers water quality and water rights laws in California, set water quality standards for the Delta in Decision 1485. To enforce the standards, D 1485 modified the water rights of the two projects referred to above. Challenges to D 1485 were addressed in United States v. State Water Res. Control Bd., 227 Cal. Rptr. 161 (Ct. App. 1986). After concluding that the Water Board had erred in setting the standards the court turned to the issue of enforcement:

"California, of course, has already combined both water resource functions within the exclusive jurisdiction of the Board. The stated purpose of this merger was to ensure that 'consideration of water pollution and water quality' would become an integral part of the appropriative rights process. In the 1978 proceedings the Board, as noted, exercised its water rights authority as a means to implement the water quality standards for the Delta. In D 1485 the Board modified the appropriation permits held by the projects to require them to reduce their exports or release more water into the Delta to maintain the water quality standards contained in the Plan. * * *

"The U.S. Bureau and federal contractors argue strongly that the Board had no authority to modify or interfere with the appropriative rights held by the U.S. Bureau for operation of the CVP. They contend that once an appropriation permit is issued, it is final and nonmodifiable. We disagree and will conclude that the Board's actions are supported on two independent grounds.

"*Reserved Jurisdiction.* In the present proceedings the Board explicitly grounded its authority to impose water quality standards on the CVP on its reserved jurisdiction. * * * The record of the Board's decisions in issuing permits for each unit of the CVP (reported in the margin) supports the court's determination that jurisdiction to coordinate the terms of project units was expressly reserved. The Board's authority to reserve jurisdiction to amend permits and to "coordinate" the terms of the permits with those of other units of the projects was expressly conferred by the Legislature in 1959. * * *

"*Unreasonable Use.* Independent of its reserved powers, we think the Board was authorized to modify the permit terms under its power to prevent waste or unreasonable use or methods of diversion of water. All water rights, including appropriative, are subject to the overriding constitutional limitation that water use must be reasonable. (Cal. Const., art. X, § 2) The Board is expressly commissioned to carry out that policy. To that end, the Board is empowered to institute necessary judicial, legislative or administrative proceedings to prevent waste or unreasonable use, including imposition of new permit terms. Moreover, all permits of the projects are subject to the continuing authority of the Board to prevent unreasonable use. * * * That independent basis of authority vests jurisdiction in the Board to compel compliance with the water quality standards insofar as the projects' diversions and exports adversely affect water quality.

"*Enforcement of Water Quality Standards for Nonconsumptive, Instream Uses.* In addition to protecting consumptive uses of the Delta, the Board formulated revised standards of water quality to protect fish and wildlife, a function expressly authorized by state and federal law. * * * In the proceedings below the Bureau argued the Board had no authority to modify an appropriation permit once issued, and that the new standards for the protection of fish and wildlife will result in impairment of its vested appropriative rights. * * *

"The issue is now clearly controlled by National Audubon Society v. Superior Court, supra, 33 Cal.3d 419, 189 Cal. Rptr. 346, 658 P.2d 709, decided after the proceedings below. In that case the Supreme Court clarified the scope of the "public trust doctrine" and held that the state as trustee of the public trust retains supervisory control over the state's waters such that no party has a vested right to appropriate water in a manner harmful to the interests protected by the public trust. * * * This landmark decision directly refutes the Bureau's contentions and firmly establishes that the state, acting through the Board, has continuing jurisdiction over appropriation permits and is free to reexamine a previous allocation decision. * * * In the new light of National Audubon, the Board unquestionably possessed legal authority under the public trust doctrine to exercise supervision over appropriators in order to protect fish and wildlife. * * *"

See also Shokal v. Dunn, supra p. 138, in which the court held that a permit cannot be issued for a new appropriation if exercise of the new right would result in a violation of water quality laws. Gregory J. Hobbs, Jr. & Bennett W. Raley, Water Quality Versus Water Quantity: A Delicate Balance, 34 Rocky Mtn. Min. L. Inst. 24–1 (1988), argues that the regulation of diversions to achieve water quality standards is contrary to the congressional policy which prohibits the use of dilution to avoid point and nonpoint source controls. Cf. Colorado Wild, Inc. v. United States Forest Service, 122 F. Supp. 2d 1190 (D. Col. 2000) (Clean Water Act permit not required for ski resort's diversions for artificial snowmaking even though diversions would increase concentration of toxic metals).

2. **Implementation of Water Quality Plans** As for the water quality and water rights issues in the Sacramento-San Joaquin Delta addressed in the preceding note, the California State Water Resources Control Board's Decision 1485 was replaced in 1995 by Decision 1641. That Decision promulgated new water quality standards for the Delta and the San Francisco Bay. Implementation of the decision on the Sacramento River threatened to spark major litigation between the state and federal projects and senior upstream water rights holders over the latter's responsibility, if any, to help meet the Decision 1641 water quality objectives. In effect, the senior rights holders argued that all of the harm caused in the Delta was attributable to the junior projects; the latter, in turn, argued that all upstream diverters bore some responsibility for meeting water quality objectives. Formal water rights hearings and inevitable litigation challenging the results of those hearings was averted, at least in the short term, by the 2002 adoption of a "Short Term Settlement Agreement" among the major upstream rights holders, the junior diverters, and the users in the export areas in the Central Valley and Southern California.

3. **Federalism.** Federalism plays a role in the conflict between water quality and water allocation. Water allocation is primarily a matter of state law; water quality law is dominated by the federal government. Conflicts between the two bodies of law inevitably raise questions about the appropriate roles of the state and federal governments. In particular, western states have long feared that water quality laws will be used by federal agencies to usurp state control of water allocation, particularly to provide instream flows. This fear was given added credence by a remark by Justice O'Connor in PUD No. 1 of Jefferson County v. Washington Department of Ecology, infra p. 651:

"Petitioners also assert more generally that the Clean Water Act is only concerned with water 'quality,' and does not allow the regulation of water 'quantity.' This is an artificial distinction. * * * [T]here is recognition in the Clean Water Act itself that reduced stream flow, i.e., diminishment of water quantity can constitute water pollution. First, the Act's definition of pollution as 'the man-made or man induced alteration of the chemical, physical, biological, and radiological integrity of water' encompasses the effects of reduced water quantity. 33 U.S.C. § 1362(19). This broad conception of pollution—one which evinces Congress' concern with the physical and biological integrity of water—refutes petitioners' assertion that the Act draws a sharp distinction between the regulation of water 'quantity' and water 'quality.' Moreover, § 304 of the Act expressly recognizes that water 'pollution' may result from 'changes in the movement, flow, or circulation of any navigable waters * * *, including changes caused by the construction of dams.' 33 U.S.C. § 1314(f)."

The Clean Water Act contains two provisions which address the relationship between the act and state water laws, sections 101(g) and 510(2), 33 U.S.C. §§ 1251(g) and 1370(2). Section 101(g) provides that "it is the policy of Congress that the authority of each State to allocate quantities of water within its jurisdiction shall not be superseded, abrogated, or otherwise impaired by this chapter." Section 510(2) states that nothing in the act shall "be construed as impairing or in any manner affecting any right or jurisdiction of the States with respect to waters * * * of such States." As *Jefferson County* and the *Riverside* case, set out below, show, these provisions may give the states less protection than initially seems apparent. The possible effect of *Jefferson County* on state control of water allocation is explored in Mark T. Pifher, Water, Watersheds and the West: The Impact of the Jefferson County Decision, 2 Envtl. Law 219 (1995). See generally Jerome C. Muys, Quality and Quantity: The Federal Water Pollution Control Act's Quiet Revolution in Western Water Rights Administration, 23 Rocky Mtn. Min. L. Inst. 1013 (1977); Gregory J. Hobbs, Jr. & Bennett W. Raley, supra p. 581, Note 1.

4. **Use of state water quality standards to avoid federal preemption.** Section 401 of the Clean Water Act, 33 U.S.C. § 1341, provides that no federal license or permit can be issued for an activity which may result in a discharge into navigable waters unless the applicant has obtained a state certification that the discharge will comply with state water quality standards. See PUD No. 1 of Jefferson County v. Washington Department of Ecology, infra p. 651 and accompanying Notes, regarding the use of this provision to prevent preemption of state environmental laws by federal agencies.

C. Wetlands Regulation (Clean Water Act Section 404)

RIVERSIDE IRRIGATION DISTRICT v. ANDREWS

United States Court of Appeals, Tenth Circuit, 1985.
758 F.2d 508.

MCKAY, CIRCUIT JUDGE. The issue in this case is whether the Corps of Engineers exceeded its authority when it denied plaintiffs a nationwide permit for deposit of dredge material for construction of Wildcat Dam and Reservoir. The Corps based its decision on the potential downstream impact on an endangered species due to the resulting increased consumptive use of water.

Plaintiffs seek to build a dam and reservoir on Wildcat Creek, a tributary of the South Platte River. Because construction of the dam involves depositing dredge and fill material in a navigable waterway,[1] the plaintiffs are required to obtain a permit from the Corps of Engineers under Section 404 of the Clean Water Act, 33 U.S.C. § 1344. The regulations under the Clean Water Act create categories of nationwide permits that provide automatic authority to place fill material if certain conditions are met. 33 C.F.R. § 330.4. If the conditions are not met, the party must seek an individual permit through a public notice and hearing process. The Corps determined that the proposed deposit did not meet the required conditions because the increased use of water that the resulting reservoir would facilitate would deplete the stream flow and endanger a critical habitat of the whooping crane, an endangered species. The Corps therefore informed the plaintiffs that they would be required to obtain an individual permit before the project could proceed.

Plaintiffs filed this suit seeking declaratory and injunctive relief and review of the agency action, claiming that the project is entitled to proceed under a nationwide permit and that the Corps exceeded its authority when it considered the effect of depletions caused by consumptive use of the water to be stored in the reservoir. An interlocutory appeal was taken from the district court's decision denying the government's motion to dismiss for lack of jurisdiction. This court affirmed the trial court, and remanded "for a determination whether the Engineer acted within his authority and to resolve whatever issues may remain." Riverside Irrigation District v. Stipo, 658 F.2d 762, 768 (10th Cir.1981). On remand, the district court held that the engineer had acted within his authority and that he was required, under the Clean Water Act and the Endangered Species Act, to deny the nationwide permit. Plaintiffs appeal.

A nationwide permit is one covering a category of activities occurring throughout the country that involve discharges of dredge or fill material that will cause only minimal adverse effects on the environment when performed separately and that will have only minimal cumulative effects. See 33 U.S.C. § 1344(e)(1). Such a permit is automatic in that if one qualifies, no application is needed before beginning the discharge activity. Riverside Irrigation District v. Andrews, 568 F.Supp. 583, 585 (D.Colo.1983). The Corps has the authority and duty, however, to ensure that parties seeking to proceed under a nationwide permit meet the requirements for such action. One condition of a nationwide permit is that the discharge not destroy a threatened or endangered species as identified under the Endangered Species Act, or destroy or adversely modify the critical habitat of such species. 33 C.F.R. §

1. We assume, for purposes of this appeal, that Wildcat Creek is a navigable waterway as defined in the Clean Water Act. While plaintiffs claim to have reserved the right to argue this point in later proceedings, they have not argued the point before this court.

330.4(b)(2).[2] The regulations thus are consistent with the Corps' obligation, under the Endangered Species Act, to ensure that "any action authorized, funded, or carried out by such agency * * * is not likely to jeopardize the continued existence of any endangered species or threatened species or result in the destruction or adverse modification of habitat of such species which is determined by the Secretary * * * to be critical." 16 U.S.C. § 1536(a)(2).

No one claims that the fill itself will endanger or destroy the habitat of an endangered species or adversely affect the aquatic environment. However, the fill that the Corps is authorizing is required to build the earthen dam. The dam will result in the impoundment of water in a reservoir, facilitating the use of the water in Wildcat Creek. The increased consumptive use will allegedly deplete the stream flow, and it is this depletion that the Corps found would adversely affect the habitat of the whooping crane.

The Endangered Species Act does not, by its terms, enlarge the jurisdiction of the Corps of Engineers under the Clean Water Act. Riverside Irrigation District, 568 F.2d at 588; cf. United States v. Stoeco Homes, Inc., 498 F.2d 597, 607 (3d Cir.1974) (federal environmental statutes do not enlarge the Corps' jurisdiction under the Rivers and Harbors Appropriations Act). However, it imposes on agencies a mandatory obligation to consider the environmental impacts of the projects that they authorize or fund. As the Supreme Court stated in TVA v. Hill, 437 U.S. 153, 173, 98 S.Ct. 2279, 2291, 57 L.Ed.2d 117 (1978):

> One would be hard pressed to find a statutory provision whose terms were any plainer than those of § 7 of the Endangered Species Act. Its very words affirmatively command all federal agencies "to *insure* that actions *authorized*, funded or *carried out* by them do not jeopardize the continued existence" of an endangered species or "result in the destruction or adverse modification of habitat of such species." 16 U.S.C. § 1536. This language admits of no exception.

(emphasis in original). The question in this case is how broadly the Corps is authorized to look under the Clean Water Act in determining the environmental impact of the discharge that it is authorizing.

Plaintiffs claim that the Corps is authorized to consider only the direct, on-site effects of the discharge, particularly the effects on water quality, and that the Corps exceeded its authority by considering downstream effects of changes in water quantity. However, both the statute and the regulations authorize the Corps to consider downstream effects of changes in water quantity as well as on-site changes in water quality in determining whether a proposed discharge qualifies for a nationwide permit. The statute explicitly requires that a permit be obtained for any discharge "incidental to any activity having as its purpose bringing an area of navigable waters into a use to which it was not previously subject, where the flow or circulation of navigable

2. When the suit began, the relevant regulation was 33 C.F.R. § 323.4-2. The Corps promulgated revised regulations during the remand to the district court. Plaintiffs do not argue that the revision had any impact on the issues in this case. Brief for Riverside at 9, n. 3.

waters may be impaired or the reach of such waters reduced." 33 U.S.C. § 1344(f)(2). The guidelines for determining compliance with section 404(b)(1), developed by the Secretary of the Army and the Environmental Protection Agency, require the permitting authority to consider factors related to water quantity, including the effects of the discharge on water velocity, current patterns, water circulation, and normal water fluctuations. 40 C.F.R. §§ 230.23, 230.24. Thus, the statute focuses not merely on water quality, but rather on all of the effects on the "aquatic environment" caused by replacing water with fill material. 33 U.S.C. § 1344(f)(1)(E). Minnehaha Creek Watershed District v. Hoffman, 597 F.2d 617, 627 (8th Cir.1979).

Plaintiffs argue that, even if the Corps can consider effects of changes in water quantity, it can do so only when the change is a direct effect of the discharge. In the present case, the depletion of water is an indirect effect of the discharge, in that it results from the increased consumptive use of water facilitated by the discharge. However, the Corps is required, under both the Clean Water Act and the Endangered Species Act, to consider the environmental impact of the discharge that it is authorizing. To require it to ignore the indirect effects that result from its actions would be to require it to wear blinders that Congress has not chosen to impose. The fact that the reduction in water does not result "from direct federal action does not lessen the appellee's duty under § 7 [of the Endangered Species Act]." National Wildlife Federation v. Coleman, 529 F.2d 359, 374 (5th Cir.1976). The relevant consideration is the total impact of the discharge on the crane. Id. at 373. In *National Wildlife Federation*, the Fifth Circuit held that the federal agency was required to consider both the direct and the indirect impacts of proposed highway construction, including the residential and commercial development that would develop around the highway interchanges. Similarly, in this case, the Corps was required to consider all effects, direct and indirect, of the discharge for which authorization was sought.

The cases cited by the plaintiffs to the contrary are not controlling. Each involves the National Environmental Protection Act (NEPA), which authorizes the government to look at environmental concerns only when there is "*major* federal action." 42 U.S.C. § 4332(2)(C) (1976). Thus, in each, the question is whether the project is sufficiently federal to require an environmental impact statement at all. The Clean Water Act does not require major federal action before the Corps must consider environmental impacts. Rather, the Corps must consider the environmental impact of each act that it authorizes, both major and minor. In creating categories of nationwide permits, the Corps has "acted" to authorize discharges. Thus, simply allowing a party to proceed under the nationwide permit is an action by the Corps triggering its obligation to consider environmental impacts.

There is no authority for the proposition that, once it is required to consider the environmental impact of the discharge that it is authorizing, the Corps is limited to consideration of the direct effects of the discharge. The reduction of water flows resulting from the increased consumptive use is an effect, albeit indirect, of the discharge to be authorized by the Corps. The discharge thus may "destroy or adversely modify" the critical habitat of an endangered species, and the Corps correctly found that the proposed project did not meet the requirements for a nationwide permit.

Plaintiffs claim that the Corps cannot deny them a nationwide permit because the denial impairs the state's right to allocate water within its jurisdiction, in violation of section 101(g) of the Act (the "Wallop Amendment").[3] Even if denial of a nationwide permit is considered an impairment of the state's authority to allocate water, a question that we do not decide, the Corps acted within its authority. As discussed above, the statute and regulations expressly require the Corps to consider changes in water quantity in granting nationwide permits. Section 101(g), which is only a general policy statement, "cannot nullify a clear and specific grant of jurisdiction, even if the particular grant seems inconsistent with the broadly stated purpose." Connecticut Light and Power Co. v. Federal Power Commission, 324 U.S. 515, 527, 65 S.Ct. 749, 754, 89 L.Ed. 1150 (1945). Thus, the Corps did not exceed its authority in denying a nationwide permit based on its determination that the depletion in water flow resulting from increased consumptive use of water would adversely affect the critical habitat of the whooping crane.

The Wallop Amendment does, however, indicate "that Congress did not want to interfere any more than necessary with state water management." National Wildlife Federation v. Gorsuch, 693 F.2d 156, 178 (D.C. Cir.1982). A fair reading of the statute as a whole makes clear that, where both the state's interest in allocating water and the federal government's interest in protecting the environment are implicated, Congress intended an accommodation. Such accommodations are best reached in the individual permit process.

We need not reach the question raised by plaintiffs of whether Congress can unilaterally abrogate an interstate compact. The action by the Corps has not denied Colorado its right to water use under the South Platte River Compact. All that has been done is to deny them the ability to proceed under a nationwide permit and to require them to apply for an individual permit under public notice and hearing procedures. As plaintiffs may receive an individual permit and be able to proceed with the project, a decision on the question of the impact of the interstate compact would be premature.

We also need not decide whether the project will, in fact, have an adverse impact on the habitat of the whooping crane. Plaintiffs are entitled to proceed under a nationwide permit only if they can show that they meet the conditions for such a permit. Thus, plaintiffs must show "that the discharge *will not* destroy a threatened or endangered species as identified in the Endangered Species Act or destroy or adversely modify the critical habitat of such species." 33 C.F.R. § 330.4(b)(2). The record supports the Corps' finding that the discharge may adversely modify the critical habitat of the

---

3. The Wallop Amendment provides that: It is the policy of Congress that the authority of each State to allocate water within its jurisdiction shall not be superseded, abrogated or otherwise impaired by this Act. It is the further policy of Congress that nothing in this Act shall be construed to supersede or abrogate rights to quantities of water which have been established by any State. 33 U.S.C. § 1251(g) (1982).

whooping crane. Thus, plaintiffs did not meet their burden of showing, as a matter of fact, that the discharge will not have such an adverse impact. The Corps acted within its authority in requiring the plaintiffs to proceed under the individual permit procedure.

Affirmed.

Notes

1. **Importance of wetlands.** Wetlands used to be called "swamps," and filling and draining them used to be encouraged as "land reclamation." Modern science, however, recognizes that wetlands perform important ecological and economic functions:

"The swamps, bogs, sloughs, marshes, bottomlands, wet meadows, prairies, ponds, seeps, potholes, dune grasses and seabeds of the American landscape are the primary pollution control systems of the nation's waters, and the primary determinants of their water quality. They remove heavy metals at efficiencies ranging from twenty to one hundred percent. They remove up to ninety-five percent of phosphorous, nutrients and conventional pollutants, the equivalent of multi-million dollar treatment systems. A recent report concludes that a loss of fifty percent of America's remaining wetlands would result in increased sewage treatment plant expenditures of up to $75 billion for the removal of a single pollutant, nitrogen, alone. These same wetlands purify and recharge groundwater, providing municipal drinking water supplies for towns and cities across the country. The loss of these wetland functions is, moreover, a phenomenon felt by states and federal off-shore waters hundreds of miles downstream. Nutrient loadings to the Mississippi River from the farm states of the American midwest have created a summer "dead zone" of anaerobic water across 6800 square miles of the Louisiana coast. Similar pollution from a half-dozen states seriously threatens the life and the economy of the Chesapeake Bay. * * *

"[W]etlands perform related functions of equal importance and of a similar, transboundary nature. Their biomass is the building block for the world's fisheries. More than seventy percent of America's commercial seafood harvest, with an estimated annual value of $3.6 billion and total economic output of $31 billion, originates in the shallow seagrasses and the salt, intermediate and brackish marshes of coastal estuaries. Up to 100 million migratory waterfowl breed in the prairie potholes, lakeshores and wet tundra of North America and winter along the coastal marshes of California, Louisiana and the Chesapeake Bay. The hydrology and nutrients of these systems are, in turn, regulated and protected by freshwater systems upstream, as is the abundance of their wildlife. Clearcutting along salmon spawning streams in Idaho degrades the commercial fisheries of Washington and Oregon. Prairie pothole drainage in North Dakota has threatened to eliminate Canvasback, Redhead and other wintering waterfowl of Virginia, Maryland and Delaware. More than seventeen million Americans own fishing licenses and generate an estimated fifteen billion dollars annually in related revenue; in 1980 another 5.3 million Americans hunted migratory birds, spending $638 million in the process. Fifty-five million Americans spent almost $10 billion in 1980 simply to watch and photograph wetland- dependent species of birds. This commerce, use and enjoyment begins, and will end, with wetlands. As parts of the American landscape, wetlands are not properly viewed as static parks or monuments, the objects of our occasional visitation. In the natural world—and in an ever increasingly unnatural one—they are aptly seen as biological factories, producing interstate goods.

"Perhaps the most dramatic of these goods is flood control. The year 1973 saw record floods along the lower Mississippi River and the first-ever test of its Atchafalaya Floodway system. A post-flood analysis concluded that the rainfall fueling this extraordinary event had not been, itself, extraordinary; flood stages had been raised by riverside development and the loss of the retention capacity of adjacent wetlands. The report concluded: '[T]he '73 flood was man made.' Twenty years later, new record floods along the upper Mississippi River led to remedial proposals based on restoring the natural floodplain. Similar findings emerge from nearly every watershed and river basin in the country. They have been the basis—although at times honored more in the breach than in the observance—of the U.S. Department of Agriculture's small watershed program, whose original mission was to 'hold the raindrop on the land.' Wetlands along the coast perform a more direct flood-proofing function, buffering storm surges and protecting interior properties. A mile of vegetated wetlands can reduce storm wave heights by one foot. There are fifty miles of marshes between New Orleans and the sea.

"These values are in jeopardy. The coastal wetlands of Louisiana are disappearing at the rate of forty square miles each year. Waterfowl breeding grounds that once spread from Minnesota to Montana have been reduced to a thin wedge in North Dakota. It seems no coincidence that of the 595 plant and animal species listed in the United States as threatened or endangered, nearly sixty percent rely on wetlands during some part of their life cycle. An estimated twelve million acres of bottomland hardwood wetlands along the Lower Mississippi River dropped to five million in a half-century. Only ten percent of California's wetlands remain.

"These losses are mirrored in every state. Of an estimated 215 million acres of wetlands found in America at the time of European discovery, fewer than half remain. They continue to disappear at a rate approaching 300,000 acres per year. * * * " Oliver A. Houck & Michael Rolland, Federalism in Wetlands Regulation: A Consideration of Delegation of Clean Water Act Section 404 and Related Programs to the States, 54 Md. L. Rev. 1242, 1244-51 (1995).

2. **Section 404.** Section 404 provides that the Army Corps of Engineers "may issue permits * * * for the discharge of dredged or fill material into the navigable waters at specified disposal sites." The term "navigable waters" in the Clean Water Act is not limited to traditionally navigable waters but includes most of the waters of the United States. Cf. infra p. 624, Note 3. Still, in Solid Waste Agency v. United States Army Corps of Engineers, 531 U.S. 159 (2001) ("SWANCC"), set out on p. 617, the Court concluded that an abandoned sand and gravel pit was not a "navigable water" of the United States, at least for purpose of the Section 404 program. The Court found no evidence of Congressional intent to extend the statute's scope to include hydrologically isolated, seasonal wetlands found wholly within a single state.

SWANCC sparked a flurry of scholarship about Section 404. For a sampling, see Michael P. Healy, Law, Policy, and the Clean Water Act: The Courts, The Bush Administration, and the Statute's Uncertain Reach, 55 Ala. L. Rev. 695 (2004); Bradford C. Mank, The Murky Future of the Clean Water Act after SWANCC: Using A Hydrological Connection Approach to Saving the Clean

Water Act, 30 Ecology L.Q. 811 (2003); Robert R. M. Verchick, Toward Normative Rules for Agency Interpretation: Defining Jurisdiction Under the Clean Water Act, 55 Ala. L. Rev. 845 (2004).

As for the other part of the statutory definition—"discharge of dredged or fill material"—the principal case demonstrates that the phrase covers much more than operations in the channel and filling of wetlands. Like "navigable waters," the phrase is carried over from earlier law but its meaning is considerably broader.

The regulations of the Corps of Engineers define "dredged material" as "material that is excavated or dredged from waters of the United States." 33 C.F.R. § 323.2(c). "Discharge of dredged material" is defined as "any addition of dredged materials into, including any redeposit of dredged materials other than incidental fallback within, the waters of the United States." 33 C.F.R. § 323.2(d)(1). "Fill material" is defined as "any material used for the primary purpose of replacing an aquatic area with dry land or of changing the bottom elevation of a waterbody. It does not include any pollutant discharged into the water primarily to dispose of waste, as that activity is regulated under section 402 of the Clean Water Act." 33 C.F.R. § 323.2(e). "Discharge of fill material" is defined as "the addition of fill material into the waters of the United States * * * [including], placement of fill that is necessary to the construction of any structure in a water of the United States; the building of any structure or impoundment requiring rock, sand, dirt, or other material for its construction; site-development fills for recreational, industrial, commercial, residential, and other uses; causeways or road fills; dams and dikes; artificial islands; property protection and/or reclamation devices such as riprap, groins, seawalls, breakwaters, and revetments; beach nourishment; levees; fill for structures such as sewage treatment facilities, intake and outfall pipes associated with power plants and subaqueous utility lines; and artificial reefs. The term does not include plowing, cultivating, seeding and harvesting for the production of food, fiber, and forest products." 33 C.F.R. § 323.2(f).

The section 404 permit system is administered by the Corps of Engineers pursuant to guidelines developed by the Administrator of EPA and regulations adopted by the Corps. Permits are issued by the Secretary of the Army, acting through the Chief of Engineers, and are subject to veto by the Administrator of EPA. Most of the routine responsibilities for administering the Corp's regulatory programs, including section 404, are delegated to thirty-six distict engineers and eleven division engineers. The states may assume administration of the section 404 permit process if they have an approved program. To date, only two states, Michigan and New Jersey, have such programs. See 43 C.F.R. §§ 233.70, -.71. The Administrator has authority to veto state-issued permits and can withdraw approval of the state program.

The rather unusual administrative arrangement established in section 404 is the result of a political compromise. The Corp, which historically has had responsibility for regulating development in navigable waters was perceived by environmental interests as too insensitive to environmental values; conversely, EPA was perceived by development interests as too environmentally-oriented. See Oliver A. Houck, supra p. 589, Note 1, at 1254-55.

The Corps of Engineers' general regulations require a "public interest review" in which, "the decision whether to issue a permit will be based on an evaluation of the probable impacts, including cumulative impacts, of the proposed activity and its intended use on the public interest. Evaluation of the probable impacts which the proposed activity may have on the public interest requires a careful weighing of all those factors which become relevant in each particular case. The benefits which reasonably may be expected to accrue from the proposal must be balanced against its reasonably foreseeable detriments. The decision whether to authorize a proposal, and if so the conditions under which it will be allowed to occur, are therefore determined by the outcome of the general balancing process. That decision should reflect the national concern for both protection and utilization of important resources. All factors which may be relevant to the proposal must be considered including the cumulative effects thereof. Among those are conservation, economics, aesthetics, general environmental concerns, wetlands, cultural values, fish and wildlife values, flood hazards, floodplain values, landuse, navigation, shore erosion and accretion, recreation, water supply and conservation, water quality, energy needs, safety, food and fiber production, mineral needs, considerations or property ownership, and, in general, the needs and welfare of the people. For activities involving 404 discharges, a permit will be denied if the discharge that would be authorized by such permit would not comply with the Environmental Protection Agency's 404(b)(1) guidelines." 33 C.F.R. § 320.4(a)(1).

The EPA guidelines allow a permit to issue only if (a) there is no practicable alternative that will have less adverse impact on the aquatic ecosystem (if an activity is not "water dependent" there is a presumption that practical alternatives exist); (b) the discharge will not violate state water quality standards or certain federal toxic pollutant prohibitions, will not jeopardize an endangered or threatened species or destroy critical habitat, and will not violate certain requirements under federal marine sanctuary legislation; (c) the discharge will not significantly degrade the waters of the United States; and (d) appropriate and practicable steps have been taken to minimize adverse impacts on the ecosystem. 40 C.F.R. § 230.10.

Although actions taken by the Administrator are exempt from the requirement of NEPA, section 404 permits issued by the Corps may be major federal actions significantly affecting the quality of the environment. The public interest review is thus not limited to direct effects of the placement of the material or structure in the stream nor to effects on water quality alone. Zabel v. Tabb, 430 F.2d 199 (5th Cir. 1970) (holding NEPA applicable to the Refuse Act permits, which were superseded by section 404 permits). The environmental assessment and environmental impact statement processes may trigger consideration of not only the Endangered Species Act (16 U.S.C. §§ 1531–1534), but also of other federal laws including, the Fish and Wildlife Coordination Act (16 U.S.C. § 662), the Wild and Scenic Rivers Act (16 U.S.C. §§ 1271–1276), the Antiquities Act (16 U.S.C. § 433), and the Coastal Zone Management Act (16 U.S.C. §§ 1451–1464).

3. **Federalism and protection of minimum stream flows under section 404.** What if the dam on Wildcat Creek would have no effect on water quality and would involve none of these federal acts, but would adversely affect trout habitat and recreational features of the creek and the South Platte River? Assume that the Colorado Water Conservation Board has not appropriated a minimum stream flow in the creek or the river under Colo. Rev. Stat. § 37–92–102(3), and the Riverside District has a conditional decree for the appropriation and storage

of the water for irrigation, municipal and industrial purposes under Colorado water law, although water is expected to be available only during fall and winter flows. May the section 404 permit be conditioned to preserve the fish and the fishing if the minimum flow release would make it impossible to store enough water to make the project feasible? What is the effect of section 101(g), discussed in *Riverside*? What does it add to the still extant section 510 of the 1972 Act, declaring that the Act was not to be construed "as impairing or in any manner affecting any right or jurisdiction of the state with respect to the waters (including boundary waters) of such states?"

Charles B. White, The Emerging Relationship Between Environmental Regulations and Colorado Water Law, 53 U. Colo. L. Rev. 597 (1982), argues that under these disclaimers state water allocation laws are controlling except where overruled to meet the specific requirements of federal legislation. Similarly, Gregory J. Hobbs, Jr. & Bennett W. Raley, supra p. 580, Note 1, assert that these provisions establish a presumption that the national public interest will be served by the issuance of a section 404 permit unless a "compelling federal interest of a preemptive nature intervenes." A. Dan Tarlock, The Endangered Species Act and Western Water Rights, 20 Land & Water L. Rev. 1, 19-20 (1985), states that "the net effect of present congressional responses to western concerns that state-created water rights will be displaced is to shift the task of striking an accommodation between state and federal interests to the courts and to give water rights holders a new but slim statutory basis to argue that a federal agency has abused its discretion," and that section 101(g) "reflects the principle that integration should take place by the least intrusive means available to the federal agency."

The Army Corps of Engineers seems to assert the Tarlock approach but carries it almost to the White/Hobbs/Raley extreme. A "Regulatory Guidance Letter" (No. 85–06, Permit Conditioning for Minimum In-Stream Flows, (1985)) stated: "(2) The primary responsibility for allocating water quantities [in the 17 western states] rests with state governments. * * * (3) The public interest review criteria require district commanders to normally issue Corps permits where all local and state permits have been issued unless there are overriding factors of national concern. * * * (4) When a conflict arises between state water quantity allocation and minimum instream flows for the purposes of maintaining viable aquatic habitat, district commanders will consider that the public interest is primarily represented by state water allocation rights or preferences. Consequently, any project alternative which supersedes, abrogates or otherwise impairs those quantities is not a practicable alternative from the Federal regulatory perspective." Although this guidance letter expired in 1989 (see Regulatory Guidance Letter 87–11 (1987),) the guidance provided in expired letters generally remains valid unless expressly superseded. See 64 Fed. Reg. 13783 (1999).

Perhaps the ultimate solution might be for the state to take over administration of the section 404 permit program by incorporating it into their state water rights granting and regulating activities and procedures, as allowed by sections 404(g)–(t), upon a showing that the laws of the state provide adequate authority to carry out the program. The Administrator of EPA would retain authority to veto a permit and turn the application over to the Secretary in case of state refusal to modify it to meet federal objectives.

4. **Standards for EPA vetoes.** In James City County v. Environmental Protection Agency, 12 F.3d 1330 (4th Cir. 1993), the EPA vetoed a section 404 permit for a dam and reservoir to be used to supply water to various political entities in Virginia's Lower Peninsula. The veto was based solely on the effect which the project would have on fish, wildlife, and natural habitat and no consideration was given to the county's need for water. There was no indication that any endangered species were involved or that any of the other acts cited supra p. 589, Note 2, were implicated.

The court noted that in making the initial decision to issue a section 404 permit the Corps of Engineers conducts a "public interest review" which includes, inter alia, the public and private need for the project. In upholding the EPA veto, however, the court said:

"Ultimately, however, recognizing the EPA's expertise and concentrated concern with environmental matters, Congress gave the final decision whether to permit a project to that agency. Its authority to veto to protect the environment is practically unadorned. It is simply directed to veto when it finds that the discharge 'will have an unacceptable adverse effect on municipal water supplies, shellfish beds and fishery areas (including spawning and breeding areas) wildlife, or recreational areas.' See 118 Cong. Rec. 33,699 (1972) (senate debate explaining that under § 404 EPA should not issue a permit if project will adversely effect the listed resources); see also S. Conf. Rep. No. 1236, 92nd Cong., 2d Sess. 142 (1972) (conference committee report explaining that § 404 grants EPA the power to veto project that will adversely affect the listed resources) * * *. This broad grant of power to the EPA focuses only on the agency's assigned function of assuring pure water and is consistent with the mission assigned to it throughout the Clean Water Act.

"We think it significant that the only mention of responsibility for the quantities of water available to communities is contained in section 101(g) entitled 'Authority of States over water' * * *. In our view, the EPA's only function relating to the quantities of available water is limited to assuring purity in whatever quantities the state and local agencies provide. For these reasons, we think its veto based solely on environmental harms was proper." Id. at 1336.

What does this decision do to the arguments of White and Hobbs/Raley, supra p. 591, Note 3, regarding a presumption in favor of the issuance of a section 404 permit unless there is "compelling" federal interest to the contrary? EPA had exercised its section 404 veto only 11 times through 1991.

5. **Judicial review of decisions to issue 404 permits.** In Preserve Endangered Areas of Cobb's History, Inc. v. Army Corp of Engineers, 87 F.3d 1242 (11th Cir. 1996), the court held that a citizens group could not challenge a decision by the Corp to issue a section 404 permit nor a decision by EPA not to veto its issuance. The court found that the CWA does not "clearly and [un]ambiguously waive sovereign immunity in regard to the Army Corps of Engineers." Id. at 1249. Section 505(a)(2), 33 U.S.C. § 1365(a)(2), authorizes suits against the Administrator of EPA for alleged failures to perform any act or duty "which is not discretionary." However, the court held that the decision not to veto a section 404 permit is a discretionary duty. But see National Wildlife Federation v. Hanson, 859 F.2d 313 (4th Cir. 1988).

For a discussion of a novel third-party beneficiary theory to support a citizen's challenge to a 404 permit, see Justin Massey, Applying the Third Party Beneficiary Theory of Contracts to Enforce Clean Water Act § 404 Permits: A California Case Study, 18 J. Envtl. L. & Litig. 129 (2003).

6. **Exemption for agricultural activities.** The CWA exempts from the permit requirements activities undertaken "for the purpose of construction or maintenance of farm or stock ponds or irrigation ditches or the maintenance of drainage ditches." (§ 404(f)(1)(C).) The regulations clarify the scope of the exemption by adding, "[d]ischarges associated with siphons, pumps, headgates, wingwalls, weirs, diversion structures and such other facilities as are pertinent and functionally related to irrigation are included in this exemption." 33 C.F.R. § 323.4(a)(3). Note that intake structures for municipal and industrial uses are not exempted.

Suppose that the Wildcat Creek Dam was a diversion structure and that irrigation was the sole beneficial use to be made of the water. Is there a "Catch 22" in section 404(f)(2)? "Any discharge of dredged or fill material into the navigable waters incidental to any activity having as its purpose bringing an area of the navigable waters into a use to which it was not previously subject, where the flow or circulation of navigable waters may be impaired or the reach of such waters be reduced, shall be required to have a permit under this section." The regulations give two examples: "[A] permit will be required for the conversion of a cypress swamp to some other use or the conversion of a wetland from silvicultural to agricultural use when there is a discharge of dredged or filled material into waters of the United States in conjunction with construction of dikes, drainage ditches or other works or structures used to effect such conversion. * * * A discharge which elevates the bottom of waters of the United States without converting it to dry land does not thereby reduce the reach of, but may alter the flow or circulation of, waters of the United States." 33 C.F.R § 323.4(c). In a discussion of amendments to the regulations, EPA stated that there was no need for "a size limitation to prevent serious fish and wildlife losses from damming of a stream to take all its water for irrigation under this exemption," with the explanation, "EPA does not believe that such a size limitation is necessary in light of the safeguards provided by section 404(f)(2)." 49 F.R. 39478–01, October 5, 1984.

7. **Federal regulation of water rights under section 404.** Many water diversions require a section 404 permit. Does section 404 provide federal authority to regulate water rights to implement water quality standards? See Environmental Protection Agency, Question & Answers on Antidegradation 11: "Where a planned diversion would lead to a violation of water quality standards, a 404 permit associated with the diversion should be suitably conditioned if possible and/or additional nonpoint and/or point source controls should be imposed to compensate." Is this policy consistent with section 101(g)? See Gregory H. Hobbs, Jr. & Bennett W. Raley, supra p. 580, Note 1.

8. **Federal regulation of water rights pursuant to use of federal lands.** Rights of way for diversion works and transmission facilities on federal lands are governed by the Forest Service Organic Act (16 U.S.C. §§ 579) and the Federal Land Policy and Management Act (43 U.S.C. §§ 1751ff). Two recent cases have upheld the Forest Service's authority to impose bypass flows as a condition of granting a right-of-way permit for a water facility. County of Okanogan v. Nat'l

Marine Fisheries Serv., 347 F.3d 1081 (9th Cir. 2003) (prior permits specifically preserved full USFS discretion to impose new conditions); Trout Unlimited v. United States Dep't of Agric., 320 F. Supp. 2d 1090 (D. Colo. 2004) (finding no abuse of discretion in failing to require bypass flows from reservoir.). See Robert V. Trout, Whose Water? Meeting New Federal Water Demands in Prior Appropriation States, 50 Rocky Mtn. Min. L. Inst. 22–1 (2004).

Bypass flows were the subject of a controversial Forest Service task force. See Janet C. Neuman & Michael C. Blumm, Water for National Forests: The Bypass Flow Report and the Great Divide in Western Water Law, 18 Stan. Envtl. L.J. 3 (1999); Lawrence J. Wolfe & Anne J. Castle, Federal Land Management Law and Their Impact on Water Development in the West, 32 Rocky Mtn. Min. L. Inst. 23–1 (1986). Cf. United States v. New Mexico, infra p. 703

D. Endangered Species

UNITED STATES v. GLENN-COLUSA IRRIGATION DISTRICT

United States District Court, E.D. California, 1992.
788 F. Supp. 1126.

LEVI, DISTRICT JUDGE. This case arises from a long-standing dispute between the Glenn-Colusa Irrigation District (the "District") and federal and state authorities responsible for the preservation of marine life. The National Marine Fisheries Service (the "Service") brought this action to protect the Sacramento River winter-run chinook salmon (the "winter-run salmon"), a species designated by the Secretary of Commerce as threatened under the Endangered Species Act. The United States now moves for an injunction prohibiting the District from taking fingerling salmon in the course of pumping water from the Sacramento River at its Hamilton City, California pumping station.

At this juncture, on the motion for injunction, the case is straightforward with few relevant disputes of fact. There is no dispute that the Endangered Species Act, and the actions of the Secretary of Commerce in designating the winter-run salmon as threatened, prohibit the taking or harming of any winter-run salmon. There is no dispute that the winter-run salmon is threatened, and in fact close to extinction—from a population in the tens of thousands only some twenty years ago to fewer than 200 adult winter-run salmon returning to the Sacramento river to spawn in 1991. There is no dispute that the District's Hamilton City pumping station and the associated fish screen kill and harm the winter-run salmon. * * *

[A]t this point, the only questions before the court are whether the winter-run salmon is protected under the Endangered Species Act and whether the District's pumping irreparably harms the species in violation of federal law. If so, an injunction must issue. The District's attack on the federal and state regulatory agencies is premature and irrelevant to the resolution of the motion for injunction now ready for decision. * * *

BACKGROUND

The District was organized in 1920 to provide irrigation water to farms located in Glenn and Colusa Counties in California. The District obtains the water for its customers from the Bureau of Reclamation through a contract which permits it to divert 720,000 acre-feet of water from the natural flow of the Sacramento River. The flow of the Sacramento River is diverted into an oxbow channel at the District's Hamilton City pumping facility. During the peak irrigation season from April to October, the District's diversions from the river range from 300 to 2900 cubic feet per second with an average rate of 2,000 cubic feet per second. At certain times nearly one third of the river flow may be diverted by the District. * * *

It has been estimated that the District's pumping operation killed approximately 800,000 to 9,100,000 fingerling chinook salmon annually prior to 1972 when the California Department of Fish and Game installed the present fish screen at the District's pumping operation. Even with the fish screen, estimates of lost juvenile chinook salmon range from 400,000 to 10,000,000 annually. The winter-run salmon approaching the District's diversion face several perils. When the District is pumping more than 1,100 feet per second, the screen approach velocity exceeds the California standard causing the winter-run salmon to be pinned or battered against the screens by the current. The screen approach velocity also increases as the water level or elevation decreases because the water needed to satisfy the draw of the District's pumps must pass through a smaller area of the screen. This condition contributes to screen approach velocities in excess of the state standard. When the screen approach velocity exceeds the state standard, some winter-run salmon are so small that they are drawn directly into the mesh of the screen becoming entrained. Others are trapped against or under the screens where they are easily preyed on by predators. In addition, the District's diversion channel is a prime aquatic habitat for predators causing additional losses of salmon. * * *

On December 3, 1990, the Service notified the District that without an incidental take permit, the District was liable for incidental takings of the winter-run salmon under the Endangered Species Act.[5] The District never applied for an incidental take permit. Further negotiations between the District and the Service were unsuccessful. On August 9, 1991, the United States filed this action and was granted a temporary restraining order. The parties stipulated to the terms of a preliminary injunction which the court ordered.

---

5. Alternatively the District could comply with the incidental take statement prepared by the Service as part of its consultation with the Army Corps of Engineers concerning the District's dredging permit. 16 U.S.C. § 1536.

ANALYSIS

A. The Endangered Species Act. The Endangered Species Act was instituted to conserve endangered[1] and threatened[2] fish and wildlife species through federal action and coordination with state programs.[3] A species is identified as threatened or endangered by the Secretary of Commerce or the Secretary of the Interior after consideration of the following factors:

> (A) the present or threatened destruction, modification, or curtailment of its habitat or range;
> (B) overutilization for commercial, recreational, scientific, or educational purposes;
> (C) disease or predation;
> (D) the inadequacy of existing regulatory mechanisms; or
> (E) other natural or manmade factors affecting its continued existence.

16. U.S.C. § 1533(a)(1). This determination must be made on the basis of the best scientific and commercial data available. 16 U.S.C. § 1533(b)(1)(A).

The Act prohibits any person from taking, possessing, selling, importing, exporting or transporting a protected species. The Act also provides for identification of a critical habitat for each species and adoption of regulations which will conserve and enhance the population of the species. 16 U.S.C. § 1533(b)(2) and (d).

In this matter, the United States asserts that the District's pumping facility "takes" the winter-run salmon. Under the Endangered Species Act "take" means "to harass, harm, pursue, hunt, capture, shoot, wound, kill, trap, capture or collect or to attempt to engage in any such conduct." 16 U.S.C. § 1532(19). However, the Secretary may permit a taking of a protected species "if such taking is incidental to, and not the purpose of, the carrying out of an otherwise lawful activity." 16 U.S.C. § 1539(a)(1)(B). The application for such an incidental take permit must contain a conservation plan that specifies—

> (i) the impact which will likely result from such taking;

---

1. A species is endangered under the Endangered Species Act if it "is in danger of extinction throughout all or a significant portion of its range." 16 U.S.C. § 1532(6).

2. A species is threatened under the Endangered Species Act if it "is likely to become an endangered species within the foreseeable future throughout all or a significant portion of its range." 16 U.S.C. § 1532(20). As noted previously in text, the Secretary invoked his authority under 16 U.S.C. § 1533(d) to apply the same protection to the winter-run salmon as if it had been designated as endangered rather than threatened. Section 1533(d) provides that "[t]he Secretary may by regulation prohibit with respect to any threatened species any [taking, importation or exportation, possession, sale, transportation or delivery]" of the species.

3. The stated purpose of the Endangered Species Act is to "provide a means whereby the ecosystems upon which endangered species and threatened species depend may be conserved, to provide a program for the conservation of such endangered species and threatened species, and to take such steps as may be appropriate to achieve the purposes of the treaties and conventions" to which the United States has pledged itself in the international community. 16 U.S.C. § 1531(b).

(ii) the steps the applicant will take to minimize and mitigate such impacts and the funding that will be available to implement such steps;
(iii) what alternative actions to such taking the applicant considered and the reasons why such alternatives are not being utilized; and
(iv) such other measures that the Secretary may require as being necessary or appropriate for purposes of the plan.

16 U.S.C. § 1539(a)(2)(A). If the Secretary finds the plan satisfactory after opportunity for public comment, and determines that the taking will not appreciably reduce the likelihood of the survival and recovery of the species in the wild, the Secretary shall issue the permit on the terms and conditions deemed appropriate. Id.

Violation of the Act's prohibition on taking is subject to civil and criminal penalties. 16 U.S.C. § 1540(a) and (b). Moreover, the Act specifically provides for injunctive relief: "the Attorney General of the United States may seek to enjoin any person who is alleged to be in violation of any provision of this chapter or regulation issued under authority thereof." 16 U.S.C. § 1540(e)(6).

In considering whether an injunction should issue under the Endangered Species Act, the court must determine whether the United States has an adequate remedy at law and whether the injury to the salmon is irreparable. The Supreme Court has indicated that the "language, history, and structure" of the Endangered Species Act "indicates beyond doubt that Congress intended endangered species to be afforded the highest of priorities." TVA v. Hill, 437 U.S. 153, 174, 98 S.Ct. 2279, 2292, 57 L.Ed.2d 117 (1978). Congress "foreclosed the exercise of traditional equitable discretion by courts" faced with a taking under the Endangered Species Act. Sierra Club v. Marsh, 816 F.2d 1376, 1383 (9th Cir. 1987). "Environmental injury, by its nature, can seldom be adequately remedied by money damages and is often permanent or at least of long duration, i.e. irreparable. If such injury is sufficiently likely" an injunction will issue. Amoco Production Co. v. People of the Village of Gambell, 480 U.S. 531, 546, 107 S.Ct. 1396, 1404, 94 L.Ed.2d 542 (1987). Congress has decided that any possible expense and inconvenience to the public cannot equal the potential loss from extinction. Sierra Club, 816 F.2d at 1386 n. 13.

Thus, the court must determine whether defendant Glenn-Colusa is violating a substantive or procedural provision of the Endangered Species Act and whether injury to the salmon is likely and irreparable; if so, the United States is entitled to an injunction. Sierra Club, at 1384.[10] The District invites the court to engage in a "detailed analysis of the mechanisms and a consideration of the social utility of ordering" the District to cease taking winter-run salmon. In light of the clear authority cited above, the court declines the

10. These cases deal with violations of section 7 rather than section 9. However, the prohibitive language in section 9 is at least as unambiguous as that in section 7. Both sections evidence Congress' intent that the balance of equities and hardships tip in favor of the endangered species.

District's invitation. Such an analysis and weighing of competing considerations is precluded by the Act and has already been undertaken by Congress.

The Secretary of Commerce has determined by duly adopted regulation that the winter-run salmon is a threatened species. The final regulation regarding the winter-run salmon invoked the Secretary's authority to accord a threatened species the protections of an endangered species. The regulation provides that "the prohibitions of section 9 of the Act (16 U.S.C. § 1538) relating to endangered species apply to the Sacramento River winter-run chinook salmon * * *" unless an incidental take permit is granted.

There is no genuine question that a taking—harming or killing—of winter-run salmon is occurring at the District's pumping station in violation of the Endangered Species Act. Rather, the District argues first, that the taking is caused by the fish screen, owned by the California Department of Fish and Game, and not by the District's pumping. Second, the District asserts that enforcement is premature since the Service has not yet determined the critical habitat of the winter-run salmon nor adopted regulations conserving the species, and has failed to comply with the National Environmental Protection Act ("NEPA").

B. The Cause and Responsibility for the Taking of Salmon. The District now urges this court to find that the fish screen, rather than the pumping, causes the taking of winter-run salmon. The court does not agree. * * * The screen itself presents no hazard to the salmon. It is because of the pumping that the screen is needed and that the screen becomes hazardous because of the force exerted by the District's pumps. The primary activity is pumping and not "fish screening" and the fish screen is present to mitigate the effects of the District's pumping. In short, it is because of the pumping that the screen exists and it is because of the District's stubborn resistance to its obligations that the California Department of Fish and Game undertook to install the screen. The District's argument that it may shift to the State all responsibility under federal law for any taking is at least brash, in light of the history, but also absurd for it is the pumping that creates the taking.

Of course, the District may have certain remedies against the California Department of Fish and Game. Under state law it may—although it apparently has not done so—contest the design, maintenance or repair of the fish screen. See Cal. Fish and Game Code §§ 5981 and 5990. But the remedies the District may have under state law against the California Department of the Fish and Game do not absolve it from its responsibility under federal law to avoid any taking of the winter-run salmon. The District has an independent responsibility to refrain from taking an endangered species, quite aside from the allocation of responsibility under California law for maintenance of the fish screen or protection of fish in general. * * *

Finally, in the same vein, the District argues that state water law rights should prevail over the Endangered Species Act. The Act provides that federal agencies should cooperate with state and local authorities to resolve water resource issues regarding the conservation of endangered species. 16 U.S.C. § 1531(c)(2). This provision does not require, however, that state water rights should prevail over the restrictions set forth in the Act. Such an interpretation would render the Act a nullity. The Act provides no exemption from compliance to persons possessing state water rights, and thus the District's state water rights do not provide it with a special privilege to ignore the Endangered Species Act. Moreover, enforcement of the Act does not affect the District's water rights but only the manner in which it exercises those rights.

The Injunction Shall Issue. The court concludes that the District is taking winter-run salmon in violation of section 9 of the Endangered Species Act, 16 U.S.C. § 1538, and that neither state or federal law exempts or excuses the District from complying with the Act. Plaintiff's motion for summary judgment is granted.

Plaintiff seeks a permanent injunction preventing the District from further violations of the Endangered Species Act. The court finds that the survival of the winter-run salmon population is jeopardized by the District's activities, and that these activities present a danger of irreparable harm to a species on the verge of extinction. The Act provides that injunctive relief is proper to prevent irreparable harm to the winter-run salmon. Accordingly, the court hereby enjoins the District from pumping water from the Sacramento River at its Hamilton City facility during the winter-run chinook salmon's peak downstream migration season of July 15 through November 30 of each year.

Notes

1. **Administrative Responsibilities.** Administration of the ESA is assigned to the Secretary of Commerce (marine species and anadromous fish) and the Secretary of Interior (all other species). See 16 U.S.C. § 1532(15). The Secretary of Interior has delegated most of his responsibilities to the U.S. Fish and Wildlife Service; the Secretary of Commerce has made a similar delegation to the National Marine Fisheries Service.

2. **Habitat modification.** Regulations promulgated by the Secretary of Interior provide that "harm" in the definition of "take" under section 9 "may include significant habitat modification or degradation where it actually kills or injures wildlife by significantly impairing essential behavior patterns, including breeding, feeding, or sheltering." 50 C.F.R. § 17.3(c)(3). In Babbitt v. Sweet Home Chapter of Communities for a Greater Oregon, 515 U.S. 687 (1995), the Supreme Court held that this regulatory definition is valid. Most exercises of most water rights result in habitat modification. Thus, the potential impact of the ESA on water law is greatly increased by the administrative definition. An example of the potential impact is found in a celebrated dispute involving the Edwards Aquifer in Texas, discussed supra p. 386, Note 1. As indicated in that note, the ESA has forced the Texas legislature to substantially modify the "rule of capture," which allowed unregulated pumping, by the enactment of legislation to manage the aquifer and limit pumping.

The impact of *Babbitt* may have been blunted by a recent 9th Circuit decision. In Arizona Cattle Growers' Association v. United States Fish & Wildlife Service, 273 F.3d 1229 (9th Cir. 2001), the Fish and Wildlife Service

(FWS) issued a Biological Opinion governing 288 livestock grazing entitlements on over 1.6 million acres of public land. The FWS issued ten Incidental Take Statements (ITS) for various listed or candidate species which it believed were present within the allotments. These statements placed substantial conditions on some grazing operations, including a complete ban on cattle grazing on certain floodplains and riparian corridors. The Ninth Circuit found that the FWS had acted arbitrarily and capriciously when it issued ITS for two species. For those species, the court found that FWS had no specific evidence that grazing would cause direct harm to the listed species. As such, it struck down FWS' assumption that habitat modification alone in the affected allotments would necessarily "take" the listed species. See Paul Stinson, Note, Arizona Cattle Growers Association v. U.S. Fish & Wildlife Service: Has the Ninth Circuit Weakened the "Take" Provisions of the Endangered Species Act?, 30 Ecology L. Q. 497 (2003).

A substantial body of scholarship has reviewed the constitutionality of the ESA in light of recent Commerce Clause jurisprudence. According to one writer, the articles break down into four groups. "One viewpoint holds that the habitat modification provisions of the ESA are unconstitutional because such regulations are land use regulations that should be governed by local governments. A second concludes that habitat modification is constitutional only if it regulates a commercial activity or if the protected species has a clear connection to commerce. A third determines that the ESA is constitutional based on the treaty Power, and a fourth finds that the ESA is constitutional based on the Commerce Clause." Omar N. White, Comment, The Endangered Species Act's Precarious Perch: A Constitutional Analysis Under the Commerce Clause and the Treaty Power, 27 Ecology L.Q. 214 (2000). See also infra, Chapter 8, Section 1.

3. **"Take" and Tort Law.** In Priority, Probability, and Proximate Cause: Lessons from Tort Law about Imposing ESA responsibility for Wildlife Harm on Water Users and Other Joint Habitat Modifiers, 33 Envtl. L. 595 (2003), Professor James Rasband argues that "the current approach of federal wildlife agencies and courts to causation of wildlife harm, particularly in cases involving water users, fails to properly account for background risks, multiple habitat modifiers, and, in prior appropriation settings, for priority." He proposes using classic tort causation principles to better address these issues. In addition, he suggests that, consistent with other tort law trends, the courts should abandon joint and several liability for ESA violations in favor of more equitable apportionment. Such an apportionment, he concludes could better adapt principles of priority and proportionality.

4. **Section 7 of the ESA.** The principal case deals with section 9 of the Endangered Species Act. Section 7, the other major substantive provision of the act, provides that "[e]ach Federal agency shall, in consultation with and with the assistance of the Secretary [of Interior or Commerce], insure that any action authorized, funded, or carried out by such agency * * * is not likely to jeopardize the continued existence of any endangered species or threatened species or result in the destruction or adverse modification of habitat of such species which is determined by the Secretary * * * to be critical." Section 7(a)(2), 16 U.S.C. § 1536(a)(2). Note that section 7 applies not just to activities undertaken by federal agencies themselves, but also to actions "authorized" by federal agencies, such as permits and licenses issued to private parties. Where the exercise of water rights is concerned, section 7 is frequently triggered by the

requirement to obtain a section 404 permit from the Army Corp of Engineers See, e.g., *Riverside Irrigation*, supra p. 583. Section 7 can also be triggered when private parties seek permits to use federal lands to divert, store, or transport water (see supra p. 594, Note 8) or when private parties seek electrical hydropower licenses from the Federal Energy Regulatory Commission (see Chapter 8, Section 2A). Section 7 may also be triggered when the EPA is asked to approve a state's water quality control plans. See Elizabeth Rosan, Comment, EPA's Approach to Endangered Species Protection in State Clean Water Act Programs, 30 Envtl. L. 447 (2000). Joint regulations of the Fish and Wildlife Service and the National Marine Fisheries Service implementing section 7 are found at 50 C.F.R. pt. 402.

To implement its mandate, section 7 requires an agency to prepare a "biological assessment" if the Secretary of Interior or Commerce (acting through the designated biological agency, the Fish and Wildlife Service or the National Marine Fisheries Service) determines that a listed species may be present in the area of a proposed action. Section 7(c), 16 U.S.C. § 1536(c). The acting agency must "formally consult" with the designated biological agency if the biological assessment determines that the action may affect a listed species. 50 C.F.R. § 402.14(a). Until the consultation process is completed, the ESA prohibits "any irreversible or irretrievable commitment of resources with respect to the agency action which has the effect of foreclosing the formulation or implementation of any reasonable and prudent alternative measures." Section 7(d), 16 U.S.C. § 1536(d).

Formal consultation results in a "biological opinion" by the designated biological agency which discusses the effect of the action on listed species or critical habitat and states whether or not the action is likely to jeopardize a listed species or result in destruction of critical habitat. If jeopardy or adverse modification is found (a "jeopardy biological opinion"), the opinion must list reasonable and prudent alternatives, if any. Section 7(b)(3), 16 U.S.C. § 1536(b)(3); 50 C.F.R. § 402.14(h)(3). The opinion may be accompanied by an "incidental take statement" if the biological agency determines that takings incidental to the proposed action or to reasonable and prudent alternatives will not violate the act. The statement must specify reasonable and prudent measures to minimize the impact on listed species and terms and conditions implementing such measures. Section 7(b)(4), 16 U.S.C. § 1536(b)(4); 50 C.F.R. § 402.14(i).

Following the issuance of a biological opinion, the agency proposing the action must determine how to proceed in light of its section 7 obligations and the biological opinion. 50 C.F.R. § 402.15(a). Although it is technically free to ignore a "jeopardy biological opinion," as a practical matter it cannot do so because the opinion makes it almost impossible to defend against claims that it has violated section 7. Similarly, it can ignore conditions in an incidental take statement, but if it does so, it and its employees do not get the protection of section 7(o)(2), 16 U.S.C. § 1536(o)(2), which provides that a taking in compliance with an incidental take statement is not a "prohibited taking."

Despite the mandatory language of section 7, few projects are actually stopped by the ESA. See Oliver A. Houck, The Endangered Species Act and Its Implementation By the U.S. Departments of Interior and Commerce, 64 U. Colo. L. Rev. 277 (1993). Professor Houck, who is quite critical of the implementation of the ESA by the Departments of Interior and Commerce, attributes this to a combination of the availability of non-jeopardizing alternatives and the extremely discretionary attitude toward jeopardy reflected in the regulations and practices of the biological agencies.

Section 7 does not confer substantive regulatory powers on federal agencies. See American Forest and Paper Ass'n v. EPA, supra p. 574, Note 5. Similarly, section 7 applies only to "discretionary" acts by federal agencies. 50 C.F.R. § 402.03; Sierra Club v. Babbitt, 65 F.3d 1502 (9th Cir. 1995). Section 7(e), 16 U.S.C. § 1536(e), creates a panel of cabinet-level federal officials (known irreverently as the "God Squad") with authority to grant exemptions to section 7.

5. **Impact of the ESA on western water activities.** A recent article, Michael R. Moore et al., Water Allocation in the American West: Endangered Fish Versus Irrigated Agriculture, 36 Nat. Resources J. 319 (1996), examines the potential impact of the ESA on irrigated agriculture in the western United States. The article notes the strong correlation between areas of extensive surface water irrigation and concentration of ESA-listed fish species and concludes that there is a high potential for disruption of irrigated agriculture because of the ESA. The article also notes that the involvement of the United States Bureau of Reclamation in western agriculture increases the potential impact of the ESA because of the Bureau's responsibilities under section 7 of the act. See O'Neill v. United States and accompanying Notes, infra p. 674. See also J. David Aiken, Balancing Endangered Species Protection and Irrigation Water Rights: The Platte River Cooperative Agreement, 3 Great Plains Nat. Resources J. 119 (1999), reviewing the impact of the ESA on water rights and water development activities in the Platte River basin and discussing the agreement entered into between the governors of Colorado, Wyoming, and Nebraska and the Secretary of Interior to develop a cooperative approach to the problem. For general discussions of the impact of the ESA on water law, see Jennie L. Bricker & David E. Filippi, Endangered Species Act Enforcement and Western Water Law, 30 Envtl. L. 735 (2000); Deborah L. Freeman & Carmen M. Sower, Emerging Conflicts between ESA Protection and Water Use, 40 Rocky Mtn. Min. L. Inst. 23–1 (1994).

The impact of the ESA could be particularly great in river basins with a heavy federal presence, such as the Colorado and Columbia River Basins. Species of native fish are endangered in both of these basins, in significant part because of water development and regulatory activities of various federal agencies. Consequently, the mandate of section 7 is particularly significant, both in its own right and as a means of implementing "recovery plans" required for listed species by section 4(f) of the ESA, 16 U.S.C. § 1533(e).

Efforts to implement the ESA in the Colorado and Columbia River Basins are examined and critiqued in Mary Christina Wood, Reclaiming the Natural Rivers: The Endangered Species Act as Applied to Endangered River Ecosystems, 40 Ariz. L. Rev. 197 (1998). Professor Wood suggests that these river basins are in a class of their own in terms of ESA implementation because of the extent and complexity of their ecosystems, the heavy federal presence in the basins, and the frontal challenge which recovery of endangered species presents to status quo operations. She finds the results in both basins disappointing and concludes that political resistance to change has seriously infected implementation of the ESA despite the strong mandate of section 7.

A similar examination, albeit of a smaller basin, was undertaken by Professors Holly Doremus and A. Dan Tarlock in Fish, Farms, and the Clash of Cultures in the Klamath Basin, 30 Ecology L. Q. 279 (2003). They reviewed the

ESA-induced complete curtailment of water from a federal project in Northeastern California in 2001. In the article, the authors focused on four issues. These included: 1) the management of the transition to a sustainable landscape; 2) the overemphasis of science in management decisions; 3) the negative consequences of longstanding denial of the fundamental conflicts in the region; and 4) the need for a more comprehensive, ecosystem approach to basin management. They concluded by offering the process that led to the Florida Everglades restoration efforts as one model for a new approach. (For another recent view of the role of the ESA in the massive Florida Everglades restoration project, see Keith W. Rizzardi, The Everglades in Jeopardy: A Drama of Water Management and Endangered Species, 27 Fla. St. U. L. Rev. 349 (2000).)

6. **The ESA and Indian water rights.** The regulations use a "first-in-time, first-in-right" approach in implementing section 7. The effects of a proposed action are not considered in isolation but include the effects of existing activities, federal actions for which section 7 consultation has been completed, and contemporaneous state and private activities. See 50 C.F.R. §§ 402.02 (definition of "effects of the action"). If the jeopardy threshold is not reached, the proposed action can proceed as proposed, except perhaps for steps to minimize the effect on listed species which may be required by an incidental take statement. See 50 C.F.R. §§ 402.14(i)(1) & (5). Conversely, if the jeopardy threshold is breached, the proposed action cannot proceed unless "reasonable and prudent alternatives" which prevent jeopardy are adopted. See supra Note 3. (In determining jeopardy, the effects of future state or private activities which are "reasonably certain to occur" must also be considered. See 50 C.F.R. §§ 402.02 (definition of "cumulative effects" and 402.14(g)(3). While this is a deviation from the first-in-time rule, it does not affect the rule as applied to competing federal actions.)

Thus, the "conservation burden" falls almost solely on actions which are proposed after the jeopardy threshold is reached, while earlier activities and actions, including other federal projects, which contribute to the problem and may have been responsible for the listing of species in the first place, bear none of the burden. In effect, each action "appropriates" part of the pool of permissible adverse effect (permissible because the jeopardy threshold has not been reached), until the pool is fully appropriated; thereafter, no new federal action can proceed unless mitigation measures are adopted which reduce the adverse effects below the jeopardy threshold.

This approach when applied in an aquatic environment is somewhat congruent with the doctrine of prior appropriation. Assume for example that a minimum stream flow of 25 cfs is required to avoid jeopardy to listed species. A proposed federal project which would reduce the flow below that level would result in jeopardy opinion and could not proceed, unless mitigative measures could be developed. The flow necessary to prevent jeopardy is like a senior appropriation, and the effect on the proposed action resembles the denial of an appropriation application because no unappropriated water is available.

Whatever its merits in general, some writers have argued that this approach is unfair when applied to Indian Tribes. See Brian A Schmidt, Reconciling Section 7 of the Endangered Species Act with Native American Reserved Water Rights, 18 Stan. Envtl. L. J. 109 (1999); Tim Vollmann, The Endangered Species Act and Indian Water Rights, 11–Fall Nat. Resources & Env't 39 (1996); Mary Christina Wood, Fulfilling the Executive's Trust Responsibilities Toward the

Native Nations on Environmental Issues: A Partial Critique of the Clinton Administration's Promise and Performance, 25 Envtl. L. 733 (1995). Under the reserved rights doctrine (discussed in Chapter 8, Section 3A), Indian tribes often have undeveloped water rights with a very early priority. Large-scale development of such rights is almost certain to involve federal agencies and federal funding, thereby triggering section 7. If the exercise of non-Indian rights, which are legally junior, has pushed a listed species to or past the threshold of jeopardy, these writers argue that the priority approach adopted by the section 7 regulations could prevent development of the Indian rights.

Comments on proposed regulations preceding adoption of the present regulations implementing section 7, 51 Fed. Reg. 19926, 19933 (1986), state: "In order to determine the effects of the action when a water project is the subject of consultation in a State which follows the prior appropriation doctrine, the project's operation plan should indicate the priority of the project's water rights under State law and account for the future effects of senior conditional water rights." Does this suggest that the effects of junior rights, whether conditional or perfected, can be ignored? In other words, when an Indian water project is the subject of consultation in jurisdictions applying the appropriation doctrine, does the quote indicate that the project should account only for the effects of rights senior to the Indian rights?

Section 9 of the ESA provides the basis for another argument for ignoring the effects of junior water rights when considering Indian water projects. Schmidt, supra, argues that priority should be used in determining which rights to regulate to maintain critical stream flows in order to prevent a "taking" of a listed species under section 9, i.e., he argues that rights should be regulated (shut off) in order of priority to maintain instream flows sufficient to prevent a "taking." Thus, Schmidt reasons, the effect of junior non-Indian water rights should be ignored in making section 7 jeopardy determinations associated with the development of Indian rights because the effects resulting from the Indian project can be eliminated by regulating the non-Indian rights under section 9. (But see Harrison C. Dunning, State Equitable Apportionment of Western Water Resources, 66 Neb. L. Rev. 76 (1987), suggesting that "equitable apportionment" should be used to allocate regulatory burdens of this sort.)

7. **Application of section 7 to federal reservoir operations.** Southwest Center for Biological Diversity v. U.S. Bureau of Reclamation, 143 F.3d 515 (9th Cir. 1998), involved an attempt to limit the storage of water in Lake Mead, a major Colorado River reservoir. In 1996, the Bureau of Reclamation issued a biological assessment which found that rising water levels in Lake Mead due to normal storage activities were inundating a stand of native willows which had grown in the Lake Mead delta during a dry period. This 1,148 acre stand, the largest contiguous stand in the Southwest, was an important nesting area for the Southwestern Willow Flycatcher, an endangered species.

In response to the Bureau's biological assessment, the Fish and Wildlife Service (FWS), issued a draft biological opinion which determined that the Bureau's activities on the Lower Colorado would jeopardize the survival of the Flycatcher. Initially, the FWS proposed a reasonable and prudent alternative (RPA) which required the Bureau to protect the delta habitat by lowering the water level in Lake Mead or, alternatively, to defer the use of conservation space in Roosevelt Lake, Arizona, to maintain Flycatcher habitat there. The Bureau informed the FWS that under the "law of the river" it lacked discretion to reduce the level of Lake Mead except for purposes of river regulation, water supply, and power generation. The Secretary of Interior, acting through the FWS, then adopted a final RPA which did not require the Bureau to protect the delta or defer the use of conservation space in Roosevelt Lake, but did require other short-term and long-term measures to protect the Flycatcher, including a program to procure and protect alternative habitat. The RPA was accompanied by an incidental take statement which permitted an "unquantifiable" take of Flychatchers at Lake Mead.

Southwest filed suit, seeking an injunction to force the Bureau to protect the delta habitat by lowering the water level in Lake Mead, an action which allegedly would have required the release of 3.5 to 5 million acre-feet of water. A second claim against the Secretary of Interior under the Administrative Procedure Act (APA) asserted that the adoption of the final RPA was arbitrary, capricious, and contrary to the ESA. The district court dismissed Southwest's claim for injunctive relief, holding that Southwest had not given sixty days notice of the alleged violation of the ESA before filing suit as required by section 1540 of the ESA, 16 U.S.C. § 1540(g)(2)(A)(i), and granted summary judgment for the Secretary on the APA claim.

The Ninth Circuit affirmed the decision of the district court on all points. With respect to the APA claim, Southwest argued that the Secretary had an obligation to make an independent review of the Bureau's claim that it has no discretion regarding water levels in Lake Mead. The district court disagreed, holding that the Bureau's alleged lack of discretion was immaterial to a review of the Secretary's decision. In affirming the district court, the Ninth Circuit said that the Secretary is not required to pick the first alternative or even the best alternative, but only an alternative which complies with the jeopardy standard and which can be implemented by the agency. The Ninth Circuit also held that the Secretary is not required to explain why one RPA is chosen over another or to base the choice solely on apolitical factors. Finally, the Ninth Circuit found that in determining whether the Secretary's adoption of the final RPA was arbitrary, capricious, or an abuse of discretion the district court only needed to determine whether the final RPA will avoid jeopardy to the Flycatcher. Reviewing the evidence, the Ninth Circuit held that the district court had not erred in finding that the final RPA will avoid jeopardy. Consequently, no review of the Bureau's claimed lack of discretion was required.

The opinion does not address the applicability of section 7 of the ESA to ongoing operations of a project to pursuant to longstanding policies and procedures. The Bureau of Reclamation apparently never questioned its applicability and the question became moot once the court concluded that the final RPA satisfied the ESA. Note, however, that section 7 refers to "any action" by a federal agency and the regulations state that "action" means "all activities or programs of any kind." 50 C.F.R. § 402.02. See also Pacific Rivers Council v. Thomas, 30 F.3d 1050 (9th Cir. 1994), holding that an ongoing policy or decision is an "agency action" each time it is applied.

8. **Transboundary Application of the ESA.** The ESA was the basis for another challenge to the Bureau of Reclamation's Colorado River operations, but one that presented an international twist. The Colorado River Delta, which begins just across the U.S.-Mexican border south of Yuma, Arizona, was once one of the richest wetlands in North America. See generally Charles Berman, Red Delta:

Fighting for Life at the End of the Colorado River (2002). Ecosystem decline in the delta began with the filling of Lake Mead and continued through the filling of Lake Powell. Several species listed by the United States as endangered make their homes in the Delta and in adjoining areas in the United States. In Defenders of Wildlife v. Norton, 257 F. Supp. 2d 53 (D.D.C. 2003), plaintiffs claimed that the impacts of the Bureau of Reclamation's management of the lower Colorado River on the Mexican habitat of the listed species violated the ESA. In particular, they alleged that the Bureau had a duty to consult with other federal agencies—e.g, the U.S. Fish & Wildlife Service and the National Marine Fisheries Service—regarding the transboundary impacts of its water management operations.

In contrast to the United States Supreme Court's decision in Lujan v. Defenders of Wildlife, 504 U.S. 555 (1992), the district court found that the plaintiffs had standing to raise their claim. Nevertheless, the court granted summary judgment on the merits to the United States. The court agreed with the defendants that "even if Reclamation's actions have extraterritorial effects on the protected species in the delta, the consultation requirements of Section 7(a)(2) have no application to non-discretionary acts." Here, the court concluded, there was no discretion for the Bureau to adjust the time or amount of its water deliveries. Rather, the court concluded, the Bureau's hands were effectively tied by the "Law of the River." (For an overview of the law governing water use in the Colorado River basin, see supra, Ch. 6, Section 3.) The court concluded that "it seems unlikely that any case will more clearly make any agency's actions nondiscretionary than this one: a Supreme Court injunction, an international treaty, federal statutes, and contracts between the government and water users that account for every acre foot of lower Colorado River." In combination, the applicable law gave the Bureau no flexibility to alter water deliveries to make more water available for species in Mexico. Absent such discretion, the court concluded that no ESA consultation obligation existed.

The international legal and political challenges presented by ecosystem restoration in the Colorado River Delta have been the subject of numerous recent articles. See, e.g., David H. Getches, Water Management in the United States and the Fate of the Colorado River Delta in Mexico, 11 U.S. Mex. L.J. 107 (2003); Robert J. Glennon & Peter W. Culp, The Last Green Lagoon: How and Why the Bush Administration Should Save the Colorado River Delta, 28 Ecol. L. Q. 903 (2002); David Parrish, Note, Where Has All the Water Gone? Water Marketing and the Colorado River Delta, 13 Transnat'l L. & Contemp. Probs. 369 (2003); Jennifer Pitt, Daniel F. Luecke, Michael J. Cohen, Edward P. Glenn, & Carlos Valdes-Casillas, Two Nations, One River: Managing Ecosystem Conservation in the Colorado River Delta, 40 Nat. Res. J. 819 (2000).

For a more general discussion of the problems presented by international rivers, see A. Dan Tarlock, Safeguarding International River Ecosystems in Times of Scarcity, 3 U. Denv. L. Rev. 231 (2000).

9. **State Endangered Species Acts.** Several states have endangered species acts which closely parallel the federal act and which have the potential to affect water rights activities. See, e.g., Dept. of Fish & Game v. Anderson-Cottonwood Irrigation Dist., 11 Cal. Rptr. 2d 222 (Cal. Ct. App. 1992), reaching results similar to the principal case under the California Endangered Species Act; and Central Platte Natural Res. Dist. v. City of Fremont, 549 N.W.2d 112 (Neb. 1996),

holding that the state water agency could not issue a permit for the appropriation of water which would jeopardize a species listed under the Nebraska Endangered Species Act. A recent survey concludes that state endangered species legislation is far less comprehensive than the federal act. Dale D. Goble et al., Local and National Protection of Endangered Species: An Assessment, 2 Envtl. Sci. & Pol'y 43 (1999).

TULARE LAKE BASIN WATER STORAGE DIST. v. UNITED STATES

United States Court of Claims, 2001
49 Fed. Cl. 313

WIESE, JUDGE. * * *

This case concerns the delta smelt and the winter-run chinook salmon—two species of fish determined by the United States Fish and Wildlife Service ("USFWS") and the National Marine Fisheries Service ("NMFS") to be in jeopardy of extinction. The efforts by those agencies to protect the fish—specifically by restricting water out-flows in California's primary water distribution system—bring together, and arguably into conflict, the Endangered Species Act and California's century-old regime of private water rights. The intersection of those concerns, and the proper balance between them, lie at the heart of this litigation.

The development of California's water system has a long and detailed history well chronicled in case law. * * * That system, in brief, involves the transport of water from the water-rich areas in northern California to the more arid parts of the state. Various water projects or aqueduct systems have been built to facilitate that goal; two—the Central Valley Project ("CVP") and the State Water Project ("SWP")—are the focus of the present litigation.

Although CVP is a federal project managed by the Bureau of Reclamation ("BOR") and SWP is a state project managed by the Department of Water Resources ("DWR"), the two projects share a coordinated pumping system that requires, as a practical matter, that the systems be operated in concert. * * *

Both BOR and DWR are granted water permits by the State Water Resources Control Board ("SWRCB" or "the Board")—a state agency with the ultimate authority for controlling, appropriating, using and distributing state waters. * * * BOR and DWR in turn contract with county water districts, conferring on them the right to withdraw or use prescribed quantities of water. Of the present plaintiffs, two—Tulare Lake Basin Water Storage District and Kern County Water Agency—have contracts directly with the [SWP], and three—Hansen Ranches, Lost Hills Water District, and Wheeler Ridge-Maricopa Water Supply District—have subsidiary contracts with Tulare and Kern County. Under its contract with DWR, Kern County's allotment of entitlement water was set at 1,153,400 acre-feet per year during the period in question (1992-1994), while Tulare's allocation was 118,500 acre-feet. * * *

Against this backdrop of water transportation and entitlements, Congress passed the Endangered Species Act in 1973 * * * ("ESA"). That act was designed to "halt and reverse the trend toward species extinction, whatever the cost." * * *.

In fulfillment of the duties assigned to it under the ESA, the [NMFS] initiated discussions with the [BOR] and [DWR] to determine the impact of the [CVP] and the [SWP] on the winter-run chinook salmon. As a result of those discussions, the NMFS issued a biological opinion on February 14, 1992, concluding that the proposed operation of SWP and CVP was likely to jeopardize the continued existence of the salmon population. Included in the agency's findings was a reasonable and prudent alternative ("RPA")[2] designed to protect the fish by restricting the time and manner of pumping water out of the Delta. As a result, water that would otherwise have been available for distribution by the water projects was made unavailable. * * *

The RPAs were thus implemented in each of the years in question, giving rise to the present claims. According to plaintiffs, the restrictions imposed by the RPAs deprived Tulare Lake Basin WSD of at least 9,770 acre-feet of water in 1992; at least 26,000 acre-feet of water in 1993, and at least 23,050 acre-feet of water in 1994. Kern County Water Agency, by contrast, is alleged to have lost a minimum of 319,420 acre-feet over that same period.

DISCUSSION The Fifth Amendment to the United States Constitution concludes * * * "nor shall private property be taken for public use, without just compensation." The purpose of that clause * * * is "to bar Government from forcing some people alone to bear public burdens which, in all fairness and justice, should be borne by the public as a whole." At issue, then, is not whether the federal government has the authority to protect the winter-run chinook salmon and delta smelt under the Endangered Species Act, but whether it may impose the costs of their protection solely on plaintiffs.

In arguing against the existence of a taking, the government offers three lines of defense. First, defendant maintains that the implementation of the RPAs merely frustrated the contract's purpose and, under Omnia Commercial Co. v. United States, 261 U.S. 502, 43 S.Ct. 437, 67 L.Ed. 773 (1923), did not therefore effectuate a taking. Second, it argues that the criteria for a regulatory taking—specifically the existence of reasonable, investment-backed expectations and of a significant decrease in economic value—have not been met. Finally, defendant contends that the federal government cannot be held liable for a taking when it does no more than impose a limit on plaintiffs' title that the background principles of state law would otherwise require. We address these arguments in turn.

---

2. Where the activities of a federal agency are seen to jeopardize the continued existence of listed species or cause the destruction or adverse modification of critical habitats, the Endangered Species Act directs the Secretary to suggest "reasonable and prudent alternatives" to avoid such harms. 16 U.S.C. § 1536(b)(3)(A)(1994).

1. Defendant argues that *Omnia* stands for the proposition that the government may not be held liable for lawful actions that, though they may injure or destroy contract rights, do not take them as that phrase is understood in the constitutional sense. No taking occurs, defendant maintains, when "expectations under a contract are merely frustrated by lawful government action not directed against the takings claimant." 767 Third Avenue Assocs. v. United States, 48 F.3d 1575, 1581 (Fed. Cir.1995). In defendant's view, the limitations imposed by the RPAs represent a legitimate exercise of federal authority that does no more than frustrate, rather than appropriate, plaintiffs' rights in water.

At issue in *Omnia* was a contract between Omnia and the Allegheny Steel Company that allowed Omnia to purchase large quantities of steel plate at a below-market price. When the government requisitioned the steel company's entire production of steel plate for the year, Omnia sued, alleging a taking of its right of priority to the steel plate. The Supreme Court denied Omnia's claim, concluding that the contract had merely been ended rather than appropriated. * * *

Contrary to the government's assertion, however, we do not believe *Omnia* governs the present case. *Omnia's* distinction between a contract that has been appropriated and one that has merely been frustrated is relevant only where the contract right that is claimed remains separate and distinct from the property that is the subject of the contract. Put differently, *Omnia* addresses those situations in which a litigant claims a contract right with regard to the property (e.g., the right to buy it at a certain price) but cannot claim ownership of the property, since title to the property has not yet passed to the party seeking compensation. * * * Under those circumstances, the contract holder can recover only if the government has actually appropriated the contract itself, i.e., stepped into the shoes of the contracting party and assumed the rights and responsibilities under the contract. But that is not our case.

Unlike the situation in *Omnia*, where the plaintiff could claim only a contract expectancy but not an ownership right in the steel, our plaintiffs can claim an identifiable interest in a stipulated volume of water. While under California law the title to water always remains with the state, the right to the water's use is transferred first by permit to DWR, and then by contract to end-users, such as the plaintiffs.[6] Those contracts confer on plaintiffs a right to the exclusive use of prescribed quantities of water, consistent with the terms of the permits. That right remains in place until formally changed by administrative process. Thus, we see plaintiffs' contract rights in the water's

---

6. We accept that plaintiffs' contracts are derivative of the permit issued to DWR, and that the permit has not yet matured into a license. (A permit establishes a conditional priority of usage; a license, in contrast, is a confirmed appropriative right.) We further acknowledge that plaintiffs possess rights not as direct appropriators of water, but as parties to a contract with an entity—DWR—entitled to appropriate water. Those observations, however, do not change our conclusion that plaintiffs' right to the use of water is a compensable contractual right outside the purview of *Omnia*.

use as superior to all competing interests. It is a property interest sufficiently matured to take it out of the realm of an *Omnia* analysis.

II. Turning then to the merits of plaintiffs' claim, we begin by determining the nature of the taking alleged. Courts have traditionally divided their analysis of Fifth Amendment takings into two categories: physical takings and regulatory takings. A physical taking occurs when the government's action amounts to a physical occupation or invasion of the property, including the functional equivalent of a "practical ouster of [the owner's] possession." * * * When an owner has suffered a physical invasion of his property, courts have noted that "no matter how minute the intrusion, and no matter how weighty the public purpose behind it, we have required compensation." Lucas v. South Carolina Coastal Council, 505 U.S. 1003, 1015, 112 S.Ct. 2886, 120 L.Ed.2d 798 (1992).

A regulatory taking, in contrast, arises when the government's regulation restricts the use to which an owner may put his property. In assessing whether a regulatory taking has occurred, courts generally employ the balancing test set forth in *Penn Central*, weighing the character of the government action, the economic impact of that action and the reasonableness of the property owner's investment-backed expectations. Penn Central Transp. Co. v. New York, 438 U.S. 104, 124-125, 98 S.Ct. 2646, 57 L.Ed.2d 631 (1978). Regulations that are found to be too restrictive, however—i.e., those that deprive property of its entire economically beneficial or productive use—are commonly identified as categorical takings and, like physical takings, require no such balancing. *Lucas*, 505 U.S. at 1015-1016, 112 S.Ct. 2886.

Plaintiffs urge us to consider this action as a case involving a physical taking of property. Under that theory, plaintiffs possessed contract rights entitling them to the use of a specified quantity of water. By preventing them from using that water, plaintiffs argue, the government deprived them of the entire value of their contract right.

Defendant sees the case differently. In defendant's view, the court must examine the government's conduct under the three-part test that *Penn Central* prescribes for the evaluation of regulatory action that interferes with an owner's use of his property. Under that rubric, defendant contends, the claim must fail because plaintiffs' reasonable contract expectations were necessarily limited by regulatory concern over fish and wildlife; and because the economic loss asserted here—a fraction of the master contract's overall value—was de minimis.

Of the two positions, plaintiffs', we believe, is the correct one. Case law reveals that the distinction between a physical invasion and a governmental activity that merely impairs the use of that property turns on whether the intrusion is "so immediate and direct as to subtract from the owner's full enjoyment of the property and to limit his exploitation of it." United States v. Causby, 328 U.S. 256, 265, 66 S.Ct. 1062, 90 L.Ed. 1206 (1946). In *Causby*, for instance, the Court ruled that frequent flights immediately above a landowner's property constituted a taking, comparing such actions to a more traditional physical taking: "If, by reason of the frequency and altitude of the flights, respondents could not use this land for any purpose, their loss would be complete. It would be as complete as if the United States had entered upon the surface of the land and taken exclusive possession of it." Id. at 261, 66 S.Ct. 1062 (footnote omitted).

While water rights present an admittedly unusual situation, we think the *Causby* example is an instructive one. In the context of water rights, a mere restriction on use—the hallmark of a regulatory action—completely eviscerates the right itself since plaintiffs' sole entitlement is to the use of the water. See Eddy v. Simpson, 3 Cal. 249, 252-253 (1853) ("the right of property in water is usufructuary, and consists not so much of the fluid itself as the advantage of its use."). Unlike other species of property where use restrictions may limit some, but not all of the incidents of ownership, the denial of a right to the use of water accomplishes a complete extinction of all value. Thus, by limiting plaintiffs' ability to use an amount of water to which they would otherwise be entitled, the government has essentially substituted itself as the beneficiary of the contract rights with regard to that water and totally displaced the contract holder. That complete occupation of property—an exclusive possession of plaintiffs' water-use rights for preservation of the fish—mirrors the invasion present in *Causby*. To the extent, then, that the federal government, by preventing plaintiffs from using the water to which they would otherwise have been entitled, have rendered the usufructuary right to that water valueless, they have thus effected a physical taking. * * *

III. Having concluded that a deprivation of water amounts to a physical taking, we turn now to the question of whether plaintiffs in fact owned the property for which they seek to be compensated. * * * Defendant argues that both the terms of plaintiffs' contracts and the background principles of state law impose limits on plaintiffs' titles that render their loss of water non-compensable. * * *

i. Contract Language as a Limitation on Title Under the terms of the water supply contracts, neither the state nor its agents may be held liable for "any damage, direct or indirect, arising from shortages in the amount of water to be made available for delivery to the Agency under this contract caused by drought, operation of area of origin statutes, or any other cause beyond its control." Para. 18(f). Defendant reads that language to mean that plaintiffs are entitled to receive water only to the extent that water is available to DWR. * * *

Paragraph 18(f) [however, only] insulates DWR from liability for circumstances beyond its control; not the federal government. The inclusion of Paragraph 18(f) in the contract does not render plaintiffs' interest in the water contingent; it merely provides DWR with a defense against a breach of contract action in certain specified circumstances. With that exception, plaintiffs' contract rights are otherwise fully formed against DWR, and certainly against a third party seeking to infringe on those rights. * * * .

ii. The Public Trust Doctrine, the Doctrine of Reasonable Use and Nuisance Law In addition to its contract-based argument, defendant offers a number of common law justifications for limiting the scope of plaintiffs' property right: specifically, that plaintiffs can have no vested right in a use or method of diverting water that is unreasonable or violates the public trust. The difficulty with defendant's argument, however, is that the water allocation scheme in effect for the period 1992-1994, as set forth in D-1485, specifically allowed for the allocations of water defendant now seeks to deem unreasonable. * * *

Whether a particular use or method of diversion is unreasonable or violative of the public trust is a question committed concurrently to the [SWRCB] and to the California courts. See National Audubon Soc'y v. Superior Court of Alpine County, 33 Cal.3d 419, 451-452, 189 Cal.Rptr. 346, 658 P.2d 709 (1983). Thus, while we accept the proposition that plaintiffs have no right to use or divert water in an unreasonable manner, nor in a way that violates the public trust, the issue now before us is whether such a determination has in fact been made.

Plaintiffs argue that the [SWRCB's] decision D-1485—a comprehensive water rights scheme balancing the needs of and allocating water rights among competing users—defines the full scope of their contract rights. In plaintiffs' view, D-1485 represents the state's determination of various water rights, thereby reflecting the amount of water, under state law, they reasonably can expect and to which they are reasonably entitled. * * *

In defendant's view, D-1485 fails to encapsulate the Board's approach to the endangerment of the delta smelt and salmon, both because it was promulgated before the fish were found to be in jeopardy, and because the [B]oard enacted D-95-1—a 1995 decision whose provisions adopt measures found in the RPAs—to protect the fish. Additionally, defendant argues that D-1485 should be read as an evolving document, one informed by later developments in water needs and altered by subsequent state actions. * * *

We cannot accept defendant's position. As an initial matter, the responsibility for water allocation is vested in the [SWRCB]. * * * Once an allocation has been made—as was done in D-1485—that determination defines the scope of plaintiffs' property rights, pronouncements of other agencies notwithstanding. While we accept the principle that California water policy may be ever-evolving, rights based on contracts with the state are not correspondingly self-adjusting. Rather, the promissory assurances they recite remain fixed until formally changed. * * *

Defendant argues against this position, urging us to anticipate how the Board or the California courts would apply the doctrine of reasonable use if the issue were before them. * * * The issue, defendant contends, is not what limitations the state in fact imposed on plaintiffs' titles, but what limitations the state could have imposed under state background principles. * * *

That the use now being challenged was not always unlawful is evident from the fact that it was specifically authorized by the state in D-1485. Were we now to deem that use a nuisance, we would not be making explicit that which had always been implied under background principles of property law, but would instead be replacing the state's judgment with our own. That we cannot do.

* * * The public trust and reasonable use doctrines each require a complex balancing of interests—an exercise of discretion for which this court is not suited and with which it is not charged.

To the extent that water allocation in California is a policy judgment—one specifically committed to the SWRCB and the California courts—a finding of unreasonableness by this court would be tantamount to our making California law rather than merely applying it. * * *

Accordingly, we conclude that plaintiffs' right to divert water in the manner specified by their contracts and in conformance with D-1485 continued until a determination to the contrary was made either by the SWRCB or by the California courts. As no such determination was made during the period 1992-1994, and subsequent amendments to policy cannot, for contract purposes, be made retroactive, plaintiffs were indeed entitled to the water use provided for in D-1485 and in their contracts.

CONCLUSION * * * It is the Board that must provide the necessary weighing of interests to determine the appropriate balance under California law between the cost and benefit of species preservation. The federal government is certainly free to preserve the fish; it must simply pay for the water it takes to do so. * * *

Notes

1. **Physical v. Regulatory Takings.** As the principal case illustrates, the impacts of environmental restrictions upon water diverters and users have led to repeated claims of compensable "takings" under the 5th Amendment. That Amendment states that private property shall not be "taken" for public use without just compensation. Under the Fifth Amendment, the Supreme Court has recognized two types of takings: physical and regulatory.

As the principal case indicates, a physical taking occurs when the government's action amounts to a physical occupation or invasion of the property. It does not matter how minute the intrusion nor the significance of the public purpose behind the intrusion. See Lorretto v. Teleprompter Manhattan CATV Corp. 458 U.S. 419 (1982); Lucas v. South Carolina Coastal Council, 505 U.S. 1003 (1992). In the context of water rights, courts have found a physical taking where the government has physically diverted water for its own consumptive use or decreased the amount of water accessible by the owner of the water rights. See Washoe County v. United States, 319 F.3d 1320, 1326 (Fed. Cir. 2003) (discussing Dugan v. Rank 372 U.S. 609, 625-26 (1963) and Int'l Paper Co. v. United States, 282 U.S. 399, 407-08 (1931).)

In contrast, a regulatory taking occurs when the government's regulation severely restricts the use to which an owner may put his property. The Supreme Court has declined to develop a precise formula for determining whether a regulatory taking has occurred, beyond the deprivation of "all economically viable use of the land." See, e.g., City of Monterey v. Del Monte Dunes at Monterey,

Ltd., 526 U.S. 687 (1999). Where some economically viable uses remain, as noted in the principal case, courts generally apply the standards set forth in Pennsylvania Central Transportation Co. v. New York, 438 U.S. 104, 124-25 (1978). Under *Penn Central,* courts weigh the character of the government action, the economic impact of that action and the reasonableness of the property owner's investment-backed expectations. Compare *City of Monterey,* supra, (finding submission of regulatory taking issue to jury appropriate when the City had repeatedly rejected the developer's application to develop a parcel of land and each time imposed more rigorous demands) with Tahoe-Sierra Preservation Council, Inc. v. Tahoe Regional Planning Agency, 535 U.S. 302 (2002) (finding that a 32-month moratorium on development did not constitute a temporary taking.)

In the principal case, the decision to label the impact of the ESA water delivery cutbacks a "physical taking" made plaintiffs' case substantially easier. As indicated above, under this doctrine, any physical intrusion, no matter how slight, is a "taking." Was the court's use of the physical takings case law here appropriate? While it is true that the specific amount of water that was not delivered to the contract holders was not available to them for their use that year, they did not suffer a complete cessation of deliveries. Is the cutback that they suffered any different from, say, land zoning requirements that require a set-aside of a portion of land for open space? These restrictions have long been upheld against regulatory takings claims. See, e.g., Gorieb v. Fox, 274 U.S. 603 (1927) (setbacks). Cf. Euclid v. Ambler Realty Co., 272 U.S. 365 (1927) (no taking even though zoning ordinance reduced overall property value75%); Hadachek v. Sebastian, 239 U.S. 394 (no taking even though property lost 87.5% of overall value) (1915). But even if this argument were sufficient to address the facts in the principal case, how would it apply to the irrigators in the Klamath Basin, supra p. 603, Note 5? In 2001, under the mandate of the ESA, the Bureau of Reclamation stopped all deliveries of irrigation water to project contractors. Shortly after their victory in the principal case, the attorneys for the successful plaintiffs filed a similar suit on behalf of Klamath Basin irrigators. Cf. Cori S. Parobek, Note, Of Farmers' Takes and Fishes' Takings: Fifth Amendment Compensation Claims When the Endangered Species Act and Western Water Rights Collide, 27 Harv. Envtl. L. Rev. 177 (2003) (discussing Klamath Basin conflict.)

Takings scholarship is rich and diverse. See, e.g., articles cited supra p. 323, Note 7. More recent articles include: James S. Burling, Private Property Rights and the Environment After Palazzolo, 30 B.C. Envtl. Aff. L. Rev. 1 (2002); Holly Doremus, Takings and Transitions, 19 J. Land Use & Envtl. L. 1 (2003); Donald C. Guy & James E. Holloway, Finding the Development Value of Wetlands and Other Environmentally Sensitive Lamds under the Extent of Interference with Reasonable Investment-Backed Expectations, 19 J. Land Use & Envtl. L. 297 (2003); Stewart E. Sterk, The Federalist Dimension of Regulatory Takings Jurisprudence, 114 Yale L.J. 203 (2004); Jeffrey A. Wilcox, Note, Taking Cover: Fifth Amendment Takings Jurisprudence as a Tool for Resolving Water Disputes in the American West, 55 Hastings L.J. 477 (2003).

2. Background Principles of California Water Law. A regulation that reflects the application of "background principles" of state property law will not trigger a taking. Lucas v. South Carolina Coastal Council, 505 U.S. 1003, 1030 (1992). In the principal case, the court notes that under both the California reasonable use and public trust doctrines, no water user can acquire a right to use water unreasonably or in violation of the public trust. And the court also notes that the both the California State Water Resources Control Board and the courts have concurrent jurisdiction to enforce both doctrines. Yet the court refused to second guess the state board's approval of the diversions in question. Was this appropriate? Did the California State Water Resources Control Board, in its Decision 1485, actually authorize deliveries of water that would themselves violate the ESA? How would a California state court have ruled on the validity of such deliveries, had a suit been brought in state court under either the reasonable use or public trust doctrines? Even if a California state court might have second guessed the state board, did the federal court in the principal case take the correct approach so that it did not have to guess what a California state court might have done? Or is such guessing part of the court's job when presented with such state law questions?

3. **Impact of Decision.** The court in the principal case is the first court to find a compensable taking for an ESA impact on a water right, albeit a contractual right to purchase water as opposed to a common law or statutory right to divert. As the first such case, it has received a lot of attention from regulators, environmentalists, and water rights holders alike. Is it a landmark decision, or is it distinguishable on its unique facts? For an article setting out the latter argument, see Melinda Harm Benson, The Tulare Case: Water Rights, The Endangered Species Act, and the Fifth Amendment, 32 Envtl. L. 551 (2002). Benson argues that the case involved a rather unique concatenation of legal relationships. In particular, it was not a suit by a project's contractor against the project's operators itself. As the principal case notes, there are usually provisions within the water delivery agreements that only obligate the project operator to deliver such water as is available to them in a given year. Suits by federal contractors against federal project operators for ESA-induced water delivery curtailments have so far been barred by such contractual provisions. E.g., O'Neill v. United States, infra p. 674. See also Rio Grande Silvery Minnow v. Keys, infra p. 677, Note 1. Moreover, as noted in the principal case, the California State Water Project at issue has a unique Coordinated Operating Agreement with the federal Bureau of Reclamation; this set of federal-state relationships is not likely to be duplicated elsewhere.

4. **Denouement.** In the article noted above, Melinda Benson argued that the principal case is both distinguishable on its facts and wrong on takings law. She concluded that the "decision will be of lasting significance only if the federal government fails, for political reasons, to appeal the decision." Benson, supra Note 3, at p. 551. If you were the relevant federal attorney charged with handling such an appeal, would you have recommended that the United States appeal? On the one hand, any damages owed to the plaintiffs will come out of the Treasury. On the other hand, would you be concerned that a decision upholding the matter by the Federal Circuit or the United States Supreme Court would make for even stronger precedent than the Court of Claims decision? Or would there be other factors influencing your decision? As it turned out, in late 2004, the United States decided not to appeal and agreed to pay plaintiffs $16.7 million dollars as compensation for the "taking."

Chapter 8

FEDERAL WATER LAW

SECTION 1. CONSTITUTIONAL POWERS

SOLID WASTE AGENCY v. UNITED STATES ARMY CORPS OF ENGINEERS

Supreme Court of the United States, 2001.
531 U.S. 159, 121 S. Ct. 675, 148 L. Ed.2d 576.

CHIEF JUSTICE REHNQUIST delivered the opinion of the Court.

Section 404(a) of the Clean Water Act (CWA or Act), 33 U.S.C. § 1344(a), regulates the discharge of dredged or fill material into "navigable waters." The United States Army Corps of Engineers (Corps) has interpreted § 404(a) to confer federal authority over an abandoned sand and gravel pit in northern Illinois which provides habitat for migratory birds. We are asked to decide whether the provisions of § 404(a) may be fairly extended to these waters, and, if so, whether Congress could exercise such authority consistent with the Commerce Clause, U.S. Const., Art. I, § 8, cl. 3. We answer the first question in the negative and therefore do not reach the second.

Petitioner, the Solid Waste Agency of Northern Cook County (SWANCC), is a consortium of 23 suburban Chicago cities and villages that united in an effort to locate and develop a disposal site for baled non-hazardous solid waste. [SWANCC located] a 533-acre parcel, bestriding the Illinois counties Cook and Kane, which had been the site of a sand and gravel pit mining operation for three decades up until about 1960. Long since abandoned, the old mining site eventually gave way to a successional stage forest, with its remnant excavation trenches evolving into a scattering of permanent and seasonal ponds of varying size (from under one-tenth of an acre to several acres) and depth (from several inches to several feet). * * *

Section 404(a) grants the Corps authority to issue permits "for the discharge of dredged or fill material into the navigable waters at specified disposal sites." The term "navigable waters" is defined under the Act as "the waters of the United States, including the territorial seas." § 1362(7). The Corps has issued regulations defining the term "waters of the United States" to include "waters such as intrastate lakes, rivers, streams (including intermittent streams), mudflats, sandflats, wetlands, sloughs, prairie potholes, wet meadows, playa lakes, or natural ponds, the use, degradation or destruction of which could affect interstate or foreign commerce * * *." 33 CFR § 328.3(a)(3). In 1986, in an attempt to "clarify" the reach of its jurisdiction, the Corps stated that § 404(a) extends to intrastate waters:

"a. Which are or would be used as habitat by birds protected by Migratory Bird Treaties; or

"b. Which are or would be used as habitat by other migratory birds which cross state lines; or

"c. Which are or would be used as habitat for endangered species; or

"d. Used to irrigate crops sold in interstate commerce."

51 Fed.Reg. 41217. This last promulgation has been dubbed the "Migratory Bird Rule."

[T]he Corps formally "determined that the seasonally ponded, abandoned gravel mining depressions located on the project site, while not wetlands, did qualify as 'waters of the United States' [because] the water areas and spoil piles had developed a natural character and * * * are used as habitat by migratory bird [sic] which cross state lines." [T]he Corps refused to issue a § 404(a) permit [because, among other things,] SWANCC had not established that its proposal was the "least environmentally damaging, most practicable alternative" for disposal of nonhazardous solid waste * * *.

Petitioner filed suit under the Administrative Procedure Act in the Northern District of Illinois challenging both the Corps' jurisdiction over the site and the merits of its denial of the § 404(a) permit. The District Court granted summary judgment to respondents on the jurisdictional issue, and petitioner abandoned its challenge to the Corps' permit decision. On appeal to the Court of Appeals for the Seventh Circuit, [the decision was affirmed.] We granted certiorari and now reverse. * * * We conclude that the "Migratory Bird Rule" is not fairly supported by the CWA.

This is not the first time we have been called upon to evaluate the meaning of § 404(a). In United States v. Riverside Bayview Homes, Inc., 474 U.S. 121, 106 S.Ct. 455, 88 L.Ed.2d 419 (1985), we held that the Corps had § 404(a) jurisdiction over wetlands that actually abutted on a navigable waterway. In so doing, we noted that the term "navigable" is of "limited import" and that Congress evidenced its intent to "regulate at least some waters that would not be deemed 'navigable' under the classical understanding of that term." Id., at 133, 106 S.Ct. 455. But our holding was based in large measure upon Congress' unequivocal acquiescence to, and approval of, the Corps' regulations interpreting the CWA to cover wetlands adjacent to navigable waters. We found that Congress' concern for the protection of water quality and aquatic ecosystems indicated its intent to regulate wetlands "inseparably bound up with the 'waters' of the United States." Id., at 134, 106 S.Ct. 455.

It was the significant nexus between the wetlands and "navigable waters" that informed our reading of the CWA in *Riverside Bayview Homes*. Indeed, we did not "express any opinion" on the "question of the authority of the Corps to regulate discharges of fill material into wetlands that are not adjacent to bodies of open water * * *." Id. at 131-32, n.8, 106 S.Ct. 455. In order to rule for respondents here, we would have to hold that the jurisdiction of the Corps extends to ponds that are *not* adjacent to open water. But we conclude that the text of the statute will not allow this. * * *

We * * * decline respondents' invitation to take what they see as the next ineluctable step after *Riverside Bayview Homes*: holding that isolated ponds, some only seasonal, wholly located within two Illinois counties, fall under § 404(a)'s definition of "navigable waters" because they serve as habitat for migratory birds. As counsel for respondents conceded at oral argument, such a ruling would assume that the use of the word navigable in the statute does not have any independent significance. We cannot agree that Congress' separate definitional use of the phrase "waters of the United States" constitutes a basis for reading the term "navigable waters" out of the statute. We said in *Riverside Bayview Homes* that the word "navigable" in the statute was of "limited import" and went on to hold that § 404(a) extended to nonnavigable wetlands adjacent to open waters. But it is one thing to give a word limited effect and quite another to give it no effect whatever. The term "navigable" has at least the import of showing us what Congress had in mind as its authority for enacting the CWA: its traditional jurisdiction over waters that were or had been navigable in fact or which could reasonably be so made. See, e.g., United States v. Appalachian Elec. Power Co., 311 U.S. 377, 407-408, 61 S.Ct. 291, 85 L.Ed. 243 (1940). * * *

Respondents * * * contend that, at the very least, it must be said that Congress did not address the precise question of § 404(a)'s scope with regard to nonnavigable, isolated, intrastate waters, and that, therefore, we should give deference to the "Migratory Bird Rule." See, e.g., Chevron U.S.A. Inc. v. Natural Resources Defense Council, Inc., 467 U.S. 837, 104 S.Ct. 2778, 81 L.Ed.2d 694 (1984) [saying that a court should accept an agency's interpretation of an ambiguous statute unless the interpretation is arbitrary, capricious, or manifestly contrary to the statute]. We find § 404(a) to be clear, but even were we to agree with respondents, we would not extend *Chevron* deference here.

Where an administrative interpretation of a statute invokes the outer limits of Congress' power, we expect a clear indication that Congress intended that result. This requirement stems from our prudential desire not to needlessly reach constitutional issues and our assumption that Congress does not casually authorize administrative agencies to interpret a statute to push the limit of congressional authority. This concern is heightened where the administrative interpretation alters the federal-state framework by permitting federal encroachment upon a traditional state power. Thus, 'where an otherwise acceptable construction of a statute would raise serious constitutional problems, the Court will construe the statute to avoid such problems unless such construction is plainly contrary to the intent of Congress." Edward J. DeBartolo Corp. v. Florida Gulf Coast Building & Constr. Trades Council, 485 U.S. 568, 575, 108 S.Ct. 1392, 99 L.Ed.2d 645 (1988).

Twice in the past six years we have reaffirmed the proposition that the grant of authority to Congress under the Commerce Clause, though broad, is not unlimited. See United States v. Morrison, 529 U.S. 598, 120 S.Ct. 1740, 146 L.Ed.2d 658 (2000); United States v. Lopez, 514 U.S. 549, 115 S.Ct. 1624, 131 L.Ed.2d 626 (1995). Respondents argue that the "Migratory Bird Rule" falls within Congress' power to regulate intrastate activities that "substantially affect" interstate commerce. They note that the protection of migratory birds is a "national interest of very nearly the first magnitude," Missouri v. Holland, 252 U.S. 416, 435, 40 S.Ct. 382, 64 L.Ed. 641 (1920), and that, as the Court of Appeals found, millions of people spend over a billion dollars annually on recreational pursuits relating to migratory birds. These arguments raise significant constitutional questions. For example, we would have to evaluate the precise object or activity that, in the aggregate, substantially affects interstate commerce. This is not clear, for although the Corps has claimed jurisdiction over petitioner's land because it contains water areas used as habitat by migratory birds, respondents now, post litem motam, focus upon the fact that the regulated activity is petitioner's municipal landfill, which is "plainly of a commercial nature." Brief for Federal Respondents 43. But this is a far cry, indeed, from the "navigable waters" and 'waters of the United States" to which the statute by its terms extends.

These are significant constitutional questions raised by respondents' application of their regulations, and yet we find nothing approaching a clear statement from Congress that it intended § 404(a) to reach an abandoned sand and gravel pit such as we have here. Permitting respondents to claim federal jurisdiction over ponds and mudflats falling within the "Migratory Bird Rule" would result in a significant impingement of the States' traditional and primary power over land and water use. Rather than expressing a desire to readjust the federal-state balance in this manner, Congress chose to "recognize, preserve, and protect the primary responsibilities and rights of States * * * to plan the development and use * * * of land and water resources * * *." 33 U.S.C. § 1251(b). We thus read the statute as written to avoid the significant constitutional and federalism questions raised by respondents' interpretation, and therefore reject the request for administrative deference. * * *

We hold that 33 CFR § 328.3(a)(3), as clarified and applied to petitioner's balefill site pursuant to the "Migratory Bird Rule" exceeds the authority granted to respondents under § 404(a) of the CWA. The judgment of the Court of Appeals for the Seventh Circuit is therefore reversed.

JUSTICE STEVENS with whom JUSTICE SOUTER, JUSTICE GINSBURG, and JUSTICE BREYER join, dissenting.

* * * In its decision today, the Court draws a new jurisdictional line, one that invalidates the 1986 migratory bird regulation as well as the Corps' assertion of jurisdiction over all waters except for actually navigable waters, their tributaries, and wetlands adjacent to each.

* * *

Because I am convinced that the Court's miserly construction of the statute is incorrect, I shall comment briefly on petitioner's argument that Congress is without power to prohibit it from filling any part of the 31 acres of ponds on its property in Cook County, Illinois. The Corps' exercise of its § 404 permitting power over "isolated" waters that serve as habitat for migratory birds falls well within the boundaries set by this Court's Commerce Clause jurisprudence.

The activity being regulated in this case (and by the Corps' § 404 regulations in general) is the discharge of fill material into water. The Corps did not assert jurisdiction over petitioner's land simply because the waters were 'used as habitat by migratory birds." It asserted jurisdiction because petitioner planned to *discharge fill* into waters "used as habitat by migratory birds." * * * There can be no doubt that, unlike the class of activities Congress was attempting to regulate in United States v. Morrison, 529 U.S. 598, 613, 120 S.Ct. 1740, 146 L.Ed.2d 658 (2000) ("[g]ender-motivated crimes"), and United States v. Lopez, 514 U.S. 549, 561, 115 S.Ct. 1624, 131 L.Ed.2d 626 (1995) (possession of guns near school property), the discharge of fill material into the Nation's waters is almost always undertaken for economic reasons. * * * Moreover, no one disputes that the discharge of fill into "isolated" waters that serve as migratory bird habitat will, in the aggregate, adversely affect migratory bird populations. Nor does petitioner dispute that the particular waters it seeks to fill are home to many important species of migratory birds, including the second-largest breeding colony of Great Blue Herons in northeastern Illinois and several species of waterfowl protected by international treaty and Illinois endangered species laws. In addition to the intrinsic value of migratory birds, it is undisputed that literally millions of people regularly participate in birdwatching and hunting and that those activities generate a host of commercial activities of great value. * * *

The power to regulate commerce among the several States necessarily and properly includes the power to preserve the natural resources that generate such commerce. Migratory birds, and the waters on which they rely, are such resources. Moreover, the protection of migratory birds is a well-established federal responsibility. As Justice Holmes noted in Missouri v. Holland, the federal interest in protecting these birds is of "the first magnitude." 252 U.S., at 435, 40 S.Ct. 382. Because of their transitory nature, they "can be protected only by national action." Ibid. * * * If, as it does, the Commerce Clause empowers Congress to regulate particular "activities causing air or water pollution, or other environmental hazards that may have effects in more than one State," [Hodel v. Virginia Surface Mining & Reclamation Assn., Inc., 452 U.S. 264, 282, 101 S.Ct. 2352, 69 L.Ed.2d 1 (1981)], it also empowers Congress to control individual actions that, in the aggregate, would have the same effect. * * *

Notes

1. **The classical Commerce Clause concept of navigable waters of the United States.** In *SWANCC*, the Court quoted language from *Riverside Bayview Homes* referring to the classical understanding of navigable waters. This under-

standing grew out of three early nineteenth century cases on the grant to Congress by Article I, Section 8 of the Constitution of power "[t]o regulate Commerce * * * among the several states." Two of the cases, Gibbons v. Ogden, 22 U.S. (9 Wheat.) 1 (1824), and Gilman v. City of Philadelphia, 70 U.S. (3 Wall.) 713 (1865), established that the power of Congress to regulate interstate commerce extends to regulation of navigable waters of the United States. The third case, The Daniel Ball, 77 U.S. (10 Wall.) 557, 563 (1870), supplied a definition of such waters. Departing from the English common law definition of navigability, which generally was limited to the sea and waters affected by the ebb and flow of the tides, the Court stated in *Daniel Ball*:

> Those rivers must be regarded as public navigable rivers in law which are navigable in fact. And they are navigable in fact when they are used, or are susceptible of being used, in their ordinary condition, as highways for commerce, over which trade and travel are or may be conducted in the customary modes of trade and travel on water. And they constitute navigable waters of the United States within the meaning of the acts of Congress, in contradistinction from the navigable waters of the States, when they form in their ordinary condition by themselves, or by uniting with other waters, a continued highway over which commerce is or may be carried on with other States or foreign countries in the customary modes in which such commerce is conducted by water.

Much later, in United States v. Appalachian Electric Power Co., 311 U.S. 377 (1940), the Court elaborated on the *Daniel Ball* statement that waters should be regarded as navigable in fact "when they are used, or are susceptible of being used, in their ordinary condition, as highways for commerce." The Court said this definition of navigability in fact is satisfied if a river either (a) presently is used or susceptible of being used for commerce, (b) in the past was so used or was susceptible of being so used though it no longer is, or (c) in the future could be so used. Thus, "[w]hen once found to be navigable, a waterway remains so." Furthermore, said the Court, a waterway's susceptibility for use in its "ordinary condition" as a highway for commerce should be judged by whether the river could be so used if reasonable improvements were made to it. The phrase "ordinary condition" thus refers to the volume of water, gradients, and regularity of flow, not to whether artificial aids are required before commercial navigation can be undertaken.

Consistent with the English common law on navigability, lower federal courts have treated the classical Commerce Clause concept of navigable waters of the United States as including not only waters meeting the *Daniel Ball* test of navigability in fact for interstate commerce but waters affected by the ebb and flow of the tide even though they are not used or usable as highways for interstate commerce. E.g., United States v. Sasser, 967 F.2d 993 (4th Cir. 1992); United States v. Stoeco Homes, Inc., 498 F.2d 597 (3d Cir. 1974) (tracing the ebb-and-flow test in the United States back to pre-1851 admiralty cases).

2. **Current significance of the classical concept.** In 1979, the Court observed that Commerce Clause jurisprudence has evolved since the early nineteenth century to make it clear Congress' power to regulate waterways and activities thereon extends far beyond the classical concept of navigable waters of the United States.

> Reference to the navigability of a waterway adds little if anything to the breadth of Congress' regulatory power over interstate commerce. [A] wide spectrum of economic activities "affect" interstate commerce and thus are susceptible of congressional regulation under the Commerce Clause irrespective of whether navigation, or, indeed, water, is involved. The cases that discuss Congress' paramount authority to regulate waters used in interstate commerce are consequently best understood when viewed in terms of [affect-interstate-commerce] analysis than by reference to whether the stream in fact is capable of supporting navigation or may be characterized as "navigable water of the United States."

Kaiser Aetna v. United States, 444 U.S. 164 (1979). Six years later, in *Riverside Bayview Homes*, the Court concluded Congress intended in CWA § 404 to reach "at least some waters that would not be deemed 'navigable' under the classical understanding of that term."

The evolution of the Commerce Clause does not mean, however, that the classical concept of navigable waters has become obsolete under existing congressional legislation. One example of its continued significance is section 10 of the Rivers and Harbors Appropriation Act of 1899 (RHA). This requires a Corps of Engineers permit to excavate, fill, or otherwise alter the channel of "any navigable water of the United States" or to build any structures in such water. Current Corps of Engineers regulations on RHA § 10 define the jurisdictional phrase "navigable water of the United States" in accordance with the classical concept, i.e., water that is navigable in fact for interstate commerce or is affected by the ebb and flow of the tide. See 33 C.F.R. §§ 322.2, 329.4.

A second example is Federal Power Act (FPA) § 23(b), 16 U.S.C. § 817. This requires a Federal Energy Regulatory Commission (FERC) license for nonfederal hydroelectric projects that either (1) are located on "navigable waters of the United States," (2) are located on other waters "over which Congress has jurisdiction under its authority to regulate commerce with foreign nations and among the several states * * * if * * * the interests of interstate or foreign commerce would be affected," (3) occupy federal public lands or reservations, or (4) use surplus water from a federal dam. The first two grounds for licensing jurisdiction are based on the Commerce Clause. (The last two grounds are based on the Property Clause, infra Note 4.) The act defines the first jurisdictional ground—"navigable waters of the United States"—by using the navigability-in-fact component of the classical concept of navigable waters of the United States. FPA § 3(8), 16 U.S.C. § 796(8).

The second jurisdictional ground—"interstate or foreign commerce would be affected"—was once thought to require a license for a project on a nonnavigable river only if that river was tributary to a navigable river and the project would impair navigation on the navigable river. In other words, it was thought that interstate commerce *in the form of navigation* would have to be affected before Congress intended to require a license for a project on a nonnavigable river. See Nantahala Power & Light Co. v. Fed. Power Comm'n, 384 F.2d 200 (4th Cir. 1967). In 1965, however, the Supreme Court ruled that Congress exercised its full Commerce Clause authority in the second jurisdictional ground, so that a license is required for a project on a nonnavigable river if it will affect interstate commerce by the generation of electric power for interstate transmission, even though it will have no impact on downstream navigability. Fed. Power Comm'n v. Union Elec. Co., 381 U.S. 90 (1965). See also U.S. Dep't of Commerce v. FERC, 36 F.3d 893 (9th Cir. 1994) (stating that effect-on-interstate-commerce jurisdiction exists if a project will have a substantial adverse effect on anadromous fish).

The modern expansive view of the second jurisdictional ground has not swallowed up the first ground, i.e., "navigable waters of the United States." If a proposed hydroelectric project will be located on a navigable waterway, that fact alone supports regulatory jurisdiction. There is no need for FERC to inquire whether the project will affect interstate commerce. Thus, in City of Centralia v. FERC, 661 F.2d 787 (9th Cir. 1981), a small municipal hydroelectric plant was not shown to impact interstate commerce enough to require a license under the effect-on-interstate-commerce basis for jurisdiction; but later the same plant was held to need a license under the "navigable waters" jurisdictional ground, 851 F.2d 278 (9th Cir. 1988). FERC's application of the "navigable waters" jurisdictional ground is critiqued in Richard J. Pierce, Jr., What Is A Navigable Water? Canoes Count But Kayaks Do Not, 53 Syracuse L. Rev. 1067 (2003).

As a final example, the classical Commerce Clause concept of navigable waters of the United States has significance beyond the role it plays in federal permitting and licensing legislation. The Supreme Court established long ago that the constitutional power of Congress to "regulate" navigable waters of the United States includes not only power to enact permitting and licensing programs but also power to authorize and fund the construction of navigation improvements on such waters. South Carolina v. Georgia, 93 U.S. 4 (1876). As the Court noted decades later, Congress developed the "custom of invoking the navigation power in authorizing [waterway] improvements" though they served multiple purposes rather than just navigation—a custom that "appears to have had its origin when the power of the Central Government to make internal improvements was contested and in doubt." United States v. Gerlach Live Stock Co., 339 U.S. 725, 738 (1950). When Congress adheres to custom and invokes the navigation power in funding waterway improvements, that can trigger the federal navigation servitude, a doctrine that is the subject of the next two principal cases. It is generally understood that the navigation servitude doctrine operates only when Congress acts under the navigation power. But cf. infra p. 631, Note 6.

3. **Clean Water Act § 404 and wetlands.** *Riverside Bayside Homes* held section 404 applies to intrastate wetlands adjacent to classically navigable waters. *SWANCC* said section 404 does not apply to intrastate wetlands that do not abut classically navigable waters and are "isolated," meaning water in the wetlands never reaches classically navigable waters. What about intrastate wetlands that do not abut classically navigable waters but ultimately flow into such waters? For example, suppose wetlands abut a nonnavigable creek that is tributary to a navigable water body. Compare United States v. Rapanos, 339 F.3d 447 (6th Cir. 2003) (holdng a section 404 permit was needed to fill intrastate wetlands abutting a man-made ditch that emptied into a creek flowing into a classically navigable waterway miles distant from the wetlands), cert. denied, Rapanos v. United States, 124 S. Ct. 1875 (2004), and United States v. Deaton, 332 F.3d 698 (4th Cir. 2003) (finding section 404 applied on similar facts), cert. denied, Deaton v. United States, 124 S.Ct. 1874 (2004), with In re Needham, 354 F.3d 340 (5th Cir. 2003) (stating section 404 does not apply to intrastate wetlands unless they abut "an open body of navigable water").

4. **Other constitutional powers.** Apart from the Commerce Clause, several other constitutional grants of power to Congress justify federal water regulation and water development. An important one is the Property Clause, Article IV, Section 3: "The Congress shall have power to dispose of and make all needful Rules and Regulations respecting the Territory or other Property belonging to the United States." Power and control over water arising out of federal ownership of the public domain sustained the Reclamation Act of 1902. The Property Clause also finds use as the connecting link between the authority of the United States under the Commerce Clause and the production of hydroelectric power at federal dams. "The power of falling water was an inevitable incident of the construction of the dam. That water power came into the exclusive control of the Federal Government. The mechanical energy was convertible into electrical energy, and the water power, the right to convert it into electric energy, and the electric energy thus produced, constitute property belonging to the United States. * * * The Government could lease or sell and fix the terms." Ashwander v. TVA, 297 U.S. 288, 330 (1936).

Article I, Sections 8 and 9 of the Constitution empower Congress to declare war and to levy taxes and appropriate money to provide for the common defense of the United States. Under the 1916 National Defense Act, Congress authorized the President to investigate means of producing nitrates and other products for munitions of war, and to designate sites on rivers and public lands suitable for generating power for the production of nitrates and other useful products. The Wilson Dam on the Tennessee River was constructed under this authority and later was incorporated into the system of the Tennessee Valley Authority. Its hydroelectric energy was sold in peacetime for distribution in the Tennessee Valley. In Ashwander v. TVA, supra, the Court ruled that the dam and power plant were "adapted to the purposes of national defense" and that their maintenance in operating condition, and the resulting assurance of abundant electric energy in the event of war, were national defense assets which the government might constitutionally construct and acquire.

Article I, Section 8 also empowers Congress to levy taxes and to appropriate funds to provide for the general welfare of the United States. Not until 1936 was it thought that these provisions delegated a separate power to the national government. In that year, United States v. Butler, 297 U.S. 1 (1936), held that the General Welfare Clause was not restricted by the specific powers enumerated in the Constitution, such as the power to regulate commerce. In United States v. Gerlach Live Stock Co., 339 U.S. 725 (1950), the Court said that one of the largest federal water development projects—the Central Valley Project in California—could be sustained under this power: "Congress has a substantive power to tax and appropriate for the general welfare, limited only by the requirement that it shall be exercised for the common benefit as distinguished from some mere local purpose. * * * Thus the power of Congress to promote the general welfare through large-scale projects for reclamation, irrigation, and other internal improvement, is now as clear and ample as its power to accomplish the same results indirectly through resort to strained interpretation of the power over navigation." Id. at 738.

Treaties made under Article II, Section 2 become under Article VI "the supreme Law of Land." Treaties of the United States with Canada and Mexico impose limitations on state action affecting boundary waters and other waters that flow across the boundary or into boundary waters. "[T]he interests of the nation are more important than those of any state," and the federal government may act to prevent a state from interfering with a national treaty obligation. Sanitary Dist. v. United States, 266 U.S. 405 (1925). Treaty obligations of the United States give the Nation an additional basis for authorizing works of improvements on international waterways. Arizona v. California, 283 U.S. 423 (1931).

UNITED STATES v. RANDS

Supreme Court of the United States, 1967.
389 U.S. 121, 88 S. Ct. 265, 19 L. Ed.2d 329.

MR. JUSTICE WHITE delivered the opinion of the Court.

In this case the Court is asked to decide whether the compensation which the United States is constitutionally required to pay when it condemns riparian land includes the land's value as a port site. Respondents owned land along the Columbia River in the State of Oregon. They leased the land to the State with an option to purchase, it apparently being contemplated that the State would use the land as an industrial park, part of which would function as a port. The option was never exercised, for the land was taken by the United States in connection with the John Day Lock and Dam Project, authorized by Congress as part of a comprehensive plan for the development of the Columbia River. Pursuant to statute the United States then conveyed the land to the State of Oregon at a price considerably less than the option price at which respondents had hoped to sell. In the condemnation action, the trial judge determined that the compensable value of the land taken was limited to its value for sand, gravel, and agricultural purposes and that its special value as a port site could not be considered. The ultimate award was about one-fifth the claimed value of the land if used as a port. The Court of Appeals for the Ninth Circuit reversed, apparently holding that the Government had taken from respondents a compensable right of access to navigable waters and concluding that "port site value should be compensable under the Fifth Amendment." 367 F.2d 186, 191 (1966). We granted certiorari because of a seeming conflict between the decision below and United States v. Twin City Power Co., 350 U.S. 222, 76 S.Ct. 259, 100 L.Ed. 240 (1956). We reverse the judgment of the Court of Appeals because the principles underlying *Twin City* govern this case and the Court of Appeals erred in failing to follow them.

The Commerce Clause confers a unique position upon the Government in connection with navigable waters. "The power to regulate commerce comprehends the control for that purpose, and to the extent necessary, of all the navigable waters of the United States * * *. For this purpose they are the public property of the nation, and subject to all the requisite legislation by Congress." Gilman v. City of Philadelphia, 3 Wall. 713, 724–725, 18 L.Ed. 96 (1866). This power to regulate navigation confers upon the United States a "dominant servitude," FPC v. Niagara Mohawk Power Corp., 347 U.S. 239, 249, 74 S.Ct. 487, 493, 98 L.Ed. 686 (1954), which extends to the entire stream and the stream bed below ordinary high-water mark. The proper exercise of this power is not an invasion of any private property rights in the stream or the lands underlying it, for the damage sustained does not result from taking property from riparian owners within the meaning of the Fifth Amendment but from the lawful exercise of a power to which the interests of riparian owners have always been subject. Thus, without being constitutionally obligated to pay compensation, the United States may change the course of a navigable stream or otherwise impair or destroy a riparian owner's access to navigable waters, even though the market value of the riparian owner's land is substantially diminished.

The navigational servitude of the United States does not extend beyond the high-water mark. Consequently, when fast lands are taken by the Government, just compensation must be paid. But "just as the navigational privilege permits the Government to reduce the value of riparian lands by denying the riparian owner access to the stream without compensation for his loss, * * * it also permits the Government to disregard the value arising from this same fact of riparian location in compensating the owner when fast lands are appropriated." United States v. Virginia Elec. & Power Co., 365 U.S. 624, 629, 81 S.Ct. 784, 788, 5 L.Ed.2d 838 (1961). Specifically, the Court has held that the Government is not required to give compensation for "water power" when it takes the riparian lands of a private power company using the stream to generate power. United States v. Chandler-Dunbar Water Power Co., 229 U.S. 53, 73-74, 33 S.Ct. 667, 676, 57 L.Ed. 1063 (1913). Nor must it compensate the company for the value of its uplands as a power plant site. Id., at 76, 33 S.Ct. at 677. Such value does not "inhere in these parcels as upland," but depends on use of the water to which the company has no right as against the United States: "The government had dominion over the water power of the rapids and falls, and cannot be required to pay any hypothetical additional value to a riparian owner who had no right to appropriate the current to his own commercial use." Ibid.

All this was made unmistakably clear in United States v. Twin City Power Co., 350 U.S. 222, 76 S.Ct. 259, 100 L.Ed. 240 (1956). The United States condemned a promising site for a hydroelectric power plant and was held to be under no obligation to pay for any special value which the fast lands had for power generating purposes. The value of the land attributable to its location on the stream was "due to the flow of the stream; and if the United States were required to pay the judgments below, it would be compensating the landowner for the increment of value added to the fast lands if the flow of the stream were taken into account." 350 U.S., at 226, 76 S.Ct., at 261.

We are asked to distinguish between the value of land as a power site and its value as a port site. In the power cases, the stream is used as a source of power to generate electricity. In this case, for the property to have value as a port, vessels must be able to arrive and depart by water, meanwhile using the waterside facilities of the port. In both cases, special value arises from access to, and use of, navigable waters. With regard to the constitutional duty to compensate a riparian owner, no distinction can be drawn. It is irrelevant that the licensing authority presently being exercised over hydroelectric projects may be different from, or even more stringent than, the licensing of port sites. We are dealing with the constitutional power of Congress completely to regulate navigable streams to the total exclusion of private power companies or port owners. As was true in *Twin City,* if the owner of the fast lands can demand port site value as part of his compensation, "he gets the value of a right that the Government in the exercise of its dominant servitude can grant or withhold as it chooses. * * * To require the United States to pay for this * * * value would be to create private claims in the public domain." 350 U.S., at 228, 76 S.Ct., at 263. * * *

For the foregoing reasons, the judgment of the Court of Appeals is reversed and the case remanded with direction to reinstate the judgment of the District Court.

Notes

1. **History and rationale of the federal navigation servitude.** In Eva H. Morreale (now Hanks), Federal Power in Western Waters: The Navigation Power and the Rule of No Compensation, 3 Nat. Resources J. 1 (1963), the development of the federal navigation servitude is recounted from its origin in an ancient English public right of passage and fishing in navigable waters: The ancient public right existed on navigable waterways whether or not they were private property in other respects. Obstruction or destruction of the public right of passage was a public nuisance abatable by the Crown, and no compensation was owed to the tortfeasor. (The Crown not only had power to abate such nuisances but also had a duty not to do anything itself to derogate the public right, a duty that evolved into the modern public trust doctrine covered supra pp. 523-45.) The ancient public right survived the American Revolution, with the new states succeeding to the power of the Crown to preserve public navigation. Then the adoption of the Constitution gave Congress the superior power to protect and to improve navigation in aid of interstate commerce. While the superior power of Congress concerning navigation does not explain why private property interests must yield without compensation, "[t]he historical notion of the paramount right of the community to navigate and fish its navigable waterways free from any interference does explain it." Id. at 30.

The Supreme Court has relied upon this history to advance the following rationale for the navigation servitude: "The owner's use of property riparian to a navigable stream long has been limited by the right of the public to use the stream in the interest of navigation. * * * There thus has been ample notice over the years that such property is subject to a dominant public interest." United States v. Kan. City Life Ins. Co., 339 U.S. 799 (1950). Professor Hanks, however, found the notice rationale insufficient to justify many modern judicial applications of the servitude: "[A] good deal of the difficulty lies in the manner in which the navigation servitude has been permitted to grow from a rule securing free and unhindered passage on navigable waterways to its present scope." 3 Nat. Resources J. at 76. She noted that originally the Supreme Court applied the federal navigation servitude only when Congress acted to protect or improve navigation in aid of interstate commerce. But over time, she reported, "[c]ongressional activity in the name of navigation has expanded—as has the concept of navigable streams. The cases have not taken account of either development and its respective effects on notice." Id. at 31.

The *Twin City* case discussed in *Rands* provides one example of expanded congressional activity. There Congress decided to develop the Savannah River with a multipurpose dam primarily to generate hydroelectric power, but also to improve navigation and provide flood control. When the United States condemned fast land for the project that had value as a future hydroelectric site, the Court held that no compensation was due for the land's hydropower value. In Professor Hanks' view, expansion of the servitude to such multimillion-dollar federal projects bearing little relation to navigation was neither constitutionally necessary nor economically desirable. She argued that the Court could have expanded the power of Congress to regulate and develop the Nation's waterways, as it eventually expanded the general Commerce Clause power, but left the navigation servitude to its historically based role of protecting or improving the public right of way for navigation.

2. **The navigation servitude and nonnavigable streams.** In United States v. Grand River Dam Authority, 363 U.S. 229 (1960), a state agency owned a power site on a nonnavigable tributary of the navigable Arkansas River. The United States condemned the site for construction of a federal dam as part of a comprehensive river basin plan to develop electric power and to improve navigation and flood control on the Arkansas River. The Court applied the navigation servitude to deny the state agency's claim of $10 million for loss of water power rights. After noting that the servitude does not become inoperative because a dam that improves navigation also serves other purposes, the Court stated: "When the United States appropriates the flow either of a navigable or a nonnavigable stream pursuant to its superior power under the Commerce Clause, it is exercising established prerogatives and is beholden to no one." Id. at 233.

3. **The navigation servitude and water rights.** Professor Hanks, in the article cited supra Note 1, also addressed whether the navigation servitude could affect western water rights:

"It should be noted that none of the previously discussed cases, whether denying or granting compensation, concerned a consumptive water right or, more narrowly, an irrigation water right. * * * But while there is no case subjecting irrigation water rights to the rule of no compensation nothing on the other hand suggests their compensability. * * *

"Finally, brief consideration shall be given to a fear that has repeatedly been voiced, namely that the full application of navigation power and servitude principles will lead to the evaluation of desert uplands as *dry* land rather than as *irrigated* land when taken in connection with a navigation power project. As was shown earlier, the evaluation of uplands excludes any consideration of their adaptability as dam sites. That was so because the value thus added to the land derived 'in the end' from the stream itself. It was, in other words, dependent on a right to the water which the United States could destroy without compensation. Similarly, of course, it could be said that such value as is added to desert land by irrigation is dependent on the consumptive use of water, a use which can be destroyed without compensation by the exercise of the navigation power. The noncompensable destruction of that which gave the land its additional value would thus lead to the noncompensable destruction of that additional value itself. On purely logical terms, therefore, the fears regarding the evaluation of irrigated desert land are justified." 3 Nat. Resources J. at 75.

4. **Congressional waiver of the navigation servitude.** Enough criticism was leveled at *Rands* to cause Congress to reverse it with section 111 of the Rivers and Harbors and Flood Control Act of 1970, 33 U.S.C. § 595a:

"In all cases where real property shall be taken by the United States for the public use in connection with any improvement of rivers, harbors, canals, or waterways of the United States, and in all condemnation proceedings by the United States to acquire lands or easements for such improvements, the compensation to be paid for real property taken by the United States above the normal high water mark of navigable waters of the United States shall be the fair market value of such real property based upon all uses to which such real property may reasonably be put, including its highest and best use, any of which uses may be dependent upon access to or utilization of such navigable waters. In cases of partial takings of real property, no depreciation in the value of any remaining real property shall be recognized and no compensation shall be paid for any damages to such remaining real property which result from loss of or reduction of access from such remaining real property to such navigable waters because of the taking of real property or the purposes for which such real property is taken."

Clearly section 111 reverses *Rands.* It seems fairly clear that section 111 also would reverse *Twin City*. *Rands* was so directly based on *Twin City* that a shot aimed at the former should hit the latter. What of *Chandler-Dunbar*, which *Rands* mentioned and was the basis of *Twin City*? There, when the federal government condemned uplands and instream hydropower generating facilities of the Chandler-Dunbar Company, the company unsuccessfully claimed compensation for the water power capacity of the rapids and falls of the river. Commonly the values attributable to a stream are incorporated into the value of the riparian land. If the *Chandler-Dunbar* facts arose today, could the company's claim be phrased as one to recover for the value of its uplands as a power plant site?

Does section 111 put an end to the fears of irrigators described by Professor Hanks in Note 3, supra?

Does section 111 apply when government regulation deprives fast land of essentially all value, but the government does not literally acquire title to the land? In United States v. 30.54 Acres of Land, 90 F.3d 790 (3rd Cir. 1996), the Corps of Engineers condemned 30.54 acres of a 132.55-acre parcel needed for construction of a lock and dam on the Monongahela River. The landowners used the remaining 102 acres as a coal loading facility for barges. This use depended upon a coal tipple that was grounded on their land but extended over the river to load the barges. Subsequently, the Corps prohibited coal loading operations in the area of the tipple because they endangered navigation on the river. The landowners claimed the prohibition deprived their remaining 102 acres of all economically reasonable use. The court held section 111 did not require compensation for the loss of use of their remaining land as a coal loading facility: "* * * Section 111 applies only to 'real property taken by the United States above the high water mark.' Here the United States did not acquire above the high-water mark real property (other than the original 30.54 acres); rather, it prohibited use of the tipple—a structure jutting one hundred feet into a navigable waterway. * * * Congress intended to modify the rule of United States v. Rands only to the extent of paying full compensation based on riparian location in cases of actual acquisition of above the high-water mark real property." Id. at 796 (alternative holding).

Long before section 111, United States v. Gerlach Live Stock Co., 339 U.S. 725 (1950), found another congressional waiver of the navigation servitude. The case involved the Central Valley Project in California, which is the Nation's largest federal reclamation project. Included as part of the project were Friant Dam on the San Joaquin River and two great canals that would divert and distribute almost the entire flow of the river to irrigators. The plaintiffs owned grass lands that had been naturally irrigated by spring high water before these works were built. Friant Dam ended the natural overflow irrigation. The plaintiffs sought just compensation for deprivation of riparian rights. Federal legislation authorizing the project spoke of the "improvement of navigation and flood control," but it also provided that the work would be undertaken by the Bureau of Reclamation and that the provisions of the federal Reclamation Act would govern. The Reclamation Act explicitly requires the Bureau to condemn and pay just compensation for water rights needed for projects. The Court held that Congress had elected to treat the project as a reclamation project and thus compensation was due.

5. **State navigation servitude.** California has a state navigation servitude that is said to arise from the state's ownership of navigable waterways in trust for the benefit of the public. In Colberg, Inc. v. State ex rel. Department of Public Works, 432 P.2d 3 (Cal. 1967), the court invoked the servitude to deny just compensation to shipyard owners when the state built two freeway bridges over a channel, thereby blocking access to the shipyards by large ships. Although the bridges impaired navigation, they facilitated commercial traffic on the freeway. The court said the servitude applies when the state acts relative to navigable waterways in any manner that improves commercial traffic and intercourse, whether or not navigation is improved.

6. **Whether or not navigation is improved?** Suppose the United States Congress, rather than the California public works department, had built the two freeway bridges over the channel in *Colberg*, and had done so under its general Commerce Clause power rather than under the classical navigation power. Would the United States owe just compensation to the shipyard owners or would the federal navigation servitude apply? In *Gerlach Live Stock*, supra Note 4, Congress invoked the navigation power in authorizing the Central Valley Project. The plaintiffs argued that Friant Dam itself had no navigation benefits. The Court acknowledged that the navigation benefits of the project as a whole were "economically insignificant" compared to the irrigation benefits. But because the Reclamation Act governed the project and required compensation, the Court was able to say: "[W]e need not ponder whether by virtue of a highly fictional navigational purpose, the Government could destroy the flow of a navigable stream and carry away its waters for sale to private interests without compensation to those deprived of them. We have never held that or anything like it, and we need not here pass on any question of constitutional power * * *." 339 U.S. at 737. In a separate opinion, Justice Douglas concurred that the Reclamation Act required compensation but read the Court's navigation servitude precedents more broadly than did the *Gerlach* majority: "[W]e have repeatedly held that there are no private property rights in the waters of a navigable river. * * * [T]he existence of property rights in the waters of a navigable stream are not dependent upon whether the United States is changing the flow of the river in aid of navigation or for some other purpose." Id. at 756.

KAISER AETNA v. UNITED STATES

Supreme Court of the United States, 1979.
444 U.S. 164, 100 S. Ct. 383, 62 L. Ed.2d 332.

MR. JUSTICE REHNQUIST delivered the opinion of the Court.

[Kuapa Pond on the island of Oahu, Hawaii, was originally a shallow 523-acre lagoon separated by a barrier beach from Maunalua Bay and the Pacific Ocean. The early Hawaiians installed sluice gates across two openings from the pond to the bay, and used the pond to raise fish. Water from the bay and ocean entered the pond through the gates during high tide, and during low tide the flow reversed toward the ocean. Kuapa Pond and similar fishponds were always considered private property by the people and government of Hawaii. In 1961 Kaiser Aetna acquired the site for development of Hawaii Kai, a marina-style subdivision. Kaiser Aetna then deepened the pond and cut a channel connecting it to the bay and the ocean. A community of 22,000 persons was developed. The marina was used by the residents of waterfront lots, many residents of back lots, and some nonresident boat owners—all of whom paid fees for maintenance, privacy, and security.

Kaiser Aetna did its initial dredging and channel cutting with the acquiescence of the U.S. Army Corps of Engineers that no permit was needed under section 10 of the Rivers and Harbors Appropriation Act of 1899 (RHA), 33 U.S.C.A. § 403, which requires a permit to excavate, fill, or otherwise alter the channel of "any navigable water of the United States" or to build any structures in such water. In 1972, however, the Corps asserted that the pond had become navigable water of the United States, thus making a RHA § 10 permit necessary for future excavation, filling, or construction in the marina. The Corps also asserted that the pond was subject to a federal navigation servitude that obligated Kaiser Aetna to allow public access to the pond. Kaiser Aetna initially disputed both assertions, but by the time the case got to the Supreme Court, the only matter still contested by Kaiser Aetna was whether the navigation servitude applied to the pond.]

* * * The question before us is whether the Court of Appeals erred in holding that petitioners' improvements to Kuapa Pond caused its original character to be so altered that it became subject to an overriding federal navigational servitude, thus converting into a public aquatic park that which petitioners had invested millions of dollars in improving on the assumption that it was a privately owned pond leased to Kaiser Aetna.

The Government contends that petitioners may not exclude members of the public from the Hawaii Kai Marina because "[t]he public enjoys a federally protected right of navigation over the navigable waters of the United States." It claims the issue in dispute is whether Kuapa Pond is presently a "navigable water of the United States." When petitioners dredged and improved Kuapa Pond, the Government continues, the pond— although it may once have qualified as fast land—became navigable water of the United States. The public thereby acquired a right to use Kuapa Pond as a continuous highway for navigation, and the Corps of Engineers may consequently obtain an injunction to prevent petitioners from attempting to reserve the waterway to themselves.

The position advanced by the Government, and adopted by the Court of Appeals below, presumes that the concept of "navigable waters of the United States" has a fixed meaning that remains unchanged in whatever context it is being applied. While we do not fully agree with the reasoning of the District Court, we do agree with its conclusion that all of this Court's cases dealing with the authority of Congress to regulate navigation and the so-called "navigational servitude" cannot simply be lumped into one basket. * * *

It is true that Kuapa Pond may fit within definitions of "navigability" articulated in past decisions of this Court. But it must be recognized that the concept of navigability in these decisions was used for purposes other than to delimit the boundaries of the navigational servitude: for example, to define the scope of Congress' regulatory authority under the Interstate Commerce Clause, to determine the extent of the authority of the Corps of Engineers under the Rivers and Harbors Appropriation Act of 1899, and to establish the limits of the jurisdiction of federal courts conferred by Art. III, § 2, of the United States Constitution over admiralty and maritime cases. Although the Government is clearly correct in maintaining that the now dredged Kuapa Pond falls within the definition of "navigable waters" as this Court has used that term in delimiting the boundaries of Congress' regulatory authority under the Commerce Clause, this Court has never held that the navigational servitude creates a blanket exception to the Takings Clause whenever Congress exercises its Commerce Clause authority to promote navigation. Thus, while Kuapa Pond may be subject to regulation by the Corps of Engineers, acting under the authority delegated it by Congress in the Rivers and Harbors Appropriation Act, it does not follow that the pond is also subject to a public right of access. * * *

In light of its expansive authority under the Commerce Clause, there is no question but that Congress could assure the public a free right of access to the Hawaii Kai Marina if it so chose. Whether a statute or regulation that went so far amounted to a "taking," however, is an entirely separate question. * * * When the "taking" question has involved the exercise of the public right of navigation over interstate waters that constitute highways for commerce, however, this Court has held in many cases that compensation may not be required as a result of the federal navigational servitude. See, e.g., United States v. Chandler-Dunbar Co., 229 U.S. 53, 33 S.Ct. 667, 57 L.Ed. 1063 (1913).

The navigational servitude is an expression of the notion that the determination whether a taking has occurred must take into consideration the important public interest in the flow of interstate waters that in their natural condition are in fact capable of supporting public navigation. Thus, in United States v. Chandler-Dunbar Co., supra, 229 U.S., at 69, 33 S.Ct., at 674, this Court stated that "the running water in a great navigable stream is [incapable] of private ownership * * *." And, in holding that a riparian landowner was not entitled to compensation when the construction of a pier cut off his access to navigable water, this Court observed:

"The primary use of the waters and the lands under them is for purposes of navigation, and the erection of piers in them to improve navigation for the public is entirely consistent with such use, and infringes no right of the riparian owner. Whatever the nature of the interest of a riparian owner in the submerged lands in front of his upland bordering on a public navigable water, his title is not as full and complete as his title to fast land which has no direct connection with the navigation of such water. It is a qualified title, a bare technical title, not at his absolute disposal, as is his upland, but to be held at all times subordinate to such use of the submerged lands and of the waters flowing over them as may be consistent with or demanded by the public right of navigation." Scranton v. Wheeler, 179 U.S. 141, 163, 21 S.Ct. 48, 57, 45 L.Ed. 126 (1900).

For over a century, a long line of cases decided by this Court involving Government condemnation of "fast lands" delineated the elements of compensable damages that the Government was required to pay because the lands were riparian to navigable streams. The Court was often deeply divided, and the results frequently turned on what could fairly be described as quite narrow distinctions. * * * [W]hen the Government acquires fast lands to improve navigation, it is not required under the Eminent Domain Clause to compensate landowners for certain elements of damage attributable to riparian location, such as the land's value as a hydroelectric site or a port site. But none of these cases ever doubted that when the Government wished to acquire fast lands, it was required by the Eminent Domain Clause of the Fifth Amendment to condemn and pay fair value for that interest. * * *

Here, the Government's attempt to create a public right of access to the improved pond goes so far beyond ordinary regulation or improvement for navigation as to amount to a taking * * *. More than one factor contributes to this result.[9] It is clear that prior to its improvement, Kuapa Pond was incapable of being used as a continuous highway for the purpose of navigation in interstate commerce. Its maximum depth at high tide was a mere two feet, it was separated from the adjacent bay and ocean by a natural barrier beach, and its principal commercial value was limited to fishing.[10] It consequently is not the sort of "great navigable stream" that this Court has previously recognized as being "[incapable] of private ownership." See, e.g., United States v. Chandler-Dunbar Co., 229 U.S., at 69, 33 S.Ct., at 674. And, as previously noted, Kuapa Pond has always been considered to be private property under Hawaiian law. Thus, the interest of petitioners in the now dredged marina is strikingly similar to that of owners of fast land adjacent to navigable water.

---

9. We do not decide, however, whether in some circumstances one of these factors by itself may be dispositive.

10. * * * Although Kuapa Pond clearly was not navigable in fact in its natural state, the dissent argue that the pond nevertheless was "navigable water of the United States" prior to its development because it was subject to the ebb and flow of the tide. This Court has never held, however, that whenever a body of water satisfies this mechanical test, the Government may invoke the "navigational servitude" to avoid payment of just compensation irrespective of the private interests at stake.

[W]hat petitioners now have is a body of water that was private property under Hawaiian law, linked to navigable water by a channel dredged by them with the consent of the Government. While the consent of individual officials representing the United States cannot "estop" the United States, it can lead to the fruition of expectancies embodied in the concept of "property"—expectancies that, if sufficiently important, the Government must condemn and pay for before it takes over the management of the landowner's property. In this case, we hold that the "right to exclude," so universally held to be a fundamental element of the property right, falls within this category of interests that the Government cannot take without compensation. This is not a case in which the Government is exercising its regulatory power in a manner that will cause an insubstantial devaluation of petitioners' private property; rather, the imposition of the navigational servitude in this context will result in an actual physical invasion of the privately owned marina. * * * Thus, if the Government wishes to make what was formerly Kuapa Pond into a public aquatic park after petitioners have proceeded as far as they have here, it may not, without invoking its eminent domain power and paying just compensation, require them to allow free access to the dredged pond while petitioners' agreement with their customers call for an annual $72 regular fee.

Accordingly the judgment of the Court of Appeals is reversed.

MR. JUSTICE BLACKMUN, with whom MR. JUSTICE BRENNAN and MR. JUSTICE MARSHALL join, dissenting.

* * * I believe the Court errs by implicitly rejecting the old and long-established "ebb and flow" test of navigability as a source for the navigational servitude the Government claims. * * * The Court begins by asking "whether * * * petitioners' improvements to Kuapa Pond caused its original character to be so altered that it became subject to an overriding federal navigational servitude." It thus assumes that the only basis for extension of federal authority must have arisen after the pond was "developed" and transformed into a marina. This choice of starting point overlooks the Government's contention, advanced throughout this litigation, that Kuapa pond was navigable water in its natural state, long prior to petitioners' improvements, by virtue of its susceptibility to the ebb and flow of the tide. * * *

I take it the Court must concede that, at least for regulatory purposes, the pond in its current condition is "navigable water" because it is now "navigable in fact." I would add that the pond was "navigable water" prior to development of the present marina because it was subject to the ebb and flow of the tide. * * *

Note

1. **Navigability for purposes of the navigation servitude.** *Kaiser Aetna* makes it clear that the test of navigability for purposes of the navigation servitude is not coextensive with the classical Commerce Clause concept of navigability, at least if the classical test is understood to include both waters that are navigable in fact for interstate commerce and waters that ebb and flow with the tide. Beyond that, *Kaiser Aetna* generates some difficult questions about the test of navigability for navigation servitude purposes.

Was the majority's implicit rejection of the ebb-and-flow test of navigability for servitude purposes based on unique facts in *Kaiser Aetna*, or was it a broader rejection that will apply in other fact situations? Earlier in the litigation, the federal district court said: "[I]f it were not for the unique legal status of Hawaiian fishponds such as Kuapa Pond as strictly private property, free and clear of any claim by the Crown either to the beds thereof or the waters thereon under Hawaiian law prior to annexation, and their protection then and thereafter as such by statute and Constitution, application of the ebb and flow test would have established a public right of access to Kuapa Pond." United States v. Kaiser Aetna, 408 F. Supp. 42, 50 (D. Haw. 1976). Was the Supreme Court referring to this statement when it said, without elaborating, "we do not fully agree with the reasoning of the District Court"?

If navigability for servitude purposes excludes at least some waters that ebb and flow with the tide, might it also exclude at least some waters that meet the navigable-in-fact branch of the classical Commerce Clause test? Justice Blackmun, in dissent in *Kaiser Aetna*, thought the majority would have to concede that Kuapa Pond had become navigable in fact under the classical test. If he was correct, the majority opinion stands for the proposition that not all waters navigable-in-fact in the classical Commerce Clause sense are navigable for purposes of the navigation servitude. But if that is so, which classically navigable-in-fact waters are subject to the servitude and which are not? Does the servitude apply to all waters that *prior to improvement* were capable of being used as continuous highways for navigation in interstate commerce? How much confusion is added by footnote 9 of the majority opinion?

2. **Private riverbed interests not deriving value from the use of or access to navigable water.** In United States v. Cherokee Nation, 480 U.S. 700 (1987), the tribe owned portions of the bed of the Arkansas River. Its submerged lands contained sand and gravel deposits that were damaged by federal navigation improvements to the river. The Tenth Circuit ruled that because the tribe's ownership interest, i.e., the sand and gravel deposits, was unrelated to any navigational use of the river, the no-compensation rule of the navigation servitude should not apply automatically, and instead a balancing of public and private interests should be used to determine whether just compensation must be paid. The Supreme Court reversed: "We think the Court of Appeals erred in formulating a balancing test to evaluate this assertion of the navigational servitude. No such 'balancing' is required where, as here, the interference with in-stream interests results from an exercise of the Government's power to regulate navigation uses of 'the deep streams which penetrate our country in every direction.' Gibbons v. Ogden, 9 Wheat. 1, 195, 6 L.Ed. 23 (1824)." Id. at 703. What, if anything, does *Cherokee Nation* do to *Kaiser Aetna*?

SPORHASE v. NEBRASKA EX REL. DOUGLAS

Supreme Court of the United States, 1982.
458 U.S. 941, 102 S. Ct. 3456, 73 L. Ed.2d 1254.

JUSTICE STEVENS delivered the opinion of the Court.

Appellants challenge the constitutionality of a Nebraska statutory restriction on the withdrawal of ground water from any well within Nebraska intended for use in an adjoining State. * * *

Appellants jointly own contiguous tracts of land in Chase County, Nebraska, and Phillips County, Colorado. A well physically located on the Nebraska tract pumps ground water for irrigation of both the Nebraska tract and the Colorado tract. Previous owners of the land registered the well with the State of Nebraska in 1971, but neither they nor the present owners applied for the permit required by § 46–613.01 of the Nebraska Revised Statutes. That section provides:

> "Any person, firm, city, village, municipal corporation or any other entity intending to withdraw ground water from any well or pit located in the State of Nebraska and transport it for use in an adjoining state shall apply to the Department of Water Resources for a permit to do so. If the Director of Water Resources finds that the withdrawal of the ground water requested is reasonable, is not contrary to the conservation and use of ground water, and is not otherwise detrimental to the public welfare, he shall grant the permit if the state in which the water is to be used grants reciprocal rights to withdraw and transport ground water from that state for use in the State of Nebraska."

Appellee brought this action to enjoin appellants from transferring the water across the border without a permit. The trial court rejected the defense that the statute imposed an undue burden on interstate commerce and granted the injunction. The Nebraska Supreme Court affirmed. It held that, under Nebraska law, ground water is not "a marketable item freely transferable for value among private parties, and therefore [is] not an article of commerce." * * *

I

In holding that ground water is not an article of commerce, the Nebraska Supreme Court and appellee cite as controlling precedent Hudson County Water Co. v. McCarter, 209 U.S. 349, 28 S.Ct. 529, 52 L.Ed. 828 (1908). [*Hudson County* held that a New Jersey statute prohibiting the transfer of water outside the state was not subject to the Commerce Clause under Geer v. Connecticut, 161 U.S. 519, 16 S.Ct. 600, 40 L.Ed. 793 (1896).]

* * * *Geer*, which sustained a Connecticut ban on the interstate transportation of game birds captured in that State, was premised on the theory that the State owned its wild animals and therefore was free to qualify any ownership interest it might recognize in the persons who capture them. One such restriction is a prohibition against interstate transfer of the captured animals. * * * In expressly overruling *Geer* three years ago, this Court traced the demise of the public ownership theory and definitively recast it as "'but a fiction expressive in legal shorthand of the importance to its people that a State have power to preserve and regulate the exploitation of an important resource.'" Hughes v. Oklahoma, 441 U.S. 322, 334, 99 S.Ct. 1727, 1735, 60 L.Ed.2d 250 (1979) (quoting Toomer v. Witsell, 334 U.S. 385, 402, 68 S.Ct. 1156, 1165, 92 L.Ed. 1460 (1948)). In *Hughes* the Court found the State's interests insufficient to sustain a ban on the interstate transfer of natural minnows seined from waters within the State.

Appellee insists, however, that Nebraska water is distinguishable from other natural resources. [W]ater, unlike other natural resources, is essential for human survival. Appellee, and the *amici curiae* that are vitally interested in conserving and preserving scarce water resources in the arid Western States, have convincingly demonstrated the desirability of state and local management of ground water. But the States' interests clearly have an interstate dimension. Although water is indeed essential for human survival, studies indicate that over 80% of our water supplies is used for agricultural purposes. The agricultural markets supplied by irrigated farms are worldwide. They provide the archetypical example of commerce among the several States for which the Framers of our Constitution intended to authorize federal regulation. The multistate character of the Ogallala aquifer—underlying appellants' tracts of land in Colorado and Nebraska, as well as parts of Texas, New Mexico, Oklahoma, and Kansas—confirms the view that there is a significant federal interest in conservation as well as in fair allocation of this diminishing resource.

The Western States' interests, and their asserted superior competence, in conserving and preserving scarce water resources are not irrelevant in the Commerce Clause inquiry. Nor is appellee's claim to public ownership without significance. Like Congress' deference to state water law, these factors inform the determination whether the burdens on commerce imposed by state ground water regulation are reasonable or unreasonable. But appellee's claim that Nebraska ground water is not an article of commerce goes too far: it would not only exempt Nebraska ground water regulation from burden-on-commerce analysis, it also would curtail the affirmative power of Congress to implement its own policies concerning such regulation. * * * Ground water overdraft is a national problem and Congress has the power to deal with it on that scale.

II

Our conclusion that water is an article of commerce raises, but does not answer, the question whether the Nebraska statute is unconstitutional. For the existence of unexercised federal regulatory power does not foreclose state regulation of its water resources, of the uses of water within the State, or indeed, of interstate commerce in water. Determining the validity of state statutes affecting interstate commerce requires a more careful inquiry:

> "Where the statute regulates evenhandedly to effectuate a legitimate local public interest, and its effects on interstate commerce are only incidental, it will be upheld unless the burden imposed on such commerce is clearly excessive in relation to the putative local benefits. If a legitimate local purpose is found, then the question becomes one of degree. And the extent of the burden that will be tolerated will of course depend on the nature of the local interest involved, and on whether it could be promoted as well with a lesser impact on interstate activities." Pike v. Bruce Church, Inc., 397 U.S. 137, 142, 90 S.Ct. 844, 847, 25 L.Ed.2d 174 (1970) (citation omitted).

The only purpose that appellee advances for § 46-613.01 is to conserve and preserve diminishing sources of ground water. The purpose is unquestionably legitimate and highly important, and the other aspects of Nebraska's ground water regulation demonstrate that it is genuine. Appellants' land in Nebraska is located within the boundaries of the Upper Republican Ground

Water Control Area, which was designated as such by the Director of the Nebraska Department of Water Resources based upon a determination "that there is an inadequate ground water supply to meet present or reasonably foreseeable needs for beneficial use of such water supply." Neb.Rev.Stat. § 46-658(1). Pursuant to § 46-666(1), the Upper Republican Natural Resources District has promulgated special rules and regulations governing ground water withdrawal and use. The rules and regulations define as "critical" those townships in the control area in which the annual decline of the ground water table exceeds a fixed percentage; appellants' Nebraska tract is located within a critical township. The rules and regulations require the installation of flow meters on every well within the control area, specify the amount of water per acre that may be used for irrigation, and set the spacing that is required between wells. They also strictly limit the intrastate transfer of ground water: transfers are only permitted between lands controlled by the same ground water user, and all transfers must be approved by the district board of directors.

The State's interest in conservation and preservation of ground water is advanced by the first three conditions in § 46-613.01 for the withdrawal of water for an interstate transfer. Those requirements are "that the withdrawal of the ground water requested is reasonable, is not contrary to the conservation and use of ground water, and is not otherwise detrimental to the public welfare." Although Commerce Clause concerns are implicated by the fact that § 46-613.01 applies to interstate transfers but not to intrastate transfers, there are legitimate reasons for the special treatment accorded requests to transport ground water across state lines. Obviously, a State that imposes severe withdrawal and use restrictions on its own citizens is not discriminating against interstate commerce when it seeks to prevent the uncontrolled transfer of water out of the State. An exemption for interstate transfers would be inconsistent with the ideal of evenhandedness in regulation. At least in the area in which appellants' Nebraska tract is located, the first three standards of § 46-613.01 may well be no more strict in application than the limitations upon intrastate transfers imposed by the Upper Republican Natural Resources District.

Moreover, in the absence of a contrary view expressed by Congress, we are reluctant to condemn as unreasonable measures taken by a State to conserve and preserve for its own citizens this vital resource in times of severe shortage. Our reluctance stems from the "confluence of [several] realities." Hicklin v. Orbeck, 437 U.S. 518, 534, 98 S.Ct. 2482, 2491, 57 L.Ed.2d 397 (1978). First, a State's power to regulate the use of water in times and places of shortage for the purpose of protecting the health of its citizens—and not simply the health of its economy—is at the core of its police power. For Commerce Clause purposes, we have long recognized a difference between economic protectionism, on the one hand, and health and safety regulation, on the other. Second, the legal expectation that under certain circumstances each State may restrict water within its borders has been fostered over the years not only by our equitable apportionment decrees, but also by the negotiation and enforcement of interstate compacts. Our law therefore has recognized the relevance of state boundaries in the allocation of scarce water resources. Third, although appellee's claim to public ownership of Nebraska ground water cannot justify a total denial of federal regulatory power, it may support a limited preference for its own citizens in the utilization of the resource. In this regard, it is relevant that appellee's claim is logically more substantial than claims to public ownership of other natural resources. Finally, given appellee's conservation efforts, the continuing availability of ground water in Nebraska is not simply happenstance; the natural resource has some indicia of a good publicly produced and owned in which a State may favor its own citizens in times of shortage. A facial examination of the first three conditions set forth in § 46-613.01 does not, therefore, indicate that they impermissibly burden interstate commerce. Appellants, indeed, seem to concede their reasonableness.

Appellants, however, do challenge the requirement that "the state in which the water is to be used grants reciprocal rights to withdraw and transport ground water from that state for use in the State of Nebraska"—the reciprocity provision that troubled the Chief Justice of the Nebraska Supreme Court. Because Colorado forbids the exportation of its ground water, the reciprocity provision operates as an explicit barrier to commerce between the two States. The State therefore bears the initial burden of demonstrating a close fit between the reciprocity requirement and its asserted local purpose.

The reciprocity requirement fails to clear this initial hurdle. For there is no evidence that this restriction is narrowly tailored to the conservation and preservation rationale. Even though the supply of water in a particular well may be abundant, or perhaps even excessive, and even though the most beneficial use of that water might be in another State, such water may not be shipped into a neighboring State that does not permit its water to be used in Nebraska. If it could be shown that the State as a whole suffers a water shortage, that the intrastate transportation of water from areas of abundance to areas of shortage is feasible regardless of distance, and that the importation of water from adjoining States would roughly compensate for any exportation to those States, then the conservation and preservation purpose might be credibly advanced for the reciprocity provision. A demonstrably arid state conceivably might be able to marshal evidence to establish a close means-end relationship between even a total ban on the exportation of water and a purpose to conserve and preserve water. Appellee, however, does not claim that such evidence exists. We therefore are not persuaded that the reciprocity requirement—when superimposed on the first three restrictions in the statute—significantly advances the State's legitimate conservation and preservation interest; it surely is not narrowly tailored to serve that purpose. The reciprocity requirement does not survive the "strictest scrutiny" reserved for facially discriminatory legislation.[18]

---

18. The reciprocity requirement cannot * * * be justified as a response to another State's unreasonable burden on commerce.

III

Appellee's suggestion that Congress has authorized the States to impose otherwise impermissible burdens on interstate commerce in ground water is not well founded. The suggestion is based on 37 statutes in which Congress has deferred to state water law, and on a number of interstate compacts dealing with water that have been approved by Congress. * * * Although the 37 statutes and the interstate compacts demonstrate Congress' deference to state water law, they do not indicate that Congress wished to remove federal constitutional constraints on such state laws. * * * In the instances in which we have found [congressional] consent [to otherwise impermissible burdens on interstate commerce], Congress' "'intent and policy' to sustain state legislation from attack under the Commerce Clause" was "'expressly stated.'" New England Power Co. v. New Hampshire, 455 U.S. [331], at 343, 102 S.Ct. [1096], at 1102 (quoting Prudential Ins. Co. v. Benjamin, 328 U.S. 408, 427, 66 S.Ct. 1142, 1153, 90 L.Ed. 1343 (1946).

The reciprocity requirement of Neb.Rev.Stat. § 46–613.01 violates the Commerce Clause. We leave to the state courts the question whether the invalid portion is severable. The judgment of the Nebraska Supreme Court is reversed and the case is remanded for proceedings not inconsistent with this opinion. It is so ordered.

Notes

1. **The negative commerce clause.** As *Sporhase* indicates, the Commerce Clause does more than grant Congress power to regulate interstate commerce. It also has a negative or dormant aspect that restricts the power of states to interfere with the national interest in interstate commerce even when Congress has not legislated on the subject. The effect of the negative commerce clause on state regulation of interstate water export is thoroughly analyzed in Richard S. Harnsberger et al., Interstate Transfers of Water: State Options After *Sporhase*, 70 Neb. L. Rev. 754 (1991).

2. **The *El Paso* cases.** The City of El Paso, Texas, sits below New Mexico's southern border. The city applied to the New Mexico State Engineer for 326 permits to appropriate 296,000 acre-feet of water annually from wells in New Mexico to serve a growing city population and to stimulate economic growth. The State Engineer denied all the applications under a New Mexico statute banning the interstate export of groundwater. New Mexico sought to defend the facially discriminatory statute by arguing that it was needed to avoid a projected statewide water shortage by the year 2020. New Mexico was relying, of course, on the *Sporhase* statement that a demonstrably arid state might be able to show a close fit between conserving and preserving water and a total ban on export. New Mexico's projected shortage was based on estimated water needs not just for public health and safety but also for a variety of economic activities. In City of El Paso v. Reynolds (*El Paso I*), 563 F. Supp. 379 (D.N.M. 1983), the court struck down the statute. It said that under *Sporhase*, "a state may discriminate in favor of its citizens only to the extent that water is essential to human survival. Outside of fulfilling human survival needs, water is an economic resource." Id. at 389.

While appeal of this decision was pending, the New Mexico Legislature repealed the statute banning export and enacted new legislation requiring a permit to appropriate underground water for export and use outside the state. The new legislation authorizes the State Engineer to issue a permit only if the proposed use would not impair existing water rights, would not be contrary to water conservation within the state, and would not be otherwise detrimental to the public welfare of New Mexico citizens. In applying these criteria, the legislation directs the State Engineer to consider six factors. The first four relate to water conditions within New Mexico—water supply, water demand, whether shortages exist, and the feasibility of transporting water from the proposed point of diversion to alleviate shortages within the state. The remaining two factors relate to water supply and demand conditions in the state of proposed export. In City of El Paso v. Reynolds (*El Paso II*), 597 F. Supp. 694 (D.N.M. 1984), El Paso argued that this legislation on its face violated the Commerce Clause. The court held, however, that requiring an exporter to meet the statutory conservation and public welfare criteria is not facially discriminatory because similar requirements apply to new appropriations for local use. And it said that comparing water supply and demand conditions in New Mexico with water supply and demand conditions in the importing state was a necessary step in applying the balancing test prescribed by *Sporhase.* "Simple economic protectionism" is still forbidden, said the court, but some burdens on commerce may be valid if outweighed by "non-economic local benefits."

The new legislation applies both to new appropriations for export and to transfers of existing appropriations from in-state to out-of-state use. El Paso sought permits to export water from four existing New Mexico wells to Texas. At the time of *El Paso II*, New Mexico allowed intrastate transfers if existing water rights would not be impaired; it did not subject intrastate transfers to the conservation and public welfare requirements applicable to interstate transfers. The *El Paso II* court held, therefore, that the portion of the new legislation dealing with transfers of existing appropriations was facially unconstitutional for imposing an extra burden on interstate transfers. The state legislature responded to *El Paso II* by adopting conservation and public welfare requirements for intrastate transfers, N.M. Stat. Ann. § 72-5-23.

After *El Paso I* and *II*, the New Mexico State Engineer invoked a completely different state statute to deny all the City of El Paso's applications. N.M. Stat. Ann. § 72-1-9 provides that a municipality cannot hold unused water rights in excess of its projected needs for the next forty years. The State Engineer found that El Paso's present water supply would meet its needs until 2020, which was forty years from the date of El Paso's applications. El Paso again sought review in federal court, asserting that the forty-year requirement unduly burdens interstate commerce. The parties ended the litigation, however, by a settlement in which El Paso withdrew its applications.

3. **Applicability of the negative Commerce Clause to new water rights for export.** The *El Paso* cases applied the negative Commerce Clause to both new appropriations and the transfer of existing appropriations. Soon thereafter, a narrower reading of *Sporhase* was urged in Frank J. Trelease, State Water and State Lines: Commerce in Water Resources, 56 U. Colo. L. Rev. 347, 351, 359 (1985): "*Sporhase* does not apply to the initial allocation of unappropriated water by the state to a person who seeks to put the water to future use; *Sporhase* deals

instead with the commerce that occurs when a person who owns a right to use water on land in one state transfers the water across the state line for use on land in a different state. When a state is doling out unappropriated water, it may place restraints upon itself; it may limit its grants of rights to develop its natural resources in such a way as to insure that at least the primary benefits of the first use are realized within the state. But further economic activity by the water user in the processing, sale, or transportation of goods or crops, or in the sale or transportation of water itself as a product, may not be regulated to keep the benefits of that activity within the state. Oil and gas captured and brought to the surface, netted shrimp, seined minnows, felled trees from state public land—all these things and creatures—were once 'natural resources,' free-roaming or at least unpossessed, subject to no private claim of ownership. All are now property in the hands of those who reduced them to possession or have acquired a property right to take them. The state has received the economic benefit from the activity that transferred them out of the public domain and into private hands, but it may not burden or prevent interstate commerce carried on by the owners of the appropriated things. *Sporhase* correctly adds water to this list."

The argument for distinguishing between the initiation of new water rights and the transfer of existing water rights was expanded in Frank J. Trelease, Interstate Use of Water—"Sporhase v. El Paso, Pike & Vermejo," 22 Land & Water L. Rev. 315 (1987). Both articles are critiqued in Douglas L. Grant, State Regulation of Interstate Water Export, in 4 Waters and Water Rights §§ 48.03(d) to -(d)(3) (Robert E. Beck ed., repl. vol. 2004).

4. **Congressional consent to state burdens on interstate commerce.** In Intake Water Co. v. Yellowstone River Compact Commission, 769 F.2d 568 (9th Cir. 1985), the water company planned a transbasin diversion of water from the Yellowstone River for use in Montana and North Dakota. The Yellowstone River Compact provides: "No waters shall be diverted from the Yellowstone River Basin without unanimous consent of all the signatory states." The compact was ratified by the three signatory states, and Congress enacted legislation consenting to it in accordance with the Compact Clause of the Constitution. The water company challenged the restriction as state action placing an unreasonable burden on interstate commerce. The court held that Congress' consent to the compact converted it into federal law and thus immunized it against attack under the negative Commerce Clause, which limits the power of the states but not of Congress.

SECTION 2. FEDERAL LEGISLATIVE PROGRAMS (AND PREEMPTION OF STATE LAW)

A. Licensing and Permitting of Nonfederal Projects

FIRST IOWA HYDRO-ELECTRIC COOPERATIVE v. FEDERAL POWER COMMISSION

Supreme Court of the United States, 1946.
328 U.S. 152, 66 S. Ct. 906, 90 L. Ed. 1143.

MR. JUSTICE BURTON delivered the opinion of the Court.

This case illustrates the integration of federal and state jurisdictions in licensing water power projects under the Federal Power Act. The petitioner is the First Iowa Hydro-Electric Cooperative, a cooperative association organized under the laws of Iowa with power to generate, distribute and sell electric energy. On January 29, 1940, pursuant to § 23(b) of the Federal Power Act, it filed with the Federal Power Commission a declaration of intention to construct and operate a dam, reservoir and hydro-electric power plant on the Cedar River, near Moscow, Iowa.

On April 2, 1941, it also filed with the Commission an application for a license, under the Federal Power Act, to construct an enlarged project essentially like the one it now wishes to build. The cost of the enlarged project is estimated at $14,600,000. It calls for an 8,300 foot earthen dam on the Cedar River near Moscow, an 11,000 acre reservoir at that point and an eight mile diversion canal to a power plant to be built near Muscatine on the Mississippi. * * *

The Cedar River rises in Minnesota and flows 270 miles southeasterly through Iowa to Moscow which is 10 miles west of the Mississippi. From there it flows southwesterly 29 miles to Columbus Junction where it joins the Iowa River and returns southeasterly 28 miles to the Mississippi. The proposed diversion will take all but about 25 c.f.s. of water from the Cedar River at Moscow. This will correspondingly reduce the flow in the Iowa River while the diverted water will enter the Mississippi at Muscatine, about 20 miles above its present point of entry at the mouth of the Iowa River. There are no cities or towns on the Cedar River between Moscow and Columbus Junction and the record indicates that the petitioner has options upon 98% of the riparian rights on the Cedar River in that area. * * *

* * * On November 4, 1941, the Commission granted the State of Iowa's petition to intervene and, since then, the State has opposed actively the granting of the federal license.

On January 29, 1944, after extended hearings, the Commission rendered an opinion including the following statements:

> "As first presented, the plans of the applicant for developing the water resources of the Cedar River were neither desirable nor adequate, but many important changes in design have been made. * * * The applicant has also agreed to certain modifications proposed by the Chief of Engineers of the War Department. The present plans call for a practical and reasonably adequate development to utilize the head and water available, create a large storage reservoir, and make available for recreational purposes a considerable area now unsuitable for such use, all at a cost which does not appear to be unreasonable. * * *

The Commission also expressly found that—

"The applicant has not presented satisfactory evidence, pursuant to § 9(b)[6] of the Federal Power Act, of compliance with the requirements of applicable laws of the state of Iowa requiring a permit from the State Executive Council to effect the purposes of a license under the Federal Power Act, and the pending application, as supplemented, should be dismissed without prejudice."

* * * The laws of Iowa which that State contends are applicable and require a permit from its Executive Council to effect the purposes of the federal license are all in Iowa Code Ann. §§ 7767-7796.1, constituting Chapter 363, entitled "Mill Dams and Races." Section 7767 of that chapter is alleged to require the issuance of a permit by the Executive Council of the State and is the one on which the Commission's order must depend. It provides:

"7767 Prohibition—permit. No dam shall be constructed, maintained, or operated in this state in any navigable or meandered stream for any purpose, or in any other stream for manufacturing or power purposes, nor shall any water be taken from such streams for industrial purposes, unless a permit has been granted by the executive council to the person, firm, corporation, or municipality constructing, maintaining, or operating the same."

To require the petitioner to secure the actual grant to it of a State permit under § 7767 as a condition precedent to securing a federal license for the same project under the Federal Power Act would vest in the Executive Council of Iowa a veto power over the federal project. Such a veto power easily could destroy the effectiveness of the federal act. It would subordinate to the control of the State the "comprehensive" planning which the Act provides shall depend upon the judgment of the Federal Power Commission or other representatives of the Federal Government. * * * For example, § 7776 of the State Code requires that "the method of construction, operation, maintenance, and equipment of any and all dams in such waters shall be subject to the approval of the executive council." This would subject to State control the very requirements of the project that Congress has placed in the discretion of the Federal Power Commission. A still greater difficulty is illustrated by § 7771. This states the requirements for a State permit as follows:

"7771 When permit granted. If it shall appear to the council that the construction, operation, or maintenance of the dam will not materially obstruct existing navigation, or materially affect other public rights, will not endanger life or public health, and *any water taken from the stream in connection with the project is returned thereto at the nearest practicable place* without being materially diminished in quantity or polluted or rendered deleterious to fish life, it shall grant the permit, upon such terms and conditions as it may prescribe." (Italics supplied.)

---

6. "Sec. 9. That each applicant for a license hereunder shall submit to the commission—

"(b) Satisfactory evidence that the applicant has complied with the requirements of the laws of the State or States within which the proposed project is to be located with respect to bed and banks and to the appropriation, diversion, and use of water for power purposes and with respect to the right to engage in the business of developing, transmitting, and distributing power, and in any other business necessary to effect the purposes of a license under this Act." 41 Stat. 1068, 16 U.S.C.A. § 802(b), 16 U.S.C.A. § 802(b).

This strikes at the heart of the present project. The feature of the project which especially commended it to the Federal Power Commission was its diversion of substantially all of the waters of the Cedar River near Moscow, to the Mississippi River near Muscatine. Such a diversion has long been recognized as an engineering possibility and as constituting the largest power development foreseeable on either the Cedar or Iowa Rivers. It is this diversion that makes possible the increase in the head of water for power development from a maximum of 35 feet to an average of 101 feet, the increase in the capacity of the plant from 15,000 kw. to 50,000 kw. and its output from 47,000,000 kwh. to 200,000,000 kwh. per year. It is this diversion that led the Federal Power Commission, on January 29, 1944, to make its favorable appraisal of the enlarged project in contrast to its unfavorable appraisal * * * of the smaller project. It is this feature that * * * gives the project its greatest economic justification.

If a state permit is not required, there is no justification for requiring the petitioner, as a condition of securing its federal permit, to present evidence of the petitioner's compliance with the requirements of the State Code for a state permit. Compliance with State requirements that are in conflict with federal requirements may well block the federal license. For example, compliance with the State requirement that the water of the Cedar River all be returned to it at the nearest practicable place would reduce the project to the small one which is classified by the Federal Power Commission as "neither desirable nor adequate." Similarly, compliance with the engineering requirements of the State Executive Council, if additional to or different from the federal requirements, may well result in duplications of expenditures that would handicap the financial success of the project. * * * On the other hand, there is ample opportunity for the Federal Power Commission, under the authority expressly given to it by Congress, to require by regulation the presentation of evidence satisfactory to it of the petitioner's compliance with any of the requirements for a State permit on the state waters of Iowa that the Commission considers appropriate to effect the purposes of a federal license on the navigable waters of the United States. This evidence can be required of the petitioner upon the remanding of this application to the Commission.

In the Federal Power Act there is a separation of those subjects which remain under the jurisdiction of the states from those subjects which the Constitution delegates to the United States and over which Congress vests the Federal Power Commission with authority to act. To the extent of this separation, the Act establishes a dual system of control. The duality of control consists merely of the division of the common enterprise between two cooperating agencies of Government, each with final authority in its own jurisdiction. The duality does not require two agencies to share in the final decision of the same issue. Where the Federal Government supersedes the state government there is no suggestion that the two agencies both shall have final authority. * * * A dual final authority, with a duplicate system of state permits and federal licenses required for each project, would be unworkable. "Compliance with the requirements" of such a duplicated system of licensing would be nearly as bad. Conformity to both standards would be impossible in some cases and probably difficult in most of them. * * *

The Act leaves to the states their traditional jurisdiction subject to the admittedly superior right of the Federal Government, through Congress, to regulate interstate and foreign commerce, administer the public lands and reservations of the United States and, in certain cases, exercise authority under the treaties of the United States. * * *

Sections 27 and 9 are especially significant in this regard. Section 27 expressly "saves" certain state laws relating to property rights as to the use of water, so that these are not superseded by the terms of the Federal Power Act. It provides:

> "Sec. 27. That nothing herein contained shall be construed as affecting or intending to affect or in any way to interfere with the laws of the respective States relating to the control, appropriation, use, or distribution of water used in irrigation or for municipal or other uses, or any vested right acquired therein." 16 U.S.C.A. §821.
>
> * * *

The effect of § 27, in protecting state laws from supersedure, is limited to laws as to the control, appropriation, use or distribution of water in irrigation or for municipal or other uses of the same nature. It therefore has primary, if not exclusive reference to such proprietary rights. The phrase "any vested right acquired therein" further emphasizes the application of the section to property rights. * * *

Section 9(b) does not resemble § 27. It must be read with § 9(a) and (c). The entire section is devoted to securing adequate information for the Commission as to pending applications for licenses. Where § 9(a) calls for engineering and financial information, § 9(b) calls for legal information. * * * It does not itself require compliance with any state laws. Its reference to state laws is by way of suggestion to the Federal Power Commission of subjects as to which the Commission may wish some proof submitted to it of the applicant's progress. The evidence required is described merely as that which shall be "satisfactory" to the Commission. The need for compliance with applicable state laws, if any, arises not from this federal statute but from the effectiveness of the state statutes themselves.

When this application has been remanded to the Commission, that Commission will not act as a substitute for the local authorities having jurisdiction over such questions as the sufficiency of the legal title of the applicant to its riparian rights, or as to the validity of its local franchises, if any, relating to proposed intrastate public utility service. Section 9(b) says that the Commission may wish to have "satisfactory evidence" of the progress made by the applicant toward meeting local requirements but it does not say that the Commission is to assume responsibility for the legal sufficiency of the steps taken. The references made in § 9(b) to beds and banks of streams, to proprietary rights to divert or use water, or to legal rights to engage locally in the business of developing, transmitting and distributing power neither add anything to nor detract anything from the force of the local laws, if any, on those subjects. In so far as those laws have not been superseded by the Federal Power Act, they remain as applicable and effective as they were before its passage.

The State of Iowa, however, has sought to sustain the applicability and validity of Chapter 363 of the Code of Iowa in this connection, on the ground that the Federal Power Act, by the implications of § 9(b), has recognized this chapter of Iowa law as part of a system of dual control of power project permits, cumbersome and complicated though it be. * * *

The inappropriateness of such an interpretation is apparent in the light of the circumstances which culminated in the passage of the Federal Water Power Act in 1920. The purposes of the Act were then so generally known as to have made such a restrictive interpretation impossible and a denial of it unnecessary. It was the outgrowth of a widely supported effort of the conservationists to secure enactment of a complete scheme of national regulation which would promote the comprehensive development of the water resources of the Nation, in so far as it was within the reach of the federal power to do so, instead of the piecemeal, restrictive, negative approach of the River and Harbor Acts and other federal laws previously enacted. * * *

The detailed provisions of the Act providing for the federal plan of regulation leave no room or need for conflicting state controls. * * * It is the Federal Power Commission rather than the Iowa Executive Council that under our constitutional Government must pass upon these issues on behalf of the people of Iowa as well as on behalf of all others.

We accordingly reverse the judgment of the court below with directions to remand the case to the Federal Power Commission for further proceedings in conformity with this opinion.

Notes

1. **Federal Power Act licensing criteria.** Key licensing criteria under the Federal Power Act (FPA) are set forth in sections 4(e) and 10(a). 16 U.S.C. §§ 797(e), 803(a). Section 4(e) authorizes the Commission to issue a license if it concludes a proposed hydroelectric project is "desirable and justified in the public interest for the purpose of improving or developing a waterway or waterways for the use or benefit of interstate or foreign commerce." A 1986 amendment provides that in making this public interest determination, "the Commission, in addition to the power and development purposes for which licenses are issued, shall give equal consideration to the purposes of energy conservation, the protection, mitigation of damage to, and enhancement of, fish and wildlife (including related spawning grounds and habitat), the protection of recreational opportunities, and the preservation of other aspects of environmental quality."

Section 10(a) requires that "the project adopted * * * shall be such as in the judgment of the Commission will be best adapted to a comprehensive plan for improving or developing a waterway or waterways for the use or benefit of interstate or foreign commerce, for the improvement and utilization of water-power development, for the adequate protection, mitigation, and enhancement of fish and wildlife (including related spawning grounds and habitat), and for other beneficial public uses, including irrigation, flood control, water supply, and recreational and other purposes referred to in section 4(e) * * *." The references in the latter part of section 10(a) to fish and wildlife, irrigation, flood control, water supply, and recreation were added in 1986.

The word "Commission" in sections 4(e) and 10(a) now refers to the Federal Energy Regulatory Commission (FERC). Congress abolished the Federal Power Commission and transferred its hydroelectric licensing functions to FERC in the Department of Energy Reorganization Act of 1977, 42 U.S.C. §§ 7171, 7172(a)(1)(A).

2. ***First Iowa* reaffirmed.** The Court reaffirmed *First Iowa* in California v. FERC, 495 U.S. 490 (1990). FERC issued a license for a hydroelectric project in California that required the licensee to maintain certain minimum streamflows for fish protection. The State Water Resources Control Board wanted to require the licensee to maintain substantially greater minimum flows for the fish. In rejecting California's argument that *First Iowa* should be overruled so that the state could require greater minimum flows, the Court stated:

"Were this a case of first impression, petitioner's argument based on [FPA § 27] could be said to present a close question. As petitioner argues, California's minimum stream flow requirement might plausibly be thought to 'relat[e] to the control, appropriation, use, or distribution of water used * * * for * * * other uses,' namely the generation of power or the protection of fish. * * * But the meaning of § 27 and the pre-emptive effect of the FPA are not matters of first impression. * * * We decline at this late date to revisit and disturb the understanding of § 27 set forth in *First Iowa*. * * * Adherence to precedent is, in the usual case, a cardinal and guiding principle of adjudication, and '[c]onsiderations of *stare decisis* have special force in the area of statutory interpretation, for here, unlike in the context of constitutional interpretation, the legislative power is implicated, and Congress remains free to alter what we have done.' Patterson v. McLean Credit Union, 491 U.S. 164, 172-73, 109 S.Ct. 2363, 2370, 105 L.Ed.2d 132 (1989). There has been no sufficient intervening change in the law, or indication that *First Iowa* has proved unworkable or has fostered confusion and inconsistency in the law, that warrants our departure from established precedent." Id. at 497-99.

3. **Preemption of state public interest review of appropriations for hydroelectric power generation.** In Sayles Hydro Associates v. Maughan, 985 F.2d 451 (9th Cir. 1993), the plaintiffs obtained a FPA license for a hydroelectric project in California but then encountered difficulty getting a state water right permit for the project. The State Water Resources Control Board refused to process Sayles Hydro's water permit application until it submitted what the court called "a shifting, expanding range of studies and reports" on how the project would affect recreation, aesthetics, archaeology, sport fishing, and cultural resources. The court interpreted *First Iowa* and California v. FERC, supra Note 2, to mean that the federal program occupies the field except for allowing the states under section 27 to "determine proprietary water rights." The court found that requiring the plaintiffs to provide the studies and reports to the State Board "has nothing to do with determining proprietary rights in water." It ruled that federal preemption barred the state requirements, explaining as follows: "[M]ost or all of the State Board's concerns were considered by the Federal Energy Regulatory Commission in granting the license, and conditions were imposed in the license to protect these multiple values. * * * There would be no point in Congress requiring the federal agency to consider the state agency recommendations on environmental matters and make its own decisions about which to accept, if the state agencies had the power to impose the requirements themselves." Id. at 456.

The State Water Resources Control Board argued the case was not ripe for the Ninth Circuit to decide because its water permit application process had not been completed, and ultimately its substantive permit requirements might not conflict with those in the federal license. The court responded that "the state process itself, regardless of the results, is preempted. * * * The hardship is the process itself. * * * Undue process may impose cost and uncertainty sufficient to thwart the federal determination that a power project should proceed."

In 1991, FERC issued a regulation requiring that every potential license applicant first "consult with the relevant Federal, State, and interstate resource agencies, including * * * the appropriate State water resource management agencies." 18 C.F.R. § 4.38(a)(1). The regulation provides further that unless the federal Office of Hydropower Licensing determines it is unnecessary, "a potential applicant must diligently conduct all reasonable studies and obtain all reasonable information requested by resource agencies * * * that are necessary for the Commission to make an informed decision regarding the merits of the application." § 4.38(c)(1). Suppose Sayles Hydro had not sought a FPA license until after this regulation became operative. Bearing in mind that FPA § 4(e) requires FERC to consider "the protection, mitigation, and enhancement of fish and wildlife (including spawning grounds and habitat), the protection of recreational opportunities, and the preservation of other aspects of environmental quality," supra p. 648, Note 1, could the State Water Resources Control Board have required that the studies and reports it desired be done for FERC?

4. **Relicensing.** FPA licenses cannot be issued for a period exceeding fifty years. When a license expires, the United States has the right to take over the project upon payment of the licensee's net investment. If the United States does not take over the project, FERC can issue a new license to the applicant whose proposal is "best adapted to serve the public interest," taking into account the requirements of section 10(a) and other specified considerations. The successful applicant may or may not be the existing licensee, and the new license may be partly or wholly for nonpower use. Insignificant differences in applications, however, must not result in the transfer of a project, and transfer requires the new licensee to compensate the old licensee for its net investment. 16 U.S.C. §§ 799, 807, 808(a), (f).

FERC has issued the following statement about relicensing:

"[G]enerally, when the license for a project expires, the Commission issues a new license to the existing licensee. However, * * * the Commission concludes that it has the legal authority to deny a new license at the time of relicensing if it determines that, even with ample use of its conditioning authority, no license can be fashioned that will comport with the statutory standard under section 10(a) of the Federal Power Act (the Act) and other applicable law. The Commission anticipates that, where existing projects are involved, license denial would rarely occur. * * * There may be instances where a new license can be fashioned, but the terms will not be acceptable to the licensee, and so the license will be rejected. This is most likely to occur where the licensee of an already marginal project is confronted with additional costs at relicensing that render the project uneconomic. The Commission concludes that this possibility will not preclude it from imposing the environmental (and other) conditions it deems appropriate to carrying out its responsibilities under the Act." Project Decommissioning at Relicensing—Policy Statement, 60 Fed. Reg. 339 (1995).

The determination of what will serve the public interest at relicensing is subject to the section 4(e) requirement, supra Note 1, that in addition to power and development purposes, the Commission must give equal consideration to fish and wildlife, recreational opportunities, and other aspects of environmental quality. Environmental groups have used this requirement to negotiate mitigation of environmental damage associated with a number of nonfederal hydropower projects up for relicensing. Bruce A. Driver, Western Hydropower: Changing Values/New Visions, Report to the Western Water Policy Review Advisory Commission 2-3, 9-10 (Aug. 1997).

5. **Small hydroelectric projects.** After the energy crisis of the 1970s, Congress enacted the Public Utilities Regulatory Policies Act of 1978 (PURPA) to stimulate electric power production by small generating facilities using various energy sources, including hydropower. The act empowers FERC to exempt from the licensing requirements (and some other requirements) of the FPA two kinds of hydropower projects. The first is "small hydroelectric power projects," defined for this purpose as projects with no more than five megawatts of capacity that are constructed at existing dams or that do not need any dam or impoundment because they utilize natural water features for head to generate electricity. 16 U.S.C. §§ 2705(d), 2708(a)(1), (b). The second is "conduit hydroelectric facilities" with a maximum capacity of fifteen megawatts (forty megawatts for certain state or municipal facilities). § 823a. A conduit hydroelectric facility is located on nonfederal land and generates electricity by using "only the hydroelectric potential of a manmade conduit, which is operated for the distribution of water for agricultural, municipal, or industrial consumption and not primarily for the generation of electricity," such as an irrigation canal. Id. FERC rules implement the statutorily authorized exemptions. 18 C.F.R. §§ 4.30(b)(2), (28), (29), 4.90-.96, 4.101-.108. To assure a market for power produced at small power projects and facilities, PURPA requires electric utilities to offer to purchase the power they produce at rates that are just and reasonable to their electricity consumers, are non-discriminatory, and do not exceed the incremental cost to the purchasing utility of alternative electric energy. 16 U.S.C. § 824a-3.

Is the owner of an exempt project or facility entitled to the preemptive effect of the Federal Power Act? In a conduit facility case, FERC said: "[T]he issuance of an exemption does not confer upon the exemptee any power to obtain the necessary water rights for the exempted project. Such water rights are therefore under the control of the administering states." Twin Falls Canal Co., 35 F.E.R.C. ¶ 62,104 (1986).

PUD NO. 1 OF JEFFERSON COUNTY v. WASHINGTON DEPARTMENT OF ECOLOGY

Supreme Court of the United States, 1994.
511 U.S. 700, 114 S. Ct. 1900, 128 L. Ed.2d 716.

JUSTICE O'CONNOR delivered the opinion of the Court.

[Petitioners, a city and a local public utility district, sought a Federal Power Act (FPA) license for a hydroelectric project on the Dosewallips River in the State of Washington. The river was subject to state water quality standards developed under federal Clean Water Act (CWA) § 303, 33 U.S.C.A. § 1313. Subsection 303(c)(2)(A) provides that state water quality standards "shall consist of the designated uses of the navigable waters involved and the water quality criteria for such waters based upon such uses." A state standard for certain rivers, including the Dosewallips, listed fish and wildlife habitat among the designated uses and also set out numerical water quality criteria for characteristics such as pH, temperature, and dissolved oxygen. Another state standard for all rivers declared an antidegradation policy calling for protection of existing beneficial water uses and disallowing degradation that would interfere with those uses. Petitioner's project as proposed would have greatly reduced the water flow in one stretch of the Dosewallips River. This in turn would have impaired salmon and steelhead habitat and degraded water quality.

CWA § 401, 33 U.S.C.A. § 1341, imposes a state certification requirement for federal licensing as follows:

> "(a) * * * Any applicant for a Federal license or permit to conduct any activity including, but not limited to, the construction or operation of facilities, which may result in any discharge into the navigable waters, shall provide the licensing or permitting agency a certification from the State in which the discharge originates or will originate * * * that any such discharge will comply with applicable provisions of sections 301, 302, 303, 306, and 307 of this Act. * * *
>
> "(d) * * * Any certification provided under this section shall set forth any effluent limitations and other limitations, and monitoring requirements necessary to assure that any applicant for a Federal license or permit will comply with any applicable effluent limitations and other limitations, under sections 301 or 302 of this Act, standard of performance under section 306 of this Act, or prohibition, effluent standard, or pretreatment standard under section 307 of this Act, and with any other appropriate requirement of State law set forth in such certification, and shall become a condition on any Federal license or permit subject to the provisions of this section."

The Washington Department of Ecology issued a certification for the project under § 401 that imposed a minimum streamflow requirement in order to protect the Dosewallips fishery and to comply with the statewide antidegradation policy. After challenging the minimum streamflow requirement in state court without success, petitioners obtained review by the United States Supreme Court.]

There is no dispute that petitioners were required to obtain a certification from the State pursuant to § 401. Petitioners concede that, at a minimum, the project will result in two possible discharges—the release of dredged and fill material during the construction of the project, and the discharge of water at the end of the tailrace after the water has been used to generate electricity. Petitioners contend, however, that the minimum stream flow requirement imposed by the State was unrelated to these specific discharges, and that as a consequence, the State lacked the authority under § 401 to condition its certification on maintenance of stream flows sufficient to protect the Dosewallips fishery.

If § 401 consisted solely of subsection (a), which refers to a state certification that a "discharge" will comply with certain provisions of the Act, petitioners' assessment of the scope of the State's certification authority would have considerable force. Section 401, however, also contains subsection (d), which expands the State's authority to impose conditions on the certification of a project. Section 401(d) provides that any certification shall set forth "any effluent limitations and other limitations * * * necessary to assure that *any applicant*" will comply with various provisions of the Act and appropriate state law requirements. (Emphasis added.) The language of this subsection contradicts petitioners' claim that the State may only impose water quality limitations specifically tied to a "discharge." The text refers to the compliance of the applicant, not the discharge. Section 401(d) thus allows the State to impose "other limitations" on the project in general to assure compliance with various provisions of the Clean Water Act and with "any other appropriate requirement of State law." * * * [Section] 401(d) is most reasonably read as authorizing additional conditions and limitations on the activity as a whole once the threshold condition, the existence of a discharge, is satisfied. * * *

Although § 401(d) authorizes the State to place restrictions on the activity as a whole, that authority is not unbounded. The State can only ensure that the project complies with "any applicable effluent limitations and other limitations, under section 301 or 302" or certain other provisions of the Act, "and with any other appropriate requirement of State law." The State asserts that the minimum stream flow requirement was imposed to ensure compliance with the state water quality standards adopted pursuant to § 303 of the Clean Water Act.

We agree with the State that ensuring compliance with § 303 is a proper function of the § 401 certification. Although § 303 is not one of the statutory provisions listed in § 401(d), the statute allows states to impose limitations to ensure compliance with § 301 of the Act. Section 301 in turn incorporates § 303 by reference. As a consequence, state water quality standards adopted pursuant to § 303 are among the "other limitations" with which a State may ensure compliance through the § 401 certification process. * * * Moreover, limitations to assure compliance with state water quality standards are also permitted by § 401(d)'s reference to "any other appropriate requirement of State law." We do not speculate on what additional state laws, if any, might be incorporated by this language. But at a minimum, limitations imposed pursuant to state water quality standards adopted pursuant to § 303 are "appropriate" requirements of state law. * * *

Having concluded that, pursuant to § 401, States may condition certification upon any limitations necessary to ensure compliance with state water quality standards or any other "appropriate requirement of State law," we consider whether the minimum flow condition is such a limitation. Under § 303(c)(2)(A), state water quality standards must "consist of the designated uses of the navigable waters involved and the water quality criteria for such waters based upon such uses." In imposing the minimum stream flow requirement, the State determined that construction and operation of the project as planned would be inconsistent with one of the designated uses of Class AA water, namely "[s]almonid [and other fish] migration, rearing, spawning, and harvesting." * * * The designated use of the river as a fish habitat directly reflects the Clean Water Act's goal of maintaining the "chemical, physical, and biological integrity of the Nation's waters." 33 U.S.C. § 1251(a). * * *

Petitioners assert, however, that § 303 requires the State to protect designated uses solely through implementation of specific "criteria." According to petitioners, the State may not require them to operate their dam in a manner consistent with a designated "use"; instead, say petitioners, under § 303 the State may only require that the project comply with specific numerical "criteria."

We disagree with petitioners' interpretation of the language of § 303(c)(2)(A). Under the statute, a water quality standard must "consist of the designated uses of the navigable waters involved *and* the water quality criteria for such waters based upon such uses." (Emphasis added.) The text makes it plain that water quality standards contain two components. We think the language of § 303 is most naturally read to require that a project be consistent with both components, namely the designated use and the water quality criteria. Accordingly, under the literal terms of the statute, a project that does not comply with a designated use of the water does not comply with the applicable water quality standards.

Consequently, pursuant to § 401(d) the State may require that a permit applicant comply with both the designated uses and the water quality criteria of the state standards. * * * A certification requirement that an applicant operate the project consistently with state water quality standards—i.e., consistently with the designated uses of the water body and the water quality criteria—is both a "limitation" to assure "compliance with * * * limitations" imposed under § 303, and an "appropriate" requirement of State law. * * *

The State also justified its minimum stream flow as necessary to implement the "antidegradation policy" of § 303. * * * EPA has promulgated regulations implementing § 303's antidegradation policy, a phrase that is not defined elsewhere in the Act. These regulations require States to "develop and adopt a statewide antidegradation policy and identify the methods for implementing such policy." 40 CFR § 131.12 (1992). * * * The State of Washington's antidegradation policy in turn provides that "[e]xisting beneficial uses shall be maintained and protected and no further degradation which would interfere with or become injurious to existing beneficial uses will be allowed." WAC 173-201-035(8)(a). The State concluded that the reduced streamflows would have just the effect prohibited by this policy. The Solicitor General, representing EPA, asserts, and we agree, that the State's minimum stream flow condition is a proper application of the state and federal antidegradation regulations * * *.

Petitioners also assert more generally that the Clean Water Act is only concerned with water "quality," and does not allow the regulation of water "quantity." This is an artificial distinction. In many cases, water quantity is closely related to water quality; a sufficient lowering of the water quantity in a body of water could destroy all of its designated uses, be it for drinking water, recreation, navigation or, as here, as a fishery. In any event, there is recognition in the Clean Water Act itself that reduced stream flow, i.e., diminishment of water quantity, can constitute water pollution. First, the Act's definition of pollution as "the man-made or man induced alteration of the chemical, physical, biological, and radiological integrity of water" encompasses the effects of reduced water quantity. 33 U.S.C. § 1362(19). This broad conception of pollution—one which expressly evinces Congress' concern with the physical and biological integrity of water—refutes petitioners' assertion that the Act draws a sharp distinction between the regulation of water "quantity" and water "quality." Moreover, § 304 of the Act expressly recognizes that water "pollution" may result from "changes in the movement, flow, or circulation of any navigable waters * * *, including changes caused by the construction of dams. 33 U.S.C. § 1314(f). This concern with the flowage effects of dams and other diversions is also embodied in the EPA regulations, which expressly require existing dams to be operated to attain designated uses.

Petitioners assert that two other provisions of the Clean Water Act, §§ 101(g) and 510(2), 33 U.S.C. §§ 1251(g) and 1370(2), exclude the regulation of water quantity from the coverage of the Act. Section 101(g) provides "that the authority of each State to allocate quantities of water within its jurisdiction shall not be superseded, abrogated or otherwise impaired by this chapter." 33 U.S.C. § 1251(g). Similarly, § 510(2) provides that nothing in the Act shall "be construed as impairing or in any manner affecting any right or jurisdiction of the States with respect to the waters * * * of such States." 33 U.S.C. § 1370. In petitioners' view, these provisions exclude "water quantity issues from direct regulation under the federally controlled water quality standards authorized in § 303."

This language gives the States authority to allocate water rights; we therefore find it peculiar that petitioners argue that it prevents the State from regulating stream flow. In any event, we read these provisions more narrowly than petitioners. Sections 101(g) and 510(2) preserve the authority of each State to allocate water quantity as between users; they do not limit the scope of water pollution controls that may be imposed on users who have obtained, pursuant to state law, a water allocation. In California v. FERC, 495 U.S. 490, 498, 110 S.Ct. 2024, 2029, 109 L.Ed.2d 474 (1990), construing an analogous provision of the Federal Power Act, we explained that "minimum stream flow requirements neither reflect nor establish 'proprietary rights'" to water. Moreover, the certification itself does not purport to determine petitioners' proprietary right to the water of the Dosewallips. In fact, the certification expressly states that a "State Water Right Permit (Chapters 90.03.250 RCW and 508-12 WAC) must be obtained prior to commencing construction of the project." The certification merely determines the nature of the use to which that proprietary right may be put under the Clean Water Act, if and when it is obtained from the State. Our view is reinforced by the legislative history of the 1977 amendment to the Clean Water Act adding § 101(g). See 3 Legislative History of the Clean Water Act of 1977 (Committee Print compiled for the Committee on Environment and Public Works by the Library of Congress), Ser. No. 95-14, p. 532 (1978) ("The requirements [of the Act] may incidentally affect individual water rights. * * * It is not the purpose of this amendment to prohibit those incidental effects. It is the purpose of this amendment to insure that State allocation systems are not subverted, and that effects on individual rights, if any, are prompted by legitimate and necessary water quality considerations").

[Petitioner's last argument is] that we should limit the State's authority to impose minimum flow requirements because FERC has comprehensive authority to license hydroelectric projects pursuant to the FPA. In petitioners' vew, the minimum flow requirement imposed here interferes with FERC's authority under the FPA.

The FPA empowers FERC to issue licenses for projects "necessary or convenient * * * for the development, transmission, and utilization of power across, along, from, or in any of the streams * * * over which Congress has jurisdiction." § 797(e). The FPA also requires FERC to consider a project's effect on fish and wildlife. §§ 797(e), 803(a)(1). In *California v. FERC*, we held that the California Water Resources Control Board, acting pursuant to state law, could not impose a minimum stream flow which conflicted with minimum stream flows contained in a FERC license. We concluded that the FPA did not "save" to the States this authority.

No such conflict with any FERC licensing activity is presented here. FERC has not yet acted on petitioners' license application, and it is possible that FERC will eventually deny petitioners' application altogether. Alternatively, it is quite possible, given that FERC is required to give equal consideration to the protection of fish habitat when deciding whether to issue a license, that any FERC license would contain the same conditions as the State § 401 certification. Indeed, at oral argument the Solicitor General stated that both EPA and FERC were represented in this proceeding, and that the Government has no objection to the stream flow condition contained in the § 401 certification.

Finally, the requirement for a state certification applies not only to applications for licenses from FERC, but to all federal licenses and permits for activities which may result in a discharge into the Nation's navigable waters. For example, a permit from the Army Corps of Engineers is required for the installation of any structure in the navigable waters which may interfere with navigation, including piers, docks, and ramps. Rivers and Harbors Appropriation Act of 1899, § 10, 33 U.S.C. § 403. Similarly, a permit must be obtained from the Army Corps of Engineers for the discharge of dredged or fill material, and from the Secretary of the Interior or Agriculture for the construction of reservoirs, canals and other water storage systems on federal land. See 33 U.S.C. §§ 1344(a), (e); 43 U.S.C. § 1761. We assume that a § 401 certification would also be required for some licenses obtained pursuant to these statutes. Because § 401's certification requirement applies to other statutes and regulatory schemes, and because any conflict with FERC's authority under the FPA is hypothetical, we are unwilling to read implied limitations into § 401. If FERC issues a license containing a stream flow condition with which petitioners disagree, they may pursue judicial remedies at that time.

In summary, we hold that the State may include minimum stream flow requirements in a certification issued pursuant to § 401 of the Clean Water Act insofar as necessary to enforce a designated use contained in a state water quality standard. The judgment of the Supreme Court of Washington, accordingly, is affirmed.

Notes

1. **State conditions unrelated to water quality.** Shortly after the Court decided *Jefferson County*, FERC declared in Tunbridge Mill Corp., 68 F.E.R.C. ¶ 61,078 (1994): "Section 401 authorizes states to impose only conditions that relate to water quality. To the extent that states include conditions that are unrelated to water quality, these conditions are beyond the scope of section 401 and are thus unlawful. We conclude that we have the authority to determine that such conditions do not become terms and conditions of the license we issue." Upon review of *Tunbridge Mill* and several related cases, the Second Circuit agreed that section 401(d) allows states to impose only conditions that relate to water quality. But the court ruled that "the Commission is bound by the language of § 401 to incorporate all state-imposed certification conditions into hydropower licenses and * * * the legality of such conditions can only be challenged by the licensee in a court of appropriate jurisdiction." American Rivers, Inc. v. FERC, 129 F.3d 99, 102 (2d Cir. 1997).

2. **FPA preemption and section 401 state certification.** The certifying agency in California for purposes of section 401 is the State Water Resources Control Board. Cal. Water Code § 13160. Sayles Hydro Associates v. Maughan, supra pp. 649-50, Note 3, held that Sayles Hydro's FPA license preempted the State Board when processing its water permit application from requiring studies and reports on how the project would affect recreation, aesthetics, archaeology, sport fishing, and cultural resources. If an essentially identical project were proposed today, could the State Board require as part of section 401 certification that studies be done on whether the project would impair water quality in ways that would harm recreation, aesthetics, and so on?

If the project would impair water quality in ways harmful to those values, could the State Board successfully impose section 401 certification conditions protecting them though FERC wants to license the project without the conditions? In *Tunbridge Mill*, supra Note 1, FERC said of *Jefferson County*: "The Court determined that there was no conflict between the state's action and the Commission's licensing authority under the FPA, because the Commission had not yet acted on the license application and might deny it altogether and, alternatively, because the Commission license might contain the same conditions as the state certification. Thus, the Court did not reach the issue of whether conditions that might otherwise be appropriate could be deemed unenforceable if they conflicted with our determination of the public interest under the FPA." In *American Rivers*, supra Note 1, the court said: "The Commission * * * argues that without the authority to reject state-imposed § 401 conditions its Congressionally mandated role under the FPA of ensuring comprehensive planning and development of hydropower would be undermined. * * * The CWA, however, has diminished [the FPA's] preemptive reach by expressly requiring the Commission to incorporate into its licenses state-imposed water-quality conditions." 129 F.3d at 107, 111.

3. **Other federal regulatory programs subject to section 401 state certification.** The penultimate paragraph of *Jefferson County* mentions three federal licensing and permitting programs in addition to the FPA that the Court assumed may trigger section 401 certification: (1) Rivers and Harbors Appropriation Act of 1899 (RHA) § 10, (2) 33 U.S.C. § 1344, which is CWA § 404, and (3) 43 U.S.C. § 1761, which is the Federal Land Policy and Management Act (FLPMA) § 501.

RHA § 10 reads: "The creation of any obstruction not affirmatively authorized by Congress, to the navigable capacity of any of the waters of the United States is prohibited; and it shall not be lawful to build or commence the building of any wharf, pier, dolphin, boom, weir, breakwater, bulkhead, jetty or other structures in any * * * navigable river, or other water of the United States, outside established harbor lines, or where no harbor lines have been established, except on plans recommended by the Chief of Engineers and authorized by the Secretary of the Army; and it shall not be lawful to excavate or fill, or in any manner to alter or modify the course, location, condition, or capacity * * * of the channel of any navigable water of the United States, unless the work has been recommended by the Chief of Engineers and authorized by the Secretary of the Army prior to beginning the same."

The first clause of section 10, running to the first semicolon, had an essentially identical predecessor in the Rivers and Harbors Act of 1890. The predecessor provision was used to enjoin construction of an irrigation dam in the nonnavigable upper reach of the Rio Grande in New Mexico. The dam would have appropriated the entire water flow at its location, thereby diminishing the flow downstream in the navigable reach of the river and impairing navigation. The Supreme Court said of the statute: "It is not a prohibition of any obstruction to the navigation, but any obstruction to the navigable capacity, and anything, wherever done or however done, within the limits of the jurisdiction of the United States which tends to destroy the navigable capacity of one of the navigable waters of the United States, is within the terms of the prohibition." The Court also said that a state's power to authorize the appropriation of water "is limited by the superior power of the General Government to secure the uninterrupted navigability of all navigable streams within the limits of the United States." United States v. Rio Grande Dam & Irrigation Co., 174 U.S. 690 (1899).

The third clause of RHA § 10, beginning after the second semicolon, was involved in *Kaiser Aetna*, supra p. 632. This clause overlaps with CWA § 404. It requires a Corps of Engineers permit to excavate, fill, or otherwise alter the channel of any navigable water of the United States, while section 404 requires a Corps of Engineers permit to discharge dredged or fill material into navigable waters. Permit applicants complete the same standard Corps of Engineers application form for section 10 and section 404. 33 C.F.R. § 325.1(a), (c). Section 10, however, applies only to waters that are navigable in the classical sense, see supra pp. 621-22, Note 2, while section 404 reaches more broadly, e.g., to wetlands abutting classically navigable waters. Another difference is that a section 404 permit application, unlike a section 10 application, must comply with guidelines developed by the Environmental Protection Agency (EPA) in conjunction with the Corps of Engineers. 33 U.S.C.A. § 1344(b).

Until 1968, the thrust of RHA § 10 as administered by the Corps was protection of navigation. Now the section 10 permit process involves broad public interest review in which the favorable and detrimental impacts on the public interest are considered. 33 C.F.R. § 320.1(a)(1). This is the same public interest review process required for section 404 permits that is described supra pp. 589-91, Note 2. Id. at § 320.1(a)(1).

Although the present materials deal with federal permitting and licensing of nonfederal projects, it might be noted that RHA § 10 and CWA § 404 permits generally are required as well for federal agency projects that are not specifically authorized by Congress. 33 C.F.R. §§ 322.3(c), 323.3(b).

The final of the three licensing and permitting programs mentioned in *Jefferson County*, FLPMA § 501, authorizes the Secretary of the Interior in the case of public lands, and the Secretary of Agriculture in the case of National Forest lands, to issue right-of-way permits through such lands for (among other things) reservoirs, canals, ditches, flumes, laterals, pipes, pipelines, tunnels, and other facilities for the impoundment, storage, transportation, or distribution of water.

4. **Federal licenses and permits not requiring section 401 state certification.** The issuance of a federal livestock grazing permit does not trigger section 401 state certification because the requirement is limited to point source discharges; it does not apply to runoff from nonpoint sources. Or. Natural Desert Ass'n v. Dombeck, 172 F.3d 1092 (9th Cir. 1998).

Although an application for relicensing under the FPA must be filed at least two years before a license expires, FPA § 15, 16 U.S.C. § 808, the relicensing proceeding might not be completed before expiration. When that happens, section 15 requires FERC to issue annual licenses to the holder of the expired license on the same terms as before until the relicensing decision is made. Since the FPA mandates this, section 401 state certification is not required for the annual licenses. Cal. Trout, Inc. v. FERC, 313 F.3d 1131 (9th Cir. 2002).

B. Construction and Management of Federal Projects

CALIFORNIA v. UNITED STATES

Supreme Court of the United States, 1978.
438 U.S. 645, 98 S. Ct. 2985, 57 L. Ed.2d 1018.

MR. JUSTICE REHNQUIST delivered the opinion of the Court.

The United States seeks to impound 2.4 million acre-feet of water from California's Stanislaus River as part of its Central Valley Project. The California State Water Resources Control Board ruled that the water could not be allocated to the Government under state law unless it agreed to and complied with various conditions dealing with the water's use. The Government then sought a declaratory judgment in the District Court for the Eastern District of California to the effect that the United States can impound whatever unappropriated water is necessary for a federal reclamation project without complying with state law. The District Court held that, as a matter of comity, the United States must apply to the State for an appropriation permit, but that the State must issue the permit without condition if there is sufficient unappropriated water. The Court of Appeals for the Ninth Circuit affirmed, but held that § 8 of the Reclamation Act of 1902, as amended, 43 U.S.C.A. §§ 372, 383, rather than comity, requires the United States to apply for the permit. We granted certiorari to review the decision of the Court of Appeals insofar as it holds that California cannot condition its allocation of water to a federal reclamation project. We now reverse. * * *

If the term "cooperative federalism" had been in vogue in 1902, the Reclamation Act of that year would surely have qualified as a leading example of it. In that Act, Congress set forth on a massive program to construct and operate dams, reservoirs, and canals for the reclamation of the arid lands in 17 western States. Reflective of the "cooperative federalism" which the Act embodied is § 8, whose exact meaning and scope are the critical inquiries in this case:

> "*[N]othing in this Act shall be construed as affecting or intended to affect or to in any way interfere with the laws of any States or Territory relating to the control, appropriation, use or distribution of water used in irrigation,* or any vested rights acquired thereunder, *and the Secretary of the Interior, in carrying out the provisions of this Act, shall proceed in conformity with such laws,* and nothing herein shall in any way affect any right of any State or of the Federal Government or of any landowner, appropriator, or user of water in, to or from any interstate stream or the waters thereof: Provided, That the right to use of water acquired under the provisions of this Act shall be appurtenant to the land irrigated, and beneficial use shall be the basis, the measure, and the limit of the right." 43 U.S.C.A. § 383 (emphasis added).

The New Melones Dam, which this litigation concerns, is part of the California Central Valley Project, the largest reclamation project yet authorized under the 1902 Act. The Dam, which will impound 2.4 million acre-feet of water of California's Stanislaus River, has the multiple purposes of flood control, irrigation, municipal use, industrial use, power, recreation, water quality control and the protection of fish and wildlife. The waters of the Stanislaus River that will be impounded behind the New Melones Dam arise and flow solely in California.

The United States Bureau of Reclamation, as it has with every other federal reclamation project, applied for a permit from the appropriate state agency, here the California State Water Resources Control Board, to appropriate the water that would be impounded by the Dam and later used for reclamation. After lengthy hearings, the State Board found that unappropriated water was available for the New Melones Project during certain times of the year. Although it therefore approved the Bureau's applications, the State Board attached 25 conditions to the permits. The most important conditions prohibit full impoundment until the Bureau is able to show firm commitments, or at least a specific plan, for the use of the water.[8] The State Board concluded that

---

8. Other conditions * * * require that a preference be given to water users in the water basin in which the New Melones Project is located; require storage releases to be made so as to maintain maximum and minimum chemical concentrations in the San Joaquin River and protect fish and wildlife; require the United States to provide means for the release of excess waters and to clear vegetation and structures from the reservoir sites; require the filing of additional reports and studies; and provide for access to the project site by the State Board and the public. Still other conditions reserve jurisdiction to the Board to impose further conditions

without such a specific plan of beneficial use the Bureau had failed to meet the California statutory requirements for appropriation. * * *

The history of the relationship between the Federal Government and the States in the reclamation of the arid lands of the western States is both long and involved, but through it runs the consistent thread of purposeful and continued deference to state water law by Congress. * * *

[R]eclamation of the arid lands began almost immediately upon the arrival of pioneers to the western States. Huge sums of private money were invested in systems to transport water vast distances for mining, agriculture, and ordinary consumption. Because a very high percentage of land in the West belonged to the Federal Government, the canals and ditches that carried this water frequently crossed federal land. In 1862, Congress opened the public domain to homesteading. Homestead Act of 1862, 12 Stat. 392. And in 1866, Congress for the first time expressly opened the mineral lands of the public domain to exploration and occupation by miners. Mining Act of 1866, 14 Stat. 251. Because of the fear that these Acts might in some way interfere with the water rights and systems that had grown up under state and local law, Congress explicitly recognized and acknowledged the local law:

> "[W]henever, by priority of possession, rights to the use of water for mining, agricultural, manufacturing, or other purposes, have vested and accrued, and the same are recognized and acknowledged by the local customs, laws, and the decisions of the courts, the possessors and owners of such vested rights shall be maintained and protected in the same." Mining Act of 1866, § 9, 14 Stat. 251, 253.

The Mining Act of 1866 was not itself a grant of water rights pursuant to federal law. Instead, as this Court observed, the Act was "a voluntary recognition of a preexisting right of possession, constituting a valid claim to its continued use." United States v. Rio Grande Dam & Irrig. Co., 174 U.S. 690, 705 (1899). Congress intended "to recognize as valid the customary law with respect to the use of water which had grown up among the occupants of the public land under the peculiar necessities of their condition." Basey v. Gallagher, 20 Wall. 670, 684 (1874).

In 1877, Congress took its first step towards encouraging the reclamation and settlement of the public desert lands in the West and made it clear that such reclamation would generally follow state water law. In the 1877 Desert Lands Act, 19 Stat. 377, Congress provided for the homesteading of arid public lands in larger tracts

> "by conducting water upon the same, within the period of three years [after filing a declaration to do so], *Provided however* that the right to the use of water by the person so conducting the same * * * shall not exceed the amount of water actually appropriated, and necessarily used for the purpose of irrigation and reclamation: *and all surplus water over and above such actual*

---

on the appropriations if necessary to protect the "beneficial use" of the water involved. Respondent did not challenge any of the conditions under state law, but instead filed the federal declaratory action that is now before us.

> *appropriation and use, together with the water of all lakes, rivers and other sources of water supply upon the public lands and not navigable, shall remain and be held free for the appropriation and use of the public for irrigation, mining and manufacturing purposes subject to existing rights.*" 19 Stat. 377 (emphasis added).

This Court has had an opportunity to construe the 1877 Desert Lands Act before. In California Oregon Power Co. v. Beaver Portland Cement Co., 295 U.S. 142 (1935), Justice Sutherland explained that, through this language, "[Congress] effected a severance of all waters upon the public domain, not theretofore appropriated, from the land itself." Id., at 158. The nonnavigable waters thereby severed were "reserved for the use of the public under the laws of the states and territories." Ibid. Congress' purpose was not to federalize the prior appropriation doctrine already evolving under local law. Quite the opposite:

> "What we hold is that following the act of 1877, if not before, all non-navigable waters then a part of the public domain became *publici juris,* subject to the plenary control of the designated states, including those since created out of the territories named, with the right in each to determine for itself to what extent the rule of appropriation or the common-law rule in respect of riparian rights should obtain. For since 'Congress cannot enforce either rule upon any state,' Kansas v. Colorado, 206 U.S. 46, the full power of choice must remain with the state. The Desert Land Act does not bind or purport to bind the states to any policy. It simply recognizes and gives sanction, in so far as the United States and its future grantees are concerned, to the state and local doctrine of appropriation, and seeks to remove what otherwise might be an impediment to its full and successful operation. See Wyoming v. Colorado, 259 U.S. 419, 465." Id., at 163-64.

* * *

It is against this background that Congress passed the Reclamation Act of 1902. * * *

From the legislative history of the Reclamation Act of 1902, it is clear that state law was expected to control in two important respects. First, and of controlling importance to this case, the Secretary would have to appropriate, purchase, or condemn necessary water rights in strict conformity with state law. According to Representative Mondell, the principal sponsor of the reclamation bill in the House, once the Secretary determined that a reclamation project was feasible and that there was an adequate supply of water for the project, "the Secretary of the Interior would proceed to make the appropriation of the necessary water *by giving the notice and complying with the forms of law of the State or Territory in which the waters were located.*" 35 Cong. Rec. 6678 (1902) (emphasis added). The Secretary of the Interior could not take any action in appropriating the waters of the state streams "which could not be undertaken by an individual or corporation if it were in the position of the Government as regards the ownership of its lands." H.R. Rep. No. 794, 57th Cong., 1st Sess., at 7B8. Thus, in response to the statement of an opponent to the bill that the Secretary would be allowed to condemn water even if in violation of state law, Representative Mondell briskly responded:

"Whereabouts does the gentleman find any such provision as he is arguing? Whereabouts in the bill is there anything that attempts to give the Federal Government any right to condemn or to take any water right or do anything which an individual could not do? Will the gentleman point out any place or any provision for the Federal Government to do anything that I could not do if I owned the public land?

"MR. RAY of New York. Do you say there is nothing in this bill that provides for condemnation?

"MR. MONDELL. *The bill provides explicitly that even an appropriation of water can not be made except under State law.*" 35 Cong. Rec. 6687 (1902) (emphasis added).

Second, once the waters were released from the dam, their distribution to individual landowners would again be controlled by state law. As explained by Senator Clark of Wyoming, one of the principal supporters of the reclamation bill in the Senate, "the control of the water after leaving the reservoirs shall be vested in the State and Territories through which such waters flow." Id., at 2222. * * * As Representative Sutherland, later to be a Justice of this Court, succinctly put it, "if the appropriation and use were not under the provisions of the State law the utmost confusion would prevail." Id., at 6770. Different water rights in the same State would be governed by different laws and would frequently conflict.[21]

For almost half a century, this congressionally mandated division between federal and state authority worked smoothly. No project was constructed without the approval of the Secretary of the Interior, and the United States through this official preserved its authority to determine how federal funds should be expended. But state laws relating to water rights were observed in accordance with the congressional directive contained in § 8 of the Act of 1902. In 1958, however, the first of two cases was decided by this Court in which private land owners or municipal corporations contended that state water law had the effect of overriding specific congressional directives to the Secretary of

---

21. Congress did not intend to relinquish total control of the actual distribution of the reclamation water to the States. Congress provided in § 8 itself that the water right must be appurtenant to the land irrigated and governed by beneficial use, and in § 5 Congress forbade the sale of reclamation water to tracts of land of more than 160 acres. * * *

In previous cases interpreting § 8 of the 1902 Reclamation Act, however, this Court has held that state water law does not control in the distribution of reclamation water *if* inconsistent with other congressional directives to the Secretary. We believe that this reading of the Act is also consistent with the legislative history and indeed is the preferable reading of the Act. Whatever the intent of Congress with respect to state control over the distribution of water, however, Congress in the 1902 Act intended to follow state law as to appropriation of water and condemnation of water rights. Under the 1902 Act, the Secretary of the Interior was authorized in his discretion to 'locate and construct' reclamation projects. As the legislative history of the 1902 Act convincingly demonstrates, however, if state law did not allow for the appropriation or condemnation of the necessary water, Congress did not intend the Secretary of the Interior to initiate the project. Subsequent legislation authorizing a specific project may by its terms signify congressional intent that the Secretary condemn or be permitted to appropriate the necessary water rights for the project in question, but no such legislation was considered by the Court of Appeals in its opinion in this case. That court will be free to consider arguments by the Government to this effect on remand.

the Interior as to the operation of federal reclamation projects. In Ivanhoe Irrigation District v. McCracken, 357 U.S. 275, 78 S.Ct. 1174, 2 L.Ed.2d 1313 (1958), the Supreme Court of California decided that California law forbade the 160-acre limitation on irrigation water deliveries expressly written into § 5 of the Reclamation Act of 1902, and that therefore, under § 8 of the Reclamation Act, the Secretary was required to deliver reclamation water without regard to the acreage limitation. Both the State of California and the United States appealed from this judgment, and this Court reversed it, saying:

> "Section 5 is a specific and mandatory prerequisite laid down by the Congress as binding in the operation of reclamation projects, providing that '[no] right to the use of water * * * shall be sold for a tract exceeding one hundred and sixty acres to any one landowner. * * * ' Without passing generally on the coverage of § 8 in the delicate area of federal-state relations in the irrigation field, we do not believe that the Congress intended § 8 to override the repeatedly reaffirmed national policy of § 5." 357 U.S., at 291-292.

Five years later, in City of Fresno v. California, 372 U.S. 627 (1963), this Court affirmed a decision of the United States Court of Appeals for the Ninth Circuit holding that § 8 did not require the Secretary of the Interior to ignore explicit congressional provisions preferring irrigation use over domestic and municipal use.[24]

Petitioners [State of California, State Water Resources Control Board, and its members] do not ask us to overrule these holdings, nor are we presently inclined to do so. Petitioners instead ask us to hold that a State may impose any condition on the "control, appropriation, use or distribution of water" through a federal reclamation project that is not inconsistent with clear congressional directives respecting the project. Petitioners concede, and the Government relies upon, dicta in our cases that may point to a contrary conclusion. Thus, in *Ivanhoe,* the Court went beyond the actual facts of that case and stated:

> "As we read § 8, it merely requires the United States to comply with state law when, in the construction and operation of a reclamation project, it becomes necessary for it to acquire water rights or vested interests therein.

---

24. "Section 9(c) of the Reclamation Project Act of 1939 * * * provides: 'No contract relating to municipal water supply or miscellaneous purposes * * * shall be made unless, in the judgment of the Secretary [of the Interior], it will not impair the efficiency of the project for irrigation purposes.' * * * It therefore appears clear that Fresno has no preferential rights to contract for project water, but may receive it only if, in the Secretary's judgment, irrigation will not be adversely affected." 372 U.S., at 630-631.

The Court also concluded in a separate portion of its opinion that "§ 8 does not mean that state law may operate to prevent the United States from exercising the power of eminent domain to acquire the water rights of others. * * * Rather, the effect of § 8 in such a case is to leave to state law the definition of the property interests, if any, for which compensation must be made." 372 U.S., at 630. Because no provision of California law was actually inconsistent with the exercise by the United States of its power of eminent domain, this statement was dictum. It also might have been apparent from examination of the congressional authorization of the Central Valley Project that Congress intended the Secretary to have the power to condemn any necessary water rights. We disavow this dictum, however, to the extent that it implies that state law does not control even where not inconsistent with such expressions of congressional intent.

> * * * We read nothing in § 8 that compels the United States to deliver water on conditions imposed by the State." 357 U.S. 275.

Like dictum was repeated in City of Fresno, 372 U.S., at 630, and in this Court's opinion in Arizona v. California, 373 U.S. 546, (1963), where the Court also said:

> "The argument that § 8 of the Reclamation Act requires the United States in the delivery of water to follow priorities laid down by state law has already been disposed of by this Court in Ivanhoe Irr. Dist. v. McCracken, * * * and reaffirmed in City of Fresno v. California * * *. Since § 8 of the Reclamation Act did not subject the Secretary to state law in disposing of water in [*Ivanhoe*], we cannot, consistently with *Ivanhoe,* hold that the Secretary must be bound by state law in disposing of water under the Project Act." Id., at 586-587.

While we are not convinced that the above language is diametrically inconsistent with the position of petitioners, or that it squarely supports respondent, it undoubtedly goes further than was necessary to decide the cases presented to the Court. *Ivanhoe* and *City of Fresno* involved conflicts between § 8, requiring the Secretary to follow state law as to water rights, and other provisions of Reclamation Acts that placed specific limitations on how the water was to be distributed. Here the United States contends that it may ignore state law even if no explicit congressional directive conflicts with the conditions imposed by the California State Water Control Board.

In *Arizona v. California*, the States had asked the Court to rule that state law would control in the distribution of water from the Boulder Canyon Project, a massive multistate reclamation project on the Colorado river. After reviewing the legislative history of the Boulder Canyon Project Act, 43 U.S.C.A. § 617 *et seq.*, the Court concluded that because of the unique size and multistate scope of the Project, Congress did not intend the States to interfere with the Secretary's power to determine with whom and on what terms water contracts would be made. While the Court in rejecting the States' claim repeated the language from *Ivanhoe* and *City of Fresno* as to the scope of § 8, there was no need for it to reaffirm such language except as it related to the singular legislative history of the Boulder Canyon Project Act.

But because there is at least tension between the above quoted dictum and what we conceive to be the correct reading of § 8 of the Reclamation Act of 1902, we disavow the dictum to the extent that it would prevent petitioner from imposing conditions on the permits granted to the United States which are not inconsistent with congressional provisions authorizing the project in question. Section 8 cannot be read to require the Secretary to comply with state law only when it becomes necessary to purchase or condemn vested water rights. That section does, of course provide for the protection of vested water rights, but it also requires the Secretary to comply with state law in the "control, appropriation, use, or distribution of water." * * * The legislative history of the Reclamation Act of 1902 makes it abundantly clear that Congress intended to defer to the substance, as well as the form, of state water law. The Government's interpretation would trivialize the broad language and purpose of § 8. * * *

Because the District Court and the Court of Appeals both held that California could not impose any conditions whatever on the United States' appropriation permits, those courts did not reach the United States' alternative contention that the conditions actually imposed are inconsistent with congressional directives as to the New Melones Project. Nor did they reach California's contention that the United States is barred by principles of collateral estoppel from challenging the consistency of the permit conditions. Assuming, *arguendo,* that the United States is still free to challenge the consistency of the conditions, resolution of their consistency may well require additional fact-finding. We therefore reverse the judgment of the Court of Appeals and remand for further proceedings consistent with this opinion. * * *

MR. JUSTICE WHITE, with whom MR. JUSTICE BRENNAN and MR. JUSTICE MARSHALL join, dissenting. * * *

[The majority has] concluded that because of § 8, the United States may not acquire water rights by appropriation or condemnation except in accordance with state law. If, for example, particular water rights are not subject to condemnation under state law by private interests, neither may they be taken by the United States. This issue, going to the acquisition by the United States of water rights by eminent domain, is not among the questions presented in this case, and the views expressed in this respect are no sounder and no less inconsistent with our prior cases than is the majority's view that the distribution of water developed by federal reclamation projects is to be governed by state law.

* * *

The short of the matter is that no case in this Court, until this one, has construed § 8 as the present majority insists that it be construed. All of the relevant cases are to the contrary. * * *

Although I do not join the Court in reconstruing the controlling statutes as it does, the Court's work today is a precedent for "setting things right" in the area of statutory water law so as to satisfy the views of a current Court majority. And surely the dicta with which the Court's opinion is laced today deserve no more or no less respect than what it has chosen to label as dicta in past Court decisions. Of course, the matter is purely statutory and Congress could easily put an end to our feuding if it chose to make it clear that local authorities are to control the spending of federal funds for reclamation projects and to control the priorities for the use of water developed by federal projects.

Notes

1. **References in California v. United States.** As the Court's references to the Secretary of the Interior imply, the Bureau of Reclamation is an agency within the Department of the Interior.

The majority opinion found Arizona v. California to be of little precedential value because it involved a federal water project of unique size and multistate scope. This case is the same Arizona v. California reprinted in part supra p. 494, where the Court addressed the allocation of lower Colorado River water among California, Arizona, and Nevada. In a portion of the opinion not included earlier, the Court ruled that state law would not control the distribution of project water to users: "All this vast interlocking machinery—a dozen major works delivering water according to congressionally fixed priorities for home, agricultural, and industrial uses to people spread over thousands of square miles—could function efficiently only under unitary management, able to formulate and supervise a coordinated plan that could take account of the diverse, often conflicting interests of the people and communities of the Lower Basin States. * * * Subjecting the Secretary to the varying, possibly inconsistent, commands of the different state legislatures could frustrate efficient operation of the project and thwart full realization of the benefits Congress intended this national project to bestow." 373 U.S. at 589-90.

Amy K. Kelley, Staging a Comeback—Section 8 of the Reclamation Act, 18 U.C. Davis L. Rev. 97 (1984), provides an exhaustive and perceptive review of California v. United States, its predecessor cases, its subsequent history, and its progeny.

2. **The Reclamation Act and the Federal Power Act contrasted regarding preemption.** In *First Iowa*, supra p. 643, the Court gave FPA § 27 extremely limited effect in saving state law from federal preemption. In the principal case, California v. United States, the Court gave Reclamation Act § 8 much greater effect in saving state law from federal preemption. More recently, in California v. FERC, supra p. 649, Note 2, California pointed out that FPA § 27 and Reclamation Act § 8 are similarly worded state-law savings clauses, and it argued that the expansive view of Reclamation Act § 8 taken in California v. United States should require abandonment of the narrow view of FPA § 27 taken previously in *First Iowa*. The Court reaffirmed *First Iowa*, however, giving the following explanation: "[A]s in *First Iowa*, the Court in *California v. United States* examined the purpose, structure, and legislative history of the entire statute before it and employed those sources to construe the statute's saving clause. Those sources indicate, of course, that the FPA envisioned a considerably broader and more active federal oversight role in hydropower development than did the Reclamation Act." 459 U.S. at 504.

3. **Federal versus state control of water—should "ownership" matter?** In the principal case, the Court noted that California Oregon Power Co. v. Beaver Portland Cement Co. relied on congressional severance of water from public domain land as the basis for state jurisdiction over water rights. The severance concept explains the source of state jurisdiction if the federal government started out "owning" all waters in the western states as an incident of its ownership of the public domain.

Major John Wesley Powell, famous explorer of the West and Director of the U.S. Geological Survey, recommended to Congress a system of federal grants of water rights coupled with reform of the federal system for disposal of the land in the public domain. Report on the Lands of the Arid Regions of the United States (1879). His proposals were never enacted.

Meanwhile the western states claimed "ownership" of the waters within their borders and argued that the United States should be subject to state control whenever it engages in water resources development activities, under federal reclamation law or otherwise. Merrill v. Bishop, 287 P.2d 620 (Wyo. 1955); National

Reclamation Assoc., Preservation of Integrity of State Water Laws (1942). Some logical and historical fallacies of this position were explored in Frank J. Trelease, Government Ownership and Trusteeship of Water, 45 Cal. L. Rev. 638 (1957), and Note, Federal-State Conflicts Over the Control of Western Waters, 60 Colum. L. Rev. 967 (1960), and it seems to have been completely demolished by B. Abbott Goldberg, Interposition—Wild West Water Style, 17 Stan. L. Rev. 1 (1964), and Eva H. Morreale, Federal-State Conflicts over Western Waters—A Decade of Attempted "Clarifying Legislation," 20 Rutgers L. Rev. 423 (1966).

Is the "ownership" concept useful in analyzing and resolving federal-state jurisdictional conflicts involving water? Consider the following:

"Better results can be reached by sticking to what the Supreme Court has said—that the [federal] government had power to dispose of the water. It had that power in 1802, when Ohio became the first state created out of the public domain, but it did not exercise it. Congress might have adopted a federal water law for disposing of water rights as it enacted laws to dispose of the lands, but it did not do so. As the western public lands states were born, they took over the function of establishing water rights by common law and statutes, as had been done in the original thirteen states in which there was no public domain. * * * They did what all states had always done, exercised what the Supreme Court has called their 'traditional jurisdiction' over water. There is no evidence that the legislators or courts of any state from Ohio to California had any thought that they were dealing with water that belonged to the federal government until California's 1886 mistake [in assuming that was so in Lux v. Haggin, 10 P. 674 (Cal. 1886)]. The states filled the vacuum left by federal inaction, and the United States gave its sanction by its 'silent acquiescence,' which means that Congress gave the matter no thought either.

"The holding of [California Oregon Power Co. v. Beaver Portland Cement Co.] gave the western states the rule they had always hoped was law, that each could decide the form of its own water law. Nevertheless, the grounds on which the decision was rested left uneasy doubts as to its universal application. The Court's use of the Desert Land Act in its reasoning creates several difficulties. The act did not cover all the appropriation law states, for it had no force in Kansas, Nebraska and Oklahoma, and it was not applied to Colorado until amended in 1891. The proviso excepts from its operation navigable waters, but surely this could not mean that landowners along the Missouri River in Montana have federal riparian rights. That state recognizes no such rights and inconceivable chaos would result if such rights were held to exist by virtue of federal law. The Act was passed in 1877 and if it in that year severed the water from the federal lands and patents, this could be taken as an indication that patents granted before its enactment did carry riparian rights. Such a ruling would raise havoc with the water law systems of all of the Colorado doctrine states. The Court did leave a way out of this construction by saying that the severance occurred in 1877 'if not before,' and it is commonly supposed that the reference is to the Act of 1866. This is only a less unsatisfactory solution, because much land had been patented in the Colorado doctrine states before that date. Only if 'if not before' refers back to the beginning of state and territorial governments and if each state or territory had from the beginning the right to determine for itself the law of water rights, can the *Beaver* holding be sustained on the reasoning of a severance. And if that is done, we are back to the original proposition here proposed, that the state laws have validity not because of an act of Congress but because of the 'silent acquiescence' of the federal government. Water law was the subject of concurrent federal and state jurisdiction. The states could exercise their traditional jurisdiction unless their laws were superseded by a federal law disposing of the water. Since the federal government never enacted such a law, the state law stood." Frank J. Trelease, Federal-State Relations in Water Law, Nat'l Water Comm'n, Legal Study No. 5, at 147b, 147g-147h (1971).

4. **Origin and evolution of federal reclamation law.** Frank J. Trelease, Reclamation Water Rights, 32 Rocky Mtn. L. Rev. 464, 465 (1960):

"The Carey Act of 1894 was the first attempt of the national government to assume an active role in the development of western irrigation. It placed a million acres at the disposal of each participating state that would build (or cause to be built by private capital) large irrigation works and would sell the lands to settlers in tracts of 160 acres. However, the Carey Act was substantially a failure. Few projects were built and on most of them the settlers found themselves in severe financial difficulties resulting from the heavy mortgages placed upon the lands to secure repayment of the cost of construction of the irrigation works.

"The Reclamation Act [of 1902] marked a departure from this pattern of private development. Since the need for large dams and canals was not being fully met by private capital, the act introduced federal financing of projects. A revolving fund was established with moneys received from the sale of public lands, and the Secretary of the Interior was directed to survey the west and locate and construct irrigation projects, opening up the improved public lands to settlement under the homestead laws. * * * Construction costs were to be repaid into the fund by the settlers and landowners in ten annual installments without interest.

"This basic statute has been amended, supplemented, and superseded by a long series of acts, some general in nature, some relating to specific projects. * * * Nowadays the Bureau of Reclamation builds multipurpose projects which include features for production of hydroelectric power, control of floods, navigation improvement, municipal and industrial water supplies, recreation, and fish and wildlife preservation, as well as for irrigation. Projects now encompass the comprehensive development of entire river basins. The revolving fund was long ago exhausted and today's projects are built with general funds. Repayment periods have been stretched out."

One of the acts supplementing the Reclamation Act of 1902 is the Reclamation Project Act of 1939, as amended, 43 U.S.C. §§ 485-485k. It authorizes the construction of multipurpose water projects, provides for allocating project costs to the various purposes undertaken, and makes costs allocated to navigation and flood control nonreimbursable. Costs allocated to the preservation and propagation of fish and wildlife are made nonreimbursable by the Fish and Wildlife Coordination Act, 16 U.S.C. §§ 661-666c. Costs allocated to power and to irrigation and municipal and industrial water supply are reimbursable. They are to be repaid to the United States from net power revenues and by the water users. Costs allocated to irrigation but beyond the irrigators' ability to pay are assigned for repayment from revenues received for power and municipal water supply.

The Colorado River Storage Project Act, 43 U.S.C. §§ 620-620o, authorizes several major dams and a number of "participating projects" in Upper Basin states. The large dams are for storage to meet the water delivery requirements to Lower

Basin states under the Colorado River Compact and to produce power. The participating projects in Upper Basin states are primarily for irrigation and municipal and industrial supply. A basin fund is created that in effect permits the use of power revenues exceeding the return of costs allocated to power to be used for reimbursement of the costs of the participating projects. These funds are assigned for use in the states of the Upper Basin in proportion to the amount of flow of the river arising in each state.

5. **Reclamation law subsidies to irrigators.** The subsidies to irrigators served by federal reclamation projects were described as follows in Nat'l Water Comm'n, Water Policies for the Future 128 (1973):

"A primary weakness of the Federal water resources development projects is that they have been heavily subsidized by the Federal Government; that is, by all the taxpayers of the Nation, to provide benefits for a few. The water users on some modern Federal Reclamation projects, for example, repay no more than 10 percent of the construction costs attributable to irrigation, the remaining cost being borne by the Federal Government in three ways: by not requiring the water users to reimburse the Treasury for the interest on the capital advanced for project construction, by permitting power revenues and sometimes other nonirrigation revenues to be credited toward irrigation reimbursement, and by allocating an unduly large part of the costs to nonreimbursable purposes."

As of 1994, the Bureau of Reclamation was managing repayment of reimbursable construction costs for 133 projects that supply water for irrigation. The total cost of these projects was $21.8 billion. The total reimbursable costs were $16.9 billion, including $7.1 billion for irrigation. Of the $7.1 billion allocated to irrigation, $3.4 billion was shifted to other project beneficiaries for repayment, primarily power consumers. The irrigators' repayment obligation was further decreased through charge offs granted by specific legislation. As a result, the repayment obligation of irrigators has been reduced to $3.4 billion—or only 47 percent of the construction costs allocated to irrigation. U.S. Gen. Accounting Office, Bureau of Reclamation: Information on Allocation and Repayment of Costs of Constructing Water Projects (1996).

6. **Acreage limitations.** President Theodore Roosevelt conceived of the Reclamation Act of 1902 as reopening the American frontier—giving a new wave of settlers the opportunity to "go West," settle on family-sized farms, and continue the "agrarian myth" that America's strength lay in its rural population. Consequently, section 5 of the Act provided that no right to the use of water would be sold for land in excess of 160 acres in one ownership.

The Omnibus Adjustment Act of 1926 ended contracts with individual settlers and water user associations and instead required the United States to enter into contracts with irrigation districts—quasi-governmental agencies that would distribute water to eligible landowners, collect charges for water and for operation and maintenance, and reimburse the United States for the allocated costs of construction of the project. The districts were required by the contracts to withhold project water from private land in excess of 160 acres in one ownership unless the owner executed a recordable contract with the Secretary of the Interior obligating the owner to sell the excess land at a price excluding incremental value attributable to the availability of project water. By administrative interpretation, landowners who executed recordable contracts to sell their excess land within ten years were allowed to receive project water for the excess land in the meantime. An owner with excess land had the choice of keeping all the land, with only its pre-project water, if any, or instead using all the land for the next ten years with a full supply of project water and then selling the excess.

On a number of projects, water users in financial straits received dispensations and extensions allowing irrigated excess lands to remain in their hands for long periods. The acreage limitation was held inapplicable to certain lands in the Imperial Valley of California supplied by Boulder Canyon Project water. Bryant v. Yellen, 447 U.S. 352 (1980). More generally, the Bureau of Reclamation treated only owned land as subject to the 160-acre limitation, and many large farms operated through leasing, trust, and multiple-ownership arrangements. This led to calls for stricter enforcement of the acreage limitation. In some areas, notably the Central Valley of California, large corporate farms and agribusinesses responded by challenging the "family farm" as an uneconomic unit for the production of food and other agricultural products. After years of debate and trial balloons, Congress finally passed the Reclamation Reform Act of 1982 (RRA), 43 U.S.C. §§ 390aa to 390zz-1, which made major changes in reclamation law, including the acreage limitation.

The RRA distinguishes between qualified recipients and limited recipients of project water. A qualified recipient is an individual (including a spouse and other dependents) or a legal entity benefiting twenty-five persons or less. § 390bb(7). A limited recipient is a legal entity benefiting more than twenty-five persons. § 390bb(9).

A qualified recipient can receive project water for no more than 960 acres of owned land, unless the land in excess of that is subject to a recordable contract to sell it. In addition, a qualified recipient can receive project water for an unlimited amount of leased land if the lease term, including exercisable options, does not exceed ten years (twenty-five years if the land is used for perennial crops). But a qualified recipient can get water at a subsidized price for no more than 960 acres of land, whether owned or leased, and must pay full cost for any additional leased acres. §§ 390bb(6), 390dd, 390ee, 390yy. A limited recipient can receive project water for up to 640 acres of owned land and for additional leased land. But a limited recipient can get water at a subsidized price for no more than 320 acres, and then only if the entity was receiving water before October 1, 1981. A limited recipient must pay full cost for all other water received. § 390ee.

The acreage limitations are based on the best lands, called Class I lands. Larger acreages are allowed for farmers with less productive lands to give them the equivalent of Class I lands. §§ 390dd, 390gg. For repayment contracts predating the RRA, the acreage limitations do not apply after the repayment obligation is discharged. The subsidized water price continues under the RRA to be based on the ability of the irrigators to pay, but for contracts made or amended after the date of the RRA, the price must at least cover all operation and maintenance costs (which often was not the case under old contracts). § 390hh. "Full cost" is a price fixed to amortize construction costs and accumulated operation and maintenance deficits, with interest based on market rates; in addition, current operation and maintenance costs must be paid. § 390bb(3). Recordable contracts to sell excess lands entered into after the date of the RRA must require their sale within five years, rather than ten years as was customary previously. §§ 390ii, 390mm. Detailed regulations implementing the RRA appear at 43 C.F.R. pt. 426.

A provision in the RRA, known as the "hammer clause," gave districts with existing contracts five years to decide whether to amend their contracts to be governed by the new law, thus gaining the benefits of the higher acreage limits but losing any old contract right to pay less than actual operation and maintenance charges. Districts that elected not to amend are subject to the prior law, and any water delivered to land in excess of 160 acres, *including leased land*, is charged at full cost. A qualified or limited recipient in a district that elected not to amend its contract could elect individually to be governed by the new law. 43 U.S.C. § 390cc.

7. **The Central Valley Project Improvement Act (CVPIA).** A decade after the RRA, Congress dramatically reshaped reclamation policy in the CVPIA, which is Title XXXIV of the Reclamation Projects Authorization and Adjustment Act of 1992, Pub. L. No. 102-575, 106 Stat. 4600, 4706. The CVPIA addresses concerns of environmentalists who had long complained of environmental damage caused by the Central Valley Project (CVP) in California. Although the Act applies only to the CVP, it is important both because of the massive size of that project and because it may signal a trend toward greater environmental sensitivity in the operation of reclamation projects throughout the West as well as changes in reclamation policy related to conservation, water pricing, and transfers.

Although the CVPIA has several stated purposes, its primary overall goal is environmental protection and restoration in areas affected by the CVP. To accomplish this goal, the Act adds mitigation, protection and restoration of fish and wildlife as a project purpose and places it on a par with domestic and agricultural water uses. In addition, it makes enhancement of fish and wildlife a project purpose and places it on a par with power production at a lower priority. Specific fish and wildlife provisions include the following: (1) dedication of 800,000 acre-feet of CVP water annually to general fish and wildlife purposes, dedication of approximately 200,000 acre-feet of water annually for wildlife refuges in the Central Valley, and instream release of 340,000 acre-feet annually to the Trinity River; (2) creation of an annual fish and wildlife restoration fund of $50 million to be provided primarily by assessments on project contractors; (3) development and implementation of a program to double populations of anadromous fish in ten years; (4) identification of a number of specific measures to be undertaken to mitigate effects of CVP operations on fish and wildlife; and (5) prohibition of new water contracts until fish and wildlife goals are met. The CVPIA required completion of a programmatic environmental impact statement within three years analyzing the impacts and benefits of implementing the CVPIA and prohibited the long-term renewal of existing contracts until the environmental impact statement was completed. The Act also limits long-term renewal contracts to 25 years rather than the 40 years previously used.

The CVPIA contains other innovative provisions. To encourage water conservation, it establishes a tiered pricing structure in which water contractors receive the first 80 percent of their contract amount at the subsidized contract rate, the next 10 percent at a rate halfway between the contract rate and full cost, and the final 10 percent at full cost. It also requires the Secretary of the Interior to develop criteria for assessing water conservation plans developed by water contractors.

To provide flexibility to meet urban water needs, the CVPIA allows the transfer of water by all individuals or districts that receive CVP water, subject to certain conditions. The conditions include requirements that all transfers must be between willing buyers and willing sellers (i.e., condemnation is forbidden), that transfers cannot adversely affect groundwater conditions or the fish and wildlife purposes of the Act, that transfers must be consistent with state law, and that proposed transfers outside the CVP service area are subject to a first right of refusal by entities within the CVP service area. Transfers must be approved by the Secretary of the Interior, and transfers involving more than 20 percent of the CVP water subject to long-term contracts within any contracting district or agency must also be reviewed and approved by the district or agency. Water transferred to an agency or district that is not a CVP contractor must be paid for at the greater of full-cost or cost-of-service rates if used for irrigation and at the greater of cost-of-service or municipal and industrial rates if used for municipal or industrial purposes.

The CVPIA is analyzed in Harrison C. Dunning, Confronting the Environmental Legacy of Irrigated Agriculture in the West: The Case of the Central Valley Project, 23 Envtl. L. 943 (1993); Brenda W. Jahns, Reforming Western Water Rights: Contemporary Vision or Stubborn Revisionism?, 39 Rocky Mtn. Min. L. Inst. 21-1 (1993).

Implementation of the CVPIA provision dedicating 800,000 acre-feet annually to fish and wildlife purposes has proved complicated and controversial. It has been complicated because of the need to estimate how much water could be provided for reallocation to fish and wildlife under varying climatic conditions—wet years, normal years, and dry years—through various changes in CVP facilities and operations such as water banking, new storage, and conservation measures. It has been controversial because the reallocation of 800,000 acre-feet annually to fish and wildlife represents a not insignificant share of the project's average yield of 5,826,000 acre-feet. Some agricultural interests fear potentially devastating consequences for themselves, especially during a drought cycle. To the dissatisfaction of environmental interests, the Department of the Interior did not finalize a plan to implement the reallocation until 1999. Upon modifying the plan in 2003, Interior commented: "Despite the fact that the CVPIA was enacted ten years ago, many of the purposes and goals of the CVPIA, including the doubling of anadromous fish populations in Central Valley rivers and streams, have yet to be realized." Dep't of the Interior, Decision on Implementation of Section 3406(b)(2) of the Central Valley Project Improvement Act 3 (May 9, 2003).

8. **Types of water contracts.** Section 9(d) of the Reclamation Project Act of 1939 states that no project water may be delivered for irrigation until the irrigation district receiving it has entered into a "repayment contract." 43 U.S.C. § 485h(d). The usual repayment contract requires payment of the irrigators' shares of project costs over a forty year period, after a ten year development period. The necessary charges are assessed to their lands by the district and collected along with annual operation and maintenance charges. According to Ickes v. Fox, 300 U.S. 82, 94 (1937), irrigators entitled to water under a repayment contract have "a vested right to the perpetual use of the waters as appurtenant to their lands." The Court made this statement after noting that the irrigators in *Ickes* had fully repaid their share of project construction costs. The opinion thus did not settle whether irrigators with executory repayment obligations have similar vested perpetual rights, provided they continue to make their payments. Nevada v. United States, 463 U.S. 110 (1983), concerned contracts for "a permanent water right" for irrigation. Apparently the contracts predated section 9(d), but the Court described them as "similar" to the *Ickes* contract. The Court declared: "Once these lands were acquired by settlers in the Project, the Government's 'ownership' of the water rights was at most nominal; the beneficial interest in the rights confirmed to the Government resided in the

owners of the land within the Project to which these water rights became appurtenant upon the application of Project water to the land." 463 U.S. at 126.

Section 9(e) creates an exception to the section 9(d) requirement of a repayment contract for water delivery. 43 U.S.C. § 485h(e). It authorizes the Secretary of the Interior to enter into "contracts to furnish water," commonly called water service contracts. These contracts obligate the United States to supply water for up to forty years at rates fixed to cover only an "appropriate share" of construction costs and annual operating and maintenance costs, as the Secretary of the Interior deems proper. They were designed for situations where total repayment of reimbursable construction costs in forty years would be beyond the financial ability of the water users. They have been widely used in the Central Valley Project in California. A statute enacted in 1956 requires section 9(e) contracts to include, if requested, a provision for renewal under "mutually agreeable" terms. The terms must, however, "provide for an increase or decrease in charges set forth in the contract to reflect, among other things, increases or decreases in construction, operation, and maintenance costs and improvement or deterioration in the party's repayment capacity." 43 U.S.C. § 485h-1(1).

Madera Irrigation District v. Hancock, 985 F.2d 1397 (9th Cir. 1993), concerned a section 9(e) contract that predated the 1956 statute and lacked an express renewal right. The court found an implicit renewal right because the contract, though for a stated term of forty years, spoke of affording the district a "permanent" supply of water. The court ruled, however, that the district's implicit renewal right did not preclude the Bureau from raising the water rate upon renewal to recoup not only operation and maintenance costs over the term of the new contract but also operation and maintenance deficits that had built up over the past forty years under the old contract.

Apart from section 9(d) and 9(e) contracts, a less permanent right to water may be obtained by nonproject landowners under the Warren Act, 43 U.S.C. §§ 523, 524. The Secretary may agree to provide water users outside the project with water from the project works when their capacity exceeds the project's needs. The contracts may provide for temporary water deliveries pending full development of the project or for the "rental" of water on terms making such use secondary and inferior to the right to use the water on the project.

O'NEILL v. UNITED STATES

United States Court of Appeals, Ninth Circuit, 1995.
50 F.3d 677.

CHOY, CIRCUIT JUDGE. Landowners and water users within "Area I" of the Westlands Water District appeal the district court's denial of their motion to enforce a stipulated judgment which required the United States to perform a 1963 long-term water service contract with the Westlands Water District. The district court held that the contract does not obligate the government to furnish to Westlands the full contractual amount of water when that water cannot be delivered consistently with the requirements of the Endangered Species Act ('ESA"), 16 U.S.C. § 1531 et seq., and the Central Valley Project Improvement Act ("CVPIA"), Pub.L. No. 102-575, 106 Stat. 4706 et seq. * * * We affirm * * *.

In 1963, the United States entered into a long-term water service contract with Westlands Water District pursuant to federal reclamation statutes. Under this contract, the United States agreed to construct the San Luis Unit of the Federal Central Valley Project ("CVP") in part to furnish water to the Westlands Water District. The CVP is the country's largest federal water reclamation project. The United States agreed to furnish, and the District agreed to pay for, 900,000 acre-feet of water annually subject to Article 11(a) which limits the government's liability for water shortages caused by "errors in operation, drought, or any other causes." * * *

In November of 1990, the Sacramento River winter-run chinook salmon was listed as a threatened species under the Endangered Species Act. * * * ESA Section 7(a)(2) requires all federal agencies Ain consultation with and with the assistance of the Secretary [of the Interior or Commerce, to] insure that any action authorized, funded, or carried out by such agency * * * is not likely to jeopardize the continued existence of any endangered species or threatened species * * * ." Accordingly, when the winter-run chinook salmon was listed as a threatened species, the Bureau of Reclamation ("Bureau") entered into ESA consultation with the National Marine Fisheries Service ("NMFS"). As a result of this consultation, NMFS issued a biological opinion which concluded that the Bureau's continued operation of the CVP in the water year 1992-1993 was likely to jeopardize the continued existence of the salmon population. The opinion noted that jeopardy to the salmon could be avoided if the Bureau operated the CVP in accordance with certain prescribed alternatives.

While the Bureau was developing its initial 1993 CVP water allocation, the United States Fish and Wildlife Service issued a notice of intent to list another species of fish indigenous to the Sacramento-San Joaquin Delta, the delta smelt, as a threatened species. The delta smelt was listed on March 5, 1993. Consultation and a biological opinion followed with a result analogous to that in the salmon case.

In October 1992, Congress enacted CVPIA, amending the 1937 CVP reauthorization statute. CVPIA seeks to achieve "a reasonable balance among competing demands for use of Central Valley Project water, including the requirements of fish and wildlife, agricultural, municipal and industrial and power contractors." Section 3402(f). Section 3406(b)(2) of the CVPIA directs the Secretary to

> dedicate and manage annually eight hundred thousand acre-feet of Central Valley Project yield for the primary purpose of implementing the fish, wildlife and habitat restoration purposes and measures authorized by this title; to assist the State of California in its efforts to protect the waters of the San Francisco Bay/Sacramento-San Joaquin Delta Estuary; and to help meet such obligations as may be legally imposed upon the Central Valley Project under State or Federal law following the date of enactment of this title, including but not limited to additional obligations under the Federal Endangered Species Act.

On February 15, 1993, the Bureau announced its initial allocation of CVP water for 1993. Under the final allocation, agricultural contractors south of the Sacramento-San Joaquin Delta, such as the Westlands District, were to receive only 50 percent of their contractual supply of water. * * * [Area I water users responded by seeking a court order requiring delivery of the full contractual amount.] The government argued that compliance with ESA and CVPIA required it to reduce the amount of water supplied to Area I and that such a reduction was covered by the liability limitation in Article 11 of the contract. The district court agreed with the government * * * .

Article 11(a) of the water service contract provides that the government shall not be held liable for "any damage, direct or indirect, arising from a shortage on account of errors in operation, drought, or any other causes." The government contends this language is broad and unambiguous and that shortages stemming from mandatory compliance with ESA and CVPIA are shortages resulting from 'any other cause." Therefore, the government concludes, it is not liable for its failure to deliver the full contractual amount of water to Area I. Area I maintains that the contract language is ambiguous, and limits the government's liability for water delivery only in the event of a "temporary emergency" such as a 'rare time[] of severe drought." Appellants' Opening Brief at 9. * * *

On its face, Article 11(a) unambiguously disclaims any liability for damages in the event the United States is unable to supply water in times of shortage. * * * Article 26 provides, in relevant part:

> In the event that the Congress of the United States * * * amends * * * provisions of the Federal reclamation laws, the United States agrees, at the option of the District, to negotiate amendments of appropriate articles of this contract, all consistently with the provisions of such * * * amendment.

The contract preamble recites that the contract was entered into pursuant to the federal reclamation laws. Area I contends that because Article 26 and the contract preamble explicitly reference statutes, whereas the phrase "any other causes" does not explicitly include the effects of subsequently enacted statutes, the scope of "any other causes" is ambiguous.

"[A]ny other causes" is a catchall phrase that does not "explicitly" include any particular causes. Contrary to Area I's position, the specific reference to reclamation law in Article 26 is not at all inconsistent with the notion that "any other causes" broadly and unambiguously contemplates the effects of subsequent Congressional mandates. We conclude that the contract's liability limitation is unambiguous and that an unavailability of water resulting from the mandates of valid legislation constitutes a shortage by reason of "any other causes."

* * *

Even if the water service contract did obligate the government to supply, without exception, 900,000 acre-feet of water, the district court correctly held that Area I would still not be entitled to prevail as the contract is not immune from subsequently enacted statutes. The Supreme Court has held that Congress's power to exercise sovereign authority "'will remain intact unless surrendered in unmistakable terms.'" Bowen v. Public Agencies Opposed to Social Sec. Entrapment, 477 U.S. 41, 52, 106 S.Ct. 2390, 2397, 91 L.Ed.2d 35 (1986) (quoting Merrion v. Jicarilla Apache Tribe, 455 U.S. 130, 148, 102 S.Ct. 894, 907, 71 L.Ed.2d 21 (1982)). "[C]ontractual arrangements, including those to which a sovereign itself is party, 'remain subject to subsequent legislation' by the sovereign." Id. (quoting Merrion, 455 U.S. At 147, 102 S.Ct. at 907). Nothing in the 1963 contract surrenders in "unmistakable terms" Congress's sovereign power to enact legislation. Rather, the contract was executed pursuant to the 1902 Reclamation Act and all acts amendatory or supplementary thereto. 1963 Contract Preamble. The contract contemplates future changes in reclamation laws in Article 26, and Article 11 limits the government's liability for shortages due to any causes. As Area I recognized in its oral argument, CVPIA marks a shift in reclamation law modifying the priority of water uses. There is nothing in the contract that precludes such a shift. * * *

Notes

1. **Executory water contracts and the ESA.** Shortage provisions like Article 11(a) are common in Bureau of Reclamation water contracts. Rio Grande Silvery Minnow v. Keys, 333 F.3d 1109 (10th Cir. 2003), concerned repayment contracts for the San Juan-Chama and Middle Rio Grande Projects in New Mexico that exculpated the government from liability for damage resulting from a shortage of available water "[o]n account of drouth or other causes." Environmental groups obtained a preliminary injunction ordering the Bureau to consult with the U.S. Fish and Wildlife Service under ESA § 7 and curtail contract water deliveries as needed to maintain river flows sufficient to avoid jeopardy to the endangered Rio Grande silvery minnow. On appeal to the Tenth Circuit, the Bureau argued that continued performance of its contractual water delivery obligations came within the exception from ESA § 7 for nondiscretionary acts. See Note 4, supra p. 601-03. The Bureau conceded that the "other causes" clause in *O'Neill* was virtually identical to shortage language in the New Mexico contracts, but it argued *O'Neill* was not on point because there the CVPIA specifically allocated water for fish and wildlife, whereas no similar specific legislation governed the reclamation facilities in New Mexico. The Tenth Circuit held, however, that general references to fish and wildlife in the New Mexico project legislation and the repayment contracts, especially a contract clause stating that water for fish and wildlife is a beneficial use, gave the Bureau discretion to determine the amount of water available to the contract holders. Therefore, the Bureau was required to consult under ESA § 7 and reduce water deliveries to contract holders if necessary to protect the silvery minnow.

The decision evoked strong protest. The Bureau denounced the decision as "just plain wrong" and an impediment to its collaborative approach to protecting the silvery minnow. New Mexico quit participating in the collaborative process. The defendants moved for reconsideration en banc. Supportive amici briefs were filed by a number of western states and large water distribution organizations outside of New Mexico. The New Mexico congressional delegation included in the Energy and Water Development Appropriations Act of 2004, Pub. L. No. 108-137, § 208(a), 117 Stat. 1827, a provision prohibiting the expenditure of funds to reallocate water from San Juan-Chama Project contracts to meet the requirements of the ESA, unless the water is purchased from a willing seller or lessor. Early in 2004, the Tenth Circuit panel that issued the *Silvery Minnow* decision undercut efforts at en banc reconsideration by vacating its opinion as moot. It found the case moot because the preliminary injunction that was the basis of the appeal covered only the latter part of 2002 and 2003, and favorable climatic conditions had produced sufficient water flows in those months that the injunction was never invoked. Rio Grande Silvery Minnow v. Keys, 355 F.3d 1215 (10th Cir. 2004).

2. **Water contract renewal and the ESA.** Natural Resources Defense Council v. Houston, 146 F.3d 1118 (9th Cir. 1998), addressed the effect of ESA § 7 on the Bureau's renewal of section 9(e) contracts for Friant Dam, a part of the Central Valley Project. The Bureau renewed the section 9(e) contracts of various water and irrigation districts for water from the dam on terms substantially similar to their previous contracts. No formal ESA consultation was done before the renewals. This was because the National Marine Fisheries Service had concluded (erroneously, it was held in *Houston*) that although the renewals likely would adversely affect a threatened species of chinook salmon, consultation was unnecessary because of an ongoing consultation for the entire Central Valley Project.

Environmental groups sued for rescission of the renewal contracts in an effort to obtain greater releases of water from the dam to improve the badly degraded downstream habitat of several listed species of fish. The water and irrigation districts defended by asserting that the renewals came within the exception from ESA § 7 for nondiscretionary acts. The districts relied on a statute providing that a section 9(d) or 9(e) contract holder "shall, during the term of the contract and of any renewal thereof * * * have a first right (to which right the rights of the holders of any other type of irrigation water contract shall be subordinate) to a stated share or quantity of the project's available water supply * * * and a permanent right to such share or quantity upon completion of payment of the amount assigned for ultimate return * * *." 43 U.S.C. § 485h-1(4). The districts argued that this statute deprived the Bureau of discretion to alter the contract terms on renewal, particularly regarding the quantity of water to be delivered. The court disagreed. Keying on the word "available" in the statute and citing *O'Neill* for the proposition that an agency can deliver less than a contractually agreed upon amount of water in order to comply with subsequently enacted federal law, it said: "[E]ven if the original contracts guaranteed the [districts] a right to a similar share of available water in the renewal contracts, the Bureau had discretion to alter other key terms in the contract, and the Bureau may be able to reduce the amount of water available for sale if necessary to comply with ESA." 146 F.3d at 1126.

The districts also argued that even if ESA consultation was required, the renewal of their contracts without consultation was valid anyway. ESA § 7(d) prohibits any irreversible commitment of resources before completion of the consultation process if that would foreclose implementing reasonable and prudent alternative measures, but the districts pointed out that Article 14 of their contracts authorized minor contract modifications needed to comply with federal law. The court again disagreed: "We do not think that an agency should be permitted to skirt the procedural requirements of § 7(d) by including such a catchall savings clause in illegally executed contracts. However, even if such a clause could preserve the contracts, Article 14 is inadequate to serve that purpose here because it limits conservation-based modification to minor adjustments and prohibits an adjustment in the amount of water delivered. Because Article 14 does not permit a reduction in the quantity of water delivered, the reasonable and prudent alternative of reallocating contracted water from irrigation to conservation is foreclosed." Id. at 1128. The court ordered rescission of the contracts.

3. **The modern Bureau of Reclamation.** In recent decades, the Bureau of Reclamation has undergone major changes in mission. Beginning with the adminis-

trations of Presidents Carter and Reagan, federal investments in water resources projects were severely curtailed, due in large part to federal budget deficits. Funding for new starts on authorized projects of the Bureau came virtually to a standstill, and funding for progress on construction of ongoing projects was slowed.

In the Reclamation Reform Act of 1982, supra p. 670-72, Note 6, Congress sought to strengthen the Bureau's role in the conservation of project water. It directed the Bureau to encourage nonfederal recipients of irrigation water to implement economically feasible conservation measures, and it required each district with a repayment contract or water service contract to develop a water conservation plan consisting of goals, conservation measures, and a time schedule for meeting the goals. 43 U.S.C. § 390jj.

Five years later, the Bureau issued a report titled "Assessment '87: A New Direction for the Bureau of Reclamation." The report's key conclusion was that "the Bureau's mission must change from one based on federally supported construction to one based on effective and environmentally sensitive resource management." In 1992, the Bureau issued Reclamation's Strategic Plan: A Long-Term Framework for Water Resources Management, Development and Protection (1992), which builds on Assessment '87 and carries forward the theme of shifting its emphasis from construction to better management of existing projects. For fiscal year 1998, the Bureau's budget was $948 million. In a dramatic change from a quarter century earlier, nearly one-third of that budget was allocated to ecosystem restoration and to fish recovery and pollution reduction projects. Western Water Policy Rev. Advisory Comm'n, Water in the West: The Challenge for the Next Century 3-51 to 3-52 (1998).

In 1995, the Bureau issued a Framework for the Transfer of Title, which provides for it to transfer title to "uncomplicated" projects or parts of projects that do not have national importance, could be efficiently and effectively managed by non-federal entities, and meet six specific criteria. See William H. Holmes, Dams for Sale: The Ins and Outs of Federal Facility Transfers, 43 Rocky Mtn. Min. L. Inst. 24-1 (1997),. The Framework is available at http://www.usbr.gov/gp/nepa/ middle _loup_ea/attachment_a.htm.

In 2003, the Department of the Interior issued a document titled "Water 2025: Preventing Crises and Conflict in the West." The document says federalism principles and fiscal realities mean that solutions to complex water problems in the West should not and cannot be driven from the federal level. It refers only briefly to building new federal water storage projects. In contrast, it identifies and stresses four tools for solving western water problems: (1) conservation, efficiency, and markets, (2) collaboration, (3) improved technology, and (4) removal of institutional barriers and increased interagency coordination.

4. **Transfer of project water.** In Chapter 2, Section 5, the transfer of water rights as a method of shifting water to new needs, particularly from agriculture to municipal and industrial use, was considered from the point of view of state law. The transferability of Bureau project water is a matter of potential importance since the Bureau delivers over twenty-five million acre-feet of water annually for irrigation. In general, reclamation law does not expressly or by clear implication restrict transfers. Reclamation Act § 8 makes water rights appurtenant to land, but the Bureau has not viewed this provision as prohibiting transfers. Practically all Bureau repayment contracts and water service contracts require Bureau consent for transfer. Historically, in the absence of any firm policy at the national level, regional

Bureau offices generally discouraged transfers. Their opposition was based in part on the theory of preventing windfall profits to farmers who might in effect sell the irrigation subsidy to the buyer, and in part on the fear of jeopardizing repayment. See Joseph L. Sax, Selling Reclamation Water Rights: A Case Study in Federal Subsidy Policy, 64 Mich. L. Rev. 13 (1965). However, in some areas, an active market was allowed to develop in project water. See Raymond L. Anderson, Windfall Gains from Transfers of Water Allotments Within the Colorado-Big Thompson Project, 40 Land Econ. 265 (1967). A penetrating study is Charles J. Meyers & Richard A. Posner, Market Transfers of Water Rights: Toward an Improved Market in Water Resources, Nat'l Water Comm'n, Legal Study No. 4 (1971).

In recent years, the Department of the Interior has begun to develop a national policy to facilitate the transfer of reclamation project water. In 1988, the Department released a policy statement titled "Principles Governing Voluntary Water Transactions that Involve or Affect Facilities Owned or Operated by the Department of Interior." In general, this document supports the transfer of reclamation water, including the transfer of agricultural water to municipal and industrial use. It states that the federal government will not burden a transfer with costs not associated with the transfer. A supplemental policy addresses the subsidy/windfall profits issue: "When a transfer of project water involves a change in the type of use from irrigation to a different beneficial use, and the capital costs allocable to a project's irrigation purpose have not been repaid, subsidies associated with the provision of project water for irrigation purposes will not follow the transferred project water. Charges payable to Reclamation for transferred project water will be consistent with the new use to which the transferred water is put. On projects where contractual obligations for the repayment of construction costs allocable to irrigation purposes have been fulfilled, charges payable to Reclamation for the transferred project water will be negotiable. In either situation, Reclamation will not attempt to recapture the value of past subsidies in setting charges for transferred project water." Reclamation Manual/Policy WTR P02, 6.G.

Congress has shown some inclination in recent years to facilitate transfers of reclamation project water. To alleviate damage from drought conditions, the Reclamation States Emergency Drought Relief Act of 1991, 43 U.S.C. §§ 2201-2247, authorizes the Secretary of the Interior to purchase project water from willing sellers for delivery to willing buyers under temporary contracts (for up to two years) and to participate in state water banks. The CVPIA authorizes and encourages the transfer of project water by districts or individuals for any purpose recognized as beneficial by state law, as described in Note 2, supra.

5. **The Corps of Engineers.** Although a number of federal agencies have water-related functions, the major agency in addition to the Bureau of Reclamation with responsibilities for water project construction and management is the U. S. Army Corps of Engineers. While the Bureau operates only in seventeen western states, the Corps operates nationwide. Its has responsibilities for improving navigation that go back to 1824, when Congress called upon it to remove snags and sandbars that were interfering with navigation on the Mississippi and Ohio Rivers. In many Rivers and Harbors bills, Congress has authorized and appropriated funds for dredging, protective works, locks, and dams to store water for release during low flows. The Corps also has flood control responsibilities. For years, these were confined primarily to the Mississippi Valley, but in 1936 Congress adopted a

national policy and continuing program for flood control in which the Corps has the predominant role through the construction of improvements on main stem rivers. 33 U.S.C. §§ 701a, 701a-1. Projects have been authorized and funded periodically in flood control bills. The Corps has no single purpose irrigation projects but supplies water from many of its multipurpose dams in the West to the Bureau of Reclamation for distribution to irrigators under the Flood Control Act of 1944, 43 U.S.C. § 390b. In the East, the Corps provides large amounts of irrigation water in central and southern Florida. Its multipurpose dams also generate hydroelectric power and provide water for municipal and industrial use. In 1990, Congress made environmental protection "one of the primary missions of the Corps of Engineers in planning, designing, constructing, operating, and maintaining water resources projects." 33 U.S.C. § 2316.

In ETSI Pipeline Project v. Missouri, 484 U.S. 495 (1988), the Court held that without approval from the Secretary of the Army, the Bureau lacked authority to remove water stored behind a Corps of Engineers dam on the Missouri River built under the Flood Control Act of 1944, water that the Bureau claimed was available for irrigation and wished to deliver instead for industrial use. The Court added in dictum that if the Bureau "wishes to remove water from an Army reservoir for *any* purpose, the approval of the Army Secretary must be secured."

6. **Sovereign immunity.** If an aggrieved person wants to sue a federal agency over its operation of a water project, does the sovereign immunity of the United States bar suit? Any of three general waivers of sovereign immunity might apply. First, the Federal Tort Claims Act, 28 U.S.C. §§ 2671-2680, allows suit for monetary relief in tort actions, such as trespass or negligence, unless the water project operation can be fitted under the "discretionary function" exception to waiver of immunity. Second, the Tucker Act, 28 U.S.C. § 1491(a)(1), allows suit for monetary relief in nontort actions such as inverse condemnation or breach of contract. The suit must be brought in the Court of Federal Claims rather than a federal district court if it is for more than $10,000. Third, the Administrative Procedure Act, 5 U.S.C. § 702, allows suit for nonmonetary relief alleging agency action or inaction in violation of a federal statute.

In addition to these general waiver statutes, which are not limited to suits concerning water projects, a specific waiver of immunity is included in the Reclamation Reform Act of 1982, § 221, 43 U.S.C. § 390uu. The waiver is for any suit concerning "the contractual rights of a contracting entity and the United States regarding any contract executed pursuant to Federal reclamation law." It authorizes suits for damages, Sumner Peck Ranch, Inc. v. Bureau of Reclamation, 823 F. Supp. 715 (E.D. Cal. 1993), and for injunctive or declaratory relief, Westlands Water District v. Firebaugh Canal, 10 F.3d 667 (9th Cir. 1993). While an irrigation district with a Bureau of Reclamation water contract can sue under this waiver of immunity, the waiver does not extend to suits by irrigators the district serves unless they are intended, rather than incidental, beneficiaries of the district's contract with the Bureau. Orff v. United States, 358 F.3d 1137 (9th Cir. 2004), cert. granted, 125 S. Ct. 309 (2004), ruled that irrigators in the Westlands Water District were only incidental beneficiaries of the district's water contract with the Bureau.

In contrast to the specific waiver of immunity in the Reclamation Reform Act, a specific assertion of immunity appears in the Flood Control Act of 1928, 33 U.S.C. § 702c: "No liability of any kind shall attach to or rest upon the United States for any damage from or by floods or flood waters at any place * * *." When a dam has multiple purposes, rather than the single purpose of flood control, the no-liability rule does not apply to damage from water released for purposes other than flood control, e.g., for hydroelectric power generation. Cent. Green Co. v. United States, 531 U.S. 425 (2001).

SECTION 3. RESERVED WATER RIGHTS

A. Indian Reserved Rights

WINTERS v. UNITED STATES

Supreme Court of the United States, 1908.
207 U.S. 564, 28 S. Ct. 207, 52 L. Ed. 340.

[By the Act of April 15, 1874, ch. 96, 28 Stat. 28 (1875), Congress "set apart" for the use and occupation of the Gros Ventre, Peigan, Blood, Blackfeet, and River Crow Indians a very large area of land in the Territory of Montana. Then, by the Act of May 1, 1888, ch. 213, 25 Stat. 113 (1889), Congress approved an agreement between federal commissioners and the Indians whereby the tribes did "cede and relinquish to the United States" all of this large area of land except for several smaller parcels specifically therein "set apart and reserved" for them. One of these parcels was the Fort Belknap Indian reservation, the northern boundary of which was the middle of the channel of the nonnavigable Milk River. The United States opened the ceded land to settlement, and portions of it upstream from the Fort Belknap reservation came into the hands of the defendants, several individuals and a cattle company. After the reservation was established but before 1898, the defendants appropriated under Montana law 5000 inches of water from the Milk River for the irrigation of hay and grain. Much of the land on the Fort Belknap reservation was usable for grazing, and some of it was suitable for irrigated agriculture. In 1898 an Indian project was constructed on the reservation that required 5000 inches from the Milk for the irrigation of hay, grass, and vegetables. The defendants' water diversions, however, left insufficient water for the Indian project. Upon suit by the United States, the lower court granted an order enjoining the defendants from interfering in any manner with use on the reservation of 5000 inches of water.]

MR. JUSTICE MCKENNA delivered the opinion of the court: * * *

The case, as we view it, turns on the agreement of May, 1888, resulting in the creation of Fort Belknap Reservation. In the construction of this agreement there are certain elements to be considered that are prominent and significant. The reservation was a part of a very much larger tract which the Indians had the right to occupy and use, and which was adequate for the habits and wants of a nomadic and uncivilized people. It was the policy of the government, it was the desire of the Indians, to change those habits and to become a pastoral and civilized people. If they should become such, the original tract was too extensive; but a smaller tract would be inadequate without a change of conditions. The lands were arid, and, without irrigation, were practically valueless. And yet, it is contended, the means of irrigation were deliberately given up by the Indians and deliberately accepted by the government. The lands ceded were, it is true, also arid; and some argument may be urged, and is urged, that with their cession there was the cession of the waters, without which they would be valueless, and "civilized communities could not be established thereon." And this, it is further contended, the Indians knew, and yet made no reservation of the waters. We realize that there is a conflict of implications, but that which makes for the retention of the waters is of greater force than that which makes for their cession. The Indians had command of the lands and the waters—command of all their beneficial use, whether kept for hunting, "and grazing roving herds of stock," or turned to agriculture and the arts of civilization. Did they give up all this? Did they reduce the area of their occupation and give up the waters which made it valuable or adequate? And, even regarding the allegation of the answer as true, that there are springs and streams on the reservation flowing about 2,900 inches of water, the inquiries are pertinent. If it were possible to believe affirmative answers, we might also believe that the Indians were awed by the power of the government or deceived by its negotiators. Neither view is possible. The government is asserting the rights of the Indians. But extremes need not be taken into account. By a rule of interpretation of agreements and treaties with the Indians, ambiguities occurring will be resolved from the standpoint of the Indians. And the rule should certainly be applied to determine between two inferences, one of which would support the purpose of the agreement and the other impair or defeat it. On account of their relations to the government, it cannot be supposed that the Indians were alert to exclude by formal words every inference which might militate against or defeat the declared purpose of themselves and the government, even if it could be supposed that they had the intelligence to foresee the "double sense" which might some time be urged against them.

Another contention of appellants is that if it be conceded that there was a reservation of the waters of Milk river by the agreement of 1888, yet the reservation was repealed by the admission of Montana into the Union, February 22, 1889, "upon an equal footing with the original states." The language of counsel is that "any reservation in the agreement with the Indians, expressed or implied, whereby the waters of Milk river were not to be subject of appropriation by the citizens and inhabitants of said State, was repealed by the act of admission." But to establish the repeal counsel rely substantially upon the same argument that they advance against the intention of the agreement to reserve the waters. The power of the government to reserve the waters and exempt them from appropriation under the state laws is not denied, and could not be. United States v. Rio Grande Ditch & Irrigation Co., 174 U.S. 702, 43 L.Ed. 1141, 19 S.Ct. 770 (1899); United States v. Winans, 198 U.S. 371, 49 L.Ed. 1089, 25 S.Ct. 662 (1905). That the government did reserve them we have decided, and for a use which would be necessarily continued through years. This was done May 1, 1888, and it would be extreme to believe that within a year Congress destroyed the reservation and took from the Indians the consideration of their grant, leaving them a barren waste—took from them the means of continuing their old habits, yet did not leave them the power to change to new ones. * * *

Decree affirmed.

Notes

1. **Who reserved the waters?** Did the Indians in *Winters* cede most of their ancestral lands to the United States but retain some of them, so that for the retained lands the tribes might claim aboriginal water rights dating back to prehistory? Alternatively, did the United States by assuming sovereign authority over the Territory of Montana extinguish prior Indian rights in all the ancestral lands and then grant the reservation lands back to the Indians, so that the tribes could claim only an implied grant of water that would date from the 1874 or 1888 legislation?

Is any light shed on this question by United States v. Winans, cited in *Winters*? That case involved an 1859 treaty between the United States and the Yakima Nation in which the Indians ceded certain lands to the United States. The treaty stated: "The exclusive right of taking fish in all streams where running through or bordering said reservation is further secured to said Confederated Tribes and Bands of Indians, as also the right of taking fish at all usual and accustomed places, in common with citizens of the territory, and of erecting temporary buildings for curing them." Thereafter, non-Indian settlers who obtained title to lands bordering the river sought to exclude the Indians from placing their "fish wheels" (salmon traps) in their accustomed places, now on private lands. The Court said: "The right to resort to the fishing places in controversy was a part of larger rights possessed by the Indians, upon the exercise of which there was not a shadow of impediment, and which were not much less necessary to the existence of the Indians than the atmosphere they breathed * * *. The treaty was not a grant of rights to the Indians, but a grant of rights from them—a reservation of those not granted." 198 U.S. at 381. Why did the Court in *Winters* cite *Winans* for the proposition that "[t]he power of the government to reserve the waters and exempt them from appropriation under the state laws is not denied, and could not be"?

2. **Arizona v. California.** After *Winters*, the Supreme Court did not issue another major Indian water rights opinion until Arizona v. California, 373 U.S. 546, 595-96 (1963): "The Government, on behalf of five Indian Reservations in Arizona, California, and Nevada, asserted rights to water in the mainstream of the Colorado River. The Colorado River Reservation, located partly in Arizona and partly in California, is the largest reservation. It was created by an Act of Congress in 1865, but its area was later increased by Executive Order. Other reservations were created by Executive Orders and amendments to them, ranging in dates from 1870 to 1907. The Special Master found that when the United States created these reservations or added to them, it reserved not only land but also the use of enough water from the Colorado to irrigate the irrigable portions of the reserved lands." The Court agreed with the Special Master, summarizing and relying on *Winters* as follows: "The Court in *Winters* concluded that the Government intended to deal fairly with the Indians by reserving for them the waters without which their lands would have been useless. * * * We follow it now and agree that the United States did reserve the water rights for the Indians effective as of the time the Indian Reservations were created." Id. at 600. The Court entered a decree fixing the priorities of the Indian reserved water rights as of the dates the reservations were created or expanded by statute or executive order. 376 U.S. 340 (1964).

The Court's 1963 opinion addressed several aspects of reserved rights not presented in *Winters*. It established that (1) the implied reservation doctrine applies to navigable waters as well as nonnavigable waters, (2) the doctrine applies to Indian reservations created after statehood as well as those created before statehood, (3) water can be impliedly reserved by executive order as well as by act of Congress, and (4) the amount of water reserved for irrigation and related purposes should be measured not by the reasonably foreseeable needs of the Indians living on the reservation, i.e., not by the number of Indians, but by the number of practicably irrigable acres (PIA) on the reservation.

In a portion of the 1963 opinion reprinted supra p. 494, the Court allocated the first 7.5 million acre-feet (m.a.f.) of mainstream Colorado River water reaching the Lower Basin each year for consumptive use as follows: California 4.4 m.a.f., Arizona 2.8 m.a.f., and Nevada .3 m.a.f. The reserved Indian water rights come out of the allocations of the states in which the Indian reservations are located. Arizona sought to minimize the Indians' share of its 2.8 m.a.f. allocation by arguing that the doctrine of equitable apportionment should be applied to divide that water between the Indians and others in the state. The Court rejected the idea: "The doctrine of equitable apportionment is a method of resolving water disputes between States. It was created by this Court in the exercise of its original jurisdiction over controversies in which States are parties. An Indian Reservation is not a State. And while Congress has sometimes left Indian Reservations considerable power to manage their own affairs, we are not convinced by Arizona's argument that each reservation is so much like a State that its rights to water should be determined by the doctrine of equitable apportionment. Moreover, even were we to treat an Indian Reservation like a State, equitable apportionment would still not control since, under our view, the Indian claims here are governed by the statutes and Executive Orders creating the reservations." Id. at 597.

Early in 1979, the Court entered a supplemental decree upon the joint motion of the parties that quantified the Indian reserved water rights as follows: 131,400 acre-feet for the California reservations, 761,562 acre-feet for the Arizona reservations, and 12,534 acre-feet for the Nevada reservations—for a total of 905,496 acre-feet per year. These quantities represent annual diversions, not consumptive use. 439 U.S. 419 (1979).

Indian tribes in the Lower Colorado River Basin were not parties to the proceedings that resulted in the 1964 and 1979 decrees. The tribes were represented by the United States. Late in 1979, the tribes were allowed to intervene, and they asked the Court to reopen its earlier determination of the amount of PIA on their reservations. They claimed additional water for (1) "boundary lands," which were lands lying outside the boundaries used in the 1964 decree that the tribes alleged should have been included within the reservations, and (2) "omitted lands," which were lands within reservation boundaries that the tribes alleged were practicably irrigable but were not inventoried as such by the United States in the earlier proceeding. The Court held that the "boundary lands" question could still be litigated because the earlier proceedings had not determined certain reservation boundaries with finality and its 1964 decree expressly contemplated future resolution of those boundary issues. It also added small amounts of disputed boundary lands to reservations, with appropriate water rights to serve them.

But the Court ruled differently on the "omitted lands" question, despite a general provision in the 1964 decree allowing the parties to file applications for its amendment or for further relief. The Court applied principles akin to res judicata to preclude reopening of the that question:

"Certainty of rights is particularly important with respect to water rights in the Western United States. The development of that area of the United States would not have been possible without adequate water supplies in an otherwise water-scarce part of the country. The doctrine of prior appropriation, the prevailing law in the western states, is itself largely a product of the compelling need for certainty in the holding and use of water rights.

"Recalculating the amount of practicably irrigable acreage runs directly counter to the strong interest in finality in this case. A major purpose of this litigation, from its inception to the present day, has been to provide the necessary assurance to states of the Southwest and to various private interests, of the amount of water they can anticipate to receive from the Colorado River system. 'In the arid parts of the West * * * claims to water for use on federal reservations inescapably vie with other public and private claims for the limited quantities to be found in the rivers and streams.' United States v. New Mexico, 438 U.S. 696, 699 (1978). If there is no surplus of water in the Colorado River, an increase in federal reserved water rights will require a 'gallon-for-gallon reduction in the amount of water available for water-needy state and private appropriators.' As Special Master Tuttle recognized, 'not a great deal of evidence is really needed to convince anyone that western states would rely upon water adjudications.' Tuttle Report at 46. Not only did the Metropolitan Water District in California and the Central Arizona Project predicate their plans on the basis of the 1964 allocations, but, due to the high priority of Indian water claims, an enlargement of the Tribes' allocation cannot help but exacerbate potential water shortage problems for these projects and their States." 460 U.S. 605, 620-21 (1983).

The Court ruled further that the absence of the Indian tribes as formal parties to the prior proceedings was not a reason to relitigate their rights. "We find no merit in the Tribes' contention that the United States' representation of their interests was inadequate whether because of a claimed conflict of interests arising from the government's interest in securing water rights for other federal property, or otherwise. The United States often represents varied interests in litigation involving water rights, particularly given the large extent and variety of federal land holdings in the West. Indeed, the substantial water allocations awarded the Tribes reflect the competency of the United States' representation. We believe the issue of practicably irrigable acreage was fully and fairly litigated in 1963."

Most recently, the Court added some more disputed boundary lands to a reservation and reserved water for them. 530 U.S. 392 (2000); 531 U.S. 1 (2000).

3. **The PIA standard and Wyoming v. United States.** In Wyoming v. United States, 492 U.S. 406 (1989), the United States Supreme Court was asked to reconsider use of the PIA standard to quantify Indian reserved water rights for irrigation and related uses. The Wyoming Supreme Court had applied the PIA standard in the Wind River Indian Reservation and awarded the reservation 500,420 acre-feet of water annually. In re General Adjudication of All Rights to Use Water in Big Horn River System (*Big Horn I*), 753 P.2d 76 (Wyo. 1988). The United States Supreme Court issued a one sentence per curiam opinion: "The judgment below is affirmed by an equally divided Court." The Court was divided 4 to 4, with Justice O'Connor not voting because she held a minority interest in a family ranch corporation that was party to a stream adjudication in Arizona involving Indian water rights.

Papers donated by Justice Thurgood Marshall to the Library of Congress after his retirement from the Court included a draft majority opinion in Wyoming v. United States written by Justice O'Connor before she learned of the family ranch matter and recused herself. The draft majority opinion is published as an appendix to Andrew C. Mergen & Sylvia F. Liu, A Misplaced Sensitivity: The Draft Opinions in Wyoming v. United States, 68 U. Colo. L. Rev. 683 (1997), an article strongly critical of the draft majority opinion. That draft opinion expressly declined to discard the PIA standard but would have modified it with a "sensitivity" doctrine and remanded the case for reconsideration in light of that doctrine. Excerpts from the draft opinion follow:

"We have not previously addressed the factors that go into determining PIA. * * * [A]rable lands which have been or are currently being irrigated should generally be considered practically irrigable. * * *[T]hree factors * * * must be considered in determining whether lands which have never been irrigated should be included as PIA: the arability of the lands, the engineering feasibility (based on current technology) of necessary future irrigation projects, and the economic feasibility of such projects (based on the profits from cultivation of future lands and the costs of the projects). * * *

"[In addition,] quantification of Indian reserved water rights must entail sensitivity to the impact on state and private appropriators of scarce water under state law. * * * The inclusion in the PIA quantification of arable lands not yet irrigated depends on the assumption that necessary future irrigation projects will be built to supply water to those lands. * * * Given that federal reserved water rights will frequently require a gallon-for-gallon reduction in the amount of water available for water-needy state and private appropriators, the existence of future projects cannot be taken for granted. Sensitivity to the impact on prior appropriators necessarily means that there has to be some degree of pragmatism in determining PIA. We think this pragmatism involves a 'practical' assessment—a determination apart from theoretical economic and engineering feasibility—of the reasonable likelihood that future irrigation projects, necessary to enable lands which have never been irrigated to obtain water, will actually be built.

"Although some have argued that the Government has a duty to assert Indian reserved water rights, no court has held that the Government is under a general legal or fiduciary obligation to build or fund irrigation projects on Indian reservations so that irrigable acreage can be effectively used. If money were plentiful, a finding of economic feasibility might suggest that the projects in question will be built. But massive capital outlays are required to fund irrigation projects, and in today's era of budget deficits and excess agricultural production, government officials have to choose carefully what projects to fund in the West. * * *

"By mentioning federal fiscal concerns, we do not mean to suggest that the practicability factor set forth above turns only on funding by the Government. It may be that the Tribes themselves, state agencies, or private investors have the means and intent to construct irrigation projects needed to bring water to future lands. Whether or not such project will be undertaken will also depend in part on the nature of the demand. Thus, the trier of fact must examine the evidence, if any, that additional cultivated acreage is needed to supply food or fibre to resident tribal members, or to meet the realistic needs of tribal members to expand their existing farming operations. The trier must also determine whether there will be a sufficient market for, or economically productive use of, any crops that would be grown on the additional acreage." (Internal citations and quotation marks omitted.)

4. **Lower court cases on reservation purposes, priority date, and the PIA standard.** United States v. Adair, 723 F.2d 1394 (9th Cir. 1983), was a suit to

declare water rights in the former Klamath Indian Reservation. The reservation was established under an 1864 treaty between the United States and the Indians. It was terminated under 1954 legislation whereby the United States purchased or condemned the tribal land. The United States then added some of the former reservation land it acquired to a national forest and made the 15,000 acre Klamath Marsh into a national wildlife refuge. For more than a thousand years, the Indians had lived near the marsh and depended upon it as a source of food in the form of game, wildfowl, and edible plants. The 1864 treaty had reserved to the Indians the exclusive right to continue their activities in the marsh, and in other litigation their hunting and fishing rights were held to have survived the termination act.

The court found that the 1864 treaty had the dual essential purposes of encouraging the Indians to take up farming and securing continuation of their traditional hunting and fishing lifestyle. Accordingly, the court held that water was impliedly reserved for both purposes. The reserved water right for hunting and fishing was a nonconsumptive right entitling the tribe to prevent upstream appropriators from depleting the streamflow below a protected level. Concerning the priority date of that right, the court said that "where, as here, a tribe shows its aboriginal use of water to support a hunting and fishing lifestyle, and then enters into a treaty with the United States that reserves this aboriginal water use, the water right thereby established retains a priority date of first or immemorial use." The court limited the aboriginal right, however, to "the amount of water necessary to support * * * hunting and fishing rights as currently exercised to maintain the livelihood of Tribe members, not as those rights once were exercised by the Tribe in 1864." In contrast, the court assigned the reserved right for irrigated agriculture a priority dating only from the 1864 treaty because there was no aboriginal water use for that purpose.

In *Big Horn I,* supra Note 3, the Wyoming court determined that the sole purpose of the 1868 treaty establishing the Wind River Indian Reservation was to encourage agriculture. Therefore, the court held that water was impliedly reserved only for agriculture and subsumed uses, including livestock, domestic, municipal, and commercial uses. The court refused to find an implied reservation of water for mineral and industrial uses, for fisheries (because when the treaty was signed the Indians neither depended on fishing for a livelihood nor had a traditional lifestyle involving fishing), or for wildlife and aesthetics (because no tradition of wildlife and aesthetic preservation was shown). The priority date of the reserved right for agriculture and subsumed uses was the date of the treaty.

State ex rel. Martinez v. Lewis, 861 P.2d 235 (N.M. Ct. App. 1993), involved the priority of reserved water rights for PIA on the Mescalero Apache Indian Reservation. In an 1852 treaty, the United States promised to create a reservation for the Apaches and also promised to give that promise a liberal construction. The boundaries of the reservation were not delineated, however, until issuance of a series of executive orders commencing in 1873. The court ruled that to establish the priority date of the tribe's water rights, the reservation should be regarded as having been created when the United States made its promises in 1852, rather than in 1873. The tribe claimed an even earlier priority of time immemorial based on aboriginal title. The court noted that the area was not settled by non-Indians until after 1852, so that a priority earlier than 1852 would make no practical difference. It declined to address the tribe's argument for a time-immemorial priority "[b]ecause we will not issue advisory opinions."

In re General Adjudication of the Gila River System, 35 P.3d 68 (Ariz. 2001), eschewed case-by-case analysis of historic documents to determine the purpose of Indian reservations, largely because the court believed those documents often do not express the true reasons for creating the reservations. Instead, the court declared that the purpose of Indian reservations is to serve as a homeland for the Native Americans living there. The court also rejected using PIA as the sole standard to quantify the amount of water reserved because that would be inconsistent with the idea of a permanent homeland and would be unfair to tribes inhabiting terrain that is mountainous or otherwise agriculturally marginal. The court provided a nonexclusive list of factors bearing on quantification, including tribal history and culture; the tribal land's geography, topography, and natural resources, including groundwater availability; the tribe's economic base and the optimal manner of creating jobs and income; past water use on the reservation; and present and projected population. Regardless of the relevant factors on a particular reservation, the court said proposed uses must be reasonably feasible both practically and economically.

5. **Lower court cases on reserved rights in groundwater.** The Wyoming Supreme Court declared in *Big Horn I*, supra Note 3, that "the reserved water doctrine does not extend to groundwater." The Montana Supreme Court ruled the reserved rights doctrine extends to groundwater necessary to accomplish the purpose of the reservation. Confederated Salish & Kootenai Tribes v. Stults, 59 P.3d 1093 (Mont. 2002). Similarly, the Arizona Supreme Court said: "The significant question for the purpose of the reserved rights doctrine is not whether the water runs above or below the ground but whether it is necessary to accomplish the purpose of the reservation." In re General Adjudication of All Rights to Use Water in Gila River System & Source, 989 P.2d 739, 747 (Ariz. 1999). But the Arizona court added a qualification for groundwater: "A reserved right to groundwater may only be found where other waters are inadequate to accomplish the purpose of a reservation." Id.

The Arizona case presented the complication that the state has the reasonable use doctrine for groundwater. Some parties argued reserved rights in groundwater were unnecessary because the reasonable use doctrine allows any overlying landowner, including the Indians, to capture at any time as much groundwater as can reasonably be used on the overlying land. The court responded as follows:

"Under the 'reasonable use' doctrine Arizona has consumed far more groundwater than nature can replenish. * * * Some Indian reservations have been entirely 'de-watered' by off-reservation pumping. We therefore cannot conclude that deference to Arizona's law—and to the opportunity it extends all landholders to pump as much groundwater as they can reasonably use—would adequately serve to protect federal rights." Id. at 748.

The Arizona court also addressed what protection should be given reserved rights in surface water and groundwater against interference from the exercise of water rights obtained under state law. Under Arizona's bifurcated state system of water rights—prior appropriation for surface streams and their subflow, reasonable use for other groundwater—a surface appropriator cannot enjoin groundwater pumping though it depletes the surface appropriator's supply. Similarly, Arizona's reasonable use doctrine does not allow an overlying owner to enjoin pumping by other overlying owners for reasonable use on their lands though the pumping interferes with the overlying owner's well. These rules apply to the holders of state water rights as against each other. The court declared that holders of federal reserved rights enjoy greater protection against interference. It said that if state law is inadequate to protect reserved rights in surface water or groundwater, the reservation may invoke federal law to preserve waters necessary to accomplish the reservation purpose. Id. at 749-50. The court quickly added that the protection for reserved rights is not without limitation:

"We do not, however, read the case law to require a zero-impact standard of protection for federal reserved rights. The Supreme Court has repeatedly acknowledged that the reserved rights doctrine 'reserves only that amount of water necessary to fulfill the purpose of the reservation, no more.' *Cappaert* [*v. United States*, 426 U.S. 128, 141 (1976)]. In *Cappaert*, the Court affirmed an injunction 'appropriately tailored * * * to minimal need, curtailing pumping only to the extent necessary to preserve an adequate water level at Devil's Hole.' Id. If injunctions should ultimately prove necessary in this case, they shall likewise be appropriately tailored to minimal need." Id. at 750.

6. **Nature of Indian reserved rights.** A water right is traditionally viewed as a usufruct—a right to use water, not "ownership" of water. In addition, a person is usually permitted to use water not being used by someone having superior rights. Consequently, it is generally assumed that non-Indians can use water that would be required to satisfy Indian reserved rights until the Indians actually begin exercising their rights. However, Confederated Salish & Kootenai Tribes v. Clinch, 992 P.2d 244 (Mont. 1999), casts doubt upon this assumption. In holding that the Montana Department of Natural Resources and Conservation could not issue permits to non-Indians to appropriate water on the Flathead Indian Reservation until the tribes' reserved rights are quantified (see supra p. 131-33, Note 5), the court rejected arguments by the department that it should be able to issue permits, first, because some new non-Indian water uses would not diminish instream flow and, second, because by state statute all permits issued before a final determination of existing water rights are only provisional and are subject to being reduced or revoked if necessary to protect senior rights:

"The idea that permits can be issued to use water on reservations where that water may have been reserved for the Tribes who occupy those reservations without interfering with tribal rights, ignores the distinction we made in State ex rel. Greely v. Confederated Salish and Kootenai Tribes of the Flathead Reservation (1985), 219 Mont. 7, 712 P.2d 754, between appropriative water rights provided by Montana's Water Use Act and Indian reserved water rights. 'Appropriative rights are based on actual use. Appropriation for beneficial use is governed by State law. Reserved rights are established by reference to the purposes of the reservation rather than to actual, present use of water.'

"We, furthermore, stated that, 'Indian reserved water rights are "owned" by the Indians.' Therefore, because under federal law, Indian tribes have an ownership interest in the water reserved for them and because that interest does not depend on use of the water it is unpersuasive that the State's permitting process might allow uses of Indian reserved water which in the long-term will not diminish in-stream flows.

"Nor do we agree that the provisional nature of permits issued by the Department is determinative. * * * [U]se of water which may have been reserved by federal law to the Tribes is no less impermissible simply because it is temporary and can be terminated following final quantification of the Tribes' right * * *."

7. **Pueblo Indian water rights.** When the Spaniards came in the sixteenth century to what is now New Mexico, they found established Pueblo Indian communities practicing irrigated agriculture along the Rio Grande and its tributaries. The Spanish and later the Mexican governments granted the Indians the right to their aboriginal lands. Then in 1848, Mexico ceded territory including New Mexico to the United States in the Treaty of Guadalupe Hidalgo. Pursuant to that treaty, the United States issued patents in 1858 to the various Indian pueblos conveying communal fee simple title to four square leagues of land surrounding the pueblos.

In a water adjudication commenced in 1966, the Indians claimed reserved rights or aboriginal rights derived from Spanish and Mexican law to as much water as needed to irrigate all the lands of each pueblo. In New Mexico v. Aamodt, 537 F.2d 1102 (10th Cir. 1976), the Tenth Circuit stated that since the Pueblo Indians held fee simple titles to their lands, which are not reservations, decisions like *Winters* were "not technically applicable." It remanded the case to the federal district court to determine what water rights the Indians did hold. The federal district court then ruled that no *Winters* rights existed in lands granted to the Pueblos by the Spanish or Mexican governments. State ex rel. Reynolds v. Aamodt, 618 F. Supp. 993 (D.N.M. 1985). Accord State ex rel. Martinez v. Kerr-McGee Corp., 898 P.2d 1256 (N.M. Ct. App. 1995). The federal district court recognized *Winters* rights only in former public land set aside in 1902 by executive order for one pueblo.

More significantly, the federal district court found that the Spanish and Mexican governments had recognized Indian property rights to the four square leagues of common lands, not subject to loss by adverse possession, and held that these pueblo lands came into the United States with aboriginal rights of *primacia*, first use, measured by the amount customarily used to grow crops for basic life support. The court ruled further that aboriginal rights attached only to lands irrigated between 1846 (when the United States first took control of the territory from Mexico) and 1924 (when, said the court, the Pueblo Lands Act terminated aboriginal water rights as to lands not previously irrigated).

The complex of Spanish, Mexican, and federal laws relating to the rights of Pueblo Indian communities is thoroughly explored in Charles T. DuMars et al., Pueblo Indian Water Rights (1984); Ed Newville, Comment, Pueblo Indian Water Rights: Overview and Update of the Aamodt Litigation, 29 Nat. Resources J. 251 (1989). The concept of water rights for Pueblo Indian communities should be distinguished from the question—explored in Note 3, supra p. 52-53—of whether modern cities in the Southwest tracing their origins to Spanish or Mexican grants have paramount rights to water for future municipal growth.

8. **Rancherias.** Rancherias are small plots of land in California purchased by the United States to provide homes for Indians not on reservations or whose reservations lacked sufficient land suitable for cultivation. 35 Stat. 70, 76 (1908); 34 Stat. 325, 333 (1906). The Secretary of the Interior was authorized to construct any necessary irrigation ditches, flumes, and reservoirs. Eighty-six such "reservations" were established, ranging in size from 640 acres to one or two acres, and any Indians, whether or not members of an organized tribe, were entitled to settle on them. Most of the lands were informally broken up into unsurveyed homesites. Many remained unoccupied. In 1958, the value of the program was questioned, and the Secretary was directed to distribute the lands and water rights on 41 rancherias to the residents or to sell the lands for their benefit, with their approval. 72 Stat. 619 (1958). Before doing so, the Secretary was instructed to install or rehabilitate

irrigation or domestic water systems as needed. When the lands were distributed, many of the plots were sold to non-Indians.

The rancheria lands were not reserved or withdrawn from public lands but, as noted above, were purchased by the United States. Section 4 of the Termination Act nevertheless provided: "Nothing in this act shall abrogate any water right that exists by virtue of the laws of the United States. To the extent that the laws of the State of California are not now applicable to any water right appurtenant to any lands involved herein they shall continue to be inapplicable while the water right is in Indian ownership for a period not to exceed 15 years after the conveyance pursuant to this act of an unrestricted title thereto, and thereafter the applicability of such laws shall be without prejudice to the priority of any such right not theretofore based on state law."

COLVILLE CONFEDERATED TRIBES v. WALTON

United States Court of Appeals, Ninth Circuit, 1981.
647 F.2d 42.

WRIGHT, CIRCUIT JUDGE. * * * In 1871 the predecessors of the Colville Confederated Tribes had no treaty with the United States and no reservation. These Indians were contemporaneously described as "good farmers, [who] raise extensive crops, make good improvements, and own stocks of cattle and horses." [1871] Report of the Commissioner of Indian Affairs, 277. After the Civil War, settlers had begun to encroach on Indian lands. The Farmer in charge of Fort Colville reported that violence was likely unless a reservation was established to protect Indian interests. In response to a request from the Commissioner of Indian Affairs, President Grant created the Colville Reservation. Executive Order of July 2, 1872. * * *

In 1906, Congress ratified an agreement with the Colvilles that provided for distribution of reservation lands to the Indians pursuant to the General Allotment Act of 1887, 24 Stat. 388, and for disposition of the remainder by entry and settlement. * * *

In 1917, a row of seven allotments was created in the No Name Creek watershed. Walton, a non-Indian, now owns the middle three, numbers 525, 2371 and 894. He bought them in 1948 from an Indian, not a member of the Tribe, who had begun to irrigate the land by diverting water for 32 acres from No Name Creek. Walton immediately procured a permit from the state to irrigate 65 acres by diverting up to 1 cubic foot per second "subject to existing rights." He now irrigates 104 acres and uses additional water for domestic and stock water purposes. The United States holds the remaining allotments in trust for the Colville Indians. * * *

The No Name Creek is a spring-fed creek flowing south into Omak Lake, which has no outlet and is saline. * * * Salmon and trout were traditional foods for the Colville Indians, but the salmon runs have been destroyed by dams on the Columbia River. In 1968, the Tribe, with the help of the Department of the Interior, introduced Lahonton cutthroat trout into Omak Lake. The species thrives in the lake's saline water, but needs fresh water to spawn. The Indians cultivated No Name Creek's lower reach to establish spawning grounds but irrigation use depleted the water flow during spawning season. The federal government has given the Indians fingerlings to maintain the stock of trout.

The trial court found that 1,000 acre feet per year of water were available in No Name Creek Basin in an average year. It calculated the quantity of the Colvilles' reserved water rights on the basis of irrigable acreage. * * * The trial court determined the Indians had a reserved right to 666.4 acre feet per year of water from the No Name Creek Basin. It held that Walton was not entitled to share in the Colvilles' reserved water rights. The trial court found, however, that the Colvilles were irrigating only a portion of the irrigable acres included in its calculation.

Under the district court's findings, in an average year there are 333.6 acre feet per year of water not subject to the Indians' reserved right. There are an additional 237.6 acre feet per year of water to which the Indians have a reserved right, but which they are not currently using. This water is available for appropriation by non-Indians, subject to the Indians' superior right. The court held that Walton had a right to irrigate the 32 acres under irrigation at the time he acquired his land, with a priority date of the actual appropriation of water for that use.

The court also held that the Indians were potentially entitled to use water to propagate trout, but refused to award water for that purpose. It concluded that spawning was unnecessary because fingerlings were provided free by the federal government. * * *

The Tribe's Water Rights

* * * We hold that water was reserved when the Colville Reservation was created. The more difficult question concerns the amount of water reserved. * * * We conclude that, when the Colville reservation was created, sufficient appurtenant water was reserved to permit irrigation of all practicably irrigable acreage on the reservation.

Providing for a land-based agrarian society, however, was not the only purpose for creating the reservation. The Colvilles traditionally fished for both salmon and trout. Like other Pacific Northwest Indians, fishing was of economic and religious importance to them. The Tribe's principal historic fishing grounds on the Columbia River have been destroyed by dams. The Indians have established replacement fishing grounds in Omak Lake by planting a non-indigenous trout. We agree with the district court that preservation of the tribe's access to fishing grounds was one purpose for the creation of the Colville Reservation. Under the circumstances, we find an implied reservation of water from No Name Creek for the development and maintenance of replacement fishing grounds. * * * We affirm the district court's holding that the Colvilles have a reserved right to the quantity of water necessary to maintain the Omak Lake Fishery.

The district court held that water for spawning could not be awarded at this time because the federal government provides the necessary fingerlings. We reverse this holding. The right to water to establish and maintain the Omak Lake Fishery includes the right to sufficient water to permit natural spawning of the trout. When the Tribe has a vested property right in reserved water, it may use it in any lawful manner. As a result, subsequent acts making the historically intended use of the water unnecessary do not divest the Tribe of the right to the water. * * * Finally, we note that permitting the Indians to determine how to use reserved water is consistent with the general purpose for the creation of an Indian reservation—providing a homeland for the survival and growth of the Indians and their way of life.

The General Allotment Act of 1887

We next consider Walton's rights as the fee owner of allotted land, and reverse the district court's judgment that he has no right to reserved water. * * *

The General Allotment Act provided that land on reservations could be allotted for the exclusive use of individual Indians. Remaining land was to be made available for homesteading by non-Indians. After holding allotted lands in trust for individual Indians for a 25-year period, the federal government could convey the land to the allottee in fee, "discharged of said trust and free of all charge or incumbrance whatsoever." 25 U.S.C. § 348.

Because the use of reserved water is not limited to fulfilling the original purposes of the reservation, Congress had the power to allot reserved water rights to individual Indians, and to allow for the transfer of such rights to non-Indians. Whether it did so is a question of congressional intent.

The General Allotment Act represented the shift in federal objectives from segregation of Indians on reservations to assimilation of them in non-Indian culture and society. Its primary sponsor, Senator Dawes, explained that "the quicker [the Indian] is mingled with the whites in every particular the better it will be." The Act was designed to encourage Indians to become self-supporting citizens by making them landowners. Allotted lands were held in trust for a 25 year period because of

> the desire to protect the Indian against sharp practices leading to Indian landlessness, the desire to safeguard the certainty of titles, and the urge to continue an important basis of governmental activity [on the Indians' behalf].

F. Cohen, Handbook of Federal Indian Law 221 (1940); U.S. Department of Interior, Federal Indian Law 788–89 (1958).

The only reference to water rights in the Act is found in section 7:

> In cases where the use of water for irrigation is necessary to render the lands within any Indian reservation available for agricultural purposes, the Secretary of the Interior is authorized to prescribe such rules and regulations as he may deem necessary to secure a just and equal distribution thereof among the Indians residing upon any such reservation; and no other appropriation or grant of water by any riparian proprietor shall be authorized or permitted to the damage of any other riparian proprietor.

25 U.S.C. § 381.

The Act was passed over 20 years before the Supreme Court announced the implied-reservation doctrine in *Winters*. There is nothing to suggest Congress gave any consideration to the transferability of reserved water rights.

To resolve this issue, we must determine what Congress would have intended had it considered it.

It is settled that Indian allottees have a right to use reserved water. United States v. Powers, 305 U.S. 527 (1939). "[W]hen allotments were made for exclusive use and thereafter conveyed in fee, the right to use some portion of tribal waters essential for cultivation passed to the owners." Id. at 532. We must determine whether non-Indian purchasers of allotted lands also obtain a right to some portion of reserved waters.

The general rule is that termination or diminution of Indian rights requires express legislation or a clear inference of Congressional intent gleaned from the surrounding circumstances and legislative history. Upon careful consideration, we conclude this principle supports the proposition that an Indian allottee may sell his right to reserved water.

The district court's holding that an Indian allottee may convey only a right to the water he or she has actually appropriated with a priority date of actual appropriation reduces the value of the allottee's right to reserved water. We think this type of restriction on transferability is a "diminution of Indian rights" that must be supported by a clear inference of Congressional intent.

By placing allotted lands in trust for 25 years, Congress evinced an intent to protect Indians by preventing transfer of those lands. But there is no basis for an inference that some restrictions survived beyond the trust period. Congress provided for extensions of the trust period, but directed that fee title be conveyed to the allottee when the period expired. We think the fee included the appurtenant right to share in reserved waters, and see no basis for limiting the transferability of that right. * * *

In determining the nature of the right acquired by non-Indian purchasers, we consider three aspects of an allottee's right to use reserved waters. First, the extent of an Indian allottee's right is based on the number of irrigable acres he owns. If the allottee owns 10% of the irrigable acreage in the watershed, he is entitled to 10% of the water reserved for irrigation (i.e., a "ratable share"). This follows from the provision for an equal and just distribution of water needed for irrigation. A non-Indian purchaser cannot acquire more extensive rights to reserved water than were held by the Indian seller. Thus, the purchaser's right is similarly limited by the number of irrigable acres he owns.

Second, the Indian allottee's right has a priority as of the date the reservation was created. This is the principal aspect of the right that renders it more valuable than the rights of competing water users, and therefore applies to the right acquired by a non-Indian purchaser. In the event there is insufficient water to satisfy all valid claims to reserved water, the amount available to each claimant should be reduced proportionately.

Third, the Indian allottee does not lose by non-use the right to a share of reserved water. This characteristic is not applicable to the right acquired by a non-Indian purchaser. The non-Indian successor acquires a right to water being appropriated by the Indian allottee at the time title passes. The non-Indian also acquires a right, with a date-of-reservation priority date, to water that he or she appropriates with reasonable diligence after the passage of title. If the full measure of the Indian's reserved water right is not acquired by this means and maintained by continued use, it is lost to the non-Indian successor.

The full quantity of water available to the Indian allottee thus may be conveyed to the non-Indian purchaser. There is no diminution in the right the Indian may convey. We think Congress would have intended, however, that the non-Indian purchaser, under no competitive disability vis-à-vis other water users, may not retain the right to that quantity of water despite non-use.

The district court's holding that Walton has no right to share in water reserved when the Colville reservation was created is reversed. On remand, it will need to determine the number of irrigable acres Walton owns, and the amount of water he appropriated with reasonable diligence in order to determine the extent of his right to share in reserved water. * * *

Notes

1. **The Allotment Act and allotment water rights.** The Supreme Court recounted the origin and the demise of the General Allotment (or Dawes) Act in South Dakota v. Yankton Sioux Tribe, 522 U.S. 329 (1998):

"[The mid-nineteenth century was] a period of rapid growth in the United States' population, increasing westward migration, and ensuing demands from non-Indians to open Indian holdings throughout the Western States to settlement. In response * * *, Congress retreated from the reservation concept and began to dismantle the territories that it had previously set aside as permanent and exclusive homes for Indian tribes. The pressure from westward-bound homesteaders, and the belief that the Indians would benefit from private property ownership, promoted passage of the Dawes Act in 1887, 24 Stat. 388. The Dawes Act permitted the Federal Government to allot tracts of tribal land to individual Indians and, with tribal consent, to open the remaining holdings to non-Indian settlement. Within a generation or two, it was thought, the tribes would dissolve, their reservations would disappear, and individual Indians would be absorbed into the larger community of white settlers. * * * [T]he policy favoring assimilation through the allotment of reservation land [was] formally repudiated with the passage of the Indian Reorganization Act in 1934, 48 Stat. 984, 25 U.S.C. § 461 * * *."

For somewhat differing analyses of Indian allotment water rights and their transferability, see Richard B. Collins, Indian Allotment Water Rights, 20 Land & Water L. Rev. 421 (1985); David H. Getches, Water Rights on Indian Allotments, 26 S.D. L. Rev. 405 (1981).

2. **"Reasonable diligence after the passage of title."** *Walton* says a non-Indian purchaser of land from an Indian allottee gets a date-of-reservation priority only for (i) water used by the Indian allottee when the title passes and (ii) water the purchaser "appropriates with reasonable diligence after the passage of title." The Wyoming Supreme Court addressed the latter criterion in In re General Adjudication of All Rights to Use Water in Big Horn River System (*Big Horn V*), 48 P.3d 1040 (Wyo. 2002). Various non-Indians bought allotted lands in the Wind River Indian Reservation from Indians after the United States commenced the Wind River Irrigation Project but ten to twenty years before the project was completed. The lands in question could not be irrigated until the project was completed. The court held the non-Indian purchasers would qualify for *Walton* rights if they irrigated their

lands "within a reasonable time and with due diligence, as defined by state law, after the federal project facilities became available to the properties." Id. at 1055.

Two properties in *Big Horn V* were sold by Indian allottees to non-Indians, then were resold to Indian purchasers, and later were resold again to non-Indians. The court ruled a reasonable time runs from the first conveyance from Indian ownership, not the most recent one.

3. **Unallotted reservation lands acquired by non-Indians.** Reserved water rights do not continue in former reservation lands not allotted to individual Indians but ceded by the tribe to the United States and then patented to non-Indians under general land grant statutes such as the Homestead Act and the Desert Land Act. In re General Adjudication of All Rights to Use Water in Big Horn River System (*Big Horn IV*), 899 P.2d 848 (Wyo. 1995). The court refused to extend *Walton* to this situation because it said the purpose for which the reserved water was recognized ceased to exist when the tribe relinquished the land to the United States.

4. **Use of reserved water on the reservation by Indians for new purposes.** The 1979 supplemental decree in Arizona v. California entered on the joint motion of the parties, supra p. 685, states that while PIA is used to quantify reserved water rights for the five Indian reservations, the reliance on that method of quantification "shall not constitute a restriction of the usage of [the water rights] to irrigation or other agricultural application. If all or part of the adjudicated water rights of any of the five Indian Reservations is used other than for irrigation or other agricultural application, the total consumptive use * * * for said Reservation shall not exceed the consumptive use that would have resulted if the diversions * * * had been used for irrigation of the number of acres specified for that Reservation * * *."

In *Big Horn I*, supra p. 686, Note 3, the Wyoming court awarded the Wind River Indian Reservation a reserved water right for agricultural and subsumed uses. The award included water for both historically irrigated lands and unirrigated PIA that would require construction of new water project facilities. But the court rejected a tribal claim for instream fishery flows. Later, in In re General Adjudication of All Rights to Use Water in Big Horn River System (*Big Horn III*), 835 P.2d 273 (Wyo. 1992), the tribes sought to change their reserved water right for future irrigation projects to the new use of maintaining instream fishery flows. They argued that the PIA standard applied in *Big Horn I* served only as a means to quantify their rights and did not restrict the purposes for which they could use the water. The district court approved the change in use they requested. Although Wyoming law prohibits anyone other than the state from owning an instream flow water right, the district court ruled that state law did not apply to the reserved right.

The Wyoming Supreme Court reversed the change approval by vote of 3 to 2. Justice Macy's lead opinion for the majority said *Big Horn I* clearly and unequivocally limited the reserved right to agricultural and subsumed uses and did not allow instream use: "If we had intended to specify what the water could be used for merely as a methodology to determine the amount of water the Tribes could use for any purpose, we would have said so." Justice Macy also said state law governs transfers of reserved rights to secondary reservation purposes, see infra p. 709, Note 2, and the requested transfer was barred by the Wyoming rule against anyone other than the state owning an instream appropriation. A second justice said state law applied to the transfer but only because of the peculiar history of the Wind River Reservation. The third justice making up the majority concluded federal law governs transfers of reserved rights. But he thought federal law barred the transfer of a right reserved for irrigation use to instream flow maintenance unless the right had first been exercised for its irrigation purpose, and the tribes were seeking transfer of an unexercised irrigation right.

United States v. Orr Water Ditch Co., 309 F. Supp. 2d 1245 (D. Nev. 2004), also involved reserved rights for irrigation that had not been fully exercised. The Nevada State Engineer issued permits to the Pyramid Lake Paiute Tribe to temporarily transfer two reserved rights for irrigation to instream fishery use. The reserved rights were decreed by the Orr Ditch Decree, a consent decree that authorized changes in the place or manner of use "in the manner provided by law." In affirming the state engineer's transfer approval, the court said "provided by law" means state law except so far as federal law preempts it, and the court found federal preemption of a state requirement that only water rights perfected by exercise can be transferred. The court also accepted the state engineer's finding that both irrigation and fishery were primary reservation purposes, thus making it unnecessary to decide whether a reserved right can be transferred from a primary to a secondary reservation purpose. Finally, the court accepted the state engineer's view that in applying the no-injury rule for transfers, the impact of the tribe's new use should be compared to the physical conditions that would have existed if the tribe had put its reserved rights fully to use as decreed, rather than to the tribe's actual past water use.

5. **Leasing of reservation land with reserved water to non-Indians.** Congress has authorized the leasing of the surplus lands of any tribe and the unallotted irrigable lands on any Indian reservation for farming purposes. 25 U.S.C. §§ 402, 402a. Congress has also authorized the leasing of tribally or individually owned restricted Indian lands (restricted, among other things, as to their alienability) for "business purposes, including the development or utilization of natural resources in connection with operations under such leases, * * * and for those farming purposes which require the making of a substantial investment in the improvement of the land for the production of specialized crops." Id. § 415. It is generally thought that these authorizations include the leasing of water rights for the lands. See Skeem v. United States, 273 F. 93 (9th Cir. 1921).

6. **Leasing of reserved water to non-Indians for off-reservation use.** Tribes with reserved waters rights measured by PIA have water supplies that might never be fully used to irrigate reservation land and, in any event, could be used more productively off the reservation by growing municipalities or by other entities. Commentators have debated whether and under what conditions a tribe can lease water to non-Indians for use off the reservation. See, e.g., David H. Getches, Management and Marketing of Indian Water: From Conflict to Pragmatism, 58 U. Colo. L. Rev. 515 (1988); Jack D. Palma, II, Considerations and Conclusions Concerning the Transferability of Indian Water Rights, 20 Nat. Resources J. 91 (1980); Lee H. Story, Comment, Leasing Indian Water Off the Reservation: A Use Consistent With the Reservation's Purpose, 76 Cal. L. Rev. 179 (1988).

7. **Indian water right settlements.** Congress has approved a number of negotiated Indian water right settlements during the last quarter century. Negotiated settlement can be faster and less expensive than litigation of unsettled issues regarding Indian reserved water rights.

Although the settlements vary in their terms, they typically resolve some of the major legal and factual issues commonly arising from claims of Indian reserved water rights: the purposes for which reserved rights exist on a particular reservation, quantification of the rights, whether reserved rights exist in groundwater, transfer of reserved rights to new uses on the reservation, and transfer for off-reservation uses. Settlements generally protect existing non-Indian uses despite also contemplating an increase in the exercise of Indian reserved rights. Often this is accomplished through water conservation requirements and new federal water storage or other federally financed measures. In a era of generally diminished congressional interest in financing water projects, federal expenditures for Indian water right settlements seem to have been an exception. Many of the settlements are analyzed in Jon C. Hare, Indian Water Rights: An Analysis of Current and Pending Indian Water Rights Settlements (1996); Reid P. Chambers & John E. Echohawk, Implementing the *Winters* Doctrine of Indian Reserved Water Rights: Producing Indian Water and Economic Development Without Injuring Non-Indian Water Users?, 27 Gonz. L. Rev. 447 (1991/92).

8. **Abrogation of Indian reserved water rights.** Congress can unilaterally abrogate Indian treaty rights, though compensation must be paid to the tribe for loss of its rights. State, Department of Ecology v. Yakima Reservation Irrigation District, 850 P.2d 1306 (Wash. 1993), concerned an 1855 treaty that established the Yakima Indian Reservation and impliedly reserved water to maintain treaty fishing rights with a priority dating from time immemorial. Non-Indian irrigation districts argued that this reserved right was abrogated or diminished by post-treaty actions of the United States in promoting water use by non-Indians for irrigation. The court applied the established rule that federal abrogation of a treaty is not to be inferred lightly. It said abrogation requires clear evidence the United States actually considered the conflict between its intended action and the treaty rights, and chose to resolve the conflict by abrogating the treaty. The court noted that during the years when the United States was promoting irrigation by non-Indians, it also was trying to protect fish runs and continuing to recognize the Indians' right to fish. In light of these inconsistent governmental actions, the court decided there was no abrogation of the treaty's implied water reservation for fishing rights. (The court found, though, that the water reservation for fishery purposes was diminished because the tribe had filed a claim with the Indian Claims Commission seeking compensation for loss of fishing rights caused by non-Indian irrigation and then accepted compensation to settle the claim and dismiss it with prejudice.)

In addition to its reserved water right associated with treaty fishing rights, the Yakima Indian Nation had a reserved water right for irrigation with a priority as of the date of the 1855 treaty. The court found Congress had abrogated this right through legislation and federal contracts to supply water to the Indians, which together had limited and quantified the reserved right, changed the priority date of part of it to 1905, and made that part of it proratable during shortage along with the water rights of non-Indians holding similar federal water supply contracts.

B. Federal Reserved Rights

CAPPAERT v. UNITED STATES

Supreme Court of the United States, 1976.
426 U.S. 128, 96 S. Ct. 2062, 48 L. Ed.2d 523.

MR. CHIEF JUSTICE BURGER delivered the opinion of the Court.

The question presented in this litigation is whether the reservation of Devil's Hole as a national monument reserved federal water rights in unappropriated water.

Devil's Hole is a deep limestone cavern in Nevada. Approximately 50 feet below the opening of the cavern is a pool 65 feet long, 10 feet wide, and at least 200 feet deep, although its actual depth is unknown. The pool is a remnant of the prehistoric Death Valley Lake System and is situated on land owned by the United States since the Treaty of Guadalupe Hidalgo in 1848, 9 Stat. 922. By the Proclamation of January 17, 1952, President Truman withdrew from the public domain a 40-acre tract of land surrounding Devil's Hole, making it a detached component of the Death Valley National Monument. Proclamation No. 2961, 3 CFR 147 (1949-1953 Comp.). The Proclamation was issued under the American Antiquities Preservation Act, 34 Stat. 225, 16 U.S.C.A. § 431, which authorizes the President to declare as national monuments "objects of historic or scientific interest that are situated upon the lands owned or controlled by the Government of the United States * * *."

The 1952 Proclamation notes that Death Valley was set aside as a national monument "for the preservation of the unusual features of scenic, scientific, and educational interest therein contained." The Proclamation also notes that Devil's Hole is near Death Valley and contains a "remarkable underground pool." Additional preambulary statements in the Proclamation explain why Devil's Hole was being added to the Death Valley National Monument:

> "WHEREAS the said pool is a unique subsurface remnant of the prehistoric chain of lakes which in Pleistocene times formed the Death Valley Lake System, and is unusual among caverns in that it is a solution area in distinctly striated limestone, while also owing its formation in part to fault action; and
>
> "WHEREAS the geologic evidence that this subterranean pool is an integral part of the hydrographic history of the Death Valley region is further confirmed by the presence in this pool of a peculiar race of desert fish, and zoologists have demonstrated that this race of fish, which is found nowhere else in the world, evolved only after the gradual drying up of the Death Valley Lake System isolated this fish population from the original ancestral stock that in Pleistocene times was common to the entire region; and
>
> "WHEREAS the said pool is of such outstanding scientific importance that it should be given special protection, and such protection can be best afforded by making the said forty-acre tract containing the pool a part of the said monument * * *."

The Cappaert petitioners own a 12,000-acre ranch near Devil's Hole, 4,000 acres of which are used for growing Bermuda grass, alfalfa, wheat, and barley; 1,700 to 1,800 head of cattle are grazed. The ranch represents an investment of more than $7 million; it employs more than 80 people with an annual payroll of more than $340,000.

In 1968 the Cappaerts began pumping groundwater on their ranch on land 2½ miles from Devil's Hole; they were the first to appropriate groundwater. The groundwater comes from an underground basin or aquifer which is also the source of the water in Devil's Hole. After the Cappaerts began pumping from the wells near Devil's Hole, which they do from March to October, the summer water level of the pool in Devil's Hole began to decrease. Since 1962 the level of water in Devil's Hole has been measured with reference to a copper washer installed on one of the walls of the hole by the United States Geological Survey. Until 1968, the water level, with seasonable variations, had been stable at 1.2 feet below the copper marker. In 1969 the water level in Devil's Hole was 2.3 feet below the copper washer; in 1970, 3.17 feet; in 1971, 3.48 feet; and, in 1972, 3.93 feet.

When the water is at the lowest levels, a large portion of a rock shelf in Devil's Hole is above water. However, when the water level is at 3.0 feet below the marker or higher, most of the rock shelf is below water, enabling algae to grow on it. This in turn enables the desert fish (*cyprinodon diabolis,* commonly known as Devil's Hole pupfish), referred to in President Truman's Proclamation, to spawn in the spring. As the rock shelf becomes exposed, the spawning area is decreased, reducing the ability of the fish to spawn in sufficient quantities to prevent extinction.

In August 1971 the United States * * * sought an injunction in the United States District Court for the District of Nevada to limit, except for domestic purposes, the Cappaerts' pumping from six specific wells and from specific locations near Devil's Hole. * * * The District Court found that if the injunction did not issue "there is grave danger that the Devil's Hole pupfish may be destroyed, resulting in irreparable injury to the United States." 375 F. Supp. 456, 460 (1974).

On April 9, 1974, the District Court entered its findings of fact and conclusions of law substantially unchanged in a final decree permanently enjoining pumping that lowers the level of the water below the 3.0-foot level. The Court of Appeals for the Ninth Circuit affirmed, 508 F.2d 313 (1974). We granted certiorari to consider the scope of the implied-reservation-of-water-rights doctrine.

This Court has long held that when the Federal Government withdraws its land from the public domain and reserves it for a federal purpose, the Government, by implication, reserves appurtenant water then unappropriated to the extent needed to accomplish the purpose of the reservation. In so doing the United States acquires a reserved right in unappropriated water which vests on the date of the reservation and is superior to the rights of future appropriators. Reservation of water rights is empowered by the Commerce Clause, Art. I, § 8, which permits federal regulation of navigable streams, and the Property Clause, Art. IV, § 3, which permits federal regulation of federal lands. The doctrine applies to Indian reservations and other federal enclaves, encompassing water rights in navigable and non-navigable streams. * * *

In determining whether there is a federally reserved water right implicit in a federal reservation of public land, the issue is whether the Government intended to reserve unappropriated and thus available water. Intent is inferred if the previously unappropriated waters are necessary to accomplish the purposes for which the reservation was created. Both the District Court and the

Court of Appeals held that the 1952 Proclamation expressed an intention to reserve unappropriated water, and we agree. The Proclamation discussed the pool in Devil's Hole in four of the five preambles and recited that the "pool * * * should be given special protection." Since a pool is a body of water, the protection contemplated is meaningful only if the water remains; the water right reserved by the 1952 Proclamation was thus explicit, not implied. * * *

The implied-reservation-of-water-rights doctrine, however, reserves only that amount of water necessary to fulfill the purpose of the reservation, no more. Here the purpose of reserving Devil's Hole Monument is preservation of the pool. Devil's Hole was reserved "for the preservation of the unusual features of scenic, scientific, and educational interest." The Proclamation notes that the pool contains "a peculiar race of desert fish * * * which is found nowhere else in the world" and that the "pool is of * * * outstanding scientific importance * * *." The pool need only be preserved, consistent with the intention expressed in the Proclamation, to the extent necessary to preserve its scientific interest. The fish are one of the features of scientific interest. The preamble noting the scientific interest of the pool follows the preamble describing the fish as unique; the Proclamation must be read in its entirety. Thus, as the District Court has correctly determined, the level of the pool may be permitted to drop to the extent that the drop does not impair the scientific value of the pool as the natural habitat of the species sought to be preserved. The District Court thus tailored its injunction, very appropriately, to minimal need, curtailing pumping only to the extent necessary to preserve an adequate water level at Devil's Hole, thus implementing the stated objectives of the Proclamation. * * *

No cases of this Court have applied the doctrine of implied reservation of water rights to groundwater. Nevada argues that the implied-reservation doctrine is limited to surface water. Here, however, the water in the pool is surface water. The federal water rights were being depleted because, as the evidence showed, the "[g]roundwater and surface water are physically interrelated as integral parts of the hydrologic cycle." C. Corker, Groundwater Law, Management and Administration, National Water Commission Legal Study No. 6, p. xxiv (1971). Here the Cappaerts are causing the water level in Devil's Hole to drop by their heavy pumping. It appears that Nevada itself may recognize the potential interrelationship between surface and groundwater since Nevada applies the law of prior appropriation to both. Nev. Rev. Stat. §§ 533.010 et seq., 534.020, 534.080, 534.090 (1973). Thus, since the implied-reservation-of-water-rights doctrine is based on the necessity of water for the purpose of the federal reservation, we hold that the United States can protect its water from subsequent diversion, whether the diversion is of surface or groundwater. * * *

Petitioners argue that the Federal Government must perfect its implied water rights according to state law. They contend that the Desert Land Act of 1877, 19 Stat. 377, 43 U.S.C.A. § 321, and its predecessors severed nonnavigable water from public land, subjecting it to state law. That Act, however, provides that patentees of public land acquire only title to land through the patent and must acquire water rights in nonnavigable water in accordance with state law. This Court held in FPC v. Oregon, 349 U.S. 435, 448, 75 S.Ct. 832,

840, 99 L.Ed. 1215, 1226 (1955), that the Desert Land Act does not apply to water rights on federally reserved land. * * * The Desert Land Act still provides that the water rights of those who received their land from federal patents are to be governed by state law. That there may be no more federal land available for homesteading does not mean the Desert Land Act now applies to all federal land. Since the Act is inapplicable, determination of reserved water rights is not governed by state law but derives from the federal purpose of the reservation; the fact that the water rights here reserved apply to nonnavigable rather than navigable waters is thus irrelevant. * * *

We hold, therefore, that as of 1952 when the United States reserved Devil's Hole, it acquired by reservation water rights in unappropriated appurtenant water sufficient to maintain the level of the pool to preserve its scientific value and thereby implement Proclamation No. 2961. Accordingly, the judgment of the Court of Appeals is Affirmed.

Note

History of federal reserved water rights. In United States v. Rio Grande Dam & Irrigation Co., 174 U.S. 690, 703 (1899), the Court declared that "a state cannot by its legislation destroy the right of the United States, as the owner of lands bordering on a stream, to the continued flow of its waters, so far at least as may be necessary for the beneficial uses of the government property." Although the Court cited *Rio Grande Dam* when it decided Winters v. United States in 1908, *Winters* was widely regarded for many years as a special quirk of Indian law. Then in 1955, the Court held that a Federal Power Act license for a dam on federal land reserved for power site purposes could not be thwarted by lack of state permission. Fed. Power Comm'n v. Oregon, 349 U.S. 435 (1955) (often called the Pelton Dam case). The majority and dissenting opinions in Pelton Dam were susceptible of being read as saying that when the United States reserves land for a power site, it impliedly reserves water needed to carry out that purpose. Since the federal licensee, a power company, had no state water permit, many observers assumed that the company must be operating the facility under some implicit assignment of the right of the United States to use water which it impliedly reserved from state jurisdiction when it reserved the power site. Frank J. Trelease, Federal Reserved Water Rights Since PLLRC, 54 Denv. L.J. 473 (1977).

The Court's first express allocation of water for non-Indian lands and purposes under the reserved rights theory came in its 1963 Arizona v. California opinion: "The Master ruled that the principle underlying the reservation of water rights for Indian Reservations was equally applicable to other federal establishments such as National Recreation Areas and National Forests. We agree with the conclusions of the Master that the United States intended to reserve water sufficient for the future requirements of the Lake Mead National Recreation Area, the Havasu Lake National Wildlife Refuge, the Imperial National Wildlife Refuge and the Gila National Forest." 373 U.S. at 601.

UNITED STATES v. NEW MEXICO

Supreme Court of the United States, 1978.
438 U.S. 696, 98 S. Ct. 3012, 57 L. Ed.2d 1052.

MR. JUSTICE REHNQUIST delivered the opinion of the Court.

The Rio Mimbres rises in the southwestern highlands of New Mexico and flows generally southward, finally disappearing in a desert sink just north of the Mexican border. The river originates in the upper reaches of the Gila National Forest, but during its course it winds more than 50 miles past privately owned lands and provides substantial water for both irrigation and mining. In 1970, a stream adjudication was begun by the State of New Mexico to determine the exact rights of each user to water from the Mimbres. In this adjudication the United States claimed reserved water rights for use in the Gila National Forest. The State District Court held that the United States, in setting the Gila National Forest aside from other public lands, reserved the use of such water "as may be necessary for the purposes for which [the land was] withdrawn," but that these purposes did not include recreation, aesthetics, wildlife-preservation, or cattle grazing. The United States appealed unsuccessfully to the Supreme Court of New Mexico. We granted certiorari to consider whether the Supreme Court of New Mexico had applied the correct principles of federal law in determining petitioner's reserved rights in the Mimbres. We now affirm.

The question posed in this case—what quantity of water, if any, the United States reserved out of the Mimbres River when it set aside the Gila National Forest in 1899—is a question of implied intent and not power. * * *

Recognition of Congress' power to reserve water for land which is itself set apart from the public domain, however, does not answer the question of the amount of water which has been reserved or the purposes for which the water may be used. Substantial portions of the public domain *have* been withdrawn and reserved by the United States for use as Indian reservations, forest reserves, national parks, and national monuments. And water is frequently necessary to achieve the purposes for which these reservations are made. But Congress has seldom expressly reserved water for use on these withdrawn lands. If water were abundant, Congress' silence would pose no problem. In the arid parts of the West, however, claims to water for use on federal reservations inescapably vie with other public and private claims for the limited quantities to be found in the rivers and streams. This competition is compounded by the sheer quantity of reserved lands in the western States, which lands form brightly colored swaths across the maps of these States.[3]

* * * While many of the contours of what has come to be called the "implied-reservation-of-water doctrine" remain unspecified, the Court has repeatedly emphasized that Congress reserved "only that amount of water necessary to fulfill the purpose of the reservation, no more." Cappaert, 426 U.S., at 141, 96 S.Ct., at 2071. Each time this Court has applied the "implied-reservation-of-water doctrine," it has carefully examined both the asserted water right and the specific purposes for which the land was reserved,

3. The percentage of federally owned land (*excluding* Indian reservations and other trust properties) in the western States ranges from 29.5% of the land in the State of Washington to 86.5% of the land in the State of Nevada, an average of about 46%. 33.6% of the land in the State of New Mexico is federally owned. Because federal reservations are normally found in the uplands of the Western States rather than the flatlands, the percentage of water flow originating in or flowing through the reservations is even more impressive. More than 60% of the average annual water yield in the 11 Western States is from federal reservations.

and concluded that without the water the purposes of the reservation would be entirely defeated.

This careful examination is required both because the reservation is implied, rather than expressed, and because of the history of congressional intent in the field of federal-state jurisdiction with respect to allocation of water. Where Congress has expressly addressed the question of whether federal entities must abide by state water law, it has almost invariably deferred to the state law. Where water is necessary to fulfill the very purposes for which a federal reservation was created, it is reasonable to conclude, even in the face of Congress' express deference to state water law in other areas, that the United States intended to reserve the necessary water. Where water is only valuable for a secondary use of the reservation, however, there arises the contrary inference that Congress intended, consistent with its other views, that the United States would acquire water in the same manner as any other public or private appropriator.

Congress indeed has appropriated funds for the acquisition under state law of water to be used on federal reservations. Thus, in the National Parks Act of August 7, 1946, 60 Stat. 885, 16 U.S.C.A. § 17j–2, Congress authorized appropriations for the "[i]nvestigation and establishment of water rights *in accordance with local custom, law, and decisions of courts,* including the acquisition of water rights or of lands or interests in lands or rights-of-way for use and protection of water rights necessary or beneficial in the administration and public use of the national parks and monuments." (Emphasis added.) * * *

The quantification of reserved water rights for the national forests is of critical importance to the West, where, as noted earlier, water is scarce and where more than 50% of the available water either originates in or flows through national forests. When, as in the case of the Rio Mimbres, a river is fully appropriated, federal reserved water rights will frequently require a gallon-for-gallon reduction in the amount of water available for water-needy state and private appropriators. This reality has not escaped the attention of Congress and must be weighed in determining what, if any, water Congress reserved for use on the national forests.

The United States contends that Congress intended to reserve minimum instream flows for aesthetic, recreational, and fish-preservation purposes. An examination of the limited purposes for which Congress authorized the creation of national forests, however, provides no support for this claim. In the mid- and late-1800's, many of the forests on the public domain were ravaged and the fear arose that the forest lands might soon disappear, leaving the United States with a shortage both of timber and of watersheds with which to encourage stream flows while preventing floods. It was in answer to these fears that in 1891 Congress authorized the President to "set apart and reserve, in any State or Territory having public lands bearing forests, any part of the public lands wholly or in part covered with timber or undergrowth, whether of commercial value or not, as public reservations." Creative Act of March 3, 1891, 26 Stat. 1095, 1103, 16 U.S.C.A. § 471 (repealed 1976).

The Creative Act of 1891 unfortunately did not solve the forest problems of the expanding Nation. To the dismay of the conservationists, the new national forests were not adequately attended and regulated; fires and indiscriminate timber-cutting continued their toll. To the anguish of Western settlers, reservations were frequently made indiscriminately. President Cleveland, in particular, responded to pleas of conservationists for greater protective measures by reserving some 21 million acres of "generally settled" forest land on February 22, 1897. President Cleveland's action drew immediate and strong protest from Western Congressmen who felt that the "hasty and ill considered" reservation might prove disastrous to the settlers living on or near these lands.

Congress' answer to these continuing problems was three-fold. It suspended the President's Executive order of February 22, 1897; it carefully defined the purposes for which national forests could in the future be reserved; and it provided a charter for forest management and economic uses within the forests. Organic Administration Act of June 4, 1897, 30 Stat. 11, 16 U.S.C.A. § 473 et seq. In particular, Congress provided:

> "*No national forest shall be established, except to improve and protect the forest within the boundaries, or for the purpose of securing favorable conditions of water flows, and to furnish a continuous supply of timber for the use and necessities of citizens of the United States*; but it is not the purpose or intent of these provisions, or of [the Creative Act of 1891], to authorize the inclusion therein of lands more valuable for the mineral therein, or for agricultural purposes, than for forest purposes." 30 Stat. 35, as amended, 16 U.S.C.A. § 475 (emphasis added).

The legislative debates surrounding the Organic Administration Act of 1897 and its predecessor bills demonstrate that Congress intended national forests to be reserved for only two purposes—"[t]o conserve the water flows and to furnish a continuous supply of timber for the people." 30 Cong.Rec. 967 (1897) (Cong. McRae). National forests were not to be reserved for aesthetic, environmental, recreational, or wildlife-preservation purposes.

> "The objects for which the forest reservation should be made are the protection of the forest growth against destruction by fire and axe and preservation of forest conditions upon which water conditions and water flow are dependent. The purpose, therefore, of this bill is to maintain favorable forest conditions, without excluding the use of these reservations for other purposes. They are not parks set aside for nonuse, but have been established for economic reasons." 30 Cong. Rec. 966 (1897) (Cong. McRae).

Administrative regulations at the turn of the century confirmed that national forests were to be reserved for only these two limited purposes.

Any doubt as to the relatively narrow purposes for which national forests were to be reserved is removed by comparing the broader language Congress used to authorize the establishment of national parks. In 1916, Congress created the National Park Service and provided that the

> "fundamental purpose of said parks, monuments, and reservations * * * is to conserve the scenery and the natural and historic objects and the wild life

therein and to provide for the enjoyment of the same * * * unimpaired for the enjoyment of future generations." National Park Service Act of 1916, 39 Stat. 535, 16 U.S.C.A. § 1 et seq.

When it was Congress' intent to maintain minimum instream flows within the confines of a national forest, it expressly so directed, as it did in the case of the Lake Superior National Forest:

> "In order to preserve the shore lines, rapids, waterfalls, beaches and other natural features of the region in an unmodified state of nature, no further alteration of the natural water level of any lake or stream * * * shall be authorized." 16 U.S.C.A. § 577b. * * *

In 1960, Congress passed the Multiple-Use Sustained-Yield Act of June 12, 1960, 74 Stat. 215, 16 U.S.C.A. § 528 et seq., which provides:

> "It is the policy of Congress that the national forests are established and shall be administered for outdoor recreation, range, timber, watershed, and wildlife and fish purposes. The purposes of this Act are declared to be supplemental to, but not in derogation of, the purposes for which the national forests were established as set forth in the [Organic Administration Act of 1897.]"

The Supreme Court of the State of New Mexico concluded that this Act did not give rise to any reserved rights not previously authorized in the Organic Administration Act of 1897. * * * While we conclude that the Multiple-Use Sustained-Yield Act of 1960 was intended to broaden the purposes for which national forests had previously been administered, we agree that Congress did not intend to thereby expand the reserved rights of the United States. * * *

The House Report accompanying the 1960 legislation * * * indicates that recreation, range, and "fish" purposes are "to be supplemental to, but not in derogation of, the purposes for which the national forests were established" in the Organic Administration Act of 1897. * * *

As discussed earlier, the "reserved rights doctrine" is a doctrine built on implication and is an exception to Congress' explicit deference to state water law in other areas. Without legislative history to the contrary, we are led to conclude that Congress did not intend in enacting the Multiple-Use Sustained-Yield Act of 1960 to reserve water for the *secondary* purposes there established. A reservation of additional water could mean a substantial loss in the amount of water available for irrigation and domestic use, thereby defeating Congress' principal purpose of securing favorable conditions of water flow. Congress intended the national forests to be administered for broader purposes after 1960 but there is no indication that it believed the new purposes to be so crucial as to require a reservation of additional water. By reaffirming the primacy of a favorable water flow, it indicated the opposite intent.

What we have said also answers petitioner's contention that Congress intended to reserve water from the Rio Mimbres for stockwatering purposes. Petitioner issues permits to private cattle-owners to graze their stock on the Gila National Forest and provides for stockwatering at various locations along the Rio Mimbres. Petitioner contends that, since Congress clearly foresaw stock-watering on national forests, reserved rights must be recognized for this purpose. The New Mexico courts disagreed and held that any stockwatering rights must be allocated under state law to individual stockwaterers. We agree.

While Congress intended the national forests to be put to a variety of uses, including stockwatering, not inconsistent with the two principal purposes of the forests, stockwatering was not itself a direct purpose of reserving the land.[23] If stockwatering could not take place on the Gila National Forest, Congress' purposes in reserving the land would not be defeated. Congress, of course, did intend to secure favorable water flows, and one of the uses to which the enhanced water supply was intended to be placed was probably stockwatering. But Congress intended the water supply from the Rio Mimbres to be allocated amongst private appropriators under state law. There is no indication in the legislative histories of any of the forest acts that Congress foresaw any need for the Forest Service to allocate water for stockwatering purposes, a task to which state law was well suited. * * *

Affirmed.

MR. JUSTICE POWELL, with whom MR. JUSTICE BRENNAN, MR. JUSTICE WHITE, and MR. JUSTICE MARSHALL join, dissenting in part.

I agree with the Court that the implied-reservation doctrine should be applied with sensitivity to its impact upon those who have obtained water rights under state law and to Congress' general policy of deference to state water law. I also agree that the Organic Administration Act of 1897 cannot fairly be read as evidencing an intent to reserve water for recreational or stockwatering purposes in the national forests.

I do not agree, however, that the forests which Congress intended to "improve and protect" are the still, silent, lifeless places envisioned by the Court. In my view, the forests consist of the birds, animals, and fish—the wildlife—that inhabit them, as well as the trees, flowers, shrubs, and grasses. I therefore would hold that the United States is entitled to so much water as is necessary to sustain the wildlife of the forests, as well as the plants. * * *

Notes

1. **Effect of the Multiple-Use Sustained-Yield Act (MUSYA).** In United States v. City of Challis, 988 P.2d 1199 (Idaho 1999), the United States asserted the discussion of MUSYA in United States v. New Mexico was "dictum because the Supreme Court did not have before it the question of whether MUSYA established a federal reserved water right with a priority date of 1960, but rather addressed whether MUSYA reached back before its enactment to expand the purposes of national forests as of the date of the Organic Act of 1897." The United States argued that MUSYA, properly viewed, re-reserved the national forests and reserved water therein as of 1960 for the purposes expressed in the act. The Idaho court disagreed. It read United States v. New Mexico as establishing that MUSYA creates no reserved water rights, of either priority date. Moreover, the Idaho court's

---

23. As discussed earlier, the national forests were not to be "set aside for non-use," 30 Cong. Rec. 966 (1897) (Cong. McRae), but instead to be opened up for any economic use not inconsistent with the forests' primary purposes. * * *

independent analysis of MUSYA was that it was not intended to reserve either land or water but only to expand the purposes for which national forests are managed.

2. **Indian reserved rights and the primary/secondary purpose distinction.** Justice Macy, who wrote the lead opinion for the three-member majority in *Big Horn III*, supra pp. 697-98, Note 4, concluded that the distinction between primary and secondary reservation purposes in United States v. New Mexico applies not only to federal land reservations but to Indian reservations. He said that although water is impliedly reserved for the primary purpose(s) of an Indian reservation, the acquisition of water rights for secondary purposes is governed by state law because of general congressional deference to state water law. And he could see no reason why state law should not also govern transfer from a primary reservation purpose (agriculture) to a secondary purpose (fish habitat). Wyoming law prevented the transfer because it bars anyone except the state from owning an instream flow water right.

Contrary to Justice Macy's view, three members of the Wyoming court concluded that federal law should govern transfer. But they failed to form a 3-2 majority in favor of allowing the transfer because, as noted earlier, one of the three thought federal law would prohibit the transfer of an unexercised irrigation right to instream flow maintenance.

In Colville Confederated Tribes v. Walton, 647 F.2d 42 (9th Cir. 1981), the Ninth Circuit also treated the primary/secondary purpose distinction of United States v. New Mexico as applicable to an Indian reservation. But the *Colville* court added a telling refinement by recognizing the existence of both general and specific reservation purposes. It found that the Colville Reservation had the general purpose of providing a homeland for the Indians, and the more specific purposes of providing for agriculture and preserving access to fishing grounds. The court concluded that while water was reserved for agriculture and fishing, the tribe could transfer the water to any new use because "permitting the Indians to determine how to use reserved water is consistent with the general purpose for the creation of an Indian reservation—providing a homeland for the survival and growth of the Indians and their way of life." This contrasts with the Wyoming court's rejection in *Big Horn I*, supra p. 686-87, Note 3, of a general homeland concept.

The Arizona court embraced the homeland concept for Indian reservations and rejected making any distinction between primary and secondary reservation purposes in In re General Adjudication of All Rights to Use Water in Gila River System & Source, 35 P.3d 68 (Ariz. 2001).

3. **Reserved rights for instream flows.** All the non-Indian federal water rights in western Colorado were at issue in United States v. City & County of Denver, 656 P.2d 1 (Colo. 1982) (hereinafter *Denver*). Among the claims asserted by the United States were reserved rights for flow maintenance in a national park, three national monuments, and seven national forests. In the national park, the court recognized reserved rights for instream flows and lake levels to conserve scenery, historic and scientific objects, and wildlife. In the national monuments, it recognized reserved rights for instream flows but limited them to flow levels needed to support the specific purposes for which the monuments were formed. Thus, the court denied a claim for a large instream flow right for recreation (river rafting) in one of the national monuments. In the national forests, the court relied on United States v. New Mexico to deny claims instream recreational, scenic, and wildlife flows.

Wilderness areas have been a battleground in the judiciary concerning reserved rights for instream flow maintenance. In Sierra Club v. Block, 622 F. Supp. 842 (D. Colo. 1985), the district court held that reserved water rights exist in wilderness areas for conservation and recreation purposes set forth in the Wilderness Act of 1964, including preservation of these areas in their natural condition. The Tenth Circuit vacated the judgment and dismissed the case on ripeness grounds without ruling on whether the Wilderness Act impliedly reserves water. Sierra Club v. Yeutter, 911 F.2d 1405 (10th Cir. 1990). More recently, the Idaho Supreme Court held the Wilderness Act impliedly reserved flows for three wilderness areas in Idaho and that the quantity reserved was all the unappropriated water within each area at the time it was established. Potlatch Corp. v. United States, No. 24546, 1999 WL 778325 (Idaho Oct. 1,1999) (3-2 decision). The justice who wrote the opinion for the three-member majority was up for re-election seven months later, and controversy over her opinion was the likely cause of her overwhelming defeat. Gregory J. Hobbs, Jr., State Water Politics Versus an Independent Judiciary: The Colorado and Idaho Experiences, 5 U. Denv. Water L. Rev. 122 (2001). The Idaho Supreme Court reheard the case after the election but before she left the bench, and the chief justice changed her vote to create a new 3-2 majority holding the Wilderness Act does not create implied reserved water rights. Potlatch Corp. v. United States, 12 P.3d 1260 (Idaho 2000). The majority decided water was not strictly necessary to accomplish the purposes of wilderness areas and also relied on remarks by Senator Frank Church of Idaho in support of the Wilderness Act during Senate debate, in which he said the act would not impede water development in the West.

Congress expressly addressed the reserved water issue in several recent acts creating wilderness areas. For example, the Nevada Wilderness Protection Act of 1989, Pub. L. No. 101-195, 103 Stat. 1784 (1989), and the Arizona Wilderness Act of 1990, Pub. L. 101-628, 104 Stat. 4469 (1990), expressly reserve a sufficient quantity of water to fulfill the purposes of the acts. These acts also direct federal officials to take steps necessary to protect the reserved rights, including filing claims in water right adjudications. However, both acts also state that their provisions reserving water shall not be construed as precedent for future wilderness designations nor constitute an interpretation of past acts or designations. The California Desert Protection Act of 1994, Pub. L. No. 103-433, 108 Stat. 4471 (1994), contains similar provisions expressly reserving water for all but two of the seventy-four wilderness area designations; for the two, it states that "no rights to water of the Colorado River are reserved, either expressly, impliedly, or otherwise." The Clark County Conservation of Public Land and Natural Resources Act of 2002, Pub. L. No. 107-282, 116 Stat. 1994 (2002), creates a number of small wilderness areas in the Mohave Desert within Nevada and declares that nothing in the act shall be construed to constitute an express or implied reservation of water or water rights for the lands.

Wild and Scenic Rivers Act § 13(c), 16 U.S.C. § 1284(c) declares: "Designation of any stream or portion thereof as a national wild, scenic or recreational river area shall not be construed as a reservation of the waters of such streams for purposes other than those specified in this chapter, or in quantities greater than necessary to accomplish these purposes." The Idaho court ruled that although Congress awkwardly expressed its intent in the negative, this language clearly reserves water to fulfill the purposes of the act. Potlatch Corp. v. United States, 12 P.3d 1256 (Idaho 2000).

4. **Other reserved right claims.** In *Denver*, supra Note 3, the United States also asserted reserved rights for two mineral hot springs on federal land and for fifteen hundred springs and water holes withdrawn from the public domain by a 1926 executive order entitled Public Water Reserve No. 107 (PWR No. 107). The court held that water was impliedly reserved in the mineral hot springs by 43 U.S.C. § 971, which authorized the Secretary of the Interior to lease lands near such springs for bathhouses, hotels, or other public accommodations. But it rejected the United States' claim that water in the hot springs was also reserved for the additional purpose of power production under leasing authority given to the Secretary by the Geothermal Steam Act of 1970, 30 U.S.C. § 1001. Finally, the court recognized reserved rights in the fifteen hundred springs and water holes withdrawn by PWR No. 107, but only to provide water for domestic and stockwatering purposes and only in amounts necessary to prevent monopolization of the supply by homesteaders, rather than for their entire yields as the United States had claimed.

The *Denver* ruling on the reservation of water for stockwatering under PWR No. 107 was followed in United States v. State, 959 P.2d 449 (Idaho 1998). The Idaho court added that "the United States has the right to administer such water rights on the public lands managed under the Taylor Grazing Act." Id. at 453.

The Federal Land Policy and Management Act of 1976 (FLPMA), 43 U.S.C. §§ 1701-1783, directed the Bureau of Land Management (BLM) to undertake a comprehensive program of planning and management of 448 million acres of federal public domain lands—lands not reserved for parks, monuments, forests, and so on—for a multiplicity of purposes. Among the act's directives is a requirement that the BLM manage the public lands in a manner "that will protect the quality of scientific, scenic, historical, ecological, environmental, air and atmospheric, water resource, and archaeological values; that, where appropriate, will preserve and protect certain public lands in their natural condition; that will provide food and habitat for fish and wildlife and domestic animals; and that will provide for outdoor recreation and human occupancy and use." Sierra Club v. Watt, 659 F.2d 203 (D.C. Cir. 1981), held that FLPMA did not create reserved water rights because it did not withdraw land from the public domain and because it expressly disclaimed making any change in federal or state jurisdiction or rights in water resources.

5. **Federal water rights acquired under state law.** In *Denver*, supra Note 3, the United States was denied instream flow reserved water rights in the national forests for watershed protection and timber production, but it did successfully assert thousands of claims for appropriations under state law, mostly for use on public domain lands administered by the BLM. In DeKay v. United States Fish & Wildlife Service, 524 N.W.2d 855 (S.D. 1994), the federal Fish & Wildlife Service was allowed to appropriate water under South Dakota law to maintain waterfowl habitat on formerly private land it purchased that is contiguous to a national wildlife refuge.

In California, the United States was held to have state-law riparian rights for the secondary purpose of wildlife enhancement in a national forest. In re Water of Hallett Creek Stream Sys., 749 P.2d 324 (Cal. 1988). The rights claimed, however, were for future wildlife enhancement and thus were unexercised riparian rights. As such, said the court, the rights were subject to the rule of In re Waters of Long Valley Creek System, supra p. 316, footnote 2, authorizing the State Water Resources Control Board to subordinate unexercised riparian rights to appropriations made before the riparian rights are exercised.

In Nevada, the supreme court and the legislature have been at odds over BLM appropriations for watering livestock owned by Taylor Grazing Act lessees or permittees. The court allowed the BLM to appropriate water for livestock in State v. Morros, 766 P.2d 263 (Nev. 1988). It said the United States did not have to own the livestock on federal range lands to appropriate water under state law because it owned the land where the water was beneficially used. The legislature responded by prohibiting the state engineer from issuing any permit for livestock watering unless the applicant "is legally entitled to place the livestock on the public lands for which the permit is sought". Nev. Rev. Stat. 533.503. But the court held in United States v. State Engineer, 27 P.3d 51 (Nev. 2001), that the BLM still could appropriate water for livestock watering because it would be illogical and unreasonable to interpret the new statute to obligate the BLM to issue itself a grazing lease for its own land before it could qualify for a livestock watering appropriation. The court said: "A plain reading of the statute indicates it requires an applicant to have some legal authority to use the public land for grazing purposes and nothing else." Id. at 54. The legislature again responded. It amended the statute to prohibit the state engineer from issuing a permit for livestock watering on public or private land unless the applicant is legally entitled to place the livestock on the land, has a legal or proprietary interest in the livestock, and the forage is not encumbered by a grazing preference, i.e., a superior right to receive a grazing permit or lease, issued by the government for the benefit of someone other than the water permit applicant.

6. **Federal nonreserved water rights.** If the United States has no reserved water rights for public domain lands or for the secondary purposes of reserved lands, is there any way for it to claim recreational and habitat flows in an appropriation doctrine state that either requires a diversion structure, does not regard such uses as beneficial, or limits instream flow appropriations to state agencies? A possible solution would be a federal nonreserved right to water. The main constitutional basis asserted for the concept is the Supremacy Clause: If a constitutional act of Congress authorizes a federal use of water, the United States must have power to make that use regardless of state water law. Another asserted constitutional basis is that the United States, by virtue of its "ownership of unappropriated water" (see supra pp. 667-68, Note 3), has power under the Property Clause to use such water as it sees fit without regard to state law. The priority of a nonreserved right would be the date of its first actual use.

The concept of federal nonreserved water rights was created, modified, and repudiated by three successive Solicitors of the Department of the Interior. Solicitor Leo Krulitz made very broad claims to federal nonreserved rights. Federal Water Rights of the National Park Service, Fish and Wildlife Service, Bureau of Reclamation, and Bureau of Land Management, 86 Interior Dec. 553 (1979). The broad claims seemingly ignored the dictum of United States v. New Mexico that where the United States has not reserved water, "there arises the * * * inference that Congress intended * * * that the United States would acquire water in the same manner as any other public or private appropriator." Later Solicitor Clyde Martz opined that federal nonreserved water rights could exist when expressly or impliedly mandated by Congress, but he found no such mandate in the two major federal acts that he addressed, FLPMA and the Taylor Grazing Act. Memorandum of the Solicitor of the Department of the Interior, 88 Interior Dec. 253 (1981). Finally, Solicitor William Coldiron came out flatly against the concept of a nonreserved right: "There is no 'federal non-reserved water right.'" Non-Reserved

Water Rights—United States Compliance with State Law, 88 Interior Dec. 1055 (1981).

The third Solicitor's opinion did not end the concept of federal nonreserved water rights. Other agencies of the United States, particularly the Department of Defense and the Forest Service in the Department of Agriculture, could benefit from nonreserved water rights if they exist, so the question of such rights was reviewed by the Department of Justice. Assistant Attorney General Theodore Olson of the Office of Legal Counsel concluded that ownership of unappropriated water was an anomaly "if ownership is understood to mean a proprietary interest in the water," and that "[c]laims of ownership of natural resources by the states or by the federal government are best understood as claims of regulatory jurisdiction over these resources, either under the states' police powers or under the federal government's constitutional powers." He acknowledged that the Supremacy Clause, coupled with the Commerce Clause, the Property Clause and other federal powers, gave ample federal authority to supersede state laws; but in the light of California v. United States, supra p. 659, and United States v. New Mexico, supra p. 703, he concluded: "[T]he federal constitutional authority to preempt state water law must be clearly and specifically exercised, * * * otherwise the presumption is that western states retain control over the allocation of unappropriated water within their borders. * * * The exercise of such power must be explicit or clearly implied, however, and federal rights to water will not be found simply by virtue of the ownership, occupation, or use of federal land, without more." Federal "Non-Reserved" Water Rights, 6 U.S. Op. Off. Legal Counsel 328 (1982). See also Frank J. Trelease, Uneasy Federalism —State Water Laws and National Water Uses, 55 Wash. L. Rev. 751 (1980).

Congress explicitly exercised its power to created a federal nonreserved water right for ecosystem protection in the Great Sand Dunes National Park and Preserve Act of 2000, Pub. L. No. 106-530, § 9(b)(2)(B), 114 Stat. 2527, 2533-34. The story of how this came about is told in John D. Leshy, Water Rights for New Federal Land Conservation Programs: A Turn-of-the Century Evaluation, 4 U. Denv. L. Rev. 271 (2001).

7. **Nonreserved rights for federal uses arising under state law.** Federal agencies, particularly the Forest Service, have made many small diversions on reserved lands over the years without a state permit. Apparently, they relied either on the theory that reserved rights were being exercised or on something like the concept of federal nonreserved rights. In 1983, the California legislature provided a modicum of recognition for such diversions made for secondary forest purposes. It adopted a state version of what it called "nonreserved water rights for federal uses." The legislation gave federal agencies until July 1, 1984, to file for "a priority of right to appropriate water" on reserved land if the water use for secondary purposes was initiated prior to July 3, 1978 (the date of decision in United States v. New Mexico holding that there are no reserved water rights for secondary purposes). Each such water right has a priority dating from its initial use, but the priority can be exercised only against other appropriations with a priority on or after July 1, 1984. In other words, a federal secondary water use initiated before July 3, 1978, that was filed by July 1, 1984, would take priority only over appropriations by others made on or after July 1, 1984. Cal. Water Code §§ 1227-1227.4.

8. **A federal regulatory approach to instream flows?** Given the difficulty the United States has had in establishing reserved rights for instream flows in national forests, would a regulatory approach be a viable alternative in some

circumstances? Suppose an irrigation company has a right-of-way permit from the Forest Service for a dam and reservoir within a national forest. When the permit comes up for renewal, could the Forest Service condition renewal upon a requirement that the company bypass, i.e., not store, some of the stream flow to provide downstream fish habitat? See Note 8, supra pp. 594-95.

C. Adjudication and Administration

COLORADO RIVER WATER CONSERVATION DISTRICT v. UNITED STATES

Supreme Court of the United States, 1976.
424 U.S. 800, 96 S. Ct. 1236, 47 L. Ed.2d 483.

MR. JUSTICE BRENNAN delivered the opinion of the Court.

The McCarran Amendment, 66 Stat. 560, 43 U.S.C.A. § 666, provides that "consent is hereby given to join the United States as a defendant in any suit (1) for the adjudication of rights to the use of water of a river system or other source, or (2) for the administration of such rights, where it appears that the United States is the owner of or is in the process of acquiring water rights by appropriation under State law, by purchase, by exchange, or otherwise, and the United States is a necessary party to such suit." The questions presented by this case concern the effect of the McCarran Amendment upon the jurisdiction of the federal district courts under 28 U.S.C.A. § 1345 over suits for determination of water rights brought by the United States as trustee for certain Indian tribes and as owner of various non-Indian Government claims. * * *

Under the Colorado [Water Rights Determination and Administration] Act, the State is divided into seven Water Divisions, each Division encompassing one or more entire drainage basins for the larger rivers in Colorado. Adjudication of water claims within each Division occurs on a continuous basis. Each month, Water Referees in each Division rule on applications for water rights filed within the preceding five months or refer those applications to the Water Judge of their Division. Every six months, the Water Judge passes on referred applications and contested decisions by Referees. A State Engineer and engineers for each Division are responsible for the administration and distribution of the waters of the State according to the determinations in each Division. * * *

The reserved rights of the United States extend to Indian reservations and other federal lands, such as national parks and forests. The reserved rights claimed by the United States in this case affect waters within Colorado Water Division No. 7. On November 14, 1972, the Government instituted this suit in the United States District Court for the District of Colorado, invoking the court's jurisdiction under 28 U.S.C.A. § 1345. The District Court is located in Denver, some 300 miles from Division 7. The suit, against some 1,000 water users, sought declaration of the Government's rights to waters in certain rivers and their tributaries located in Division 7. In the suit, the Government asserted reserved rights on its own behalf and on behalf of certain Indian tribes, as well as rights based on state law. It sought appointment of a water master to administer any waters decreed to the United States.

Prior to institution of this suit, the Government had pursued adjudication of non-Indian reserved rights and other water claims based on state law in Water Divisions 4, 5, and 6, and the Government continues to participate fully in those Divisions.

Shortly after the federal suit was commenced, one of the defendants in that suit filed an application in the state court for Division 7, seeking an order directing service of process on the United States in order to make it a party to proceedings in Division 7 for the purpose of adjudicating all of the Government's claims, both state and federal. On January 3, 1973, the United States was served pursuant to authority of the McCarran Amendment. Several defendants and intervenors in the federal proceeding then filed a motion in the District Court to dismiss on the ground that under the Amendment, the court was without jurisdiction to determine federal water rights. Without deciding the jurisdictional question, the District Court, on June 21, 1973, granted the motion in an unreported oral opinion stating that the doctrine of abstention required deference to the proceedings in Division 7. On appeal, the Court of Appeals for the Tenth Circuit reversed, United States v. Akin, 504 F.2d 115 (1974), holding that the suit of the United States was within district-court jurisdiction under 28 U.S.C.A. § 1345, and that abstention was inappropriate. We granted certiorari. * * *

We first consider the question of district-court jurisdiction under 28 U.S.C.A. § 1345. That section provides that the district courts shall have original jurisdiction over all civil actions brought by the Federal Government "[e]xcept as otherwise provided by Act of Congress." It is thus necessary to examine whether the McCarran Amendment is such an Act of Congress excepting jurisdiction under § 1345.

The McCarran Amendment does not by its terms, at least, indicate any repeal of jurisdiction under § 1345. * * * Beyond its terms, the legislative history of the Amendment evidences no clear purpose to terminate any portion of § 1345 jurisdiction. * * * Accordingly, we hold that the McCarran Amendment in no way diminished federal-district-court jurisdiction under § 1345 and that the District Court had jurisdiction to hear this case.

We turn next to the question whether this suit nevertheless was properly dismissed in view of the concurrent state proceedings in Division 7.

First, we consider whether the McCarran Amendment provided consent to determine federal reserved rights held on behalf of Indians in state court. This is a question not previously squarely addressed by this Court, and given the claims for Indian water rights in this case, dismissal clearly would have been inappropriate if the state court had no jurisdiction to decide those claims. We conclude that the state court had jurisdiction over Indian water rights under the Amendment.

United States v. District Court for Eagle County, 401 U.S. 520, 91 S.Ct. 998, 28 L.Ed.2d 278 (1971), and United States v. District Court for Water Div. 5, 401 U.S. 527, 91 S.Ct. 1003, 28 L.Ed.2d 284 (1971), held that the provisions of the McCarran Amendment, whereby "consent is * * * given to join the United States as a defendant in any suit (1) for the adjudication * * * or (2) for the administration of [water] rights, where it appears that the United States is the owner * * * by appropriation under State law, by purchase, by exchange, or otherwise," subject federal reserved rights to general adjudication in state proceedings for the determination of water rights. More specifically, the Court held that reserved rights were included in those rights where the United States was "otherwise" the owner. Though *Eagle County* and *Water Div. 5* did not involve reserved rights on Indian reservations, viewing the Government's trusteeship of Indian rights as ownership, the logic of those cases clearly extends to such rights. Indeed, *Eagle County* spoke of non-Indian rights and Indian rights without any suggestion that there was a distinction between them for purposes of the Amendment.

Not only the Amendment's language, but also its underlying policy, dictates a construction including Indian rights in its provisions. *Eagle County* rejected the conclusion that federal reserved rights in general were not reached by the Amendment for the reason that the Amendment "[deals] with an all-inclusive statute concerning 'the adjudication of rights to the use of water of a river system.'" Id., at 524, 91 S.Ct., at 1002, 28 L.Ed.2d, at 282. This consideration applies as well to federal water rights reserved for Indian reservations. * * * Thus, bearing in mind the ubiquitous nature of Indian water rights in the Southwest, it is clear that a construction of the Amendment excluding those rights from its coverage would enervate the Amendment's objective. * * *

The Government argues that because of its fiduciary responsibility to protect Indian rights, any state-court jurisdiction over Indian property should not be recognized unless expressly conferred by Congress. * * * [T]he Government's argument rests on the incorrect assumption that consent to state jurisdiction for the purpose of determining water rights imperils those rights or in some way breaches the special obligation of the Federal Government to protect Indians. Mere subjection of Indian rights to legal challenge in state court, however, would no more imperil those rights than would a suit brought by the Government in district court for their declaration, a suit which, absent the consent of the Amendment, would eventually be necessitated to resolve conflicting claims to a scarce resource. The government has not abdicated any responsibility fully to defend Indian rights in state court, and Indian interests may be satisfactorily protected under regimes of state law. * * * The Amendment in no way abridges any substantive claim on behalf of Indians under the doctrine of reserved rights. Moreover, as *Eagle County* said, "questions [arising from the collision of private rights and reserved rights of the United States], including the volume and scope of particular reserved rights, are federal questions which, if preserved, can be reviewed here after final judgment by the Colorado court." 401 U.S., at 526, 91 S.Ct., at 1003, 28 L.Ed.2d, at 283.

Next, we consider whether the District Court's dismissal was appropriate under the doctrine of abstention. We hold that the dismissal cannot be supported under that doctrine in any of its forms. * * *

Although this case falls within none of the abstention categories, there are principles unrelated to considerations of proper constitutional adjudication and regard for federal-state relations which govern in situations involving the contemporaneous exercise of concurrent jurisdictions, either by federal courts or by state and federal courts. These principles rest on consideration of "wise judicial administration, giving regard to conservation of judicial resources and comprehensive disposition of litigation." Kerotest Mfg. Co. v. C-O-Two Fire Equipment Co., 342 U.S. 180, 183 (1952). * * *

Turning to the present case, a number of factors clearly counsel against concurrent federal proceedings. The most important of these is the McCarran Amendment itself. The clear federal policy evinced by that legislation is the avoidance of piecemeal adjudication of water rights in a river system. * * * The consent to jurisdiction given by the McCarran Amendment bespeaks a policy that recognizes the availability of comprehensive state systems for adjudication of water rights as the means for achieving these goals.

Beyond the congressional policy expressed by the McCarran Amendment and consistent with furtherance of that policy, we also find significant (a) the apparent absence of any proceedings in the District Court, other than the filing of the complaint, prior to the motion to dismiss, (b) the extensive involvement of state water rights occasioned by this suit naming 1,000 defendants, (c) the 300-mile distance between the District Court in Denver and the court in Division 7, and (d) the existing participation by the Government in Division 4, 5, and 6 proceedings. We emphasize, however, that we do not overlook the heavy obligation to exercise jurisdiction. We need not decide, for example, whether, despite the McCarran Amendment, dismissal would be warranted if more extensive proceedings had occurred in the District Court prior to dismissal, if the involvement of state water rights were less extensive than it is here, or if the state proceeding were in some respect inadequate to resolve the federal claims. But the opposing factors here, particularly the policy underlying the McCarran Amendment, justify the District Court's dismissal in this particular case.

The judgment of the Court of Appeals is reversed and the judgment of the District Court dismissing the complaint is affirmed for the reasons here stated.

Notes

1. **Arizona v. San Carlos Apache Tribe.** A sequel to *Colorado River* is Arizona v. San Carlos Apache Tribe, 463 U.S. 545 (1983). This was a consolidated appeal of cases concerning Indian reservations in Arizona and Montana. These two states, like many other western states, have clauses in their statehood enabling acts and state constitutions providing that the state disclaims all right to lands of any Indian or Indian tribe and acknowledges that such lands shall be under the jurisdiction and control of Congress. The tribes argued that the disclaimer clauses barred state court adjudication of their water rights. The Court ruled, however, that the McCarran Amendment removed any barrier to state adjudication possibly arising from disclaimer clauses in the statehood enabling acts. The Court left the meaning of the disclaimer clauses in the state constitutions to the state courts. Subsequently, the Arizona and Montana courts held that their respective state disclaimer provisions

did not bar state court adjudication of Indian water rights. United States v. Superior Court for Maricopa County, 697 P.2d 658 (Ariz. 1985); State ex rel. Greely v. Confederated Salish & Kootenai Tribes, 712 P.2d 754 (Mont. 1985).

San Carlos also addressed another post-*Colorado River* issue. In *Colorado River*, the concurrent federal suit had been brought by the United States and was for the adjudication of both Indian and non-Indian reserved rights. In *San Carlos*, the Court held that the *Colorado River* criteria for dismissal of concurrent federal suits apply with full force to federal suits that are brought directly by the tribes, rather than by the United States, and that seek only the adjudication of Indian rights.

2. **Consent to a "suit" adjudicating water rights.** The McCarran Amendment consents to joinder of the United States in a "suit" for the adjudication of water rights. The Oregon adjudication statutes require water right claims to be submitted to an administrative agency, the Oregon Water Resources Department, rather than to a court. The agency accepts objections to claims and holds hearings on contested claims. It then makes findings and issues an order determining the parties' water rights. The order is filed with a court. If no objections are timely filed, the court must enter judgment affirming the order. If objections are filed, a hearing is held, and then the court enters a judgment affirming or modifying the order. In United States v. Oregon, 44 F.3d 758 (9th Cir. 1994), the United States argued this process did not constitute a "suit" within the meaning of the McCarran Amendment. The court disagreed: "Congress had in mind not only traditional suits in equity but also hybrid adjudications taking advantage of the expertise of nonjudicial officials. In fact, the active participation of administrative agencies is at the core of most of the 'comprehensive state systems for adjudication of water rights' contemplated by the McCarran Amendment." Id. at 766.

3. **Consent to adjudication of rights in "a river system or other source."** Another requirement of the McCarran Amendment is that the suit must be to adjudicate rights to use water of "a river system or other source." Dugan v. Rank, 372 U.S. 609 (1963), held that the waiver of immunity does not extend to a private suit to determine the water rights of only some users on a river. Rather, the suit must be a general adjudication of all the rights in "a river system or other source." *Dugan* spawned much litigation about constitutes a river system or other source.

United States v. District Court for Eagle County, 401 U.S. 520 (1971), popularly known as *Eagle County*, concerned a Colorado adjudication of the Eagle River and its tributaries. The Court rejected an argument by the United States that the Eagle River and its tributaries by themselves were not a "river system" under the McCarran Amendment because the Eagle River was in turn tributary to the Colorado River. The Court said: "No suit by any State could possibly encompass all of the water rights in the entire Colorado River, which runs through or touches many states. The 'river system' must be read as embracing one within the particular State's jurisdiction." Id. at 523.

In re General Adjudication of Rights to Use of Water from Snake River Basin Water System, 764 P.2d 78 (Idaho 1988), held that the "river system" requirement meant that immunity would be waived in the Snake River adjudication only if it included all tributaries of the river within Idaho. The court distinguished *Eagle County*, where the Eagle River adjudication did not include all tributaries of the Colorado River within Colorado. It said *Eagle County* involved a unique system of water adjudication existing in Colorado whereby other tributaries of the Colorado River within that state were the subject of other ongoing adjudication proceedings in the state. (See supra p. 164, Note 2, regarding the Colorado adjudication system.) The court also refused to treat the main stem Snake River as a separately adjudicatable "other source" under the McCarran Amendment, saying that this phrase refers to sources like lakes or groundwaters.

Elephant Butte Irrigation District v. United States, 849 P.2d 372 (N.M. Ct. App. 1993), involved adjudication of only part of the Rio Grande (and hydrologically connected sources) in New Mexico, specifically, the part between Elephant Butte Dam and the New Mexico/Texas state line. Elephant Butte Dam is approximately 100 miles above of the state line. The United States objected that the McCarran Amendment did not permit its joinder unless the entire stretch of the Rio Grande in New Mexico was included rather than just the portion below Elephant Butte Dam. The court disagreed. It said an adjudication of part of the main stem of a river ordinarily must include all of the river system within the state, but the unique terms of the Rio Grande Compact justified an exception. The compact requires New Mexico to deliver a specific quantity of water at Elephant Butte Dam, rather than at the state line. Apparently this was done because the federal Rio Grande Project independently apportions water below the dam between Texas and New Mexico users. The court said that by requiring a specific quantity of water to be delivered to Elephant Butte Dam, the compact in effect bifurcates the Rio Grande within New Mexico. New Mexico water uses are allowed below the dam, and those are totally independent of the rights of New Mexico users above the dam. Therefore, said the court, the portion of the Rio Grande within New Mexico below the dam could be considered a separate "river system" for purposes of the McCarran Amendment.

In United States v. Oregon, supra Note 2, the United States and the Klamath Tribe asserted that the Klamath River Basin adjudication was not comprehensive enough to comply with the McCarran Amendment for two reasons. First, they objected because rights represented by water certificates issued under the Oregon permit system and rights recognized in earlier statutory adjudications could not be challenged in the adjudication, and holders of those rights did not have to appear unless they wished to contest other claims. The Ninth Circuit saw no merit in this objection: "As was true in *Eagle County*, all existing water rights claims will have been determined when the adjudication is finished. * * * The comprehensiveness standard requires the consolidation of existing controversies, not the reopening of settled determinations." Id. at 768. Additionally, in response to fears of the United States and the tribe that their rights would be insufficiently protected because they would not be allowed in the adjudication to challenge water right certificates issued under the permit system, the court quoted the following passage from *Eagle County*: "The absence of owners of previously decreed rights may present problems going to the merits, in case there develops a collision between them and any reserved rights of the United States. All such questions, including the volume and scope of particular reserved rights, are federal questions which, if preserved, can be reviewed here after final judgment by the [state] court." Id.

Second, the United States and the tribe objected that the adjudication was insufficiently comprehensive because it did not include claims to hydrologically related groundwater. After noting that the McCarran Amendment requires the adjudication of "a river system or other source," the court stated: "Groundwater may be included as an 'other source,' but the use of 'or' strongly suggests that the adjudication may be limited to either a river system or some other source of water, like groundwater, but need not cover both. * * * [W]hile the adjudication must avoid excessively piecemeal litigation of water rights, it need not determine the rights of users of all hydrologically-related water sources." Id. at 769. To explain why the "river system" requirement should not be read to mandate inclusion of hydrologically related groundwater, the court said: "While the trend has been toward a greater legal recognition of the connection between ground and surface waters, that recognition is too recent and too incomplete to infer that Congress intended to require comprehensive stream adjudications under the McCarran Amendment [passed in 1952] to include the adjudication of groundwater rights as well as rights to surface water." Id. at 769-70.

In Arizona, streams and their subflow are subject to the appropriation doctrine, while percolating groundwater is governed by different rules. The exclusion of percolating groundwater from a stream adjudication was approved in In re General Adjudication of All Rights to Use Water in Gila River System & Source, 857 P.2d 1236, 1248 (Ariz. 1993): "The McCarran Amendment was not intended to impose on the states a federal definition of 'river system or other source.' * * * We believe that the trial court may adopt a rationally based exclusion for wells having a de minimis effect on the river system. Such a de minimis exclusion effectively allocates to those well owners whatever amount of water is determined to be de minimis. It is, in effect, a summary adjudication of their rights."

4. **Review of federal agency decisions regarding reserved rights claims.** Suppose an environmental group alleges a federal agency entitled to a reserved right is violating federal law by seeking too small a quantity of water in a state court adjudication. Judicial review of the agency's decision about how much water to claim lies exclusively in federal court. The McCarran Amendment's waiver of immunity is not broad enough to allow the state court conducting the adjudication to evaluate the federal agency's decision making processes regarding quantification. In re Application for Water Rights of United States, 101 P.3d 1072 (Colo. 2004).

5. **The role of state law under the McCarran Amendment.** The McCarran Amendment does more than consent to the joinder of the United States in general adjudication suits. It also addresses what law governs: "The United States, when a party to any such suit, shall * * * be deemed to have waived any right to plead that the State laws are inapplicable or that the United States is not amenable thereto by reason of its sovereignty, * * * Provided, That no judgment for costs shall be entered against the United States in any such suit."

United States v. Idaho ex rel. Director, Idaho Department of Water Resources, 508 U.S. 1 (1993), held that Idaho could not require the United States to pay filing fees under state law in the Snake River adjudication. An Idaho statute obligated each water right claimant to pay a filing fee to help finance the cost of the adjudication. The amount of the fee varied with the size of the claim. The United States estimated that the filing fees for its various claims could exceed $10 million. It argued that the McCarran Amendment waiver of "any right to plead that the State laws are inapplicable" should not be construed to subject it to state adjective law governing procedure, fees, and the like. The Court disagreed because the United States' view "would render the amendment's consent to suit largely nugatory, allowing the Government to argue for some special federal rule defeating established state-law rules governing pleading, discovery, and the admissibility of evidence at trial." Nonetheless, the Court held for the United States on the ground that the McCarran Amendment proviso prohibiting any "judgment for costs" against the United States exempted it from payment of filing fees. The state argued that fees are not the same as costs. The Court acknowledged that generally there is a distinction between fees and costs: Fees are amounts paid to a public official for particular charges typically delineated by statute, and costs are expenses incurred in litigation that a prevailing party is allowed by rule to tax against the losing party. But in this case, said the Court, the line was blurred. Before Idaho revised its system for recovering adjudication expenses in 1986, Idaho courts upon entering final judgment in an adjudication had taxed the costs against all parties, not just the losing parties. Moreover, many of the items that Idaho had formerly taxed as costs were now denominated as fees to be paid upon filing a claim. The court therefore concluded that the McCarran Amendment does not subject "the United States to the payment of the sort of fees that Idaho sought to exact here." 508 U.S. at 8.

In United States v. Bell, 724 P.2d 631 (Colo. 1986), the United States sought to amend a reserved water right claim it filed eleven years earlier in an ongoing Colorado adjudication. The United States wanted to change its claimed point of diversion from small tributaries of the White and Colorado Rivers to the main stem Colorado River. This change would have enabled a substantial increase in the amount that could be diverted. The trial court applied a state rule of civil procedure on the relation back of pleading amendments. The court denied relation back under that rule because the original claim gave no notice to persons who would be adversely affected that the United States claimed a large quantity of main stem water. Without relation back under the pleading rule, a state adjudication statute then required that the enlarged portion of the claim be postponed in priority to the date when the pleading was amended rather than the date the reservation was created. The Colorado Supreme Court approved application of the state pleading rule and the postponement statute to the federal claim. It viewed the McCarran Amendment as being intended to "promote certainty in water allocation by subjecting undeclared and unquantified federal water rights to state adjudication." It reasoned that without application of the pleading rule and postponement statute, "the purposes of the McCarran Amendment would be frustrated, and the United States would have avoided the equivalent of a filing deadline."

United States v. Oregon, supra Note 2, dealt not only with the Klamath Basin adjudication but with an Oregon statute requiring the United States to register and describe its reserved right claims to waters *outside* of the Klamath Basin by December 31, 1992. Outside of the Klamath Basin, no suits were under way to adjudicate the water rights of the United States. The Ninth Circuit held that the McCarran Amendment did not consent to make the United States subject to the Oregon registration statute. "While the information obtained by the registration system regarding claims not yet at issue in any proceeding may be useful in future comprehensive adjudications, the process cannot accurately be described as part of the state's adjective law for the adjudication of water rights. * * * It is * * * possible that many years will pass before a registered claim is adjudicated, if it is ever adjudicated at all. The connection between registration and adjudication is too tenuous for the registration provisions to be characterized as part of the adjudications to which the United States has consented to be joined." 44 F.3d at 771.

6. **Water right administration suits.** The McCarran Amendment, as set out at the beginning of the principal case, contains two waivers of sovereign immunity. Clause (1) consents to joinder of the United States in suits to adjudicate water rights in a river system or other source. Clause (2), which has been less in the spotlight, consents to joinder of the United States in suits "for the administration of such

rights." The phrase "such rights" in clause (2) refers only to water rights previously adjudicated in a general adjudication. It does not include rights decreed in private suits. South Delta Water Agency v. Bureau of Reclamation, 767 F.2d 531 (9th Cir. 1985).

In State Engineer v. South Fork Band of Te-Moak Tribe of Western Shoshone Indians, 339 F.3d 804 (9th Cir. 2003), a state district court had issued a general adjudication decree for the Humboldt River. Later, the United States purchased five ranches with decreed water rights to create an Indian reservation. Decades after that, the tribe challenged the state engineer's authority to administer the river on the reservation by handcuffing a state water official and charging him with trespass. The state engineer responded by filing contempt proceedings against the tribe in the state court that issued the adjudication decree. The tribe sought removal to federal district court. The Ninth Circuit ruled the McCarran Amendment waiver of immunity from suit in state court to administer adjudicated water rights applied even though the state adjudication predated that statute. (The Ninth Circuit ruled further that the federal district court lacked subject matter jurisdiction because of the state court's prior exclusive jurisdiction arising from its earlier adjudication of the water rights, supra Note 6, pp. 175-76.

7. **Res judicata effect of previous adjudication of reserved rights.** Nevada v. United States, 463 U.S. 110 (1983), involved the effect of an earlier adjudication of Indian reserved rights in the Orr Ditch decree. The Truckee River flows from the Sierra Nevada, through Lake Tahoe, to Pyramid Lake, home of the Lahontan cutthroat trout and the unique cui-ui sucker. Surrounding the lake is the 1859 reservation of the Paiute Indians, who have always looked to the lake fish as an important source of food. Long ago a large portion of the Truckee's waters were diverted by the U.S. Bureau of Reclamation to serve an irrigation project now managed by the Truckee-Carson Irrigation District. A number of private landowners also acquired water rights to the Truckee. In 1913, the United States instituted the Orr Ditch litigation in federal district court to assert and protect its water rights for the Indian reservation and the reclamation project. A master's report proposed awarding the Indian reservation an 1859 right for 58.7 c.f.s. to irrigate 3,130 acres and the reclamation project a 1902 priority for 1500 c.f.s. In 1926, the district court put this award in force for an experimental period. In 1934 settlement negotiations, the United States demanded an increase in the Indian rights to enable irrigation of an additional 2,745 acres of reservation land. This was accepted and a decree adopting the settlement was signed in 1935.

Over the years, the level of Pyramid Lake dropped, its surface acreage decreased, and the river formed a delta that prevented the trout from leaving the lake to spawn upstream. In 1973, the United States instituted a new suit against all users of Truckee water, asserting that the former decree determined only the Indians' reserved rights for irrigation water. It claimed on behalf of the Indians an additional reserved right for water to maintain and preserve Pyramid Lake and maintain the lower Truckee as a natural spawning ground. The Court held, however, that res judicata barred the United States from asserting this claim. The Court found that the same cause of action was litigated in both proceedings and that all of the parties in the second suit were bound by the original Orr Ditch decree, including the United States and the tribe.

The government had represented both the Indian tribe and the reclamation project landowners in the original suit. The Court acknowledged the government owed a fiduciary duty to the tribe but said it also had obligations to those who held beneficial ownership of project water. Regarding the dual duties, the Court said:

"Today, * * * it may well appear that Congress was requiring the Secretary of the Interior to carry water on at least two shoulders when it delegated to him both the responsibility for the supervision of the Indian tribes and the commencement of reclamation projects in areas adjacent to reservation lands. But Congress chose to do this, and it is simply unrealistic to suggest that the Government may not perform its obligation to represent Indian tribes in litigation when Congress has obliged it to represent other interests as well. In this regard, the Government cannot follow the fastidious standards of a private fiduciary, who would breach his duties to his single beneficiary solely by representing potentially conflicting interests without the beneficiary's consent. The Government does not 'compromise' its obligation to one interest that Congress obliges it to represent by the mere fact that it simultaneously performs another task for another interest that Congress has obligated it by statute to do." 463 U.S. at 128.

UNITED STATES v. ANDERSON

United States Court of Appeals, Ninth Circuit, 1984.
736 F.2d 1358.

J. BLAINE ANDERSON, CIRCUIT JUDGE: * * * The plaintiffs [United States and Spokane Tribe of Indians] sought an adjudication of water rights in the Chamokane Basin, a hydrological system including Chamokane Creek, its tributaries and its ground water basin. The waters of the Chamokane Basin are not wholly within the Spokane Indian Reservation; Chamokane Creek originates north of the reservation and flows south along the eastern boundary. The creek leaves the reservation by discharging into the Spokane River which, in turn, joins with the Columbia River and flows into the Pacific Ocean. * * *

The Spokane Indian Reservation is not exclusively owned and resided upon by Indians. Non-Indian settlement has occurred there, encouraged by various federal programs authorizing allotment of reservation lands to individual Indians and opening excess land to homesteading by non-Indians. * * *

In the case before us, the district court determined that it was permissible for the State of Washington to exercise regulatory jurisdiction over non-Indian use of excess Chamokane Basin waters on lands owned by non-Indians within the Spokane Indian Reservation. The Spokane Tribe takes issue with this determination, arguing that it, not the state, has jurisdiction by virtue of our decision in Colville Confederated Tribes v. Walton.

Regulatory jurisdiction of a state over non-Indian activities on a tribal reservation "may be barred either because it is pre-empted by federal law, or because it unlawfully infringes on the right of reservation Indians to self-government." *Walton*, 647 F.2d at 51. These barriers to regulation, although independent, are related by the concept of tribal sovereignty. * * *

Of course, tribal sovereignty is not absolute. In particular, the power to regulate generally the conduct of nonmembers on land no longer owned by or held in trust for the tribe is impliedly withdrawn as a necessary result of tribal dependent status. Montana v. United States, 450 U.S. 544, 564, 101 S.Ct. 1245,

1257, 67 L.Ed.2d 493 (1981). Some exceptions to this implied withdrawal of tribal regulatory authority do exist.

> A tribe may regulate, through taxation, licensing or other means, the activities of nonmembers who enter consensual relationships with the tribe or its members, through commercial dealing, contracts, leases, or other arrangements * * * A tribe may also retain inherent power to exercise civil authority over the conduct of non-Indians on fee lands within the reservation when that conduct threatens or has some direct effect on the political integrity, the economic security, or the health or welfare of the tribe.

Montana v. United States, 450 U.S. at 565-66, 101 S.Ct. at 1258-59. * * *

Applying these standards, we conclude that the State, not the Tribe, has the authority to regulate the use of excess Chamokane Basin waters by non-Indians on non-tribal, i.e., fee, land. Our review reveals no consensual agreement between the non-Indian water users and the Tribe which would furnish the basis for implication of tribal regulatory authority. We find no conduct which so threatens or has such a "direct effect on the political integrity, the economic security, or the health or welfare of the Tribe," as to confer tribal jurisdiction. Montana v. United States, 450 U.S. at 566, 101 S.Ct. at 1258. The water rights adjudication which furnishes the basis for the instant inquiry quantifies and preserves tribal water rights. The district court appointed a federal water master whose responsibility is to administer the available waters in accord with the priorities of all the water rights as adjudicated. * * * The state may regulate only the use, by non-Indian fee owners, of excess water. Any permits issued by the state would be limited to excess water. If those permits represent rights that may be empty, so be it.

It is evident, however, that the political and economic welfare of the Tribe will not suffer adverse impact from the state-regulated use of surplus waters by nonmembers on non-Indian lands. Instead the factual situation points in favor of state regulation. First, no direct federal preemption of state regulation has occurred. No federal statute or regulatory scheme expressly or impliedly governs water use by non-Indians on the Spokane Reservation. Second, the balance of interest weighs most heavily in favor of the state.

The instant situation is contrary to that addressed by this circuit in Colville Confederated Tribes v. Walton, 647 F.2d 42 (1981). [In *Walton*, reprinted in part supra p. 692, the court held that the power of the State of Washington to issue permits to appropriate "water in the No Name system was pre-empted by the creation of the Colville Reservation." 647 F.2d at 52.] The *Walton* decision was compelled by the geography and hydrology of the No Name Basin and its relationship to the Colville Reservation. The reservation lands in question were allotted, not opened for entry and settlement. The No Name hydrological system is non-navigable and is located entirely within the reservation. Validation of the state-issued permits claimed by Walton could have jeopardized the agricultural use of downstream tribal users as well as the existence of the tribal fishery. In essence, the interest of the Tribe in regulation of the waters of the No Name Basin was "critical to the lifestyle of its residents and the development of its resources."

The district court noted, and we agree, that because water per se lies within the exterior boundaries of an Indian reservation does not necessarily negate a state's interest in overseeing its usage along with the other in-state water systems. Washington is obligated to regulate and conserve water consumption for the benefit of all its citizens, including those who own land within a reservation in fee. Therefore, the state's special concern is shared with, not displaced by, similar tribal and federal interests when water is located within the boundaries of both the state and the reservation. The weight of the state's interest depends, in large part, on the extent to which waterways or aquifers transcend the exterior boundaries of Indian country. * * * Chamokane Creek arises outside of the Spokane Indian Reservation and its course, for a good deal of its length, continues outside of that reservation. * * *

The facts in this case are readily distinguishable from the facts in the *Walton* decision. By weighing the competing federal, tribal and state interests involved, it is clear that the state may exercise its regulatory jurisdiction over the use of surplus, non-reserved Chamokane Basin waters by nonmembers on non-Indian fee lands within the Spokane Indian Reservation. Central to our decision is the fact that the interest of the state in exercising its jurisdiction will not infringe on the tribal right to self-government nor impact on the Tribe's economic welfare because those rights have been quantified and will be protected by the federal water master. Additionally, in view of the hydrology and geography of the Chamokane Creek Basin, the State of Washington's interest in developing a comprehensive water program for the allocation of surplus waters weighs heavily in favor of permitting it to extend its regulatory authority to the excess waters, if any, of the Chamokane Basin. State permits issued for any such excess water will be subject to all preexisting rights and those preexisting rights will be protected by the federal court decree and its appointed water master. We do not believe there is any realistic infringement on tribal rights and protected affairs. If there is any intrusion, it is minimal and permissible under all of the circumstances of this case. * * *

Notes

1. **State versus tribal jurisdiction over non-Indian appropriation of surplus water.** Non-Indians own about 8% of the land within the external boundaries of the Yakima Indian Reservation. The Yakima Indian Nation adopted a water code purporting to regulate all waters that underlie, arise upon, flow through, or border upon the reservation, including waters used by non-Indians on fee lands both within and outside the reservation. The code required all persons using or claiming the right to divert water to apply for a permit. A tribal water resources council was empowered to issue ten-year permits. Any person using water who failed to apply for a permit waived all right to the water. The code established priorities among uses in the following order: (a) tribal or public use dedicated by the Tribal Council, (b) use for tribal enterprises, (c) farming use on Yakima allotments, (d) non-farm use on Yakima allotments, (e) use on allotments held by nonresident Yakimas, (f) use on lands held by non-Yakima Indians, and (g) use on formerly allotted lands now in non-Indian ownership. Within each class, individual users were to receive a just and equitable distribution.

The State of Washington sued to have the tribal water code declared invalid. The parties stipulated that surplus water existed over that needed to satisfy the Yakima Nation's *Winters* rights, though the amount of the excess was not fully quantified. The court granted summary judgment that the code was invalid to the extent it asserted civil regulatory jurisdiction over non-Indian use of the surplus water on fee lands inside or outside the reservation. Holly v. Confederated Tribes & Bands of Yakima Indian Nation, 655 F. Supp. 557 (E.D. Wash. 1985), aff'd sub nom. Holly v. Totus, 812 F.2d 714 (9th Cir. 1987) (without reported opinion). The federal district court applied the rule of Montana v. United States, discussed in the principal case, that tribal regulatory authority over non-Indians on nonreservation land has been impliedly withdrawn subject to two exceptions. The court concluded: "The defendants [the tribes] have not come forward with facts to show [the] existence of a material factual question with respect to whether non-Indian conduct related to non-Indian use of excess waters threatens the political integrity, economic security, or health and welfare of the Tribes. Nor have the non-Indians entered into agreements or dealings with the Tribes with a result of subjecting themselves to tribal civil jurisdiction." 655 F. Supp. at 559.

The Montana court held in In re Application for Beneficial Water Use Permits, supra pp. 131-32, Note 5, that the state water code precluded issuing permits for non-Indian appropriation of surplus water on Indian reservations until the Indian reserved rights were quantified. In a concurring opinion, Justice Leapheart found a different basis for limiting state authority to issue permits to non-Indians, a basis that has potential implications for state administration of Indian reserved water rights. He said a tribe's sovereign immunity gives it sole regulatory authority over waters within reservation boundaries absent waiver of the immunity. But he then noted that the McCarran Amendment waives tribal sovereign immunity not only for suits to adjudicate water rights but also for suits to administer previously adjudicated water rights. From this, he concluded that once a tribe's water rights are quantified in a general adjudication under the McCarran Amendment or by negotiation with the tribe, tribal immunity is waived for the purpose of administering those rights. This waiver, he said, enables the state to issue permits to use surplus, nonreserved waters within reservation boundaries. Would this waiver also bear on the issue discussed in the next Note?

2. **Integrated administration of Indian reserved rights and appropriative. rights.** In *Big Horn III*, supra p. 697, Note 4, the Wyoming Supreme Court by vote of 3 to 2 reversed a trial court order substituting the tribal water agency for the state engineer as the administrator of both the reserved and the state-permitted water rights within the Wind River Indian Reservation. The tribes sought this relief because they believed the state engineer was not adequately recognizing their rights. Justice Macy's lead opinion for the fragmented three-member majority relied on the separation of powers in the state constitution: The state engineer is a constitutionally designated water administration official subject to removal only by the governor, not the judiciary. In apparent recognition of tension between the state engineer and the tribes, he admonished the state engineer that if he failed to protect the tribes' reserved rights, the courts have power to take appropriate enforcement action. He also limited the state engineer's power by saying that if the state engineer thinks the tribes are violating the terms of their water rights, he cannot directly shut down their headgates but must seek judicial enforcement. The other two justices making up the majority, in separate concurrences, expressed their conviction that dual management would be unworkable, though their individual reasons for putting management in

the state engineer rather than the tribal water agency seem to turn more on quirks of the case than on any broadly applicable principle.

The two dissenting justices each proposed different approaches. One favored dual state and tribal administration of all water rights on the reservation, with judicial resolution of disputes between the joint administrators. He acknowledged, however, that this might result ultimately in judicial administration of the river. The other dissenter urged allowing tribal "monitoring" of non-Indian water use on the reservation. He called this a "lesser regulatory activity" than full tribal administration because non-Indians would not be subject to the jurisdiction of the tribal water agency. Since he thought the state engineer had shown reluctance to enforce the Indian reserved rights, he also urged allowing the tribes to seek judicial enforcement of their rights without first having to request relief from the state engineer.

Compare United States v. City & County of Denver, 656 P.2d 1, 35 (Colo. 1982), which involved the adjudication and integration of non-Indian reserved rights into the water rights systems of several Colorado rivers: "[The United States] agrees that water rights ultimately adjudicated to it are subject to administration by the State Engineer." Should Indian and non-Indian federal reserved rights be treated differently regarding water right administration? If the United States were later to conclude that the state engineer was inadequately protecting its rights, would it have any recourse (would it need any recourse) other than that suggested in *Eagle County*, supra p. 718, Note 3, where the Court said that questions arising from collision of reserved rights and state-created water rights "are federal questions which, if preserved, can be reviewed here after final judgment by the [state] court"? 401 U.S. at 526.

3. **Tribal water quality regulation.** Issues of tribal jurisdiction over activities of nonmembers arise with water quality regulation under the Clean Water Act (CWA). The states have various functions under the CWA, such as development of water quality standards under section 303 and certification in federal licensing or permitting proceedings under section 401. See PUD No. 1 of Jefferson County v. Washington Dep't of Ecology, supra p. 651. With Environmental Protection Agency (EPA) approval of their programs, states can issue National Pollutant Discharge Elimination (NPDES) permits under section 402 and, in some circumstances, permits for dredged or fill material under section 404. See supra p. 516 and pp. 589-91, Note 2. CWA § 518, 33 U.S.C. § 1377, authorizes EPA to treat an Indian tribe as a state for purposes of performing these functions. EPA takes a case-by-case approach to approving tribal jurisdiction over activities on lands within reservation boundaries held in fee by nonmembers. Whether the tribe has regulatory jurisdiction depends on how seriously the activity to be regulated affects the tribe's political integrity, economic security, or health and welfare. E.g., Montana v. EPA, 137 F.3d 1135 (9th Cir. 1998); 58 Fed. Reg. 67966, 67970-67971 (various CWA sections); 58 Fed. Reg. 8172, 8173-8176 (CWA § 404); 56 Fed. Reg. 64877-64878 (CWA §§ 303, 401). State ownership of a lake bed does not preclude tribal regulation under CWA § 518. Wisconsin v. EPA, 266 F.3d 741 (7th Cir. 2001).

Tribal water quality standards can impact the activities of nonmembers on lands outside the reservation. The Isleta Pueblo in New Mexico issued water quality standards under section 518 for waters of the Rio Grande River flowing through its reservation. The standards protected use of the river for ceremonial purposes involving human immersion and ingestion of water. They were more stringent than the state water quality standards for the river. About five miles upstream from the reservation, the City of Albuquerque discharged treated wastes into the river under a NPDES permit. These discharges lowered water quality within the reservation. When EPA undertook to revise the city's permit to ensure compliance with the tribal water quality standards, the city challenged EPA's approval and enforcement of the standards. In City of Albuquerque v. Browner, 97 F.3d 415 (10th Cir. 1996), the court held that (a) a tribe can establish water quality standards more stringent that those required by federal law and (b) EPA can enforce the tribal standards against point source dischargers located outside the reservation boundaries. Section 518 directs EPA to "provide a mechanism for the resolution of any unreasonable consequences that may arise as a result of differing water quality standards that may be set by States and Indian tribes located on common bodies of water." The court held that EPA complied with this directive even though it provided only for resolution by mediation or nonbinding arbitration and furthermore authorized only states and tribes, not interested third parties, to initiate the process.

Index

References are to Pages

References are to Pages

References are to Pages

References are to Pages

References are to Pages

References are to Pages

References are to Pages

References are to Pages

References are to Pages